Kap Stann

Kap Stann is the author of a guide to Georgia and South Carolina. Originally from New York, Kap traveled to Washington, DC, almost every year of her childhood. In addition to these starched-shirt school field trips through the Capitol, she also enjoyed long beach vacations at the Eastern Shore, where she watched the wild horses run along Assateague Island. During her research for the DC chapter, Kap was able to reunite with many fond memories and introduce old friends to her eight-year-old daughter, Corinne. Cory's favorite part of Washington, DC? 'Staying in a hotel!'

Jeff Williams

Jeff Williams was born in New Zealand and currently lives with his wife Alison and son Callum in a seaside/fishing village near Brisbane in the Australian state of Queensland. He is the author of Lonely Planet's guide to Western Australia, and coauthor of Lonely Planet's guides to Australia; South Africa, Lesotho & Swaziland; New Zealand; Tramping in New Zealand; and contributor to Africa on a shoestring, and Outback Australia. He has had a love affair with Virginia since his first trip there over 20 years ago and has a special interest in the Civil War of 1861 – 65. He had fun combing the far-flung parts of the state while researching this book.

Randy Peffer

As a boy Randy hopped a freight train out of Pittsburgh, Pennsylvania, his home town, in search of the King of the Hoboes. He's been traveling ever since. He has nearly died as a commercial pilot, Chesapeake Bay waterman, and a teacher in the Portsmouth, NH, Naval Prison (see *Five Easy Pieces*). Now Randy teaches at Phillips Academy in Andover, MA, and has written for *National Geographic*, *Smithsonian*, *Islands*, *Travel Holiday*, and *Sail*. Randy's book *Watermen* (Johns Hopkins) about Chesapeake fishermen won the *Baltimore Sun's* Critic's Choice award and almost got him shot by a pirate whose cover got blown in the book. Every summer Randy and his wife Jackie study whales off Cape Cod on the research schooner *Sarah Abbot*.

Eric Wakin

Eric Wakin was born in New York City and grew up there and in Maryland. After completing a BA in English at Columbia University, he traveled in South and Southeast Asia. He has since studied at Chiang Mai University, earned MAs in Asian studies and political science at the University of Michigan, and written *Anthropology Goes to War: Professional Ethics and Counterinsurgency in Thailand* (University of Wisconsin/Center for Southeast Asian Studies). He is now back in New York working on a doctorate in American history.

FROM THE AUTHORS

From Kap Stann

Thanks to the Merkels, lifelong family friends without whom Washington, DC, would not be always remembered as an inviting and exciting place to be. And thanks to the San Francisco expatriate tribe – particularly Andrea Torrice, David, and Mikkel and Rebecca – and also to Lisa E. Thanks also to DC's hospitality industry, most notably Lisa Holland.

From Jeff Williams

First of all thanks to Caroline Liou who entrusted this project to me over a few beers in Fitzroy, Australia, and to her able offsider Carolyn Hubbard who put up with queries at odd times (which were complicated by the tyranny of distance) – thanks for your humor. To Russ Hubbard of Washington state (Carolyn's Dad) who nursed the technical piece on the Civil War through its infancy and offered invaluable suggestions on how to cram four vital years of history into a few pages; I wish I had you as a professor at university. A special thanks to Tom Downs for persevering in adversity, and to Randy, my coauthor, who let forth the secrets of outdoor Maryland and Delaware, a big 'ta.'

Thanks also to the many Virginians who sat back and persevered as a bedraggled Aussie fired questions at them – the state owes you a debt. In particular, much thanks to all the tourism staff in Richmond, Virginia Beach, Norfolk, Alexandria (and Mount Vernon), Williamsburg, Newport News, Hampton, Portsmouth, Fredericksburg, Petersburg *thanks Lee*, Winchester, Strasburg *the buffs at Hupp's Hill*, Staunton, Lexington, Roanoke *thanks Richard for the tour along the Blue Ridge and Cockram's General Store*, Abingdon *I hope you are still surfing*, Big Stone Gap, Charlottesville (and Monticello), Lynchburg and Danville. To those who shared conversation, a beer or a game of pool after 8 pm, I am 'externally ingrateful'.

Lastly, but not least, to my minders at home – Ali and Callum – thanks for putting up with late nights, a table covered in brochures and maps, and my forgetfulness (especially the promised meals I never cooked) and general lack of attention.

From Randy Peffer

Mindy Schneeberger of Maryland's Department of Business and Economic Tourism, and Ivy Allen, formerly of the Delaware Tourism Office, provided endless counsel and logistical support. Captain Bart Murphy of Tilghman Island bought the beer and made us laugh. My wife, Jackie Peffer, organized the files, made calls, drove, sang, and kept the wolf from the door.

From Eric Wakin

Thanks to Kate Bunting; Elizabeth Forero; Jackie Gotthold; Katie Meskill; Therese Murdza; Scotty Oliver of the Maryland Room of the Talbot County Library; Sig Sauer; Jeff & Darlene Seitz; Nancye Staff-Messore of the Washington County, Maryland, CVB; Allan & Cyndi Stam; Carl Taylor of Backcountry Publications; and especially family members and close friends Daniel, Edward, Francesca, Jeanette, and Lawrence Wakin.

This Book

This guide is the work of dedicated and patient authors. Kap Stann dove into DC and wrangled with the introductory chapters; for the latter she had assistance from Jeff and Randy. Jeff Williams brought much enthusiasm to his writing of the outdoor activities chapter, the Virginia chapters, and Civil War section. Randy Peffer imbued his writing of the Maryland and Delaware chapters with his love of the bays and the people who work them. Eric Wakin provided manuscript from which portions of this first edition were written, particularly for the Delaware and Maryland chapters. Dr Russ Hubbard consulted with Jeff on the Civil War section and relevant sidebars.

From the Publisher

Kate Hoffman, Tom Downs, and Carolyn Hubbard edited the pages and maps with regular help from Don Gates, and Kate saw the book through production. Kim (Eagle Eyes) Haglund proofed it.

A slew of cartographers turned their talents to creating the maps: Beca Lafore, Chris Salcedo, Cyndy Johnsen, Alex Guilbert, Mark Williams, Melissa J Webster, and Blake Summers. Alex oversaw map production. Hugh D'Andrade, Hayden Foell, Rini Keagy, John Fadeff, and Mark Butler put pen and paint to paper in creating the illustrations. And when all the pieces were ready, Scott Summers and Hugh designed them into book form.

Thanks also to Neil Tilbury for providing manuscript from which portions of this first edition were written.

Warning & Request

Things change – prices go up, schedules change, good places go bad and bad places go bankrupt – nothing stays the same. So, if you find things better or worse, recently opened or long since closed, please tell us and help make the next edition even more accurate and useful.

We value all of the feedback we receive from travelers. Julie Young coordinates a small team that reads and acknowledges every letter, postcard and email, and ensures that every morsel of information finds its way to the appropriate authors, editors and publishers. Everyone who writes to us will find their name in the next edition of the appropriate guide and will also receive a free subscription to our quarterly newsletter, *Planet Talk*. The very best contributions will be rewarded with a free Lonely Planet guide.

Excerpts from your correspondence may appear in updates (which we add to the end pages of reprints); new editions of this guide; in our newsletter, *Planet Talk*; or in the Postcards section of our Website – so please let us know if you don't want your letter published or your name acknowledged.

Contents

FACTS ABOUT DELAWARE . . . 547

WILMINGTON . . . 558

NORTHERN DELAWARE . . . 570

CENTRAL DELAWARE . . . 585

DELAWARE SEASHORE . . . 597

INDEX . . . 615

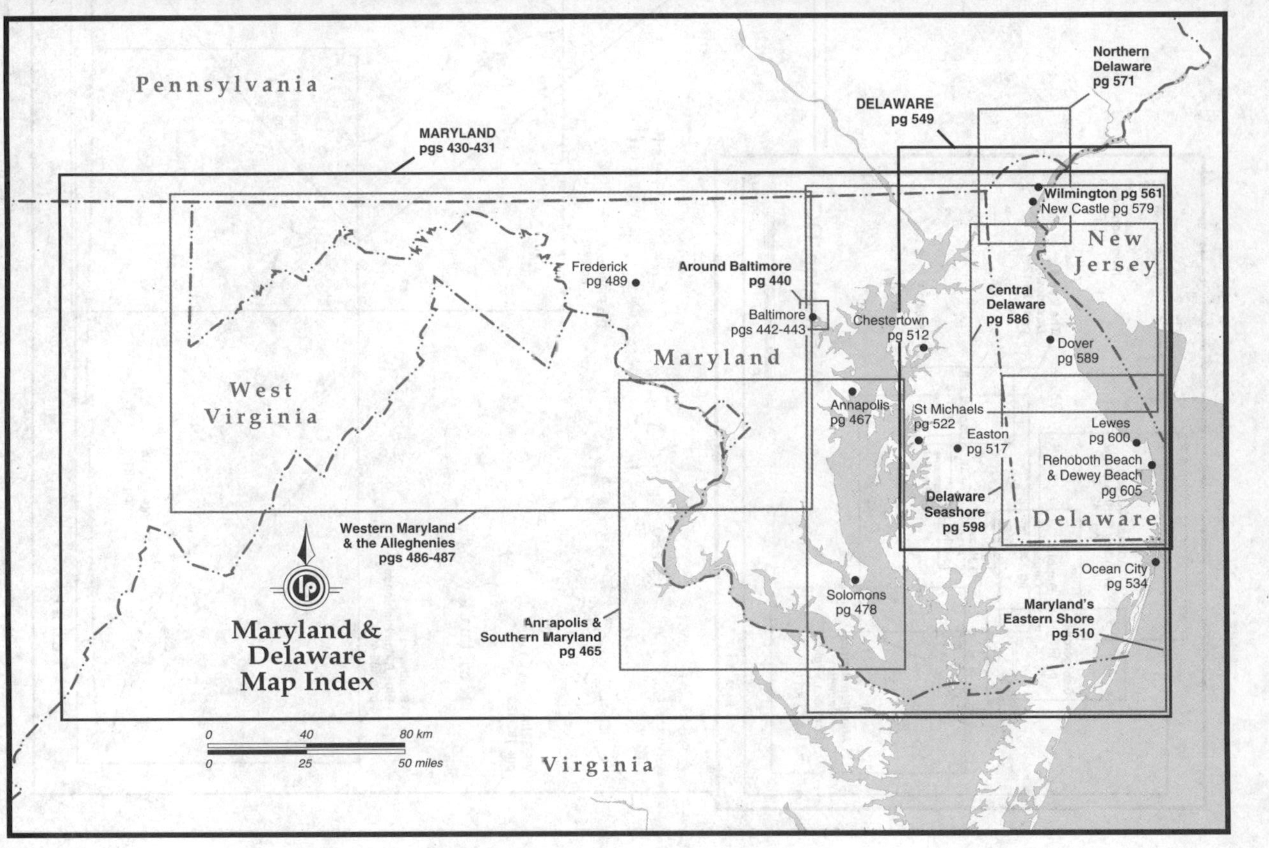
Maryland & Delaware Map Index
Pennsylvania
MARYLAND pgs 430-431
DELAWARE pg 549
Northern Delaware pg 571
Wilmington pg 561
New Castle pg 579
New Jersey
Frederick pg 489
Around Baltimore pg 440
Baltimore pgs 442-443
Chestertown pg 512
Central Delaware pg 586
Dover pg 589
Maryland
West Virginia
Annapolis pg 467
St Michaels pg 522
Easton pg 517
Lewes pg 600
Rehoboth Beach & Dewey Beach pg 605
Delaware Seashore pg 598
Delaware
Western Maryland & the Alleghenies pgs 486-487
Ocean City pg 534
Solomons pg 478
Maryland's Eastern Shore pg 510
Annapolis & Southern Maryland pg 465
0 40 80 km
0 25 50 miles
Virginia

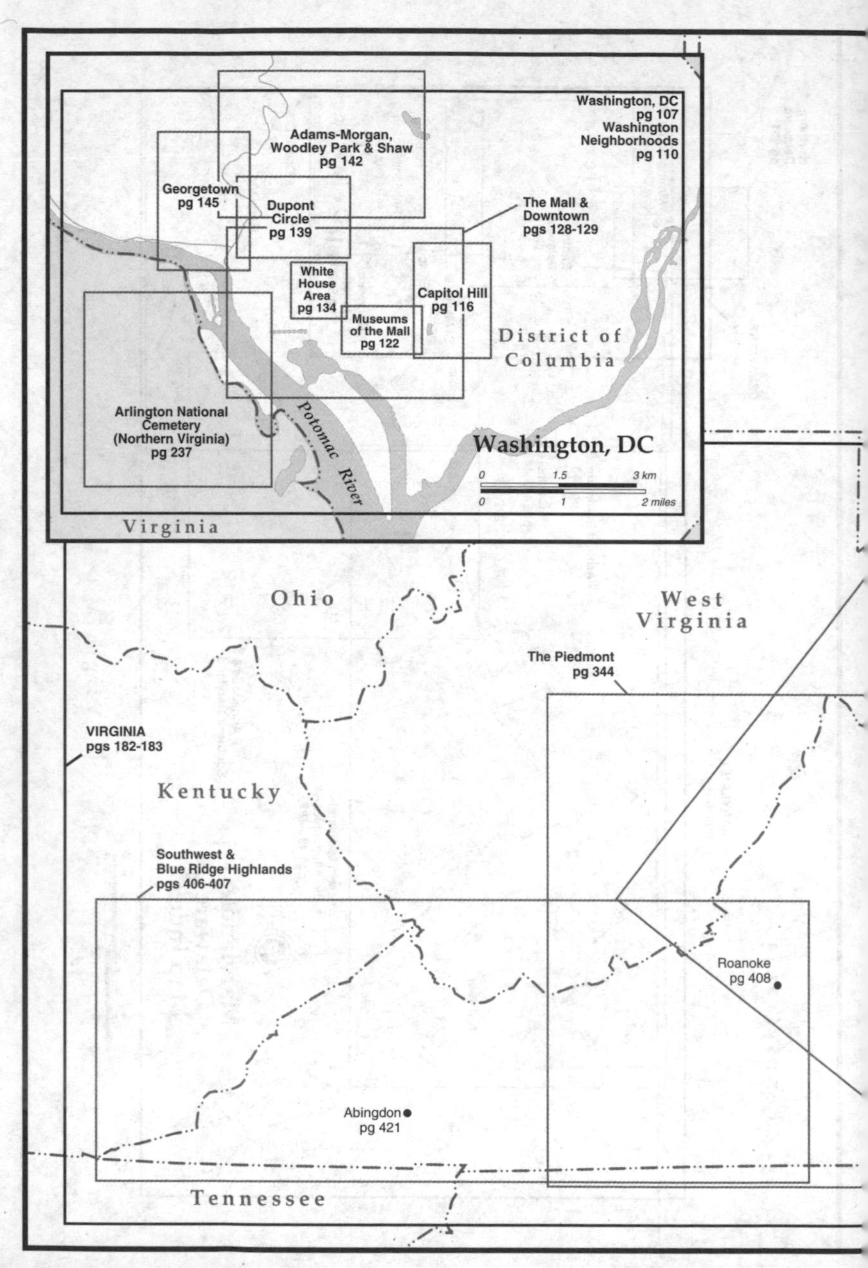
Washington, DC
pg 107
Washington
Neighborhoods
pg 110
Adams-Morgan,
Woodley Park & Shaw
pg 142
Georgetown
pg 145
Dupont
Circle
pg 139
The Mall &
Downtown
pgs 128-129
White
House
Area
pg 134
Capitol Hill
pg 116
Museums
of the Mall
pg 122
District of
Columbia
Arlington National
Cemetery
(Northern Virginia)
pg 237
Potomac River
Washington, DC
0 1.5 3 km
0 1 2 miles
Virginia
Ohio
West
Virginia
The Piedmont
pg 344
VIRGINIA
pgs 182-183
Kentucky
Southwest &
Blue Ridge Highlands
pgs 406-407
Roanoke
pg 408
Abingdon
pg 421
Tennessee

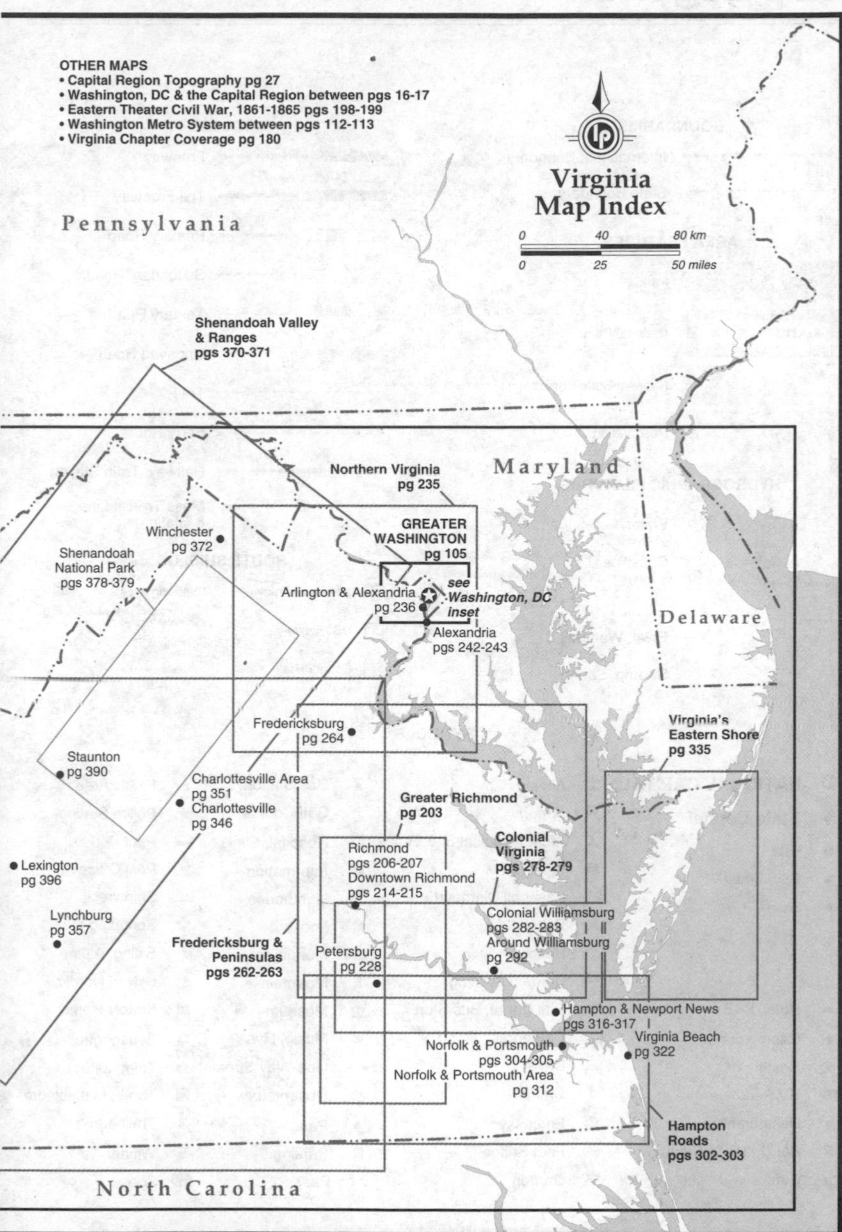

OTHER MAPS
• Capital Region Topography pg 27
• Washington, DC & the Capital Region between pgs 16-17
• Eastern Theater Civil War, 1861-1865 pgs 198-199
• Washington Metro System between pgs 112-113
• Virginia Chapter Coverage pg 180
Virginia
Map Index
0 40 80 km
0 25 50 miles
Pennsylvania
Maryland
Delaware
North Carolina
Shenandoah Valley
& Ranges
pgs 370-371
Northern Virginia
pg 235
GREATER
WASHINGTON
pg 105
Winchester
pg 372
Shenandoah
National Park
pgs 378-379
Arlington & Alexandria
pg 236
see
Washington, DC
inset
Alexandria
pgs 242-243
Fredericksburg
pg 264
Virginia's
Eastern Shore
pg 335
Staunton
pg 390
Charlottesville Area
pg 351
Charlottesville
pg 346
Greater Richmond
pg 203
Colonial
Virginia
pgs 278-279
Lexington
pg 396
Richmond
pgs 206-207
Downtown Richmond
pgs 214-215
Lynchburg
pg 357
Colonial Williamsburg
pgs 282-283
Around Williamsburg
pg 292
Fredericksburg &
Peninsulas
pgs 262-263
Petersburg
pg 228
Hampton & Newport News
pgs 316-317
Norfolk & Portsmouth
pgs 304-305
Norfolk & Portsmouth Area
pg 312
Virginia Beach
pg 322
Hampton
Roads
pgs 302-303

Map Legend

Note: Not all symbols displayed above appear in this book.

Introduction

From the Blue Ridge Mountains to the Chesapeake Tidewater, the mid-Atlantic states of Virginia, Maryland, and Delaware, along with the District of Columbia, constitute a geographically and culturally distinct region that joins the traditions of north and south. Its people are Southerners or Quakers or shrimpers, faintly Elizabethan or Appalachian or Republican, diplomats, Redskins fans, hunters, and hikers. Its history is the history of the new American nation.

Washington, DC, is today a beautiful city, studded with monuments, memorials, colossal architecture, and inviting public spaces. Its museums and galleries – most notably the always-free Smithsonian – offer unparalleled access to some of the world's best art, artifacts, and cultural touchstones. But DC is far from being solely ornamental; as a seat of global power it's always enlivened by the latest controversy or scandal. With some of the best-informed, most intelligent, opinionated, and politically savvy residents on the planet, you're never far from spirited debate on topics ranging from public policy to which Eritrean restaurant serves the best *injera* in town.

Some of the country's earliest heritage can be glimpsed in Virginia. Nearly every river landing, mountain pass, field, or town tells stories of English colonies, American independence, or the Civil War. Visit Jamestown, the first successful English settlement in the New World; the Yorktown battlefield; and Richmond, the former capital of the Confederate States of America. Travelers can tour the graceful estates of Monticello, the home of Thomas Jefferson, and Mount Vernon, George Washington's manor. Small reservations still retain some traditions of early Native American nations.

Throughout the state, from tidy lawns to wild woods, you can see the flowering landscapes for which the South is famous, hear the languid Southern dialect, and sample grits, hush puppies, collards, and pecan pie.

The Southern Appalachian traditions of the Blue Ridge Mountains in western Virginia reflect a distinct heritage. Bluegrass music fills country stores on Saturday nights, and hand-sewn quilts hang for sale from the porches of tin-roof mountaineer cabins. The Appalachian Trail is the most famous of many footpaths through beautiful backcountry, but even without leaving your car, you can take in stunning vistas along the Blue Ridge Highway and Skyline Drive.

The Chesapeake Bay defines the Tidewater region that dominates Maryland; nearly every family has a boat for exploring bay waters and its many tributaries. Visitors can easily sample the bay's bounty by ordering a plate of soft-shell crab, oysters, and Maryland rockfish. And the state's major cities are right on the bay: Baltimore offers a new waterfront development, and Annapolis, the attractive capital, is where sailors converge.

Maryland's eastern shore is dotted with old-time rural towns surprisingly unaffected by their close proximity to the urban corridor; stable communities here trace their lineage back to British, African, or Native American roots.

Delaware tops the 'Delmarva' Peninsula (portions belong to DEL-aware, MARyland, and VirginiA), offering some of the best Atlantic Coast beaches in the region, including the popular resorts at Rehoboth Beach and Fenwick Island. Northern Delaware prides itself on the 'chateau country' of the inland Brandywine Valley with its regal estates, formal gardens, and outstanding art collections.

Across the Capital Region you'll find outdoor recreation in each season, from surfing at Atlantic Coast beaches to skiing on Appalachian mountain slopes. In between, by boat or on foot, you can discover the serene tidal lowlands and lushly wooded uplands that led Captain John Smith (of Pocahontas fame) to exclaim about the region, 'Heaven and earth never agreed better to frame a place for man's habitation.' Now those were certainly romantic days, but there's plenty in the Capital Region to take you back.

MDT

Fly-fishing in western Maryland

MDT

Fells Point in Baltimore, MD

ROBERT DE GAST

Thomas Point Lighthouse in Chesapeake Bay

RICK GERHARTER

Spring on Capitol Hill, DC

ROBERT DE GAST

Nordic skiing at New Germany State Park, MD

MDT

Kite festival on the beach at Ocean City, MD

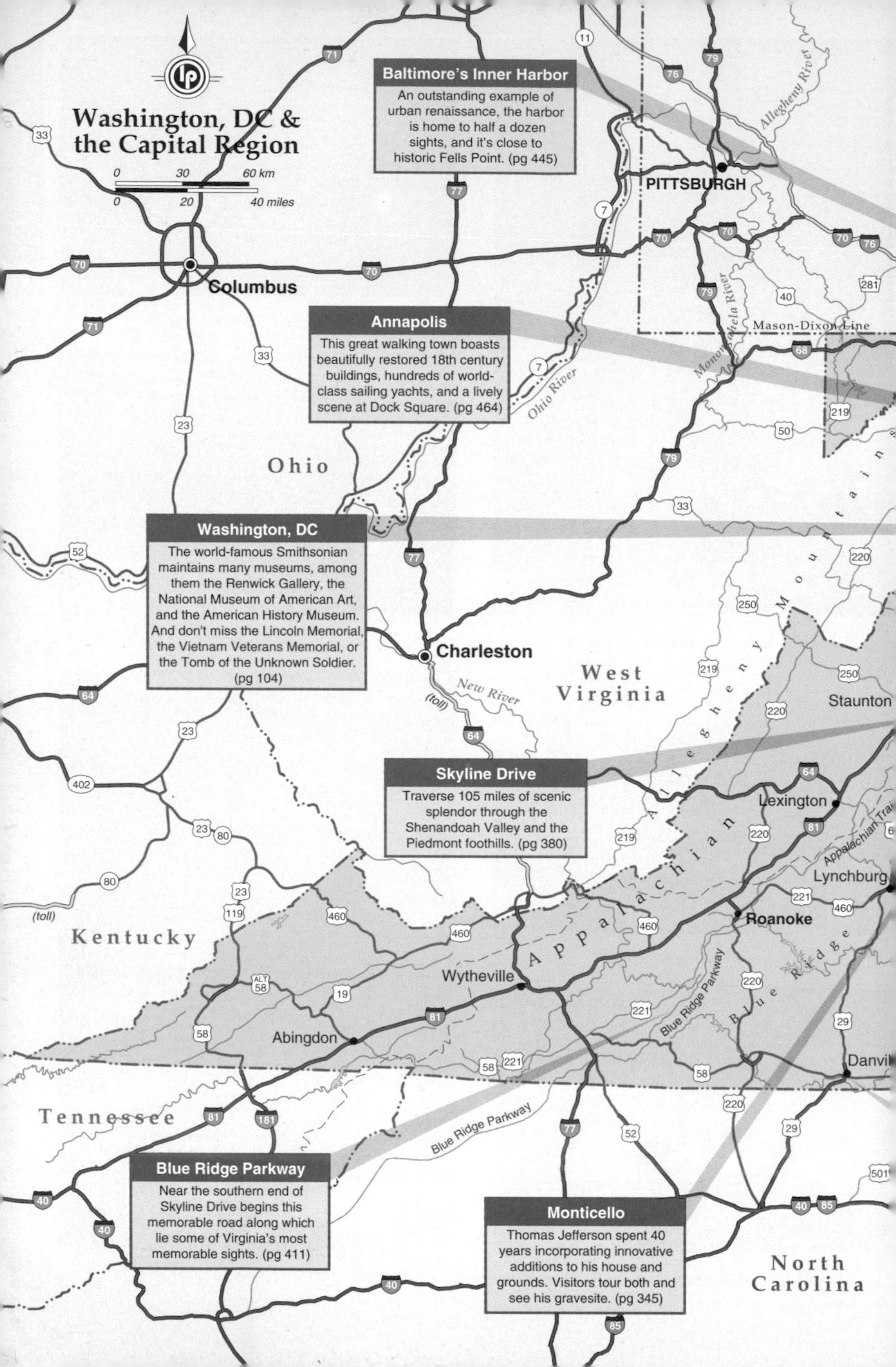

Washington, DC & the Capital Region
0 30 60 km
0 20 40 miles
Baltimore's Inner Harbor
An outstanding example of urban renaissance, the harbor is home to half a dozen sights, and it's close to historic Fells Point. (pg 445)
Annapolis
This great walking town boasts beautifully restored 18th century buildings, hundreds of world-class sailing yachts, and a lively scene at Dock Square. (pg 464)
Washington, DC
The world-famous Smithsonian maintains many museums, among them the Renwick Gallery, the National Museum of American Art, and the American History Museum. And don't miss the Lincoln Memorial, the Vietnam Veterans Memorial, or the Tomb of the Unknown Soldier. (pg 104)
Skyline Drive
Traverse 105 miles of scenic splendor through the Shenandoah Valley and the Piedmont foothills. (pg 380)
Blue Ridge Parkway
Near the southern end of Skyline Drive begins this memorable road along which lie some of Virginia's most memorable sights. (pg 411)
Monticello
Thomas Jefferson spent 40 years incorporating innovative additions to his house and grounds. Visitors tour both and see his gravesite. (pg 345)
PITTSBURGH
Columbus
Charleston
Staunton
Lexington
Lynchburg
Roanoke
Wytheville
Abingdon
Danvi
Ohio
West Virginia
Kentucky
Tennessee
North Carolina
Allegheny River
Monongahela River
Ohio River
New River
Mason-Dixon Line
Allegheny Mountains
Appalachian
Appalachian Trail
Blue Ridge
Blue Ridge Parkway
(toll)

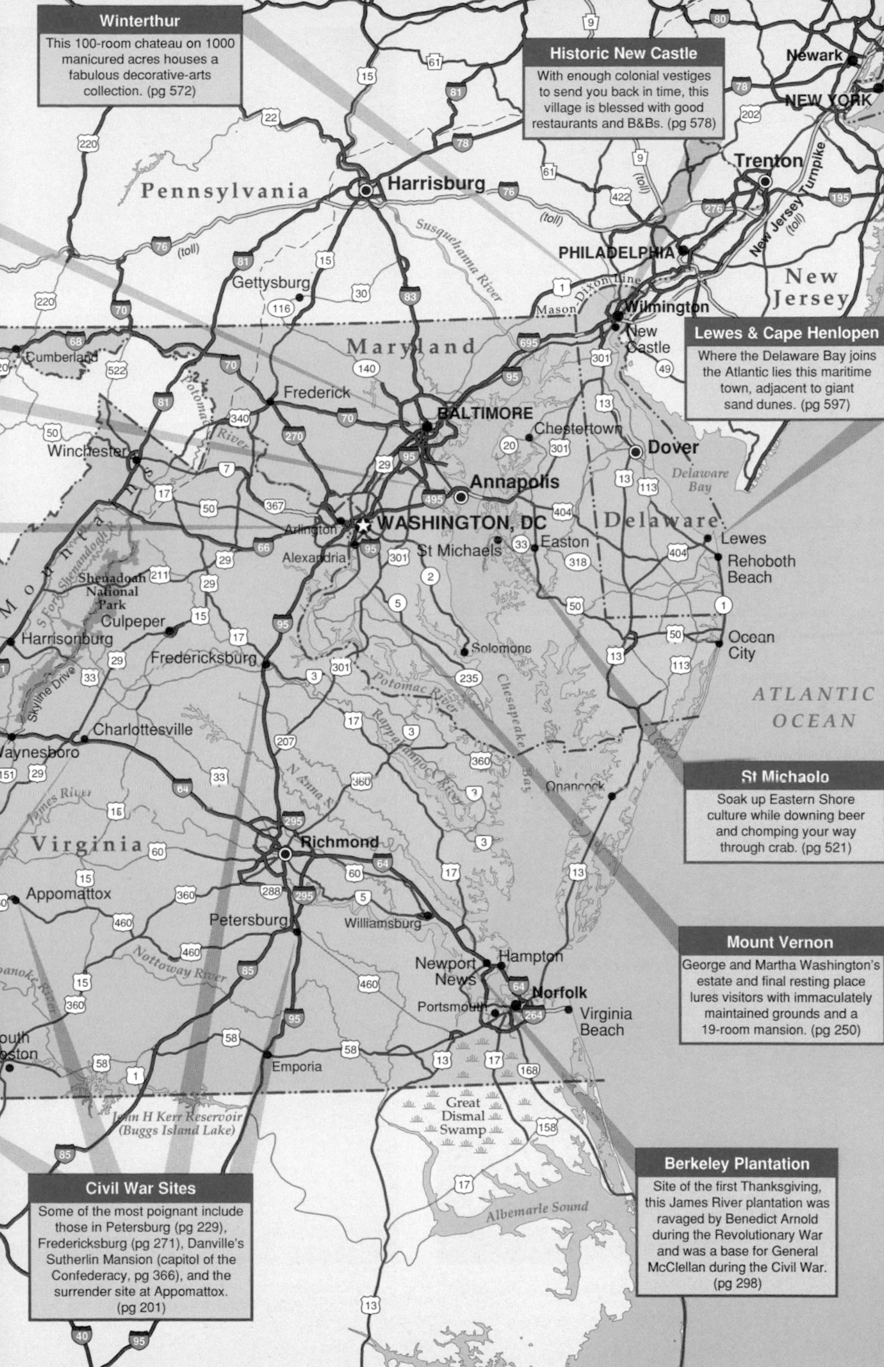
Winterthur
This 100-room chateau on 1000 manicured acres houses a fabulous decorative-arts collection. (pg 572)
Historic New Castle
With enough colonial vestiges to send you back in time, this village is blessed with good restaurants and B&Bs. (pg 578)
Lewes & Cape Henlopen
Where the Delaware Bay joins the Atlantic lies this maritime town, adjacent to giant sand dunes. (pg 597)
St Michaels
Soak up Eastern Shore culture while downing beer and chomping your way through crab. (pg 521)
Mount Vernon
George and Martha Washington's estate and final resting place lures visitors with immaculately maintained grounds and a 19-room mansion. (pg 250)
Berkeley Plantation
Site of the first Thanksgiving, this James River plantation was ravaged by Benedict Arnold during the Revolutionary War and was a base for General McClellan during the Civil War. (pg 298)
Civil War Sites
Some of the most poignant include those in Petersburg (pg 229), Fredericksburg (pg 271), Danville's Sutherlin Mansion (capitol of the Confederacy, pg 366), and the surrender site at Appomattox. (pg 201)
Pennsylvania
Harrisburg
Newark
NEW YORK
Trenton
New Jersey Turnpike (toll)
PHILADELPHIA
New Jersey
Gettysburg
Susquehanna River
Mason-Dixon line
Wilmington
New Castle
Maryland
Cumberland
Frederick
BALTIMORE
Chestertown
Dover
Delaware Bay
Annapolis
WASHINGTON, DC
Arlington
Alexandria
Delaware
St Michaels
Easton
Lewes
Rehoboth Beach
Winchester
Potomac River
Shenandoah National Park
Culpeper
Harrisonburg
Fredericksburg
Solomons
Ocean City
ATLANTIC OCEAN
Skyline Drive
Charlottesville
Waynesboro
Potomac River
Rappahannock River
Chesapeake Bay
Onancock
James River
N Anna R
Virginia
Richmond
Appomattox
Petersburg
Williamsburg
Nottoway River
Newport News
Hampton
Norfolk
Portsmouth
Virginia Beach
Emporia
Great Dismal Swamp
John H Kerr Reservoir (Buggs Island Lake)
Albemarle Sound

RICK GERHARTER

It's a long climb to the top at the Capitol.

DCCVA

The Constitution is on display at the National Archives.

DCCVA

The Jefferson Memorial honors the 3rd US President.

DCCVA

Glorious gilt on the Capitol's Rotunda

RICK GERHARTER

The West Wing of the National Gallery of Art

RICK GERHARTER

Visitors search for names on the Vietnam Veterans Memorial (Washington Monument in background).

Facts about the Capital Region

HISTORY

The Capital Region is most closely identified with the development of the United States – as numerous Revolutionary battlefields, colonial architecture, and Civil War monuments attest – yet its story started much earlier than 200-odd years ago.

Prehistory of the Americas

Nearly 20,000 years ago, when the accumulated ice of the great polar glaciers of the Pleistocene Epoch lowered sea levels throughout the world, the ancestors of Native Americans crossed from Siberia to Alaska via a land bridge across the Bering Strait. Over millennia, subsequent migrations distributed the population southward and eastward through North and Central America and down to the southern tip of South America.

Native Peoples

The first inhabitants of North America were nomadic hunter-gatherers who lived in small bands. Some of the earliest evidence of human habitation on the continent – dating back as much as 11,500 years – was unearthed in the Capital Region. At the Williamson site in southern Virginia (just north of the North Carolina border), archaeologists found a variety of tools used to shape projectile points, indispensable weapons against such ancient large game as mammoth and bison, which were present in the Paleo-Indian period. Researchers also concluded that in addition to large game such early communities relied heavily on small game and vegetable foods, and that they held some notion of an afterlife – but without strong evidence these claims remain speculative.

Further south the development of pottery around 8000 BC is often considered a hallmark of the Archaic period that followed, but mid-Atlantic region inhabitants continued through this period to shape containers out of steatite (soapstone). This soft, easily worked mineral is readily found in the region – in fact, one soapstone quarry can be seen right in Washington, DC's northwest district in Soapstone Valley Park. During this time increased efficiency in hunting and gathering techniques enabled Archaic communities to pursue more than subsistence tasks, and adornments and ritual objects began to appear.

Around 1000 BC, a transition period occurred during which woodland hunting and gathering traditions grew, supported by the rudiments of agriculture. Nuts and seeds were among the first foods to be collected and cultivated, and for the first time they were stored in underground pits for later use. Along with such developments, settlements grew more sedentary, and communities constructed relatively permanent housing and discovered the utility of banding together in organized chiefdoms.

These were the prehistoric antecedents to the Native American nations of the modern period. The mid Atlantic region became the southernmost territory of the great Algonquin Nation that stretched north to New England along the Eastern Seaboard. The Iroquois Nation presided over areas farther inland. When survivors of smaller bands in the region fled the decimation wrought by European-borne diseases, the Iroquois Nation absorbed many and grew in strength and number. Fear of the stronger Iroquois may have been a compelling factor in forcing the Algonquin tribes into later alliances with the arriving English.

At the time of European contact, many native peoples lived at the water's edge around cornfields and gardens of squash, beans, and potatoes – as they had for many centuries. Villages consisted of longhouses constructed from bent branches and woven grass mats, and these tribes depended heavily on fish and shellfish for their diet. They dressed in deerskin decorated with seashells, bones, porcupine quills, and paint, and used paints and tattoos to decorate their skin. For religious rituals they wore headdresses made of snakeskin stuffed with grass and shook hollow gourds filled with pebbles. They called their god Okewas and for generations prophesied that strangers from across the sea would come and destroy their people.

Captain John Smith was the first European to reach the navigable head of the Potomac River (a name derived from the Algonquian word meaning variously 'place to which tribute is brought' or 'trading place'). The hostile reception Smith received, his subsequent capture, and ultimate rescue by Pocahontas (daughter of the tribal leader Powhatan) is today a favorite American legend.

Early Exploration

The Chesapeake Bay found its way onto the map of European exploration six years after Christopher Columbus landed at San Salvador. Englishman John Cabot sailed past the Virginia capes in 1498 as he searched for the fabled Northwest Passage. That same year Italian Amerigo Vespucci sailed northward on his own mapping expedition.

During the next century dozens of other European expeditions (mostly Spanish) passed the entrance to Chesapeake Bay as they followed the trade winds along the Gulf Stream up the North American coast and back to Europe. In some of these mariners' accounts, they called this great inland sea the 'Madre de Aguas' (Mother of Waters), which some historians believe is a corruption of the Algonquian words for the region, possibly 'Chesupioca' or 'Chissapiacke,' which translates as 'great saltwater' or 'country on a great river.' But in spite of regular visits to the great estuary, no serious efforts to colonize the area occurred until 1585, when the English adventurer Sir Walter Raleigh established his famous lost colony of Roanoke just south of the Chesapeake in modern North Carolina. Although the colony vanished within a year (probably due to Native American attacks), Raleigh's name for the region stuck. He called this tidewater region 'Virginia' for Queen Elizabeth, the virgin queen, and England eventually called all its Eastern Seaboard territory by that name. From that expanse England would carve smaller colonies such as Maryland and Delaware, and the area known as Virginia would shrink.

First Colonies

During the European Age of Exploration (the 16th and 17th centuries), the nations of Western Europe subscribed to the political-economic philosophy of 'mercantilism.' Mercantilists believed that the nations of the world were in unstoppable struggle to define and assert their national identities at the expense of rival nations. A nation furthered its interests by creating a network of economically dependent colonies that might supplement the national treasury, industry, army, and navy.

Portugal and Holland took a strong early lead by establishing trading colonies in Africa and the East Indies, but after Columbus' discovery of America, Spain hit pay dirt by wresting gold and silver mines from the native peoples of Mexico and South America. Fear of Spain's potential domination of the world spurred northern European countries like France, Holland, England, and Sweden to redouble their efforts at colonizing the New World. Everybody wanted a piece of El Dorado (the fabled city of gold).

On April 10, 1606, King James I granted the Virginia Company the right to establish settlements of English colonists in America. The Virginia Company comprised two subgroups: the London and Plymouth Companies. The London Company was allowed to colonize the southern half of the grant, and the Plymouth Company the northern half. A number of other conditions applied. Provisions were made for a president to be elected annually and for a constitution by which the settlers and their children 'would forever . . . enjoy all liberties, franchises and immunities enjoyed by Englishmen in England.'

Sir Thomas Smith, treasurer of the London Company, supervised arrangements for the colonization. Led by Christopher Newport, 104 English colonists sailed for America and arrived at Cape Henry (near modern-day Virginia Beach) on April 26, 1607, after a four-month voyage on three small ships *(Susan Constant, Godspeed* and *Discovery).* After an initial exploration of Chesapeake Bay, Newport and his colonists entered the James River and on May 14 founded Jamestown, the first permanent English settlement in America (named after England's king). Although the stockholders, as well as some of the 100 men who sailed with Newport, claimed to be on a mission to deter Spanish and Roman Catholic domination of the New World, the men of the Virginia Company hoped that the Jamestown venture would make them all rich.

Newport left his colonists at Jamestown and returned to England, and at first, the colonists were sorely disappointed. Life went badly at Jamestown for a multitude of reasons, chief among them the 'entitled' attitude of the colonists. More than a third of the original settlers, and an even greater number of subsequent arrivals, were gentry; most of the other colonists were personal servants to the gentry. Local tribes under the powerful chief Powhatan warned the colonists they would need to plant corn to sustain them through the cold months when hunting and fishing were difficult, but few of the colonists had the inclination or skill to plant, tend, and harvest corn. The Jamestown colony verged on starvation many winters.

Instead of planting corn, colonists like the legendary Captain John Smith fussed about in boats looking for gold, silver, and the Northwest Passage and antagonized the Chesapeake's Native Americans until a state of regular guerrilla skirmishing defined the relationship between the two camps. By the time Newport returned to the colony on January 12, 1608, only 38 of the 100 colonists remained. One of these was John Smith, who became president of the colony in 1608. The following year the newly incorporated London Company expanded to include even more territory. The charter fixed the boundaries of Virginia at 200 miles north and 200 miles south of Old Point Comfort, and west and northwest from sea to sea. Additionally, government was now vested in the treasurer and council of the company in London.

On July 30, 1619, the first representative assembly in the New World, the House of Burgesses, was elected by free colonists. The king revoked the London Company's charter and Virginia became a royal colony – England's first – in 1624.

Low on funds and without direction and initiative, the Jamestown colony verged on collapse, when John Rolfe, who had married Powhatan's famous daughter Pocahontas, discovered that this weed his father-in-law dried and smoked held an addictive charm for European libertines looking for a new thrill.

Tobacco – the 'Sot Weed' Factor

Rolfe received news with the arrival of trading ships that showed up every spring to resupply the rum lockers of the Jamestown gentry. He learned that the British were paying big money for tobacco that the ship captains purchased from West Indian planters who could only supply small quantities. The captains encouraged Rolfe to supply some native weed for the folks back home, but the quality of the local variety did not meet the standards of Europe's growing legion of 'sot weed' connoisseurs. Rolfe obtained seeds of the preferred West Indies plants and planted them in the rich tidewater soil. Voilà! Good smoke.

Suddenly, ship captains were begging Virginians to plant the sot weed and paying three shillings a pound. While tobacco profits couldn't meet the expectations of gold-hungry investors, a man who tended 1000 tobacco plants a year might get rich. He might even get rich in a hurry if he could locate cheap labor; once a planter drove off the Indians, the land for tobacco plantations was limitless, but the labor supply was not.

The population of the colony amounted to some 4000, including indentured servants, apprentices, and a handful of petty criminals dispatched by an increasingly hostile king.

Colonists sent to England offered to pay passage for anyone willing to work on a tobacco plantation for some years (typically five to seven) in exchange for room and board. After working the contracted years, the indentured servant gained his freedom and received a parcel of land to grow corn and tobacco. Tobacco plantations began spreading all along the shores of the southern Chesapeake and its tributaries. Thousands left England for Virginia seeking fortune and a new life, however the influx of people did not meet the demand for plantation labor.

Slavery

In the early colonial period, Europeans tried enslaving Indians as a cheap source of labor, but many escaped back into familiar terrain. Indentured servants were then lured from Europe and after serving their time, they easily blended into the colonist population.

In 1619 a Dutch merchant ship sailed to Jamestown with a load of indentured English servants to 'sell' to local plantation owners striving to produce more tobacco. On board the ship were 20 Africans the captain had picked up in his travels, and the Virginians bought these Africans as indentured servants, too. The Africans found it nearly impossible to escape their servitude due to their distinctive appearance and unfamiliarity with local languages and

The Slave Trade

The gruesome slave trade that brought over millions of Africans (estimates vary from at least 10 million to upwards of 20 million) to the New World (South America, the Caribbean, and North America) reached its height in the 18th century; yet its legacy continues to shape (and haunt) contemporary society throughout the Americas.

From the 1400s to the 1800s, the slave trade operated from Africa's west coast in the region stretching from Senegal to Angola, principally the central 'Gold Coast' region (now Ghana, Togo, Benin, and Nigeria). At first, captives were largely prisoners of local wars sold by the chieftains of victorious tribes. Later, as demand soared, raiders throughout West Africa kidnapped men, women, and children, and drove them to the coast, where they were held in stockades before being loaded onto ships bound for the Americas. An overwhelming number – 95% – were brought to the Caribbean and Central and South America; the remaining 5% arrived in North America.

During the 'Middle Passage' across the Atlantic, captives were packed shoulder-to-shoulder in inhumane and unsanitary conditions for six to 12 weeks before reaching shore. One-third of the captives did not survive the ordeal (sharks commonly followed slave ships in anticipation of the bodies thrown overboard). The ones who did endure were fattened as they reached port and oiled upon arrival to appear healthy for auction.

In addition to having their labor exploited, most basic human liberties were also denied. In the American South, clans and families were separated, slave marriages were not recognized, and women were routinely exploited sexually. African culture was likewise suppressed: Any expression of African languages, religious worship, and cultural rituals were strictly prohibited. It was a crime to teach a slave to read. Though some slaves rose in stature by learning trades or becoming house servants, the great majority were field workers whose legal status was roughly equivalent to that of domestic animals.

It would take centuries and the costliest war the country has ever fought before slavery was abolished in the US. One century later full civil rights for the descendants of slaves were legally affirmed. But it may take a century more before the crippling consequences of slavery are fully overcome. ■

terrain, and planters soon surmised they could be ruthlessly exploited beyond the years of their servitude. As oversupply of tobacco began to lower prices and cut into profits, ruthless planters conspired to keep servants in bondage.

From here the transition to outright slavery was swift; the first laws addressing slave labor appeared in 1662. In the following decades, tens of thousands of Africans were captured, deported, and enslaved to fuel the ambitions of colonial planters. This practice continued unabated over the next century, and Africans soon made up half the colonial population.

Because slaves were expensive – a skilled worker might cost more than a prized racehorse in a farming community where few even owned mules – slave owning was beyond the reach of the great majority of Southern farmers. The overwhelming number of farms – over two-thirds – held no slaves. Of those that held slaves, the greatest proportion held only one slave. The popular image of huge plantations with hundreds of slaves (such as in *Gone With the Wind)* actually accounted for only a small number of Southern farms. Yet enriched by slave labor, this elite ruling class dominated the economy, society, and political life of the South far out of proportion to their number.

Lord Baltimore & the Religious Idealists

Not every European who came to the Chesapeake in the early 1600s came specifically for profit. In 1634 George Calvert (Lord Baltimore), having received a grant from the king for vast lands in northern Virginia, encouraged his brother Leonard Calvert to gather a group of religiously tolerant families to start a society founded on religious freedom in the New World. No doubt Baltimore saw the potential for profits in such a colony, but having suffered religious persecution in England because of his Roman Catholic faith, Baltimore also saw that his royal grant and wealth gave him the opportunity to establish a utopian community free from the persecution and prejudice common in England.

In 1634 Leonard Calvert and about 200 religious idealists – Catholics, Puritans, and Anglicans – sailed up the Chesapeake to an island they called St Clements. They prayed and negotiated with local Native Americans to occupy a great hill overlooking the horseshoe bend in a tributary of the Potomac River. They called this settlement St Mary's City and immediately set about putting their religious tolerance into practice and law. They also cleared the land and planted corn and tobacco. Calvert named the new colony 'Maryland' after Queen Henrietta Maria, wife of King Charles I. It wasn't long before more shiploads of immigrants came to this colony on the Chesapeake north of the Potomac River to pursue religious freedom and plant the sot weed. Slave traders came, too, and trade was brisk in agricultural boom towns like Port Tobacco, Oxford, and Annapolis.

The Dutch & the Swedes

Not to be outdone by the British colonial initiatives, the Dutch and the Swedes sent mapmakers and colonists to North America as well, and they too focused on the area of the mid-Atlantic coast that the English called Virginia. Sailing under the Dutch flag, Henry Hudson reached the mouth of Delaware Bay, a hundred miles north of the Virginia capes, in 1609 while scouting New World territory for Holland. Finding the bay shallow and rough, Hudson sailed northeast and found the river that today bears his name. It proved a more welcoming place to begin the colony of New Amsterdam, but destiny was to bring the Dutch back to Delaware 45 years later.

In 1610 Captain Samuel Argall, sailing aboard the pinnace *Discovery* from the Jamestown colony, anchored in Delaware Bay and named it for the governor of Virginia, Lord De La Warre. But the English did not return here for years. In 1631, 28 Dutch whalers built a fishing colony in the lee of Cape Henlopen and named the place Zwaanendael. Less than a year passed before the Dutch quarreled with the local

Nanticokes, who killed the intruders and scattered the bones of the men and their cattle over present-day Lewes.

In 1638 a shipload of Swedes braved the Delaware and built Fort Christina at the site of today's Wilmington. They claimed an area that stretched from south of Wilmington to near Philadelphia as 'New Sweden' with 1000 Swedish and Finnish colonists (their remarkable 400-pound governor Johan Prinz was known as the 'Big Tub'). Accomplished farmers and millers, they found the northern shores of the Delaware Bay/River a good place to grow grains that they could process at water-driven mills along the swift-flowing Brandywine Creek.

In 1655 jealousy of the Swedish colony on the Delaware reached its peak among the Dutch at New Amsterdam. They charged up Delaware Bay with ships and armed men under the direction of Peter Stuyvesant and intimidated the Swedes into surrender. A few years later, a British naval vessel sailed within firing range of the Dutch settlement at Fort Casimir (later New Castle); the Dutch surrendered without a fight. Now the shores of a second great bay along America's mid-Atlantic coast were under English control. The English did not drive out the earlier settlers; they simply absorbed them and made them pay taxes. The proud settlers, Swedes and Dutch alike, consoled themselves with the conviction that the British were just another wave of brash immigrants who had yet to prove themselves.

New English immigrants arrived and began clearing plantations south of the old Swedish/Dutch colonies on the Delmarva Peninsula. The English tried raising tobacco, and they introduced slavery. British kings and politicians, watching from afar, thought the time had come for the so-called Tidewater colonies to begin carrying the mother country toward a position of wealth and power on the world stage.

Early Rebellions

Relations between the New World colonies and England became strained under the political troubles and turmoil in the motherland. When the government of Oliver Cromwell replaced the monarchy of Charles I at the end of the Great Rebellion of England, the colony of Virginia mounted a very brief resistance. That was soon put down when in 1652 a fleet was sent to quell any trouble. The House of Burgesses played a major role in the development of the colony, and on occasion exercised its independent streak – they determined that it was the colony, and not Britain, that had the right to elect its own officers.

When the Commonwealth collapsed in England, Sir William Berkeley was elected governor of the colony of Virginia. After being crowned, Charles II introduced the burdensome Navigation Acts, encouraged the slave trade, and showed considerable favoritism in the form of large land grants to his cronies. In addition, Governor Berkeley refused to dispatch soldiers to protect the colony's frontier from Indians, and the Virginia government was controlled by a privileged few who levied intolerable export duties. The right to vote was determined by a property qualification.

All this led to a popular uprising of Virginian farmers, servants, and slaves spearheaded by Nathaniel Bacon, a plantation owner and democratic member of the Governor's Council who had arrived in the colony in 1673. At first the rag-tag army of 300 marched against the Indians on the frontier. The defeat of the Indians was inspirational to the whole colony. As a result Berkeley was forced to dissolve the Virginia Assembly (the colony's elected body) and order a new election. Bacon was arrested, released on parole, and then offered a commission which he didn't receive until his army occupied Jamestown, the colony's capital.

While Bacon was marching against the Indians once more and about to participate in the Battle of Bloody Run, Berkeley was raising a force against him. Bacon marched on Jamestown again and on September 19, 1676, he captured and torched it. Bacon's rebellion collapsed a month later with his untimely death from malaria just as his force was marching to meet Berkeley's forces.

With no leader to rally the opposition forces, Berkeley regained power and his revenge was swift. He executed 23 rebels, an act that drew this remark from the king: 'That old fool has hanged more men in the naked country than I have done for the murder of my father.' Charles recalled the governor, but Berkeley died before he felt the king's wrath. Many historians see Bacon's rebellion as the forerunner of the American Revolution.

Following Bacon's Rebellion, Virginia became a channel of expansion into the 'wilderness' – the region beyond the Blue Ridge Mountains – and even as far as the Ohio Valley.

Colonial Struggles

In addition to political squabbles, the Tidewater colonies were also subject to the economic troubles rooted in the overproduction and falling prices of tobacco. Throughout the region more and larger plantations competed for decreasing tobacco profits. England exacerbated the situation by requiring the colonies to sell their tobacco to the mother country and pay import duties on crops. These economic problems led to a series of confrontations between Marylanders and Virginians, Puritans and Catholics, planters and laborers, Indians and Europeans.

One major border dispute erupted after William Penn won his grant to Pennsylvania north of Maryland in 1681. The debate between Maryland and Pennsylvania over territory grew so heated that in 1763 the Crown called in the famous English astronomers Mason and Dixon to settle the conflict. The resulting border – the Mason-Dixon Line – has been popularly considered the dividing line between North and South in the US ever since. (This notion would later be reinforced by the Missouri Compromise, which used the line to divide slaveholding states from free states.) Mason and Dixon also established firm borders for Delaware. Maryland had wanted to annex Delaware, but Delaware's citizens had enjoyed basic autonomy under William Penn's aegis for more than half a century and wished to be fully independent.

In spite of the economic and regional problems, locally colonists tried to transform their frontier culture into a civilized society that mirrored England's. The colonies established assembly-style governments (with an appointed governor, an appointed chamber of deputies and an elected representative assembly), a vigorous constable/magistrate system to uphold the laws, strong churches, and rigorous schools/colleges. Health conditions in the colonies improved, longevity increased, and the population of the colonies reached over one million before the start of the 18th century.

In 1699, the Virginia capital was moved from Jamestown to Middle Plantation (now Williamsburg) after a major fire (and also because the new site was far more suitable). For the next 70 years the colony prospered with the capital as its social and cultural hub. The number of slaveholding plantations increased.

Prelude to Revolution

As a second century of English colonization began, many planters in Maryland and Delaware reacted to the diminishing returns on tobacco by converting their farms to the production of corn and wheat. They also planted orchards and financed their own merchant fleets in order to overcome their dependence on European and New England shippers. However, England continued to retard the growth of an American infrastructure by prohibiting the use of gold and silver money in the colonies and reducing colonial businesses to barter or trade in paper script of questionable value.

To the north the French alliance with the native Huron and Algonquin peoples and its fur-trading empire (extending from eastern Canada south to the valley of the northern Ohio River) led France and Britain into four wars between 1689 and 1764. The last of these wars, called the 'French and Indian War' in America and

'King George's War' in England, erupted in 1754 and lasted nine years, during which the colonists assisted the British. The French were establishing outposts in the Ohio Valley when a small force led by young George Washington was dispatched by the governor of Virginia to warn the French to keep off British claims. In the first clash of the war in July 1754, Washington surrendered Fort Necessity in western Pennsylvania. When the British commander Edward Braddock was defeated at Fort Duquesne in 1755, Washington was appointed commander of Virginia's army on the frontier, which the colonial army successfully defended. The colony had found in Washington an able commander, and the colonial forces had proved themselves in the campaigns with minimal help from the British.

During this time, English colonists and militia, some under the leadership of young George Washington, fought protracted battles in the Appalachian Mountains north and west of Maryland against Native Americans organized and armed by the King of France. Britain finally prevailed when General James Wolfe captured Quebec in 1759. But when the war ended in 1763, England found itself nearly bankrupt from the fighting.

The war and the terror it had inspired did a lot to realign Americans' patriotism with Britain, but Britain, which had dug deep into the colonial coffers to support their war against the French, was desperate to replenish the national treasury, and did so with a series of new taxes that undercut the colonists' patriotism. And in a time of economic hardship, the British Parliament set about to enforce the old Navigation Acts, which restricted colonies in their trade with other nations.

In the course of the next 18 years, the British government imposed new taxes on imports to America on everything from sugar to tea. In 1765 the British Parliament passed the Stamp Act to defray the costs of maintaining a British defense force in the colonies. This revenue-raising measure required that just about all paper documents issued in the colony had to bear stamps sold by the British. Protest against this act, seen as a form of 'taxation without representation,' was almost instantaneous. In Virginia, Patrick Henry delivered his 'If this be treason, make the most of it' speech, inspiring the General Assembly to oppose many provisions of the act. The Virginia Resolves stated emphatically that Virginians could only be taxed by their own legislature.

Yielding not so much to the colonists but to the demands of their own merchants, the British repealed the act in 1766. The Crown continued to legislate for the colonies, however, and in 1767 passed the Townshend Acts, another revenue-raising measure that included the abhorred tax on tea. Colonists protested against 'taxation without representation,' but the English government did not listen. King George III simply ordered his governors to grow more persistent in collecting the taxes and sent more companies of armed British 'Red Coats' to stand as visible reminders of the royal authority.

The American Revolution

By 1773 the colonists had had enough. To protest English taxes on American imports, they threw a shipload of English tea into Boston Harbor. After word reached Maryland that Bostonians had filled their harbor with British tea, Marylanders staged 'tea parties' of their own in 1774 when they burned the tea ship *Peggy Ann* in Annapolis and ransacked another tea ship in Chestertown.

In subsequent revolutionary events, Virginia played a pivotal role. In 1774 the British Parliament passed a series of laws aimed at punishing the people of Massachusetts for their defiance. These restrictive measures, known as the Coercive or Intolerable Acts, aroused the sympathy of the other colonies, and at a revolutionary convention held at Raleigh Tavern in Williamsburg in 1774, Virginia called for a meeting of the thirteen colonies (and Canada) to discuss the issue of colonial rights. (The Virginia legislature had previously been dissolved by the Governor Dunmore, who was infuriated by the continuous revolutionary utterances from the House of Burgesses.)

In response to Virginia's call, representatives of the colonies met at the First Continental Congress in Philadelphia in September 1774. In attendance was Virginia's Richard Henry Lee, Patrick Henry, George Washington, and four others – all representatives of the former Virginia legislature. The delegates to the First Congress petitioned King George III to ensure that their rights as Englishmen be maintained and they also resolved to meet again in May 1775.

A second revolutionary convention met in Richmond, Virginia, in March 1775. At this gathering Patrick Henry delivered a fiery speech to give impetus to the arming of a colonial militia. He concluded with the now famous words: 'Is life so dear or peace so sweet as to be purchased at the price of chains and slavery? Forbid it, Almighty God! I know not what course others may take, but, as for me, give me liberty or give me death!' A committee, headed by Henry, was established to prepare Virginia's military defense.

Less than a month after Patrick Henry uttered these words, the war had commenced in Massachusetts. In mid-April 1775 the British moved to prevent the colonial militia from stockpiling munitions at Concord, 18 miles from Boston. The British advance guard bumped into the militia at Lexington on April 19 and eight Americans were killed. At Concord, the militia ('minutemen'), alerted by mounted messengers such as Paul Revere, resisted and turned the British advance into retreat. The Americans, joined by more militia forces, pursued and boxed up the British force in Boston, where it remained until being evacuated in March 1776.

In Virginia, committees of safety were hurriedly organized and militias formed. In April 1775, Dunmore, Virginia's royal governor, seized the colonial powder supply in Williamsburg and transferred part of it to the warship *Magdalen*. After a near riot in the Virginia legislature, Dunmore fled to the awaiting man-of-war *Fowey* anchored in Chesapeake Bay. The burgesses saw his flight as a virtual abdication and with him went the last royal government in Virginia.

On May 10, the Second Continental Congress met in Philadelphia as planned. Now the colonies were engaged in war and the deliberations of the congress reflected the new crisis. The congress proclaimed itself the government of the 'United Colonies of America'; heightened the conflict in the vicinity of Boston by adopting the colonial forces as the 'Continental Army'; and unanimously chose Washington as commander-in-chief.

By the end of 1775, Maryland had a militia of well-disciplined soldiers called the Old Line (earning Maryland the nickname 'The Old Line State') fighting alongside other patriots in northern colonies. In addition, more than 250 privateers sailed from Chesapeake ports to cripple British shipping.

Divided under William Penn into the three counties of New Castle (north), Kent (central), and Sussex (south), with a colonial assembly separate from Pennsylvania, Delaware joined the other American colonies in revolution against England in 1776. In September 1777 the British under General Howe sailed up the Chesapeake, invaded Delaware, and marched across the state on their way to attack Philadelphia. The British met a band of American patriots south of Newark at Cooch's Bridge, where they skirmished on September 3. Forty Delaware men fell dead before the Delaware forces retreated, and the British pressed forward into Pennsylvania. Eight days later the British went on to defeat General George Washington at the Battle of Brandywine just across the Pennsylvania border. On September 12 the English returned to Delaware and occupied Wilmington.

British naval ships patrolled the Delaware Bay and River, making the rebellious colony vulnerable to attack at any time. Tory sympathizers (colonists who supported British rule) in New Castle County systematically raided the farms of those who favored independence. Because of these threats, Delaware moved its capital away from riverside New Castle to safer, southern, inland Dover in Kent County. No further revolutionary battles took place in Delaware, but Delaware's renowned 'Blue Hens' (so called for the fighting cocks they kept for entertainment) won distinction on the front lines throughout the war and hundreds of Delaware's young men died for the cause of freedom.

Virginia did not see Revolutionary War fighting until the war's closing stages – ultimately Richmond was attacked three times and Yorktown was laid under siege. More important than combat on Virginia soil was the intellectual impetus – the 'brain power' – provided by many of its great thinkers, who articulated the rationale behind the revolution and spurred the militias on.

The Declaration of Independence

In June 1776, the Virginia Convention met in Williamsburg to discuss issues for the next Continental Congress. The intellectuals had been hard at work and the first fruits of their labor were seen in the work of George Mason. His revolutionary Virginia Declaration of Rights (later described as the embryonic 'Bill of Rights') was adopted, and Virginia's representatives to the next Continental Congress were told to forward it as a proposal for independence. In his Declaration Mason proposed that 'all men are created free and independent, and have certain inherent rights' that include 'the enjoyment of life and liberty, and the means of acquiring and possessing property' (as well as a number of other now accepted freedoms).

Thomas Jefferson then went to work, and with enhancements to Mason's Declaration, produced the Declaration of Independence. While a British expeditionary force hovered off the American coast, the Continental Congress, again meeting in Philadelphia, adopted on July 4, 1776, a Declaration of Independence emphasizing that the colonies 'are of right and ought to be free and independent states.'

Thomas Jefferson

France, which had been secretly supporting the revolutionary cause since the beginning of the war, openly recognized the independence of the colonies in February 1778. The way was now clear for the French to provide Washington with naval support off the American coast, but the much needed assistance did not materialize until 1781 when the French fleet of Admiral de Grasse combined with Washington's Continental Army to lay siege to Yorktown. On October 19, Lord Cornwallis' army, which constituted a third of the British troops in America at the time, surrendered (see the Yorktown Campaign sidebar in the Colonial Virginia chapter).

Hostilities on American soil were effectively over, but it was not until the signing of the Treaty of Paris in September 1783, that the British finally accepted the independence of its old colonies, now known as the United States of America. Washington, wishing at that stage to retire quietly from public office, resigned as commander-in-chief in December – but in April

1789 this Virginian was later persuaded to be the first president of the new democracy. (See the introductions to the state chapters for history beyond the signing of the Constitution.)

GEOGRAPHY

The contour of the Capital Region slopes downward from the rounded summits of the Appalachian Mountains in the west, to the central Piedmont Plateau, to the flat Coastal Plain region of tidewater and beach at the Atlantic Coast.

Appalachian Mountains

The Appalachian Mountains run along the Eastern Seaboard from Maine to Alabama. Historically, the mountains served as a wilderness frontier, and even today, while threatened by increasing encroachment, the range maintains a wild spirit despite its proximity to one of the most densely populated urban corridors in the US.

In the Capital Region, the Southern Appalachians consist of three geological provinces. The first, or front range, is the famed Blue Ridge Mountains, a region of legendary beauty and rich folk history and heritage. This land of forested coves, rounded summits, and waterfalls can be easily seen on a scenic drive along the Blue Ridge Parkway and Skyline Drive, or explored on foot. One of the most popular trails is the Appalachian Trail, the 2086-mile route along the spine of the Appalachians that runs through Virginia and Maryland (the Trail Conference Headquarters is located in Harpers Ferry, at the juncture of West Virginia, Virginia, and Maryland – see the Activities chapter for headquarters information).

To the west is the Ridge-and-Valley province, a fertile belt between the Blue Ridge and the Allegheny Mountains. In Virginia, this lush region holds the celebrated and historic Shenandoah Valley.

Piedmont Plateau

The Piedmont Plateau, named by early settlers who likened it to the 'foot of the mountain' regions of southern Europe, is a large undulating plateau that holds most of the urban development along the Eastern Seaboard. It is separated from the lower Coastal Plain region by the 'fall line,' the point at which mountain rivers drop from

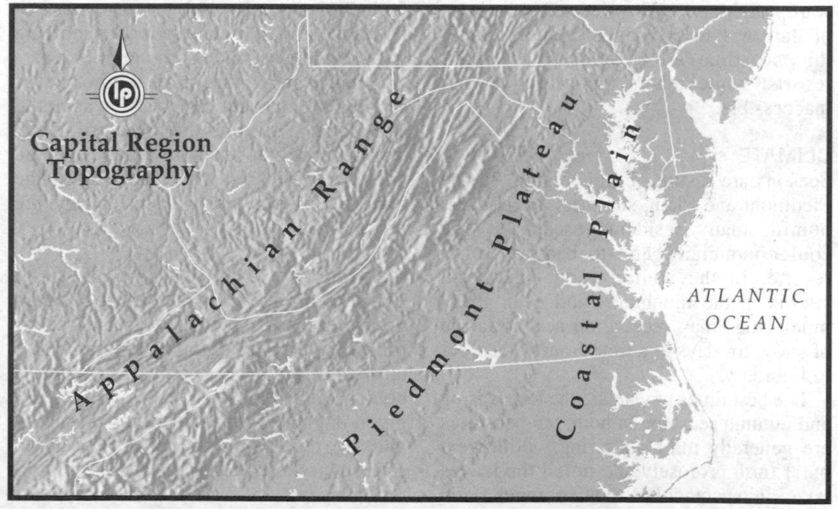

the plateau to the plain in a series of waterfalls, beyond which they are easily navigable to the Atlantic Ocean. This convenient access to both the interior and sea attracted humans from the earliest Paleo-Indian settlements on. Today the plateau is home to the region's biggest cities – including Richmond, Washington, DC, and Baltimore.

Coastal Plain

The low, flat, hundred-mile-wide Coastal Plain of the Capital Region lies between the fall line and the Atlantic Coast. The plain is dotted with marshy wetlands. The best of these, the Great Dismal Swamp in Virginia's southeast corner, is a national wildlife refuge harboring an impressive variety of wildlife, particularly birds. Yet this mid-Atlantic region of the Plain is most dominated by the ecology and riparian history of its two famous bays, the Chesapeake and the Delaware.

The Chesapeake Bay, more accurately described as an estuary (where saltwater and freshwater mix), is in a long, wide delta of 48 navigable rivers and countless smaller streams that create an area known ecologically and culturally as the Tidewater.

The Atlantic Coast in Virginia, Delaware, and Maryland is protected by a series of narrow barrier islands. Some parts of this coastline are developed as beach resorts, while others are primitive and inaccessible.

CLIMATE

Seasons are distinct in this region. In the Piedmont and Plain, summers are hot and humid; many residents escape to the cooler mountains and to beaches for a respite. In the winter, snow opens ski resorts in the mountains and even Piedmont cities may receive an accumulation of snow for days at a time from December to February.

The best times to visit are the long spring and autumn seasons. In both, temperatures are generally mild; in spring wildflowers burst forth profusely and in fall the leaves take on spectacular reds, oranges, and yellows. Expect rain in the spring, and days that vary from hot one day to frosty the next. The early fall is more consistently dry, and warm summer temperatures linger long into mid-October.

Washington, DC

The most comfortable times are in spring and fall. Summers are hot and humid (oppressively hot midday in July and August) with warm summer nights. Enough snow falls in winter to collect on the ground for days at a time, mostly from December to February.

Virginia

Virginia experiences four very distinct seasons. The climate is characterized by warm, humid summers (except in the mountainous regions) and mild winters. Spring and autumn are relatively long and pleasant. In winter, snowfall, which rarely stays on the ground for long, ranges from about 10 inches at the coast to 30 inches in the western mountains (the state average is 18 inches).

Richmond experiences measured precipitation some 115 days per year, Norfolk 116, and Roanoke 121 days. General precipitation is variable, ranging from 36 to 50 inches annually (with a state average of 46 inches), with by far the most occurring in the southwest and south-central areas.

Even though Virginia's highest-ever recorded temperature of 110°F was noted at Balcony Falls and the lowest of -29°F was recorded at Monterey, the expected annual range is no where near that. The lowest temperatures occur in January, the highest in July.

Maryland

The Chesapeake Bay and Atlantic Ocean give the eastern part of Maryland fairly mild winters and humid summers. The climate in the western half of the state is colder with more snow in winter. On any given day average temperatures in eastern and western Maryland differ by about 10°F. Maryland sees 42 inches of precipitation a year.

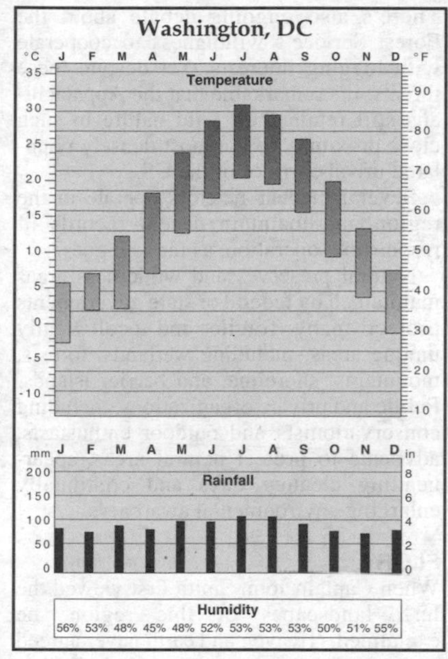
Washington, DC
°C J F M A M J J A S O N D °F
35 30 25 20 15 10 5 0 -5 -10
90 80 70 60 50 40 30 20 10
Temperature
mm J F M A M J J A S O N D in
200 150 100 50 0
8 6 4 2 0
Rainfall
Humidity
56% 53% 48% 45% 48% 52% 53% 53% 53% 50% 51% 55%

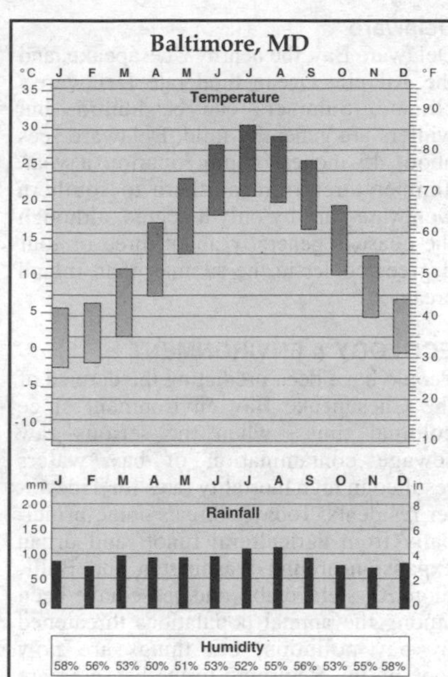
Baltimore, MD
°C J F M A M J J A S O N D °F
35 30 25 20 15 10 5 0 -5 -10
90 80 70 60 50 40 30 20 10
Temperature
mm J F M A M J J A S O N D in
200 150 100 50 0
8 6 4 2 0
Rainfall
Humidity
58% 56% 53% 50% 51% 53% 52% 55% 56% 53% 55% 58%

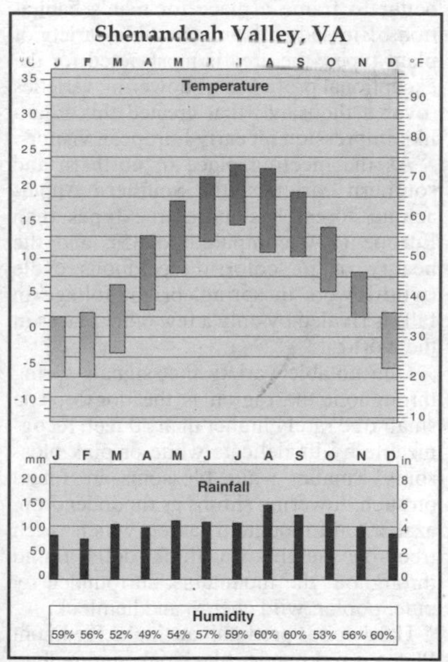
Shenandoah Valley, VA
°C J F M A M J J A S O N D °F
35 30 25 20 15 10 5 0 -5 -10
90 80 70 60 50 40 30 20 10
Temperature
mm J F M A M J J A S O N D in
200 150 100 50 0
8 6 4 2 0
Rainfall
Humidity
59% 56% 52% 49% 54% 57% 59% 60% 60% 53% 56% 60%

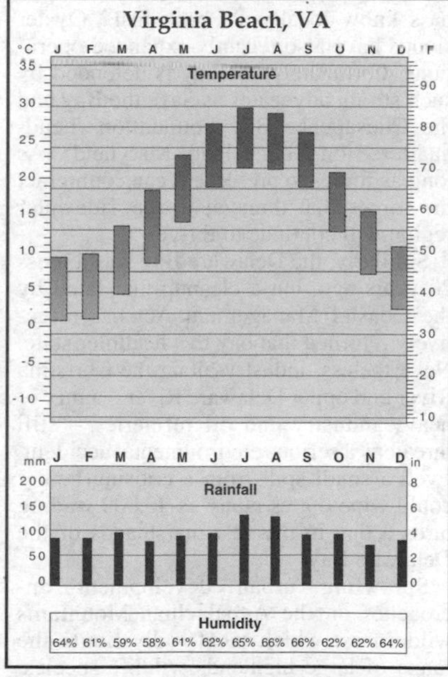
Virginia Beach, VA
°C J F M A M J J A S O N D °F
35 30 25 20 15 10 5 0 -5 -10
90 80 70 60 50 40 30 20 10
Temperature
mm J F M A M J J A S O N D in
200 150 100 50 0
8 6 4 2 0
Rainfall
Humidity
64% 61% 59% 58% 61% 62% 65% 66% 66% 62% 62% 64%

Delaware

Delaware Bay, the nearby Chesapeake, and the Atlantic Ocean moderate Delaware's climate. Summers can be humid, but winters are generally mild. Delaware sees about 45 inches of precipitation a year. Temperatures from northern to southern Delaware vary by only a degree, although the coast is generally about three or four degrees cooler in the summer than inland areas.

ECOLOGY & ENVIRONMENT

People have been predicting the demise of the Chesapeake Bay environment since colonial times, when the serious raw sewage contamination of bay waters resulted in high mortality rates for Tidewater residents. Today's threats come principally from agricultural runoff and urban expansion around Washington and Baltimore. Oysters, crabs, and geese have been among the animal populations threatened by bay pollution, but things are now looking up. Returning to the bay area are osprey, eagles, and a near-extinct striped bass know locally as 'rock fish.' Oyster sloops have also recently expanded operations. Fortunately, the bay is defended by such strong advocates as Save the Bay and the Chesapeake Bay Foundation (headquartered on Kent Island, Maryland). As long as forces to preserve it can counteract the forces that threaten it, the Tidewater region will continue to thrive.

Similarly, the Delaware Bay was a mess 20 years ago, but a cleanup mandated by the Coastal Management Act has effectively returned that bay to a healthier state. Nevertheless, industry along the Christina River and upper Delaware River – a mix of heavy industry and oil refineries – still threatens a serious environmental accident. Even a small spill from a cruising tanker could wipe out as many as 40,000 wading birds a day in the vast marshlands of the Delaware Bay.

Sprawling urban development encroaches on the Appalachian Mountains wilderness, which most sadly limits the range of large highlands wildlife species. There's also ongoing debate about the Forest Service's willingness to cooperate with logging interests. Yet despite these threats, it's remarkable that the Appalachians still retain their wild nature in such close proximity to the most densely populated urban corridor of the US.

Several nuclear reactors operate in the region and maintain decent records of responsible operation, as far as it goes.

Natural preserves and wilderness areas maintained by federal or state governments protect many fragile and ecologically unique areas, including wetlands, forests, mountains, shoreline, and barrier islands. Public and private organizations, including conservationists and outdoor enthusiasts, advocate to protect natural areas, spearheading cleanup days and continually enlarging environmental awareness.

FLORA

When Captain John Smith first viewed the lush landscapes of this region, he exclaimed, 'Heaven and earth never agreed better to frame a place for man's habitation.' Blessed with an incredible variety of plant types, the area is most noted for the exceptional profusion of flowering varieties (over a thousand) that created this Eden-like impression on early European visitors.

As the meeting place of northern and southern varieties, the Southern Appalachian forest has more tree types than Europe (130 compared to 85), and the beauty of its colorful deciduous cycle (wildflowers in spring, bright foliage in fall) is rivaled by only a few other places in the world.

One notable variety that signals spring throughout the region is the dogwood, a small tree rarely higher than 30 feet, recognizable by its delicate white or pink blossoms. Smaller white blossoms are found on such flowering shrubs as rhododendron, azalea, and mountain laurel, which reach tree-size heights in thick dells found throughout the mountains, surrounded by pine, poplar, wild cherry, and hemlock.

Hardwoods predominate in the Piedmont Plateau; red maple, black oak, and redbud can be found throughout the region. In Maryland, varieties such as ash, black locust, and American elm thin as you go south, while pine and cedar varieties increase. In Virginia you'll find sassafras, persimmon, redbud, tulip, and sweet gum trees, as the forest makes a transition from the deciduous northern varieties to the southern conifers – commonly such pine varieties as Virginia pine and loblolly. Hemlock, borvitae, and hawthorn grow in the limestone valleys among groups of beautiful wildflowers.

Along the Coastal Plain pines grow in abundance and birches thrive near streams. In Virginia you will also find alder, holly, wisteria, trumpet vine, myrtle, cranberry, wild yam, and wild rice. In the southwest walnut, hickory and chestnut are found in groves. The Great Dismal Swamp, around 30 miles inland from the Atlantic at the North Carolina border holds impressive stands of bald cypress in its moody landscapes as well as black gum and sweet gum trees.

FAUNA

A remarkable diversity of fauna lives in the region, which is surprising considering its proximity to the large cities on the Eastern Seaboard. The Shenandoah, for instance, has 1100 species.

When the Great Valley of Virginia was first settled by Europeans in the 1730s, herds of bison grazed along the Shenandoah, but these have long since disappeared. Current large species of animals include the black bear *(Ursus americanus)* in the mountains and in Great Dismal Swamp, and Virginia white-tailed deer *(Odocoileus virginianus)*.

More common are the small mammals found in abundance throughout the region – opossum, raccoons, muskrats, gray squirrels, striped skunks, eastern cotton-tailed rabbits, and bats. You may also come across gray and red foxes, and the more elusive wildcats. Beavers, otter, and mink are present but uncommon (there are only three active beaver dams in Shenandoah National Park).

The many wetland environments of the Coastal Plain harbor such amphibians as snapping turtles and many varieties of frogs, toads, and newts. Of course, the most feared inhabitant of the wetlands is an insect: the mosquito. As for feared reptiles, poisonous copperheads are present but rarely encountered.

The Tidewater region of the Chesapeake and Delaware Bays is a primary winter haven for migratory waterfowl; Canada geese and snow geese arrive in the Tidewater each fall in numbers exceeding hundreds of thousands. Wading birds, such as egrets and many varieties of heron, are common species in the summer.

Ruffed grouse, wild turkey, bobwhite (quail), ducks, and geese are among many game varieties present throughout the year. The many songbirds include the cardinal. Raptors (birds of prey) include owls, hawks, and the golden and American bald eagle.

Anglers find such freshwater fish as pike, catfish, bream, and carp, or saltwater rock fish (striped bass), menhaden, bluefish, weakfish, butterfish, herring, and shad. The Chesapeake Bay is rich in scallops, clams, and oysters.

Endangered Species

Rare and threatened plants and animals include the dwarf trillium, pirate bush, rockcress, the Virginia big-eared bat *(Corynorhinus townsendii virginianus)*, the northeastern beach tiger beetle, the grizzled skipper, the regal fritillary, the flypoison borer moth, and the Shenandoah salamander *(Plethodon shenandoah)*. The main culprits? Sewage and agricultural runoff, among other pollutants.

GOVERNMENT

The USA has a federal system with a president and a bicameral Congress, consisting of the 100-member Senate and the 435-member House of Representatives. Each of the 50 states has two senators and a number of congressional representatives, which is determined by the size of its population.

The president, whose term is four years,

'I'd love to dance, but who's gonna lead?'

is chosen by individual electors of the Electoral College. Each state has a number of electors equal to its number of senators and congressional representatives. A candidate receives all of a state's electoral votes if he or she wins a simple majority of the popular vote. To be elected, the president must obtain a majority of 270 of the total 538 electoral votes (the District of Columbia, which has no voting representatives in Congress, nevertheless, has three electoral votes). The president may only serve two terms. The next presidential election is scheduled to occur in the year 2000.

The seat of the US government is in Washington within the federal enclave of the District of Columbia. The municipal government of the District, which is overseen by the federal body, has recently been as scandal-ridden as the federal government. As a federal protectorate, DC has a political life that more closely resembles that of a colony than a state. District residents won the right to vote in presidential elections only in 1961, and their hard-fought struggle for Congressional representation earned them only non-voting representatives. Despite calls for statehood, the raise in status seems a long way off – made longer still by the District government's local reputation for inefficiency and fiscal irresponsibility. There's also talk of incorporating DC into Maryland, but Maryland's governor wants no part of it.

As for the states, a governor presides over state government, and a bicameral legislature consisting of a senate and a house delegation enacts laws.

ECONOMY

Even though the US has the largest annual gross national product in the world ($6350 billion), the average Belgian, Norwegian, or Kuwaiti has a higher per capita income than the average US resident. In addition, the USA's national debt, created by a truly breathtaking spate of overspending that began in the early 1980s, stands at a rough $4350 billion and keeps growing. A trade deficit of $254 billion has also been a point of concern.

US citizens pay taxes on a sliding scale, with the poorest paying around 15% of personal earnings and the richest fifth paying around 40%. Average Americans can expect to pay out 20% of their earnings.

Although TV programs and Hollywood movies foster an impression that Americans are flashy and wealthy, the US is as diverse in its economic circumstances as it is in its cultures. Whole regions of the USA are wealthier than others, and within a city the standard of living can vary considerably from neighborhood to neighborhood. The lowest 20% of the population receives only 4.4% of the national income distribution, while the top 5% receive 17.6%. In the Capital Region, some of the most disadvantaged communities are in the inner city of the nation's capital itself; the rest of the region has its pockets of poverty but is on the whole one of the most developed and economically stable regions in the nation.

During colonial times the economic mainstay of the region was tobacco. Since the 18th century the region has diversified its agricultural produce, and today important cash crops include corn, apples, dairy products, poultry, livestock, peanuts, and Virginia ham. Within the urban corridor of the region, high-tech industries predominate; Maryland is the home of an enormous electronics industry, while Delaware is the base for the giant chemical producer Du Pont. The military, as well as federal and state governments, are among the largest employers.

POPULATION & PEOPLE

The greatest proportion of the region's population is found in an urban corridor stretching along the Piedmont, a portion of the larger urban crescent of development concentrated along the mid-to-northern part of the Eastern Seaboard. In these areas, and in cities, you will find a wide mix of people, most particularly in the nation's cosmopolitan capital with its many international influences. This ethnic diversity decreases outside these areas.

As a whole, the region is over two-thirds white and slightly less than one-third African American, with other races accounting for much smaller proportions (figures vary dramatically from place to place; DC, for example, is over two-thirds African American). The same racial/class dynamics at work in the nation at large are also at work here, which is to say that centuries of oppression and discrimination against non-whites continue to take their toll. Fortunately, visitors intent on accessing the riches of diverse cultures can do so without too much trouble. For example, black heritage tours provide an alternative perspective to mainstream history and insights to the local culture. Ethnic festivals are also offer a chance to explore multicultural activities – from Scottish Highland games to Greek dancing.

Remnants of the region's original Native American communities survive today. In Virginia, there are two state reservations, the Mattaponi and Pamunkey in King William County (see West Point in the Fredericksburg chapter for Mattaponi); five other Native American communities do not have trust land – the Rappahannock, Upper Mattaponi, Chickahominy, and groups in Amherst County and Person County. In Maryland, a few thousand people on the lower Eastern Shore claim Pocomoke and Assateague ancestry; south of DC in Waldorf, the Piscataways gather for big powwows at Maryland's Indian Cultural Center each June and September. In Delaware, a small but strong community of Nanticokes live along the Indian River (see the Delaware Seashore chapter).

EDUCATION

Public elementary and secondary education in all but affluent suburban areas is commonly underfunded in the region (as in many regions throughout the US); as parents increasingly opt out of the system in favor of private education, the gap between the haves and have-nots widens dramatically. With far fewer minority families able to opt out of the system, underfunded public education exacerbates de facto segregation between the races as well.

Beyond the many well-regarded private independent schools and traditional parochial schools in the region, Virginia has lately seen an increase in private schools funded by the Christian right. These schools are often criticized for a lack of tolerance and diversity.

Students who flourish despite these pitfalls face greater options in higher education in the region. Many public and private colleges and universities thrive in the region. Affirmative action (a policy mandating systematic approaches for achieving a diverse student body and faculty) is hotly debated on many campuses.

Among the best known schools in Virginia are the College of William and Mary in Williamsburg (the second-oldest college in the nation, founded in 1693) and the University of Virginia in Charlottesville (Thomas Jefferson's model 'academical village,' founded in 1819). The largest tertiary institution is Virginia Tech in Blacksburg. Dating to before emancipation, Hampton Institute (in Hampton) is a preeminent black college that counts Booker T Washington among its graduates.

In Maryland, Annapolis is the home of not only the US Naval Academy, but also of St Johns College, a so-called 'Great Books School.' Baltimore is the site of the prestigious Johns Hopkins University, and the University of Maryland is located outside of DC in College Park. In Delaware, the mammoth state-run University of Delaware is located in Newark.

Of the many colleges and universities located in the District of Columbia, among the most distinguished are Georgetown

University (the first Roman Catholic university in the nation), American University, George Washington University, Catholic University, historic Howard University (largely African American), and Gallaudet College (the only liberal arts school for the deaf in the world).

RELIGION

While today the region is represented by a wide variety of religious communities (dominated by Protestant sects such as Baptists, United Methodists, Presbyterians, and Episcopalians), the religious origins of Virginia, Maryland, and Delaware are very distinct.

Virginia was founded on strict Anglican roots – all nonconformists were strongly encouraged to take up residence elsewhere. Maryland was founded in part as a refuge for persecuted Roman Catholics from Europe. Delaware's earliest European settlers – Swedes and Finns – were Lutherans. Dutch immigrants were members of the Reformed Church. Later immigrants were mostly Quakers – a group whose views on ethnic pluralism, slavery, and liberty were a sharp contrast to the beliefs of many slave-holding Anglicans. Subsequent English immigrants belonged to the Church of England and later reorganized as Episcopals. Jesuits brought Roman Catholicism to Maryland and Virginia, but the real increase in Catholics (as well as Jews and Greek Orthodox) came with the 19th century European immigrants.

Today Protestants dominate in numbers in the region as a whole. Roman Catholics are the single largest religious denomination in Maryland, although Protestant sects together outnumber Roman Catholics. Amish and Mennonites call southern Maryland home, and in Virginia there are Mennonite communities in Dayton (near Harrisonburg) and in Stuarts Draft (west of Charlottesville). The majority of Delaware's citizen's identify themselves as Christian (85%); those who claim no religion account for 7.2% and Jews make up 1.4%.

In general, people in this part of the country take their religion very seriously – Virginia is an intrinsic part of the conservative Southern 'Bible Belt' – and many attend church services (note business closures and 'blue laws' restricting alcohol sales on Sunday). Respectfully attending a local service offers insight into local culture and will usually gain visitors fast friends – and you may hear good gospel music besides. You'll want to dress well and check with an usher about participating in the communion ceremony (generally this is OK at Protestant churches, but Catholics restrict the ritual to Catholics). Attend services at Washington, DC's National Cathedral for the most modern, diverse, and 'religiously correct' ceremony; the program walks visitors through the expected etiquette.

The nonprofit Christian Broadcasting Network (CBN), part of a worldwide network of Christian television stations, tapes its popular '700 Club' in hi-tech studios in Virginia Beach (to be in the studio audience call ☎ 757-424-7777).

LANGUAGE

In the late 1700s, a Pennsylvanian offered this description of a gentleman from Maryland: 'He has the softest voice – never pronounces the R at all.' Distinctive regional dialects and speech patterns can be heard in great variety throughout the region. From the black dialect and bureaucratese heard in urban DC to the gentrified drawl of Tidewater Virginia to the faintly Elizabethan strains of Eastern Shore Maryland to an Appalachian twang, the variations of English spoken within this compact geographical region are dramatic. Many locals can readily pinpoint a particular local accent down to a 50-mile radius. Yet few other language minorities exist in the region beyond the rich diplomatic community in DC.

Tricky pronunciation of place names may further confuse visitors, for example: Suffolk ('suffik'), Staunton ('stanton'), Chincoteague ('shincoteege'), Baltimore ('balmer'), and Tilghman ('tillmun').

Facts for the Visitor

PLANNING

As with many destinations, a trip to the Capital Region is best made with some advance planning, especially if you are heading for popular resorts or cities during the high season. You'll want to be aware of the climate and local holidays and events that can embellish your trip if you plan to participate or which may impede a trip designed around a different purpose. And of course, extensive backcountry travel or backpacking always requires advance preparation.

When to Go

As noted under Climate (in Facts about the Capital Region), spring and fall are the most temperate and scenic seasons regionwide, though many visitors are naturally drawn to beaches in the summer and mountain ski areas in winter (the mountains are also a cool destination in summer). The tourist season in Washington, DC, runs from April (early spring cherry blossoms kick off the high season) through September, and it's wise to purchase advance tickets to popular attractions whenever possible to avoid long lines. Note also that because DC business travel slumps dramatically during the summer, vacationers can find good lodging bargains if they can tolerate the heat.

What Kind of Trip?

This guide is largely intended for travelers planning their own trips. Those looking to participate in outdoor activities such as hiking, biking, and backpacking should refer to the Outdoor Activities chapter, where we list relevant organizations and tour groups.

Visitors interested in group tours of the Shenandoah Valley, colonial Williamsburg, and other historic areas should contact Wayfaring Travelers (☎ 410-666-7456, 27 Sunnyview Drive, Phoenix, MD 21131-2036), which organizes two-week trips.

Maps

Maps of excellent quality are available throughout the USA. Depending on your interests, and the way in which you intend to travel, there are many sources, a few of which are listed below.

Highway Maps The American Automobile Association (AAA) issues the most comprehensive and dependable highway maps, which are free with AAA membership (sce Car & Motorcycle in the Getting Around chapter). These range from national, regional, and state maps to very detailed maps of counties, cities, and even relatively small towns; AAA also prepares suggested travel routes for its members, and issues a regional TourBook and CampBook that contain equally useful maps, also free of charge to members.

Topographic Maps The US Geological Survey (USGS), an agency of the federal Department of the Interior, publishes very detailed topographic maps of the entire country at different scales up to 1:250,000. Maps at 1:62,500, or approximately 1 inch:1 mile, are ideal for backcountry hiking and backpacking. Fortunately, some private cartographers are producing updated versions of old USGS maps at 1:62,500 that give hikers a much clearer notion of mountain terrain.

Many bookstores and outdoor equipment specialists carry a wide selection of topographic maps.

Atlases The DeLorme Mapping series of atlases and gazetteers includes state atlases containing detailed topographic and highway maps at a scale of 1:250,000. Readily available in good bookstores, these are especially useful for car and mountain-bike travel off the main highways and cost about $20 each.

What to Bring

When packing, bear in mind that this is a fairly conservative part of the country. Casual dress is fine for beach areas, and it's standard tourist wear even in the cities, but you'll stand out less and earn the gratitude of locals if you trade in shorts and T-shirts for something slightly less casual. City folk wear jackets and closed shoes even in the sweltering summer, and no matter where you are, exceptionally revealing or sloppy dress (sleeveless, backless, too short or strappy, patched) will attract negative attention from locals – this isn't California. It may be wise to pack a dressy outfit for any unexpected business, church, or formal social encounter; you might also make use of a rain jacket or parka depending on the season.

For health precaution items, see Health below. For camping items, see the Outdoor Activities chapter.

THE BEST OF THE REGION

Washington, DC's Best

Museums & Galleries The classic DC pursuits are popular for good reason: The Smithsonian museums and DC's art galleries offer unparalleled *free* access to some of the world's best art, science, historical, and cultural exhibits. Consider checking out the craftwork at the Renwick Gallery, folk art at the National Museum of American Art, and kitsch at the American History Museum. And while you're at it, grab a coffee in the National Building Museum's wondrous atrium.

Memorials DC's powerful memorials are important cultural and historic icons. Many are best seen on a clear night, particularly the view from the top of the Washington Monument. Don't miss the larger-than-life Lincoln, the grippingly poignant Vietnam Memorial, and the changing of the guard at the Tomb of the Unknowns in Arlington National Cemetery.

Political Milieu The political scene in Washington – who's in, who's out, the often absurd machinations and fluctuations of the American democratic process – generates a highly charged political atmosphere. Residents are very sophisticated and opinionated about politics – you'll find cashiers debating foreign policy and political junkies watching Congressional hearings at C-SPAN bars on Capitol Hill. Also, the concentration of diplomats creates a vibrant international community offering many multicultural events.

Virginia's Best

Civil War Sites No Union or Confederate state experienced more of the tumult of the Civil War (1861 – 1865) than Virginia. In recent years interest in the Civil War has surged, resulting in many annual battle reenactments, museums, battlefield memorials, monuments, and other associated historic sites. The war is 'in' and the buffs and would-be buffs comb battlefields with the fervor of Victorian-era explorers.

Some of the finest Civil War sites include New Market in the Shenandoah Valley, Petersburg (both town and surrounds), Fredericksburg (the stone wall in town and Chatham House across the river), Sutherlin House (the last capitol of the Confederacy) in Danville, and the surrender site at Appomattox.

Colonial Virginia Virginia offers an astonishing variety of colonial sites. In the Historic Triangle, between the York and the James Rivers, are the almost sacred sites of Williamsburg, Jamestown, and Yorktown (and a circus of amusement parks and 'living history' places in between). But this historical trio is only the beginning. Many more estates, such as the James River plantations, and many other points of interest lure history-hungry visitors. Where to head? I fear incarceration in the stocks and a face full of rotting vegetables for this – Berkeley Plantation on the James River, Mount Vernon near Alexandria, the George Washington birthplace on

Northern Neck, and sublime Monticello (the zenith of Jefferson's achievements) near Charlottesville.

Shenandoah National Park & the Skyline Drive Few magnificent drives in the world are free of billboards and commercial vehicles. The 105 miles of the Skyline Drive, from Front Royal in the north to Waynesboro in the south, is one of the most pristine places you could ever visit. So avail yourself of the opportunity and gaze in awe from the summits of the Blue Ridge upon the beautiful Shenandoah Valley and Piedmont foothills. It costs $5 for a week per car – paradise on the cheap.

Blue Ridge Parkway When you reach Waynesboro at the southern end of the Skyline Drive, you can continue south on an equally beautiful road, the unforgettable Blue Ridge Parkway – for no charge. Some of Virginia's most memorable sights – Mabry Mill, interlocked wooden fences, and picture-postcard farms – line the Virginian section of the parkway. (It continues south through North Carolina to the Great Smoky Mountains in Tennessee.) A short drive away is an unforgettable Friday night jamboree at Cockram's General Store in Floyd or an impromptu fiddle session in Galax.

Maryland's Best

Annapolis Maryland's capital tops the list of 'must sees' because it is a great place to walk in almost any weather. On a stroll you will see the city's collection of 18th century buildings, matchless in their scope and restoration. In addition, the city's sailing scene – including the US Naval Academy and the thousands of sailing yachts – is unrivaled even in Sydney, Monte Carlo, or San Francisco Bay. Finally, the Dock Square area of Annapolis has an extensive collection of restaurants, bars, and musical entertainment that draws a lively crowd.

Baltimore Inner Harbor & Fells Point This area is an outstanding example of urban renaissance. Around the Inner Harbor you will find a half dozen major attractions such as the National Aquarium, museums, historic watercraft, food courts, shopping, and a waterfront promenade. Historic Fells Point, Baltimore's restored historic district, is a short water-taxi ride from the Inner Harbor.

St Michaels & the Chesapeake Bay Maritime Museum Although the town has become gentrified, St Michaels is still the one place to come if you are short on time and still want to soak up Eastern Shore culture or put away beer and crabs. The maritime museum's exhibits, lectures, and collection of watercraft give a vivid picture of the bay's maritime culture. Of course, you need only look around the harbor shores to find a representative collection of working watermen or travel up the road to Tilghman Island to see America's last fleet of working sailboats, the skipjacks.

Delaware's Best

Winterthur Museum With 1000 acres of manicured fields and forest, a 100-room chateau, and the world's best collection of American decorative arts, Winterthur ranks with Rosecliff in Newport, Rhode Island, and Hearst Castle in California as one of the most fabulous personal estates in America. You don't have to love mansions and antiques to love Winterthur: The grounds make for entertaining hiking and excellent picnicking.

Historic New Castle It is no exaggeration to say that when you walk the cobblestone streets of New Castle you get the feeling you have stepped back in time to colonial America. Yet New Castle is a breathing, working village, not a living history museum.

The restaurants here are good; the Green Frog Pub is a particularly good value. The B&Bs are even better – restored historic homes with expansive views of Delaware Bay and River. Best of all, New Castle is not crowded with tourists, and it makes a good starting point for a bicycling tour down Delaware's historic and scenic Route 9, the Coastal Heritage Greenway.

Lewes & Cape Henlopen Poised at the foot of giant sand dunes at the junction of Delaware Bay and the Atlantic Ocean, Lewes/Cape Henlopen could hardly have a more dramatic landscape. Delaware's first European settlement, Zwaanendael, is here, amid 300 years of maritime tradition. Whalers, fishermen, and Delaware Bay pilots have all sailed from here. The pilots still do, as do a host of big-game fishing boats and the Cape May-Lewes Ferry, which can carry you across Delaware Bay to America's premier Victorian resort, Cape May, New Jersey. Lewes has historic homes, shady streets, romantic B&Bs, creative restaurants, a vineyard, and Cape Henlopen State Park, where you can swim and camp free from most of the crowd that funnels into Rehoboth Beach next door.

THE WORST OF THE REGION

Washington, DC's Worst

The 'Mint' When you consider the average length of the wait (typically measured in hours), the Bureau of Printing and Engraving (mistakenly called 'the Mint') offers little more than a short factory tour through an overrated press shop. Skip it unless the kids are adamant and head straight for the souvenir stand for bags of shredded money.

Long Lines Unless you travel during the winter off season, you'll find yourself standing in long lines to see Washington's most popular attractions (the downside of free admission). Make the most of the advance-ticket option at some sights. Prepare yourself for a wait: Take along a hat or an umbrella to shield yourself from sun exposure, and carry snacks and water.

Few Whimsical Pursuits Washington is a serious place, with many 'Type A' residents bearing the burdens of responsibility for domestic and international policy. Such weighty matters and preoccupied folk can make it a tough place to just cut loose and have aimless fun. Most diversions are Important or Significant, too few pointlessly fanciful or whimsical. To break the spell, take all opportunities to fly kites on the Mall (in winter, skate at its homey little ice rink), and dance yourself silly at lively clubs all night long.

Virginia's Worst

Virginia Beach Virginia Beach earns a place on this list for pretending to be what it isn't – a 'family' destination. Virginia's biggest city is an agglomeration of bad taste: high-rises along a beleaguered stretch of beach; 'theme-park' mini golf courses, paint-ball shooting galleries, amusement parlors, expensive souvenir shops, and tacky wax museums; an overstaffed and zealous police force; overpriced, run-of-the-mill restaurants; and crowded bars notable only for their poor service, loud noise, and cramped confines. If you want to take the family somewhere more rewarding, try the Eastern Shore, Shenandoah Valley, or Blue Ridge Mountains. It's almost not worth braving Hampton Roads' tunnels to get to this place.

All that said, there are some oases in this concrete jungle of artificiality, among them the nearby state parks, the Edgar Cayce Association for Research & Enlightenment, and The Jewish Mother restaurant.

Theme Parks & Outlet Malls The last thing this history-rich state needs is 'living history' parks and pastiche European villages complete with 'adrenaline rides.' These incongruities often stand near absorbing places of historic interest such as Jamestown, Yorktown, Williamsburg, and Richmond, for example.

Equally bad are the outlet malls. These monstrosities are often more popular than their historic neighbors, and more often than not, they're not a good value (slick advertising may convince you otherwise).

Drinking Laws If the legal drinking age (21) wasn't bad enough, those who can legally drink are tossed out of bars by 2 am, just when they are getting into it – a big turnoff for those who relish the freedom to punish their bodies and go where they please. Just experience the 'Ten minutes to go, finish up!' demand once and you'll agree. This is one drawback that's unlikely to change in the short term in this prohibition-minded Bible Belt.

Maryland's Worst

Waldorf Once a country town in rural southern Maryland, Waldorf has degenerated into five miles of malls, traffic lights, and gridlock on Hwy 301. There is almost no good time of day to escape Waldorf's congestion, except perhaps between 2 and 5 am.

Kent Island Another victim of commercialism, Kent Island fell prey to rampant development after the Annapolis Bay Bridge crossed to this rural Eastern Shore community. Now, this onetime watermen's and farmer's community is a collection of outlet malls, roadhouses, and marinas, most adorned with surreal images of blue crabs.

Delaware's Worst

Hwy 13 between I-95 & the C&D Canal Here's traffic straight out of your nightmares: lots of trucks, a fog of exhaust vapor, every fast-food chain known to humankind, traffic lights every half mile. Avoid this place: Take scenic Route 9 along the Delaware Bay or the newly opened thruway, Route 1.

Wilmington Waterfront Heavy industry, including petroleum refining, has overwhelmed the potentially beautiful banks of the Christina and Delaware Rivers. The city claims a Baltimore Inner Harbor-like restoration is in the works, but there are no material signs of such regeneration. Oil spills and smelly stack emissions rule.

TOURIST OFFICES

Local Tourist Offices

State tourist offices can often provide a package of useful information that includes an official highway map, a scenic-route map, an events calendar, an outdoor recreation guide, a B&B guide, a state-park directory with camping/cabins price list, a list of accommodations (hotels and motels), and sundry other publications.

Delaware Tourism Office
99 Kings Hwy, PO Box 1401, Dover, DE 19903 (☎ 302-739-4271, 800-441-8846)

Maryland Dept of Tourism
217 E Redwood St, Baltimore, MD 21298-6349, (☎ 410-583-7313, 800-543-1036)

Virginia Division of Tourism
901 E Byrd St, Richmond, VA, 23219 (☎ 804-786-2051, 800-847-4882; fax 804-786-1919, TTY/TTD 804-371-0327)

Washington, DC, Convention and Visitors Association
1212 New York Ave NW, Suite 600, Washington, DC 20005-3992 (☎ 202-789-7099)

For information about federally managed sites and lands, as well as helpful federal offices call the Federal Information Center (☎ 800-688-9889, in Virginia, ☎ 703-440-1713).

Tourist Offices Abroad

The USTTA has closed its doors worldwide. Your best bet for getting information on the US is your travel agency.

In the UK, you can find information on a number of US cities, states, and regions through specialized tourism offices in the country, but these can only be contacted by phone. Delaware has such an office (☎ 0171-470-8802), as does Washington, DC (☎ 0181-392-9187). A complete list of phone numbers is available from the US embassy or consulates in the UK.

Maryland maintains an office in Belgium (☎ 32-2-775-8450). Virginia has offices in Germany (☎ 49-69-273-9900) and Hungary (☎ 36-1-267-9701).

VISAS & DOCUMENTS

All foreign visitors besides Canadians are required to have a passport (Canadians must have proper proof of citizenship); many foreign visitors will also need a US visa. All visitors should bring a driver's license and health-insurance or travel-insurance cards, if available. You'll also need photo identification proving you're over 21 to purchase alcohol or to gain admission to bars and clubs.

It's a good idea to photocopy your passport (the photo page); carry around the copy and store the original in a secure hotel safe. It's similarly wise to photocopy your airline tickets.

Visas

Apart from Canadians and those entering under the visa-waiver program (see below), all foreign visitors must obtain a visa from a US consulate or embassy. In most countries the process can be handled by mail or through a travel agent.

Your passport should be valid for at least six months longer than your intended stay in the USA, and you'll need to submit a recent photo (37 x 37 mm) with the application. Documents of financial stability and/or guarantees from a US resident are sometimes required, particularly for travelers from developing countries.

Visa applicants may be required to 'demonstrate binding obligations' that will ensure their return back home. Because of this requirement, those planning to travel through other countries before arriving in the USA are generally better off applying for their US visa while they are still in their home country – rather than on the road.

The most common visa is a Non-Immigrant Visitors Visa, of which there are two types: B1 for business purposes, and B2 for tourism or visiting friends and relatives. A visitor's visa is good for one or five years with multiple entries, and it specifically prohibits the visitor from taking paid employment in the USA. The validity period depends on what country you're from. The length of time you'll be allowed to stay in the USA is ultimately determined by US immigration authorities at the port of entry. If you're coming to the USA to work or study, you will probably need a different type of visa, and the company or institution that you'll be joining should make the arrangements. Allow six months for processing the application.

Entering the USA If you have a non-US passport and a visa, you must complete an Arrival/Departure Record (Form I-94) before you present yourself at the immigration desk. It's usually handed out on the plane, along with the customs declaration. It's a rather badly designed form, and many people fill out more than one before they get it right. Some airlines suggest you start at the last question and work upwards. Answers should be written *below* the questions. For question 12, 'Address While in the United States,' give the address of the location where you will spend the first night. Complete the Departure Record, too (the lower part of the form), giving exactly the same answers for questions 14 to 17 as for questions 1 to 4.

Despite the smiling pictures of the president welcoming you to the USA at the immigration area, the staff of the Immigration & Nationalization Service (INS) can be less than welcoming and there's usually a line at the immigration desk. The main concern of the INS is excluding those who are likely to work illegally or overstay, so visitors will be asked about their plans and sometimes about whether they have sufficient funds for their stay. If they surmise you're OK, a six-month entry is usually approved, even if you say you only want to enter for a few weeks.

It's a good idea to be able to list an itinerary that covers the period for which you ask to be admitted. You should also to be able to show you have $300 or $400 for every week of your intended stay: A couple of major credit cards will go a long way towards establishing 'sufficient funds.' Don't make too much of having friends, relatives, or business contacts in the USA – the INS official may decide that this will encourage you to overstay.

Visa-Waiver Program Citizens of certain countries may enter the USA without a US visa, for stays of 90 days or less, under the reciprocal visa-waiver program. Currently these countries are Andorra, Argentina, Australia, Austria, Belgium, Brunei, Denmark, Finland, France, Germany, Iceland, Ireland, Italy, Japan, Luxembourg, Liechtenstein, Monaco, the Netherlands, New Zealand, Norway, San Marino, Spain, Sweden, Switzerland, and the UK. Under this program you must have a roundtrip

HIV & Entering the USA

Everyone entering the USA who is not a US citizen is subject to the authority of the Immigration & Naturalization Service (INS). The INS can prevent someone from entering or staying in the USA by excluding or deporting them. This is especially relevant to travelers with HIV (human immunodeficiency virus). Though being HIV-positive is not grounds for deportation, it is a 'ground of exclusion' and the INS can invoke this rule and refuse to admit visitors to the country.

Although the INS doesn't test people for HIV at the point of entry into the USA, agents may try to exclude anyone who answers yes to this question on the nonimmigrant visa application form: 'Have you ever been afflicted with a communicable disease of public health significance?' INS officials may also stop people if they seem sick, are carrying AIDS/HIV medicine, or, sadly, if the officer happens to think the person looks gay, though sexual orientation is not legally a ground of exclusion. A visitor may be deported if the INS later finds that he or she has HIV but did not declare it. Being HIV-positive is not a 'ground for deportation' but failing to provide correct information on the visa application is.

If you do have HIV but can prove to consular officials you are the spouse, parent, or child of a US citizen or legal permanent resident (green-card holder), you are exempt from the exclusionary law.

It is imperative that visitors know and assert their rights. Immigrants and visitors who may face exclusion should discuss their rights and options with a trained immigration advocate within the USA before applying for a visa. For legal immigration information and referrals to immigration advocates, contact the National Immigration Project of the National Lawyers Guild (☎ 617-227-9727), 14 Beacon St, Suite 506, Boston, MA 02108; or Immigrant HIV Assistance Project, Bar Association of San Francisco (☎ 415-267-0795), 685 Market St, Suite 700, San Francisco, CA 94105. ■

ticket that is nonrefundable in the USA, and you will not be allowed to extend your stay beyond 90 days.

Visa Extensions & Re-Entry If you want, need, or hope to stay in the USA longer than the date stamped on your passport, go to the local INS office (or call ☎ 800-755-0777, or look in the local white pages telephone directory under US Government) *before* the stamped date to apply for an extension. Applying after that date usually leads to an unamusing conversation with an INS official who assumes you want to work illegally. If you find yourself in that situation, it's a good idea to bring a US citizen with you to vouch for your character. It's also a good idea to have verification that you have money to support yourself.

Travel Insurance

No matter how you're traveling, take out travel insurance that covers you not only for medical expenses and luggage theft or loss, but also for unavoidable cancellation or delays in your travel arrangements. In addition, everyone should be covered for worst-case scenarios, such as an accident that requires hospital treatment and a flight home. Coverage varies from policy to policy, so ask both your insurer and your ticket-issuing agency to explain the finer points. STA Travel offers a variety of travel-insurance options at reasonable prices. Keep a photocopy of your ticket separate from the original.

Buy travel insurance as early as possible. If you buy it the week before you fly, you may find, for instance, that you're not covered for delays to your flight caused by strikes or other industrial action that may have been in force before you took out the insurance.

If you plan to travel for a long time, the insurance may seem very expensive – but if you can't afford it, you certainly won't be able to afford a medical emergency in the USA.

Driving Documents

An International Driving Permit is a useful accessory for foreign visitors in the USA.

EMBASSIES

Embassies Abroad

US diplomatic offices abroad include the following:

Australia
21 Moonah Place,
Yarralumla ACT 2600
(☎ 6-270-5000)

Level 59 MLC Center
19-29 Martin Place,
Sydney NSW 2000
(☎ 2-373-9200)

553 St Kilda Rd,
Melbourne Victoria
(☎ 3-9526-5900)

There are also consulates in Perth and Brisbane.

Austria
Boltzmanngasse 16,
A-1091, Vienna
(☎ 1-313-39)

Belgium
Blvd du Regent 27, B-1000,
Brussels
(☎ 2-513-38-30)

Canada
100 Wellington St,
Ottawa, Ontario K1P 5T1
(☎ 613-238-5335)

1095 W Pender St,
Vancouver, BC V6E 2M6
(☎ 604-685-1930)

1155 rue St-Alexandre,
Montreal, Quebec
(☎ 514-398-9695)

There are also consulates in Toronto, Calgary, and Halifax.

Denmark
Dag Hammarskjolds Allé 24,
Copenhagen
(☎ 31-42-31-44)

Finland
Itainen Puistotie 14A,
Helsinki
(☎ 0-171-931)

France
2 rue Saint Florentin,
75001 Paris
(☎ 01-42-96-1202)

There are also consulates in Bordeaux, Lyon, Marseille, and Toulouse.

Germany
Deichmanns Aue 29,
53179 Bonn
(☎ 228-33-91)

Greece
91 Vasilissis Sophias Blvd,
10160 Athens
(☎ 1-721-2951)

India
Shanti Path, Chanakyapuri
110021, New Delhi
(☎ 11-60-0651)

Indonesia
Medan Merdeka Selatan 5,
Jakarta
(☎ 21-360-360)

Ireland
42 Elgin Rd,
Ballsbridge, Dublin
(☎ 1-687-122)

Israel
71 Hayarkon St, Tel Aviv
(☎ (3-517-4338)

Italy
Via Vittorio Veneto
119a-121, Rome
(☎ 6-46-741)

Japan
1-10-5 Akasaka Chome,
Minato-ku, Tokyo
(☎ 3-224-5000)

Korea
82 Sejong-Ro,
Chongro-ku, Seoul
(☎ 2-397-4114)

Malaysia
376 Jalan Tun Razak,
50400 Kuala Lumpur
(☎ 3-248-9011)

Mexico
Paseo de la Reforma 305,
Cuauhtémoc,
06500 Mexico City
(☎ 5-211-0042)

Netherlands
Lange Voorhout 102,
2514 EJ The Hague
(☎ 70-310-9209)

Museumplein 19,
1071 DJ Amsterdam
(☎ 20-310-9209)

New Zealand
29 Fitzherbert Terrace,
Thorndon, Wellington
(☎ 4-722-068)

Norway
Drammensvein 18, Oslo
(☎ 22-44-85-50)

Philippines
1201 Roxas Blvd,
Ermita Manila 1000
(☎ 2-521-7116)

Russia
Novinskiy Bulivar 19/23,
Moscow
(☎ 095-252-2451)

Singapore
30 Hill St, Singapore 0617
(☎ 338-0251)

South Africa
877 Pretorius St, Box 9536,
Pretoria 0001
(☎ 12-342-1048)

Spain
Calle Serrano 75, 28006
Madrid (☎ 1-577-4000)

Sweden
Strandvagen 101,
S-115 89 Stockholm
(☎ 8-783-5300)

Switzerland
Jubilaumsstrasse 93,
3005 Berne (☎ 31-357-70 11)

Thailand
95 Wireless Rd, Bangkok
(☎ 2-252-5040)

UK
5 Upper Grosvenor St,
London W1
(☎ 0171-499-9000)

3 Regent Terrace,
Edinburgh EH7 5BW
(☎ 31-556-8315)

Queens House, Belfast
BT1 6EQ,
(☎ 232-328-239)

Foreign Embassies in USA

Most nations' principal diplomatic representation is in Washington, DC; see the DC chapter for a selected list. To find others, look in the local phone directory under 'Consulates' or call DC directory assistance at ☎ 202-555-1212.

Local traffic police are more likely to accept it as valid identification than an unfamiliar document from another country. Your national automobile association can provide one for a small fee, and these permits are usually valid for one year.

If you plan on doing a lot of driving in the USA, you should consider joining your national automobile association. Members of the American Automobile Association (AAA) and affiliated automobile clubs can get car-rental and sightseeing admission discounts with membership cards. More importantly, it gives you access to AAA road service in case of emergency (from locking your keys in the car to major break-downs).

Hostel Card

Most hostels in the USA are members of Hostelling International (formerly American Youth Hostels), which is affiliated with the International Youth Hostel Federation (IYHF). You can purchase membership on the spot when checking in, although it's probably advisable to purchase it before you leave home. Most hostels allow non-members to stay, but they charge them a few dollars more.

Student & Youth Cards

If you're a student, get an international student ID or bring along a school or university ID card to take advantage of student discounts.

Seniors' Cards

Travelers over the age of 65 get discounts throughout the USA. All you need is ID with proof of age should you be carded. There are organizations such as AARP (see the Senior Travelers section below) that offer membership cards for further discounts (available to US residents only).

CUSTOMS

US Customs allows each person over the age of 21 to bring one liter of liquor and 200 cigarettes duty free into the USA. US citizens are allowed to import $400 worth of gifts from abroad duty free, and non-US citizens are allowed to bring in $100 worth.

US law permits you to bring in, or take out, as much as $10,000 in US or foreign currency, traveler's checks, or letters of credit without formality. Larger amounts of any or all of the above must be declared to customs (there are no limits).

MONEY

Costs

The cost of accommodations – whether in the city or country, at beach or ski resorts – may vary by season, weekday/weekend, and during special holiday or festival periods. At all but the ski areas, prices are generally lowest in winter. The cheapest motel rates are usually around $20 to $30. Rustic camping is inexpensive at only about $5 or so per night, but only costlier formal sites (from $10 to $20) offer such amenities as hot showers.

Food prices may seem reasonable by European standards, but DC prices are higher than in most other American cities outside New York. A splurge at a first-rate restaurant in the Capital Region costs anywhere between $25 and $50 per person, but good restaurant meals can be found for $10 – half that at lunch. Purchase food at markets to get by even more cheaply.

Public transportation within a city is relatively inexpensive; bus or subway fares vary by system and distance traveled, but expect fares to start around a dollar a trip. Owning or renting a car is much less expensive than in other parts of the world, and in some areas a car is the only way of getting around. Rentals are fairly inexpensive in large cities, and gasoline costs a fraction of what it does in Europe and most of the rest of the world. For more information on purchasing and operating a car, see the Getting Around chapter.

Carrying Cash & Traveler's Checks

It's unwise and unnecessary to carry large amounts of cash; any currency beyond a day's worth of spending cash is most safely stored in a money belt or in a secure hotel safe. Traveler's checks are safer and can be readily cashed at most banks.

Visitors from outside the US can save themselves trouble and expense by buying traveler's checks in US dollars. While you may lose some money in the foreign exchange rates, you'll spare yourself the hassle of finding a foreign exchange. Restaurants, hotels and most stores accept US dollar traveler's checks as though they were cash, so if you're carrying traveler's checks in US dollars, odds are you'll never have to use a bank or pay an exchange fee.

ATMs

ATMs are a convenient way of obtaining cash from a bank account back home (within the USA or from abroad); you can readily find ATMs at banks, shopping malls, and in certain chain stores (many supermarkets and convenience stores, for example). Even small backcountry towns usually have ATMs with access to many major networks (such as Exchange, Accel, Plus, and Cirrus), and many are accessible 24 hours a day. You may, however, be charged one or two dollars per transaction.

For a nominal service charge, you can withdraw cash from an ATM using a credit card or a charge card. Credit cards usually have a 2% fee with a $2 minimum, so using bank cards linked to your personal checking account is usually far cheaper. Check with your bank or credit-card company for exact information.

Credit & Debit Cards

Major credit cards are accepted at hotels, restaurants, gas stations, shops, and car-rental agencies throughout the USA. In fact, you'll find it hard to perform certain transactions without one. Ticket buying services, for instance, won't reserve tickets over the phone unless you offer a credit-card number, and it's virtually impossible to rent a car without one. Even if you loathe credit cards and prefer to rely on traveler's checks and ATMs, it's a good idea to carry one for such occasions and for emergencies. Visa and MasterCard are the two most widely accepted, followed by Discover and American Express.

Places that accept Visa and MasterCard are also likely to accept debit cards. Unlike a credit card, a debit card deducts payment directly from the user's checking account. Instead of an interest rate, users are charged a minimal fee for the transaction. Be sure to check with your bank to confirm that your debit card will be accepted in other states; debit cards from large commercial banks can often be used worldwide. For information on what to do if you lose a credit card, see the Emergency section below.

International Transfers

Money can be wired to and from the main branches of most banks, as well as through Western Union and American Express, but inquire about the charges for the service beforehand. A better option may be to have someone add funds to your credit card, from which you can request a cash advance.

Currency

The US dollar is divided into 100 cents (¢). Coins come in denominations of 1¢ (penny), 5¢ (nickel), 10¢ (dime), 25¢ (quarter), and 50¢ (the rare half dollar). Quarters are the most commonly used coins for airport luggage-cart machines, and for vending machines and parking meters, so it's handy to have a stash of them (self-service laundries have change machines that dispense quarters). Notes, commonly called bills, come in $1, $2, $5, $10, $20, $50, and $100 denominations – $2 bills are rare, but perfectly legal. Unfortunately for poor-sighted folks, all bills are the same size and color. There is also a $1 coin that the government has tried unsuccessfully to bring into mass circulation; you may get them as change from ticket and stamp machines. Be aware that they look similar to quarters.

Currency Exchange

Most banks will exchange cash or traveler's checks in major foreign currencies, though the process may take some time. Banks in outlying areas rarely exchange cash, so it's less of a hassle to exchange foreign currency in larger cities. Additionally, Thomas Cook, American Express, and exchange windows in airports offer exchange (although you'll get a better rate at a bank).

At press time, exchange rates were:

Australia	A$1	=	US$0.79
Canada	C$1	=	US$0.75
France	Fr1	=	US$0.20
Germany	DM1	=	US$0.66
Hong Kong	HK$10	=	US$1.29
Japan	¥112	=	US$1
New Zealand	NZ$1	=	US$0.71
United Kingdom	UK£1	=	US$1.65

Tipping

Tipping is expected in restaurants and better hotels, and by taxi drivers, hairdressers, and baggage carriers. In restaurants, servers are paid minimal wages and rely upon tips for their livelihoods. Tip 15% unless the service is terrible (in which case a complaint to the manager is warranted) or up to 20% if the service is great. Never tip in fast-food, take-out, or buffet-style restaurants where you serve yourself.

Taxi drivers expect 10% and hairdressers get 15% if their service is satisfactory. Baggage carriers (skycaps in airports, bellhops in hotels) get $1 for the first bag and 50¢ for each additional bag. In budget hotels (where there aren't bellhops anyway) tips are not expected. In 1st-class and luxury hotels, tipping can reach irritating proportions – door attendants, bellhops, parking attendants, and cleaning staff are all tipped at least $1 for each service performed. However, saying 'thank you' to an attendant who merely opens a door when you could just as easily have done it yourself is sufficient.

Taxes & Refunds

Almost everything you pay for in ...or is taxed. Occasionally, the tax ... meals the advertised price (and this is added and most drinks in a bar. Unless otherwise museum... and ... ot...

stated, the prices given in this book don't reflect local taxes.

When inquiring about hotel or motel rates, be sure to ask whether taxes are included or not.

In Virginia a 4.5% state sales tax is added to most purchases, and in some places 0.5% is added to this, bringing it up to 5%. In hotels you are likely to pay an additional 5% hotel tax, meaning the total tax on a bill amounts to about 10%. Restaurant taxes are applied in some areas (fortunately not all), and meal and drink bills may reflect 8% to 10% tax. Delaware has no sales tax, but room tax is 8%. Maryland sales tax is 5% and the room tax is 10%. In DC, the sales tax is 5.75%, the restaurant tax is 10% (as it is for rental cars and liquor), and the hotel tax is 13% plus $1.50 per room per night.

Special Deals

The USA is probably the most promotion-oriented society on Earth. Though the bargaining common in many other countries is not generally accepted in the US, you can work angles to cut costs. For example, at hotels in the off-season, casually and respectfully mentioning a competitor's rate may prompt a manager to lower the quoted rate. Artisans may consider a negotiated price for large purchases. Discount coupons are widely available – check circulars in Sunday papers, at supermarkets, tourist offices, or chambers of commerce.

POST & COMMUNICATIONS

Postal Rates

Postage rates increase... in 1997, ...few years. The next increase ... probably go up by about ... when ... rates for 1st-class mail postage USA are 32¢ for letters up to one ... 23¢ for each additional ounce) and ...¢ for postcards.

International airmail rates (except to Canada and Mexico) are 60¢ for a half-ounce letter, 95¢ for a one-ounce letter, and 39¢ for each additional half ounce. International postcard rates are 40¢. Letters to Canada cost 46¢ for a one-ounce lett...

or each additional ounce, and 30¢ for a postcard. Letters to Mexico are 35¢ for a half-ounce letter, 45¢ for a one-ounce letter, and 30¢ for a postcard. Aerogrammes are 45¢.

The cost for parcels airmailed anywhere within the USA is $3 for two pounds or less, increasing by $1 per pound up to $6 for five pounds. For heavier items, rates differ according to the distance mailed. Books, periodicals, and computer disks can be sent by a cheaper 4th-class rate.

Sending Mail

If you have the correct postage, you can drop your mail into any blue mailbox. These are found at many convenient locations including shopping centers, airports, and street corners. However, due to concerns over terrorism, packages weighing 16 ounces or more must be mailed from a post office. The times of the next mail pickup are written on the inside of the lid of the mailbox. This sign also indicates the location of the nearest mailbox with later or more frequent pickup.

If you need to buy stamps or weigh your mail, go to the nearest post office. The address of each town's main post office is given later in the text. In addition, larger towns have branch post offices and post-office centers in some supermarkets and drugstores. For the address of the nearest one, call the main post office listed under 'Postal Service' in the US Government section of the white pages of the telephone directory.

Usua[illegible] post offices in main towns are open from [illegible] and 8 am to [illegible] to 5 pm Monday to Friday [illegible] vary. Post offices [illegible] Saturday, but hours do [illegible] hour Express Mail se[illegible]ities offer a 24- in the city's main post offi[illegible] item[illegible] higher cost)

If you wish to send items [illegible] packaging, consider using the s[illegible] local packaging stores such as Mail [illegible] Etc. In addition to fax, mailbox, and sh[illegible]ping services, these stores pack items and also sell packaging materials. Check the yellow pages telephone directory under 'Packaging Services.'

Receiving Mail

You can have mail sent to you c/o General Delivery at any post office that has its own zip (postal) code. Mail is usually held for 10 days before it's returned to the sender; you might request your correspondents to write 'hold for arrival' on their letters. Alternatively, have mail sent to the local representative of American Express or Thomas Cook, which provide mail service for their clients. Stores such as Mail Boxes Etc (see above) also receive and hold mail for customers.

Telephone

All phone numbers within the USA consist of a three-digit area code followed by a seven-digit local number. If you are calling locally, just dial the seven-digit number. If you are calling long distance, dial 1 + the three-digit area code + the seven-digit number.

If you're calling from abroad, the international country code for the USA is 010.

The 800 or 888 area code designates a number that is toll free within the USA and sometimes from Canada as well. These toll-free numbers usually aren't available for local calls.

The 900 area code designates a call for which the caller pays a premium rate. They are often associated with sleazy operations – a smorgasbord of phone sex at $2.99 a minute is typical.

Directory assistance can be reached locally by dialing 411. For directory assistance outside your area code, dial 1 + the three-digit area code of the place you want to call + 555-1212. For example, to obtain directory assistance for a toll-free number, dial 1-800-555-1212 (be aware, however, that not all businesses have 800 numbers).

This guide lists the local area code with every phone number. Here are the major [illegible]des in the region; if you need the code for [illegible] location, ask an operator:

A[illegible]

Bethe[illegible]

Virginia
Arlington 703
Hampton, Newport News & Richmond 804
Roanoke 540
Norfolk & Williamsburg 757
Washington, DC
202

Area codes for places outside the region are listed in the front of telephone directories. That's where you'll find country codes as well.

Local calls usually cost 25¢ at pay phones, although some telephone companies charge more.

Long-distance rates vary depending on the destination and telephone company – call the operator (0) for rate information. Don't ask the operator to put your call through, however, because operator-assisted calls are much more expensive than direct-dial calls. Generally, nights (11 pm to 8 am), all day Saturday, and from 8 am to 5 pm Sunday are the cheapest times to call (60% discount). Evenings (5 to 11 pm Sunday to Friday) are mid-priced (35% discount). Day calls (8 am to 5 pm Monday to Friday) are the most expensive within the USA.

Many businesses use letters instead of numbers for their telephone numbers in an attempt to make them snappy and memorable. Sometimes it works, but sometimes it is difficult to read the letters on the keyboard. If you cannot read the letters, here they are: 1 – no letters; 2 – ABC, 3 – DEF, 4 – GHI, 5 – JKL, 6 – MNO, 7 – PRS, 8 – TUV, 9 – WXY. There are no Qs or Zs.

Hotel Phones Many hotels (especially the more expensive ones) add a service charge of 50¢ to $1 for each local call made from a room phone, and they also add hefty surcharges for long-distance calls. Public pay phones, which can be found in most lobbies, are always cheaper. For public phones, you pay either with coins or a phone credit card. You can also make collect calls.

Phone Debit Cards A recent long-distance alternative is phone debit cards, which allow purchasers to pay in advance for long-distance calls, with access through a toll-free 800 number. In amounts of $5, $10, $20, and $50, cards are available from Western Union and some other sources. As a precaution when using phone credit cards in conspicuous public places, be discreet when punching in your credit-card number so that no one else can learn it.

Fax, Telegraph & Email

Fax machines are easy to find in the USA – at such private shipping companies as Mail Boxes Etc, photocopy stores, and hotel business service centers, but be prepared to pay over $1 a page. Telegraphs can be sent from Western Union (☎ 800-325-6000). Email is quickly becoming a preferred method of communication; however, unless you have a laptop and modem that can be plugged into a telephone socket, it's difficult to get online. Hotel business service centers may provide connections, and some trendy restaurants and cafes may offer Internet service as well. Some public libraries also provide access.

BOOKS

Lonely Planet

If you are planning to travel north of the Capital Region, check out our guide to New England and guide to New York, New Jersey & Pennsylvania.

Guidebooks

The Smithsonian's Historic America series on Virginia and the Capital Region contains the most exhaustive architectural review of regional historic sites, along with luxurious color photographs. *Maryland: A Guide to the Old Line State* by the Federal Writer's Project (reissued in 1976) provides the most comprehensive guide to the state.

Virginia's Shenandoah Valley by Greg Mock is a word-and-photographic tour of the valley with a focus on history and attractions. *Blue Ridge Parkway: The Story Behind the Scenery* by Margaret Rose Rives tells you all you need to know about th[e] history, building of, and tours throug[h] parkway, and it includes maps. Published by the US National Park Service, *Guide to Shenandoah National Park and Skyline Drive* is known as the 'bible' for those visiting this national park. It includes descriptions cross-referenced to milepost markers.

The Guide to Black Washington by Sandra Fitzpatrick provides comprehensive information about DC's African American heritage. Bookworms should look through *Literary Washington* by David Cutler.

History

The first American literature consisted of accounts of exploration and discovery in the New World. Captain John Smith's *The Generall Historie of Virginia, New-England, and the Summer Isles* (1624) displayed the largeness of vision and vigorous style of Elizabethan writers. The works of William Byrd (1674 – 1744), a Virginia plantation owner, were among the first to exhibit an emerging provincialism. His diaries, published as *Secret Diary* and *Another Secret Diary* (in 1941 and 1942, respectively) have been compared to the works of the great English diarist Samuel Pepys.

Great pieces of political writing, remembered for their felicity rather than imaginative content, are Jefferson's Declaration of Independence (1776) and *Notes on the State of Virginia* (1787). Alexis de Toqueville's *Democracy in America* describes what a radical experiment in social and political systems the founding of the United States represented in its time.

Even today *Colonial Virginia* (two volumes, 1960) remains as one of the best accounts of the history of an American colony. *Patriotic Gore* by Edmund Wilson is an absorbing account and narrative in its own right of the literature of the Civil War.

For more recent DC history, read Woodward and Bernstein's *All the President's Men*, for the nitty-gritty on the Watergate scandal of the Nixon administration.

Autobiographies & Biographies

Fawn M Brodie's *Thomas Jefferson: An Intimate Portrait* reveals a side of this great intellectual's private life. It includes some surprising discussions on his relationships with some of his slaves. For more in-depth coverage of this statesman, Dumas Malone's *Jefferson and His Times* (six volumes) is a monumental work by a Pulitzer Prize winner.

Douglas Southall Freeman's *George Washington* (seven volumes) and *Lee* (four volumes), both Pulitzer Prize winners, survey the lives of two of Virginia's most famous personages (both works have been abridged into more digestible single-volume histories). The Lee biography is especially important, as Lee never penned his own memoirs, but it has come under considerable criticism in recent years.

The diaries of Mary Chesnut, gathered in the 400,000-word *Diary from Dixie* (1905), were considered one of the greatest personal eyewitness accounts of the war and life in the Confederacy until recently. Many historians now contend that much of it may have been 'remembered' and written during Reconstruction. Historian C Vann Woodward edited the diaries and published them as *Mary Chesnut's Civil War* in 1982, an effort that earned him a Pulitzer Prize. Despite the controversy the end result is captivating.

Booker T Washington's autobiography, *Up from Slavery* (1903), focuses on the life of this great black educator who was born into slavery in Virginia and rose to become one of the first African American reformers.

The Life of John Marshall by Albert J Beveridge is a Pulitzer Prize-winning book that examines the life of the powerful Virginia politician and the nation's chief justice for 34 years.

Richard C Davids' *The Man Who Moved a Mountain* recounts the life and work of the Reverend Bob Childress and the people of Buffalo Mountain and other parishes in the Blue Ridge Mountains whom he served for so many years.

Natural History

A good natural history is Jane Scott's *Between Ocean & Bay: A Natural History of Delmarva* (Tidewater Press, 1991).

Christopher P White's *Endangered and Threatened Wildlife of the Chesapeake Bay Region* (Tidewater Press, 1982) deals more with the Maryland Eastern Shore and has some Delaware information.

For a look at the Maryland watermen's quarry, the blue crab, read William Warner's *Beautiful Swimmers*. Tom Horton's *Bay Country* makes a readable reflection on the environmental issues challenging the Chesapeake and its people.

Novels

Read Gore Vidal's *Washington DC, Burr,* or *Lincoln* to put you in the mood for a DC visit. Elliott Roosevelt, FDR's son who died in 1990, wrote a series of murder mysteries in which First Lady Eleanor Roosevelt solves crimes committed inside the White House during the Depression.

Though a fictionalized account, William Styron's *The Confessions of Nat Turner* was a bestseller and won the Pulitzer Prize. The novel has been widely praised for its narrative construct (in which the white author puts himself in black Nat Turner's shoes) but criticized for its somewhat stilted view of the African American.

James Michener lived for years on Maryland's Eastern Shore where he wrote the blockbuster *Chesapeake*. Anne Tyler's popular novels like *The Accidental Tourist* unfold the bittersweet world of contemporary Baltimore life.

Photography

Delaware Discovered by Kevin Fleming (Portfolio, 1992) is a terrific coffee table book of photographs that capture the First State and its residents in all their glory.

The latest book from longtime bay author/photographer Robert DeGast is *Five Rivers* (Johns Hopkins, 1995), a tale of solo exploration on the bay's main tributaries by small sailboat.

ONLINE SERVICES

For DC, basic tourist information can be found at *www.wash.org*.

An amazing array of Internet sites are devoted to Virginia and its towns. Click on the Virtual Library of Hampton Roads (after a simple Web search for 'Virginia'), and you get a list of the Virginia towns/cities in alphabetical order that have home pages on the World Wide Web. These days you need hardly leave your keyboard to visit Virginia, and the fine pictures mean that you'll always see the sights in the best of weather! In fact, the first two US towns fully experimentally online were Virginia's Blacksburg and Abingdon. Some towns have comprehensive Web sites; these include Richmond, Charlottesville, Norfolk, Alexandria, and Williamsburg. Among the weirder sites is put up by a peanut outlet in Wakefield (between Petersburg and Hampton Roads on US Route 460).

The home page for Maryland's Office of Tourism Development *(www.mdisfun.org)* is currently a rather primitive site, but it's slated for major upgrading. You can find basic information on Delaware at *www.state.de.us*.

There are a host of related sites, such as the US National Parks' home page, 'Best Brew Pubs,' restaurant guides, and accommodations (many of which now have their own home page).

MEDIA

Newspapers & Magazines

The dominant regional news source, the *Washington Post*, is also one of the nation's best newspapers. In addition, you can also readily find the *Wall Street Journal*, *USA Today*, and the *New York Times*. Larger city newsstands sell some international newspapers, including the *International Herald Tribune*. See regional chapters for information on the local alternative and ethnic press.

Radio & TV

All rental cars have car radios, and travelers can choose from hundreds of stations. Most stations have a range of less than 100 miles, and in and near major cities scores of stations crowd the airwaves with a wide variety of news, music, and entertainment.

Listen for National Public Radio (NPR), whose signal is usually on the left side of the FM dial, for sophisticated news and feature programming. NPR's *Morning Edition* and its afternoon *All Things Considered* are the country's best national news programs.

All major TV networks have affiliated stations throughout the USA, including ABC, CBS, NBC, FOX, and PBS. Most hotels also offer cable programming, including continuous news coverage on Cable News Network (CNN), other news networks, and the Weather Channel. CNN's C-SPAN airs live broadcasts of Congress.

PHOTOGRAPHY & VIDEO

Film & Equipment

Print film for amateur photography is widely available at photo shops, supermarkets, and discount drugstores throughout the region. Color print film has a greater latitude than color slide film (that is, it can handle a wider range of light and shadow); however, slide film, particularly the slower speeds (under 100 ASA), has better resolution than print film. Slide film at the exact speed you want and B&W film may be harder to find and more expensive outside of cities. It's wise to carry a spare camera battery.

Drugstores are a good place to get your print film processed cheaply. If you drop it off by noon, you can usually pick it up the next day. A roll of 100 ASA 35 mm color film with 24 exposures will cost about $6 to get processed; B&W film is often double that. Many one-hour photo processing shops offer a quicker turnaround for a higher price.

Video

Overseas visitors considering a video purchase should note that the USA uses the National Television System Committee (NTSC) color TV standard, which is incompatible with other standards (PAL or SECAM) used in Africa, Europe, Asia, and Australasia unless converted.

Restrictions

Museums and galleries may prohibit or restrict photography and videography – check their policy before shooting.

Airport Security

All checked and hand-carried luggage passes through X-ray machines, which is supposedly safe enough for all but high speed film (request a hand search on 1600 ASA or above). Leave yourself extra time to pass through security if your camera equipment or computer equipment needs to be hand searched.

TIME

The Capital Region operates on Eastern Standard Time. When it is noon in DC it is 5 pm in London, 3 am in Sydney, and 9 am in Los Angeles. Daylight Saving Time (one hour ahead of standard time) is in effect from 1 am on the first Sunday in April until 2 am on the last Sunday in October.

ELECTRICITY

In the USA voltage is 110V and the plugs have two (flat) or three (two flat, one round) pins. Plugs with three pins don't fit into a two-hole socket, but adapters are easy to buy at hardware or drugstores. Two-pin plugs, especially ones with equal dimensions, can easily slip out of the socket. Should this happen a quick remedy is to pull the prongs apart a bit for a tighter fit.

WEIGHTS & MEASURES

Distances are measured in feet (ft), yards (yds), and miles (m or mi). Three feet equal one yard (which is 0.914 meters); 1760 yards or 5280 feet are one mile. Dry weights are in ounces (oz), pounds (lbs), and tons (16 ounces equal one pound; 2000 pounds are one ton).

Liquid measures differ from dry measures. One pint equals 16 fluid ounces; two pints equals one quart, a common measure for liquids like milk. (Milk is also sold in half gallons – two quarts – and gallons – four quarts.) Gasoline is dispensed in US gallons, which is about 20% less than the imperial gallon. (US pints and quarts are also 20% less than imperial ones.) The most significant exception to the use of US customary measures is the wine industry, which employs a standard size 750ml bottle, but the labels of canned and liquid supermarket foods usually list both US customary measures and their metric equivalents. (For conversion formulas, see the chart on the inside back cover of the book.)

LAUNDRY

There are self-service, coin-operated laundry facilities in most towns of any size and in better campgrounds. Washing a load costs about $1 and drying it another $1. Coin-operated vending machines sell single-wash–size packages of detergent, but it's usually cheaper to pick up a small box at the supermarket. Some laundries have attendants who will wash, dry, and fold your clothes for you for an additional charge. To find a laundry, look under 'Laundries' or 'Laundries – Self-Service' in the yellow pages of the telephone directory. Dry cleaners are also listed under 'Laundries' or 'Cleaners.'

RECYCLING

Traveling in a car seems to generate large numbers of cans and bottles. If you'd like to save these for recycling, you'll find recycling centers in the larger towns. Materials accepted are usually plastic and glass bottles, aluminum and tin cans, and newspapers. Some campgrounds and a few roadside rest areas also have recycling bins next to the trash bins.

Perhaps better than recycling is to reduce your use of these products. Many gas stations and convenience stores sell large plastic insulated cups with lids that are inexpensive and ideal for hot and cold drinks. Bringing your own cups will usually get you a discount at cafes and gas stations.

Despite the appearance of many large cities, littering is frowned upon by most Americans. Travelers should respect the region even though some locals think it's OK to trash their territory. Some states have implemented anti-littering laws (which impose fines for violation) to try to curb the problem. When hiking and camping in the wilderness, take out everything you bring in – in some wilderness areas this includes *any* kind of garbage you may create.

HEALTH

Generally speaking, the USA is a healthy place to visit. There are no prevalent diseases or risks associated with traveling here, and the country is well served by hospitals. However, health care costs in the US are astronomical, so international travelers should take out comprehensive travel insurance before leaving home. If you're from a country with socialized medicine, you should find out what you'll need to do in order to be reimbursed for out-of-pocket money you may spend for health care in the USA.

Also, go to the emergency rooms of hospitals for emergencies only. Although these are often the easiest places to go for treatment, they are also incredibly expensive. Many city hospitals have 'urgent care clinics,' which are designed to deal with walk-in clients with less than catastrophic injuries and illnesses. You'll pay a lot less for treatment at these clinics. Likewise, you could simply look up a doctor in the yellow pages telephone directory under 'Doctors' or 'Physicians,' and try to make an appointment. Be aware, however, that many doctors have very busy schedules. Nonetheless, they may be able to refer you elsewhere. If you know someone in the area, consider asking them to recommend a doctor.

Predeparture Preparations

Health Insurance A travel insurance policy to cover theft, loss, and medical problems is a good idea, especially in the USA, where some hospitals will refuse care without evidence of insurance. There are a wide variety of policies and your travel agent should have recommendations. International student travel policies handled by STA Travel or other student travel organizations are usually a good value. Some policies offer lower and higher medical expenses options; the higher one is chiefly for countries like the USA with extremely high medical costs. Check the small print:

- Some policies specifically exclude 'dangerous activities' like scuba diving, motorcycling, and even trekking. If these activities are on your agenda, avoid this sort of policy.
- You may prefer a policy that pays doctors or hospitals directly, rather than your having to pay first and claim later. If you do have to file a claim later, keep all documentation. Some policies ask you to call back (reverse charges) to a center in your home country for an immediate assessment of your problem.
- Check whether the policy covers ambulance fees or an emergency flight home. If you have to stretch out on the plane, you will need two seats and somebody has to pay for them!

Medical Kit A useful small medical kit might include:

- Aspirin, acetaminophen, or panadol, for pain or fever.
- Antihistamine (such as Benadryl), which is useful as a decongestant for colds. It also eases the itch from allergies, insect bites, or stings, and minimizes motion sickness.
- Antiseptic, mercurochrome, and antibiotic powder or similar 'dry' spray, for cuts and grazes.
- Calamine lotion to ease irritation from bites or stings.
- Bandages for minor injuries.
- Scissors, tweezers, and a thermometer (airlines prohibit mercury thermometers).
- Insect repellent, sunscreen, and lip balm.

Health Preparations The best way to stay healthy during your travels is to start out that way. If you are embarking on a long trip, make sure your teeth are in good shape. If you wear glasses, take a spare pair and your prescription. You can get new spectacles made up quickly and competently for well under $100, depending on the prescription and frame you choose. If you require a particular medication, take an adequate supply and bring a prescription in case you lose the medication.

Immunizations No vaccinations are required to enter the US unless you are coming from a country that has had outbreaks of cholera or yellow fever. However, you might consider being immunized against hepatitis A. Plan ahead – some vaccinations require an initial shot followed by a booster, and others should not be given together – seek medical advice at least six weeks prior to travel.

Basic Rules

Care in what you eat and drink is paramount. When you're traveling, it's easy to forget to vary your diet or to skip meals altogether, but such oversights usually catch up with you either on the road or when you get home. Stomach upsets are the most likely travel health problem (between 30% and 50% of travelers experience this in a two-week stay). However, the majority of these upsets are relatively minor.

Don't become paranoid; trying the local food is part of the experience of travel, after all. If a restaurant is clean, the food should be OK. At buffet-style restaurants, be cautious of foods made with mayonnaise; these should be well chilled. Also make sure that burgers at fast-food joints are cooked thoroughly. If something smells or tastes like it has gone bad, don't take a chance.

Bottled drinking water, both carbonated and noncarbonated, is widely available in the USA, but most locals drink tap water.

Climatic & Geographical Ailments

The Capital Region has few extremes to merit serious caution, except for the summer heat and humidity, which can be disarming to people from colder or drier climates. Of course, backcountry adventures carry their own health risks and those heading to remote regions should know how to treat such conditions as hypothermia and giardia. Wilderness travelers should leave a detailed itinerary with someone at home and at a local ranger station and carry an emergency kit stocked with first-aid supplies, spare clothing, food and water, matches, a compass, a flashlight, and a whistle (three toots signals distress, as does a triangle of three smoky fires).

Sunburn To avoid painful sunburn, use sunscreen and wear a hat. For added protection apply zinc cream or some other barrier cream for your nose and lips. Calamine lotion soothes mild sunburn as does aloe lotion.

Heat Exhaustion Dehydration or salt deficiency can cause heat exhaustion. Take time to acclimatize to high temperatures and make sure that you drink plenty of liquids. Always carry – and use – a water bottle on long trips. Salt deficiency is characterized by fatigue, lethargy, headaches, giddiness, and muscle cramps. Salt tablets may help.

Vomiting or diarrhea can also deplete your liquid and salt levels. Anhydrotic heat exhaustion, caused by the inability to sweat, is quite rare. Unlike the other forms of heat exhaustion it is likely to strike people who have been in a hot climate for some time, rather than newcomers.

Heat Stroke Long, continuous periods of exposure to high temperatures can leave you vulnerable to this serious, sometimes fatal, condition, which occurs when the body's heat-regulating mechanism breaks down and body temperature rises to dangerous levels. Avoid excessive alcohol intake or strenuous activity when you first arrive in a hot climate.

Symptoms include feeling unwell, a lack of perspiration, and a high body temperature of 102°F to 105°F (39°C to 41°C). Hospitalization is essential for extreme cases, but meanwhile get out of the sun, remove clothing, wrap yourself in a wet sheet or towel, and fan continually.

Hypothermia Hypothermia results from the inability to maintain sufficient body heat. Though commonly associated with cold weather, overexertion coupled with coldness, wetness, and wind in almost any climate carries the risk of hypothermia. Symptoms include shivering and poor coordination. Avoid it by keeping clothing warm and dry, staying in motion, and of course, seeking shelter. Woolen clothing and special synthetics retain warmth even when wet, unlike cotton. If you'll be heading to the wilderness, a quality sleeping bag is a worthwhile investment, but be aware that goose down loses much of its insulating qualities when wet. Carry high-energy, easily digestible snacks, such as chocolate or dried fruit.

Get hypothermia victims out of the wind or rain, remove wet clothing, and replace with dry, warm clothes. Offer hot liquids – not alcohol – and high-calorie, easily digestible food. In advanced stages it may be necessary to place victims in warm sleeping bags and get in with them. Do not rub victims but place them near a fire or, if possible, in a warm (not hot) bath.

Motion Sickness Eat lightly before and during a trip to reduce the chance of motion sickness. Also try to find a place that minimizes disturbance, for example, near the wing on aircraft, near the center on buses. Fresh air usually helps, while reading or cigarette smoke doesn't. Commercial anti-motion sickness preparations, which can cause drowsiness, have to be taken before the trip commences; if you're feeling sick, it's too late. Ginger, a natural preventative, is available in capsule form.

Jet Lag Jet lag occurs when a person travels by air across more than three time zones (each time zone usually represents a one-hour time difference). It occurs because many of the functions of the human body (such as temperature, pulse rate, and emptying of the bladder and bowels) are regulated by internal 24-hour cycles called circadian rhythms. When we travel long distances rapidly, our bodies take time to adjust to the 'new time' of our destination, and we may experience fatigue, disorientation, insomnia, anxiety, impaired concentration, and loss of appetite. These effects will usually be gone within three days of arrival, but there are ways of minimizing the impact of jet lag:

- Rest for a couple of days prior to departure; try to avoid late nights and last-minute dashes for traveler's checks, passport, and other important items.
- Try to select flight schedules that minimize sleep deprivation; arriving late in the day means you can go to sleep soon after you arrive. For very long flights, try to organize a stopover.
- Avoid excessive eating (which bloats the stomach) and drinking alcohol and caffeinated beverages (which cause dehydration) during the flight. Instead, drink plenty of noncarbonated, nonalcoholic drinks such as fruit juice or water.
- Avoid smoking, as this reduces the amount of oxygen in the airplane cabin even further and causes greater fatigue.
- Make yourself comfortable by wearing loose-fitting clothes and perhaps bringing an eye mask and ear plugs to help you sleep.

Giardiasis Commonly known as giardia, and sometimes 'beaver fever,' this intestinal parasite often contaminates water in rivers and streams, even apparently pristine rushing streams in the backcountry. Symptoms are stomach cramps, nausea, a bloated stomach, watery, foul-smelling diarrhea, and frequent gas. Giardia can appear several weeks after exposure to the parasite; symptoms may disappear for a few days and then return, a pattern that may continue. Tinidazole, known as Fasigyn, or metronidazole (Flagyl), are the recommended drugs for treatment. Either can be used in a single treatment dose. Antibiotics are useless.

Hepatitis Hepatitis is a general term for inflammation of the liver. There are many causes of this condition: drug use, alcohol, and infections are but a few. Viral hepatitis is an infection of the liver, which can lead to jaundice (yellow skin), fever, lethargy, and digestive problems. It may have no symptoms at all, with the infected person not knowing that they have the disease. Travelers need not be too paranoid about the apparent proliferation of hepatitis strains. The main routes of transmission are via contaminated water, shellfish contaminated by sewage, or foodstuffs sold by food handlers with poor standards of hygiene.

The symptoms for Hep A are fever, chills, headache, fatigue, feelings of weakness and aches and pains, followed by loss of appetite, nausea, vomiting, abdominal pain, dark urine, pale feces, and jaundiced skin. The whites of the eyes may turn yellow. You should seek medical advice, but in general there is not much you can do apart from resting, drinking lots of fluids, eating lightly, and avoiding fatty foods. People who have had hepatitis must forgo alcohol for six months after the illness, as hepatitis attacks the liver and it needs that amount of time to recover.

Tetanus Tetanus is difficult to treat but is preventable with immunization. Tetanus occurs when a wound becomes infected by a germ that lives in the feces of animals or people, so carefully clean all cuts, punctures, or animal bites. Tetanus is also known as lockjaw, and the first symptom may be discomfort in swallowing or stiffening of the jaw and neck; this is followed by painful convulsions of the jaw and whole body.

Sexually Transmitted Diseases Sexual contact with an infected sexual partner spreads these diseases. While abstinence is the only 100% preventative, using condoms is also effective. Gonorrhea and syphilis are the most common of these diseases; sores, blisters, or rashes around the genitals, discharges, or pain when urinating are common symptoms. Symptoms may be less marked or not observed at all in women. Syphilis symptoms eventually disappear completely, but the disease continues and can cause severe problems in later years. Gonorrhea and syphilis are treated with antibiotics.

There are numerous other sexually transmitted diseases, and for most of them effective treatment is available. However, there is no cure for herpes, and there is also no cure for AIDS.

HIV/AIDS HIV (human immunodeficiency virus) may develop into AIDS (acquired immune deficiency syndrome). HIV is a major problem in many countries including the USA. Any exposure to blood, blood products, or bodily fluids may put you at risk. Infection can also arise from practicing unprotected sex or sharing contaminated needles. Apart from abstinence, the most effective preventative is always to practice safe sex using condoms. It is impossible to detect the HIV-positive status of an otherwise healthy-looking person without a blood test.

HIV/AIDS can also be spread through infected blood transfusions, but the blood supply in the USA is routinely screened for the virus. Vaccinations, acupuncture, tattooing, and body piercing can potentially be as dangerous as intravenous drug use if the equipment is not clean. A good resource for help and information is the US Center of Disease Control AIDS hotline (☎ 800-343-2347).

Insect-Borne Diseases & Bites

Ticks Ticks are a species of parasitic arachnid that suck blood from hosts by burying their head into skin. Hikers may encounter ticks in forest and grasslands; avoid them by wearing insect repellent and covering exposed skin on your legs and feet. By checking thoroughly after hiking, you can generally brush off any you might find before they become attached. If a tick has become attached, resist yanking it out; this will likely break off the body and leave the head in, increasing the risk of infection, and worse yet, the risk of Lyme disease. Rather, you want to induce the tick to remove itself completely: Try covering it with Vaseline, alcohol, or oil, or press something hot (say, a match or the lit end of a cigarette) against the tick until it backs out. If you fall ill in the next couple of weeks, consult a doctor.

Bedbugs & Lice Bedbugs live in a variety of places but particularly in dirty mattresses and bedding. In a hotel room (most often a very cheap one), spots of blood on bedclothes or on the wall around the bed can be taken as a suggestion to find other accommodations. Bedbugs leave itchy bites in neat rows. Calamine lotion may help.

All lice cause itching and discomfort. They make themselves at home in your hair (head lice), your clothing (body lice), or in your pubic hair (crabs). You catch lice through direct contact with infected people or by sharing combs, clothing, and the like. Special powder or shampoo available at drugstores will kill the lice. Infected clothing should then be washed in hot water.

WOMEN TRAVELERS

When traveling, women often face different situations than men do. If you are a woman traveler, especially a woman traveling alone, it's not a bad idea to get in the habit of traveling with a little extra awareness of your surroundings.

The USA is such a diverse and varied country that it's difficult to make accurate generalizations. People are generally friendly and happy to help travelers, and you will probably have a wonderful time unmarred by dangerous encounters. To ensure that this is the case, consider the following suggestions, which should reduce or eliminate your chances of problems. The best advice is to trust your instincts.

In general, you must exercise more vigilance in large cities than in rural areas. Try to avoid the 'bad' or unsafe neighborhoods or districts. If you are unsure which areas are considered unsafe, ask at your hotel or telephone the tourist office for advice. If you must go into or through these areas, it's best to go in a private vehicle (car or taxi). It's more dangerous at night, but in the worst areas crime can occur even in the daytime. Be aware that tourist maps can sometimes be deceiving, compressing areas that are not tourist attractions and making the distances look shorter than they are.

Men may interpret a woman drinking alone in a bar as a bid for male company, whether you intend it that way or not. If you don't want the company, most men will respect a firm but polite 'no thank you.'

While there is less to watch out for in rural areas, women may still be harassed by men unaccustomed to seeing women traveling solo. Try to avoid hiking or camping alone, especially in unfamiliar places. Hikers all over the world use the 'buddy system' not only for protection from other humans, but also for aid in case of any accident or injury.

Don't hitchhike alone, and don't pick up hitchhikers if driving alone. If you get stuck on a road and need help, it's a good idea to have a premade sign to signal for help. At night avoid getting out of your car to flag down help; turn on your hazard lights and wait for the police to arrive. Be extra careful at night on public transit, and remember to check the times of the last bus or train before you go out at night.

To deal with potential dangers, many women protect themselves with a whistle, mace, cayenne-pepper spray, or some karate training. If you do decide to purchase a spray, contact a police station to find out about regulations and training classes. Laws regarding sprays vary from state to state, so be informed based on your destination. One law that doesn't vary is carrying sprays on airplanes – due to their combustible design, it is a federal felony to carry them on board.

Women must also contend with the extra threat of rape, not only in urban but also in rural areas, albeit to a lesser degree. The best way to deal with the threat of rape is to avoid putting yourself in vulnerable situations. Conducting yourself in a common-sense manner will help you to avoid most problems. For example, you're more vulnerable if you've been drinking or using drugs than if you're sober; you're more vulnerable alone than if you're with company; and you're more vulnerable in a high-crime urban area than in a 'better' district.

If despite all precautions you are assaulted, call the police; in any emergency situation, telephoning '911' will connect you with the emergency operator for police, fire, and ambulance services. (In some rural areas where 911 is not active, just dial '0' for the operator.) Most cities and larger towns have rape crisis centers and women's shelters that provide help and support; they are listed in the telephone directory, or if not, the police should be able to refer you to them.

Organizations

The headquarters for National Organization for Women (NOW; ☎ 202-331-0066), 1000 16th St NW, Suite 700, Washington, DC 20036, is a good resource for women-related information; it can also refer you to state and local chapters. Planned Parenthood (☎ 212-541-7800), 810 7th Ave, New York, NY 10019, can refer you to clinics throughout the country and offer advice on medical issues. Check the yellow pages of the phone directory under 'Women's Organizations and Services' for local resources. Women's bookstores, which can be found in the yellow pages under 'Bookstores,' are good places to find out about gatherings, readings, and meetings, and often have bulletin boards where you can find or place travel and short-term housing notices.

GAY & LESBIAN TRAVELERS

There are gay people everywhere in the USA, but by far the most visible are in the major cities, where it is easier for gay men and women to live their lives with a certain amount of openness. In rural areas discrimination often forces them to lead closeted lives. In such areas, it would be wise to exercise discretion.

Gay travelers will particularly enjoy the lively and open gay community in Washington, DC (see the DC chapter for gay press, bookstores, bars, clubs, and businesses welcoming gay travelers). Baltimore has a vital gay scene, too. Rehoboth Beach in Delaware is a popular beach resort for gay/lesbian couples, with many gay-owned and gay-friendly establishments. See Baltimore and Rehoboth for more details.

Apart from the Virginia cities close to

Washington, DC, Charlottesville and Richmond are about the only other places in the state that have good services for gay and lesbian travelers. In Charlottesville, the Lesbian, Gay & Bisexual Union (LGBU) Helpline number is ☎ 804-982-2773; it operates Sunday to Wednesday from 7 to 10 pm. In Richmond, the Gay Information Line is ☎ 804-353-3626.

Resources

A couple of good national guidebooks are *The Women's Traveller*, which provides listings for lesbians, and *Damron's Address Book*, directed at gay men. Both are published by the Damron Company (☎ 415-255-0404, 800-462-6654), PO Box 422458, San Francisco, CA 94142-2458. *Ferrari's Places for Women* and *Places for Men* are also useful. These can be found at any good bookstore as can guides to specific cities (for example, check out *Betty & Pansy's Severe Queer Review of Washington, DC)*.

In Search of Gay America by Neil Miller is a good book about gay and lesbian life across America in the 1980s. It's a bit dated but gives a good view of life outside of the major cities. For a pre-plague view Edmund White's *States of Desire* focuses on gay men in the 1970s and is quite good.

Another good resource is the Gay Yellow Pages (☎ 212-674-0120), PO Box 533, Village Station, NY 10014-0533, which has a national edition and also regional editions. For online information, America Online hosts the Gay and Lesbian Community Forum and also the online home of National Gay/Lesbian Task Force (NGLTF), GLAAD, Parents-Friends of Lesbians and Gays (P-FLAG), and other regional, state, and national organizations. Michelle Quirk, host of AOL's Gay & Lesbian Community Forum, can be contacted at quirk@aol.com.

Organizations

Some national resource numbers that may prove useful include: National AIDS/HIV Hotline (☎ 800-342-2437), Washington, DC-based National Gay/Lesbian Task Force (☎ 202-332-6483), and Lambda Legal Defense Fund (☎ 212-995-8585 New York City office, 213-937-2727 Los Angeles office).

DISABLED TRAVELERS

Travel within the USA is becoming easier for people with disabilities. Of course, the more populous the area, the greater the likelihood of finding facilities for the disabled, so it's important to call ahead to see what is available. Washington, DC, is one of the most accessible cities on the planet. Public buildings (including hotels, restaurants, theaters, and museums) are now required by law to be wheelchair accessible and to have accessible restroom facilities. Public transportation services (buses, trains, and taxis) must be accessible to all, including those in wheelchairs, and telephone companies are required to provide relay operators for the hearing impaired. Many banks now provide ATM instructions in Braille, and you will find audible crossing signals as well as dropped curbs at busier roadway intersections.

Larger private and chain hotels (see Accommodations below for listings) include accessible rooms, though definitions of 'accessible' may vary from standard ground floor rooms to fully equipped suites. Main car-rental agencies offer hand-controlled models at no extra charge. All major airlines, Greyhound buses, and Amtrak trains will allow service animals to accompany passengers and will frequently sell two-for-one packages when seriously disabled passengers require attendants. Airlines will also provide assistance for boarding and deplaning the flight, as well as for making connections – just ask for assistance when making your reservation. (Note: Airlines must accept wheelchairs as checked baggage and have an onboard chair available, though some advance notice may be required on smaller aircraft.)

Resources

A DC advocacy organization for the disabled publishes *Access Washington*, a guide to metro DC for people with physical disabilities ($6 from IPACHI, ☎ 202-547-8081, 300 Eye St NE, Suite 202, Washington, DC 20002).

Virginia's main visitor information guide and official visitor map (see Tourist Offices above) includes notes on attractions with handicapped facilities. The *Virginia Travel Guide for the Disabled* (2nd edition) is a first-rate publication that treats all the facilities, restaurants, and accommodations in turn. It is published by the Opening Door, Inc ($5, ☎ 540-633-6752), 8049 Ormesby Lane, Woodford, VA 22580.

The *Handicapped Travel Newsletter* is a nonprofit publication with good information on traveling around the world and updates on US government legislation. Subscriptions are $10 annually (☎/fax 903-677-1260, PO Drawer 269, Athens, TX 75751).

US residents who are medically blind or permanently disabled and who are planning to visit national park sites should apply for Golden Access Passports, which offer free admission to all sites in the national park system and a 50% reduction on camping fees. You can apply in person at any national park or regional office of the USFS or NPS or call ☎ 800-365-2267 for information.

Organizations

There are a number of organizations and tour providers that specialize in the needs of disabled travelers:

Access
The Foundation for Accessibility by the Disabled, PO Box 356, Malverne, NY 11565 (☎ 516-887-5798)

Information Center for Individuals with Disabilities
Free listings and travel advice. Fort Point Place, 1st Floor, 27-43 Wormwood St, Boston, MA 02210 (☎ 617-727-5540, TTY 617-345-9743 or 800-248-3737)

Mobility International USA
Advises disabled travelers on mobility issues and runs an exchange program. PO Box 3551, Eugene, OR 97403 (☎ 503-343-1284)

Moss Rehabilitation Hospital's Travel Information Service
1200 W Tabor Rd, Philadelphia, PA 19141-3099 (☎ 215-456-9600, TTY 215-456-9602)

SATH
Society for the Advancement of Travel for the Handicapped
347 Fifth Ave No 610, New York, NY 10016 (☎ 212-447-7284)

Twin Peaks Press
Publishes several handbooks for disabled travelers. PO Box 129, Vancouver, WA 98666 (☎ 360-694-2462, 800-637-2256)

SENIOR TRAVELERS

When retirement leaves the time clock behind and the myriad 'senior' discounts begin to apply, the prospect of exploring the USA tempts foreigners and native-born alike. Though the benefits begin at various ages depending on the attraction, travelers from 50 years and up can expect to receive cut rates and benefits unknown to (and the envy of) their younger fellows. Be sure to inquire about such rates at hotels, museums, and restaurants.

US citizens age 62 and over who are planning to visit national parks and campgrounds can cut costs greatly by using the Golden Age Passport, a card that allows seniors (and those traveling in the same car) free admission to all sites in the national park system and a 50% reduction on camping fees. You can apply in person at any national park or regional office of the USFS or NPS or call ☎ 800-365-2267 for information and to place orders.

Organizations

Some national advocacy groups that can help in planning your travels include the following:

American Association of Retired Persons
AARP, an advocacy group for Americans 50 years and older, is a good resource for travel bargains. A one-year membership is available to US residents for $8. 601 E St NW, Washington, DC 20049 (☎ 800-424-3410)

Elderhostel
Elderhostel is a nonprofit organization that offers seniors the opportunity to attend

academic college courses throughout the USA and Canada. The programs last one to three weeks, include meals and accommodations, and are open to people 55 years and older and their companions. 75 Federal St, Boston, MA 02110-1941 (☎ 617-426-8056)

Grand Circle Travel
This organization offers escorted tours and travel information in a variety of formats and distributes a free useful booklet, *Going Abroad: 101 Tips for Mature Travelers*. 347 Congress St, Boston, MA 02210 (☎ 617-350-7500, fax 617-350-6206)

National Council of Senior Citizens
Membership (open to both nonresidents and US residents) in this group gives access to added Medicare insurance, a mail-order prescription service, and a variety of discount information and travel-related advice. Fees are $13/30/150 for one year/three years/lifetime. 1331 F St NW, Washington, DC 20004 (☎ 202-347-8800)

TRAVEL WITH CHILDREN

With its many historical, cultural, and recreational attractions, the Capital Region is a popular destination for families with children. In Washington, DC, many of these attractions are free, offering budget travelers unsurpassed opportunities for kid-friendly entertainment and enrichment. Many hotels catering to families offer such incentives as special discounts, baby-sitting services, and children's activities and menus; check package specials for economical and convenient perks.

For information on enjoying travel with kids, read *Travel with Children* by Lonely Planet cofounder Maureen Wheeler. Those heading to DC with kids age eight and up may want to look through *Kidding Around Washington, DC* by A Anderson.

DANGERS & ANNOYANCES

Personal Security & Theft

In urban areas here as well as around the world it is wise to exercise caution to avoid trouble. Muggings can occur and some cities, like Richmond, Virginia, have drug problems. Stay out of dangerous districts, and check with your hotel staff or the visitors center to identity which areas are safe to visit and travel through and which are not. Secure your cash in a front pocket, money belt, or hotel safe; leave other valuables home. Maintain an awareness of your surroundings and try not to look hopelessly lost and confused (even if you are). Of course, you will likely find more friendly people eager to help you than people trying to take advantage, so be prepared for both – trust your instincts.

Always lock cars and put valuables out of sight, whether leaving the car for a few minutes or longer, and whether you are in a town or in the remote backcountry. Rent a car with a lockable trunk. If your car is bumped from behind in a remote area, it's best to keep going to a well-lit area or service station.

In hotels, don't leave valuables lying around your room. Use safety-deposit boxes or at least place valuables in a locked bag. Don't open your door to strangers – check the peephole or call the front desk if unexpected guests try to enter. Throughout the region call ☎ 911 in case of an emergency.

Street People The USA has a lamentable record in dealing with its most unfortunate citizens, who often roam the streets of large cities in the daytime and sleep by store fronts, under freeways or in alleyways and abandoned buildings. Street people and panhandlers may approach visitors in the larger cities and towns; nearly all of them are harmless. It's an individual judgment call whether it's appropriate to offer them money or anything else.

Guns The USA has a widespread reputation as a dangerous place because of the availability of firearms. This reputation is partly deserved, but it's also propagated and exaggerated by the media. In rural areas, do be careful in the woods (wear bright colors) during the fall hunting season, when unsuccessful or drunken hunters may be less selective in their targets than one might hope.

Recreational Hazards

In wilderness areas the consequences of an accident can be very serious, so inform someone of your route and expected return. Backcountry adventurers should be prepared for sudden changes in weather conditions; carry emergency survival equipment and know the symptoms of and treatment for hypothermia. Avoid driving after heavy snowfalls; surprisingly few local drivers have developed the expertise of driving in these conditions.

A major summer annoyance in the Tidewater (especially Chincoteague, Assateague, and the Eastern Shore) are the swarms of mosquitoes. Make sure you bring plenty of repellent (some locals swear by an Avon product with repellent qualities called 'Skin So Soft'; readily available locally).

EMERGENCY

Throughout most of the USA dial ☎ 911 for emergency service of any sort; in large cities or areas with substantial Hispanic populations, Spanish-speaking emergency operators may be available, but other languages are less likely. This is a free call from any phone. A few rural phones might not have this service, in which case dial 0 for the operator and ask for emergency assistance – it's still free. Each state also maintains toll-free numbers for traffic information and emergencies.

Lost or Stolen Documents

Carry a photocopy of your passport separately from your passport. Copy the pages with your photo and personal details, passport number, and US visa. If it is lost or stolen, this will make replacing it easier. In this event, you should call your embassy. You can find your embassy's telephone number by dialing ☎ 202-555-1212, which is directory inquiries for Washington, DC.

Similarly, carry copies of your traveler's check numbers and credit-card numbers separately. If you lose your credit cards or they are stolen, contact the company immediately. Following are toll-free numbers for the main credit cards. Contact your bank if you lose your ATM card.

Visa . . . . ☎ 800-336-8472
MasterCard . . . . ☎ 800-826-2181
American Express . . . . ☎ 800-528-4800
Discover. . . . . ☎ 800-347-2683
Diners Club . . . . ☎ 800-234-6377

LEGAL MATTERS

If you are stopped by the police for any reason, bear in mind that there is no system of paying fines on the spot. For traffic offenses, the police officer will explain your options to you. Attempting to pay the fine to the officer is frowned upon at best and may lead to a charge of bribery to compound your troubles. Should the officer decide that you should pay up front, he or she can exercise their authority and take you directly to the magistrate instead of allowing you the usual 30-day period to pay the fine.

If you are arrested for more serious offenses, you are allowed to remain silent and are presumed innocent until proven guilty. There is no legal reason to speak to a police officer if you don't wish to. All persons who are arrested are legally allowed (and given) the right to make one phone call. If you don't have a lawyer or family member to help you, call your embassy. The police will give you the number upon request.

For information on driving laws, car rental, insurance, and other automobile related concerns, see the Getting Around chapter.

Drinking Laws

The drinking age is 21 and you need an ID (identification with your photograph on it) to prove your age if anyone asks for it. Stiff fines, jail time, and penalties could be incurred if you're caught driving under the influence of alcohol. During festive holidays and special events, road blocks are sometimes set up to deter drunk drivers.

BUSINESS HOURS

Generally speaking, business hours are from 9 am to 5 pm, but there are certainly no hard and fast rules. In any large city, a few supermarkets, restaurants, and the main post office are open 24 hours. Shops are usually open from 9 or 10 am to 5 or 6 pm, but in shopping malls they're often open until 9 pm, except on Sunday when hours are noon to 5 pm. Post offices are open from 8 am to 4 or 5:30 pm Monday to Friday, and some are open from 8 am to 3 pm on Saturday. Banks are usually open from either 9 or 10 am to 5 or 6 pm Monday to Friday. A few banks are open from 9 am to 2 or 4 pm on Saturdays. Basically hours are decided by the individual branch so if you need specifics, give the branch a call.

PUBLIC HOLIDAYS

National public holidays are celebrated throughout the USA. Banks, schools, and government offices (including post offices) are closed, and transportation, museums, and other services are on a Sunday schedule. Holidays falling on a Sunday are usually observed the following Monday.

January

New Year's Day, January 1

Martin Luther King, Jr Day, the third Monday of the month. Celebrates this civil rights leader's birthday (January 15, 1929).

February

Presidents' Day, the third Monday of the month. Celebrates the birthdays of Abraham Lincoln (February 12, 1809) and George Washington (February 22, 1732).

April

Easter, the first Sunday in spring after a full moon, usually in April. Those who observe the holiday may go to church, eat a holiday meal, dye eggs, eat chocolate eggs, or do any combination of the above. Travel during this weekend is usually expensive and crowded. Incidentally, Good Friday (the Friday before Easter) is not a public holiday.

May

Memorial Day, the last Monday in the month. Honors the war dead (and also marks the unofficial first day of the summer tourist season).

July

Independence Day, July 4. Commemorates the adoption of the Declaration of Independence on that date in 1776; celebrated throughout the country with parades, fireworks displays, and a huge variety of other events.

September

Labor Day, the first Monday of the month. Honors working people (and also unofficially marks the end of the summer tourist season).

October

Columbus Day, the second Monday of the month. Commemorates the landing of Christopher Columbus in the Bahamas on October 12, 1492. Though it is a federal holiday, many Native Americans do not consider this event to be cause for celebration.

November

Veterans Day, the 11th. Honors war veterans.

Thanksgiving, the fourth Thursday. Commemorating the Jamestown colonists' first harvest, this holiday is one of the most important annual family gatherings. The holiday is celebrated with a bounty of food, parades, and televised football games. The following day is the biggest shopping day of the year – everyone burns off pumpkin pie by running shopping relays through the malls in search of Christmas presents and sales.

December

Christmas. The night before the 25th is as much an event as the day itself with church services, caroling in the streets, people cruising neighborhoods looking for the best light displays, and stores full of procrastinators.

Besides the above holidays, the USA celebrates a number of other events. Retailers remind the masses of coming events with huge advertising binges running for months before the actual day. Because of this tacky overexposure some of these events are nicknamed 'Hallmark Holidays' after the greeting card manufacturer. In larger cities with diverse cultures, traditional holidays of other countries are also celebrated with as much, if not more, fanfare. Unlike the above, however, most businesses stay open for the following:

January

Chinese New Year, begins the end of January or beginning of February and lasts two weeks. The first day is celebrated with parades, firecrackers, fireworks, and lots of food.

February

Valentine's Day, the 14th. No one knows why St Valentine is associated with romance in the USA, but this is a day of roses, sappy greeting cards, and packed restaurants. Some people wear red and give out candies imprinted with the invitation to 'Be My Valentine.'

March

St Patrick's Day, the 17th. The patron saint of Ireland is honored by all those who feel the Irish in their blood and by those who want to feel Irish beer in their blood. Everyone wears green (or you may be pinched), stores sell green bread, bars serve green beer, and towns and cities put on lively parades of marching bands and frolicking community groups. Wearing orange on this day may earn you hard stares.

April

Passover, either in March or April, depending on the Jewish calendar. Families get together to honor persecuted forebears, partake in the symbolic seder dinner, and eat unleavened bread.

May

Cinco de Mayo, the 5th. Originally a commemoration of the day the Mexicans wiped out the French Army in 1862, it's now the day all Americans get to eat lots of Mexican food and drink margaritas.

Mothers Day, the second Sunday. Honors moms with lots of cards, flowers, and dinners out (many of the nicer restaurants are packed for early family dinners).

June

Fathers Day, the third Sunday. Same idea as Mothers Day, different parent.

October

Halloween, the 31st. Kids and adults dress in costumes. In safer neighborhoods children go 'trick-or-treating' door to door for candy. Adults go to parties to act out their alter egos.

November

Day of the Dead, the 2nd. Observed in areas with Mexican communities, this is a day for families to honor dead relatives and make breads and sweets resembling skeletons, skulls and such.

Election Day, the 2nd Tuesday of the month. This is the chance for US citizens to perform their patriotic duty. Even more flags are flown than on July 4 and signs with corny photos of candidates decorate the land.

December

Hanukkah, eight days in December, according to the Jewish calendar. Also called 'The Feast of Lights.'

Kwanzaa, starts on the 26th and ends on the 31st. With the purpose of giving thanks for the harvest, this seven-day African American holiday is celebrated with families joining together for a feast and the elder men burying a plate of food to give back to the earth. Throughout the week people visit the homes of various families and practice seven different principles for which the dates are symbolic.

New Year's Eve, the 31st. Some folks dress up, head out to parties, and drink champagne, and others stay home, watch the festivities on TV, and drink champagne. The following day everyone stays home to nurse their hangovers and watch college football on TV.

SPECIAL EVENTS

The following is only a smattering of the many events that take place annually throughout the region. See the state chapters for expanded lists.

Washington, DC

Washington's major festivals are the Smithsonian's *Kite Festival* in March, the *Cherry Blossom Festival* in April (two weeks of festivities culminating in a grand parade), the *Easter Egg Roll* hosted by the First Lady on the White House lawn the day after Easter, the Smithsonian's *Folklife Festival* in late June/early July, the celebrations on Independence Day, and a great international block party on Adams Morgan Day in early September.

Virginia

With such a rich history there is no shortage of anniversaries, centennials, and regular festivals to celebrate. A trip to Virginia at any time will allow you to be witness to at least one or two. Local celebrations are described with the towns and cities themselves, but a few are worthwhile enough to merit special consideration.

January

Lee-Jackson Day, third Monday of January. Celebrated throughout Virginia but with special emphasis in Lexington, this holiday marks the birthdays of Robert E Lee (January 19) and Stonewall Jackson (January 21).

February

Washington's Birthday, late February. Celebrated in Alexandria with a parade complete with Revolutionary War reenactments. Also celebrated in Fredericksburg and at Mt Vernon.

April

Historic Garden Week, late April. Celebrated throughout Virginia, this holiday sees private houses opened to the public for ogling.

May

Tour Du Pont, early May. This famous cycling event passes through Fredericksburg, Richmond, Emporia, Roanoke, Salem, Blacksburg, and Bristol.

Shenandoah Apple Blossom Festival, early May. This four-day celebration attracts over 250,000 visitors with parades, arts and crafts shows, live music, races, and even a circus. Many concurrent activities take place in nearby valley towns.

June

Folklore Week, early June. Held at Smith Mountain Lake State Park near Roanoke, this festival (☎ 703-297-5998) includes displays of Appalachian arts and crafts.

Virginia Indian Heritage Festival, mid June. This event (☎ 804-253-4838) at Jamestown Settlement brings together the state's original inhabitants in a celebration of song and dance.

July

Virginia Highlands Festival (☎ 703-628-8141), late July. This event in Abingdon celebrates all that is Appalachia (arts, crafts, livestock, antique sales, and good ol' country music).

August

Manassas (Bull Run) Reenactments, late August. Witness reenactments (☎ 703-491-4045) of the two Civil War battles that took place at Manassas.

September

Virginia State Fair (☎ 804-228-3200), last week of September and first week of October. This state tradition at Strawberry Hill (Richmond) entertains with carnival rides, exhibitions of livestock and produce, and a variety of food.

October

Virginia Festival of American Film (☎ 804-924-3378), late October. Charlottesville hosts recent releases with stars in attendance.

November

Waterfowl Week, last week of November. The national wildlife refuge in Chincoteague (☎ 804-336-6122) sensitively opens nature trails to the public so they can observe the southward migration of Canada and snow geese.

December

Thanksgiving at Berkeley Plantation (☎ 804-272-3226), December 4. Virginia celebrates the original holiday (in 1619) at Charles City with a reenactment involving music and performances.

Maryland

April

Maryland Hunt Cup Race, third weekend. At Glyndon, the gentry go at it again; you'll likely see senators, congressional reps, and Presidential cabinet members if the weather is good.

World Championship Wildfowl Carving Competition, late April. Ocean City sees simply thousands of decoys.

May

William Paca House & Garden Tour, late in the month. This is really the best time all year to get behind the scenes and into Annapolis's historic homes.

July

Annapolis Rotary Club Crab Feast, late in the month. Eat crabs and drink beer with 10,000 people in a football stadium.

August

Rocky Gap Music Festival, early in the month. Make plans early – this event in Cumberland is the Woodstock of bluegrass music and draws a host of young people to dance, sing, footstomp, swim, camp and party on.

Maryland State Fair, late in the month. In a state that still likes to think of itself as rural, this is a great state fair. It takes place in Timoniumin.

September

National Hard Crab Derby, first weekend. It's hard to believe that crab racing can attract a cast of tens of thousands, but here's the proof. The derby at Crisfield is a weird hybrid of carnival, rodeo, and feast; locals love it.

October

United States Sailboat and Powerboat Shows, first and second weeks. During Annapolis's equivalent to Mardi Gras, hundreds of demo boats are in view in the waters around City Dock. The event draws legions of boat lovers and the simply curious for eating, drinking, and merrymaking.

November

Chesapeake Appreciation Days, last weekend. Do not miss this event at Sandy Point State Park if you want to see most of the bay's remaining working skipjacks testing their boats and crews in races before the opening of oyster season.

Waterfowl Festival, early in the month.

People from around the country go to Easton to buy decorative duck decoys, see master decoy carvers at work, and see or compete in retrieving dog trials.

December

Baltimore's New Year's Eve Extravaganza, December 31. A great fireworks display lights the sky.

First Night Annapolis, December 31. City-wide fine arts and music entertainment at nominal prices draws thousands to this big booze-free function – of course the city pubs are packed (as usual) with First Night dropouts.

Delaware

May

Tour Du Pont, mid-May. Great athletes flock to Wilmington for the official start of this premier cycling competition.

June

Clifford Brown Jazz Festival, mid-June to July. Wilmington's downtown jumps each evening.

July

Delaware State Fair, late July. Families descend on Harrington to enjoy this enormous event.

August

Nanticoke Powwow, early September. You can find traditional dances, storytelling, food and crafts at this powwow in Millsboro, but it does have a commercial carnival atmosphere.

Mid-November through December

Artists' Open Studio Tour. Many artists make their homes in Wilmington, and this event offers a festive way to see their work and get out on the town for wine, cheese, and conversations.

December

Festive Christmas in Old New Castle, middle weekends in December. Enjoy holiday festivities: candlelight, carolers, extended shopping hours, decorated evergreens, mulled cider, and hot, spiced wine.

WORK

Seasonal work is possible in national parks and other tourist sites, especially ski areas; for information, contact park concessionaires or local chambers of commerce. The beach resorts of Ocean City, Maryland, and Rehoboth Beach, Delaware, hire lots of young people to work in hotels, restaurants, and beach attractions. If you are in search of temporary summer employment in a setting with good daytime and nighttime attractions, consider the beach.

If you are a foreigner in the USA with a standard non-immigrant visitors visa, you are expressly forbidden to take paid work in the USA and will probably be deported if you're caught working illegally. Legislation passed in the 1980s makes it an offense to employ an illegal worker, so employers are required to establish the status of their employees. This requirement makes it much tougher for a foreigner to get work.

For foreigners to work legally, they need to apply for a work visa before they leave home, but such visas aren't easy to get. A J-1 visa, for exchange visitors, is issued mostly to young people who are going to work in summer camps; an H-2B visa, which you get when being sponsored by a US employer, is not easy to obtain since the employer has to prove that no US citizen or permanent resident is available to do the job.

ACCOMMODATIONS

Camping

Camping is the cheapest approach to a vacation. Visitors with a car and a tent can take advantage of hundreds of private and public campgrounds and RV parks at relatively low prices. The down side is having to hunker down amid the monster RVs that German-speaking visitors eloquently call *Campingschiffe* (camping ships); however, some campgrounds segregate tent and RV sites.

AAA's annually updated *Mid-Atlantic CampBook* covers public and private RV and tent sites in Delaware, Maryland, Virginia, and West Virginia; it's free to AAA members, but nonmembers can purchase it for $5.50 at AAA offices.

Public Campgrounds These are on public lands such as national forests, and national and state parks (also see Useful Organizations in the Outdoor Activities chapter).

Backcountry Camping Free dispersed camping (meaning you can camp almost anywhere) is permitted in many public backcountry areas. Sometimes you can camp right next to your car along a dirt road, especially in national forest areas (expect no facilities other than a bush). In other places, you can pack your gear in to a cleared campsite. Information and detailed maps are available from many local ranger stations (addresses and telephone numbers are given in the text) and may be posted along the road. A free camping permit is sometimes required in national forests and commonly so in national parks.

Camping in an undeveloped area, whether from your car or backpacking, entails basic responsibility. Choose a camp site at least 200 yards (approximately 70 adult steps) from water and wash up at camp, not in the stream, using biodegradable soap. Dig a six-inch-deep hole to use as a latrine and cover and camouflage it well when leaving the site. Burn toilet paper unless fires are prohibited. Carry out *all* trash. Use a portable charcoal grill or camping stove; don't build new fires. If there already is a fire ring, use only dead and fallen wood or wood you have carried in yourself. Make sure to leave the campsite as you found it.

Developed Sites The most basic developed areas usually have pit toilets, fire pits (or charcoal grills), and picnic tables. Many have drinking water (this is mentioned in the text), but it's always a good idea to have a few gallons of water when venturing out to the boonies. These basic campgrounds usually cost about $5 to $7 a night.

More developed sites usually have flush toilets, fire pits, picnic tables, and water, and some may have showers and/or recreational vehicle (RV) hookups. These cost several dollars more than basic sites. On the whole, national forest campgrounds tend to be of the less developed variety, and national park and state park campgrounds are more likely to have showers or RV hookups available. The less-developed sites are often available on a 'first-come, first-served' basis, so plan on an early arrival. Note that if you arrive early on Saturday or around a holiday, you may find campgrounds already full with people who arrived on Friday and are spending the weekend. More-developed areas may accept or require reservations. In popular parks, reservations are a good idea. When making a reservation, you will have to pay with Visa, MasterCard or Discover Card; call ☎ 800-365-2267 for national park reservations.

Costs given in the text for public campgrounds are per site. A site normally accommodates up to six people (or two vehicles). If there are more of you, you'll need two sites; however, some campgrounds have group sites. Public campgrounds often have seven- or 14-night limits.

Private Campgrounds These are on private property and are usually close to or in a town. Most are designed with recreational vehicles (RVs) in mind; tenters can camp in them, but fees are several dollars higher than in public campgrounds. Also, fees given in the text are for two people per site. There is usually an extra person charge of $1 to $3 per person. In addition, state and city taxes apply. However, they may offer discounts for week or month stays.

Facilities can include hot showers, coin laundry, swimming pool, full RV hookups, game area, playground, and convenience store. Kampgrounds of America (KOA) is a national network of private campgrounds with sites usually ranging from $12 to $15, depending on hookups. You can get the annual directory of KOA sites by calling or writing (☎ 406-248-7444, PO Box 30558, Billings, MT 59114-0558).

Hostels

The US hostel network is less widespread than in Canada, the UK, Europe, and Australia, and it's predominately in the north and coastal parts of the country. In the Capital Region, you can find hostels at the HI headquarters in Washington, DC; in Virginia at three locations (Virginia Beach, Bluemont, and Galax); and in Baltimore, Maryland. Not all of them are affiliated with Hostelling International (formerly American Youth Hostels). HI hostels offer discounts to HI members and usually allow nonmembers to stay for a few dollars more. Dormitory beds cost about $10 to $12 a night; private rooms cost in the $20s for one or two people, sometimes more.

HI hostels expect you to rent or carry a sheet or sleeping bag to keep the beds clean. Dormitories are segregated by gender and curfews may exist. Kitchen and laundry privileges are usually available in return for light housekeeping duties. There are information and advertising boards, TV rooms, and lounge areas. Alcohol may be banned.

Reservations are accepted and advised during the high season, and there may be a limit of a three-night stay then. You can call HI's national office (☎ 202-783-0552, 800-444-6111) to make reservations.

Motels & Hotels

Motel and hotel prices vary tremendously from season to season. A hotel charging $40 for a double in the high season may drop to $25 in the low; likewise, it may raise its rates to $55 for a special event when the town is overflowing. A $200-per-night luxury resort may offer special weekend packages for $79 in the low season. So be aware that prices in this guide can only be an approximate guideline at best. Also, be prepared to add room tax to prices.

Children are often allowed to stay free with their parents, but rules for this vary. Some hotels allow children under 18 to stay free with parents, others allow children under 12, and still others may charge a few dollars per child. You should call and inquire if traveling with kids.

Hotels' advertised prices are referred to as 'rack rates,' and these are not written in stone. If you simply ask about any specials that might apply, you can often save quite a bit of money. Booking through a travel agent may also result in significant savings. Members of AARP and AAA can qualify for a 'corporate' rate at several hotel chains. If you are in a resort area like Virginia Beach or Williamsburg, don't be afraid to ask for weekday or weeklong rates, and off-season discounts. If the owners exhibit disdain, then go somewhere else – there is ample choice.

If you're a resident of the USA or plan to spend more than a couple of months here, there's a discount program called Entertainment Publications that offers discounts for hotels. (See the Special Deals section above for more details.)

Making phone calls directly from your hotel room is usually a losing proposition. Hotels charge around 75¢ for local calls that cost only 20¢ at a pay phone. Long-distance rates are surcharged from 100% to 200%! The best plan of action is simply to carry a fistful of quarters and use a pay phone for all your calls.

Special events and conventions can fill up a town's hotels quickly, so call ahead to find out what will be going on. The chamber of commerce is always a good resource.

Budget Cheap hotels are hard to come by in this region, especially in Virginia. You'll often find motels with $20 rooms in small towns along major highways and in larger towns along the motel strips. A quick drive through one of these will yield a selection of neon-lit signs advertising '$19.95 for Two.' The few towns currently experiencing great popularity just won't have cheap motels, so what passes for a bottom-end motel in one town may pass for a middle hotel in another (at least in quality).

Budget rooms are usually small and beds may be soft or saggy, but the sheets should be clean. A minimal level of cleanliness is usually maintained, but expect scuffed walls, atrocious decor, old furniture and strange noises from your shower and even the heater and air conditioner. These places do normally have a private shower and toilet and a TV in each room. Some of even the cheapest motels may advertise kitchenettes: These may cost a few dollars more but give you the chance to cook a simple meal for yourself. Kitchenettes vary from a two-ring burner to a spiffy little mini-kitchen and may or may not have utensils. If you plan on doing a lot of kitchenette cooking, carry your own set.

Chains There are many motel and hotel chains in the USA. These offer a certain level of quality and style that tend to be consistent throughout the chain. People may say 'If you've stayed in one, you've stayed in them all!' This is partially true, but there are certainly individual variations depending on location. Some travelers prefer a particular chain and stay there repeatedly, expecting and generally finding a familiar level of comfort and service. These travelers should investigate the chain's frequent-guest program – discounts and guaranteed reservations are offered to faithful guests.

The following is only a rough guide: Prices vary dramatically by location and date, and the same chain may charge twice as much for a room in a popular city or resort as it does for one off a freeway exit in the middle of nowhere.

Generally the cheapest national chain is Motel 6. Rooms are small and very bland, but the beds are usually OK, every room has a TV and phone (local calls are free), and most properties have a swimming pool. Rooms start in the $20s for the lowest-priced single in a small town, in the $30s in larger towns. There's usually a flat $6 charge for each extra person.

Several motel chains compete with one another at the next price level, with rooms starting in the $30s or $40s. The main difference between these and bottom-end hotels is the size of each room – more space to spread out in. Beds are always reliably firm, decor may be a little more attractive, a 24-hour desk is often available, and perks may include free coffee, a table, cable or rental movies, or a bathtub. If these sorts of things are worth an extra $10 or $15 a night, then you'll be happy with the Super 8 Motels, Travelodge, Econo Lodge, or Quality Inn. Not all of these have pools, however; Super 8 Motels are especially lacking in this regard. Days Inns also start in this price range.

Motel chains with rooms in the $45 to $80 range (depending on location) offer noticeably nicer rooms; cafes, restaurants, or bars may be on the premises or adjacent to them; and the swimming pool may be indoor with a spa or exercise room also available. The Best Western chain offers good rooms in this price range, as do Comfort Inns, Ramada Inns, and Howard Johnsons (with conveniently attached coffee shops).

Privately Owned There are, of course, non-chain establishments in these price ranges. Some of them are funky historical hotels, full of turn-of-the-century furniture. Others look similar to the motel chains but just don't want to belong to one. In smaller, more rural towns, complexes of cabins are available – these often come complete with fireplace, kitchen, and an outdoor area.

Luxury Full-service hotels, with bellhops and door attendants, restaurants and bars, exercise rooms and saunas, room service and concierge, are found in the major cities. Some of the finest resorts in the US are in Virginia. These include Homestead in Bath County, Mountain Lake, Camberley's Martha Washington Inn in Abingdon, the Jefferson Hotel in Richmond, Tides Inn on the Northern Neck, and the Hotel Roanoke & Conference Center.

Reservations The cheapest places may not accept reservations, but at least phone from the road to see what's available; even if they don't take reservations, they'll often hold a room for an hour or two.

All chain hotels take reservations days or months ahead. Chains often have a toll-free number, but their central reservation system might not be aware of local special discounts. Booking ahead, however, gives you the peace of mind of a guaranteed room when you arrive.

Normally, you have to give a credit-card number to hold the room. If you don't show and don't call to cancel, you will be charged the first night's rental. Cancellation policies vary – some let you cancel at no charge 24 hours or 72 hours in advance, while others are less forgiving. Inquire about cancellation penalties when you book. Also alert the hotel if you plan on a late arrival – many will give your room away if you haven't arrived or called by 6 pm.

Here are reservation numbers of some of the best known chains:

Best Western	☎ 800-528-1234
Comfort Inn	☎ 800-221-2222
Days Inn	☎ 800-329-7466
Econo Lodge, Rodeway Inn	☎ 800-424-4777
Howard Johnson	☎ 800-446-4656
Motel 6	☎ 800-466-8356
Quality Inn	☎ 800-228-5151
Ramada Inns	☎ 800-272-6232
Travelodge	☎ 800-578-7878
Super 8 Motel	☎ 800-800-8000

B&Bs

You could travel all over the Capital Region and stay in a different B&B every night. If you can afford them, they are a good option. You get to meet locals and usually receive a monster of a breakfast that sets you up for the day.

European visitors should be aware that North American B&Bs are not quite the casual, inexpensive sort of accommodations found on the continent or in Britain. While they are usually family-run, many if not most B&Bs require advance reservations, though some will be happy to oblige the occasional drop-in. A large majority of B&Bs prohibit smoking, if not entirely at least in guests' rooms (stepping outside in winter to smoke is a true test of tobacco addiction!). B&B rates usually include a substantial breakfast, but lighter continental breakfasts are not unheard of.

Beyond the similarities mentioned above, B&Bs vary tremendously. The cheapest establishments, with rooms in the $30s and $40s, may have clean but unexciting rooms with a shared bathroom. Pricier places have rooms with private baths and, perhaps, amenities like fireplaces, balconies, and dining rooms with enticingly grand breakfasts and other meals. They may be in historical buildings, quaint country houses, or luxurious urban townhouses. Most B&Bs fall in the $50 to $100 price range, but some go over $100. The best are distinguished by owner-hosts who evince a friendly attention to detail and who can provide you with local information and contacts.

Reservations services include Bed & Breakfast Association of Virginia (☎ 540-672-4893), PO Box 791, Orange, VA 22960; and Bed & Breakfast of Maryland (☎ 410-269-6232, 800-736-4667), PO Box 2277, Annapolis, MD 21404. In Virginia you can also use the Division of Tourism reservation service (☎ 800-934-9184) to book country inns and B&Bs.

Condominiums

Like house and apartment rentals, these self-catering accommodations turn up in beach and ski resort areas. While they are often very expensive, several people can lodge for the same price, so they can be more economical than motels or hotels for larger groups. Contact the chamber of commerce in resort towns for information on condominium listings.

FOOD

Throughout the region the cuisine ranges from plentiful and cheap fast food choices (as little as $2 for a meal but not necessarily a very nutritious or tasty one) to elaborate steak houses where a three-course meal and wine costs $50 per person and up. The more distinctive cuisine of the region is served at the coast and around the Tidewater, where seafood and fish specialties predominate, and further south into Virginia, where you'll find Southern cuisine.

Restaurants serve breakfast from around 6 to 11 am; some budget motels put out a simple complimentary breakfast bar (juice, pastries, cold cereals) from around 7 to 9 am, and this can be a good way to save time as well as money. Standard breakfast choices range from a hurried bagel and coffee for under $2 to a full Southern-style breakfast of eggs, breakfast meat (bacon, ham, or beef), 'grits' (a hot cereal of ground hominy seasoned with butter and salt), and biscuits-and-gravy (around $7 for everything including juice and coffee). Several fast-food coffee shop chains, such as the Waffle House, offer breakfast around the clock.

Lunch is served from around 11:30 am to 2 or 3 pm (in cities the office-worker rush is from noon to 1 pm); sandwiches, salads, hamburgers, and other short orders go for around $4 to $5. At better restaurants, many lunch menus are identical to dinner menus, but lunch entrees cost about half (a $7 pasta plate at lunch might go for $12 at dinner). Many restaurants also serve all-you-can-eat lunch buffets, which are a good value for larger appetites.

Dinner is the largest (also the most expensive, most formal, and most varied) meal of the day. It's served from around 6 to 10 pm (dinners start later in the cities, but many restaurants offer bargain 'early bird' specials to fill seats around 5 pm). Traditionally, Sunday dinner is eaten as early as midday in the South (typically after church services, so the dress is most formal). In many cities, a large Sunday brunch served from 10 am to 2 pm has supplanted this tradition; many hotels and restaurants offer elaborate brunch buffets from which people graze for hours.

Budget travelers will want to seek out farmers markets for the freshest produce at the lowest prices. Many of these markets also offer prepared foods, deli meats, and bread, and some have inexpensive restaurants or cafeterias on-site. Grocery stores and deli counters also commonly have prepared foods for cheap takeout. Restaurants often offer discounts on meals for children and seniors.

Most restaurants have both nonsmoking and smoking areas; some prohibit smoking.

Seafood Specialties

The Tidewater and coastal regions are famous for fleet-fresh fish and shellfish. The most famous regional specialty is crab cakes – small tasty patties of crab meat lightly browned in oil, often offered as an appetizer or as an entree with a side order. At a typical Maryland crab house, plates of uncracked shellfish – oysters, crabs, clams, mussels, and shrimp – are served to tables covered with brown paper or newsprint. You'll be offered cracking tools and plastic bibs, and when you're done the server will collect the whole mess in the paper and toss it away in one quick swipe. A newer local tradition is the 'raw bar,' typically situated in a saloon, where you can sample local shellfish at a per-item cost.

Southern Cuisine

Classic Southern country cookin' means heaps of crispy fried chicken, a thick slice of baked Virginia ham, or hickory-smoked barbecue ribs, all served with several vegetables and your choice of biscuits or cornbread (called 'hushpuppies' in golf-ball-size form or 'corn pone' if it's cylindrical or triangular). If you can forgo the meat, you can order an inexpensive 'vegetable plate' with your choice of three or four vegetables – fried okra, corn-on-the-cob, black-eyed peas, and collard greens are typical selections. (Strict vegetarians should ask if the vegetables have been cooked with meat products.)

Southerners have more of a sweet tooth than other Americans. You will find such wonderful desserts as pecan pie, banana pudding, and peach cobbler, and some popular meats and vegetables are also laced with sugar (honey-roasted ham and sweet-potato soufflé are typical examples).

Not only is Southern food unique and the portions large, but the style of service may also differ in the South. Luncheon and dinner buffets are much more common (cafeterias are also much more popular), and many restaurants serve 'family-style,' seating unrelated groups at the same table and having patrons pass plates around and serve themselves. Note that many Southern families may say a prayer before eating; restaurant patrons would not be expected to join in (guests *would* be expected to do so at a family's home), but it's respectful to wait until they're done before serving or eating. You might also notice that many Southerners prefer food served less that piping hot, and many restaurants oblige. Server tips are slightly lower at buffet-style and family-style restaurants (around 10%); at cafeterias it's kind to leave a tip for the table clearer (a dollar or two).

Traditional soul food, the ethnic cuisine of African Americans, includes all the above plus exotic meats the preparation of which began in slavery days. Common examples include chitterlings (fried tripe, called 'chitlins') and pigs' feet. Okra was brought to the US from Africa by slaves.

Barbecue (BBQ) is a particularly revered Southern cuisine; pork is the he-man meat of choice (offered chopped, sliced, or in ribs), but BBQ chicken and beef are also available. 'Cue is served with either a mustard, vinegar, or tomato-based sauce, along with a slice of white bread and a side of coleslaw or baked beans. The classic venue is a no-frills roadside stand with long picnic tables out front and a hickory-scented smoking chimney out back.

Packages of gift-wrapped Southern foods make inexpensive souvenirs – you'll easily find fancy stone-ground grits in small canvas sacks, jars of local fruit preserves and syrups daintily topped with calico-print fabric, and colorful pickled relishes made of corn, cucumber, and red pepper.

DRINKS

Nonalcoholic Drinks

Most Americans start the day with a cup of coffee, and this ritual has expanded in recent years to include the full array of European choices – espresso, cappuccino, and caffé latte (though Americans prefer weaker roasts than Europeans). Beware of popular 'gourmet' coffees strangely flavored with such things as mint, anise, hazelnut, and cinnamon. Brewed decaffeinated coffee is widely available in restaurants. Orange juice often comes with breakfast.

Iced tea, sweetened or unsweetened and topped with a slice of lemon, is a popular nonalcoholic drink considered the 'house wine' of the South. This is what a server will bring if you ask for 'tea' in Virginia; in Delaware the same request will get you hot tea, so be sure to specify which you want. Sugared sodas – Coca-Cola, 7-Up, root beer, and the like – are also common nonalcoholic choices; lemonade is a popular summer drink. Milk comes in 'whole' or low-fat varieties. Restaurants serve iced tap water (safe to drink) on request at no charge with a meal.

Alcoholic Drinks

Wine is commonly served at dinner but not exclusively so; in the South in particular it's not uncommon for iced tea to be the dinner beverage. Microbrewed beer is growing increasingly popular, and you'll find cozy brew pubs in most cities. Hard liquor is widely available, but less commonly consumed than beer and wine. In general, Southerners are not big consumers of alcohol. This contrasts sharply with cities in the northern part of the region that have reputations as 'party towns,' such as Annapolis, Baltimore, and Ocean City in Maryland, along with Delaware's beach resorts.

Beverage laws vary from state to state, and liquor sales in stores and restaurants may be restricted on Sunday throughout the region. In Maryland and Delaware, only liquor stores sell alcoholic beverages; in Delaware the sale of spirits on Sunday is limited to establishments serving food. In DC and Virginia, beer and wine are sold at most markets, convenience stores, and even at gas stations; hard liquor is sold in liquor stores.

The minimum drinking age is 21 throughout the region and a photo identification card (driver's license, passport, etc) is often requested at stores and restaurants as proof of age (this ritual is known as being 'carded'). It's illegal to drive with open containers of alcohol in the car, and drunk driving is a serious offense. Public drinking is officially prohibited outdoors, but a discreet bottle of wine with a picnic is generally overlooked. Some outdoor venues allow alcohol but prohibit glass containers.

ENTERTAINMENT

The Capital Region offers many opportunities for live entertainment in music and the performing arts, from costumed 18th century drama and dance to contemporary political satire and experimental theater. Arts festivals are a great way to sample the cultural arts of the region for free or for only a small charge. These festivals showcase the region's most popular music, dance, and drama (not to mention food), and you'll likely find children's activities or performances too. Many bars and coffeehouses also feature a wide variety of live music – particularly jazz, folk, and rock – for inexpensive casual entertainment.

First-run, revival, or international films shown at cinemas throughout the region are both a popular and inexpensive way to entertain yourself. Bar- and cafe-hopping, billiard-shooting, and grazing at exotic restaurants are all inexpensive diversions as well.

Traditional Performing Arts

Historic cities such as Williamsburg often feature period performances of old English dramas and dance in keeping with their colonial character; characteristic venues include Elizabethan-style playhouses and English-style taverns. In the mountains, you can hear traditional Appalachian bluegrass music (a descendent of Elizabethan musical styles, on occasion accompanied by dulcimer) and country-western music in country stores, church halls, and saloons. You may even see square dancing or a regional form of flat-footin' called clogging.

Contemporary Performing Arts

In the Capital Region, DC features the most impressive variety of nationally and internationally renowned arts and artists, led by the preeminent programs of the John F Kennedy Center for the Performing Arts. The symphony, opera (led by Placido Domingo), and ballet are all tops in their fields. The large theaters downtown run long seasons of mainstream theater and musicals, while a small alternative theater district offers more experimental productions. Political satire and comedy are also popular diversions in the politically driven capital.

Throughout the region, larger cities host their own symphonies, ballet, and theater companies – some of which are quite good – along with cultural arts programs and venues. Many universities and colleges also offer a full calendar of performing-arts events and lectures open to the public.

Nightclubs and concert venues throughout the region attract nationally known jazz, rock, pop, and alternative musical performances for a cover charge (or equivalent drink minimum) or admission fee. In many dance clubs, the DJ becomes the performer, playing canned music accompanied by a running commentary designed to incite the crowd.

SPECTATOR SPORTS

American sports developed separately from those played in the rest of the world and, consequently baseball (with its clone softball), football, and basketball dominate the sports scene, both for spectators and participants. Football and basketball are sponsored by high schools and universities, which gives them a community foundation that reinforces their primacy. Basketball has the additional advantages of requiring only limited space and equipment, making it a most popular pastime among inner-city residents.

Baseball is so embedded in the American psyche that, despite complex rules and labor-management conflicts at professional levels, it continues to flourish. Many of the most meaningful metaphors in American language and political discourse come from the sport – such as 'getting to first base' or the recently debased 'three strikes and you're out.'

Building on the success of the 1994 World Cup, soccer has made limited inroads in the US. Many high schools and colleges have teams, and many folks, especially immigrants, play recreationally. In 1996 Major League Soccer began playing a full-length season. Despite naysayers initially predicting lack of interest, the games won national cable television coverage and attracted record numbers of fans, all boding well for the fledgling league. In 1996 the team based in Washington – DC United – won the national championship before a stadium packed with ecstatic fans.

Professional major league teams have loyal followers in the region – the Baltimore Orioles (baseball), the Washington Redskins and the new Baltimore Ravens (football), and the Washington Capitals (ice hockey). Minor league and college competitions are also very popular.

Not long ago recreational, intercollegiate, and professional sports were dominated by men, but in the last 25 years this has changed drastically due in large part to the passage of Title IX, a federal law prohibiting gender-based inequities in programs receiving federal funding. Each year more women and girls participate in sports. The fruits of this surge in interest were evident at the 1996 Olympics when the US women's basketball, softball, soccer, and gymnastics teams brought home gold medals. Visitors to Richmond, Virginia, may wish to see the Richmond Rage play – it's one of the teams in the women's American Basketball League.

THINGS TO BUY

The region's many urban areas offer most anything you might need (necessities or luxuries or such specialty items as recreational equipment) at a wide variety of stores and shopping malls, but the region is not known for exceptional bargains or unusual goods.

Among the most distinctive items the region has to offer are Appalachian crafts made in the mountains. Highland crafts well known for quality workmanship include woodwork, quilts, basketry, and folk art. Checking out small cabin shops and meeting artisans selling their wares are some of the pleasures of traveling in the mountains. Visitors restricted to the DC area can find high-end Highland crafts at Appalachian Spring stores, one of which is at Union Station.

Southern food specialties – stone-ground grits, handmade fruit preserves, local berry wines – are also popular souvenirs from Virginia and parts of Maryland.

Outdoor Activities

History may well be the biggest draw in the Capital Region, but the active traveler will not be disappointed with the wide range of outdoor activities available. We have read that California is the only place in the USA where you can surf in the morning and ski in the afternoon, but the surfers who hit Virginia Beach on a winter 'am' and shred the rad on their snowboards at Massanutten or Wintergreen (in the Appalachians) in the 'pm' will probably retort 'Bulldust!' (or something a little more emphatic).

Not that we are boasting! But throw in the Appalachian Trail, Shenandoah National Park, Blue Ridge, and the Allegheny Mountains for hiking, cycling, and camping; the James, Shenandoah, Maury, and Youghiogheny Rivers for rafting, tubing, and kayaking; the world-class sailing center of Annapolis; fishing and boating possibilities on Chesapeake Bay; bird watching at Chincoteague and Assateague Islands; and horseback riding in Hunt Country and along many mountain trails – just to mention a few activities – and you will soon realize that you are not exactly in 'couch-potato' country.

Read the suggestions in this chapter, and then refer to the regional chapters for specifics such as how to get to the parks and sites and what facilities you'll find there.

Useful Organizations

National Park Service & US Forest Service The NPS, part of the Department of the Interior, administers the use of parks, including many of the national monument sites in Washington, DC. The US Forest Service (USFS) is under the Department of Agriculture and administers the use of national forests. National forests are less protected than parks, and commercial exploitation occurs in some areas (usually in the form of logging or privately owned recreational facilities).

National parks most often surround spectacular natural features and cover hundreds of square miles, and visitors usually find a full range of accommodations in and around national parks. National park campground and reservations information can be obtained by calling ☎ 800-365-2267 or writing to National Park Service Public Inquiry, US Department of the Interior, 18th & C Sts NW, Washington, DC 20013. General information can be obtained from the National Park Service Public Information Officer (☎ 202-619-7222), US Department of the Interior, 1100 Ohio Drive SW, Washington, DC 20242. Contact individual parks for more specific information.

For current information about national forests, contact local ranger stations, which are also listed in the text. National forest campground and reservation information can be obtained by calling ☎ 800-280-2267. General information about federal lands is also available from the Fish & Wildlife Service (see below).

A very good source of information is the National Parks Service (NPS) home page on the Internet. There are also useful pages on the Appalachian Trail, state parks, publications, and wilderness areas. For a good, handy index try a search for GORP (Great Outdoor Recreation Pages).

The *Guide to National Park Areas: Eastern States* by David L Scott and Kay Scott describes all the major parks east of the Mississippi and has 80 maps.

You can apply in person for several types of passes at any national park or regional office of the USFS or NPS (or call the number above for information and ordering). Golden Eagle Passports cost $25 annually and allow one-year entry into national parks to the holder and accompanying guests. US citizens age 62 and over who are planning to visit national park sites should refer to the Senior Travelers section in the Facts for the Visitor chapter for information about Golden Age Passports. US residents who are medically blind or permanently disabled should refer to the Disabled Travelers section in the Facts for the Visitor chapter for information on Golden Access Passports.

Fish & Wildlife Service Each state has a few regional Fish & Wildlife Service (FWS) offices that can provide information about viewing local wildlife. Their phone numbers appear in the blue section of the local phone directory's white pages under 'US Government, Interior Department,' or you can call the Federal Information Center (☎ 800-688-9889, in Virginia ☎ 703-440-1713).

HIKING & BACKPACKING

Virginia, without doubt, is one of the nation's best hiking areas, offering over 2000 trails of varying levels of difficulty and a good mix of coastal, foothill, and mountain regions to suit hikers of all abilities.

The 2159-mile Appalachian Scenic National Trail, the East Coast's premier hiking path running from Maine to Georgia, passes through 14 states. In the Capital Region, it follows the mountain ridges of western Maryland, Shenandoah National Park, Jefferson and George Washington National Forests, Mount Rogers National Recreation Area, and the Blue Ridge Mountains of Virginia (see The Appalachian Trail in Virginia's Southwest & Blue Ridge Highlands chapter). The Virginia section of the trail is 544 miles. The Appalachian Trail Conference Headquarters (☎ 304-535-6331), PO Box 807, Harpers Ferry, WV 25425-0807, is the place to pick up maps/regulations as well as to log on/off the trail.The Potomac Appalachian Trail Club (PATC; ☎ 703-242-0693) is another useful organization.

In addition to this famous trail there are myriad other opportunities for hiking and backcountry camping in Virginia. Shenandoah National Park has over 300 miles of trails, and the extensive network of trails in the George Washington and Jefferson National Forests is almost limitless. Peak baggers scramble up the sides of Mount Rogers (5729 feet), Virginia's highest peak, in the national recreation area of the same name – and up the sides of many other southwestern Virginian peaks.

The eastern shore of Virginia and Maryland includes many fine coastal walks. Near Virginia Beach, better known for fleshy displays than for getting away from it all, there are a few great, undeveloped natural areas for hiking and backcountry camping, among them False Cape and Seashore State Parks, the Great Dismal Swamp, and Back Bay National Wildlife Refuge. Cross the Chesapeake Bay Bridge-Tunnel, and you find even more great coastal wilderness hiking in the beautiful Assateague Island National Seashore, accessible from both Virginia and Maryland. Jay Abercrombie's *Walks & Rambles on the Delmarva Peninsula* is a good choice (Countryman Press, ☎ 800-245-4151, PO Box 175, Woodstock, VT 05091).

Head north and west of Harpers Ferry (West Virginia) and you will find yourself entering Maryland's rugged sector of the Allegheny Mountains. Although these mountains can't match the Rockies or Cascades for height or extensive wilderness, the Alleghenies and their trails can take you a long way from civilization into pristine mountains and valleys. Green Ridge State Forest and Rocky Gap State Park are two popular trailheads in Allegany County. Further west is the Savage River State Forest south of Grantsville. Flatland hikers love to follow segments (or all) of the Chesapeake & Ohio (C&O) Canal bed that leads 185 miles along the edge of the Potomac River from Washington, DC, to Cumberland, Maryland.

Delaware's flat, marshy terrain is not conducive to backcountry hiking. Those who are in the know escape civilization in small boats.

National Parks & Wilderness Areas

The Capital Region is well endowed with parks and wilderness areas and, compared to parks in other heavily populated states in the US, some see few visitors.

Within Virginia lies Shenandoah (☎ 540-999-2266), the country's most visited national park; two huge national forests, George Washington (☎ 540-564-8300) and Jefferson (☎ 540-265-6054) with over 2000 miles of trails; and the Mount Rogers National Recreation Area (☎ 540-783-5816). Some other contact numbers are: Assateague Island National Seashore (☎ 757- 336-6577); Blue Ridge Parkway (☎ 540-298-0398); Chincoteague National Wildlife Refuge (☎ 757-336-6122). Maryland has over 25 state parks and recreation areas, and Delaware boasts more than 10 such areas.

Virginia has a very enlightened environmental policy. There is a network of Natural Area preserves designed to protect rare habitats and species; over 900 conservation sites protecting one or more communities; and wilderness areas (most lying within the two major national forests).

State Parks

Virginia has about 40 state parks and natural areas, including Grayson Highlands and Smith Mountain Lake. The Division of Parks and Recreation (☎ 804-786-1712, TDD 804-786-2121), 203 Governor St, Suite 302, Richmond, VA 23219, has a range of information on the parks. For camping and cabin reservations in any of these areas call ☎ 804-225-3876, 800-933-7275. Another good source of camping information is the Virginia Campground Association (☎ 804-288-3065, 800-922-6782), 2101 Libbie Ave, Richmond, VA 23230.

You can obtain similar information on Maryland camping from the Department of Natural Resources, State Forest, and Park Service (☎ 410-974-3771), Tawes State Office Building E-3, 580 Taylor Ave, Annapolis, MD 21401. For information on Delaware camping contact the Division of Parks and Recreation (☎ 302-739-4702), 89 Kings Highway, PO Box 1401, Dover, DE 19903, or the Delaware Campground Association, PO Box 156, Rehoboth Beach, DE 19971.

Treading Lightly

Backcountry areas are composed of fragile environments and cannot support an inundation of human activity, especially any insensitive and careless activity. A new code of backcountry ethics is evolving to deal with the growing numbers of people in the wilderness. Most conservation organizations and hikers' manuals have their own set of backcountry codes, all of which outline the same important principles: minimizing the impact on the land, leaving no trace, and taking nothing but photographs and memories. Above all, stay on the main trail, stay on the main trail, and, lastly, even if it means walking through mud or crossing a patch of snow, *stay on the main trail.*

Wilderness Camping

Camping in undeveloped areas is rewarding for its peacefulness but raises special concerns. Take care to ensure that the area you choose can comfortably support your presence and leave the surroundings in at least as good condition as on arrival. The following list of guidelines should help:

- Camp below timberline, since alpine areas are generally more fragile. Good campsites are found, not made. Altering a site shouldn't be necessary.
- Camp at least 200 feet (70 adult steps) away from the nearest lake, river, or stream.
- Bury human waste in cat holes dug six to eight inches deep, at least 200 feet from water, camp, or trails. The salt and minerals in urine attract deer; use a tent-bottle (funnel attachments are available for women) if you are prone to middle-of-the-night calls by Mother Nature. Camouflage the cat hole when finished.
- Use soaps and detergents sparingly or not at all, and never allow these things to enter streams or lakes. When washing yourself (a backcountry luxury, not necessity), lather up (with biodegradable soap) and rinse yourself with cans of water 200 feet away from your water source. Scatter dish water after removing all food particles.

- Some folks recommend carrying a lightweight stove for cooking and using a lantern instead of a campfire.
- If a fire is allowed and appropriate, dig out the native topsoil and build a fire in the hole. Gather sticks no larger than an adult's wrist from the ground. Do not snap branches off live, dead, or downed trees. Pour waste water from meals around the perimeter of the campfire to prevent the fire from spreading, and thoroughly douse it before leaving or going to bed.
- Establish a cooking area at least 100 yards away from your tent and designate cooking clothes to leave in the food bag, away from your tent.
- Burn cans to remove odors, and then take them from the ashes and pack them out.
- Pack out what you pack in, including all trash – yours *and* others'.

Safety

The major forces to be reckoned with while hiking and camping are the weather (which is uncontrollable) and your own frame of mind. Be prepared for unpredictable weather especially in the mountainous areas – Maryland's Alleghenies, the Blue Ridge Mountains, and other areas of the Appalachians such as Mount Rogers. Carry a rain jacket and light pair of long underwear at all times; in spring and fall, take this precaution even on short afternoon hikes. Backpackers should have a pack-liner (heavy-duty garbage bags work well), a full set of rain gear, and food that does not require cooking. A positive attitude is helpful in any situation. If a hot shower, comfortable mattress, and clean clothes are essential to your well-being, don't head out into the wilderness for five days – stick to day hikes.

The most stringent safety measures suggest never hiking alone, but solo travelers should not be discouraged, especially if they value solitude. The important thing is to always let someone know where you are going and how long you plan to be gone. Use sign-in boards at trailheads or ranger stations. Travelers looking for hiking companions can inquire or post notices at ranger stations, outdoors stores, campgrounds, and youth hostels.

Fording rivers and streams is another potentially dangerous but often necessary part of being on the trail. In national parks and along maintained trails in national forests, bridges usually cross large bodies of water (this is not the case in designated wilderness areas, where bridges are taboo). Upon reaching a river, unclip all of your pack straps – your pack is expendable. Avoid crossing barefoot – river cobbles suck body heat right out of your feet, numbing them and making it impossible to navigate. Bring a pair of lightweight canvas sneakers to avoid sloshing around in wet boots for the rest of your hike.

Although cold water will make you want to cross as quickly as possible, don't rush things: Take small steps, watch where you are stepping, and keep your balance. Using a staff for balance is helpful, but don't rely on it to support all your weight. Don't enter water higher than mid-thigh; when water is higher than that, your body gives the current a large mass to work against.

If you should get wet, wring your clothes out immediately, wipe off all the excess water on your body and hair, and put on any dry clothes you (or your partner) might have. Special synthetic fabrics and wool retain heat when they get wet, but cotton does not.

People with little hiking or backpacking experience should not attempt to do too much too soon, or they might end up being non-hikers for the wrong reasons. Know your limitations, know the route you are planning to take, and pace yourself accordingly. Remember, there is absolutely nothing wrong with turning back or not going as far as you originally planned.

What to Bring

The following list is meant only to be a general guideline for backpackers, not an 'if-I-have-everything-here-I'll-be-fine' checklist. Know yourself and what special things you may need on the trail; consider the area and climatic conditions you will be traveling in. This list is inadequate for snow country or winter.

Boots
Light to medium weight are recommended for day hikes, while sturdy boots are necessary for extended trips with a heavy pack. Most importantly they should be well broken in and have a good heel. Waterproof boots are preferable. All this said, some experienced walkers prefer not to wear boots at all, choosing lightweight running shoes instead.

Alternative footwear
Thongs or sandals or running shoes for wearing around camp and canvas sneakers for crossing streams.

Socks
Heavy polypropylene or wool will stay warm even when it gets wet. Frequent changes during the day reduce the chance of blisters, but this is usually impractical.

Shorts, light shirt
Everyday wear should be in subdued colors, but if you're hiking during hunting season, wearing blaze orange is a necessity. Remember that heavy cotton takes a long time to dry and is very cold when wet.

Long-sleeve shirt
Light cotton, wool, or polypropylene. A button-down front makes layering easy and can be left open when the weather is hot and your arms need protection from the sun.

Long pants
Heavy denim jeans take forever to dry. Sturdy cotton or canvas pants are good for trekking through brush, and cotton or nylon sweats are comfortable to wear around camp. Long underwear with shorts over them is the perfect combo – warm but not cumbersome – for trail hiking where there is not much brush.

Sweater or pullover
Wool, polypropylene, or polar fleece; essential in chilly or cold weather.

Rain gear
Light, breathable, and waterproof is the ideal combination. If nothing else is available, use heavy-duty trash bags to cover you and your packs.

Hat
Wool or polypropylene is best for cold weather, while a cotton hat with a brim is good for sun protection. About 80% of body heat escapes through the top of the head. Keep your head (and neck) warm to reduce the chances of hypothermia.

Bandanna or handkerchief
Good for a runny nose, dirty face, unmanageable hair, picnic lunch, and flag (especially a red one).

Small towel
Pick one that is indestructible and will dry quickly (for example, 'chamois' cloth).

First-aid kit
Should include self-adhesive bandages, disinfectant, antibiotic salve or cream, gauze, small scissors, and tweezers. See Health in Facts for the Visitor.

Knife, fork, spoon & mug
A double-layer plastic mug with a lid is best, as it can function as an eating and drinking receptacle, mixing bowl, and wash basin, and the handle protects you from getting burned. Bring an extra cup if you like to eat and drink simultaneously.

Pots & pans
Aluminum cook sets are best, but any sturdy one-quart pot is sufficient. True gourmands who want more than pasta, soup, and freeze-dried food will need a skillet or frying pan. A pot scrubber is helpful for removing stubborn oatmeal, especially when using cold water and no soap.

Stove
One that is lightweight and easy to operate is ideal. Most outdoors stores rent propane or butane stoves; test the stove before you head out – even cook a meal on it – to familiarize yourself with any quirks it may have.

Water purifier
Optional but really nice to have. Alternatively, water can be purified by boiling for at least 10 minutes.

Matches or lighter
Waterproof matches are good, but it's still smart to have several lighters on hand.

Candle or lantern
Candles are easy to use, but do not stay lit when wet, and they can be hazardous inside a tent. Outdoors stores rent lanterns; test it before you hit the trail.

Flashlight
Each person should have one. Be sure the batteries have plenty of power.

Sleeping bag
Goose-down bags are warm and lightweight but worthless if they get wet; most outdoors stores rent synthetic bags.

Sleeping pad
This is strictly a personal preference. Use a sweater or sleeping bag sack stuffed with clothes as a pillow.

Tent
Make sure it is waterproof or has a waterproof cover, and know how to put it up *before* you reach camp. You'll need one big enough for you and your pack.

Camera & binoculars
Don't forget extra film and waterproof film canisters (sealable plastic bags work well).

Compass & maps
Each person should carry both.

Eyewear
Contact-lens wearers should always bring a back-up set.

Sundries
Toilet paper, small sealable plastic bags, insect repellent, sunscreen, lip balm, unscented moisturizing cream, moleskin for foot blisters, dental floss (burnable and good when there is no water for brushing), sunglasses, deck of cards, pen or pencil, paper or notebook, books, and nature guides.

Food
Basic staples include packaged instant oatmeal, bread (the denser the better), rice or pasta, instant soup or ramen noodles, dehydrated meat (jerky), dried fruit, energy bars, chocolate, trail mix, and peanut butter or honey or jam (in plastic jars or squeeze bottles). Don't forget the wet-wipes, but be sure to dispose of them properly or pack them out.

Keeping your energy up is important, but so is keeping your pack light. Backpackers tend to eat a substantial breakfast and dinner and snack heavily in between. If you pack loads of food, you'll probably use it, but if you have just enough, you probably won't wish for more.

Books

There are plenty of books describing the hiking possibilities in Virginia; for those relating to the Appalachian Trail, Shenandoah National Park, and other major hiking areas, see the relevant chapters. Just ask at an outdoor gear shop; the staff will guide you to the best and most current publications.

But two good general books on Virginia stand out: Randy Johnson's pocket-size *The Hiker's Guide to Virginia* and Allen de Hart's more up-to-date *The Trails of Virginia: Hiking the Old Dominion*.

The Potomac Appalachian Trail Club (☎ 703-242-0315, fax 703-242-0968), 118 Park St SE, Vienna, VA 22180, publishes *The Big Blue: A Trail Guide*, a full description of the 144-mile trail that runs from Shenandoah National Park via the George Washington National Forest and West Virginia to Hancock, Maryland, where it becomes the Tuscarora Trail. As of early 1997, the Big Blue Trail was officially renamed; it now is also called the Tuscarora Trail.

Chris Camden's *Backpacker's Handbook* (Ragged Mountain Press) is a beefy collection of tips for the trail. More candid is *A Hiker's Companion*, written by Cindy Ross and Todd Gladfelter, who hiked 12,000 miles before sitting down to write. *How to Shit in the Woods* is Kathleen Meyer's explicit, comic, and useful manual on wilderness 'toilet' training for adults.

Maps

A good map is essential for any hiking trip. NPS and USFS ranger stations usually stock topographical maps that cost $2 to $6. In the absence of a ranger station, try the local stationery, hardware, or bookstore.

Longer hikes require two types of maps: USGS Quadrangles and US Department of Agriculture-Forest Service maps. To order a map index and price list, contact the US Geological Survey, PO Box 25286, Denver, CO, 80225. For general information on maps, also see the Facts for the Visitor chapter; for information regarding maps of specific forests, wilderness areas, or national parks, see the appropriate geographic entry.

There are many free planning maps, such as the excellent little Forest Service map, *Jefferson National Forest*, available from Forest Service and National Park Headquarters. The staff will advise which more detailed topographical maps you will need.

A handy compendium of topographic maps can be found in the *Virginia Atlas & Gazetteer* (available from DeLorme Mapping Company, PO Box 298, Freeport, Maine 22312).

Organized Tours

If you'd rather venture into the woods in good company, a number of operators can help. All Adventure Travel (☎ 303-440-4160, 800-537-4025), 5589 Arapahoe, Suite 208, Boulder, CO 80303, offers six-day hiking/cycling tours to the Shenandoah Valley and Wine Country near Charlottesville. Hiking Holidays (☎ 802-453-4816), PO Box 750, Bristol, VT 05443, runs five-day, five-night hiking trips in the Shenandoah National Park and beautiful sections of the Blue Ridge Parkway. New England Hiking Holidays (☎ 800-869-0949, 407-778-3806), PO Box 164B, North Conway, NH 03860, has five-day hiking trips in the Shenandoah National Park and Blue Ridge Mountains. North Wind Touring (☎ 800-496-5571), PO Box 46, Waitsfield, VT 05673, advertises five-day hiking trips in the Blue Ridge Mountains and Rockfish Valley, with some hiking along the Appalachian Trail.

Getting There & Away

The beauty of hiking in Virginia and Maryland is the easy accessibility of the trailheads. The 300 miles of trails in Shenandoah National Park can all be easily reached from the Skyline Drive. But for these hikes, and those in the national forests and recreation areas, you are going to need your own car, as there is very little public transport away from the main cities. In the southwest there are a couple of useful shuttle services catering mainly to mountain bikers (and their bikes): New River Bicycles (☎ 540-980-1741) in Draper and Blue Blaze Shuttle Service (☎ 540-475-5095) in Damascus.

Some of the trailheads in the national forests are hard to find, but the NFS in these areas provides plenty of information, free maps, and, occasionally, personal advice.

BIKING & MOUNTAIN BIKING

Many of the popular hiking trails in the region are either partially or wholly open to cyclists, but there are notable exceptions. It pays to check with the authorities before gearing down and steering your bike along a tempting path.

Virginia is a real gem with all types of cycling terrain and a comprehensive network of trails. The state is crisscrossed by three major bicycling routes: sections of the TransAmerica Bicycle Trail from Oregon to Virginia (500 miles from Breaks Interstate Park on the Kentucky border to Yorktown); the Maine to Virginia Bicycle Route (150 miles from Washington, DC, to Richmond); and the Virginia to Florida Bicycle Route (130 miles from Richmond to Suffolk on the North Carolina state line). Strip maps are available from the Adventure Cycling Association (see below).

In addition to these long routes there is the 105-mile Shenandoah Skyline Drive, 214 miles of the Blue Ridge Parkway, the 22-mile Colonial Parkway, the 17-mile Mount Vernon Trail, the 33-mile Virginia Creeper Trail, and a 20-mile route around the Fredericksburg battlefields. The latter is one of nine rails-to-trails bikeways statewide. Many overnight cycling adventures are offered by national tour companies such as Backroads.

Mountain bikers can go 'wild' in Virginia's two national forests; in the Grayson Highlands State Park and the Mount Rogers National Recreation Area; and just about anywhere along some of the mountain roads. The 57 miles of the New River Trail, in the state park of the same name, would be manageable for someone used to clicking 21 gears (there is a good map and user's guide to the New River Trail).

Washington, DC, and nearby Arlington County have a good collection of bicycle routes. The 45-mile paved Washington and Old Dominion (W&OD) Trail runs from the Potomac River to Leesburg through the

Virginia centers of Falls Church, Vienna, and Herndon.

Maryland is also an excellent place for bike touring and mountain biking. Some of the best tours pass through Kent and Talbot Counties on the Eastern Shore, and Calvert and St Mary's Counties in Southern Maryland. Wisp Ski Resort in McHenry (western Maryland) is a good place for summer mountain biking. Lots of off-road bikers follow the C&O Canal path and camp at designated sites along the way. John R Wennersten's *25 Bicycle Tours on Delmarva* provides helpful touring suggestions (Countryman Press, P O Box 175, Woodstock, VT 05091, ☎ 800-245-4151).

Delaware's Tour du Pont, one of America's premier grand-prix bicycle races, has awakened to the possibilities for recreational bike touring as well. The Tour du Pont follows Route 9 (the Heritage Coastal Greenway) through historic New Castle and the farms and marshlands of Delaware Bay to the south, and you can do the same. This is historic and scenic flatland cycling, but plan your itinerary carefully so you can end your day at a B&B or campground.

Just as picturesque but more hilly and wooded are roads like Route 100 and Route 52 that wind through the Brandywine Valley. Be careful here since the roads have narrow shoulders and heavy traffic during morning and evening commutes to and from Wilmington.

Information

Local bike shops have the best information on bike routes and conditions – the staff will tell you about places to go (and not to go) and regulations and will sell the maps you need. The small but detailed *Virginia: A Great Place to Bike*, available from information centers, has all you need to know about contacts in that state. If you wish to avoid traffic, the secondary routes (those numbered over 600) are the best choices. Maps of county routes are available from the Virginia Department of Transportation. *Bicycling on Virginia Roads – Laws and Safety Tips*, a brochure detailing Virginia's laws as they affect cyclists, is available from the State Bicycle Coordinator (see below). Mountain bikers will find good ideas in Scott Adams' *Mountain Bike Virginia*, which has plenty of detailed maps. The numerous southwestern Virginia trails, including the humongous ups and downs of the single tracks of Mount Rogers, are covered in Lori Finley's *Mountain Biking the Appalachians: Northwest North Carolina/Southwest Virginia*. Due out soon is Randy Porter's *A Mountain Biker's Guide to Western Virginia*.

Washington, DC, routes are indicated on the map *Bicycle Routes in the Washington Area*. The *Greater Washington Area Bicycle Atlas* is published by the Washington Area Bicyclist Association in conjunction with American Youth Hostels.

Many of the counties on Maryland's Eastern Shore as well as in the south of the state offer comprehensive trail guides. You can also check the county-by-county maps in *Best Bike Routes in Maryland: A County-by-County Guide*. Also useful is *Bicycling in Maryland: A Quick Reference Guide* (☎ 410-333-1633).

You can get information on bicycling and mountain biking from most visitor centers. Some useful Getting There & Away information (which applies equally to bikers) appears in the Hiking & Backpacking section (above). Other important contacts include:

Adventure Cycling Association
PO Box 8308, Missoula, MT 59807, (☎ 406-721-1776)

State Bicycle Coordinator
Virginia Department of Transportation, 1401 E Broad St, Richmond, VA 23219, (☎ 804-786-2964)

United States Cycling Federation – Virginia/DC District
946 Shillelagh Rd, Chesapeake VA 23323, (☎ 757-547-7905)

Virginia Department of Transportation
Address as above, (☎ 804-786-2838)

Metropolitan Washington Council of Governments
For maps and advice write 777 North Capitol St NE, Ste 300, Washington, DC 20002-4201, (☎ 202-962-3200)

Richmond Area Bicycling Association
9013 Prestondale Ave, Richmond, VA 23294

Organized Tours

For a good introduction to the biking possibilities of the region, consider joining a bike tour organized by one of these companies. All Adventure Travel (☎ 303-440-4160, 800-537-4025), 5589 Arapahoe, Suite 208, Boulder, CO 80303, runs six-day hiking/cycling tours to the Shenandoah Valley and Wine Country near Charlottesville. Backroads (☎ 800-462-2848), 1516 5th St, Suite L101, Berkeley, CA 94710-1740, has five-day cycling and country-inn tours of the Shenandoah Valley. Classic Adventures (☎ 800-777-8090, 716-964-8488), PO Box 153, Hamlin, NY 14464-0153, has five-night cycling tours of Fredericksburg and the Virginia horse country.

SKIING & SNOWBOARDING

In this region, no ski terrain rivals Jackson Hole or Aspen, but in winter it does snow! Keen skiers not willing to board a plane to live out their fantasies can win ample satisfaction from Virginia's Appalachians and Maryland's Alleghenies.

Usually snow-covered from December to March, Virginia has the most choices for downhill and cross-country skiers and snowboarding enthusiasts. There are five main areas: Bryce, the Homestead, Massanutten, and Wintergreen for lift-assisted snow play (as well as half-pipes for the snowboarders); and Mount Rogers National Recreation Area for the most sublime 'skinny' skiing, comparable to anywhere in the world when conditions are right (see the relevant chapters for more information). And snowboarders, often the pariahs at many resorts, are much loved in Virginia.

All of these ski areas have a wide range of accommodations and conduct special races (followed by the requisite après-ski activity, with 'hoopla' to rival the western and Rockies states). The four downhill areas have state-of-the-art snow-making equipment. As for Washington, DC, you may well get the perennial 'snow job' but nothing you can ski on! There is an information service, however; try the Ski Club of Washington, DC (☎ 703-536-8723). For more Virginia skiing information, call ☎ 800-843-7669.

Occasionally, the east sneaks into *Ski* and *Skiing*, year-round and widely available travel magazines, and there are always the latest stats in *Snow Country*, which looks at difficulty of runs, ski-school facilities, lodging, and dining.

Although western Maryland has some dramatic mountains and significant snowfalls, you can't count on sustained periods of cold weather. Downhill skiing and snowboarding in the Allegheny Mountains tends to rely on snow making and is expensive, crowded, and only moderately challenging when compared to other mountain ranges in the country. If it is a snowy winter, and you can beat the high prices and crowds by going on a weekday, head for either Wisp at Grantsville or the more-challenging Whitetail at Mercersburg, Pennsylvania, for downhill. New German State Park at Grantsville has good ski-touring trails.

ROCK CLIMBING & CAVING

This region ain't no Yosemite or Joshua Tree but the keen climber can ferret out the odd vertical challenge. Sadly, a number of the modern climbs are in gyms (much cherished by Generation-Xers these days), but there are still a few routes, exposed to the elements, that attract a slower group of pot-bellied baby-boomers.

Virginia has a few climbing areas (although the choicest routes are in neighboring West Virginia, for example, at Seneca Rocks). Notable are those near Great Falls of the Potomac, along the Skyline Drive, and in Arlington County. In Richmond you'll find good practice routes on the old Manchester Bridge ruins on the south side of the James River. For more information on climbing, contact the antonymic Outdoor Insights Inc (☎ /fax 540-456-8742), 6370 Midway Rd, Crozet, VA 22932. Artificial climbing walls in Virginia include the Wall at Bodyworks in Fredericksburg and the Rock Gym in Virginia Beach.

Adventure caving possibilities abound, even in a state heavily pockmarked by commercial caverns. A couple of good Virginia caving contacts are Highland Adventures (☎ 540-468-2722), PO Box 151, Monterey, VA 24465; and Richmond Area Speleological Society (☎ 804-673-2283), 5300 W Marshall St, Suite 10, Richmond, VA 23230.

A number of good technical climbs and an extensive network of caves are in the vicinity of Cumberland in Allegany County, Maryland. To find these climbs and caves and get up to speed on local conditions, consult Allegany Expeditions (☎ 301-722-5170, 800-819-5170) in Cumberland.

For artificial walls in Maryland, try the City of Rockville Climbing Gym and the Baltimore Clipper City Rock Gym; in Delaware, claw up the university climbing wall in Newark.

A couple of handy publications are the *Climbers' Guide to Great Falls of the Potomac*, which covers both the Maryland and Virginia shorelines of the Potomac, and *Carderock, Past and Present: A Climbers' Guide*.

Safety & Minimum Impact

Climbing is potentially a hazardous activity, though serious accidents are more newsworthy than frequent; driving to the climbing site can be more dangerous than the climb itself. Nevertheless, climbers should be aware of hazards that can contribute to falls and very serious injury or death.

Weather is an important factor, as rain makes rock slippery and lightning can strike an exposed climber; hypothermia is an additional concern. In dry weather, lack of water can lead to dehydration.

Many climbers are now following guidelines similar to those established for hikers to preserve the resource on which their sport relies. These include concentrating impact in high-use areas by using established roads, trails, and routes for access; dispersing use in pristine areas and avoiding the creation of new trails; refraining from creating or enhancing handholds; and eschewing the placement of bolts wherever possible. Climbers should also strive to respect archaeological and cultural resources, such as rock art, and refrain from climbing in such areas.

HORSEBACK RIDING & HORSERACING

Horseback riding is extremely popular in Virginia's mountainous areas where there are many liveries and access to trails of all levels of difficulty. Probably the most famous area is Hunt Country in Northern Virginia, which is crossed with many miles of public trails. The Virginia Horse Council (☎ 540-382-3071), PO Box 72, Riner, VA 24149, publishes the free *Virginia Horse Riding Trail Guide*, a list of public horse trails with useful contact numbers and addresses, and notes on type of trail.

The George Washington and Jefferson National Forests have many designated and unmarked trails. The Skyland Lodge (☎ 540-999-2210) in Shenandoah National Park conducts one-hour and 2½-hour guided rides. There are many operators in the Shenandoah Valley – for example, Virginia Mountain Outfitters (☎ 540-261-1910) in Buena Vista provides half-day and full-day rides for $50/85. The Magnolia Centre for Special Equestrians (☎ 804-273-0813) near Richmond organizes programs for people with disabilities.

It is in the southwest of the state, however, that you will see experienced riders trailering their horses. In this region are the New River and Virginia Creeper Trails, and the famous Virginia Highlands Horse Trail (with its three special horse camps with hitching and watering facilities in the Mount Rogers National Recreation Area and Grayson Highlands State Park.

Horse racing is popular in Hunt Country, especially point-to-point and steeplechase races. On the first Saturday in May the Virginia Gold Cup is run at Great Meadow near the Plains; Great Meadow also hosts the International Gold Cup on the third Saturday in October. At Foxfield near Charlottesville, two major steeplechase meetings are held each year (late April and late September); contact the Virginia Steeplechase Association, PO Box 1158, Middleburg, VA 22117, for information on other events.

Another equestrian sport is combined training (also called three-day eventing and horse trials). You can watch this at the Virginia Horse Center at Lexington, at Morven Park in Leesburg, and at Glenwood Park at Middleburg. The whole horsey gamut is rounded off with polo at Middleburg and endurance riding near Front Royal.

Believe it or not: Maryland's state sport is jousting. The knights in shining armor are long gone, but the modern-day jousters need a fair amount of skill to catch rings of decreasing size with their lances. In Virginia, jousting tournaments are held at the Natural Chimneys Recreation Area in June and August.

RAFTING, KAYAKING & CANOEING

The Capital Region is blessed with plenty of free-flowing rivers and streams to satisfy all types of paddlers. There are also huge estuaries (Chesapeake Bay is the nation's largest) and hundreds of miles of coastline for canoeists and sea kayakers.

In spring and late fall, when the river flows are greatest in Virginia, whitewater rafters hurtle down the James River (at Scottsville to the south of Charlottesville, and right in the city limits of Richmond); the Maury River near Goshen Pass; the Shenandoah River south of Front Royal; and, farthest west, the Russell Forks River in the Breaks Interstate Park on the Kentucky border (see detailed entries in the relevant chapters).

In summer, when the river flows are much less, tubing (floating downstream on inner tubes) is a popular local pastime. Sometimes tubers tow along a 'refreshment' tube stacked with drinks.

Not so well known places for whitewater kayaking in Virginia are the Moormans River; the Rappahannock watershed; streams in Carroll County; the New River near the North Carolina border; the Chickahominy and North Anna Rivers; and streams on the slopes of the Blue Ridge Mountains. For detailed descriptions of some canoe and kayak trips, see Richard Corbett's *Virginia Whitewater*.

The Youghiogheny River, which threads its way between the mountains of Pennsylvania and Maryland, offers world-class whitewater. The Upper Yough has class V+ rapids near Friendship and has been the site of numerous national and international kayaking events. The lower parts of the river are a bit tamer (as are the rapids of the nearby Savage River). Working with a number of outfitters in Ohiopyle, Pennsylvania, you can plan a rafting adventure to meet your personal skills and courage. The offices of the rafting companies are in the village on or near Route 381. Rates are lower during the week and vary according to the season. Laurel Highlands River Tours (☎ 412-329-8531, 800-472-3846) conducts guided trips on the Middle Yough and Upper Yough (trips include lunch). Other companies offering guided trips are Wilderness Voyageurs (☎ 800-272-4141), Mountain Streams (☎ 800-723-8669), and White Water Adventurers (☎ 412-329-1488, 800-992-7238).

For a slightly less 'gung ho' experience, kayakers, tubers, and canoeists head for the Potomac and Shenandoah Rivers near

River Rankings

Class I – easy
The river ranges from flatwater to occasional series of mild rapids.

Class II – medium
The river has frequent stretches of rapids with waves up to three feet high and easy chutes, ledges, and falls. The best route is easy to identify and the entire river can be run in open canoes.

Class III – difficult
The rivers feature numerous rapids with high, irregular waves and difficult chutes and falls that often require scouting. They are suitable for experienced paddlers who either use kayaks and rafts or have a spray cover for their canoe.

Class IV – very difficult
These rivers have long stretches of irregular waves, powerful back eddies, and even constricted canyons. Scouting is mandatory and rescues can be difficult in many places. Suitable for rafts or whitewater kayaks with paddlers equipped with helmets.

Class V – extremely difficult
Rivers with continuous violent rapids, powerful rollers, and high, unavoidable waves and haystacks. These rivers are only for whitewater kayaks and paddlers who are proficient in the Eskimo roll.

Class VI – highest level of difficulty
These rivers are rarely run except by highly experienced kayakers under ideal conditions. ■

Harpers Ferry and navigate toward Washington, DC. This trip is not without rapids, but it's nothing like the 115-feet-per-mile descents you get on the Youghiogheny.

All of the tidal tributaries of the Chesapeake make for excellent canoe and sea kayak adventuring. Favorite Maryland cruising grounds are the St Mary's and Patuxent Rivers in Southern Maryland, the Tred Avon River around Oxford, the Chester and Sassafras Rivers on the upper Eastern Shore, and the Pocomoke River on the lower Eastern Shore.

Delaware has scenic but rarely dangerous waters for kayaking, canoeing, and tubing along the Brandywine River from Chadds Ford, Pennsylvania, south almost to Wilmington. A more serene site for canoeing is along the hundreds of miles of tidal rivers such as the Leipsic that wind through extensive coastal marshes and wildlife refuges on the fringe of Delaware Bay. In the southern part of the state you can explore the Indian River, Rehoboth Bay, and Assawoman Bay with a canoe or sea kayak. On weekends and in summer these waters can get congested with speedboats, jet-skis, and water-skiers. But you'll only share the place with migratory waterfowl in September or May. Take plenty of insect repellent during hot weather.

There are 15 or so outfitters/trip operators in Virginia; many of them are mentioned in the Virginia chapters. If you plan to stick to familiar waters, many outfitters will provide canoes and kayaks, paddles, life jackets, maps, and shuttle service – short trips cost about $25 and all-day trips around $45. For more information contact the Virginia Professional Paddlesport Association, 352 Shenandoah Heights Rd, Front Royal, VA 22630. One company in particular, Atlantic Canoe & Hire Company (☎ 800-297-0066), PO Box 405, Oakton, VA 22124, runs kayaking tours/trips to parts of the Northern Neck and Assateague and Chincoteague Islands on the Eastern Shore.

Get an issue of the *Coastal CaNews* (outfitters should have copies) for information on current coastal and sea-kayaking activities.

SURFING & WINDSURFING

Virginia Beach, with eight dedicated areas nearby, is the hub of surfing in this region and host to the annual East Coast Surfing Championships. There are restrictions placed on where you can take your board, and it must be leashed at all times; an untethered board can earn you a $50 fine. For a surf report, ring Wave Riding Vehicles (☎ 757-422-8823) and for surfing regulations, call ☎ 757-428-9133.

Ocean City in Maryland also has a big surf scene. Legal surfing beaches change daily, but you'll probably find the best surf and riders around the pier and inlet at the south end of town before eight in the morning while the offshore breeze is shaping and glassing off the waves. Surfing is not nearly as popular in Delaware as it is in Ocean City because the beach breaks around Rehoboth and Dewey tend to close out in a hurry.

Windsurfing is fast growing in popularity, and there are plenty of suitable boardsailing spots in the Capital Region. In Virginia, popular centers are Belle Haven Marina near Alexandria (☎ 703-768-0018), and Fort Belvoir and Mason Neck State Park along the Potomac River. At Virginia Beach, you can get lessons and rentals at the Chick's Beach Sailing Center; also, those up to wave jumping can try Wave Riding Vehicles (see above).

The Chesapeake's rivers, coves, and harbors can be superb venues for windsurfing particularly in the spring and fall when the wind is up and the sea nettles (stinging jellyfish) are south of the Potomac River. At these times of year Sandy Point State Park is a popular site for board sailing. In Ocean City, head for Assawoman Bay. In Delaware, the board-sailing crowd congregates at Dewey Beach around Rehoboth Bay, and in DC you will see them at the Washington Sailing Marina.

SAILING

Annapolis, Maryland, is the sailing capital of the United States in title and fact. There are thousands of racing and cruising sailboats berthed at the marinas that line the city's shores. If you know your way around a sailboat, you can probably find a place aboard someone's boat for the Wednesday evening or weekend races. Such acquaintances can lead to an invitation for some vacation cruising to the backwaters of the Eastern Shore.

Annapolis also has a large collection of head boats to carry tourists on daylong sails. More than a dozen yacht charter companies rent bareboats out of Annapolis. Other places to find bareboat cruising sailboats for charter are Rock Hall near Chestertown on the upper Eastern Shore, Oxford on the central Eastern Shore, and Solomons Island in southern Maryland. Good publications are the *Guide to Cruising Chesapeake Bay* and the Department of Natural Resource's *Cruising Guide to Maryland Waters*.

Virginia shares the waters of Chesapeake Bay and there are many opportunities for sailing in that state; a good place to start is at the Chesapeake Sailing Association (☎ 757-588-2022) at Willoughby Harbor, Norfolk; it has five-day 'learn to sail' packages. Chick's Beach Sailing Center (☎ 757-481-3067) at Virginia Beach is a good place to rent a boat. Don't be surprised if you see some large sailing craft in the inland lakes such as Smith Mountain, Buggs Island, and Claytor.

FISHING

Saltwater

Its proximity to the massive Chesapeake Bay and to the Atlantic Ocean means that Virginia is well situated for saltwater fishing enthusiasts. From July through September the wealthy are in pursuit of the white marlin. The poorer anglers could probably afford to potter around Wachapreague or Chincoteague on the Eastern Shore. Wachapreague, the so-called 'flounder fishing capital,' is also a good place to chase black and red drum, kingfish, spot, gray trout, bluefish, and croaker. The seaward beaches of the Barrier Islands, accessible only by boat, are great for surfcasting. Knowledgeable anglers reckon that the Sea Gull Fishing Pier on the Chesapeake Bay Bridge Tunnel is one of the hottest spots in the state – you will still have to pay the $10 crossing fee.

You do not need to have a license for saltwater fishing in Virginia, and this applies to the bay, ocean, and up to the freshwater line. This is good news as there are nearly 20 catchable species in the bounds of Chesapeake Bay including the seasonal cobia, black and red drum, bluefish, and striped bass (which can be caught year round). A valuable resource is the *Guide to Virginia Saltwater Fishing* published by the Virginia Saltwater Fishing Tournament (☎ 757-491-5160), 968 S Oriole Dr, Suite 102, Virginia Beach, VA 23451.

Oddly, Maryland's saltwater fishing regulations differ from Virginia's. Even nonresidents used to be able to fish the Chesapeake without a license, but those days are gone. However, you can by a five-day Chesapeake fishing permit for $4 at almost any bayside venue. The catches are similar to those in Virginian waters. Ocean City is the place to go if you want to head offshore for marlin, tuna, mako, or swordfish. Within range of the surf angler on Assateague Island are seabass, flounder, and tautog. Head for the northern bay if you're after striped bass. Off Tilghman Island you will find bluefish, rockfish, and the huge (35 to 60 lbs) drum fish.

In Delaware, as in Virginia, you don't have to pay a thing to fish in the saltwater of Delaware Bay or in the ocean. Currently, bluefish, flounder, and weakfish have been strong throughout the bay. Look for tautog around wrecks and rock piles in the ocean and the mouth of the bay. In recent years strong runs of yellowfin tuna and marlin have been seen offshore.

Freshwater

Virginia is an ideal destination for the keen angler; over 25 freshwater species live in state waters. And there is no shortage of idyllic rivers, streams, and lakes where the canny quarry can be snagged – nearly a million trout are annually released into the 2800 miles of the 180 plus trout streams.

Look for brown and rainbow trout, largemouth and smallmouth bass, and crappie in Lake Moomaw; striper (including the state's largest at over 45 lbs), smallmouth bass, and walleye in Smith Mountain Lake;

crappie, bream, and channel cats in the Rivanna Reservoir just outside Charlottesville; flathead catfish and white bass in Claytor Lake southwest of Roanoke; catfish and smallmouth bass in the Rappahannock; and largemouth bass, crappie, and bluegill in Hungry Mother State Park.

For general freshwater fishing information read the *Virginia Fishing Guide* by Bob Gooch. If it's trout you're after, check out *A Fly Fisherman's Blue Ridge* by Christopher Camuto, *Trout Fishing in Shenandoah National Park* by Harry Murray, or *Virginia Trout Streams* by Harry Slone. Residents pay $5 for five consecutive days of fishing in rivers not stocked with trout ($12 more if they are after trout); nonresidents pay $6 (and an extra $30 for the five days for trout fishing). The days of the first weekend in June are free fishing days throughout Virginia.

In Maryland, a freshwater permit for five days will cost thc traveler $7 ($5 extra for a trout stamp). The lakes and slow-moving streams of western Maryland are well stocked with largemouth bass. The faster streams have pike, walleye, and trout. The Gunpowder River in Baltimore County may have the best brown and rainbow trout fishing in the state.

You'll have to buy a Delaware fishing license to fish for trout in freshwater streams like Brandywine Creek. More than four dozen inland lakes are well stocked with crappie, perch, trout, bass, and bluegill. A seven-day nonresident freshwater license costs $5.50.

For more information on licenses, seasons, size, and limits contact:

Virginia Department of Game & Inland Fisheries
4010 W Broad St, Richmond, VA 23230,
☎ 804-367-1000

Maryland Department of Natural Resources – Tidewater Administration
580 Taylor Ave, Annapolis, MD 21401,
☎ 410-974-3987
For saltwater fishing information, call
☎ 800-688-3467.

Delaware Division of Fish & Wildlife
89 Kings Highway, PO Box 1401, Dover, DE 19903, ☎ 302-739-4431

Charter Fishing

If you wish to head out to sea in search of the big fish (in Virginia waters), you will find operators at Wachapreague and Chincoteague on the Eastern Shore; at Reedville and Smiths Point on the Northern Neck; and at Norfolk and Virginia Beach. You can get on board a head boat (so called because they charge per person) for about $300 per day; triple this plus if you are after marlin.

In Maryland, head for Ocean City, but expect that a half day on the water will cost you $400 to $500 for the boat and tackle. For about half that price you can go fishing on the Chesapeake Bay. There are large fleets of charter fishing boats working out of Chesapeake Bay and Solomons and Tilghman Islands.

Important billfish tournaments bring a host of fancy sport fishing rigs to Lewes, Delaware, and you can charter one of these boats if you don't mind spending over $1000 a day. Lewes also has some head boats that fish around the mouth of the bay. For bargain bay fishing take one of the boats out of Bowers Beach for the day. The fishing for blues, weakfish, and flounder is good. Fishing for the whole day will cost you less than $30, and you will never forget the woebegone look of this town presided over by the ruins of the Heartbreak Hotel.

Clamming & Crabbing

Clamming and crabbing for personal consumption require no license in Maryland. If you are at the Atlantic shore, try Assawoman Bay for both activities. Clams love intertidal sand flats and crabs like brackish water. Any dock, pier, or sea wall along the Chesapeake will likely have a colony of catchable blue crabs. (Virginia has its share of spots along the Chesapeake shore – when you find them, however, reveal them to no one!)

In Delaware from May to November the shores of Indian River and the Little Assawoman and Rehoboth Bays are good places to look for clams and crabs. You also find blue crabs in the tidal rivers of Delaware Bay.

GOLF

Virginia's golf courses have played a huge part in world affairs – this recreation has given a number of presidents the chance to slip a friendly word of advice into the ears of foreign visitors. It may not exactly constitute an 'adventure' outdoor sport, but it is certainly popular as is evident on the state's more than 150 courses, including some of the nation's finest: those at The Homestead (Cascades is rated among America's 100 best golf courses), Wintergreen, Massanutten, Bryce, the Shenandoah Country Club, Meadows Farm in Orange County, Tides Inn, the courses at the Williamsburg Inn and Kingsmill Resort (home of the PGA Anheuser Busch Golf Classic), Honey Bee and Hell's Point in Hampton Roads, and the Country Club of Virginia in Richmond.

For more information contact the Golf Resorts Association (☎ 800-932-2259) and the Virginia Golf Association (☎ 804-378-2300). A good place to start reading is *Virginia's Fairways Annual Golf Guide*.

BIRD & WILDLIFE WATCHING

During the fall, winter, and early spring, the Chesapeake, located right on the Atlantic Flyway, is host to one of the world's greatest collection of waterfowl including Canada geese, snow geese, and swans. In Virginia, great 'twitching' areas are the Chincoteague, Eastern Shore, Plum Tree Island, and Back Bay National Wildlife Refuges, Assateague Island, and the Great Dismal Swamp, all on the east coast. The Caledon Natural Area on the Potomac has one of the East Coast's greatest concentrations of bald eagles. Many bird species, as well as other wildlife, can be seen in Shenandoah National Park, Assateague Island, the Great Dismal Swamp, and in the many forests and recreation areas of the mountainous southwest of Virginia.

Maryland's biggest collections of waterfowl as well as fish hawks and eagles gather at Eastern Neck National Wildlife Refuge near Chestertown, the Blackwater National Wildlife Refuge near Cambridge, and Point Lookout in Southern Maryland.

In Delaware, the Bombay Hook and the Prime Hook National Wildlife Refuges have immense populations of snow geese in season. Fort Delaware/Pea Patch Island is a good place to look for large populations of wading birds like snowy egrets.

Getting There & Away

AIR

Major Airlines

Most major airlines offer service to the Capital Region. Here's a partial list of the ones with toll-free telephone numbers (free within the US); major domestic carriers are noted with an asterisk:

Air Canada	☎ 800-776-3000
Air France	☎ 800-237-2747
Air New Zealand	☎ 800-262-1234
American Airlines*	☎ 800-433-7300
British Airways	☎ 800-247-9297
Canadian Airlines	☎ 800-426-7000
Continental Airlines*	☎ 800-525-0280
Delta Air Lines*	☎ 800-221-1212
Japan Air Lines	☎ 800-525-3663
KLM	☎ 800-374-7747
Northwest Airlines*	☎ 800-447-4747
Qantas Airways	☎ 800-227-4500
TWA*	☎ 800-221-2000
United Airlines*	☎ 800-241-6522
USAir*	☎ 800-428-4322

Major Airports

There are three major airports in the Capital Region; all three are within 35 miles of Washington, DC. (See later chapters for regional airports and local transit information.)

Baltimore-Washington International Airport (BWI; ☎ 410-859-7111, 800-435-9294) is located in Linticum, Maryland, 10 miles south of downtown Baltimore and 30 miles northeast of Washington, DC. From BWI, you can find limousine, van shuttle, taxi, and train service to either city and other points.

Washington Dulles International Airport (pronounced 'dull-ess', ☎ 703-661-2700) is in Herndon, Virginia, 25 miles east of Washington. From here, limousine, van shuttle, and taxi service is available to downtown Washington; shuttles also connect with outlying Metro subway stations.

By far the most convenient airport for Washington visitors is Washington National Airport (☎ 703-417-8000), which is right on the Potomac River near Arlington National Cemetery. A terminal subway station offers easy access to all Metro points; you can also find quick shuttle and taxi service downtown.

Travelers heading straight for Delaware, especially Wilmington, should consider flying into Philadelphia International Airport (☎ 215-492-3181), eight miles southwest of downtown Philadelphia. It is served by direct flights from Europe, the Caribbean, and Canada, and offers connections to Asia, Africa, and South America. There is shuttle-bus service to Wilmington (see the Wilmington chapter).

Buying Tickets

Finding Airfare Bargains Airfare will likely be the highest priced item in your travel budget, and with so many airfare options and packages to US destinations available from a variety of vendors, it pays to do research and shop around. One of the factors to consider is how much flexibility you want your ticket to have; for example, would you be willing to pay more for a ticket that allowed a certain number of stopovers or schedule changes, than one set in stone with penalties for changes?

Start shopping for a ticket early – some of the cheapest tickets must be bought months in advance, and some popular flights sell out early. Talk to recent travelers (who can steer you towards good deals and away from common mistakes), examine newspaper and magazine ads, consult reference books, and watch for special offers.

Airfare in the US can vary tremendously by season, day of the week, duration of stay, and flexibility for flight changes and refunds. High season in the USA is mid-June to mid-September (summer), and the one week before and after Christmas. The best rates for travel to and in the USA occur from November 1 to March 31. Yet nothing determines fares more than demand, and when things are slow, regardless of the season, airlines will lower their fares to fill empty seats. Competition is fierce, and at any moment any of the airlines could have the cheapest fare.

International travelers might peruse the travel sections of such magazines as *Time Out* and *TNT* (in the UK) or the Saturday editions of such newspapers as the *Sydney Morning Herald* and *The Age* (in Australia). Ads in these publications offer cheap fares, but don't be surprised if they're sold out when you call: They're typically low-season fares on obscure airlines limited by lots of conditions.

If you're departing from the UK, you will probably find that the cheapest flights are advertised by obscure bucket shops so new that their name hasn't yet reached the telephone directory. Though many are honest and solvent, watch out for the few rogues that collect money and disappear only to reopen elsewhere a month or two later under a new name. It's wise to avoid giving a firm all the money for a ticket at once – try leaving a deposit of 20% or so and paying the balance upon receipt of the ticket (if they insist on cash in advance, go elsewhere). Once you have the ticket, ring the airline to confirm that you are booked on the flight.

It may be worth spending more for the security of a well-known travel agent. Established firms like STA Travel, which has offices worldwide, Council Travel in the USA (☎ 800-226-8624), or Travel CUTS in Canada are good alternatives.

Domestic travelers can check the *Washington Post*, *New York Times*, *Chicago Tribune*, and other major newspapers for their ad-filled travel sections. The magazine *Travel Unlimited* (PO Box 1058, Allston, MA 02134) publishes details of the cheapest airfares and courier possibilities.

Phone around to various travel agents for bargains (airlines can supply information on routes and timetables, but they do not supply the cheapest tickets except at times of fare wars. Airlines often have competitive low-season, student, and senior citizens' fares. Always inquire about the fare, the route, the duration of the journey, and any restrictions on the ticket.

Cheap tickets are available in two distinct categories: official and unofficial. Official ones have a variety of names including advance-purchase fares, budget fares, Apex, and super-Apex. Unofficial tickets are simply discounted tickets that the airlines release through selected travel agents (not through airline offices). The cheapest tickets are often nonrefundable and require an extra fee for changing your flight. Many insurance policies will cover this loss if you have to change your flight for emergency reasons. Return (roundtrip) tickets are generally much less expensive than two one-way fares.

Use fares quoted in this book as a guide only. They are approximate and based on the rates advertised by travel agents and airlines at press time. Quoted airfares do not necessarily constitute a recommendation for the carrier.

Once you have your ticket, record the number and flight information (better yet, make a photocopy), and keep the copy in a safe place; if your ticket is lost or stolen, this will make it much easier to have it replaced.

Round-the-World Tickets Round-the-world (RTW) tickets have become very popular in the last few years. Airline RTW tickets are often real bargains and can work out to be no more expensive or even cheaper than an ordinary return ticket. Prices start at about UK£850, A$1800, or US$1300.

The official airline RTW tickets are usually put together by a combination of two airlines and permit you to fly anywhere you want on the route systems of these two airlines as long as you do not backtrack. Other restrictions are that you must usually book the first sector in advance and cancellation penalties apply. There may be restrictions on the number of stops permitted, and tickets are usually valid from 90 days up to a year. An alternative type of RTW ticket is one put together by a travel agent using a combination of discounted tickets.

Although most airlines restrict the number of sectors that can be flown within the USA and Canada to four, and some airlines black out a few heavily traveled routes (like Honolulu to Tokyo), stopovers are otherwise generally unlimited. In most cases a 14-day advance purchase is required. After the ticket is purchased, dates can be changed without penalty and tickets can be rewritten to add or delete stops for US$50 each.

The majority of RTW tickets restrict you to just two airlines. British Airways and Qantas Airways offer a RTW ticket called the Global Explorer that allows you to combine routes on both airlines to a total of 28,000 miles for US$2999 or A$3099. Qantas also flies in conjunction with American Airlines, Delta Air Lines, Northwest Airlines, Canadian Airlines, Air France, and KLM. Qantas RTW tickets, with any of the aforementioned partner airlines, cost US$3247 or A$3099.

Canadian Airlines offers numerous RTW combinations. One with Philippine Airlines (C$2790) could include Manila, Dubai, Pakistan, and Europe; another with KLM (C$3149) could include Cairo, Bombay, Delhi, and Amsterdam; and a third with South African Airways (C$3499) could include Australia and Africa.

Many other airlines also offer RTW tickets. Continental Airlines, for example, links up with either Malaysia Airlines, Singapore Airlines, or Thai Airways for US$2570. TWA's lowest priced RTW, linking up with Korean Air, costs US$2087 and allows stops in Honolulu, Seoul, Tel Aviv, Amsterdam, and Paris or London.

Visit USA Passes Non-US citizens can purchase 'Visit USA' passes from nearly all domestic carriers. Each pass is made up of coupons, and each coupon is good for one flight. The following airlines are the most representative, but check with your travel agent about other airlines that offer the service.

Continental Airlines' Visit USA pass can be purchased outside the US in all countries except Canada and Mexico. All travel must be completed within 60 days of the first flight into the USA or 81 days after arrival in USA. You must have your trip planned out in order to purchase the coupons; if you decide to change destinations once you're in the USA, you will be charged $50. High-season prices are $479 for three coupons (minimum purchase) and $769 for eight coupons (maximum purchase).

Northwest offers the same deal, but it lets you fly standby or reserve seats in advance. American Airlines uses the same coupon structure and also sells the passes in all other countries except Canada and Mexico. You must declare where you want to go on your first flight and stick to that schedule or be penalized. You must also reserve flights one day in advance, and if a coupon only takes you halfway to your destination, you will have to buy the remaining ticket at full price.

Delta has two different systems for travelers coming to the US across the Atlantic. Visit USA gives travelers a discount, but you need to have your itinerary mapped out to take advantage of this. The other option is Discover America, in which a traveler buys coupons good for standby travel anywhere in the continental USA. One flight equals one coupon. Only two transcontinental flights are allowed – Delta prefers that your travels follow some sort of circular pattern. Four coupons cost about $550, 10 cost $1250. Children's fares are about $40 less. In order to purchase coupons, you must pay for the transatlantic flight in advance.

When flying standby, call the airline a day or two before the flight and make a 'standby' reservation. This way you get priority over all the others who just show up hoping to get on the flight.

Baggage & Other Restrictions

On most domestic and international flights you are limited to two checked bags or three if you don't have a carry-on. You may pay a charge if you bring more or if the size of the bags exceeds the airline's limits. It's best to check with the specific airline if you are worried about this. On some international flights the luggage allowance is based on weight, not number of bags; again, check with the airline.

If you arrive but your luggage is delayed (which is rare), some airlines will give you a cash advance to purchase necessities. If the airline misplaces sporting equipment, it may pay for rentals. If the luggage is lost, you must submit a claim. The airline is not required to pay the full amount of the claim; rather, it can estimate the value of your lost items. The airline may take anywhere from six weeks to three months to process the claim and pay you.

Smoking Smoking is prohibited on all domestic flights within the USA. Many international flights are following suit, so be sure to call to check. (Incidentally, the restriction applies to the passenger cabin and the lavatories but not the cockpit.) Many airports in the USA also restrict smoking, but they compensate by having 'smoking rooms.'

Illegal Items Items that are illegal to take on a plane, either as checked or carry-on luggage, include aerosols of polishes, waxes, etc; tear gas and pepper spray; camp stoves with fuel; and divers' tanks that are full. Matches should not be checked.

Getting Bumped

When airlines overbook flights, they may need to 'bump' some passengers, which can be a tremendous inconvenience if waiting for the next flight upsets your travel plans. If you aren't on a tight schedule, however, it can be a boon, because airlines offer a variety of perks to people who volunteer to be bumped. Depending on the airline's desperation and quality, it may offer anything from a roundtrip ticket to anywhere the airline flies to a $200 voucher towards your next flight; if you need to wait overnight, the airline should provide vouchers for lodging and meals. If you wouldn't mind being bumped (and compensated), ask if they will need volunteers when you check in and leave your name if they do. Be sure to ask when they can get you on a flight to your destination, and try to confirm that flight so you aren't stuck in the airport for too long.

To/From Canada

Travel CUTS has offices in all major cities. The *Toronto Globe & Mail* and *Vancouver Sun* carry travel agents' ads; the magazine *Great Expeditions* (PO Box 8000-411, Abbotsford BC V2S 6H1) is also useful. Air Canada charges C$416 (US$312) for a flight from Toronto to Washington, based on a 14-day advance purchase and a maximum stay of a year.

To/From Australia & New Zealand

In Australia, STA Travel and Flight Centres International are major dealers in cheap airfares; check the travel agents' ads in the yellow pages, and ring around. Qantas flies to Los Angeles from Sydney, Melbourne (via Sydney or Auckland), and Cairns. United flies to San Francisco from Sydney and Melbourne (via Sydney) and also flies to Los Angeles. Connector flights are available to the East Coast.

In New Zealand, STA Travel and Flight Centres International are also popular travel agents.

The cheapest tickets have a 21-day advance-purchase requirement, a minimum stay of seven days, and a maximum stay of 60 days. Qantas flies from Melbourne or Sydney to Los Angeles for A$1470 (US$1156) in the low season and A$1820 (US$1432) in the high season. Qantas flights from Cairns to Los Angeles cost A$1579 (US$1243) in the low season and A$1919 (US$1510) in the high season. Flying with Air New Zealand is slightly cheaper, and both Qantas and Air New Zealand offer tickets with longer stays or stopovers, but you pay more. United also flies to Los Angeles.

Full-time students can save A$80 (US$63) to A$140 (US$110) on roundtrip fares to the USA. Roundtrip flights from Auckland to Los Angeles on Qantas cost NZ$1720 (US$1223) in the low season (this is the quoted student fare).

To/From the UK & Ireland

Check the ads in magazines like *Time Out*, the Sunday papers, and *Exchange & Mart*. Also check the free magazines widely available in London – start by looking outside the main railway stations.

Most British travel agents are registered with the ABTA (Association of British Travel Agents). If you have paid an ABTA-registered agent for your flight and the agent then goes out of business, ABTA will guarantee a refund or an alternative. Unregistered bucket shops are riskier but sometimes cheaper.

London is arguably the world's headquarters for bucket shops, which are well advertised and can usually beat published airline fares. Two good, reliable agents for cheap tickets in the UK are Trailfinders (☎ 0171-938-3366), 46 Earls Court Rd, London W8 6EJ, and STA Travel (☎ 0171-937-9962), 74 Old Brompton Rd, London SW7. Trailfinders produces a lavishly illustrated brochure including airfare details.

American Airlines has a roundtrip fare from London to Washington of UK£515 (US$850), which allows a six-month maximum stay and requires a seven-day advance purchase.

Virgin Atlantic has a roundtrip high-season fare from London to New York for UK£448 (US$739), which allows a one-month maximum stay and requires a 21-day advance purchase. Off-season (winter) flights from London to New York range from UK£240 (US$396) to UK£508 (US$838) and to Los Angeles starting at UK£280 (US$462).

The Globetrotters Club (BCM Roving, London WC1N 3XX) publishes a newsletter called *Globe* that covers obscure destinations and can help you find traveling companions.

To/From Continental Europe

The most common route to the Capital Region is through Washington or via a connection from New York. If you're interested in heading east with stops in Asia, it may be cheaper to get a round-the-world ticket instead of returning the same way.

American Airline's high-season roundtrip fare between Paris and Washington is FF4096 (US$804); it requires a seven-day advance purchase and is good for a stay of up to 21 days. Virgin Atlantic flights from Paris to New York are somewhat cheaper; a ticket purchased at least seven days in advance ranges from FF3790 (US$744) to FF4530 (US$889). United, Delta, and Continental have similarly priced service from a number of European cities.

In Amsterdam, NBBS is a popular travel agent. In Paris Transalpino and Council Travel are popular agencies. The newsletter *Farang* (La Rue 8 à 4261 Braives, Belgium) covers exotic destinations, as does the magazine *Aventure du Bout du Monde* (116 rue de Javel, 75015 Paris, France).

To/From Africa

At press time, there were no nonstop flights between Africa and the Capital Region. Direct connecting flights are available through major international carriers – British Airways, for example, flies daily from its London hub to seven cities in Africa, including Nairobi, Capetown, and Johannesburg. Its standard rate for a flight between BWI and Nairobi runs around $2760.

To/From Asia

Hong Kong is the discount plane ticket capital of the region, but its bucket shops can be unreliable. Ask the advice of other travelers before buying a ticket. STA Travel, which is dependable, has branches in Hong Kong, Tokyo, Singapore, Bangkok, and Kuala Lumpur. Many if not most flights to the USA are routed via Honolulu, Hawaii.

To/From Central & South America

Most flights from Central and South America are routed via Miami, Houston, or Los Angeles, though some fly via New York. Most countries' international flag carriers (some of them, such as Aerolíneas Argentinas and LANChile, recently privatized), as well as US airlines like United and American, serve these destinations, with onward connections to the Capital Region. Continental has flights from about 20 cities in Mexico and Central America, including San Jose, Guatemala City, Cancún, and Mérida.

Arriving in USA by Air

Even if you are continuing immediately to another city, the first airport that you land in is where you must carry out immigration and customs formalities. Even if your luggage is checked from, say, London to Baltimore, you will still have to take it through customs if you first land in New York.

Passengers aboard the airplane are given standard immigration and customs forms to fill out. The cabin crew will help you fill them out if you have any questions (see the Entering the USA section in the Facts for the Visitor chapter), but the forms are quite straightforward. After the plane lands, you'll first go through immigration. There are two lines: One is for US citizens and residents, and the other is for nonresidents. Immigration formalities are usually straightforward if you have all the necessary documents (passport and visa). Occasionally, you may be asked to show your ticket out of the country, but this doesn't happen very often.

After passing through immigration, you collect your baggage and then pass through customs. If you have nothing to declare, there is a good chance that you can clear customs quickly and without a luggage search, but you can't rely on it. After passing through customs, you are officially in the country. If your flight is continuing to another city or you have a connecting flight, it is your responsibility to get your bags to the right place. Normally, there are airline counters just beyond the customs area that will help you. Also see the information under Customs in the Facts for the Visitor chapter.

Air Travelers with Special Needs

If you have special needs of any sort – a broken leg, dietary restrictions, dependence on a wheelchair, responsibility for a baby, fear of flying – you should let the airline know as soon as possible so that it can make arrangements accordingly. You should remind the airline when you reconfirm your booking (at least 72 hours before departure) and again when you check in at the airport. It may also be worth ringing round the airlines before you make your booking to find out how they can handle your particular needs.

Airports and airlines can be surprisingly helpful, given enough advance warning. Most international airports can provide escorts from check-in desk to plane, and there should be ramps, lifts, accessible toilets, and reachable phones. Aircraft toilets, on the other hand, are likely to present a problem; travelers should discuss this with the airline at an early stage and, if necessary, with their doctor.

Guide dogs for the blind will often have to travel in a specially pressurized baggage compartment with other animals, away from the owner, though smaller guide dogs may be admitted to the cabin. Guide dogs are not subject to quarantine as long as they have proof of being vaccinated against rabies.

Deaf travelers can ask that attendants write down airport and in-flight announcements for them.

Children under two travel for 10% of the standard fare (or free on some airlines), as long as they don't occupy a seat. (They don't get a baggage allowance either.) 'Skycots' should be provided by the airline if requested in advance; these will take a child weighing up to about 22 lbs. Children between two and 12 can usually occupy a seat for half to two-thirds of the full fare and do get a baggage allowance. Strollers can often be taken on as hand luggage.

Departure Taxes

Airport departure taxes are normally included in the cost of tickets bought in the USA, although tickets purchased abroad may not include this. A $6 airport departure tax is charged to all passengers bound for a foreign destination. There's also a $6.50

North American Free Trade Agreement (NAFTA) tax charged to passengers entering the USA from a foreign country.

LAND

Bus

Greyhound (☎ 800-231-2222), a private bus carrier, is the only company that operates nationwide bus service in and out of most cities of any size. Greyhound runs cross-country between New York and San Francisco (via Denver and Chicago); Seattle (via Minneapolis-St Paul and Chicago); and Los Angeles (via Las Vegas, Denver, and Chicago). Bus service also connects such Capital Region cities as Baltimore, Washington, and Richmond (Virginia) with destinations along the Eastern Seaboard. Trailways also provides service to eastern cities.

Buses are not the most comfortable way to travel – the most common complaints are monotonous rides, questionable fellow passengers, and run-down bus stations in lousy parts of town – but they can be a cheap alternative for some long-distance travel. Compare costs closely – sometimes a great airfare deal or rental-car rate will get you there a lot more comfortably for not that much more.

To inquire about regular fares and routes, contact Greyhound International ☎ 800-246-8572. For information about local stations and schedules, see the following chapters.

International Ameripass Greyhound offers a special fare available only to foreign tourists and foreign students and lecturers (with their families) staying less than one year. These prices are $89 for a four-day pass for unlimited travel Monday to Thursday, $149 for a seven-day pass, $209 for a 15-day pass, and $289 for a 30-day pass. The International Ameripass is usually for sale abroad at travel agencies or it can be purchased in the USA through the Greyhound International depot in New York City (☎ 212-971-0492) at 625 8th Ave at the Port Authority Subway level (open Monday to Friday from 9 am to 4:30 pm). New York Greyhound International accepts MasterCard and Visa, traveler's checks and cash, and allows purchases to be made by phone. Those buying an International Ameripass must complete an affidavit and present a passport or visa (or waiver) to the appropriate Greyhound officials.

There are also special passes for travel in Canada that can be purchased only through the New York City office or abroad.

Train

Amtrak (☎ 800-872-7245, 800-872-7245) provides nationwide rail service, most comprehensively along the busy Eastern Seaboard corridor from Boston to Washington, DC. You'll generally find efficient, well-maintained trains, and convenient stations. Rates and travel times between many destinations along this route are competitive with air travel, especially considering that train stations are centrally located in major cities. Union Station in Washington, DC, is Amtrak's 'flagship' station, and offers a variety of convenient travel resources to visitors.

Amtrak service to and through other parts of the US is more limited, less convenient, and not as good a value – long-distance fares are often higher than the cost of airfare or car rentals for covering the same distance, so beyond the East Coast corridor, train travel is an option that appeals mostly to dedicated rail lovers.

Special discount fares and package rates may make rail travel more economical. The best value overall is Amtrak's *All Aboard America* fare (US$278 for adults low season, US$338 between mid-June and late August). It enables you to travel to any city you choose. There are restrictions, however: Travel must be completed in 45 days, and you are allowed a maximum of three stopovers (additional stopovers can be arranged at extra cost). Your entire trip must be reserved in advance; since seats are limited, book as far ahead as possible. These tickets are for reclining seats; sleeping cars cost extra. If you want to travel just in the eastern portion of the country, $178 All Aboard America fares are available.

For further travel assistance, call Amtrak or ask your travel agent. Note that most small train stations don't sell tickets; you have to book them with Amtrak over the phone. Some small stations have no porters or other facilities, and trains may stop there only if you have bought a ticket in advance.

Car & Motorcycle

Most people get around the region (and the rest of the nation) by private automobile. For information on buying or renting a car, or using a drive-away (driving a car for someone else) see the Getting Around chapter. Drivers of cars and riders of motorcycles will need the vehicle's registration papers, liability insurance, and an international driver's permit in addition to their domestic license. Canadian and Mexican driver's licenses are accepted.

If you're considering shipping a car, note that air-cargo planes do have size limits, but a normal car or even a Land Rover can fit. For motorcyclists, shipping the bike by air is probably the easiest option; you may be able to get a special rate for air cargo if you are flying with the same airline. Start by asking the cargo departments of the airlines that fly to your destination. Travel agents can sometimes help as well.

WARNING

The information in this chapter is particularly vulnerable to change: Prices for international travel are volatile, routes are introduced and canceled, schedules change, special deals come and go, and rules and visa requirements are amended. Airlines and governments seem to take a perverse pleasure in making price structures and regulations as complicated as possible. You should check directly with the airline or a travel agent to make sure you understand how a fare (and ticket you may buy) works. In addition, the travel industry is highly competitive and there are many pitfalls and perks.

The upshot is that you should get opinions, quotes, and advice from as many airlines and travel agents as possible before you part with your hard-earned cash. The details given in this chapter should be regarded as pointers and are not a substitute for your own careful, up-to-date research.

Getting Around

Though private automobile remains the most common way to traverse the Capital Region beyond city-to-city connections, air, train, and bus service is readily available throughout the region.

AIR

Beyond the three major international airports (Baltimore-Washington, Washington Dulles, and Washington National – see Getting There & Away), many smaller airports serve parts of Delaware, Maryland, and Virginia. Regional airports are discussed under the cities and towns that they service.

Commuter Flights

Several airlines run short commuter flights between the major airports and smaller regional airports. If you're coming from outside the Capital Region, they may prove useful, but they aren't necessarily the most practical way to travel inside the region nor the most economical. USAir (☎ 800-428-4322) is the main carrier with commuter services from all three major airports. It flies from BWI to Richmond, for example, three times a day; the standard fare is $365 roundtrip. Also contact United Express (☎ 800-241-6522) or Continental Express (☎ 800-525-0280).

BUS

Buses are the budget alternative for getting to many smaller cities not served by air or rail service (though again, check car-rental rates and packages to compare costs). Nearly every city of any size has its Greyhound bus station or stop; Trailways is another bus line that often uses the same terminals. See Getting There & Away for more information about bus transit and toll-free numbers for route and schedule information.

Greyhound Fares

Tickets can be bought over the phone with a credit card (MasterCard, Visa, or Discover) and mailed if purchased 10 days in advance or picked up at the terminal with proper identification. Greyhound terminals also accept American Express, traveler's checks, and cash. Note that all buses are nonsmoking, and reservations are made with ticket purchases only.

Greyhound occasionally introduces a mileage-based discount-fare program that can be a bargain, especially for very long distances, but it's a good idea to check the regular fare anyway. As with regular fares, these promotional fares are subject to change.

Greyhound's Ameripass is potentially useful, depending on how much you plan to travel, but the relatively high prices may motivate you to travel more than you normally would simply to get your money's worth. There are no restrictions on who can buy an Ameripass; it costs $179 for seven days of unlimited travel year round, $289 for 15 days of travel and $399 for 30 days of travel. Children under 11 travel for half price. You can get on and off at any Greyhound stop or terminal, and the Ameripass is available at every Greyhound terminal.

Bus vs Train Rates in the Capital Region
(Fares for 10/96, traveling on a Saturday, one-way/roundtrip)

From Washington, DC, to:	*Greyhound*	*Amtrak*
Baltimore, MD	$8/13	$15/30
Wilmington, DE	$14/26	$33/66
Richmond, VA	$16/31	$18/36
Charlottesville, VA	$25/49	$34/68

TRAIN

Amtrak's *Metroliner* route carries passengers from New York and other cities along the Eastern Seaboard through the region from Delaware to Virginia's Atlantic coast, including major stops in Wilmington, Baltimore, BWI Airport, Washington, DC, and Richmond. For more information on train travel, see Getting There & Away.

CAR & MOTORCYCLE

The Capital Region is well served by major interstate freeways. Interstate 95 runs north-south along the Eastern Seaboard and connects with major east-west routes in Baltimore, Washington, and Richmond. Around major cities, a three-digit interstate extension bypasses the central city for through-travelers (in Baltimore, it's I-695; in Washington it's the I-495 Beltway).

The region offers two exceptionally scenic two-lane highway routes for leisurely driving adventures: the Appalachian route through Maryland and Virginia via the Blue Ridge Highway and Skyline Drive (most scenic, and crowded, during the fall foliage season); and the old Atlantic Coast Highway (Hwy 17), which detours from the urban corridor and runs through the old-time beach towns of the Delmarva Peninsula, the 18-mile-long Chesapeake Bay tunnel, and mainland Virginia's corner coast and Dismal Swamp before continuing south to Florida.

For information on road conditions, call ☎ 800-367-7623 in Virginia, ☎ 800-642-3282 in Maryland, ☎ 800-732-8500 in Delaware, and ☎ 202-727-5745 in the District of Columbia. (For beach conditions in Maryland call ☎ 800-541-9595.)

Driving Laws

State driving laws vary, but these general rules apply: Drivers must be at least 16 years of age, and speed limits are 65 mph on interstate highways and freeways unless otherwise posted. You can drive five mph over the limit without much likelihood of being pulled over, but if you're doing 10 mph or more over the limit, you'll be

Accidents Do Happen

In an auto-dependent country like the USA, accidents are fairly common. It's important that a visitor knows the appropriate protocol when involved in a 'fender-bender.'

- DON'T TRY TO DRIVE AWAY! Remain at the scene of the accident; otherwise, you may spend some time in the local jail.

- Call the police (and an ambulance, if needed) immediately, and give the operator as much specific information as possible (your location, the number of vehicles involved, whether injuries were sustained). The emergency phone number is ☎ 911.

- Get the other driver's name, address, driver's license number, license plate number, and insurance information. Be prepared to provide any documentation you have, such as your passport, international driver's license, and insurance documents.

- Tell your story to the police carefully. Refrain from answering any questions until you feel comfortable doing so (with a lawyer present, if need be). That's your right under the law. The only insurance information you must reveal is the name of your insurance carrier and your policy number.

- Always comply with a request that you undergo an alcohol breathalyzer test. If you refuse, you'll almost certainly find yourself with an automatic suspension of your driving privileges.

- If you're driving a rental car, call the rental company promptly.

caught sooner or later. Speed limits on other highways are 55 mph or less, and in cities they can vary from 25 to 45 mph. Watch for school zones, which can be as low as 15 mph during school hours – these limits are strictly enforced. Seat belts and motorcycle helmets must be worn in most states (see also Driving Documents in the Facts for the Visitor chapter).

American Automobile Association

With offices in all major cities and many smaller towns, AAA (referred to as 'Triple A') provides emergency roadside service in the event of an accident, breakdown, or keys locked in the car. Service is free within a given radius of the nearest service center, and trucks will tow your car to a mechanic if the driver can't fix it. The nationwide toll-free roadside assistance number is ☎ 800-222-4357, 800-AAA-HELP; service is available to members only.

AAA also provides great travel information, free road maps, and guide books, and sells American Express traveler's checks without commission. Showing the AAA membership card often qualifies members for discounts on accommodations, car rentals, and admission charges. If you plan to do a lot of motoring – even in a rental car – it is usually worth joining AAA. It costs $56 for the first year and $39 for subsequent years.

Members of foreign affiliates, like the Automobile Association in the UK, are entitled to the same services if they bring their membership cards and/or a letter of introduction.

Rental

Major international rental agencies like Hertz, Avis, and Budget have offices throughout the region, but there are also local agencies. To rent a car, you must have a valid driver's license, be at least 25 years of age, and present either a major credit card like MasterCard or Visa or a large cash deposit.

Many rental agencies have bargain rates for weekend or weeklong rentals, especially outside the peak summer season or in conjunction with airline tickets. Prices vary greatly among companies and according to region, season, and type or size of the car.

Basic liability insurance, which covers damage you may cause to another vehicle, is required by law and comes with the price of renting the car. (Liability insurance is also called third-party coverage.)

Collision insurance (also called the Liability Damage Waiver) is optional; it covers the full value of the vehicle in case of an accident, except when caused by acts of nature or fire. The cost of collision insurance varies among rental companies but ranges from $12 to $15 per day. You are not required to buy this waiver to rent the car, but rental companies will encourage you to do so. Most agencies also tack on a daily fee per each additional driver in the car unless the additional driver is the renter's spouse; however, some companies are beginning to cover domestic partners as well.

Some credit cards, such as the MasterCard Gold Card, offer a collision insurance benefit, which kicks in when you rent a car for 15 days or less and charge the full cost of rental to your card. If you opt to do that, you'll need to sign the waiver, declining the coverage. If you already have collision insurance on your personal auto policy, the credit card covers the large deductible. To determine what coverage your credit card offers and the extent of the coverage, contact the credit card company.

Major car rental agencies and national toll-free numbers include the following:

Avis Rent-A-Car	☎ 800-831-2847
Budget Car & Truck Rental	☎ 800-527-0700
	TDD 800-826-5510
	Spanish 800-992-2776
Dollar Rent-A-Car	☎ 800-800-4000
Enterprise Rent-A-Car	☎ 800-325-8007
Hertz Rent-A-Car	☎ 800-654-3131
	TDD 800-654-2280
National Car Rental	☎ 800-227-7368
Thrifty Car Rental	☎ 800-367-2277

Purchase

If you're planning to spend several months in the USA, you might consider purchasing a car which is more flexible than public transport and likely to be cheaper than rentals, but buying one can be a very complicated process and requires plenty of research.

It's possible to purchase a viable car in the USA for about $1500, but you can't expect to go too far before you'll need some repair work that could cost several hundred dollars or more. It doesn't hurt to spend more to get a quality vehicle. It's also worth spending $50 or so to have a mechanic check it for defects before purchasing it (some AAA offices have diagnostic centers where they can do this on the spot for members and those of foreign affiliates). You can check out the official valuation of a used car by looking it up in the *Blue Book* (published quarterly), a listing of cars by make, model, year issued, and average resale price. Local public libraries have copies of the *Blue Book*, as well as back issues of *Consumer's Report*, a magazine that annually tallies the repair records of common makes of cars.

If you want to purchase a car, the first thing to do is contact AAA (☎ 800-222-4357) for some general information. Then contact the state's motor vehicle bureau to find out about registration fees and insurance, which can be very confusing and expensive. As an example, say you are a 30-year-old non-US citizen and you want to buy a 1984 Honda. If this is the first time you have registered a car in the USA, you'll have to fork over some $300 first and then about $100 to $200 more for general registration.

Inspect the title carefully before purchasing the car; the owner's name that appears on the title must match the identification of the person selling the car. If you're a foreigner, you may find it very useful to obtain a notarized document authorizing your use of the car, since the motor vehicle bureau in the state where you buy the car may take several weeks or more to process the change in title.

Insurance While insurance is not obligatory in every state, all states have financial responsibility laws and insurance is highly desirable; otherwise, a serious accident could leave you a pauper. In order to get insurance some states request that you have a US driver's license and that you have been licensed for at least 18 months. If you meet those qualifications, you may still have to pay anywhere from $300 to $1200 a year for insurance, depending on the make and value of the car and the address where you register it. Rates are generally lower if you register it at an address in the suburbs or in a rural area rather than in a central city. Collision coverage has become very expensive, with high deductibles, and is generally not worthwhile unless the car is somewhat valuable.

Obtaining insurance, however, is not as simple as walking into an agency, filling out a form, and paying for it. Many agencies refuse to insure drivers who have no car insurance (a classic Catch-22!); those who will sell insurance to uninsured drivers often charge much higher rates because they presume a higher risk. Male drivers under the age of 25 will pay astronomical rates. The minimum term for a policy is usually six months, but some insurance companies will refund the difference on a prorated basis if the car is sold and the policy voluntarily terminated. It is advisable to shop around, and always read the fine print.

Drive-Aways

Drive-aways are cars that belong to owners who can't drive them to a specific destination but are willing to allow someone else to drive for them. For example, if somebody moves from Boston to Portland, he may elect to fly and leave the car with a drive-away agency. The agency will find a driver and take care of all necessary insurance and permits. If you happen to want to drive from Boston to Portland, have a valid driver's license, and a clean driving record, you can apply to drive the car. Normally, you have to pay a small refundable deposit. You pay for the gas (though sometimes a gas allowance is given). You are allowed a set number of days to deliver the car – usually based on driving eight hours a day.

You are also allowed a limited number of miles, based on the best route and allowing for reasonable side trips, so you can't just zigzag all over the country. However, this is a cheap way to get around if you like long-distance driving and meet eligibility requirements.

Drive-away companies often advertise in the classified sections of newspapers under 'Travel.' They are also listed in the yellow pages of telephone directories under 'Automobile Transporters & Drive-Away Companies.' You need to be flexible about dates and destinations when you call. If you are going to a popular area, you may be able to leave within two days or less, or you may have to wait over a week before a car becomes available. The routes most easily available are coast to coast, although shorter trips are certainly possible.

BICYCLE

The region's terrain offers a variety of experiences for bike touring, from mountain biking along rugged Forest Service roads and trails through the Appalachian forest to leisurely trips along the two-lane blacktop at the remote peninsular coast. Spare parts and repair shops are readily available. For more information, see the Outdoor Activities chapter.

If you're flying to the region and bringing your bike with you, ask the airline about requirements, restrictions, and any additional fees before purchasing a ticket.

HITCHHIKING

Hitchhiking is not safe, not recommended, and often not legal. Both hitchers and the drivers who pick them up should recognize that they are taking a small but potentially serious risk. If you do choose to hitch, reduce your risk by traveling in pairs, letting someone know where you are planning to go, keeping your bags with you, and sitting by a door.

WALKING

You can cross the region on foot along the Appalachian Trail, part of the 2159-mile route along the spine of the mountain range. Another well-traveled hike is the 185-mile trail that follows the old Chesapeake and Ohio Canal towpath, stretching from Washington, DC, to Cumberland, Maryland (see the Outdoor Activities chapter for more information). Dedicated city walkers will be most drawn to Washington, DC, for long safe walks through neighborhoods filled with monuments and notable architecture.

BOAT

The Delaware Bay, Chesapeake Bay, and Atlantic Coast are all connected by the Intracoastal Waterway, the navigable channel along the Eastern Seaboard. Small craft can traverse and explore the region off this route. The government publishes the *Coast Pilot* guide for navigation information. It's available from government bookstores, by mail order, or from many marine supply shops in the region. The *Waterbury Guide* is the bible for intracoastal travelers.

Hundreds of marinas line the Chesapeake Bay and its fringed waterways. The major yachting centers are in Annapolis and the Solomons, on the Eastern Shore on the Sassafras River, Rock Hall/Gratitude, St Michaels, and Oxford. In Virginia, the main marinas are the York River and in the Norfolk area. On the Delaware Bay, Lewes is the major yachting center.

LOCAL TRANSPORT

Bus

Each city operates its own municipal bus service, and these services vary considerably from system to system in reliability, cost, and safety. Commonly, passengers pay upon boarding and exact change is required (some more modern buses can accept paper money). Seats up front are often reserved for disabled or elderly passengers.

Train

Besides the Amtrak service in the region (see the Getting There & Away chapter), regional rail service is also available. Maryland's MARC trains connect with Union Station in Washington, DC, and BWI Airport, and service points in eastern Maryland.

Subway

Washington, DC, operates a modern efficient subway system called the Metro, with service throughout the District, to the airport, and into outlying suburban communities. Baltimore has a metro, too, but while the system is efficient, it only services a narrow corridor of suburban towns north and south of downtown.

Taxi

Even small towns usually offer taxi service. Relative to other forms of transit, taxis are an expensive way to get about, but for convenient point-to-point service they can't be beat. In cities such as Washington, DC, taxis can be the most sensible way for newcomers to get about – fares for short distances may be comparable to the Metro (especially if you share cabs), and driving and parking are sometimes not worth the hassle.

ORGANIZED TOURS

Local tours by bus or 'trolley' (a bus disguised as a trolley) are available in many cities, historic towns, and resorts. They can be useful for providing an overview of major sights. Washington, DC, has the widest variety of tour possibilities, including 'duck' tours on recycled military amphibious vehicles that glide through the streets and river, helicopter tours, and theme tours, such as the popular 'Scandal Tours' of DC.

Throughout the region, tours focusing on Civil War sites are available from several operators (see the special Civil War section). For outdoor adventure tours, see Outdoor Activities.

Washington, DC

Washington, DC

From the top of the 555-foot Washington Monument (the tallest point in DC), you can see miles of the long, flat Potomac River basin, which was selected for the permanent seat of the US government over 200 years ago. About two miles east of the river, the land rises to form a low shelf, a contour the city's chief architect Pierre L'Enfant recognized as 'a pedestal awaiting a monument'; today it's known as Capitol Hill.

Broad avenues radiate from the stately Capitol like wheel spokes, intersecting at geometric angles with an alphabetized grid and roundabouts designed for defense. The corridor from the Capitol to the river forms a vast green centerpiece – a national lawn – called the Mall. The great majority of the city's world-famous sights – the grand monuments, memorials, and museums – are located around this compact area. You could walk it in 30 minutes flat or spend days without getting bored.

Downtown Washington surrounds the Mall with massive federal buildings, courthouses, bureaus, and libraries, around which lie graciously landscaped courtyards, squares, and plazas. With all the statues, fountains, and flowers, it's nice just to wander around.

Beyond downtown you'll find DC's varied neighborhoods, from swank Embassy Row at Dupont Circle and Georgetown's prim row houses to funky ethnic, bohemian, and soulful enclaves in the northwestern neighborhoods of Adams-Morgan and Shaw. Throughout the District, you can find plenty of colorful places catering to DC's distinct cultural communities – its vibrant gay community, political activists, the cultural elite, the black vanguard, artists, the international population – but naturally the best spots are the ones that mix it up the most.

For outdoor recreation, Washington residents head to the bike paths and trails in Rock Creek Park and along the C&O Canal and to the shores of the Potomac. The Mall's a great place to fly kites in warm weather; in winter there's a small ice rink across from the sculpture garden.

The height of visitor season runs from April 1 to September 30, and at any time visitors may have to wait in long lines for hours to see the newest and most popular attractions. In terms of weather the most comfortable times are spring (when millions of pale-pink cherry blossoms bloom) and fall. Summers are hot and humid,

HIGHLIGHTS

- The always-free, always-awesome Smithsonian Institution museums – not only the heavy-hitters on the Mall but also the Renwick's craft works and American Art's folk-art collection
- The monumental sights – paddle-boating by the Jefferson Memorial, the view from the top of the Washington Monument by night, and the poignant Vietnam Memorial and Lincoln Memorial
- The political tour – the Capitol Rotunda and statue hall (skip the tour and line), protests outside the Supreme Court, Jackie O's Blue Room in the White House, and the political debate heard at Irish pubs on the Hill
- Adams-Morgan's international restaurant scene along the 18th St strip, especially the jazzy bohemian Cafe Lautrec
- Ben's Chili Bowl, the granddaddy of the New U District for food, and the Black Cat down the street for music

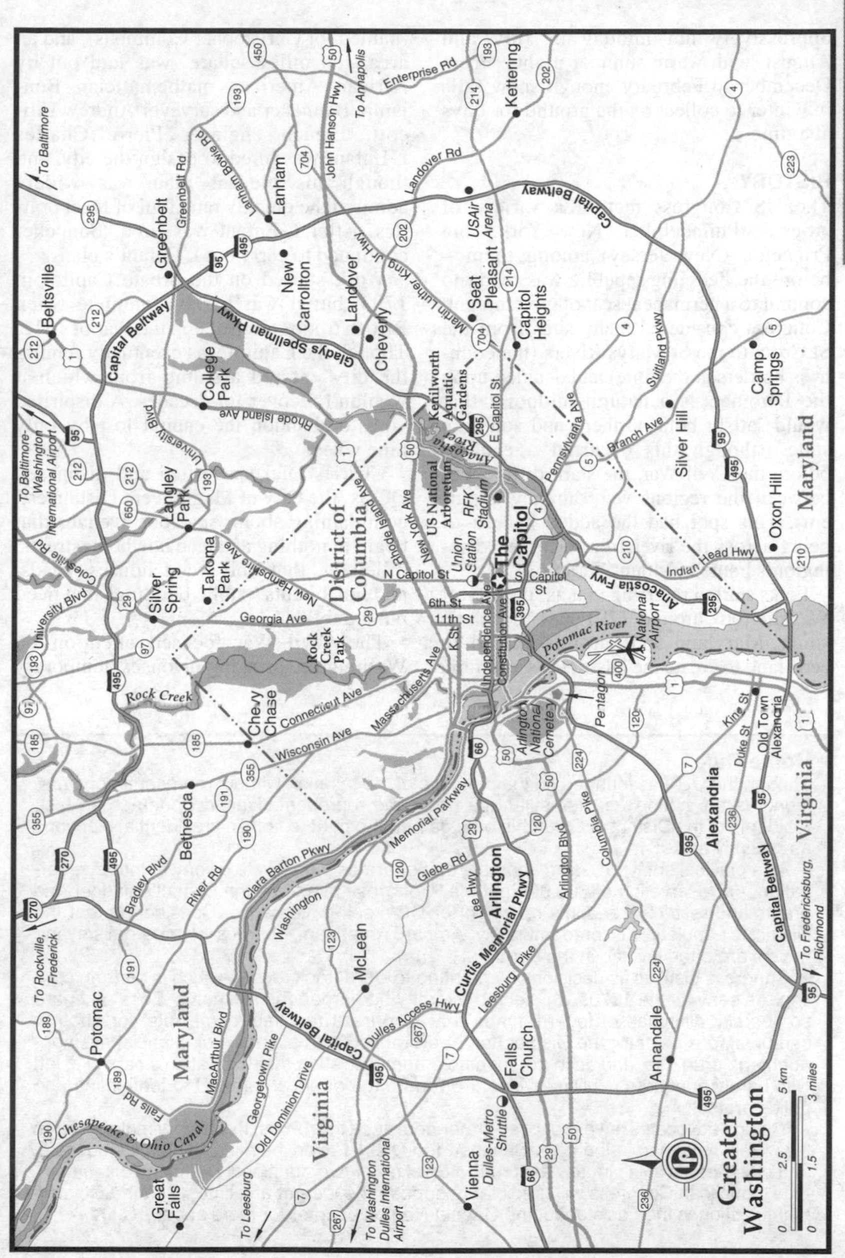
Greater Washington
0 2.5 5 km
0 1.5 3 miles
District of Columbia
Maryland
Virginia
The Capitol
Union Station
US National Arboretum
RFK Stadium
Kenilworth Aquatic Gardens
Anacostia River
Potomac River
National Airport
Pentagon
Arlington National Cemetery
Rock Creek Park
Rock Creek
Chesapeake & Ohio Canal
Capital Beltway
Gladys Spellman Pkwy
Anacostia Fwy
Curtis Memorial Pkwy
Memorial Parkway
Clara Barton Pkwy
Dulles Access Hwy
Georgetown Pike
Old Dominion Drive
Great Falls
Potomac
Bethesda
Chevy Chase
Silver Spring
Takoma Park
Langley Park
College Park
Beltsville
Greenbelt
Lanham
New Carrollton
Landover
Cheverly
Seat Pleasant
Capitol Heights
Kettering
USAir Arena
Silver Hill
Camp Springs
Oxon Hill
Alexandria
Old Town Alexandria
Arlington
McLean
Falls Church
Vienna
Annandale
Dulles-Metro Shuttle
To Baltimore
To Baltimore-Washington International Airport
To Annapolis
To Rockville, Frederick
To Leesburg
To Washington Dulles International Airport
To Fredericksburg, Richmond

oppressively hot midday in July and August, with warm summer nights. From December to February enough snow falls in winter to collect on the ground for days at a time.

HISTORY

The US Congress met in a variety of cities – Philadelphia, New York, and Princeton (New Jersey) among them – before the fledgling republic was ready to commit to a permanent seat of government. Congress considered many sites from the St Croix to the St Marys Rivers (the country's borders at the time) and decided upon the Potomac as a natural midpoint that would satisfy both northern and southern states (though this occurred a century before the Civil War, the stark differences between the regions were already apparent). This spot had the added benefit of being across the river from George Washington's home in Mount Vernon.

Folks started referring to it as 'the city of Washington' around 1791 and the name stuck. Maryland and Virginia agreed to cede land to create the District of Columbia (named for Christopher Columbus), and an area 'ten miles square' was laid out by African American mathematician Benjamin Banneker and surveyor Andrew Ellicott. French engineer Pierre Charles L'Enfant was hired to design the city, and though his elegant plan was widely admired, he quickly ran afoul of local politics. After L'Enfant was fired, Banneker continued to carry out L'Enfant's plans.

Work started on the ornate Capitol in 1793, but it was barely complete when British troops torched it in the War of 1812. Though the Capitol was eventually rebuilt, the city entered a slump from which it wouldn't recover for decades. A dispirited vote to abandon the capital lost by only nine votes.

Charles Dickens visited and dismissed DC as 'the City of Magnificent Distances,' complaining about 'spacious avenues that begin in nothing and lead nowhere; streets, milelong, that only want houses, roads, and inhabitants; public buildings that need but a public.'

The Civil War focused attention on Washington, bringing bivouacs, temporary

Home Rule

Though the US was founded on the principle of 'no taxation without representation,' residents of the nation's capital still have no voting representatives in Congress. In fact, residents of the District of Columbia only gained the right to vote in presidential elections as recently as 1964.

As a political entity, DC is an anomaly that operates more like a colony or Indian reservation – a reservation of 600,000 people. Congress oversees the District's budget and grants and restricts freedoms on whim for DC's self-governance. Considering that the District's population is predominantly African American, charges of paternalism and racism are often leveled in the debate.

Congress justifies its decisions by pointing to DC's track record, which is far from sterling. As early as the 1870s, an elected mayor who earned the nickname 'Boss' Shepard so liberally disposed of federal funds that Congress revoked 'home rule' for another century. More recently, the District has been rocked with scandals of financial mismanagement, drug use, and such irresponsible administration that the nation's capital is left with barely adequate public services, from garbage or snow removal to firefighting and police protection.

Though advocates have proposed statehood since the 1960s, this history makes it even less likely now than in the past. Because the District overwhelmingly votes Democratic, and statehood would virtually assure the election of two additional Democratic senators, the Republican Congress will predictably oppose the idea at any time. (See the Government section in the Facts about the Capital Region chapter for more about DC.) ■

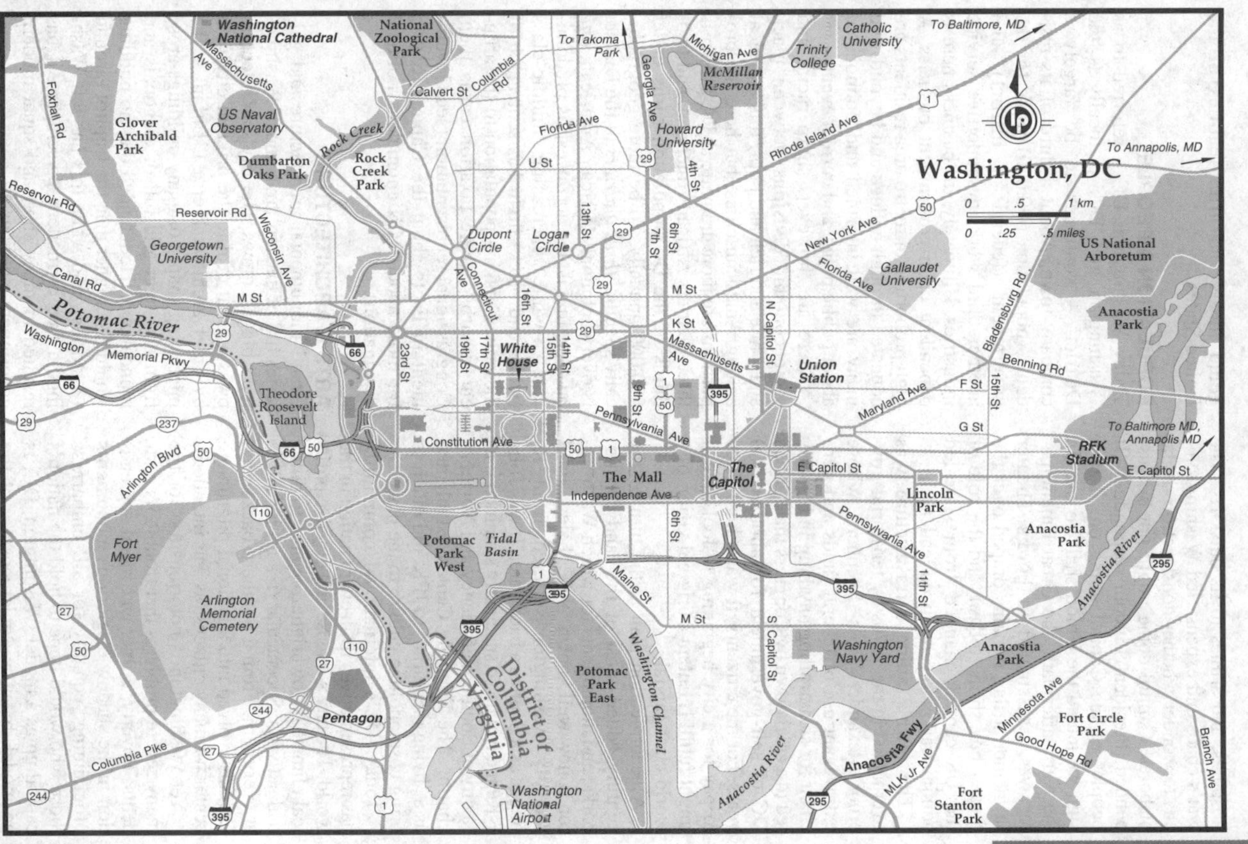
Washington, DC
0 .5 1 km
0 .25 .5 miles
To Baltimore, MD
To Annapolis, MD
To Baltimore MD, Annapolis MD
To Takoma Park
Washington National Cathedral
National Zoological Park
Catholic University
Trinity College
Michigan Ave
McMillan Reservoir
Georgia Ave
Howard University
Rhode Island Ave
Massachusetts Ave
Calvert St
Columbia Rd
Foxhall Rd
Glover Archibald Park
US Naval Observatory
Rock Creek
Rock Creek Park
Dumbarton Oaks Park
Florida Ave
U St
4th St
Reservoir Rd
Wisconsin Ave
Georgetown University
Dupont Circle
Logan Circle
13th St
7th St
6th St
New York Ave
Florida Ave
Gallaudet University
Bladensburg Rd
US National Arboretum
Anacostia Park
Canal Rd
M St
Potomac River
Washington
Memorial Pkwy
Connecticut Ave
16th St
K St
23rd St
19th St
17th St
15th St
14th St
White House
Massachusetts Ave
N Capitol St
Union Station
Benning Rd
F St
15th St
Theodore Roosevelt Island
9th St
Pennsylvania Ave
Maryland Ave
G St
Constitution Ave
Arlington Blvd
The Mall
Independence Ave
The Capitol
E Capitol St
RFK Stadium
Lincoln Park
Pennsylvania Ave
Anacostia Park
Anacostia River
Fort Myer
Potomac Park West
Tidal Basin
Maine St
11th St
Arlington Memorial Cemetery
M St
S Capitol St
Washington Navy Yard
Anacostia Park
Potomac Park East
Washington Channel
District of Columbia
Virginia
Pentagon
Columbia Pike
Washington National Airport
Anacostia River
Anacostia Fwy
MLK Jr Ave
Minnesota Ave
Good Hope Rd
Fort Circle Park
Fort Stanton Park
Branch Ave
1
29
50
66
110
237
27
244
295
395

hospitals, and armies to its outskirts. The war's chaos and expense led Washingtonians to wonder whether construction of the elaborate Capitol dome might not be suspended. President Lincoln responded, 'If people see the Capitol going on, it is a sign we intend the Union shall go on.' In the war's aftermath, the Great Emancipator was assassinated in Ford's Theater (a memorial flag remains draped over the theater box shrine today), and the role of the US capital changed from state-led administration to centralized leadership.

The town's ailing infrastructure was overhauled in the 1870s by territorial governor Alexander 'Boss' Shepherd, whose extravagant use of federal funds and penchant for steamrolling anything in his way led to a crackdown by Congress that robbed DC of self-government for another 100 years. For the citizenry, it was a high price to pay for a city beginning to look like it might fulfill L'Enfant's original vision of a world-class capital.

A beautification plan at the turn of the century added most of the landscaping, parks, and monuments for which Washington is now well known. Nevertheless, until recently Washington suffered from its image as a Southern backwater. It was John F Kennedy who so succinctly slammed it as 'a city of Southern efficiency and Northern charm.' The Kennedy Center, established as a 'living memorial' to JFK, did much to bring cosmopolitan culture to the place.

Today, DC's international community has representatives from every nation in the world. The city's intense and divisive political climate is downright *romantic* to political activists. Spectacular *free* art is visible at every turn. From a Southern backwater, DC has evolved into a national pilgrimage center for many citizens (as was intended).

Yet Washington is notorious too for the many severe problems that trouble its residents. Poverty, crime, and racial segregation in the shadow of glorious monuments proclaiming 'equality for all' embarrass those who would hope to hold the nation's capital up as a model. Washington, DC, is no model, but it is a microcosm – of the grand ideals and grim realities of the United States.

POPULATION & PEOPLE

Today Washington, DC – referred to as 'Washington' and 'DC,' or locally as 'the District' – continues to be largely a company town. About a third of its residents (population 600,000) work for the government (federal or district), and another third work in supportive service industries. Ultimately, *all* business here is dependent upon government business. A high proportion of metro area residents are educated through college and beyond, and many are well informed and opinionated about public policy and current events.

There are, however, sharp racial and socioeconomic divisions between black and white and rich and poor; this is typical among American cities, but here the proportions are more dramatic as DC proper is three-quarters African American, and two-thirds of the DC population earns under $30,000 annually. To be more geographically specific, *three quarters* of the District is overwhelmingly African American; *one quarter*, that is, the northwest, is predominantly white. Increasing middle-class (white and black) flight has sent much of the policy-making population to the affluent suburbs, where taxation earns them Congressional representation (see Government in Facts about the Capital Region for more about DC's anomalous political designation).

ARTS & ARCHITECTURE

Grand monumental architecture and galleries full of fine arts are some of Washington's biggest draws. The city's architecture owes a great deal to the original city plan by chief architect Pierre L'Enfant – the interesting shapes of many buildings arose from his street grid full of diagonals and roundabouts. He intended that no building would rise higher than the Capitol (around 13 stories), and while this has left Washington free of modern skyscrapers, it has resulted in many short and squat modern government buildings.

Borrowed Roman and Grecian architectural styles – columns and marble everywhere you turn – reflect the ambition to create a classical capital (the Capitol, Archives, and Lincoln Memorial are ready examples). The Victorian era is best reflected in Washington's lavish churches and houses, though the Old Executive Office Building is a fine example of Victorian excess. The post-WWII building boom can be seen in the many monolithic modern buildings that easily overwhelm their surroundings (the Housing and Urban Development building in the southwest quadrant might be the best example or the row of glass looming behind Lafayette Square). The 1978 East Wing of the National Gallery of Art is one of the best examples of modern design. Exhibits at the National Building Museum examine Washington's architectural choices.

As for arts, Washington's galleries hold astounding classical and modern masterpieces (though they're not best known for their innovation); DC's ready and free access to so many collections in such a compact area is near unparalleled in the world.

ORIENTATION

Washington is bounded on one side by the Potomac River (across which lies the city of Arlington and the city of Alexandria, Virginia) and by Maryland on all other sides. Its original neat diamond shape has shifted over the years as DC has dropped and added territory, and the city now measures 69 sq miles.

The Grid

Washington is ringed by a freeway bypass called 'the Beltway' (I-495), which is as much of a cultural boundary as a geographical one, dividing the urban insiders from suburbanites.

The Capitol is the center of Washington in more than a strictly symbolic way. From the Capitol building, the city is divided into four quadrants (northwest, northeast, southeast, and southwest) along axes following N Capitol St, E Capitol St, S Capitol St, and the Mall (the equivalent of W Capitol St). Identical addresses appear in all four quadrants, so you *must* know the directional component of most addresses (11th St NW and 11th St NE, for example, are in opposite parts of town). Most sights of interest to visitors are centrally located around the Capitol, along the Mall, and in the northwest quadrant.

Streets are arranged on a grid of north-south numbered streets and east-west lettered streets (from A to W with no B, J, X, Y, or Z Sts; note also that I St sometimes appears as 'Eye' St). Addresses on lettered streets generally reveal their cross street; for example, Sholl's Colonial Cafeteria at 1900 K St NW lies at the corner of 19th and K, and the main library at 901 G St NW can be found on G between 9th and 10th Sts.

This grid is overlaid by broad diagonal avenues. Pennsylvania Ave is best known as the president's address; it connects the White House and the Capitol; Connecticut Ave is also a major thoroughfare. The main east-west arteries through town are K and M Sts; 16th is a good north-south route. The geometric pattern is further interrupted by traffic circles that add to the city's scenic appeal but can make DC a challenging place for outsiders to navigate by car.

DC Neighborhoods

Capitol Hill is the only area that has sights in all four quadrants; it's a business and residential area. Most other sights of major interest to visitors are located in the northwest quadrant.

Downtown includes the Mall and is strictly business, with many hotels and few residences. **Foggy Bottom** is mostly business with some residential areas; it's not as much a university neighborhood as you might expect with the presence of the large George Washington University campus.

Dupont Circle is an upscale business and residential address, with a funky fringe. **Adams-Morgan** is bohemian and international, mostly residential but with a popular business strip along 18th St. **Shaw** varies from historically elite residential areas near Howard University to rundown businesses

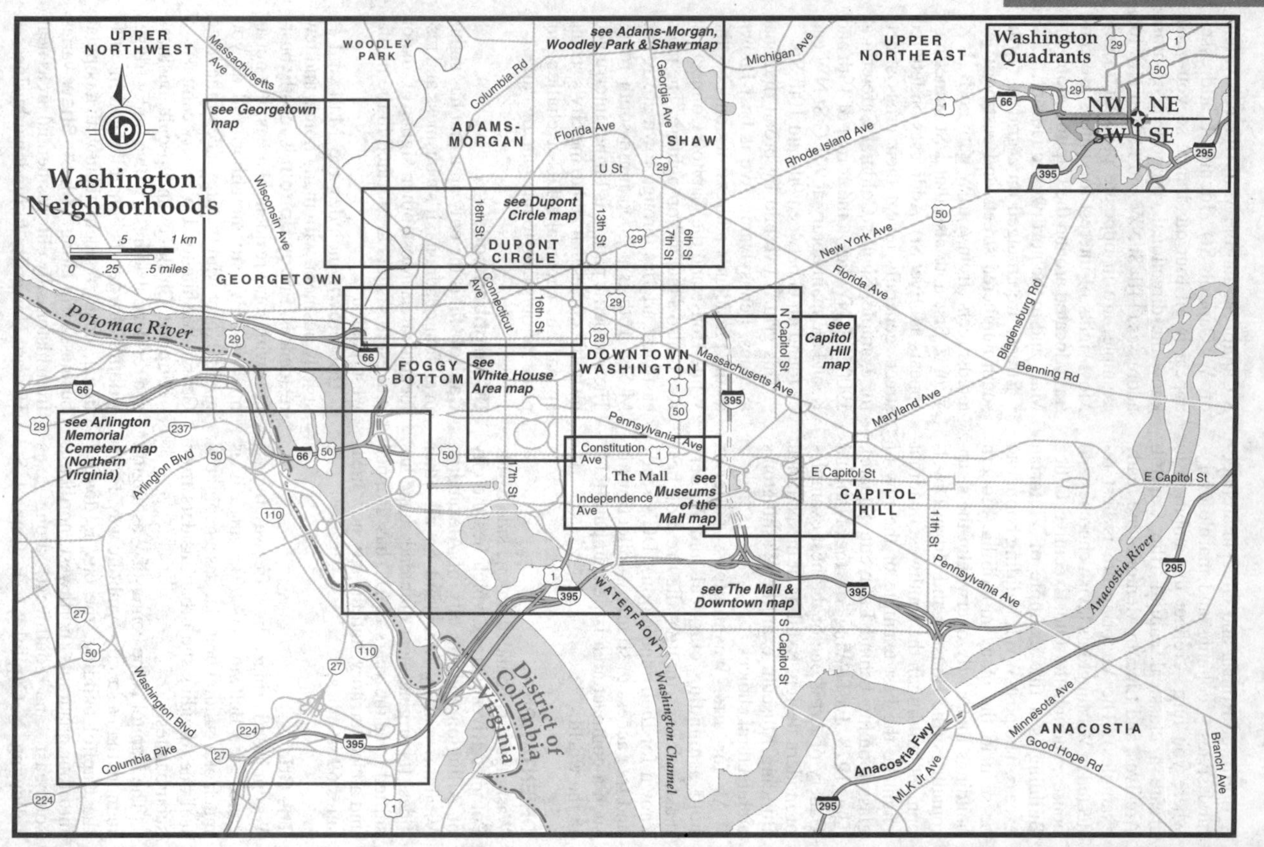
Washington Neighborhoods
Washington Quadrants
NW
NE
SW
SE
UPPER NORTHWEST
UPPER NORTHEAST
WOODLEY PARK
ADAMS-MORGAN
SHAW
DUPONT CIRCLE
GEORGETOWN
FOGGY BOTTOM
DOWNTOWN WASHINGTON
CAPITOL HILL
WATERFRONT
ANACOSTIA
see Adams-Morgan, Woodley Park & Shaw map
see Georgetown map
see Dupont Circle map
see White House Area map
see Capitol Hill map
see Museums of the Mall map
see The Mall & Downtown map
see Arlington Memorial Cemetery map (Northern Virginia)
The Mall
District of Columbia
Virginia
Potomac River
Anacostia River
Washington Channel
Massachusetts Ave
Wisconsin Ave
Columbia Rd
Florida Ave
U St
18th St
13th St
7th St
6th St
16th St
17th St
Connecticut Ave
Georgia Ave
Michigan Ave
Rhode Island Ave
New York Ave
Bladensburg Rd
Benning Rd
Maryland Ave
N Capitol St
E Capitol St
S Capitol St
11th St
Pennsylvania Ave
Constitution Ave
Independence Ave
Arlington Blvd
Washington Blvd
Columbia Pike
Minnesota Ave
Good Hope Rd
MLK Jr Ave
Anacostia Fwy
Branch Ave
0 .5 1 km
0 .25 .5 miles

and housing, to the emerging 'New U' business district. **Georgetown** has businesses, lively bars, and pristine historic houses appealing to more upscale students and residents. Other sights are scattered through the remaining three quadrants.

Maps

For maps try the Map Store (☎ 202-628-2608), 1636 I St NW. A small Washington, DC, pop-up map, convenient for downtown and Metro travel, is widely available locally. Most bookstores sell local maps (see Bookstores below) as do major museum gift shops.

INFORMATION

Tourist Offices

The Washington DC Convention and Visitors Association (☎ 202-789-7038) distributes information (including events calendars and an African American heritage guide) by mail or from its 6th-floor offices at 1411 K St NW. It's open weekdays 9 am to 5 pm.

Two visitors centers are to the east of the White House. The White House Visitor Center is located in the Commerce Building at 1450 Pennsylvania Ave NW. The National Park Service Visitor Pavilion is in the northeast corner of the Ellipse.

The International Visitors Information Service (☎ 202-939-5566) operates from the Meridien International Center at 1630 Crescent Ave. You can pick up brochures and maps there weekdays 9 am to 5 pm. The service provides a 'language bank' (☎ 202-939-5538) to answer visitors' questions in 54 languages; hours are from 8 am to 10 pm, and possibly beyond those times in an emergency.

Call the National Park Service at Dial-a-Park (☎ 202-619-7275) for information about events in and around Washington's parks and monuments (NPS operates most of the federal sights open to the public in DC).

Money

During business hours major banks exchange money and cash traveler's checks. Also try American Express, which has four locations in Washington: 1150 Connecticut Ave NW in the Dupont Circle district (☎ 202-457-1300); 1001 G St NW (☎ 202-393-0095); 1776 Pennsylvania Ave NW (☎ 202-289-8800); and 5300 Wisconsin Ave (☎ 202-362-4000) in the Mazza Gallery Mall, third floor. Most are open business hours on weekdays only; the Mall location keeps extended evening hours till 6 pm weeknights and offers Saturday service from 10 am to 5 pm.

Another reliable exchange is Thomas Cook (☎ 202-237-2229), with currency service desks at 1800 K St NW (weekday business hours only) and in Union Station across from Gate G (weekend service available). They also have several desks at Dulles and National airports.

Teletrip operates currency exchanges at National Airport (☎ 703-417-3200) and Dulles Airport (☎ 703-661-8864) daily 6 am to 9 pm. Look for signs reading 'Business Service Center, Foreign Currency Exchange' in the main terminals. At Baltimore-Washington International Airport, go to Travelex (☎ 410-859-5997) on the upper level at the entrance to Pier C; it's open daily 6:30 am to 8:30 pm.

Post & Communications

The main post office (☎ 202-636-1532), where all general delivery mail is directed, is out near the Maryland border at 900 Brentwood Rd NE, Washington, DC, 20066 (near the Rhode Island Ave Metro stop). It is open Monday to Friday 8 am to 8 pm, Saturday 10 am to 6 pm, and Sunday and holidays noon to 6 pm. The more conveniently located post office across from Union Station also has the longest hours, Monday to Friday 7 am to midnight and weekends 7 am to 8 pm. It's at 2 Massachusetts Ave next to the Postal Museum. Throughout town, you can easily find other US post offices, as well as many private mailing outlets (such as Mail Boxes Etc) where you can send faxes and packages via United Parcel Service or Federal Express (including overnight delivery). To send a telegram call Western

Embassies & Consulates

(Visa services are generally available during hours listed.)

Australia
1601 Massachusetts Ave NW, 20036
(☎ 202-797-3000)
Open 8 am to 4:30 pm
Metro: Dupont Circle

Austria
3524 International Court NW, 20008
(☎ 202-895-6700)
Open 9 am to 1 pm
Metro: Van Ness

Belgium
3330 Garfield St NW, 20008
(☎ 202-333-6900)
Open 9:30 am to noon
Metro: Woodley Park

Canada
501 Pennsylvania Ave NW, 20001
(☎ 202-682-1740)
Open 9 am to 1 pm
Metro: Archives

Denmark
3200 Whitehaven St NW, 20008
(☎ 202-234-4300)
Open 10:30 am to noon
Metro: Dupont Circle

France
4101 Reservoir Rd NW, 20007
(☎ 202-944-6000)
Open 9 am to 1 pm
Metro: Dupont Circle

Germany
4645 Reservoir Rd NW, 20007
(☎ 202-298-4000)
Open 9 am to noon
Metro: Foggy Bottom or Dupont Circle

Ireland
2234 Massachusetts Ave NW, 20008
(☎ 202-462-3939)
Open 9 am to 1 pm
Metro: Dupont Circle

Israel
3514 International Dr NW, 20008
(☎ 202-364-5500)
Open 9 am to 4:30 pm
Metro: Van Ness

Italy
1601 Fuller St NW, 20009
(☎ 202-328-5500)
Open 10 am to 12:30 pm
Metro: Woodley Park

Japan
2520 Massachusetts Ave NW, 20008
(☎ 202-939-6700)
Open 10 am to noon and 2 to 4 pm
Metro: Dupont Circle

Mexico
2827 16th St NW, 20006
(☎ 202-736-1000)
Open 8:30 am to 2 pm
Metro: Farragut North

The Netherlands
4200 Linnean Ave NW, 20008
(☎ 202-244-5300)
Open 10 am to noon
Metro: Van Ness

New Zealand
37 Observatory Circle NW, 20008
(☎ 202-328-4800)
Open 8:30 am to 5 pm
Metro: Dupont Circle

Philippines
1617 Massachusetts Ave NW, 20036
(☎ 202-467-9300)
Open 9 am to 5 pm
Metro: Dupont Circle

Singapore
3501 International Place, 20008
(☎ 202-537-3100)
Open 9 am to noon and 2 to 5 pm
Metro: Van Ness

South Africa
3051 Massachusetts Ave NW, 20008
(☎ 202-232-4400)
Visa services: 3201 New Mexico Ave NW, open 9 am to 12:30 pm
Metro: Dupont Circle

Spain
2375 Pennsylvania Ave NW, 20009
(☎ 202-265-0190)
Open 9 am to noon
Metro: Foggy Bottom

Sweden
1501 M St NW, 20037
(☎ 202-467-2600)
Open 9 to 11:30 am
Metro: McPherson Square

Switzerland
2900 Cathedral Ave NW, 20008
(☎ 202-745-7900)
Open 9 am to noon
Metro: Woodley Park

Thailand
1024 Wisconsin Ave NW, 20007
(☎ 202-944-3600)
Open 9 am to 12:30 pm and 2 to 4 pm
Metro: Foggy Bottom

United Kingdom
3100 Massachusetts Ave NW, 20008
(☎ 202-462-1340)
Open 9 am to 5:30 pm
Metro: Dupont Circle

RICK GERHARTER

The Smithsonian Castle on the Mall

KAP STANN

An aerial view in the Smithsonian Air & Space Museum

DCCVA

Moving along on the Metro

RICK GERHARTER

Names Project quilt on display near the White House

RICK GERHARTER

General McPherson guarding the tulips

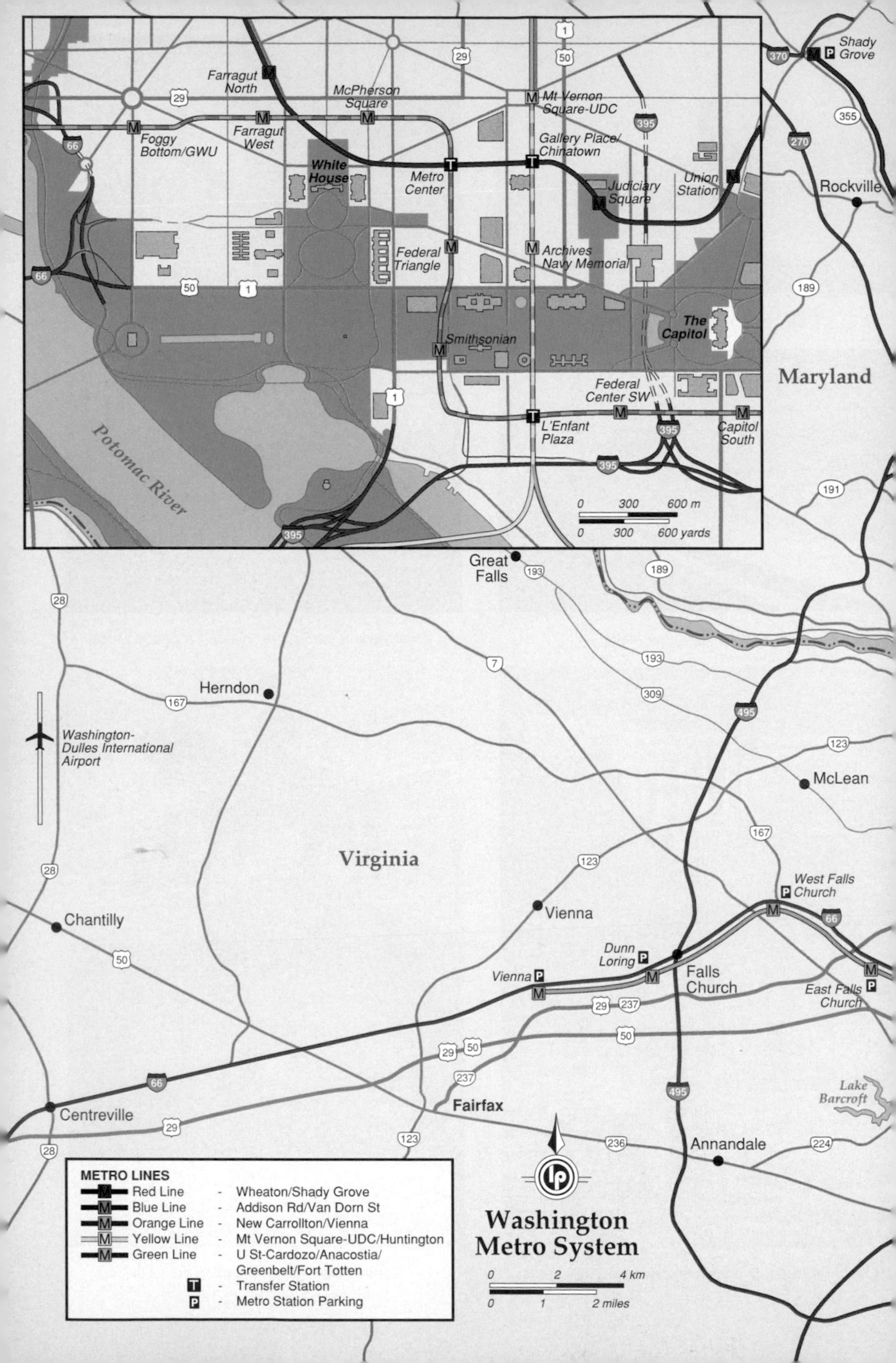

Farragut North
McPherson Square
Mt Vernon Square-UDC
Foggy Bottom/GWU
Farragut West
Gallery Place/ Chinatown
White House
Metro Center
Judiciary Square
Union Station
Federal Triangle
Archives Navy Memorial
The Capitol
Smithsonian
Federal Center SW
L'Enfant Plaza
Capitol South
Potomac River
0 300 600 m
0 300 600 yards
Shady Grove
Rockville
Maryland
Great Falls
Herndon
Washington-Dulles International Airport
Virginia
McLean
West Falls Church
Vienna
Chantilly
Dunn Loring
Falls Church
East Falls Church
Centreville
Fairfax
Lake Barcroft
Annandale
METRO LINES
Red Line - Wheaton/Shady Grove
Blue Line - Addison Rd/Van Dorn St
Orange Line - New Carrollton/Vienna
Yellow Line - Mt Vernon Square-UDC/Huntington
Green Line - U St-Cardozo/Anacostia/ Greenbelt/Fort Totten
T - Transfer Station
P - Metro Station Parking
Washington Metro System
0 2 4 km
0 1 2 miles

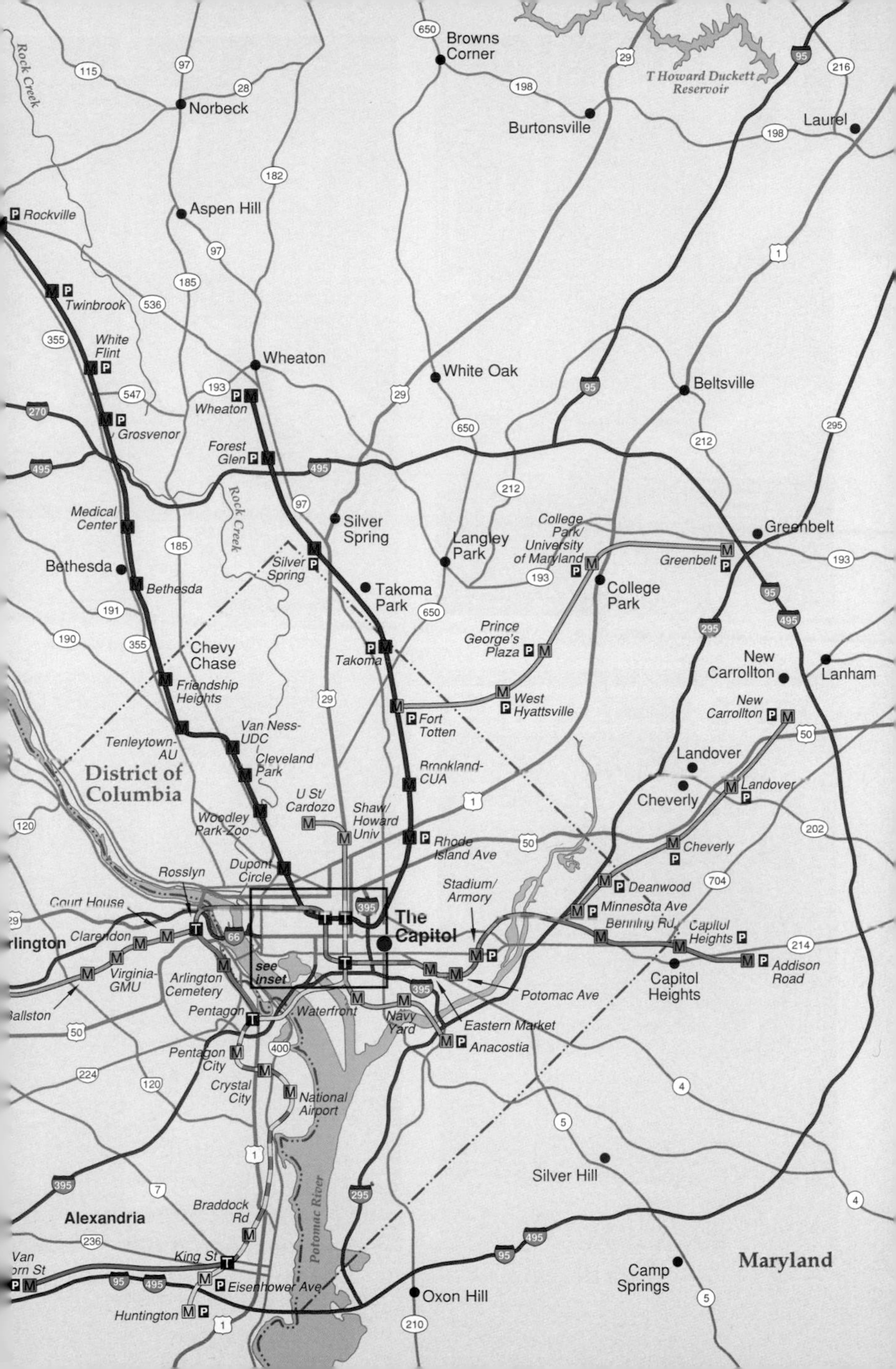
Browns Corner
Norbeck
Burtonsville
T Howard Duckett Reservoir
Laurel
Rock Creek
Rockville
Aspen Hill
Twinbrook
White Flint
Wheaton
White Oak
Beltsville
Grosvenor
Forest Glen
Medical Center
Silver Spring
Langley Park
College Park/ University of Maryland
Greenbelt
Bethesda
Takoma Park
College Park
Prince George's Plaza
Chevy Chase
Takoma
New Carrollton
Lanham
Friendship Heights
West Hyattsville
Fort Totten
Van Ness-UDC
Tenleytown-AU
Cleveland Park
District of Columbia
Brookland-CUA
Landover
Cheverly
U St/ Cardozo
Shaw/ Howard Univ
Woodley Park-Zoo
Rhode Island Ave
Dupont Circle
Rosslyn
Stadium/ Armory
Deanwood
Court House
Minnesota Ave
The Capitol
Benning Rd
Capitol Heights
Clarendon
Arlington
Virginia-GMU
Arlington Cemetery
see inset
Addison Road
Ballston
Potomac Ave
Pentagon
Waterfront
Navy Yard
Eastern Market
Anacostia
Pentagon City
Crystal City
National Airport
Silver Hill
Potomac River
Braddock Rd
Alexandria
King St
Van Dorn St
Eisenhower Ave
Camp Springs
Maryland
Oxon Hill
Huntington

RICK GERHARTER
Lively Cafe Lautrec in Adams-Morgan

RICK GERHARTER
Saturday farmers market in Adams-Morgan

KAP STANN
The chili dogs are barkin' at Ben's Chili Bowl.

KAP STANN
The National Building Museum, site of the presidential inaugural balls

Union (☎ 800-325-6000) and ask for the nearest office.

The area code for Washington is 202. Local calls cost 25¢. Note that some hotels charge up to a dollar a call for guests to make local calls.

Travel Agencies

Hostelling International's American Youth Hostel Travel Center (☎ 202-783-4943), at 1108 K St NW, and Council Travel (☎ 202-337-6464), at 3300 M St NW, both specialize in low-budget and student-oriented travel resources. They help find airfare discounts and sell Eurail passes; the Travel Center hosts travel seminars and maintains a library and bookstore as well. The Travel Center's hours are Monday to Friday from 10 am to 6 pm, Saturday from 10 am to 5 pm, and they are located diagonally across from the hostel near Domino's Pizza. Council Travel's hours are Monday to Friday 10 am to 6 pm, except Wednesday when it opens at 11 am.

See the Sunday Travel section of the *Washington Post* for advertisements of discount travel agents in DC and the surrounding suburbs.

Bookstores

Washington's bookstores are more than places to buy books and periodicals. The ones with attached cafes encourage casual meetings and conversation. Many bookstores sponsor readings, open mike poetry nights, and other literary events; some feature live music, and many are open late.

Across the street from the Washington Flyer shuttle terminal is Chapters (☎ 202-347-5495), 1512 K St NW, a friendly literary bookstore just blocks from the White House that sponsors author events and poetry readings.

Dupont Circle has a wonderful selection. Kramerbooks (☎ 202-387-1400), 1517 Connecticut Ave NW, features the popular Afterwords Cafe and live entertainment. Olsson's (☎ 202-785-1133), 1307 19th St NW, sells records too. Also see Vertigo (☎ 202-429-9272), 1337 Connecticut Ave NW; MysteryBooks (☎ 202-483-1600), 1715 Connecticut Ave NW; and Lambda Rising (☎ 202-462-6969), 1625 Connecticut Ave NW, specializing in gay and lesbian titles. Lammas (☎ 202-775-8218), 1426 21st St NW, bills itself as 'Washington's only feminist bookstore.' The International Language Center (☎ 202-332-2894) and Newsroom (☎ 202-332-1489) feature books and periodicals in 100 languages; both are located at 1753 Connecticut Ave NW near S St.

In Adams-Morgan head to Bick's Books (☎ 202-328-2356), 2309 18th St NW, for new titles; for used books go to Idle Times (☎ 202-232-4774), 2410 18th St NW. Near the Maryland border in Upper Northwest is Politics & Prose (☎ 202-364-1919), 5015 Connecticut Ave NW, which sponsors author readings and serves great coffee.

In Georgetown, there's another Olsson's (☎ 202-338-9544), 1239 Wisconsin Ave NW; Bridge Street Books (☎ 202-965-5200), 2814 Pennsylvania Ave NW; and Lantern Bryn Mawr Bookshop (☎ 202-333-3222), 3160 O St NW, for used books. Barnes and Noble (☎ 202-965-9880), 3040 M St NW, features literary events, music, and a third-floor cafe overlooking M St.

Pyramid Books (☎ 202-328-0190), 2849 Georgia Ave NW across from Howard University, specializes in Afrocentric books. Also see museum bookstores for titles related to their collections.

On Capitol Hill, you can stop by the Government Printing Office & Bookstore (☎ 202-512-0132), 710 N Capitol St between G and H Sts (open weekdays only). Here they sell 15,000 titles published by the US government, including the blockbusters *Selling to the Military*, *Cooking for People with Allergies*, and *Nest Boxes for Wood Ducks*. Near the Capitol, Trover Shops (☎ 202-543-8006), 227 Pennsylvania Ave SE, is a DC institution for books, cards, and gifts.

Libraries

The Martin Luther King Jr Memorial Library (☎ 202-727-1111), 901 G St NW, is the city's central library. In addition to its stacks, the library hosts community events, displays an African American heritage mural, and operates a small gift kiosk. It's open Monday to Thursday from 9 am to 5 pm, Friday and Saturday 9 am to 5:30 pm, and Sunday 1 to 5 pm. See the phone book for the more than two dozen other branch libraries around town.

Media

Newspapers Besides being the major local newspaper, the *Washington Post* is one of the top newspapers in the nation. The smaller circulation *Washington Times*, owned by Reverend Sung Myung Moon's Unification Church, is more conservative. The alternative weekly *Washington City Paper*, distributed free throughout the city, scrutinizes District politics and trends and contains excellent entertainment coverage, including listings for the upcoming week's new movies, concerts, exhibits, readings, and special events.

For news and events of particular interest to the gay and lesbian population, look for the free weekly *Washington Blade* in stores around Dupont Circle and elsewhere. The *Washington Afro-American* is the city's newspaper for African Americans.

Television The federally supported Public Broadcasting System (PBS) based here in DC operates a superior national news program as well as arts, entertainment, and children's programming. (Not only highly regarded, PBS is also hotly contested; conservatives who consider it too liberal aim to decimate its budget.) Find *The News Hour*, *Sesame Street*, and *Mr Rogers Neighborhood* on WETA Channel 26. All national networks (ABC, CBS, NBC, and CNN's all-news station) are represented on the dial, and C-SPAN broadcasts live from the floor of Congress (aired at bars across Capitol Hill).

Radio Tune in to locally produced National Public Radio at either WAMU (88.5 FM) or WETA (90.9 FM) for the most thoughtful local and national news coverage and features (they also play jazz). The Voice of America prepares news reports for international broadcast in 44 languages; they also offer studio tours (see Other Mall Sights below).

Online Services Find visitor information at *www.washington.org*. The Planet Earth home page on the Web can be found at *nosc.mil/planet_earth/washington.html*; there you can get information on government agencies, the Metro system and area airports, and all that's new in DC. For the update on Socks and other pressing White House information, check out *www.whitehouse.gov*. If your computer can handle the graphics, see *www.ustreas.gov* for a virtual tour of the Bureau of Printing and Engraving.

Laundry

Many budget hotels and hostels offer coin-operated washers and dryers; higher-priced hotels provide higher-priced laundry and dry-cleaning services. You can readily find self-service laundromats and wash-and-fold laundries in residential neighborhoods and around college campuses, a few open 24 hours.

Medical Services & Emergencies

Anywhere in the US, the free number to call for any emergency – police, fire, or accident – is 911. In DC, *know your quadrant*; without the correct coordinates, emergency services can easily head to the wrong side of town. Round-the-clock telephone service is also available from the Traveler's Aid Society hotline (☎ 202-546-3120), 512 C St NE; drop-in service is available at their desks at branch offices in Union Station (☎ 202-371-1937, TDD 202-684-7886), at National Airport (☎ 703-684-3472, TDD 202-684-7884), and at Dulles Airport (☎ 703-661-8636, TDD 202-471-9776). The George Washington University Medical Center is at 901 23rd St NW (24 hours, ☎ 202-994-3211).

Other useful numbers include: Ask-A-Nurse (☎ 703-760-8787); DeafPride (☎ 202-675-6700 Voice/TTY); Disabled Persons Hotline (☎ 202-727-3323); DC Rape Crisis Center (☎ 202-333-7273); Gay and Lesbian Hotline (☎ 202-833-3234); and Poison Control (☎ 202-625-3333).

Dangers & Annoyances

DC has earned a reputation for high crime, violence (75 murders per 100,000 residents, the highest of any city in the Americas), and drug use (in 1990, Mayor Marion Barry was arrested for using crack cocaine). Wide swaths of the inner city are bleak, which might be ironic for the capital of such a prosperous nation were it not such a travesty. Fortunately for visitors, these are areas that tourists are unlikely to stumble upon by accident. The areas where most tourist sights are located show Washington at its best and are as safe as anywhere (though standard urban precautions apply).

Standard urban precautions for travelers in DC include the following: Leave valuables home, store your identification and cash securely in a money belt or neck pouch, avoid walking alone through poorly lit areas late at night, and, if you're lost and confused, try not to look lost and confused. Though the city's high-crime reputation should not be downplayed, neither should it be overblown; most violent crime occurs outside tourist areas.

The hot and humid summer weather can be a health concern; exposure and dehydration may cause heat stroke, especially in July and August. This is particularly a concern at the many Washington attractions where visitors stand outside in the sun in long lines. In these months, plan your travel for the cooler mornings and late afternoons (advance planning can also reduce your time in lines), aim to be inside in air conditioning through the midday heat, carry water and snacks, and wear hats and loose, light clothing.

CAPITOL HILL

Three years after Thomas Jefferson and Alexander Hamilton decided that Washington should house the nation's capital in 1790, construction began on the grand Capitol that was to grace the hill east of the Potomac. During the Civil War, the rise now known as Capitol Hill was nicknamed 'Bloody Hill' for all the injured soldiers moved into legislative buildings that served as temporary hospitals.

Today the residential areas east of the Capitol are home to a cross section of Washingtonians, poor living near rich, longtime residents next to transplanted staffers.

Be aware that east of 11th St and south of D St, the neighborhoods become higher crime areas. Keep your eyes open, go where you feel comfortable, and remember that neighborhoods change.

Walking Tour

The US Capitol is the epicenter of Washington, DC; all the city's avenues intersect at an imaginary point under its dome.

Although it may appear to face the Mall, you actually see the back of the Capitol from the Potomac side. It opens out eastward (note the direction of the 'Armed Liberty' statue up top) onto a small shady plaza surrounded by monolithic government landmarks.

A particularly nice approach to the Capitol is from **Union Station**. As you exit the station, you see the impressive vista of the Capitol dome framed in the station's huge archways. Walk south past fountains, statues, and an arc of flags from every state along landscaped paths. The **Taft Memorial** on your right houses carillon bells that ring every quarter hour.

If you approach the Capitol from the Mall, you'll pass the gigantic statue of **General Grant** on horseback, poised in front of the reflecting pool. The **US Botanic Gardens** are on the south side of Maryland Ave; behind the conservatory on the other side of Independence Ave SW you'll see the grand **Bartholdi Fountain**. In the northwest corner of the Capitol's back lawn you'll find a shady **grotto**.

After touring the inside of the Capitol and seeing the view of the Mall, cross the plaza to climb the marble steps of the **Supreme Court** building and visit the historic **Library of Congress** buildings on either side of E Capitol St. On the north

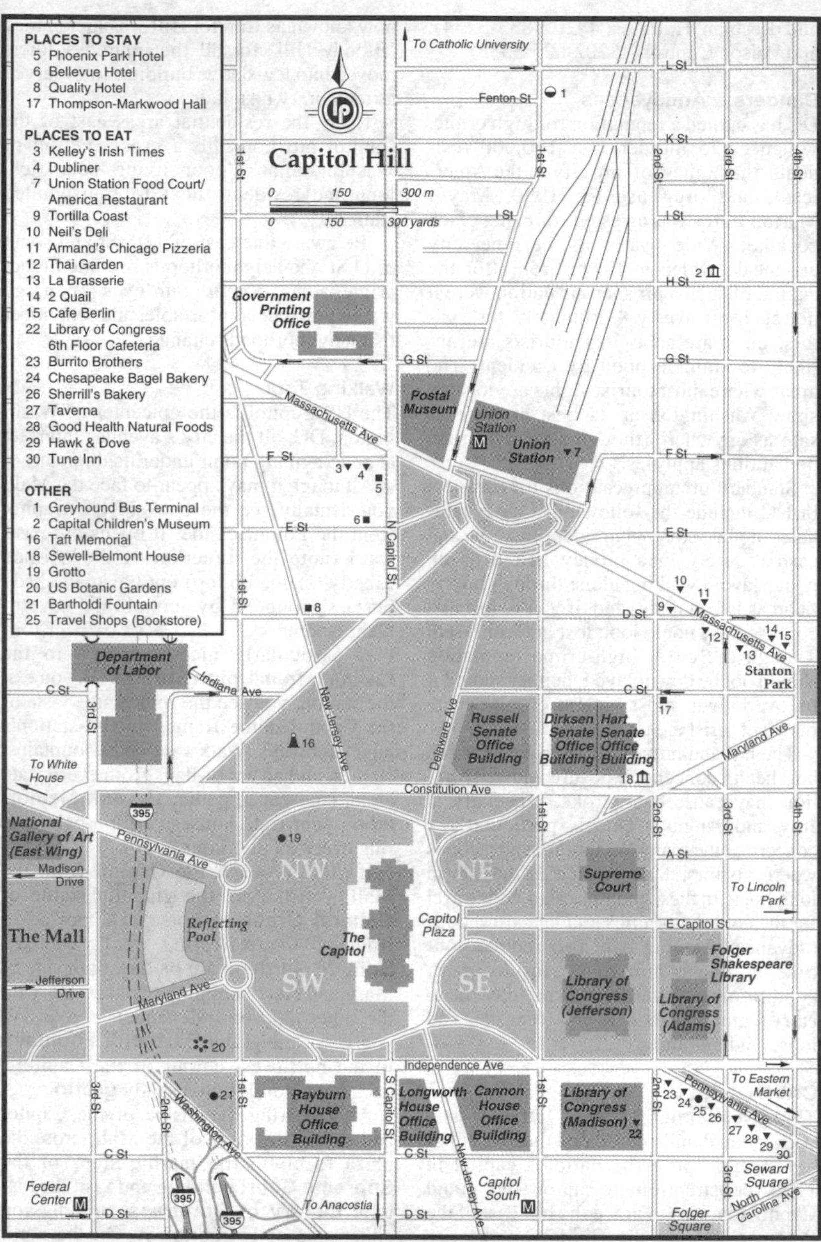

PLACES TO STAY
5 Phoenix Park Hotel
6 Bellevue Hotel
8 Quality Hotel
17 Thompson-Markwood Hall
PLACES TO EAT
3 Kelley's Irish Times
4 Dubliner
7 Union Station Food Court/ America Restaurant
9 Tortilla Coast
10 Neil's Deli
11 Armand's Chicago Pizzeria
12 Thai Garden
13 La Brasserie
14 2 Quail
15 Cafe Berlin
22 Library of Congress 6th Floor Cafeteria
23 Burrito Brothers
24 Chesapeake Bagel Bakery
26 Sherrill's Bakery
27 Taverna
28 Good Health Natural Foods
29 Hawk & Dove
30 Tune Inn
OTHER
1 Greyhound Bus Terminal
2 Capital Children's Museum
16 Taft Memorial
18 Sewell-Belmont House
19 Grotto
20 US Botanic Gardens
21 Bartholdi Fountain
25 Travel Shops (Bookstore)
Capitol Hill
0 150 300 m
0 150 300 yards
To Catholic University
L St
Fenton St
K St
I St
H St
G St
F St
E St
D St
C St
A St
E Capitol St
1st St
2nd St
3rd St
4th St
N Capitol St
S Capitol St
Government Printing Office
Postal Museum
Union Station
Massachusetts Ave
New Jersey Ave
Delaware Ave
Indiana Ave
Maryland Ave
Constitution Ave
Pennsylvania Ave
Independence Ave
Washington Ave
North Carolina Ave
Department of Labor
To White House
National Gallery of Art (East Wing)
Madison Drive
Jefferson Drive
The Mall
Reflecting Pool
The Capitol
Capitol Plaza
NW
NE
SW
SE
Russell Senate Office Building
Dirksen Senate Office Building
Hart Senate Office Building
Stanton Park
Supreme Court
To Lincoln Park
Folger Shakespeare Library
Library of Congress (Jefferson)
Library of Congress (Adams)
Library of Congress (Madison)
Rayburn House Office Building
Longworth House Office Building
Cannon House Office Building
To Eastern Market
Seward Square
Folger Square
Federal Center
Capitol South
To Anacostia
395

side of Constitution Ave are the three **Senate office buildings**; the three **House office buildings** are located on the south side of Independence Ave. (A mini-subway – like coal cars with seats – connects these buildings to the Capitol.) In session, the Hill is the hectic scene of rushed government staffers dangling security passes from their necks, pods of well-dressed school groups, placard-carrying protesters, and microphone-wielding journalists hoping for impromptu interviews.

For a quiet walk through the Hill's historic residential district, follow E Capitol St out past the **Folger Shakespeare Library** to the right and the **Sewell-Belmont House** (home of the National Women's Party) one block to your left. Among the 19th century row houses, brownstones, and old corner shops, you'll find **Jimmy T's** at 5th St for diner coffee. Then head over to **Lincoln Park**, a lively neighborhood center with historic statues and a nice view of the Capitol (unobstructed by trees in winter).

Within the park you'll find two historic statues. The **Emancipation Memorial** (1876) portrays a kneeling slave (the likeness of Archer Alexander, the last man captured under the Fugitive Slave Law) breaking the chains of slavery as President Lincoln holds his Proclamation in an outstretched hand. African American soldiers raised all the funds to erect it, and it served as the principal tribute to President Lincoln in DC until the Lincoln Memorial opened. The other statue, the **Mary McLeod Bethune Memorial** (1974), honors the African American educator and founder of the National Council of Negro Women (it was the first statue of an African American woman in DC).

You have all sorts of food choices north along Massachusetts Ave or south along Pennsylvania Ave. Your best bet may be **Eastern Market** at 7th St SE at C St. This colorful produce market, which dates back to 1873, has a popular food counter inside and a choice of restaurants across the street. On weekends, the market spills outside and offers crafts and a flea market in addition to fresh foods and flowers. The handy Eastern Market Metro stop is a block away, or you could return to the Capitol by walking up Pennsylvania Ave.

Union Station

Union Station (☎ 202-289-1908), 40 Massachusetts Ave NE, is the most impressive gateway into Washington. The massive 1908 Beaux Arts building was beautifully restored in 1988 and transformed into a contemporary city center and transit hub, with Amtrak connections to destinations throughout the East, a Metro station, an octoplex cinema (☎ 202-842-3757), and a 200,000-sq-foot complex of shops, newsstands, restaurants, and cafes. Many travelers resources – including Travelers' Aid, transit information, currency exchange, and automatic tellers, with late-night and weekend hours – can also be found.

The huge main hall was modeled on the Roman Baths of Diocletian. (Strategically placed shields were added to the legionnaire statues lining the second-story balcony.)

The Capitol

The Capitol (☎ 202-224-3121), Washington's most prominent landmark, was designed by William Thornton. The cornerstone was laid by George Washington in 1793, and Congress moved in seven years later. The British nearly burned it to the ground during their 1814 invasion of Washington. The dispiriting destruction tempted people to abandon the whole DC experiment altogether, but it was finally rebuilt from 1817 to 1819.

The House and Senate wings were added in 1857, and in 1863 a nine million-pound iron dome was set atop, replacing a smaller one. With a 32.5-foot extension of the east face in the late 1950s, the Capitol is now over twice as large as the original building. Most presidents have been inaugurated on its East Terrace (Reagan preferred the West Terrace).

The House of Representatives meets in the south wing and the Senate in the north wing. When either body is in session, a flag

The Capitol Building, almost synonymous with DC

is raised above the appropriate wing. A light in the dome at night means one group is working late.

You enter from the east side *(not* the Mall side) into the dramatic **Rotunda**. The fresco inside the dome by Italian immigrant Constantino Brumidi, entitled *The Apotheosis of Washington*, depicts Washington as he's welcomed into heaven by 13 angels representing the original 13 states (the story goes that Brumidi used local prostitutes as models for the angels). Brumidi and his successors also painted the murals and ceilings in the hallways, which picture the nation's great heroes and their great deeds (the most recent is a group portrait of the Challenger astronauts). Bare spaces await future heroes and their deeds. Similarly, a marble statue of suffragists has one missing face awaiting the first woman president.

To the right of the Rotunda is **Statuary Hall**, where the House convened until 1857. In 1864 Congress asked each state to send statues of two distinguished citizens for display in this room, but the weight of so much marble was eventually deemed too heavy for the floor, and several of these now grace other parts of the Capitol. Yet what remains is a an impressive assemblage of giant stone men in a room of tile and drapery all gold and red.

The Supreme Court originally met in the Capitol in the **Old Supreme Court Chamber** and then later in the **Old Senate Chamber**. Here the great Senate debates over slavery took place prior to the Civil War.

The Capitol is open daily 9 am to 4:30 pm and from Easter to Labor Day till 8 pm. You could skip the tour (and another line) by wandering around on your own. There are special tours for those with disabilities (☎ 202-224-4048, TDD 202-224-4049).

Congress Watching Free tours of the Capitol stop at the visitors galleries overlooking the House and Senate floors, but only when they are *not* in session. To watch Congress in action, you must first call to find out when Congress is in session (☎ 202-224-3121) and determine where you need to go to get a pass to the visitors gallery. American citizens can request passes (good for two years) from their Congressional representatives. Foreign visitors can get passes from the Sergeant-At-Arms in Room S-321 for the Senate gallery or just show their passport at the House gallery for admission. Committee hearings are often more interesting than open session, and some of these are open to the public. Check the *Washington Post*'s 'Today in Congress' notice (in section A) to find an open hearing.

US citizens can meet with their Congressional representatives in the House and Senate by calling or writing to request an appointment (as early as three months in advance of your visit).

Supreme Court

The Supreme Court (☎ 202-479-3000), directly across the plaza from the Capitol at 1st and E Capitol Sts, holds court in an imposing 1935 building designed by

Supreme Justice

The US Supreme Court is the highest judicial body in the land. The court consists of nine justices appointed for life terms, and it is referred to by the name of its presiding chief justice, such as the 'Warren Court' or the 'Rehnquist Court.' While the image of stately justices cloaked in black robes is a familiar one, only recently have the faces of women and African Americans appeared.

The rise in stature of the court came with the appointment of John Marshall as chief justice in 1801. Where previously justices had given separate opinions, Marshall established the single 'opinion of the court,' which carried much more weight. The Marshall Court issued a number of decisions that upheld the power of Congress over the states and affirmed the court's right to declare unconstitutional actions of the other branches of government.

The most notorious case of the 19th century was *Dred Scott v Sanford* in 1857, a major precursor to the Civil War. In this case the court ruled that African Americans could not be citizens of the US, and Congress had no right to prevent territories in the American West from allowing slavery.

In 1896 in *Plessy v Ferguson* the Court upheld the segregation of the 'white and colored races' under a doctrine of 'separate but equal.' In a powerful dissent Associate Justice and former slave owner John Marshall Harlan of Kentucky wrote that 'the white race deems itself to be the dominant race,' but the Constitution recognizes 'no superior, dominant, ruling class of citizens . . . . Our Constitution is colorblind . . . . In respect of civil rights all citizens are equal before the law.' It wasn't until almost 60 years later that the court said in *Brown v Board of Education of Topeka* that separate but equal was not, in fact, equal.

One of the most important and most controversial rulings of the 20th century is the 1975 *Roe v Wade* decision that negated all laws preventing the right to an abortion in early pregnancy. The opinions of prospective Supreme Court justices on *Roe v Wade* are invariably sought out and considered a condition of appointment.

Today protesters and advocates continue to gather on the marble steps of the Supreme Court atop Capitol Hill to try and sway judicial and public opinion.■

Cass Gilbert and constructed entirely of marble. Gilbert used himself and his friends as models for the justices carved into the building pediment; other marble figures represent Confucius, Solon, and Moses. The Court is in session from the first Monday in October through June. The justices hear oral arguments and ask questions generally from Monday to Wednesday for two weeks every month, but the schedule varies considerably. Check the *Washington Post* or call before you visit and get there by 8 am to get a seat – first-come, first-served.

Library of Congress

A block east of the Capitol are the three buildings of the Library of Congress (☎ 202-707-5000). The library contains approximately 100 million items – including more than 26 million books, 36 million manuscripts, maps, photographs, sheet music, and musical instruments – making it the largest library in the world. The British used the books from the original library to burn the Capitol in 1814. Retired President Jefferson then sold his collection to the library to rebuild it.

Wander into the historic **Jefferson Building** (built in 1897) to see its impressive **Main Reading Room** and the **Great Hall**, with vaulted ceilings and ornate decoration; it's the one on the plaza, on 1st St SE between E Capitol St and Independence Ave.

The library's two modern annexes are nearby. The **Adams Building** is behind the Jefferson Building, between 2nd and 3rd Sts SE. Like the Capitol, a series of underground hallways connect these two. The **Madison Building**, located immediately south of the Jefferson Building between

Independence Ave and C St SE, holds the library's central visitors center and a low-cost cafeteria with a view.

The library screens classic films for no charge, and occasionally there are concerts performed on the library's five Stradivarius violins (call ☎ 202-707-8000 for special events and exhibitions information). For reading room hours, call ☎ 202-707-6400.

Legislative Office Buildings

Members of the House of Representatives and Senate do business in six legislative office buildings surrounding the Capitol. The three Senate office buildings – Russell (its Senate Caucus Room was the familiar scene of the prolonged Watergate hearings), Hart, and Dirksen – are on the north side of Constitution Ave. The three House office buildings – Rayburn, Longworth, and Cannon – are on the south side of Independence Ave.

US Botanic Garden

The conservatory (☎ 202-225-7099) on the far eastern end of the Mall (downhill from the Capitol) was designed in 1931 to resemble London's Crystal Palace; the Botanic Garden's history in other locations dates back to 1842. Iron-and-glass greenhouse rooms provide a beautiful setting for displays of exotic and local plants, including cycad trees that produce 50-lb cones. It's a good place to relax and cool off (free and open daily 9 am to 5 pm, until 9 pm during the summer).

Folger Shakespeare Library

The Folger research library and museum (☎ 202-544-4600; events 202-544-7077), 201 E Capitol St SE, houses the world's largest collection of works by Shakespeare and sponsors changing exhibits, concerts, and plays. Its **theater** is modeled after the one at Stratford-on-Avon. The museum is free and open Monday to Saturday 11 am to 4 pm.

Sewall-Belmont House

The historic house from which Alice Paul and the National Women's Party led the struggle for equal rights for women is at 144 Constitution Ave SE (☎ 202-546-3989) on the corner of 2nd St. The heroines

The National Women's Party

'If we get freedom for women, then they are probably going to do a lot of things that I wish they wouldn't do. But it seems to me that it isn't our business to say what they should do with it. It is our business to see that they get it.' – Alice Paul

Firebrand Alice Paul, born into a Quaker family in 1885, gained notoriety as one of the nation's first and foremost feminists. In 1914 Paul cofounded the Congressional Union, an organization that advocated for a Constitutional amendment granting women the right to vote. By picketing Congress and the White House and through hunger strikes the group lobbied for the 19th Amendment, which passed in 1920. It states that 'the right of citizens of the United States to vote shall not be denied or abridged . . . on account of sex.'

Paul and her cohorts went on to form the National Women's Party (NWP) to work for total equality for women. Their primary goal was the Equal Rights Amendment (ERA), first proposed by the NWP in 1923. The most recent version of the ERA – 'Equality of rights under the law shall not be denied or abridged by the United States or any state on account of sex' – was approved by two-thirds of the House of Representatives and the Senate in 1971 and 1972, but failed to get ratification by the required 38 states and thus never became law.

The National Women's Party is now headquartered in the house of Alice Paul, who died in 1975, and displays mementos of the women's rights movement throughout the century. ■

of the women's rights movement are the focus of historical exhibits, portraits, sculpture, and a library. The 1800 building has been the headquarters for the party since 1929. It's free and open Monday to Friday 10 am to 3 pm and Saturday and Sunday noon to 4 pm.

Capital Children's Museum

The Children's Museum (☎ 202-543-8600), 800 3rd St NE at H St, holds three floors of inviting hands-on, interactive exhibits, including a do-it-yourself TV studio, a cave, a miniature Mexican village, a fire station, a what's-under-the-street exhibit, and the always popular maze and bubble shroud. It's open daily from 10 am to 5 pm; admission is $6 for everyone over the age of two.

The museum is only a three-block walk northeast of Union Station, but the neighborhood is somewhat ragged and some families may prefer to take a cab.

National Postal Museum

In the post office building across from Union Station, the newest Smithsonian museum (opened in 1994) features kid-friendly exhibits on postal history from the Pony Express to Cliff Clavin postal carrier uniform (from the sitcom *Cheers*). There are plenty of philatelic displays and souvenirs. It's open daily 9 am to 5:30 pm.

THE NATIONAL MALL

The 400-foot-wide expanse of green stretching two miles from the Potomac River to Capitol Hill is called the Mall. Lined with gravel paths and shade trees along its bordering streets (Constitution Ave to the north and Independence Ave to the south), the Mall is home to the capital's most famous monuments and museums.

It has taken on this role only relatively recently. Between 1791 and 1972, the area had held variously a swamp, a cow pasture and slaughter site, a Civil War hospital, a train station, a stagnant canal, and temporary government buildings that lasted from WWI to 1972.

When Pierre L'Enfant designed it, he imagined the Mall as a grand promenade lined with mansions and embassies, like an American Champs-Elysées, but it evolved in a more American way into a national lawn lined with family-friendly museums. On sunny days the Mall attracts people who jog, walk dogs, play soccer and Frisbee, and pose for photographs. The Smithsonian's Kite Festival in late March and its Festival of American Folklife in June are two highlights among many popular public events that take place annually on the Mall.

But perhaps the Mall is best known for the political gatherings and rallies held here. Antiwar protesters demonstrated against the Vietnam War during the 1960s, and in 1963, Martin Luther King, Jr, delivered his world-famous 'I Have a Dream' speech on the steps of the Lincoln Memorial. Three decades later, the Million Man March returned to question how that dream had progressed.

When the Vietnam Veterans Memorial first opened in 1982, it generated tremendous controversy, but its subsequent popularity sparked a monument binge around the Mall memorializing American military history with congressionally approved

After delivering his 'I Have a Dream' speech, King began planning the Poor People's March on Washington, which took place after his assassination.

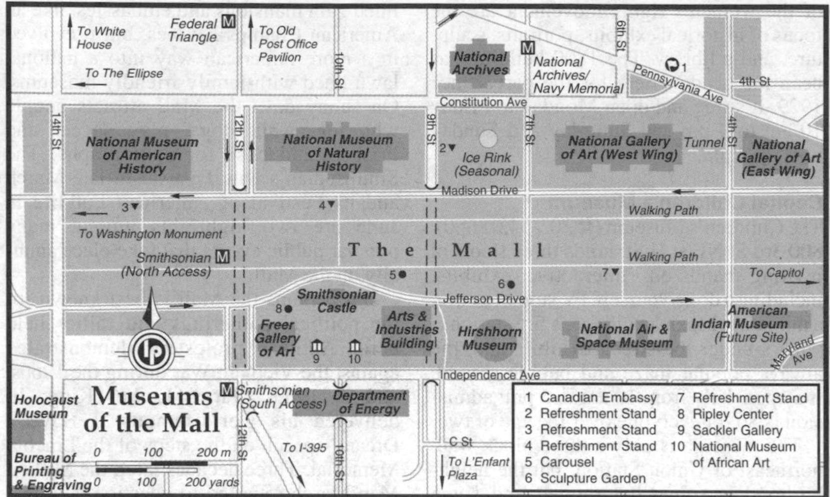

monuments (in various states of completion) to WWII, the Korean War, women in Vietnam, black Revolutionary War patriots, African American Union soldiers, and a Japanese American patriots memorial. (Proposals such as a monument to the Army's canine corps did not win Congressional approval.)

Metro riders can use the Smithsonian station for all Mall sights (though the Mall's north side is actually a bit closer to the Archives and Federal Triangle stations).

During his historic four-term presidency Franklin Delano Roosevelt entreated that no memorial be built in his honor 'any larger than his desk.' Despite this request, a 7.5-acre **FDR Memorial** is under construction in West Potomac Park near the Jefferson Memorial. The planned opening date is May 1, 1997.

Smithsonian Institution

Among the world's finest research centers, the Smithsonian Institution administers thirteen phenomenal museums and galleries in DC as well as the National Zoo. It maintains a collection so large (138,843,570 pieces at last count) that only 1% of it is ever on display.

In 1826 James Smithson, a Brit who had never been to America, willed £4,100,000 to the US to found an 'establishment for the increase and diffusion of knowledge' in the event that his only heir, a nephew, die childless. That happened six years later, and the gift of $508,318 came when the entire yearly budget of the US was less than $34 million. In 1846 Congress decided to use the funds to create a museum and research center.

Nine of the Smithsonian museums are on the Mall (listed individually below); families shouldn't miss the Air & Space, Natural History, and American History museums. (For Smithsonian museums in other districts – such as the Renwick Gallery and Women in the Arts museum downtown, the National Zoo in the Upper Northwest, and the Anacostia Museum in Anacostia – see those sections.) The Smithsonian also maintains the Museum of the American Indian in New York City; future plans call for moving this to a new home on the Mall.

The Smithsonian museums are open from 10 am to 5:30 pm (with exceptions noted in text) daily except Christmas. Admission is always free.

Call ☎ 202-357-2700, TDD 202-357-1729 for general information on any of the Smithsonian museums. For activity information (concerts, films, and lectures are among the many special events scheduled), call Dial-a-Museum at ☎ 202-357-2020, or 202-633-9126 for Spanish. Request a 'Smithsonian Access' brochure for a guide to the museums for people with physical disabilities.

Smithsonian Castle

The original Smithsonian museum now houses the Visitor Information Center as a clearinghouse for information about the institution. Referred to as the 'Castle,' the turreted red brick building (☎ 202-357-2700) is on the south side of the Mall at 10th St SW, and it serves as the most recognizable landmark as you surface from the Metro station. Inside, a 20-minute film provides an overview; the 1855 castle also houses the crypt of Smithsonian benefactor James Smithson. The center is open daily from 9 am (an hour before the museums) to 5:30 pm.

The small round building directly west is the above-ground access to the largely underground **Ripley Center**. Public lectures, classes, and temporary exhibits take place in the center's classrooms and meeting spaces.

Freer Gallery of Art

Named for founder Charles Lang Freer, the Freer Gallery (☎ 202-357-2700) was built in 1923 to hold Freer's collection of American and Asian art, including an extensive collection of paintings by James McNeill Whistler. Its Middle Eastern and Asian exhibits are the most evocative, especially those in the Peacock Room. The gallery is next to the Castle.

National Museum of African Art

One of two twin 'bookends' behind the castle, the Museum of African Art Museum (☎ 202-357-2700) starts to entertain before you even see the collection. When you enter the foyer, you discover the museum is underground (built to conserve open space), and tunnels connect to the three other underground galleries and to the Freer Gallery. (Kids will enjoy tossing pennies three stories down into the fountain.) Devoted to sub-Saharan African art, the museum displays masks, textiles, ceramics, and other examples of the visual traditions of a continent of 900 distinct cultures.

Arthur M Sackler Gallery

Twin to the Museum of African Art above ground and connected below, the Sackler (☎ 202-357-2700) exhibits Asian arts, including Chinese ritual bronzes, jade ornaments, and other objects reflecting the aesthetic heritage of half the world's population – some of which date back to the 3rd millennium BC.

Arts & Industries Building

This odd little museum (☎ 202-357-2700) beside the Castle houses Victorian Americana, mainly the inventions and products of the 1876 Philadelphia Centennial Exposition. Wurlitzer-era carriages, machinery, and bric-a-brac are displayed with a ghostly carnival-type ambiance; there's also a full-size locomotive.

The museum also shows children's performances here in the Experimental Gallery and Discovery Theater; check at the desk to see what's playing.

The antique carousel in front of the building takes children for old-fashioned rides for $1. It's open from 10 am to 5:30 pm.

Hirshhorn Museum

East of the Castle, this modern doughnut-shaped museum (☎ 202-357-2700) with a view of the Mall (enter from Independence Ave) houses the extensive modern and contemporary art collection of Latvian American millionaire Joseph Hirshhorn. With one of the largest collections of 20th century sculpture in the world, the museum displays works by Rodin, Brancusi, Calder, and Henry Moore. Also exhibited are paintings by Dubuffet, O'Keeffe, Warhol, Pollock, Stella, and de Kooning.

From September to June, the museum airs independent films Thursday and Friday at 8 pm; art documentaries are featured Thursday at noon and Saturdays at 1 pm.

The museum's sunken **sculpture garden** on the Mall holds a rich collection of works in a beautiful setting, including Rodin's *Monument to the Burghers of Calais*. There's an outdoor cafe nearby in the summer.

National Air & Space Museum

Since its bicentennial opening on July 4, 1976, the Air & Space Museum (☎ 202-357-2700) has grown to be the world's most popular museum. Its cavernous halls hold full-size air and spacecraft, from the Wright brothers' *Flyer* and Charles Lindbergh's *Spirit of St Louis* to the Apollo IX command module.The museum actively engages all visitors big and small. You can touch a moon rock, walk through a DC-7 and Skylab, or join a volunteer-led tour to hear the stories behind the impressive flying machines on display.

The museum's Langley Theater shows IMAX films on a 50-by-75-foot screen. Of the four shows, the best is still *To Fly*. Get a ticket ($3.25 adults; $2 kids/seniors/students) as soon as you arrive, enjoy the exhibits, and then see the film later when you're tired of walking. Or come back after hours for evening screenings, usually at 6 pm.

The **planetarium** presents astronomy programs several times a day for an extra charge.

The gift shops sell model planes and spacecraft, personalized dog tags, and freeze-dried astronaut food among other space paraphernalia. The museum cafeteria and restaurant are in a spacious greenhouse-like setting overlooking the Mall.

The museum opens at 9:45 am. In July and August the museum has extended summer hours from 9:30 am to 7:30 pm.

National Gallery of Art

The National Gallery (☎ 202-737-4215) consists of two buildings: the original neoclassical building across the Mall from the Air & Space Museum, now called the West Wing, and the modern angular East Wing across 4th St. The two are connected by an underground tunnel.

The **West Wing** exhibits primarily European works from the Middle Ages to the early 20th century, including masterpieces by Rembrandt, Vermeer, El Greco, Renoir, Monet, and Cézanne. It's the only gallery in America that owns a da Vinci (the *Ginevra de Benci)*, and it hosts such blockbuster exhibitions as the Vermeer collection in 1996. You can customize your own tour of the collection with the museum's multimedia computers.

The spacious **East Wing** features a Calder mobile as the centerpiece of its four-story atrium, along with other abstract and modern works.

Though affiliated, the National Gallery is not part of the Smithsonian Institution; note the different hours. It's open Monday to Saturday from 10 am to 5 pm and Sunday from 11 am to 6 pm; admission is free. The West Wing operates the Terrace Cafe; a buffet cafeteria and espresso bar is in the tunnel across from the underground fountain. There are big bookshops too. Check at the desk for a calendar of events (concerts, lectures, activities).

National Museum of Natural History

The Natural History Museum (☎ 202-357-2700) holds many awesome highlights: the 45-carat Hope Diamond, a suspended life-size model of the largest blue whale ever seen, the 13-foot-tall mammoth elephant that greets you at the entrance, dinosaur skeletons, an insect zoo, and a newly renovated hall of geology, gems, and minerals. Other exhibits examine various ecosystems and Native American cultures.

The hands-on exhibits in the Discovery Room enable children to closely examine shells, bones, geodes, costumes, and more. The small room is open afternoons only and requires tickets for a specific time; get your passes when it first opens for the widest choice of times.

The museum's two windowless cafeterias (one for Smithsonian members only) are among the least desirable of the ready options – it's better to wander over to

American History Museum or up to the Old Post Office Pavilion at lunchtime.

National Museum of American History

From such venerated cultural touchstones as the original American flag to such kitsch Americana icons as Dorothy's ruby slippers from *The Wizard of Oz*, the original Kermit the Frog, and Fonzie's *(Happy Days)* jacket, the eclectic collection of the American History Museum (☎ 202-357-2700) celebrates American culture. The original whites-only lunch counter from the Woolworth's in Greensboro, North Carolina, tells the story of the sit-ins that led to the desegregation of the South; the poignant Vietnam Memorial collection exhibits the touching mementos left at 'the Wall' over the years. The First Ladies' inauguration ball gowns are a perennial favorite.

A lively gift shop sells specialty items from all over the US: Vermont maple syrup, Appalachian quilts, Charleston tea, Harlem Boys Choir cassettes, and Navaho jewelry. There are also wonderful books, guides, toys, and trinkets. The recently remodeled cafeteria has an updated menu; the Palm Court restaurant offers sit-down service in an ice-cream parlor setting.

US Holocaust Memorial Museum

Opened in 1993, the Holocaust Museum (☎ 202-488-0400, TTD 202-488-0406) is a hauntingly powerful memorial to victims of Nazi tyranny from 1933 to 1945. The three-floor permanent exhibit chronologically traces the rise of Hitler's Germany and graphically documents Nazi atrocities against six million Jews and millions of others – including homosexuals, the disabled, Jehovah's Witnesses, and political dissidents and resistors – with the use of film footage, audio and video recordings, photographs, and recovered personal belongings. The museum's literature recommends the main exhibit for children over the age of 11 and the separate children's exhibit for children 8 and up. However, all the exhibits very vividly convey the scope and nature of Holocaust atrocities, and parents would do well to overestimate rather than underestimate the impact of such horrific history on children.

The museum is a half block south of the Mall. Though its official address is 100 Raoul Wallenberg Place SW, you enter from the 14th St side. Admission is free, but crowds necessitate that they hand out admission tickets. The box office distributes all tickets available that day starting at 10 am till they run out (limit four per person). They admit you that day only at a specific time (for example, at 10 am you may end up with tickets for admission at 2:30 pm), but once in you can stay as long as you like. (Visitors may see the children's exhibit, a computer room featuring a multimedia Holocaust encyclopedia, and the memorial room without a ticket.) The museum is open daily from 10 am to 5:30 pm except on Yom Kippur and Christmas. The cafe opens at 9 am for folks waiting in line for tickets.

Bureau of Engraving & Printing

Often mistakenly called the 'Mint,' the bureau (☎ 202-874-3019), at 14th and C Sts SW one long block south of the Mall, is where they design, engrave, and print all US paper currency. Tour guides lead groups on raised walkways through what is, essentially, a print shop; kids are excited by it, so many families wait hours in line for their turn. You do learn fun money trivia, though, and you can buy such souvenirs as shredded money and uncut sheets of one or two dollar bills. The bureau's open Monday to Friday from 9 am to 2 pm. This is a popular tour, and from July through August you need to pick up free tickets at the kiosk on 15th St, and then go to the 14th St entrance for the tour (tickets are often gone by late morning). The nearest Metro stop is Smithsonian station.

Washington Monument

The Washington Monument (☎ 202-426-6839), the 555-foot white obelisk rising above the center of the Mall, offers a wonderful view of the Potomac basin, especially at night (it's open until midnight from spring to fall). The monument has had a checkered history: Construction began in 1848 but was not completed until 37 years later. The first glitch occurred when Pope Pius IX contributed a stone that was subsequently stolen by antipapists who then undermined fundraising efforts. The project was then abandoned during the Civil War; after the war the Army Corps of Engineers resumed construction. The two separate phases of construction are evident in the slightly different shade of stone you see about a quarter of the way up.

An elevator ride takes visitors to an observation landing inside, where you may stay as long as you like. You can even walk down (on your own or on a ranger-led tour); the inside of the shaft is decorated with decorative plaques from different states (also from the Cherokee Nation). The monument is open September to March from 9 am to 5 pm and April to August from 8 am to midnight. Admission is free, but expect long lines.

You can get advance tickets through Ticketmaster (☎ 800-551-7328) for a 'convenience charge' of $1.50 per ticket.

Sylvan Theater

Downhill from the Washington Monument, this outdoor theater (☎ 202-426-6841) features free military (and sometimes big band) concerts from June to August at 8 pm, Sunday through Friday. (Who was it that said military justice is to justice as military music is to music?)

Vietnam Veterans Memorial

Downhill from the Lincoln Memorial, two walls of polished black marble that come together in a V shape are inscribed with the names of 58,202 veterans killed as a result of the Vietnam War (including 1150 officially listed as Prisoners of War/Missing in Action, denoted by a cross). The stark, powerful memorial (☎ 202-634-1568) – the most visited memorial in DC – was designed by Maya Ying Lin, a 21-year-old architecture student at Yale University, whose design was selected from a national competition. Names are inscribed chronologically from date of death; alphabetical rosters are available nearby. On request, volunteers will help you get rubbings of names from 'The Wall.' The most moving remembrances are the notes, medals, and mementos left by survivors, family, and friends since the memorial was completed in 1982 (see many such items on exhibit at the American History Museum). The monument is open 24 hours, and the ranger station is staffed till midnight.

Opponents to the design insisted on a more traditional sculpture that was added nearby in 1984; a memorial to women who served in the war was recently unveiled as well.

Lincoln Memorial

The Lincoln Memorial (☎ 202-426-6895), at the west end of the Mall, is much more than a monument to the 16th US President; its symbolic power became apparent immediately upon its completion in 1922. Invited to speak at the dedication was Dr Robert Moton, president of Tuskegee Institute (a historical African American college in Alabama), yet instead of being seated at the speakers' platform Dr Moton was ushered to a segregated section across from the white audience. Indignant African Americans protested and transformed the memorial into a symbol of America's commitment to civil rights. From its steps in 1963 Martin Luther King, Jr, preached 'I have a dream – that one day this nation will rise up and live out the true meaning of its creed: "We hold these truths to be self-evident, that all men are created equal." '

Designed to resemble a Greek temple, the monument's 36 columns (representing the 36 states in Lincoln's union) tilt slightly inward to avoid the optical illusion of a bulging top.

The hands of the 19-foot-tall marble statue of the Great Emancipator are positioned to read 'A' and 'L' in American Sign Language to honor Lincoln's support for Gallaudet College for the Deaf. Under the memorial is a stalactite-filled cave now closed to the public. The monument is open 24 hours and offers a neat view at night.

Tidal Basin

A ring of cherry trees, a gift from Japan in the early 1900s, surrounds the Tidal Basin and the Jefferson Memorial. When they bloom in late March and early April, the perimeter is lined with their pale-pink blossoms. The Cherry Blossom Festival is timed to coincide with this event – the first two weeks of April draw 100,000 visitors to DC for the festivities, which climax with the Cherry Blossom Parade.

The Tidal Basin boathouse (☎ 202-479-2426), just south of the Bureau of Printing and Engraving, rents **paddleboats** daily 10 am to 7 pm from March to September (depending on the weather). The cost is $7 per hour for a two-seater and $14 per hour for a four-seater.

Jefferson Memorial

This memorial (☎ 202-426-6822) south of the Washington Monument and Tidal Basin honors Thomas Jefferson, the third US President, drafter of the Declaration of Independence, and founder of the University of Virginia. Designed by John Russell Pope to resemble Jefferson's Virginia home, the rounded, domed monument was initially derided by critics as 'the Jefferson Muffin.' Inside, there's a 19-foot bronze likeness and excerpts from Jefferson's writings etched into the walls. In spring, sit on the steps and admire the cherry blossoms; there's also a beautiful moonlight reflection over the Tidal Basin at night. It's open 24 hours.

Other Mall Sights

Each winter, the humble **Sculpture Garden Ice Rink** (☎ 202-371-5340) next to the natural history museum offers ice skating, skate rental, and lockers from November to March (depending on the weather). Refreshments are available here year round (on the Mall, you're never too far from a stand selling hot dogs, sodas, ice cream, and other snack foods).

The stone **Korean War Memorial** on the south side of the Reflecting Pool near the Lincoln Memorial depicts a troop of soldiers taking a hill. One local speechwriter relates how 'walking among the soldiers early on a rainy morning is spooky . . . like being in a cinéma vérité before the talkies were invented.'

The **Voice of America** (☎ 202-619-4700) broadcasts US and world news in 44 languages from its studios at 330 Independence Ave SW. Free 45-minute tours are offered Monday to Friday at 40 minutes past the hour from 8:40 am to 2:40 pm.

DOWNTOWN

Downtown began in what is now called Federal Triangle, east of the White House and bordered by Pennsylvania and Constitution Aves. This area was a thriving marketplace throughout the 19th century, though by midcentury it became known as 'Hooker's Division' due to the presence of General Hooker's Union troops. The strong commercial district began to decline after WWII, when residents started moving out to the suburbs. President Kennedy encouraged a revitalization effort in the 1960s, which resulted in the renovation and transformation of the Old Post Office Pavilion, a Romanesque structure that escaped demolition in the 1930s. Federal Triangle is now characterized by its many red-roofed government buildings, including the National Archives at its tip.

Since then downtown has spread north and east. Though definitions vary, its boundaries roughly encompass the area east of the White House to Judiciary Square at 4th St, and from the Mall north up to around K or M St.

The following downtown section traces a path east from the White House to the Federal Triangle, north to Metro Center, and east to Gallery Place, Chinatown, and Judiciary Square.

The **Federal Triangle** area (Metro: Federal Triangle or National Archives) from 14th St east to 6th St includes the National Archives and the Old Post Office (an easy place to take a break from touring; food and shops are in an interior courtyard). The FBI building is across the street and Ford's Theater a block and some north.

The **Metro Center** area, contrary to its

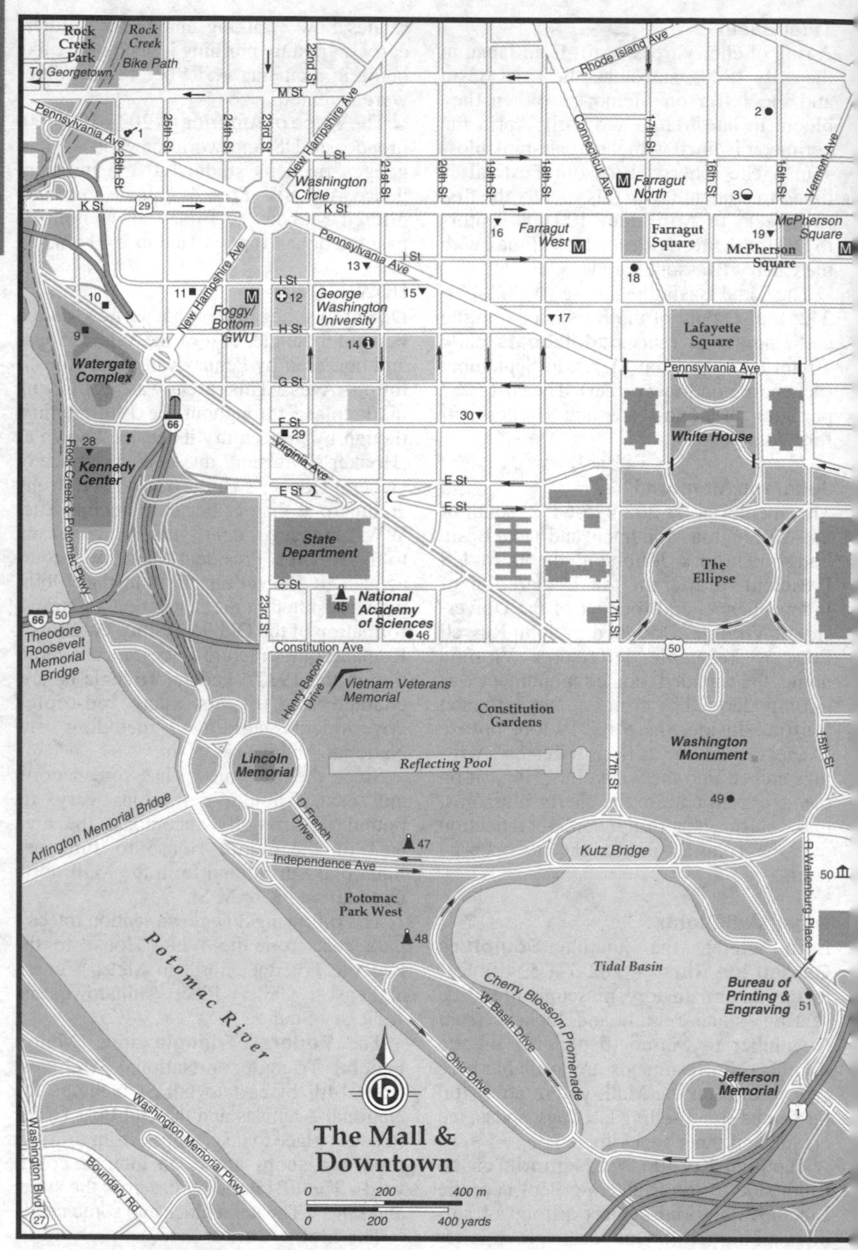

The Mall & Downtown
Rock Creek Park
Rock Creek Bike Path
To Georgetown
Pennsylvania Ave
26th St
25th St
24th St
23rd St
22nd St
21st St
20th St
19th St
18th St
17th St
16th St
15th St
M St
L St
K St
I St
H St
G St
F St
E St
C St
New Hampshire Ave
Rhode Island Ave
Connecticut Ave
Vermont Ave
Virginia Ave
Washington Circle
Foggy Bottom GWU
George Washington University
Farragut North
Farragut West
Farragut Square
McPherson Square
Lafayette Square
White House
The Ellipse
Watergate Complex
Kennedy Center
Rock Creek & Potomac Pkwy
State Department
National Academy of Sciences
Constitution Ave
Theodore Roosevelt Memorial Bridge
Henry Bacon Drive
Vietnam Veterans Memorial
Constitution Gardens
Reflecting Pool
Washington Monument
Lincoln Memorial
Arlington Memorial Bridge
D French Drive
Independence Ave
Kutz Bridge
Potomac Park West
Tidal Basin
R Wallenburg Place
Bureau of Printing & Engraving
Cherry Blossom Promenade
W Basin Drive
Ohio Drive
Jefferson Memorial
Potomac River
Washington Memorial Pkwy
Washington Blvd
Boundary Rd
0 200 400 m
0 200 400 yards

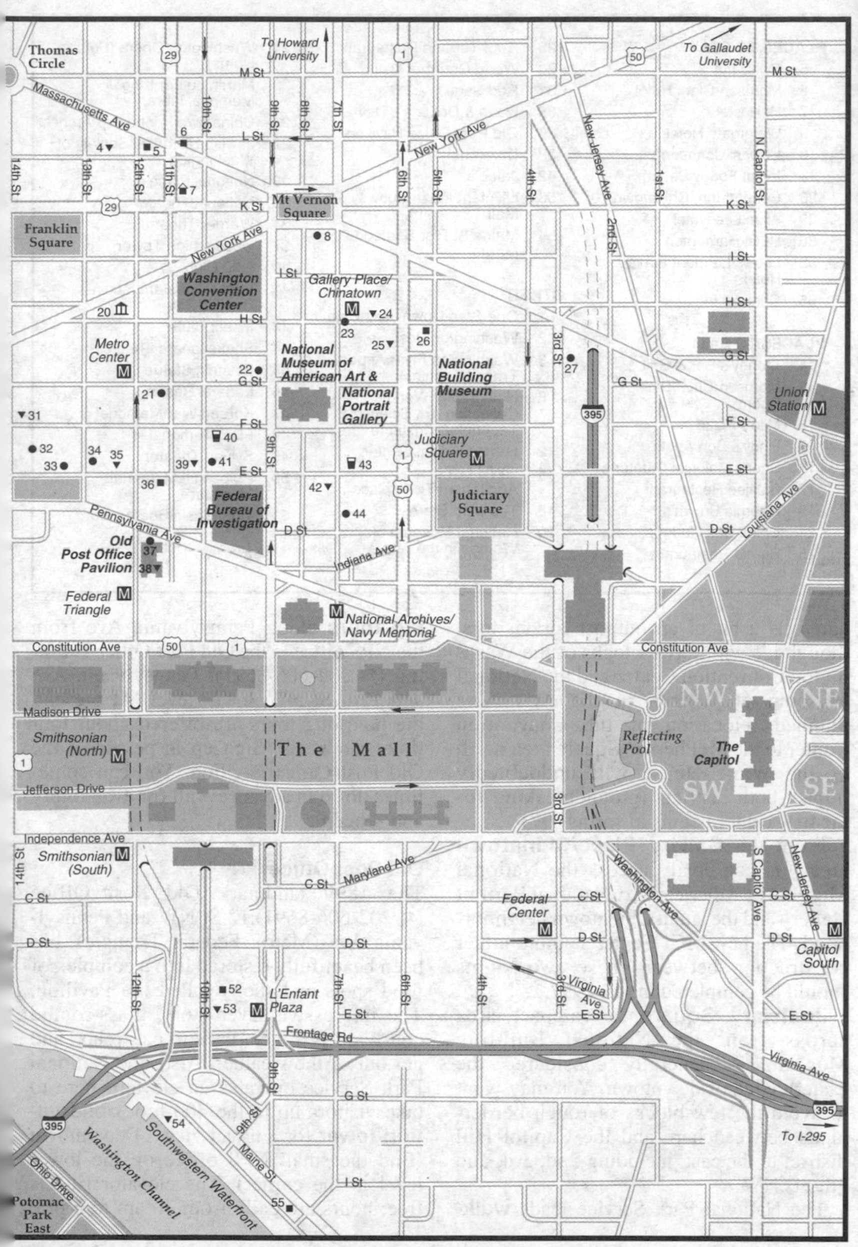
Thomas Circle
Massachusetts Ave
To Howard University
To Gallaudet University
M St
L St
K St
I St
H St
G St
F St
E St
D St
C St
E St
G St
I St
14th St
13th St
12th St
11th St
10th St
9th St
8th St
7th St
6th St
5th St
4th St
3rd St
2nd St
1st St
N Capitol St
S Capitol St
New York Ave
New Jersey Ave
Mt Vernon Square
Franklin Square
Washington Convention Center
Gallery Place/ Chinatown
Metro Center
National Museum of American Art & National Portrait Gallery
National Building Museum
Judiciary Square
Union Station
Federal Bureau of Investigation
Pennsylvania Ave
Old Post Office Pavilion
Federal Triangle
Indiana Ave
Louisiana Ave
National Archives/ Navy Memorial
Constitution Ave
Madison Drive
Smithsonian (North)
The Mall
Reflecting Pool
The Capitol
NW
NE
SW
SE
Jefferson Drive
Independence Ave
Smithsonian (South)
Maryland Ave
Washington Ave
Federal Center
Capitol South
Virginia Ave
L'Enfant Plaza
Frontage Rd
To I-295
Washington Channel
Southwestern Waterfront
Maine St
Ohio Drive
Potomac Park East

PLACES TO STAY

5 Swiss Inn
6 Morrison-Clark Hotel
7 HI Hostel
9 Watergate Hotel
10 Howard Johnson's
11 Inn at Foggy Bottom
26 Comfort Inn, Chinatown
29 Allen Lee Hotel
36 Hotel Harrington
52 Loews L'Enfant Plaza Hotel
55 Channel Inn

PLACES TO EAT

4 Stoney's Bar & Grill
6 Morrison-Clark Dining Room
13 Milo's Pizza
15 Lindy's Bon Apetit
16 Sholl's Colonial Cafeteria
17 Balajee Restaurant
19 Georgia Brown's
24 China Doll Gourmet
25 Burma Restaurant
28 Roof Terrace Restaurant
30 World Gourmet Deli
31 Red Sage
35 Dean & DeLuca's Deli
38 Old Post Office Pavilion
39 Dixie Grill
42 Jaleo's
53 L'Enfant Plaza Subway Mall
54 Maine St Pier Seafood Market

OTHER

1 One Step Down Jazz Club
2 Washington Post
3 Washington Flyer Airport Transit Terminal
8 Holography World Collection Art, Science & Technology Institute
12 GWU Medical Center
14 GWU Lisner Auditorium/Ticketplace
18 The Map Store
20 National Museum of Women in the Arts
21 Washington Opera (Future Home)
22 Martin Luther King Jr Memorial Library
23 Chinatown Friendship Arch
27 Jewish Historical Society of Washington
32 National Place
33 National Theater
34 Warner Theatre
37 Observation Tower
40 9:30 Club
41 Ford's Theater/Lincoln Historic Site
43 Insect Club
44 Shakespeare Theater
45 Einstein Statue
46 Federal Reserve
47 Korean War Memorial
48 FDR Memorial
49 Sylvan Theater
50 Holocaust Memorial Museum
51 Tidal Basin Boathouse

name, is a bit of an outpost for visitors, though it's within two blocks of the Washington Convention Center and the National Museum of Women in the Arts. The planned relocation of the Convention Center to the McPherson Square area north of the White House will undoubtedly impact both districts (groundbreaking for the new center begins in spring '97).

From the **Gallery Place/Chinatown** area you can easily access the National Museum of American Art/National Portrait Gallery and the small Chinatown neighborhood. The new MCI Center stadium under construction between these two sights should be completed in fall 1997.

Judiciary Square, a compact area across from the National Building Museum, is generally considered the eastern edge of downtown. You may want to avoid the few blocks of rough borderlands between here and the Capitol Hill district to the east, including 2nd, 3rd, and 4th Sts NW.

The National Park Service leads **walking tours** along Pennsylvania Ave from the NPS office in the Old Post Office Building (☎ 202-606-8691), Pennsylvania Ave and 12th St NW, lower level. At present, the hourlong tours are offered about four times per week. Sign up in person at the Old Post Office Pavilion. You can sometimes do so in advance; call for availability and schedule.

Old Post Office

The 1899 landmark Old Post Office (☎ 202-606-8691),12 St NW and Pennsylvania Ave (Metro: Federal Triangle), has been beautifully restored into a complex of food spots and shops called the Pavilion. The impressive seven-story, glass-roofed courtyard is a nice place to eat, relax, and get out of the weather. Also, the National Park Service operates an elevator here to take visitors up to the 400-foot **observation tower** for a broad view of downtown (find the small NPS office on the lower level in the corner). The elevator ride is free; hours are daily from 10 am to 6 pm;

expanded summer hours are daily 8 am to 10:45 pm (closed Thursdays 6:30 to 9:30 pm). There's also a post office.

National Archives

The grand neoclassical building on Constitution Ave between 7th and 8th Sts (Metro: Archives, see Museums on the Mall map) houses the national archives (☎ 202-501-5205). Inside, a dimly lit rotunda displays the original documents upon which the US government is founded – the Declaration of Independence, the Constitution, and the Bill of Rights. Also here is one of four remaining versions of the 1297 Magna Carta, courtesy of H Ross Perot, who purchased it upon its discovery in 1974. These precious documents are sealed in airtight cases filled with helium that sink nightly into an underground vault to protect them from nuclear attack or theft.

The archives are free and open daily September to March from 10 am to 5:30 pm and April to August from 10 am to 9 pm. Guided tours of the 55-ton steel vault and other documents are given daily at 10:15 am and 1:15 pm to people with reservations (call at least 10 days in advance). Researchers first make arrangements with an archivist (☎ 202-501-5400) and enter on the Pennsylvania Ave side. Visitors must pass through x-ray security.

Federal Bureau of Investigation

The honeycomb-like FBI building (☎ 202-324-3447), 10th and Pennsylvania Sts NW (Metro: Federal Triangle or Archives) is officially named the J Edgar Hoover FBI Building in honor of the notorious director who led the bureau for 48 years (1924 – 1972) and transformed it from a tiny force into a huge crime-fighting bureaucracy. The FBI tour is one of the most popular in Washington, and it ends with a bang – actually the many bangs of a live machine gun demonstration. You also get to see crime laboratories, DNA testing, and a forfeiture unit (items the FBI has confiscated). Free 45-minute tours run Monday to Friday 8:45 am to 4:15 pm. Line up at the E St entrance between 9th and 10th Sts; people start lining up by 7:30 am in busy seasons.

Ford's Theater

On April 14, 1865, lone gunman John Wilkes Booth assassinated Abraham Lincoln while the President and Mrs Lincoln watched *Our American Cousin* in the Presidential box in Ford's Theater (☎ 202-426-6924), 511 10th St NW. The scene of the crime remains draped with a period flag to this day. You can have a look around on your own, catch a tour, or, to fully enjoy the beautifully restored theater, attend one of the many live performances the operating theater puts on seasonally. The basement's **Lincoln Museum** maps out the details of the assassination and displays related artifacts.

Across the street, the **Peterson House** is today immortalized as the 'house where Lincoln died.' The tiny, unassuming little group of rooms creates a movingly personal memorial. The national historic area encompassing all three sites is open daily from 9 am to 5 pm (the theater may occasionally be closed for rehearsals or matinees). The closest Metro stop is Metro Center, but you could also take the slightly longer but well-worn path from the Federal Triangle stop.

National Museum of Women in the Arts

This museum (☎ 202-783-5000) is at 1250 New York Ave NW at the corner of 12th St (Metro: Metro Center or McPherson Square). In it you'll find displays of works by women artists from 28 countries, including Judy Chicago, Mary Cassat, and Georgia O'Keeffe. The impressive 1911 building – once a Masonic lodge open only to men – features a grand foyer and cozy mezzanine (the mezzanine cafe serves such arty sandwiches such 'the Frida Kahlo' – grilled cheese with dill havarti and sautéed spinach). On a recent visit the displays were largely paintings and mostly portraits at that – not as rich a scope as you might hope. And the location is a bit out of the way – go for lunch or dessert to make a trip of it.

The gift shop sells handmade pottery, jewelry, and other women-made crafts. Admission is free (donations encouraged), and hours are Monday to Saturday from 10 am to 5 pm and Sunday from noon to 5 pm.

Martin Luther King Memorial Library

DC's main library (☎ 202-727-1221), 901 G St NW (Metro: Metro Center), holds a popular mural portraying the Civil Rights Movement. In addition, the library is an important community and cultural center, and it sponsors many readings, concerts, films, children's activities, and more. There's a gift kiosk as well, with specialty periodicals. Hours are Monday to Thursday 9 am to 9 pm, Friday and Saturday 9 am to 5:30 pm, and Sunday 1 to 5 pm.

National Museum of American Art & National Portrait Gallery

These Smithsonian museums (☎ 202-357-2700) are both housed in the old 1867 US Patent Office building between 7th and 9th and F and G Sts NW (Metro: Gallery Place/Chinatown). You'll recognize them by the gleaming *Vaquero* out front by Luis Jimenez, Jr. One highlight of the American Art Museum is a spirited, colorful collection of American folk art, including a giant bottlecap giraffe, a Coca-Cola-icon quilt, and James Hampton's 1964 *Throne of the Third Heaven of the Nations Millennium General Assembly* – a room-size shrine constructed from gold and silver tin foil and colored craft paper.

The Portrait Gallery contains portraits of important Americans and frequent biographical exhibits. Both are free and open daily from 10 am to 5:30 pm. There's a nice little cafeteria with courtyard seating between the two museums.

Chinatown

Enter DC's small Chinatown under **Friendship Arch**, the ornate golden gate on H St at 8th St NW constructed in 1986 – it's the largest of its kind outside China and easily the sad little Chinatown's most appealing feature. Chinese shops and restaurants line the next couple blocks of 8th St north and dot the intersecting streets.

Supposedly they're developing the area to attract tourists. The addition of a new stadium nearby (to be completed in fall 1997) is sure to affect the area one way or the other. For the moment, travelers can readily find dim sum and inexpensive trinkets conveniently accessible above the Gallery Place/Chinatown Metro station.

National Building Museum

The National Building Museum (☎ 202-272-2448), 401 F St NW (Metro: Judiciary Square) takes up an entire city block. The main room is the Great Hall where rows of massive pink marble Corinthian columns – among the largest in the world – rise 75 feet high. The dramatic 300-foot-wide interior courtyard is banked by four stories of ornately ornamented balconies – a grand setting for inaugural balls since the Cleveland administration.

The building was constructed in 1887 to house the Pension Office (note the frieze of terracotta soldiers outside) and now holds a museum dedicated to architectural arts. The showy space easily overshadows the exhibits, but they're provocative nonetheless – the one on *Washington: City and Symbol* examines the deeper significance and symbolism of DC's architecture. Concerts here make the most of the natural acoustics, and there's also a coffee bar. The museum shop is great, with furnishings, crafts, and rich coffee table books. Admission is free, and hours are Monday to Saturday 10 am to 4 pm and Sunday noon to 4 pm. (The museum is across the street from the Law Officers Memorial, a stark memorial to police officers slain in the line of duty).

Other Downtown Sights

The **Metropolitan AME Church** at 1518 M St NW was built in 1886 by African Americans. The funeral of Frederick Douglass was held here in 1895.

The **National Jewish Historical Society of Greater Washington** (☎ 202-789-0900), 701 3rd St NW (Metro: Judiciary Square), has an archive and museum. Open Sunday to Thursday from 11 am to 3 pm.

The **Wilderness Society** (☎ 202-833-2300), 900 17th St NW, has a permanent collection of 70 Ansel Adams photographs on display. It's open Monday to Friday 10 am to 5 pm.

The **Holography World Collection Art, Science & Technology Institute** (☎ 202-667-6322), 800 K St NW, displays holographic art from around the world. Hours are Monday to Friday from 11 am to 6 pm, $8 per person.

The **Federal Reserve** (☎ 202-452-3000), on C St between 20th and 21st Sts, has tours of the place that is as close to a central bank as there is in the US. Admission is free, but it's only open Thursdays at 2:30 pm.

THE WHITE HOUSE AREA

The site for the White House – originally called the President's House – was selected by George Washington in 1791. The hope was that the President and Congress could keep a eye on one another along the unobstructed sight line of Pennsylvania Ave, but later the **Treasury Building** was built immediately east of the White House, blocking the view. Flanking the White House's west side is the **Old Executive Office Building**, a French Second Empire palace that could have been designed by cartoonist Charles Addams.

Pennsylvania Ave crosses in back of the White House (which faces the Washington Monument). Until recently it served as a central thoroughfare, but after threats from gunmen in 1995, the portion across from the White House was blocked to car traffic. The ramshackle look of the concrete blockades and the heightened security presence add an imposing imperial air to the White House; nevertheless, the area is more pleasant as a pedestrian walkway.

Across from the White House to the north you will find the **Renwick Gallery** on Pennsylvania Ave at the corner of 17th St – it's the Smithsonian museum dedicated to American crafts – and several doors down there's the 1824 **Blair House**, presidential guest quarters since 1948 (note the plaque out front commemorating the bodyguard killed in action while protecting Truman in 1950).

Lafayette Square, named for American Revolutionary War hero the Marquis de Lafayette, is the statue-studded park just north of the White House. It's a nice spot to walk around, play at chessboard tables, or observe tourists, undercover security police, and placard-carrying demonstrators. Once an orchard, the area around the square was lined in the 19th century with the mansions of the rich and powerful. Among the beautiful Victorian homes that remain is **Decatur House**, where tour guides tell stories of the square's high society. In the 1960s, the government proposed tearing down these historic houses and erecting government buildings, but the appeals of First Lady Jacqueline Kennedy spared the houses – though the modern government monoliths now loom directly behind. Today the area is home to the office buildings of the rich and powerful.

North of the square on opposite sides of 16th St there's the exclusive **Hay-Adams Hotel** to the west and the beautiful little **St John's Church** to the east, where pew 54 is reserved for presidential families to worship.

South of the White House, an expansive park called the **Ellipse** borders the Mall and is surrounded by more sights. The southernmost point of the semicircular presidential lawn provides the classic photo opportunity of the front of the White House, across from the zero milestone marking the site. The National Christmas Tree is decorated here in December, and whimsical urban visionaries have also proposed the installment of a 'national sofa' here across from a large screen that would allow two-way communication with White House residents. The National Park Service operates a **visitor pavilion** in the northeast corner of the Ellipse (snacks and restrooms available).

The elegant row of monumental buildings at the west side of the Ellipse from E St south includes the wonderful Corcoran Gallery (the Octagon House is directly behind), the Red Cross, Constitution Hall of the Daughters of the American Revolution (DAR), and the Organization of American States at the corner of Constitution Ave.

The **Department of the Interior** (☎ 202-343-2743), on C St NW at 19th St, displays dioramas of American wildlife, maintains a nice garden out back, and runs a gift shop featuring Native American crafts.

On the east side of the Ellipse, the Hotel Washington and Willard Hotel bank a power-broker block of Pennsylvania Ave. Here too **Pershing Park** attracts brown-bag lunchtime crowds, and there's an outdoor cafe in summers (and plenty of cart vendors offer fast food nearby). The **Department of Commerce Building** along the Ellipse's east side – at its opening in 1931 the government's largest building – contains two significant resources for tourists: the **White House Visitor Center** on the north side, which distributes tour tickets, and the humble **National Aquarium** (enter from 14th St).

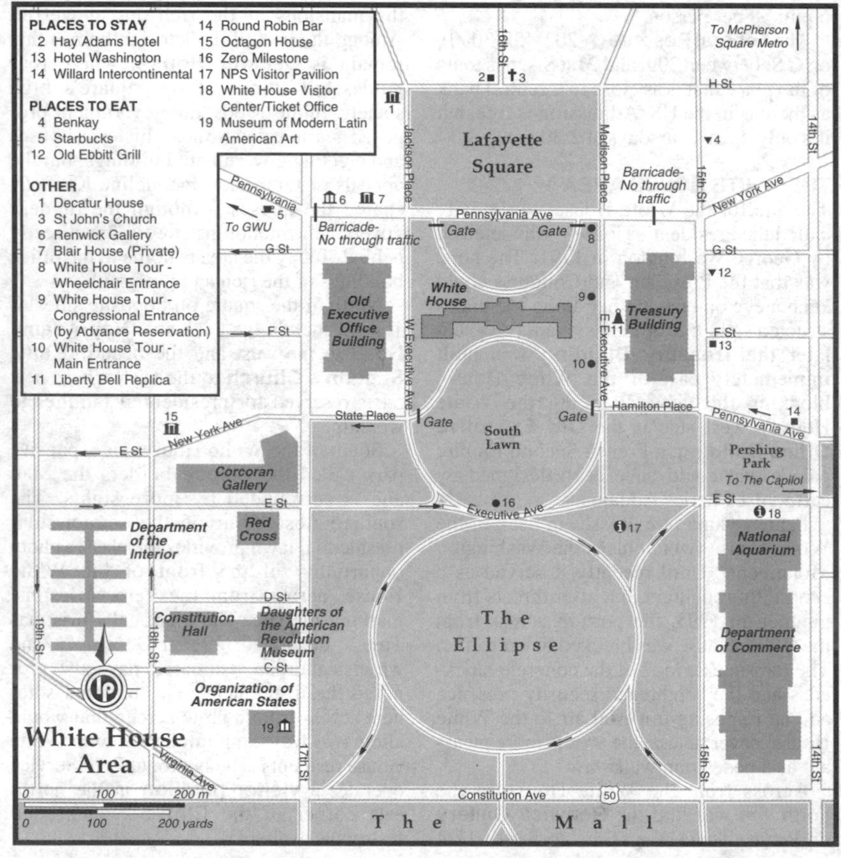

The National Park Service offers **free walking tours** of the White House area. Tours begin at the Ellipse directly south of the White House; sign up at the ranger office at the visitor pavilion (☎ 202-523-3780). Tours are scheduled Tuesday to Saturday mornings, at 8, 8:30, and 9 am.

White House

Since 1800, every president since John Adams has lived in the White House (☎ 202-456-7041) at 1600 Pennsylvania Ave (the most famous address in the nation), and it has grown in size and stature from a presidential residence to a symbol of the power of the President.

It was torched by the British in 1814 and reopened in 1818. An overhaul in 1950 gutted almost the entire interior, and Jacqueline Kennedy's extensive redecoration campaign in the 1960s replaced the previous hodgepodge with more tasteful furnishings. Presidents have customized the property over time: Franklin Delano Roosevelt put in a pool, Truman installed a second-story porch, Bush added a horseshoe-throwing lane, and Clinton put in a jogging track. Some residents never leave: It's said that Eleanor Roosevelt and Harry Truman both sighted the ghost of Abe Lincoln in Lincoln's old study.

On the tour you see eight interior rooms, including the China Room, Blue Room, and Red Room. Guides go through the usual perfunctory details of the decor, but it's more interesting to personalize this powerful symbol of American democracy by envisioning the resident personalities that shaped it. Free guided tours are offered 10 am to noon Tuesday to Saturday. In fall and winter just line up at the east entrance; in spring and summer first obtain tickets (up to six per person) at the White House Visitor Center at 1450 Pennsylvania Ave (a block southeast of the White House on the ground floor of the Commerce Building). The ticket booth opens at 7:30 am and distributes all tickets available that day until the supply is exhausted; no advance tickets are available here.

US citizens can shortcut the lines by making an **advance request** of their congressional representative to be put on one of the early morning congressional tours. Disabled visitors can forgo ticketing and go directly to the Pennsylvania Ave driveway starting at 10 am on tour days.

The White House is also open for garden tours on selected weekends in April and October, and for candlelight tours during the Christmas season. On Easter Monday the traditional Easter Egg Roll takes place on the South Lawn (the only time the grounds are wide open to the public).

The home of Bill, Hillary, Chelsea, and Socks

To find out the president's schedule, call the White House press office for the recorded press announcement (☎ 202-456-2343).

Department of the Treasury
The squat monolith of the Treasury (☎ 202-622-0896, TDD 202-622-0692) occupies a city block next door to the White House at Pennsylvania Ave and 15th St. To end the debate on where to build it (they hadn't wanted to block the view of Congress), President Andrew Jackson stood on the lawn, stuck his cane in the ground, and declared, 'Here.' The 1833 Greek Revival landmark (each of the 30 36-foot columns were carved from a single block of granite) is decorated as befits a treasury, with golden eagles, ornate balustrades, and a two-story marble Cash Room constructed with eight types of marble. There's even a Liberty Bell replica on the White House side. US currency was printed in the basement here from 1863 to 1880. Free guided tours are offered Saturday mornings only at 10, 10:20, and 10:40 am (call for reservations). The staff is extremely security-conscious (your name, birth date, and photo identification are required for admission).

Old Executive Office Building
The imperially elaborate 1888 OEOB (☎ 202-395-5895) immediately west of the White House was designed by Alfred Mullet to house State, War, and Navy Department staff. Two years after its completion, Mullet committed suicide after not being paid and facing criticism over its lavish design. Today the OEOB is used as offices for White House staff (during the Reagan administration, Colonel Oliver North led covert efforts to raise funds for the Nicaraguan contras from Room 392 in the basement). Take a free tour of this beautifully restored French Second Empire building Saturday mornings by appointment (call Tuesday to Friday 9 am to noon). The Indian Treaty Room murals are worth a look.

Renwick Gallery
The Smithsonian's Renwick Gallery (☎ 202-357-2700) on Pennsylvania Ave near the White House (at the corner of 17th St next to Blair House) invites you up the regal stairs of the 1859 mansion, through its dignified Grand Salon, then startles you with some really wild pieces of craftwork, whimsy, and abstraction. Don't miss Larry Fuente's *Game Fish* (1988), a sailfish trophy meticulously adorned with beads, buttons, badminton birdies, Scrabble tiles, dominoes, yo-yos, Pez dispensers, and more. The gallery's collection focuses on crafts – after a close look you can recognize some of the pieces as furniture, jewelry, dishes, and lampshades. It's free and open daily from 10 am to 5:30 pm.

Corcoran Gallery
Housed in a beautiful 1897 Beaux Arts building overlooking the Ellipse, the private Corcoran (☎ 202-638-1439) on 17th St NW houses an esteemed collection of American art – Hudson River School, Ashcan, Pop, Abstract Expressionism – as well as some French and Dutch works. Elegant, contemplative rooms and halls are full of master paintings and sculpture (including *Dancer and Gazelles*, a favorite). Jazz performances are held in the atrium Wednesdays at lunchtime, and a jazz/gospel brunch is offered some Sundays (check current schedule); it's a great place to linger over coffee. They have an art school out back and occasional student shows. Admission is free (donations encouraged); hours are Friday to Monday and Wednesday 10 am to 5 pm, Thursday until 9 pm, closed Tuesdays.

Historic Buildings
Two historic houses near the White House offer a glimpse of the area's early-1800s residential district. Facing Lafayette Square at 748 Jackson Place NW, the 1818 **Decatur House** (☎ 202-842-0920) features mannerly tours detailing the life and lifestyles of the residents along with architectural and decor highlights. It's open

Tuesday to Friday 10 am to 2 pm, Saturday and Sunday noon to 4 pm; admission is $3 for adults, half price for students and seniors.

West of the White House, the eight-sided **Octagon House** (☎ 202-638-3105), 1799 New York Ave NW, was the temporary home of President and Dolley Madison while the White House was repaired after being burned by British troops. The 1801 Federal-style mansion now houses the American Institute of Architects and its museum of architecture and the interior arts. Hours are 10 am to 4 pm Tuesday to Sunday; admission to the exhibition galleries is $2 adults, $1 students/seniors.

The **Daughters of the American Revolution Museum** (☎ 202-879-3254), 1778 D St NW, contains 33 period rooms and genealogical information dating to the Revolutionary War. Admission is free, and hours are Monday to Thursday 8:30 am to 4 pm and Sunday from 1 to 5 pm. The adjacent 4000-seat **Constitution Hall** is a popular venue for concerts and performances.

The **Organization of American States** (OAS) (☎ 202-458-3000), 17th St NW between C St and Constitution Ave, is dedicated to promoting political and economic cooperation between the nations of North and South America. Founded in 1890, the OAS's 1910 Beaux Arts building features **Aztec Gardens** and the **Museum of Modern Art of Latin America**. Admission Museum of Modern Art of Latin Americais free, and hours are Tuesday to Saturday 10 am to 5 pm.

Other White House Area Sights

The small **National Aquarium** (☎ 202-482-2825) in the basement of the Commerce Building (enter on 14th St south of Pennsylvania Ave) has a touch tank and a sampling of ecosystems from the Chesapeake Bay to the Pacific Ocean. Staff feeds the piranhas and sharks at 2 pm on alternating days. Entrance fees are $2 adults, 75¢ children and seniors (it would take a considerably spruced-up aquarium to compete with DC's many free museums). It's open daily 9 am to 5 pm.

The **National Press Club** and **National Press Building** at the corner of 14th and F Sts NW houses journalists from around the world. In the same block below ground you'll find food, newsstands, shops, and a place to rest your feet at the **National Place** complex.

FOGGY BOTTOM

DC's West End district (see Downtown & the Mall map) was nicknamed 'Foggy Bottom' after the emanations of a long-lost gasworks – the term has also been used to metaphorically describe the bureaucratic gobbledygook emanating from the district's government agencies. It falls roughly between 17th St NW and Rock Creek Park, the Mall to the south, and K or M St to the north where it bumps up against the Dupont Circle neighborhood. (For sights at the 17th St Ellipse boundary, see the White House Area section above).

The area was first founded in the mid-18th century and called Funkstown after its first settler or Hamburgh by its mostly German residents (some church services are still offered in German). By the 19th century K St divided the wealthy in north Foggy Bottom from the laboring classes in the south, where the riverside was lined with factories making beer and cement. Many African Americans settled south of K St after the Civil War. In 1912 **George Washington University** was built here. Today the neighborhood is a mix of workers, professionals, and students.

State Department & National Academy of Sciences

The State Department (☎ 202-641-3241), 2201 C St NW at 23rd St, offers tours of its diplomatic reception rooms by advance reservation only. The National Academy of Sciences, facing the Mall on Constitution Ave between 21st and 22nd Sts NW, features an appealing statue of Albert Einstein set in a shady spot to the west of the building at 22nd St and Constitution Ave. The larger-than-life smiling figure sits cross-legged, inviting children to climb all over. (And who knows? Maybe a bit of genious will rub off.)

John F Kennedy Center for the Performing Arts

Overlooking the Potomac River, the Kennedy Center (☎ 202-467-4600, 2700 F St NW, Metro: Foggy Bottom/GWU) was dedicated as a 'living memorial' to Kennedy in 1964. The center's three theaters, concert hall, opera house, and movie theater almost single-handedly turned around Washington's reputation as a cultural desert. There are also nice views (particularly at sunset), several shops, a cafe, and the Roof Terrace restaurant. You could take a tour (☎ 202-416-8341), but the best way to see the center is to attend one of the many performances, festivals, films, and concerts held here year round.

This site once housed the Christian Heurich Brewery, makers of Senate brand beer until 1956 (now 'Old Heurich' is a local homebrew). History and scandal lovers will thrill to learn that the Kennedy Center's parking garage is where *Washington Post* reporters Bob Woodward and Carl Bernstein met with their Watergate informant 'Deep Throat.'

Watergate

The riverfront Watergate complex, 2650 Virginia Ave NW (Metro: Foggy Bottom/GWU), is a posh private community encompassing residential apartments, designer boutiques, the deluxe Watergate Hotel, and the notorious office buildings that gave Nixon's Watergate scandal its name. Here in 1972, a break-in at Democratic National Committee headquarters was linked to CREEP – the Committee to Re-elect the President – leading to the unprecedented resignation of a sitting president.

DUPONT CIRCLE

The Dupont Circle area north of the White House was once a marshland called the Slashes after Slash Creek, which flowed through it. In the early 1870s a group of developers calling themselves the California Syndicate bought up most of the land, improved it, and named it Pacific Circle. By the early 1900s, the area was home to Washington's wealthiest citizens. Though many were forced to abandon their mansions during the Depression, the area later began to regain its luster when many mansions were converted to elegant embassies along the northwest stretch of Massachusetts Ave. As other embassies followed, nearby Sheridan Circle became the center of Washington's diplomatic community, now referred to as Embassy Row.

Today the eclectic neighborhood ranges from plush ambassadorial estates, exclusive art galleries, and refined museums to gay bars, yuppie pool parlors, and anarchist bookstores. It's generally considered the place to go to find a wide variety of civilized restaurants, cafes, pubs, clubs, and trendy boutiques. Patio seating on wide sidewalks, window tables, and park benches offer some of the best people-watching roosts in the city.

The scenic park with the marble statues and fountain that makes up Dupont Circle is at the intersection of Connecticut and Massachusetts Aves, though when people direct you to Dupont Circle they're generally referring to the entire neighborhood. The Dupont Circle Metro station underneath the circle (a modest underground food court is whimsically designed to resemble train cars) provides the best access to everything in this area, and it's a very lively and safe place to walk around.

For a view of the grand architecture of the area, head north up Massachusetts Ave's **Embassy Row** from the Circle to Sheridan Circle, around which you'll see the elegant flag-waving embassies of many countries. Continue north on Massachusetts Ave to see the exceptional Embassy of Japan, the Islamic Center (on Belmont Rd off Massachusetts), and the embassies of Brazil and Great Britain (few of these allow visitors). If you wander up by the Textile Museum, look for the steps leading down S St to 22nd – it's a scenic little spot.

A few blocks north of the White House,

you can tour the publishing operations of the *Washington Post* (☎ 202-334-7969) at 1150 15th St NW.

Phillips Collection

America's first modern-art museum (☎ 202-387-2151), 1600 21st St NW (at Q St northwest of the Circle), exhibits an outstanding collection in a casually intimate setting; from room to room you can see great works by the likes of Renoir (the huge *Luncheon of the Boating Party*, for one), Cézanne, Monet, Degas, van Gogh, Klee, Rothko, O'Keeffe, Diebenkorn, Jacob Lawrence, and others. You enter through the modern extension wing and work your way back to the Victorian home that originally housed the collection; now there's a small cafe and bookstore. The galleries are open Tuesday to Saturday 10 am to 5 pm, Sunday noon to 7 pm (closed Monday). Donations are requested during the week; weekend admission is $6.50 for adults, $3.25 for students and seniors (children and teens under 18 are free). On Thursday night the museum extends its hours from 5 to 8:30 pm and requires an admission of $5 adults. Sunday afternoon concerts and

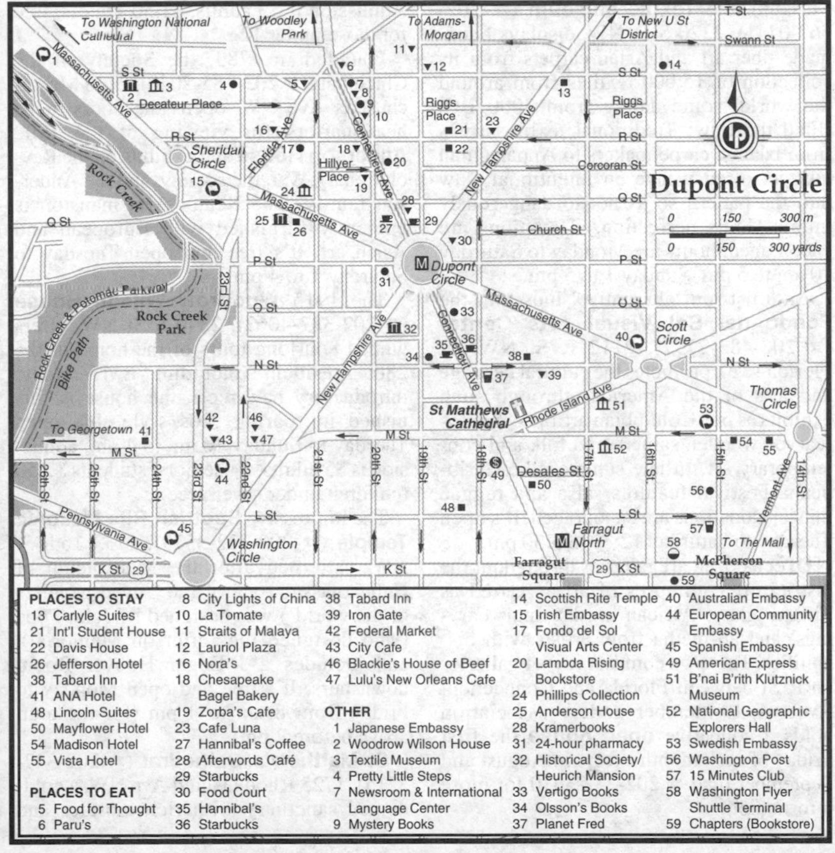

lunchtime lectures are among many scheduled special events.

B'nai B'rith Klutznick Museum
This museum (☎ 202-857-6583), 1640 Rhode Island Ave NW, maintains one of the largest collections of Judaica in the nation, from archaeological artifacts and early Jewish American settlements to exhibits on contemporary arts, sports, and culture. Donations are encouraged; it's open Sunday to Friday 10 am to 5 pm, closed Saturday.

Other Museums & Galleries
Housed in two historic residencesTextile Museum, the **Textile Museum** (☎ 202-667-0441), 2320 S St NW, displays handmade fiber art and Asian carpets from its collection of 15,000 textiles from around the world, some dating from 3000 BC. (Find the flaw: Traditional textile artists from Islamic carpetmakers to Appalachian quilters often weave an intentional flaw into the pattern so as not to dangerously mimic God's perfection.) Donations are encouraged; hours are Monday to Saturday 10 am to 5 pm, Sunday 1 to 5 pm.

An artist-run 'alternative' museum, the **Fondo del Sol Visual Arts Center** (☎ 202-483-2777), 2112 R St NW (at Florida Ave), promotes the cultural heritage and arts of the Americas through such exhibits as pre-Columbian artifacts, Santos (carved wooden saints), and folk and contemporary art. In late summer, the Caribbeana Festival features salsa and reggae music. Donations are encouraged; it's open Tuesday to Saturday 12:30 to 5:30 pm.

Over a dozen art galleries throughout the district offer glimpses of art as varied as Tiffany glass, African masks, Inuit carvings, and all-media from artists with disabilities. There's a compact row of galleries on R St between Florida and Connecticut Aves. A 19-member gallery association holds a collective **open house** the first Friday of each month except in August and September (call ☎ 202-232-3610 for more information).

Historic Homes & Buildings
The headquarters of the Historical Society of Washington, DC (☎ 202-785-2068) are in the **Heurich Mansion** on 1307 New Hampshire Ave NW (at 20th St). Docents guide visitors through 14 rooms of the medieval-inspired 1894 Victorian home of local brewing magnate Christian Heurich, but you can wander about on your own if you'd rather (look for the small garden refuge). The society is dedicated to preserving the history of Washington, and it operates a library on DC history and sells Washingtoniana in its bookstore. The mansion is open Wednesday to Saturday 10 am to 4 pm (call for tour schedule). Admission is $3 adults, $1.50 seniors, free for those under 12.

Founded in 1783, the Society of the Cincinnati (☎ 202-785-2040), 2118 Massachusetts Ave NW, opens the doors of its headquarters for viewing of the 1902 **Anderson House** and exhibits on the Revolutionary War, the society, and the Anderson family. The Beaux Arts mansion is opulently furnished with European and Asian art. It's free and open Tuesday to Saturday 1 to 4 pm.

The 1915 **Woodrow Wilson House** (☎ 202-387-4062), 2340 S St NW, offers guided hourlong tours of the home of the 28th President (including a 15-minute introductory newsreel); the house is furnished in roaring '20s style. It's open Tuesday to Sunday 10 am to 4 pm; admission is $5 adults, $4 seniors, students $2.50 (children under seven free).

The impressive **Scottish Rite Masonic Temple** (☎ 202-232-3579), 1733 16th St NW, patterned after the Mausoleum of Halicarnassus (one of the 'seven wonders of the world') was designed by John Pope (who designed the Jefferson Memorial), and includes a J Edgar Hoover Room downstairs. It's free and open Monday to Friday from 8 am to 4 pm (for the tour, arrive before 2 pm).

St Matthew's Cathedral (☎ 202-347-3215), 1725 Rhode Island Ave NW, a gold-domed sanctuary with rich mosaics and yellow-and-ironwork globes, is where JFK's funeral was held. Catholic masses are offered in Spanish and Latin as well as English; guided tours are offered Sunday 2:30 to 4:30 pm (donations accepted).

National Geographic Society

Kids enjoy the National Geographic Society's Explorers Hall (☎ 202-857-7588) at the headquarters at 1145 17th St NW (at M St), where there's a simulated orbital flight, a moon rock under glass, an 11-foot globe, and many interactive video displays. It's free and open Monday to Saturday 9 am to 5 pm, Sunday 10 am to 5 pm.

ADAMS-MORGAN

The funky, ethnic, bohemian neighborhood of Adams-Morgan, north of Dupont Circle, is centered along 18th St and Columbia Rd – this winding, climbing route was once a major trail for Native Americans. Before 1955, the neighborhood was called Lanier Heights, but after Washington became the first major city to voluntarily integrate its public schools residents elected to change the name by combining the names of two area elementary schools, historically white 'Adams' and historically African American 'Morgan.' Adding to this blend today are residents from Central and South America, the Caribbean, Central Africa, Southeast Asia, and many other lands.

The lively district is lined with restaurants, cafes, bars, and clubs – a funkier version of Dupont Circle. It's a great place to hang out, people-watch, browse, and eat. The long hilltop blocks of 18th St between Florida Ave and Columbia Rd are packed with new and secondhand bookstores, record stores, retro and nouveau clothing boutiques, sidewalk cafes, and rooftop restaurants.

Note that the neighborhood is not too convenient to the Metro, though in decent weather it's a nice walk from the Woodley Park station along Calvert St. At night you'd be better off in a cab to avoid the hassle of gridlocked streets and little parking.

Meridian Hill

Occupying two historic houses near Meridian Hill Park, the **Meridian International Center** (☎ 202-939-5568), 1624 and 1630 Crescent Place NW, presents three-month exhibits focusing on the cultural and artistic heritage of a particular country or region (Morocco, Russia, and Palestine were among recent subjects). The International Visitors Information Service operates out of here.

Meridian Hill Park (unofficially dedicated to Malcolm X) scales the slope from the lower Shaw neighborhood (see below) to the upper reaches of Adams-Morgan. Waterfalls grace this contour and provide a needed bit of scenery to an uneven area (for safety's sake, avoid visiting alone or at night).

SHAW

Named for Colonel Robert Gould Shaw, a white Bostonian who commanded the famous African American 54th Massachusetts Regiment (as related in the 1990 film *Glory)*, the Shaw neighborhood stretches south to north from around Thomas Circle to Meridian Hill Park, and east to west from roughly N Capitol St to 15th St NW.

Anchoring the neighborhood is **Howard University**, a traditionally African American school founded in 1867. The university's elite settled in an attractive adjacent area called **LeDroit Park**; where some fine examples of Victorian homes remain around U St NW between 4th and 5th Sts.

Its heyday was in the 1930s, when Shaw was a high point on the country's renowned 'chitlin' circuit' of African American entertainment centers. Here Shaw's 'Great Black Way' hosted such celebrities as Ella Fitzgerald, Eubie Blake, and homeboy Duke Ellington (born at 1212 T St NW).

One of the highlights of the neighborhood's many contributions to the Civil Rights Movement occurred in the 1950s, when Washington's Committee for School Desegregation first met here at **John Wesley African Methodist Episcopal Church**, the 1850s sanctuary at 1615 14th

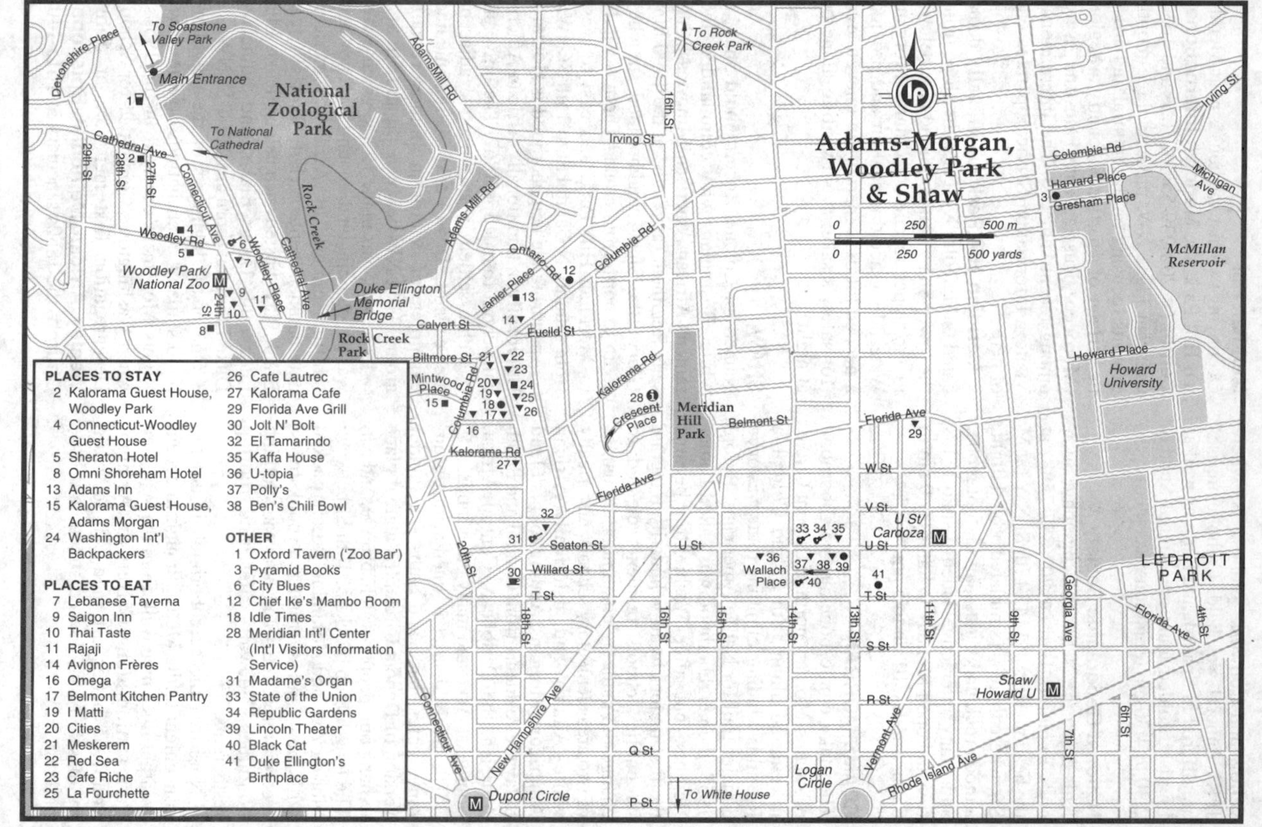
Adams-Morgan, Woodley Park & Shaw
0 250 500 m
0 250 500 yards
PLACES TO STAY
2 Kalorama Guest House, Woodley Park
4 Connecticut-Woodley Guest House
5 Sheraton Hotel
8 Omni Shoreham Hotel
13 Adams Inn
15 Kalorama Guest House, Adams Morgan
24 Washington Int'l Backpackers
PLACES TO EAT
7 Lebanese Taverna
9 Saigon Inn
10 Thai Taste
11 Rajaji
14 Avignon Frères
16 Omega
17 Belmont Kitchen Pantry
19 I Matti
20 Cities
21 Meskerem
22 Red Sea
23 Cafe Riche
25 La Fourchette
26 Cafe Lautrec
27 Kalorama Cafe
29 Florida Ave Grill
30 Jolt N' Bolt
32 El Tamarindo
35 Kaffa House
36 U-topia
37 Polly's
38 Ben's Chili Bowl
OTHER
1 Oxford Tavern ('Zoo Bar')
3 Pyramid Books
6 City Blues
12 Chief Ike's Mambo Room
18 Idle Times
28 Meridian Int'l Center (Int'l Visitors Information Service)
31 Madame's Organ
33 State of the Union
34 Republic Gardens
39 Lincoln Theater
40 Black Cat
41 Duke Ellington's Birthplace
National Zoological Park
Main Entrance
To Soapstone Valley Park
To National Cathedral
Rock Creek
Rock Creek Park
Duke Ellington Memorial Bridge
Woodley Park/ National Zoo
Meridian Hill Park
McMillan Reservoir
Howard University
LEDROIT PARK
U St/ Cardoza
Shaw/ Howard U
Dupont Circle
Logan Circle
To White House
To Rock Creek Park
Connecticut Ave
New Hampshire Ave
Florida Ave
Columbia Rd
Adams Mill Rd
Georgia Ave
Vermont Ave
Rhode Island Ave
16th St

Duke Ellington

Born and raised in DC's Shaw district, Edward Kennedy Ellington (1899–1974) developed his keyboard skills while listening to local ragtime pianists. His first piece was the *Soda Fountain Rag*, composed at age 16. He became successful in Washington by the early 1920s and left for New York City in 1923, where he went on to play at Harlem's Cotton Club. His collaborated with many artists – trumpeters Bubber Miley and Cootie Williams and saxophonists Johnny Hodges and Otto Hardwick among them. But the most famous of his collaborators was composer Billy Strayhorn, who gave the Ellington Band their theme *Take the A Train* in 1941. Strayhorn worked with Ellington throughout his life and collaborated on later numbers like *Such Sweet Thunder* (1957) and *Far East Suite* (1966).

Ellington is best known for his big-band jazz compositions. But his broad range and huge volume of work – over 1500 pieces – set him above everyone else in the field. The entire Duke Ellington collection is preserved at the Smithsonian Institution. ■

St NW. Their work led to the landmark civil rights case *Brown v Board of Education* that mandated school desegregation.

In 1968, the DC riots following the assassination of Martin Luther King, Jr, hit the neighborhood hard; fires destroyed many buildings and devastated the historically strong black commercial district.

Today the district is undergoing a renaissance, particularly the 'New U' area along U and 14th Sts NW. The reopening of the historic Lincoln Theater and the appearance of many new cafes, clubs, and shops alongside familiar neighborhood joints make this area the most up-and-coming area in DC. The U St Metro station provides convenient access to the area.

Howard University

Since it was founded to educate African Americans in 1867, Howard University (☎ 202-806-6100) at 2400 6th St NW has grown to one of the nation's finest schools. Its distinguished alumni include Supreme Court Justice Thurgood Marshall, Ralph Bunche, and Nobel Laureate Toni Morrison.

Today it has over 12,000 students in 18 different schools. Campus tours are available by calling ☎ 202-806-2900. You may also wish to visit the **Moorland-Springarn Research Center** (☎ 202-806-7239) with the nation's largest collection of African American literature (open Monday to Friday 9 am to around 4:30 pm) and the **James Herring Gallery of Art** (☎ 202-806-7070, open Monday to Friday 9:30 am to 4:30 pm, Sunday 1 to 4 pm). There's no charge. From the Shaw/Howard U Metro, walk north on 7th St.

Other Shaw Sights

The **Mary McLeod Bethune House** (☎ 202-332-1233), 1318 Vermont Ave NW between 13th and 14th Sts, is a national historic site devoted to African American

Howard alumnus Thurgood Marshall

women's history housed in the former home of educator Mary McLeod Bethune (founder of the National Council of Negro Women and the first African American women's college in the US). It's free and open Monday to Friday from 10 am to 4 pm and for tours on weekends (call for schedule).

The restored historic **Lincoln Theater** (☎ 202-328-6000), 1215 U St NW, has regained its position as the preeminent cultural institution of DC's African American community. The best way to see it is to attend one of the many performances held here, from flamenco dance to hip hop.

GEORGETOWN

Georgetown was an established town in Maryland before the capital moved in. In fact, its history stretches back much further: It was the Native American settlement of Tohoga when British fur trader Henry Fleet arrived in 1632.

Once the decision was made to site the new nation's capital between here and the town of Alexandria further downriver, Georgetown drew DC's gentry and thrived on a flourishing tobacco exporting industry. Georgetown University, the country's first Roman Catholic university, was founded in 1789. Throughout the campus and district, many 18th century buildings can still be seen.

Although Georgetown was a Confederate bastion during the Civil War, it was also a stop on the Underground Railroad that smuggled slaves to freedom. An antebellum free black community settled in Herring Hill (between 29th St and Rock Creek Park, north of P St), later supplanted by Georgetown's expanding affluent white community. Some historic African American churches remain, and their services continue to draw worshippers from other parts of DC.

In 1871 Georgetown became part of the District of Columbia. During the 1930s New Deal Democrats bought up much of the housing and reshaped the neighborhood. The Kennedys moved in during the 1950s (to Marbury House on N St NW at 33rd St, exterior view only) and Georgetown grew more fashionable, developing since then into a very popular district for shopping, dining, and entertainment. The largely white, mostly affluent community is a mix of college students and longtime residents.

Georgetown stretches west from Rock Creek Park along the Potomac River, and north past T St NW. M St NW is its main drag, and its epicenter is the intersection of M St NW and Wisconsin. These downtown streets are lined wall-to-wall with popular eateries, trendy clothing boutiques, record stores, bookstores, bars, and clubs.

Movie buffs will want to visit the steep steps at 3600 Prospect Ave (west of 36th St); that's where the priest goes tumbling down in the 1973 movie *The Exorcist*.

The community resisted the plan for a Metro station, and as a result Georgetown is not easily accessible by public transit (though it's a nice walk west along Pennsylvania Ave from the Foggy Bottom station in decent weather). It's often congested – gridlocked at peak times – and street parking can be near impossible (off-street parking is both limited and expensive). If you must drive, look for spots on O, P, or Q Sts near Dumbarton Oaks or on the same streets to the east by Georgetown University.

Georgetown University

Founded in 1789 America's first Roman Catholic college (☎ 202-687-5055), 37th St NW, was first directed by America's first black Jesuit. Notable alumni include Bill Clinton. Its attractive shaded campus of cobblestone lanes retains some of its original 18th and 19th century buildings. Enter at O and 37th Sts NW.

Dumbarton Oaks

Here in 1944 (☎ 202-339-6401), at 1703 32nd St NW (at S St), the agreement to create the United Nations was reached. The estate has a small but excellent collection of pre-Columbian and Byzantine art (open Tuesday to Sunday 2 to 5 pm). A $1 donation 'would be appreciated.'

The 16-acre **Dumbarton Oaks Garden**

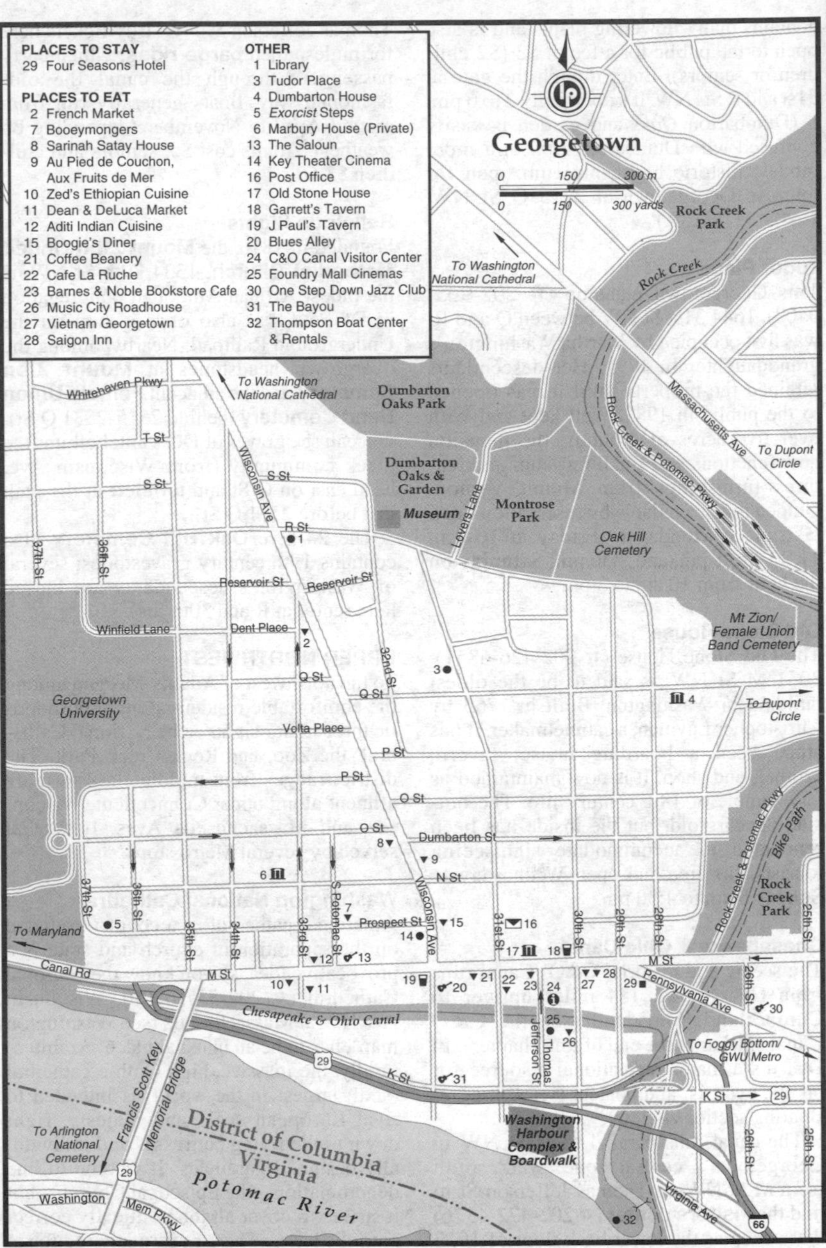

Georgetown
PLACES TO STAY
29 Four Seasons Hotel
PLACES TO EAT
2 French Market
7 Booeymongers
8 Sarinah Satay House
9 Au Pied de Couchon, Aux Fruits de Mer
10 Zed's Ethiopian Cuisine
11 Dean & DeLuca Market
12 Aditi Indian Cuisine
15 Boogie's Diner
21 Coffee Beanery
22 Cafe La Ruche
23 Barnes & Noble Bookstore Cafe
26 Music City Roadhouse
27 Vietnam Georgetown
28 Saigon Inn
OTHER
1 Library
3 Tudor Place
4 Dumbarton House
5 Exorcist Steps
6 Marbury House (Private)
13 The Saloun
14 Key Theater Cinema
16 Post Office
17 Old Stone House
18 Garrett's Tavern
19 J Paul's Tavern
20 Blues Alley
24 C&O Canal Visitor Center
25 Foundry Mall Cinemas
30 One Step Down Jazz Club
31 The Bayou
32 Thompson Boat Center & Rentals
0 150 300 m
0 150 300 yards
Rock Creek Park
To Washington National Cathedral
Rock Creek
Whitehaven Pkwy
Dumbarton Oaks Park
Massachusetts Ave
Rock Creek & Potomac Pkwy
To Dupont Circle
T St
S St
Wisconsin Ave
Dumbarton Oaks & Garden
Museum
Lovers Lane
Montrose Park
Oak Hill Cemetery
R St
37th St
36th St
Reservoir St
Winfield Lane
Dent Place
32nd St
Mt Zion/ Female Union Band Cemetery
Q St
Georgetown University
Volta Place
P St
O St
Dumbarton St
N St
Bike Path
Rock Creek Park
To Maryland
35th St
34th St
33rd St
S Potomac St
Prospect St
31st St
30th St
29th St
28th St
25th St
M St
Canal Rd
Pennsylvania Ave
26th St
Chesapeake & Ohio Canal
Jefferson St
Thomas St
To Foggy Bottom/ GWU Metro
K St
Washington Harbour Complex & Boardwalk
To Arlington National Cemetery
Francis Scott Key Memorial Bridge
District of Columbia
Virginia
Potomac River
Washington Mem Pkwy
Virginia Ave

contains many flowering plants and is also open to the public for a fee of $3 ($2 children or seniors). Enter though the gate at 31st and R Sts NW. It's open daily 2 to 6 pm.

(Dumbarton *Oaks* and garden is easily confused with Dumbarton *House*, a more modest historic house museum open for tours in Georgetown at 2715 Q St NW, ☎ 202-337-2288.)

Tudor Place

This Georgetown mansion (☎ 202-965-0400), 1644 31st St NW between Q and R, was first occupied by Martha Washington's granddaughter in 1794. Her descendants retained the property until it was opened to the public in 1983. Well kept and with over five acres of grounds, the mansion now functions as a small museum and features furnishings from Mount Vernon. Guided tours, available by reservation only, take place Monday to Friday at 10 am, 11:30 am, 1 pm, and 2:30 pm; Saturday on the hour from 10 am to 3 pm.

Old Stone House

The Old Stone House (☎ 202-426-6851), 3051 M St NW, is said to be the oldest building in Washington. Built in 1765 by Christopher Layman, a cabinetmaker, it has since been a boarding house, tavern, brothel, and shop. It is now maintained as an example of 18th century life. The outside appears old, but the inside has been renovated to accommodate sightseeing tourists. It's free and open Wednesday to Sunday 8 am to 4:30 pm.

Chesapeake & Ohio Canal

The scenic and historic 'C&O' Canal runs from Georgetown 184 miles upriver to Cumberland, Maryland (see the C&O Canal sidebar at the end of this chapter). In DC, it's a major recreational resource for hikers, cyclists, and boaters (see Biking & Boating sections below).

The canal runs parallel to M St NW in Georgetown's central zone; walk south from M St NW on Thomas Jefferson St to find the **visitors center** (☎ 202-472-4376) that occupies the lower back floor of 1057 Thomas Jefferson St NW. Buy tickets here for mule-pulled **barge rides**, which carry passengers through the canal the old-fashioned way. Boats generally run from around April to November (depending on weather). Adults cost $5, seniors and children $3.50.

Religious Sights

Founded in 1816, the **Mount Zion United Methodist Church**, 1334 29th St NW, is the oldest African American congregation in DC and was also once a stop on the Underground Railroad. Nearby, among the overgrown headstones at **Mount Zion Cemetery** and the adjacent **Female Union Band Cemetery** (behind 2515-2531 Q St), you can see graves of DC's antebellum free black community (from Wisconsin Ave, head east on Q St and turn left at the path just before 2531 Q St).

The 24-acre **Oak Hill Cemetery** also contains 19th century gravestones; several of Washington's descendants are buried here (enter at R and 30th Sts).

UPPER NORTHWEST

To the northwest of Adams-Morgan among the comfortable residential neighborhoods lie three major sights – the National Cathedral, the Zoo, and Rock Creek Park. The district ranges from middle-class to more affluent along upper Connecticut, Wisconsin, and Massachusetts Aves. It is well served by several Metro stops.

Washington National Cathedral

A national cathedral in a country founded on the separation of church and state is a provocative idea, so you know the National Cathedral (☎ 202-537-6200), Wisconsin Ave NW at Massachusetts (see Washington map), has to be an unusual place. Architecturally, the massive, high Gothic cathedral (sixth largest in the world) is intended to rival European scale and majesty, right down to the flying buttresses and individually designed gargoyles. It's home to one denomination – the Episcopal Church – but it strives to cover all the politically correct patriotic bases: There's affirmative action at the altar, a stained-glass window of Apollo 11, and each week prayers are devoted to a different state and religious tradition.

The national church was originally George Washington's idea, but took 83 years to complete. Martin Luther King, Jr, gave his last sermon here before being assassinated; now it's the standard place for state funerals and other high profile events.

Take the elevator to the **tower overlook** for a great view of Washington. The landscaped grounds include a fragrant herb garden and garden shop, and there's a great gift shop downstairs with many wonderful icons. Daily tours are offered, but the best way to experience the cathedral is to attend a service – all are invited and made welcome (the program cues you when to sit, stand, and other protocol). There are three services daily (donation requested). Take the Metro to the Tenleytown station, and then hop on the No 30, 32, 34, or 36 bus to the cathedral.

National Zoological Park

The Smithsonian zoo (☎ 202-357-2700, tape 202-673-4800), 3000 Connecticut Ave NW (see the Adams-Morgan map), was beautifully designed by Frederick Law Olmsted, who designed New York's Central Park. It follows the natural contour of its woodland canyon setting. The zoo's 130 acres hold lions, tigers, bears, and many other exotic residents, most in natural-habitat environments set along two sloping paths. The most famous resident is *Hsing-Hsing*, the giant panda, who, along with his former companion Ling-Ling (now dead) were gifts from China in 1972 (millions of visitors turned out to watch them mate).

The dozen zoo buildings include the Great Ape House, an aviary, a reptile house, and the newest additions, **Amazonia** (a replica of the Brazilian rain forest), and the **Think Tank**, which explores animal intelligence. From May to mid-September, buildings are open daily 9 am (some open at 10 am) to 6 pm, till 4:30 pm the rest of the year. The grounds are open longer; you can see the animals outside from 8 am to either 8 pm (May to mid-September) or 6 pm (rest of year). Parking is extremely limited. There is a great 'Zoo Bar' across the street. The closest Metro stop is Woodley Park/National Zoo, a nice third of a mile walk north from the station.

Rock Creek Park

Rock Creek Park drops a slice of wilderness into the center of urban Washington. The national park starts at the Potomac River and extends north through DC, first confined to the narrow corridor of Rock Creek until it expands to wide parkland in the Upper Northwest district. Terrific bike and hiking trails extend along its entire length, but most major recreational services (including park headquarters) are in the zone north of the zoo. Some sights can be reached by foot from a Metro station; most require a car to access easily.

Recreational services include guided nature walks and astronomy programs at the **nature center** and **planetarium** (☎ 202-426-6829), near Missouri and 27th Sts NW; they're open Wednesday to Sunday 9 am to 5 pm. There are also hiking and biking trails, an 18 hole golf course, tennis courts, and a rental horse stable (see Activities for details).

Historic sights in the park include the remains of Civil War forts (at Oregon Ave and Military Rd, and at 13th and Quackenbush Sts NW). On the creek at Tilden St, the 1820 **Pierce Mill** (☎ 202-426-6908, Metro: Van Ness/UDC) is open to visitors Wednesday to Sunday 8 am to 4:30 pm. The park's western **Soapstone Valley Park** extension (off Connecticut Ave at Albemarle St) preserves quarries where the area's original Algonquin residents obtained soapstone for shaping cookware.

The park's **Carter Barron Amphitheater** (☎ 202-426-6837), 16th St and Colorado Ave NW, holds summertime concerts. An **Art Barn** studio presents works by local artists. Park headquarters (☎ 202-426-6832), 5000 Glover Rd NW, are located near the nature center (open daily 9 am to 5 pm).

Nat'l Museum of Health & Medicine

On the grounds of the Walter Reed Army Medical Center at 6825 16th St N (at Aspen adjacent to Rock Creek Park), this peculiar collection (☎ 202-576-2348) includes such medical oddities as a gangrenous foot, a mummified two-headed infant, a tattooed human torso skin, and bone chips from Abe Lincoln's head, along with more conventional medical exhibits. It's free and open daily 10 am to 5:30 pm.

Hillwood Museum & Gardens

Heiress Marjorie Merriweather Post (of Post Toasties fame), once wed to the ambassador to the Soviet Union, amassed an imperial collection of Russian art now on display at her Hillwood estate (☎ 202-686-5807), 4155 Linnean Ave NW. A cafe serves Russian specialties (borsht, blintzes, cabbage) and an English afternoon tea. Guided tours are by advance reservation.

UPPER NORTHEAST

The upper northeast district is a largely uneventful residential district with neighborhoods that range from OK to not so great. It's dominated by the large campuses of Gallaudet University to the south and Catholic University further north (Trinity College is also nearby).

Gallaudet University

Established in 1864, Gallaudet University (☎ 202-651-5000; TDD 202-651-5359), 800 Florida Ave NE, is the world's only accredited liberal arts school for the hearing impaired. Student protests here in 1989 led to the appointment of the college's first hearing-impaired president. Few sports fans know that in 1894, Gallaudet football players invented the American football huddle to prevent their opponents from reading the sign language used to call the plays. Tours are available by advance reservation. Enter from 8th St.

National Shrine of the Immaculate Conception

This huge, strange church (☎ 202-526-8300), adjacent to Catholic University at Michigan Ave and 4th St NE, accommodates 6000 worshipers in what is the largest Catholic church in the Western Hemisphere. In addition to the church's unearthly size, the Marian shrine is a bizarre mix of Romanesque and Byzantine styles – from classical towers to a mosque-like dome, and minarets besides. Yet the mosaics, the stained glass, and a little grotto chapel downstairs taken singly are lovely. It's open daily 7 am to 7 pm.

Take the Metro to Brookland/CUA. When you exit the station, hook back around to Michigan Ave, and walk southwest up the hill till you spot the basilica looming on the horizon.

Brookland Gallery

The gallery (☎ 526-2927), 3624 12th St NE, displays African American art. It's open Tuesday to Saturday from noon to 6 pm. From the Brookland/CUA Metro stop, walk up Newton St to 12th St NE. Make a left and you'll see a green building that is the gallery.

Franciscan Monastery

The Franciscan Monastery (☎ 202-526-6800), 1400 Quincy St NE, maintains 44 acres of grounds that invite contemplation. In spring thousands of tulips bloom, and in June it's roses. Holy sights dot the grounds; there are catacombs too. The monks in residence lead tours Monday to Saturday, every hour on the hour except noon from 9 am to 4 pm.

From the Brookland/CUA Metro station, walk east on Monroe St to 14th St NE; go north on 14th St to Quincy. The monastery is on the right.

US National Arboretum

You can drive, bike, or walk through 400 acres of beautifully landscaped native and exotic plants at the 440-acre National Arboretum (☎ 202-475-4815; see the Washington map). Also see the **National Bonsai and Penjing Museum** (open 10 am to 3:30 pm). The grounds are open Monday to Friday 8 am to 5 pm, weekends 10 am to 5 pm. The flowering season from March through May is the best time to visit.

From the Stadium/Armory Metro station, take the B2 or B4 bus to the intersection of Bladensburg Rd and R St, and walk to the gate from there.

Kenilworth Aquatic Gardens

Kenilworth Aquatic Gardens (☎ 202-426-6905), 900 Anacostia Drive NE (see Greater Washington map), is the only national park devoted to aquatic plants. Displays include a beautiful selection of water lilies and other varieties of aquatic vegetation on over 40 ponds. The best time to see blooms is mid-July to mid-August; the water lily festival is the last Saturday in July. Admission is free.

From the Deanwood Metro station, walk along Douglas St to the pedestrian overpass, continue to Anacostia Ave, and turn right. By car, take New York Avenue (US 50) east across the Anacostia River; at the highway split, stay right towards Annapolis. Exit at Kenilworth Ave south (US 295), turn right on Douglas St, and follow signs to the gardens.

RIVERFRONT

The original site for the nation's capital was identified as the confluence of the Potomac and Anacostia Rivers. Today DC's southern riverfront ranges from the upscale waterfront at the Potomac side in southwest DC to the rough streets of southeastern DC along the Anacostia. Directly south of the Capitol there's the Navy Yard (home of the Navy Museum and Marine Corps Museum); directly east along E Capitol St is RFK Stadium (home of the Redskins).

Southwestern Waterfront

A riverside promenade runs along the Washington Channel parallel to Maine Ave SW from the vicinity of around 6th St to around 11th St SW. One side is lined with yachts, sailboats, and houseboats in a narrow marina, the other with park benches (a great spot to watch the sunset), a hotel, and several big and popular seafood restaurants (note the tour buses parked outside), a few with patio seating. More adventurous visitors continue past the end of the promenade to the open-air **seafood market**, where fisherfolk hawk the day's catch from floating barges. The **Arena Stage**, a popular theatrical venue, is near the southern end of the promenade. The theater is close to the Waterfront Metro stop, but to go to the seafood market you could also take the equally long walk from the L'Enfant Plaza station. The rugged walk south from the Jefferson Memorial or the Mint crosses under several imposing freeways and is not recommended (a cab is a better bet).

Across the channel there's **Potomac Park East**, a long narrow strip of green running from the Jefferson Memorial to the scenic promontory at Hains Point. (For Potomac Park *West*, see Mall sights.)

Military Sights

The **Washington Navy Yard**, built in 1800, stretches along the Anacostia River from 1st to 11th Sts SE. Here you'll find the **Navy Museum** (☎ 202-433-4882), the **Marine Corps Museum** (☎ 202-433-3534), and tours of the decommissioned destroyer USS *Barry*. Featuring submarines, guns, uniforms, and scale ship models, the Navy Museum is the more interesting of the two. It's open Monday to Friday 9 am to 4 pm, weekends 10 am to 5 pm. The Marine Museum is open Monday to Saturday 10 am to 4 pm, and Sunday from noon to 5 pm (possibly extended hours in summer). Both museums are free. From the Navy Yard Metro, exit onto M St, and walk east to 9th St to enter.

For an offbeat sight, check out the entombed leg of Colonel Ulric Dahlgren nearby. Dahlgren, son of a Washington Navy Yard commander, lost his leg at Gettysburg. His father made sure his son's leg was given full honors at its interment. A plaque marks the site on Isaac Hull Ave. (From the Navy Museum exit, walk to the right three blocks, turn right on Isaac Hull, and walk down to the fire hydrant.)

The Eighth & Eye **Marine Corps Bar-**

racks are home to the Marine Corps commandant (☎ 202-433-6060), where you can catch a two-hour parade drill Friday evenings at 8:45 pm during the summer. Call at least three weeks in advance for reservations, or send a request to the Adjutant, Marine Corps Barracks, Washington, DC 20390, or just show up at the general admission line at 7 pm before the drill. The closest Metro stop (three blocks south) is Eastern Market.

ANACOSTIA

A district of DC across the Anacostia River, Anacostia is named after its Native American inhabitants – recorded by Europeans as Nacothtant or Anaquashtank, the name was later corrupted to Anacostia. A European settlement here predated Washington – in fact, the Native American trading village here drew famed Captain John Smith as early as 1608.

Before the Civil War, it was the home of a large free black community, and after the war, many freed slaves settled here. The village was incorporated into DC in 1854, and in 1877 abolitionist Frederick Douglass moved in. Parts of Anacostia developed into a middle-class African American community by the end of the century, and a few quiet middle-class neighborhoods remain.

Yet years of decline have now earned the district a reputation for violent crime (over a quarter of the murders in DC happen here). Visitors should use extra caution; you might want to consider an organized tour.

Frederick Douglass National Historic Site

Cedar Hill (☎ 202-426-5960), 1411 West St SE, was the home of abolitionist, author, diplomat, and former slave Frederick Douglass from 1877 until his death in 1895. Here Douglass wrote *The Life and Times of Frederick Douglass*, and today the house still contains most of his original furnishings, right down to his wire-rim eyeglasses on the roll-top desk. After his first wife died, Douglass sealed off her room, and Douglass was the last one to use it for 80 years until it was opened again in 1962.

Start at the visitors center embedded in the foot of the hill; here you can see a short biographical film and buy related books and gifts. Admission and house tours are free. From April 15 to October 15, it's open daily 9 am to 5 pm, the rest of the year until 4 pm.

From the Anacostia Metro, you can take

From Slave to Statesman: Frederick Douglass

Born a slave in 1817 on a plantation outside of Easton in Maryland, Frederick Douglass lived a life that eventually led him to prominent government posts such as US Marshal for the District of Columbia and US minister to Haiti. Aside from these prominent positions, Americans remember Douglass as the country's most outstanding African American leader during the 19th century.

When he was 21 years old, he escaped wretched treatment at the hands of Maryland planters and established himself as a freeman among a community of sympathetic Quakers in the booming whaling port of New Bedford, Massachusetts. Largely self-educated, Douglass had a natural gift for eloquence. In 1841 he won the admiration of New England abolitionists when he delivered an impromptu speech at an antislavery convention, introducing himself as 'a recent graduate from the institution of slavery with his diploma [whipping marks] on his back.' Thereafter, abolitionists hired Douglass as an agent for the Massachusetts Anti-Slavery Society for which he traveled the free states speaking a B2 or B4 bus right to the house, but the bus stop and route for the return trip is less convenient. It's better to take a cab.

Anacostia Museum

This Smithsonian museum (☎ 202-357-2700), 1901 Fort Place SE, expanded from a neighborhood museum to a regional heritage center celebrating African American history and culture in the 'Upper South' through exhibitions, education, and interpretive programs. It's free and open daily 10 am to 5 pm.

From the Anacostia Metro stop, you can take the W1 or W2 bus to the museum.

ACTIVITIES

For outdoor recreation, residents head primarily to Rock Creek Park and the C&O Canal (see C&O sidebar), both in the northwest section. You can also find boating activities on the Potomac River and some activities on the Mall.

Biking

A 10-mile paved bike path runs from below the Kennedy Center to Pierce Mill, largely along the wooded creek in Rock Creek Park. (The park's Beach Drive between Military and Broad Branch Rds is closed to vehicles from 7 am Saturday to 7 pm Sunday.)

The C&O Canal towpath also makes a great bike route, particularly for mountain bikes – it starts in Georgetown and stretches nearly 185 miles (barring flood damage – see C&O sidebar below).

Bike rentals are available at Thompson Boat Center (see Boating section below and Georgetown map).

Big Wheel Bikes, at 1034 33rd St NW in Georgetown (☎ 202-337-0254) and 315 7th St SE in Capitol Hill (☎ 202-543-1600), rents racing bikes by the hour/day for $4/20 and mountain bikes for $5/25 (three-hour minimum rental). Both stores open weekdays 10 am to 8 pm and weekends to 6 pm.

Several good books describe local bike tours, such as *Short Bike Rides in and around Washington, DC* by Michael Leccese (Globe Pequot Press) and *25 Bicycle Tours in and around Washington* by Ann M. Oman (Backcountry Publications). Another good source is *ADC's Washington Area Bike Map* by the Metropolitan Washington Council of Governments. You can find this and other good maps and guides at the Map Store (☎ 202-628-2608), 1636 I St NW.

memorably for the abolition of slavery and energizing the Underground Railroad to carry runaway slaves to freedom.

Douglass so angered the proslavery establishment in America that his friends urged him to flee to England to escape seizure and punishment under the recently enacted Fugitive Slave Law. Douglass continued lecturing against slavery in England and became so popular that admirers contributed money to purchase his freedom in the States. After Douglass returned to the US in 1847 he became the self-proclaimed 'station master and conductor' of the Underground Railroad in Rochester, New York. During the decade preceding the Civil War, Douglass worked with other prominent abolitionists like Harriet Tubman and John Brown. But Douglass broke with Brown when he learned of the zealot's disastrous plans to attack the federal armory at Harpers Ferry, West Virginia.

In 1860 Douglass campaigned for Abraham Lincoln's election to the Presidency. When war broke out Douglass helped raise two regiments of black soldiers, the Massachusetts 54th and 55th (see the film *Glory* with Denzel Washington) to fight for the Union cause. After the Union won the war, Douglass went to Washington to lend his support to the 13th, 14th, and 15th Constitutional Amendments, which abolish slavery, grant citizenship to former slaves, and guarantee all citizens the right to vote exclusive of their race or color.

His Anacostia hilltop residence is now a national historic site open to the public and operated by the National Park Service. ■

Hiking & Jogging

Fifteen miles of well-marked day-hike trails traverse Rock Creek Park's 2100 acres in DC. These range in difficulty from easy to strenuous; loop trips are possible. The C&O Canal National Historical Park also has many trails and the towpath (see C&O sidebar); a popular four-mile roundtrip runs between Fletcher's Boathouse and Key Bridge in Georgetown. The Mall is also a popular jogging route. Of course, the most exclusive jog in town is the track on the White House lawn installed at President Clinton's request. A 1.5-mile **Parcourse** exercise trail runs behind the Omni Shoreham Hotel (Metro: Woodley Park), stopping at 18 exercise stations.

Boating

Boaters head to the Potomac River and the C&O Canal. Rent canoes (and bikes) at Thompson Boat Center (☎ 202-333-4861), 2900 Virginia Ave NW (on the Potomac north of the Kennedy Center; see Georgetown map). It's open weekdays 6:30 am to 6 pm, weekends 8 am to 5 pm. Canoes, rowboats, and bikes can also be rented from Fletcher's Boathouse (☎ 202-244-0461), upriver at 4940 Canal Rd NW.

Golf

DC has two public golf courses, one near downtown and one in the Upper Northwest district. The East Potomac Park Golf Course (☎ 202-863-9007) south of the Jefferson Memorial on Potomac Park East offers a par 72 18-hole course and two nine-hole courses (open dawn to dusk year round, first-come, first-served). Greens fees for nine/18 holes are $6/11, club rental $5/9. It also offers a driving range and miniature golf. The Rock Creek Golf Course (☎ 202-882-7332) offers two nine-hole courses that may be played as one 18-hole course (open daily from dawn to dusk, first-come, first-served). Fees for nine/18 holes are $6/11 for weekdays, $7/13 for weekends; cart $9/15; club rental $5/7.

Horseback Riding

Rock Creek Park has 11 miles of bridle paths. The Rock Creek Park Horse Center (☎ 202-362-0117), at Military and Glover Rds NW, rents horses for guided trips. It's open Tuesday to Friday from 1 to 8 pm, weekends from 10 am to 6 pm.

Swimming

Of the 35 outdoor and 11 indoor free public pools in Washington, try the one in Georgetown (☎ 202-282-2366) at 34th St and Volta Place NW; the indoor Capitol East pool (☎ 202-724-4495) at 635 North Carolina Ave SE in Capitol Hill; or the Marie Reed pool (☎ 202-673-7771) at 2200 Champlain St NW near the foot of 18th St in Adams-Morgan.

Ice Skating

The small Sculpture Garden Ice Rink (☎ 202-371-5340) on the Mall at Constitution Ave and 7th St NW (across from the National Archives) offers a homey ice-skating scene from November to March (weather depending), generally from 10 am to 11 pm. The rink plays tinny oldies music and attracts languid teens – a pretty whimsical touch to the monumental Mall. Admission is $4 to $5 adults, $3 to $4 children and seniors. Skate rentals cost $2.50 per two-hour session.

If the ice is thick enough, you can also skate on the Reflecting Pool and on the C&O Canal in Georgetown; bring your own skates.

Tennis

The city maintains more than 50 free public tennis courts throughout DC; for information and a permit, call the DC Department of Parks and Recreation (☎ 202-673-7671), 3149 16th St NW.

ORGANIZED TOURS

Bus & Shuttle

Tourmobile Sightseeing (☎ 202-554-7950) regularly runs trams around major monuments and museums; their running commentary focuses on practical information (what it is, when it's open, does it have food service, how to get elsewhere). You can just regard it as convenient transit (or a scenic mobile rest while you eat a takeout lunch from Union Station) if you don't mind being among throngs of camera-swinging tourists. Get on and off as often as you like for an all-day fee ($12 adults, $6 children – get a day and a half of use by purchasing after 2 pm).

Other general and specialty tours include Gray Line (☎ 202-289-1995), offering a black heritage tour and the largest number of foreign-language tours (Japanese, French, Italian, German, and Spanish); Old Town Trolley Tours (☎ 301-985-3020), on-off service available; and Scandal Tours (☎ 301-587-4291), which delivers the dirt on DC's infamous spots.

Land, Water & Sky

DC Ducks (☎ 202-966-3825) recycles amphibious vehicles into land/water city tours. For river tours, try Spirit Cruises (☎ 202-554-8000), departing from 6th and Water Sts SW (this runs tours to Mount Vernon). Liberty Helicopter Tours (☎ 202-863-0455), 1724 S Capitol St SE, does fly-overs of the city at a premium.

SPECIAL EVENTS

The city is best known for its Cherry Blossom Festival in March–April and for the Smithsonian's Folklife Festival in June. And of course, Independence Day is always a big event. For a full calendar, contact the Washington Visitors Center (☎ 202-789-7038). Here are some highlights:

January

Martin Luther King's Birthday, third Monday. Orators recite King's 'I Have a Dream' speech at the Lincoln Memorial (☎ 202-619-7222).

Robert E Lee's Birthday, January 22. 19th century festivities, a tour, and cake at Arlington House. Admission fee (☎ 703-548-8454).

February

Abraham Lincoln's Birthday, February 12. Hear the Gettysburg Address read at the Lincoln Memorial (☎ 202-619-7222).

Chinese New Year's Parade, mid-February. Dances and firecrackers light up Chinatown.

March

St Patrick's Day Parade, around March 17. Revelers parade down Constitution Ave NW.

Smithsonian Kite Festival, late March. Kite designers, flyers, and competitors gather on the Mall for this rite of spring (☎ 202-357-3244).

National Cherry Blossom Festival, late March to early April. This two-week-long arts and culture fest celebrates the blooming of thousands of DC's cherry trees. It all culminates in a parade extravaganza (☎ 202-737-2599).

April

White House Easter Egg Roll, Easter Monday. The Easter Egg roll on the White House grounds is hosted by the First Lady for children under 8. Enter at the East Gate on E Executive Ave (☎ 202-619-7222).

American College Theater Festival, late April. The best college shows appear at the Kennedy Center. Tickets are free (☎ 202-416-8850).

Washington Craft Show, mid-month. Crafts people show their work at the Smithsonian Department Auditorium, 14th St and Constitution Ave NW (☎ 202-357-4000).

May

Georgetown House Tour. Historic houses are opened to the public (☎ 202-338-4678).

Filmfest DC, early May. Local and international art films premier in area cinemas (☎ 202-727-2396).

Goodwill Embassy Tour, mid-month. Daylong open house of embassies (☎ 202-636-4225).

Greek Spring Festival, mid-month; also in mid-September. A celebration of Greek food and culture is held at Saints Helen and Constantine Church, 4115 16th St NW (☎ 202-829-2910).

Memorial Day, late May. Commemorative programs at Arlington Cemetery and the Vietnam Memorial.

June

Gay Pride Day, date varies. Gays, lesbians, and their friends and families march through DC (☎ 202-298-0970).

Festival of American Folk Life, last weekend in June and first weekend in July. The Smithsonian hosts this famous gathering of American regional groups. Crafts, food, music, and dance on the Mall (☎ 202-357-2700).

July

Independence Day, July 4. Colonial troops parade, the Declaration of Independence is read aloud, musicians play concerts, and fireworks explode over the Potomac (☎ 202-357-2700).

Latin American Festival, late July. Salsa and samba surround the Washington Monument. There's plenty of music, food, and shows (☎ 202-319-1340).

September

Adams-Morgan Day, first Sunday after Labor Day. A huge international block party with global music, food, and crafts along and around 18th St NW and Columbia Rd (☎ 202-332-3292).

National Frisbee Festival, early September. Folks toss Frisbees on the mall, so watch your head (☎ 202-485-7275).

Greek Fall Festival, mid-month; also in mid-May. A celebration of Greek food and culture at Saints Helen and Constantine Church, 4115 16th St NW (☎ 202-829-2910).

African Cultural Festival. A celebration of Africa, with crafts, food, music, and dance at Freedom Plaza on 14th St and Pennsylvania Ave NW (☎ 202-667-5775).

DC Blues Festival. Free blues concerts take place in outdoor venues around town (☎ 202-724-4091).

November

Veterans Day, November 11. Special programs at Arlington Cemetery and the Vietnam Memorial honor veterans.

December

Kennedy Center Holiday Celebration, December 1 to January 1. Plenty of free seasonal music and activities, including gospel and a *Messiah* sing-along (☎ 202-416-8000).

National Christmas Tree Lighting, second Thursday in December. The President illuminates the national Christmas tree and lights a menorah on the Ellipse (☎ 202-619-7222).

New Year's Eve, December 31. Outdoor partying at the Old Post Office (☎ 202-289-4224).

PLACES TO STAY

DC offers the complete range of accommodations, from dormitory-style hostels to five-star hotels. When inquiring about room rates, bear in mind that DC is overall a business town, so hotel rates will be highest during the business week and will drop dramatically (sometimes by as much as half) on weekends and during summer (guesthouses or B&Bs, on the other hand, maintain fairly constant rates year round). The tourist season runs roughly from April 1 through September – with a peak start in April for the cherry blossom spell and a drop in August due to the heat. The business season starts earlier in spring and runs later in fall, virtually disappearing in the summer. Play any card for a discounted rate – even *museum* membership can earn you a discount at some DC motels (mention professional associations, veteran status, any government or NGO affiliation). The city assesses an 11% tax plus $1.50 per room per night on accommodations.

Wherever you choose to stay, close proximity to a Metro station greatly increases your ability to get around with ease. See below for lodging downtown and in neighborhoods at the low end (hostelries and hotels under $55), middle (rates under $100), and top end ($100 and up). Some rates include tax, and prices do vary depending on shared versus private baths, so categories are approximate.

Convenient Areas

Though downtown prime locations (including Capitol Hill and the Mall area) are convenient to major sites, most become fairly lifeless once the workers have gone home. The northwestern neighborhoods are lively at night, but you'll need transportation to major sights. You could stay around Dupont Circle and seek out the many less-traveled sights right in the area. The Adams-Morgan neighborhood offers the most reasonable rates at several guesthouses not too far from the Metro, but it might be too far out or raggedy for some. The Foggy Bottom district has less neighborhoody appeal, but it's closer in and right on the Metro – and consequently more pricey. Then there's Georgetown, which isn't convenient to the Metro; it's also pricey and quite congested, though this doesn't seem to diminish its popularity. You could also consider budget motels at the outskirts of town.

Referrals

For citywide B&B lodging, you can find referrals through Bed & Breakfast Accommodations (☎ 202-328-3510) and the Bed & Breakfast League (☎ 202-363-7767). For foreign students, the Foreign Student

Service Council (☎ 202-232-4979), 3259 Prospect St in Georgetown, can arrange two- to three-day homestays with American families ($15 processing fee, and the council can fax applications). For homestays for $20 a night and up including kitchen privileges, call and drop by the Women's Information Bank (also known as Bed & Bread; ☎ 202-338-1863), at 3918 W St NW above Georgetown in the Glover Park neighborhood off the D2 bus line, one block southeast of 39th and Benton Sts NW; ring the bell.

Places to Stay – bottom end

Camping There are no campgrounds in DC. The nearest one is in *Cherry Hill Park* (☎ 301-937-7116) northeast of town in College Park, Maryland. It has 360 sites and a pool; sites cost $25 for two tent campers ($3 each additional person) and $34 for RVs. It's open year round; call for reservations in the summer. The minimum drive time into downtown DC is 15 minutes, but expect longer. A better bet is taking a bus from the campground to the College Park Metro stop; both the bus and the Metro run throughout the day.

Greenbelt Park (☎ 301-344-3948), 12 miles northeast of DC at 6565 Greenbelt Rd, operates a 168-site campground (no hook-ups). Sites cost $10 per night. A city pool and showers are available down the road for a minimum charge.

Hostels The *Washington International AYH/HI Hostel* (☎ 202-737-2333), 1009 11th St NW at K St, is the main hostel for the worldwide Hostelling International organization headquartered here in DC. The eight-story hostel (24-hour access) provides dormitory lodging for 300 on men's and women's floors (eight-bunk rooms, some handicapped access, sleepsacks required, available by loan). Facilities include modern, clean bathrooms and kitchen, coin-operated laundry, a tiny store, comfortable common dining and lounging rooms (with TV), and a dank smokers' room in the basement. It's a central gathering place and resource for many traveling students and other HI-types, though it's isolated four blocks north of Metro Center in a nothing-happening area (safe enough). The charge is $18 members, $21 nonmembers, with a $5 deposit, reservations and ID required. From the Metro Center station, go north on 11th St NW to the flag-flying hostel.

On Capitol Hill, *Thompson-Markwood Hall* (☎ 202-546-3255) 235 2nd St NE at C St, is open to women 18 to 34 years old in DC for work or study. The minimum stay is two weeks; the charge of $138.95 per week ($595 per month) includes two meals a day (one on Sunday) and covers a small comfortable room with a phone and a shared bath. There's a spacious patio and yard. No alcohol, smoking, or male guests above lobby-level common areas.

In Adams-Morgan, *Washington International Backpackers* (☎ 202-667-7681), 2451 18th St NW, provides no-frills dormitory lodging in a worn walk-up building, four small bedrooms (six to eight beds per room, triple bunks, linen provided), three OK bathrooms, a comfortable common room with cable TV, makeshift kitchen facilities, bike rentals, and a small breakfast. It's upstairs from one of the liveliest blocks in DC (cafes, stores, clubs). It costs $15 a night per person – the cheapest place in town – and you come and go as you please with your own key. Free pickup from train or bus station is available by advance request.

In Dupont Circle, *Davis House* (☎ 202-232-3196, fax 202-232-3197), 1822 R St NW, is an older row house on a quiet residential street run by the American Friends Service Committee for international visitors, AFSC staff, and those 'working on peace and justice concerns' by advance reservation. No private baths, smoking, or alcohol, and no kitchen. Singles/doubles cost $35/60.

Across the street, the *International Student House* (☎ 202-387-6445, fax 202-387-4115), 1825 R St NW, offers 90 guests an 'in-depth experience in international living.' You're expected to stay a minimum of three months during the summer and four otherwise. Rates include breakfast and dinner and start at $600 a month for shared rooms with phones (higher for single room, private bath, parking). There are comfortable common areas (library, piano room) with Tudor accents, and a walled courtyard.

In the Upper Northwest (a four-mile bus trip from downtown), the *International Guest House* (☎ 202-726-5808), 1441 Kennedy St NW, offers five neat and clean guest rooms with two beds each for $25 per adult, $12.50 for children six to 16 (under six free). The cost includes a breakfast of cereal and homemade muffins and evening tea. There's a common room, large backyard, and some off-street parking. But note the early curfew: The house shuts at 11 pm and opens back up at 7 am. Sunday it closes midday 10 am to 2 pm. No drinking or smoking. To get there from the White House area, take the S2 or S4 bus up 16th St to Kennedy St.

Guesthouses In Adams-Morgan, the *Adams Inn* (☎ 202-745-3600, 800-578-6807), 1744 Lanier Place NW, converted two side-by-side townhouses and a carriage house on a shady residential street into a welcoming guesthouse with cozy common areas (porch, living rooms, patio). Homey walk-up rooms are modestly furnished with old Asian carpets, and there are modern bathrooms; no phones or TVs in rooms. You can get coffee and doughnuts around the clock and access to kitchen facilities, coin laundry, and pay phones. Room prices include continental breakfast and run from $55 for a single/double with shared bath to $70 for private bath. It's a half block from the intersection of Calvert and 18th Sts, a 10-minute walk from the Woodley Park Metro.

A few blocks away off Columbia Rd, the *Kalorama Guest House* (☎ 202-667-6369) at 1854 Mintwood Place NW (a couple blocks south of 18th St) offers continental breakfast and afternoon sherry along with comfortable rooms in a brick townhouse with some Victorian frills. Rooms range from $55 to $105, and half have private baths.

Across Rock Creek Park from Adams-Morgan, the compact Woodley Park neighborhood is convenient to the Metro, Zoo, and a dozen places to eat and gather (even a local blues club). The Sheraton and Omni Hotels are here, along with such lower-priced guesthouses as another *Kalorama Guest House* (☎ 202-328-0860), 2700 Cathedral Ave NW (similar to above).

Also in Woodley Park, the old-fashioned *Connecticut-Woodley Guest House* (☎ 202-667-0218), 2647 Woodley Rd NW, looks like grandma's house – metal awnings, flowery water-stained wallpaper, worn carpets and furniture arranged haphazardly, sunken twin beds with chenille spreads, tidy but not super-clean. It's friendly and overlooks the Sheraton's green lawn. Free parking too. Singles/doubles with shared bath are $42 to $46/48 to $51; add around $14 for a private bath. Group rates are a real bargain: A triple with shared bath is $55, a quadruple $57. From the Woodley Park/National Zoo Metro station exit, turn around, walk to Woodley Rd and turn left; it's on your right.

Hotels In Foggy Bottom, the *Allen Lee Hotel* (☎ 202-331-1224), 2224 F St NW, offers friendly service and clean rooms with phones, TVs, and worn furnishings. Rates include taxes – singles/doubles without bath are $35/46; with bath, $46/57 (extra cots $5.65). From the Foggy Bottom Metro station, go right and walk three blocks south on 23rd St; it's at the corner of 23rd and F Sts.

In Chinatown, the *Comfort Inn* (☎ 202-289-5959, 500 H St N, Metro: Gallery Place/Chinatown) has a sauna, coin laundry, paid parking, and a plodding elevator (opt for a walkable floor). Singles/doubles start at $79/89; the weekend rate is $59. Both the hotel and neighborhood were recently undergoing much-needed renovation.

The *Hotel Harrington* (☎ 202-628-8140, 800-424-8532), at the corner of 11th and E Sts NW in downtown, is a favorite budget choice a block from Ford's Theater. It's popular with scout troops, school groups, marching bands, tourist families, and small-time salespeople. The 12-story hotel offers basic rooms with private baths for $69/79 single/double.

Located strategically across from the Watergate complex (just across the creek from Georgetown; see Mall & Downtown map), *Howard Johnson's* (☎ 202-965-2700; fax 202-965-2700, ext 7910), 2601 Virginia Ave NW, is notorious as the Plumbers' lookout (ask for Room 723 to be part of history); rates start at $79. A much-needed renovation was recently in progress.

If you have a car, you're striking out elsewhere, and you don't mind the lousy area, there's a strip of cheap chain motels along the tracks of New York Ave NE. Predictable presences include the *Super 8 Motel* (☎ 202-543-7400), 501 New York Ave NE, with singles/doubles around $55/65; *HoJo Inn* (☎ 202-546-9200), 600 New York Ave, with singles/doubles $60/65; *Budget Motor Inn* (☎ 202-529-3900), 1615 New York Ave NE, with singles/doubles $45/55; and *Days Inn* (☎ 202-832-5800), 2700 New York Ave NE, singles/doubles $71/78 (including tax).

Places to Stay – middle

Unfortunately, midrange hotels in DC often charge around $100 a night for a room with private bath (though again, you can find lower weekend rates, special discounts, and packages). Kitchenettes can help you lower the cost of eating out.

Downtown On Capitol Hill, the *Bellevue Hotel* (☎ 202-638-0900, fax 202-638-5132), 15 E St NW near N Capitol St, is a good midrange choice where singles run $89 to $109 and doubles $109 to $134. Nearby on the Hill, the *Quality Hotel* (☎ 202-638-1616), 415 New Jersey Ave NW, offers rates of $99-159 single or double. Find both a block east of Union Station.

Downtown near the hostel, the *Swiss Inn* (☎ 202-371-1816, 800-955-7947), 1204 Massachusetts Ave NW, operates out of a worn but homey brownstone house in a somewhat isolated area four blocks from Metro Center. Rooms with kitchenettes, private baths, telephones, TVs, laundry access, and a manager bilingual in Swiss-German range from $98 to $108.

More centrally located *Lincoln Suites Downtown* (☎ 202-223-4320, 800-424-2970, fax 202-223-8546), 1823 L St NW, was remodeled in 1996 to provide rooms with kitchens, TVs, coffee and tea. Rates starting at $109 single or double include free continental breakfast on weekends and free access to a nearby health club. Lincoln Suites is 1½ blocks west of Connecticut Ave on the border of Dupont Circle (see Dupont Circle map).

Set apart at DC's waterfront, the modern *Channel Inn* (☎ 202-554-2400, fax 202-863-1164), 650 Water St SW at 9th St SW, offers spacious rooms, many with balconies overlooking the channel (particularly nice at sunset), and a seasonal pool. The hotel anchors a strip of seafood restaurants that attracts busloads of senior tourists. Singles/doubles are $110/120; weekend rates start at $85.

Neighborhoods In Dupont Circle, the *Tabard Inn* (☎ 202-785-1277, fax 202-785-6173), 1739 N St NW, retains the original quirky charm of an old Victorian townhouse – separate hot and cold faucets, armoires, iron bedsteads, vintage overstuffed couches, and maybe even an old upright in the corner of your room. The style is hippie tweed, rustic gentility. There's a great restaurant and bar downstairs, with a lounge seemingly designed for fomenting armchair revolutions over glasses of vintage port. Rooms with shared bath are $59 to $79; with private bath, $99 to $140. Lots of complaints about the service add to its mystique.

In a more removed residential area in Dupont, the *Carlyle Suites* (☎ 202-234-3200, fax 202-387-0085), 1731 New Hampshire Ave NW (at S St), has 170 small suites (some would say cozy, others might think cramped) with kitchenettes, all in a mod Art Deco style; downstairs there's a gleaming cafe/bar. Rates for singles/doubles hover around $119/129 (children under 18 stay free with parents). They advertise quite a bit in gay newspapers.

In the west end, the *Inn at Foggy Bottom* (☎ 202-337-6620), 824 New Hampshire Ave NW, is a nice centrally located choice. Rates begin at $79/94 for singles/doubles during the summer; $90/105 in the winter; weekend rates are $49/99.

Places to Stay – top end

South of the Mall, *Loews L'Enfant Plaza Hotel*, (☎ 202-484-1000, 800-243-1166), 480 L'Enfant Plaza SW, provides upscale family-friendly lodging above a central Metro station two long blocks south of most Smithsonian museums, which offers tremendous convenience for visitors to popular DC sights. Rates may range from single/double $149/169 to $99 specials for a three-day minimum stay (inquire about packages). The hotel hosts an annual Bark Ball for dogs and gives kids a Back House hotel tour. A heated bubble converts an outdoor pool for year-round use.

On Capitol Hill across from Union Station, the *Phoenix Park Hotel* (☎ 202-638-6900, fax 202-393-3286), 520 N Capitol St NW, offers Irish hospitality along with 88 neatly appointed rooms. It's owned by an Irish firm, along with the brogue-filled *Powerscourt* cafe and the *Dubliner* pub downstairs. The high 'rack' rate of $169 drops to $100 for government business, down to $88 to $118 on weekends.

A couple blocks north of the Washington Convention Center, the *Morrison Clark* (☎ 202-898-1200, 800-332-7898), Massachusetts Ave NW at 11th St, is an elegant historic hotel set in an expansive 1864 mansion with a well-regarded Southern dining room. Its 54 rooms and suites are tastefully appointed with Victorian accents and all modern conveniences. Singles/doubles cost $135/155, more for suites. It's in a somewhat isolated area.

Of the many big business-oriented hotels clustered north of Washington Circle in Foggy Bottom, the *ANA Hotel* (that's A-N-A, ☎ 202-429-2400), 2401 M St NW, offers a comprehensive health club on site. The Japanese-owned hotel (note traditional Japanese breakfast offerings) has large rooms, a fancy restaurant, and a large atrium lobby; weekend packages start at $149 a night, standard weekday rates are more like $265.

Right across the creek in Georgetown, the lively *Four Seasons Hotel* (☎ 202-342-0444), 2800 Pennsylvania Ave NW, caters to the upscale (room rates start at $290), but it's less stiff than ritzy hotels downtown – at Sunday brunch you might find a mix of college couples, blue-blood families in sporty Land's End separates, and international corporate executives.

DC's most exclusive hotels (including also the Hotel Washington, the Ritz-Carlton, the Madison, and the Jefferson) cater to dignitaries and the corporate aristocracy; on a walk through their lobbies or at the bar you may spot celebrity power-brokers sealing deals.

In fact, President Grant originally coined the term 'lobbyist' (so the story goes) for the political wranglers hanging out in the lobby of the historic Willard Hotel. Today known as the *Willard Intercontinental* (☎ 202-628-9100, 800-327-0200, fax 202-637-7326), 1401 Pennsylvania Ave NW, the luxuriously restored 1904 marble hotel (the third on this site) has housed 10 American presidents in its various incarnations, including Lincoln, Harding, and Coolidge; and Julia Ward Howe wrote the lyrics to the 'Battle Hymn of the Republic' here during the Civil War. The Willard has a great Round Robin bar, Nest Lounge jazz nights (hotel guests receive jazz CDs), and afternoon tea. It's been recognized for outstanding handicapped access. Standard weekday rates for singles/doubles of $290/320 can drop to $139 on the weekend.

Another landmark on DC's political landscape is across from the White House – the refined *Hay Adams Hotel* (☎ 202-636-6800, fax 202-638-2716), 800 16th St NW, overlooking Lafayette Square. Reportedly Colonel Oliver North solicited contributions for the Contras while dining here with interested parties. Rooms start at $180.

The claim to fame of the *Vista Hotel* (☎ 202-429-1700), 1400 M St NW near

Dupont Circle, is that it was where federal agents caught Mayor Marion Barry smoking crack with an ex-girlfriend. Though some weekend rates start at $89, standard weekday rates are around $230 (if that notoriety is worth it to you).

Dating from 1924 but less exclusive than in years past, the *Mayflower Hotel* (☎ 202-347-3000, fax 202-466-9082), 1127 Connecticut Ave NW, remains a regal landmark south of Dupont Circle. During the Kennedy administration, the Secret Service reportedly knew Suite 812 as 'JFK's playpen.' There's a Starbucks coffee stand in the grand lobby; also check out the inaugural ballroom. Room rates start at $195.

The *Watergate Hotel* (☎ 202-965-2300, fax 202-337-7915), 2650 Virginia Ave NW, housed the notorious 'Plumbers' of the Watergate scandal in 1972, but the elite hotel takes such infamy in stride. The modern building is decorated with antiques and checkerboard marble; amenities include its acclaimed restaurant, health club, and service. Rooms start at $230 single, $255 double; most overlook the Potomac.

PLACES TO EAT

Relative to other costs, food is pretty expensive in DC – not as expensive as New York, for example, but more expensive than San Francisco. In general, you'd be lucky to find a decent dinner plate of sauced pasta for under $9, and even takeout deli lunches with a soda can climb to $7 or $8 in a hurry. So you really have to seek out the bargains. Fortunately, plenty of ethnic eateries offer hearty low-priced meals, many of them vegetarian. Shop at markets and carry your own snacks, water, and picnic tools to keep expenses to the barest minimum.

Congressional ethics laws designed to blunt the power of lobbyist largess limited Washington's revered 'gift lunch' tradition to $10 as of January 1996 – expect a sudden profusion of entrees in the $9.95 range at DC restaurants popular with politicos.

Farmers Markets DC's farmers markets are great places to find fresh produce, meats, seafood, and flowers, and they often offer interesting sights besides. You can usually find prepared foods there or nearby too. Most open at 7 or 8 am, and close around 5 or 6 pm (with shorter hours on Sunday).

Eastern Market (☎ 202-543-7293), 7th St SE at North Carolina Ave on Capitol Hill, encloses food stalls selling produce, meats, and fish; there's also a popular greasy spoon breakfast joint inside, a crafts and flea market on weekends, and cafes all around.

Hawkers at the floating barge market at the Waterfront's *Maine St Pier* (off Maine St SW under the freeway overpass), advertise fresh seafood on ice, including ready-to-eat cracked crab.

The small open-air *farmers market* (☎ 717-573-4527) at Columbia Rd and 18th St NW in Adams-Morgan, open Saturdays from 7 am to 5 pm year round, draws an international crowd.

Also look for the *DC Farmers Market* (☎ 202-547-3142), 5th St and Neal Place NE, open daily year round; and the *DC Open Air Farmers Market* (☎ 202-728-2800) at RFK Stadium (Oklahoma Ave and Banning Rd NE) on Thursday and Saturday year round (also Tuesday July to September).

A couple of excellent grocery stores merit mention. In Georgetown, try the *French Market* at 1632 Wisconsin Ave NW for wine, cheese, meat, and other provisions, or *Dean & DeLuca* at 3276 M St for (higher priced) produce and imported products. There's another Dean & DeLuca downtown on E St between 12th and 13th Sts NW.

Food Courts Although 'food courts' have a bad name in the US (associated with the chain restaurant junk food found in generic shopping malls), DC's best food courts are decent places where you can find a variety of inexpensive food to eat quickly (particularly with kids in tow). You can commonly find vegetarian Indian curries, sushi, burritos, Chinese stir-fry, and fruit smoothies among more traditional American choices. Downtown, you'll find popular food courts on Capitol Hill at *Union Station*, at the *Old*

Post Office (Pennsylvania Ave at 12th St), and at the shops at *National Place* (Press Club Building on 14th St at F St). South of the Mall, L'Enfant Plaza Metro station also connects directly with subterranean delis, cafes, markets, and shops.

Large government buildings typically have cafeterias designed for their employees that are also open to the public for inexpensive American fare (you may have to pass through security, and the ambiance is usually fluorescent and utilitarian). Exceptional spots include the 6th floor cafeteria at the *Library of Congress Madison Building*, catered by different DC restaurants, and the exclusive *Senate dining room* in the Capitol (obtain passes in advance from your Congressional representative). Or befriend a Congressional staffer to hook into the free-hors-d'oeuvres circuit, compliments of one reception or another.

Capitol Hill

On Capitol Hill, you will find your greatest food choices in and around Union Station off Massachusetts Ave NE, along Pennsylvania Ave SE between 2nd and 4th Sts, and around Eastern Market southeast of the Capitol (the following guide roughly follows that north-to-south order).

Budget to Middle Besides the great food court on Union Station's lower level (cheap eats from dahl and chiles rellenos to Chesapeake Bay oysters), upstairs find *America*, a restaurant with seating at the bar, on a narrow mezzanine, or at tables spilling out into the cavernous station. Regional specialties (Mississippi fried catfish, Midwestern patty melt, Boston cream pie) run around $10 per entree.

A block west of Union Station, the *Dubliner* (☎ 202-737-3773), 520 N Capitol St at F St, is DC's best Irish pub (in the 'classic' category; find *Kelly's Irish Times* next door for a younger crowd), offering live Irish music, Guinness on tap, and all the corned beef and cabbage ($10) or Irish stew ($8) you can eat.

The clump of cafes and restaurants along Massachusetts Ave NE (between 2nd and 4th Sts, getting more expensive as you go east) includes takeout at *Neil's Deli* (☎ 202-546-6970), 208 Massachusetts Ave NE; decent Tex-Mex at *Tortilla Coast* (☎ 202-546-6768), 201 Massachusetts Ave NE; and *Armand's Chicago Pizzeria*, 226 Massachusetts Ave NE (☎ 202-546-6600), for build-your-own pizzas and a lunch buffet. For all-you-can-eat Thai, *Thai Garden* (☎ 202-546-5900), 301 Massachusetts Ave NE, serves a 10-item lunch buffet for $7 weekdays only 11 am to 3 pm (menu selections offered daily until 10:30 pm).

Five blocks east of the Capitol, *Jimmy T's* on E Capitol St at 5th St SE is a down-home corner diner that serves breakfast all day (waffles $3.85) and other short orders to neighborhood regulars at red Formica tables.

On Pennsylvania Ave SE between 2nd and 3rd Sts, you'll find Mexican food at *Burrito Brothers* (☎ 202-543-6835), 205 Pennsylvania Ave SE; *schmerred* (with a spread) bagels at *Chesapeake Bagel Bakery* (☎ 202-546-0994), 215 Pennsylvania Ave SE; and meat-and-two plates (around $5) at *Sherrill's Bakery* (☎ 202-544-2480) at 233 Pennsylvania Ave, a neighborhood institution.

Between 3rd and 4th Sts, try the Greek dishes at *Taverna* (☎ 202-547-8360), 307 Pennsylvania Ave SE; cheap Japanese takeout at *Good Health Natural Foods* (☎ 202-543-2266), 325 Pennsylvania Ave SE; or the bar-and-grills popular with staffers, the *Hawk & Dove*, 329 Pennsylvania Ave SE, and *Tune Inn*, 331½ Pennsylvania Ave SE.

At Eastern Market (☎ 202-546-2698) on 7th St SE at North Carolina Ave, people line up with butchers and fishmongers for breakfast and lunch at the *Market Lunch* stand inside. They've got some of the best crab cakes in the city (under $5).

Among several eateries along 7th St SE across from Eastern Market, *Misha's Deli* (☎ 202-547-5858), 210 7th St SE, serves traditional Russian food – mushroom-caviar dip ($6 a pound), black bread, broccoli-cheese knishes ($2), 'baboushka soup' – all in a stylish deli setting (a skyline silhouette adorns the rafters) for takeout or eat-in.

For good coffee and espresso, muffins, sweets, and modern sandwiches, there's *Bread and Chocolate* (☎ 202-547-2875), 666 Pennsylvania Ave SE at 7th St.

Top End *La Brasserie*, 239 Massachusetts Ave NE, serves duck confit, salmon, and squid in its own ink for around $15 for lunch (dinner higher). *2 Quail* (☎ 202-543-8030), 320 Massachusetts Ave NE, is a bit precious with all the wicker and pillows (very Lady Legislator), but the food is good: paella one day, the next it's penne pasta with seafood in spicy macadamia nut cream sauce ($16).

Cafe Berlin (☎ 202-543-7656) 322 Massachusetts Ave NE, serves hearty German dishes, such as wiener or paprika schnitzel ($17).

Around the Mall

Many visitors stick to inexpensive museum cafeterias on the Mall to conserve time for sightseeing. Note that museum food-service hours are generally restricted to lunchtime, and expect crowds. Cafeteria fare costs from $3 up, restaurant entrees around $7 to $10. You'll find exceptional settings at the Air & Space Museum and the National Gallery's West Wing; the worst is at Natural History. The most trendy, healthy, very uninstitutional food-court menu is at the American History Museum (for those who crave a fat fix, there's also an ice cream parlor here). There's an outdoor cafe overlooking the Hirshhorn's sculpture gardens in summer, and an espresso bar in the tunnel at the National Gallery year round. (And you have to wonder what possessed them to install a cafe at the Holocaust Museum.) Refreshment stands and hot dog carts are never far away for cheap snacks.

Downtown

Budget to Middle Scores of inexpensive downtown eateries serving familiar American and deli food cater to office workers. Markets also typically sell some prepared food (sandwiches, fruit salads, soup-to-go) at lower prices than delis, and many also tuck full-blown hot-food buffets and salad bars in the back behind the aisles, where you might find anything from country-fried steak to broccoli chicken.

At *Sholl's Colonial Cafeteria* (☎ 202-296-3065), 1990 K St NW in the Esplanade Mall, you pay per item for such regional cafeteria fare as baked chicken ($2.65), liver and onions ($2.35), mashed potatoes and gravy ($.65), desserts, and drinks. For ambiance, little homilies are scattered throughout: 'The family that prays together stays together.' Open daily, Sholl's serves three meals – breakfast 7 to 10:30 am, lunch 11 am to 2:30 pm, dinner 4 to 8 pm; open Sunday 8:30 am to 6 pm.

Though all-you-can-eat sushi is a cultural oxymoron, you can find buffet-style sushi along with hot entrees at *Benkay* (☎ 202-737-1515), downstairs at 727 15th St NW near the White House (see the White House Area map). Though of course it's less fresh than made-to-order, you can't beat the price, the sumo-wrestling on cable, the Japanese rebels, and the rare opportunity for sushi gluttony (lunch $10.50, dinner $13.50, children half-price).

Balajee (☎ 202-682-9090), 917 18th St NW, serves an all-you-can-eat Indian lunch buffet that includes soup, dahl, rice, vegetarian curry, and poori for $6.49; lassis $1. The buffet is served weekdays only 11:30 am to 2:30 pm; or order off the menu daily till 8 pm.

Near the youth hostel, *Stoney's* (☎ 202-347-9163), 1307 L St NW, looks like a dive from the outside, but inside, it's a cozy burger joint that draws neighborhood regulars and Secret Service agents from their headquarters across the street for 'dude burgers' ($5.75), half a fried chicken with cornbread ($7.25), Philly cheesesteak ($6.50), and cheap beer.

If you're looking to eat around Ford's Theater, the *Dixie Grill* (☎ 202-628-4800), 518 10th St NW, serves Southern lunches and dinners, such as okra-and-sausage beggar's gumbo ($4.95 bowl) and hickory-smoked Carolina pulled pork ($6.95) – there's a great pool hall upstairs too.

At *Jaleo's* (☎ 202-628-7949), 480 7th St NW at the corner of E St, you can put together a meal from 40 choices of tapas. It's across from the Shakespeare Theater.

The classic choice near the White House is the *Old Ebbitt Grill*, (☎ 202-347-8881), 675 15th St NW, a watering hole dating back to 1856 that serves a daily menu of such local grill favorites as Maryland rockfish, crab cakes, steak, and burgers, along with grilled chicken salad and pasta plates (entrees $8 to $16, also a Sunday brunch).

For convenience and economy you could also consider the chains, such as *Au Bon Pain* for sandwiches and bakery items (inside the shopping mall at 2000 Pennsylvania Ave NW), or *China Cafe* for no-MSG takeout from four northwest locations: 2009 K St, 1411 K St, 1018 Vermont Ave, and 1990 M St.

Top End The trendy *Red Sage* (☎ 202-638-4444), 405 14th St NW at F St, is as acclaimed for its lavish decor as for its innovative cuisine. The style is all Southwestern, spicy red walls and chili-laced plates. Entrees start at $10; to economize go for lunch or opt for their adjacent Chili Bar or Cafe knockoffs. *Georgia Brown's* (☎ 202-637-2077), 950 15th St NW, offers high-style low-country cuisine and hospitality particularly popular with the city's African American elite. On Sunday there's a live R&B brunch.

Chinatown

If you find yourself near Chinatown, you can choose from among several inexpensive Asian restaurants along H St NW between 5th and 7th Sts, but the neighborhood's not worth going out of your way for. *China Doll Gourmet* (☎ 202-289-4755) at 627 H St serves dim sum for takeout or eat-in on white tablecloths (dim sum served daily 11 am to 3 pm, other menu items available thereafter).

The only Burmese food in DC is served at the *Burma Restaurant* (☎ 202-638-1280), upstairs at 740 6th St NW. It's a quiet place with good prawn appetizers, papaya salad, and Burmese curries (entrees around $6 to $8). It's open daily 11 am to 3 pm and 6 to 10 pm.

Foggy Bottom

For a university neighborhood, there are surprisingly few places to eat, though you can find more choices towards Dupont Circle to the north (and Georgetown is right across the bridge). For burgers, there's *Lindy's Bon Appétit* (☎ 202-452-0055), 2040 I St NW, offering 22 different takeout choices for $2.85 each (you can eat in the *Red Lion* bar upstairs). For pizza, try *Milo's* (☎ 202-338-3000), 2142 Pennsylvania Ave NW; prices range from $6 to $12 depending on size and toppings (bands sometimes play here during the school year).

The *World Gourmet* (☎ 202-371-9048), a deli/market at the corner of 19th and F Sts, sells sandwiches, salads, and Middle Eastern vegetarian dips like hummus and baba ghanoush that you can eat at the counter or at outside tables. It's a good coffee stop too.

Further up towards the Dupont Circle side of the West End, *Federal Market* (☎ 202-293-0014), 1215 23rd St NW, hides a buffet and salad bar behind its aisles; pay by the ounce and picnic in the park a block away. Nearby, *Bread & Chocolate* (☎ 202-833-8360), 2301 M St NW, serves daily French specials, but come here for the baked goods and hot chocolate.

Riverfront

Pass up the overpriced, overcrowded, mediocre seafood restaurants that dominate the waterfront, and continue up Maine St SW (or the boardwalk if you're on foot) to the freeway overpass around 9th St to find the *floating fish market*. A handful of barges here sell fresh seafood (with all the smells and tentacles, it's a sensory spectacle even if you don't buy anything) and some prepared foods, like softshell crab sandwiches (in season) at $3 to $5, fish platters with fries for $5 to $6, and great crab cakes for about $5. Unfortunately, no tables are provided; you can sit on the curb or amble back down to boardwalk benches.

Dupont Circle

Dupont Circle is the main restaurant district for everyone who considers Adams-Morgan too funky and Georgetown too young. It's also the center of DC's gay community. Weekend nights bring in many out-of-town license plates from surrounding suburbs. Many restaurants are found along Connecticut Ave NW on either side of the Circle and on side streets all around.

Budget to Middle *Afterwords Cafe*, attached to Kramerbooks at 1517 Connecticut Ave NW, is a good place to meet someone to decide where to go, or you can just eat there. It's a morning cafe for espresso and muffins, al fresco brunch spot or mezzanine hideaway, and late-night bar with live music most nights. Tucked away at 1633 P St NW, *Cafe Luna* (☎ 202-387-4005) serves cafe food and sticky desserts to a worldly set. Other coffee stops (over-represented in the neighborhood both sides of the Circle) are *Hannibal's* and *Starbucks*. There's a *Chesapeake Bagel Bakery* outlet at 1636 Connecticut Ave NW.

City Lights of China (☎ 202-265-6688), 1731 Connecticut Ave NW, is one of the best Chinese restaurants in the city; try the asparagus-and-crabmeat soup or spicy eggplant with garlic sauce ($5.95 at dinner).

Authentic Southern Indian vegetarian plates at *Paru's* (☎ 202-483-5133), 2010 S St NW off Connecticut Ave, include paratha, two curries, a samosa, and lassi for around $7, served in a small dining room across a counter from the kitchen.

On the Dupont Circle end of 18th St, *Lauriol Plaza* (☎ 202-387-0035), 1801 18th St NW, graciously serves Mexican, Spanish, and South American dishes – a ceviche Peruano appetizer costs $6.45, paella $15.95, fajitas $6.95 – on white tablecloths in a window-lined corner restaurant. (You'll find that the cooked salsa commonly served on the East Coast more closely resembles a bland marinara sauce than true spicy Mexican salsa – bring your own.)

You'll find Malaysian and Singaporean dishes, such as nasi goreng and satay with peanut sauce at the *Straits of Malaya* (☎ 202-483-1483), 1836 18th St NW.

Vegetarian and health-food specialties are served at *Food for Thought* (☎ 202-797-1095), 1738 Connecticut Ave NW; the menu includes sunburgers (rice and sunflower seed patties) for $5.50, and veggie reubens (Swiss, sauerkraut, green pepper, onion, mushrooms, and tomato on rye) for $6.95. It's open for dinner daily, for lunch Monday to Saturday.

La Tomate (☎ 202-667-5505), 1707 Connecticut Ave, offers pasta plates and Italian dishes (entrees $9 to $12) in a bright and airy dining room or out on the patio.

Zorba's Cafe (☎ 202-387-8555), 1612 20th St NW off Connecticut Ave, serves such Greek specialties as moussaka for $5 and gyro for $3.75 with piped-in Greek music (sit outside).

If you stray into the West End in lower Dupont, you'll find a few more choices around 22nd and M Sts NW. *Lulu's New Orleans Cafe* (☎ 202-861-5858), 1217 22nd St NW, makes a good turtle soup ($3.25), catfish and oyster po'boy sandwiches ($8), and decent jambalaya ($8.25).

Top End Set in a historic inn, the *Tabard Inn* (☎ 202-785-1277), 1739 N St NW, offers an arty daily menu of appetizers like smoked trout cakes with red cabbage relish ($7.50), entrees like grilled shrimp with fennel-garlic cream ($19), or things in puff pastry. Service is often indifferent; to New Yorkers it's ambiance.

Across from the Tabard, the *Iron Gate* (☎ 202-737-1370), 1734 N St NW, has a storybook setting under trellises outside or inside by the fire. It serves high-end romantic food, like lamb chops with ruffly paper garters ($17.50 dinner). Closed Sunday.

Nora's (☎ 202-462-5143), 2132 Florida Ave NW (at the corner of R), offers organic gourmet dinners in an elegant intimate corner bistro.

In the West End part of lower Dupont, *City Cafe* (☎ 202-797-4860), 2213 M St NW, also promotes an organic menu that includes fish, seafood salad, spring rolls, and carrot juice (entrees reach to $13).

Steak lovers head to *Blackie's House of Beef* (☎ 202-333-1100) at 22nd and M Sts NW for large steaks ($20 to $25).

Adams-Morgan

This district has the greatest concentration of the widest variety of cuisines, particularly in a compact stretch of 18th St NW south of Columbia Rd. It's an international smorgasbord – find mee goreng, shish kabobs, yebeg alecka, calzone, jerk chicken, burritos, empanadas, and of course, Happy Meals. Parking becomes impossible from dinnertime on. The menus and ambiance of all these places are low-end to middle, though you can find selected entrees towards the top end.

There's a dozen Ethiopian restaurants here (some say Eritrean, bone up on your African history before dinner); many feature live jazz in the evenings. Two good ones are at the top of the hill: *Meskerem* at 2434 18th and the *Red Sea* across the street at 2463 18th. The food at Meskerem is slightly better and the prices are slightly higher; it also offers authentic seating on camel-hide hassocks at woven-straw drum tables upstairs (don't let them consign you to the basement). If you prefer less exotic seating, go to Red Sea. At both you can order spicy stews of lamb, beef, chicken, seafood, and lentils, braised and simmered for hours (small portions under $5, large portions under $10). Meals are commonly served with two vegetable side dishes and a plate of *injera*, a spongy sourdough bread used to scoop up food in place of silverware.

For French, *Cafe Lautrec* (☎ 202-265-6436), 2431 18th, is the granddaddy of DC's bohemian cafes. Its two-story mural of Parisian singer Aristide Bruant that mimics Toulouse-Lautrec is a neighborhood landmark. Though many come just for the jazz or tap-dancing bartender, you can eat good French food with a Moroccan twist. A less predictable French Moroccan-ish experience is to be had at *Cafe Riche* up the street, if the eccentric bartender/owner ('the Sultan of 18th St') is in the mood to let you in or serve you. The more normal French bistro *La Fourchette* (☎ 202-332-3077), 2429 18th St, makes a great bouillabaisse along with other daily specials.

Cities (☎ 202-328-7194), 2424 18th, changes its 'city' theme every three months or so, recreating its menu, wine list, and decor in the style of, say, Rio, Istanbul, Bangkok, or lately, Firenze (Tuscan specialties cost around $13.50 to $19.95). There's a disco upstairs.

For Italian, *I Matti* (☎ 202-462-8844), 2436 18th, is a bright and airy spot on the fashionably dark street, with red-tile floors, blond-wood tables, and big picture windows for good people-watching. A locally renowned chef invents pasta plates and modern Italian fare garnished with fried radicchio or fava beans ($12.95 and up) for power-lunchers and dinner crowds.

For Latin food, *El Tamarindo* (☎ 202-328-3660) at 1785 Florida Ave NW serves excellent Salvadoran and Mexican dishes 24 hours in a checkered vinyl-tablecloth setting off 18th St. Enchiladas, tacos, and flautas fall in the $7 range. The Cuban *Omega* at 1858 Columbia Rd was one of the first restaurants in the neighborhood, and rumor goes that the Bay of Pigs invasion was planned here.

For breakfast and treats try *Jolt N' Bolt*, 1918 18th St; it's a great perch for coffee, tea, and bakery things. Other good breakfast spots in the late-to-rise neighborhood are the *Belmont Kitchen Pantry* (☎ 202-667-1200) at 2400 18th St, and *Avignon Frères* (☎ 202-462-2050) at 1775 Columbia Rd. The *Kalorama Cafe*, 2228 18th, has good cheap natural and vegetarian foods.

Woodley Park

The compact little triangle above the Woodley Park/National Zoo Metro station is packed with a lot of good places to eat. The clientele is a diverse mix of locals and tourists from several neighborhood hotels. All are low-end to middle.

At *Lebanese Taverna* (☎ 202-483-3007), 2641 Connecticut Ave NW, you can make a meal of the many good Middle Eastern appetizers that run under $5 – baba ghanoush, falafel, moussaka, grape leaves, tabouleh. Entrees are $11.50 and up.

Thai Taste (☎ 202-387-8876), 2606 Connecticut Ave NW, serves several good soups for under $3 and curry dishes for $6.50 each. *Rajaji* (☎ 202-265-7344), 2603 Connecticut Ave, serves Indian dishes; try to sit outside.

The *Saigon Inn* chain (☎ 202-483-8400), 2614 Connecticut Ave NW, has good Vietnamese food, including clear spring rolls for $3.25 and skewered lemon chicken for $6 at lunch (dinner prices higher).

Also handy within the triangle are a bakery cafe, an Irish pub, and a gourmet market (across from the Omni Hotel).

Shaw

There's an intriguing mix of great soul-food landmarks and avant-garde cafes within walking distance of the U St Metro. Recent neighborhood revitalization along U St and a bohemian enclave centered at U and 14th Sts make this neighborhood the most emerging place in DC – anything can happen. All the following are suitable for travelers on a tight budget.

Ben's Chili Bowl (☎ 202-667-0909), 1213 U St NW, is such a neighborhood institution that it appears on the Metro station maps as a local landmark. The old guard, trim Muslims, and regulars gather here for chili dogs ('Our chili will make a hot dog bark!'), scrapple, shakes, TV, and conversation. It opens at 6 am every day but Sunday, when it opens at noon; the chili flows till at least midnight every night.

The vanguard collects across the street at the *Kaffa House* (☎ 202-462-1212), 1212 U St NW, a collective named for the region in Ethiopia where the coffee bean was first discovered, according to the owners. Howard University students, poets, and dreadlocked slackers come for vegetarian soups, muffins, and coffee, as well as for readings and live jazz.

U-topia (☎ 202-483-7669), 1418 U St NW, is one of the neighborhood's new arty restaurants. It serves an uneven assortment of experimental dishes, the most local of which is called U-Street Shrimp-and-Rice. The colorful abstract interior, out-there patrons, and great bar are big draws.

Polly's (☎ 202-265-8385), 1343 U St NW, offers morning-after brunches on weekends with eggs, strong coffee, and mimosas by the pitcher.

The *Florida Avenue Grill* (☎ 202-265-1586), 1100 Florida Ave NW, serves down-home Southern-style breakfasts, lunches, and dinners – grits, meatloaf, and barbecued ribs (entrees $6 to $9). From the U St Metro station, walk north on 11th St for three blocks.

Georgetown

Georgetown is like one giant outdoor food court, with see-me perches in every storefront along its central (clogged) arteries of M St and Wisconsin Ave NW. It's the most easily overrated part of town unless you're real young and hungry and like crowds. There's no Metro service here, but if you can make your way across Rock Creek (from the Foggy Bottom/GWU Metro), you'll find the commercial zone in a compact walkable area.

Budget to Middle For starters and rest stops, there's the *Coffee Beanery* at 3110 M St NW, and the second-story overlook cafe at *Barnes & Noble* bookstore, 3040 M St NW.

Next door to one another on M St NW at 30th are two good Vietnamese restaurants, *Saigon Inn* (☎ 202-337-5588) at 2928 M St NW and *Vietnam Georgetown* next door at 2934 M St NW. Though some patrons swear by one or the other, to others they're interchangeable. The Saigon Inn chain is a bit cheaper at around $6 for lunch and $7 for dinner dishes.

Zed's Ethiopian Cuisine (☎ 202-333-4710), 3318 M St NW, is comparable to Ethiopian restaurants in Adams-Morgan (that means good). Vegetarian dishes are about $6, meats $7 to $8.

Aditi (☎ 202-625-6825), 3299 M St NW, has good Indian food, but come for the more reasonably priced lunch instead of the pricey dinner (meat curries $10, vegetable $7 at lunch).

Sarinah Satay House (☎ 202-337-2955), down under at 1338 Wisconsin Ave NW, serves chicken and beef satay with gado gado peanut sauce ($8.80) along with other Indonesian dishes for lunch and dinner (closed Mondays).

Popular American diner fare (sandwiches, burgers) can be found at *Booeymonger* (☎ 202-333-4810), 3265 Prospect St NW at S Potomac, and at *Boogie's Diner* (☎ 202-298-6060), 1229 Wisconsin Ave NW.

'Put the South in your mouth' at the *Music City Roadhouse* (☎ 202-337-4444), on 30th St NW at the canal, a smoker-friendly saloon that offers Southern plates and a gospel brunch on Sundays.

The *Burrito Brothers* chain at 3273 M St NW (☎ 202-965-3963) serves filling California-style burritos (around $5) and tacos.

Top End *Cafe La Ruche* (☎ 202-965-2684), 1039 31st St, set away from crowds near the canal, offers a sunny dining room full of colorful tile tables alongside a garden. Caribbean-French entrees such as moules and saucisses (small sausages) start at $9.95. Also worth a splurge: *Aux Fruits de Mer* (☎ 202-333-2333) and *Au Pied du Cochon* (☎ 202-333-5440), both at 1335 Wisconsin Ave NW (seafood from $14, land food from $12), open 24 hours.

ENTERTAINMENT

There's always a lot going on in DC, and the best place to find out what's happening where and when is the weekly tabloid *Washington City Paper*, issued each Thursday afternoon and distributed free in corner racks and at bookstores, restaurants, and clubs around the city. A more mainstream resource is the Weekend tabloid that appears in Friday's edition of the *Washington Post*, as well as listings in the *Post*'s daily Style section and Sunday's Show section. The weekly *Washington Blade* tabloid, distributed free at many city outlets, includes events of particular interest to DC's gay community.

Keep the number of Time Out Washington (☎ 202-364-8463) handy; it's an automated guide to who's playing at which bars and clubs (including a CD sampler of popular local bands), concerts, performing arts, and special events, conveniently indexed by club, band, and neighborhood. Leave your fax number and they'll fax back an up-to-the-minute club list.

For advance planning, you can request a seasonal calendar (produced quarterly) of major cultural events from the DC Convention and Visitors Association (☎ 202-789-7000), 1212 New York Ave NW, Suite 600, Washington, DC 20005-3992.

Free or Cheap In addition to being free all day long, DC's museums also present special evening events, many of which are free (some do carry a small fee). There are many lectures and readings, but also wonderful and unusual concerts and performances from bluegrass jams to art films to puppet shows. Call Dial-a-Museum (☎ 202-357-2020) for an updated recording, or pick up a calendar of events at museum desks. The Library of Congress and Washington churches are dramatic venues for regularly scheduled concerts (usually jazz and classical); call or pick up calendars.

Street fairs and festivals provide great local entertainment; they're scheduled throughout the more temperate months (see Special Events above or check papers for listings).

Note also that many of the major memorials are most dramatic at night, and you can avoid crowds and conserve your time for day-only museums by covering such sights as the Lincoln Memorial, Jefferson Memorial, and Washington Monument in the evening (the elevator rides to the top until midnight from around April through September).

Discount Tickets In the Lisner Auditorium on the George Washington University campus, Ticketplace (☎ 202-842-5387), 730 21st St NW at the corner of H St, sells tickets to citywide concerts and shows on the day of performance at half price plus 10%. Available tickets are listed on a board at the office. It's open Tuesday to Friday noon to 6 pm, Saturday 11 am to 5 pm, closed Sunday and Monday (tickets for Sunday and Monday shows are sold on Saturday). Ticketplace accepts cash only; full-price advance sales are also available.

You can also check with theaters directly on the day of the performance to see if tickets are available for less than face value.

Kennedy Center

The *Kennedy Center* (☎ 202-467-4600), 25th St and New Hampshire Ave NW, is an important cultural touchstone largely credited with transforming DC from a cultural backwater to a contender. The massive building overlooking the Potomac holds two theaters, a theater lab, a cinema, an opera house, and a concert hall (and a good rooftop restaurant besides). Nationally recognized artists and companies appear here, and film festivals and cultural fairs are also common. Tickets to the main events can be steep; inquire about half-price tickets sometimes available on the day of performance. (Renovations scheduled for the next few years may temporarily close certain venues.)

Theater

The *National Theater* (☎ 202-628-6161, 800-233-3123), 1321 Pennsylvania Ave, established in 1835 and renovated in 1984, is Washington's oldest continually operating theater. This is where they'd show *Les Misérables* (and have). The *Warner Theater* (☎ 202-628-1818), 1299 Pennsylvania Ave NW, is a 1924 Art Deco theater that hosts headliner concerts and the annual *Nutcracker*.

Arena Stage (☎ 202-488-3300), at the waterfront on 6th St and Maine St SW, is actually three theaters, among them a theater-in-the-round where they host both mainstream and more experimental performances.

The *Shakespeare Theater* (☎ 202-393-2700), 450 7th St NW, is home to a Shakespearean troupe. Shakespearean and other performances are also held in the Elizabethan theater of the *Folger Shakespeare Library* on E Capitol Ave at 3rd St SE.

Ford's Theater (☎ 202-347-4833), 511 10th St NW, is not only a historic site but an inviting performance venue. You sit in wooden chairs downstairs or up in the balcony; the flag-draped box where Lincoln was sitting when he was shot is reserved as a memorial. Expect the likes of the *Fantasticks* and other mainstream performances.

The *Lincoln Theater* (☎ 202-328-6000), 1215 U St NW, is another historic theater. The center of the 1930s 'Black Broadway' strip in the neighborhood's heyday, the theater was recently renovated by the city and it's now a main factor in the area's resurgence.

DC's theater district (such as it is) is centered east of Dupont Circle around 14th St NW between P and Q Sts. Here you'll find smaller repertory companies, alternative theater, and cheaper seats. Check listings for the *Woolly Mammoth Theatre Co* (☎ 202-393-3939) at 1401 Church St NW off 14th St; the *Source Theatre Co* (☎ 202-462-1073) at 1835 14th St NW; and *Studio Theatre* (☎ 202-332-3300) at 1333 P St NW.

Music

There's symphonic music here, and opera has gotten a huge shot in the arm with plans for building a new opera house, but DC's music scene really excels in more modern music, particularly jazz and blues.

Classical The National Symphony and the Washington Chamber Symphony perform at the *Kennedy Center* (☎ 202-467-4600). The Symphony also holds summertime concerts at an outdoor amphitheater at *Wolf Trap Farm Park for the Performing Arts* (☎ 703-255-1827), a 40-minute drive away in Vienna, Virginia (see the Northern Virginia chapter).

In town, other classical performances take place at acoustically monumental venues such as the *National Gallery of Art*, the *National Building Museum*, the *Corcoran Gallery*, and the *Library of Congress*, as well as at local universities and churches.

Opera The Washington Opera is going places. Famed tenor Placido Domingo was named its conductor in 1996, and the company purchased an $18.1 million building near Metro Center (G St at 11th St NW) with plans to sink another $105 million into exterior renovation and interior reconstruction. Until the move (scheduled for the year 2000), the opera continues to appear at *Kennedy Center*, where it's been housed for the past 25 years.

Jazz DC really excels in live blues and jazz. The preeminent *Blues Alley* (☎ 202-337-4141) in Georgetown at 1073 Rear Wisconsin Ave (in an alley south of M St) has attracted such nationally known artists as Dizzy Gillespie and Ahmed Jamal to its elegant candlelit supper club. The cover charge is steep ($13 to $40), and so are the drinks and Creole specialties. For a more casual and less expensive evening, the *Saloun* (☎ 202-965-4900), 3239 M St NW, features blues on Saturday and live jazz all other nights (slip in before 9 pm to evade the $3 cover). Its clientele is much more varied than the usual M St prowlers. Across the bridge in Foggy Bottom, *One Step Down* (☎ 202-331-8863), 2517 Pennsylvania Ave NW, features out-of-town talent on the weekends and local artists and a great jukebox the rest of the time.

In Woodley Park, *City Blues* (☎ 202-232-2300) is at 2651 Connecticut Ave NW facing the Woodley Park/National Zoo Metro entrance. It occupies an old Victorian townhouse where you can wander from room to room through the smoky haze listening to the blues and nursing your $5 drink (the minimum; a cover charge may also apply).

In Adams-Morgan, *Cafe Lautrec* (☎ 202-265-6436), 2431 18th St NW, voted best jazz club by local critics, is a small restaurant also infamous for its wild bartender Johne Forget, who tap dances on the bar most weekends. The cafe asks for a $6 food/drink minimum. Plenty of other restaurants in the neighborhood feature live jazz too.

Out at the DC border, *Takoma Station* (☎ 202-889-1999), 6914 4th St NW across from the Takoma Park Metro station, is a great old tavern that plays down-home blues and jazz to a mixed crowd of jazz lovers.

So much for the classics. The *New Vegas Lounge* (☎ 202-483-3971), 1415 P St NW, plays the blues in the pioneering 'New U' district, with an anything-goes jam on Tuesday and Wednesday (no cover). *Madame's Organ* (a play on Adams-Morgan; ☎ 202-667-5370), 2003 18th St NW, is a raunchier blues club anchoring the bottom of the 18th St strip. The best new place is *Twins Lounge* (☎ 202-445-8038), way out at 5516 Colorado Ave NW near nothing else, a casually stylish supper club that books jazzy crooners.

The *Corcoran Gallery* features a jazz brunch on Sunday. The *Willard Intercontinental* hosts jazz nights in its Nest Lounge downtown. You can hear jazz outdoors in Rock Creek Park's 4200-seat amphitheater on summer weekends (it's near 16th and Colorado Sts NW). And the annual DC Blues Festival (☎ 202-828-3028) is scheduled for early September.

Rock/Contemporary The 400-seat *Bayou* (☎ 202-333-2897), 3135 K St, is the mainstream venue in Georgetown for hearing a wide variety of rock and pop, jazz, reggae, and even comedy acts. Two of DC's most established downtown rock venues are the *930 Club* (☎ 202-393-0930), 930 F St NW (near Metro Center) and *15 Minutes* (see Dupont Circle map; ☎ 202-408-1855), 1030 15th St NW – both darker, clubbier, more alternative dance clubs. Also check out the *Insect Club* (☎ 202-347-8884), 625 E St NW for its bug-infested decor.

The newest major venue is the *Capitol Ballroom* (☎ 703-549-7625), 1015 Half St SE, which opened in 1995 in an old boiler works that can hold crowds of 2000. Get the lineup off their Web site: *harborside.com/cdp/ballroom* (watch for 'Buzz'). Shows tend to wrap up before midnight so that patrons can catch the last train (Navy Yard Metro station).

The New U District has some of the city's best venues for alternative music, offering mixed-up styles and crowds. The *Black Cat* (☎ 202-667-7960), 1831 14th St, hosts the likes of Girls Against Boys, the Zimmermans, and Jimmie's Chicken Shack; the back room is reserved for poetry readings and other groovy events. The *State of the Union* (☎ 202-588-8810), 1357 U St NW, books many of the same artists, and weird DJs run the garagelike back room for dancing. The sickle-studded Soviet decor is a nostalgic look back at the Cold War (there's Russian food too). *Republic Gardens* (☎ 202-232-2710) is another modern scene a few doors down at 1335 U St.

DC grabbed its 15 minutes of musical infamy by introducing go-go (roots rap) to the national scene years back. Nowadays the go-go scene has such a reputation for violence that many locals steer clear of even favorite clubs when go-go's playing; outdoor venues are your best bet.

World Music *Kilimanjaro* (☎ 202-328-3838), 1724 California St NW in Adams-Morgan, draws a cosmopolitan mix of locals and globals for world-beat bands and dancing.

Cinemas

First-run movies play at cinemas throughout DC; for starters, there's the octoplex cinema at *Union Station* and the *Foundry Mall Cinemas* at the C&O Canal in Georgetown (see the newspaper for complete listings). Alternative and foreign films are regularly shown at the Kennedy Center's *American Film Institute* cinema; the Cineplex Odeon's *Outer Circle* (☎ 202-244-3116) at 4849 Wisconsin Ave NW (north on Wisconsin Ave at the DC border); and at *Key* (☎ 202-333-5100), 1222 Wisconsin Ave NW in Georgetown. Also check for film showings at museums (the Hirshhorn regularly shows art films) and the Library of Congress (more classic films).

Bars

Great bars are scattered all over the city, but the greatest concentration of nightlife and streetlife for walkable bar-hopping is in Adams-Morgan (mostly 18th St NW between Florida Ave and Columbia Rd) and in Georgetown (mostly M St NW between 29th and 33rd Sts). All around Dupont Circle there are bars catering especially to gay drinkers. Many bars commonly also feature live music, DJs, and dancing, and there's often food as well (also see jazz bars and rock bars above).

Capitol Hill bars cater to the congressional crowd. Look along Pennsylvania Ave between 2nd and 5th Sts SE for the *Hawk 'n' Dove* (☎ 202-543-3300), 329 Pennsylvania Ave SE, an institution since the late 1960s, and the *Tune Inn* (☎ 202-543-2725), 331½ Pennsylvania Ave SE. Hear some Irish music at the *Dubliner* and *Kelly's Irish Times* on M St NW at N Capitol St.

Gay bars around Dupont Circle include *JR's* (☎ 202-328-0090), 1519 17th St NW; *Mr P's* (☎ 202-293-1064), 2147 P St NW; and *Badlands* (☎ 202-296-0505), 1415 22nd St NW, near P St. *Hung Jury* (☎ 202-279-3212) is a lesbian bar downtown at 1819 H St NW. But the biggest gay-oriented club is on Capitol Hill at *Tracks* (☎ 202-488-3320), 1111 1st St SE, which welcomes all kinds for dancing to DJ music and pick-up volleyball in good weather. (It's in a seedy part of town; take a cab.)

A body-pierced clientele slips into Dupont Circle to *Planet Fred* (☎ 202-296-9563), 1221 Connecticut Ave, with its loony sci-fi/hi-fi/lava lamp interior for regular 'drag freak bingo,' rockabilly, and 'Female Trouble' lesbian dance nights (every other Sunday).

In Adams-Morgan, *Cafe Heaven and Cafe Hell* (☎ 202-667-4355), 2327 18th St NW, and *Chief Ike's Mambo Room* (☎ 202-332-2211), 1725 Columbia Rd NW, are among the many nightclubs, bars, and restaurants with bars where people can hang out and listen to live music.

Like most of Georgetown, a string of bars along the neighborhood's Wisconsin Ave NW corridor cater mostly to a white, 20- to 40-year-old crowd, and some are strictly college joints. *J Paul's*

(☎ 202-333-3450), 3218 M St NW, and *Winston's* (☎ 202-333-3150), 3295 M St, are popular, as is *Garrett's* (☎ 202-333-1033), 3003 M St NW.

SPECTATOR SPORTS

The popular Redskins football team plays in Robert F Kennedy (RFK) Stadium at E Capitol and 22nd Sts SE, Metro: Stadium/Armory. (The team is due to move into a new $160 million, 78,600-seat stadium now under construction in suburban Maryland by September 1997.) Games are nearly always sold out, but you can buy scalped tickets around the stadium at exorbitant prices or buy tickets to the two pre-season games that usually take place towards the end of the summer. For Redskins tickets call ☎ 202-546-2222; for other sports events at the stadium call ☎ 202-547-9077.

The NBA Wizards (☎ 202-432-7328), formerly the too-violent-sounding Bullets, play basketball at the USAir Arena (☎ 301-350-3400) in Landover, Maryland (take the Beltway to Exit 17A and follow signs). This is also the current home of the Capitals (☎ 202-432-7328), Washington's NHL ice hockey team.

Plans call for both the Wizards and the Capitals to move into a new 20,000-seat arena currently under construction at Gallery Place near Chinatown in downtown DC. The estimated completion date is October 1997.

Since the Washington Senators left DC for Texas some 20 years back, the city has had no professional baseball team, and fans adopted the Baltimore Orioles for hometown-vicinity favorites.

DC's favorite college team is Georgetown's Hoyas. Competitive crew racing attracts large crowds to the shores of the Potomac around Thompson Boat Center. You can sometimes watch local and embassy teams play soccer, rugby, polo, and cricket games on the Mall; call the National Park Service (☎ 202-619-7222) for dates.

A recent addition to the sports scene is DC United, a Major League Soccer team. The team won the first national soccer championship in 1996. Check the sports sections of the local papers for the team's current venue.

THINGS TO BUY

People don't come to DC for the shopping, but you can find some good items. Classic DC souvenirs include shredded money from the Bureau of Printing and Engraving, copies of the Declaration of Independence from the National Archives, and stuffed pandas from the National Zoo.

Museum gift shops sell a wonderful selection of things related to their specialty. At Air & Space you can buy sophisticated model airplanes and freeze-dried astronaut food. The Museum of American Art sells oddball handmade jewelry. The National Gallery of Art sells art prints for as little as two dollars. The National Building Museum sells arty interior furnishings, the Renwick Gallery sells handblown glass and other craftwork, and the American History Museum sells products from every region of the US – from Vermont maple syrup and stone-ground Carolina grits to Navaho pottery and Inuit icons. Also look for fun and arty mobiles, great children's toys and trinkets, and, of course, fabulous books on art, architecture, history, science, and culture.

Along 18th St in Adams-Morgan you'll find great vintage and modern clothing boutiques, music stores, and thrift stores with weird retro finds. Ethnic markets and stores may yield votive candles and frilly crinoline party dresses for little girls. The New U area at U St NW around 14th St has a much smaller but similar collection of shops, several of which specialize in African items such as masks and wooden carvings.

The upscale Dupont Circle district has dozens of art galleries exhibiting paintings, sculpture, and artifacts for sale. This is also where you'll find Benetton, Gap, and Polo.

Georgetown along M St NW (from around 30th to 35th Sts) also has trendy boutiques and national chains like Urban Outfitters, Victoria's Secret, and the Body

Shop. Georgetown Park is a huge shopping mall at 3222 M St NW with Eddie Bauer-type clothing.

Shopping complexes downtown are good places to get out of the weather and have a snack, but you'd hardly head there just to shop. However, Union Station does have a few nicer clothing stores and also an Appalachian Spring store with regional crafts.

Of course, the bookstores – new, used, historical, political, arty – are wonderful (see Bookstores under Information above).

GETTING THERE & AWAY

Air

Flights into Washington land at one of three area airports: Washington National Airport, Dulles International Airport, or Baltimore-Washington International Airport (BWI). National is by far the most convenient; it's just across the river from DC and the Metro stops right there. Dulles is 26 miles west, and BWI 35 miles north. Major car-rental agencies are well represented at all three airports. (See also the Getting There & Away chapter for more information on travel in the region.)

Washington National Airport For general information about National Airport dial ☎ 703-685-8000. To get to town from National, follow signs to the Metro station; this may be a circuitous route during the next few years of airport expansion. At the station take either the westward Blue Line or eastward Yellow Line – both end up downtown. The fare will probably be under $2, depending on your destination and time of travel (see the Metrorail section below for additional information).

A taxi to/from downtown will cost between $12 and $15. Taxis leaving from the airport tack on an additional $1 fee.

The Washington Flyer Express (☎ 703-685-1400) runs shuttle buses to/from the terminal at 1517 K St NW (see Downtown & the Mall map); the closest Metro stop is McPherson Square 2½ blocks southeast. Airport shuttle buses run every half hour weekdays from early morning to around 9:30 pm and less frequently on weekends (call for exact schedule). The trip takes about 30 minutes and costs $8 one-way and $14 roundtrip (kids under six ride free), cash only. No reservations are necessary from National; just hop on.

Washington Dulles Airport For Dulles Airport general information, call ☎ 703-471-4242. The Washington Flyer (see above) runs Dulles shuttle buses to/from the downtown terminal every half hour weekdays from early morning to around 9:30 pm and less frequently on weekends (call for exact schedule). The fare is $16 one-way and $26 roundtrip, cash only. Buses also take people to/from the Metro stop at West Falls Church for $8 one-way.

A taxi to/from Dulles will be around $47.

Baltimore-Washington International Airport For general airport information, call ☎ 410-859-7111. There are many options for getting to and from BWI. For complete information see the Getting There & Away chapter. For BWI ground transport dial ☎ 410-859-7545. A taxi between BWI and downtown Washington costs about $57. Airport Connection (☎ 301-441-2345) takes people to/from the airport to the terminal it shares with the Washington Flyer at 1517 K St NW. Shuttle buses run every hour and a half most days, fewer on Saturday. *Call for reservations* at least two hours in advance. The fare is $14 one-way and $25 roundtrip (kids under six ride free).

You can also take the MARC commuter train (☎ 800-325-7245) between DC's Union Station and a terminal near BWI; once there you'll be shuttled to and from the airport free of charge. The fare is $4.25 one-way and $7.75 roundtrip. Amtrak also stops at BWI (see the Getting There & Away chapter).

Bus

Greyhound buses stop at the Greyhound terminal (☎ 800-232-2222) at 1005 1st St NE, on the corner of L St (see Capitol Hill map). Peter Pan Trailways buses (☎ 202-371-2111, 800-343-9999) stop in a lot across the street from Greyhound. Take note that the rundown neighborhood becomes deserted at night, and the nearest Metro station is eight blocks south (via 1st St SE) at Union Station. Cabs are usually available at the station, or call one.

Train

Passenger trains from around the country arrive directly downtown into Union Station, the 'flagship' terminal of the Amtrak network – it's the best way to arrive in the capital. Located at 50 Massachusetts Ave NE on Capitol Hill, Union Station (☎ 202-371-9441) connects directly to DC's Metro subway system. Call ☎ 800-872-7245 for Amtrak information, or pick up schedules at Union Station.

Amtrak's express Metroliner (☎ 800-523-8720) runs between DC and New Haven, Connecticut. It'll get you to major cities in less time for premium fares. It's an extremely civilized – near clubby – way for serious visitors to travel conveniently from downtown Manhattan to downtown DC for around $106 one-way.

Also from Union Station, the MARC commuter train (☎ 800-325-7245) runs to Baltimore weekdays only.

Car

I-95 runs north-south to DC, merging into the I-495 Beltway that surrounds the metro region. Approaching from the northeast, Hwy 1 leads into Rhode Island Ave, and the Baltimore-Washington Expressway (Route 295) leads to Route 50 and New York Ave. From the south, I-395 takes you to downtown near the Mall by the Memorial Bridge or the 14th St Bridge. From the west, I-66 runs from Virginia to the Mall area, but you should avoid congested rush hours here unless you have at least two passengers and can use the zippy carpool lane (drivers are ticketed for driving in the carpool lane with less than three people per vehicle). From the north on the Beltway, take the Connecticut Ave Exit marked Chevy Chase to get to Adams-Morgan and Dupont Circle or the Wisconsin Ave Exit to get to Georgetown.

GETTING AROUND

Most major sights and hotel districts are efficiently served by the Metro subway system, and DC's bizarre street grid can be difficult to navigate by car (not to mention parking) but wonderful to explore on foot. Given these factors, your best bet is to forget the car altogether or leave it at an outlying neighborhood. (For information on getting to and from the airports, see the specific airport under Getting There & Away above.)

Cabs are plentiful and (relatively) cheap for getting around town day or night (for groups of three or four, taking a cab may be near comparable in price to everyone taking the Metro, and a whole lot more convenient). For cycling information, see the Biking section above.

Metrorail

DC is served by a sleek modern subway network (call ☎ 202-637-7000 for route information 6 am to 11:30 pm). The 'Metro' runs conveniently to most major sights, hotel and business districts, and out to the Maryland and Virginia suburbs (see the color Washington Metrorail System map). Trains and stations are well marked, well maintained, well lit, climate-controlled, reasonably priced, decently staffed, reliable, and safe. Trains run daily – from 5:30 am to midnight Monday to Friday and 8 am to midnight on weekends. Plentiful parking is available at certain outlying stations. The time limit is 24 hours, and there's a $2.25 charge between 2 pm and 10:30 pm (no charge if you arrive before or leave after these times).

The network consists of five color-coded lines – blue, yellow, orange, green, and red – that intersect at a total of seven transfer points. The trickiest part of navigating the system is determining and remembering the final destination of the train you want, because trains and platforms are identified by their outlying terminus (names that are otherwise irrelevant to intown travelers).

To ride the subway, buy a computerized paper fare card in any amount from self-service machines inside the station entrance (buy one for each passenger). Keep the card handy; you'll need it to both enter *and* exit Metro stations. To exit, slip your fare card in the slot on the turnstile.

If the card's value is the same as the fare, the turnstile keeps the card and the gates open. If the card's value is greater, the turnstile returns the card to you with the remaining value printed on it and the gates open. If the card's value is less than the fare, the turnstile returns the card to you and the gates don't open; if this happens you need to use an 'Addfare' machine that tells you how much to add. Other machines inside the gates dispense free bus transfers – remember to get these before exiting if you need a bus connection.

Rates are determined by the distance traveled and time of day (there's a premium for traveling at rush hour). The minimum fare is $1.10. The maximum value card the machines can dispense is $30; there's a 10% 'bonus' on purchases of $20 or more. Machines give up to$4.95 change in coins. A one-day excursion rail pass costs $5, and it's good for unlimited travel weekdays from 9:30 am or weekends all day. A Fast Pass is good for two week's unlimited travel. Senior discounts are available to holders of the free Metro Senior Citizen ID Card. All these special cards are available from the Sales & Information office in the Metro Center station at 12th and F Sts NW (call above number for nine other branches and information about additional local outlets).

Metrobus

DC's Metrobus system provides relatively clean and efficient bus service throughout the city and to outlying suburbs. Call ☎ 202-637-7000 for route information, schedules, and fares (minimum fare $1.10, $.25 with a Metro transfer). Automatic fare machines accept paper dollars; you need the exact fare.

Some handy routes are the L2, which runs along 18th St in the heart of Adams-Morgan (connecting to Metro stations at Woodley Park and Foggy Bottom), and the D5, which runs from Union Station to Georgetown's central M St strip (board along K St downtown).

Car

Driving & Parking In addition to the city's bizarre geometric street pattern and many confusing traffic roundabouts, certain lanes of some streets change direction during rush hour, and some two-way streets become one-way. But still, it's not New York – outside of rush hours driving around town during the day is no big deal. Finding street parking can, however, be a big hassle in certain congested neighborhoods, most notably in Georgetown and around the Mall.

Rentals All major car-rental agencies are represented in town and at the airports, and most have offices at Union Station (see the Getting Around chapter for national toll-free numbers). Weekly rates are often the best deal.

Unfortunately for young drivers, most national agencies in DC won't rent to anyone under 25. Some local car-rental companies will rent to drivers over 21 with a major credit card, but their rates may not be competitive. One exception is Petrocci Auto Rentals (☎ 703-643-2006), but they're 30 miles south of DC in Woodbridge, Virginia. Their daily/weekly rates start at $18.95/133 with unlimited local mileage.

Taxi

Taxicabs are plentiful in the central city and are generally easy to find; hail them with a wave of the hand. They are relatively inexpensive under the present zone-fare system, but that may change once they switch over to a meter system in late 1997.

Under the zone system, the city is cut into concentric zones (zone maps posted in cabs) and rates are determined by how many zones you cross, and also by the number of passengers and time of day (evening rush-hour surcharge). With this static system, drivers can quote the exact fare as soon as you say your destination.

The minimum fare is $2.60 for travel within one 'subzone.' There are additional fees for extra services (large bags, ordering a cab by phone, traveling during snow emergency).

Rates under the meter system will be less predictable and may be influenced by route and length of time waiting in traffic.

To call a cab, call Diamond (☎ 202-387-6200), Yellow (☎ 202-544-1212), or the conglomeration Taxi Transportation Service (☎ 202-398-0500).

Around DC

The District of Columbia is at the heart of a metropolitan region that expands into suburban Maryland and Virginia; a few sights closely associated with Washington – most notably Arlington National Cemetery and the Pentagon – are actually located beyond DC's boundary. A few more nearby attractions – particularly Alexandria's historic district and upriver reaches of the C&O Canal – are also worth exploring, but the metro region largely consists of bedroom communities most appealing to residents.

Beyond the metro region, Washington's visitors can access more distinct areas of Virginia and Maryland. In Virginia, you'll find George Washington's home in Mount Vernon within an hour's drive from DC. In Maryland, the state capital of Annapolis can be reached in an hour, and an hour's drive to the Eastern Shore gets you to surprisingly remote country communities.

Atlantic beaches are a three- to four-hour drive from Washington (not too practical for a day trip). You can reach Chesapeake Bay beaches in under an hour from DC. Time your trips out of the city to avoid major routes leaving DC on Friday afternoon and reentering on Sunday afternoon to bypass predictable delays and congestion (as well as typical morning and evening rush hours).

Below you'll find summaries of the regional offerings not far from DC proper. Highlights of other areas that may be of most interest to DC visitors are also included (see the Virginia and Maryland chapters for more information).

BELTWAY VIRGINIA

Within the Beltway (the interstate highway bypass that surrounds Washington, DC), Virginia offers several attractions worth a trip out of urban Washington. See the Northern Virginia chapter for more information on all the sights listed below.

One of the DC area's most-visited sights is **Arlington National Cemetery**, which is best known for its Tomb of the Unknowns, where a ritualized changing of the guard takes place periodically throughout the day. Visitors also make a pilgrimage to the Kennedy gravesites, the final resting place of John F Kennedy (memorialized with an eternal flame), Robert Kennedy, and most recently, Jacqueline Kennedy Onassis.

The **Pentagon**, also located in Arlington, is the headquarters of the powerful Department of Defense. The massive five-sided structure – said to be the largest office complex in the world – can be visited on a guided tour designed around security measures.

The **city of Arlington** itself offers resources nearby for Metro area visitors. In fact, there's a cluster of budget motels off I-495 in Arlington, just south of the Potomac River, that are inexpensive and convenient for visitors traveling by car.

Alexandria is also a popular destination for DC visitors looking for a short day trip out of the city. The compact riverside 'Old Town' lures walkers with its colonial architecture, beautiful historic houses, churches, storefronts, and taverns, alongside modern boutiques, restaurants, and cafes.

BELTWAY MARYLAND

Besides Bethesda (see the Western Maryland chapter), Maryland's Beltway suburbs have little to offer travelers in the way of culture, history, recreation, or cheap/distinctive lodging. Until the end of WWII, places like Takoma Park, Rockville, and Landover were country

C&O Canal National Historic Park

The C&O Canal was envisioned as a western passage joining the Chesapeake Bay and the Ohio River. The 184-mile section between DC's Georgetown district and Cumberland, Maryland, contains 74 lift locks that rise from near sea level to an elevation of 605 feet. A dusty towpath alongside the canal was trod by children (paid four cents a day by some accounts) leading mules, who in turn pulled barges through the canal. The advent of the railroads rendered the canal obsolete, and by 1848 the western passage idea was abandoned.

Today the historic canal corridor along the Potomac is preserved as a national park, and it is a major recreational resource for hiking, bicycling, boating, backpacking, horseback riding, and historic touring. Mule-pulled barge rides run along the canal from Great Falls and from Georgetown.

The Georgetown **visitors center** sells tickets for mule-pulled barge rides and distributes maps. A half mile away, **Thompson's Boat Center** rents canoes, kayaks, and bicycles. (See the Chesapeake & Ohio Canal section under Georgetown above.)

You can also rent canoes and bicycles at **Fletcher's Boathouse**, around 2½ miles upriver from Georgetown on Canal Rd, and around 16 miles upriver at Swain's Lock (☎ 301-299-9006), a concession that has been in the Swain family for generations.

Near the Maryland town of Potomac (ten miles northwest of DC), a visitors center operates out of the historic **Great Falls Tavern** (☎ 301-299-3613, 301-299-2026), 11710 MacArthur Blvd. The tavern (first built as a lock house) is open daily 9:30 am to 5 pm. Hiking trails here lead along an exciting stretch of river falls and to an old gold mine. Barge rides aboard the *Canal Clipper* operate from April to November (depending on weather) for $5 adults and $3.50 children. To reach Great Falls, take I-495 to Exit 41, exit onto the Clara Barton Pkwy towards Carter Rock, and then turn west on MacArthur Blvd to the park entrance. There's an entrance fee of $4.

At the canal's northern terminus, you'll find the **Canal Visitor Center** on Canal St in Cumberland (☎ 301-722-8226), open Tuesday to Sunday, except in winter when it's open Tuesday to Saturday. Nearby **Canal Park** on PPG Rd (☎ 301-729-3136) features a canal boat replica with period furnishings from the canal's 1828 to 1924 heyday near three original canal locks and a restored lock house (a donation is requested). Here the annual C&O Canal Boat Festival is held each July.

Off Route 51 28 miles south of Cumberland, the **Paw Paw Tunnel** cuts 3118 feet through a mountain – a major engineering feat when it was built in the 1800s. Located on the C&O Canal towpath, the tunnel is open year round for hiking and biking; the **Tunnel Hill Trail** is around two miles long and crosses over the top of the tunnel (flashlights suggested).

Note that all canal activity is dependent upon local conditions. Seasonal flooding chronically damages the canal, and there's pressure and threats of closure because the constant upkeep and restoration strains the national park budget. Check on conditions before heading out. (For more information, see the Cumberland section in the Western Maryland and Alleghenies chapter.) ■

towns with individual identities. With the onset of urban flight and construction of the Beltway in the 1960s, housing developments sucked up all of the farms. Older suburban towns like Cheverly, Seat Pleasant, and Silver Hill have since become the choice residence for middle-class families escaping the urban jungle of southeast Washington, while newer suburbs like Potomac are upper-class enclaves. The salient differences between these places are the sizes of the houses, the number of shopping malls, and the colors of residents' skin.

Sites of interest to day-trippers include the Paul Garber Facility, the Smithsonian's Air & Space Museum's restoration and storage facility, and Surratt House, where John Wilkes Booth and his accomplice planned Lincoln's assassination.

BEYOND THE BELTWAY

Airport Areas

Baltimore Washington National Airport (BWI) is 30 miles northeast of Washington in Linthicum, Maryland. Dulles Washington International Airport is 25 miles west of Washington near Herndon, Virginia (and not far from Leesburg). Major chain hotels such as Comfort Inn, Holiday Inn, and Marriott are near both airports. Many major chains and local budget motels typically offer van shuttle service from the airport. By the baggage claim you can also find a bank of phones that connect directly to local hotels.

Beaches

Atlantic Ocean beach resorts such as **Rehoboth** in Delaware, and **Ocean City** and wild **Assateague Island** in Maryland are a three- to four-hour drive from Washington on highways that can be congested on summer weekends. Because of the distance and potential traffic, day-tripping to Atlantic beaches is barely feasible, and travelers headed for the coast should plan on spending at least a night at the shore. Day-trippers looking for a beach might consider the two following Chesapeake Bay spots, both within an hour's drive of Washington.

Sandy Point State Park sits near the foot of the Bay Bridges to the Eastern Shore just off Hwy 50/301, 35 miles east of Washington. A broad beach overlooks an offshore lighthouse and the bay's main shipping lanes; the state provides changing facilities, a vending area, boat ramps, and fishing jetties. The beach can get packed in July and August, and swimming can be hazardous if the Chesapeake's infamous stinging jellyfish – sea nettles – are around.

The small resort of **Chesapeake Beach** lies 25 miles south of Annapolis and 35 miles southeast of Washington on the Chesapeake's Western Shore.'CB' boasts a yacht basin, an extensive sport-fishing charter boat fleet, attractive condos, good restaurants, two new boardwalks, and a small but lively night scene. The beach here is far less crowded than the bay beach at Sandy Point. Of course, there may be sea nettles during summer months. From the Washington Beltway take Route 4 east to Lyons Creek, and then head east on Route 260 to Chesapeake Beach (see the Southern Maryland chapter).

Countryside

Poised on the Chesapeake Bay's Western Shore 30 miles east of Washington on Hwy 50/301, **Annapolis** has been the capital of Maryland since colonial times. A national landmark, the city has one of the largest concentrations of 18th century homes and public buildings (many open to the public) in the country. The Annapolis harbor, along with its connecting tidal creeks, shelters dozens of marinas where thousands of cruising and racing sailboats moor. Restaurants, bars, and inns are clustered on the city's waterfront. Today, Annapolis has a well-deserved reputation as a party town.

If you only have a day to spend outside of Washington, and you want to see something of the Chesapeake's Eastern Shore, which is fabled for its 'long-ago-and-far-away' ambiance, consider visiting **Chestertown**. Lying on the upper Eastern Shore 75 miles northeast across the Chesapeake from Washington, Chestertown is an architectural and historic gem on Route 213 N. The town's restored colonial grand houses, along with some churches and public buildings, rival those of Annapolis, but Chestertown remains a quiet country town largely overlooked by the tourist hordes.

The port town of **St Michaels**, on Bay Hundred Peninsula 75 miles across the Bay Bridge from Annapolis, is the most popular destination for day-trippers who want to get a feel for the Eastern Shore. Thickly settled around a trio of coves on the Miles River, St Michaels has been a vital port on the Chesapeake since the 1700s. Today, the town maintains its colonial feel with red brick, Georgian buildings, bed & breakfast inns, and historic watercraft tied at the wharf of the Chesapeake Bay Maritime Museum. The watermen still unload their catches at harborside. St Michaels lies nine miles west of Easton on Hwy 33.

If you really want to see how Eastern Shore watermen work and live, visit **Tilghman Island**. This thriving watermen's community is home to hundreds of oystering, clamming, fishing, and crabbing boats and the rough-and-ready men and women who, as they say, 'follow the water.' You will find this small island at the end of Hwy 33, 14 miles southwest of St Michaels.

Mountains

Harpers Ferry is a small town at the confluence of the Shenandoah and Potomac Rivers in West Virginia about 50 miles from Washington. The town's notoriety stems from fiery abolitionist John Brown's raid on the federal armory here in 1859, but Harpers Ferry was also in the thick of conflict during much of the Civil War. Most of the town falls within a national historic park that encompasses the Maryland and West Virginia sides of the Potomac. The Appalachian Trail also passes through town. From DC, the town is easily accessed by car via I-270 and Hwy 340 W.

Facts about Virginia

At first read you will find the following chapters replete with history. There will be no apologies, as Virginia oozes history – every town seems to have some association with great events and people. Virginia was the cradle of American civilization and the predominant battleground of the cataclysmic Civil War between North and South. Hardly a village, patch of forest, river, or geographical feature escaped the ravages of the war and there are many mementos left for the traveler to see and reflect on.

Virginia is also endowed with tremendous natural features, from mountains and foothills to coastal beaches, and many of the state's regions are identified accordingly.

HISTORY

From the earliest beginnings of English settlement in the New World, Virginia has played an important and influential role, almost unproportionally large for its size, in the shaping of the nation's history.

Consolidation of the New Nation

Virginians played a major role in establishing the constitutional basis for the newly independent nation. In fact, four of the first five presidents were born and raised in the state.

In 1778, Virginia abolished further trade in African slaves, but slavery still constituted an important pillar of the state's plantation economy. Many of the nation's leaders, such as Washington and Jefferson, who wrote of the importance of individual liberty, still kept slaves – Washington, for example, owned 277 slaves at the time of his death.

The impotent provisions of the Articles of Confederation, which loosely bound the new nation together, needed thorough reexamination. These matters were considered in detail at a Constitutional Convention begun in Philadelphia on May 25, 1787. Twelve of the 13 states sent representatives (Rhode Island declined) and the convention lasted 16 weeks.

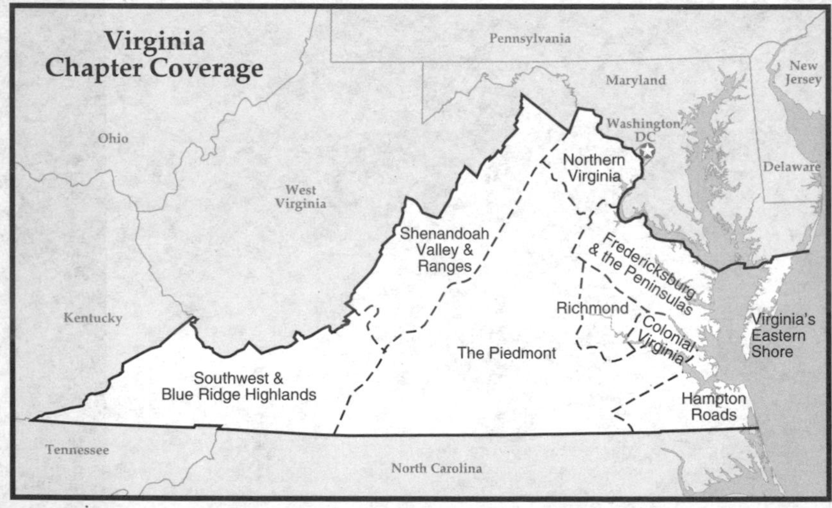

A number of prominent Virginians – George Mason, James Madison, Edmund Randolph, and Washington (who was elected the convention president) – attended. Thomas Jefferson was overseas on government business and Patrick Henry, who opposed strong central government, did not attend.

After lengthy and sometimes bitter debate the Virginia Plan was accepted and a bicameral legislature established. Throughout the proceedings both Washington and Madison fought to include a Bill of Rights and ensure the gradual phasing out of slavery. They were unsuccessful, but acquiesced to the document in its early form, feeling that they could achieve these changes at a later date.

On September 17, 1787, the Constitution was signed by 39 delegates and sent to the states for ratification. The Virginia convention struggled to ratify it after the influential Patrick Henry and James Monroe argued that it was undemocratic. John Marshall and James Madison eventually garnered enough support for the Constitution, and Virginia ratified it by a slim majority. Virginia officially entered the Union as the 10th state on June 25, 1788.

The first Congress of the US met in March 1789 to consider amendments and the two bills of rights forwarded by Virginia and New York. Ten of the amendments (of twelve submitted) were adopted and came to be known as the Bill of Rights. Nine of the amendments are attributable to Madison and the tenth to another Virginian, Richard Henry Lee.

Fighting for Freedom

Two of the most powerful uprisings against slavery occurred in Virginia. In Southampton in 1831, a 30-year-old slave named Nat Turner led around 70 men towards the county seat's store of arms and ammunition. Along the way they slew about 60 white masters and their families (they spared a poor white family) before they were suppressed by federal troops. Nat Turner initially escaped, then surrendered; he was sentenced to death and was hung. The nightmare of all slaveowners, Nat Turner's revolt rocked the institution of slavery throughout the South.

In Harpers Ferry (now West Virginia), white abolitionist John Brown further shocked the nation by demonstrating that some whites so opposed slavery they were willing to die for the abolitionist cause. In 1859, Brown with his band of 22 men attempted to seize the federal arsenal, but he was trapped by US troops. Ten of the band were killed, five escaped; Brown and six others were captured. Brown was executed. Though he failed to incite a regionwide slave rebellion, his raid and the national response to it did prefigure the coming civil war. ■ *– KS*

Virginian Presidents

Washington was the first president elected under the terms of the new constitution; he was inaugurated in April 1789. He was persuaded to run for re-election in 1792, and served a second term of four years. He declined a third term, preferring instead to retire to his beloved Mount Vernon on the Potomac River. During his presidency Virginia ceded part of its territory for the new national capital, which would eventually bear Washington's name.

Thomas Jefferson was the second Virginian to be elected president. He was the nation's third president (1801–1808) and the first to take up the post in Washington, DC. Although Jefferson will be remembered more for his intellectual achievements than his deliberations when in office, it should not be forgotten that his purchase from Napoleon of the Louisiana Territory almost doubled the size of the US. He also encouraged exploration of this new territory, the Mississippi River and the Southwest, and carefully steered the nation away from involvement in further damaging wars.

The next Virginian to become president was James Madison. Fully supported by his friend Jefferson, who had declined a third term, Madison took office in 1809. Pressured by hawkish elements in Congress

Madison, unlike Jefferson, was not able to avoid entry into another war, and much of his second term was spent embroiled in the so-called War of 1812. During this war some Virginia plantations were attacked by British naval forces, and at one stage (in 1814) Madison and his wife had to flee Washington, DC. The city was subsequently burned by the British in retaliation for the earlier burning of York (now Toronto) in Canada in 1812.

In 1817, the already 'elder' statesman (and Virginian) James Monroe succeeded Madison as president. During his two-term presidency Monroe oversaw expansion into the West, helped to determine the boundary with British North America (Canada), and signed the Missouri Compromise (which admitted Missouri to the union as a slave-holding state). His most significant achievement – the first clear statement of US foreign policy, now called the Monroe Doctrine – was delivered to Congress in 1823. In the 36 years since Washington's inauguration as president, Virginians had occupied the post for 32 years.

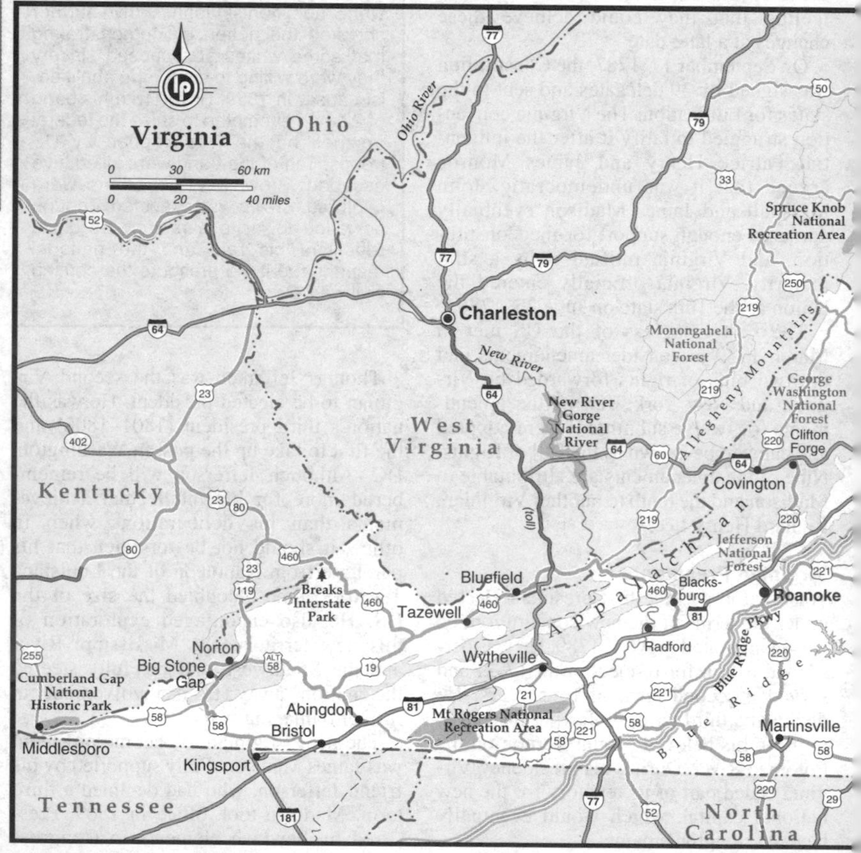

The Coming of War

Prior to the Civil War the state was roughly divided into two camps. The eastern camp, based in the Tidewater, was reliant upon slavery to reap the maximum out of its tired soil. The western counties, with a more diverse economic base, were undergoing rapid development.

An attempt in 1830 by democratic forces within the legislature to achieve the gradual phasing out of slavery failed, and with the subsequent failure of Nat Turner's brief slave revolt in Southampton County in August 1831, the entrenched slave-holding forces in the legislature won out. Feeding on the fear of the white population, who saw such revolts as a consequence of abolition, these forces were able to pass more oppressive laws, and the anti-slavery forces in the state were effectively silenced from then onward.

Following John Brown's 1859 raid on Harpers Ferry (then part of Virginia; see the Western Maryland chapter for more on this raid), the state surprisingly opposed secession, proposed a peace convention, and

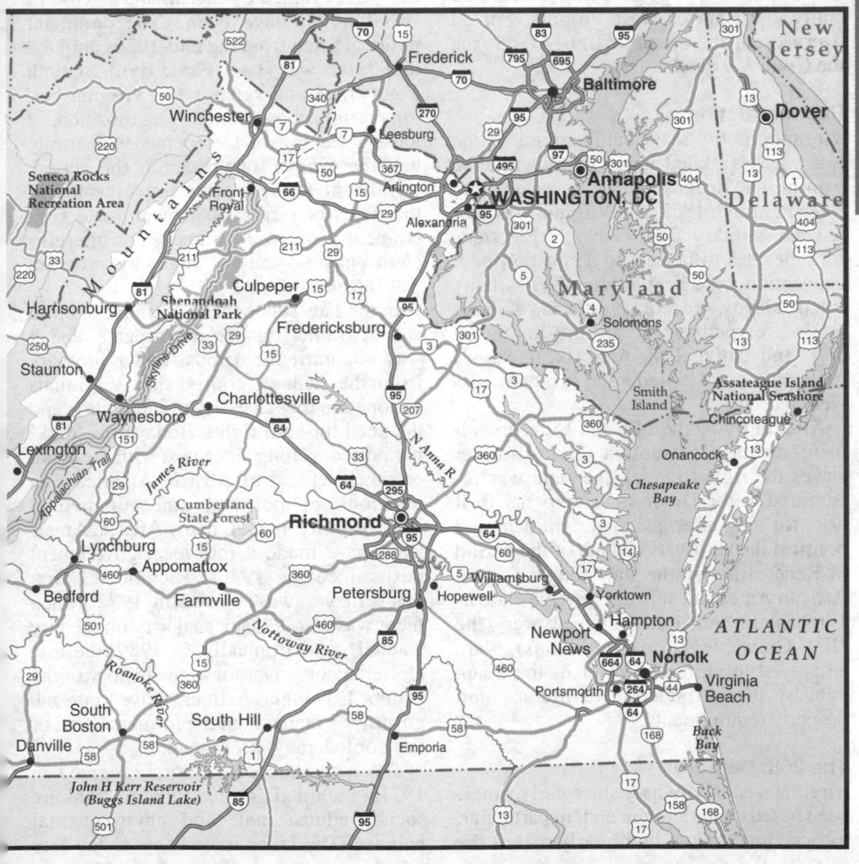

even dispatched a delegation to Washington with the intention of avoiding hostilities at all costs.

As late as February 1861 the state convention voted against secession. It was after Lincoln's call for troops, which followed the firing on Fort Sumter, that the state finally seceded on April 17, 1861. With Virginia went the military genius of Robert E Lee (see the sidebar on Lee in the Northern Virginia chapter) and the future Confederate capital, Richmond. The northwestern portion of the state had little to do with secession and, during the course of the war, on June 20, 1863, was recognized in Washington, DC, as being a separate entity, the state of West Virginia. For an overview of the events of 1861–1865, see the Civil War sidebar.

Reconstruction

Virginia, as the main battleground of the war, was devastated and recovery was to be painful. The Reconstruction Acts came into force in March 1867, and Virginia was designated Military District No 1. Elections for delegates to be sent to a constitutional convention were held in late 1867 – many freed slaves, recent Northern arrivals (called 'carpetbaggers' by the Southerners), and native Unionists ('scalawags') took part but Confederate sympathizers were barred.

After ratifying the 14th and 15th Amendments to the Constitution (giving former slaves the right to vote), the state was readmitted to the Union in January 1870. It was, for long after, plagued with debt and political instability. For much of the period of Reconstruction the state fought against African American suffrage. Even as late as 1902, state constitutional measures (the 'Jim Crow' legal manipulations) were employed to curb the power of the black vote by the introduction of literacy and property requirements.

The 20th Century

Virginia's economy had, since early times, been based on agriculture and, in particular, tobacco production. In the early part of the 20th century many Virginians left the state to seek work elsewhere. But the network of railroads connecting urban centers expanded, spurring industrial growth and gradually reversing the population exodus. The importance of Virginian ports (and the shipbuilding industry) supported industrailization, as steamships carried more and more freight.

By this point the importance of Virginia as a source of motivating intellectual thought had all but faded. No longer was the state important in the determination of national affairs. In fact, the state seemed to head in an opposite direction, clutching to old values fueled by racism and a sense of 'what might have been.' The dominant political force from the mid-1920s until the mid-1960s was Harry Flood Byrd, Sr, both a governor and senator for Virginia but, importantly, boss of the 'Organization,' a loose grouping of Democrats who firmly held the reins of state power. In this period, significant reforms were implemented in the fields of city management, state government costs were pruned, and the efficient 'pay-as-you-go' highway program was introduced.

In the late 1950s the state chose to close schools rather than to desegregate, and it was not until the 1960s, under pressure from the Federal courts, that Virginians cottoned to the necessity of integration and the need for civil rights. Today, this 'dark' period seems long since past with the equal enfranchisement of African Americans in positions of political and commercial responsibility. In fact, many African Americans have made it into local government posts since the 1970s. Richmond's first black mayor was elected in 1977 (when there was also a black majority on the city council), and ironically, in 1989, the first elected black governor in the history of the nation, L Douglas Wilder, moved into the governor's mansion in the former capital of the Confederacy, Richmond.

The new state constitution, adopted in 1971, included some forward-thinking social, educational, and environmental policies. The latter issue came to the fore in the mid-1970s with the Kepone pesticide disaster near Hopewell on the James River – a consequence was the introduction of stricter controls over the disposal of toxic waste.

The state's economic 'risorgimento' came with WWII, in part because of its new role as the 'military base' for the US. Northern Virginia, the back doorstep of DC, assumed importance as a bedroom community for government employees. Thus the fastest growing areas in the state today are the counties near the nation's capital and the area around the many military bases of Hampton Roads – and now the large majority of the population is urban based.

GEOGRAPHY

Virginia is roughly triangular in shape, measuring about 200 miles from north to south and 425 miles from west to east. A portion of the state lies on the Delmarva Peninsula, cut off from the rest of the state by Chesapeake Bay.

The main part of Virginia can be divided into three very distinct topographical regions. These are the Appalachian Mountains at the western border of the state, the Piedmont plateau running down the middle, and the Tidewater region, a coastal plain about 100 miles wide that comprises about a quarter of the state. The average elevation of the state is 950 feet.

The Appalachian region is again divided into three parts – the Blue Ridge Mountains, the Allegheny Mountains, and the Great Valley in between. The Blue Ridge Mountains, immortalized in folklore and song, run in a southwest direction, vary from three miles to 20 miles in width and include the highest point in Virginia, Mt Rogers at 5729 feet. These mountains are composed of ancient granitic and metamorphic volcanic formations, some over one billion years old.

The Blue Ridge Mountains are separated from the Allegheny Mountains by the Great Valley, which varies from 25 miles to 30 miles in width. It is in turn intersected by five river valleys which drain the high ground to either side. The Allegheny Mountains of Virginia vary from 1500 to 4000 feet in elevation – much of this range is in West Virginia.

The Piedmont, a large undulating plateau, extends from the Potomac River in the north of the state, where it is about 40 miles wide, to the border with North Carolina in the south, where it is about 175 miles wide. At its western edge it is about 1000 feet in elevation but it slopes down almost to sea level in the east.

Occupying about one quarter of the state is the low-lying coastal plain or 'Tidewater' on the eastern fringe. It is about 100 miles wide and is about 100 feet in elevation at its western edge where it meets the Piedmont, dropping to sea level in often marshy regions to the east. The marshlands are typified by the Great Dismal Swamp in the state's southeast corner. The general coastline is only 112 miles in length but if measured to take in all the indentations of bays, inlets, and estuaries it is over 3200 miles.

The state is intersected by a number of rivers and drainage is in two main directions. The rivers and their tributaries which drain the Piedmont – the Potomac, Rappahannock, James, and York – head into Chesapeake Bay in a southeasterly direction. Most of Virginia's Tidewater region is divided into three peninsulas ('necks') by these rivers.

The one anomaly, the Roanoke, in the south of the Piedmont, meets the Atlantic in North Carolina. The main watershed is in the west of the state. Here the North Fork of the Holston River and the New River flow in a southwest direction, to the south of the Great Valley, into Tennessee.

ECONOMY

The state's economic base has traditionally been agricultural, with tobacco being the most important crop. In spite of its recent bad press, the 'sot weed' is still important, along with other farm produce such as apples, dairy products, poultry, livestock, peanuts, and the famed Virginia ham.

Virginia's proximity to Washington, DC, means that there are many parts of the north of the state that are dormitory cities. The military is a major employer, in the DC region (the Pentagon is in Arlington), at Virginia's many forts and military installations, and at Hampton Roads, where the world's largest naval facility is located.

The primary employer is the manufacturing sector, however, with transportation equipment, clothes, furniture, and chemicals and allied products being important industries. Third and fourth largest employers are the wholesale and retail trades and services – the booming travel industry gets included with services.

GOVERNMENT & POLITICS

Virginia's General Assembly is the oldest continuous law-making body in the 'New World' as it dates from the House of Burgesses, established in Jamestown in 1619. The General Assembly, consisting of the 40-member Senate, elected for four-year terms, and the 100-member House of Delegates, elected for two-year terms, exercises legislative authority. Currently the speaker is Thomas W Moss, Jr, a Demo-crat, the majority leader is C Richard Cran-well, also a Democrat, and the minority leader is S Vance Wilkins, Jr, a Republican.

The current governor, the young Republican George Felix Allen – son of the professional football coach of the Washington Redskins – was elected in 1993 after a short period in the House of Representatives.

POPULATION & PEOPLE

The population of the state is 6,552,000 and well over 60% of this is concentrated in an 'urban corridor' that stretches from the Northern Virginia cities south of Washington, DC, through Richmond to its greatest concentration in Hampton Roads. This concentration is often seen as an extension of the 'Megalopolis,' or great mass of population, which arches in a crescent from Boston to Washington, DC. There are other concentrations of population in the west of the state, in Lynchburg, Charlottesville, and Roanoke; the mountainous southwest of the state and much of the Piedmont remain essentially rural enclaves.

There is a really interesting mix of people in Virginia, and approximately 80% are Caucasian. Some 20% of the population is African American, reflecting the time when black slaves played an important part in the development of the region. There is an increasing number of foreign-born people, especially in the region of Northern Virginia which lies to the south of Washington, DC. The ethnic mix found in places such as Arlington has created tremendous diversity in restaurants and choices of entertainment. Generally, relations between the various groups have been much less violent than in other parts of the US, and there seems a conscious attempt for all to work together for the common good.

An interesting series of pamphlets called *Heritage* focuses on minority groups such as Native Americans, Hispanic Americans, and African Americans. It's produced by The Pepper Bird Foundation (☎ 757-220-5761), PO Box 1071, Williamsburg, VA 23187-1071. These pamphlets outline pertinent museums and sites, festivals, events, history, and resources, such as publications and organizations.

There are many African American sites and Black Heritage walking tours, including the Alexandria Black History Resource Center, Alexandria Archaeology, the Fredericksburg Black Heritage walking tour, Hampton University, the Little England Chapel in Hampton, the Booker T Washington National Monument in Hardy (south of Roanoke), the Black Soldiers Memorial in Norfolk, the Harrison Museum of African American Culture in Roanoke, and The Other Half Tours of Colonial Williamsburg.

In Richmond, there is a gallery of African art in the Virginia Museum of Fine Arts, the colorful Jackson Ward Historic District, the Black History Museum and Cultural Center of Virginia, the Maggie L Walker National Historic Site, The Valentine Museum, and Virginia Union University.

Important Native American sites include Jamestown Settlement and Island, the Pamunkey and Mattaponi Indian museums in King William County, the Historic Crab

Orchard Museum in Tazewell County, and the Virginia Historical Society in Richmond. For more information about these contact the Virginia Council on Indians, Virginia Department of Health & Human Resources, PO Box 1475, Richmond, VA 23219. They will advise on the many powwows and festivals which are open to the public.

ARTS

Literature

Virginia has a rich literary history, with many of the best works linked to either the colonial or Civil War period of its history. Perhaps the best known of Virginian novelists is Ellen Glasgow (1874–1945), born into an aristocratic family in Richmond just after the Civil War. In her writings she eschews her privileged background and attempts to make a realistic assessment of the South and its problems in the period following the war. All of Glasgow's novels mix romantic sensibility and tough reality but give insight into a 100-year period of Virginia history, particularly as it relates to Richmond at the turn of the century. Her most important works are *The Voice of the People* (1900), *Virginia* (1913), *Barren Ground* (1925), *The Romantic Comedians* (1926), *They Stooped to Folly* (1929), and *In This Our Life* (1941), for which she won the Pulitzer Prize.

A contemporary of Glasgow's, Willa Cather (1873–1947), was born in Winchester, Virginia. Most of her best known works centered on life on the Midwestern prairie; she received the first Prix Femina Americana in 1933 for her novel *Shadows on the Rock* (1931). *Sapphira and the Slave Girl* (1940) is one of Cather's few novels to include Virginia as a setting; most of the others were based in Nebraska.

James Branch Cabell (1879–1958) was also born in Richmond and, like Ellen Glasgow, came from a distinguished family. He was very prolific, writing over 50 novels and two collections of autobiographical essays. His first novel, published in 1904, was *The Eagle's Shadow*, the first in an 18-volume series called *The Biography of Manuel* – a series which related the fantastic tales of Manuel in the medieval land of Poictesme.

Writers not born in Virginia but who spent some time in the state include William Faulkner, winner of the 1919 Nobel Prize for Literature (while a writer-in-residence at the University of Virginia in Charlottesville), and the famous poet, short-story writer, and essayist Edgar Allan Poe. After his parents died in his early childhood, Poe was raised for some years by John Allan, a Richmond businessman. He studied in private schools in Virginia, and at the University of Virginia for one year.

John William Fox, Jr (1863–1919), for many years a resident of Big Stone Gap in the Appalachians, may not have been the most prolific writer but his novels were certainly popular. Though once described as an 'antediluvian Ozarkian melodrama,' *The Trail of the Lonesome Pine* (1908) was the nation's first novel to sell a million copies. Based on firsthand experiences of the author, this novel paints a sentimental picture of life in the southwest Virginian mountains. His fiction has been adapted very successfully for the movies and theater.

Anne Spencer (1882–1975), an African American poet of the Harlem Renaissance period of the 1920s, lived and wrote in Lynchburg. Spencer had an international reputation and her works have been anthologized in *The Norton Anthology of American Literature*.

Many popular American novelists moved to rural parts of Virginia in the 1980s and 1990s – for example, John Grisham of *The Rainmaker* fame lives in Covesville, just south of Charlottesville.

Fine Arts

Virginia is well represented in all of the fine arts. The first state museum of the arts in the US was the Virginia Museum of Fine Arts in Richmond. The Chrysler Museum in Norfolk has one of the largest art collections south of Washington, DC, and Roanoke has the Art Museum of Western Virginia with a southern mountain folk art collection.

All forms of music are well represented throughout the state. In the southwest, there is an opera and a symphony in Roanoke; the Garth Newel Music Center, for chamber music, in Bath County; Cockram's General Store on a Friday night for mountain music; and Galax, where the fiddle reigns supreme. Throughout the southwest and Shenandoah old dance forms are kept alive by square dance groups and 'flatfoot cloggers.'

Richmond has performances of opera and symphonic music at the Shanghai Quartet at the University of Richmond; the Carpenter Center; the Big Gig Musicfest in summer; and a host of choirs. The Richmond Ballet is the state ballet of Virginia, but the Concert Ballet of Virginia, also based in Richmond, is the state's oldest.

Hampton Roads, the most populous part of the state, is also well served with the fully professional Virginia Opera and the very busy Virginia Symphony.

Jefferson designed the state's architectural gems: Monticello, Poplar Forest, the Rotunda and Academical Village (the University of Virginia), and the State Capitol in Richmond. Other places of interest the Pope-Leighey House, designed by Frank Lloyd Wright, in Alexandria; the garden layout of Mount Vernon; the many Georgian-style plantation mansions; and the preserved colonial city of Williamsburg.

Folk Arts

The Appalachian region is best known for its highly evolved arts and crafts, most notably woodworking, including fine cabinetry to rough-hewn works, in addition to quilting, basketry, and self-taught artwork that draws on the Highland heritage. The music and dancing of the region is also distinctive – bluegrass music emanates from Highland fiddles, and occasionally Elizabethan ballads can be heard on mountain dulcimers, traditions retained from the residents' English ancestry. A flat-footin' style of dancing called clogging can be seen – it's thought to have derived from black dance styles earlier this century – and square dancing is also popular.

Theater

There is a rich tradition of live theater in the state. In 1932, the Barter Theater, so called because produce was traded for admission, was established by out-of-work actors in Abingdon in the southwest. At this, the oldest professional repertory theater in the US, actors such as Gregory Peck and Ernest Borgnine got their start. Other southwestern theatrical events are the outdoor dramas *Trail of the Lonesome Pine* in Big Stone Gap and *The Long Way Home* in Radford. Another outdoor venue is Lexington's Lime Kiln Theatre, with its unique setting in a limestone quarry.

The state's second oldest theater, the Wayside Theatre in Middletown, has a season from May through December. Actors getting their start here include Peter Boyle and Susan Sarandon.

The main centers have quite an assortment of theaters and players. Richmond has the Theatre Virginia (the state's flagship professional company), Theatre IV, and two well known theater restaurants. In Norfolk, the Virginia Stage Company performs in the historic Wells Theatre; Broadway productions are performed at Chrysler Hall.

Films & Video

Virginia has been fertile ground for the setting of films. Movies filmed in Richmond include *Doc Hollywood* (1991) with Michael J Fox, Woody Harrelson, and Bridget Fonda; *True Colors* (1991) with John Cusack, Mandy Patinkin and Richard Widmark; *Miss Rose White* (1992) with Maximilian Schell and Maureen Stapleton; and *Love Field* (1992) with Michelle Pfeiffer.

In other parts of the state, *Trail of the Lonesome Pine* (1937) was set in the Appalachians in the southwest of the state and starred Fred MacMurray, Henry Fonda, and Sylvia Sidney; *Brother Rat* (1938), starring Ronald Reagan and Jane Wyman, was set in the Virginia Military Institute in Lexington; *Dirty Dancing* (1987), with Jennifer Grey and Patrick Swayze, was filmed at Mountain Lake Resort; the chilling *Silence of the Lambs* (1990), starring Anthony Hopkins and Jodie Foster, was filmed at Quantico, in Northern Virginia; *Sommersby* (1993), with Jodie Foster and Richard Gere, was filmed in Lexington and Bath County (Sommersby, watched by his wife, was hanged behind 'Stonewall' Jackson's house); and the final scenes of *Broadcast News* (1987) with William Hurt, Albert Brooks, and Holly Hunter, were filmed in the boxwood hedge gardens of Gunston Hall.

A video you might want to get your hands on is the one-hour *National Parks of the Appalachians: Great Smoky Mountains, Blue Ridge Parkway, Shenandoah* ($29.95). It's a comprehensive tour over the mountains, with a background of mountain music.

INFORMATION

Tourist Offices

Besides the Virginia Division of Tourism (see Facts for the Visitor, Tourist Offices) Virginia has 10 welcome centers throughout the state on interstate highways. These have brochures about regional sites, accommodations in the area and more specific information. They are listed in the text.

Area Codes

The telephone area codes have undergone considerable change recently. There are four codes: 703 for the area of Northern Virginia around Washington, DC; 540 for the Blue Ridge Mountains and Shenandoah Valley; 804 for Richmond and the Piedmont; and 757 for Hampton Roads, Williamsburg, and the Eastern Shore.

Time

Virginia operates on Eastern Standard Time. Daylight Saving Time (one hour ahead of standard time) is in effect from 1 am on the first Sunday in April until 2 am on the last Sunday in October.

Taxes

In Virginia a 4.5% sales tax is added to most purchases, and in some places 0.5% is added to this, bringing the tax up to 5%. In hotels you are likely to pay an additional 5% hotel tax meaning a total tax of about 10%. There are restaurant taxes applied in some areas (fortunately not all), and meal and drink bills may run from 8% to 10% in total tax.

Media

All of the major cities in Virginia have their own daily newspapers, and these are usually of a high standard. In Hampton Roads *The Virginia Pilot/Ledger Star* is the pick of the dailies, in Richmond the *Richmond Times-Dispatch* has a daily circulation of over 250,000, copies and *The Roanoke Times* serves the southwest. There are some fine African American weekly papers in Richmond – *Richmond Afro-American*, *Richmond Free Press*, and *The Voice*.

There are radio stations galore in Virginia with a smattering of everything on the airwaves – gospel, country & western, traditional country, and religious music are commonplace.

Liquor Laws

You can buy beer and wine in most grocery and convenience stores and at many gas stations. 'Hard' liquor (spirits) is only sold in stores approved by the Alcoholic Beverage Control (ABC). Licensed establishments, including restaurants, sell all types of drinks by the glass to patrons who can prove (with valid IDs) that they are 21 or older. The law requires all places that sell unpackaged liquor – bars included – to serve food.

THE CIVIL WAR, 1861–1865

In April 1861 a divided Union plunged into four dark years of bloody conflict – brother pitted against brother, families divided and often on opposing sides, widespread destruction, and an horrific toll in both military and civilian casualties. It is an almost impossible task trying to describe the cataclysmic events of 1861–65 in a few pages – some 100,000 books and articles have been written about it since! With numerous asides and maps, located in the chapters where the events took place, you may come a little closer to an understanding of the war.

IT ALL FALLS APART . . .

The path to war was essentially a long and complex struggle to save the Union. The actual state of war represented the boiling over of differences that had been simmering for some time.

One of the clearest factors was sectionalism, occasioned by the very different economic bases of the primarily agricultural South and the increasingly industrialized North. The South by the end of the 1850s produced nearly all of the world's cotton, and the viability of this one-crop economy was based on cheap black slave labor. How was it, in America, which feted itself as being a country founded on the premise of freedom from oppression, that the practice of human bondage won acceptance?

Following the establishment of the Union there had been opposition to slavery in both the South and North. But opposition in the South had almost vanished by the 1830s, as any abolitionists there were threatened, tarred and feathered, and generally ostracized. In the North there was a growing abolitionist presence and a definite sense that slavery was contrary to true liberal ideals – all Northern states had outlawed slavery by 1846. A landmark was the publication in 1852 of Harriet Beecher Stowe's novel *Uncle Tom's Cabin*, which hardened opposition to slavery in the North but was met with derision in the South.

The 1850s saw a number of developments that strengthened the divisions. A bill sponsored by Stephen A Douglas of Illinois in 1854 introduced the concept that settlers in the new territories, such as Kansas and Nebraska, had the right to choose whether or not their territory would allow slavery. Douglas' bill was passed into law, effectively ending the provisions of the Missouri Compromise, which for 30 years had successfully held the lid on the powder-keg issue of states' rights by allowing for twelve free states and twelve slave states and forbidding slavery in the Louisiana Purchase area north of latitude 36°30'N.

Once passed, Douglas' act had the very effect its opponents feared. Although Nebraska remained relatively unscathed, Kansas received a torrent of settlers from both the South and North who intended to influence the future of slavery in the territory. The opposing sides were soon at each other's throats and there were several bloody encounters.

In one week in May 1856 there was an attack on the 'free-stater' town of Lawrence, Kansas, which was followed up by an 'eye-for-an-eye' massacre of pro-slavery settlers by a band led by the fanatical Northern abolitionist, John Brown. 'Bleeding Kansas' intensified the divisions between anti-slavery and pro-slavery lobbies and, importantly, politicized the issue and polarized the various political groups. In the same week in May, Senator Charles Sumner, an abolitionist from Massachusetts, was beaten senseless with a cane by Congressman Preston Brooks, a pro-slavery supporter from South Carolina, in the Senate chamber. Not long before the beating, Sumner in a speech to the Senate had predicted that the fighting in Kansas would spread out from the western plains to a greater stage, 'where every citizen will be not only spectator but actor.'

In the national election of 1856 the new Republican party, opposed to the expansion of the number of slave-holding territories, won valuable experience and recognition, but failed to gain office. Northern hopes that the issue of states' rights not be settled in favor of the South were dashed with the Southern-dominated Supreme Court's ruling in the Dred Scott Case in 1857 – the court effectively ruled that Congress could not interfere with states' determinations in regard to the issue of slavery. The territories would be allowed to decide by 'popular sovereignty,' that is, a vote by the settlers.

Lincoln Enters the Picture

Before hope of resolving these divisive issues on the political level disintegrated, a little-known, rangy politician named Abraham Lincoln entered the picture. In 1858, Lincoln ran against Douglas in a Senate election. He debated the issue of slavery with Douglas; later he uttered the immortal words, 'A house divided against itself cannot stand. I believe this government cannot endure permanently half slave and half free.' Lincoln was defeated in the Senate election but won the recognition that would set him up for later battles.

In October 1859 John Brown was captured and hung for his raid on the arsenal at Harpers Ferry. Though Virginia slaves did not heed Brown's call for insurrection, his action sharpened the lines of division between the abolitionist North – which saw him as a martyr – and the pro-slavery South – which feared a wider slave revolt.

Abraham Lincoln

ELECTION OF 1860

All of these issues came to a head in the critical election of 1860, with sectionalism again the most critical divider. At a convention in Chicago, the Republicans nominated Lincoln to run for president, rejecting the distinguished politician William H Seward, whose strong anti-slavery stance was seen as a liability. The Democrats were fielding two slates of candidates – after two conventions they split into Northern and Southern sections. The Southern Democrats found in John C Breckinridge a candidate willing to protect slavery in the territories. Stephen A Douglas, who had mostly Northern and border state support, had been rejected by Southern Democrats, who felt his notion of 'popular sovereignty' was not clear-cut enough. A third group, the Constitutional Union Party, led by John Bell, gathered in the extremes of the Southern/Northern split.

The November 1860 election resulted in a Republican victory – Lincoln won a plurality of the popular vote (just over 40%) and over half of the electoral college votes (180 to 123) and therefore would take office the following March.

Once it became clear that Lincoln had been elected president, the Union began to fall apart. South Carolina had threatened to secede if this was the result – they feared that the Republicans, predominantly representing non-slave holding states, would now act to keep slavery out of the territories. To them Lincoln was the worst type of 'black' Republican and they had already witnessed his anti-slavery stance in earlier debates.

At a state convention, held on December 20, it was declared 'that the Union now subsisting between South Carolina and other states under the name of the 'United States of America' is hereby dissolved.' The other states of the lower south were not far behind – by February 8, Georgia, Alabama, Florida, Louisiana, Mississippi, and Texas had joined with South Carolina at a meeting in Montgomery, Alabama, to form the Confederate States of America. Jefferson Davis (a West Point graduate and senator from Mississippi) was elected president and Georgian Alexander Stephens vice-president.

Between the time of Lincoln's election and inauguration, very little of practical value was done by the then incumbent president, the Democrat James Buchanan, or his administration to avoid secession. Concerted attempts at compromise failed – even the proposal by John J Crittenden to extend the line of the Missouri Compromise from the Atlantic to the Pacific was rejected. Meanwhile the Southerners took control of the eleven forts and several other military installations in their territory, which they would need in time of war.

So by Lincoln's inauguration, on March 4, 1861, he had inherited a no win situation. On one side the hardened secessionists were unwilling to compromise and on the other, the successful Republicans were not about to squander the fruits of their electoral victory. Lincoln was willing to compromise on all issues demanded by the Southern states, except one – the division of the Union. When he learned that his Federal troops in Fort Sumter, in Charleston Harbor, South Carolina, needed to be supplied or withdrawn he ordered that supplies be sent to them. This provoked the Confederates into firing the first shots of the war on April 12–13, 1861.

With those shots the issues were now crystal clear – those who had had lingering doubts took sides. More states aligned with the Confederacy – Virginia on

April 17, 1861, then Arkansas, North Carolina, and Tennessee a month later. Slave-owning border states, with stronger ties to the Union – Delaware, Maryland, Kentucky, and Missouri – aligned with the North. These developments complicated matters for Lincoln – how could he outlaw slavery without alienating the loyal border states?

After Virginia's secession the capital of the Confederacy moved to Richmond, and with Virginia went the military genius Robert E Lee. Lincoln had offered Lee command of the Union forces, but the general would not turn his back on his beloved state. Lincoln called for volunteers 'to cause the laws to be duly executed' and the South did likewise, brandishing the ideals of defense of homeland and white supremacy.

The 'Political' War

Underlying all of the verbal sparring that preceded the war (and the battles to be waged later) was the issue of slavery. Remarkably, when the war started the two sides appeared to maintain similar stances. Lincoln feared any attempt at emancipation would alienate the Union's slave-holding border states, while the South enshrined the concept of Negro slavery in its new constitution by prohibiting the African slave trade but permitting the interstate trade of slaves. But slowly Lincoln realized that there were distinct advantages to officially oppose slavery. As the correct moral choice, it was hoped that emancipation would win support for the Northern cause in Europe. It also meant potential black recruits for the Union forces. But he really needed a victory before he could proclaim such a strong stance – otherwise, his actions would have been seen as born of desperation. The victory Lincoln was waiting for came at Antietam, Maryland, in mid-September 1862.

As soon as Lee had departed Union soil, Lincoln acted swiftly and on September 23 issued his preliminary Emancipation Proclamation, which promised to free all slaves in the Confederacy by January 1, 1863, unless the rebel states had by then returned to the Union. The border states were not affected – it was thought that after the war slavery could easily be abolished in these.

This symbolic proclamation had the desired result. By the end of the war there were nearly 180,000 black soldiers in the Union army and many had experienced combat – a great number distinguished themselves in battle and joined the list of war heroes. Furthermore, the move was greeted warmly by the European powers. Even in Britain, where textile industries were hungry for the South's cotton crop, sympathy for the Southern cause dwindled.

Towards the end of the war the South even made moves that faintly resembled a begrudging acceptance of emancipation. In March 1865, bowing to pressure from the Confederate generals, the Confederacy allowed the recruitment of black regiments. These never really came into play as the war was concluded swiftly.

Two victories in July 1863 – at the battle of Gettysburg and in the capitulation of Vicksburg – further strengthened Lincoln's political position. The midterm congressional elections of 1862 had been a rebuff to the Republicans – the Democratic Party, replete with anti-war forces (known as 'Copperheads'), nearly seized control of the House of Representatives – but with these victories on the battlefield pro-Lincoln sentiment returned. In dedicating the battlefield cemetery at

Gettysburg he enunciated his feelings simply. Regarding the preservation of the Union, he expressed his belief 'that these dead shall not have died in vain, that this nation under God shall have a new birth of freedom, and that the government of the people by the people for the people shall not perish from the earth.' The election of 1864 loomed and Lincoln agonized over it. Battle casualties in 1864 had been particularly heavy and there were elements in the Republican Party that opposed his renomination. The Democrats, with a platform of immediate peace, nominated General George McClellan (who conversely insisted that peace was dependent on preservation of the Union). Lincoln got the nomination for the Union Party, a loose alliance of Republicans and War Democrats. Thanks to another string of victories on the battlefield, especially Sherman's capture of Atlanta, he won the election of November 1864 with an electoral college vote of 212 to 12 (but in most states his plurality was only slightly more than his opponent). At his inauguration in 1865 he urged the American people to forget about vengeance and to 'do all which may achieve and cherish a just and lasting peace.'

The Congress had abolished slavery with the 13th Amendment to the Constitution on January 31, 1865. So, at the fall of Richmond, as Jefferson Davis and his cabinet fled south, Lincoln was greeted by hundreds of 'free' slaves. One elderly slave fell to his knees before Lincoln and praised him as a messiah. Lincoln responded: 'Don't kneel to me. You must kneel to God and thank Him for your freedom.' Lincoln did not live to see the 13th Amendment finally ratified (that happened on December 6, 1865). On April 9, five days after Lee surrendered to Grant at Appomattox, Lincoln was assassinated in a Washington theater by the Southern partisan John Wilkes Booth who believed that 'this country was formed for the *white* not for the black man.'

The thankless task of Reconstruction and the implementation of the objectives of the Emancipation Proclamation passed to Andrew Johnson, Lincoln's vice-president in the 1864 campaign. Reconstruction was made difficult by extremists on both sides, including Radical Republicans who had opposed Lincoln's sensible Reconstruction plans, the corrupt Northern opportunists known as 'carpetbaggers,' and the two Southern organizations that had developed in response to the Southern defeat – the Ku Klux Klan and the Knights of the White Camellia. The spirit of the generous terms which Grant and Sherman had offered to the armies of their defeated enemies, Lee and Joseph E Johnston, faded amid calls for retribution. Reconstruction was to be a bitter and painful process.

The Military War

It was never a 'dead cert' that the North would bulldoze the South into submission. The North's strength lay in a roughly two-to-one advantage in manpower, greater financial resources, and a far greater capacity to produce munitions (estimated by some sources then to have been 30-1). But as defender the South had the advantage of fighting on a system of interior lines, it had a huge coastline that proved hard to blockade, and there was always the possibility of foreign aid (from cotton-hungry European powers).

The South had Lee and, as they soon discovered, several other brilliant generals such as Stonewall Jackson. And the volunteer 'Rebels' seemed initially to have a far greater sense of brotherhood – the 'brothers-in-arms' strength of the underdog – which united them on the battle-field. Early on, the blood-curdling 'Rebel yell' put the fear of God into the hearts of the opposing Yankees. Only a few sound victories by the Federal forces redressed the balance.

Ulysses S Grant

After several minor battles in 1861, the two armies of volunteers, which had been gathering around their respective capitals, clashed at Manassas Junction, in northern Virginia, in July. The victory of the Southern forces in this battle was a precursor of events to come. The North initially suffered heavy losses in the ensuing battles because of poor and hesitant generalship, especially in the eastern theater (centered on Virginia).

The strategy of the war was simple – and certainly never grand. The South was essentially on the defensive, but there were times when their early forays into Federal territory could have easily been turned into victorious offensives – especially at the point when the North had not yet found a good land-battle commander. The Battle of Antietam in September 1862 spelled out the horrendous cost in casualties for unsuccessful offensives and also illustrated the difficulties of maintaining a large military force in hostile territory. If there were any doubts, the debacle of Gettysburg in July 1863, in which the Confederates suffered more casualties than the larger Northern forces, confirmed that further offensive action would be suicidal for the South.

The North's strategy had to be the offensive. It was outlined to a certain extent in the Anaconda Plan of Wilfred Scott, the first supreme commander of the Union forces, in May 1861. Roughly it proposed that the Confederate coastline be blockaded and control of the Mississippi be wrested, thus surrounding and strangling the South and facilitating Union invasions. The trouble was, it took enormous losses and four years to achieve the desired result.

Towards the end of the war, when US Grant dogged Lee through Virginia, there is no doubt that 'attrition' came into play. Despite greater losses on the battlefield, Grant maintained the offensive, attempting to isolate his foe from the supply base of Richmond and to sever the 'interior lines.' When Grant eventually trapped Lee in the Confederate capital and the war settled down to a siege it was only a matter of time before the North won. Interestingly, both sides had to resort to conscription – the South in 1862 and the North in 1863.

Lee knew that a set-piece defensive action with no room to maneuver was anathema to an army seasoned to making surprising and bold tactical moves. The biggest army would eventually stretch the defensive perimeter to its breaking point and then move in for the kill. Lee even said that with the Army of Northern Virginia besieged 'it will be a mere question of time.' And while Lee's troops were bottled up in the Richmond defenses Union General William Tecumseh Sherman was permitted to wage war in the west (Tennessee) and to eventually march triumphantly through Georgia and the Carolinas.

And of the oft forgotten naval effort, there is no doubt that the Federal navy – called 'Uncle Sam's web feet' by Lincoln – eventually provided a means to help win the war, although its actions and the blockade of the coastline did not really have an impact until the end of 1863. Early in the war, about 10% of the blockade runners were captured, but by the end of 1864 it was about one in three. Towards the end of the war, the only Confederate port that remained open to blockade runners was Galveston, Texas.

And with the Civil War came revolutionary changes in the nature of naval warfare. The most vaunted change at the time was the introduction of ironclad ships – the *Monitor* and *Merrimack/Virginia* battle highlighted this watershed. The use of steam and marine torpedoes ('mines'), and the sinking of a battleship by submarine (the Confederate *Hunley* sank the *Housatonic* in February 1864), presaged the major sea battles of WWI.

There was also a transitional revolution in the nature of land warfare. Innovations that would become de rigueur in later wars included the gathering of military intelligence (albeit misinformation, a lot of the time, in this war); aerial reconnaissance by balloon (and thus anti-balloon measures such as camouflage and 'anti-aircraft' fire); communication in the field by telegraph; the movement of troops and material by railroad and the use of rail guns (such as those at the siege of Petersburg); the establishment of field hospitals and the treatment of diseases in the field; a change in the weaponry (repeating magazine rifles, machine guns, shells, and rifled artillery); and the widespread appearance of journalists and photographers on the battlefield.

And what was it all for? For the South it was probably the defense of their homeland against an invading army; for the North the preservation of the Union and the survival of a form of democratic government ('of, by, and for the people') then only eighty years old. Interestingly, before the war the states were referred to as a plural noun (eg, the United States *are* . . .) and after, as a singular entity. For the slaves, of course, the war resulted in freedom.

The loss of over 600,000 lives and the half million or so other casualties was a gaping wound in the Union – a wound which even to this day has not fully healed. The Confederate flags still strewn over the cemeteries of Virginia and other Southern states indicate that the 'rebel' sentiment is still strong. Talk to many Southerners and touch on the subject of the war and you are likely to receive an emotional tirade. Sherman's 'March to the Sea,' Sheridan's razing of the Shenandoah, and the merciless shelling of the civilian populations in Vicksburg and Petersburg are still remembered by the descendants of those who felt the brunt of these actions, and the specter of the emaciated Union prisoners-of-war in the Confederate prison of Andersonville still arouses intense emotion in the North.

The defeated Lee expressed the purest of hopes when he implored that the sins of the past be forgotten and that Southern supporters should 'make your sons Americans.'

EASTERN THEATER CHRONOLOGY

1861 There were a few minor engagements in northwestern Virginia in June and July, won by the Federals. Sizable armies gathered around Washington, DC, and Richmond, and the first major engagement of the war took place at Manassas Junction (see Manassas in the Northern Virginia chapter), 26 miles southwest of Washington, DC, on July 21. The result of the **1st Battle of Manassas (Bull Run)** was a total rout of the Federal troops. A stalemate ensued, giving the new Union commander, George B McClellan, valuable time to train his Army of the Potomac. The combined actions of 1861, however, do not equal in losses and size a day of the later major battles of the war.

1862 On March 9 the USS *Monitor* dueled with the CSS *Virginia* (formerly the *Merrimack*) in Hampton Roads, the first clash of **ironclad vessels** in the history of naval warfare.

The Confederates under Joe Johnston abandoned their lines around Manassas and moved toward Richmond. McClellan geared up his new army and moved by water to the Federal strongholds of Fort Monroe and Newport News. He then mounted his **Peninsula Campaign** on April 4, a march on Richmond to the northwest. Both Confederate resistance and the mud caused by heavy rains slowed McClellan's advance, and he did not come within sight of Richmond for two months.

The Confederates attacked the Union force at Seven Pines (Fair Oaks) from May 31 to June 1, but the Federals stood fast. The most significant event was the wounding of Johnston and the subsequent assumption of command by Robert E Lee.

The **Seven Days Battles** raged around Richmond from June 25 to July 1 (see the Richmond chapter). The Union troops, after several defeats in these battles, successfully disengaged at Harrison's Landing.

Before and during the Peninsula Campaign the Confederate tactical genius Thomas 'Stonewall' Jackson had played a cat-and-mouse game with Union forces in the **Shenandoah Valley.** His victories and forays successfully prevented the Union forces from reinforcing McClellan's troops around Richmond (see the Shenandoah Valley chapter).

On August 9, Jackson clashed indecisively with the Federal forces of General John Pope at Cedar Mountain. When Lee learned that the Army of the Potomac was moving by water to join Pope, he moved to bolster Jackson's forces. The war returned to Manassas and on August 28 – 30 the **2nd Battle of Manassas (Bull Run)** was fought, resulting in another Confederate victory (see Manassas in the Northern Virginia chapter). Lee had, in nine weeks, succeeded in moving the war

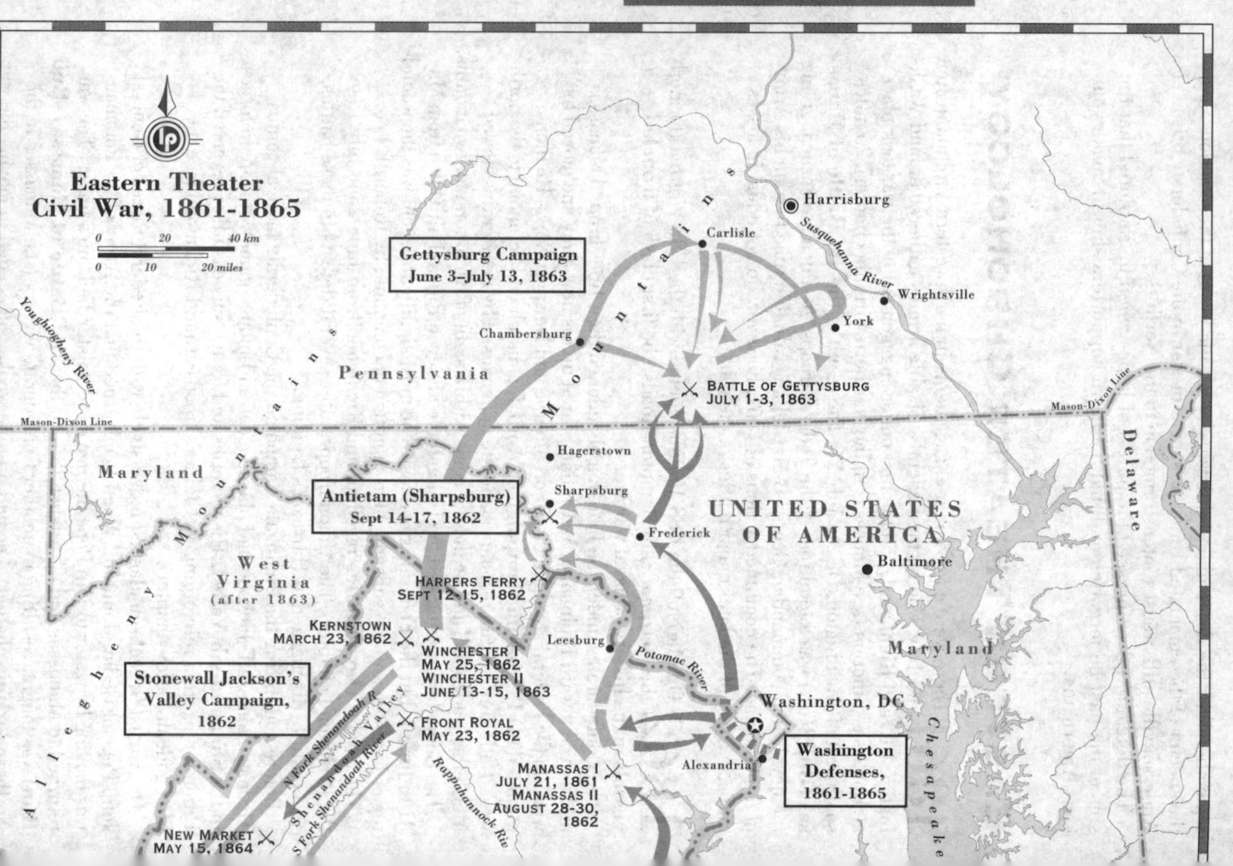
Eastern Theater
Civil War, 1861-1865
0 20 40 km
0 10 20 miles
Gettysburg Campaign
June 3–July 13, 1863
Antietam (Sharpsburg)
Sept 14-17, 1862
Stonewall Jackson's
Valley Campaign,
1862
Washington
Defenses,
1861-1865
BATTLE OF GETTYSBURG
JULY 1-3, 1863
UNITED STATES
OF AMERICA
Pennsylvania
Maryland
West
Virginia
(after 1863)
Maryland
Delaware
Chesapeake
Mason-Dixon Line
Mason-Dixon Line
Youghiogheny River
Harrisburg
Susquehanna River
Carlisle
Wrightsville
York
Chambersburg
Hagerstown
Sharpsburg
Frederick
Baltimore
Leesburg
Potomac River
Washington, DC
Alexandria
HARPERS FERRY
SEPT 12-15, 1862
KERNSTOWN
MARCH 23, 1862
WINCHESTER I
MAY 25, 1862
WINCHESTER II
JUNE 13-15, 1863
FRONT ROYAL
MAY 23, 1862
MANASSAS I
JULY 21, 1861
MANASSAS II
AUGUST 28-30,
1862
NEW MARKET
MAY 15, 1864
N Fork Shenandoah R
Shenandoah Valley
S Fork Shenandoah River
Rappahannock Riv
Mountains
Allegheny Mountains

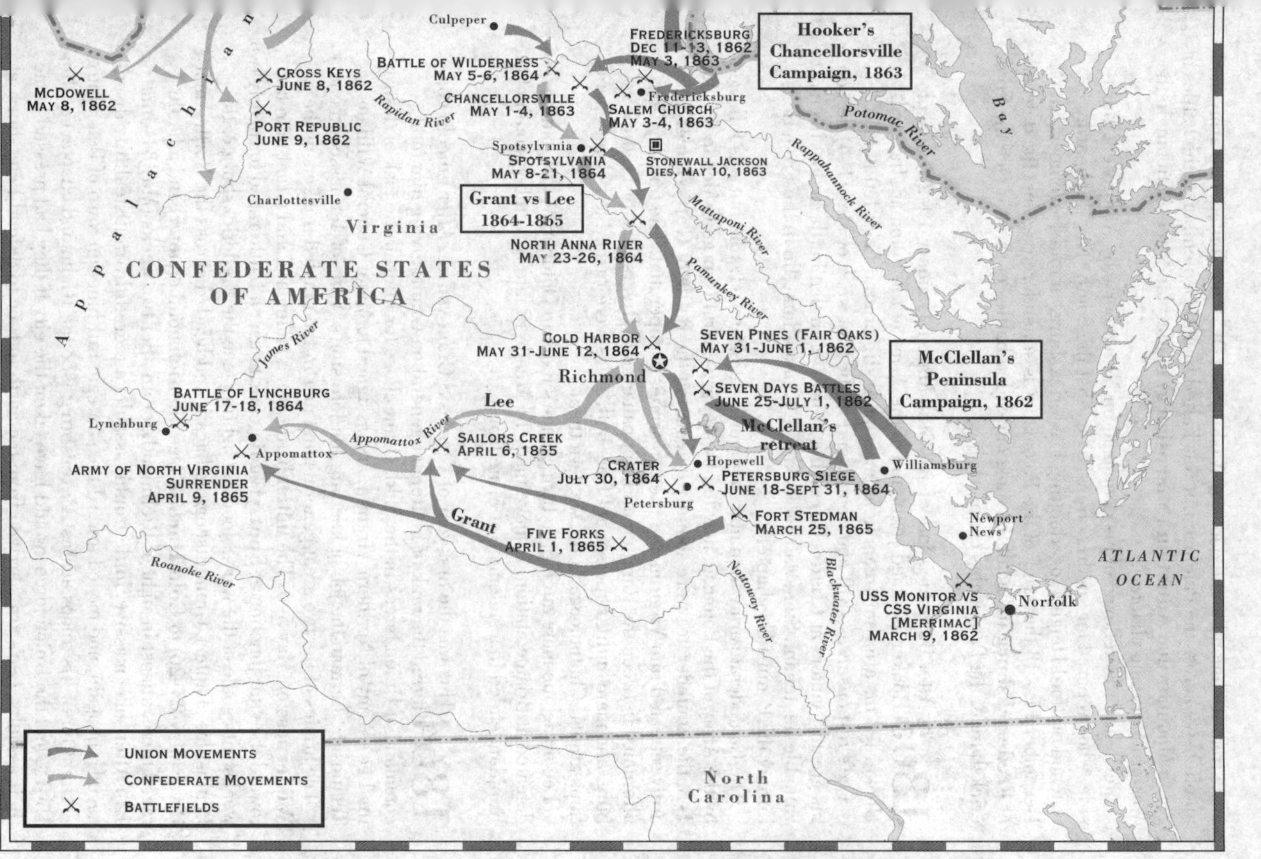
Hooker's Chancellorsville Campaign, 1863
McClellan's Peninsula Campaign, 1862
Grant vs Lee 1864-1865
Bay
ATLANTIC OCEAN
Potomac River
Rappahannock River
Mattaponi River
Pamunkey River
Rapidan River
James River
Appomattox River
Blackwater River
Nottoway River
Roanoke River
Appalachian
Culpeper
Fredericksburg
Spotsylvania
Charlottesville
Lynchburg
Appomattox
Richmond
Petersburg
Hopewell
Williamsburg
Newport News
Norfolk
FREDERICKSBURG DEC 11-13, 1862 MAY 3, 1863
SALEM CHURCH MAY 3-4, 1863
STONEWALL JACKSON DIES, MAY 10, 1863
CHANCELLORSVILLE MAY 1-4, 1863
BATTLE OF WILDERNESS MAY 5-6, 1864
SPOTSYLVANIA MAY 8-21, 1864
NORTH ANNA RIVER MAY 23-26, 1864
COLD HARBOR MAY 31-JUNE 12, 1864
SEVEN PINES (FAIR OAKS) MAY 31-JUNE 1, 1862
SEVEN DAYS BATTLES JUNE 25-JULY 1, 1862
McClellan's retreat
CRATER JULY 30, 1864
PETERSBURG SIEGE JUNE 18-SEPT 31, 1864
FORT STEDMAN MARCH 25, 1865
FIVE FORKS APRIL 1, 1865
SAILORS CREEK APRIL 6, 1865
Lee
Grant
ARMY OF NORTH VIRGINIA SURRENDER APRIL 9, 1865
BATTLE OF LYNCHBURG JUNE 17-18, 1864
CROSS KEYS JUNE 8, 1862
PORT REPUBLIC JUNE 9, 1862
McDOWELL MAY 8, 1862
USS MONITOR VS CSS VIRGINIA [MERRIMAC] MARCH 9, 1862
Virginia
CONFEDERATE STATES OF AMERICA
North Carolina
UNION MOVEMENTS
CONFEDERATE MOVEMENTS
BATTLEFIELDS

away from Richmond to the doors of Washington, DC. The Confederate army made an offensive across the Potomac but was halted in mid-September at the battles of South Mountain and **Antietam (Sharpsburg)** in Maryland (see Antietam in the Western Maryland chapter).

McClellan was relieved of his command on November 7 by Ambrose E Burnside, who prepared for another offensive against the South. The Union army reached Stafford Heights, overlooking Fredericksburg, in mid-November, but on December 11 – 13 the Army of the Potomac was squandered against the defenses of **Fredericksburg** in one of the most one-sided battles of the war (see the Fredericksburg & the Peninsulas chapter).

1863 After Burnside's indecisive 'Mud March' (January 19–23), Joseph Hooker assumed command of the Army of the Potomac. In April, Hooker led his army upstream in an attempt to slip around Lee's left flank.

Lee's response was swift and deadly and in the first week of May (1–4) he won his greatest victory at **Chancellorsville**. However, in that battle he lost his most valuable lieutenant, Stonewall Jackson (see Chancellorsville in the Fredericksburg & the Peninsulas chapter).

The Confederate army then marched north into Pennsylvania but was followed by the Army of the Potomac, now led by Major General George G Meade. On July 1–3, the Confederates were soundly defeated at the Battle of **Gettysburg.** Lee's army retreated into Virginia and the two armies recuperated. The military lines alternated between the Rapidan and Rappahannock Rivers west of Fredericksburg, and many military personnel from both sides were rushed to bolster operations around Chattanooga in the western theater.

Lee made one more attempt to turn Meade's flank in October (9–22), but he was defeated at Bristoe Station. A move made by Meade in late November, south of the Rapidan, ended in a stalemate at Mine Run.

1864 This was the first year of Ulysses S Grant vs Lee. After Lincoln conferred the rank of lieutenant general on Grant, giving him total command of Union forces in the field, Grant chose for himself the task of destroying Lee's Army of Northern Virginia, and assigned to Major General William Tecumseh Sherman the job of keeping Joe Johnston's Army of Tennessee in check.

The armies of the two great generals first met in the tangled thickets of the **Wilderness** on May 5–6. The initial battle was a stalemate, and Grant marched toward the vital junction at **Spotsylvania** courthouse; a battle raged for nearly two weeks with some of the war's bloodiest fighting (see the Fredericksburg & the Peninsulas chapter). Grant disengaged again and headed across the North Anna River (May 23–26) to **Cold Harbor** (see the Richmond chapter) and a battle raged there, almost in sight of Richmond, for another two weeks (May 31–June 12). After some massive, futile frontal assaults a regretful Grant stealthily disengaged, yet again, and moved toward the strategic rail junction town of Petersburg.

Grant threw his troops against **Petersburg** (see the Richmond chapter) on June 15–18, and the Union forces would have taken the city if they had pressed home their assaults. Lee's army arrived from the north in time to defend Petersburg, at which point a protracted siege of the city began. The Union forces tried to breach a gap in the Confederate lines after the huge explosion of the **Battle of the Crater** on July 30 but were unsuccessful. Lee's defenses were stretched thin as the Union forces peppered away and captured and fortified ground between Richmond and Petersburg, such as at **Fort Harrison** (September 29–30) on the James River (see the Richmond chapter). Winter brought a halt to major operations, but skirmishing, sniping, and shelling continued.

1864 was an active year in the **Shenandoah Valley.** First there was the Battle of **New Market,** on May 15, in which students from Lexington's Virginia Military Institute participated in charges against the Federal lines. Jubal Early's Maryland Campaign began in late June, and after expelling Union troops from the Shenandoah his forces threatened Washington. They were turned around at the Battle of **Fort Stevens** on July 12. The Rebels returned to the valley, but in a series of hard-fought battles against the Union forces of General Philip Sheridan they were soundly defeated, the last major battle being the Battle of **Cedar Creek** on October 19.

1865 At the beginning of the year the armies of Grant and Lee still faced each other in entrenchments around Petersburg. In February, Grant dispatched his infantry and cavalry to the south and west of the city in an attempt to outflank the city. Lee, realizing that each passing day increased the likelihood of Federal success, attempted to break the impasse by attacking **Fort Stedman** (March 25), to the east of the city. The attack failed and Lee reported to Jefferson Davis, 'I fear now that it will be impossible to prevent a junction between Grant and Sherman . . . .'

The stretched Confederate defenses were broken at **Five Forks,** southwest of Petersburg, on April 1 and Petersburg fell the next day. Richmond fell on April 3. Lee extricated his forces in the dark of the night, but Grant, rather than savor victory, pursued his old adversary. After the Battle of **Sailor's Creek** on April 6, the end was in sight. The remnants of the Army of Northern Virginia were cut off at **Appomattox Courthouse** – Lee surrendered to Grant on April 9 and the war was all but over (see Appomattox in the Piedmont chapter). In late May the Union victory was celebrated with a grand review of Federal troops in Washington, DC.

Richmond

VIRGINIA

Richmond (population 203,100), strategically positioned at the very heart of Virginia, is an intriguing city with a rich history. While history, especially that of the antebellum, is proudly thrust in front of the visitor, there is a heartening 20th century feel, best experienced in The Fan, Shockoe Slip, and Shockoe Bottom enclaves.

Many visitors come expecting a dour, conservative, almost bleak city but are soon surprised by its rejuvenation, vibrancy, and multifaceted nature. In addition to its true 'Southern' feel (it was the capital of the Confederacy after all) there is a real sense that this city is the birthplace of African American entrepreneurship, as a contemplative stroll through the city's revitalized Jackson Ward will reinforce. After wandering through Capitol Square, Shockoe Bottom, Shockoe Slip, the Court End, The Fan, Monument Ave, and the Museum District you'll get a feel for the diversity of neighborhoods, the extraordinary amount of green open spaces, the vitality, and the bright future of this city.

HIGHLIGHTS

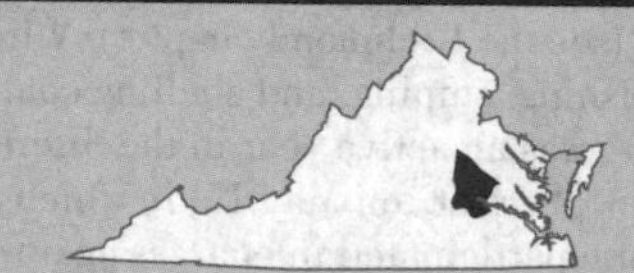

- The African American heritage of historic Jackson Ward
- The Valentine Museum & myriad other museums – surely one of the country's best historical repositories
- Civil War battlefields
- Whitewater rafting on the falls of the James River – a wilderness in the heart of a city
- The lively nightlife of Shockoe Slip, Shockoe Bottom, Carytown, and The Fan
- Petersburg – a fascinating tour through one of the last battlefields of the Civil War

History

Richmond's early colonial history is linked to its strategic position on the James River at the furthest navigable point up the river. Founded in 1637 as a small outpost, a fort was constructed there in 1644 as protection against Native American attacks. Richmond had its beginnings as a town when William Byrd, a colonial statesman, made projections in 1733; it was later incorporated in 1742. It became the Virginia capital in 1779 and was chartered as a city in 1782.

Richmond was important during the American Revolution. As the vulnerability of Williamsburg (then state capital) became apparent those Virginians seeking independence moved the capital a further 50 miles up the James River. It was in this city, in St John's Church, on Church Hill, on March 23, 1775, that Patrick Henry delivered his immortal 'give me liberty or give me death!' speech at the Second Virginia Convention. A month later the Revolutionary War began. On three occasions during the war the city was attacked by the British. The second attack was repulsed by Continental Army troops led by Lafayette and von Steuben, but on the other occasions the town was occupied and burned.

As capital of the Confederacy from 1861 to 1865 Richmond became the prime military objective of the Federal forces. At the commencement of the Civil War the city had over 40 tobacco curing plants and a population of some 100,000. The first major threat to the city, and probably the most serious threat of the entire war, was in 1862. The Federal troops were repulsed in the Seven Days' Battle (see the sidebar Battles for Richmond, in this chapter). When Petersburg fell on April 2, 1865, the Confederate government evacuated the city. Its fleeing occupants set fire to most of the warehouses, bridges, and other installations – the resulting conflagration destroyed much of the old city. On April 4, Abraham Lincoln walked into a city that was still smoldering from the fires. Virginia wasn't readmitted to the Union for another five years following the war, and for two of these the city was under military occupation.

The economy boomed in the 1890s with many types of manufacturing including a stable iron industry and, of course, tobacco. The population grew rapidly in the early 20th century with banking and finance a new growth area. During the Great Depression of the 1930s, the number of unemployed waiting in food lines across the nation with cigarettes in their mouths ensured that Richmond would survive such an economic catastrophe. Now it is a major finance and distribution center that boasts 14 of the US's Fortune 500 corporate headquarters.

Orientation

Richmond is bisected by the James River and most of its attractions lie to the north. The central access to downtown is along Broad St, not Main St which is three streets to the south. The numbered streets which cross Broad St increase from west to east. Foushee St, which runs north-south, is the dividing line for east and west markings.

Richmond's heart is the **Court End** district, in downtown, which has more than 20 significant old buildings (on the historic register) and museums. Main St, which runs west from the Court End, has most of the banks. Northeast of Broad St is the colorful **Jackson Ward** (see the later description).

Also fashionable is Cary St, which between 12th and 15th Sts forms an area of converted warehouses known as **Shockoe Slip** in the city's oldest mercantile district. The buildings now housing the many shops and restaurants were mostly built between 1868 and 1888, as much of this area was burned to the ground in the Great Evacuation Fire of April 2–3, 1865. It is called a 'slip' because of its proximity to the once

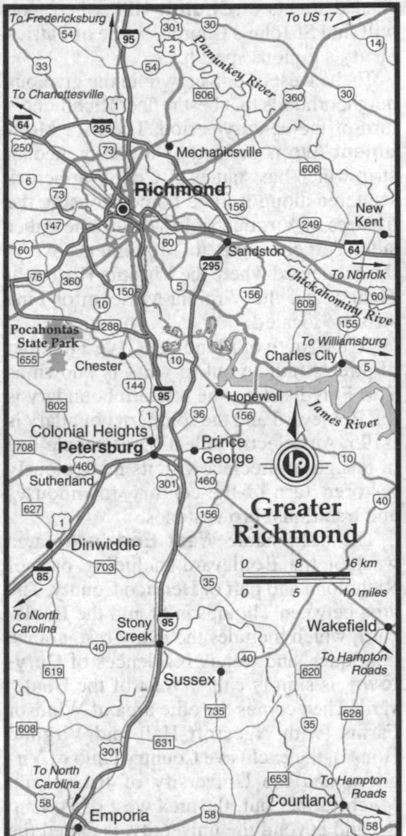

bustling Great Turning Basin of the James River Canal (which no longer exists).

Shockoe Bottom is a popular restaurant and nightclub area further to the east of Shockoe Slip. The most recognizable feature is Main Street Station, which dominates the warehouses and the 400-year-old 17th St Farmers Market, possibly the nation's oldest. Some 15 city blocks between 20th and Pear Sts, along the James River, have been in the process of slow revitalization in the **Tobacco Row** redevelopment (it started in the mid-1980s). To the north of Shockoe Bottom and perched above the James River are the narrow, shaded streets of **Church Hill**, where you will find St John's Church, scene of Patrick Henry's famous speech.

To the west of downtown lie the gracious neighborhoods that best reflect Richmond's turn-of-the-century period. The wide **Monument Ave** is divided by a grassy median strip which has statues of Civil War heroes scattered along it. Fine homes housing the trustees of Virginia's old wealth line either side. Perpendicular to Monument Ave is the Boulevard where the Virginia Historical Society and the Virginia Museum of Fine Arts are located.

To the south of Monument Ave a number of streets radiate out in what is known as **The Fan** district – the western boundary is the Boulevard and the southern boundary is I-195. An eclectic collection of people live in this gaslit precinct with its meticulously restored turn-of-the-century townhouses and traditional brownstones.

The fashionable **West End** is the area west of the Boulevard including part of Richmond and part of Henrico County. The area between Thompson St and the Boulevard, which includes the many restaurants, boutiques, and trendy residences of **Carytown**, is simply called West of the Boulevard. Then comes the elite area of Windsor Farms (with Agecroft Hall and Virginia House), the exclusive Country Club of Virginia, and the University of Richmond. Much further out, the area west of Parham Rd and beyond the university, is called the **Far West End**.

Information

Tourist Offices The Virginia Division of Tourism (☎ 800-932-5827), at 1021 E Cary St, Richmond, VA 23219, produces a good map and state guide. If you need information on a particular attraction, your best bet is the Richmond Information Center (☎ 804-786-4484) in the Old Bell Tower on the Capitol grounds on Capitol Square (corner of 9th and Bank Sts). It is open from 9 am to 5 pm, Monday to Saturday, and on Sunday from noon to 5 pm.

The Metro Richmond Visitors Center (☎ 804-358-5511), at 1710 Robin Hood Rd, is housed in a converted train depot (Exit 78 off I-95/I-64). After watching an informative eight-minute video covering the city's main attractions you can obtain information on downtown and metro walks, and pick up maps of the same. There is a gift shop and exhibits on the premises. They are open daily, Memorial Day to Labor Day, from 9 am to 7 pm, otherwise 9 am to 5 pm.

The Satellite Visitors Center (☎ 804-236-3260), at Richmond International Airport (Exit 197 off I-64) is open Monday through Saturday from 9 am to 5 pm, and Sunday noon to 5 pm.

The Metro Richmond Convention and Visitors Bureau (☎ 804-782-2777, 800-365-7272) is on the second floor of the 6th St Marketplace, 550 E Marshall St. For lodging reservations and information throughout the metro area ring ☎ 800-444-2777; for a weather report call ☎ 804-268-1212. There are two Traveler's Aid lines – ☎ 804-643-0279 and 804-648-1767.

Good free publications are the *Metropolitan Richmond Visitor's Guide* and *Metro Richmond Restaurant Guide* (available from the visitor centers), *Do the Town* and *Richmond Guide* (free at accommodations), and the *GRTC Route Map* (for buses).

Money As headquarters of the Fifth Federal Reserve District there are plenty of financial institutions here. The Crestar Bank (☎ 804-343-9262) in the 6th St Marketplace, NationsBank (☎ 804-788-2496) in the 6th and Grace Banking Center (601 E Grace St), and a 'wealth' of banks on Main St between 10th and 12th all have full facilities. The Central Fidelity National Bank (☎ 804-697-6700), in the James Center at 1021 E Cary St, Shockoe Slip, has an ATM accessible 24 hours.

The Central Fidelity National Bank at the airport also has a foreign exchange facility.

Post & Communications The main post office (☎ 804-783-0825), on the corner of 7th and Main Sts, is open weekdays from

7:30 am to 5 pm. There are a number of other post offices downtown. There is a business center at the airport and places downtown where you can send faxes.

Travel Agencies Covington International Travel (☎ 804-344-3244) is in the James Center at 901 E Cary St; and Travel Agents International (☎ 804-358-5800) is at 5004 Monument Ave. Both agents have a number of other Richmond locations.

Bookstores Bookpeople (☎ 804-288-4346), 536 Granite Ave, is a good general bookstore.

The Valentine Museum has an excellent bookstore. Barnes & Noble and Walden-Books are in most of the malls and Cokesbury Books, in the West End, is a great place to browse.

Media There are five local TV stations. These are Channels 6, 8, 12 (the most 'Richmond' of the stations), 23 (PBS), and 35 Community.

Probably the most popular of the drive-time radio shows is WRVA's 1140 AM. Also worth tuning in to are WKHK 95.3 FM for continuous country; WCDX 92.7 FM (urban contemporary); WRVQ 94.5 FM for contemporary hits; and WTVR 98.1 FM for 'easy listening.' There is good fare on WCVE 88.9 FM, the public radio station.

The main newspaper is the daily *Richmond Times-Dispatch*; the Sunday edition's 'Arts & Entertainment' and 'Sport & Recreation' sections are most useful.

There are three popular weekly African American papers – *The Voice*, *Richmond Free Press*, and *Richmond Afro-American*. *The Richmond State*, a popular off-beat weekly with heaps of opinion pieces, defies categorization; it is available free from distribution points in the city or by mail to subscribers. *Style Weekly*, for the 'in' crowd wishing to know where it's all happening, comes out on Tuesday and is free.

Laundry Main Street Cleaners (☎ 804-644-3310), at 1806 E Main St, is open for dry cleaning and laundry, weekdays from 7:30 am to 6:30 pm, Saturday 9 am to 2 pm. Eggleston's Laundromat (☎ 804-648-0541), at 514 N 2nd St is self-service or drop-off; it is open daily from 9 am to 6 pm. In the Virginia Commonwealth University there is *The Lost Sock* where you can have a beer while your laundry spins.

Emergency The Medical College of Virginia Hospital (☎ 804-786-9151), at 401 N 12th St, is open 24 hours. CVS (☎ 804-359-2497), 2730 W Broad St, is a 24-hour pharmacy. The Rape Crisis Center number is ☎ 804-643-0888.

Walking Tour

The best place to start a walk through historic Richmond is the Court End, where there are heaps of attractions within eight city blocks – at last count, nine National Landmarks, four museums, and 11 other notable buildings. A discount block ticket ($9 for adults, $8.50 for seniors, $4 for children seven to 12) will get you admission into most of the museums (it is valid for 30 days); with it you get a map of a self-guided walking tour.

Valentine Museum

The Valentine, also known as the Museum of Life and History of Richmond (☎ 804-649-0711), at 1015 E Clay St, is a good place to start a tour. Once the home of a 19th century businessman and arts benefactor, it now features changing exhibitions on American urban and social history, costumes, decorative arts, toys, and architecture. The main emphasis, however, is on the history of the city from the 17th to the 20th century.

Included in the complex is the stately 1812 **Wickham House**, a Federal-style building built by John Wickham, one of Richmond's wealthiest citizens at the time. Its rare neoclassical decorative wall paintings, Oval Parlor ('one of the 100 most beautiful rooms in America'), and Palette Staircase all indicate the lavish lifestyle of its owner.

The museum is open daily from 9 am to 5 pm with tours of Wickham House from

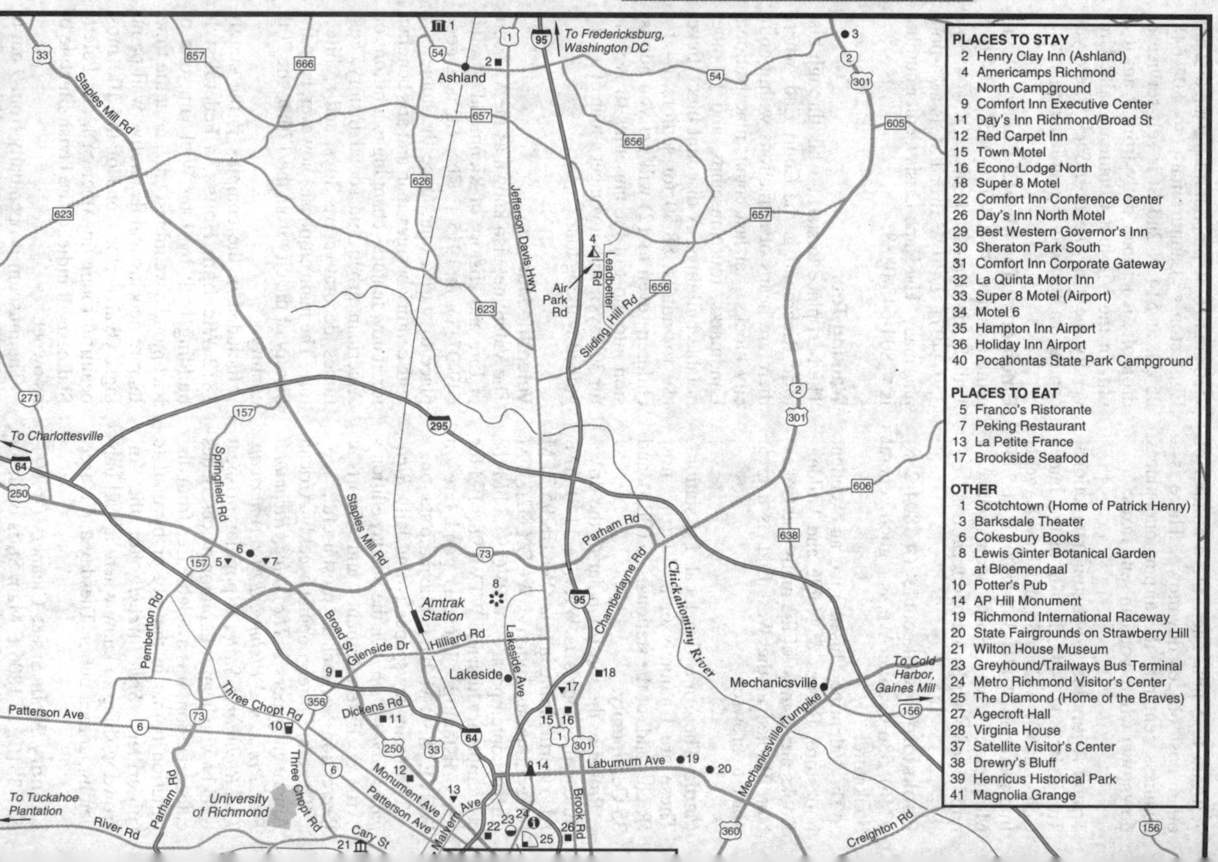
PLACES TO STAY
2 Henry Clay Inn (Ashland)
4 Americamps Richmond
North Campground
9 Comfort Inn Executive Center
11 Day's Inn Richmond/Broad St
12 Red Carpet Inn
15 Town Motel
16 Econo Lodge North
18 Super 8 Motel
22 Comfort Inn Conference Center
26 Day's Inn North Motel
29 Best Western Governor's Inn
30 Sheraton Park South
31 Comfort Inn Corporate Gateway
32 La Quinta Motor Inn
33 Super 8 Motel (Airport)
34 Motel 6
35 Hampton Inn Airport
36 Holiday Inn Airport
40 Pocahontas State Park Campground
PLACES TO EAT
5 Franco's Ristorante
7 Peking Restaurant
13 La Petite France
17 Brookside Seafood
OTHER
1 Scotchtown (Home of Patrick Henry)
3 Barksdale Theater
6 Cokesbury Books
8 Lewis Ginter Botanical Garden
at Bloemendaal
10 Potter's Pub
14 AP Hill Monument
19 Richmond International Raceway
20 State Fairgrounds on Strawberry Hill
21 Wilton House Museum
23 Greyhound/Trailways Bus Terminal
24 Metro Richmond Visitor's Center
25 The Diamond (Home of the Braves)
27 Agecroft Hall
28 Virginia House
37 Satellite Visitor's Center
38 Drewry's Bluff
39 Henricus Historical Park
41 Magnolia Grange
To Fredericksburg, Washington DC
Ashland
Jefferson Davis Hwy
Leadbetter Rd
Air Park Rd
Sliding Hill Rd
Chickahominy River
Chamberlayne Rd
Parham Rd
Mechanicsville
Mechanicsville Turnpike
To Cold Harbor, Gaines Mill
Creighton Rd
Laburnum Ave
Brook Rd
Lakeside Ave
Lakeside
Hilliard Rd
Amtrak Station
Glenside Dr
Staples Mill Rd
Broad St
Dickens Rd
Monument Ave
Patterson Ave
Malvern Ave
Cary St
Three Chopt Rd
University of Richmond
Springfield Rd
Pemberton Rd
Parham Rd
River Rd
Patterson Ave
To Tuckahoe Plantation
To Charlottesville
Staples Mill Rd

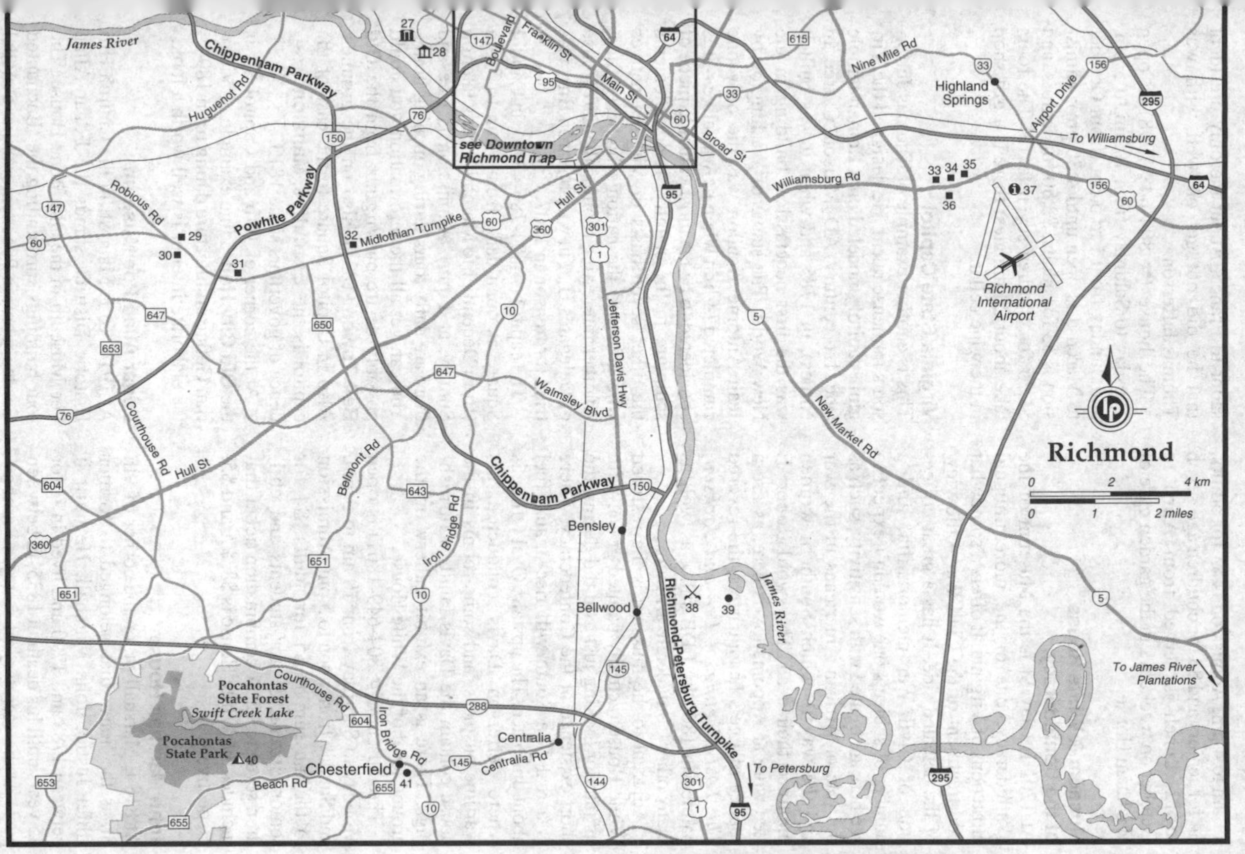
Richmond
0 2 4 km
0 1 2 miles
James River
Chippenham Parkway
Huguenot Rd
Boulevard
Franklin St
Main St
see Downtown Richmond map
Nine Mile Rd
Highland Springs
Airport Drive
To Williamsburg
Broad St
Williamsburg Rd
Richmond International Airport
Robious Rd
Powhite Parkway
Midlothian Turnpike
Hull St
Jefferson Davis Hwy
Walmsley Blvd
New Market Rd
Courthouse Rd
Belmont Rd
Iron Bridge Rd
Bensley
Bellwood
Richmond-Petersburg Turnpike
To Petersburg
To James River Plantations
Pocahontas State Forest
Swift Creek Lake
Pocahontas State Park
Chesterfield
Centralia
Centralia Rd
Beach Rd

11 am to 4 pm. Admission is $5 for adults, $4 for seniors and $3 for children age seven to 12. Lunch is served from April to October on weekdays in the garden cafe of Wickham House.

Museum & White House of the Confederacy

At 1201 E Clay St is the Museum of the Confederacy, one of the more unusual attractions of Virginia. It offers a somewhat odd treatment of the Civil War – the view of the defeated side. It has a great collection of Civil War memorabilia, and a number of subjects one wouldn't expect to see here are treated with sensitivity, such as the role of African Americans in the war and the way in which Southern women mourned their dead. The sword Robert E Lee wore at Appomattox is here, as are a replica of Lee's headquarters, the revered *The Last Meeting of Lee and Jackson*, painted in 1869 by EDB Julio, as well as many other Confederate artifacts.

Adjacent to the museum is the restored White House (actually painted gray), with its interior looking just as it did during the short existence of the Confederacy. There is a real 'the South will rise again' feel about this place. The upstairs Oval Office is where Jefferson Davis conducted his wartime business, and some rooms in the house contain the Davis family's furnishings. There is an exhibit gallery on the ground level of the White House.

The museum (☎ 804-649-1861) is open Monday to Saturday from 10 am to 5 pm, and Sunday from noon to 5 pm. Admission to the museum is $5 for adults, $4 for senior citizens, $3 for students and children seven to 12. A combination ticket that includes the White House is $8, $7, and $5, respectively.

John Marshall House

At 818 E Marshall St, on the corner of 9th St, is the house that belonged to former Chief Justice John Marshall. He built it between 1788 and 1790 and lived in it for 45 years until his death in 1835, in between posts as the secretary of state and ambassador to France. About the only president that he did not get on well with was Thomas Jefferson.

The house (☎ 804-648-7998) is open Tuesday to Saturday from 10 am to 5 pm, and Sunday from 1 to 5 pm (from October to March it is open until 4:30 pm); admission is $3 for adults, $2.50 for seniors, and $1.25 for children seven to 12. The tours take about 20 minutes; there is a gift shop in the wine cellar.

Virginia State Capitol

This is another example of Thomas Jefferson's immense talent. He designed the Virginia capitol, modeled on a Roman temple (the 1st century AD Maison Carrée in Nîmes), in 1785 and when it was built it was the first neoclassical building in the New World. The statue of Washington by Jean Antoine Houdon was the only one completed of him when he was alive – it is considered to be the most valuable piece of sculpture in the country. It complements the other seven busts of Virginia natives who achieved the nation's highest office. Another interesting room is the Old House of Delegates Hall in which Aaron Burr was tried for treason in 1807.

The capitol (☎ 804-786-4344), in Capitol Square, is open daily from 9 am to 5 pm (from December to March it opens later on Sunday, at 1 pm). Admission is free and there are daily tours during opening hours. You can get all the information you could possibly desire on Virginia from the **Old Bell Tower** (1824), also on the grounds. Also in Capitol Square to the east of the capitol is the **Executive Mansion**, residence of governors since 1813.

At the corner of 10th and Capitol Sts is the **Old City Hall**, a fine example of Victorian Gothic architecture dating from 1894 – the elaborate interior is well worth a look.

Edgar Allan Poe Museum

At 1914–16 E Main St, in the Church Hill Historic District, stands the Edgar Allan Poe Museum in the Old Stone House. The four buildings surrounding the 'Enchanted Garden' contain Poe memorabilia, a model

RICK GERHARTER

Virginia State Capitol, designed by Thomas Jefferson

RICK GERHARTER

Robert E Lee Monument in Richmond, VA

RICK GERHARTER

The fashionable Fan District in Richmond, VA

ROBERT DE GAST

Berkeley Plantation in Virginia, site of the first Thanksgiving celebration

JEFF WILLIAMS

Stonewall Jackson Monument at Manassas National Battlefield Park, VA

JEFF WILLIAMS

Chatham Manor in Fredericksburg, VA

JEFF WILLIAMS

Church ruins are all that remains standing of 17th century Jamestown, VA.

RICK GERHARTER

The *rat-a-tat-tat* of the Williamsburg Fife & Drum Corps

RICK GERHARTER

Governor's Palace, Williamsburg, VA

RICK GERHARTER

RICK GERHARTER

At living history sites many Williamsburg residents work and dress as the colonists did.

of Richmond in Poe's time, and the Raven Room with James Carling's illustrations inspired by Poe's poem. It is the largest collection of Poe publications and other artifacts in existence. Although Poe grew up in Richmond, he never actually lived in this house.

The museum (☎ 804-648-5523) is open Tuesday to Saturday from 10 am to 4 pm, and Sunday and Monday from 1 to 4 pm; admission is $5 for adults, $4 for seniors and $3 for students (and tours are available).

St John's Episcopal Church

This colonial church, at 2401 E Broad St at the corner of 24th St, was built in 1741. It was the site of the rebellious Second Virginia Convention where Patrick Henry, on March 23, 1775, uttered the immortal and oft quoted words 'give me liberty or give me death!'

The church (☎ 804-648-5015) is open year round from 10 am to 4 pm; admission is $2 for adults, $1.50 for seniors, and $1 for children. There are Sunday reenactments of Henry's speech at 2 pm (from the last Sunday in May to the first in September).

Jackson Ward

One of the most fascinating parts of Richmond is Jackson Ward, which at the turn of the century was a thriving African American community at the forefront of cultural, religious, and business progress. Then it was simply known as 'Little Africa,' but today the remaining 40 city blocks (or parts thereof) represent the nation's largest National Historic Landmark district associated primarily with African Americans. The best way to see this district, with its many row houses with cast-iron porches, is on foot. Get a copy of the excellent free brochure *Experience Historic Jackson Ward, Richmond, Virginia*.

The best place to start is at the **Black History Museum & Cultural Center of Virginia** (☎ 804-780-9093), in a fine Greek Revival building on Clay St in the heart of the ward. Highlighting the lives and achievements of black Virginians, it was opened as a repository for oral, visual, and written records relating to African American life in the city and the state. It is open Tuesday, Thursday, Friday, and Saturday from 11 am to 4 pm; entry is $2 for adults, $1 for children and senior citizens.

Southeast of the center, on the corner of Marshall and N 1st St, is the **Consolidated Bank and Trust Co**, the nation's oldest continuously owned African American bank. Northeast of the center, on 'The Deuce' – 2nd St – is the **Hippodrome Theater**, 528 N 2nd St, one of the places that gave this ward the nickname 'Harlem of the South.' In this neighborhood the likes of Bill Robinson ('Mr Bojangles'), Cab Calloway, Lena Horne, Billie Holliday, James Brown, and Nat King Cole honed their skills.

Just to the north of this area is the **Maggie Lena Walker National Historic Site** (☎ 804-780-1380), at 110½ E Leigh St. This place commemorates the life of a progressive and talented African American, the daughter of an ex-slave. She was the first black woman to found and serve as the president of a bank (the St Luke Penny Savings Bank, 1903), despite a physical disability and poverty in her early years. The site includes her 22-room brick residence of 30 years (1904 to 1934), restored to its 1930s appearance. It is open daily from 9 am to 5 pm and admission is free.

Two blocks west on Leigh St, at the corner of Adams St, is the **statue of 'Mr Bojangles'** (see the aside on the next page). Further down W Leigh St, at No 216, is the **Ebenezer Baptist Church** (1856), where public education for African Americans began. To the northeast, at 114 W Duval St, is the **Sixth Mount Zion Baptist Church** (1867), organized by a former slave, John Jasper, known for his 'The Sun Do Move' sermon, which he delivered on request more than 250 times during his lifetime.

Hollywood Cemetery

This is an extremely beautiful and historic place, perched above the rapids of the James River. The main entrance is near the corner of Albemarle and Cherry Sts. Get a

The Happiest Feet in Richmond

The famous dancer and actor Bill Robinson, better known as 'Mr Bojangles,' was born May 25, 1878, on N 3rd St in Richmond's Jackson Ward. There is a larger-than-life aluminum statue of him at the corner of Adam and Leigh Sts, near the intersection to which he once donated a traffic light so kids from his old neighborhood could safely cross the street. This statue is one of the only major monuments in the city that relates to someone actually born in the city (another is the Arthur Ashe statue on Monument Ave).

Bojangles was well known for his famous staircase tap routine, which he performed in films of the 1930s. He appeared in six movies with Shirley Temple and in the first African American talkie, *Harlem Is Heaven*. In 1937 he was named the 'outstanding stage and screen star of the year.' This talented man died in 1949. In 1989, the US Congress designated May 25 as National Tap Dancing Day. ■

copy of *Historic Hollywood Cemetery* ($1) from the cemetery office – it will make the search through the labyrinthine pathways much easier.

I visited Hollywood Cemetery in the driving rain. It was eerie, foreboding, and, as premature darkness fell, a little scary. (Lone trips through cemeteries seem to have this effect on me.) Statues of winged angels, fresh grave mounds of orange dirt and clay wasting away down drains, and the brooding holly woods dripping with raindrops set the mood. Suddenly it cleared, just near the President's Circle, and the rapids on the fall line of the James River came into view below. The sun reflected from many angles off the granite tombs, the groves of trees, and the asphalt paths. It was as if one had chanced upon and opened a box of glittering treasure. Surely it is one of the most serene places of repose left in this world!

Gravesites to look for are those of presidents James Monroe and John Tyler; Confederate president Jefferson Davis; novelists James Branch Cabell and Ellen Glasgow; sculptor EV Valentine; historian Douglas E Freeman; six state governors; 22 Confederate generals including James Ewell Brown (JEB) Stuart and George E Pickett (who led the ill-fated charge on Cemetery Hill in Gettysburg); 'Pathfinder of the Seas' Matthew Fontaine Maury; and over 18,000 Confederate soldiers, buried near a 90-foot-high granite pyramid.

The cemetery is open Monday to Saturday from 7 am to 6 pm, Sunday 8 am to 6 pm.

Monument Ave

There is no doubt that this tree-lined boulevard is beautiful, but in its role as a shrine to the Confederacy it cannot help but be controversial. The latest controversy was sparked by the plan to erect a monument to Arthur Ashe, the first African American to win the Wimbledon tennis tournament. The other statues commemorate revered personages who, unlike Ashe, were on a losing side.

Comment in Richmond, at the time that Ashe's monument was mooted, was along the lines that he didn't need a statue as he already had an athletics center named after him, or that the other statues commemorate soldiers who carry swords, not sportspersons with tennis racquets. Just about everyone carefully sidestepped the race issue, which was obviously the most vexing point to those who wished to maintain the status quo.

Anyway, from east to west you will now find: General JEB Stuart, facing north; Robert E Lee atop his horse Traveller, the first monument to be dedicated (1890), facing south; Jefferson Davis, by the sculptor EV Valentine; General 'Stonewall' Jackson, like Stuart facing north as he died from wounds received in battle; next, Matthew Fontaine Maury, the scientist and oceanographer; and lastly, but not without a 'swordless fight,' the gentle, quiet achiever, Arthur Ashe.

Some distance north of Monument Ave is a statue of the popular Confederate general, AP Hill – he has put down his sword and spurs at the junction of Laburnum Ave and Hermitage Rd.

Belle Isle

This 60-acre island in the James River, the site of industry for centuries, is better known for the notorious Civil War prison camp that was established on its east end. It is thought that some 30 Union soldiers (then prisoners) died each day during the harsh winter as a result of poor shelter and little food.

To get there, head down Byrd St and 7th St S to the river, turn right at Tredegar St, and pass the iron works on the right. Access is from a pedestrian bridge under Hwy 1/301 (Lee Bridge). It is open only in daylight.

Other Historic Places

At 1700 Hampton St, between Route 161 and Meadow St, is the 100-acre intact Victorian-Romanesque mansion **Maymont** (see also the sidebar 'Richmond for Kids'). The estate (☎ 804-358-7166) features formal Japanese and Italian gardens, a children's farm, carriage rides, and tram tours. It is open daily, April to October, from 10 am to 7 pm (November to March, until 5 pm); admission is free.

The **Wilton House Museum** (☎ 804-282-5936), at 215 S Wilton Rd, is on a bluff overlooking the James River. This impressive 18th century Georgian mansion was constructed in 1753 some 14 miles further south on the James River; it was resurrected on its present site in 1933. The rooms have fine pine paneling and cornices. The house is open Tuesday to Saturday from 10 am to 4:30 pm, and Sunday from 1:30 to 4:30 pm; admission is $4 for adults, $3 for students, and children under six (who may wonder why they were brought here in the first place) are free.

Agecroft Hall (☎ 804-353-4241), at 4305 Sulgrave Rd in the fashionable Fan District, is a 15th century Tudor manor house uplifted from Lancashire, England, and reconstructed here in 1928 (another transplanted London Bridge or *Queen Mary* perhaps?). The house, furnished with artifacts reflecting the life of Tudor and early Stuart England, is surrounded by 23 acres of lawns, gardens, and woodlands. Agecroft Hall is open Tuesday to Saturday from 10 am to 4 pm, and Sunday from 12:30 to 5 pm; admission is $4.50 for adults, $4 seniors, and $2.50 students.

The castle-like **Virginia House** (☎ 804-353-4251), also on Sulgrave Rd (at No 4301), is more of the 'transplanted Englishness' that seemed to grip those Virginians who made substantial sums of money in the last couple of centuries. Parts of the original structure date back to the English priory of St Sepulchre but it is the elegant furnishings, a real potpourri of European art, tapestries, and furniture, and the eight acres of beautiful gardens, which make a visit worthwhile. It is open Tuesday to Saturday from 10 am to 4 pm, Sunday from 12:30 to 5 pm; admission is $4 for adults, $2 for students and children.

The **Lewis Ginter Botanical Garden at Bloemendaal** (☎ 804-262-9887) is at 1800 Lakeside Ave; take I-95N to Brook Rd/Hwy 1N (Exit 80), turn left at Hilliard Rd, then right onto Lakeside Ave.

Lewis Ginter, founder of the American Tobacco Company, established the Lakeside Wheel Club in the 1880s for Richmond's well-to-do. When he died, his niece, Grace Arents, converted the area to much more humanitarian uses. She set about developing the gardens and changed their name to Bloemendaal, after Ginter's Dutch home. On her death she bequeathed the gardens to the city of Richmond for everyone to enjoy. The Lora Robins Teahouse in the grounds serves succulent meals. The garden is open Monday to Saturday from 9:30 am to 4 pm, and Sunday from 1 to 4:30 pm; admission is $3 for adults, $2 for seniors, and $1 for children age two to 12.

The **Tuckahoe Plantation** (☎ /fax 804-784-57360), at 12601 River Rd, seven miles west of Richmond, is an early Thomas Randolph mansion. On the grounds is the school in which Thomas Jefferson studied as a boy. The plantation is open daily by appointment from 8:30 am to 4 pm; admission is $5 for groups of fewer than 10, $3.50 for groups of more than 10, and admission to the grounds is free.

At 10020 Ironbridge Rd in Chesterfield there is the 1822 Federal-style plantation house **Magnolia Grange** (☎ 804-796-1479), which interprets early 19th century rural life in Virginia. It is open weekdays from 10 am to 4 pm, Sunday from 1 to 4 pm; admission is $2 for adults, $1.50 for seniors, and $1 for students.

The **Henricus Historical Park** (☎ 804-748-1623), in Chesterfield County on the banks of the James River, is the site of the second English New World settlement (1611). The short-lived settlement was decimated in a Native American massacre in 1622. Now known as Farrar's Island, it is open year round from sunup to sundown; entry to the park, currently accessible by a mile-long path along the river, is free.

The 18th century home of Patrick Henry, **Scotchtown**, built in 1719 by Charles Chiswell, is near Beaverdam in western Hanover County, about nine miles northwest of Ashland. The wood-frame house, Patrick Henry's home during the Revolutionary War (1771-78), is furnished with period antiques. There are special 'hands-on' tours for children's groups and occasional living history presentations. Scotchtown (☎ 804-227-3500) is open April to October, Tuesday to Saturday from 10 am to 4:30 pm, and Sunday from 1:30 to 4:30 pm; admission is $5 for adults, $2 for children age six to 12. To get there take Hwy 1N through Ashland. Turn off onto County Rd 738 and then take County Rd 685.

VIRGINIA

Science Museum of Virginia

This museum (☎ 804-367-0000) and the OmniMax Theater are housed in the old Richmond, Fredericksburg & Potomac Railroad W Broad St station (at No 2500). The station, with its massive dome, was designed by John Russell Pope and finished in 1919. There are over 250 permanent hands-on exhibits covering such diverse fields as aerospace, astronomy, chemistry, computers, electricity, illusions, and physics. The Ethyl Universe Theater provides the biggest spectacle with movies or a planetarium star show on the giant OmniMax screen.

Richmond for Kids

So it's time to get rid of the kids or at least preoccupy them for a while. The **Science Museum of Virginia** (see above) has many exhibits that will interest the kids, but perhaps a more suitable choice is the **Children's Museum** (☎ 804-788-4949), on Navy Hill Drive. It's a great place with its own cave and plenty of hands-on activities. The museum is open Tuesday to Friday from 10 am to 4:30 pm, Saturday from 10 am to 5 pm, and Sunday from 1 to 5 pm; admission is $2 for kids and $3 for adults (only if they are accompanied by a responsible child).

Maymont House & Garden (☎ 804-358-7166), at 1700 Hampton St, West End, has a children's farm with many animals native to Virginia. The grounds are open daily and admission is free.

About 22 miles north of town on I-95 (Doswell Exit) is the fantastic **Paramount King's Dominion** (☎ 804-876-5000), a theme park with all manner of rides, including a Days of Thunder racing simulator, stand-up roller coaster, simulated whitewater rafting, and a monorail ride. Opening times meet the holiday demand: July to August, daily from 9:30 am to 10 pm, Sunday to Friday from 9:30 am to 8 pm (open till 10 pm on Saturday nights in June); and April to May and September to October, weekends only, from 9:30 am to 8 pm. And the bad news: Admission is $25 for adults, $17 for children under six! (They should throw in a nanny for that price.) This is the most popular attraction in the Richmond area, however, with some two million visitors annually, so be prepared for crowds. ■

The museum is open September to May, Monday to Saturday from 9:30 am to 5 pm, Sunday from noon to 5 pm; Memorial Day to Labor Day, Monday to Thursday from 9:30 am to 5 pm, Friday and Saturday from 9:30 am to 9 pm, and Sunday from noon to 5 pm; admission is $4.50 for adults, $4 for seniors and youths. The OmniMax shows and planetarium are open daily and on Friday and Saturday evenings. With one theater show, admission to the exhibit area is $6.50 for adults, $6 for seniors and youths.

Virginia Historical Society

This museum (☎ 804-342-9676) is on the corner of Kensington St and the Boulevard. It has museum galleries displaying rare Virginia-related treasures and changing exhibits on Virginia history. 'Arming the Confederacy' is the finest collection of Confederate-made weapons in existence. It is open daily from 10 am to 5 pm, Sunday from 1 to 5 pm; admission is $4 for adults and $2 for students.

Virginia Museum of Fine Arts

This excellent museum (☎ 804-367-0844), at 2800 Grove Ave, has a superb collection containing a wide range of works of art – as diverse as Monet's *Iris by the Pond*, Warhol's *Triple Elvis,* Goya's portrait of *General Nicholas Guye*, and Picasso's *Circus Life*. There are many other works representing numerous civilizations, such as a fine collection of Himalayan (Indian, Nepalese, and Tibetan) pieces. Many people will be coming to see the shimmering jewel-encrusted Easter eggs, treasures of Imperial Russia, created by Peter Carl Fabergé. The collection here is believed to be the world's largest public display outside Russia.

The museum is open Tuesday to Sunday from 11 am to 5 pm, on Thursday evening until 8 pm (tours on Thursday evening are at 6 and 7 pm); admission is free. There is a public cafeteria and sculpture garden, a gift shop, and free parking.

Hiking

There are over 200 miles of trails in the Richmond-Petersburg area, including many through the surrounding battlefields. For those who like the terrain a bit tougher there are many wildlife areas within an hour's drive of the city. For trail information in specific counties call:

Richmond	☎ 804-780-5704
Hanover	☎ 804-537-6165
Chesterfield	☎ 804-748-1623
Henrico	☎ 804-672-5100

Bicycling

Many of the hiking trails are open to cyclists. Two interstate bike routes, the north-south Bike Route 1 and the east-west Bike Route 76, pass through Richmond; also see Getting Around in this section.

Horseback Riding

There are more than 270 miles of public trails near the city, and some two dozen riding academies and stables. The nearest public equestrian trail is in Pocahontas State Park.

Fishing

The Game and Inland Fisheries Department (☎ 804-367-1000), 4010 W Broad St, provides the brochure *Fishing Access to the James River in Richmond*. From Covington to the fall line at Richmond the James River is great for smallmouth bass fishing. The lower James, more tidal and saline, is good for largemouth and striped bass.

Golf

Judging by the many courses in metro Richmond – 13 public and 11 private – golf is really popular, probably due to the fact that it can be played year round. The busy time, of course, is summer and on weekends. Public courses include Glenwood (☎ 804-226-1793), 3100 Creighton Rd ($15 weekdays, $25 weekends), and The Crossings (☎ 804-266-2254), at 800 Virginia Center Parkway, Glen Allen ($37, $42).

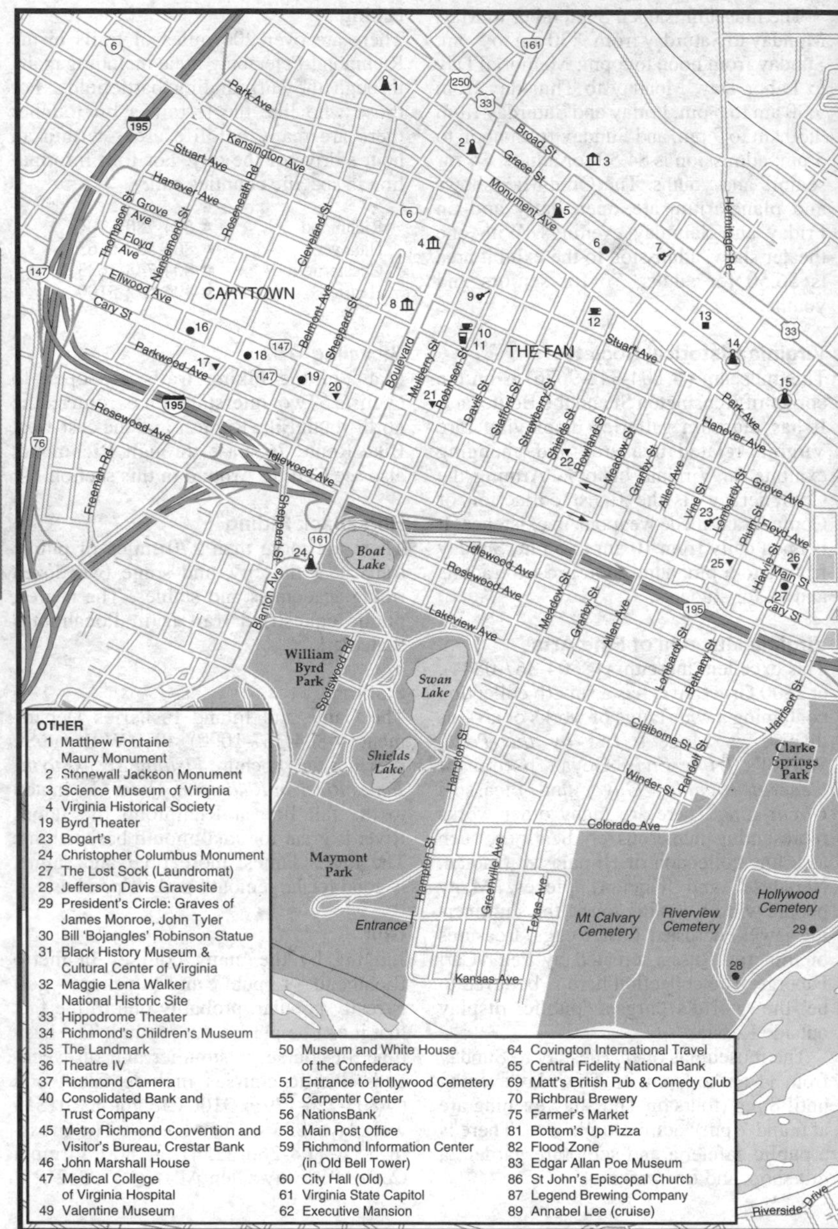

CARYTOWN
THE FAN
Park Ave
Kensington Ave
Stuart Ave
Hanover Ave
Grove Ave
Floyd Ave
Ellwood Ave
Cary St
Parkwood Ave
Rosewood Ave
Idlewood Ave
Lakeview Ave
Broad St
Grace St
Monument Ave
Thompson St
Nansemond St
Roseneath Rd
Cleveland St
Belmont Ave
Sheppard St
Boulevard
Mulberry St
Robinson St
Davis St
Stafford St
Strawberry St
Shields St
Rowland St
Meadow St
Granby St
Allen Ave
Vine St
Lombardy St
Plum St
Harvie St
Main St
Hermitage Rd
Freeman Rd
Blanton Ave
Sheppard St
Spotswood Rd
Hampton St
Greenville Ave
Texas Ave
Kansas Ave
Colorado Ave
Claiborne St
Winder St
Randolph St
Bethany St
Harrison St
Riverside Drive
Boat Lake
Swan Lake
Shields Lake
William Byrd Park
Maymont Park
Entrance
Clarke Springs Park
Mt Calvary Cemetery
Riverview Cemetery
Hollywood Cemetery
OTHER
1 Matthew Fontaine Maury Monument
2 Stonewall Jackson Monument
3 Science Museum of Virginia
4 Virginia Historical Society
19 Byrd Theater
23 Bogart's
24 Christopher Columbus Monument
27 The Lost Sock (Laundromat)
28 Jefferson Davis Gravesite
29 President's Circle: Graves of James Monroe, John Tyler
30 Bill 'Bojangles' Robinson Statue
31 Black History Museum & Cultural Center of Virginia
32 Maggie Lena Walker National Historic Site
33 Hippodrome Theater
34 Richmond's Children's Museum
35 The Landmark
36 Theatre IV
37 Richmond Camera
40 Consolidated Bank and Trust Company
45 Metro Richmond Convention and Visitor's Bureau, Crestar Bank
46 John Marshall House
47 Medical College of Virginia Hospital
49 Valentine Museum
50 Museum and White House of the Confederacy
51 Entrance to Hollywood Cemetery
55 Carpenter Center
56 NationsBank
58 Main Post Office
59 Richmond Information Center (in Old Bell Tower)
60 City Hall (Old)
61 Virginia State Capitol
62 Executive Mansion
64 Covington International Travel
65 Central Fidelity National Bank
69 Matt's British Pub & Comedy Club
70 Richbrau Brewery
75 Farmer's Market
81 Bottom's Up Pizza
82 Flood Zone
83 Edgar Allan Poe Museum
86 St John's Episcopal Church
87 Legend Brewing Company
89 Annabel Lee (cruise)

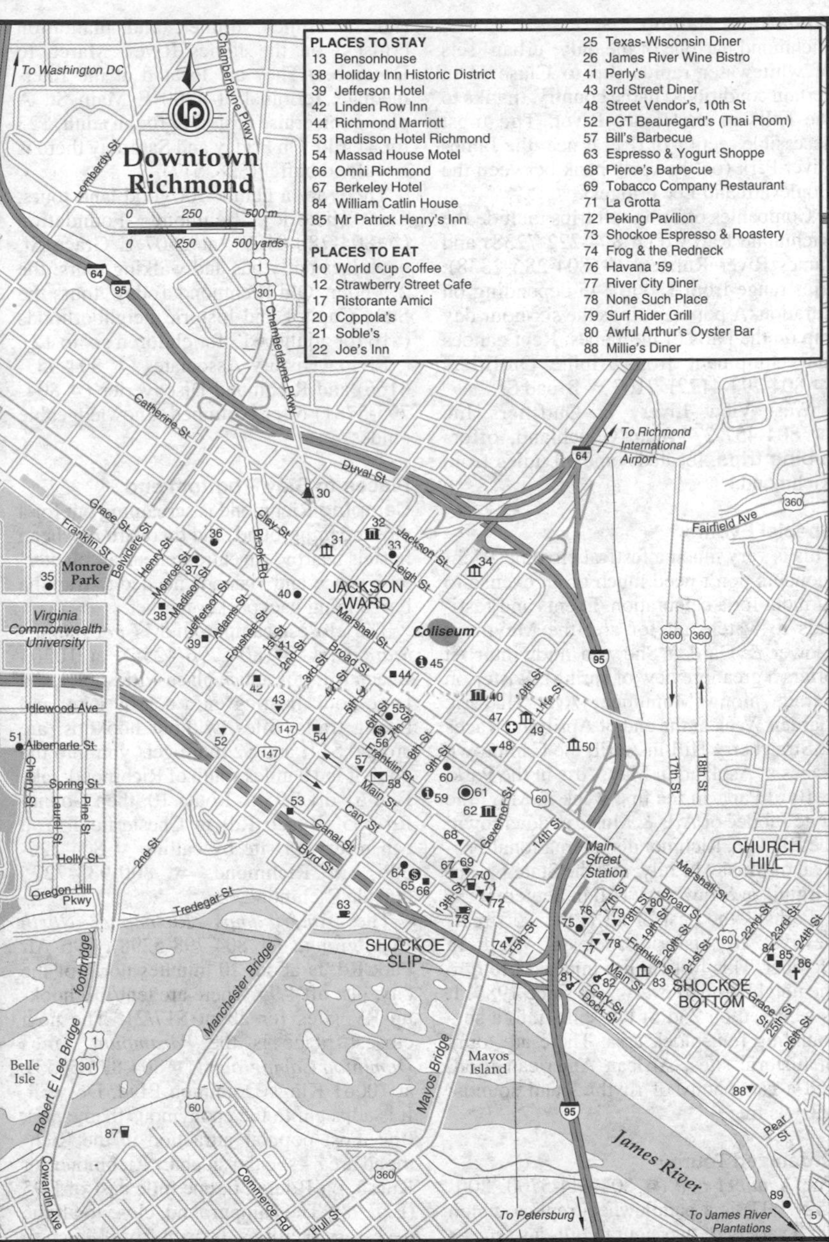

Downtown Richmond
PLACES TO STAY
13 Bensonhouse
38 Holiday Inn Historic District
39 Jefferson Hotel
42 Linden Row Inn
44 Richmond Marriott
53 Radisson Hotel Richmond
54 Massad House Motel
66 Omni Richmond
67 Berkeley Hotel
84 William Catlin House
85 Mr Patrick Henry's Inn
PLACES TO EAT
10 World Cup Coffee
12 Strawberry Street Cafe
17 Ristorante Amici
20 Coppola's
21 Soble's
22 Joe's Inn
25 Texas-Wisconsin Diner
26 James River Wine Bistro
41 Perly's
43 3rd Street Diner
48 Street Vendor's, 10th St
52 PGT Beauregard's (Thai Room)
57 Bill's Barbecue
63 Espresso & Yogurt Shoppe
68 Pierce's Barbecue
69 Tobacco Company Restaurant
71 La Grotta
72 Peking Pavilion
73 Shockoe Espresso & Roastery
74 Frog & the Redneck
76 Havana '59
77 River City Diner
78 None Such Place
79 Surf Rider Grill
80 Awful Arthur's Oyster Bar
88 Millie's Diner
To Washington DC
To Richmond International Airport
To Petersburg
To James River Plantations
Monroe Park
Virginia Commonwealth University
JACKSON WARD
Coliseum
SHOCKOE SLIP
SHOCKOE BOTTOM
CHURCH HILL
Main Street Station
Belle Isle
Mayos Island
James River

VIRGINIA

Whitewater Rafting

Richmond has one of the only 'urban' sets of whitewater rapids (up to Class V in certain conditions) in the country, thanks to the Falls in the James River. The most accessible section of river is near the James River Park (on the south bank between the Boulevard and Lee bridges).

Companies offering raft trips include the Richmond Raft Co (☎ 804-222-7238) and James River Runners (☎ 804-286-2338); trips range from $30 to $45 depending on duration. A popular trip is the six-hour day trip on the Falls of the James. Rent canoes and equipment from Alpine Outfitters (☎ 804-794-4172), 7107 W Broad St.

West View Livery & Outfitters Inc (☎ 804-457-2744), in Goochland, offers **tubing trips**, located some 30 miles from Richmond.

Special Events

This is very much a festival city and Richmonders don't need much of an excuse to turn out for a celebration. Events and festivals to watch out for are: the Maymont Flower & Garden Show in midwinter (it offers a great preview of spring); Easter on Parade along Monument Ave; Historic Garden Week at the end of April; the Races at Strawberry Hill in April; the Camptown Races at Ashland in May; Arts in the Park, at Byrd Park, in the first week in May; the June Jubilee of Arts & Music in downtown; the Big Gig, Richmond's International Festival of Music, in July; and the State Fair of Virginia at Strawberry Hill in September.

Perhaps the best of all is the '2 Street' Festival in historic Jackson Ward in October. This festival has injected life into the neighborhood every year since 1989. It is centered on 2nd St but spills into a surrounding four-block area. There are tours of historic sites, African American food, and a cacophony of rhythms and sounds; entry is free.

Organized Tours

The *Annabel Lee* (☎ 804-644-5700, 800-752-7093) is a paddlewheel replica which has a variety of two-hour to full-day cruises (lunch, brunch, dinner, and plantation cruises) on the James River, March to December. They are located at the Intermediate Terminal at 4400 E Main St. A plantation cruise costs $43 for an adult, $23 for a child. On Friday and Saturday there is a seafood buffet ($28, $17).

There are a number of good land tours. The Historic Richmond Foundation (☎ 804-780-0107), at 2407 E Grace St, organizes daily bus and walking tours; the 2½-hour 'Old Richmond Today' tours the State Capitol and historic neighborhoods ($16 for adults, $13 for children six to 12).

Living History Associates (☎ 804-353-8166) and Richmond Discoveries (☎ 804-795-5781) offer costumed, knowledgeable guides.

Places to Stay – bottom end

Camping Richmond is screaming out for a closer campground, and there are no cheap hostels nearby. An entrepreneurial 'planter' with space and vision is needed to trap the burgeoning backpacker market.

The closest campground is *Pocahontas State Park* (☎ 804-796-4255), at 10301 Beach Rd. It is a nice place with showers, a large pool, boating on a nearby lake, and biking trails. Sites, without hookups, are around $11, and $2 more gets you into the pool. It is 10 miles south of Richmond; take Exit 61 off I-95 to Route 10, then County Rd 655 (Beach Rd) in Chesterfield. You can reserve a site by calling ☎ 804-225-3867 in Richmond, ☎ 800-933-7275 outside Richmond.

The *Americamps Richmond North Campground* (☎ 804-798-5298), 396 Air Park Rd, is about 20 minutes north of the city, just off I-95. There are tent/full hookup RV sites for about $17/21. The next closest place is the *Paramount Kings Dominion Campground* (☎ 804-876-5355), at 10061 Kings Dominion Blvd, Doswell. It is adjacent to the eponymous theme park (the most popular attraction in the Richmond area – see the sidebar 'Richmond for Kids'), on Route 30, one mile east of I-95 (Exit 98). The campground, close to all the necessary facilities, is open from March to

October; camp sites are $18 per night (up to five people), electricity/water hookups are $22.

Hotels & Motels This is the way to go, even for budget tourists. Search along Williamsburg Rd, at the edge of town, and also along the Midlothian Turnpike (Hwy 60), south of the river, and if this fails ask at the visitors center. The cost decreases proportionally with the distance from downtown. There are at least 100 accommodations of various sorts in and around Richmond – you are bound to find something to suit your tastes and budget.

At 5215 W Broad St is the *Red Carpet Inn* (☎ 804-288-4011), just three miles from downtown. The rooms don't exactly live up to the 'red carpet' tag but it is good by motel standards; singles/doubles are $41/44. Only the brave would try the *Town Motel* near the corner of Azalea Ave and Brook Rd (Hwy 1); a seasoned traveler may like the eclectic company, but watch out for illegal activity. Apart from that, it's cheap at $33 for singles.

The ubiquitous *Motel 6* (☎ 804-222-7600), at 5704 Williamsburg Rd, Sandston, is six miles east on Hwy 60 and not far from the airport. You can reach it on GRTC bus No 7 (Seven Pines); singles/doubles in this good value stalwart are $30/34.

Out on Chamberlayne Ave, at No 5615, is a quiet *Super 8 Motel* (☎ 804-262-8880) where a double will cost about $44; if you are heading north you will get a traffic-free start. There is another *Super 8 Motel* (☎ 804-222-8008) at 5110 Williamsburg Rd, near the airport; singles/doubles are about the same as the one on Chamberlayne.

The *Econo Lodge North* (☎ 804-266-7603), at 5221 Brook Rd, has doubles from $45. The *Massad House Motel* (☎ 804-648-2893), at 11 N 4th St, is quite close to downtown, only four blocks away from the Capitol, and about the best value this close to town. The rooms, reached by a quaint elevator, are spacious and clean; singles/doubles are $34/38.

The red-brick *Days Inn North Motel* (☎ 804-353-1287, 800-325-2525) is two miles northwest of downtown at 1600 Robin Hood Rd, in an office area. You enter the adequate rooms from the parking area. The cost of singles/doubles in low season is $38/40 (otherwise $39/45), good value when you consider there is a restaurant and pool. The *Days Inn Richmond/Broad St* (☎ 804-288-2145), at 2100 Dickens Rd (Exit 183 off I-64), close to downtown, is more expensive at $46/52.

Places to Stay – middle

The *Comfort Inn Conference Center* (☎ 804-359-4061), at 3200 W Broad St near The Fan, is good value with singles/doubles from $55/62. The colonial-style *Comfort Inn Executive Center* (☎ 804-672-1108), 7201 W Broad (Exit 183 off I-64), has singles/doubles from $55/61. The *Holiday Inn Historic District* (☎ 804-644-9871) at 301 W Franklin St, is very popular and has a restaurant with a great view over Franklin St; doubles are from $65 to $70 and it is wheelchair accessible.

South of the river there are a few midrange choices. The *Best Western Governor's Inn* (☎ 804-323-0007), at 9848 Midlothian Turnpike, has a restaurant, outdoor pool, and, for those who are into it, a whirlpool; singles/doubles are from $58/61 to $85/90. The *Comfort Inn Corporate Gateway* (☎ 804-320-8900), at 8710 Midlothian Turnpike, has singles and doubles from $56 in the off season (otherwise, from $59). *La Quinta Motor Inn* (☎ 804-745-7100), at 6910 Midlothian Turnpike, has a pool, restaurant, and handicapped access; singles and doubles are from $50. The *Sheraton Park South* (☎ 804-323-1144), at 9901 Midlothian Turnpike, is much more expensive, but it is a classy place with indoor pool, sauna, jacuzzi, and health club; weekend doubles are from $75 and mid-week doubles begin at $100.

Also, out at the airport there are a couple of midrange places. The *Hampton Inn Airport* (☎ 804-222-8200), at 5300 Airport Square Lane, has an outdoor swimming pool and free continental breakfast; doubles are from $65. About the same price is the *Holiday Inn Airport* (☎ 804-222-6450) at 5203 Williamsburg Rd, Sandston – this is the largest of the airport hotels.

The *Radisson Hotel-Richmond* (☎ 804-788-0900, 800-333-3333), at 555 E Canal St in the business district is quite expensive at $69/79 for singles/doubles in the low season (otherwise $89/99). Rooms on one side overlook the river and on the other side the city skyline; you may be lucky enough to get a room which overlooks both.

Places to Stay – top end

Hotels Richmond has a wide range of upmarket accommodations. The *Linden Row Inn* (☎ 804-783-7000, 800-348-7424), at 100 E Franklin St, is in a group of nice converted antebellum terrace houses. This revitalized place is worth it with singles and doubles from $99 to $149. The *Berkeley Hotel* (☎ 804-780-1300) is a small but elegant place at 1200 E Cary St, on Shockoe Slip, with valet parking for guests and a health club; singles/doubles are from $120/124 to $140/154.

The *Omni Richmond* (☎ 804-344-7000, 800-843-6664), at 100 S 12th St, is in the James Center complex, close to Shockoe Slip. The comfortable rooms, furnished in contemporary style, are expensive at $79 for singles or doubles on the weekend, from $99 to $159 during the week. You get what you pay for, however, and guests can enjoy the three restaurants, bar, indoor and outdoor pools, racquetball and squash courts, whirlpool, sauna, and even an indoor track!

Near the 6th St Marketplace, at 500 E Broad St, is the 400-room *Richmond Marriott* (☎ 804-643-3400) with expensive singles or doubles, many with stunning city views, for about $115 (an extra person is $10); there are weekend packages available. A peek into the ostentatious lobby will give you an idea of what this place is about. There are three restaurants, an indoor pool, nightclub, and gymnasium (with tanning parlor!).

The *Jefferson Hotel* (☎ 804-788-8000, 800-424-8014), appropriately on the corner of Franklin and Adams Sts, is the most famous of the downtown hotels with a magnificent rotunda or lower lobby. Its 26-step staircase was, they say, used as a model for the staircase in the movie *Gone with the Wind*. But frankly, Scarlett, I don't give a damn – it is the rooms I am after. These live up to the required antebellum splendor, but are relatively small and very expensive with singles and doubles from $99 to $140 on weekends, $145 to $185/$165 to $205, Monday to Thursday.

B&Bs The bed and breakfast options in the historic quarters may well be worth trying. Recommended is the pricy *William Catlin House* (☎ 804-780-3746), a small B&B on Church Hill at 2304 E Broad St (across from St Johns Church); the cost is from $85/95 for singles/doubles. *Mr Patrick Henry's Inn* (☎ 804-644-1322), at 2300 E Broad St, is similar to the Catlin Inn in most respects; it is from $85/95 but its best room is much more expensive. The restaurant (closed Sunday) has a local reputation so bookings are advised. The *Be My Guest B&B* (☎ 804-358-9901), 2926 Kensington Ave, in The Fan, makes it in here because of its quaint name; it is expensive.

The *Henry Clay Inn* (☎ 804-798-3100), at 114 Railroad Ave, Ashland, almost doesn't make it into this category as it has 14 rooms. Doubles with all the creature comforts are from $80 to $145.

There is a reservation service for Richmond and Williamsburg B&Bs operated by Bensonhouse (☎ 804-353-6900), 2036 Monument Ave, Richmond, VA 23220. Ms Benson's *Emmanuel Hutzler House* (☎ 804-355-4885) has been carefully restored (the address and telephone is as above).

Places to Eat

Fortunately, Richmond has plenty of options for cheap dining and the area around Virginia Commonwealth University is the place to go for cheap student eateries. For good old-fashioned Southern fare head to downtown. There are plenty of upmarket places in downtown, Shockoe Slip &

Bottom, and The Fan. A spoiler for male travelers is the occasional need to dress up with a jacket and tie.

The best synopsis of eateries is to be found in *The Insiders' Guide to Greater Richmond*, written by people who appreciate their food.

Coffeehouses Sipping cappuccinos has become a lot more popular these days and many coffeehouses are now sprinkled throughout Richmond; this a small selection.

Sip away at *Espresso & Yogurt Shoppe* (☎ 804-782-8619) at 951 E Byrd St in the Riverfront Plaza; the *Shockoe Espresso & Roastery* (☎ 804-648-3734) at 104 Shockoe Slip; *The Bidder's Suite* (☎ 804 355-5707), at 917 W Grace St, a place with a sniff of 'cafe revolution' in the wings that stays open till 2 am; and *World Cup* (☎ 804-359-5282), at 204 N Robinson St, serving an aromatic FIFA brand.

Picnic Fare Richmonders love to grab take-out lunches and then sit in one of their many parks to enjoy it. *Ukrop's* (☎ 804-379-3663), a distinctly Richmond grocery chain that's revered for both freshness and quality, has 15 or so carry-out places in the city. Try those in the Heritage Building at 10th and Main Sts, 9645 W Broad St, or in the Village Shopping Center.

Other good picnic places are *Coppola's* (see The Fan & Carytown below); *Padow's Ham & Deli* at four city locations, including one (☎ 804-354-1931) at 1110 E Main St; *Fantaste* (☎ 804-355-1642), open 24 hours, at 1201 W Main St; *Sally Bell's Kitchen* (☎ 804-644-2838), at 708 W Grace St; and *New York Delicatessen* (☎ 804-355-6056), at 2920 W Cary St, for bagels, deli meats, and fish.

Downtown & Shockoe Slip A convenient way to grab a snack at lunchtime in downtown is from street vendors, who have their carts set up on weekdays from 11 am until 3 pm. Search along 10th St and you will 'smell out' carts operated by some of Richmond's most popular restaurants.

The breakfast special for $2.25 at the *3rd St Diner* (☎ 804-788-4750), on the corner of 3rd and Main Sts, in downtown, makes this odd place well worth the visit; it is open 24 hours, and the eclectic staff will draw your gaze away from the food. Another reliable cheapie is *Perly's* (☎ 804-649-2779), at 111 E Grace St. It is open weekdays from 7 am to 3 pm and is a good choice for breakfast (from $1.50 to $5) and lunch ($5 to $7). Lunch ranges from sandwiches to gazpacho.

La Grotta (☎ 804-644-2466), at 1218 E Cary St, owned by the people who own Ristorante Amici (see The Fan & Carytown, below), is a perfect choice for good old Italian salads and pasta; it is open Monday to Saturday from 11:30 am until midnight.

The *Chicken's Snack Bar* on the lower level of the Capitol building is a Richmond institution and the haunt of Virginia's hungry legislators. There's a good selection of bagels and sandwiches, but it is the limeade that attracts visitors. Buy one and sip it slowly on the steps of the Capitol.

Barbecue is a popular Richmond dining choice and there are two beauties downtown. *Pierce's* (☎ 804-643-0427), at 1116 E Main St, on the edge of Shockoe Slip, has been voted 'best BBQ' a number of times; it is open for lunch and take-out from 10 am to 6 pm. They have a branch (☎ 804-674-4049) south of the river, at 10825 Hull St, Midlothian. *Bill's* (☎ 804-643-9857), 700 E Main St, has all the favorites such as pork barbecue, soups, salads, strawberry pie, and limeade; it is open daily from 7 am to 10 pm. A la Pierce's, there's a branch (☎ 804-270-9722) in the West End at 8820 W Broad St.

The *Dining Room at the Berkeley Hotel* (☎ 804-780-1300) has been consistently voted one of Richmond's best restaurants. The food is American-European, there's an extensive wine list, and lunch is from $8 to $14, dinner from $17 to $25. It is open for breakfast from 7 to 10:30 am, lunch from 11:30 am to 2 pm, dinner from 6 to 10 pm.

The *Lemaire Restaurant* (☎ 804-788-8000), in the Jefferson Hotel, is a great dining experience with a Southern-inspired menu with a number of regional dishes. It is open daily from 11 am to 10 pm and lunch is from $10 to $20, dinner from $25 to $50, and the magnificent Sunday brunch is $27. If you just want to sample the ambiance of this place, have afternoon tea in the *Palm Court*.

If you are after a Chinese meal, especially an inexpensive lunch, then *Peking Pavilion* (☎ 804-649-8888), at 1302 E Cary St in Shockoe Slip, is recommended (not to be confused with the Peking Restaurant, also good – see West End, below). The food is superb, the accent on Hunan, Szechuan, and Mandarin, and their lunch platters (about $6) are tops. They open for lunch weekdays from 11:30 am to 2:15 pm, for dinner, Monday to Thursday 5 to 9:30 pm (on weekends to 10:30 pm).

For Thai food there is only one place – upstairs at PGT Beauregard's, at 103 E Cary St, is the *Thai Room* (☎ 804-644-2328), open for dinner Tuesday to Saturday from 5 to 10 pm. It serves ginger beef, green curry chicken, and vegetarian dishes at moderate prices (two can eat for less than $30). The other parts of *PGT Beauregard's* serve what you would expect from the old South.

Sam Miller's Warehouse (☎ 804-644-5465), a comfortable place at 1210 E Cary St, is known for its seafood (Maine lobsters, Chesapeake Bay delights) and steaks. It is open daily from 11 am to 11 pm and its Sunday brunch is served from 11 am to 5 pm. Across the road, at No 1201, is the immensely popular *Tobacco Company Restaurant* (☎ 804-782-9555), furnished with antiques and one of the places to be 'seen' in Richmond. The menu is extensive, with an accent on contemporary cuisine, and all comers should be well satisfied. If you finish a serving of prime rib then you get the next one free, and no one in the house will utter 'Oink, oink!' It is open for lunch and dinner daily, except Sunday (dinner only).

The Frog and the Redneck (☎ 804-648-3764), at 1423 E Cary St, Shockoe Slip, gets its name from its owners, a Southerner and an accomplished French chef. The $35 'tasting menu,' incorporating French touches with regional cuisine, is good value if your appetite is up to it. It is open Monday through Thursday from 5:30 to 10 pm, Friday and Saturday 5:30 until 10:30 pm; reservations are strongly recommended on the weekend.

Shockoe Bottom & Church Hill At 1721 E Franklin St is one of Richmond's best restaurants – *None Such Place* (☎ 804-644-0832) with an eclectic menu ('now' Virginia cuisine as well as enlightened treatment of old favorites such as salads, steaks, seafood, and mouthwatering desserts). It is open for lunch on weekdays from 11:30 am to 2:30 pm, for dinner Monday to Thursday 5:30 to 10:30 pm (weekends until 2 am); lunch is from $4 to $8, dinner from $7 to $20.

Millie's Diner (☎ 804-643-5512), at 2603 E Main St, Church Hill, looks plain from the outside but you will be happy once you are seated (there is usually a wait and reservations are not accepted). Large portions of their self-titled 'Fusion cuisine' (cooked before your eyes), a great wine selection, yummy desserts, and jukeboxes attract the locals back again and again. It is open for lunch and dinner daily, except Monday. The *River City Diner* (☎ 804-644-9418), at 1712 E Main St in Shockoe Bottom, is a good 24-hour alternative (except on Monday, when it too is closed).

The inexpensive *Main Street Grill* (☎ 804-644-3969), at 17th and Main Sts, across from the Farmer's Market, has a comprehensive vegetarian menu in the evenings (much of the fresh produce having been purchased just across the road). It too is open daily, except Monday.

Not far from the Farmer's Market in Shockoe Bottom are a handful of consistently good eateries. *Awful Arthur's Oyster Bar* (☎ 804-643-1700), at 101 N 18th St, is now a chain (with fish-house compatriots in Charlottesville and Roanoke) but it's still awfully good. They have consistently good seafood repasts – steamed crabs, oysters, shrimp, clams, and fish in gigantic portions, especially if you choose the specials – and burgers that would be too much for Attila the Hun. It is open, roughly, from midday to 2 am daily (Sunday till midnight).

The *Surf Rider Grill* (☎ 804-644-8704), at 1714 E Franklin St, is an oh-so-casual place with a delectable blackboard lunch menu that avoids fancy extras (11 am to 3 pm). (Surf is but a memory at the forlorn second branch of *Surf Rider* (☎ 804-744-8446), 13548 Genito Rd.)

The *Island Grill* (☎ 804-643-2222), at 14 N 18th St, mixes the best of contemporary American, Caribbean, and Latin cuisine, and their mixed grill entree with tropical sauces is well worth trying; the main dishes, from $12 to $25, are perfectly topped off with a 'cafe Antigua.' Dinner is served from 5:30 pm to closing, Monday to Saturday.

If you can't stand acrid cigar smoke, you will probably want to avoid *Havana '59* (☎ 804-649-2822), at 16 N 17th St, in Shockoe Bottom. But if you have been anywhere that is anywhere lately you will realize that this is an in place these days – just look at the pavement outside for the profusion of cigar butts the morning after. (Launder that business suit or sexy black number later – a small price to pay for a top night out.) The food is a mix of Cuban and 'advanced American diner' (steaks, seafood, pasta), the decor transports you to the Caribbean, and '59 is open from 5 pm (from 9 pm on weekends) until 2 am.

The Fan & Carytown The *Texas-Wisconsin Border Cafe* (☎ 804-355-2907) is somewhat geographically confused at 1501 W Main St, in Richmond. More than just steak is on offer here. The lunches are from $5 to $7 and dinners from $6 to $10. As it is a popular bar at night, the hours are from 11 am to 2 am.

Much more expensive but a good choice for northern Italian cuisine is the *Ristorante Amici* (☎ 804-353-4700), at 3343 W Cary St, Carytown. The decor feebly attempts to recreate a little piece of Italy but is made tolerable by the quality of the food (at dinner the entrees are from $14); reservations are advised. *Coppola's* (☎ 804-359-6969), at 2900 W Cary St, has a good selection of cheap, hearty Italian meals and great sandwiches (from $3 to $6), and heaps of ingredients with which to fashion the perfect picnic lunch; you can dig right into your purchase on indoor or outdoor tables. It is open from 10 am to 8 pm Monday to Wednesday, until 9 pm Thursday to Saturday, and is closed on Sunday.

You'll get good spaghetti at the modestly priced *Joe's Inn* (☎ 804-355-2282), at 205 N Shields Ave in The Fan. It is very busy at night and is open daily from 7 am to 2 pm.

The *Strawberry Street Cafe* (☎ 804-353-6860), at 421 Strawberry St (between Park and Stuart Aves), is a casual place frequented by locals. Its reputation is widespread for an inexpensive 'bathtub' salad bar, burgers, beef, chicken, quiche, and pasta dishes (quiche and burgers are half-price Monday nights). Lunch is from 11:30 am to 2:30 pm weekdays, brunch is served until 4:30 pm on weekends, and dinner is from 5 pm, Sunday to Thursday.

Grace Place (☎ 804-353-3680), in a Victorian home at 826 W Grace St (between Schaeffer and Laurel Sts), is a good, casual vegetarian haunt with daily specials, a selection of breads, and homemade desserts (some sugarless, including apple crisp). It is open for lunch and dinner daily, except Sunday.

There is much more to The Fan than the above and the adventurous will be well rewarded at *Soble's* (☎ 804-358-7843), 2600 W Main St, with its well-stocked raw bar and deli; the *James River Wine Bistro* (☎ 804-358-4562), 1520 W Main St, with classic and modern cuisine and a copious selection of wine; *Helen's* (☎ 804-358-4370), at the corner of Robinson and Main Sts, with an eclectic dinner menu (entrees from $16); a local hangout *Not Betty's* (☎ 804-359-4404); and classy *Avalon* (☎ 804-353-9709), 2619 W Main St, for innovative cuisine and microbrewery beers.

West End & North of Downtown At 2108 Maywill St, in the West End, a group of conservative diners are bound to be seen enjoying the mainly formal and certainly expensive traditional French cuisine of *La Petite France* (☎ 804-353-8729). The house specialty is lobster meat in puff pastry with a whisky sauce, but old favorites, such as chateaubriand, are also served. It is closed Sunday and Monday.

Franco's Ristorante, 9031-1 W Broad St in the West End, is the place for authentic Italian cuisine – good enough to satisfy Frank Sinatra. It is open weekdays for lunch from 11:30 am to 2:30 pm, for dinner from 5:30 to 10 pm.

For Chinese food, *Peking Restaurant* (☎ 804-270-9898), at 8904 W Broad St, is fairly good.

It is hard to keep a secret in this business, so we'll (without deliberation) let another one out of the bag. The best seafood place north of downtown is *Brookside Seafood* (☎ 804-262-5716), at 5221 Brook Rd (see the Greater Richmond map). During happy hour you can help yourself to a selection of finger food while enjoying a pre-dinner drink. Then comes the Brookside Special (a platter of scallops and shrimp with mushrooms and onions) for about $10.

VIRGINIA

Entertainment

A visitor to Richmond who thinks that the town is representative of the staid old South will be surprised to find that the town buzzes these days. There's a lot going on in the city and the free *Style Weekly* lists it all.

Cinemas & Theaters On no account should you miss the fabulous old *Byrd Theater* (☎ 804-353-9911), at 2908 W Cary St, where the movie is preceded by a concert on an old (but fully functional) Wurlitzer organ that rises, Phoenix-like, from the floor. Shows are an amazingly low $1; access to the balcony is another $1.

There are a couple of dinner theaters in the Richmond region. The Hanover Tavern houses the *Barksdale Theatre* (☎ 804-537-5333). It's on Hwy 310 some 13 miles north of town. It was the first of this ilk (dinner theaters) in the country putting on Broadway musicals, comedies, and drama. It is open year round from 6 to 11 pm. The tavern's three colonial dining rooms are separate from the theater.

In Colonial Heights, 11 miles south of downtown on Hwy 1, is the *Swift Creek Mill Playhouse* (☎ 804-748-5203), another dinner theater – an unlikely mix of Southern fare and Yankee entertainment. The theater is in a 17th century gristmill, believed to be the oldest in the country.

Theatre Virginia (☎ 804-367-0831), at 2800 Grove Rd in the Museum of Fine Arts, is a professional repertory theater, and probably the best choice for live theater. Its season runs from September to April and the box office is open Monday to Saturday from 11 am to 5 pm; dining is available.

Theatre IV (☎ 804-344-8040), a resident professional outfit, performs in the historic Empire Theatre (the oldest in Virginia), at 114 W Broad St, year round. Performances are at 8 pm, matinees at 2:30 pm.

Performing Arts There is plenty for those seeking the 'yarts.' The *Carpenter Center* (☎ 804-782-3900), at 600 E Grace St, is a performing arts center where you are likely to see or hear opera, ballet, or classical music. *The Landmark* (☎ 804-780-4213), formerly The Mosque, at the corner of Main and Laurel Sts, also features a range of performances. This architectural incongruity is worth seeing for its Moorish-influenced design, even if no performances are on offer.

The *Richmond Symphony* (☎ 804-788-1212) has built up a substantial reputation in its relatively short 30-year existence. Apart from performances of classical symphonic works there's a good chamber outfit and the Richmond Pops. The *Shanghai Quartet* (formed in Shanghai, China, in 1982) has been in residence at the University of Richmond since 1989. This talented quartet often performs during the fall and winter months.

The *Virginia Opera* (☎ 804-644-8168) is based in the Carpenter Center; call the box office between 10 am and 4:30 pm for their season (September to April) schedule.

Ballet lovers have the choice of modern and experimental works performed by the *Concert Ballet of Virginia* (☎ 804-780-1279) or more classical works by the *Richmond Ballet* (☎ 804-359-0906), 614 N Lombardy St. The latter has a program of five productions from September to May.

Nightlife This scene changes daily but there are always listings in the free weekly papers *Night Moves* and *Style Weekly*, and in the *Richmond Times-Dispatch*. If you are in Shockoe Bottom you will have no trouble finding a venue with entertainment. Much of the action is centered on restaurants because Virginia licensing laws dictate that any place that serves drinks must serve food. Shockoe Slip and The Fan are also pretty busy most nights. Rockin' Daddy and Mad Dog prepare a weekly telephone listing of events. Phone ☎ 804-353-7625 for details.

If you want a laugh centered on understatement rather than hyperbole, try *Matt's British Pub and Comedy Club* (☎ 804-643-5653) in Shockoe Slip at 109 S 12th St on weekend nights; shows start at 8 and 11 pm. The last joke is 'played' around 2 am.

For folk music, a few venues have a good feel: *Potter's Pub* (☎ 804-282-9999), at 7007 Three Chopt Rd, Village Shopping Center; *Main Street Grill* (☎ 804-644-3969), at 1700 E Main St (see Places to Eat – Shockoe Bottom & Church Hill); and *Castle Thunder Cafe & Taco Bottom* (☎ 804-648-3038), at 1724–26 E Main St. *Poe's Pantry & Pub* (☎ 804-648-2120), at 2706 E Main St, is open until 2 am every night but not for poetry readings; there is acoustic music on weekend nights and an open mike on Sunday from 4 pm.

Jazz lovers will probably want to head for cozy *Bogart's* (☎ 804-353-9280), at 203 N Lombardy St, or *Benjamin's* (☎ 804-355-3667), at 2053 W Broad St. Country and bluegrass is likely to be found out in the suburbs. *Dakota's Saloon* (☎ 804-346-2100) in Innsbrook is open until 1:30 am Monday to Saturday and has Southern-style rock and country music; the cover is from $3 to $4.

Rock aficionados (do they come by any other name?) have heaps of choice. Just about everyone recommends the hip *Flood Zone* (☎ 804-643-6006), at the corner of S 18th and E Main Sts, in Shockoe Bottom, for a 'bloody' good night out – dance to the music or jive alone as you watch from the balcony. Tickets are from $6 to $20 depending on who's playing (expect the moderately famous to complete unknowns). The ticket office is open Tuesday to Friday from 10 am to 6 pm.

Otherwise, try the *Tobacco Company Club* (☎ 804-782-9555), mentioned earlier under Places to Eat, a haunt for those seeking top-40 music ($3 cover downstairs). Not far from the Tobacco Company, at 9 N 17th St, is the *Moon Dance Saloon* (☎ 804-343-1757) with acoustic musicians on Wednesday and Thursday nights, and blues and rock and roll on Friday and Saturday. *Bottoms Up Pizza* (☎ 804-644-4400), at 1700 Dock St, Shockoe Bottom, is open until 2 am Friday and Saturday and has live music most days of the week, sometimes on the outside deck if weather permits. Those who dig blues and rockabilly are likely to find it at the *Memphis Bar & Grill* (☎ 804-783-2608), 119 N 18th St, which has live music, Tuesday to Saturday.

The happening venue, judging by the nightly queues, is *Havana '59* in Shockoe Bottom (see Places to Eat) – this place really moves to the antics of a DJ who mixes up an eclectic sound while perched above the crowd and cigar smoke in an old Jeep eyrie.

In the Fan District are the *James River Wine Bistro* (☎ 804-359-6324), mentioned above, and *Buddy's Place* (☎ 804-355-3701), at 325 N Robinson St, a popular place with students – both have live music.

Popular gay clubs are *Feilden's* (☎ 804-359-1963), at 2033 W Broad St, and *Babe's* (☎ 804-355-9330), at 3166 W Cary St. *The Pyramyd*, at 1008 N Boulevard, may reopen in a new guise.

Bars The locals love their beer and have plenty of bars in which to imbibe. In Shockoe Slip is the *Richbrau Brewery* (☎ 804-644-3018), at 1214 E Cary St, a shrine for those who enjoy microbrews – in this case Richmond's own 'richbrau.' Other great microbreweries include *The Legend Brewing Co* (☎ 804-232-8871), at 323 W 7th St on the south side of James River, which also serves vegetarian fare, and the *Commercial Taphouse & Grill* (☎ 804-359-6544), at 111 N Robinson St in The Fan. British-style pubs, with steak & kidney pie and Cornish pasties, include *Matt's* and *Potter's* (see Nightlife in this section), the *Fox and Hounds* (☎ 804-272-8309) at 10455 Midlothian Turnpike, and *Penny Lane* (☎ 804-780-1682) at 207 N 7th St.

A favorite of travel writers is the *Lakeside Tavern*, Lakeside Drive, for a bunch of real working-class Richmonders, a game of pool, passable food, cheap beer, and a return to boozy normality. Other places where you can play pool and billiards are the cleverly named *Breakers* (☎ 804-747-7665) at 4032-A Cox Rd, Innsbrook; *Rack 'n' Roll* (☎ 804-644-1204) at 1713 E Main St; and *Side Pocket* (☎ 804-353-7921) at 2012 Staples Mill Rd – all are open until 2 am every night with full-service bars and full menus.

VIRGINIA

Spectator Sports

Richmond has no NFL or NBA teams – you will have to go to Baltimore or Washington, DC to see those.

The Coliseum (☎ 804-780-4956), which seats 12,000, is the main venue for a host of other spectator sports such as basketball, wrestling, and tennis. The Richmond Braves are a Triple-A farm **baseball** team for Atlanta's Braves – they play at the 12,000-plus-seat Diamond (☎ 804-359-4444), 3001 N Boulevard (Exit 78 off I-64 and I-95 junction) – you can't miss it as it has a gigantic sculpture of Native American warrior, Connecticut, peering over a wall. Their home schedule runs from April through August.

For **basketball**, devoid of big names but not big hearts, try Randolph-Macon College, Virginia Commonwealth University (which appeared in five NCAA tournaments in the 1980s), and the University of Richmond. Also check out the Richmond Rage, a team in the women's American Basketball League. Game times are listed in the *News Leader* and *Times-Dispatch*. The local **soccer** team is the Richmond Kickers, who play in the US Interregional Soccer League (☎ 804-644-5425), and the local **ice hockey** team is the Richmond Renegades (☎ 804-643-7825) from the East Coast Hockey League.

The **Richmond International Raceway** (☎ 804-329-6796) in the east at the Virginia State Fairgrounds, between Henrico Turnpike (Meadowbridge Rd) and Laburnum Ave, is a 0.75-mile track which seats 90,000 fans. Each year it hosts two Grand National Series and two Winston Cup races – the Miller Genuine Draft 400 in September and the Pontiac Excitement 400 in March.

There must be an abundance of 'revheads' here because the **Southside Speedway** (☎ 804-744-1275), at Genito Rd in Midlothian, attracts them in droves. On Friday nights, from April to September, expect to find NASCAR/Winston-sanctioned races.

In May, Richmonders line the streets to watch some of the world's top cyclists speed through the city blocks in the **Tour du Pont**. The women cyclists race through town just before the men. For more information, call Medalist Sports Inc (☎ 804-354-9934).

Things to Buy

The Very Richmond Shop in the Jefferson Hotel has a range of Richmond prints and ephemera. For photographic supplies go to *Richmond Camera* on W Broad St.

Getting There & Away

Air About a dozen airlines serve Richmond International Airport with over 150 flights daily – these include Delta (☎ 804-800-221-1212), American (☎ 800-433-7300), and United (☎ 800-241-6522). USAir (☎ 800-428-4322) is the major regional carrier.

Bus The Greyhound/Trailways terminal (☎ 804-254-5910, 800-231-2222) is at 2910 N Boulevard, Exit 78 off I-95. You will need to take a GRTC bus to get into town. Here are some fares and travel times from Richmond:

Charlottesville	$18	1.5 hours
Norfolk	$13	3 hours
Washington	$27	2.5 hours
Williamsburg	$10	1 hour

Train Richmond is well served by Amtrak (☎ 804-264 9194, 800-872-7245) but is some distance away at 7519 Staple Mills Rd; it is open 24 hours and has handicapped access. A taxi fare to downtown is about $12. The closest bus is GRTC No 27 which passes Glenside Park 'n' Ride.

Within the state, there are services to Washington, DC, a two-hour trip that costs $22; Williamsburg (1¼ hours, $10); and Virginia Beach (three hours, $20, the last part on a bus shuttle). There are interstate services to New York ($85), Philadelphia ($45), and Baltimore ($30).

Car Richmond is at the junction of I-95 (north-south) and I-64 (east-west) and is about a two-hour drive away from Washington, DC, Hampton Roads, or the Blue Ridge Mountains. Also bisecting the city east-west is Hwy 60, and Hwys 1 and 301 run through it north-south. I-295 bypasses the city on its eastern side. The Highway Helpline (☎ 800-367-7623) has info on the state's major highways. See the Driving Distances Chart in Getting Around.

Getting Around

To/From the Airport A taxicab to downtown is $16 to $18. There is no GRTC bus service but Groome Transportation (☎ 800-552-7911) offers 24-hour service into downtown; the cost is $13 for one person, $18 for two, and a carload for around $26.

At the airport, short-term parking is $1 per hour or $8 for 24 hours; long-term parking is $5 for 24 hours; and satellite parking is $4 per day with a shuttle running every 10 minutes from the parking area.

All the major rental car companies are at the airport. In the Richmond area, you can get info on road conditions by calling ☎ 800-367-7623, and on weather by calling ☎ 804-268-1212.

Bus & Trolley The city bus service is provided by the Greater Richmond Transit Company (GRTC), 101 S Davis St (☎ 804-358-4782). There are infrequent services out to the suburbs but plenty in downtown. You can get a route map from the basement of City Hall, 99 E Broad St. Most buses leave from on or near Broad St. Bus No 24 is a good service for getting south into downtown and Broad St. Fares are from 75¢ to $1.20 and transfers cost 10¢ (request these when you first get on); the exact change is required.

Taxi There are over 40 taxicab companies in the city. Three 'road-tested' cab companies are Town and Country Taxi (☎ 804-271-2211), Veterans Cab Association (☎ 804-329-1414), and Colonial Cab (☎ 804-264-7960). Cabs are metered and the charge is $1.50 per mile with a $1.50 drop charge.

Bicycle There are several good bike tours in the Richmond area. Two Wheel Travel, at 2934 W Cary St in Carytown, does repairs, rents bikes (from $15), and provides maps and information on bike tours in the area. Other info sources are the Richmond Area Bicycling Association (☎ 804-266-7562), which publishes *Rides Around Richmond*, listing 50 tours; and Rowlett's, at the corner of Broad St and Staples Mill Rd, for info and repairs.

Around Richmond

RICHMOND BATTLEFIELD PARK

Richmond was always seen by the Federal forces as the main prize of the Civil War, and a few campaigns came within miles of the city. These battles are

The Battles for Richmond

Three major Civil War campaigns were fought in the vicinity of Richmond – the Seven Days Battles (June 25 to July 1, 1862), the Battle of Cold Harbor (June 1864), and the Battle of Fort Harrison (September 1864).

Seven Days Battles By early June 1862, General George B McClellan's Peninsula Campaign had ground to a halt just short of the Richmond defenses and Robert E Lee had assumed command of Confederate forces in the field. On June 25 McClellan inched his skirmish lines forward, planning a major attack for the next day.

But Lee acted quickly and decisively, recalling Stonewall Jackson's troops from the Shenandoah Valley, and on June 26 with a combined force of 90,000, he counterattacked, thus beginning the Seven Days Battles. First the Union troops were flushed out of the village of Mechanicsville. The following day at Gaines' Mill, in the biggest assault of the war to that point, 55,000 Confederates attacked the lines of blue. They were repulsed time and time again but kept coming and, in a last ditch attack, overwhelmed the Union lines, capturing whole regiments and artillery.

McClellan ordered the Army of the Potomac to move to another base on the James River and Lee tried to get around it to head it off. There were furious battles as the armies dodged and weaved – at Savage Station on June 29, and at White Oak Swamp and Frayser's Farm (Glendale) on June 30 – all contributing to the mounting casualty lists on both sides.

The Federal troops reached the James at Harrison's Landing and came under the protection of gunboats with large-caliber guns. McClellan ordered Major General Fitz-John Porter to occupy Malvern Hill with as many forces as he needed and protect the withdrawal. Lee attacked Malvern Hill in the afternoon of July 1, but the Union position, with its vast array of artillery and clear field of fire, slaughtered the assaulting troops – over half the 6000-plus casualties were caused by cannon fire. McClellan, cautious as ever, did not follow up the reversal of Confederate fortunes, and secured his army in the lines at Harrison's Landing. Lee had saved Richmond and the possibility for a short war had been lost.

commemorated in the Richmond National Battlefield Park (☎ 804-226-1981), a collection of eleven sites (altogether over 760 acres) including Gaines' Mill, Malvern Hill, Cold Harbor, and Fort Harrison. The Chimborazo Visitors Center, at 3215 E Broad St, is in a former Civil War hospital (a giant complex built in 1862 in which over 75,000 patients were treated). It has free maps and shows a 30-minute movie about the city during the war called *Richmond Remembered,* and a slide show about the battlefields. It is open daily from 9 am to 5 pm and there is no admission fee.

At the small Cold Harbor visitor center is an electric map of the battle. The Fort Harrison visitor center, open June to August, is close to the well preserved fortifications.

There are interpretative facilities at Chickahominy Bluff, Malvern Hill, Fort Harrison, and Drewry's Bluff. You'll find historical trails at Gaines' Mill (Watt House), Fort Brady, and Drewry's Bluff. There are also tour roads (and picnic areas) at Cold Harbor and Fort Harrison, and an audio cassette is available for a four-hour self-driving tour of the Seven Days Battles. Other sites to visit are Savage's Station, Yellow Tavern, Hanover Junction, Haw's Shop, Howlett and Bermuda Hundred lines, and River Road – ask for directions and a free map at the Chimborazo visitors center – and the Museum of the Confederacy.

PETERSBURG

This historic town (population 38,400), on the Appomattox River 23 miles south of Richmond (on I-95), was the scene of the last great battle of the Civil War. When this vital junction center fell to Union troops in

VIRGINIA

Cold Harbor In March 1864 General US Grant assumed command of the Union forces and by May was engaged in an overland campaign against Lee's army. After several battles in which Grant attempted to outflank Lee, the two generals finally faced each other directly in June, at Cold Harbor and again near the Chickahominy to the northeast of Richmond.

In the sweltering heat, Grant massed his soldiers for what he hoped would be the final blow against the Confederates. On June 1 the Union troops made old-fashioned frontal assaults and gained scant ground. The next day the two worn armies, which for a solid month had been in close contact, attempted to rest. On June 3 the Union troops again attacked frontally, but in just half an hour they incurred several thousand casualties. For the next 24 hours the two sides engaged in bloody trench warfare. It is estimated that Grant lost over 12,000 troops in these days; Lee's losses were much lighter.

Battle of Fort Harrison After Cold Harbor Grant stealthily moved his army across the James River and concentrated his efforts on the important rail center of Petersburg. Throughout late summer and fall the Union forces peppered away at the outer defenses of Richmond and Petersburg. On September 29, 1864, Federal troops attacked and captured Fort Harrison, in a move designed to prevent Lee from freely moving his troops between sectors of operations.

Several African American regiments participated in the fierce fighting for the fort, and their gallantry is reflected in the awarding of Medals of Honor to 14 black soldiers. Once occupied, Fort Harrison was enlarged by the Union troops and a line of fortifications was extended south to Fort Brady, which strategically dominated a bend in the James River.

During the winter, active operations slowed down and the soldiers suffered the privations of cold, boredom, and hunger. The Confederate lines were being stretched to the breaking point, and on April 2, 1865, the siege of Petersburg was over. Lee's army retreated westwards and the war neared its end. ■

early April 1865, after a 10-month siege, the nearby capital of Richmond was evacuated by the Confederates. Much earlier it had changed hands in the Revolutionary War – it fell in the spring of 1781 to a British force.

The Old Towne, the most interesting part of Petersburg with many fine antebellum buildings, is easy to walk around. At the town visitors center you can purchase passes to five Old Towne attractions – the Siege Museum, Trapezium House, Blandford Church, Centre Hill Mansion, and the Farmers Bank.

The city's many local industries include a large optical plant. The giant military installation of Fort Lee is nearby. In August 1993, a tornado tore through Old Towne destroying many buildings – locals say it did more damage in five minutes than Grant managed in his entire siege!

Information

The I-95 Petersburg Visitors Center (☎ 804-246-2145), at the Carson Rest Area on I-95S (20 miles south of the city), and the Petersburg Visitors Center – Old Towne (☎ 804-733-2400, 800-368-3595), at 425 Cockade Alley off Old St, have lots of info and exhibits on battlefield tours and accommodations. The *Petersburg Community Info Guide* has a detailed map of the town.

The most fascinating freebie is the pamphlet *African-American Historic Sites in Petersburg*. Few know that a group of free blacks left Petersburg in 1829 for Liberia on the West African coast. One of them, Joseph Jenkins Roberts, became the first president of Liberia. He served as president from 1848 to 1855, then from 1871–76. There is a marker at the corner of Sycamore and Wythe Sts.

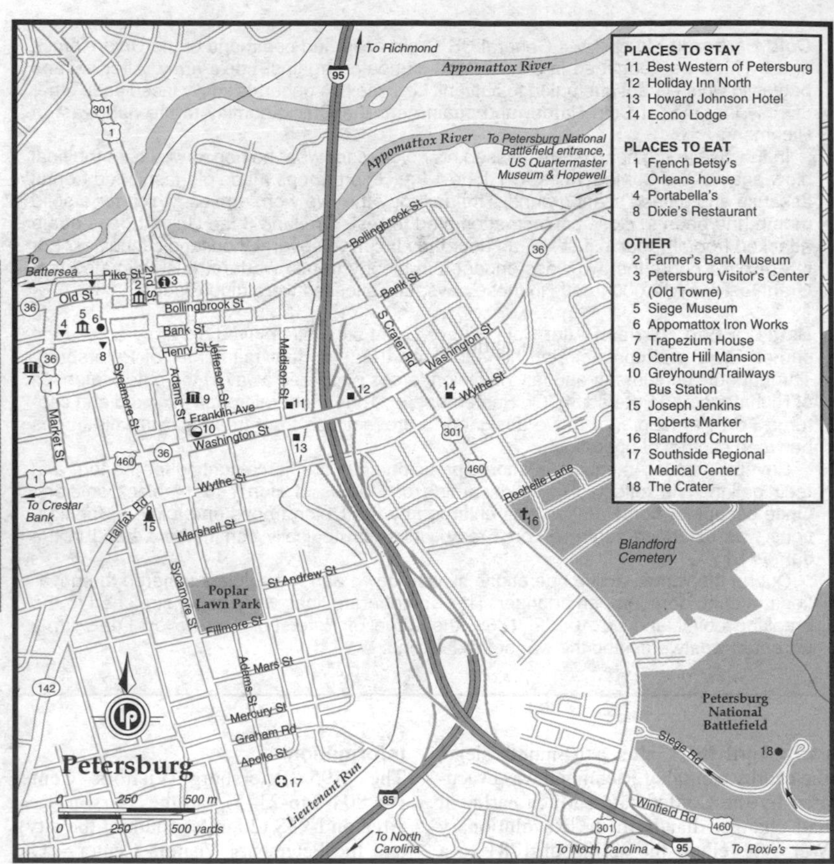

VIRGINIA

Old Towne

One of the more interesting parts of Old Towne is the **Appomattox Iron Works** at 20-28 Old St (☎ 804-733-7300, 800-232-4766). The complex reminds us of life in the early industrial age, when an element of brute strength and a leather apron were essential ingredients in the preparation of iron objects. This building was severely damaged in the '93 tornado and will reopen in spring of 1997.

At the **Siege Museum** (☎ 804-733-2404), 15 W Bank St, you get a glimpse of what life was like for those under siege here during the Civil War. The exhibits focus on the lot of the civilians, rather than the warring troops, and there are several poignant examples of the will to survive. A film, narrated by Joseph Cotton, evokes some of the sense of the time. The museum is open daily from 10 am to 5 pm. The cost of admission is $3 for adults, $2 for seniors and children.

The intriguing **Trapezium House** of 1817 (☎ 804-733-2400, 800-368-3595), at 244 N Market St, would be a challenge for any modern builder. Its construction is said to have been influenced by

Caribbean superstitions that the builder learned from one of his servants. Evil spirits lurked in parallel lines and right angles, the sort that *feng shui* could not remove. It is open Monday to Saturday from 10:30 am to 3:30 pm, Sunday 12:30 to 3:30 pm (February to November); admission is $3 for adults, $2 for children. All tours begin from the Siege Museum.

The **Centre Hill Mansion** (☎ 804-733-2401) on Centre Hill Court has undergone several remodelings since it was built in 1823. Furnished with Victorian antiques, including a huge 100-year-old Knabe grand piano, it is well worth a visit. It is open from Monday to Saturday from 9 am to 5 pm, Sunday from 12:30 to 5 pm; admission is $2 for adults, $1.50 for children.

At 19 Bollingbrook St is the **Farmers Bank** of 1817 (☎ 804-733-2400), one of the oldest bank premises in the nation. It is open April to September, Monday to Saturday from 10 am to 5 pm; entry is $3 for adults, $2 for seniors and children. Tours also start at the visitors center. **Battersea** (☎ 804-733-2400), Upper Appomattox St, is a 1770 Palladian house. It is undergoing restoration but you can walk past it.

At 319 S Crater Rd is the historic **Blandford Church**, built in 1735 and now a memorial to the Confederate soldiers who died during the Civil War. It features 15 stained glass windows by Louis Comfort Tiffany, 13 of them memorials donated by the Confederate states.

Let's face it, you probably don't know how Memorial Day got started, do you? Not long after the war ended, Mary Logan, wife of the politician and Union General John Alexander Logan, saw schoolgirls placing flowers on the gravesites of some of Petersburg's war dead, near Blandford Church. She saw the observance repeated the following year. Very moved, she told her husband, who was by then head of the Grand Army of the Republic, the major body of Union veterans. At his instruction Memorial Day was instituted as a national holiday, first celebrated on May 30, 1868, for the purpose of decorating the graves of Civil War dead. The church is open daily from 10 am to 5 pm; admission is $3 for adults, $2 for children.

Free Black Communities

A small but fascinating sidelight to slavery arose in the antebellum South. Slaves who either bought their freedom or were 'manumitted' (released from slavery) quietly formed small 'Free Black' communities throughout the South. Though their freedom was severely limited, free blacks nevertheless enjoyed liberties denied to their enslaved peers: They organized in largely self-regulated communities, raised families, formed churches, learned trades, inherited property (though most supported abolition, some wealthier free blacks even owned slaves), and established a social elite of their own. One such community was located on Pocahontas Island on the north side of the Appomattox River near Petersburg. Though visitors can stroll around the island, no monument or museum recalls the former community. ■ *– KS*

The **Slo-Pitch Softball Hall of Fame** (☎ 804-733-1005), at 3935 S Crater Rd, houses memorabilia of players inducted into the US Slo-Pitch Softball Hall of Fame. There are numerous exhibits, photographs, and displays. It is open on weekdays from 9 am to 4 pm, Saturday from 10 am to 4 pm, Sunday from noon to 4 pm; admission is $1.50 for adults, $1 for students and seniors, and children under 12 are admitted free.

Petersburg National Battlefield

This 2650-acre park is just to the northeast of the city. It was the site of the 10-month siege of Petersburg – June 1864 to April 1865 (see the aside in this section).

At the War Room in the visitors center (☎ 804-732-3531) there are maps and models to assist those going on a self-guided four-mile driving tour (where you park and walk out to points of interest). There is a living history program (mid-June

Siege of Petersburg, 1864–1865

Following the tumultuous battles around Richmond in June 1864, US Grant's Union forces struck out to take the vital rail center of Petersburg, 23 miles south of Richmond on the Appomattox River.

Grant handled the move around the Confederate right with skill. His army stole from their trenches and, thanks to a 2100-foot pontoon bridge across the James River constructed by George Meade's engineers, got close to Petersburg before Robert E Lee knew what was happening.

Petersburg at that stage was held by a small Confederate force led by PGT Beauregard. Twice Union forces attacked, only to fail to make the most of the opportunity, perhaps because the troops were exhausted. Lee got the Army of Northern Virginia into position just in time and Grant called off further attacks; on June 20 Grant's forces settled down to a partial siege. It was exactly the situation Lee had hoped to avoid, as his army was now pinned to a fixed position.

In July a Union regiment, the 48th Pennsylvania composed largely of coal miners, dug in opposite a Confederate stronghold. Their plan, which was quite a long shot, was to build a 500-foot-long tunnel under the Confederate lines, pack it with eight tons of blasting powder, and blow it up, thus breaching the Confederate defenses. At dawn on July 30, after a harrowing moment when a brave soldier crawled into the tunnel to splice the broken fuse, the biggest bang of the war occurred, creating a 150-foot crater (which you can still see today). Massive bungling by the attacking forces failed to take the advantage and by midday the attack was thwarted and the stalemate resumed. A division of black soldiers, sent in to breach the Confederate line, had been butchered and the hapless General Burnside was removed from command.

After this blunder the siege continued, and Grant and Meade gradually extended their lines on the southern flank, attempting to cut off supply lines to Petersburg and Richmond. Eventually the Union lines were more than 50 miles long, stretching from northeast of Richmond in an arc to southeast of Petersburg. In response, Lee stretched his lines taut; his only hope was to break the siege and try to join Joseph Johnston in North Carolina, where his army might have a chance of success against Sherman's forces.

Lee's infantry attacked the Union stronghold of **Fort Stedman**, due east of Petersburg, on March 25, hoping to break the Union line in two, but the attack failed, with a loss of about 5000 men. Grant responded swiftly, moving a full corps against the farthest end of the Confederate line and moving Phil Sheridan's cavalry to the crossroads at Five Forks.

The next day Grant led a concerted assault along Lee's main lines and on the night of April 2-3 Lee evacuated Petersburg and Richmond to begin his final retreat. Sheridan's cavalry, supported by infantry, chased the retreating Southerners towards Appomattox and the war's end. The next day Lincoln, transported down the James River by gunboat, walked into a burning Richmond with an escort of sailors and witnessed firsthand the collapse of the Confederacy. ■

VIRGINIA

to late August) in which costumed interpreters construct earthworks and portray the life of an ordinary soldier. A 17,000-pound Federal seacoast mortar (similar to 'Dictator' which shelled the town from 2.5 miles away) is on display.

The park is open daily, mid-June to August, from 8 am to 7 pm; September to mid-June, 8 am to 5 pm. Admission is $4 for a car, $2 for cyclists or pedestrians. To get there take Exit 52 off I-95 on to Route 36 – the entrance to the park is signed.

Quartermaster Corps Museum

The US Army's Quartermaster Museum (☎ 804-734-4203) is on E Washington St (Route 36), three miles east of old Petersburg in **Fort Lee**. It includes uniforms and equipment dating back to 1775, Civil War memorabilia, Eisenhower's uniforms, President Franklin Pierce's saddles, and General George Patton's jeep, specially fitted out with its Mercedes car seat. The museum is open Tuesday to Friday from 10 am to 5 pm, weekends from 11 am to

5 pm; admission is free and you don't need a pass to enter the fort.

Special Events

Two special events in Petersburg are designed to raise the hair on your back. In late January, visitors await the appearance of a 'ghost' brigade from the Civil War in the Ghost Watch at Centre Hill Mansion. In late October there's the Hallows Eve Tour of Historic Blandford Cemetery.

Places to Stay

The *South Forty KOA* (☎ 804-732-8345), at 2809 Courtland Rd (Exit 41 off I-95), has over 100 campsites. In winter, sites are from $15 to $17 for two people, otherwise $16 to $20 (an extra person is $3); there are 'kamping kabins' from $28 to $35.

There are plenty of cheap chain accommodations, especially near Exit 52/50D off I-95 and Exit 45 near the intersection of I-95 and I-295. The *Econo Lodge Interstate* (☎ 804-732-2000) is at 12002 S Crater Rd (Exit 45 off I-95 at Hwy 301); singles and doubles are from $33 to $50. The *Holiday Inn North* (☎ 804-733-0730), at 501 E Washington St (Exit 50D northbound and 52 southbound, off I-95), has a pool and exercise room; singles are from $49 to $59, doubles from $55 to $67.

Also in this enclave is the *Best Western Petersburg* (☎ 804-733-1776) with a restaurant; the rooms all have free movies and TV, the price includes continental breakfast, and singles/doubles are from $42/47 in the winter low season, and $51/57 otherwise. The *Howard Johnson Hotel* (☎ 804-732-5950), at 530 E Washington St (Exit 52 off I-95), has mostly balcony rooms (all with movies and cable TV), a restaurant, and a pool and wading pool; singles are from $39 to $56, doubles from $44 to $58.

The *Mayfield Inn B&B* (☎ 804-861-6775), an 18th century brick building, is at 3348 W Washington St. The large rooms, furnished with antiques, are from $65 to $70 for a double. To get there take Exit 52 off I-95 to Washington St (Hwy 1/460) and travel west for about three miles.

Places to Eat

The *Dixie Restaurant* (☎ 804-732-5761), at 250 N Sycamore St, is an unpretentious place that serves Southern-style fare to poor and rich alike; a lunch costs from $2.50 to $4.50.

Annabelle's (☎ 804-732-0997), in a converted barn at 2733 Park Ave (just off S Crater Rd), serves good old-fashioned American dishes; a steak dinner is from $8 to $15. *Portabella* (☎ 804-732-6233), at 105 Bank St, is a small intimate French/Italian restaurant.

At 3221 W Washington St (Hwy 1S) is the immensely popular *King's Barbecue* (☎ 804-732-5861) where beef and pork are served directly from a dining room smoking pit. Other Southern favorites are on the menu and side orders include fried potato cakes and barbecued beans – eat a huge meal here for less than $10. There is another branch of King's (☎ 804-732-0975) at 2910 S Crater Rd. Both are open daily from 7 am to 9 pm.

French Betsy's Orleans House (☎ 804-732-8888), at 21 W Old St in Old Towne, serves all of the Louisiana Cajun and Creole favorites. It's more expensive than King's (their Sunday buffet brunch is $12). There is often live music on nights towards the end of the week. It's open daily for lunch and dinner, until midnight Thursday to Saturday.

Roxie's (☎ 804-861-3470), in the Flagship Inn, is the place to listen to a little country music while you enjoy a meal.

Getting There & Away

The closest major airport is Richmond International (see Richmond for details). Greyhound/Trailways runs daily service, and the depot is on the southeast corner of Washington and Adams Sts. The Amtrak stop is in Ettrick just across the river on Route 36. You will have to get a taxi to accommodations from here; it is about $5 per person.

Petersburg Area Transit (☎ 804-733-2413) serves the city and the surrounding area. A ride is 70¢ (10¢ for a transfer) but you must have exact change.

HOPEWELL

The city of Hopewell, north of Petersburg on the James River, is an outgrowth of Old City Point, founded by Sir Thomas Dale in 1613. It was the one of the earliest English settlements in America but was wiped out in a Native American attack in 1622. Its strategic location in the Civil War led to a revival in its importance. In the mid-1970s it was the scene of one of the nation's worst pesticide contaminations.

The Hopewell Visitors Center (☎ 804-541-2206), at 201-D Randolph Square, has info on this suburb. The **City Point National Historic Site** (☎ 804-458-9504) was the site of Ulysses S Grant's army headquarters for over nine months. Included on the site are two rooms with original furnishings, Grant's cabin, and wayside exhibits. The dozens of other pre–Civil War houses at the confluence of the James and Appomattox rivers that survived war use as commissaries, lodgings, and munitions stores for the Federal army during the siege of Petersburg, can be seen in self-guided tours. There is a national cemetery nearby where many Confederate and Union soldiers are buried. City Point is open daily from 8:30 am to 4:30 pm; entry is free.

At 1617 Flowerdew Hundred Rd, off Route 10 near Hopewell, is an interesting archaeological excavation. **Flowerdew Hundred** was founded in 1619. The archaeological site (☎ 804-541-8897) now includes a museum, detached plantation kitchen, and intriguing outdoor excavations. It is open, April to November, Tuesday to Sunday from 10 am to 5 pm (by appointment only on Monday); admission is $4 for adults, $3.50 for seniors, and $2 for students.

On Crescent and Prince George Aves in Crescent Hill-Oakwood there is a display of the **Sears, Roebuck & Co Houses by Mail**, 44 diverse examples of house-building kits, ranging from executive housing to English cottages, which you could order in the 1920s and '30s. There is a self-guided tour of the neighborhood or you can take a 30-minute guided tour (available from 9 am to 5 pm; call ☎ 804-863-8687 to find out costs).

The **Weston Plantation** (☎ 804-541-2206), at 21st Ave and Weston Lane (off Route 10), is also worth a visit. The three stories of the house are furnished with antiques, and there are extensive gardens. Particularly interesting is the history in the Civil War journals left by 12-year-old Emma Wood. The plantation is open April to October, weekdays from 9 am to 5 pm, Sunday 1 to 5 pm; admission is $5 for adults, $4 for seniors, and children under 12 are free.

The *Pocahontas II* (☎ 800-405-9990) leaves from the marina, 906 Riverside Ave, for tours of the James River. It operates from April to November and the cost varies depending on the nature and length of cruise; the shortest cruise is $10.50 for adults, $5.50 for children.

WAKEFIELD

Peanut lovers head southeast of Petersburg on Hwy 460 to Wakefield, self-proclaimed 'peanut capital of the world.' The reason for a trip that could only be described as 'Nuts!' is the idiosyncratic *Virginia Diner* (☎ 804-899-3106), which pays homage to the humble goober and which has been open since 1929. The restaurant, once housed in a railroad car, has expanded as its notoriety has grown. The peanuts, cooked in vendor roasters, are free and a sumptuous breakfast of ham, eggs, hot cakes, omelets, hash browns, Southern grits, biscuits, and sausage is less than $6.

The diner is open from 6 am to 9 pm in summer, and until 8 pm in winter. You can take some peanuts away. Melvin, the chef, has been cooking them since he was big enough to mount a crate and peer into a fryer.

PAMPLIN PARK CIVIL WAR SITE

This private park (☎ 804-861-2408), at 6523 Duncan Rd (County Rd 670, Exit 63A off I-85), southwest of Petersburg in Dinwiddie County, is at the site where the Union forces broke through the Confederate defenses on April 2, 1865. Fifteen hours after the breakthrough here, Lee was forced to abandon Petersburg (Richmond was evacuated soon after).

The interpretative center, designed to reflect the shape of the Confederate defensive line at the time, has a fiber-optic battle map, interactive video programs, and well-presented displays of artifacts; outside is a one-mile trail that leads to some of the fortifications and to a reconstruction of one of the huts in which Confederate soldiers wintered over in 1864–65.

The National Museum of the Civil War Soldier is expected to open here in 1999.

Northern Virginia

At first glance you could be forgiven for thinking that Northern Virginia is just a huge dormitory for the juggernaut of Washington, DC. Sure, its future is linked to the nation's capital and it is physically connected by the Metro and road bridges across the Potomac River. Also, Washingtonians fan out into nearby counties to relax on weekends. But cross to the south side of the river, and you're in Virginia where the people will proudly call themselves Virginians.

This chapter covers the main cities, towns, and counties within an easy drive south of the nation's capital. Alexandria and Arlington are both fascinating cities in their own right – the former has its quaint and well-preserved Old Town, the latter the world's most famous cemetery and the Pentagon. Both also shelter high tech industries and a fair slice of the US's brain power (some of it atrophying in bureaucratic service!).

Travel a little further beyond these boundaries and you reach Fairfax, Prince William, Loudoun, and Fauquier counties (the last two called 'Hunt Country'). These are replete with historical associations (eg, Manassas), pleasant rural scenery, and such treasures as Mount Vernon and Gunston Hall.

HIGHLIGHTS

- Cobblestone streets and an aura of history in Old Town Alexandria
- Arlington National Cemetery – the most famous final resting place in the world
- Mount Vernon – home of George and Martha Washington and one of America's most visited estates
- Hunt and Horse Country – a little bit of England in the heart of America
- Manassas Battlefield – the first major battle of the Civil War

Getting Around

To/From the Airport Dulles International Airport (☎ 703-661-2700) is a 40-minute drive from Alexandria). Washington's National Airport (☎ 703-358-5720) is a five- to ten-minutes drive away from Old Town Alexandria and not much farther away from the major sites in Arlington.

From Dulles you can take Washington Flyer Airport Shuttles (☎ 703-685-1400) to the West Falls Church Metro stop ($8). From here you can take one of the Metrorail or Metro bus links to the parts of Northern Virginia near DC. The Washington Flyer also runs from National Airport to various northern Virginia destinations, but even more convenient is the Metrorail (☎ 202-637-7000, TDD 202-638-3780), which stops right at National. A copy of *StationMasters* indicates possible destinations. Metro buses (☎ 202-637-7000) conveniently interconnect with Metrorail services. The fare on Metrorail or Metro bus from National to Alexandria or Arlington is about $1.25.

Reliable cab companies are Yellow (☎ 202-544-1212), Diamond (☎ 202-387-6200), and Capitol (☎ 202-546-2400); a taxi fare into Alexandria or Arlington from Dulles may cost up to $45, from National probably about $12. (We are cagey about costs because of the possibility of gridlock, which can raise fares.)

Train From Union Station (☎ 202-484-7540) in DC (see the DC chapter for further information) you can catch the Metrorail to Arlington, Alexandria, and points beyond

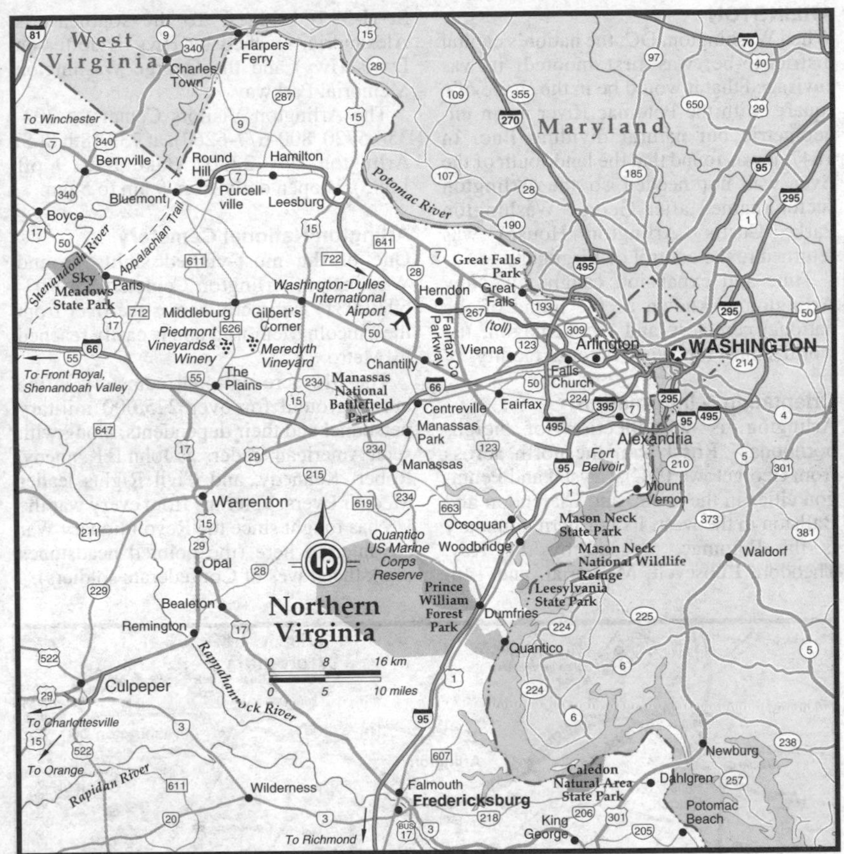

in northern Virginia. Amtrak passes through Alexandria on its East Coast route; it stops at the station (☎ 703-836-4339) at 110 Callahan Drive.

Bus Greyhound/Trailways (☎ 703-998-6312) passes through Arlington.

Car Driving within the Beltway can be a real headache – traffic congestion can be maddening and once you reach a destination, parking is extremely limited. That said, northern Virginia has a sophisticated road system – I-95 (which connects with the I-495 Beltway) passes to the east and south of the region. A feeder freeway, I-395, cuts north-south through both Alexandria and Arlington to reconnect with I-95S. Hwy 50W connects the city areas to the northwest, I-66W leads to the west and Shenandoah Valley, Hwy 29 to Manassas, and Hwy 1 is a slower but more relaxed alternative to the north-south I-95 (and gives access to many of the historic attractions such as Mount Vernon). Just watch out for HOV-3 (high occupancy vehicle) routes, and if you find yourself alone in an HOV lane in peak hour, expect a fine.

ARLINGTON

When Washington, DC, the nation's capital district-to-be, was first mooted, it was envisaged that it would be in the shape of a square, with the Potomac River as an ungeometric but natural dividing line. In 1847, it was found that the land south of the river was not needed so the Arlington sector (named after George Washington Parke Custis' Arlington House) was returned to the control of Virginia.

Time and expansion caught up. Now Arlington is known as the home of the national cemetery and the Pentagon, the world's most renowned defense facility.

Orientation & Information

Arlington is a collection of neighborhoods – Rosslyn in the north across from Georgetown (DC), Crystal and Pentagon cities in the south, and Clarendon and Ballston in the west. Its northern boundary is the Potomac, crossed by the Key, Theodore Roosevelt, Memorial, and 14th St (I-395) bridges. To the southeast is Alexandria, reached by Hwy 1 (Jefferson Davis Hwy) and the George Washington Memorial Parkway.

The Arlington Visitors Center (☎ 703-358-5720, 800-677-6267), at 735 18th St S, Arlington, VA 22202 (take Exit 9 off I-395), is open daily from 9 am to 5 pm.

Arlington National Cemetery

One of the most-visited sights around Washington, Arlington Cemetery (☎ 703-692-0931) is directly across the river from the Lincoln Memorial and is easily reached by Metro.

The 612-acre national cemetery is the burial ground for over 225,000 military personnel and their dependents, along with such American leaders as John F Kennedy, Robert Kennedy, and Civil Rights leader Medgar Evers. Veterans from every war the US has fought since the Revolutionary War are interred here (the pointed headstones mark the graves of Confederate soldiers).

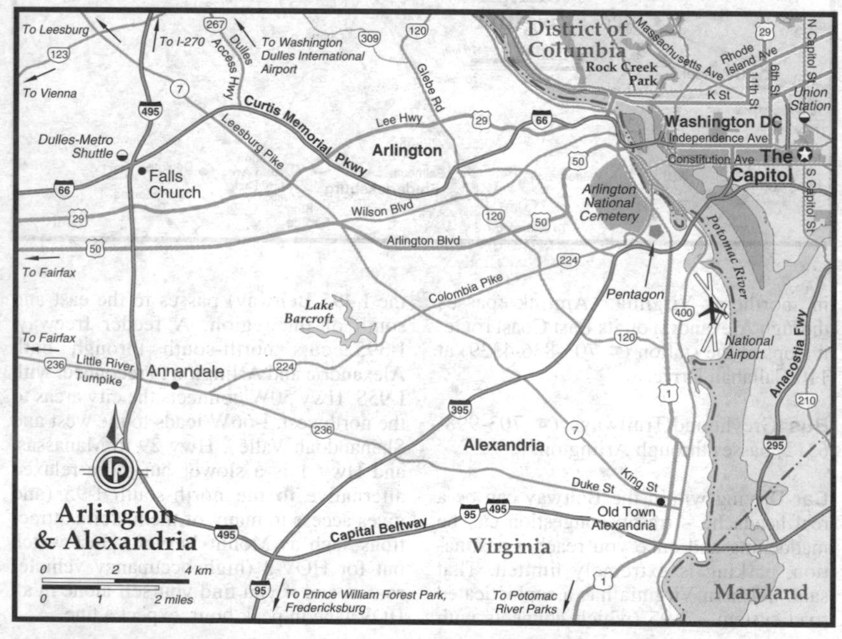

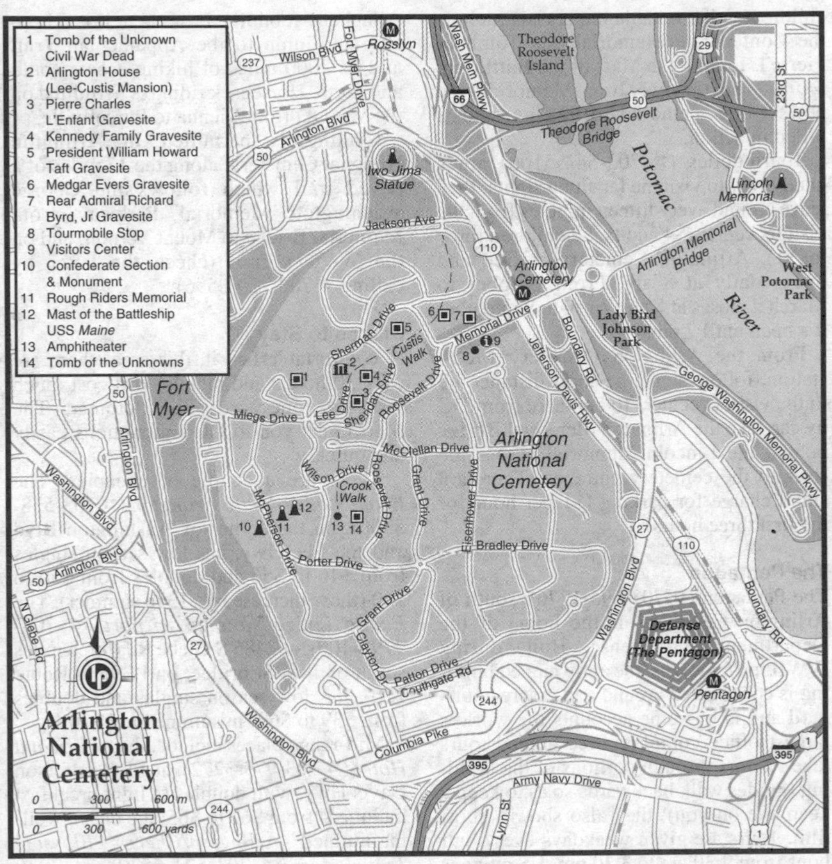

Arlington House is the former home of Confederate General Robert E Lee, whose wife was the great-granddaughter of Martha Washington and her first husband (before George). The house and part of the 1100-acre property was confiscated after Lee left to command the Army of Virginia, and bodies of Union soldiers were buried around the house to spite Lee. When Lee returned, the family sued the federal government to be reimbursed for the property; Arlington Cemetery was born and eventually the historic house was opened for public tours.

The **Tomb of the Unknowns** holds an unknown soldier from WWI, WWII, and the Korean and Vietnam Wars. Visitors come to pay their respects and to watch the changing of the guard; soldiers march ritualistically in front of the memorial 24 hours a day. During the day, the guard changes every half hour from April to September, every hour during the rest of the year. At night it's every two hours, year round.

Near the eternal flame that marks the **grave of John F Kennedy** lie gravestones for Robert Kennedy, and Jacqueline Kennedy Onassis and her two infant children. Other notable memorials include the Confederate Memorial, the Tomb of Pierre L'Enfant, the Mast of the Battleship *Maine,* and the Iwo Jima Memorial; the newest is a memorial to 934 journalists killed in action.

Tourmobiles (☎ 703-544-5100) are a handy way to visit the far-flung sights; they leave around every fifteen minutes from the visitors center ($4 adults, $2 children three to 11). Arlington Cemetery is free and opens daily at 8 am. From October to March it closes at 5 pm; April to September it's open until 7 pm.

From the Arlington Cemetery Metro station, follow signs the short distance up to the visitors center. To get there from DC by car, take the Arlington Memorial Bridge behind the Lincoln Memorial across the river to the cemetery entrance. There's a small charge for parking ($1 per hour for the first three hours).

VIRGINIA

The Pentagon

The Pentagon (☎ 703-695-1776), south of Arlington Cemetery, is the home of the Department of Defense. Built during WWII in 16 months, the aptly named building is constructed around a five-acre courtyard and is by some accounts the world's largest office complex. Free guided tours take visitors through portions of the building (guides walk backwards so as to keep a keen eye on you); they also show a short film. Tours are given weekdays every half hour from 9:30 am to 3:30 pm. US citizens should bring a photo identification and foreigners a passport. Take the Metro to the Pentagon station and at the top of the escalator you will see a window with a sign about tours.

Hiking, Bicycling & Horseback Riding

It is almost possible to walk from Washington, DC, to Maine or to the Great Smoky Mountains in Tennessee. The 45-mile **Washington & Old Dominion Trail** follows an old railway bed from Shirlington, in southern Arlington, to Purcellville, in far eastern Loudoun County in the Allegheny foothills. From here it is a hop-skip-and-jump to the Appalachian Trail and its 2000 miles of hiking access south and north. Horseback riding is permitted on the W&OD from Vienna to Purcellville.

Cycling is permitted in Arlington National Cemetery; along the 17 miles of a paved trail which follows the George Washington Memorial Parkway from Memorial Bridge to Mount Vernon; and on the W&OD Trail (check the latter by calling ☎ 703-729-0596).

Places to Stay

A comfortable bed in this area (there are over 30 hotels and motels) will cost much less than one across the Potomac. The Metro gets you to DC's attractions easily and quickly.

There are a couple of cheapies. The *Econo Lodge-Metro Arlington* (☎ 703-538-5300), on the corner of Washington Blvd and the Lee Hwy, has low season singles from $46 to $56 and doubles from $50 to $60 (these increase by $13 in summer). The *Econo Lodge-National Airport* (☎ 703-979-4100), at 2485 S Glebe Rd (three miles south of 14th St bridge, on I-395 at Route 120), has low season singles and doubles from $39 to $69 (in summer add $10).

Mid-range places include: the *Americana Hotel* (☎ 703-979-3772), at 1400 Jefferson Davis Hwy, with doubles (a light breakfast included) from $60 to $65; the clean, well-maintained *Arlington/Cherry Blossom Travelodge* (☎ 703-521-5570), at 3030 Columbia Pike, with low season singles and doubles from $57 to $69 (add $6 in high season); the huge *Best Western Arlington Inn & Tower* (☎ 703-979-4400), at 2480 S Glebe Rd, with comfortable singles and doubles from $60 to $100; and the *Days Inn Crystal City* (☎ 703-920-8600), at 2000 Jefferson Davis Hwy (1.3 miles south of 14th St bridge on Hwy 1), close to the Crystal City Metro station, with singles from $59 to $119 (doubles are $10 extra).

Slightly more expensive are the *Howard Johnson National Airport Hotel* (☎ 703-684-7200), at 2650 Jefferson

Davis Hwy near Washington Blvd, which has transportation to the airport included in the singles/doubles price of $119/129; the *Comfort Inn Ballston* (☎ 703-247-3399, 800-221-2222), at 1211 N Glebe Rd, with spacious doubles from $100; and the *Holiday Inn Arlington at Ballston* (☎ 703-243-9800), at 4610 N Fairfax Drive (Exit 71 off I-66), which has pool, sauna, exercise room, and single and double rooms from $89 on weekends, and $124 weekdays.

Expensive choices, with all the facilities you would expect for the price, are the *Ritz-Carlton Pentagon City* (☎ 703-415-5000), at 1250 S Hayes St, one mile south of the 14th St bridge, with singles/doubles from $175/195 and parking at a mere $15; and the *Crystal Gateway Marriott* (☎ 703-920-3230), at 1700 Jefferson Davis Hwy (1.3 miles south of 14th St bridge on Hwy 1 – the entry is on S Eads St at S 18th St), which has weekend specials from $119 and a weekday singles/doubles price of $172/192.

Places to Eat

There are restaurant enclaves at Crystal City, Clarendon, Shirlington, and Rosslyn; inquire at the visitors center, and they'll add many more to this list. All of the brew pubs mentioned under Entertainment serve meals.

Shirlington Village There are three good choices at the Village, S 28th St, just west of I-395 (southbound Exit 7, northbound Exit 6). *Charlie Chiang's* (☎ 703-671-4900), specializing in Hunan and Szechuan dishes, just creeps into the moderate bracket with main courses from $11 to $20; it is open for lunch and dinner daily.

The *Carlyle Grand Cafe* (☎ 703-931-0777) is a lively bistro with great rotisserie and grilled meals (there are early-bird dinner specials); it is open daily for lunch and dinner, and for Sunday brunch.

Bistro Bistro (☎ 703-379-0300) serves innovative American cuisine. Lunch is served till 5 pm and, if you are lucky with the weather, you can eat it at one of the sidewalk tables; the cafe is open daily, except Sunday.

Crystal City There is *Ruth's Chris Steak House* (☎ 703-979-7275), in Crystal Park building No 3 at 2231 Crystal Drive (two miles south of the 14th St bridge). This is an upmarket place for which you have to dress up to eat – a true carnivore's delight – and as you dine you get magnificent views of the Washington skyline; it is open for dinner daily and a meal for two will cost well over $60.

Other Crystal City favorites, both open for dinner daily, are *Ristorante Portofino* (☎ 703-929-8200), at 526 S 23rd St, for expensive home-style Italian pastas (and taped opera); and *Chez Froggy* (☎ 703-979-7676), close by at 509 S 23rd St, for less expensive Froggy dishes such as the ubiquitous legs sautéed in butter and garlic.

Rosslyn The *Red Hot & Blue* (☎ 703-276-7427), at 1600 Wilson Blvd (at N Pierce St), open daily for lunch and dinner, gets rave reviews from everyone who eats there. Sample Memphis-style wet and dry ribs, barbeque, chicken, smoked ham, and all the Southern accessories you could wish for; entrees are from $7 to $15. Another local favorite, *Tom Sarris' Orleans House* (☎ 703-524-2929), at 1213 Wilson Blvd, is open for lunch weekdays and dinner daily, and is, as its name suggests, a little slice of New Orleans; the $8 beef dinner (with a baked potato and a big salad) should be enough, but if you are feeling especially peckish, then elevate to the $10 or $14 dinners – oink!

Other Rosslyn delights are the *Star of Siam* (☎ 703-524-1208), at 1735 N Lynn St, opposite the Metro Center, which has a fabulous selection of Thai curries and seafood dishes, and the *Tivoli* (☎ 703-524-8900), near the Metro at 1700 N Moore St, an upmarket place serving delectable northern Italian cuisine. The 'Tiv' is not cheap, as a meal costs about $25 per person, and they also expect you to dress appropriately for dinner.

Clarendon Good restaurants in this enclave include the *Queen Bee* (☎ 703-527-3444), at 3181 Wilson Blvd, for inexpensive and sumptuous Vietnamese dishes such as a filling *pho*; the casual 'in-spite-of-the-title' *Hard Times Cafe* (☎ 703-528-2233), at 3028 Wilson Blvd, for Tex-Mex chilis, cornbread, and beans (no entree is over $6.50); and the *Chesapeake Seafood Crab House* (☎ 703-528-8888), at 3607 Wilson Blvd near Glebe Rd, for reasonably priced meals including tasty steamed blue crabs.

Entertainment

Brew pubs are really big in Arlington (and in DC also). Several have been recommended, including *Bardo Rodeo* (☎ 703-527-1852), at 2000 Wilson Blvd, just across the Key Bridge and a block from the Court House Metro. Deemed to be the largest such place in the US, it has its own microbrew (a pitcher of Bardo is $6 at happy hour).

Others are *Strangeways*, at 2830 Wilson Blvd, near the Clarendon Metro, with 15 brews on tap, a pool table, a jukebox, and appropriate dark and dank atmosphere; the *Galaxy Hut*, at 2711 Wilson Blvd (between Strangeways and Bardo), with passable pub grub and a well-stocked bar of 12 taps; and the *Gourmet Pizza Deli*, on Washington Blvd, halfway between Tysons Corner and Bardo, with 150 beers!

For other nighttime activities check in the Friday 'Weekend' section of the *Washington Post* and in the *Where Washington* magazine. If you are here, you are practically in DC and will no doubt cross the river to party.

Getting Around

Unlike Alexandria, Arlington does not have its own bus system, but it is well served by Metrorail's (☎ 202-637-7000) Yellow, Blue, and Orange lines, and by Metro buses.

Metrorail Blue Line connects DC with Rosslyn, Arlington Cemetery, the Pentagon, Pentagon City, and Crystal City; the Yellow Line links into Alexandria and connects Arlington destinations with National Airport; and the Orange Line heads west through Rosslyn, Court House, Clarendon, and Ballston (all the way to Vienna).

Metrorail's hours of operation are 5:30 am to midnight weekdays, 8 am to midnight on weekends; consider buying a Metro one-day pass if you use the services throughout the day. Metro bus fares require exact change (minimum fare is $1.10, transfer 25¢).

ALEXANDRIA

'Still making history' is the slogan of this fascinating city (population 117,000), and ongoing archaeological projects are an important part of its allure. The natural barrier of the Potomac allows this now suburban city to retain a distinct, historic charm. In the early pre-Revolutionary days Alexandria was bigger than Georgetown, modern DC's oldest precinct.

Orientation

The main streets dividing the city are north-south Washington St (George Washington Parkway) and east-west King St. Streets are simply divided by the 100 system – eg, Cameron to Queen is the 200 block north.

The historic area, Old Town, is a square marked by the King St Metro in the west, Slaters Lane in the north, the Potomac River to the east, and South St – most historic sights lie to the east of Washington St.

Saturday parking costs $2 all day or $3 if you are still there after 6 pm. Visitors can park free at any two-hour parking meter in the city by picking up a pass from Ramsay House (the visitors center).

Information

Tourist Offices The Alexandria Convention & Visitors Bureau (☎ 703-838-4200), in Ramsay House, at 221 King St, Alexandria, VA 22314, is the best place to start a tour of the town, if for no other reason than they will give you a free 24-hour parking permit. The yellow clapboard Ramsay House, built in Dumfries 25 miles to the south in 1724 (and moved here in 1749), once belonged to William Ramsay, Alexandria's first Lord Mayor. It is open daily

JEFF WILLIAMS
Relaxing on the waterfront in Norfork, VA

JEFF WILLIAMS
Cobblestoned Prince St in Old Town Alexandria, VA

JEFF WILLIAMS
Woodlawn Plantation, south of Alexandria, VA

JEFF WILLIAMS
The view at Otter Lodge and Lake, VA

JEFF WILLIAMS
e *Norwegian Lady* on the boardwalk in Virginia Beach

ROBERT DE GAST
Chincoteague Harbor, VA

JEFF WILLIAMS

Farmers market in Roanoke, VA

JEFF WILLIAMS

Local color on the Blue Ridge Parkway, VA

JEFF WILLIAMS

Thomas Jefferson designed and oversaw the construction of Monticello (near Charlottesville) for 40 years.

JEFF WILLIAMS

After designing the Academical Village of the University of Virginia, Jefferson oversaw its construction by telescope from Monticello.

from 9 am to 5 pm. Get a copy of the free *Walking Tour Guide: Old Town*.

You can purchase a block ticket from the visitors center for $12 ($5 for students and children six to 17) which gives discounted entry to five of Alexandria's attractions: the Stabler-Leadbeater Apothecary Museum & Shop, Carlyle House, Lee's Boyhood Home, the Lee-Fendall House, and Gadsby's Tavern. A ticket to three of these attractions is $7 for adults, $3 for students and children six to 17.

Money Good banks for foreign exchange are Burke & Herbert, on the corner of King and Fairfax (it has ATMs); and Crestar, in the 500 block of King St (No 515).

Post The main post office (☎ 703-549-4201) is at 1100 Wythe St; stamps are also sold at the visitors center.

Bookstores Gilpin House (☎ 703-549-1880), at 208 King St, and Super Crown Books (☎ 703-548-3432), at 501 King St near the Crestar Bank, are good bookstores for browsing. The aptly named kid's bookstore A Likely Story (☎ 703-836-2498) is at 1555 King St.

Laundry There is a self-serve laundromat, West End Coin-Op (☎ 703-370-1727), at 4623 Duke St in the Fox Chase shopping center.

Medical Services Alexandria Hospital (☎ 703-379-3000), at 4320 Seminary Rd, has a 24-hour facility.

Torpedo Factory

This collection of buildings, at 105 N Union St, was built during WWI for the manufacture of torpedo parts (and reused again during WWII as a munitions factory). Today, it is the centerpiece of a revamped waterfront with marina, shops, parks and walkways, residences, offices, and restaurants. The **Torpedo Factory Art Center** (☎ 703-838-4565), is dedicated to nearly 200 artists and craftspersons who sell their creations directly from their studios. It is open daily from 10 am to 5 pm; there is no admission fee.

Also in this complex is **Alexandria Archaeology** (☎ 703-838-4399), an interesting place where archaeologists, engaged in a number of local urban digs, clean and catalog the artifacts they have unearthed. The real appeal is seeing the current work in progress; there are also informative videos. This museum is open Tuesday to Friday from 10 am to 3 pm, Saturday 10 am to 5 pm, Sunday 1 to 5 pm; admission is free.

Fort Ward Museum & Historic Site

This fort, at 4301 W Braddock Rd, was one of the largest of the 162 Civil War fortifications known as the Defenses of Washington.

The northwest bastion of the fort has been completely restored and the remaining earthwork walls are well preserved to reflect the original state of the defenses. The museum on site has interpretative displays and features exhibits on Civil War topics. Tours, lectures, and living history programs are offered, and there are services for the disabled. The museum (☎ 703-838-4848) is open Tuesday to Saturday from 9 am to 5 pm, Sunday noon to 5 pm, and the historic site is open 9 am to sunset; admission is free.

Gadsby's Tavern Museum

This museum (☎ 703-838-4242), at 134 N Royal St, consists of two tavern buildings built in 1770 and 1792, and named after John Gadsby who operated them from 1796 to 1808. As the center of political, business, and social life in early Alexandria they were visited by George Washington and Thomas Jefferson. Lafayette stayed here during a visit in 1824 and the tavern ballroom was the scene of Washington's last two birthday celebrations.

The rooms of the tavern and hotel have been restored to their 18th century appearance. There are guided tours and services for the disabled. The museum is open April through September, Tuesday to Saturday from 10 am to 5 pm, Sunday from 1 to

5 pm; otherwise Tuesday to Saturday from 11 am to 4 pm, Sunday from 1 to 4 pm. Admission is $3 for adults, $1 for students (11 to 17), and kids are free if accompanied by an adult.

The Lyceum

The Lyceum (☎ 703-838-4994), at 201 S Washington St, is Alexandria's history museum, housed in a Greek Revival building that was restored in the 1970s. The changing exhibits focus on Alexandria since its founding. There are prints, photographs, ceramics, silver, and Civil War memorabilia on display.

The Lyceum is open Monday to Saturday from 10 am to 5 pm, Sunday 1 to 5 pm; admission is free.

Stabler-Leadbeater Apothecary Museum

This museum (☎ 703-836-3713), at 105-7 S Fairfax St, is an 18th century apothecary shop (founded in 1792 by Quaker pharmacist Edward Stabler). It features a fine collection of 900 hand-blown apothecary bottles in their original site. (Don't know why, but I have never been inspired by such jars.) Of greater interest was learning that here on October 17, 1859, Lieutenant

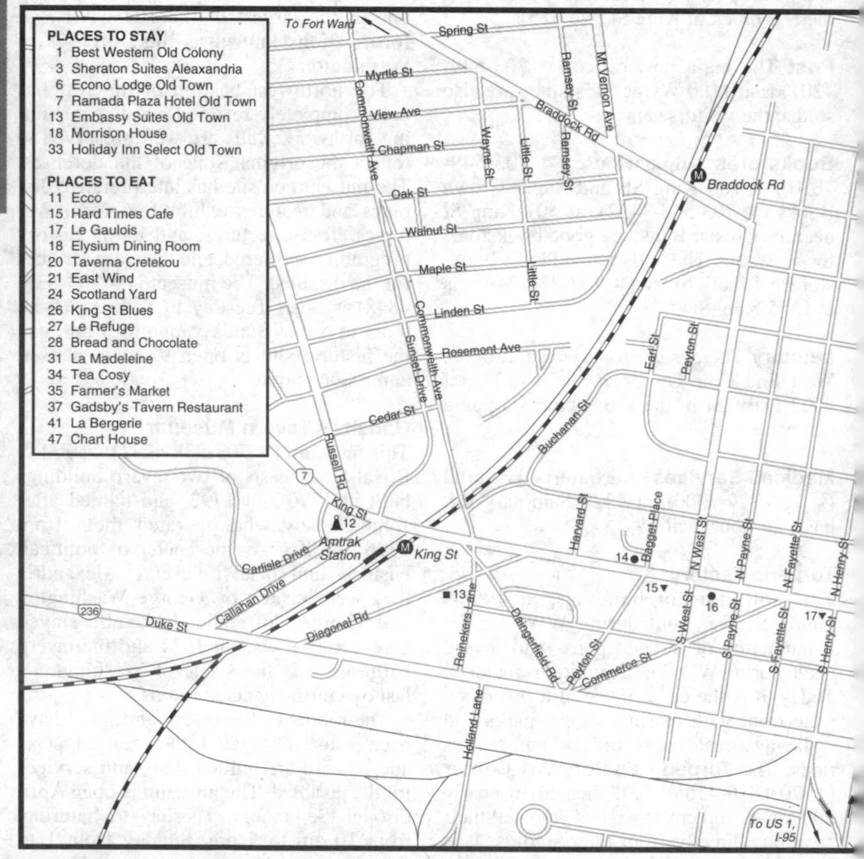

Colonel Robert E Lee received his orders to move to Harpers Ferry to put down John Brown's insurrection.

The bottles in the museum are displayed Monday to Saturday from 10 am to 4 pm, Sunday 1 to 5 pm; admission is $2 for adults, $1 for students, and children under 11 are admitted free.

Prince St

The 100 block of Prince St, called **Captain's Row**, is one of two remaining cobblestone streets in Alexandria. The cobblestones were the ballast of English ships, and the street was laid by Hessian prisoners of war. There are lovely private homes, including one once owned by a Captain John Harper. It is said that his wife died in self-defense after the birth of her 15th child!

Gentry Row is the 200 block of Prince St, named after the number of imposing private dwellings. The pumpkin-colored **Athenaeum** (☎ 703-548-0035), the Greek Revival building at 201 Prince St, is now a museum of fine art. It started life as a bank in 1850 and was used as a hospital during the Civil War. It is open Tuesday to Saturday from 10 am to 4 pm, Sunday from 1 to 4 pm; admission is free.

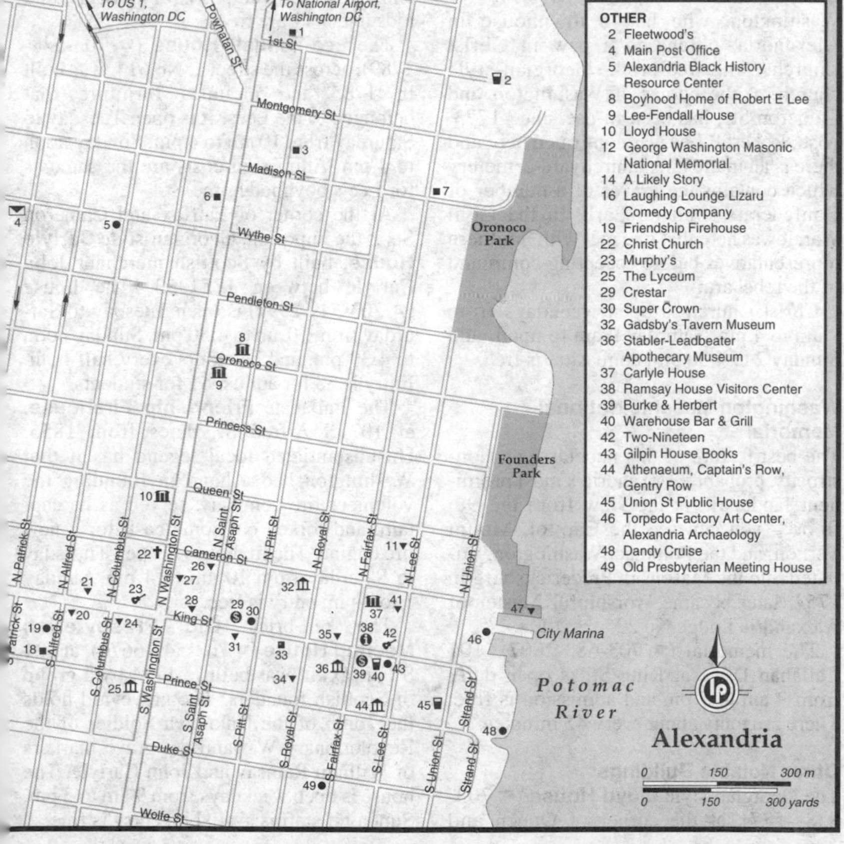

Black History Resource Center

This center (☎ 703-838-4356), at 638 N Alfred St in the Parker-Gray Historical District (entrance on Wythe St), presents lectures, tours, and other activities relating to the accomplishments and history of African American Alexandrians. On display are paintings, photographs, books, and other memorabilia that document black experience in Alexandria and Virginia from 1749 to the present. The center is open Tuesday to Saturday from 10 am to 4 pm. They have an annex, the Watson Reading Room, with a wealth of books and documents relating to African American topics.

Christ Church

Washington, who had a townhouse in Alexandria, purchased a pew in Christ Church. The red-brick Georgian-style church, at the corner of Washington and Cameron Sts, has been in use since 1773. Also, Robert E Lee was confirmed here and there is an interesting churchyard cemetery which contains the graves of a number of Confederate soldiers. Early in the Civil War, it was here that Lee met with Southern representatives before accepting command of the rebel army.

Christ Church is open weekdays from 9 am to 4 pm, Saturday 9 am to noon, and Sunday 2 to 4:30 pm; admission is free.

Washington Masonic National Memorial

The best feature of this neoclassical monstrosity, probably Alexandria's most prominent landmark, is the view from the 9th floor – you can see the Capitol, Mount Vernon, and the Potomac. Washington, initiated into the Masons in Fredericksburg in 1752, later became Worshipful Master of Alexandria Lodge No 22.

The memorial (☎ 703-683-2007), 101 Callahan Drive at King St, is open daily from 9 am to 5 pm and admission is free. There are tours about every 45 minutes.

Other Notable Buildings

The Georgian-style **Lloyd House** (☎ 703-838-4577), at the corner of Queen and Washington Sts, dates from 1794. As part of the Alexandria library service, it has a collection of rare documents and books which cover the city's history and genealogy. It is open Monday to Saturday from 9 am to 5 pm; entry is free.

The Georgian-style townhouse at 607 Oronoco St was the **boyhood home of Robert E Lee**. It was built in 1795. Lee's father Henry, known as 'Lighthorse Harry,' a Revolutionary War commander and governor of Virginia from 1792 to 1795, moved his family to Alexandria in 1810. The house (☎ 703-548-8454) is open February to December, Monday to Saturday from 10 am to 4 pm, Sunday 1 to 4 pm; entry is $3 for adults, $1 for students, and kids under 11 are free.

The **Lee-Fendall House** (☎ 703-548-1789), across the street at No 614, was built in 1785 and includes furniture that belonged to the Lees. It is open Tuesday to Saturday from 10 am to 4 pm, Sunday noon to 4 pm. Admission costs are the same as for Lee's boyhood home.

At the corner of Fairfax and Cameron Sts is the imposing, Georgian-style **Carlyle House**, built by Scottish merchant John Carlyle between 1751–53. The house (☎ 703-549-2997) is open Tuesday to Saturday from 10 am to 4:30 pm, Sunday noon to 4:30 pm, and has tours every half hour. Entry is $3 for adults, $1 for students.

The Italianate **Friendship Firehouse**, at 107 S Alfred St, dates from 1855. Unsubstantiated local legend has it that Washington had a hand in founding the volunteer fire company, served as its captain, and forked out some cash for a new fire engine. The firehouse is open Thursday to Saturday from 10 am to 4 pm, Sunday 1 to 4 pm; entry is free.

The red-brick **Old Presbyterian Meeting House** (☎ 703-549-6670), at 321 S Fairfax St, was built in 1774 by a group of Scottish founders. The graveyard holds the Tomb of the Unknown Soldier of the Revolutionary War and the grave markers of William Ramsay and John Carlyle. The house is open weekdays from 9 am to 3 pm, Sunday if staff is available; entry is free.

Robert E Lee

Robert Edward Lee is one of the most famous Virginians and, in this guidebook, it is hard to escape his name. Lee was born in Stratford, Virginia, in 1807, the son of Henry Lee – 'Lighthorse Harry,' himself a representative of an already very distinguished Virginia family.

Lee was educated at the US Military Academy at West Point, where he graduated second in his class (one must wonder, who was first?) as a second lieutenant in the engineers. In the battles of the Mexican War he distinguished himself and was wounded in the storming of Chapultepec in 1847.

He was assigned to the US Military Academy as superintendent and later promoted to the rank of colonel in the cavalry. In 1861, when he was in command of the Department of Texas and war between the states seemed imminent, Lincoln summoned him to Washington and offered him command of the Union forces. Lee declined, and on April 21, three days after his beloved Virginia seceded from the Union, he resigned from the US Army and became commander in chief of the Confederate Forces of Virginia.

After a year as military advisor to Jefferson Davis he assumed command of the Army of Northern Virginia. Many battles followed, in which Lee proved himself a master strategist and a tactical genius with his use of field fortifications and defensive entrenchments to facilitate outflanking maneuvers (see the numerous sidebars in this book describing Civil War battles). In February 1865 he was elevated to commander of all the forces of the South, but two months later he surrendered to the numerically far superior Union forces of Ulysses S Grant at Appomattox, virtually ending the Civil War. He applied for a post-war amnesty, but it was granted posthumously, more than a century later, by an Act of Congress in 1975. In 1865 he became president of Washington College (now Washington and Lee University) in Lexington, and he remained there until his death in 1870.

Lee was revered by both Southerners and Northerners, and the places he was associated with still attract visitors from both camps in large numbers. In Virginia, these include Stratford Hall (his birthplace), his boyhood home in Alexandria, his antebellum home Arlington House (now the Robert E Lee Memorial), Appomattox, Washington and Lee University, the Lee Chapel and Museum (where Lee is buried) in Lexington, and a host of battlefields where he brilliantly defied the odds stacked up against him. Perhaps the best image of him is the portrait by American artist William Edgar Marshall. Lee seems to epitomize historic Virginia and the modern visitor will sense his spirit throughout the state. ■

Organized Tours & Cruises

There are really informative **walking tours** of Old Town Alexandria, conducted daily from late March to November. They commence at Ramsay House (☎ 703-838-4200), at 221 King St; the cost is $3 per person. There are also ghost tours on weekend nights at 9 pm; these are $4 for adults and $3 for students.

There are several cruise options on the Potomac. The Potomac Riverboat Co (☎ 703-548-9000) docks its boats at the city marina, behind the Torpedo Factory at Cameron and Union Sts. The *Admiral Tilp* and *Matthew Hayes* operate from April to October and charge $13 for adults, $10 for seniors, and $6 for children from two to 12.

The *Dandy* (☎ 703-683-6090) is a restaurant/cruise ship renowned for its food and service. On weekdays, lunch is $26 and the Sunday champagne brunch is $30.

Special Events

Alexandria always seems to have something to celebrate or commemorate. The town's associations with Washington and Robert E Lee are given thorough annual workouts. Lee's birthday is celebrated in the third week of January, and Washington's birthday in February with a much vaunted parade, banquet, and ball.

VIRGINIA

On the second weekend in June the Red Cross Waterfront Festival is celebrated with ship tours, art shows, and entertainment. The Scottish nexus is recalled on the fourth weekend of July with the annual Virginia Scottish Games and, in early December, with the Scottish Christmas Walk – featuring wailing bagpipes and kilted pipers. Another December event is a candlelight tour of Alexandria, where music and food accompany your sojourn – call ☎ 703-463-3777.

Places to Stay – bottom end

The nearest budget accommodations are at the youth hostel (☎ 202-737-2333) in Washington, DC (see the DC chapter). The *Econo Lodge Old Town* (☎ 703-836-5100), at 700 N Washington St, is the best close-to-town bet for the impecunious; doubles are from $50 to $65. The *Econo Lodge-Mount Vernon* (☎ 703-780-0300), on Hwy 1, 7.5 miles south of the I-95/I-495 Beltway, is a better cheapie; singles/doubles are from $62/68. There are dives along this strip, so beware.

The *Days Inn Alexandria* (☎ 703-354-4950), at 110 S Bragg St (Exit 3B off I-395 at Route 236W), is one of the more reasonable places; singles/doubles are from $46/52 in winter, otherwise add $4.

Places to Stay – middle

The *Holiday Inn Eisenhower Metro* (☎ 703-960-4300), at 2460 Eisenhower Ave, 0.3 miles north of I-95/I-495, is handy to the Metro station. It has a heated indoor pool, sundeck, and exercise room; singles are from $72 to $103 and doubles from $87 to $118.

The *Best Western Old Colony* (☎ 703-739-2222), at 615 First St on the George Washington Memorial Parkway, includes a free breakfast in its weekday/weekend double rate of $64/69.

The *Ramada Plaza Hotel Old Town* (☎ 703-683-6000), at 901 N Fairfax St just to the east of Hwy 1 Alt, is an excellent, well-located choice with a rooftop pool and a restaurant – singles and doubles are $75 in low season (otherwise add $10).

Princely B&B (☎ 703-683-2159) has 30 houses in and around Old Town; expect to pay about $80 for a double. The central office is at 819 Prince St.

Places to Stay – top end

The *Embassy Suites-Old Town* (☎ 703-684-5900), at 1900 Diagonal Rd, adjacent to King St Metro and the Amtrak terminal, is a trusted favorite that offers all the facilities – indoor pool, sauna, sundeck, exercise room, and restaurant; on weekdays rooms are from $149 to $250 and on weekends from $109 to $154. Similarly, the *Sheraton Suites Alexandria* (☎ 703-836-4700), at 801 N Saint Asaph St, a block east of Washington St, has facilities similar to the Embassy. On weekends, rooms are from $99 to $129 and on weekdays from $149 to $164.

The *Holiday Inn Select Old Town* (☎ 703-549-6080), at 480 King St, half a block from the City Hall, has all the facilities including a restaurant. Some rooms have a balcony overlooking a central courtyard and would be the best value; all rooms fall within the range of $145 to $160 for a double.

The four-star, boutique-style *Morrison House* (☎ 703-838-8000, 800-367-0800), at 116 S Alfred St, is the town's most expensive choice but worth the luxury if you can afford it. It includes the aid of a butler, two excellent restaurants (see Places to Eat), and a library where afternoon tea is served. The rooms, furnished with Federal-style reproductions, have marble baths; singles are from $185 to $220, doubles from $205 to $240.

Places to Eat

Breakfast & Lunch Wandering around Alexandria's many attractions is bound to build up an appetite and, fortunately, there are many eateries in Old Town, most arrayed along King St. If you are short on cash then stock up for the week at the Saturday *Farmer's Market* (☎ 703-838-4770), at No 301; all manner of cheap fresh produce, baked goods, and meats are sold here.

Bread and Chocolate (☎ 703-548-0992), at No 611, has a wonderful selection of sandwiches, and desserts to keep any sweet tooth satisfied. A hearty breakfast will cost from $3 to $6, and $7 should see you happy at lunchtime. The *Hard Times Cafe* (☎ 703-683-5340), at No 1404, is inexpensive and casual and open for lunch and dinner. As one discerning local food critic opined, 'two can eat silly here for $20.' They have a selection of Texas beers, onion rings for $3, five-way chilis (including Cincinnati with a hint of cinnamon), Mexican dishes ('all-the-way wet' with mucho sauce), and corn bread.

Several thousand miles away in terms of flavor is the Vietnamese *East Wind* (☎ 703-836-1515), at No 809, a good choice for those after a vegetarian lunch or hot soup – surely a steaming *pho* is the best lunch selection in any country or temperature. If you don't get here for lunch, sneak back at night; it is open for lunch weekdays, for dinner daily.

Other lunch possibilities are the *Tea Cosy* (☎ 703-836-2236), at 119 S Royal St, a comfortable English tearoom that serves breakfast and lunch; *La Madeleine* (☎ 703-739-2854), at 500 King St (at the corner of Pitt St), a French bakery/cafe which concocts fresh breads and pastries from its wood-burning oven; and *King Street Blues* (☎ 703-836-8800), at 112 N Saint Asaph St, a Southern 'roadhouse' diner, where you can expect beef stew and garlic potatoes, hot salad, and yummy chicken – the lunch and dinner special is only $5 and they have a 'Little Dudes' kids menu for $2.

Dinner *Taverna Cretekou* (☎ 703-683-5340), at 818 King St, is a delightful eatery, a real slice of Athens – it has an outside grapevine arbor, waiters spontaneously dance for you à la Zorba after supper, and the Sunday brunch is legendary. Expect to pay from $20 to $25 for a full meal.

Le Gaulois (☎ 703-739-9494), at 1106 King St, is the perfect dinner choice. It has great ambiance, the cost is reasonable, and, understandably, it wins local acceptance. Francophiles also gravitate towards *Le Refuge* (☎ 703-548-4661), at 127 N Washington St. It's open daily (except Sunday) for lunch and dinner; their early-bird dinner, which includes salad, a main course, and dessert, is a mere $20. This special is offered nightly from 5:30 to 7 pm (all night Monday). With the preponderance of French eateries, Lafayette's spirit apparently still rules.

Get past its terrible motto – 'Endless Pastabilities' – and you will probably enjoy the Italian fare at *Ecco* (☎ 703-684-0321), 220 N Lee St. It is open seven days.

Gadsby's Tavern Restaurant (☎ 703-548-1288), at 138 N Royal St, tries hard to emulate an 18th century hostelry. Once the finest public house in America, its new life of kitschy charm destroys any such ambiance. (S'pose if I had wanted colonial entertainment I should have been born 300 years ago!) The 'tav' is open for lunch from 11:30 am to 3 pm, dinner from 5:30 to 10 pm, Sunday brunch 11 am to 3 pm; kitsch costs – around $15 for lunch, $16 for brunch, and $30 for dinner (men must wear jackets and ties).

Scotland Yard (☎ 703-683-1742), at 728 King St, struggles to create the culinary masterpieces of Scotland (a struggle made especially difficult by the fact that, notwithstanding the haggis, which is certainly different, there are few such delights!). The Yard is not open at lunchtime, but at dinner the lace curtains, highland menu, and cozy, intimate atmosphere (plus tasty 'Bramble Mist' dessert) ring an echo from the glens.

Alexandria's best dining choice by far is the marvelous *La Bergerie* (☎ 703-683-1007), at 218 N Lee St, in the Crilley shops. They serve Basque-style (French and Spanish-influenced) cuisine and a full meal will cost from $20 to $25 for lunch, $35 for dinner; it is open Monday to Saturday for lunch from 11:30 am to 2:30 pm, and for dinner from 6 to 10 pm. There is convenient parking across the street.

More expensive is *The Chart House* (☎ 703-684-5080), at 1 Cameron St on the waterfront, which is open for dinner only. The views justify the considerable cost; main courses are from $16 to $25, and

Sunday champagne brunch (11 am to 2:30 pm), a little more than eggs & bacon, is around $18.

The *Elysium Dining Room* (☎ 703-838-8000), in Morrison House (see Places to Stay), is bloody expensive but, by all reports, well worth the hefty check; it is open daily for breakfast and dinner, and on Sunday for brunch.

Entertainment

The *West End Dinner Theatre* (☎ 703-370-2500), at 4615 Duke St, has the largest dinner theater stage in the area and is only minutes from DC. It features Broadway musicals and comedies. From Tuesday to Sunday dinner is served at 6 pm and the curtain rises at 8 pm; there are matinees on Wednesday and Sunday with lunch at noon and curtain up at 2 pm. It costs about $25 per person.

Fleetwood's (☎ 703-548-6425), at 44 Canal Center Plaza, a club part-owned by Mick Fleetwood, serves good suppers and is lots of fun. Most nights there is blues and Sunday features a gospel brunch.

For a quiet beer in true drinking environments, try the *Union Street Public House* (☎ 703-548-1785), at 121 S Union St; and *The Warehouse Bar & Grill* (☎ 703-683-6868), at 214 King St.

Birchmere (☎ 703-549-5919), at 3901 Mount Vernon Ave, just south of Glebe Rd, is the place for bluegrass, folk, and country. Other live music venues can be found along King St: *Murphy's* (☎ 703-548-1717), at No 713, lives up to its Irish name; and *Two-Nineteen* (☎ 703-549-1141), a Creole/New Orleans–flavored place at No 219, has jazz nightly.

Getting Around

The King St Metro station – which doubles as the Amtrak station (connected by DC's Metrorail Yellow and Blue lines) – is Alexandria's main transport hub and from here you can take Metrorail AT-2 or DASH bus AT-5 directly to the visitors center. Other Metrorail stations, all connected to the Yellow and Blue lines, are Braddock Rd and Eisenhower Ave.

Alexandria's bus transit system, DASH (☎ 703-370-3274), operates daily. The cost of travel is 75¢ for a four-hour pass; the brochure *DASHing Around Alexandria* explains how to easily get from sight to sight.

OUTER FAIRFAX COUNTY

Fairfax County (population 865,000) has been absorbed into the DC metropolitan area, and life here is dogged by all the attendant inconveniences of living on the edge of a big city. The biggest draw for visitors is Mount Vernon, George Washington's estate.

Old Town Fairfax

The Fairfax Museum & Visitors Center (☎ 703-385-8414), at 10209 Main St (Route 236), is open daily from 9 am to 5 pm. The museum, in an 1873 brick schoolhouse, has exhibits on local, colonial, and Civil War history; entry is free and local volunteers often give tours.

The **Center for the Arts** (☎ 703-993-8788), at George Mason University, 4400 University Drive, is a concert hall where symphonies, dance companies, chamber music groups, and jazz artists perform. There is an adjoining professional theater. The **Fairfax Symphony Orchestra** (☎ 703-642-7200) has a seven-concert Classic Series; check at the box office. The center is open September to May for performances.

The county, so close to DC, has many accommodations. In the town of Fairfax, on Route 123 opposite the courthouse, is the *Bailiwick Inn* (☎ 703-691-2266), a fine restored 19th century residence. The comforts are not cheap: singles and doubles are from $130 to $295. The dining room is open in the evening from Wednesday to Saturday; the prix fixe menu is $45 on weekdays, $55 on weekends. Cheaper choices in the Fairfax region are the *Hampton Inn-Fairfax* (☎ 703-385-2600) at the intersection of Hwys 50 and 29; the *Holiday Inn Fairfax City* (☎ 703-591-5500) on Route 123; and the *Comfort Inn University Center* (☎ 703-591-5900) on Hwy 50.

VIRGINIA

Good dining options are the Tuesday morning *Farmer's Market* (May to November), near Truro Church parking lot, for fresh produce; the *Black-eyed Pea* (☎ 703-352-0588), 3971 Chain Bridge Rd; and *Havabite Eatery* (☎ 703-591-2243), 10416 Main St, for home-style cooking.

The City of Fairfax bus (☎ 703-385-7859), 50¢ per sector, runs daily until 9 pm.

Vienna & Reston

Vienna is a sizable suburban city between Dulles Airport and DC. Reston, one of the nation's prototypes for a planned community (first occupied in 1964), has **Terraset**, the country's first earth-sheltered school.

The unique **Wolf Trap Farm Park for the Performing Arts** (☎ 703-255-1860), at 1624 Trap Rd, Vienna, is the US's only national park for the performing arts. During the summer all types of performances are given in two 18th century barns, a partial outdoor amphitheater, and the outdoor Theater in the Woods. On Labor Day weekend, an International Children's Festival features local and overseas performers. Why Wolf Trap? Records from 1632 show that wolves caused much damage here, and tobacco was offered as a reward to those who trapped them.

Ticket order forms for events at Wolf Trap Farm regularly appear in the *Washington Post*. The cost is from $24 for an in-house show; a picnic space on the lawn is from $16. To get there, turn off I-495 onto Route 7. Then follow Towlston Rd for one mile; the park is on the left and is well marked.

The **Reston Animal Park** (☎ 703-759-3637), at 1228 Hunter Mill Rd, is a 56-acre children's zoo with a variety of domestic and exotic animals. There are lots of rides to be had on ponies, horses, and elephants, and plenty of fluffy animals to pet, feed, and watch. It is open daily from mid-June to Labor Day from 10 am, closing at 5 pm on weekdays and 6 pm on weekends; the rest of the year it closes at 3 pm on weekdays and 5 pm on weekends. Admission is $8for adults, $7 for seniors and children (two to 12).

Also in Reston is the **US Geological Survey** (☎ 703-648-4748), 12201 Sunrise Valley Drive, where data on minerals and land and water resources is collected and distributed; there are tours on Monday, Tuesday, and Thursday, year round.

McLean

In McLean, the **Claude Moore Colonial Farm at Turkey Run** (☎ 703-442-7557), 6310 Georgetown Pike, is a living history farm demonstrating a working low-income Virginia tenant homestead of 1770. Interpreters explain the 18th century animals, crops, and farming methods. There are also craft sessions, fairs, and harvest celebrations. It is open April to mid-December, Wednesday to Sunday from 10 am to 4:30 pm; admission is $2 for adults, $1 for seniors and children three to 12. To get there take Route 123 to the intersection of Route 193.

Chantilly

In Chantilly, near Dulles International Airport and well marked with signs is the **Sully Historic Site**. This house (built in 1794) was once the home of Richard Bland Lee, uncle of Robert E and Northern Virginia's first congressman. It was saved from bulldozers expanding Dulles for 'jumbo duty' in the late 20th century.

The site (☎ 703-437-1794) is open daily (except Tuesday) from 11 am to 5 pm; in winter from 11 am to 4 pm. On weekdays the last tour is at 3 pm, on weekends at 3:30 pm; admission is $4 for adults, $2 for seniors and children. The easiest way to get here from DC is to take Hwy 66W and turn onto Route 28; Sully is 2.5 miles further on.

Great Falls

The **Colvin Run Mill Historic Site** (☎ 703-759-2771), at 10017 Colvin Run Rd in Great Falls, includes a restored 19th century grist mill (still producing corn meal and whole wheat flour) and is open March to December, Wednesday to Monday (the rest of the year on weekends only) from 11 am to 5 pm; entry is $4 for adults, $2 for seniors and kids.

Off the I-495 Beltway at Exit 13 and northwest along Route 193 is the scenic 800-acre **Great Falls Park**. Here, the Potomac River cascades some 77 feet in a series of falls and rapids. A canal system was constructed in 1785 by George Washington's Patowmack Company to circumvent the falls – a 0.75-mile stretch of this remains and you can explore it on foot. Across the river, in Maryland, is the Chesapeake & Ohio Canal Historical Park.

The park grounds are open daily from 7 am until dusk and admission is $4 for a private vehicle and $2 for pedestrians. The visitors center (☎ 703-285-2966), open daily from 10 am to 5 pm, has audiovisual exhibits and conducts historical programs. Be careful – the slippery rocks on the cliffs around the river can be dangerous.

Mount Vernon

A visit to fascinating Mount Vernon, George Washington's home for many years, is a must for those coming to Virginia, and it is second in popularity only to the White House as a visited historic house. The country estate of this quintessential country gentleman has been meticulously restored and affords a glimpse of life as it was when Washington 'took to the farm.' All is not ostentation, however, and there are many glimpses of the farm's working nature and regular living history presentations.

On my first visit to Virginia in 1976 I visited Mount Vernon. I purchased an illustrated handbook to the estate and assiduously thumbed through it as I looked around. Twenty years hence I had the same book in my hand and, to my surprise, little had changed. The place has maintained its essence as a late 18th century plantation – only the entry price has increased.

Much of Mount Vernon's allure has to do with the fact that both George and his wife Martha (née Custis) are buried here in an enclosure on the south side of the house. The entrance to the family vault has the brief legend 'Within this Enclosure Rest the remains of General George Washington.' There are two sarcophagi with the simple inscriptions 'Washington' and 'Martha, Consort of Washington.' George Washington died here in a four-poster bed in the bedchamber on December 14, 1799.

Mount Vernon is pleasantly situated on the banks of the Potomac and has immaculate gardens, a preserved 19-room mansion, and several outbuildings. Work on the main building commenced in 1754, on land that had belonged to the family for 80 years. George and Martha lived here for 15 years from 1759 to 1775 when George assumed command of the Continental Army. After his eight years as president he finally retired here in 1797. The Mount Vernon Ladies' Association purchased it in 1858 from the Washington family, commenced restoration and operated it as a national shrine.

The white, colonnaded facade of the main building faces the Potomac, and the kitchen and slaves' and workers' quarters are detached. In the main reception room you can see the key to the Bastille, presented to Washington by Thomas Paine on behalf of Lafayette (and which has only

George Washington

left the building once, when it was taken to Paris for the bicentennial of the storming of the Bastille).

The library, with its ornate fireplace, terrestrial globe, and revolving desk chair and secretary desk, exudes an air befitting the nation's first president.

The estate (☎ 703-780-2000) is open daily from 9 am to 5 pm in March, September, and October, 8 am to 5 pm from April to August, otherwise 9 am to 4 pm. There is an adjoining museum which highlights the uncoverings of an archaeological dig of the blacksmith's shop and slave quarters. Admission is $8 for adults, $4 for children. In summer, go early as there are usually long lines of people waiting to get in.

Mount Vernon is only 16 miles south of DC on Route 235 (the George Washington Memorial Parkway) – you can also take Hwy 1 to Route 235 to reach the south entrance. You can take public transport – the Yellow or Blue Metrorail to Huntington, then bus No 11P to the estate.

A great place to eat is the Colonial-style *Mount Vernon Inn* (☎ 703-780-0011), located on the estate. It serves colonial fare for lunch and dinner daily and wine by the glass; a lunch is around $6.50 and dinner is $18 (there is a fixed price dinner for $14). For the inappropriately dressed, there is a snack bar near the entrance to the estate.

Gunston Hall – George Mason's Home

George Mason, a contemporary of Washington, penned the lines 'all men are by nature equally free and independent and have certain inherent rights' – words adapted by Thomas Jefferson for incorporation into the Declaration of Independence. Later, Mason, one of the main framers of the Constitution, refused to give the document his support because it did not include a Bill of Rights, it failed to prohibit slavery, and did not provide a system of checks and balances for curbing the power of federal government. He penned the Virginia Declaration of Rights in May 1776, which became the basis for what was later adopted as the Bill of Rights. Mason, unlike Jefferson and Washington, avoided political office, preferring life at Gunston Hall with his family.

Gunston Hall, which dates from 1755, is an architectural masterpiece with elegant carved wooden interiors. It is surrounded by meticulously kept formal gardens with boxwood hedges (where the last scene of the film *Broadcast News* was filmed).

The brick home (☎ 703-550-9220) is only six miles in a straight line from Mount Vernon on a bend in the Potomac River (about 15 minutes' drive via Hwy 1 and Route 242). It is open daily from 9:30 am to 5 pm, and admission is $5 for adults, $4 for senior citizens, and $1.50 for students six to 18.

Woodlawn Plantation

Woodlawn Plantation (☎ 703-780-4000) features two houses of very different styles, both splendid examples of their respective eras. Woodlawn, a typical plantation home once belonging to Lawrence and Eleanor ('Nelly') Custis Lewis (nephew and granddaughter of George and Martha Washington) was built between 1800 and 1805. The building was supervised by William Thornton, one of the architects of the Capitol in Washington, DC. Today it is furnished with period antiques, and outside there is a formal garden with a stunning collection of roses.

It is open daily March to December from 9:30 am to 4:30 pm, January and February on weekends only from 9:30 am to 4:30 pm. Admission is $6 for adults, $4 for seniors and children (five to 12); tours are conducted on the half hour. To get there take Hwy 1 from Washington, DC; the entrance is opposite the turn off to Route 235.

Frank Lloyd Wright's **Pope-Leighey House**, a 1940s middle-class Usonian dwelling of cypress, brick, and glass, is also on the grounds of Woodlawn (where it was moved from Falls Church after being saved from destruction in 1964). Furnished with Wright pieces, the house is utilitarian in structure but quite beautiful. It is open daily March to December from 9:30 am to 4:30 pm (weekends only in January and February). Admission is $6 for adults, $4 for everyone else. A combined pass to Woodlawn and this house is $10 for adults, $7 for seniors and students.

Potomac River Parks

About one mile west of Mount Vernon on Route 235 is **Washington's Gristmill State Historic Park**. The restored mill (☎ 703-780-3383), used by Washington when he was a farmer, is open Memorial Day to Labor Day, Thursday to Monday from 9 am to 5 pm; admission is $1.25 for adults, $1 for children six to 12. About 4.5 miles south of the mill, on Hwy 1, is the **Pohick Church**, built in the 1770s from plans drawn up by Washington and with an interior designed by George Mason. It is open daily from 9 am to 4 pm.

There are a couple of riverfront parks near Gunston Hall. **Mason Neck State Park** (☎ 703-550-0960) is seven miles northeast of Woodbridge on Route 242. It has a range of outdoor activities and programs and many bird watchers come for the extremely popular weekend bald eagle counts.

The **Pohick Bay Regional Park** is also northeast of Woodbridge on Route 242 (the Lorton exits off I-95 – No 163 southbound, No 161 northbound). The park has a large pool ($3.25 for adults, $2.75 for seniors and children), boat access to the Potomac, nature trails, and a golf course. Pohick Park (☎ 703-339-6104) is open daily from 8 am until sunset; entry per car is $4. Over 100 of the 150 sites in the campground have electricity hook-ups. These cost from $12 to $14 for four persons and are available year round.

PRINCE WILLIAM COUNTY

Perhaps the greatest appeal of Prince William County is the fact that it is so close to DC yet so far away in terms of feeling – a close 'escape' half an hour from the capital.

The Prince William County/Manassas Tourist Information Center (☎ 703-491-4045, 800-432-1792) is at 200 Mill St in Occoquan – the name comes from the Dogue Indian word meaning 'at the end of the water.' The **Mill House** (☎ 703-491-7525), at 413 Mill St, is yet another restored 18th century gristmill. It also houses Historic Occoquan, Inc, with local history exhibits, audiovisuals, and a gift shop; it is open daily from 11 am to 4 pm, and entry is free. Occoquan has other treasures and a visit to this small part of Prince William County can turn into a sojourn of several hours.

And if you are hungry stop by at the *Bistro Belgique Gourmande* (☎ 703-494-1180), at 302 Poplar Alley, for great continental delights, or *Toby's Cafe* (☎ 703-494-1317), at 201 Union St, for fresh baked goods.

Shoppers will love the **Potomac Mills** (☎ 703-643-1605, 800-826-4557), a value outlet mall (one of the world's largest) at Exit 156 off I-95. There are over 220 stores open year round, Monday to Saturday, from 10 am to 9:30 pm, Sunday 11 am to 6 pm.

Just beyond the county line is the *Lazy Susan Dinner Theatre* (☎ 703-550-7384), at the junction of Hwy 1 and I-95. It is known for its Pennsylvania Dutch buffet and theatrical performances. It opens at 6 pm, the dinner buffet is served from 7 to 8 pm and the curtain goes up at 8:30 pm (an hour earlier on Sunday). The cost for adults is $29, for children $15.

Prince William Forest Park (Quantico)

This 18,570-acre park consists of pine and hardwood forests in the Quantico Creek watershed. The area was set aside as a national park in 1948 and now offers 35 miles of hiking trails, playing fields, fishing streams, picnic areas, and scheduled naturalist programs (run by the staff of the NPS Pine Grove visitors center – ☎ 703-221-7181).

The *Oak Ridge Campground* (☎ 703-221-7181) is one mile west of the town of Triangle on County Rd 619 (Exit 150 off I-95); basic sites are $7 for up to six people. The *Prince William Travel Trailer Village* (☎ 703-221-2474) is 2.5 miles north of I-95 (Exit 152) on Route 234 – a very busy road; sites, with electric/water hook-ups are from $16.50 to $19.50 for two.

The park is open dawn to dusk year round. To get there from I-95, take Exit 150 or 152; there is a private vehicle entrance fee of $4, valid for seven days. Only campers are allowed in the park in the evenings, unless there is a scheduled interpretive program.

Marine Corps Air Ground Museum

This interesting museum (☎ 703-640-2606), housed on the US Marine base at Quantico, shows the development of the US Marine Corps from 1900 to the present.

It is open April through November, Tuesday to Saturday from 10 am to 5 pm, Sunday noon to 5 pm; admission is free. Take the Quantico exits off I-95.

Dumfries

This small town on Hwy 1 has the **Weems-Botts Museum** (☎ 703-221-3346) at 300 Duke St. The original building was the bookstore of Parson Weems, Washington's first biographer and perpetuator of the 'cherry tree' myth. Later, a local attorney named Benjamin Botts used the building as a law office. It is open April to October, Tuesday to Saturday from 10 am to 5 pm, Sunday from 2 to 5 pm, otherwise Tuesday to Saturday from 10 am to 4 pm, Sunday 1 to 4 pm. Admission is by donation.

Leesylvania State Park (☎ 703-670-0372), in Prince William County, is two miles east of Hwy 1 on County Rd 610 (Neabsco Rd). This park, once the home of the Lee family, is now a popular place for hiking, picnicking, fishing, and boating.

Manassas

The city of Manassas (population 30,000) lies south of the battlefield and suffers some of the busiest rush hour traffic that you could ever imagine. The Virginia Welcome Center (☎ 703-361-2134) is on I-66W at 9915 Vandor Lane.

The **Manassas Museum** (☎ 703-368-1873), at 9101 Prince William St, is the regional history museum for the Northern Virginia Piedmont. The Civil War is emphasized but there are also collections of photographs and artifacts, and videos covering community history. The museum is open daily, except Monday, from 10 am to 5 pm; admission is $2.50 for adults, and $1.50 for children six to 17 (on Tuesday it is free).

There is a daily commuter link between Manassas (9451 West St) and Union Station in Washington, DC, via Alexandria and Arlington; for information contact Virginia Railway Express (☎ 703-497-7777, 800-743-3843). A single ride to DC is $5.55.

Manassas National Battlefield Park

This Civil War battlefield will probably be known even to those who have very little interest in the Civil War. To keen historians, on the other hand, a visit will be an absolute must. Arrayed over grassy hills on the very edge of modern DC, there is little left to remind one of the cataclysmic to-ings and fro-ings of the battles of July 1861 and August 1862 – see the sidebars in this section. These battles are referred to as Manassas in the south, Bull Run in the north. Bull Run is the stream which forms a semicircle around the north and east of the battlefield.

There is a good self-guided tour which commences from the park's visitors center (☎ 703-361-1339). The center also has a number of exhibits, a captivating audio-visual program, and an excellent pamphlet which shows all the points of interest. In August, reenactments of the two Civil War battles of Manassas (Bull Run) are staged – call ☎ 703-491-4045 for information.

The park is open daily from daylight to dusk, the visitors center from 8:30 am to 6 pm (except June 15 to Labor Day when it closes at 5 pm); admission is $2, children under 17 are free.

To get to Manassas, a 26-mile drive from DC, take I-66W to Route 234 (Exit 47B); the battlefield is half a mile along this road on the right. Two heavily used highways cross the park so use caution when driving along or turning into these.

FAUQUIER COUNTY

This predominantly agricultural county of rolling hills, picturesque villages, and vineyards is nicknamed 'Horse Country' or 'Hunt Country.' The small junction town of

The Battles of Manassas

Not long after the first shots were fired at Fort Sumter, South Carolina, on April 12, 1861, sizable armies of both Federal and Confederate troops began to gather around the capitals of Richmond and Washington, DC.

The first significant battle resulted when a Confederate army, commanded by PGT Beauregard, camped near the rail junction of Manassas, perilously close to the national capital. The battle that Northerners hoped would end the war, **First Battle of Manassas (Bull Run),** started with an air of ebullience. Under orders from Abraham Lincoln, Brigadier General Irvin McDowell roused his 32,000 poorly trained troops on the afternoon of July 16 and marched to Centreville, 20 miles west of Washington. McDowell's men skirmished and scouted near Bull Run, gathering scanty intelligence, and on July 21 the general committed two divisions, including cavalry and artillery, against the Confederate lines.

McDowell's first assault on the right flank was checked by Stonewall Jackson's soldiers and driven back. Then, what was meant to be an organized retreat turned into a rout: The Federal troops knew tactical drilling techniques well enough but had not been taught the essentials of withdrawal under fire.

On the supposedly 'safe' side of Bull Run there had been a macabre picnic in progress, with Washington civilians coming down to witness the fray. As the soldiers fled in panic they intermingled with this now befuddled crowd of onlookers and there was a melee, especially when a strategic bridge across Cub Run collapsed (see the 'Battle Hymn of the Republic' sidebar). When the counting ended, the Confederates, who incurred about 2000 casualties as opposed to McDowell's 3000, could claim victory. Both groups were so ill-trained at this early stage of the war, however, that any advantage could not be followed up.

More than a year later the war returned to Manassas. Following McClellan's Peninsula Campaign and the Seven Days Battle (see the sidebar in the Richmond chapter), Federal troops had withdrawn to the safety of Washington and many of McClellan's soldiers were handed over to a new commander, John Pope. By the time Pope was ordered to move against Richmond, Robert E Lee was in command of the Confederates.

Pope advanced south towards the Rappahannock River and Lee advanced north to confront Pope's troops before they could be reinforced by McClellan. Lee brilliantly split his force and consigned an attack on Pope's supply base at Manassas to Stonewall Jackson's men. Jackson's force came up against a numerically inferior force commanded by Nathaniel Banks at Cedar Mountain and, after a seesawing battle, the Union troops were forced back with heavy losses.

Pope's main body came up the next day and the **Second Battle of Manassas (Bull Run)** commenced on August 29 with Pope making concerted but futile attacks on Jackson's troops, who were in defense behind the bed of an unfinished railroad.

The following day Lee unexpectedly arrived in force with the 30,000-strong force of James Longstreet, which in devastating flank assault on the Federals' left (combined with Jackson's attacks on the other flank) caused a repeat of First Manassas, with the Northerners fleeing back across Bull Run to the security of Washington, DC. At this stage almost all of Virginia had been returned to the hands of the Confederates.

When you wander across the hills of Manassas contemplate these terrible losses. Pope lost his job when it was revealed that he had lost about a quarter of his force of 70,000 (the remainder of which were then incorporated into the Army of the Potomac) while Lee had lost only 10,000 of his force of 60,000. ■

Stonewall Jackson

One of the greatest figures of the Civil War, General Thomas Jonathan Jackson, a true soldier in every sense of the word, was born in Clarksburg, Virginia (now West Virginia) on January 21, 1824. A devout fire-and-brimstone Presbyterian, he had been a professor of natural philosophy for ten years at the Virginia Military Institute in Lexington when the Civil War broke out.

He was soon in the service of the South and at the First Battle of Manassas (July 21, 1861) earned the nickname 'Stonewall' when his brigade acted as an anchor in a vital part of the battle. Barnard Bee, a Confederate brigadier had shouted: 'There stands Jackson like a stone wall!' – perhaps the most famous phrase of the war.

Jackson proved his tactical genius in the Shenandoah Valley Campaign in the spring of 1862. Even though vastly outnumbered, Jackson's force, employing surprise attacks and unusual battle tactics, was able to rid the valley of Union troops. More importantly, they prevented the reinforcement of the Union armies threatening Richmond (see the Shenandoah Valley chapter). General Richard Taylor, who joined Jackson in May 1862, gives us the best description of the man: 'I (saw) a pair of cavalry boots covering feet of gigantic size, a mangy cap with visor drawn low, a heavy, dark beard, and weary eyes – eyes I afterward saw filled with intense but never brilliant light.'

At Chancellorsville, in May 1863, in one of the boldest strokes of the war, Jackson marched his 30,000 men 12 miles westward across the front of General Joseph Hooker's positions, and then initiated a surprise attack on the Federal army. On the evening of May 2, Jackson rode out to reconnoiter the battlefield. As he returned to his lines he was shot and mortally wounded by his own pickets. He died at Guinea Station a week later and was buried in Lexington, Virginia. ■

Warrenton has a population of 5300. It was established when a trading post, Read Store, opened on the Falmouth-Winchester-Alexandria-Culpeper road. The **Old Jail Museum** (☎ 540-347-1545), on Ashby St at Court House Square, has a small eclectic collection. It is open daily, May to October, from 11 am to 4 pm; entry is free. The Warrenton-Fauquier County Visitor Center (☎ 540-347-4414), at 183A Keith St, is open daily from 9 am to 5 pm.

At **Bealeton**, on County Rd 644, The Flying Circus Airshows (☎ 540-349-8942) relive the 1930s era of **barnstorming** – you know, wing walking, parachutes, balloons, biplanes, aerobatics, formation flying, general aerial idiocy. The airstrip is open on Sunday, May to October, from 10 am to dusk. Shows start at 2:30 pm; ring to find out costs.

The *Black Horse Inn* (☎ 540-349-4020), at 8393 Meetze Rd, Warrenton, is a gracious old country home with doubles from $95 to $150. The place to eat and party is *Fat Tuesday's Raw Bar* (☎ 540-347-5757), 573 Frost Ave, open daily for Creole and Cajun food (and live entertainment most nights).

Wineries

There are several small vineyards in Fauquier and Loudoun counties. *Piedmont* (☎ 540-687-5528), south of Middleburg on County Rd 626, has tours and tastings daily from 10 am to 5 pm; *Meredyth* (☎ 540-687-6277), also south of Middleburg, on County Rd 628, has tours and tastings from 10 am to 4 pm; *Oasis Vineyards* (☎ 540-635-7627), north of the junction of Hwy 211W and Hwy 522N on County Rd 635, has tours and tastings from 10 am to 4 pm; and *Swedenburg Estate* (☎ 540-687-5219), on Hwy 50 east of Middleburg, has daily tours from 10 am to 4 pm.

Sky Meadows State Park

This park, close to the Appalachian Trail in the northwest corner of Fauquier County, is rich in history. Mount Bleak House has been restored to reflect the lifestyle of an 1850s middle-class family. From spring to fall, nature and history programs are offered, and hiking, picnicking, and horseback riding on a bridle trail are all popular. There are primitive walk-in camping sites ($7 per night).

The park (☎ 703-592-3556) is two miles south of Paris on County Rd 710W; from DC take Hwy 50 to Hwy 17S or I-66 to Hwy 17N.

LOUDOUN COUNTY

Loudoun County proudly wears the mantle 'Hunt and Horse Country.' Weekends out here can get a little frustrating with ostentatious displays by black-jacketed, jodhpured, leather-booted Washingtonians in search of that English brand of finesse and class. Midweek, however, the county is a fascinating destination with several picturesque towns, replete with history and fine old buildings.

Leesburg

The hub of Loudoun County, Leesburg (population 10,500) is on the Maryland border, just to the northwest of Washington Dulles International Airport, and is one of the oldest towns in Northern Virginia. There are many colonial-era buildings in the town and a number of fine plantations in the vicinity.

Leesburg was a staging area during the French and Indian War, and it was to here that James and Dolly Madison fled (with copies of the Declaration of Independence and the US Constitution) when the British torched Washington in 1812. In 1861, a major battle of the Civil War was fought at nearby Ball's Bluff. The Union troops were forced back across the Potomac by the Confederates and houses on Leesburg's King St were used as hospitals; one of the patients was the young Oliver Wendell Holmes, later a justice of the Supreme Court.

Tourist Offices The Leesburg tourist office, in Market Station on Loudoun St, is open daily 9 am to 5 pm. For information in advance, contact the Loudoun Tourism Council (☎ 703-777-0519, 800-752-6118), 108-D South St SE, Leesburg, VA 20175.

Loudoun Museum This museum (☎ 703-777-7427) at 16 Loudoun St, covers the time from early Native American settlement, through the Civil War (which is given special emphasis) to the present. There is a daily video presentation and the museum is the starting point of an interesting walking tour. It is open daily Monday to Saturday from 10 am to 5 pm, Sunday 1 to 5 pm; admission is by donation and the walking tour booklet costs $1.

Morven Park Just one mile north of Leesburg on Old Waterford Rd is this park (☎ 703-777-2414), a 1500-acre historic property that was once the home of Virginia governor Westmoreland Davis. The Greek Revival mansion with its manicured boxwood gardens, looking a little like a transplanted White House, is the main reason to visit but there is also an antique carriage museum with over 100 horse-drawn vehicles.

Places to Stay There is no real camping option near Leesburg and no close budget accommodations. About halfway between Winchester and Leesburg, at Bluemont on the Appalachian Trail, is the spectacularly situated stone lodge *Bears Den (HI-AYH) Hostel* (☎ 540-554-8708, or for reservations write Postal Route 1, Box 288, Bluemont, VA 22012). The hostel has a kitchen, a dining room, on-site parking, and a laundry room, and the friendly staff provides heaps of information on activities such as hiking, canoeing, and mountain biking. Check-in is from 5 to 9 pm and the place is quiet from 10 pm; check-out is by 9:30 am. It costs $9 for HI members ($12 for nonmembers) and camping is $4 per person.

From Leesburg, head west on Route 7 for 18 miles, then turn onto County Rd 601S at the top of the Blue Ridge. Follow this for half a mile uphill to a signed stone-gate entrance on the right; follow this road for half a mile. If coming from the Appalachian Trail take the signed trail to Bears Den Rocks; the hostel is 300 feet away.

There are a couple of reliable B&Bs in Leesburg. The renovated, red brick *Norris House Inn* (☎ 703-777-1806, 800-644-1806), at 108 Loudoun St, has singles/doubles from $90/105 (an extra person is $25). *Fleetwood Farm B&B* (☎ 703-327-4325, 800-808-5988), at the junction of County Rds 621 and 722, eight miles south of Leesburg, is a working sheep farm; doubles are from $110.

The *Leesburg Days Inn* (703-777-6622), at 721 E Market St, has budget rooms from $39/43 for singles/doubles in the low season, $46/49 otherwise. All rooms have cable TV.

One very popular place, always requiring advance booking, is the historic *Laurel Brigade Inn* (☎ 703-777-1010), at 20 W Market St, in the center of town. (Dating from 1766, it takes its name from a Civil War brigade led by a local colonel.) It has lovely gardens, a restaurant that is open for lunch and dinner, and pleasantly furnished rooms with no phones; a double is from $50 to $75.

The *Landsdowne Resort* (☎ 703-729-8400) is at 44050 Woodridge Parkway (about 10 minutes' drive from Dulles Airport and 45 minutes from DC) via Route 7. Nestled in a secluded spot on the banks of the Potomac, it has a Robert Trent Jones–designed golf course, tennis courts, pools, fitness center, and two restaurants. This place is not cheap with singles/doubles costing $149/169 ($20 for an extra person).

Places to Eat The *Lightfoot Cafe* (☎ 703-771-2233), at 2 W Market St, is a progressive American bistro with an à la carte menu and freshly baked breads. At the other end of the time scale there's *The Green Tree* (☎ 703-777-7246), at 15 S King St, which serves Colonial American fare (from authentic 18th century recipes) in colonial surroundings. It is open daily from 11:30 am until 10 pm, Sunday 11:30 am to 4 pm.

The *Laurel Brigade Inn* (see Places to Stay), featuring steak and seafood dishes, opens for lunch and dinner; lunch entrees are from $11 and a fixed price dinner is from $12.50.

The *Tuscarora Mill* (☎ 703-771-9300), at 203 Harrison St, in Market Station, is housed in a turn-of-the-century mill. The lunches average about $10 and are well worth it; dinner features a number of innovative entrees and the Sunday brunch is very popular. The mill is open daily from 11:30 am to 2:30 pm and 5:30 to 9:30 pm; light snacks are served until about 11 pm.

JR's Festival Lakes (☎ 703 821-0545) on E Fort Evans Rd, puts on sumptuous lunch and dinner barbecues. There are heaps of activities to keep you (and the kids) amused between meal times. There are two restaurants in the Landsdowne Resort (see Places to Stay) – the *Potomac Grill* and the *Riverside Hearth*, both open from 6 am to 10 pm; an average dinner costs from $20.

Waterford

This 18th century Quaker village has established a reputation for being a crafts center – an annual fall tour of local homes, combining a craft fair (and those ubiquitous battle reenactments), is held in early October.

The Waterford Foundation (☎ 540-882-3018), in the Tin Shop at Clarkes Gap Rd, 2.4 miles north of Route 9W on County Rd 662, has more information on local walking tours and the craft fair; it is open daily from 9 am to 5 pm but the village is open 24 hours.

Thirsty? Then head out of Waterford on Route 7W to Route 9W; the entrance to **Loudoun Valley Vineyards** (☎ 540-882-3375) is four miles along on the right. There are great views of the Blue Ridge Mountains from here and it is a relaxing place to sit and enjoy a European-style wine. The vineyard is open on weekends from 11 am to 5 pm.

VIRGINIA

Oatlands

Some six miles south of Leesburg on Hwy 15S is the National Trust historic plantation Oatlands (☎ 703-777-3174). The plantation was established by a great-grandson of Robert 'King' Carter, the wealthy pre-Revolutionary planter. The carefully restored Greek Revival-style mansion, which dates from 1803, is surrounded by neat fields that feature in local hunt events such as the Loudoun Hunt Point-to-Point. (You know: The sound of bugles and barking hounds and 'Tailgates down! . . . Champers, sweetie?') More to my liking is the Draft Horse & Mule Day with associated arts & crafts show, the sheep dog trials in May, or an August Civil War reenactment.

The plantation is open April to December, Monday to Saturday from 10 am to 4:30 pm, Sunday 1 to 4:30 pm. Admission is $6 for adults, $5 for seniors and students, children under 12 are free.

Middleburg

This quaint little town is right on the border between Loudoun and Fauquier counties and is fringed with tree-lined roads, horse farms, and wineries. A popular retreat for visitors wanting to escape DC for the day, it is 35 minutes from Dulles International Airport.

It was established in 1787 by the Revolutionary War soldier Colonel Leven Powell, who purchased the land from George Washington's cousin, Joseph Chinn – it had previously been called Chinn's Crossroads (because it is midway between Alexandria and Winchester on the Ashby Gap trade route, now Hwy 50). The **Windsor House Inn** (1824) was operated by a Southern sympathizer during the Civil War but she happily served Union troops when Middleburg was occupied in 1862. The **Red Fox Inn** is believed to be the oldest continuously operating inn in North America.

The region has become known for fox-hunting and steeplechasing. Now over 25 horse meets are held each year and while the majority are amateur point-to-point races there are several professional steeplechases, including the Virginia Gold Cup (☎ 703-253-5001) in early May. Polo matches (☎ 540-777-0775) are played on Sundays, June through August. Expect to see a well-heeled, genteel crowd loaded up with 'champers' buckets and dainty sandwiches.

A good time to visit is late August, when you have the choice of 'wine, women, mirth, and laughter' at the Middleburg Wine Festival (☎ 703-687-5219). The vintages of at least 20 Virginia wineries are on display, accompanied by entertainment.

For tourist information contact the Pink Box Visitor Information Center (☎ 540-687-8888), at 12 N Madison St; they sell a self-guided walking-tour pamphlet ($1).

Places to Stay The *Middleburg Country Inn* (☎ 540-687-6082, 800-262-6082), at 209 E Washington St, was the former rectory of John's Parish Church. It is a small place but the rooms are large and furnished with antiques. Rooms are quite expensive at $145 for doubles on weekdays, $145 to $275 on weekends. Guests can borrow from the extensive video library and enjoy a complimentary country breakfast and afternoon tea.

B&Bs are numerous – there are at least 10 such fine establishments in the area. Expect to pay around $100 for a weekday double, much more on weekends. The *Red Fox Inn* (☎ 540-687-6301), at 2 E Washington St, Middleburg, is a great place with traditional character (doubles are from $135 to $225); the *Ashby Inn* (☎ 540-592-3900), on County Rd 701 near Paris, has doubles from $90 to $200 (they accept 'well-behaved children over 10'); and the *Little River Inn* (☎ 703-327-6742), in Aldie on Hwy 50, is a lovely country inn in a pleasant rural setting (doubles are from $80 to $210).

Places to Eat Middleburg has some fine eateries, catering to the many visitors. For the kids there is *Scruffy's Ice Cream Parlor*, and the *Coach Stop* (☎ 540-687-5515),

9 E Washington St, specializes in the type of meals Mom used to make.

Nobel House (☎ 540-686-6800), at 2 W Washington St, is suitably decorated in hunt club style with appropriate antique furniture. There is a good selection of continental food and a wine list featuring local vintages. It is open for lunch from 11 am to 3 pm and for dinner from 5 to 10 pm daily; the Piano Bar is open seven days from 11 am to midnight, Friday and Saturday until 2 am.

Fredericksburg & the Peninsulas

The historic town of Fredericksburg, on I-95, is midway between the national capital of Washington, DC, and the state capital of Richmond. In addition to it being a great base for exploring the numerous Civil War battlefields, it also makes an ideal base for trips down into the Northern Neck and Middle Peninsula, which radiate in two fingers out to the southeast. Directly below the Middle Peninsula is a third peninsula, covered in the Colonial Virginia (Historic Triangle) chapter.

HIGHLIGHTS

- Antiques, historic tours, and battlefields in historic Fredericksburg
- Spotsylvania, the Wilderness, and Chancellorsville battlefield tours – essential for Civil War buffs
- The birthplaces of George Washington and Robert E Lee
- Northern Neck 'getaways' – Reedville, Smith Point, and Irvington – that are light years from DC
- Native American museums and reservations on the Middle Peninsula

FREDERICKSBURG

Fredericksburg (population 20,000) has a real sense of history. It once was an important inland port where tobacco and other crops were loaded for transportation down the Rappahannock River – the waterfront is still lined by 18th and 19th century buildings.

The site was visited by John Smith as early as 1608 and many luminaries followed him. Washington spent his childhood, from age six to 16, at Ferry Farm, just across the Rappahannock in Stafford County; Mary Washington, George's mother, lived there before she died; and the fifth president, James Monroe, practiced law in the town. It was in Fredericksburg, in 1777, that the Virginia Statute of Religious Freedom (which later became the main plank of the First Amendment) was drafted by Thomas Jefferson and George Mason, among others.

During the Civil War, between 1862 and 1864, the town changed hands seven times (see the sidebars in this section). Fredericksburg is now a major distribution center, and very much an antiquing spot and weekend-escape for Washington, DC, folk.

Orientation

Fredericksburg is split into two parts (no, not Blue and Gray). The old town area (a 40-block national historic district) has as its main access route Caroline St where you will find the visitors center and other historic buildings. Places to stay and eat are strewn around the intersection of Route 3 and I-95. Hwy 1 also passes north-south through the city.

Information

Tourist Offices The Fredericksburg Visitor Center (☎ 540-373-1776, 800-678-4748), at 706 Caroline St, has lots of information including maps of walking tours. Their two-part guide for the Battle of Fredericksburg covers the bombardment, river crossings, the tenacious street fighting, and the calamitous Union assault on Marye's Heights. There are also maps for bike tours of three, nine, and 20 miles that feature historical attractions. The center is open 9 am to 5 pm, with hours extended in summer until 7 pm. You can purchase a Hospitality Pass for $16/6 for adults/students which allows entry to seven major historic sites;

the Pick Four Pass costs $11.50/4. The buildings included are the area museum, Belmont, Rising Sun Tavern, Mary Washington House, Kenmore, Monroe Museum, and the Hugh Mercer Apothecary.

The free *Fredericksburg, Spotsylvania & Stafford Visitor Guide* is available from this office. Accommodations and restaurants are listed near the highway exits where they are clustered. There is also a Virginia Welcome Center (☎ 540-786-8344) on I-95S.

Money For foreign exchange try the Central Fidelity Bank (☎ 540-899-0131), 614 Princess Anne St, and the Union Bank & Trust (☎ 540-371-0108), 700 Kenmore Ave.

Laundry The Wash & Fold Laundry (☎ 540-899-6515) is at 503½ Jefferson Davis Hwy.

Medical Services For emergencies, Medic 1 Clinic (☎ 540-371-1664), at 3429 Jefferson Davis Hwy, is open from 9 am to 9 pm; ring in advance.

Fredericksburg Area Museum & Cultural Center

This museum (☎ 540-371-5668), at 907 Princess Anne St, concentrates on the history of Fredericksburg and the surrounding region. The exhibits are located in the historic town hall/market house, dating from 1816. There are exhibits of prehistory, Native American culture, the colonial period, the Civil War, and recent history. It is open daily, March to November, from 9 am to 5 pm (Sunday 1 to 5 pm), otherwise 10 am to 4 pm (Sunday 1 to 4 pm); admission is $3 for adults, $1 for students age six to 18.

Kenmore

This elegant colonial mansion (☎ 540-373-3381), at 1201 Washington St, was built circa 1775 for Fielding Lewis and his wife Betty, the only sister of George Washington. The elaborately carved interiors and decorative plasterwork are considered more lavish than Mount Vernon, and one of the rooms is on a list of America's '100 most beautiful rooms.' Outside there are lovingly tended boxwood gardens. In the colonial-style kitchen next door you can sample tea and gingerbread.

Kenmore is open March to December, Monday to Saturday from 10 am to 5 pm, Sunday from noon to 5 pm; the rest of the year on Saturday from 10 am to 4 pm, Sunday from noon to 4 pm. Admission is $5 for adults, $2.50 for students and children six to 18.

James Monroe Museum

This museum (☎ 540-654-1043), at 908 Charles St, holds the biggest collection of 'Monroe-abilia' in the country – included are White House furnishings like the desk on which the Monroe Doctrine was written, books, documents, and decorative arts. Before becoming the nation's fifth president Monroe practiced law here from 1787 to 1789. The museum is open daily, November to February from 10 am to 4 pm, March to October from 9 am to 5 pm; admission is $3 for adults, $1 for students six to 18.

Mary Washington House

This house (☎ 540-373-1569), at 1200 Charles St, is the 18th century cottage that Washington purchased for his mother. She lived there for the last 17 years of her life until she died in 1789 at the age of 81. Once she greeted Lafayette there. The gardens, meticulously tended today, reflect the time when Mary arranged them over 200 years ago. Her grave and monument are on Washington Ave (west end of Pitt St).

The cottage and gardens are open March to November, daily from 9 am to 5 pm, December to February from 10 am to 4 pm; admission is $3 for adults, $1 for students and children six to 18.

Rising Sun Tavern

This tavern (☎ 540-371-1494), at 1306 Caroline St, opened its doors for business in 1760 and has been going strong ever since. Not everyone's 'mug of ale,' it is one of those places (of the type that plague Williamsburg) with 'buxom wench' serving

VIRGINIA

staff. It was built by George Washington's brother Charles, and Patrick Henry, Washington, and Jefferson are believed to have met here. Pity, these days you can't buy an ale here – a spiced tea perhaps? It is open daily, March to November from 9 am to 5 pm, December to February, 10 am to 4 pm; admission is $3 for adults, $1 for children, and night tours (book in advance) are $4.

Hugh Mercer Apothecary Shop
Not far from the tavern, at 1020 Caroline St, is the Hugh Mercer Apothecary Shop (☎ 540-373-3362), an 18th century building fitted out to represent the medical office and apothecary shop of one Scottish Dr Mercer, a Revolutionary War brigadier general who was killed at the Battle of Princeton in 1776. Half the fun of this place is finding out about antiquated medical and dental techniques which will make you think you have walked into a torture chamber, not a doctor's office.

The shop is open March to November, daily from 9 am to 5 pm, December to February from 10 am to 4 pm; admission is $3 for adults, $1 for students and children six to 18.

Belmont – Gari Melchers Estate
The internationally renowned Detroit painter Gari Melchers (1860-1932) purchased this 18th century estate when he returned from Europe in 1916, at the time the US entered the war. In the adjoining stone studio, built in 1924, there is an exhibition of Melchers' work, the largest concentration of his paintings in the US.

The estate (☎ 540-654-1015), at 224 Washington St in Falmouth, is open daily, March to November, from 10 am to 5 pm (Sunday 1 to 5 pm), otherwise from 10 am to 4 pm (Sunday 1 to 4 pm); admission is $4 for adults, $1 for students and children six to 18. To get there, take the Hwy 1 bypass across the river, then Hwy 17 Business to County Rd 1001 (Washington St).

Chatham Manor
This fine Georgian building (☎ 540-373-4461), at 120 Chatham Lane, across the

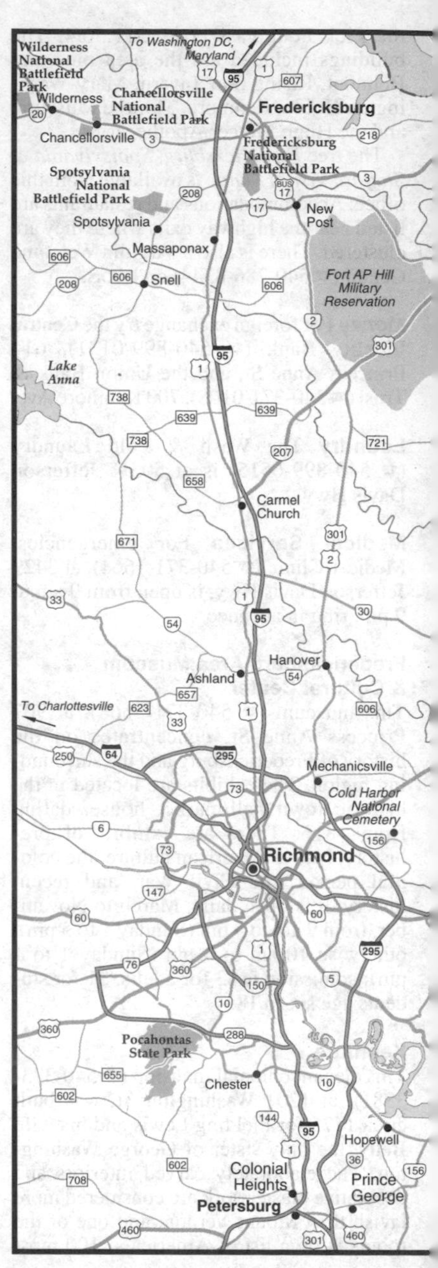

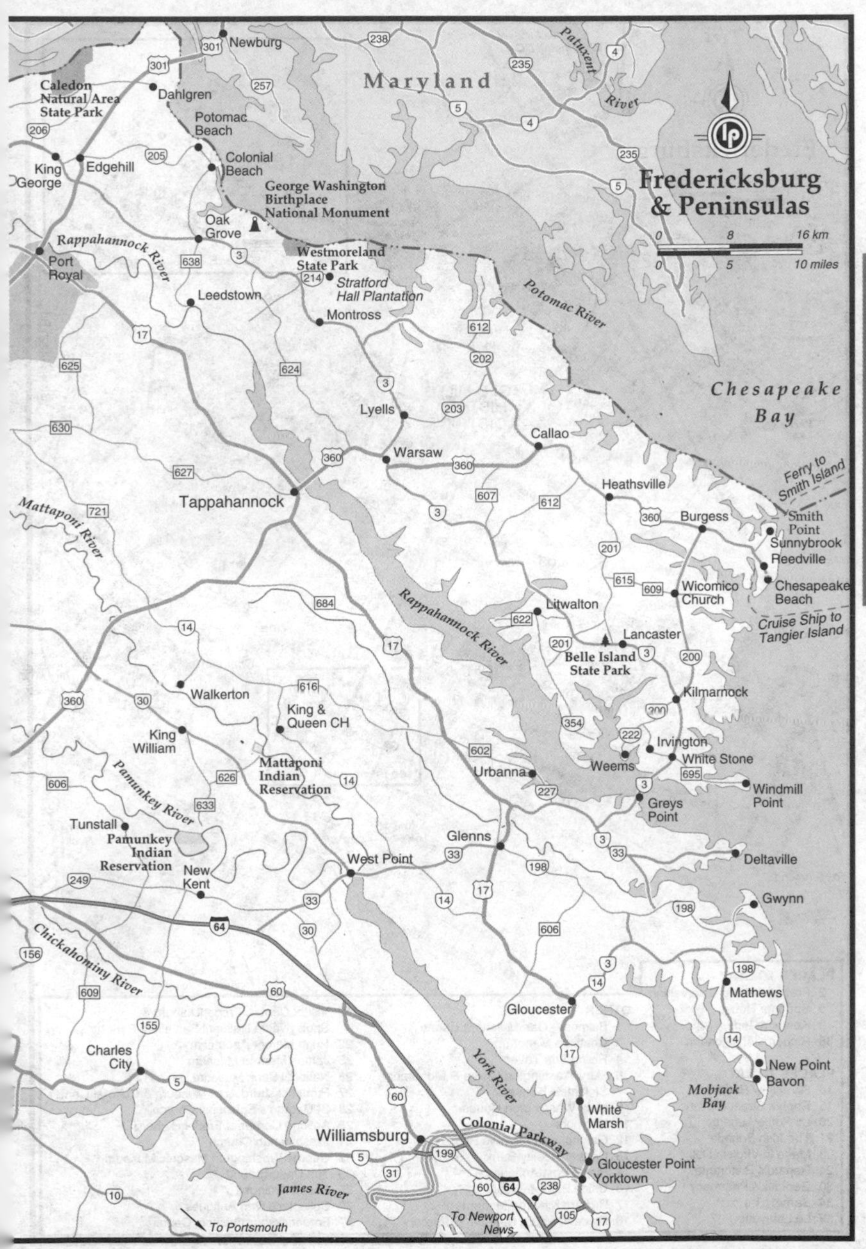
Fredericksburg & Peninsulas
Maryland
Chesapeake Bay
Potomac River
Patuxent River
Rappahannock River
Mattaponi River
Pamunkey River
Chickahominy River
York River
James River
Mobjack Bay
Caledon Natural Area State Park
George Washington Birthplace National Monument
Westmoreland State Park
Stratford Hall Plantation
Belle Island State Park
Mattaponi Indian Reservation
Pamunkey Indian Reservation
Colonial Parkway
Newburg
Dahlgren
Potomac Beach
Colonial Beach
King George
Edgehill
Oak Grove
Port Royal
Leedstown
Montross
Lyells
Warsaw
Callao
Tappahannock
Heathsville
Burgess
Smith Point
Sunnybrook
Reedville
Chesapeake Beach
Wicomico Church
Litwalton
Lancaster
Kilmarnock
Irvington
White Stone
Weems
Windmill Point
Urbanna
Greys Point
Deltaville
Gwynn
Mathews
New Point
Bavon
Walkerton
King & Queen CH
King William
Tunstall
New Kent
West Point
Glenns
Gloucester
White Marsh
Gloucester Point
Yorktown
Williamsburg
Charles City
Ferry to Smith Island
Cruise Ship to Tangier Island
To Portsmouth
To Newport News
0 8 16 km
0 5 10 miles
VIRGINIA

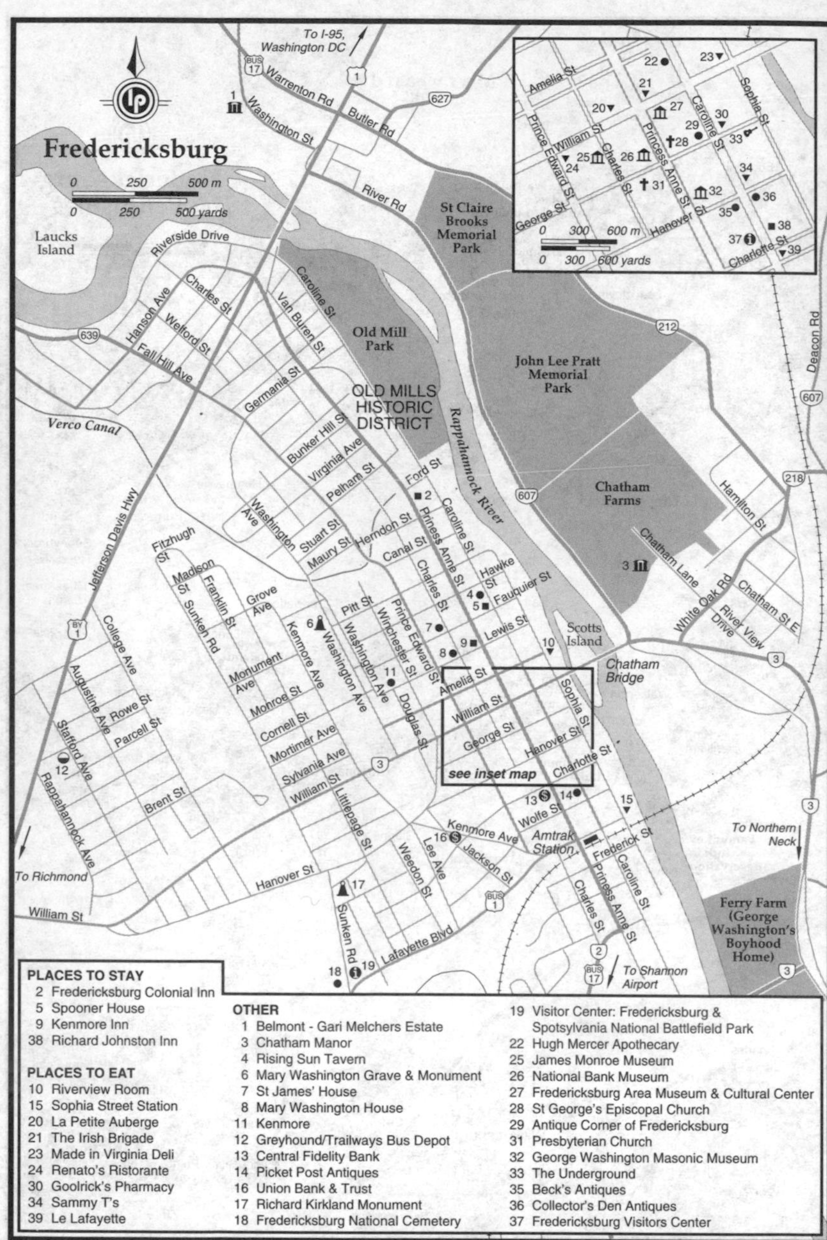

Fredericksburg
0 250 500 m
0 250 500 yards
To I-95, Washington DC
Warrenton Rd
Washington St
Butler Rd
River Rd
Riverside Drive
Laucks Island
St Claire Brooks Memorial Park
Old Mill Park
OLD MILLS HISTORIC DISTRICT
John Lee Pratt Memorial Park
Chatham Farms
Rappahannock River
Verco Canal
Jefferson Davis Hwy
Charles St
Hanson Ave
Welford St
Fall Hill Ave
Caroline St
Van Buren St
Germania St
Bunker Hill St
Virginia Ave
Pelham St
Ford St
Washington Ave
Stuart St
Maury St
Herndon St
Canal St
Princess Anne St
Hawke St
Fauquier St
Lewis St
Fitzhugh St
Madison St
Franklin St
Sunken Rd
Grove Ave
Pitt St
Prince Edward St
Winchester St
Kenmore Ave
Monument Ave
Monroe St
Cornell St
Mortimer Ave
Sylvania Ave
William St
Littlepage St
Douglas St
Amelia St
George St
Hanover St
Sophia St
Charlotte St
see inset map
Wolfe St
Kenmore Ave
Amtrak Station
Frederick St
Jackson St
Lee Ave
Weedon St
Lafayette Blvd
College Ave
Augustine Ave
Rowe St
Parcell St
Stafford Ave
Rappahannock Ave
Brent St
To Richmond
Hanover St
William St
Scotts Island
Chatham Bridge
Chatham Lane
White Oak Rd
Chatham St E
River View Drive
Hamilton St
Deacon Rd
To Northern Neck
Ferry Farm (George Washington's Boyhood Home)
To Shannon Airport
0 300 600 m
0 300 600 yards
PLACES TO STAY
2 Fredericksburg Colonial Inn
5 Spooner House
9 Kenmore Inn
38 Richard Johnston Inn
PLACES TO EAT
10 Riverview Room
15 Sophia Street Station
20 La Petite Auberge
21 The Irish Brigade
23 Made in Virginia Deli
24 Renato's Ristorante
30 Goolrick's Pharmacy
34 Sammy T's
39 Le Lafayette
OTHER
1 Belmont - Gari Melchers Estate
3 Chatham Manor
4 Rising Sun Tavern
6 Mary Washington Grave & Monument
7 St James' House
8 Mary Washington House
11 Kenmore
12 Greyhound/Trailways Bus Depot
13 Central Fidelity Bank
14 Picket Post Antiques
16 Union Bank & Trust
17 Richard Kirkland Monument
18 Fredericksburg National Cemetery
19 Visitor Center: Fredericksburg & Spotsylvania National Battlefield Park
22 Hugh Mercer Apothecary
25 James Monroe Museum
26 National Bank Museum
27 Fredericksburg Area Museum & Cultural Center
28 St George's Episcopal Church
29 Antique Corner of Fredericksburg
31 Presbyterian Church
32 George Washington Masonic Museum
33 The Underground
35 Beck's Antiques
36 Collector's Den Antiques
37 Fredericksburg Visitors Center

Fredericksburg 1862

After the Battle of Antietam (near Sharpsburg, Maryland) in mid-September 1862, Union general McClellan was replaced by Ambrose E Burnside (whose bushy muttonchop hair in front of his ears came to be known as 'sideburns'), one of McClellan's corps commanders at Antietam. Lee's Confederate forces had retreated back into Virginia, and McClellan went home and took no further part in the war.

Burnside, after delaying for a number of weeks, moved his Army of the Potomac, numbering 120,000, through bleak late-November weather down the Rappahannock towards Fredericksburg. He reached Falmouth, just across the Rappahannock from the city, where he waited for pontoons to arrive so his army could cross intact. Lee learned of the move and used Burnside's hesitation to his advantage, secreting his troops in Fredericksburg where they occupied the best high ground. On December 11 everything was in place, including the pontoons, and Burnside ordered his engineers down to the river to assemble the bridges.

The Federal artillery shelled the town as the Confederate sharpshooters picked off the engineers at the river. The battle seesawed at the river before some of Burnside's infantry began to fan out into the town. The Federals soon moved across the river freely, setting up a bloody endgame on December 13.

In the morning Burnside committed his army, in a two-pronged attack, to do the impossible. One objective of his attack was to breach the stone wall where the Confederate infantry lay in wait, and the other was to go a mile to the south. Lee looked down from the heights as the morning mist cleared and uttered: 'It is well that we know how terrible war really is, else we would grow too fond of it . . . . '

Burnside's men thrust up against the stone wall and the survivors of the assault crawled their way back dripping blood, falling, and dying. Burnside, miles away in both distance and realization, sent his divisions forward again and again to be cut to ribbons.

To the south, the troops of George Gordon Meade penetrated the defenses but were denied reinforcement. After a spirited counterattack by Stonewall Jackson's troops, the hole in the Confederate line was plugged.

Burnside dreamed of continuing the battle, but reality bit, and the Army of the Potomac retreated in wind and sleeting rain across their pontoon bridges. Many Confederate troops sneaked into the piles of 12,000 dead Union troops (Lee had lost less than half that number) and stole away with their still-warm uniforms.

After the defeat, morale on the Union side was low and many of the soldiers deserted. Less than a month later Lincoln replaced Burnside with General Joseph ('Fighting Joe') Hooker and both armies wintered over near Fredericksburg. (See the sidebar Chancellorsville 1863 for ensuing events.) ■

Rappahannock River from Fredericksburg, was built between 1768 and 1771 by William Fitzhugh, a plantation owner. Many famous people have passed through the house in its 200-year history, including Clara Barton, founder of the American Red Cross, and poet Walt Whitman, who treated the wounded here during the Civil War. Lincoln also met his generals here on two occasions during the war.

From the building there is a superb view of the many-steepled city of Fredericksburg. One of the park staff may relate the history of the battles of 1862 and 1863.

The house, administered by the NPS, is open daily 9 am to 5 pm and admission is free. To get there, follow William St (Route 3) across the Rappahannock and make the tricky left turn onto Chatham Drive; a loop road in the park returns you to Route 3.

Other Historic Buildings The **George Washington Masonic Museum** (☎ 540-373-5885), at 803 Princess Anne St, relates to the time that Washington was active in the Freemasons in lodge No 4 AF & AM in 1752. He was later Worshipful

VIRGINIA

Master of Alexandria Masonic Lodge No 22. The Masonic memorabilia includes a portrait by Gilbert Stuart and the Bible upon which Washington swore his Masonic oath. It is open daily from 9 am to 4 pm, Sunday 1 to 4 pm; admission is $2 for adults, $1 for students (or by secret handshake?).

Not far up the same street (at No 900) is the **National Bank Museum** (☎ 540-899-3243), one of the oldest buildings in the US to have continuously served as a bank. Wander in for a scintillating 30-minute discovery of 200 years of banking – not! It is open weekdays from 9 am to 1 pm; admission (unusual for any banking activity) is free.

St George's Episcopal Church, on Princess Anne St (between George and William Sts), has a number of famous people buried in its graveyard, including Martha Washington's father and the Revolutionary War generals George Weedon and Hugh Mercer. The **Presbyterian Church**, at the corner of George and Princess Anne Sts, like St George's, was hit during the Civil War.

The **Saint James House** (☎ 540-373-1569), at 1300 Charles St, is an 18th century gentleman's home that has been carefully restored and furnished with antiques. The house was once owned by James Mercer, attorney for Mary Ball Washington. It is open by appointment only, except during Garden Week in April and in the first week in October, when it is open to all.

Those retracing the lives of US presidents will undoubtedly make a trip to **Ferry Farm** in Falmouth, which was George Washington's home from age six to 20. He inherited it when he was 11 and kept it until he was 42, a year before he became commander of the Continental Army. This was supposedly the site of the cherry tree chopping and coin throwing incidents. The farm (☎ 540-372-4485) is open Monday through Saturday from 10 am to 4 pm, Sunday noon to 4 pm; there is no admission charge. To get there follow Kings Hwy to Ferry Rd.

VIRGINIA

Hiking & Biking

For information on and equipment for outdoor activities, especially hiking and cycling, contact *Outdoor Adventures* (☎ 540-786-3334), at 4721 Plank Rd. They are open weekdays from 10 am to 8 pm, Saturday 10 am to 6 pm, and Sunday noon to 5 pm; they rent bicycles (to adults only).

Canoeing & Kayaking

Rappahannock Outdoors (☎ 540-371-5085) has kayaks and canoes for hire and offers instruction on canoeing, tubing, rafting, and kayaking. Another canoeing and tubing outfitter is *Clore Bros* (☎ 540-786-7749), 5927 River Rd. *Friends of the Rappahannock* (☎ 540-373-3448) offer half-day and two-day canoe tours, accompanied by naturalists and historians, on the Rappahannock and Mattaponi Rivers.

Golf

The *Lees Hill Golfer's Club* (☎ 540-891-0111), off Hwy 1, has an 18-hole public golf course. *Meadows Farm Golf Course* (☎ 540-854-9890), at 4300 Flat Run Rd, boasts the longest hole in the United States, the 841-yard, par-6 12th hole.

Organized Tours

Fredericksburg is very much a museum and 'old house' town, and many of the features are associated with the Washington family. You could easily spend an entire day here traipsing from one old building to the next. The Living History Company (☎ 540-899-1776) has a variety of tours (eg, history and romance walks, 'Feel the Fury' Civil War tours, the 'Phantoms of Fredericksburg'); contact them for costs and details.

Special Events

Fredericksburg hosts a number of special events, some honoring past illustrious citizens. In late February President's Day and George Washington's birthday are celebrated and, in late April, it is James Monroe's birthday. Mother's Day in mid-May takes on special meaning in Fredericksburg as George Washington's mother is given top billing. In early June there is the Fred-

Chancellorsville 1863

While wintering over after the Battle at Fredericksburg, 'Fighting Joe' Hooker reorganized and refitted the Army of the Potomac, now numbering 132,000. On April 27, 1863, Hooker's army (not wishing to repeat Burnside's mistake) skirted around to the northwest of Fredericksburg, crossing the Rappahannock and Rapidan, with the intention of coming around on the Confederate rear. By April 30 three corps of the army had traversed the second-growth timber of the trackless Wilderness and was in bivouac near the Chancellorsville mansion.

A smaller Union force of two corps under General John Sedgwick began to cross the river near where Burnside had crossed in 1862; they were to form the 'wall' that Hooker would force Lee's Confederates up against. There were another two corps in reserve. On May 1 Fighting Joe confidently moved his forces east towards Fredericksburg. Lee left about 10,000 troops to hold off Sedgwick and turned to meet Hooker's troops head on. This bold move unsettled Hooker and he withdrew his forces into improvised lines around Chancellorsville.

That night Lee conferred with Jackson and hatched a brilliant and daring plan. On May 2 Jackson's force of 25,000 was to march across Hooker's front and attack the weak Union right flank. Meanwhile Lee, with a force of 20,000, enacted a charade in front of Hooker's army of 80,000, giving the impression that the Army of Northern Virginia had much stronger offensive capability than it really had at that time.

Just before sundown Jackson's troops struck and drove the Federal corps of Oliver O Howard off in rout. Darkness and the resulting disorganization saved the Federals from further destruction. Jackson, accidentally wounded by one of his own men, was carried off to a field hospital and the Confederate advance was stalled. Hooker still didn't take advantage of the fact that the Confederate army was split into two.

The next morning Lee went on the offensive again, assigning the cavalier JEB Stuart to command Jackson's forces. Stuart's artillery pounded Chancellorsville and wounded Hooker, literally knocking the fight out of him. Hooker's troops were pushed back to a defensive horseshoe around the Rappahannock bridgeheads.

In Fredericksburg, Sedgwick's men attacked Marye's Heights and drove Jubal Early's Southerners from the defenses that Burnside had failed to take the previous December. Sedgwick then tried to rescue Hooker. Calmly, Lee left a small force to check Hooker's army and moved his weary troops against Sedgwick at Salem Church. Soon he had boxed the Union soldiers into a small bend on the Rappahannock between Fredericksburg and Chancellorsville. These Union forces retreated across the river, lucky to escape.

Not content to call a halt, Lee methodically moved his army back to take on Hooker's main force in Chancellorsville but Hooker, although he had 40,000 troops in reserve, had crossed the Rappahannock on May 5 and retreated into the camps opposite Fredericksburg. The Union forces had been depleted by 17,000 and the Confederates by about 12,000. But for Lee and the South, victory had a hollow ring as on May 10 one of their finest tacticians, Stonewall Jackson, died of his wounds at Guinea Station. ■

ericksburg Arts Festival, which has been going strong for well over 20 years.

There are many and varied celebrations at Christmastime including parades, open houses each with a different theme, and candlelight tours of the historic area.

Places to Stay

Camping There are a number of campgrounds in the region. The *Fredericksburg DC South KOA* (☎ 540-898-7252) is at 7400 Brookside Lane, in Massaponax (Exit 126 southbound and Exit 118 northbound off I-95); sites are $20 for two and electricity and water hook-ups are $3 extra. There are also a couple of campgrounds on the shores of Lake Anna southwest of Fredericksburg (see the Piedmont chapter).

Hotels & Motels Lodgings are found at all of the four main exits off I-95 – 118, 126, 130, and 133. The *Econo Lodge Central*

VIRGINIA

Virginia Battles of 1864

Ulysses S Grant arrived in Washington, DC, on March 8, 1864, to become general in chief of all Federal forces. The war was now being fought on two major fronts – Sherman marched against Johnston and Atlanta, while Grant sought to engage Lee in Virginia.

On May 4, Grant's army (as a number of Federal armies had previously attempted) surged across the Rapidan and Rappahannock Rivers into the second-growth forest of the **Wilderness**, hoping to fall on Lee's forces in open country before Lee had time to react.

Lee wouldn't be drawn into a fight on Grant's terms, on ground of Grant's choosing; instead, responding swiftly, he went after Grant, sending his seasoned troops against the numerically superior Army of the Potomac. The Confederate forces appeared from the west and engaged the Federals in the trackless forest of the Wilderness, where artillery was rendered useless. For two days general utter confusion commanded the battlefield. The forest caught fire and the two sides fought blindly, the course of the battle abandoned to the whims of fate. Even the usual comforting blanket of nightfall didn't ameliorate the melee.

Timely intervention, in a small clearing at Tapp's Farm, by General James Longstreet's 1st Corps and the Texas Brigade ('the Grenadier Guard of the Confederacy') saved Lee's army from defeat by Union General Winfield Scott Hancock's 2nd Corps. An agitated Lee rode up and down, swinging his hat, but was requested by the Texans to go back to safety. The Confederate artillery, at point blank range, then stunted the Federal charge, and Longstreet followed up with a flank attack. Hancock, cool in crisis, had his men establish a defensive log breastwork and held back the attacking Confederates. Longstreet was wounded by his own men and the assault fizzled out.

Meanwhile Lee moved to attack the Federals' right flank, where Union General John Sedgwick, with the use of reserve troops, stabilized the line. Night fell and the firing stopped, and amidst the screaming and moaning of the wounded, men collapsed to get what sleep they could.

Grant had lost more than twice as many men as Lee (18,000 as opposed to 8000), but his army in numbers was still double that of the Confederates. He would not admit defeat and decided to march his army southeast to the crossroads at **Spotsylvania Courthouse**, and keep the battle alive by cutting Lee off from Richmond.

(☎ 540-786-8374), on Route 3 at the junction of I-95 (Exit 130B), has low-season singles/doubles for $29/34 (otherwise $33/38). The *Best Western-Thunderbird Inn* (☎ 540-786-7404) is also reached from the same exit off I-95; in winter it is $36/41 for singles/doubles (otherwise add $5).

The *Best Western Johnny Appleseed* (☎ 540-373-0000, 800-528-1234), at 543 Warrenton Rd near the intersection of I-95 and Hwy 17, is a two-story motel with a restaurant, an outdoor pool, volleyball court, playground, and nature trail. The cost of a basic single/double room is $40/46. The *Hampton Inn* (☎ 540-371-0330), at 2310 Plank Rd, off Exit 130A of I-95, has over 160 rooms (two are handicapped equipped), a pool, and many restaurants nearby; a single/double room is $54/60 year round.

The *Ramada Inn* (☎ 540-786-8361) is another place off Exit 130B of I-95; singles/doubles in this comfortable family-owned place are $50/55, year round.

The *Sheraton Fredericksburg Inn* (☎ 540-786-8321) is also on Route 3 at Exit 130B off I-95. In this large place, in which the rooms have a balcony or patio, there is a pool, wading pool, exercise room, tennis courts, dining room, and one of the city's most popular lounges (which has live entertainment most nights); singles/doubles are $79/89 all year.

Inns & B&Bs There are many B&Bs in old town, including *Spooner House* (☎ 540-371-1267), at 1300 Caroline St; *Selby House* (☎ 540-373-7037), at 226 Princess Anne St; and *Mary Josephine Ball* (☎ 540-371-9276), at 1203 Prince Edward St.

Lee's advance guards beat Grant to the crossroads and after the two armies skirmished a bloody battle ensued. For the next 10 uninterrupted days (May 8–19) Grant repeatedly tried to encircle the Confederates. On May 12 the fight degenerated to hand-to-hand combat at a stretch of Confederate breastworks near the principal road crossing, from then on known as the **Bloody Angle**. There, in torrential rain, the wounded were trodden into the mud, bayonets and clubs were thrust against almost unidentifiable foes, and trees were cut down by the incessant rifle and gun fire.

Nothing but the piled-up logs or breastworks separated the combatants. Our men would reach over the logs and fire into the faces of the enemy, would stab over with their bayonets; many were shot and stabbed through crevices and holes between the logs; men mounted the works and with muskets rapidly handed them kept up a continuous fire until they were shot down, when others would take their places.

– Brigadier General LA Grant, Union forces, Bloody Angle

A lad in Harris's brigade was shot down – a little, smooth-faced fellow, very out of place in this carnage. He raised his eyes, with the sweetest, saddest smile I think I ever saw on earth, and died almost on the instant.

– A South Carolinian combatant at Bloody Angle

Grant's force had been depleted by another 18,000 men and gained a mile of useless ground; Lee had lost half that number. Yet these numbers mattered little now as the Army of Northern Virginia could not afford to be in such close contact. Such attrition would ensure the success of the Union army.

The two armies then side-slipped via the North Anna, Pamunkey, and Chickahominy Rivers, towards Richmond (see the sidebars in the Richmond chapter), where the war entered its final phases. ■

A good inexpensive inn is the *Fredericksburg Colonial Inn* (☎ 540-371-5666), at 1707 Princess Anne St. This place exudes the perfect antebellum atmosphere for the Civil War buffs who gravitate to the area; doubles are $55 and two-room units are $65.

The *Richard Johnston Inn* (☎ 540-899-7606), at 711 Caroline St, across from the visitors center, is two 18th century row townhouses joined together (with a total of nine guest rooms); doubles are from $90 to $130. The inn has parking in the rear and a couple of the suites open onto a patio.

The 18th century *Kenmore Inn* (☎ 540-371-7622), at 1200 Princess St, has 14 rooms furnished with antiques and reproduction furniture (such as four-poster beds); double rooms (with complimentary sherry) are from $95 to $125, and the one suite is $150.

Places to Eat

Nostalgia buffs will like the 1940s *Goolrick's Pharmacy* (☎ 540-373-3411), at 901 Caroline St, an old original soda fountain. They make great milkshakes, soup, and sandwiches and you should be well satisfied for under $5; it is open Monday to Saturday from 8:30 am to 7 pm.

For exactly what the title suggests try *The Made in Virginia Deli* (☎ 540-371-2233), at 101 William St – they have a selection of yummy desserts, an extensive sandwich selection, and Brunswick stew (poultry stew with vegetables, corn, tomatoes, lima beans, and potatoes) for $2.

Try *Sammy T's* (☎ 540-371-2008), at 801 Caroline St, for vegetarian offerings, economical lunches and dinners, and a friendly bar. A bean and grain burger costs about $4, and a pocket sandwich chock full of sauteed vegetables is $5. This friendly, relaxed pub is open Monday to Saturday from 7 am to midnight, Sunday 11 am to 9 pm.

A great Italian place is *Ristorante Renato* (☎ 540-371-8228), at 422 William St in the center of town. It's open daily for lunch and dinner. Some of the specials include veal, chicken, and shrimp scampi; entrees are around $15, with a $6 lunch special (includes pasta, salad, and bread) and an $11 early-bird dinner (with dessert and half carafe of wine).

The *Kenmore Inn* (see Places to Stay) has a predominantly 'surf 'n' turf' (fish and meat) daily dinner menu, and a hearty brunch from 11:30 am to 2:30 pm on Sunday. There is occasionally live music in *The Pub* on weekend evenings.

The *Irish Brigade* (☎ 540-371-9413), at 1005 Princess Anne St, is named in honor of a Union brigade that made a suicidal assault against the infamous stone wall. It is well known as a late-night venue, but you can also get great food there. Salads are about $4, large burgers $5, sandwiches around $4.50, and entrees, available from 5 pm, cost from $6 to $11. Remember, 'Ní geal an gáire ach san aít a mbionn an biadh' ('Laughter is gayest where the food is best').

The Riverview Room (☎ 540-373-6500), at 1101 Sophia St in a setting overlooking the Rappahannock, is known for its sumptuous beef and seafood meals (about $15 to $20 per person); it is open daily from 11:30 am to 3 pm and 4 to 10 pm. *Sophia St Station* (☎ 540-371-3355), at the corner of Lafayette Blvd and Sophia St, also overlooking the Rappahannock River, is best known locally for its $10 ($4 for children) Sunday brunches and Thursday night raw bar.

La Petite Auberge (☎ 540-371-2727), at 311 William St (between Princess Anne and Charles Sts), has a strictly French menu that changes daily. There are great early-bird dinner specials (soup, entree, and salad for $13) and main courses are about $12; it is open weekday mornings from 11:30 am to 2:30 pm, evenings (including Saturday) from 5:30 to 10 pm.

More upmarket is *Le Lafayette* (☎ 540-373-6895), at 623 Caroline St, housed in a 1771 Georgian-style building. Interesting things are done to local seafood and produce to add a twist to conventional French and continental cuisine; two could expect to pay about $40 for dinner, without wine. It is open Tuesday to Saturday from 11:30 am to 2:30 pm and 6 to 10 pm; on Sunday it is open for brunch, from 11:30 am to 3 pm, and for dinner, from 5:30 to 9 pm.

Entertainment

The *Irish Brigade Pub* (see Places to Eat) rollicks at night with folk and rhythm and blues. You can get a sandwich or burger and draft Guinness or Harp to wash it down with. It is open from 5 pm until 2 am nightly, and there is live entertainment from Wednesday to Saturday.

Other live music venues are *The Underground* (☎ 540-371-9500), at 106 George St, for thrashy stuff, and the *Sophia St Station* for jazz on Thursday nights (see Places to Eat). A more sophisticated crowd is likely to be seen at the *lounge* at the Sheraton Inn, a place that caters to thirty-somethings (and up).

You can hear symphonic and chamber music at the *Colonial Theatre*, at 907 Caroline St, several times a season. Call the visitors center (☎ 800-678-4748) to find out what's on. Plays are performed at the *Klein Theatre* in du Pont Hall, Mary Washington College.

Spectator Sports

Probably the most famous spectator sport in Fredericksburg is the Tour du Pont cycle race in early May; the second stage of this prestigious event starts at the Kenmore Plantation.

Things to Buy

There are many shops in town selling expensive Federal and Victorian antiques. All of the following are on Caroline St, where there are at least a dozen shops and 100 dealers.

The Picket Post (☎ 540-371-7703), at No 602, open Monday to Saturday from 10 am to 6 pm, specializes in Civil War antiques; Becks Antiques Inc (☎ 540-371-1776), at No 708, open Monday to Saturday from 10:30 to 5 pm, Sunday 12:30 to 5 pm, sells rare books on the Civil War and Virginia; the Collector's Den (☎ 540-373-2430), at No 717, specializes in old baseball and sports cards; and the Antique Corner of Fredericksburg (☎ 540-373-0826), at No 900, also sells Civil War items.

Getting There & Away

Air The nearest airports are those that serve Washington, DC – Washington National and Dulles International. Shannon Airport, reached by Hwy 17 Business, is for smaller planes.

Bus Greyhound/Trailways (☎ 540-373-2103, 800-231-2222), at 1400 Jefferson Davis Hwy, has regular service to Washington, DC, Baltimore, and Richmond.

Train Amtrak (☎ 800-872-7245) has scheduled stops in Fredericksburg at the station near the junction of Caroline St and Lafayette Blvd, as part of its East Coast service running from Maine to Florida.

There is a commuter link between the Fredericksburg station at 200 Lafayette Blvd and Union Station, Washington, DC, via Alexandria, with several trains daily; for information contact Virginia Railway Express (☎ 703-497-7777, 800-743-3843). The cost for a single ride to Quantico is $3.20, to Washington, DC, $6.70.

Car I-95 and Hwy 1 bisect Fredericksburg in a north-south direction making it easily accessible by car – but, be warned, it is 'cloverleaf hell' and most confusing. Hwy 17 passes the city on its northern side and continues south through the Middle Peninsula via Hampton Roads all the way to North Carolina. East-west Route 3, the best access to the Northern Neck, also passes through the city.

Getting Around

A public bus service, which will cover the Greater Fredericksburg area, is under discussion and may be available in the near future. Until then, Historic Trolley Tours (☎ 540-898-0737), outside the tourist center on Charlotte St, operate April through December; the cost is $7 for adults and $4 for children for a 75-minute tour.

FREDERICKSBURG & SPOTSYLVANIA NATIONAL BATTLEFIELD PARKS

Fredericksburg's central location, and its closeness to the strategic Potomac and Rappahannock rivers, made it a vital prize during the Civil War. It is estimated that nearly 100,000 soldiers were killed in and around the city during the course of the war. Some of the bloodiest battles, all complete or partial Confederate victories – Fredericksburg (December 1862), Chancellorsville (May 1863), the Wilderness (early May 1864), and Spotsylvania (mid-May 1864) – were fought within a 20-mile radius of the city.

The main visitors center for the Fredericksburg & Spotsylvania National Battlefield Parks (☎ 540-373-6122) is at 1013 Lafayette Blvd to the south of town. It is open daily in summer from 8:30 am to 6 pm, otherwise 8:30 am to 5 pm; admission is free. There are a number of informative

VIRGINIA

exhibits, and you can rent 2½-hour audio tours of the battlefield sites ($3 for each battlefield tape and a cassette player, $4.25 to buy each tape). Highlights are the Sunken Road, the Kirkland monument, and the national cemetery on Marye's Heights. There is a great bookshop at the Chancellorsville battlefield visitors center (☎ 540-786-2880) on Route 3W.

The NPS provides a good map of Fredericksburg and Spotsylvania that has a self-guided 75-mile, 16-stop driving tour. There are many other points of interest you can add to this list, such as Chatham, Guinea Station (the Stonewall Jackson shrine), and Old Salem Church (the site of the battle of May 3–4, 1863).

NORTHERN NECK

The Northern Neck, a peninsula which extends from Fredericksburg to Chesapeake Bay, is bounded by the Potomac River in the north and the Rappahannock River in the south. Today it includes King George, Westmoreland, Richmond, Northumberland, and Lancaster counties.

The poorly maintained Route 3 runs almost through the center of the peninsula making it the best means of access. There are some interesting historical sites, such as the birthplaces of Washington, Monroe, and Lee, but it is the quiet, rural feel of the peninsula, the numerous quaint fishing villages, and the opportunity for quiet, relaxed hiking which attract most people.

For more information contact Virginia's Potomac Gateway Travel Center (☎ 540-663-3205) in King George, or Northern Neck Travel Council (☎ 800-453-6167), PO Box 312, Reedville, VA 22539. All you need to know can be found in the free *Riverviews* and the *Northern Neck Visitors Guide*.

Caledon Natural Area

This is bird-watching heaven. In summer this area of forests and marshes is home to a large concentration of American bald eagles. Access to the area is restricted, but ranger-guided tours are offered from time to time – these are immensely popular so book ahead at the visitors center (☎ 540-663-3861). There are no accommodations in the park but there are picnic facilities and a self-guided trail.

To get to Caledon from Fredericksburg take Route 218 east. If you are coming from Hwy 301 turn off onto Route 206. Follow this for four miles to Route 218. The reserve entrance is one mile farther along.

Colonial Beach & Monroe Hall

Colonial Beach, on the shores of the Potomac River at the northern end of Route 205, is nothing like the beaches you come to expect on the Atlantic Coast. Instead it has some fine restaurants serving traditional Southern-style food and tasty seafood, probably the main reason to make a diversion there. Try the *Dockside* (☎ 804-224-8726), at the Point, and *Wilkerson's* (☎ 804-224-7117), on Route 205, for seafood; or *Ola's Country Kitchen*, on Route 205, for old-fashioned fare.

A few miles south of Colonial Beach, on Route 205, is James Monroe's birthplace, **Monroe Hall**; it is a private dwelling so you can look only from outside on the birthplace of the 5th president and one of the fathers of US foreign policy (the Monroe Doctrine was based on his seminal speech delivered to Congress in 1823).

George Washington Birthplace National Monument

Washington's birthplace, adjoining Westmoreland State Park in Westmoreland County, is reached via Route 3 and Route 204. The national monument (538 acres), Pope's Creek Plantation, evokes the spirit of an 18th century Virginia tobacco farm with its buildings, gardens, groves of trees, livestock, and creeks and rivers. It remains as the young George would have experienced it as he went from boyhood to maturity. The house in which Washington was born no longer stands, but archaeologists have given us a thorough picture of what it looked like – the foundations are marked by oyster shell.

The visitors center (☎ 804-224-1732) has some interesting exhibits and artifacts, and screens a 14-minute film, *A Childhood Place*, relating to the Washington family history.

It is open from 9 am to 5 pm (the best time to visit is after 2 pm) and there are regularly scheduled guided tours. The cost of entry is $2 per person aged 17 and over. The center is accessible to the disabled. After visiting the colonial farm area you can hike to the beach or through the woods as Washington may well have once done. The free NPS pamphlet *George Washington Birthplace* spells out all the history you will need.

Westmoreland State Park

There is a campground at this popular park (☎ 804-493-8821), near Lee's Stratford Hall and Washington's birthplace. There are hook-ups for RVs, boat rentals and ramps, and a visitor center. Basic sites are $10.50; hook-ups with electricity and water are $15; and one-room, one-bedroom, and two-bedroom cabins cost $55, $62, and $82 respectively. To get there follow Route 3 to Baynesville then turn off onto Route 347; the park is five miles northwest of Montross.

Ingleside Plantation Winery

About 2.5 miles south of Oak Grove, not far from Washington's birthplace, is the 2500-acre Ingleside Plantation Winery (☎ 804-224-8687), which has daily tours and tastings, a picnic area, and a museum featuring Native American artifacts and Chesapeake waterfowl carvings. It is open Monday to Saturday from 10 am to 5 pm, Sunday from noon to 5 pm, and admission is free.

Stratford Hall Plantation

This working plantation of 1600 acres, dating from the 1730s, was the birthplace of Robert E Lee (his crib is on display). The restoration includes the magnificent H-shaped mansion (with its paneled Great Hall), several outbuildings, store, and gristmill. It was built by Thomas Lee, a governor of the Virginia colony, whose progeny played a major part in the development of the nation – Richard Henry Lee and Francis Lightfoot Lee were the only brothers to sign the Declaration of Independence.

Stratford Hall (☎ 804-493-8038), on the Potomac River, is open daily from 9 am to 4:30 pm and costs $7 for adults, $6 for seniors and $3.25 for students and children age six to 18. The rustic dining room serves breakfast and plantation lunches ($8/4 for adults/children). There is handicapped access to the reception center and museum only. The plantation, 45 miles east of Fredericksburg, is reached by Route 3 and Route 214.

Heathsville

This small, historic town is to the east of Warsaw on Hwy 360. The Northumberland County Historical Society (☎ 804-580-8581) operates a small museum that features the history of the county; it is open Monday, Wednesday, Thursday, and every second Saturday and fourth Sunday. Other places of interest include the courthouse and grounds, St Stephens Church, the old jail, and the old tavern grounds.

Smith Point

Smith Point, at the top Chesapeake-bound edge of Northern Neck, is the setting for *Smith Point RV Hideaway/KOA Campground* (☎ 804-453-3430). Its shaded sites are from $18 to $21 for two (electricity is $2 extra); 'kamping kabins' are from $33 for four persons. Waterfront sites, on the Potomac River, are $2.50 extra. To get to this camp from Route 3, take Hwy 360 via Warsaw, then County Rd 652.

For those who have cooking facilities, get a sack of pan-ready crabs from the *Deli at Smith Seafood* (☎ 804-453-3430).

See Cruises, below, for information about how to get to Smith and Tangier Islands from Smith Point.

Reedville

This quiet little town (population of 400), at the end of Hwy 360, has one restaurant, no bars or alcohol, no traffic lights or police. It has a number of Victorian-era homes on 'Millionaire's Row' and the cute little **Fisherman's Museum** (☎ 804-453-6529) in the diminutive but historically rich main street. The museum commemorates the fishers who went in search of the menhaden (a small, toothless fish). It is open daily May through October from 10 am to 4:30 pm, otherwise on weekends from 1 to 3 pm. (Check, as hours depend on availability of volunteer staff). Admission is by donation.

VIRGINIA

Cruises There are a couple of cruises available from Reedville and Smith Point to Smith and Tangier Islands. Island & Bay Cruises (☎ 804-453-3430) has a narrated five-hour scenic cruise, May to October, across to Smith Island, Maryland. Once there, you get the chance to tour a fishing village, Ewell, where there are crabbing shanties and a few crusty watermen; this is followed by a seafood luncheon. It costs $25 for the cruise, luncheon, and tour.

Tangier & Chesapeake Cruises (☎ 804-453-2628) have a five-hour cruise aboard the *Chesapeake Breeze* to remote Tangier Island with its quaint, narrow streets, gift shops, and unusual local dialect. Cruises are from May to October and cost $18.50 for adults, about $10 for children 13 and under.

Places to Stay & Eat There are a few fine B&Bs on or near Millionaire's Row (Main St) in Reedville; doubles cost from $65 to $100. *Cedar Grove* (☎ 804-453-3915), at 2535 Fleeton Rd (County Rd 657), is an elegantly appointed Colonial Revival building; the *Bailey-Cockrell House* (☎ 804-453-5900), on the waterfront, has its own beach. *The Gables* (☎ 804-453-5209), at the end of Main St, has a built-in 1800s schooner mast, while the *Magnolia Tree* (☎ 804-453-4720), is in a restored sea captain's home on Main St. The superb *Morris House* (☎ 804-453-7016), a magnificently renovated 1895 Victorian and pick of the B&Bs, has friendly owners (ask about their waterside cottage).

For those who haven't got the inclination to 'shuck' their own seafood, go to *Elijah's* (☎ 804-453-3621) on Main St overlooking Cockrells Creek. It's open Tuesday to Saturday for dinner, Sunday for brunch.

Tangier Island

Tangier Island is most easily accessed from Maryland's Eastern Shore – see Maryland's Eastern Shore chapter.

Warsaw & Lancaster

At the junction of Route 3 and Hwy 360 is Warsaw, a small community with a smattering of historic buildings. The **Richmond County Museum** (☎ 804-394-4901), in the Old Clerk's Office, next to the courthouse, has exhibits highlighting the rural lifestyle. (Beware, the local sheriff is a stickler for county stickers on cars. If you are driving a car with Virginia plates, and do not have a county sticker on your car, you might be pulled over. Explain to the sheriff that you are not a local resident.)

To the east of Warsaw, on Route 3, is the town of Lancaster with a fascinating historic district. The seven buildings of the **Mary Ball Washington Museum & Library** (☎ 804-462-7280) focus on the history of the Northern Neck from the colonial period through to the present. The museum is open Wednesday to Friday from 10 am to 5 pm, Saturday from 10 am to 3 pm.

Irvington

This small town near the southern tip of the Northern Neck is a popular getaway. In addition to the famous Tides Inn Resort and Tides Lodge there is the historic **Christ Church**. This church, cruciform in shape, was built around 1735 by Robert 'King' Carter and is Virginia's only colonial church which retains its original structure in unaltered form. It looks nothing like a modern church as there is no spire or bell tower. King Carter's descendants include seven governors of Virginia, three signatories to the Declaration of Independence, two Presidents (the Harrisons), several bishops, General Robert E Lee, and a chief justice of the US Supreme Court. Interesting features of the church include the three-decker pulpit tower, enclosed high-backed pews, marble baptismal font, and Carter family tombs.

The church and visitors center (☎ 804-438-6855) is open roughly April until Thanksgiving, weekdays from 10 am to 4 pm, Saturday 1 to 4 pm, and Sunday 2 to 5 pm; admission is free. From Irvington, take County Rds 646 and 709, off Route 200.

The *Tides Inn Resort* (☎ 804-438-5000, 800-843-3746), on King Carter Drive overlooking the Rappahannock River, has been rated one of the US's top 20 resorts by *Condé Nast Traveler* magazine. You can play golf and tennis, cruise on a yacht, row a small boat, cycle, swim in the salt-water pool, or dine in either of the two fine restaurants. It is open from the third week of March to January 2; the least expensive single/double rooms are from $130/220 in the low season, rising to $145/240 in the high season.

On its own private peninsula with a marina is *The Tides Lodge* (☎ 804-438-6000, 800-248-4337), at 1 St Andrews Lane. It has just about every amenity imaginable, including championship golf course, tennis, spa facilities, yacht cruises, and a superb seafood restaurant. It too is open from mid-March to January. Singles are from $130 to $211, and doubles $195 to $225 in low season; in April and May it costs $169 to $199 for a single, $259 to $285 for a double.

Activities

There is plenty of opportunity on the Northern Neck to go **fishing** in the rivers or out at sea on Chesapeake Bay. Boats are available for charter, usually between May and December. A popular choice is Captain Billy Pipkin's Charters at Ingram Bay Marina (☎ 804-580-7292), at the end of County Rd 609 east of Wicomico Church; they supply charters on *Liquid Assets*, boat rentals, bait, tackle (a day charter is from $350). Other choices are Danny Crabbe's *Kit II* (☎ 804-453-3251); Ted Curtis' *Gypsy* (☎ 804-435-2919); and Pittman's Charters' *Mystic Lady II* (☎ 804-453-3643); the latter supplies licenses.

There are a couple of **canoeing and kayaking** liveries in the region. River Rats (☎ 804-453-3064) rents kayaks and small boats and conducts tours. Tidewater River Adventure (☎ 804-769-1602), based at Walkerton on the Middle Peninsula, has guided trips and excursions around the Northern Neck.

There are many easy and moderate **hiking and walking** trails on the Northern Neck, and photographers, birders, or those seeking a quiet hour alone will all find that they're looking for. There are six miles of trails in Westmoreland State Park (see earlier); three easy trails in Belle Isle State Park (☎ 804-462-5030), off Route 354 and County Rd 683 near Litwalton; the 1.6-mile Chesapeake-Corrotoman River Nature Trail through upland and marshland terrain, near Lancaster; and a two-mile jaunt in Hughlett's Point Nature Preserve (☎ 804-462-5030), on County Rd 605 and off Route 200, north of Kilmarnock.

VIRGINIA

MIDDLE PENINSULA

The Middle Peninsula is not as isolated as the Northern Neck. The defining feature to the north is the Rappahannock River and in the south it is the York River and its tributary, the Mattaponi. Rural scenery and glimpses of the waterways are the region's attractions.

From the Northern Neck you reach the Middle Peninsula by Route 3, and from Hampton Roads, Hwy 17 crosses the York River via the Coleman Memorial Bridge connecting Yorktown to Gloucester Point.

Tappahannock

People come to this small town to go antiquing, and then to eat. The Tappahannock Essex Chamber of Commerce (☎ 804-443-5241), open weekdays from 8:30 am to 4:30 pm, has more information.

Rappahannock River Cruise (☎ 804-453-2628) leaves Tappahannock for full-day **cruises** upstream to the Ingleside Winery (see earlier) where there is a tour and wine tasting, and later a stop at Wheatland Plantation; a buffet lunch is available. With luck you will see bald eagles and many varieties of water birds. Cruises operate daily (except

Monday) from May to October, leaving at 10 am, returning 5 pm. The cost is $18.50 for adults, $9.25 for children.

Hungry? *Ferebee's* (☎ 804-443-5715), at the corner of Church Lane and Price St, has large servings of delicious home-style food. A real gem is *Lowery's Seafood* (☎ 804-443-5715), at the intersection of Hwy 17 and Hwy 360, where you can sample soft-shell crabs (in season). They must have kids as they try hard to entertain the lil' darlins.

Urbanna

This historic port town is well worth visiting, if only to wander nonchalantly around the wharves where the watermen will be busy unloading their daily catch. It advertises itself as Virginia's 'most beautiful waterfront community' and we'd agree it comes close.

About half a mile outside of town via County Rds 602 and 615 is the 66-acre **Hewick Plantation**. The manor house (☎ 804-758-4214) was built in 1678 by Christopher Robinson, a member of the Houses of Burgesses and the King's Council. The plantation includes a family cemetery and archaeological dig. It is open daily March to November from 10 am to 4 pm, and there is a nominal entry fee.

In Urbanna, the *Bethpage Camp Resort* (☎ 804-758-4349), a campground well suited to RVs, has full hook-ups at $19.50 for two. There are also some great B&Bs: Close to Hewick is *On the Plantation* (☎ 804-758-4214), offering antique-furnished rooms with private baths and fireplaces; and in Urbanna are *Atherson Hall* (☎ 804-758-2809) and the *Inn at Levelfield* (☎ 804-435-4887).

For a nearby hostel, *Sangraal-by-the-Sea*, see Williamsburg in the next chapter.

Mathews County

This county is the smallest in Virginia, separated from neighboring Gloucester County by North River and Mobjack Bay. Historic sights in the town of Mathews (on Route 14) include the **Courthouse on the Village Green** which has been in continuous use since 1792. North of Mathews, via Routes 223 and 644, is **Gwynn Island** in Chesapeake Bay. There is a small museum which, among other things, tells of the flight of the last royal governor, Lord Dunsmore. To the south of Mathews is the restored New Point Comfort **lighthouse**.

The *New Point Campground* (☎ 804-725-5120), seven miles southeast of the courthouse via Route 14 and County Rd 602, has sites with electricity, water, and sewage hook-ups from $20 to $22. A good B&B is the six-room, moderately priced *Ravenswood Inn* (☎ 804-725-7272), at Todd's Point; and a comfortable motel is the 40-bed *The Islander* (☎ 804-725-2151), on Gwynn Island, with swimming pool, tennis courts, and a beach.

West Point

West Point is a junction town where rivers (the Pamunkey, Mattaponi, and York) and roads (Routes 30 and 33) meet. The **Mattaponi Indian Museum** (tel 804-769-2194) site includes a museum (which houses Pocahontas' necklace) and a learning trail. There you can attend lectures, visit burial grounds and cemeteries, and learn about traditional medicines, dances, pottery, songs, and religion. It is open daily from 10 am to 5 pm by appointment; there's an admission fee. The Mattaponi tribe occasionally has dances that are open to the public. Call the Tribal Office (☎ 804-769-2229) for dates and sites.

Colonial Virginia (Historic Triangle)

The pearl of already 'chronically historic' Virginia is the Historic Triangle on the peninsula between the York and James rivers. It consists of Williamsburg, a recreated 18th century American city; Jamestown Island, the site of the first English settlement in North America; Yorktown, where the closing stages of the Revolutionary War were enacted; and the wealthy tobacco plantations to the north of and along the south banks of the James River. Williamsburg is a must if you have limited time to visit (it is the US's biggest historic tourist attraction), but all of these locales are truly rewarding.

There is more to the Triangle than history. World-class theme parks like Busch Gardens and Water Country USA, and a number of factory outlet shopping malls (all of which surpass historical sites in visitor numbers), ensure a blend of activities for families.

HIGHLIGHTS

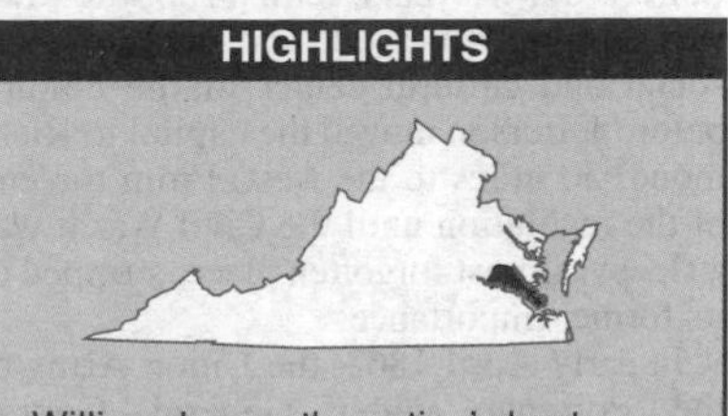

- Williamsburg – the nation's best preserved colonial city
- Jamestown Settlement, site of the state's first English occupation, a fascinating walk/drive through history
- Yorktown – a picturesque town in the heart of the last major battlefield of the Revolutionary War
- Plantation Country where the stately homes are replete with history
- World-famous theme parks, Busch Gardens and Water Country USA – something for the kids to shout about

WILLIAMSBURG

These days Williamsburg (population 11,500) is a major tourist center, because of the authenticity of its many buildings and numerous historic associations. Some visitors, hardened by travel in 'rough' parts of the world, may find the overall treatment 'syrupy' and soon hanker for other parts of the state that are less infested with tourists bedecked with Patriot Passes, raucous school groups, blasé interpretative staff, and an almost oppressive sense of organization.

But if you want to experience, albeit for a short time, the Colonial beginnings of the earth's most powerful nation, then you have to visit. It does, after all, represent the world's most authentic historic 'theme park.'

History

Here we go again! The area was first settled in 1632 as Middle Plantation. As early as 1676 the rebel Nathaniel Bacon and his followers held a convention here, and a year later, after Bacon had burned the statehouse at Jamestown, the General Assembly met in this town for the first time (see the aside on Bacon's Rebellion). Because the site, six miles inland, was strategically superior to Jamestown (the colony's first capital) it was nominated colonial capital in 1699. Later, it was renamed Williamsburg after the reigning King of England, William of Orange.

The town site was carefully laid out by Royal Governor Francis Nicholson, ensuring that there were public greens and a flourishing mercantile center. Half-acre lots were given to householders for the raising of livestock and growing vegetables.

The Governor's Palace, completed in 1720, was the residence of royal governors from 1714 until 1775 (when Lord Dunmore was forced to flee). It then housed the

Commonwealth of Virginia's first two governors, Patrick Henry and Thomas Jefferson, during the first years of the Revolution. So for 81 years, until 1780, the town was Virginia's capital, and definitely the social and cultural center of the colony, before Jefferson moved the capital to Richmond, 50 miles to the west. From the end of the revolution until the Civil War it was a sleepy, almost forgotten place, stripped of its former importance.

In early April 1862, the Union Army of the Potomac under General George McClellan commenced its Peninsula Campaign, then to be the 'last' advance on Richmond. McClellan's army, after besieging Yorktown, ran into a Confederate rearguard near old Williamsburg. After a battle near a line of fieldworks near the city, which did nothing more than produce 2200 Union casualties, Williamsburg fell on May 5.

The city's modern history has much to do with its preservation as a historic district. In the mid-1920s, WAR Goodwin, the local priest at Bruton Parish Church, saw the potential to restore the collection of 18th century buildings. He had an antipathy towards motor vehicles, seeing them as the bane of American towns. Ironically, he approached Henry Ford for funds but was given the cold shoulder. John D Rockefeller, inspired by Goodwin's vision, contributed some $70 million to the restoration program over the years. He and his wife Abby Aldrich even moved into 18th century Bassett Hall in the mid-1930s so that they could see how their legacy was being spent. He established an endowment so that restoration would continue long after he died (in 1960).

Orientation

Roughly, the Williamsburg Historic Area is bounded by Lafayette St on the north, Waller St on the east, Francis St in the south, and Henry St in the west. Just outside of this quadrangle is the College of William and Mary, in a 'V' created by Richmond and Jamestown Rds, and the DeWitt Wallace Gallery and the Abby Aldrich Rockefeller Folk Art Center.

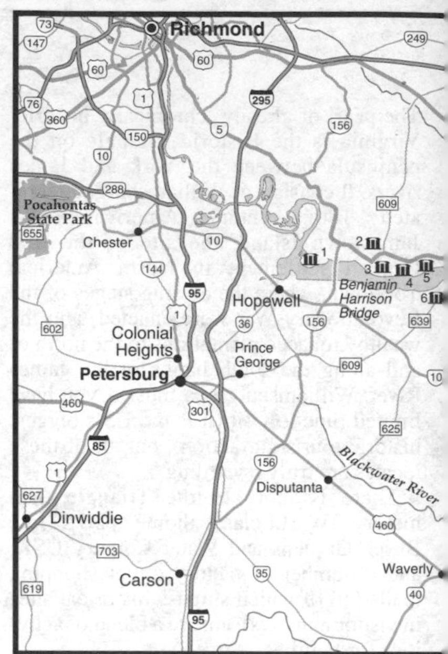

The Colonial Parkway passes roughly north-south through the center of the city (via a tunnel) as does Hwy 60 east-west. Route 5 gives access to the James River plantations to the west, and I-64 passes to the east.

The best way to see this area is on foot or by bicycle.

Information

Tourist Offices The main visitors center is to the north of the Historic District in the 'V' formed by Route 132 and the Colonial Parkway. There is also an information station at Merchants Square, at the west end of Duke of Gloucester St.

The Williamsburg Area Convention and Visitors Bureau (☎ 757-253-0192, 800-368-6511), PO Box 3585, 201 Penniman Rd, Williamsburg, VA 23187, has general info.

The Colonial Williamsburg Tourist Visitors Center (☎ 800-447-8679), Box 1776, Williamsburg, VA 23187, is one mile northeast of the train station on Route 132

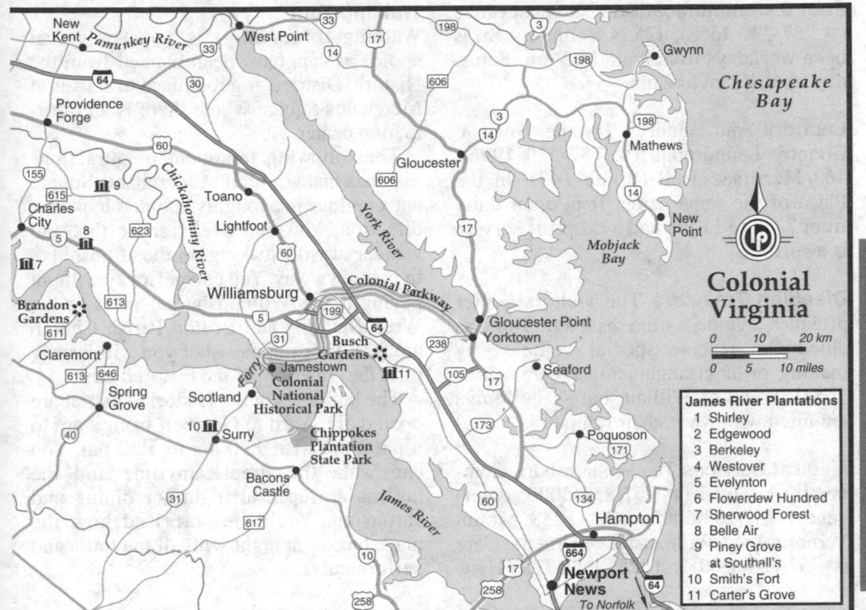

(Exit 238 off I-64). Upstairs they sell tickets to Colonial Williamsburg, and downstairs the Virginia Attractions desk covers the rest of the state and has info on prices and discounts for all Virginia's attractions. The center is open daily from 8:30 am to 6 pm.

Free publications that may be of use include the *Colonial Guide*, the *Williamsburg Magazine*, *Williamsburg Great Entertainer*, and *Colonial Williamsburg Visitor's Companion*. The Internet site, 'Williamsburg On-line,' is worth checking out.

Tickets The first thing you have to do on getting to Williamsburg is buy a ticket. These can be purchased from the main visitors center off the Colonial Parkway or from the smaller office in Merchants Square. With your ticket, you get the *Visitor's Companion*, which has listings of special exhibitions and outdoor performances such as the midday cannon firing. The ticket gives you access to the free shuttle bus, which stops around the Historic District (you'll want to use this shuttle, as parking is abysmal in the area). There are three levels of pass (all include an introductory guided tour):

Basic Ticket – This costs $25 (children $17) and is valid for one day only. It allows entry into everything except the Winthrop Rockefeller Archaeology Museum, Bassett Hall, Carter's Grove Plantation, the Abby Aldrich Rockefeller Folk Art Center, and the DeWitt Wallace Decorative Arts Gallery.

Basic Plus Ticket – This two-day pass is $29 for adults and $17 for children. It gets you into everything in the Historic District, the museums (except Bassett Hall), and Carter's Grove.

Patriot's Pass – This unlimited pass, valid for one year, gets you into everything in Williamsburg, including the Other Half tour. It is $33 for adults, $19 for children, and entitles holders to a 50% discount on evening events.

Museums Ticket – This allows entry to the Folk Art Center, DeWitt Wallace Gallery, and Bassett Hall; the cost is $10 for adults, $6.50 for children.

Post & Communications The post office (☎ 757-229-4668), 425 N Boundary St, is open weekdays from 8 am to 5 pm, Saturday from 10 am to 2 pm.

Laundry And laundry? Try the Town & Country Laundromat (☎ 757-229-4996), 463 Merrimac Trail (Route 143), in the Plaza of the same name. It is open daily from 7 am to 11 pm and a drop-off service is available.

Disabled Travelers The visitors center provides a guide for the disabled. The disabled can reserve special vehicles by making prior arrangements (☎ 757-220-7644). Some of Williamsburg's buildings are fitted with wheelchair ramps.

Medical Services The Williamsburg Community Hospital (☎ 757-253-6000, emergency: 757-253-6005) is at 1238 Mount Vernon Ave. Williamsburg Urgent Care (☎ 757-220-8300) is at 5251 John Tyler Hwy.

Walking Tour

Walking (or cycling) is your only real choice as cars have been banned from the Historic District. A good place to start is at Merchants Square where there is an information center.

The following treatment of attractions assumes that you start at Merchants Square and continue in a roughly counterclockwise direction. You may well ignore this and wander at will, soaking up the atmosphere in your own way. You can get away without paying to see Williamsburg – entry to the Wren Building and Bruton Parish Church are free, for example – but you will largely miss the 'interior' of the restored city.

The buildings in the Historic District are open daily, April to October, from 9 am to 6 pm, otherwise 9:30 am to 5:30 pm. You can walk the streets anytime and the taverns are open at night for dining and carousing. You'll be surprised how the place buzzes at night with all the tours and performances.

Bacon's Rebellion

A hundred years before the American Revolution, a Virginian named Nathaniel Bacon led a rebellion that many see as a forerunner to the independence movement.

In the years leading up to the rebellion, Virginia's colonial government was controlled by a privileged few who levied intolerable export duties. The right to vote was determined by a property qualification. White farmers, ignored as King Charles II doled out generous land grants to his cronies, settled Virginia's western frontier, where they were not welcomed by Indians. The colony's governor, Sir William Berkeley, demonstrated his indifference to the fears of these settlers by refusing to dispatch soldiers to counter Indian attacks.

Bacon, a plantation owner and democratic member of the Governor's Council, had arrived in the colony in 1673. He assembled his ragtag army of 300 in early 1776, when they fought the Indians on the frontier. The defeat of the Indians was inspirational to the whole colony, and Bacon's popularity was such that he followed up by marching his militia on Jamestown, the colony's capital, and occupying it. As a result, Berkeley was forced to dissolve the Virginia Assembly and order a new election. Bacon, initially arrested, was released on parole and then elected to the House of Burgesses.

Against Berkeley's orders, Bacon marched against the Indians once more. Berkeley raised a force against him, but Bacon marched on Jamestown nonetheless and in September he captured and torched it. Just a month later, however – as his militia marched to meet Berkeley's forces – Bacon died of malaria and his rebellion collapsed.

With no popular leader to oppose him, Berkeley regained power. His revenge was swift and he executed 23 of the rebels, an act which drew this remark from the king: 'That old fool has hanged more men in the naked country than I have done for the murder of my father.' Charles recalled the governor, but Berkeley died before he suffered the king's wrath. ■

College of William & Mary

The College of William and Mary is the second oldest college in the US, chartered in 1693 (the oldest is Harvard). Some famous students were Jefferson, Monroe, and Tyler.

The **Sir Christopher Wren Building**, at the west end of Duke of Gloucester St, is purported to be the oldest academic building in continuous use in America. Although it echoes Wren's style, and is similar to buildings in England, the architect never visited America.

Also in the College of William and Mary is the **Muscarelle Museum of Art** (☎ 757-221-2703), a fine arts museum with a permanent collection featuring European and American old master paintings, colonial Virginia portraits, and contemporary works (eg, the 'world's first solar painting' by artist Gene Davis). It is open year round on weekdays from 10 am to 4:45 pm, weekends from noon to 4 pm; admission is free.

Public Hospital & DeWitt Wallace Decorative Arts Gallery

At the junction of S Henry St (Route 132) and Francis St is the public hospital of 1773 and the modern (1985) structure that houses the DeWitt Wallace Decorative Arts Gallery. The hospital is a reconstructed insane asylum, the first in North America (isn't Williamsburg just full of firsts and seconds!), and serves as the lobby for the underground gallery. It includes reconstructions of the wretched wire cages in which some of the mental patients were locked.

The gallery is a gem and has a fine collection of furniture, ceramics, and textiles dating from the 17th to 19th centuries. One treasure is the portrait of Washington by Charles Willson Peale, and there are 150 other masterworks. The gallery (☎ 757-220-7724) is open daily from 10 am to 6 pm.

Abby Aldrich Rockefeller Folk Art Center

This is another conventional museum built with the funds of a public benefactor, in this case Rockefeller's wife, Abby. Seen as one of the country's finest collections of folk art, it includes household implements, bric-a-brac, children's toys, paintings and sculpture, and special exhibitions, like 'Folk Art in American Life' and 'Meet the Makers.'

The entrance is off S England St, opposite the entrance to Williamsburg Lodge. The center (☎ 757-220-7670) is open daily from 10 am to 8 pm.

Magazine & Guardhouse

At the northwest end of S England St (on the south side of Duke of Gloucester St) in Market Square is the octagonal 1715 magazine, used to store guns and ammunition. It was kept busy – first by the British, then by troops of the Continental Army, and later by Confederate soldiers during the Civil War. It now houses 18th century arms and ammunition.

Near the magazine is the guardhouse where troops were stationed to protect the magazine. Inside is the replica fire engine (1750) which makes it out on Williamsburg's streets in summer. The magazine and guardhouse are on the south side of Market Square, where there was once a regular produce market and occasional slave auctions.

The Capitol

At the east end of Duke of Gloucester St is the imposing Capitol, the 1945 reconstruction of the original 1705 building, which burned down in 1747. The building, with its 'H' shape, consists of an open-air arcade joining two wings, both with ornate interiors. The **Houses of Burgesses** – the elected house of the colonial government – occupied the east wing and the **General Court**, where felons were tried, was in the west wing.

In the House of Burgesses, a guide explains the evolution of English democracy from its parliamentary beginnings (when it was dominated by the landed gentry) to the pre-Revolutionary deliberations seen as the seeds of rebellion.

The justices of the General Court, all appointed by the King, acted as a second

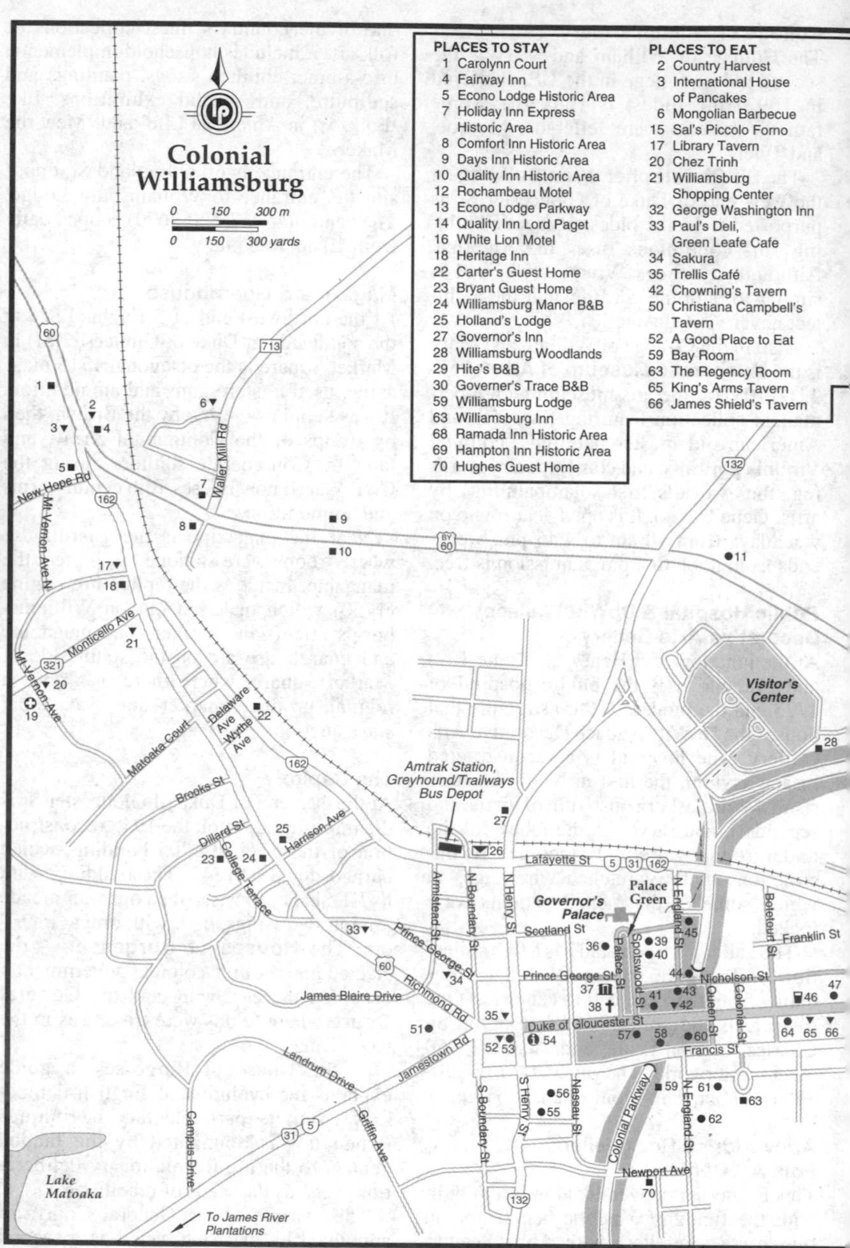
Colonial Williamsburg
0 150 300 m
0 150 300 yards
PLACES TO STAY
1 Carolynn Court
4 Fairway Inn
5 Econo Lodge Historic Area
7 Holiday Inn Express Historic Area
8 Comfort Inn Historic Area
9 Days Inn Historic Area
10 Quality Inn Historic Area
12 Rochambeau Motel
13 Econo Lodge Parkway
14 Quality Inn Lord Paget
16 White Lion Motel
18 Heritage Inn
22 Carter's Guest Home
23 Bryant Guest Home
24 Williamsburg Manor B&B
25 Holland's Lodge
27 Governor's Inn
28 Williamsburg Woodlands
29 Hite's B&B
30 Governer's Trace B&B
59 Williamsburg Lodge
63 Williamsburg Inn
68 Ramada Inn Historic Area
69 Hampton Inn Historic Area
70 Hughes Guest Home
PLACES TO EAT
2 Country Harvest
3 International House of Pancakes
6 Mongolian Barbecue
15 Sal's Piccolo Forno
17 Library Tavern
20 Chez Trinh
21 Williamsburg Shopping Center
32 George Washington Inn
33 Paul's Deli, Green Leafe Cafe
34 Sakura
35 Trellis Café
42 Chowning's Tavern
50 Christiana Campbell's Tavern
52 A Good Place to Eat
59 Bay Room
63 The Regency Room
65 King's Arms Tavern
66 James Shield's Tavern
Visitor's Center
Amtrak Station, Greyhound/Trailways Bus Depot
Governor's Palace
Palace Green
Lake Matoaka
To James River Plantations
New Hope Rd
Mt Vernon Ave N
Mt Vernon Ave
Monticello Ave
Waller Mill Rd
Matoaka Court
Delaware Ave
Wythe Ave
Brooks St
Dillard St
College Terrace
Harrison Ave
Lafayette St
Armistead St
N Boundary St
N Henry St
N England St
Scotland St
Prince George St
Richmond Rd
James Blaire Drive
Duke of Gloucester St
Francis St
Nicholson St
Franklin St
Boteourt St
Colonial St
Queen St
Spotswood St
Palace St
Nassau St
S Henry St
S Boundary St
Landrum Drive
Jamestown Rd
Campus Drive
Griffin Ave
Colonial Parkway
Newport Ave
VIRGINIA

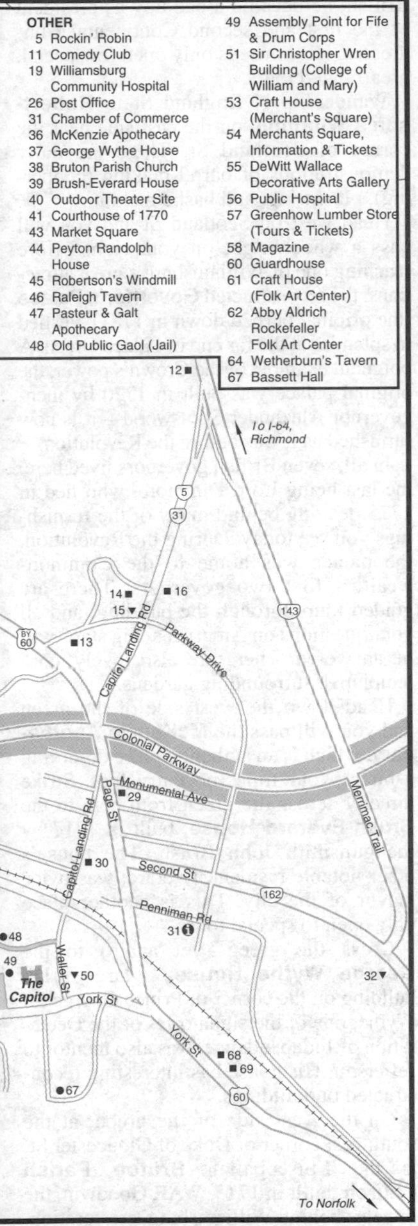

legislature, much in the way that the Senate and House of Representatives do today. The House of Burgesses and justices would meet in a special conference chamber linking the two wings if there was a need to resolve a deadlocked issue. Thirteen of Blackbeard's pirates were tried here and the guide tells of the horrendous punishments that felons received for now seemingly small offenses.

In the evening, the fife-and-drum corps assemble in front of the Capitol before marching down Duke of Gloucester St. (The starting point is marked on the Colonial Williamsburg map.)

If you have time, from the Capitol turn left into Blair St and follow it to Francis St. Turn left on Francis St and follow it until it kinks and becomes Waller St; on the right-hand side is the 18th century **Christiana Campbell's Tavern**, now a popular restaurant. Continue up Waller St and left into Nicholson St to see the **old public jail**, up on the right-hand side about 400 yards along. Then head back to the Capitol.

VIRGINIA

East End, Duke of Gloucester St

Walk west down Duke of Gloucester St, where you will see taverns and shops, some worth a look but others full of tacky souvenirs of suspect historical authenticity.

On the south side of the street, near the corner of Blair St, are a couple of taverns. **Shield's** is a recent reconstruction of an 18th century dwelling and the **King's Arms** works hard to reproduce the fare Jefferson and Washington would have enjoyed.

Across the road is the Pasteur & Galt Apothecary shop. A little ways from that is the **Raleigh Tavern**, where the first meeting of Phi Beta Kappa was said to have been held in the Apollo Room in 1776. The original building burned down in 1859. A bakery, millinery, and silversmith's are nearby.

Across the road, near the southeast corner of Botetourt St, is **Wetherburn's Tavern**, which dates from 1743 and has been meticulously restored to reflect its appearance in 1760. The carefully excavated outbuildings include a kitchen and dairy. Next door is Tarpley's store, on the corner of Botetourt St. To the right of the tavern is a wigmaker.

Cross Botetourt St and on the south side is **Anderson's Blacksmith Shop** where smiths still forge essentials, such as nails and tools, used in the town's reconstruction. Across the road you will find a printer-bookbinder and colonial post office.

Central Williamsburg

This is a fascinating area and attractions are arrayed along Duke of Gloucester St and to the north of it near Palace Green. At the corner of Queen and Duke of Gloucester Sts is the 1766 **Chowning's Tavern**, a reconstructed alehouse that is the most popular dining place these days, probably because of its location. Opposite Chowning's is Market Square and the magazine and guardhouse, mentioned earlier. There is also the disused **Market Square Tavern**, where Thomas Jefferson rented a room when he was a student at the College of William and Mary.

On the north side of Duke of Gloucester St, a few steps from Chowning's, is the site of the original, restored **Courthouse of 1770**. If you did something really bad you ended up in the Capitol and were probably executed. If you did almost nothing, but it incurred the displeasure of the ruling elite, you may have ended up in the stocks here. Today, lots of tourists, who have done little more than exceed the speed limit on the way to Williamsburg, end up in the stocks for a voluntary photo opportunity.

Wander up the delightful and broad **Palace Green**, which runs from Duke of Gloucester St to the Governor's Palace; there are a number of interesting places nearby.

Around Palace Green

Head up Palace Green on its east side and take the first right turn onto Nicholson St. On the northeast corner of N England St is the **Peyton Randolph House**, home of a prominent colonist and revolutionary. He was attorney general when the British ruled but later became Speaker of the House of Burgesses. From then on, in the eyes of the British, he became a bad boy as president of the first and second Continental Congresses. His house is only open for special, prearranged tours.

Wander up N England St to **Robertson's Windmill**, on the east side near the corner of Scotland St. There are daily demonstrations of barrel-making (coopering), pit sawing, and basketmaking.

Head west on Scotland St and you will pass a wheelwright on your right before reaching one of Williamsburg's great attractions, the reconstructed **Governor's Palace** (the original burned down in 1781), nestled in splendor at the far end of Palace Green. A poignant example of the Crown's power, the original palace was built in 1720 by then-governor Alexander Spotswood – it is now furnished as it was before the Revolution.

In all, seven British governors lived here, the last being Lord Dunmore, who fled in 1775, leaving behind many of the furnishings you see today. During the Revolution, the palace was home to the Commonwealth's first two governors. There are guided tours through the building, and all your questions on America's 'big start' will be answered. There are also lovely, contemplative surrounding gardens.

Head down the west side of the green and you will pass the **McKenzie Apothecary**, which is an authentic place deserving a bit of your time (no entry fee). Strike directly across the green from here to the **Brush-Everard House**, built in 1717 by the gunsmith John Brush. The house's other notable resident, Everard, was twice mayor of the city. This is another place only open to special tours.

Cross the green (yet again) to the **George Wythe House**, a large brick building on the corner of Prince George St. Wythe, one of the signatories of the Declaration of Independence, was also mentor to Jefferson. His house has interesting reconstructed outbuildings.

On the west side of the green, at the southwest corner of Duke of Gloucester St, is the Episcopalian **Bruton Parish Church**, built in 1715. WAR Goodwin, the impetus behind Williamsburg's restoration,

Kids, the History Lesson Is Over

If you've already taken the kids to Busch Gardens and they still need to be entertained there are other possibilities. America's Railroads (☎ 757-220-8725), in the Village Shops at Kingsmill, has some 30 model trains operating on the tracks at any one time; admission is $5 for adults, $2.50 for kids under 11. Family Fun Land (☎ 757-220-1400), at 801 Merrimac Trail in James York Plaza, is free to enter, but you pay for the activities and rides. Go Karts Plus (☎ 757-564-7600), on Richmond Rd northwest of the Williamsburg Pottery, has a Kiddie Land with Space Train, Super Playport, and battery-powered mini-cars; admission is free and rides cost from one to three tickets (tickets are $1.25 each).

In York River State Park there are two-hour guided and interpreted canoe rides every Saturday from 8:30 to 10:30 am and Sunday from 4 to 6 pm. The cost is $5 for adults, $2 for children under 12 (the minimum age is three) and reservations are recommended.

Afterwards, the kids probably deserve a dash of Ben & Jerry's Vermont natural ice cream and yogurt – there are two locations: 3044 Richmond Rd (☎ 757-565-3800) and 7097 Pocahontas Trail (☎ 757-253-0180). ■

preached here. Entry is free (donations are appreciated) and the church is open Monday to Saturday from 9 am to 5 pm, Sunday noon to 5 pm.

From here return to Merchants Square; chances are that if you visited all of these places you will have been on the go all day.

Organized Tours

The oldest tour company in Williamsburg is Interpre-Tours (☎ 757-785-2010, 800-486-9624), which specializes in personal tours. Lanthorn Tours (☎ 757-220-7645) leads night walks that visit selected trade shops from 8:30 pm (get tickets from the visitors center or Greenhow Store; it costs $10, or $5 with a Patriot Pass).

One of the most interesting tours is the 'Other Half,' conducted daily, March to September, at 10 am and 1 pm. This tour tells of the experience of African Americans and Africans; a separate ticket is required. Also available from Greenhow Store are carriage and wagon rides, weather permitting.

The 'Ghosts of Williamsburg' candlelight tour by Maximum Guided Tours (☎ 757-565-4821) takes place nightly at 8 pm and is extremely popular. The cost of the 90-minute tour is $6 per person (children under six free). Maximum's (☎ 757-220-2487) 'Pirates, Patriots & Punnery' tour, at 7:30 pm nightly, is $5 per person.

There are hour-long guided walks of the Historic District which depart from Greenhow Store, daily from 9 am to 5 pm; reserve on the day of the tour. Tours are free if you have purchased a pass.

Special Events

Williamsburg is one big year-round historical festival, but there are plenty of other celebrations. Major festivals and events include:

- Military through the Ages (mid-March)
- President John Tyler's Birthday at Sherwood Forest (March 29)
- Garden Week (late April)
- Jamestown Landing Day & Jamestown Weekend (mid-May)
- Civil War Weekend (late May)
- Virginia Indian Heritage Festival (mid-June)
- Independence Day (early July)
- Children's Colonial Day Fair (early July)
- First Assembly Day Commemoration (late July)
- General Muster/Publick Times (late August), a revival of 18th century market days
- Yorktown Day & Victory Weekend (mid-October), celebrating the defeat of the British in October 1781
- Williamsburg's Grand Illumination (early December)
- Jamestown Christmas (late December)

Places to Stay

There are nearly 100 places to stay in the immediate Williamsburg area, so a small selection has been made to indicate the range, cost, and services available.

Camping The nearest campground, *Anvil Campground* (☎ 757-526-2300), at 5243 Moreton Rd, is a small place in a rural setting, three miles north of the Colonial Williamsburg information center on Hwy 60. There is a pool, bathhouse, store, and rec room. Sites are $17 for two people, and full hook-ups are $21. There are over 600 sites at the *Jamestown Beach Campsites* (☎ 757-229-7609), on Route 31 (take Exit 242A off I-64, then drive 5.3 miles west on Route 199), very close to the settlement and Colonial National Historic Park. A site is from $13.50 to $20.50 for two people; electric/water hook-ups are $5 extra.

Near the Williamsburg Pottery in Lightfoot, there are four campgrounds near Exit 234 off I-64. The cheapest is *Kin Kaid Campground* (☎ 757-565-2010), at 559 E Rochambeau Drive, which has sites from $10 to $12 for four persons, electricity $1 extra. The *Best Holiday Trav-l Park Fair Oaks Family Campground* (☎ 757-565-2101), at 901 Lightfoot Rd, has sites from $13 to $16.50 for four (electricity and water are $2 extra); it has a pool, playground, fitness trail, and rec room. *Colonial Campgrounds* (☎ 757-565-2734), at 4000 Newman Rd, has sites for four from $16.50 to $20.

More expensive is the *Williamsburg KOA* (☎ 757-565-2907), at 5210 Newman Rd; it has all the expected facilities and more, even cable TV hook-ups – hardly roughing it! Off season rates for four are from $22 to $30, otherwise May to September it is $26 to $33.

Hostels The *Sangraal-by-the Sea Youth Hostel (HI-AYH)* (☎ 804-776-6500) is inconveniently located about 40 miles away near Urbanna. They will transport you to the Saluda and Gloucester bus stations (eight and 10 miles away from the hostel, respectively) during business hours, but the station in Williamsburg is too far away. The cost of a bed for members is $10, nonmembers $14, and there is a day-use fee of $2; breakfast/lunch/dinner are provided for $3/4/6. Ring ahead to reserve, or write PO Box 187, Urbanna, VA 23175.

To get to the hostel from Williamsburg take Hwy 60 to the junction of Route 33. Follow this north and cross the York River near West Point. Continue along this road, past Saluda for 10 miles, towards Deltaville. Turn north onto County Rd 626 for about half a mile to a junction. Head to the right and keep following County Rd 626 for 1.4 miles to the Waken post office. Turn left here and follow County Rd 626 to its end; the hostel is by Hill Creek on the Rappahannock.

Hotels & Motels The Williamsburg Hotel/Motel Association (☎ 757-220-3330, 800-446-9244) will find accommodations for you at no extra charge. The following list progresses roughly from cheaper to more expensive establishments.

As can be expected in a North American tourist destination, Williamsburg has many national chain hotels and motels offering rooms in the budget and middle range. Hostelries owned, managed, or franchised by chains are generally required to maintain certain standards of quality – for an idea of what to expect from the chains, see Accommodations in the Facts for the Visitor chapter. (Many appear on maps in this chapter.)

The *Bassett Motel* (☎ 757-229-5175), at 800 York St (Hwy 60), a mile from the Historic District, has large, clean doubles from $27 in the off season, rising up to $39 in the high season. Costing about the same are the *Fairway Inn* (☎ 757-229-8551), at 1413 Richmond Rd (a good 'cheapie'), and *Carolynn Court* (☎ 757-229-6666), at 1446 Richmond Rd (a clean and comfortable place).

The *White Lion Motel* (☎ 757-229-3931), at 912 Capitol Landing Rd, is close to the Historic District and a lovely place to stay with landscaped gardens, pool, and picnic area. Singles/doubles cost from $30/34 in low season, $44/46 in the high season. Further north on the same road, at No 929, is the *Rochambeau*

Motel (☎ 757-229-2851), also with landscaped grounds (rates are from $28 to $52).

Family Inns of America (☎ 757-565-1900), at 5413 Airport Rd, has a heated pool and is close to the factory outlets to the north of Williamsburg. A room, depending on size, facilities, and season, will cost anywhere from $30 to $120 (low family rates are offered). Another place with low rates is *Heritage Inn* (☎ 757-229-6220), at 1324 Richmond Rd, with rooms from $32 to $70.

The *Hampton Inn* (☎ 757-220-3100), at 505 York St, has a heated pool; singles/doubles are $45/49 in low season, $90 to $100 in summer.

Another great little mid-range place is the *Courtyard by Marriott* (☎ 757-221-0700), at 470 McLaws Circle (2.5 miles east of the old town on Hwy 60E). It has a breakfast cafe with full buffet (6 am to noon); doubles are from $59 to $69 in low season, $99 in summer.

The luxurious country club–style *Kingsmill Resort* (☎ 757-253-1703), at 1010 Kingsmill Rd, is adjacent to Busch Gardens, two miles from Williamsburg, and has 2900 acres of resort facilities including three golf courses (the Plantation Course was designed by Arnold Palmer and the River Course is host to the annual Anheuser-Busch Classic), tennis courts, indoor and outdoor pools, exercise rooms, four dining rooms, activities for the kids, and a free shuttle to Williamsburg. The budget double rooms are from $120 to $155, and the suites escalate rapidly from $160 to $450.

The *Marriott Hotel-Williamsburg* (☎ 757-220-2500), at 50 Kingsmill Rd, close to Busch Gardens on Hwy 60E, has heated pools, health club, racquetball, tennis, games room, and two restaurants; rates in this very classy establishment are from $79 to $150 for doubles.

There are four hotels operated by the Colonial Williamsburg Foundation (☎ 757-229-1000) – packages are available from $150 person for two nights' lodging, in restored colonial homes, meals, and admission to the area's attractions. All guests in Colonial Williamsburg hotels get a free two-hour guided tour of the Historic District. The *Governor's Inn*, on N Henry St, the least expensive of the foundation's hotels, charges from $60 to $90. *Williamsburg Woodlands*, on Visitor Center Drive, is a good choice for families (with nearby eateries and plenty of activities for the kids); rooms cost from $65 to $117.

The *Williamsburg Lodge*, on S England St, close to the Historic District, charges from $99 for the least expensive doubles in low season, $129 in high season (the rooms in the Tazewell and West wings are much more expensive). Most luxurious of all is the *Williamsburg Inn*, on Francis St. One of the best hotels in the nation (and certainly very expensive), this hotel charges from $235 to $300 for a single or double. The Inn also has a fine restaurant (see Places to Eat in this section) and three international-class golf courses, including the Golden Horseshoe; the latter has attracted many VIPs (golfing presidents) and their guests.

Guest Homes & B&Bs The *Carter's Guest Home* (☎ 757-229-1117), at 903 Lafayette St, has singles/doubles for $25/30; it is run by the redoubtable Mrs Carter. Further down the street, at No 809, the *Lewis Guesthouse* (☎ 757-229-6116) has rooms for $25 for one or two people. Other private guest homes include: the *Hughes Guest Home* (☎ 757-229-3493), at 106 Newport Ave ($50 for two), *Bryant Guest Home* (☎ 757-229-3320), at 702 College Terrace (from $30 to $50 for two), and *Johnson's Guest Home* (☎ 757-229-3909), at 101 Thomas Nelson Lane (from $26 to $30 for two).

There are 20 B&Bs close to Williamsburg. They range in price from *Holland's Lodge* (☎ 757-253-6476), 601 Richmond Rd, at $70 to $80 for two; to the superb *Edgewood Plantation* (☎ 804-829-2962), 4800 John Tyler Memorial Hwy, which charges from $110 to $188; to the 70-year-old *Liberty Rose* (☎ 757-253-1260), 1022 Jamestown Rd, a four-star place touted as Williamsburg's 'most romantic B&B,' with delightfully furnished rooms from $115 to $185.

Three good choices, close to the old city, are *Governor's Trace* (☎ 757-229-7552), at 303 Capitol Landing Rd (from $95 to $115); *Hite's* (☎ 757-229-4814), at 704 Monumental Ave ($80 to $90); and *Williamsburg Manor* (☎ 757-220-8011), at 600 Richmond Rd two blocks from the Historic District, with doubles from $90 to $150.

Places to Eat

Budget & Buffets Those strapped for cash should fuel up at the *Williamsburg Shopping Center* (☎ 757-282-1359), on the corner of Richmond Rd and Monticello Ave.

Don't hesitate to tear the discount coupons out of the many free publications. Many of these have 'all-you-can-eat' and 'free with the purchase of an entree' specials. One of the best buffets can be found at the *Country Harvest* (☎ 757-229-2698), at 1425 Richmond Rd. All the Southern-style favorites and at least eight seafood items are included in the buffet; lunch is $5 (children $3), dinner $10 (children $5). The *George Washington Inn* (☎ 757-220-1410), at 500 Merrimac Trail, is also good for smorgasbords. All meals include Virginia ham and a massive choice at the salad bar. Dinner is $16 for adults, $10 for children; Sunday brunch is $10 and $7.

Paul's Deli Restaurant & Pizza (☎ 757-229-8976), at 761 Scotland St, is a friendly student place with a huge range of 42 subs, stromboli, and burgers for around $5. It is open daily from 11 am to 2 am. It gets the nod from just about everyone who goes there. Next door to Paul's at No 765 is the *Green Leafe Cafe* (☎ 757-220-3405), a good sandwich ($3.50 plus) place. There is folk music on Tuesday evening ($2 cover) and the cafe is open daily from 11 am to 2 am.

Beethoven's Inn (☎ 757-229-7069), at 467 Merrimac Trail, has beautiful subs (around $4.50), homemade soups, and New York-style deli sandwiches; it is open Monday to Saturday from 11 am to 9 pm, Sunday noon to 8 pm.

A mile out of town, the *Old Chickahominy House* (☎ 757-229-4689), at 1211 Jamestown Rd (corner of Routes 199 and 31/5), has a $4.50 lunch special. It is open daily, serving breakfast from 8:30 to 10:15 am, and lunch from 11:30 am to 2:15 pm.

The *Bay Room* (☎ 757-220-7685), on S England St in the Williamsburg Lodge, has a huge buffet on weekend nights and a Sunday brunch (but it isn't cheap). The *Garden Lounge* is the spot for drinks and entertainment.

Breakfast The kids will be happy at *Sammy & Nick's* (☎ 800-841-9100), on Route 60E, one mile from Williamsburg. All the favorites are here – pancakes, eggs, and French toast (all $1.95), and pig in a blanket ($2.45). The cafeteria-style *A Good Place to Eat* (☎ 757-229-4370), at 410 Duke of Gloucester St, is good for breakfast ($3 to $4) or lunch ($2.50 to $6.50). There is an outdoor dining area, which, on a good day, makes it an even better place to eat! If you have risen late, the *National Pancake House* (☎ 757-229-2135) at 800 Capitol Landing Rd serves breakfast until 2 pm. The *International House of Pancakes* (☎ 757-229-9628), at 1412 Richmond Rd, is open 24 hours.

Asian For Vietnamese food try the excellent *Chez Trinh* (☎ 757-253-1888), at 157 Monticello Drive; lunch costs less then $5 and the restaurant is open daily from 11:30 am. The best known of the Chinese places is *Dynasty* (☎ 757-220-8888), at 1621 Richmond Rd (Hwy 60W), 1.5 miles from the Historic District. It features Hunan, Cantonese, Mandarin, and Szechuan styles, vegetarian dishes and a kid's menu; it is open from noon to midnight.

The *Mongolian Barbecue* (☎ 757-220-1118), in the Kingsgate Green shopping center, on Waller Mill Rd, off the Hwy 60 Bypass Rd (near the K-Mart), offers sumptuous banquets in which you select ingredients and sauces; lunch is $5, dinner $7 (desserts and salads are included in the price). The *Sakura* (☎ 757-253-1233), at 601 Prince George St, is a Japanese steak and seafood place with teppanyaki tables; lunch is $5.50 and a dinner for two is $27.

Italian *Marino's* (☎ 757-253-1844), at 1338 Richmond Rd, opens at 4 pm daily and offers all-you-can-eat spaghetti and salad for $8. *Luigi's* (☎ 757-220-3544), at 1665 Richmond Rd, matches Marino's price for spaghetti and salad and also serves steak dishes; it is open daily from 11 am to 11 pm. The two branches of Sal's, *Sal's Piccolo Forno* (☎ 757-221-0443), at 835 Capitol Landing Rd, and *Sal's the Original* (☎ 757-565-0085), at 2021 Richmond Rd, serve tasty pizza and traditional pasta dishes. Out of town near the Ewell railway station (in the shopping center at 5601 Richmond Hwy) is *Giuseppe's* (☎ 757-565-1977), open for lunch and dinner. All entrees come with soup; main courses range from $5 to $17.

Regional Cuisine West of the Historic District, in Merchants Square, is the upmarket *Trellis Cafe* (☎ 757-229-8610), touted as the 'best restaurant in this part of Virginia' by the *New York Times*. The main chef, Marcel Desualniers, author of a number of cookbooks, has won many awards for his treatments of regional cuisine. Reservations are suggested year round; a memorable fixed price dinner will cost $20.

Chowning's Tavern (☎ 800-447-8679), in the heart of the Historic District at 100 Duke of Gloucester St, is a reconstructed 18th century alehouse. It has a selection of old-fashioned food (eg, stew, Welsh rarebit). It is one of the cheaper options in this part of town, especially if you go after 9 pm and dine on sandwiches. You can also learn to play some of the traditional games on offer and listen to music. Chowning's is open daily from 11 am to 3:30 pm, 4 pm to 1 am. At all four of the Historic District's taverns (see Entertainment, below) dinner costs from $15 to $22; reservations are strongly advised in the high season.

The *Regency Room* (☎ 757-229-2141), in the Williamsburg Inn, 136 E Francis St, is the pinnacle of the town's dining choices and a Mobil five-star winner. The style is classic American (with a French flair) and for the impeccable service and million-dollar atmosphere, lunch is reasonable at $20 to $25, dinner from $50 to $60. After 6 pm you will need to dress for dinner (coat and tie) and a jacket is mandatory if you wish to visit the *Regency Lounge*, where cocktails and a light supper are served.

For those touring the plantations on the north side of the James River there are a couple of places where you can dine in style. At Berkeley the *Coach House Tavern* (☎ 804-829-6003) serves lunchtime sandwiches, salads, and soups; and between Sherwood Forest and Evelynton is the restored Victorian farmhouse *Indian Fields Tavern* (☎ 804-829-5004), where crab cakes, fish and chicken salads, and a host of other dishes are served for lunch or dinner.

Entertainment

Taverns The taverns are a must for most visitors to Williamsburg. They usually serve Colonial-style (English) food, prohibit smoking, accept casual dress, and provide information on a central reservations number (☎ 800-828-3767). Three options in E Duke of Gloucester St are *Chowning's* (at No 100), the *King's Arms* (at No 409), and *James Shield's* (at No 417). Another good one is *Christiana Campbell's Tavern* (George Washington's favorite?), at 120 Waller St.

Theater Every evening there are 18th century plays, dance, and drama (☎ 757-220-7645) performed in the open-air Colonial playhouse (where the first theater in the country once stood), out in the streets, or near or in one of the historic buildings. The accent of the company's performances is definitely English and mostly 18th century in character. Check times in the *Visitor's Companion*.

Music Williamsburg has a couple of rock venues. *Rockin' Robin Restaurant & Lounge* (☎ 757-253-8818), in the Econo

Lodge at 1402 Richmond Rd, has a good selection of music from the 1950s and 1960s. While listening you can have a sandwich or a meal in the restaurant.

The cozy *Library Tavern* (☎ 757-229-1012), at 1330 Richmond Rd, is immensely popular for lunch, dinner, late night specials, or a game of pool; it is open daily from 11 am to 2 am.

JB's Lounge (☎ 757-220-2250), in the Fort Magruder Inn at 6945 Pocahontas Trail (Hwy 60E), has live music in the evenings most nights. The *Copper Top Lounge* (☎ 757-565-2600), in the Holiday Inn Patriot at 3032 Richmond St, also has live entertainment on some evenings.

The *Comedy Club* (☎ 757-220-1776), in the Holiday Inn 1776, Hwy 60 Bypass Rd, has shows Wednesday through Friday and Sunday at 9:30 pm, and twice on Saturday, at 8 and 11 pm.

The *Old Dominion Opry* (☎ 757-564-0200, 800-282-6779), at 3012 Richmond Rd (Hwy 60W), is a country and western show that features visiting artists in a two-hour show. It is open mid-January to December, Monday to Saturday and shows commence at 8 pm. Hand-clappers will love it, as it is a hand-clapping sort of show. Admission is $15 for adults, $7 for children from six to 12.

Things to Buy

There is plenty of shopping in and around Williamsburg. The Berkeley Commons Outlet Center (☎ 757-565-0702), at 5711 Richmond Rd, has more than 50 top designer outlet stores, and its Book Cellar (☎ 757-565-6212) has over 50,000 books in stock.

The Williamsburg Outlet Mall (☎ 757-565-3378), on Hwy 60 (Exit 234 off I-64), has over 60 outlets specializing in clothing and gifts for all ages; the shops are open Monday to Saturday from 9 am to 9 pm and Sunday from 9 am to 6 pm.

The Williamsburg Pottery Factory (☎ 757-564-3326), five miles northwest of Williamsburg on Hwy 60, has 32 buildings spread over 200 acres. It offers bargains from all over the world as well as china and salt glaze pottery produced on site. Some three to four million people visit the pottery annually – compare this to the one million tickets sold each year for Colonial Williamsburg. It is open from 8 am to dusk.

Merchants Square, nestled between the College of William and Mary and the Historic District, is a collection of 40 distinctive specialty shops (and restaurants) which sell everything from hand-stitched quilts to Christmas decorations. There are nine restored or reconstructed stores in Colonial Williamsburg where you can buy reproductions of 18th century wares. There are two Craft Houses run by the Colonial Williamsburg Foundation – one is in Merchants Square and the other near the Folk Art Center; they sell reproductions of colonial furnishings and many other items.

For souvenirs such as caps and T-shirts emblazoned with 'Williamsburg,' go to Souvenirs 'N' Stuff, at 1505B Richmond Rd, in the middle of Jefferson Walk; or Everything Williamsburg (☎ 757-221-8880), at 427 Prince George St.

Getting There & Away

Air The nearest airport of note is Norfolk International Airport (☎ 757-857-3351) because it has the most incoming flights. An airport shuttle (☎ 757-587-6958) from there to Williamsburg is $14.

The Newport News/Williamsburg International Airport (☎ 757-877-0221) is in Newport News, 14 miles east of Williamsburg. The main service is provided by USAir. A taxi from the airport to Williamsburg costs from $15 to $20, and a shuttle can be anything from $9 to $20. Richmond International Airport (☎ 804-226-3052) is 45 miles west and reached by I-64.

Bus Williamsburg is the only site in the Historic Triangle easily reached by public transport. The Greyhound/Trailways depot (☎ 767-229-1460) is in the Transportation Center on the corner of Lafayette and N Boundary Sts. The ticket office is open weekdays from 7:30 am to 5:30 pm, and weekends from 7:30 am to 3 pm. Service to Richmond costs $9 (one hour); to Washington, DC, $28 (four hours); and to Norfolk $12 (two hours). There are about seven daily trips from Richmond to Norfolk, and these pass through Williamsburg.

Train The Amtrak station (☎ 757-229-8750, 800-872-7245) is at 408 N Boundary St (the Transportation Center). It is open Friday to Monday from 7:15 am to 9:30 pm, Tuesday to Wednesday from 7:15 am to 2:45 pm, and Thursday from 7:15 am to 3:45 pm.

Costs (and travel times) are: Virginia Beach $13 (two hours), Richmond $9 (1.5 hours), Washington, DC, $29 (3.5 hours), and New York City $82 (seven hours).

Car I-64, connecting Hampton Roads with Richmond (51 miles away), almost passes through Williamsburg; to get to the visitors center and the Historic District the best exit is No 238. The Historic Triangle – Colonial Williamsburg, Yorktown (to the southeast), and Jamestown (to the southwest) – are linked by the scenic Colonial Parkway.

West of Williamsburg, Hwy 60 is known as Richmond Rd (and leads to the capital); Route 5 passes the James River plantations.

Ferry Daily ferry service (☎ 757-294-3354, 800-823-3779) crosses the James River from Jamestown to Scotland. The ferry operates 24 hours, and the trip takes 15 minutes across. Fare is $4 for cars, pickups, and campers (with a trailer, up to $8) one way.

Getting Around

Bus The easiest way to get around Williamsburg is with the James City County Transit (JCCT, ☎ 757-220-1621). The service along Hwy 60 goes from the Historic District to Williamsburg Pottery and Busch Gardens. Jamestown and York are not served by JCCT from here. JCCT operates Monday to Saturday, from 6:15 am to 6:20 pm. The cost is $1 plus 25¢ per zone change, and exact change is needed. If you have a ticket for Colonial Williamsburg, use their shuttle bus to get around the Historic District.

Taxi The local taxicab service is Colonial Cab (☎ 757-565-1240).

Bicycle This is a good option for getting around the Historic Triangle, especially along the Colonial Parkway to Jamestown or Yorktown. There are a couple of places where you can rent bikes. Bikes Unlimited (☎ 757-229-4620) is open weekdays from 9 am to 7 pm, Saturday 9 am to 5 pm, and Sunday noon to 4 pm; they rent bikes for $10 per day ($5 deposit). Also recommended is Bikesmith (☎ 757-229-9858). The Williamsburg Lodge has bikes for guests.

AROUND WILLIAMSBURG

Carter's Grove

This plantation (☎ 757-220-7645) is six miles east of Williamsburg on Hwy 60 (see the Colonial Virginia map). The site has been settled since 1619, when it was called Wolstenholme Towne, and the mansion was built in 1755 by Carter Burwell, grandson of 'King' Carter, the powerful landowner. The interior of the mansion has intricate carvings and exquisite wood paneling, but the building has undergone many facelifts.

Recently the plantation has had an extensive archaeological dig that endeavors to discover more of the plantation's 400-year history, and the **Winthrop Rockefeller Archaeological Museum** (built into a hillside) is a good place to see the results. There are also reconstructed 18th century slave dwellings where guides in costume tell of the role of slaves on the plantations.

The plantation is open daily from 9 am to 5 pm (October to December from 9 am to 4 pm). The archaeological museum and slave quarters are open daily from 9 am to 5 pm. The cost of entry to Carter's Grove is $13 for adults, $8 for children, but it is free if you have a Basic Plus or Patriot's Pass.

The seven-mile, one-way **Carter's Grove country road** leads back through scenic woods to S England St in Williamsburg; this road is open for cyclists daily from 8 am to 4 pm (November to December 8:30 am to 3 pm). Another means of

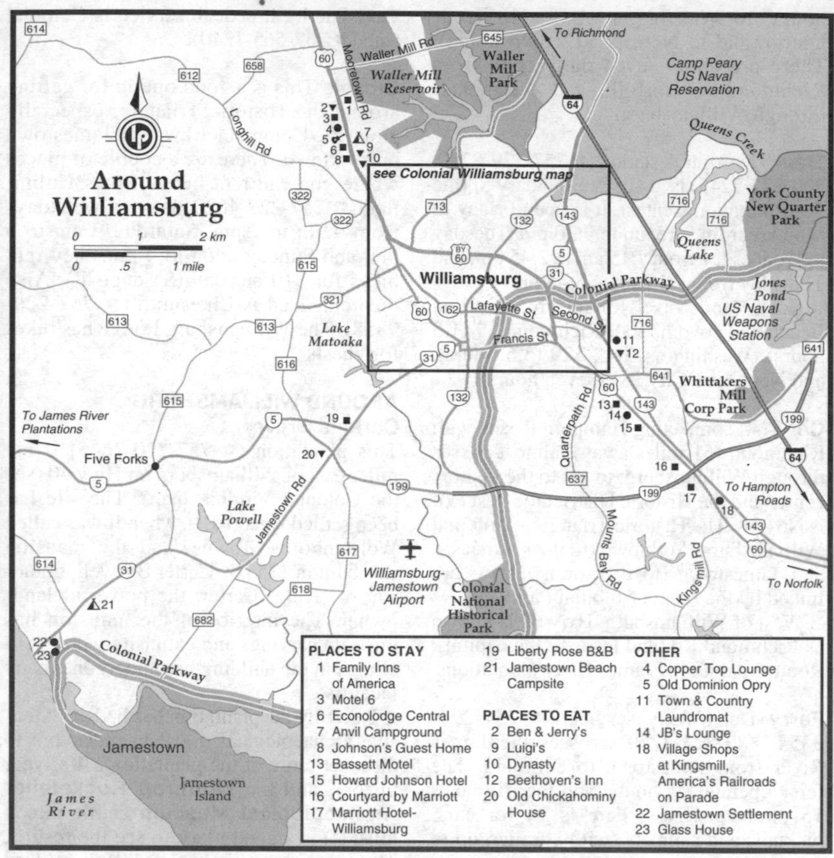

getting there is with Williamsburg Limousine (☎ 757-877-0279), which charges $8 per person from the Historic District.

Busch Gardens

The clientele here has come for an adrenaline rush on one of the 30 or so rides or to escape, for a moment, 'another bloody historical site.' The kids have persevered with all that historical stuff, so now it is their turn.

Busch Gardens: The Old Country (☎ 757-253-3350), three miles east of Williamsburg on Hwy 60, is a theme park divided up into European nations. Entrance costs a hefty $29.95 for adults and most children (kids from three to six only cost $22.95 each!); after 5 pm it's $6 cheaper. This fee lets you cross as many national borders as you care to.

Granted, a day at Busch Gardens is nearly as expensive as a year-long Patriot Pass to the Historic Triangle. But the Triangle hasn't got the large flight simulator Questor, the Roman Rapids water adventure, Wild IZZY ride, Battering Ram, the Loch Ness Monster, Drachen Fire, and Big Bad Wolf roller coasters, or the unforgettable 'Escape from Pompeii.'

This theme park is open mid-March to mid-June, daily from 10 am to 7 pm; mid-June to August, Sunday to Friday from 10 am to 10 pm, Saturday 10 am to midnight; September to October, daily from 10 am to 7 pm.

Water Country USA

This is Virginia's largest family water park with slides, rides such as the Amazon and Big Daddy Falls, pools (including a wave pool that has a 13-minute wave period followed by a 10-minute lull), and various shows. It is about three miles east of Williamsburg at 176 Water Country Parkway, just off Route 199, north of I-64. Water Country (☎ 757-229-9300, 800-343-7946) is open daily Memorial Day to Labor Day from 10 am; in May and September it is open some weekends; admission is $21.95 for adults, $15.95 for children from three to six.

JAMESTOWN

This historic site at the western end of the Colonial Parkway existed for a relatively short time in the span of history but it holds an important place in both history and American folklore. The NPS oversees exhibits and visitors centers on Jamestown Island and at Yorktown Battlefield; the state of Virginia operates Jamestown Settlement and the Yorktown Victory Center.

Jamestown was founded in May 1607 when *Discovery*, *Godspeed*, and *Susan Constant* moored in deep waters off the peninsula between the James and York rivers and 104 boys and men disembarked. It was the first permanent English settlement on the continent but was doomed to failure because of starvation, disease, and attacks by Native Americans.

In 1619 the first representative assembly met and Jamestown served as Virginia's capital from then until 1699. When the statehouse had been burned for a fourth time, the settlers accepted that they had chosen a poor site and they moved inland to what is now Williamsburg. At the end of the 19th century all that was left, after the encroachment of nature, was an overgrown churchyard and church tower.

It is almost 400 years since the town was founded, and the original Jamestown is now a collection of ruins, historical markers, visitors centers, and ongoing archaeological 'digs.' Jamestown Rediscovery, an archaeological search by the Association for Preservation of Virginia Antiquities (APVA), is endeavoring to find the site of the original 1607 fort (they now think that they have got it!) and learn more of the lives of the original settlers and their Algonquin neighbors.

Nearby, at the entrance to Jamestown Island, there is a 'living history' settlement, only of partial interest to the keen historian. Accommodations, restaurants, and shops will be found in and around Williamsburg.

Jamestown Island National Historic Site

This site is run by the Colonial National Historic Park – their visitors center (☎ 757-229-1733) screens a poor film but has pretty decent 'living history' tours. On site, there are paintings, models, dioramas, and a collection of interesting 17th century objects unearthed in the many archaeological excavations.

From the visitors center there are paths fanning out into 'James Cittie,' where you will find the only standing structure from the 17th century town, the old **church tower** (dating from the 1640s), part of the original brick church. There are a number of statues and monuments, including statues of Pocahontas and John Smith, the Hunt shrine (dedicated to the first Anglican minister), the memorial cross relating to the bleak 'starving time' (winter 1609-10), and Tercentenary and House of Burgesses monuments.

Near the park entrance there is a reconstructed **glasshouse** where artisans demonstrate 17th century glassblowing techniques; they sell their wares and these make excellent souvenirs.

There are three- and five-mile **loop drives** around the island (which was connected to the mainland by a narrow isthmus at the time of the original settlement); markers and illustrations relate the

Pocahontas

Thanks to the Walt Disney Co, the Historic Triangle now has the ultimate attraction to keep kids amused – the story of Pocahontas – and her appeal may actually inspire them to begin to understand a small aspect of Native American heritage. It is not uncommon to see parents cajoling their preschooler through the Jamestown site with promises such as 'There is a statue of Pocahontas here, can you help us find her?'

The following account of Pocahontas' life is extracted from the narrative by Nancy Elgoff of the staff of Jamestown Settlement.

The real Pocahontas (meaning 'playful one' or 'little wanton'; she was formally called Amonute and Matoaka) was born about 1596, the daughter of the powerful Powhatan, potentate of over 30 Algonquian-speaking tribes in the coastal Virginia region.

Rendition of Pocahontas, from a portrait painted in London by a young Dutch artist, Simon Van de Pass, in 1616

When she was about 11 she met John Smith near the York River in 1607. Fiction probably blends with history in the account of how she saved Smith's life when she 'got his head in her armes, and laid her owne upon his to save him from death.' The following year Pocahontas took food to the settlement at Jamestown in an effort to secure the release of Indian prisoners, and the next year she warned Smith of a plot to take his life.

In 1613 she was kidnapped by one Samuel Argall for ransom. It took her father Powhatan some time to agree to the terms of the ransom and the result was that Pocahontas remained with the English, was converted to Christianity, and baptized with the name of Rebecca. Soon after conversion, in 1614, she was married to the planter John Rolfe, who introduced tobacco as a cash crop in Virginia.

In 1616, Pocahontas, John Rolfe, and their son Thomas traveled to England, in an effort to recruit more colonists for Virginia. While there she was feted. She became ill on the return trip and died at Gravesend in March 1617. (Thomas returned to Virginia in the 1630s.)

Pocahontas now 'lives' as the most famous Native American (more famous even than Sitting Bull or Geronimo) and your knowledge of her life better be up to scratch or your kids will let you know! From now on there are many 400th anniversary events associated with Pocahontas – yes it was about 400 years ago since she was born – so there will be something for the kids to see. There are several interpretations of the way she looked: see the portraits by Mary Ellen Howe (1994), Jean Leon Ferris (c 1921), Robert Matthew Sully (1850s), and the Walt Disney Co (1994). The latter bears no resemblance, with her eyes well removed from her nose, but it is the one kids now recognize! ■

early story. For great views of the James River estuary walk out to Black Point. Get a copy of the free *Loop Drive: Jamestown Island*.

The Jamestown entrance station is open daily in summer from 8:30 am to 5:30 pm, spring and fall from 8:30 am to 5 pm, otherwise 8:30 am to 4:30 pm. The park opens and closes one hour before the visitors center, and entry is $8 per vehicle, $2 for a cyclist or pedestrian. The visitors center is open daily year round from 9 am to 5 pm (to 5:30 in spring and fall, to 6 in summer).

Jamestown Settlement

The Jamestown Settlement (☎ 757-229-1607) has a museum with changing exhibits, reconstructions of the 1607 James Fort, a Native American (Powhatan) village, full scale replicas of the three ships that carried the earliest settlers to Jamestown, and 'living history' demonstrations. It is amazing how many people visit this 'settlement' but do not cross into the original Jamestown to really imbibe history. Advice from many locals is that there is nothing to see on the 'island,' just ruins and swamp – how wrong they are.

The modern 'settlement' is open daily from 9 am to 5 pm; admission is $9 for adults, $4.25 for children under 13. A combination ticket that includes the Yorktown Victory Center costs $12.50 for adults, $6 for children six to 12.

YORKTOWN

This small town, at the east end of the Colonial Parkway some 14 miles northeast of Williamsburg, combines all you want in history and, certainly, in isolation. It is a getaway from 'touristy' Williamsburg.

Founded in 1691, when the General Assembly in Jamestown passed the Port Act, Yorktown became a busy tobacco port. In the early autumn of 1781 the most important battle of the Revolutionary War (where 'The World Turned Upside Down' was played by the surrendering British military band) was enacted here – see the Yorktown Campaign sidebar. From here, on October 19, 1781, Washington reported back to the Continental Congress: 'I have the Honor to inform Congress, that a Reduction of the British Army under the Command of Lord Cornwallis, is most happily affected.'

During the Civil War the town was besieged by Union troops led by General George McClellan from April 5 to May 4, 1862. Before the anticipated barrage commenced, the Confederates had stolen away. (At one stage, an elaborate charade by the Confederates under the command of General John Magruder had convinced McClellan that he was facing a much larger force.) Many of the fortifications from this time, and indeed from the Revolutionary War, remain intact.

Today Yorktown, perched precariously above the York River, basks in the glow of its historical past.

Orientation & Information

Yorktown is at the northeast apex of the Historic Triangle and at the east end of the Colonial Parkway. It is also reached from the Middle Peninsula via the Coleman Memorial Bridge or from Hampton Roads, on Hwy 17.

The Colonial National Historic Park (☎ 757-898-3400), PO Box 210, Yorktown, VA 23960, is open daily in summer from 8:30 am to 6 pm, spring and fall from 8:30 am to 5:30 pm, and in winter from 8:30 am to 5 pm.

The park's visitors center has an intriguing collection of displays and aids which help you understand this last major battle of the Revolutionary War. Included are a 16-minute documentary film, a replica of the quarterdeck of HMS *Charon*, the tent Washington used as his headquarters, a diorama, and a well-constructed electric map. It is open daily from 9 am to 6 pm and provides free pamphlets, including one with a simplified town map.

You can also rent a cassette recorder ($2) for the seven-mile battlefield drive and a 10.2-mile Encampment Route (for Washington and Rochambeau's headquarters); the last tape is rented out at 5 pm. Occasionally you have to get out of your car on the battlefield route to further imbibe the sense of history, such as at the Grand French Battery, Moore House, and at Surrender Field.

For info on the region contact the York County Public Information Office (☎ 757-890-3300), at 224 Ballard St, Yorktown.

Yorktown Victory Center

The Yorktown Victory Center (☎ 757-887-1776) is a flashier version of the NPS's offerings, but it tells essentially the same story. One block from Hwy 17 and just off old Route 238, the museum has a

28-minute film, *The Road to Yorktown*, and lots of Revolutionary War items. The 'living history' exhibits, featuring actors dressed as Continental troops and 18th century farmers, recreate daily life before, during, and after the Revolution.

The center is open daily from 9 am to 5 pm; admission is $3.75 for adults, $1.75 for children under 13. (See Jamestown Settlement for details of combination tickets.)

Other Sites

Three other places in Yorktown proper fall under the aegis of the Colonial National Historical Park: Moore House, the Poor Potter of Yorktown, and the Waterman's Museum. For information on all three, call ☎ 757-898-3400.

Moore House, on Yorktown Battlefield Tour Rd, is the site where the surrender terms were negotiated between the French/American force and the British in October 1781. It is open spring and fall on weekends from 1 to 5 pm, summer daily from 10 am to 5 pm, and entry is free. The Georgian-style **Nelson House**, on Main St at the corner of Nelson St, was the former home of Thomas Nelson, Jr, a signatory to

Victory at Yorktown 1781

The last major battles of the Revolutionary War were fought in and around Yorktown, on the peninsula between the James and York Rivers, during October 1781.

In July 1781 George Washington and French commander Comte de Rochambeau massed their armies and moved towards Sir Henry Clinton's British forces in New York. Washington and Rochambeau had no definite plan of attack; they were counting on the anticipated support of a French fleet under Admiral de Grasse. But then de Grasse informed him that he would only sail with his 3000 troops to Chesapeake Bay, and would leave there before the hurricane season began in October. At the same time, Washington learned that Lord Cornwallis and his 9000 troops had established a British naval depot in Yorktown. Washington left half his force to lock up Clinton in New York and, hoping to pin Cornwallis down with the help of Rochambeau and de Grasse, he began to march the rest of his army to Virginia.

It was the action at sea that made victory at Yorktown possible. De Grasse reached the Chesapeake on August 26 and landed his 3000 troops, where after a few days they joined Americans commanded by Lafayette. The French fleet of Admiral de Barras, equipped with siege artillery, sailed down from Newport, Rhode Island. When the British learned of this move their fleet set sail from New York to intercept. De Grasse engaged the British navy in the **Battle of the Capes** on September 5, allowing de Barras to slip into the Chesapeake. The sea battle was inconclusive but by the 10th the British navy had been forced back to New York. By September 26 the Allied armies were in position, and the French blockade in the Chesapeake prevented any escape by the British by water. The noose could now be tightened around Cornwallis' neck. The siege of **Yorktown** began on October 6.

Washington was overall commander of a force of 20,000 with formidable siege artillery at his disposal. He was opposed by Cornwallis' army, dug in around Yorktown, and a further 1000 troops under Sir Banastre Tarleton across the York River on Gloucester Point. The Continental engineers opened up a parallel opposite the British lines at Yorktown and the artillery pounded the defenses mercilessly. On the 14th, two key British redoubts were stormed at bayonet point, allowing the Continentals to open a second parallel on the night of October 14–15.

Cornwallis attempted to extricate his force to Gloucester Point on the night of October 16–17 but was thwarted by a storm and a shortage of boats. The heaviest cannonade of the war rained down on the British on the 17th and that evening the British petitioned for terms. On the 20th the British prisoners marched out to the 'Surrender Field' and England's part in the Revolutionary War was over. The Continentals had lost about 300 men. Washington returned to the Hudson Highlands and remained there for two more years while peace negotiations dragged on. But independence had been won. ■

the Declaration of Independence. It is open mid-June to mid-August from 10 am to 4:30 pm and entry is free.

The **Poor Potter of Yorktown** is the remains of an 18th century pottery factory, the largest of its type known to have existed in colonial America. It operated from 1720 to 1745 at a time when British mercantile trade laws made such an operation illegal. The pottery is open spring and fall on weekends, daily in summer from 11 am to 4 pm.

The **Watermen's Museum** (☎ 757-877-2641), at 309 Water St, tells of the folk who have for generations worked along the rivers and tributaries of Chesapeake Bay. It is open April to December, Tuesday to Saturday from 10 am to 4 pm, Sunday 1 to 4 pm; entry is $2.50 for adults, 50¢ for children (six to 18).

Other historic buildings in Yorktown include **Grace Church**, on Church St, built in 1697 of native marl (clay, sand, limestone, and fragmented sea shells); **Sessions House** (1693), on Main St, the oldest house in town, used as headquarters by the Union's George McClellan during the Civil War Peninsula campaign; the York County **courthouse**, which maintains records dating from 1633 (open weekdays from 8:30 am to 5 pm); and the reconstructed **Swan Tavern** of 1722, on the corner of Main and Ballard Sts, which is now an antiques shop (the original buildings were destroyed in December 1863 when a Federal powder magazine across the road exploded).

Not quite a historic house is **Cornwallis Cave**, at the foot of the Great Valley, where the British general is said to have sat out the siege while contemplating his escape.

In 1884, over one hundred years after the revolutionary battle, an imposing 98-foot **Victory Monument** with a crowning figure of Liberty was completed overlooking the York River; beneath the 13 female figures, symbolizing the 13 colonies, is the inscription 'One Country, One Constitution, One Destiny.'

Places to Stay & Eat

The *Duke of York Motor Hotel* (☎ 757-898-3232), at 508 E Water St, has bargain rooms with views of the York River – singles/doubles are $45/50 in low season and rise to $69 a double in the high season.

The *Yorktown Motor Lodge* (☎ 757-898-5451), at 8829 George Washington Hwy, three miles south of Yorktown (on Hwy 17), is cheaper, with doubles from $37.

The *Yorktown Pub* (☎ 757-898-8793), on Water St, is an absolute delight and the perfect place to take a break between redoubts and fortifications. They have great daily specials, plenty of beer, and are open daily from 11 am to 2 am. Also on Water St, *Nick's Seafood Pavilion* (☎ 757-887-5269) specializes in interesting treatments of fish and shellfish such as a seafood shish kebab; lunch entrees are from $8 but dinner is far more expensive – $20 and up. Across the road is the *Beach House* (☎ 757-890-2804) for deli sandwiches, salads, and ice cream.

Getting There & Away

There is no cheap way to get to Yorktown without your own car, but there are a number of guided tours. If a group of four gets together, then Williamsburg Limousine (☎ 757-877-0279) is an option: A morning trip to Jamestown is $20 per person, an afternoon trip to Yorktown $18, or a full day trip to both places $38 (including admission fees).

JAMES RIVER PLANTATIONS

Many of the homes of the slaveholding Virginian aristocracy were built along the banks of the James River (see Colonial Virginia map). A plantation tour, from Richmond to Williamsburg along Route 5 (the John Tyler Hwy) is not that long in distance, but if you visit most of the grand plantations and take time out to relax along the way, expect to spend a full day. Block tickets to Shirley, Berkeley, Evelynton, and Sherwood Forest are available from any of these plantations; the cost is $25 for adults. Other plantations, south of the James River, are reached by the Jamestown-Scotland ferry.

Places to Stay & Eat Most people visiting the plantations south of the James will be staying in Williamsburg but there are some good accommodations south of the river, including those in nearby Smithfield (see the Hampton Roads chapter for more details). For traditional southern-style and Virginia dining there is the *Surrey House* (☎ 757-294-3389), in the heart of Surry. Its menu features the state's famous smoked ham, peanut soup, crab cakes, and peanut-raisin pie.

Berkeley Plantation

Berkeley Hundred (☎ 804-829-6018) is southeast of Richmond, just off Route 5 and along Farm Road 633. It has many historical associations and was the place where Thanksgiving was first celebrated in the New World in 1619 (a year before the Pilgrims arrived in New England). President (for a brief period in 1841) William Henry Harrison was born here as was Benjamin Harrison, a signatory to the Declaration of Independence. (William Henry's grandson, another Benjamin Harrison, was elected president 47 years after his grandfather filled the office.)

During the Revolutionary War, in 1781, the plantation was ravaged by British troops led by Benedict Arnold. During the Civil War, in 1862, Union General George McClellan used the buildings as his headquarters and one of his subordinate generals, Daniel Butterfield, composed the famous bugle tune 'Taps,' the 'lights out' tattoo, here. Butterfield's bugler, Oliver W Norton, was the first to sound the haunting tune, also at Berkeley – it was then taken up by both Union and Confederate forces. Another world first was the use of observation balloons, just before the Seven Days Battles around Richmond in 1862. It was here that McClellan was relieved of his command.

Terraced boxwood hedges stretch up from the river to the 1726 brick building, which has a restaurant, where you can dine outside and enjoy the view, and a museum in the basement, where an interesting audiovisual is screened. Another first for the area: The first corn whiskey in America was distilled at Berkeley.

The house is open daily from 9 am to 5 pm, and the grounds open daily at 8 am. Admission to the house and grounds is $8.50 for adults, $7.65 for seniors, and $4 for children; admission to the grounds only is $5 for adults, $2 for children.

Shirley

This plantation (☎ 804-829-5121), at 501 Shirley Plantation Rd in Charles City (just off Route 5), is the oldest plantation in Virginia, dating from the 1660s. The fine brick outbuildings, which form a Queen Anne forecourt and mansion, have been in the hands of one family, the Carters, for over eleven generations. Edward Hill, a Carter relative, was the first to settle here, and Robert E Lee's mother, Anne Hill Carter, was born here. Ever since, it has been the preserve of Virginia's wealthy landed gentry.

Inside the mansion is the famous carved walnut 'hanging' staircase which goes up three stories with no apparent support, original family furniture, rare books, silver, and portraits. Other original structures are the smokehouse, stable, and dovecote.

Shirley (☎ 804-829-5121) is open daily from 9 am to 5 pm, and the last tour is at 4:30 pm. Admission is $7.50 for adults, $6.50 for seniors, $4 for students, and $3.75 for children (six to 12). It is located off Route 5, on a small peninsula jutting out into the James River.

Westover

This plantation epitomizes the efforts of the English/American aristocracy. William Byrd II (1674–1744), a member of both the lower and upper colonial legislatures of Virginia (in Williamsburg at the time), had the plantation house built in 1730, but after it was finished he spent much of his time away from it, seemingly preferring the high life of London.

Unfortunately the mansion (☎ 804-829-2882) is only open during Garden Week in April (or by appointment), but it is worth being there at the right time to see the magnificent interior with its moldings and carvings and the wrought iron gates which Byrd brought out from England, resplendent with their eagles atop the post aeries. The outbuildings and beautiful gardens are open daily from 9 am to 6 pm and admission is $2 for adults, $1.50 for children. To get there take Route 5, then Farm Route 633 to its end.

Evelynton

This plantation, once part of the original Westover Plantation land grant, is named after William Byrd's daughter Evelyn and was believed to have been part of the dowry she never got to use. Since 1847 it has been the home of the Ruffin family, whose patriarch Edmund fired the first shot of the Civil War at Fort Sumter. During the Peninsula Campaign of 1862 many of the buildings were destroyed and the present colonial-style mansion was rebuilt years later. The house is furnished with antiques and the surrounding gardens, known for brilliant displays of flowers, are still lovingly tended by descendants of the Ruffin family.

The plantation (☎ 804-829-5075, 800-473-5075) is open daily from 9 am to 5 pm and admission is $7 for adults, $6 for seniors, and $3.50 for children (from six to 12). There are tours of the house and gardens, and a gift shop. The plantation, at 6701 John Tyler Memorial Hwy (five miles west of the Charles City courthouse), is reached by Route 5.

Sherwood Forest

With neither a Sheriff of Nottingham nor a Robin Hood in sight, Virginia's Sherwood Forest instead celebrates a couple of America's famous sons – the ninth president William Henry Harrison and his successor John Tyler. Built in the 1730s, and still owned by Tyler's direct descendants, the house is today the longest wooden framed structure remaining in America (300 feet). Harrison once owned it and Tyler retired here until his death in 1862. He wished to be buried here but as he died during the Civil War, when the region was occupied by Union troops, he was buried in Richmond's Hollywood Cemetery instead.

The house (☎ 804-829-5377), at 14501 John Tyler Memorial Hwy, is surrounded by immaculate grounds and original outbuildings (with an authentic tobacco barn). The grounds are open daily from 9 am to 5 pm; admission to the grounds is $3 for adults, $1 for children. Entry to the house, open April to December from 9 am to 5 pm, January to March by appointment, is $7.50 for adults, $7 for seniors, $4.50 for students, and children under five are free. To get there take Route 5 through Charles City and New Hope; a sign marks the entrance.

Belle Air Plantation

This frame plantation home dating from 1670 is the only surviving example of its type in the South, a Virginia and national historic landmark. It is furnished with 18th century antiques and includes an old kitchen, smokehouse, and herb garden.

The house (☎ 804-829-2431), at 11800 John Tyler Memorial Hwy near Charles City, is open year round by appointment only (except for the last five days of Garden Week). To get there take Route 5 for five miles east of the Charles City courthouse.

Edgewood Plantation

This plantation, at 4800 John Tyler Memorial Hwy near Charles City, dates from 1849 and is an historic landmark. Particularly beautiful is the Christmas tree display from November 1 to January 1, when women in Victorian garb guide you through the house.

The Gothic-style house (☎ 804-829-2962) is open from February to December, Tuesday to Sunday from 11 am to 5 pm, and admission is $6 for adults, $3 for children (seven to 10). Admission to the Victorian Christmas celebration is $9 for adults, $5 for children.

Piney Grove at Southall's Plantation

Yet another property in James River plantation country, Piney Grove is a rare early

Tidewater log structure and the oldest country store in the area. Also nearby is the 1857 Ladysmith House and a nature trail. Piney Grove (☎ 804-829-2480), 16920 Southall Plantation Lane, is open year round by appointment; contact them for entry fees.

Brandon Gardens

This plantation (☎ 757-866-8486), at 23105 Brandon Rd in Spring Grove, was originally a large land grant to John Martin, companion of Captain John Smith. It is a magnificent example of a James River estate, with superb gardens spanning from the mansion to the river. The gardens are open daily from 9 am to 5:30 pm; you can visit the house by appointment or during Garden Week; admission to the gardens is $5 for adults.

To get there from Williamsburg take the Jamestown-Scotland ferry to Surry County. Then take Route 31 and turn northwest onto Route 10. Follow this into Prince George County and take County Rd 611 north to Brandon Gardens.

Smith's Fort Plantation

This plantation is also reached by the Jamestown-Scotland ferry. It is a brick colonial dwelling on land given by the Indian chief Powhatan to John Rolfe when he married Pocahontas. Included on the site are the ruins of the 'new fort' built by John Smith in 1609.

The plantation (☎ 757-294-3872) is at 217 Smith's Fort Lane on Route 31, halfway between Surry Court House and the Jamestown ferry landing. It is open April to October, Tuesday to Saturday from 10 am to 4 pm, Sunday noon to 4 pm; admission is $4 for adults, $3 for senior citizens, $2 for college students, and $1 for children six to 18.

Bacon's Castle

This is the oldest documented brick house (1665) in English North America and the only surviving high Jacobean structure. It is surrounded by a sophisticated garden, believed to be the oldest on the continent.

The castle (☎ 757-357-5976), 6.5 miles east of Surry Courthouse, off Route 10 on County Rd 617, is open April to October, Tuesday to Saturday from 10 am to 4 pm, Sunday noon to 4 pm; entry is $5 for adults, $3 for senior citizens, $2 for children.

Other Sites South of the James

There is a real potpourri of attractions in this region, making it well worth a visit. The **Chippokes Plantation State Park** (☎ 757-294-3625), on County Rd 633 (off Route 10), includes one of the oldest continuously farmed plantations in America, an 1854 manor house, formal gardens, and a Farm & Forestry museum (in which a rooter and a bull tongue plow take pride of place). It is open Memorial Day to Labor Day, Wednesday to Sunday from 1 to 5 pm. Admission to the mansion is $2 for adults ($1 for children); museum admission is the same. There are bicycles for hire, and a pool is open Memorial Day to Labor Day, Thursday to Sunday from 10 am to 7 pm.

More unusual are **Edward's Virginia Ham Shoppe** (☎ 757-294-5378), at 11381 Rolfe Hwy in Surry, where you can see Virginia hams being made; and, in quite a different category, the **Surry Nuclear Information Center** (☎ 757-357-5410).

There is a combination ticket for sites south of the James River. Included are Smith's Fort Plantation, Bacon's Castle, Chippokes mansion and museum, and the Edwards smokehouse tour, as well as a number of Hopewell attractions; the cost for adults is $17.

Hampton Roads

The extended region of Hampton Roads, from Williamsburg down to Virginia Beach, contains some 1.5 million people. It includes Chesapeake, Hampton, Newport News, Norfolk, Portsmouth, Poquoson, and Suffolk. You will most probably hear locals refer to Norfolk, Portsmouth, and Chesapeake as being on the 'southside' and Newport News and Hampton being on the 'peninsula.'

Hampton Roads is the name of the waterway that is the outlet of the James, Nansmond, and Elizabeth rivers into the Chesapeake Bay and, by proximity, of the land region around that waterway. The area is a bustling maritime area, pocked with military bases, but don't come expecting just a conglomeration of concrete towers, overcrowded ports, and the incessant roar of powerful military jets. The cities of Hampton Roads are fringed by beaches and tidal wetlands, and, in parts, the region has charming historic precincts dating from the time of first English settlement.

HIGHLIGHTS

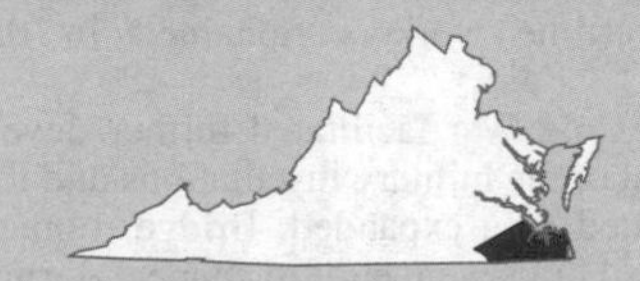

- Norfolk – a buzzing city with a great waterfront and the superb space-age Nauticus museum
- Hampton for the Virginia Air & Space Center and the Casemate Museum, Fort Monroe, and a host of African-American heritage sites
- The Chesapeake Bay Bridge-Tunnel – one of the modern wonders of the world
- The small historic town of Smithfield – a perfect getaway with many historic attractions nearby
- Boat trips in Hampton Roads and out onto expansive Chesapeake Bay
- Virginia Beach – for those seeking sun, sand, surfing, and nightlife, with a pleasant seaside boardwalk
- The Great Dismal Swamp, which is really not so bad

History

Fittingly, the *Susan Constant*, *Godspeed*, and *Discovery* first landed on the southern shore of Chesapeake Bay in 1607 before sailing up the James River to where Jamestown was established – this important connection with ships and the sea continues today.

The Revolutionary War highlighted the importance of the region and its proximity to the sea. On New Years Day 1776, over two-thirds of Norfolk was destroyed in a fire set by the British. Later, the rest was destroyed at the order of the Revolutionaries so that the British could not use it, and only the brick walls of St Paul's Church remained. In 1779, the British returned to ransack Portsmouth.

Norfolk was reconstructed after the war and resumed its status as an important world port. A yellow fever outbreak in 1855 lasted for over four months, and 100 residents succumbed to the disease each day.

In 1861, Virginia seceded from the Union and the Hampton Roads region was embroiled in war again. The historic battle between *Monitor* and *Merrimack* was fought in March 1862 (see the Battle of the Ironclads sidebar), and a month later the region was the focus of McClellan's Peninsula Campaign (see the special Civil War section).

Reconstruction commenced in earnest after the war and Norfolk prospered again. It was now linked by rail to other states and, importantly, to the coalfields of western Virginia. WWI and WWII added to the prosperity of the port – the shipbuilding facilities of Hampton Roads were expanded, more military bases were established or refurbished to respond to the changes of modern warfare, and many of the wartime workers remained in the region.

The Cold War facilitated further development of the military installations and the populated area expanded. Bridge, tunnel, and road links were built to connect dormitory suburbs to places of work. If anything, Hampton Roads now reflects the United States' new role as a peacekeeper/enforcer in the post-Cold War world. It was from here that some 40,000 military personnel embarked for the Middle East in 1991 during the Gulf War.

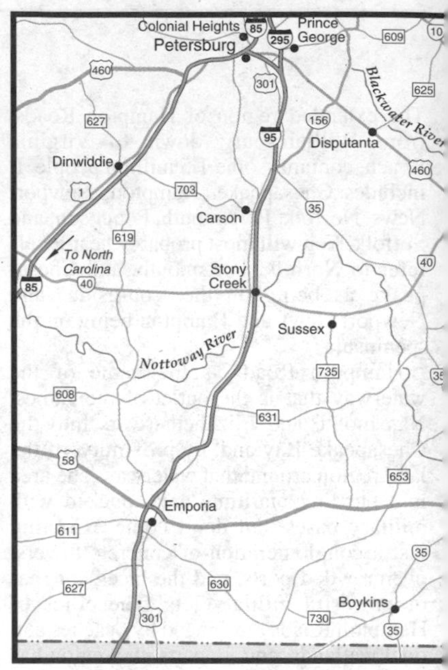

NORFOLK

Norfolk (population 262,000), on the broad waters of Hampton Roads, has a vibrant city skyline and a wealth of attractions, such as The Waterside Festival Marketplace and the futuristic Nauticus, the late 20th century equivalent of the Louvre (in its own technocratic way).

Transcending the fleshy delights of nearby Virginia Beach, Norfolk is enlivened by a revitalized downtown and the fashionable restaurant/shopping precinct of Ghent. It's a pity that most travelers pass through it, rather than stopping off in a 'real' destination that oozes history.

Orientation

Norfolk is the hub of the Hampton Roads metropolitan area. On its north shore is Ocean View; across the Hampton Roads waterway is the 'peninsula' (Newport News and Hampton); to the east is Virginia Beach; and to the southwest, Portsmouth. The main access routes are I-64 and I-664 (and the two bridge-tunnels) from Richmond and Williamsburg, Hwy 13 from the Eastern Shore and major cities to the north (via the Chesapeake Bay Bridge-Tunnel), Hwy 17 from North Carolina, Hwy 460 from Petersburg and Richmond, and Route 44 (which becomes I-264) from Virginia Beach.

Most of the attractions are arrayed along the east-west Waterside Drive, which becomes Boush St when it curves to the north. At the top of Boush St, turn west to reach trendy Ghent, an enclave of fancy shops and restaurants (in particular, 21st St and Colley Ave).

Information

Tourist Offices The Norfolk Visitor Information Center (☎ 757-441-1852, 800-368-3097) at the end of 4th View St (at Exit 273 off I-64) is open daily in summer from 9 am to 7 pm; otherwise, 9 am to 5 pm. They provide lots of information, including an audiovisual presentation. Behind the visitors center is the Monkey Bottom Wetland walkway, which is also worth exploring.

At the downtown visitors center (☎ 757-441-1852), at 232 E Main St, you can pick up brochures and information; there is also an information booth in the Waterside Festival Marketplace. Get their free *Greater*

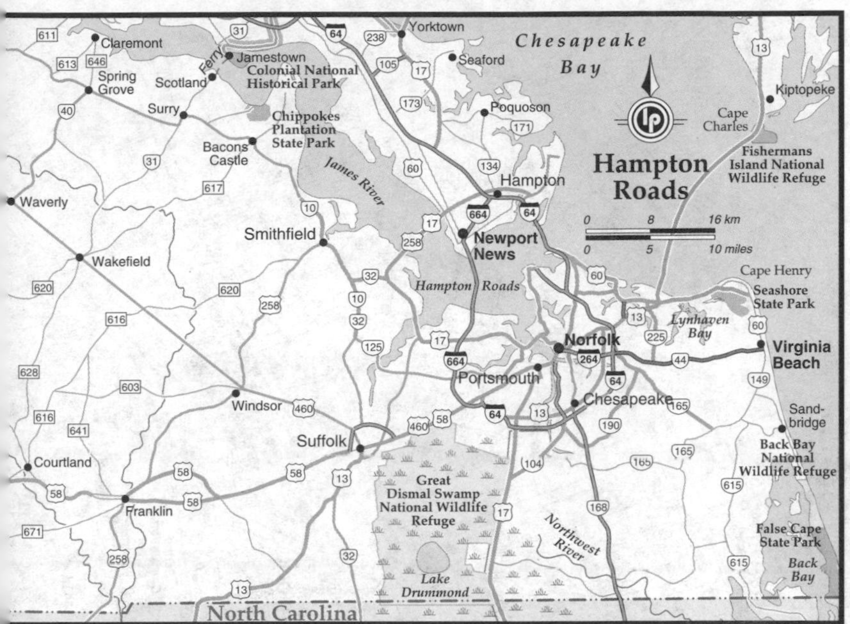

Norfolk Visitor's Guide and the *Dine Downtown* pamphlet.

There is a Travelers Aid Line (☎ 757-662-7017); the Red Cross language bank (☎ 757-446-7760) can also assist.

Money Two handy banks with foreign exchange are Crestar (☎ 757-624-5559), at the corner of Commercial Place and E Main St, and NationsBank (☎ 757-441-4707), at the corner of Atlantic and E Main Sts.

Post & Communications The main post office (☎ 757-640-8777 is at 600 Church St at the corner of Brambleton Ave. There is a subpost office (☎ 757-622-4751) at 126 Atlantic St on the corner of E Main St.

Media The main daily, the *Virginian Pilot*, has a Friday gig guide, *Preview*. The monthly entertainment magazine *Flash* is for 'Jumpin' Jacks,' and there's a free weekly lifestyle magazine, *Portfolio*.

On the radio, the local favorites are WFOG 92.9 FM (easy listening), WKOC 93.7 FM (they have a 'Dead Head' hour!), and WNIS 850 AM (talk radio with the likes of Rush Limbaugh). WHRO-TV (Channel 15) is a Public Broadcasting affiliate with exceptional children's shows.

Laundry At Sudsy's Wash & Pub laundromat (☎ 757-623-7837), at 738 W 22nd St (next to the supermarket), you can sip the foam while your wash is foaming!

Medical Services The Sentara Norfolk General Hospital (☎ 757-668-3551) is northwest of the city at 600 Gresham Drive, an extension of Brambleton Ave; it provides 24-hour emergency facilities.

Waterside Festival Marketplace
The Waterside Festival Marketplace (☎ 757-627-3300), on the scenic waterfront, has over 20 specialty food shops and

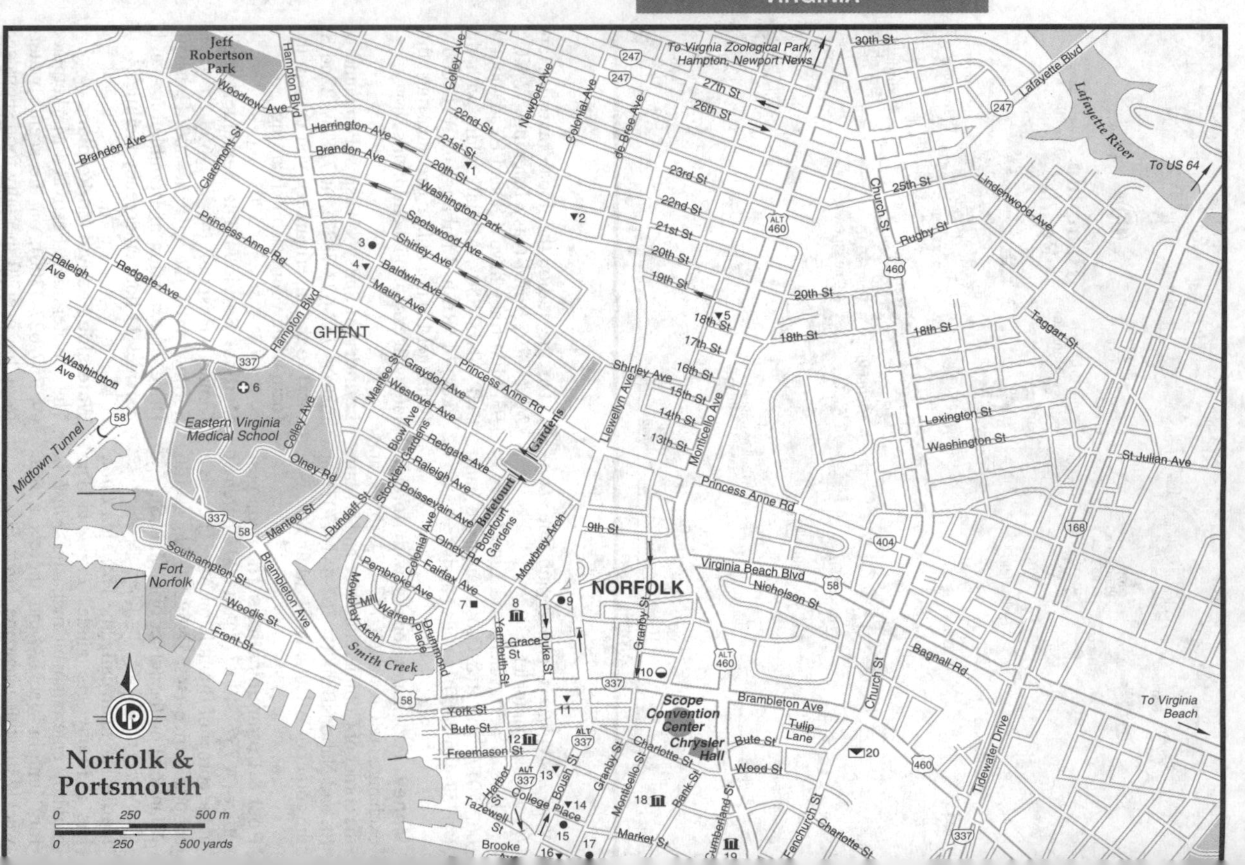
Norfolk & Portsmouth
0 250 500 m
0 250 500 yards
Jeff Robertson Park
Woodrow Ave
Hampton Blvd
Colley Ave
Newport Ave
Colonial Ave
de Bree Ave
To Virgnia Zoological Park, Hampton, Newport News
30th St
Lafayette Blvd
Lafayette River
To US 64
27th St
26th St
Harrington Ave
22nd St
21st St
Brandon Ave
20th St
23rd St
25th St
Lindenwood Ave
Claremont St
Washington Park
22nd St
21st St
Church St
Rugby St
Princess Anne Rd
Spotswood Ave
Shirley Ave
20th St
Baldwin Ave
Maury Ave
19th St
20th St
Raleigh Ave
Redgate Ave
18th St
18th St
18th St
Taggart St
GHENT
17th St
Washington Ave
Manteo St
Graydon Ave
Westover Ave
Princess Anne Rd
Shirley Ave
16th St
15th St
14th St
13th St
Llewellyn Ave
Monticello Ave
Eastern Virginia Medical School
Colley Ave
Blow Ave
Stockley Gardens
Redgate Ave
Raleigh Ave
Gardens
Lexington St
Washington St
St Julian Ave
Midtown Tunnel
Olney Rd
Boissevain Ave
Boteourt
Botetourt Gardens
Princess Anne Rd
Dundaff St
Manteo St
Colonial Ave
Olney Rd
Mowbray Arch
9th St
Southampton St
Brambleton Ave
Pembroke Ave
Fairfax Ave
Virginia Beach Blvd
Fort Norfolk
NORFOLK
Nicholson St
Woodis St
Mowbray Arch
Mill Warren
Drummond Place
Yarmouth St
Duke St
Grace St
Granby St
Front St
Smith Creek
Bagnall Rd
Church St
Scope Convention Center
Brambleton Ave
To Virginia Beach
York St
Bute St
Freemason St
Chrysler Hall
Charlotte St
Bute St
Tulip Lane
Wood St
Tidewater Drive
Harbor St
College Place
Boush St
Granby St
Monticello St
Bank St
Tazewell St
Brooke
Market St
Cumberland St
Fenchurch St
Charlotte St

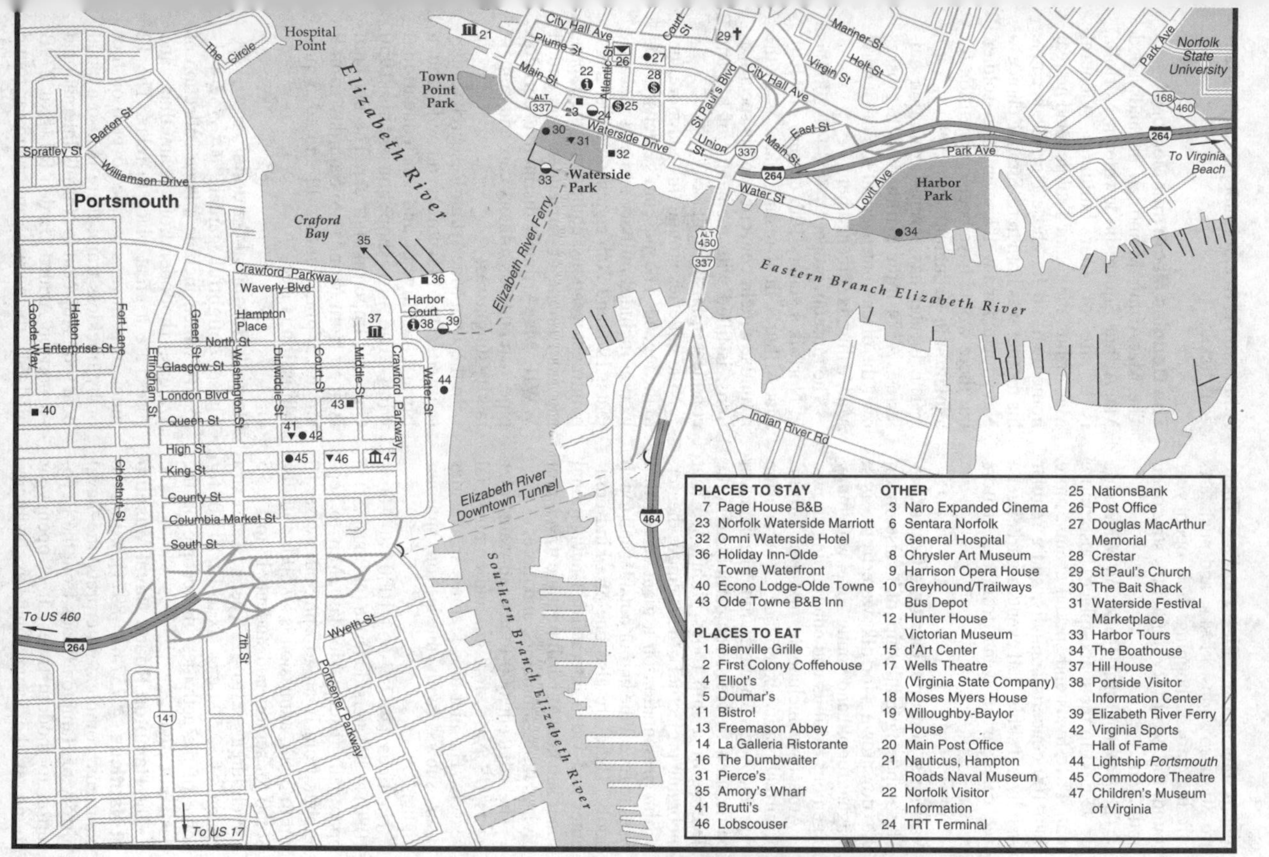

Portsmouth
Hospital Point
The Circle
Barton St
Spratley St
Williamson Drive
Elizabeth River
Town Point Park
Craford Bay
Crawford Parkway
Waverly Blvd
Hampton Place
Harbor Court
North St
Enterprise St
Glasgow St
London Blvd
Queen St
High St
King St
County St
Columbia Market St
South St
Goode Way
Hatton
Fort Lane
Effingham St
Green St
Washington St
Dinwiddie St
Court St
Middle St
Water St
Chestnut St
7th St
Wyeth St
Portcenter Parkway
To US 460
To US 17
Elizabeth River Ferry
Elizabeth River Downtown Tunnel
Southern Branch Elizabeth River
Eastern Branch Elizabeth River
Waterside Park
Waterside Drive
City Hall Ave
Plume St
Main St
Atlantic St
Court St
St Paul's Blvd
Union St
Mariner St
Virgin St
Holt St
East St
Park Ave
Water St
Lovit Ave
Harbor Park
Indian River Rd
Norfolk State University
To Virginia Beach
PLACES TO STAY
7 Page House B&B
23 Norfolk Waterside Marriott
32 Omni Waterside Hotel
36 Holiday Inn-Olde Towne Waterfront
40 Econo Lodge-Olde Towne
43 Olde Towne B&B Inn
PLACES TO EAT
1 Bienville Grille
2 First Colony Coffehouse
4 Elliot's
5 Doumar's
11 Bistro!
13 Freemason Abbey
14 La Galleria Ristorante
16 The Dumbwaiter
31 Pierce's
35 Amory's Wharf
41 Brutti's
46 Lobscouser
OTHER
3 Naro Expanded Cinema
6 Sentara Norfolk General Hospital
8 Chrysler Art Museum
9 Harrison Opera House
10 Greyhound/Trailways Bus Depot
12 Hunter House Victorian Museum
15 d'Art Center
17 Wells Theatre (Virginia State Company)
18 Moses Myers House
19 Willoughby-Baylor House
20 Main Post Office
21 Nauticus, Hampton Roads Naval Museum
22 Norfolk Visitor Information
24 TRT Terminal
25 NationsBank
26 Post Office
27 Douglas MacArthur Memorial
28 Crestar
29 St Paul's Church
30 The Bait Shack
31 Waterside Festival Marketplace
33 Harbor Tours
34 The Boathouse
37 Hill House
38 Portside Visitor Information Center
39 Elizabeth River Ferry
42 Virginia Sports Hall of Fame
44 Lightship Portsmouth
45 Commodore Theatre
47 Children's Museum of Virginia

nine restaurants (see Places to Eat). There are 80 or so shops, kiosks, and pushcarts offering varied shopping. It is open year round; the two lively nightclubs stay open until 2 am.

The **Town Point Park**, on Waterside Drive next to the marketplace, hosts more than 45 festivals and special events, more than 100 concerts annually, and a regular visit by tall ships – all events are free; get a free calendar of events from the visitors centers.

Nauticus, National Maritime Center

This imposing 'battleship' of a museum, on the downtown Norfolk waterfront, is a magnet for old and young alike, with many ingenious exhibits and entertaining shows.

Attractions include the first-ever 'group' of virtual reality experiences; a submarine ride; the Aegis Theater, a multimedia naval battle show in which you participate in the defense of a ship (oops, didn't see that incoming projectile!); the Nauticus theater, a film presentation on a giant screen that rises to reveal the harbor outside; and touch pools. There are also one-of-a-kind computer and video interactives: navigational sonar sub hunt, oil drilling, time travel, reef diving, flight simulators, and more.

The adjacent 600-foot deep-water pier hosts US Navy, foreign, and commercial vessels. The pier also features spectacular laser shows (with music) on summer nights.

Nauticus (☎ 757-664-1000, 800-664-1080) at 1 Waterside Drive (at Boush St) is open daily (except Monday), May to September, from 10 am to 7 pm; otherwise, 10 am to 5 pm; admission is $7.50 for adults, $6.50 for seniors and students 13 to 17, $5 for children six to 12. There is an extra charge of $2.50 (ages six to 12, $1.50) for some of the activities; the people on the desk will advise.

The **Hampton Roads Naval Museum at Nauticus** (☎ 757-444-8971), within the Nauticus complex, interprets the naval history of Hampton Roads from the Revolution to modern times. It is open year round at the same times as Nauticus. Admission is free; it is not part of the Nauticus ticket.

The Douglas MacArthur Memorial

The MacArthur Memorial, in landscaped MacArthur Square in downtown Norfolk, is a site of four buildings. General MacArthur, the son of a soldier, had no real hometown, so he chose Norfolk because his mother was born here. Strange choice, a Navy town, for a well known Army soldier, but there would have been competition for adulation in Arlington!

The theater has several exhibition galleries. A 24-minute film, which glosses over the often controversial life of General MacArthur, is screened here.

The museum proper (☎ 757-441-2965) is in Norfolk's stately 19th century city hall. MacArthur's final resting place is in the rotunda, which, converted to his specifications, is filled with mementos of life and conquest in far-flung places.

Nine galleries around this add more fuel to the legend. The museum's extensive collection includes military and personal artifacts: 19th and 20th century medals, flags, paintings, weapons, equipment, the Japanese instrument of surrender that ended WWII, MacArthur's distinctive corncob pipe, ostentatious military cap, and, importantly, sunglasses.

In the Jean MacArthur Research Center (named after his wife) you will find a library, archives, and an educational wing. The gift shop houses his 1950 Chrysler Imperial staff car. The museum is open from Monday to Saturday from 9 am to 5 pm, Sunday 11 am to 5 pm; admission is free.

Norfolk Botanical Gardens

These delightful gardens (☎ 757-441-5830), which include a large collection of azaleas, rhododendrons, camellias, and roses, are a great place to relax. The 12 miles of pathways can be covered on foot or by trackless train; there is also a canal boat tour. Adjacent to Norfolk International Airport on Azalea Garden Rd (Exit 279B off I-64), the gardens are open year round from 8:30 am until sunset. Admission is $3 for adults, $2 for seniors, and $1 for youths (those 6 to 18). The boat/train tours, $2.50 each ($1.50 for youths), operate mid-March to October from 10 am to 4 pm (combination boat/train tickets are $4.50).

Virginia Zoological Park

This 55-acre zoo (☎ 757-441-2706), at 3500 Granby St, has over 300 animals, a horticultural conservatory, and a nearby park. It is open daily from 10 am to 5 pm; admission is $2 for adults, $1 for seniors and children.

Fort Norfolk

At 810 Front St, on the banks of the Elizabeth River near Ghent, is a military fort first commissioned by George Washington in 1794. The original brickwork and buildings date from 1810 and the powder magazine was built in 1854 by the navy.

Today it represents one of the best preserved and most original War of 1812 sites in America and is the oldest fort in the Hampton Roads area. Military reenactments are held here annually. The fort (weekends call ☎ 757-625-1720) is open Sunday from 1 to 4 pm, admission is $2 per person, $5 for a family.

Moses Myers House

This 18th century brick building, combining late-Georgian/early-Federal architectural styles, was built in 1792 by a wealthy Jewish resident and shipping magnate. The majority of the furnishings are original, with rare pieces from England, China, Virginia, and elsewhere. The Myers family, who kept the house for six generations, were prominent members of Norfolk society.

The house (☎ 757-664-6283), at 331 Bank St (corner of Freemason St), is open January to March, Tuesday to Saturday from noon to 5 pm; otherwise, Tuesday to Saturday 10 am to 5 pm and Sunday noon to 5 pm. Admission is $3 for adults, $1.50 for seniors and students. A combination ticket with the Willoughby-Baylor House and the Adam Thoroughgood House (see the Virginia Beach section) is $6 for adults, $4.50 for children.

Willoughby-Baylor House

This red-brick townhouse, built in 1794 by Captain William Willoughby, also combines Georgian and Federal architectural styles. It is furnished with period furniture (not original to the house) and enhanced by a garden of herbs and flowers. The house (☎ 757-664-6283), 601 E Freemason St, is open by appointment only within these hours – January to March, Tuesday to Saturday from noon to 5 pm; otherwise, Tuesday to Saturday 10 am to 5 pm, Sunday noon to 5 pm. Admission is $3 for adults, $1.50 for students. See the Moses Myers House, above, for combination-ticket prices.

St Paul's Episcopal Church

St Paul's was built in 1739 on the site of an earlier church (1641). It was the only building of note left after the burning of Norfolk on New Year's Day, 1776, by Lord Dunmore's troops. There is still a cannonball, fired from a British ship, embedded in the wall. The graveyard is interesting; the church itself has been added to over the years, representing a number of styles.

The church (☎ 757-627-4353), 201 St Paul's Blvd (corner of City Hall Ave), is open by appointment daily (except Monday) from 10 am to 4 pm; admission is by donation.

The Chrysler Museum

Five minutes from Waterside, at 245 W Olney Rd in Ghent, is the superb Chrysler Museum, a fine collection of paintings, photographs, sculpture, drawings, and decorative arts. Included are paintings by Gainsborough, Renoir, Picasso, and American artists such as Jackson Pollock and Andy Warhol. One of the finest collections of glass (8000 pieces) in the country is displayed in the Institute of Glass, ranging from Ancient Roman to Tiffany pieces.

The museum (☎ 757-664-6200) is open Tuesday to Saturday from 10 am to 4 pm, Sunday 1 to 5 pm; admission is $3 for adults, $2 for students and seniors, and children 12 and under are free.

Hunter House Victorian Museum
This 1894 Victorian/Romanesque brick townhouse, at 240 W Freemason St, once belonged to a doctor. It now features stained glass, original furnishings, and a collection of early 20th century medical memorabilia. The house (☎ 757-623-9814) is open year round, Monday to Saturday from 10 am to 4 pm, Sunday noon to 4 pm; admission is $3 for adults, $2 for seniors, $1 for children.

Other Attractions
The **Hermitage Foundation Museum**, on 13 wooded acres alongside the Lafayette River at 7637 North Shore Rd, was once owned by a textile tycoon. The Tudor-style mansion, built in 1908, houses one of the largest private collections of Oriental art in the country, and also has several fine examples of decorative arts. The museum (☎ 757-423-2052) is open year round, Monday to Saturday from 10 am to 5 pm, Sunday 1 to 5 pm; admission is $4 for adults, $1 for children under 18.

The **d'Art Center** (☎ 757-625-4211) at 125 College Place is your chance to see art in the making. It consists of 30 studios where artists create, display, and sell their original artwork – drawings, paintings, ceramics, jewelry, photography. The center is open Tuesday to Saturday from 10 am to 6 pm, Sunday 1 to 5 pm; admission is free.

Organized Cruises
The *American Rover* (☎ 757-627-7245), a magnificent 135-foot, three-masted topsail schooner, cruises Hampton Roads and the Norfolk naval base. These trips depart daily (April through October) from Waterside, take from two to three hours, and cost about $14 for adults, $7 for children.

The *Spirit of Norfolk* (☎ 757-627-7771) does daytime narrated cruises and evening dinner cruises of Hampton Roads and the naval base; it departs from Waterside and costs from $20.50 to $34 for adults, depending on the meal.

Special Events
In mid-April, Norfolk hosts the Azalea Festival (☎ 757-622-2312) to celebrate the city's role as headquarters for NATO's Supreme Allied Commander Atlantic. It includes a parade and an air spectacular; events, which take place throughout the city, are usually free.

In early June, the Harborfest/Seawall Festival (☎ 757-627-5329) is held at Town Point Park and along the downtown waterfront. There is music, food, entertainment, a tall ships display, air shows, nautical races, and fireworks – all are free. There are many other festivals in and around Hampton Roads; see the list in the *Greater Norfolk Visitor's Guide*.

Places to Stay
Hotels & Motels Most of the cheap places are at Ocean View, a considerable distance from downtown Norfolk. The *Holiday Sands Motels & Apartments* (☎ 757-583-2621) at 1330 E Ocean View Ave (four miles east of the Hampton Roads Bridge-Tunnel) is on the beach and has a pool; in low season, rooms are from $50 to $90 (add $5 in high season). The *Econo Lodge W Ocean View Beach* (☎ 757-480-9611), at 9601 4th View St, close to the fishing piers, has off-season singles/doubles for $44/52 ($51/56 in season) and efficiencies (apartments with kitchenettes) from $50 to $64 for two to four persons. Also in Ocean View, the *Super 8 Motel* (☎ 757-588-7888), 7940 Shore Drive (Hwy 60), is another budget choice; rooms are from $39 to $66 in the off season, $56 to $81 in season. Close by is the *Rodeway Inn Little Creek* (☎ 757-588-3600) at 7969 Shore Drive; rooms are from $32 in the low season and between $60 to $75 in summer.

A mid-range choice is the *Best Western-Center Inn* (☎ 757-461-6600) at 235 N Military Hwy (a block north of the junction of I-264 and Hwy 13); singles are from $50 to $58 and doubles from $60 to $68 in low season (add $8 in summer). The *Doubletree Club Hotel* (☎ 757-461-9192), in the Military Circle shopping center just south of the junction of Hwys 58 and 13, is an impeccable place and is justifiably popular. There's a pool and dining room, and they offer homebaked cookies (the recipe is kept under lock and key); singles are from $73 to $88 and doubles from $88 to $98 in low season (add $5 in high season).

The *Quality Inn-Lake Wright* (☎ 757-461-6251), 6280 Northampton Blvd, has a lounge, restaurant, pool, tennis courts, and a golf course and driving range; singles are from $55 to $80 and doubles from $60 to $85 in winter (about $10 more in high season).

There are three excellent but expensive places. The *Omni Waterside Hotel* (☎ 757-622-6664), 777 Waterside Drive, is on the promenade next to the Waterside Festival Marketplace. Their lounge looks out over the water, and there is al fresco dining in the Riverwalk Restaurant; singles or doubles range from $89 to $139, not including parking. Across the road from the downtown visitors center, at 235 E Main St, is the *Norfolk Waterside Marriott* (☎ 757-627-4200). The hotel has al fresco dining, an upstairs restaurant with adjoining piano lounge, a rooftop pool, and a health club; singles and doubles are from $114 in low season, $119 in high season (ask about specials/ AAA discounts).

The *Norfolk Airport Hilton* (☎ 757-466-8000), 1500 N Military Hwy (at Hwy 13 and Route 165), is near a lot of corporate offices, and its restaurants are known for award-winning cuisine; singles are from $79 to $129 and doubles from $89 to $139.

B&Bs The classy *Page House Inn B&B* (☎ 757-625-5033, 800-599-7750), 323 Fairfax Ave (across from the Chrysler Museum), is in a restored Georgian home with magnificently furnished suites (check out the cappuccino machine imported from Italy); doubles are from $85 to $145.

Places to Eat

Check *Portfolio* for the Dining listings, which indicate price-range information and whether or not a place has won a Golden Fork or achieved Hall of Fame status. The *First Colony Coffee House* (☎ 757-622-0149), at 2000-1 Colonial Ave, is open daily for inexpensive meals (and coffee, of course); there are acoustic and folk performances some nights.

The *Bienville Grille* (☎ 757-625-5427), at 723 W 21st St, has a great dinner menu incorporating crawfish, Louisiana oysters, gumbo, and Sunday brunch enjoyed by all.

Bistro! (☎ 757-622-2310), at 210 W York St, has those California-trend (contemporary) meals, combined with a little bit of continental, into which are tossed seafood and farm products; entrees are from $7 to $13. *The Dumbwaiter – An American Bistro* (☎ 757-623-3663) at 117 Tazewell St, a fun place with its distinctive 'warehouse' decor, has Mississippi influenced meals. The affordable wine in-flights and half bottles include a 'Dumbtraminer.' It is open for lunch and dinner weekdays, and for dinner on Saturdays; entrees are from $7 to $13. This place defies description – check it out.

Elliot's (☎ 757-625-0259), at 1421 Colley Ave in trendy Ghent, is a consistent local favorite, with meatless entrees, seafood, a children's menu, and the great hamburgers on which it has built its reputation. It is open Sunday to Thursday from 11 am to 10 pm, Friday and Saturday to midnight; entrees are from $9 to $14.

The *Taphouse Grill* (☎ 757-627-9172), at 931 W 21st St, is open daily for 'beer friendly' food and a fine selection of microbrews; entrees are about $10.

Bobbywood (☎ 757-440-7515), at 7515 Granby St, is a husband-and-wife affair, painted neon green, with an open kitchen and stone hearth oven from an old bakery. The food is 'fun' nouvelle American, such as soft shelled crab, great mashed potatoes, thin fried onions, pasta, and gourmet pizza.

Freemason Abbey (☎ 757-622-3966), in an old renovated (and deconsecrated?) church building at 209 W Freemason St, has a traditional American menu that includes seafood and prime rib steaks; it is open daily for lunch ($5 to $8) and dinner ($10 to $18).

Are They Screamin' for Ice Cream?

At 919 Monticello Ave in Norfolk, *Doumar's* (☎ 757-627-4163) is home of the world's original ice cream cone-making machine. Abe Doumar invented the ice cream cone at the St Louis Exposition in 1904, and today his nephew still makes ice cream cones with the old cone-making machine at his Norfolk drive-in.

Doumar's is open year round but is closed on Sundays. There are tours at 10 am and 3 pm or by appointment; the fee for the tour is $2 and includes an ice cream with . . . *the* cone! Favorite flavors are chocolate, butter pecan, vanilla, strawberry, lime and orange sherbet – basically, that is it. It has curbside service. ■

At the *Grate Steak* (☎ 757-461-5501) in the Best Western-Center Inn (see Places to Stay) is one of those places where you pick your own steak and cook it yourself (don't burn it or you will pay for it); a meal for two will cost about $25 to $30. And for barbecue, you can't do much better than the minced pork, cole slaw, and beans at *Pierce's* (☎ 757-622-0738) at the Waterside.

La Galleria Ristorante (☎ 757-623-7111), a great Italian eatery at 120 College Place, has an authentic wood-burning pizza oven; it is open for lunch on Friday and for dinner from Monday to Saturday and has live entertainment nightly.

For seafood, the *Ship's Cabin* (☎ 757-583-4659), at 4110 E Ocean View Ave, is superbly situated with views of Chesapeake Bay. Its famous oysters Bingo (sautéed in butter, shallots, and wine), breads, crab soup and cakes, and whiskey pudding entice the locals to return. It is not cheap (a dinner for two costs up to $50), but it is well worth it.

Antiquities (☎ 757-466-8000), at the Airport Hilton (see Places to Stay), is the pinnacle of fine candlelit dining. It consistently makes it into the region's top 10.

Entertainment

Music There is plenty of choice in this part of the world, as many of the bands on the way to Virginia Beach stop off here. It includes jazz, blues, country, folk/acoustic, bluegrass, and rock in all their modern manifestations. For current entertainer and venue listings, see the periodicals listed under Media, above.

The (Fifth National) Banque (☎ 757-480-3600) at 1849 E Little Creek Rd has country and western music and free dancing lessons. Jazz and blues are featured at the *Naro Expanded Cinema* (☎ 757-625-6276), on Colley Ave, and occasionally at the *Bienville Grille*. Acoustic/folk music can be heard at the *First Colony Coffee House* (see under Places to Eat, above).

Rock music is widespread: Try *The Boathouse* (☎ 757-671-8100), 119 Bessie's Place at the Waterside (cover is from $5 to $20); *The Bait Shack* at the Waterside; and *Chrysler Hall* (☎ 757-627-2314) for international headliners. Ask around.

Performing Arts There are regular opera performances by the *Virginia Opera*, one of the top regional opera companies in the country, in the Harrison Opera House (☎ 757-623-1223), near the corner of Virginia Blvd and Llewellyn Ave; there have even been world premieres of operas here. The season is October to March, and the box office hours are Monday to Friday from 9 am to 5 pm.

There are classical music performances by the *Virginia Symphony* at Chrysler Hall (☎ 757-623-6959), part of the Scope Convention Center complex, and at the Chandler Recital Hall of the Diehn Fine & Performing Arts Center (☎ 757-683-4061). The Virginia Symphony has performed for over 75 years, and their Peanut Butter & Jam family series is very popular.

The *Virginia Stage Company* (☎ 757-627-6988) performs at the Wells Theatre, on the corner of Tazewell St and Monticello Ave, from September to May (performances are from Tuesday to Sunday).

Spectator Sports

The Norfolk Tides, a Class AAA baseball farm club for the New York Mets, play at Harbor Park (☎ 757-622-2222); box seats are about $7 and reserved seats $4.50. The Hampton Roads Admirals are part of the East Coast Hockey League with a 'league' of the most boisterous and vocal fans you can ever hope to hear. They play at the Scope (☎ 757-640-1212), on the corner of St Paul's Blvd and Brambleton Ave. The season commences in October and continues through to March.

Norfolk State University fields the Spartans and Lady Spartans in CIAA men's and women's basketball games; for ticket information call NSU Sports (☎ 757-455-3303).

Getting There & Away

Norfolk International Airport (☎ 757-857-3351) is served by American, Delta, Northwest, Southeast, TWA, United, and USAir. There is a shuttle service (☎ 757-8571231) from the airport to town.

The Greyhound/Trailways terminal (☎ 757-627-5641, 800-231-2222) is at Monticello and Brambleton Aves. From here, there are services to Williamsburg; Richmond; Washington, DC; and to Maryland via the Chesapeake Bay Bridge-Tunnel.

The nearest Amtrak (☎ 757-245-3589, 800-872-7245) terminal is 21 miles away at 9304 Warwick Blvd, Newport News, but there is a free Thruway bus to and from downtown Norfolk.

Getting Around

The TRT (Tidewater Regional Transit, ☎ 757-640-6300) bus system serves all of the southside of Hampton Roads (Chesapeake, Portsmouth, Virginia Beach, and Norfolk). You can get a timetable from the main bus office at 1500 Monticello Ave, open weekdays from 7:30 am to 5 pm, or at the Waterside terminal, which is open daily. The cost within one zone is $1.10, an additional zone is 55¢. There are Crossroads connections to the PENTRAN system of Newport News and Hampton.

TRT runs the Norfolk trolley tour throughout downtown and into Ghent. The trolley stops at most city attractions on its one-hour circuit; you can alight and then catch a later trolley. The trolley trundles late May to early September, from 11 am to 4 pm daily (for the rest of September it commences at noon); the cost is $3.50 for adults, $1.75 for seniors and children under 12.

The Elizabeth River Ferry (☎ 757-627-9291) plies between the Norfolk Waterside and Portside daily (see Portsmouth).

PORTSMOUTH

Portsmouth (population 104,000), across the Elizabeth River from Norfolk, is the nation's oldest and largest naval shipyard (see map in Norfolk Section). It has a long and fascinating history. As early as 1620, King's grants were offered to mariners to encourage them to settle here and build ships. By 1636, a ferry linked Portsmouth to Norfolk, and, in 1716, one William Crawford donated land for a market, church, courthouse, and jail.

The Gosport naval shipyard was established in 1767, and the first warship built here was the *Chesapeake*. In 1801, the Gosport naval shipyard was renamed Norfolk naval shipyard – it was, by then, the largest such facility in the country.

Portsmouth was affected by war on several occasions. During the Revolutionary War, the town was bombarded by British ships. Benedict Arnold set up a line of defenses at Fort Nelson, now Hospital Point (site of the US Naval Hospital). The town was abandoned by the British when Cornwallis moved his HQ to Yorktown.

In 1861, Union troops captured and burned the port, but it was later recaptured by the Confederates. They raised the sunken *Merrimack*, refitted it as the first ironclad battleship, and renamed it CSS *Virginia* (see the Battle of the Ironclads sidebar).

Orientation & Information

Portsmouth can be reached from Norfolk via the Midtown Tunnel (Hwy 58), the

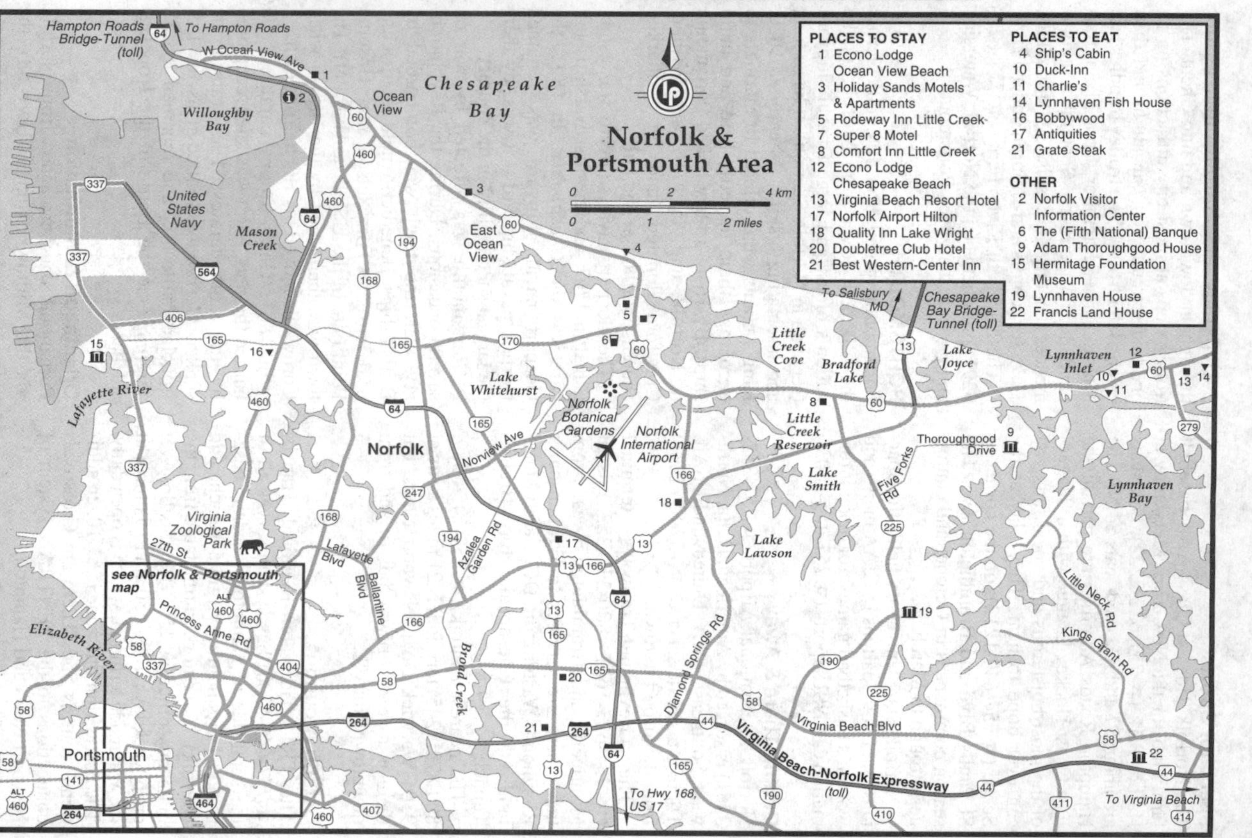

Norfolk & Portsmouth Area
0 2 4 km
0 1 2 miles
PLACES TO STAY
1 Econo Lodge
Ocean View Beach
3 Holiday Sands Motels & Apartments
5 Rodeway Inn Little Creek
7 Super 8 Motel
8 Comfort Inn Little Creek
12 Econo Lodge Chesapeake Beach
13 Virginia Beach Resort Hotel
17 Norfolk Airport Hilton
18 Quality Inn Lake Wright
20 Doubletree Club Hotel
21 Best Western-Center Inn
PLACES TO EAT
4 Ship's Cabin
10 Duck-Inn
11 Charlie's
14 Lynnhaven Fish House
16 Bobbywood
17 Antiquities
21 Grate Steak
OTHER
2 Norfolk Visitor Information Center
6 The (Fifth National) Banque
9 Adam Thoroughgood House
15 Hermitage Foundation Museum
19 Lynnhaven House
22 Francis Land House
Hampton Roads Bridge-Tunnel (toll)
To Hampton Roads
W Ocean View Ave
Chesapeake Bay
Ocean View
Willoughby Bay
United States Navy
Mason Creek
East Ocean View
Lafayette River
Lake Whitehurst
Norfolk Botanical Gardens
Norfolk International Airport
Norview Ave
Norfolk
Little Creek Cove
Bradford Lake
Little Creek Reservoir
Lake Smith
Lake Lawson
Lake Joyce
To Salisbury MD
Chesapeake Bay Bridge-Tunnel (toll)
Lynnhaven Inlet
Thoroughgood Drive
Five Forks Rd
Lynnhaven Bay
Little Neck Rd
Kings Grant Rd
Virginia Zoological Park
27th St
Lafayette Blvd
Ballantine Blvd
Azalea Garden Rd
see Norfolk & Portsmouth map
Princess Anne Rd
Elizabeth River
Broad Creek
Diamond Springs Rd
Virginia Beach Blvd
Virginia Beach-Norfolk Expressway (toll)
Portsmouth
To Hwy 168, US 17
To Virginia Beach

Battle of the Ironclads

When Union forces evacuated Norfolk naval yard in the spring of 1861, they failed to fully immobilize the steam frigate USS *Merrimack*, even though it had been burnt and scuttled. When the Confederates captured the yard, they raised the hulk, covered it with a superstructure of 24 inches of oak topped with four inches of steel plating, and rechristened the steel monster CSS *Virginia*.

After *Virginia* had sunk a few wooden ships and mocked the Federal shore batteries, authorities in Washington, DC, began to panic. But, in one of the war's great coincidences, less than 24 hours after *Virginia* had first run amok, the recently commissioned and unorthodox-looking USS *Monitor*, with its revolving turret sporting two 11-inch guns, steamed into Hampton Roads.

The ensuing battle – on March 9, 1862 – was indecisive; the ships withdrew to opposite sides of Hampton Roads, each with a few dents, but both were still operational.

After their initial battle, the two ironclads faced each other across Hampton Roads for two months but no shots were fired. *Virginia*, just by being there, paralyzed free movement by Union forces up and down the James River. Just before McClellan ordered the systematic bombardment of the Norfolk defenses on May 4, 1862, Joe Johnston withdrew the Confederate forces and since the ship's deep draught prevented escape up the James River they were forced to abandon it. The Confederates blew the ship up on May 10. Not long afterwards the *Monitor* sank in a heavy storm. It was rediscovered only in the last few decades.

Because of these two ships, the wooden ships in all the world's navies were rendered obsolete and the face of naval warfare was changed forever.■

Downtown Tunnel (I-264) or the Elizabeth River ferry. Most of the attractions are near the Portside Market; historic 'Olde Towne' is close by.

The Portside Visitor Information Center (☎ 757-393-5111), at 6 Crawford Parkway, is open daily, late May to early September, from noon to 4 pm. It has a gift shop and lots of information on Olde Towne. Get a copy of the free *Portsmouth Visitor's Guide* and *Olde Towne Walking Tour* (with its good glossary of architectural terms).

Olde Towne

There is still a large concentration of noteworthy 18th and 19th century dwellings in Olde Towne, but most are not open to the public. The TRT **Olde Towne Trolley Tour**, which covers all the major buildings of interest, leaves from the Portside Information Center (☎ 757-393-5111). It operates daily, late May to early September, from noon to 4 pm, and the cost is $2.50 for adults and $1.25 for seniors and children under 11.

Particularly significant is the **Hill House** (☎ 757-393-8591) at 221 North St, an English basement-style house built around 1830. It is open April to December, Wednesday and weekends from 1 to 5 pm; admission is $3 for adults, $1 for children.

Portsmouth Naval Shipyard Museum

This museum (☎ 757-393-8591), on the waterfront at 2 High St, has many models of 18th century warships (including the CSS *Virginia* and the USS *Delaware)* and exhibits on all aspects of shipbuilding. It is open Tuesday to Saturday from 10 am to 5 pm, Sunday 1 to 5 pm; admission is $1.

Portsmouth (☎ 757-393-8983), at the London Slip, is a retired Coast Guard lightship (No 101). Used to guide mariners away from dangerous shoals, the ship was commissioned in 1915 – the last of its class – and has been restored to its original condition. Board it Tuesday to Saturday from 10 am to 5 pm, Sunday 1 to 5 pm; admission is $1.

Organized Cruises

A Mississippi-style paddlewheeler called *Carrie B* departs daily from April to October for a narrated 1½-hour cruise of the naval dockyards and the site of the *Monitor/Merrimack* battle. Carrie B Harbor Tours (☎ 757-393-4735) is at the end of Bay St, Portside. The cost is $12 for adults, $6 for children.

Places to Stay & Eat

The *Econo Lodge-Olde Towne* (☎ 757-399-4414) at 1031 London Blvd, the best budget option in town, is close to restaurants and the ferry; doubles are from $30 in low season. The *Holiday Inn-Olde Towne Waterfront* (☎ 757-393-2573, 800-465-4329), 9 Crawford Parkway, is near the waterfront and Olde Towne. The rooms are a good value at $75/81 for singles/doubles, and some have water views. There is a pool, and a restaurant, *Harborside*, which overlooks the Elizabeth River.

Good B&Bs include the appropriately named *Olde Towne B&B Inn* (☎ 757-397-5462), a gracious 1885 Victorian home at 420 Middle St; for others, ask at the visitors center.

Portsmouth is known for its fine seafood restaurants. *Amory's* (☎ 757-483-1518), at 5909 High St, is a family-run place with a popular raw bar; there are good-value specials on weekday nights. *Amory's Wharf* (☎ 757-399-0991), 10 Crawford Parkway, is a clone of the aforementioned and just a little trendier in appearance, but, truth is, many of the dishes are the same. A favorite is *Lobscouser* (☎ 757-397-2728), 337 High St, which is open daily for lunch and dinner; the seafood is fresh and the desserts homemade.

A good cafe in which to while away time is *Brutti's* (☎ 757-393-1923) at 467 Dinwiddie St (just off High St) – it is known for its yummy 'bagelnutz' (cream cheese baked inside a bagel).

Entertainment

The restored Art Deco *Commodore Theatre* (☎ 757-393-6962) at 421 High St was built in 1945. You can have a meal here as you enjoy the movie (on the main floor), and there is the usual theater seating in the balcony. It is open for a Wednesday matinee at 2 pm, daily in the evenings at 6 and 9 pm. Patrons can ring the kitchen for snacks and drinks.

Kids will be easily entertained at the *Children's Museum of Virginia* (☎ 757-393-8983) at 400 High St. This hands-on participatory museum, focusing on science, art, music, and technology, is open Tuesday to Saturday from 10 am to 5 pm, Sunday from 1 to 5 pm; admission is $3 and this includes entry to the planetarium.

Getting There & Away

The Elizabeth River Ferry (☎ 757-627-9291), at Waterside in Norfolk and Portside in Portsmouth, is a Mississippi-style riverboat that plies the harbor daily. The five-minute trip costs 75¢ for adults, 35¢ for seniors and the disabled, and 50¢ for children.

TRT bus Nos 41, 45, 46, 47, and 50 pass near the Portside Visitors Center.

HAMPTON

The city of Hampton, north of Hampton Roads, has a rich history. Two years after first settlement at Jamestown, a fort was established here. Some say the infamous pirate Blackbeard met his end here in 1718 (or was it at Ocracoke Island, North Carolina?).

Hampton was razed by retreating Confederates during the Civil War, and many of its old buildings were destroyed. Fort Monroe remained in Union hands throughout the war. Today, Hampton has a major NASA research center, Hampton University Museum, Buckroe Beach, and a number of other interesting attractions.

Orientation & Information

Hampton is easily reached from I-64 and Hwy 60 as both pass through the city before reaching the Hampton Roads Bridge Tunnel. Alternatively, access to the southside of Hampton Roads is possible via I-664 and Monitor-Merrimac Tunnel (the 'M&M').

The Hampton Visitors Center (☎ 757-727-1102, 800-800-2202) at 710 Settlers Landing Rd (Exit 267 off I-64) has an audiovisual presentation and gift shop.

It provides information on Hampton's attractions.

Fort Monroe & Casemate Museum

On the north side of Hampton Roads on Old Point Comfort sits Fort Monroe, America's largest stone fort. It was built between 1819 and 1834, with thick brick walls meant to withstand bombardment from the sea and a moat intended to repel ground attacks. Throughout the Civil War it remained in Union hands, although the surrounding territory was controlled by the Confederates.

Today, its exhibits include the prison cell of Jefferson Davis, in a casemate (chamber) set in the walls, Civil War artifacts including a description of the *Monitor/Merrimack* battle, and details of the military careers of Robert E Lee and Edgar Allan Poe, both of whom served here in the antebellum period.

The casemate museum (☎ 757-727-3391), in Casemate No 20 on Bernard Rd, is open daily from 10:30 am to 4:30 pm; admission is free. To get there, take Hwy 258 (an extension of Mercury Blvd) to its end and enter the fort through the fort wall.

Virginia Air & Space Center

This, the official visitors center for the NASA Langley Research Center, is at 600 Settlers Landing Rd. There are interactive exhibits, suspended aircraft, a space gallery with the Apollo 12 command module and lunar lander, a moon rock, and a 300-seat IMAX theater. The theme is the history of flight and the exploration of space.

The center (☎ 757-727-0800, 800-296-0800) is open from Memorial Day to Labor Day, Monday to Wednesday from 10 am to 5 pm, Thursday to Sunday 10 am to 7 pm; otherwise, 10 am to 5 pm. Admission to the space center only is $6 for adults, $4 for seniors and children ages three to 11; add the IMAX theater (two movies) and it is $9 and $7.

Hampton University Museum

This museum in the Academy Building of Hampton University campus is an absolute must. The outstanding collection, which was started in 1868, has examples of traditional art from African, Asian, Pacific Islander, and Native American cultures. The university was originally established as a freedmen's school and an early student was Booker T Washington (see the sidebar in the Piedmont chapter). Today, there are contemporary works by African American artists. The museum (☎ 757-727-5308) is open weekdays from 8 am to 5 pm, weekends from noon to 4 pm; admission is free.

Little England Chapel & St John's Church

There are two churches of note in Hampton. The Little England Chapel at 4100 Kecoughtan Rd was built circa 1879. It is the only known remaining African American missionary chapel in Virginia and is a state and national historic landmark. The chapel's sanctuary holds a permanent exhibit of the religious lives of post-Civil War African Americans in Virginia. The chapel (☎ 757-723-6803) is open Tuesday to Saturday from 10 am to 4 pm, Sunday by appointment only.

One of the few surviving buildings from the pre-Revolutionary era is St John's Church at 100 W Queens Way and High Court Lane in Old Hampton. Built in 1728, it is believed to be the oldest English-speaking parish in continuous use in the US. Of interest is a stained-glass window depicting the baptism of Pocahontas. The church (☎ 757-722-2567) is open Monday to Friday from 9 am to 3:30 pm, Saturday from 9 am to noon; admission is free.

Other Attractions

The city's most bizarre attraction is **Air Power Park** (☎ 757-727-1163), proof that people still have a macabre fascination for missiles and firepower. Self-destruct, mid-flight at 413 W Mercury Blvd, Wednesday to Sunday from 9 am to 5 pm. Kpow! Boom! &£@%!

At the other end of the sensibility scale is the **Hampton Carousel**, a beautifully restored wooden 1920 carousel with 48 horses and two chariots, carved by a real melting pot of European immigrants. Having stood at Buckroe Beach Amusement Park for 60 years before restoration, it now revolves at 22 Lincoln St, off Settlers Landing Rd, in a waterfront park near the Virginia Air & Space Center. It is open daily, April to October, Monday to Saturday from 10 am to 8 pm, Sunday noon to 6 pm; otherwise, November to mid-December, Saturday 10 am to 6 pm, Sunday noon to 6 pm; admission is 50¢. No missiles here, Strangelove!

The **Langley Raceway** (☎ 757-358-9980), at North Armistead Ave and Commander Shepard Blvd, seats 6500 and has the Saturday-night sanction for NASCAR races. **Buckroe Beach**, at the eastern end of Route 351, is the haunt of swimmers, and for those not wanting to get into the water, there are parks and picnic facilities. North of Buckroe Beach is the pristine **Grandview Park Natural Reserve** (☎ 757-727-6347), an estuarine wildlife refuge which will satisfy the avid birder. Its entrance is at the corner of Beach Drive and State Park Rd.

If you take the Mallory St exit off I-64 you come to **Phoebus**, a fascinating little enclave with bookstores, craft shops, and a couple of great eateries (try the Victorian Station or Clyde's for lunch).

Organized Tours & Cruises

The Downtown Trolley Shuttle (☎ 757-727-1102) is an authentic reproduction of an 1888 trolley. It takes you from the visitors center through downtown, past the Air & Space Center, St John's Church, Hampton Carousel, and Charles H Taylor Arts Center. It operates April to December, Monday to Saturday from 9:30 am to 6:30 pm, Sunday 12:10 to 5:30 pm and is free.

The *Miss Hampton II* (☎ 757-727-1102) cruises down Hampton River and passes by Norfolk Naval Base, the Hampton University campus, and Fort Monroe (it is the only boat allowed to visit historic Fort Wool, a pre-Civil War fort situated on an artificial island). Cruises operate daily, April to October, at 10 am, also June to August at

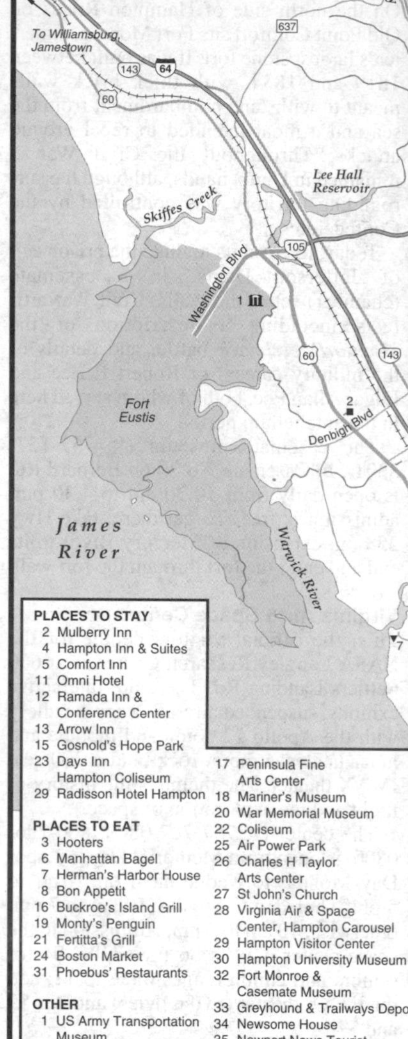

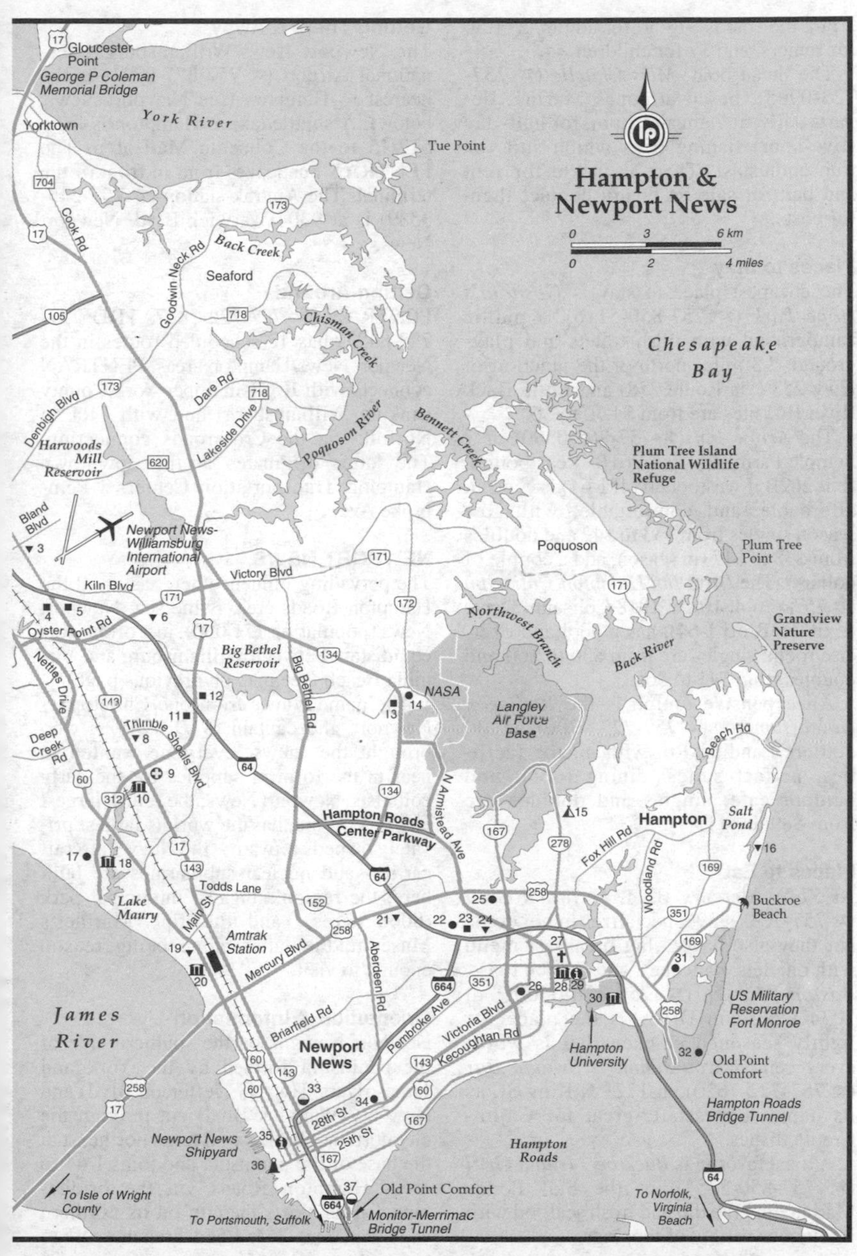
Hampton & Newport News
0 3 6 km
0 2 4 miles
Gloucester Point
George P Coleman Memorial Bridge
Yorktown
York River
Tue Point
Cook Rd
Goodwin Neck Rd
Back Creek
Seaford
Chisman Creek
Dare Rd
Denbigh Blvd
Lakeside Drive
Poquoson River
Bennett Creek
Chesapeake Bay
Harwoods Mill Reservoir
Plum Tree Island National Wildlife Refuge
Bland Blvd
Newport News-Williamsburg International Airport
Poquoson
Plum Tree Point
Victory Blvd
Kiln Blvd
Oyster Point Rd
Nettles Drive
Northwest Branch
Back River
Grandview Nature Preserve
Big Bethel Reservoir
Big Bethel Rd
NASA
Langley Air Force Base
Deep Creek Rd
Thimble Shoals Blvd
Beach Rd
N Armistead Ave
Hampton Roads Center Parkway
Hampton
Salt Pond
Fox Hill Rd
Woodland Rd
Todds Lane
Buckroe Beach
Lake Maury
Main St
Amtrak Station
Mercury Blvd
Aberdeen Rd
US Military Reservation Fort Monroe
James River
Briarfield Rd
Pembroke Ave
Victoria Blvd
Kecoughtan Rd
Hampton University
Newport News
Old Point Comfort
Hampton Roads Bridge Tunnel
28th St
25th St
Newport News Shipyard
Hampton Roads
To Isle of Wright County
Old Point Comfort
To Portsmouth, Suffolk
Monitor-Merrimac Bridge Tunnel
To Norfolk, Virginia Beach
VIRGINIA

2 pm; the cost is $13.50 for adults, $11.50 for seniors, and $7 for children

The 'head-boat' *Miss Charlie* (☎ 757-723-0998), based at Jones Marina, departs daily, at 7 am and 1 pm, for half-day (five-hour) fishing trips which suit the true enthusiast. There is tackle for rent and bait for sale on board; contact them for costs.

Places to Stay

The cheapest place to stay is *Gosnold's Hope Park* (☎ 757-850-5116), a public campground with flush toilets and playground, 2.3 miles north of the junction of Hwy 258 (via Route 278) and Little Back River Rd; sites are from $4.70 to $6.

The *Arrow Inn* (☎ 757-865-0300) at 7 Semple Farm Rd (Exit 261B if eastbound, Exit 262B if westbound off I-64) is central, affordable, and comfortable, with low season singles from $33 to $42 and doubles from $38 to $47 (in season, add a couple of dollars). The *Days Inn Hampton Coliseum* (☎ 757-826-4810), at 1918 Coliseum Drive (Exit 263B off I-64), has a pool and exercise room; singles are from $36 to $60 and doubles from $41 to $65.

An expensive option is the *Radisson Hotel Hampton* (☎ 757-727-9700), at 700 Settlers Landing Rd, with all the facilities, perfect suites, dining room, and outdoor cafe; singles and doubles are from $89 to $115.

Places to Eat

At 57 W Mercury Blvd, *Fertitta's Grill* (☎ 757-723-9939) specializes in hot dogs, but they also have a big breakfast menu with omelets, pancakes, and French toast. *Boston Market* (☎ 757-838-0300), at 2034 Coliseum Drive, is the place for lightly seasoned chicken that is worth every cent. *Bayou Johnny's Swamp Bar* (☎ 757-722-7620), at 1721 N King St, as its name suggests, is great for Cajun-Creole dishes.

A local favorite is *Buckroe's Island Grill* (☎ 757-850-5757), at the Salt Ponds Marina, for crab dip and fresh seafood with a delicious variety of toppings.

Getting There & Away

The Newport News/Williamsburg International Airport (☎ 757-877-0221) is the nearest to Hampton (see Newport News, below). A shuttle/taxi to Hampton is from $12/15 to the Coliseum Mall area. The PENTRAN bus leaves from in front of the terminal. The Amtrak station (☎ 757-245-3589) is at 9304 Warwick Blvd, Newport News.

Getting Around

PENTRAN (☎ 757-722-2837, TDD 757-722-8427) has 12 scheduled routes in the Newport News/Hampton areas. PENTRAN connects with JCCT in upper York County (linking Williamsburg) and with TRT in Norfolk via the Crossroads connection. The latter originates at the downtown Hampton Transportation Center, 2 Pembroke Ave.

NEWPORT NEWS

The pervading influence here, as in all the Hampton Roads area, is the sea. Newport News (population 171,000), just off I-64, is equidistant between Williamsburg and Virginia Beach (see map on previous page).

The name comes from one Christopher Newport, the captain of *Discovery*, who brought the 'news' everyone wanted to hear in the form of supplies for the early colonists. Newport News, the fourth largest city in Virginia, has the world's largest privately owned shipyard – the Navy's aircraft carriers and nuclear submarines are built here; the region's biggest municipal park (8000 acres); and the fine Mariner's Museum, the latter alone being reason enough to visit.

Orientation & Information

Newport News is on the southern side of the peninsula formed by the York and James rivers. Hwy 17 (Jefferson Blvd) and Hwy 60 (Warwick Blvd) cut through the city north-south; Hwy 60 turns northeast at the base of the peninsula and joins I-64 to cross Hampton Roads via the bridge-tunnel. I-64 skirts the city on its northern edge – at Exit 264, I-664 branches off to

Suffolk/Chesapeake via the Monitor-Merrimac Tunnel ('M&M'). Downtown (Washington Ave) near the shipyards is an austere place – the attractions are several miles north. The one point of interest here is the Victory Arch, a marble memorial to those who served overseas in the world wars.

The Newport News Tourist Development Office (☎ 757-928-6843, 800-333-7787), at 2400 Washington Ave, provides the *Newport News Visitor Guide* and the small publication *Civil War Sites of Newport News.*

The Riverside Regional Medical Center (☎ 757-594-3100) is at 500 J Clyde Morris Blvd. Foreign exchange is not done easily on the peninsula, so bring traveler's checks.

Mariner's Museum

This fascinating museum, at 100 Museum Drive, has America's most extensive international maritime collection. It includes intricately carved figureheads, steam engines, maps, scrimshaw (whalebone etchings), paintings, ship models (eg, SS *United States* and RMS *Queen Elizabeth*), films and videos – designed to put a whiff of sea air in your nostrils – and a display on the *Monitor.*

Especially interesting are the tiny carvings by August Crabtree, viewed through magnifying glasses. At the other end of the scale, are over 50 full-sized craft, from a Venetian gondola to a WWII Japanese submarine.

The museum (☎ 757-596-2222) is open daily from 10 am to 5 pm; admission is $6.50 for adults, $5.50 for seniors, and $3.25 for students and children. To get there, take Exit 258A off I-64.

Other Attractions

The **War Memorial Museum of Virginia** (☎ 757-247-8523), at 9285 Warwick Blvd in Huntington Park, looks at US military history from 1775 up through 'Operation Desert Storm.' There are uniforms, weapons, art (paintings, posters), vehicles, and a special treatment of the role of African Americans and women. It is open Monday to Saturday from 9 am to 5 pm, Sunday from 1 to 5 pm; admission is $2 for adults, $1 for children. To get there, take Exit 263A (Mercury Blvd) off I-64.

Newsome House, a museum and cultural center (☎ 757-247-2360) at 2803 Oak Ave, was once owned by Joseph Thomas Newsome, a prominent black lawyer, editor, founder of an area church and the Colored Voters League of Warwick County, and one of the first black lawyers to represent cases before the Virginia Supreme Court. The house is open year round, by appointment only; a free tour takes about an hour.

The **Peninsula Fine Arts Center** (☎ 757-596 8175) at 101 Museum Drive, an affiliate of the Virginia Museum, has changing exhibits ranging from national traveling exhibitions to the work of regional artists and craftspersons. It is open Tuesday to Saturday from 10 am to 5 pm, Sunday 1 to 5 pm; admission is free.

The **Virginia Living Museum** is one of the best places to see the state's wildlife – everything from eagles and otters to bullfrogs and bobcats – close up and in natural settings. Kids will love the proximity of the critters, and everyone seems to enjoy the planetarium and aquarium. The museum (☎ 757-595-1900), at 524 J Clyde Morris Blvd, is open Memorial Day to Labor Day, Monday to Saturday from 9 am to 6 pm (Thursday until 9 pm), Sunday from 10 am to 6 pm; otherwise, Monday to Saturday from 9 am to 5 pm (Thursday 7 to 9 pm), Sunday from 1 to 5 pm. Admission is $5 for adults and $3.25 for children; add 50¢ for the planetarium.

The **US Army Transportation Museum** (☎ 757-878-1183) is in Building 300, Besson Hall at Fort Eustis. Trucks, uniforms, differentials, dip sticks, mud flaps, torque, all forms of horsepower and rpm, clad in khaki and camouflage, are here. It is open daily from 9 am to 4:30 pm, as the staff keep federal public service hours; entry is free.

Organized Cruises

Harbour Cruises at Watermen's Wharf (☎ 757-245-1533, 800-362-3046), 530

VIRGINIA

12th St, cruise all of Hampton Roads; they have the only boat that covers the whole harbor. Two-hour cruises depart daily from April to October; the cost is $12.50 for adults, $11 for seniors, and $6.25 for children three to 11.

Special Events

The Celebration in Lights (☎ 757-247-8451) is held in Newport News Park from Thanksgiving through January 1; access to the twinkling displays costs $7. The Newport News Fall Festival, a two-day celebration of traditional crafts, is held in Newport News Park in early October. In mid-March, there is a reenactment of the *Monitor/Merrimack* naval battle (see the Battle of the Ironclads sidebar) at the Monitor-Merrimack Overlook.

Places to Stay

The *Mulberry Inn* (☎ 757-887-3000), 16890 Warwick Blvd (Exit 250A off I-64), has a pool and exercise room; doubles are $48/64 in winter/summer.

There are a couple of reasonable places near Exit 255A off I-64. The *Comfort Inn* (☎ 757-249-0200) is a mid-range place at 12330 Jefferson Ave; singles are from $58 to $65 and doubles from $65 to $72; this includes a 'free' breakfast. The *Hampton Inn & Suites* (☎ 757-249-0001), at 12251 Jefferson Ave, also has breakfast included, plus in-room movies and airport transportation; singles and doubles are from $69 to $99.

The *Omni Hotel* (☎ 757-873-6664) at 1000 Omni Blvd (Exit 258A off I-64), has a heated pool and dining room; singles/doubles are $69/79. The *Ramada Inn & Conference Center* (☎ 757-599-4460) at 950 J Clyde Morris Blvd also has all the facilities and the in-house *Chatfield's Restaurant*; in low season, singles/doubles are from $58/63, and in high season $94/99.

Places to Eat

Bon Appétit (☎ 757-873-0644), at 11710 Jefferson Ave, blends tasty French and Vietnamese dishes; large entrees cost from $10 to $20. *Monty's Penguin* (☎ 757-595-2151), 9607 Warwick Blvd, is an old-fashioned drive-in that serves family-style food for under $10 per person (and nostalgia for free).

At the *Manhattan Bagel* (☎ 757-988-1988), another Jefferson Ave venue (No 12783), you can get a hearty meal for under $10; it is open daily for breakfast and lunch.

Herman's Harbor House (☎ 757-930-1000), at 663 Deep Creek Rd, is the place for seafood dishes; it is open for lunch and dinner, and main courses are from $10 to $20.

Getting There & Away

The Newport News/Williamsburg International Airport (☎ 757-877-0221) is in Newport News. The main service is provided by USAir/USAir Express, United Express, and ValuJet. A taxi or shuttle to Newport News is from $6 to $15. The PENTRAN bus is available from in front of the terminal building (see Getting Around).

The Amtrak station (☎ 757-245-3589) is at 9304 Warwick Blvd, at Lafayette Square. There is a shuttle bus to Norfolk and Virginia Beach from this, the closest station to Hampton Roads.

The Greyhound/Trailways (☎ 757-599-3900) terminal is at 9702 Jefferson Ave. There is service to most East Coast cities.

Getting Around

PENTRAN (☎ 757-722-2837, TDD 722-8427) has scheduled routes in the Newport News/Hampton areas. PENTRAN services connect with JCCT in upper York County (going to Williamsburg) and with TRT in Norfolk via the Crossroads service. The latter originates at the downtown Newport News Transportation Center, 150 35th St.

SMITHFIELD

Across the James River from Newport News is the sizable community of Smithfield, in Isle of Wight County (one of the state's eight original shires). It was once called Warrosquoyacke, after the original Native American inhabitants, but was changed as many of its first English settlers hailed from the Isle of Wight. It is a pleasant, relaxed option for those visitors who don't mind 'commuting' to the attractions of Hampton Roads. The visitors center (☎ 757-357-5182) at 130 Main St is open daily from 9 am to 5 pm.

There are a number of historic buildings, and entry to all of them is free. **Fort Boykin**, in a park at 7410 Fort Boykin Trail, was built in 1623 to protect settlers against Native Americans and Spaniards. The fort (☎ 757-357-2291), shaped as a seven-point star, has featured in every major war fought on mainland American soil. It is open daily from 9 am to 6 pm.

St Luke's Shrine (☎ 757-357-3367) at 14477 Benn's Church Blvd, is the oldest existing church of English foundation in the country (1632) and the only surviving example of original Gothic design. It is open from February to December, Tuesday to Saturday from 10 am to 4 pm, Sunday 1 to 4 pm.

The **Isle of Wight Museum** (☎ 757-357-7459) at 103 Main St has an odd collection focusing on county history, eg, the world-famous Smithfield hams (the edible variety, not amateur theater). The museum is open Tuesday to Thursday and Saturday from 10 am to 4 pm, Friday 10 am to 2 pm, and Sunday 1 to 5 pm.

Places to Stay & Eat

The *Smithfield Station Waterfront Inn* (☎ 757-357-7700) at 415 S Church St (Route 10) has a picture-postcard waterfront setting, and overlooks the Pagan River. Single and double rooms in the 'station' are from $59 to $89 in the low season (up to $125 in the high season) and the suites in the quaint lighthouse range from $175 to $225.

The *Smithfield Inn* (☎ 757-357-1752) at 112 Main St dates from 1752; singles and doubles in this elegant establishment (with its renowned restaurant) are $125. Much cheaper, but not lacking in facilities, is the *Isle of Wight Inn* (☎ 757-357-3176) at 1607 S Church St; singles are from $52 to $89 and doubles from $59 to $119.

All of the restaurants serve the famous Virginia dry-cured hams, made from peanut-fed hogs. The *Smithfield Station* (see above) is a local favorite and is open daily for lunch and dinner – there is a Sunday-brunch omelet bar and outdoor raw bar.

For good old-fashioned country fare, there is the *Twins Ole Towne Inn* (☎ 757-357-3031), at 220 Main St, so named because it is run by twin sisters. *Ken's Bar-B-Q Place* (☎ 757-357-5601), on Hwy 258, prepares a North Carolina-style barbecue that will make pit-cooked meat-lovers' mouths water. At 208 Main St is the kid's favorite, *Smithfield Confectionery & Ice Cream* (☎ 757-357-6166), for sandwiches and a classic soda fountain.

VIRGINIA BEACH

Virginia Beach (population 431,000) is the fastest growing city on the East Coast (and Virginia's largest). It has been described by some observers as 'the boom town of the 1990s.' The city is everything it unashamedly attempts to be – a magnet for young revelers, a carefully spun web of tackiness, and an almost impenetrable concrete palisade that often prevents the sun's rays from reaching the beach.

There has been a concerted attempt near the high rises to 'tart up' the city and to make it more 'family friendly.' Six miles of crowded beach has been renovated with the addition of parkland, benches, lighting, and a two-mile long bike trail.

So what are the city's good points? Probably its proximity to some truly beautiful parts of Virginia, such as the Great Dismal Swamp and Seashore and False Cape state parks, and to the excellent Virginia Marine Science Museum, Edgar Cayce's ARE, and a host of other activities removed from the glitz.

History

The first settlement along this strip of coast was at Lynnhaven Bay in 1621. One of the first settlers' homes from that time, the Adam Thoroughgood House, still stands (see below). The coast has always been famous for shipwrecks, and the increasing

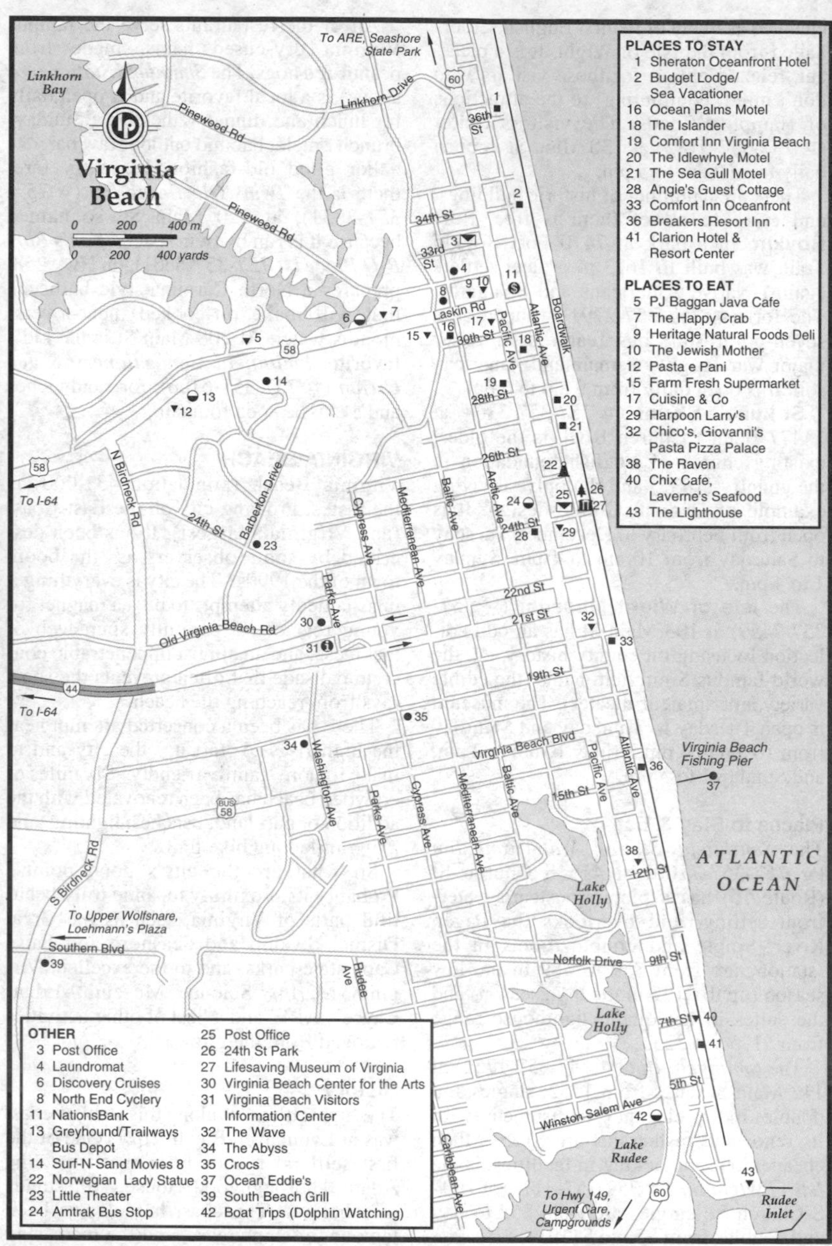
Virginia Beach
PLACES TO STAY
1 Sheraton Oceanfront Hotel
2 Budget Lodge/ Sea Vacationer
16 Ocean Palms Motel
18 The Islander
19 Comfort Inn Virginia Beach
20 The Idlewhyle Motel
21 The Sea Gull Motel
28 Angie's Guest Cottage
33 Comfort Inn Oceanfront
36 Breakers Resort Inn
41 Clarion Hotel & Resort Center
PLACES TO EAT
5 PJ Baggan Java Cafe
7 The Happy Crab
9 Heritage Natural Foods Deli
10 The Jewish Mother
12 Pasta e Pani
15 Farm Fresh Supermarket
17 Cuisine & Co
29 Harpoon Larry's
32 Chico's, Giovanni's Pasta Pizza Palace
38 The Raven
40 Chix Cafe, Laverne's Seafood
43 The Lighthouse
OTHER
3 Post Office
4 Laundromat
6 Discovery Cruises
8 North End Cyclery
11 NationsBank
13 Greyhound/Trailways Bus Depot
14 Surf-N-Sand Movies 8
22 Norwegian Lady Statue
23 Little Theater
24 Amtrak Bus Stop
25 Post Office
26 24th St Park
27 Lifesaving Museum of Virginia
30 Virginia Beach Center for the Arts
31 Virginia Beach Visitors Information Center
32 The Wave
34 The Abyss
35 Crocs
37 Ocean Eddie's
39 South Beach Grill
42 Boat Trips (Dolphin Watching)
To ARE, Seashore State Park
Linkhorn Bay
Linkhorn Drive
Pinewood Rd
To I-64
To Upper Wolfsnare, Loehmann's Plaza
Southern Blvd
To Hwy 149, Urgent Care, Campgrounds
Virginia Beach Fishing Pier
ATLANTIC OCEAN
Lake Holly
Lake Rudee
Rudee Inlet
Boardwalk
Atlantic Ave
Pacific Ave
Arctic Ave
Baltic Ave
Mediterranean Ave
Cypress Ave
Parks Ave
Washington Ave
Caribbean Ave
Rudee Ave
N Birdneck Rd
S Birdneck Rd
Barberton Drive
Laskin Rd
Old Virginia Beach Rd
Virginia Beach Blvd
Norfolk Drive
Winston Salem Ave
0 200 400 m
0 200 400 yards
VIRGINIA

number of tragedies led Congress to establish a lifesaving station here. In 1791, the Cape Henry Lighthouse was built to guide ships into Chesapeake Bay. One of the worst wrecks was that of the *Dictator*, which foundered in March 1891.

The first hotel was built on the oceanfront in 1883, and the Beach quickly developed as a holiday retreat. In 1970, there were 172,000 people living in the city, but in 1980 the beach was 'found' and the resulting influx of residents meant that the population by 1990, in a mere 10 years, had doubled to 393,000. The population is now expected to surpass half a million by the year 2000.

Orientation

You can find your way around Virginia Beach easily. The numbered streets run east-west, while named avenues run north-south, parallel to the beach. If you enter the beach area via Route 44 (the Virginia Beach-Norfolk Expressway), you reach the center of the resort area at 22nd St, not far from the visitors center. Alternatively, Hwy 58 emerges at the beach at 31st St (Laskin Rd), and from the Eastern Shore (via the Chesapeake Bay Bridge-Tunnel and Hwy 13) you can follow Hwy 60 (Shore Drive) to reach the resort area from the north.

Information

Tourist Offices The Virginia Beach Visitors Information Center (☎ 757-437-4888, 800-822-3224) is at the east end of Route 44 (Exit 284 off I-64) about half a mile west of the beach on 21st St (2100 Parks Ave). Its enthusiastic staff advise on sights in the area and budget and other accommodations. The center is open daily in season from 9 am to 8 pm, Labor Day to Memorial Day from 9 am to 5 pm. There are information kiosks at 17th, 24th, and 27th Sts, on Atlantic Ave. There is also a Virginia Beach self-guided auto tour; a tape can be rented for $6 (with a $10 deposit).

Useful publications, available free from the visitors centers and accommodations, include *Virginia Beach Visitors Guide*, *Vacationer's Guide*, an accommodations directory, and *Sunny Day Guide*.

Money Use the Norfolk International Airport exchange facilities before coming to the beach, as the banks charge hefty fees to exchange currencies. The NationsBank (☎ 800-880-5454), at the corner of Pacific Ave and 31st St (Laskin Rd), is convenient for other banking services.

Post Office The post office (☎ 757-428-2821), at the corner of 24th St and Atlantic Ave, is open Monday to Friday from 8 am to 4:30 pm. There is also a post office (☎ 757-428-4826) at 33rd St and Arctic Ave.

Laundry The Ocean Front laundromat is on 32nd St at Arctic Ave, beside the 7-11.

Medical Services The cheapest emergency medical option is Urgent Care (☎ 757-481-2333), at 1120 First Colonial Rd, next to the Virginia Beach General Hospital. The Virginia Beach General Hospital (☎ 757-481-8181), 1060 First Colonial Rd, has 24-hour emergency facilities. There are no all-night pharmacies at the beach; you have to go to the hospital. There are a couple of handy pharmacies – Ingram's, at 25th St and Pacific Ave, and Rite Aid, at 31st St and Arctic Ave.

Virginia Marine Science Museum

This great museum, at 717 General Booth Blvd, two miles inland from the mouth of Rudee Inlet, is one of the city's highlights. There are over 200 exhibits focusing on the sea, and many of them are of the hands-on variety. You can observe waders in a nearby salt marsh, handle crabs, simulate exploration undersea in a submarine, and gaze into endless aquaria. The Owls Creek Salt Marsh building houses an indoor/outdoor otter habitat and an outdoor aviary.

The museum (☎ 757-425-3474) is open Labor Day to mid-June, Monday to Sunday from 9 am to 5 pm; otherwise, Monday to Saturday from 9 am to 9 pm, Sunday from 9 am to 5 pm. Admission is about $5.25 for adults, $4.75 for seniors, and $4.50 for children four to 12. New rates are soon to be announced (prices are likely to double), as there are many more attractions planned for the future, among them an IMAX theater and a much larger aquarium.

You can go **dolphin watching** out at sea with the VMSM (☎ 757-437-4949) from mid-June to September. You will see the pods feeding, swimming, and playing near the shore. Trips in the *Miss Virginia Beach* depart during the season, from the Virginia Beach Fishing Center at Rudee Inlet, 200 Winston Salem Ave, Monday to Saturday between 9 am and 4:30 pm. The cost is $12 for adults, $10 for children; pay at the dock.

The bottlenose dolphins return here in ever increasing numbers from May to November. On one July Saturday, in an orchestrated search, there were 407 dolphins sighted. Cape Henry has taken on the deserved title of 'Dolphin Disneyland.' Farther south, at Cape Hatteras, dolphins are seen year round – this half-year migration has yet to be explained.

On an **ocean collections boat trip**, also conducted by the VMSM (☎ 757-437-4949), you can see all types of marine creatures hauled aboard the *Miss Virginia Beach*. These creatures are placed in temporary tanks and then discussed by the knowledgeable staff. Trips are conducted on Wednesdays from 12:45 to 2 pm for three months between late June and late August. The cost is $10 for adults, $8 for children.

Lifesaving Museum of Virginia

This interesting museum (☎ 757-422-1587) is by the oceanfront in the 1903 Seatack Lifesaving Station, on the corner of 24th St and Atlantic Ave. It has many exhibits about shipwrecks along this part of the coast, ship models, and displays of lifesaving equipment. Particularly interesting is the exhibit in the upper gallery relating to the Battle of the Atlantic, fought during WWII.

It is open Monday to Saturday from 10 am to 5 pm, Sunday noon to 5 pm (closed Monday from October to Memorial Day); admission is $2.50 for adults, $2 for senior citizens, and $1 for children 6 to 18.

A block north, on the boardwalk, is the **Norwegian Lady statue**, commemorating the wreck of the Norwegian ship *Dictator* off Virginia Beach in March 1891.

Virginia Beach Center for the Arts

This center (☎ 757-425-0000), at 2200 Parks Ave hosts workshops, performances, and exhibitions related to the extensive collection of 20th century art. The center sponsors the popular June Boardwalk Art Show. It is open Tuesday to Saturday 10 am to 4 pm and Sunday noon to 4 pm; admission is free.

Adam Thoroughgood House

This brick house, at 1636 Parish Rd, inland from the bay shore, dates from 1680. It is named after a plantation owner, Adam Thoroughgood, an indentured servant who settled in Virginia in 1621. Thoroughgood's grandson probably constructed the small, four-roomed building. It was built of brick and oyster shell mortar and made to resemble an English cottage. The house was fully restored in 1957 and is furnished with antiques.

Thoroughgood House (☎ 757-460-0007) is open January through March, Tuesday to Saturday from noon to 5 pm; otherwise, Tuesday to Saturday from 10 am to 5 pm and Sunday noon to 5 pm. Admission is $3 for adults, $1.50 for seniors and students. A combination ticket ($6, $4.50) also gets you into the Moses Myers and Willoughby-Baylor houses, both in Norfolk (see that section).

Association for Research & Enlightenment

New Age meets the beach at the Association for Research and Enlightenment (ARE), founded by the psychic Edgar Cayce (see the sidebar opposite). The association's building seems an incongruity, tucked away here at the corner of 67th St and Atlantic Ave (near the sun-tanned paradise of the beach), but some revelers may feel the time is ripe for rejuvenation.

Visitors can have their own psychic ability (ESP quotient) tested on electronic equipment, watch an informative video on the life of Cayce, meditate in a tranquil garden or in a 3rd-floor room that overlooks the ocean, attend a lecture, watch a movie on the paranormal, or just practice skepticism. A full library concentrates on Cayce's voluminous philosophies.

The center (☎ 757-428-3588) is open Monday to Saturday from 9 am to 8 pm, Sunday from 11 am to 8 pm, but believers can travel through the ether at any time they like; admission to this 'other world' is free.

Historical Sites

The **Cape Henry Memorial** marks the site of the first landing of Jamestown's colonists on April 26, 1607, and where they '. . . set up a Crosse at Chesupioc Bay.' The memorial, at the northern end of Virginia Beach in Fort Story (☎ 757-898-3400), can be visited daily from 8 am to 5 pm; admission is free (you may need to show the military guard a picture identification). At the end of a small boardwalk, a relief map indicates the disposition of opposing French and British forces during the Battle of the Capes (see the Battle of Yorktown sidebar in the Colonial Virginia chapter).

The nearby old **Cape Henry Lighthouse** (☎ 757-422-9421), one of the first public works authorized by Congress, operated continuously from 1791 until 1881. It is open daily from mid-March through October, 10 am to 5 pm; admission is $2 for adults, $1 for seniors and students seven to 18.

The **Francis Land House** (☎ 757-340-1732), 3131 Virginia Beach Blvd, is an 18th century plantation structure with a fine example of a gambrel roof (a ridged roof with the slope broken on each side). It is open daily from 9 am to 5 pm (Sunday noon to 5 pm); admission is $2.50 for adults, $1.50 for seniors, and $1 for students and children.

At 4401 Wishart Rd, **Lynnhaven House** (☎ 757-460-1688) is a small, stately early 18th century structure which typified middle-class living at the time. From May to October, special events, which recreate aspects of 18th century life, are held here. It is open Tuesday to Sunday from noon to 4 pm; admission is $2.50 for adults, $2 for seniors, and $1 for children.

Upper Wolfsnare (☎ 757-491-3490), at 2040 Potters Rd, was built in 1759 by Thomas Walke III, a signer of the Constitution. A Virginia landmark, it has been lovingly preserved by the Princess Anne-Virginia Beach Historical Society. It is open May through October, Wednesday and Thursday from 10 am to 4 pm; admission is $2 for adults and $1 for children six to 12.

Amusement Parks

Some holidaymakers, especially those who choose the beach for a holiday, seek this sort of entertainment. The **Ocean Breeze**

The Sleeping Prophet

Edgar Cayce (pronounced KAY-see), the 'sleeping prophet,' is probably best remembered for his dire prophecies of wars and calamities – the outbreak of WWII, the reemergence of Atlantis, the disappearance of the US west of Nebraska – but these were the smallest part of his work. In fact, of the 14,000 readings he gave from 1923 to 1945, about 65% were on medical problems, and of the rest only 17 concerned changes to the planet! In the sleep state, Cayce could diagnose an individual's physical state and outline treatment just by knowing the individual's name and address (the person could be anywhere in the world).

In 1925, Cayce moved to Virginia Beach following advice received in one of his own psychic readings. In 1932, he reinforced his decision by adding, 'of all the resorts that are in the East Coast, Virginia Beach will be the first and the longest-lasting . . . the future is good.' As this was well before the Beach took off, it was pity he wasn't into real estate.

And as for Cayce, he was born in Hopkinsville, Kentucky, in 1877, died at Virginia Beach in 1945, and may reappear in 2158 on the sea coast of Nebraska. ■

Fun Park (☎ 757-422-6628, 800-678-9453) is at 849 General Booth Blvd. It combines four themes in one – Wildwater Rapids, Motorworld, Shipwreck Golf, and Strike Zone (a baseball simulation). The last thing you would probably want to do after a shipwreck is play golf! The park is open daily, and entry to the Rapids is $16 for adults and $11 for children ($11 for all after 4 pm). Motorworld, Shipwreck Golf, and Strike Zone are $2 each, or $1 with a Rapids ticket.

Admission to the **Fun Spot Action Park** (☎ 757-422-1401), at the corner of Virginia Beach Blvd and Birdneck Rd, is free, but you pay for the rides individually. A free shuttle connects the resort strip and the park from 10 am to 11 pm. The **Atlantic Fun Center** (☎ 757-422-1742), at the corner of 25th St and Atlantic Ave, features the Haunted Fun House, the Virginia Dinosaur Museum (kids love it), and an arcade/video area. There are a plethora of time-wasters on Atlantic Ave, between 15th and 30th Sts.

Surfing & Swimming

Surfing is not permitted on the main part of the beach, but skeg-heads and grommets hang out at the south end, near Rudee Inlet, and on either side of the 14th St pier. Each year in August, Virginia Beach is host to a leg of the Bud Surf Tour (East Coast Surfing Championships), which attracts professionals from all over the world. Wave Riding Vehicles (☎ 757-422-8823) will provide a local surf report and information on the main surf areas. Another number to try is ☎ 757-428-0404.

In summer, the beach is patrolled by lifeguards from 2nd to 42nd Sts. There are more remote beaches to the south at Sandbridge, False Cape State Park, and Back Bay National Wildlife Refuge; to get there, take General Booth Blvd then Sandbridge Rd. These places are all signed.

Bicycling

The beach is a great place to bike, as there are many bike paths in the vicinity of the boardwalk or along it. The boardwalk is probably the best place for a visitor to pick up a bike (about $5 per hour, see Getting Around in this section). The visitors center provides the *Virginia Beach Bikeway Map* for planning before you set off.

If you want to venture farther afield (get the bike for a day), the ride south to Sandbridge Beach is recommended and offers a respite from the crowds. Once there, you can bike through to the trail at Back Bay. North of Virginia Beach is the Seashore State Park, with its six-mile Cape Henry cycler's trail.

Fishing

There are a couple of fishing piers where you may be rewarded for your patience. The Lynnhaven Fishing Pier (☎ 757-481-7071), at Starfish Rd off Hwy 60 (Shore Drive), and the Virginia Beach Fishing Pier (☎ 757-428-7211), nestled between 14th and 15th Sts, have bait for sale and rent rods and reels – advice is free. For private charters, contact the Virginia Beach Fishing Center (☎ 757-422-5700) at 200 Winston Salem Ave.

Other Activities

As a resort, the beach caters to just about every outdoor taste. For **scuba diving** information contact Lynnhaven Dive Center (☎ 757-481-7949), at 1413 Great Neck Rd, or Atlantic Dive Charters (☎ 757-482-9777), 1324 Teresa Drive, in Chesapeake.

Other popular pastimes along the boardwalk are **jogging** and **in-line skating**. For skates, advice, and safety equipment, contact Cherie's Bicycle Rentals (☎ 757-437-8888). There are rental stands at 8th, 22nd, 24th, and 37th Sts.

Also popular is **golf**, and there are several public and private courses. The visitors center's pamphlet *Virginia Beach: Golf* lists all details, such as length, par, and addresses. All levels of ability and budget are accommodated.

Organized Cruises

Virginia Beach Fishing Center/Cruise (☎ 757-422-5700), at 200 Winston Salem Ave in Virginia Beach, operates an oceanfront cruise in the *Miss Virginia Beach* from Rudee Inlet. There are views of the skyline, the old Coast Guard station, Cape Henry, and the lighthouses. They have scheduled sightseeing tours, Memorial Day through Labor Day, at 11 am and 2:30 pm; the cost is $10 for adults, $8 for children.

Discovery Cruises (☎ 757-422-6487) operates scheduled luxury yacht cruises on Virginia Beach's inland waterways, including Broad Bay, May through October; a lunch cruise is $16.75 for adults and $10.50 for children, and a dinner cruise $28 and $16.

Special Events

Virginia Beach hosts a number of popular annual events and festivals. These include the Memorial Day Weekend Celebration (☎ 757-437-4800); the Saltwater Fishing Tournament and the Pungo Strawberry Festival in May; Boardwalk Art Show in June; and the Neptune Festival (☎ 757-498-0215), the biggest of the beach events, in September.

Places to Stay – oceanfront

There are plenty of choices, but most places are expensive; rates sometimes drop if you book for an extended period (don't be afraid to bargain in the off season). On Atlantic and Pacific Aves, parallel to the beach, is where you will find most of the accommodations. The visitors center's free *Virginia Beach: Accommodations* lists 140 places!

Camping The *Virginia Beach KOA Campground* (☎ 757-428-1444), at 1240 General Booth Blvd (2.5 miles from the resort), is a quiet place. Basic sites start at $15 and hook-ups from $20 in low season ($24 and $33 in high season) and comfortable one-room cabins are $46. The *Best Holiday Trav'l Park* (☎ 757-425-0249), on 120 acres at 1075 General Booth Blvd (almost across the road from the KOA), is a huge place with some 1200 sites; these cost from $15 to $18 in low season, $23 to $25 in high season (electricity/water hook-ups are $2/4, respectively). Both camps operate free bus services to the beach.

The campsites amid the sand dunes and cypresses at *Seashore State Park* (☎ 757-481-2131), just off Shore Drive (Hwy 60) at Cape Henry, are very popular. The park has standard sites for $10.50, RV sites without hook-ups for $19.25, and two-bedroom cabins for $82 per night ($510 per week).

Hostels The only reasonably cheap place at the beach is *Angie's Guest Cottage-Bed & Breakfast and HI-AYH Hostel* (☎ 757-428-4690) at 302 24th St, just one block from the beach. The owner, Barbara Yates, and her friendly staff have done a lot to make this one of the best places to stay on the Virginia coast. In the busy season, late May to early September, dorm beds are $11.50 for Hosteling International members and $14.50 for nonmembers; otherwise, the cost is $8.50 and $11.50. Sheet rental is $2. Rooms in the B&B section are from $40/48 for singles/doubles (cheaper in the low season). Check-in is between noon and 9 pm only, as the owners need their sleep. The spacious barbecue area behind the rooms makes up for the cramped kitchen.

Hotels & Motels – bottom end The *Ocean Palms Motel* (☎ 757-428-8362), at the corner of 30th St and Arctic Ave, has two-room singles and double apartments from $245 to $420 for a week's stay. Another good budget option (if there are a few of you) is the *Islander* (☎ 757-425-8300), at the corner of 29th and Pacific Ave; from $60 to $82 secures a two-room apartment with cooking facilities and enough mattresses for six.

At the utilitarian *Idlewhyle Motel* (☎ 757-428-9341), at 2705 Atlantic Ave, you get a choice of a pool or ocean view. The rooms, from $30 a day in winter (but $85 in summer), are not flash, but this place is well located.

The *Budget Lodge/Sea Vacationer* (☎ 757-428-4413), at 3309 Atlantic Ave, has all the amenities, including a heated pool with diving board; rates are $25 to $35 in winter, $74 to $88 in high season.

Hotels & Motels – middle The *Comfort Inn Virginia Beach* (☎ 757-428-2203), at 2800 Pacific Ave, includes a free breakfast in its winter rates for doubles; the cost ranges from $38 to $69 (in high season it is from $89 to $159). The *Comfort Inn Oceanfront* (☎ 757-425-8200), at 20th St and Atlantic Ave, is more expensive – it's on the beach – with winter singles and doubles from $45 to $115. The *Sea Gull Motel* (☎ 757-425-5711), on the oceanfront at 27th St, has a rooftop deck and indoor pool; the comfortable double rooms are from $45 to $70 in winter, almost double that in summer.

The more upmarket *Clarion Hotel & Resort Center* (☎ 757-422-3186, 800-345-3186) overlooks the ocean at 501 Atlantic Ave and has a heated pool and sauna. It has attractive single/double rooms from $40/50 in winter, $125/135 in summer.

The *Breakers Resort Inn* (☎ 757-428-1821), at 1503 Atlantic Ave on the oceanfront, is a small, family-operated place with over 50 rooms, 15 two-room efficiencies, and a pool; rooms are from $40 to $110 in winter, $116 to $195 in high season.

Hotels & Motels – top end The *Ramada Plaza Resort* (☎ 757-428-7025, 800-365-3032), on the oceanfront at 57th St, caters to the convention crowd, who expect all the facilities their companies have paid for. Facilities include a restaurant, indoor and outdoor pools, and a fully equipped gym. Singles and doubles are from $34 to $79 in winter, $79 to $189 in summer.

The *Sheraton Oceanfront Hotel* (☎ 757-425-9000), on the oceanfront at 36th St, has all the facilities including two pools and a dining room; in winter singles/doubles are from $56/66 and in summer from $114.

The resort *Cavalier Hotels* (☎ 757-425-8555, 800-446-8199), at the corner of 42nd St and Atlantic Ave in a quiet part of town, is a gargantuan place with just about every facility imaginable and a price tag to match (rooms in summer are from $125 to $169). It combines an old red-brick building – the original 1927 Cavalier Hotel (on 42nd St and Pacific Ave) – with an adjacent 1973 high-rise with its own beach. Facilities include three restaurants; indoor, outdoor and children's pools; aerobics facilities; and croquet, tennis, and volleyball areas.

Places to Stay – Lynnhaven Inlet

There are a number of places near the Lynnhaven Inlet Bridge, to the east of the Bay Bridge-Tunnel. The *Econo Lodge-Chesapeake Beach* (☎ 757-481-0666), at 2968 Shore Drive (Hwy 60), has winter rates from $35 to $60 and summer rates from $65 to $79.

The *Comfort Inn Little Creek* (☎ 757-427-5500), at 5189 Shore Drive (just west of Independence Blvd), is a good mid-range choice. In winter, singles and doubles are from $38, in summer around $75.

The expensive choice (but a great one for those who have discovered the delights of the Duck-Inn – see Places to Eat) is the *Virginia Beach Resort Hotel* (☎ 757-481-9000, 800-468-2722) at 2800 Shore Drive; singles are from $89 and doubles from $99 in winter, rising to at least $150 and $160 in summer.

Places to Eat

You may at first think that there is little else but fast/junk food at the Beach. If you look carefully, you'll find more healthy, delicious, and elegant alternatives. Get a copy of *Virginia Beach: Dining* from the visitor center.

For those on a tight budget, the *Virginia Beach Farmers' Market* (☎ 757-427-4395), at 1989 Landstown Rd, is a good choice. It is open daily from 9 am to 6:30 pm, until dusk in winter, and sells dairy products, jams, spices, nuts, meats, and country-style food. Note that there is no public transport here.

Another good place, the 24-hour *Farm Fresh Supermarket*, at 521 Laskin Rd (31st St), has a preservative-free salad bar where you can buy fresh fruit and frozen yogurt. You can get organic salads, sandwiches, and vegetarian entrees at the *Heritage Natural Foods Deli* (☎ 757-428- 0500), at 314 Laskin Rd; it is open for lunch and dinner daily. Open daily, *Bagelworks* (☎ 757-496-2596), at 1268 Great Neck Village Rd, is the place to go for a bun with a hole in the middle.

The *Jewish Mother* (☎ 757-422-5430), at 3108 Pacific Ave, is the first place you should try – you and all the other budget travelers. During the day, it is worth it for the delicious crepes ($5 to $9), pitas ('frisbees for grandchildren' – $4.35), sandwiches ($4 to $6), salads, and desserts. At night it metamorphoses into a late-night beer bar, often with free live music (sometimes there's a cover of $2 to $15). It is open Monday to Thursday 9:30 am to 2 am, Friday 9:30 am to 3 am, Saturday 8:30 am to 3 am, and Sunday 7:30 am to 2 am. There is no cover charge at the bar, and the free take-home menu contains a handy guide to Jewish culinary terms.

At *The Raven* (☎ 757-425-1200), at 1200 Atlantic Ave, you can eat inside in the tinted greenhouse or outdoors when the weather permits. There is a range of seafood and steak meals (from $12), as well as sandwiches and burgers ($5 to $7). It is open daily from 11 to 2 am. Brunch is always a delight, especially the Raven champignon.

Chix Cafe (☎ 757-428-6836), next to the Hilton at the corner of Atlantic Ave and 7th St, is a fab little outdoor cafe with music; it's now an ex-best-kept secret. *Laverne's Seafood*, the sister restaurant (why sister?) of Chix, offers the same menu; it's known for its 'build-your-own' seafood platters.

Coffeehouses Caffeine addicts can get a fix at several locations. *Cuisine & Co* (☎ 757-428-6700), at 30th St and Pacific Ave, is open for breakfast, lunch, and dinner daily, with sandwiches, soup, salads, and delicious homemade desserts. The *First Colony Coffee House* (☎ 757-428-2994), at Hilltop East, Laskin Rd, has good coffee and live acoustic/folk music; it is open daily and serves a great brunch on Sunday.

Other places are the *Happy Hog Espresso Bar* (☎ 757-340-4144), 3101 Virginia Beach Blvd, which is open Tuesday to Saturday; and *PJ Baggan Java Cafe* (☎ 757-491-8900), at 960 Laskin Rd, which is open daily from 8 am to 10 pm for espresso, sandwiches, and a selection of fine wines.

Continental There are a number of Italian places. *Chico's* (☎ 757-422-6011), on Atlantic Ave between 20th and 21st Sts, serves lashings of spaghetti to a youngish crowd. It too stays open long after the plates have been cleared away as a popular, frenetic bar. The hours are weekdays from 5 pm to 2 am, weekends from 1 pm to 2 am. *Giovanni's Pasta Pizza Palace* (☎ 757-425-1575), at 2006 Atlantic Ave, has a good selections of pastas, pizzas, and grinders; it is open daily from noon to 11 pm. *Pasta e Pani* (☎ 757-428-2299), at 1065 Laskin Rd, wins lots of friends with great homemade pasta (seasoned with lemon and black pepper), terrific seafood specials, hearty fresh breads, and a tempting, tiered dessert cart.

Le Chambord (☎ 757-498-1234), at 324 N Great Neck Rd, is a popular institution with food that is anything but 'institutionalized.' The Belgian chef serves up masterpieces, such as sweetbread with lobster sauce and wild boar tenderloin with marinated dried figs, as well as great desserts. A meal for two with wine costs about $55. Next door is the *Bistro and Rotisserie at Le Chambord* (☎ 757-486-3636), a budget version of its neighbor, with a more casual atmosphere. You select from pork, lamb, and chicken rotating in huge glass cases. The excellent desserts are the same as next door.

Asian For cheap bento (box lunches), sushi, and tempura, try the delightful *Aji-Ichiban* (☎ 757-490-0499) at 309 Aragona Blvd where you can see one of the few female sushi chefs in action. The *Shogun* (☎ 757-422-5150), 550 First Colonial Rd, is a popular place for sushi and Japanese cuisine prepared at your table; an entree will cost about $11.

If you're looking for Thai food, you have a couple of choices. The *Bangkok Garden*

(☎ 757-498-5009) at Loehmann's Plaza, open for lunch and dinner daily, serves an excellent tom yum talay; and the *New Bangkok* (☎ 757-523-2900), at 5313 Indian River Rd, has a great pad thai (stir-fried noodles). Two people can eat at either of these places for less than $20.

The impecunious will revel in the fare at the cheap *Asian Buffet* on Laskin Rd, on the right just after First Colonial Rd.

Seafood This is a logical dining choice in these parts, and there are plenty of opportunities to sample it. One of the best raw bars around is *Harpoon Larry's* (☎ 757-422-6000) in the converted rail carriage at 216 24th St at the corner of Pacific Ave; it is open for lunch and dinner, and most diners will be well satisfied for $10 or less.

At 1st St and Atlantic Ave is the expensive *Lighthouse* (☎ 757-428-7974). This place is furnished simply, but all tables have a view of either the inlet or the ocean. Once the food is served (crab, shrimp, scallops, Maine lobsters), however, the view is secondary. The all-you-can-eat buffet is $25 for adults, $11 for kids (if they can handle a little shucking).

At 550 Laskin Rd is the *Happy Crab* (☎ 757-437-9200) – a happiness, I suppose, that depends upon the perspective . . . the crab's or yours. But if crab-cracking and shucking any form of steamed seafood interests you, you will not be disappointed. A bucket of crabs is $25 for two and a less threatening seafood platter is $16. It is open from 11 am to 10:30 pm daily.

There are a number of seafood places near the Lynnhaven Inlet. The *Lynnhaven Fish House* (☎ 757-481-0003), 2350 Starfish Rd at the top of the fishing pier, is good for oysters and chowders; entrees, such as swordfish and salmon steaks, average about $20. Also good for oysters, chowder (with crab meat, shrimp, and mushrooms), and a host of other tasty seafood dishes (crab cakes included) is the *Duck-Inn* (☎ 757-481-0201), just off Shore Drive at the east side of the Lynnhaven Bridge. In summer, dine on the outdoor deck (Friday evenings are an absolute must – dress as if you have just come from the office).

Charlie's (☎ 757-481-9863), on the south side of Shore Drive (No 3139) near the Lynnhaven Inlet, is an inexpensive seafood place that has fabulous crab. They even sell she-crab soup packed in ice to go, and on most nights there is an all-you-can-eat shrimp special. Oh, almost forgot *Henry's* (☎ 757-481-7300) at 3319 Shore Drive (also Lynnhaven), which is open until about 10:30 pm most nights. The food is almost secondary to the aquarium and other nautical delights until you bite into the fresh fish.

Entertainment

Music Entertainment listings can be found in the free *Portfolio* and *Vacationers Guide*.

Oh, to be young again, fading youth return to me now! There is a multiplicity of singles bars and flashy clubs between 17th and 23rd St along Pacific and Atlantic Aves. *Chico's* (see Places to Eat) is one such place. *The Wave*, if you are willing to take the plunge, is also between 20th and 21st Sts on Atlantic Ave. The dress code is 'show as much tantalizing flesh as possible without giving the impression that you are near nude.' It is open daily from 4:30 pm to 1:30 am, and there is no cover charge. *The Abyss* (☎ 757-422-0480), on 19th St, is the new 'in' place, probably because under-21s can go in.

If you are not out in search of Mr or Ms World and just want to enjoy some music, there are a couple of clubs worth checking out. *Ocean Eddie's* (☎ 757-425-7742), on the 14th St pier, has a wild Friday-night bash where many of the town's young and not-so-young end up dancing on the tables to the strains of a country/R&B band. It is a bit quieter on other nights but a good place for a meal and views of the beach.

Other rock or pop venues are *Scullys* (☎ 757-468-7625), at 3472 Holland Rd; the *South Beach Grill* (☎ 757-428-0820), at 1091 Norfolk Ave, home of local legends, the Snard Bros; and the *Sunset Grille* (☎ 757-481-9815), at 2973 Shore Drive, catering to those reliving the '50s and '60s with performances by the Barflys and Snuff.

For country and bluegrass, there is *Sonny's 2-Step Inn* (☎ 757-486-3873) at 172 S Plaza Trail. Acoustic/folk performances are often the backdrop when having a meal at *Abbey Road* (☎ 757-425-6330), at 203 22nd St; the *First Colony Coffee House* (see earlier); and *Hot Tuna Grill* (☎ 757-481-2888), at 2817 Shore Drive. The latter has wall-to-wall yuppies and sailors. *Crocs*, at the corner of 19th St and Cypress Ave, is for a slightly more seasoned bunch, and there is live music and DJs. It gives a new meaning to the saying 'old croc.'

For classical music, the *Virginia Symphony* occasionally plays at the 24th St Stage on the boardwalk.

From April through Labor Day weekend, there is free nightly entertainment at the 17th and 24th St stages. Someone quipped that there was free entertainment – people watching – all year round.

Cinemas There are plenty of cinemas, including the *AMC Lynnhaven 8* (☎ 757-463-2628), next to the mall on Lynnhaven Parkway; the *Cinema Cafe* (☎ 757-499-6165), at 758 Independence Blvd; and the *Surf-N-Sand Movies 8* (☎ 757-425-3838), at 941 Laskin Rd.

Theater The *Little Theater of Virginia Beach Inc* (☎ 757-428-9233), at the corner of 24th St and Barberton Drive, is the place to see local talent perform theatrical productions ranging from dramas to musicals. Performances happen year round, Friday and Saturday evenings at 8 pm and Sunday matinees at 3 pm.

Getting There & Away

Virginia Beach is served by Norfolk International Airport (☎ 757-857-3351). There is a shuttle service (☎ 757-857-1231) from the airport to the resort area, 15 miles away (30 minutes by car).

The Greyhound/Trailways terminal (☎ 757-422-2998, 800-231-2222) is at 1017 Laskin Rd. Make sure, when you book your tickets, that the Greyhound terminus is specified as Virginia Beach. The downtown Norfolk terminal is not a nice place late at night. The TRT has only two bus services to the oceanfront/resort area, Nos 20 and 37, but realize it takes about two hours to get here from Norfolk.

The Amtrak agent in Virginia Beach is Great Atlantic Travel (☎ 757-422-0444) at 1065 Laskin Rd (Suite No 101). Amtrak does not have a station at the beach; the nearest is in Newport News at 9304 Warwick Blvd (☎ 800-872-7245). There is free bus service from Newport News to the Amtrak shelter at the corner of 24½th St and Pacific Ave (you will need a valid train ticket to get on the bus).

Getting Around

The Atlantic Ave Trolley (☎ 757-428-3388) operates in summer, from noon to midnight, from Rudee Inlet to 42nd St; the fare is 50¢ for adults and children and 25¢ for seniors and disabled. There are other trolleys that run along the beach boardwalk, the North Seashore (for Seashore State Park), and Lynnhaven Mall. Ask for a free schedule.

There are a number of taxis serving Virginia Beach, including Diamond (☎ 757-460-0607), Beach (☎ 757-486-6585), and Yellow Cab (☎ 757-460-0605). Car rentals at the beach include SNAPPY (☎ 757-464-2900) and Budget (☎ 757-486-0050).

Perhaps the best way to get around is by bike. North End Cyclery (☎ 757-428-4235), on the corner of Arctic Ave and Laskin Rd, rents bikes for $3.50 per hour or $15 per day; hours are 10 am to 7 pm daily. Tom's Bike Rentals (☎ 757-425-8454) will drop off bikes for 24-hour rentals complete with locks for $15 ($3 discount if you are staying at Angie's – see Hostels).

AROUND VIRGINIA BEACH

Fortunately, there are many natural areas within easy reach of the bustle of the beach, and several inlets and beaches (eg, Lynnhaven, Broad Bay, and Rudee) where you can fish, swim, boat, or bird watch.

Back Bay National Wildlife Refuge

This 7700-acre refuge was established in 1938 to provide habitat for migratory birds and other wildlife. It also protects habitats of beach, dunes, woodlands, and marsh. Birders are treated to a variety of species on this major Atlantic flyway. The park is only open during daylight hours, and access is limited to the beach shore and to designated trails, such as the Dune and Seaside trails.

You are not allowed to swim or sunbathe on the beach, but surf-casting is permitted. There is a canoe-launching spot for those who want to explore on water; canoes can be rented at Sandbridge Boat Rentals (☎ 757-721-6210) at 3713 Sandpiper Rd.

The entrance is at 4005 Sandpiper Rd, Virginia Beach; take General Booth Blvd then follow the signs via Sandbridge to the refuge. It is open daily from sunrise to sunset; the visitors center is open Monday to Friday from 8 am to 4 pm, Saturday and Sunday from 9 am to 4 pm (it is closed from December to March). Admission is $4 for vehicles, $2 for cyclists or walk-ins. Remember to bring insect repellent!

False Cape State Park

Not much of the Atlantic Coast has escaped the bulldozer and developer, so it is nice to see this undisturbed six-mile stretch of beach that is accessible only by cycle, by boat, or on foot. The park is the southern section of the barrier spit that separates Back Bay from the Atlantic. On the north side is the Back Bay National Wildlife Refuge (five miles of which you have to walk through if you are here on foot) and the southern edge is the North Carolina border.

Primitive camping is allowed in the park ($7 per site), but you will need to get a permit from the visitors center at Seashore State Park – and, most importantly, bring drinking water. Once here, you will realize it was worth the effort.

Seashore State Park & Natural Area

It is such a blessing having this unique environment of sand dunes, salt marsh, and freshwater cypress ponds so close to Virginia Beach – its proximity makes it the state's most visited state park. There are nearly 30 miles of trails (including one accessible to the handicapped) within the park's 2770 acres. Open from sunrise to sunset, the park encourages visitors to learn a lot about the environment and animal habitats.

The visitors center (☎ 757-481-4836) is open daily, April to November, from 9 am to 6 pm. It has scheduled interpretative programs, a book sales area, and exhibits. Daytime visitors (for day use, there is a $2.50 parking fee from Memorial Day to Labor Day; otherwise, it is $1) can use the picnic areas and the self-guided nature trail; bikers have their own six-mile Cape Henry Trail, which connects to the beach's numerous other bike paths. Admission to the park is $2.50 per vehicle, but it is free for walkers or cyclists. You can also take the North Seashore Trolley.

For information on camping in the park area, see Places to Stay in the Virginia Beach section.

Chesapeake & Suffolk

Suffolk and Chesapeake are included here as they are easily reached from Virginia Beach. The **Chesapeake Planetarium** (☎ 757-547-0153), at 300 Cedar Rd, is open daily from 9 am to 4 pm, on Thursday until 8 pm when there are free programs.

In nearby Suffolk, at 510 N Main St, is **Riddick's Folly** (☎ 757-934-1390), a huge Greek Revival house dating from 1837. It has a small museum covering Civil War history. It is open Tuesday to Friday from 10 am to 5 pm, Sunday 1 to 5 pm; entry is by donation.

Lock's Pointe at Great Bridge (☎ 757-547-9618), at 136 N Battlefield Blvd, is a traditional old seafood house with a large wooden deck outside. Its traditional specialty is lightly baked crawfish cake, and they serve a great Sunday brunch.

Great Dismal Swamp

This swamp, a national wildlife refuge of 107,000 acres, is anything but dismal. The region is rich in flora and fauna, and exploration – though allowed only by day – is rewarding.

Evidence of human occupation of the swamp area dates from some 13,000 years ago, but by 1650 there were few Native Americans in the area. Being a swamp, the earliest settlers showed little interest, until in 1665 one William Drummond discovered the lake which still bears his name. In 1728, William Byrd II led a surveying party into the swamp to draw the dividing line between Virginia and North Carolina. Washington examined it in 1763 and then organized the Dismal Swamp Land Co with a view to future draining and logging. It was subsequently logged right through to 1976, and the draining has left the swamp at half of its original size. The 140 miles of logging roads greatly contributed to huge areas of stagnated water.

There are five major forest types (pine, Atlantic white cedar, maple-blackgum, tupelo bald cypress, and sweetgum-oak-poplar) and three nonforested types of plant communities (remnant marsh, sphagnum bog, and evergreen shrub). The dwarf trillium, silky camellia, and log fern – all endangered species – are found here. The dwarf trillium, found in the northwest section of the swamp, blooms briefly each year for a two-week period in March. The log fern, one of the rarest American ferns, is more common in the Dismal Swamp than anywhere else.

Over two hundred species of birds are found in the swamp, and of these species, 93 are nesting. **Bird watching** is best from April to June (spring migration), when the greatest diversity of species occurs. The Swainson's warbler and Wayne's warbler are more common here than in any other coastal locations. Also visible are the wood duck, pileated woodpecker, barred owl, and prothonotary warbler. Local mammals include otters, bats, raccoons, minks, gray and red foxes, and gray squirrels. The white-tailed deer is common, but black bears and bobcats are rarely observed.

There are three species of poisonous snake (cottonmouth, canebrake, and copperhead) and 18 nonpoisonous species. There are yellow-bellied and spotted turtles and an additional 56 species of turtles, lizards, salamanders, frogs, and toads.

Hiking and **biking** are options on the many timber roads in the swamp; the Washington Ditch Rd is the best for bikes. Also near Washington Ditch Rd, the Boardwalk Trail passes through a mile of representative swamp. Boating and fishing are possible on Lake Drummond (a Virginia license is required), and access is via the Feeder Ditch which connects the lake with the Dismal Swamp Canal. White-tailed deer are legally hunted in autumn.

The refuge (☎ 757-986-3705) is open daily from 30 minutes before sunrise until 30 minutes after sunset, and overnight use is not permitted. The Washington Ditch entrance is open April to September from 6:30 am to 8 pm and October to March until 5 pm. To get to the swamp, which is south of Suffolk, take Hwy 13 to Route 32 then follow the signs for 4.5 miles. To get to the Boardwalk Trail, take White Marsh Rd (County Rd 642) to the Washington Ditch.

In North Carolina, there is the Dismal Swamp Canal Visitor/Welcome Center (☎ 919-771-8333) at 2356 Hwy 17N, South Mills, NC 27976. For boaters, it is five miles from the South Mills Locks.

Virginia's Eastern Shore

The slender peninsula that separates Chesapeake Bay from the Atlantic Ocean is a wild, undeveloped, and intriguing destination. It is the southerly finger of Delmarva, the peninsula which also includes Delaware and a sizable chunk of Maryland. Hwy 13 starts in Wilmington, Delaware, and heads due south to Salisbury, Maryland. It crosses the Virginia border and heads down the center of the southern peninsula and across the Chesapeake Bay Bridge-Tunnel to Hampton Roads.

The peninsula itself is a place to relax, hide in peaceful harbor villages, tour quiet country roads that lead to the bay or ocean, visit pristine and wild Assateague Island and Kiptopeke State Park, watch the famous pony penning, or swim. (A good guidebook is *Off 13 – The Eastern Shore of Virginia* by Kirk Mariner.)

The first town across the Maryland-Virginia state border is **New Church**. For those traveling down Hwy 13 and the Eastern Shore to Hampton Roads, the Virginia Welcome Center (☎ 757-824-5000), on Hwy 13 near the Maryland border, is open daily and has a wealth of information on the state.

HIGHLIGHTS

- Chincoteague – a compact fishing village and home of wild ponies, close to a national wildlife refuge and great for bird watching
- Assateague Island – one of the country's best national wildlife areas, with remote beaches, endangered species, and wilderness walking
- Picturesque and historic villages, wildlife refuges, and remote fishing spots along Hwy 13

VIRGINIA

CHINCOTEAGUE ISLAND

This island (population 1600), just seven miles long and 1.5 miles wide, is one of the highlights of the Eastern Shore. Many people know it from the 1940s novel *Misty of Chincoteague* by Marguerite Henry, but it has changed markedly from the description in that book. It has developed swiftly and has all the necessary facilities to meet the tourist influx – the road across the causeway has the most prolific billboard collection you are ever likely to see. Still, the island retains a distinct charm and parts of it, such as some pristine beaches and dilapidated piers, have escaped the auctioneer's gavel and the developer's lack of taste.

In July, wild ponies from nearby Assateague Island are herded across the intervening channel to Chincoteague (see the sidebar in Maryland's Eastern Shore chapter).

Orientation & Information

From Hwy 13 turn off at Oak Hall onto Route 175, which takes you via a causeway across the channel into the center of Chincoteague. Main St runs north-south along the western shore, and the main drag, Maddox Blvd (which changes to Beach Rd at the roundabout), continues to the Assateague Channel.

The Chincoteague Chamber of Commerce (☎ 757-336-6161) is in the center of the roundabout on Maddox Blvd. It is open June to October, Monday to Saturday from 9 am to 4:30 pm, Sunday from noon to 4:30 pm; otherwise weekdays from 9 am to 4:30 pm. Don't forget to get a copy of the free *Virginia's Chincoteague Island Adventure* and the map *Where to Go, Dine & Stay on Chincoteague Island*.

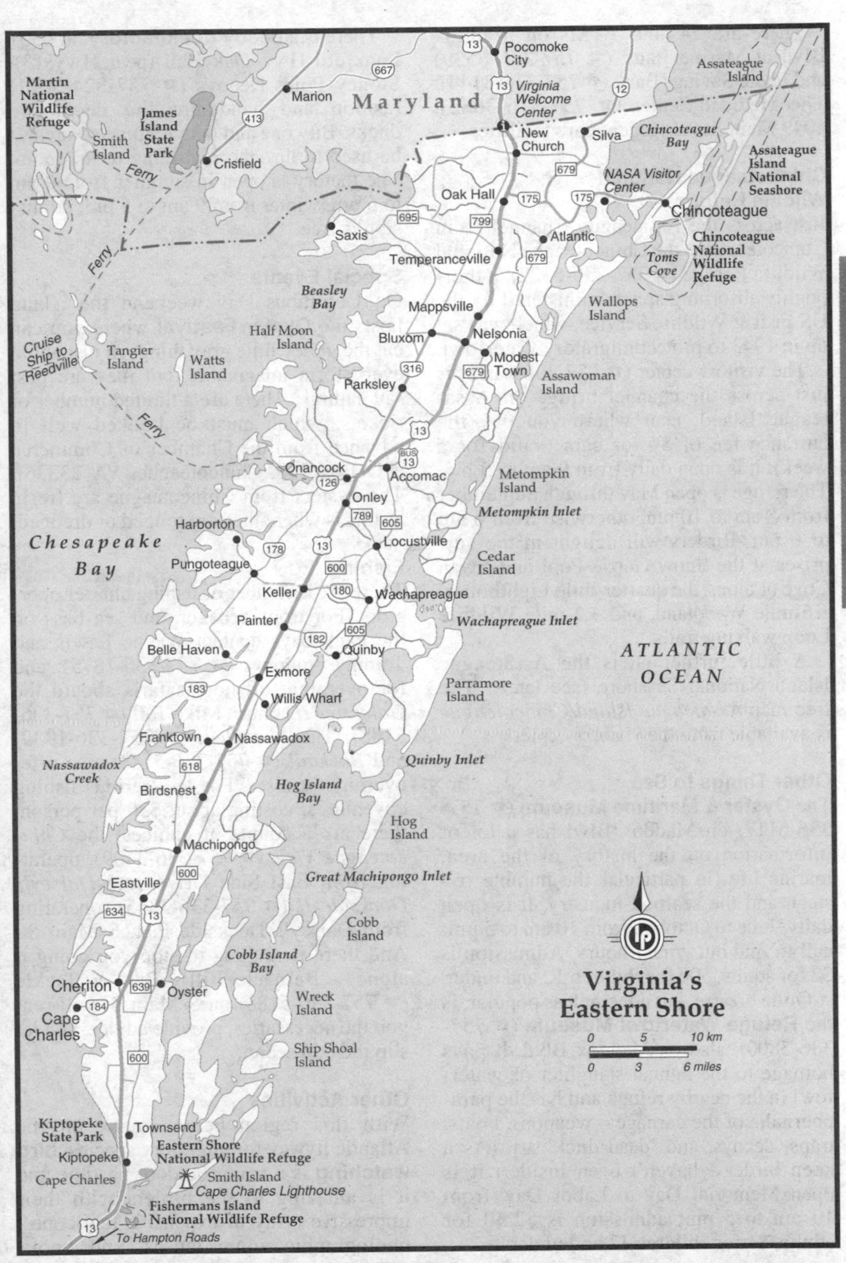
Pocomoke City
Virginia Welcome Center
Maryland
Marion
Martin National Wildlife Refuge
James Island State Park
Smith Island
Crisfield
Ferry
Assateague Island
Chincoteague Bay
Silva
New Church
Assateague Island National Seashore
NASA Visitor Center
Chincoteague
Oak Hall
Atlantic
Chincoteague National Wildlife Refuge
Toms Cove
Saxis
Temperanceville
Wallops Island
Beasley Bay
Mappsville
Half Moon Island
Bluxom
Nelsonia
Modest Town
Cruise Ship to Reedville
Tangier Island
Watts Island
Assawoman Island
Parksley
Onancock
Accomac
Metompkin Island
Onley
Metompkin Inlet
Harborton
Locustville
Chesapeake Bay
Pungoteague
Cedar Island
Keller
Wachapreague
Painter
Wachapreague Inlet
Belle Haven
Quinby
ATLANTIC OCEAN
Exmore
Willis Wharf
Parramore Island
Franktown
Nassawadox
Nassawadox Creek
Quinby Inlet
Birdsnest
Hog Island Bay
Hog Island
Machipongo
Great Machipongo Inlet
Eastville
Cobb Island
Cobb Island Bay
Cheriton
Oyster
Wreck Island
Cape Charles
Ship Shoal Island
Kiptopeke State Park
Townsend
Eastern Shore National Wildlife Refuge
Kiptopeke
Cape Charles
Smith Island
Cape Charles Lighthouse
Fishermans Island National Wildlife Refuge
To Hampton Roads
Virginia's Eastern Shore
0 5 10 km
0 3 6 miles
VIRGINIA

There are 24-hour ATMs on Maddox Blvd at Marine Bank (☎ 757-336-6539) and Shore Savings Bank (☎ 757-336-3144). The Medical Center (☎ 757-336-3682), 4049 Main St, has urgent care facilities.

Chincoteague National Wildlife Refuge

Just across the Assateague Channel from Chincoteague is the Chincoteague National Wildlife Refuge (☎ 757-336-6122), a thoroughly absorbing area administered by the US Fish & Wildlife Service, which was set up in 1943 to protect migratory waterfowl.

The visitors center (☎ 757-336-6122) is just across the channel bridge on Assateague Island, near where you pay the entrance fee of $4 for cars (valid for a week); it is open daily from 9 am to 5 pm. The refuge is open May through September from 5 am to 10 pm, otherwise from 6 am to 6 pm. Birders will delight in the surprises at the Snow Goose Pool and Swan Cove or along the quarter-mile Lighthouse, 1.6-mile Woodland, and 3.2-mile Wildlife Loop walking trails.

A little further on is the Assateague Island National Seashore (see later). The free map *Assateague Island/Chincoteague* is available from the visitors centers.

Other Things to See

The **Oyster & Maritime Museum** (☎ 757-336-6117) on Maddox Blvd has a lot of information on the history of the area, marine life (in particular the humble oyster), and the seafood industry. It is open daily, June to October, from 10 am to 5 pm; call to find out winter hours. Admission is $2 for adults, 50¢ for children 12 and under.

Quite bizarre, but nonetheless popular, is the **Refuge Waterfowl Museum** (☎ 757-336-5800), also on Maddox Blvd. It pays homage to the annual slaughter of waterfowl in the nearby refuge and has the paraphernalia of the carnage – weapons, boats, traps, decoys, and 'dead duck' art. (As a keen birder I haven't been inside.) It is open Memorial Day to Labor Day, from 10 am to 5 pm; admission is $2.50 for adults, $1 for children 12 and under.

There is a **decoy duck factory**, at 6301 Lankford Hwy, Oak Hall (near Hwy 13). Stoney Point Decoys (☎ 757-824-5621) fashion and handpaint the decorative ducks. Buy one and take it home so it can't be used to lure the real thing to its doom. The factory is open in summer from 9 am to 6 pm, winter from 9 am to 5 pm; admission is free.

Special Events

On Columbus Day weekend the island hosts the **Oyster Festival** where you can eat the gooey little gray things in just about every form imaginable, but they are best 'au natural.' There are a limited number of tickets, which must be booked well in advance from the Chamber of Commerce (PO Box 258, Chincoteague, VA 23336). The oysters from Chincoteague are fresh, as this is where they are tonged or dredged.

Fishing

There are a number of fishing charter operators. For trout, croaker, and sea bass on the back bays contact Wayne Lewis and Tommy Andrews (☎ 757-336-1875); and for overnight offshore safaris aboard the *Galeforce II* contact Mike Toff (☎ 757-336-5188). The *Mar-Shell* (☎ 757-336-1939) and *Bucktail* (☎ 757-336-5188) also offer overnight cruises. For less serious fishing adventures, costing about $30 per person, there are a couple of choices: the *Chincoteague View* (☎ 757-336-3409), operating from East Side Drive, and *Daisey's Dockside II* (☎ 757-336-3345), operating from Daisey's Dockside Pier, S Main St. And there is nothing to stop you going it alone – Barnacle Bill's Bait & Tackle (☎ 757-336-5188) on S Main St will rent you the necessaries, provide advice, and let slip the odd secret.

Other Activities

With this region being smack on the Atlantic flyway for migratory species, **bird watching** is a major outdoor pastime and it is amazing to see birders with their impressive array of expensive telescopes, photographic zoom lenses, and books (scattered over the hoods of their cars) in search of the 'buzz' twitch.

On the water, **kayaking** is an ideal way to explore the waterways. Tidewater Expeditions (☎ 757-336-3159), on East Side Drive, has instruction days where you can learn the skills you need to begin exploring the back bays ($65). They also rent kayaks and canoes (from $10 per hour) and have shorter organized trips for $21 per person in single kayaks, $37 in doubles.

A great way to see this flat area is on a **bicycle**; the Bike Depot, at the Refuge Motor Inn (☎ 757-336-5511), rents out good quality bikes. If they have nothing left, try the Piney Island Country Store (☎ 757-336-5188) on Maddox Blvd.

And, of course, there is nothing to stop you from walking wherever you want.

Organized Tours

You can tour this fascinating region by land or water. Assateague Wildlife Safari Tours (☎ 757-336-6155) has 1.5-hour tours of a 7.5-mile section of the wildlife refuge. There is a good chance that you will see sika deer, wild ponies, many species of shore and song birds, and maybe (only maybe) the endangered Delmarva Peninsula fox squirrel and the piping plover. The tours run April to mid-June, Wednesday, Friday, and Saturday at 1 pm, Sunday at 10 am; otherwise daily at 8 am, 10:30 am, and 5 pm ($7 for adults, $3.50 for children).

The owners of *Osprey* (call the Refuge Motor Inn at ☎ 757-336-5511) offer a fully narrated two-hour nature cruise through the Chincoteague channel, passing bird nesting sites. It operates most evenings, Memorial Day to Labor Day ($10 for adults, $5 for children, and you need to book). The *Osprey* departs from the town wharf, across from the fire station.

Recommended are Barry Frishman's Back Bay Cruises (☎ 757-336-6508), which depart from Landmark Plaza on Main St. He has a variety of excursions, including a 1.5-hour early morning bird watching cruise ($15) and a full morning or afternoon trip (to a private island) where you look for shellfish, and clams ($30).

Places to Stay

Camping & Cottages Camping is possible right on the beach in *Assateague State Park* (☎ 410-641-3030) in Maryland (see that chapter) but not in the Virginia section of the park. On Chincoteague there are many campgrounds and rental cottages. *Toms Cove Campground* (☎ 757-336-6498), at 8128 Beebe Rd (1.5 miles south on Main St), has sites with hook-ups from $23.50 to $25.50 for four (it is closed in December); it has bicycles for rent.

The *Pine Grove Campground* (☎ 757-336-5200), on Deep Hole Rd (reached via N Main St and Maddox Blvd), has sites from $17.50 for four. The *Inlet View Waterfront Campground* (☎ 757-336-5126), in a beautiful waterside location, caters to campers, mobile homes, and travel trailers; rates start at $16. The *Maddox Family Campground* (☎ 757-336-3111), at 6742 Maddox Blvd, is a really large campground with well over 500 sites. There are full hook-ups, pool, bathhouses, a playground, and a store; rates start at $19 and rise to $27 for full hook-ups. *Campers Ranch Campground* (☎ 757-336-6371), at the corner of Bunting and Ridge Rds in the heart of Chincoteague, has full facilities for tents and trailers and RVs, as well as a swimming pool and a fishing pond.

There are a number of cottages for rent; check at the Chamber of Commerce. To give you an idea, *Snug Harbor Marina & Cottages* (☎ 757-336-6176), at 7536 East Side Drive, has them from $56 to $59 in summer, $49 to $53 in fall and spring (their motto: 'Fishing is spoken here'). *Uncle Joe's Cabins* (☎ 757-336-6176) are $45 in summer, dropping to $30 at other times of the year.

Hotels & Motels There are plenty of such places to stay on Chincoteague. The *Beach Road Motel* (☎ 757-336-6562), at 6151 Maddox Blvd, is a well-kept place with friendly, helpful owners; singles and doubles are from $35 and $38 in the off season, rising to a range of $48 to $72 and $60 to $79 in summer. The *Mariner Motel* (☎ 757-336-6565, 800-221-7490),

6273 Maddox Blvd, has singles/doubles for $35/45.

The *Assateague Inn* (☎ 757-336-3738) is just off Maddox Blvd on Chicken City Rd. Bird watchers will love this place as it overlooks a saltwater marsh and is nestled amongst loblolly pines (each room has access to the balcony); it is reasonable with singles and doubles from $40 to $52 in low season, and $62 to $92 in high season. The comfortable *Sea Shell Motel* (☎ 757-336-6589), corner of Cleveland and Willow Sts, has a screened outdoor kitchen; singles/doubles are $37/41 in low season, rising to $58/62 in summer (two-night minimum stay).

The *Waterside Motor Inn* (☎ 757-336-3434), at 3761 S Main St, has a great location with views from private balconies out over the Chincoteague Channel. It has a waterfront pool, a fishing and crabbing pier, tennis court, and solar health spa with a Jacuzzi; singles and doubles are from $46 to $78 in low season, $90 to $145 in summer.

The *Island Motor Inn* (☎ 757-336-3141, 800-832-2925), at 4391 N Main St on the Intracoastal Waterway, has heaps of views. It is a homey place with pool, health and fitness room, restaurant, and outdoor barbecue – well worth the $68 to $125 for doubles in winter, or $98 to $150 in summer.

B&Bs The *Watson House* (☎ 757-336-1564), at 4240 Main St, is a restored country Victorian residence with tastefully decorated rooms; afternoon tea is provided on the verandah and bicycles are included in the price of $59 to $95 for singles and $69 to $105 for doubles in low season (add another $10 in summer). The *Island Manor House* (☎ 757-336-5436), 4160 Main St, is two clapboard houses joined by a garden room with delightful patio. The rooms, tastefully furnished in Federal style, cost from $66 to $120 for a double (afternoon tea is included).

For those familiar with Marguerite Henry's *Misty of Chincoteague* there will be no other choice in town except *Miss Molly's Inn* (☎ 757-336-6686), a gray wooden house at 4141 N Main St. Marguerite wrote the novel in the master bedroom. There is no smoking and they don't take credit cards. It ranges from $69 to $145 for doubles (with breakfast and afternoon tea) and is closed from January to mid-February. Good golly, stay, write a bestseller.

Near the Maryland state line, the quaintly and appropriately named *Garden and the Sea Inn* (☎ 757-824-0672) is part of a great little B&B. Turn off Hwy 13 onto Route 710 (near the First Virginia Bank) and follow it for a quarter of a mile. It is quite expensive but well worth it with doubles from $75 to $160. Specialties from the kitchen include bouillabaisse, fish from Chesapeake Bay, and scallops.

Places to Eat

The best food choices are the fruits of the sea. The *Russel Fish Company* (☎ 757-336-6986), on Main St next to the Coast Guard station, sells fresh fish and live lobsters, and seafood to go hot or cold. Grab something to eat and sit by the wharf, close to dusk if possible. Magic! Then move the kids down the street to *Muller's Ice Cream Parlor*, in the historic Cropper House at 4034 Main St. They have soda-fountain treats, splits, malts, and Belgian waffles coated in the cold stuff and whipped cream. *Steamers* (☎ 757-336-6236), 6251 Maddox Blvd, serves treats for the kids and seafood for the adults.

As for seafood restaurants, *Don's* (☎ 757-336-5715), at 4113 Main St, has the dubious motto (these are popular on the island) 'If it smells like fish eat it.' They have an excellent breakfast menu including a $6 crab omelet, clam chowder for $1.50/3 for a cup/bowl, and seafood platter with fish, shrimp, oysters, clams, scallops, and crab cake for $14.95. Fish of the day is $10.

A place with great views on three sides is the *Landmark Crab House* (☎ 757-336-5552) on N Main St on the bay. Apart from various combinations of crab on offer, there are also beef specials and a large salad bar; six clams or oysters on the half shell cost $5, a crabmeat cocktail $7, hot steamed crabs are $1.50 each, a crab cake, soft crab, or scallop entree is $14, and the children's menu is $5.50. The bar in here is reputedly from Al Capone's Chicago speakeasy and the lighting fixtures from *Gone with the Wind* – gazing at them, and at beautiful sunsets from the outdoor dining area, is free.

Other seafood places include the reliable *Etta's Family Restaurant* (☎ 757-336-5644), at 7452 East Side Drive, known for its oyster stew and crab soup; the *Shucking House Café* (☎ 757-336-5145), at 6162 Main St (next to the Landmark Crab House), has a seafood brunch on Sunday from 11:30 am to 3 pm ($10); the *Village* (☎ 757-336-5120), at 6576 Maddox Blvd, has calamari appetizers and huge seafood platters; and five miles west of Chincoteague in Atlantic, *Wright's* (☎ 757-824-4012), has a Crab Galley where you get clam strips, steamed crab, and Alaskan crab legs.

The *Channel Bass Inn* (☎ 757-336-6148), a three-story beige clapboard house at 6228 Church St, was once the pick of the B&Bs. It is open daily for delicious English-style afternoon teas, except from January to mid-February, when it is open on weekends only (check to see if they still provide bed and breakfast).

Entertainment

This is scanty. *Chatties Bar* (☎ 757-336-5715), at 4113 Main St on top of Don's Seafood, has entertainment of some form on most nights – comedy, a DJ, darts tourney, or pool competition; the food is merely passable. *AJs . . . on the Creek* (☎ 757-336-5888), at 6585 Maddox Blvd, is another place to go for a late night drink. Most of the locals sneak across the island to *Poney Pines* (☎ 757-336-9746), East Side Drive, for a quiet drink.

For videos for the kids, and beer and wine for yourself, try Steve's Mini Market (☎ 757-336-1958) on Maddox Blvd.

ASSATEAGUE ISLAND NATIONAL SEASHORE

Most of this pristine, wildly beautiful, and windswept 37-mile-long barrier island is in Maryland. The southern portion belongs to Virginia. It can be reached on Route 175 via Chincoteague. It would have to rate as one of the most remote and alluring wilderness areas in the US, which is to say that a visit is a highly recommended. Bird watchers will be well satisfied with around 300 species passing through the area (on the Atlantic migratory pathway), including swans, egrets, and migrant geese.

The Toms Cove Visitor Center (☎ 757-336-6577), operated by the NPS, is on the beach at the south end of the island. This is an information center for the Chincoteague National Wildlife Refuge and Virginia's section of the Assateague Island National Seashore. The visitors center has displays, exhibits, and a small sales area.

There are bathhouses near the beach, access to the beach via boardwalks, an off-road vehicle area (for which a permit is required), and the Toms Cove Nature Trail.

If you want to progress north along the beach to the six backcountry camping areas, see the chapter Maryland's Eastern Shore.

NASA Wallops Flight Center

Wallops Island, near Chincoteague Inlet, houses a NASA flight facility and has been the site of several rocket launchings. There is now a visitors center (☎ 757-824-2298) that highlights current NASA and Wallops space programs; it is across the road from the Wallops Flight Center (the runway encircled by a huge fence) on Route 175. It has space suits, a moon rock, special films of rocket launches, and a videotaped presentation (all of which are likely to be popular with the kids).

The exhibit is open daily, July to Labor Day, from 10 am to 4 pm, otherwise Thursday to Monday from 10 am to 4 pm; admission is free and there is handicapped access.

VIRGINIA

CENTRAL PENINSULA

Chincoteague and Assateague dominate the Eastern Shore as destinations but there are a number of interesting things to do and see in the center and south of the peninsula – a trip to either side of Hwy 13 will be rewarding.

Parksley & Accomac

The small Victorian town of Parksley, just off Hwy 13 on Route 176, is worth a side trip to see the **Eastern Shore Railway Museum** (☎ 757-665-6271), at 18468 Dunne Ave in Railroad Square. Here a 1907 New York, Philadelphia & Norfolk Railroad passenger station, maintenance-of-way tool shed, and myriad artifacts (including seven railcars) have been set out on 10 acres with a pavilion and picnic grounds. The museum is open weekdays from 10:30 am to 4 pm, Sunday 1 to 4 pm; admission is $1 for adults and children. The museum also organizes excursions (☎ 800-852-0335).

Accomac, about six miles south of Parksley, is an historic little town with many examples of restored colonial architecture (a walking tour guide is available). The **debtor's prison** dates from 1784 when it was built as a jailer's residence and remains essentially unaltered. There is no admission fee; call ☎ 757-787-2462 to arrange a visit.

Onancock

This pretty little bayside town (population 7500), once a Native American village, was founded in 1680 as Port Scarburgh. Large ships and ferries, plying between Baltimore and Norfolk, stopped in at the port and added to the town's wealth.

For more info, see the Onancock town office (☎ 757-787-3363) on weekdays. In mid-July Onancock hosts the annual **Harborfest**.

Kerr Place (☎ 757-787-8012), at 69 Market St, is a 1799 Federal period home dating from the shipping boom. There is a museum, research library, and carefully manicured colonial gardens. The museum is open year round, Tuesday to Saturday from 10 am to 4 pm; admission is $3 for adults and children under 18 are free. Also worth a look is **Hopkins & Bros** (☎ 757-787-8220), 2 Market St, one of the oldest general stores on the East Coast (built in 1842) and still operating as a dry goods store and restaurant.

From early June to mid-September there are daily five-hour **cruises** from the town wharf to Tangier Island (lunch is at the famous Hilda Crockett's Chesapeake House). The tour costs $18 for adults, $9 for children aged six to 12; contact Tangier Island Cruises (☎ 757-891-2240).

Places to Stay & Eat The *Colonial Manor Inn* (☎ 757-787-3521), at 84 Market St, five blocks from the marina, dates from 1882. The only telephone is the one mentioned above but all rooms have TV. It is a very reasonable place with friendly owners; rooms are $45 for doubles. The *76 Market St B&B* (☎ 757-787-7600) is a restored Victorian dwelling close to the shops and harbor; a double is $65. *The Spinning Wheel B&B* (☎ 757-787-7311), at 31 North St, is a wood-frame Victorian with comfortable rooms (each with a spinning wheel); the single/double rate is $75/85.

There are a surprising number of good quality places to eat considering the town's size. The *Hungry Duck* (☎ 757-787-8700), on the corner of Market and North Sts, is open daily for lunch and dinner, and for breakfast on weekends. *Hopkins & Bros Store* (☎ 757-787-4478) is good for seafood and steaks, as is *LJ Street Sports Bar/Restaurant* (☎ 757-787-2144), 20250 Fairgrounds Rd, which is open for lunch and dinner, and has bands on weekend nights.

The trendiest place (probably on the whole of the Eastern Shore) is the Argentine-run *Armando's* (☎ 757-787-8044), at 10 North St, known for its innovative pastas and seafood dishes; entrees range from $9 to $16. There is jazz here on many weekends.

Wachapreague

This small fishing village is the self-titled 'Flounder Capital of the World' – don't you just love these 'capitals?' Flounder aside, it's a picturesque spot with great views out over the waterway between the mainland and the barrier islands, Cedar and Parramore. The village is at the eastern end of Route 180, and to get there exit Hwy 13 at Keller.

From May to October, you can book bird watching tours and barrier island **cruises** on *Skimmer I*. At the Wachapreague Marina (☎ 757-787-4110) you can arrange to get dropped off on either Cedar or Parramore islands for about $60, or they will rent you a boat (and provide fuel and a chart) for $60 so you can select your own fishing spots.

Places to Stay The Hotel Wachapreague, which once attracted the rich and famous keen on hunting and fishing nearby, burnt down 20 years ago, but there are still a few accommodations in town. Locals own and run the *Hart's Harbor House* (☎ 757-787-4848) and *Burton House B&B* (☎ 757-787-4560), two cottages together on the water's edge at 9 Brooklyn Ave; a double room is from $65 to $85. The *Wachapreague Motel & Marina* (☎ 757-787-2105), at 15 Atlantic Ave, was once part of the old hotel and has a private beach; doubles are about $40. The *Island House Restaurant* is attached.

In **Pungoteague**, almost at the western end of Route 180, is the *Pungoteague Junction B&B* (☎ 757-442-3581), housed in an 1869 house with a wraparound porch. They provide toys for your children to play with (a big change when you consider kids aren't welcome at many B&Bs); a double with full breakfast is $50.

Exmore & Nassawadox

Exmore is seven miles south of Keller, close to Willis Wharf, which gives access to the barrier islands. The *Gladstone House* (☎ 757-442-4614), at 12108 Lincoln Ave, Exmore, is a brick Georgian residence with doubles (including breakfast and dinner) for $95. Nearby at 12224 Lincoln Ave is *Martha's Inn* (☎ 757-442-4641), another grand Georgian-style B&B, where singles/doubles are $65/85. On Hwy 13, the *Trawler Restaurant* (☎ 757-442-2092), is known for its she-crab soup and sweet potato biscuits.

In Nassawadox you can take a four-hour tour of the working **Custis Farms** (☎ 757-442-9071) on a hay wagon pulled by a tractor. The tour visits the greenhouse and Victorian gardens of nearby Maplewood and lunch is at *EL Willis Store* (☎ 757-442-4225), a seafood place at Willis Wharf, on the water. The tours operate April to October, Tuesday, Thursday, and Saturday between 10 am and 2 pm; it costs $25 for adults, $15 for children.

Places to Stay The *Anchor Motel* (☎ 757-442-6363) on Hwy 13 has singles and doubles from $44 to $54 in low season, $49 to $59 in summer (there are some efficiencies). For authentic Italian food try *Little Italy* (☎ 757-442-7831), at 10237 Rogers Drive, just off Hwy 13.

SOUTHERN PENINSULA

Eastville & Cheriton

Hwy 13 bisects Eastville, a historic 18th century town well worth a stop, especially to see the old courthouse and debtor's prison. The oldest continuous court records in the US (1632) are stored in the clerk's office and visitors may inspect them. Not far south of Eastville is the magnificent old house **Eyre Hall**, built in 1735 and extended in 1765.

To the west of Cheriton, on Chesapeake Bay (reached by Route 680), is the 300-acre *Cherrystone Family Camping & RV Resort* (☎ 757-331-3063) with every camping facility imaginable; low season rates are $15 for two, high season rates $19 for two (add $2 for each of the hook-ups).

Cape Charles

This 19th century town, west of Hwy 13 on Route 184, was once an important railroad terminus. It has delightful residential streets and a downtown with many antique shops.

The *Days Inn* (☎ 757-331-1000, 800-331-4000), on Hwy 13 close to the Chesapeake Bay Bridge-Tunnel, has a pool;

singles are $35 in low season, more in summer.

Cape Charles House (☎ 757-331-4920), at 645 Tazewell St, is a Colonial-style B&B close to the bay with a crabbing and fishing pier and boating facilities; singles/doubles are $75/85. Another Colonial-style lodging, *Nottingham Ridge* (☎ 757-331-1010), borders Chesapeake Bay and serves breakfast on the porch. The *Sea Gate B&B* (☎ 757-331-2206), 9 Tazewell Ave, also has a porch with spectacular views and bikes for guests; singles/doubles are $60/75.

Costing about the same is the *Sunset Inn B&B* (☎ 757-331-2424), 106 Bay Ave, open year round. In nearby Townsend, on Route 600 (off Route 13), the clapboard and brick *Pickett's Harbor* (☎ 757-331-2212) overlooks sand dunes and has a private beach.

Those looking for a hearty meal ignore the name and go to *Someplace Else* (☎ 757-331-8430), a roadside diner known for its seafood and steak dinners.

Kiptopeke State Park & Eastern Shore of Virginia National Wildlife Refuge

These two excellent bird-watching locations are at the southern end of the peninsula. Kiptopeke, just west of Hwy 13 and a few miles north of the tunnel, is a 375-acre park bordering on Chesapeake Bay that is suitable for families as there are some safe swimming spots. The park (☎ 757-331-2267) is open from mid-March to early December and campsites range from $15 for a developed site to $21 for full hook-ups for six people (it is one of the most expensive of the state parks but worth it); there is a day use fee for picnickers.

The 651-acre Eastern Shore of Virginia Wildlife Refuge (☎ 757-331-2760) has a great visitors center with all sorts of hands-on items for the kids to touch. There are also bird watching facilities – over 290 species have been spotted here, as it is one of the major stopovers for migratory birds before they cross the wide mouth of Chesapeake Bay. Also on the premises is a fine collection of waterfowl carvings. There is no admission fee, making this place one of the best value stops on the Eastern Shore (and a great way to rest before or after crossing the bridge-tunnel).

Chesapeake Bay Bridge-Tunnel

This engineering marvel connects Hampton Roads and Virginia's Eastern Shore via Hwy 13. It is said to be one of the seven wonders of the modern world and the 17.6-mile two-lane link is the world's largest bridge-tunnel complex. It saves motorists 95 miles of driving and 90 minutes between Hampton Roads and New York City. There is a restaurant, gift shop, and fishing pier located on the southernmost of four constructed islands, four miles from the southerly end.

The toll facility and fishing pier (☎ 757-624-3511) is open 24 hours all year round; the gift shop is open April 1 to September 30, from 6 am to 10 pm, otherwise from 7 am to 6 pm. The toll of $10 for cars includes a free Pepsi.

The Piedmont

Were it not for Charlottesville, the rolling Piedmont plateau would be the most unsung part of Virginia, an area to be rushed through on the east-west I-64, the north-south Hwy 29, or the host of other roads that intersect it. Virginia's heartland is sandwiched between, and thus very close to, the scenic Blue Ridge and the historic Richmond and Tidewater regions, so that is often overlooked. (Richmond and Petersburg are actually part of the Piedmont but have been covered in a separate chapter.)

The gem of the region is Monticello, Thomas Jefferson's magnificent home near Charlottesville. The region includes other Jefferson architectural masterpieces, James Monroe's home Ash Lawn-Highland, the 'real Virginia' cities of Lynchburg and Danville, and many historic monuments and Civil War battlefields such as Appomattox.

HIGHLIGHTS

- Monticello, Jefferson's home and greatest architectural achievement
- Charlottesville – a pleasant university town with a rich history and sophisticated nightlife
- Lynchburg's many historical buildings, monuments, and Jefferson's Poplar Forest
- Appomattox – where the Civil War ended
- Booker T Washington National Monument, honoring the former slave and respected spokesman

State Welcome Centers

There are two Virginia Welcome Centers in the Piedmont and both are near the North Carolina border: Skippers (☎ 804-634-4113) is on I-95 (Emporia is to the north) and Bracey (☎ 804-689-2295) is on I-85 near Buggs Island Lake (South Hill is to the north).

CHARLOTTESVILLE

This town (population 41,000) is a must if you are visiting Virginia. It has some of the state's finest architectural masterpieces and has an altogether Southern feel with its magnolia-lined streets and the scenic Blue Ridge Mountains as a backdrop. The locals call the place 'C-ville,' or 'Mr Jefferson's Country' (a nod to Thomas Jefferson, whose influence is pervasive, especially at the University of Virginia and Monticello). One wag described it as the 'sort of place you like if you like that sort of place,' but I'd rate it as one of the most delightful and sophisticated destinations in the state. And surrounding the city is the pastoral Albemarle County, a delightful rural area that attracts the rich and famous who can afford to live there.

Orientation

There are two downtowns: the one on the west side near the university is called The Corner; the more historic downtown is a mile east of The Corner and connected to it by University Ave and Main St. The intersecting streets are numbered east to west.

Information

Tourist Offices The well-signed Charlottesville/Albemarle Convention and Visitors Bureau (☎ 804-977-1783) is on Route 20S near Exit 121 of I-64 (PO Box 161, Charlottesville, VA 22902). To get there take bus No 8 ('Piedmont College') from the corner of 5th and Market Sts. As well as arranging accommodations, they sell

VIRGINIA

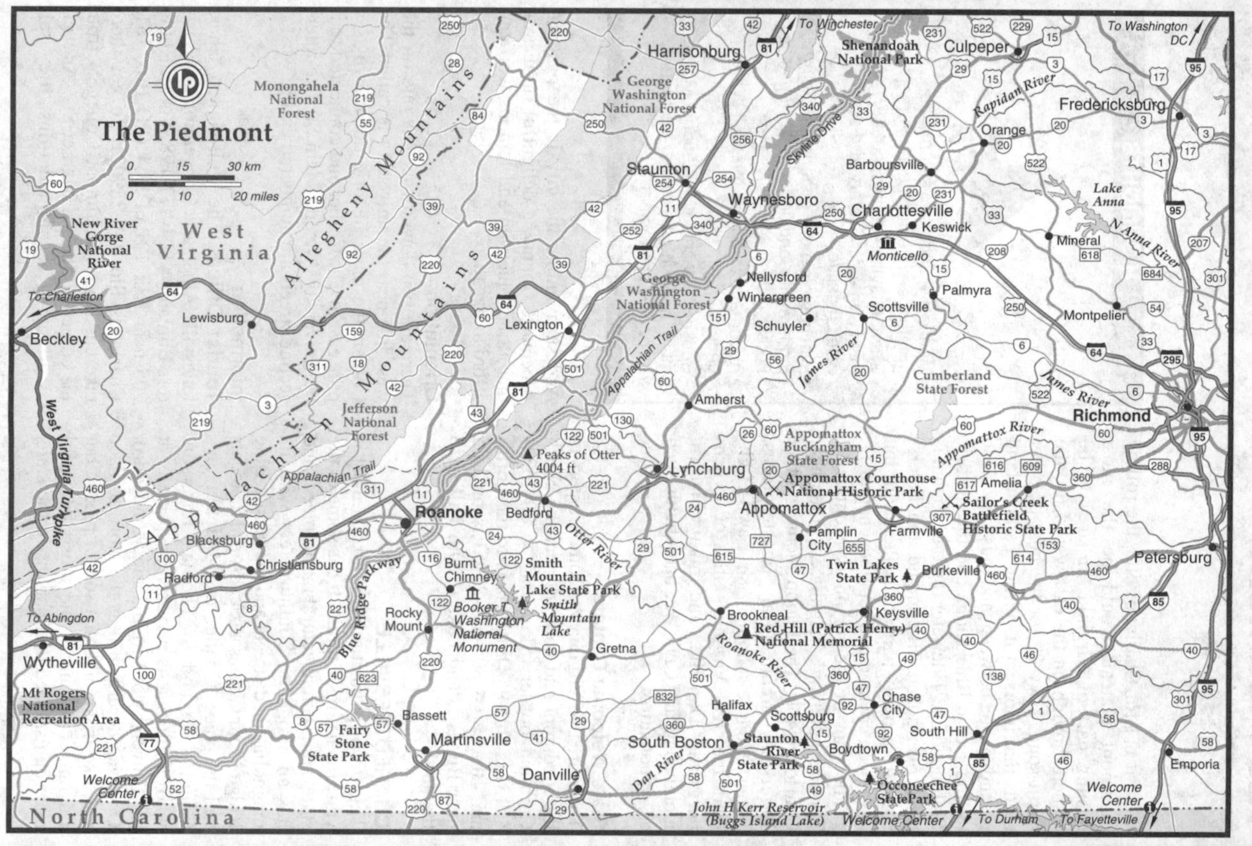
VIRGINIA
The Piedmont
0 15 30 km
0 10 20 miles
West Virginia
North Carolina
Allegheny Mountains
Appalachian Mountains
Monongahela National Forest
New River Gorge National River
George Washington National Forest
Jefferson National Forest
Shenandoah National Park
Skyline Drive
Blue Ridge Parkway
Appalachian Trail
West Virginia Turnpike
Mt Rogers National Recreation Area
Cumberland State Forest
Appomattox Buckingham State Forest
Appomattox Courthouse National Historic Park
Sailor's Creek Battlefield Historic State Park
Twin Lakes State Park
Red Hill (Patrick Henry) National Memorial
Staunton River State Park
Occoneechee State Park
Smith Mountain Lake State Park
Smith Mountain Lake
Booker T Washington National Monument
Fairy Stone State Park
Peaks of Otter 4004 ft
Monticello
Lake Anna
John H Kerr Reservoir (Buggs Island Lake)
James River
Appomattox River
Roanoke River
Dan River
Otter River
Rapidan River
N Anna River
To Winchester
To Washington DC
To Charleston
To Abingdon
To Durham
To Fayetteville
Welcome Center
Richmond
Petersburg
Fredericksburg
Culpeper
Orange
Barboursville
Charlottesville
Keswick
Mineral
Montpelier
Palmyra
Scottsville
Schuyler
Nellysford
Wintergreen
Harrisonburg
Staunton
Waynesboro
Lexington
Lewisburg
Beckley
Amherst
Lynchburg
Appomattox
Pamplin City
Farmville
Amelia
Burkeville
Keysville
Brookneal
Roanoke
Bedford
Blacksburg
Christiansburg
Radford
Burnt Chimney
Rocky Mount
Gretna
Wytheville
Bassett
Martinsville
Danville
Halifax
South Boston
Scottsburg
Boydtown
Chase City
South Hill
Emporia

discounted combination tickets for attractions near C-ville including Monticello (adults $17, seniors $15.50; for kids it is cheaper to pay individual entry at each of the attractions). The 'Thomas Jefferson at Monticello' exhibit, in the north wing of the building, is well presented, and entry is free. A visit is a must either before or after you go to Monticello. The center is open March to October, daily from 9 am to 5:30 pm; the rest of the year they close at 5 pm.

At Newcomb Hall (☎ 804-924-3363) on the UVa grounds (reached from McCormick Rd where there is no parking), students are mustered daily to answer questions and to give guided tours of the Rotunda and central grounds (daily at 10 and 11 am and 2, 3, and 4 pm). More info is available from the University Information Center (☎ 804-924-7166), off Hwy 250W – it is well signed and is open 24 hours.

Online Services There is a veritable wealth of information about Charlottesville on the Internet – the city's Web site is probably one of the most accessible and productive sites in the world. Search 'Virginia' and select COMET (Charlottesville Community On-line Metropolitan Network under 'Monticello Avenue') and be engrossed.

For performing arts information and schedules of events, browse the Charlottesville Guide On-line at *www.cjp.com/guide.*

Money The Central Fidelity Bank (☎ 804-979-2250), corner of Jefferson and Ninth Sts, and the First Virginia Bank (☎ 804-978 3041), on Barracks Rd, are good for foreign exchange.

Post The main post office (☎ 804-978-7648), 513 E Main St, is open weekdays from 8:30 am to 5 pm, Saturday 10 am to 1 pm.

Travel Agencies Enterprise Travel is in the Downtown Mall (☎ 804-296 7500), at 400 E Main St, and at the airport (☎ 804-974-1515).

Laundry There is Brown's self-service laundromat at 1326 E High St and many of the motels have their own laundry facilities.

Medical Services The emergency room at the UVa Hospital (☎ 804-924-2231), on Lee Ave (west of downtown near The Corner), and the Martha Jefferson Hospital (☎ 804-982-7150), on Locust Ave east of downtown, have 24-hour facilities.

Monticello

Everybody knows Monticello, Thomas Jefferson's home, probably because it is on the back of the nickel coin (the perfect souvenir?). It is three miles southeast of C-ville on Route 53. It is an absolute must to visit if you make it to this part of the world.

And the house is very much the embodiment of its creator, Jefferson, who oversaw all stages of its development over a period of 40 years and incorporated many of his fascinating ideas in the design. Jefferson, third president of the US and one of the nation's founding fathers, was an intriguing character – perhaps somewhat eccentric, but with a prodigious output. His private chambers were set up so that he got out of the right side of his bed to write and on the left side to get dressed. This puts a new accent on 'getting up on the wrong side of the bed.'

Unusual features include a passage linking the kitchen to the dining room so that weather conditions would not interfere with the meals, a concave mirror in the entrance hall that greets visitors with their own upside down image, fossilized bones and elk antlers from Lewis and Clark's expedition, hidden and narrow staircases (as ordinary staircases were considered by Jefferson to be unsightly space wasters) and outbuildings at the back of the main building. All of these innovations deviated from the usual English Georgian style. (Jefferson's 'essay in architecture' was based on the ancient temple of Vesta in Rome, illustrated in the 16th century Italian architect Andrea Palladio's *I Quattro Libri*.)

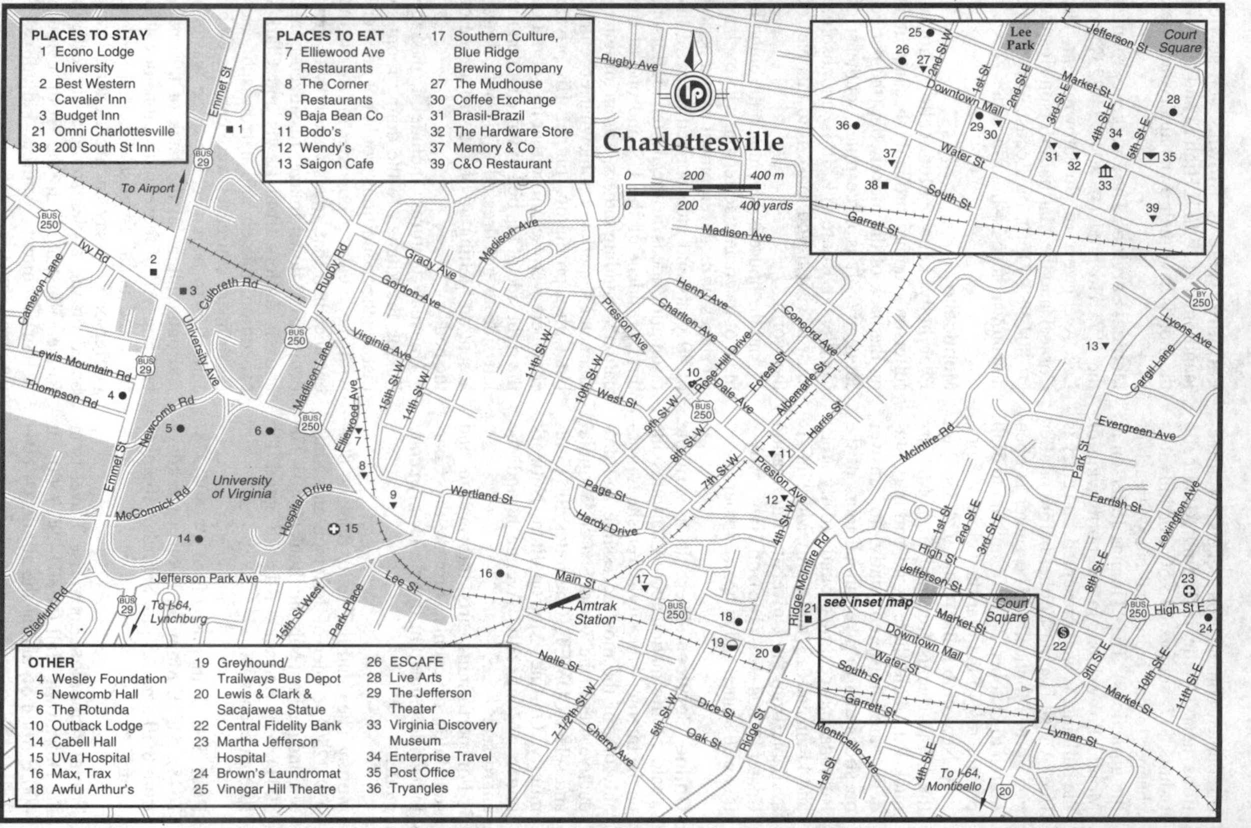
Charlottesville
0 200 400 m
0 200 400 yards
PLACES TO STAY
1 Econo Lodge University
2 Best Western Cavalier Inn
3 Budget Inn
21 Omni Charlottesville
38 200 South St Inn
PLACES TO EAT
7 Elliewood Ave Restaurants
8 The Corner Restaurants
9 Baja Bean Co
11 Bodo's
12 Wendy's
13 Saigon Cafe
17 Southern Culture, Blue Ridge Brewing Company
27 The Mudhouse
30 Coffee Exchange
31 Brasil-Brazil
32 The Hardware Store
37 Memory & Co
39 C&O Restaurant
OTHER
4 Wesley Foundation
5 Newcomb Hall
6 The Rotunda
10 Outback Lodge
14 Cabell Hall
15 UVa Hospital
16 Max, Trax
18 Awful Arthur's
19 Greyhound/ Trailways Bus Depot
20 Lewis & Clark & Sacajawea Statue
22 Central Fidelity Bank
23 Martha Jefferson Hospital
24 Brown's Laundromat
25 Vinegar Hill Theatre
26 ESCAFE
28 Live Arts
29 The Jefferson Theater
33 Virginia Discovery Museum
34 Enterprise Travel
35 Post Office
36 Tryangles
To Airport
To I-64, Lynchburg
To I-64, Monticello
see inset map
University of Virginia
Amtrak Station
Court Square
Lee Park
Downtown Mall
Emmet St
University Ave
Rugby Rd
Rugby Ave
Preston Ave
Main St
Market St
Water St
South St
Garrett St
Jefferson St
High St
High St E
Madison Ave
Jefferson Park Ave
Ridge-McIntire Rd
McIntire Rd
Monticello Ave
Cherry Ave
Stadium Rd
Ivy Rd
Lewis Mountain Rd
Thompson Rd
Cameron Lane
Newcomb Rd
McCormick Rd
Hospital Drive
Culbreth Rd
Madison Lane
Elliewood Ave
Wertland St
Lee St
Park Place
15th St West
Grady Ave
Gordon Ave
Virginia Ave
Henry Ave
Charlton Ave
Rose Hill Drive
Dale Ave
Forest St
Albemarle St
Harris St
Concord Ave
West St
Page St
Hardy Drive
Nalle St
Dice St
Oak St
Ridge St
Lyman St
Lexington Ave
Evergreen Ave
Cargil Lane
Lyons Ave
Farrish St
Park St

Other inventions are scattered throughout the house – his seven-day clock, the two-pen 'polygraph' used to reproduce correspondence, as well as an indoor compass used to indicate wind direction (which is connected to a weather vane on the roof).

Jefferson died here in 1826 (on July 4, exactly 50 years after the Declaration of Independence) and he is buried on the estate in a nearby tomb surrounded by hardwood trees. The inscription on the obelisk above his tomb, under his favorite oak tree, reads: 'Here was buried Thomas Jefferson, Author of the Declaration of American Independence, Of the Statute of Virginia for Religious Freedom, and Father of the University of Virginia.'

The grounds are well laid out and a great place for a stroll before or after touring the house. The view from the 'mountaintop' is nothing short of spectacular and visitors often stop here for a day, rather than the planned half day. The remains of Mulberry Row, the old slave quarters, reflect the darker past of Monticello. Jefferson was opposed to slavery – an 'abominable crime' he called it – but he owned over 200 slaves (one of whom he was reputedly romantically attached to – see the sidebar on Dashing Sally on the next page).

Monticello (☎ 804-984-9822) is open daily from 8 am to 5 pm in summer (March to October) and 9 am to 4:30 pm otherwise. Entry is $8 for adults, $7 for seniors, $4 for children six to 11 ($3 for students in groups).

Get there before 9 am if you want to go on a tour. You may get the feeling that you are being shoved along as there are so many tours to get through. In the busy seasons there is usually a wait of an hour.

Virginia Discovery Museum

This museum (☎ 804-977-1025), at the east end of the Downtown Mall, is a hands-on place for children and adults alike. It is open, Tuesday to Saturday, from 10 am to 5 pm, Sunday 1 to 5 pm; admission is $4 for adults, seniors and children are $3. On the last Sunday of the month it is free for all.

Gay & Lesbian Charlottesville

With enlightened UVa close by there are good services for gay and lesbian travelers. The Lesbian, Gay & Bisexual Union (LGBU) meets 9 pm every Thursday at the Wesley Foundation near the corner of Emmet St and Lewis Mountain Rd; their Helpline number is ☎ 804-982-2773 and is available Sunday to Wednesday from 7 to 10 pm.

Men2Men (☎ 804-979-7714) is a social group interested in the prevention of HIV/AIDS. The Region 10 24-hour Crisis Hotline is ☎ 804-972-1800.

Tryangles (☎ 804-296-8783), at 212 W Water St, is about the only real gay bar in C-ville; it is open Thursday to Saturday in the evening. The Eastern Standard Cafe (ESCAFE, ☎ 804-295-8668) is a local restaurant frequented by gays and lesbians; it is at the west end of the Downtown Mall near the C-ville Omni.

Bookstores with gay and lesbian information are Barnes & Noble Bookstore (☎ 804-984-0461), Quest Bookshop (☎ 804-295-3377), and the UVa Bookstore. ■

The University of Virginia

The University of Virginia (UVa) grounds, at the west end of town, include the original 'Academical Village,' which was designed by Jefferson and includes a beautiful Rotunda (a scale replica of the Pantheon in Rome), original classroom, and a library in the dome room. Adjacent to the Rotunda are student rooms, faculty pavilions, and gardens. Woodrow Wilson and an absolute antithesis, Edgar Allan Poe, spent student time in the west range of the village. Jefferson supervised building via telescope from Monticello.

The 'Village' (☎ 804-924-7969) is open daily from 9 am to 4:45 pm and tours are at 10 and 11 am, 2, 3, and 4 pm; admission is free (but watch out for parking fines). It closes for three weeks during December.

Vineyards

The 'cognoscenti of the grape' have a good choice in this region. Jefferson Vineyards

**Dashing Sally:
Jefferson's Little Secret**

With the release of the film *Jefferson in Paris*, the American public has had to reckon with the possibility that Thomas Jefferson, the 'Father of Independence,' kept a slave mistress, Sally Heming, for more than 35 years.

The story has been around since Jefferson ran for a second term as president in 1803. At that time the opposition press attacked Jefferson's character by accusing him of a sexual liaison with a beautiful mulatto, nicknamed 'Dashing Sally,' who was 30 years younger than the president. But Jefferson's cadre of male biographers have ignored, repressed, or dismissed the story for almost two centuries in spite of circumstantial evidence and Fawn M Brodie's 1974 biography *Thomas Jefferson: An Intimate History*, which details her case for Jefferson's miscegenation.

As the story goes, Jefferson began his liaison with his daughter Mary's slave nurse between 1787 and 1789 while Jefferson was America's ambassador to France. At the time, Jefferson was the widowed father of two daughters – a lonely man who had promised his dying wife that he would never remarry. Heming was the half sister of his wife, a mulatto child of Martha Jefferson's father and a slave whom Martha's father had given to Jefferson as a part of Martha's dowry. When the Paris interlude began, Heming was about 14, Jefferson at least 44. And when they returned to Virginia in 1789, Heming was pregnant. According to the Brodie biography, Jefferson and Heming continued their relationship until Jefferson died in 1826, by which time there were five children, some of whom bore a striking resemblance to the master of Monticello. These children (but not their mother) were among the handful of slaves Jefferson freed when they became adults. In addition to filmmakers, fiction writers have aired the story in Barbara Chase-Riboud's *Sally Heming* (1979) and in Steve Erickson's *Arc d'X* (1994).

Given what we know about the rampant abuse of slave women at the hands of white planters and the subsequent legions of mulatto offspring, the Heming-Jefferson story – if true – might be little more than an interesting footnote in a text on slavery in America . . . except for one thing: the persisting tendency among a wide range of writers and commentators to continue to romanticize Jefferson.

Conservative historians have argued staunchly against the existence of any liaison between their hero and Heming, protesting that such goings on would be incomprehensible to a man of Jefferson's enlightened, moral character. More liberal observers have looked at the Sally Heming story as yet another example that Jefferson was a man ahead of his time, unafraid to sustain a monogamous, interracial romance for decades while living in a racist society. Even Brodie has felt compelled to describe the Heming-Jefferson relationship as 'a serious passion.' The novels and film show Sally Heming as the one person who could draw out the emotions of a man who had dedicated his life to worshipping the power of reason. Yet amidst all the romantic speculation, few commentators notice that Dashing Sally would have been a slave child when Tom Jefferson called her to bed . . . and that she would have had little choice but to comply.

The researchers of the Thomas Jefferson Memorial Foundation (at Monticello) have assembled a packet of information describing what is and isn't known about the Sally Heming story and are actively pursuing contacts with African American descendants of Jefferson's slaves in hopes of giving visitors a more complete picture of life at Monticello in Heming and Jefferson's day. ■

– RP

(☎ 804-977-5459), on the Thomas Jefferson Memorial Parkway, is known for its vinifera (American/French varietal) wines; it is open daily from 11 am to 5 pm. Montdomaine Cellars Winery (☎ 804-971-8947), on Route 20S near C-ville, has 10 acres of vineyards, a gift shop, and a picnic area. They are known for their chardonnay, cabernet sauvignon, and Jefferson white (he has cropped up again). It is open March to November, Monday to Saturday from 10 am to 5 pm.

The Oakencroft Vineyard (☎ 804-296-4188), 3.5 miles west of Hwy 29 on Barracks Rd, has tours and tastings. It is open daily, April to December, from 11 am to 5 pm.

Statues of Explorers

On the corner of Ridge and Main Sts in Midway Park is the Meriwether Lewis, William Clark, and Sacajawea statue honoring the two explorers of the Louisiana territory and their Native American guide. On W Main St, east of UVa, is the statue of George Rogers Clark, explorer of the Northwest Territory and elder brother of William.

Special Events

Every year, for two weeks in April, C-ville celebrates the annual Dogwood Festival, with opening night fireworks, musical performances, carnival, and parade.

Independence Day (July 4) is celebrated at Monticello with a naturalization ceremony. In October, at the Virginia Festival of American Film, movie stars come to Charlottesville to view screenings of new releases – call ☎ 804-924-3378 for information. Around Christmas Day, A Merrie Olde England Christmas Festival is held at the Boar's Head Inn.

Places to Stay – bottom end

Camping If you want to camp, the *Charlottesville KOA* (☎ 804-296-9881, reservations: 800-336-9881) is south of the city on County Rd 708 (if eastbound on I-64, take Exit 118A to Hwy 29, if westbound take Exit 121 to Route 20). It is open from March 15 to November 15 and there are shady campsites, a pavilion, recreation hall, and pool (which is open Monday to Saturday from 10 am to 8 pm). It is good value with sites/hook-ups for $18/24 for two, 'kamping kabins' for $31.

Hotels & Motels Strangely, for a university town, there are no budget hostels in C-ville. There are, however, a couple of value motels on Emmet St (Hwy 29S). The *Budget Inn* (☎ 804-293-5141), at No 140, is near the university and the CSXT railway line. Singles/doubles are from $36/38 with $1 off in winter (an extra person is $5). The office is open from 8 am to midnight.

The basic but adequate *Econo Lodge University* (☎ 804-296-2104), at No 400, is open 24 hours; singles/doubles are from $37/40. The *Econo Lodge-North* (☎ 804-295-3185), at 2014 Holiday Drive (Hwy 250 at the junction of Hwy 29N), has singles/doubles for $39/43 in low season, rising a few dollars in summer (an extra person is $5).

Places to Stay – middle

The *Best Western-Cavalier Inn* (☎ 804-296-8111), at 105 Emmet St N (on Hwys 29 and 250 Business), is well within earshot of the railway line. They have a deluxe room special of $64 for a double that includes breakfast, wine on arrival, and a ticket to one of the attractions. Otherwise, singles/doubles are from $56/66 (no frills) and this includes a free airport shuttle. It also has a restaurant and outdoor pool.

The *English Inn* (☎ 804-971-9900), at 2000 Morton Drive (a block south of the junction of Hwys 29 and 250 Bypass), combines a motel with the B&B theme. Some of the rooms are furnished in colonial style, others are more modern in appearance. The full breakfast is enjoyed in the 'olde worlde' dining room. The rooms are worth it and cost from $59/64 for singles/doubles in winter, otherwise from $65/70.

The *Holiday Inn-Monticello* (☎ 804-977-5100), at 1200 5th St SW (at the junction of I-64 and 5th St, Exit 120), has a pool, dining room, and cocktail bar; singles/doubles in low season are from $60/70, otherwise $65/75. About the same price is the *Courtyard by Marriott* (☎ 804-973-7100, 800-321-2211), at 638 Hillsdale Drive, a really comfortable place with a large grassy patio; a double is $69 on weekdays and $75 on weekends but breakfast is extra.

The *Sheraton Inn Charlottesville* (☎ 804-973-2121) is at 2350 Seminole Trail, on Hwy 29N, three miles north of the junction of the Hwy 250 Bypass and seven

VIRGINIA

miles from town. Although it is relatively expensive, it is worth the $67/72 for single/double rooms in the low season. It has a full range of facilities and two restaurants.

Places to Stay – top end

Hotels At the west end of the Downtown Mall is the *Omni Charlottesville* (☎ 804-971-5500), another hotel trying to marry the colonial with the modern. Single rooms are from $94 to $150 and doubles from $109 to $169; an extra person is $15 (packages and weekend rates are available). The hotel has all the necessary additions: restaurant, spacious lounge on two levels, indoor and outdoor pools, and a fully equipped exercise room.

The *Boar's Head Inn & Sports Club* (☎ 804-296-2181, 800-476-1988), on a 53-acre estate 1.5 miles west of the junction of I-64 and Hwy 250W, is known both for its fine lodging and food. An overnight stay is for the active with golf course, 20 tennis courts, pools, fitness center, and squash courts available for their use. Single rooms are from $115 to $170, doubles from $125 to $180. There are two fine restaurants and hot-air balloon flights depart from the club.

One of the instigators of the interior decorating 'rash' of the 1980s and 1990s, Laura Ashley (purveyors of wallpapers and fabrics) has established an exclusive country house hotel, *Keswick Hall* (☎ 804-979-3440), at 701 Country Club Drive, Keswick. Likely the rooms have more of the wallpaper and fabric (and why not?) but you will have to pay from $175 to $580 for a single, from $195 to $645 a double, to peek inside. Dinner is a mere $55 per head (with the appropriate tablecloths and napkins).

B&Bs The local B&B private service is Guesthouse Bed & Breakfast Inc (☎ 804-979-7264; PO Box 5737, Charlottesville, VA 22905). Most local B&Bs are expensive.

The Inn at Sugar Hollow Farm (☎ 804-823-7086), on Sugar Hollow Rd, is a quaint little country B&B in a lovely mountain setting; singles are from $85 to $130 and doubles from $95 to $140 (an extra person is $25). The cozy, small *Inn at Monticello* (☎ 804-979-3593), off Route 20S, has delightful rooms furnished with antiques, canopy beds, fireplaces, and each has a private porch; singles are from $100 to $130 and doubles from $110 to $140. Two historic houses (one a former house of ill repute) have been combined into the *200 South Street Inn* (☎ 804-979-0200). The rooms are from $95 to $180 for two (an extra person is $20).

Clifton-The Country Inn (☎ 804-973-0579), at 1296 Clifton Drive (just off Hwy 250E, five miles from C-ville), is a large B&B with all the facilities (pool, heated spa, nature trails, tennis court, and a lake) and additional comforts such as afternoon tea at 4 pm. In winter, Sunday to Thursday, all rooms are $145, otherwise they are from $165 to $225. It gets good press – it's rated in the nation's 'top 12' by *Country Inns*.

There are a couple of places near Scottsville, south of C-ville off Route 20S. The *High Meadows Vineyard/Mountain Sunset Inn* (☎ 804-286-2218) is a large place with rooms and suites, set in 50 acres of vineyard. There are nightly candlelit dinners (by prior arrangement) and wine tastings; singles are $80 and doubles from $95 to $145, depending on whether or not you have a room or suite. *Chester* (☎ 804-286-3960), at 2783 James River Rd in Scottsville (County Rd 726), is a comfortable B&B (with bicycles for guests); singles and doubles are from $100 to $130.

Places to Eat

There are a couple of eating enclaves, downtown and in the University Corner area. Near the university are burger places like *The Virginian* (☎ 804-293-2606), at 1521 W Main St, and *Martha's Cafe* (☎ 804-971-7530), at 11 Elliewood Ave, which is great for lasagna, crab cakes, and beer.

Next door to Martha's is *Coupe de Ville's* (☎ 804-977-3966), at No 9; chicken (half a bird) is $6.50, or you can order pasta, seafood, sandwiches, or soup. It is open weekdays from 11:30 am to 2 pm and 5:30 pm to 10 pm, Saturday 5:30 to 10 pm.

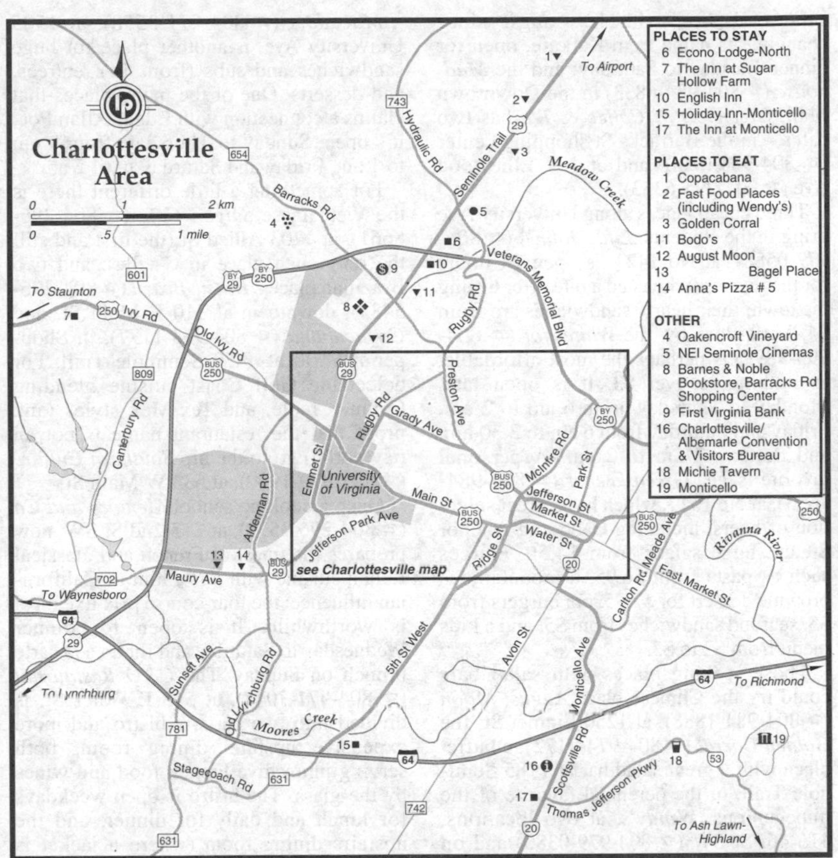

If you crave a pizza (large \$8.25, medium \$7.50, and small \$5.95) you can't go past *Anna's Pizza No 5* (☎ 804-977-6228), at 115 Maury Ave (near Sud's). It is open daily from 11 am until about 11 pm. They also have grinders, calzone, and salads, and imported olives.

Bagels are really big in this town. *Bodo's Bagel Bakery*, where they bake their own, has two locations, at Emmet and Hwy 250 Bypass (☎ 804-977-9598) and Preston Ave and Harris St (☎ 804-293-5224). The *Bagel Place* (☎ 804-971-1619), at 2408 Fontaine Ave, is another good choice.

For delicious Californian-style Mexican food there is the *Baja Bean Co* (☎ 804-293-4507), at 1327 W Main St. An entree of five delicious tacquitos is \$2.75, soup of the day is \$2.50, burgers are from \$4.25, cheap desserts \$3.50, and vegetable chimichangas \$5.50. You can select from 12 Mexican beers and 15 tequilas. Ay, caramba!

And coffee – the air in C-ville exudes the aroma. Some favorites are the *Coffee Exchange* (☎ 804-295-0975), downtown at 120 E Main St, which includes its own bakery and an impressive array of croissants; *Café Noelle* (☎ 804-296-1175), at 20

Elliewood Ave, with less angst since changing its name from Kafkafé, open for dinner Tuesday to Saturday; and the *Mudhouse* (☎ 804-984-6833) in the Downtown Mall. *Greenberry's Coffee & Tea* has two cafes – in the Barracks St shopping center (☎ 804-984-0200) and at 107 Elliewood Ave (☎ 804-295-6333).

Three cheap places along University Ave bring in the students. *Little John's* (☎ 804-977-0588), at No 1427, is open 24 hours for the revelers who need a bite after hitting the town; their hearty sandwiches are from $4. Very close by, the *Whitespot* (☎ 804-295-9899) is perhaps the most affordable, as nothing is over $3. It is open late, Monday to Thursday, from 6 am to 2 am, Friday and Saturday from 6 am to 2:30 am, and Sunday 7 am to 2 am. A personal favorite is *The Greenskeeper* (☎ 804-984-4653), at No 1517, which has a great selection of beers, including Cabo and Anchor Steam, huge salads from $4.50, entrees such as pasta from $6.95, a mountainous brownie dessert for $2.95, big burgers from $5, seafood sandwiches from $5, and a kids menu from $2 to $3.

VIRGINIA

Those seeking places with salad bars could try the Chinese place *August Moon* (☎ 804-984-1888), at 1250 Emmet St; the *Golden Corral* (☎ 804-974-7172), a buffet place with a great salad bar at 1185 Seminole Trail; or the perennial favorite of the impecunious, *Wendy's*, at two locations, 416 4th St SW (☎ 804-979-0380) and on Hwy 29N (☎ 804-973-3324).

The Hardware Store (☎ 804-977-1518), downtown at 316 E Main St, a city landmark since 1895, is a must for first-timers to C-ville. Apart from the interesting memorabilia relating to its days as a store and its 'lit up' mall entrance, the place is good for inexpensive meals – barbecued ribs, hamburgers, sandwiches (one is called 'the Pavarotti'), pasta, fish, salads, and baked potatoes; you can eat well here for less than $10 or just come in for a malt from the old soda fountain. The 'store' opens daily at 11 am and closes Monday at 5 pm, Tuesday through Thursday at 9 pm, and Friday and Saturday at 10 pm. There is free parking on Water St.

Macado's (☎ 804-971-3558), at 1505 University Ave, is another place for huge sandwiches and subs (from $4), entrees, and desserts. One of the many places that claims a connection with Edgar Allan Poe, it's open, Sunday to Thursday, from 9 am to 1 am, Friday and Saturday until 2 am.

For something a little different there is the Vietnamese *Saigon Cafe* (☎ 804-296-8661), at 1703 Allied St (the first and still the only such place in C-ville); and two Brazilian places: *Brasil-Brazil* (☎ 804-296-5485), downtown at 310 E Main St, and *Copacabana* (☎ 804-973-1177), in Shopper's World at 1420 Seminole Trail. For delectable Gulf Coast cuisine blending Cajun, Creole, and Tex-Mex styles (and proof that the restaurant name is not an oxymoron) go to the hip *Southern Culture* (☎ 804-979-1990), at 633 W Main St.

Once a cooking school *Memory and Co* (☎ 804-296-3539), at 213 2nd St SW, now prepares the finest of French and classical Italian cuisine with just a hint of Californian influence; the four-course prix fixe meal is worthwhile. It is open for dinner Wednesday to Saturday and for an à la carte brunch on Sunday. The *C&O Restaurant* (☎ 804-971-7044), at 515 E Water St, is divided into two parts, a bistro and more expensive upstairs dining room, both serving innovative French food and wines by the glass. The bistro is open weekdays for lunch and daily for dinner, and the upstairs dining room (where a jacket is required) is open for two seatings, Monday to Saturday, at 6:30 and 9:30 pm. Two diners are likely to spend $50 downstairs and up to $100 upstairs.

In the Boar's Head Inn (see Places to Stay earlier) there are two restaurants, the cheaper *Racquets* and more expensive *Old Mill Room* (☎ 804-296-2181). The latter, housed in an 1834 grist mill, serves breakfast, lunch, and dinner every day, and offers Sunday brunch; reservations are advised.

Entertainment

Get copies of the free *C'ville Weekly* and *Charlottesville Review* to find out what is on and where. There are heaps of venues for jazz, rock, and just 'chugging.' For current info, ring the free daily Happenings Line (☎ 804-980-8000).

Cinema The pick of the cinemas is *The Jefferson*, at 110 E Main St near the Downtown Mall; current movies can be seen for a mere $2. The *UVa Cinematheque* (☎ 804-924-7900), in the Newcomb Hall Theatre on campus, has a good art-house component. Other possibilities are the *Vinegar Hill Theatre* (☎ 804-977-4911), at 220 W Market St, and *NEI Seminole Cinemas* (☎ 804-980-3333), on Hwy 29N (behind the K-Mart).

Nightlife There is ample nightlife in C-ville. Students flock to *Awful Arthur's* (☎ 804-296-0969), at 333 W Main St (which has an extensive raw bar and seafood menu), and *Trax* (☎ 804-295-8729), at 127 S 11th St. *Max* on W Main St is a bit rougher but they have a C&W night for good ol' boys & girls on Wednesday night.

Far better than Max is the *Outback Lodge* (☎ 804-979-7211), in the Plaza at 917 Preston Ave, about the most happening place in C-ville at the moment. The cover charge is from $4 to $5. (I would tell you more about the place if only I remembered what happened that night! The band, I think, was the absolutely together Unified Funk Theory . . . .)

The *Blue Ridge Brewing Co* (☎ 804-977-0017), at 709 W Main St, is Virginia's first brewery restaurant (it opened 1988), and is the place for serious imbibing of the amber fluid. They serve steak, seafood, pasta, and desserts; the bar is open to 2 am every night.

Performing Arts First get a copy of the free *Charlottesville Arts Monthly*, which lists venues, has a pull-out calendar and two good maps, of downtown and The Corner. Also contact the Artsline (☎ 804-980-3366).

The *Charlottesville and University Symphony Orchestra* (☎ 804-925-6505) play an annual season. The McIntire Department of Music (☎ 804-924-3984) at UVa has information about performances by the orchestra, the University Singers, Collegium Musicum, Jazz Ensemble, and brass and wind ensembles. These performances are usually in *UVa's Cabell Hall*, although some are held 'on the lawn' near the steps of the Rotunda.

The *UVa Department of Drama* (☎ 804-924-3376) conducts a variety of performances by local and visiting companies. A good place to see live theater is at Live Arts (☎ 804-963-8400), at 609 E Market St.

Getting There & Away

USAir Express, United Express (Atlantic Coast), and Comair (Delta's service) serve Charlottesville-Albemarle Airport, 14 miles north of the city on Hwy 29N. Colgan Air (☎ 800-272-6488) services C-ville from New York. The free Charlottesville-Albemarle Airport Flight Guide has all the details.

The regular Amtrak services to New York and Chicago stop at Charlottesville's Union Station (☎ 804-296-4559, 800-872-7245), 810 W Main St. There is a daily New York to New Orleans service.

The Greyhound/Trailways bus terminal (☎ 540-295-5131) is at 310 W Main St, a few blocks away from the train station. There are daily buses to Richmond ($18) and Norfolk ($32), and two daily to DC ($28).

Charlottesville is easy to find by car. It is where Hwy 29 (north-south) meets I-64 (east-west); the latter joins I-95 and I-81.

Getting Around

You have the choice of walking around this pleasant city or renting a bike. A rental from Blue Wheel (☎ 804-977-1870), 19 Elliewood Ave, is about $10 per day. Other cycle shops at The Corner include the Go Pal Bicycle Shop (☎ 804-295-1212), at 107 14th St; and across the road, Blazing Saddles (☎ 804-293-3868), at 104 14th St.

For a cab, call Yellow Cab (☎ 804-295-4131). The cost is 90¢ for the first one-sixth of a mile and $1.50 each mile thereafter. A cab out to Monticello will cost about $8.

AROUND CHARLOTTESVILLE

Ash Lawn-Highland

James Monroe's 535-acre estate on the James Monroe Parkway (County Rd 795), includes Monroe's house, farm craft demonstrations, outbuildings, and boxwood gardens. Jefferson selected the site for his friend and had his gardeners plant orchards there while Monroe was overseas for three years as minister to France. Only 'some' Monroe items are found here. His debts had mounted by the time he retired from office, to a point where he had to sell his farm (on which he had hoped to retire) and many of his possessions.

A colonial crafts weekend, called Plantation Days, is held in early July and an outdoor summer festival of concerts, family entertainment, dramas, and opera on the grounds is held in late August. The estate (☎ 804-293-9539), administered by the College of William and Mary, is open daily, March to October, from 9 am to 6 pm, November to February, 10 am to 5 pm; admission is $7 for adults, $6.50 for seniors, and $3 for children.

Michie Tavern

Just down the road from Monticello, on the Thomas Jefferson Parkway (Route 53), is the 200-year-plus Michie Tavern, dating from 1784 (it was moved here from a well-traveled stagecoach route in 1927). It is still operating and guests can eat colonial-style cooking in 'The Ordinary,' then tour the tavern and circa-1797 Meadow Run Gristmill.

The tavern museum (☎ 804-977-1234) is open daily from 9 am to 5 pm, and lunch is served daily from 11:30 am to 3 pm. The adult cost for the 45-minute tour only is $6 for adults, $5.50 for seniors, $2 for children. A hearty lunch costs about $11.

Lake Anna State Park

Information about this state park, on one of Virginia's most popular lakes, can be obtained from Lake Anna visitors center (☎ 540-854-5503). The park features a beach, bathhouse, boat ramps, picnic areas, and hiking trails. The visitors center highlights past gold mining activity and the present natural features of the park. You can pan for gold or join one of the nature programs.

There are a couple of commercial campgrounds on the shores of Lake Anna: *Rocky Branch Marina* (☎ 540-895-5475), at 5153 Courthouse Rd, has tent and electric/water hook-ups; and *Dukes Creek Marina* (☎ 540-895-5065) has 50 sites.

The park is adjacent to County Rd 601 off Route 208. It's 25 miles southwest of Fredericksburg, 50 miles northwest of Richmond.

North Anna Nuclear Information Center

The North Anna Nuclear Information Center (☎ 540-894-4394), 8.5 miles north of Mineral, is a concerted attempt to alleviate the fear of a potential Three Mile Island or Chernobyl. Films, slides, lectures, and a picnic area all combine to lull the frightened into a sense of security in the present and post-nuclear world. Gaze at the structure and imagine the results if it was built on the San Andreas fault! And think of the carbon rods glowing quietly 24 hours a day – the public can get close weekdays from 9 am to 4 pm (bring your own dosimeter).

Nelson County

This county is best known as the birthplace of *The Waltons* TV series – such is the power of television. The **Walton's Mountain Museum** (☎ 804-831-2000), on County Rd 617 in Schuyler (pronounced 'Sky-lar'), includes all those oh-so-familiar locales of the series – the Walton's living room and kitchen, John-Boy's bedroom and Ike Godsey's store in the rural village where the series was set. A Hollywood screenwriter, Earl Hamner, Jr, based the characters on people from this district whom he remembered from his childhood. The museum, in the old elementary school not far from where Hamner lived as a youngster, is open

March to November from 10 am to 4 pm; admission is $4 for adults, $3 for seniors and children six to 12.

And before you say 'good night' to John-Boy you can also visit the **Swannanoa Marble Palace** (☎ 540-942-5161), built in 1912 and modeled on the Villa de Medici in Italy, with its original Italian frescoes and a Tiffany stained-glass window. It is now the New Age, transcendental University of Science and Philosophy. You might also stop at the 1900 **Oak Ridge Estate** with its gracious 50-room mansion, Italian gardens, carriage house, railroad station, and rotunda greenhouse (all currently being restored).

There are at least three **wineries**, including Afton Mountain Vineyards (☎ 540-456-8667), in Afton, and Wintergreen Vineyard & Winery (☎ 804-361-2519), in Nellysford. These are open from 10 am to 6 pm in summer and fall for tours and tastings.

Canoeing on the James River

There is really good canoeing on the James River near Scottsville and the chance to fish, explore, and bird watch as you paddle along. For all canoeing, tubing, and rafting equipment contact James River Runners Inc (☎ 804-286-2338) at their base camp at Hatton Ferry; it is well signed. There are three-, seven-, and nine-mile trips on the James for $15/21/21 per person and overnight trips for $42, all inclusive (minimum age for canoe trips is 10; for raft or tube trips it is six). From Hwy 20S take County Rds 726 and 625 to Hatton Ferry.

ORANGE COUNTY

This picturesque county is characterized by its gently rolling hills and a number of historical attractions including Montpelier, lifelong home of James and Dolley Madison, and the famous Barboursville vineyards. The St Thomas Episcopal Church in Orange is the only surviving example of a Jeffersonian effort at religious architecture. To the east of the county are the Wilderness battlefields, scene of the first confrontation between Generals Robert E Lee and Ulysses S Grant in May 1864. For more information contact the visitors bureau (☎ 540-672-1653), at 154 Madison Rd, Orange.

James Madison Museum

This museum (☎ 540-672-1776), at 129 Caroline St in Orange, commemorates the fourth president of the US (who served during the difficult times of the War of 1812) and the 'father' of the Constitution. The museum also covers the history of the county and has a hall of agriculture with an 18th century homestead.

It is open March to November, weekdays 9 am to 4 pm, weekends 1 to 4 pm; otherwise weekdays from 9 am to 4 pm. Admission is $4 for adults, $3 for seniors, and $1 for students and children over six.

Montpelier

The lifelong home of President James Madison is now owned by the National Trust. The main house of 55 rooms is still undergoing preservation and restoration (it was substantially modified by the du Pont family), but you can see parts of it. The formal garden and grounds overlooking the Blue Ridge Mountains are a real delight. James and Dolley and other Madisons are interred nearby. It is hoped that Montpelier will one day stand as a monument to Madison, with special emphasis placed on his contribution to the Constitution and Bill of Rights.

The house and grounds (☎ 540-672-2728) are open daily, mid-March to December, from 10 am to 4 pm, January to mid-March, Friday and Saturday from 10 am to 4 pm; admission (which includes a 10-minute video, bus tour of the grounds, and house tour) is $6 for adults, $5 for seniors, and $1 for children six to 11.

Montpelier is six miles south of Orange on Route 20 at Montpelier Station. In late April/early May, the Montpelier Wine Festival is held here. The Montpelier Hunt, initiated by Marion du Pont Scott (who built the original steeplechase course) is held in November.

Barboursville

The rural scenery around Barboursville makes the diversion along Route 20 worthwhile. Just near where Hwy 33 intersects with Route 20 (follow the signs) are the **Barboursville Vineyards** (☎ 540-832-3824) and the ruins of Governor James Barbour's mansion.

The mansion, designed for Barbour (governor of Virginia from 1812 to 1814) by Jefferson to resemble his own Monticello, was burned on Christmas 1884 and the ruins are now a registered Virginia historic landmark.

The vineyard (and ruins on the property) is open Monday to Saturday from 10 am to 5 pm, Sunday 11 am to 5 pm; there are tours on Saturday from 10 am to 4 pm and admission is free.

LYNCHBURG

This city and its surrounding area, rightly advertised as the 'real' Virginia, is 60 miles southwest of Charlottesville on Hwy 29. It was founded by a Quaker, John Lynch, who from 1757 operated a ferry across the James River. In 1785 he built the region's first tobacco warehouse. For the next 100 years, the production of cigarettes and plugs of chewing tobacco ensured the city's prosperity.

During the Civil War it was a major storage depot that at one point was saved by the quick thinking of Confederate General Jubal Early. On June 18, 1864, the general, by use of a clever ruse, convinced the approaching Union troops that the city had been reinforced and thus saved it from destruction.

Today Lynchburg (population 66,000) is a regional center and a college town. It is known as the city of churches, as there are over 130 of them in the region. The town has many fine architectural highlights arrayed around the city's seven hills and nearby are the important historical sites of Jefferson's Poplar Forest, Patrick Henry's Red Hill, Booker T Washington's birthplace, and Appomattox Court House, where Robert E Lee surrendered to Ulysses S Grant in 1865.

Orientation

The northeastern boundary of the city is the James River and across the river is Madison Heights in Amherst County. To the southeast of the city is Candlers Mountain with Lynchburg Regional Airport to the west of that. Two roads divide the city into rough quarters – Hwy 29 is the north-south artery and Hwy 501 runs roughly northwest-southeast. Hwy 460 skirts the city on its southern boundaries.

Information

Tourist Offices The Lynchburg Visitors Information Center (☎ 804-847-1811, 800-532-7821) is at 216 12th St on the corner of Church St. They screen a 10-minute audio-visual and have exhibits and a gift shop. Get free copies of intersting brochures on history, and walking tours there. The center is open daily from 9 am to 5 pm. The Greater Lynchburg Chamber of Commerce has an information line (☎ 800-732-5821).

Money There are plenty of suitable banks for foreign exchange (and other banking necessaries) in The Plaza, River Ridge Mall, and the Boonsboro shopping center.

Bookstores On a rainy day in Lynchburg, try Inkling's across from Percival's Isle, Givens on Lakeside Drive (Hwy 221), or The Bookstore in the Boonsboro shopping center (on Hwy 501 Business).

Medical Services The Lynchburg General Hospital (☎ 804-947-3000), off Tate Springs Rd, has emergency and critical care facilities. For the Doctor's Answering Service call ☎ 804-847-4466.

Monument Terrace

This is Lynchburg's most famous landmark, a war memorial consisting of 139 limestone and granite steps leading up to the old city courthouse. At the foot of the steps is a statue of a WWI 'doughboy' *(The Listening Post)*, at the top a statue of a Confederate soldier. Even if you don't climb to the top, the view from the base at the corner of Main and 9th Sts is worthwhile.

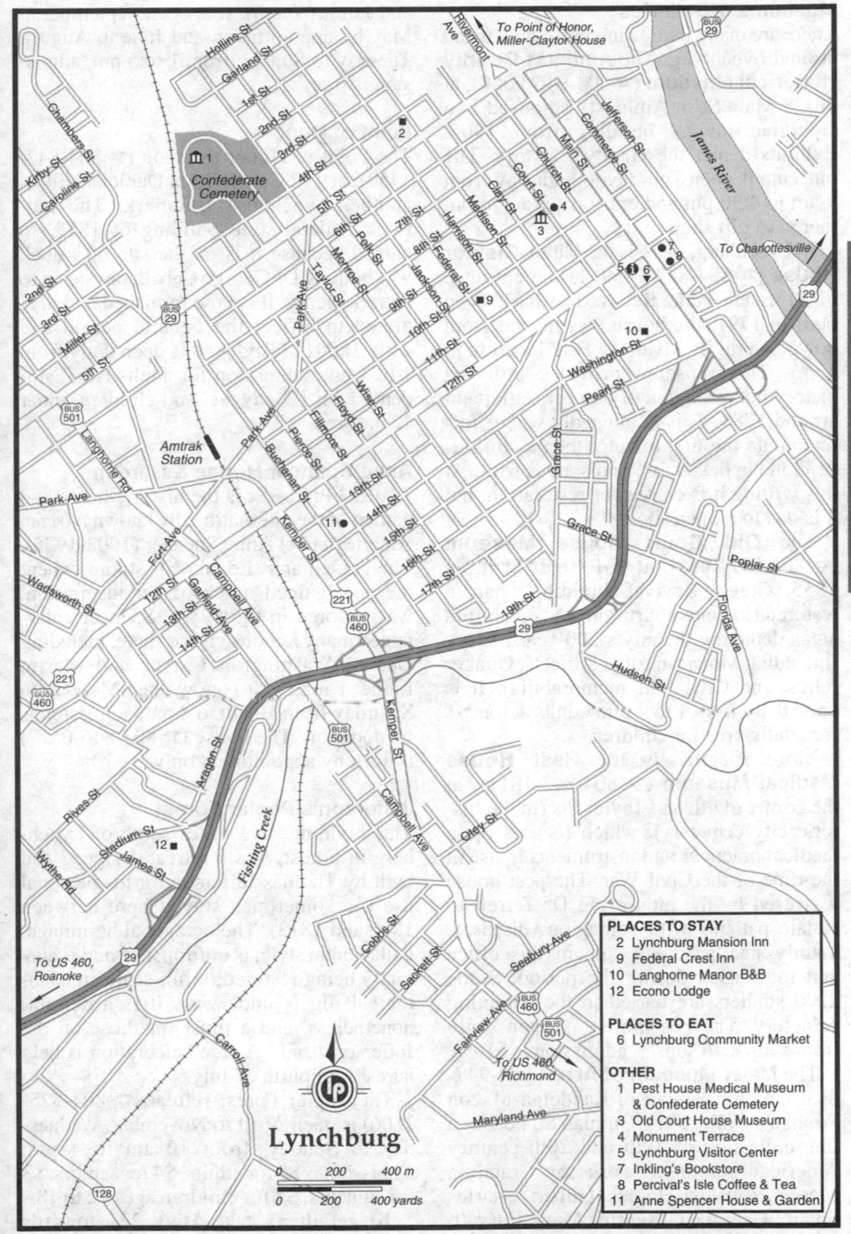
Lynchburg
PLACES TO STAY
2 Lynchburg Mansion Inn
9 Federal Crest Inn
10 Langhorne Manor B&B
12 Econo Lodge
PLACES TO EAT
6 Lynchburg Community Market
OTHER
1 Pest House Medical Museum & Confederate Cemetery
3 Old Court House Museum
4 Monument Terrace
5 Lynchburg Visitor Center
7 Inkling's Bookstore
8 Percival's Isle Coffee & Tea
11 Anne Spencer House & Garden
To Point of Honor, Miller-Claytor House
To Charlottesville
To US 460, Roanoke
To US 460, Richmond
Confederate Cemetery
Amtrak Station
James River
Fishing Creek
Rivermont Ave
Hollins St
Garland St
1st St
2nd St
3rd St
4th St
5th St
6th St
7th St
8th St
9th St
10th St
11th St
12th St
13th St
14th St
15th St
16th St
17th St
19th St
Jefferson St
Commerce St
Main St
Church St
Court St
Clay St
Madison St
Harrison St
Federal St
Jackson St
Polk St
Monroe St
Taylor St
Park Ave
Wise St
Floyd St
Fillmore St
Pierce St
Buchanan St
Kemper St
Campbell Ave
Washington St
Pearl St
Grace St
Poplar St
Florida Ave
Hudson St
Otey St
Cobbs St
Sackett St
Seabury Ave
Fairview Ave
Maryland Ave
Carroll Ave
Chambers St
Kirby St
Caroline St
Miller St
Langhorne Rd
Fort Ave
Garfield Ave
Wadsworth St
Aragon St
Rives St
Stadium St
James St
Wythe Rd
0 200 400 m
0 200 400 yards

Museums & Galleries

There are many interesting museums in and around Lynchburg. The **Amherst County Historical Museum** (☎ 804-946-9068), at 301 S Main St in Amherst, is housed in a Georgian revival building from 1905. Exhibits depict the county's history. The museum is open Tuesday to Saturday from 9 am to 4:30 pm and entry is by donation; there is a gift shop.

In Lynchburg, there is the **Miller-Claytor House** (☎ 804-847-1459) at the entrance of Riverside Park. Believed to have been built in 1791, the house was moved from downtown to its Riverside Park location in 1936. This museum provides a living history interpretation of pioneer settlement around 1786. This is allegedly where Jefferson ate the first tomato, then a 'forbidden' and believed to be poisonous fruit. At this writing it is closed for restoration, but it is due to reopen soon.

The **Old Court House Museum** (☎ 804-847-1459), at 901 Court St in an 1855 Greek Revival building, has a restored Hustings courtroom and exhibition areas depicting the city's 200-year history (including Monacan tribal artifacts, Quaker relics, and Civil War memorabilia). It is open daily from 1 to 4 pm; admission is $1 for adults, free for children.

More specific is the **Pest House Medical Museum** (☎ 804-847-1811), at the corner of 4th and Taylor Sts (in the historic city cemetery), which focuses upon medical practices and instruments in use at the time of the Civil War. The pest house was used by the pioneering Dr Terrell to isolate patients with contagious diseases, mainly smallpox, and contains his office and tools used during the period. Some 2200 soldiers are buried in the adjoining cemetery. The pest house is open daily from sunrise to sunset; admission is $1.

The **Maier Museum of Art** (☎ 804-947-8136), on the campus of Randolph-Macon Woman's College at 1 Quinlan St, houses a fine collection of 19th and 20th century American paintings (works by Grandma Moses, Winslow Homer, Gilbert Charles Stuart, Georgia O'Keeffe, Mary Cassatt, and Jamie Wyeth). It is open September to May by appointment, and June to August, Tuesday to Sunday from 1 to 5 pm; admission is free.

Point of Honor

The Point of Honor mansion (☎ 804-847-1459), at 112 Cabell St on Daniel's Hill, is another Lynchburg landmark. The red-brick Federal-style building of 1815, so named because it is on the site of a duel, was built by Dr George Cabell, physician to Patrick Henry. It is now furnished and decorated to reflect the Federal period and early 1800s lifestyles. It is open daily from 1 to 4 pm; admission for adults is $3, students with ID pay $1, and children under 12 are free.

Anne Spencer House & Garden

At 1313 Pierce St is the historic home and garden of the internationally known African American poet Anne Spencer (1903-1975). The garden and 'Edankraal' studio, where the poet gained much of her inspiration, was restored in the 1980s. Spencer entertained many famous visitors here, including George Washington Carver and Martin Luther King, Jr. It is now open Monday to Saturday from 10 am to 4 pm; admission is by donation. The house (☎ 804-846-0517) is open by appointment only.

Jefferson's Poplar Forest

This building, five miles south of Lynchburg in Forest, was a retreat designed and built by Thomas Jefferson for his personal use (he sometimes stayed here between 1806 and 1813). The octagonal hermitage, Palladian in style, is unfurnished and is currently being restored; a full-scale archaeological dig is underway. It is a delight, nonetheless, and a must for those on the Jefferson 'trail.' A free celebration is held here each Fourth of July.

The Poplar Forest retreat (☎ 804-525-1806) is open April to November, Wednesday to Sunday, from 10 am to 4 pm; admission is $5 for adults, $4 for seniors, $3 for students, $1 for children ages 12 to 18.

To get there, take Hwy 221 towards

Bedford. Turn off on County Rd 661; the entrance to Poplar Forest is one mile along County Rd 661.

Special Events

The city celebrates its river location in June in the Festival by the James and the James River Bateau Festival with authentic boats ('bateaux'), which once plied the river carrying tobacco and other goods. Call ☎ 804-845-5966 for information.

Places to Stay

Camping The nearest camping areas are close to Appomattox. The *Holliday Lake State Park* (☎ 804-248-6308) has developed sites for $10.50; it is open from January to April and late May to early December. To get there take Route 24 through the national historic park, turn south onto County Rd 626 then take County Rd 692. Six miles west of Appomattox on Hwy 460, and adjacent to Paradise Lake, is *Yogi Bear's Jellystone Camp Resort* (☎ 804-993-3332). It is open all year and fully serviced sites are from $14 to $18 for two.

Hotels & Motels Perhaps one of the cheapest accommodations is the *Thomas Motor Inn* (☎ 804-845-2121) on Hwy 29, three miles north of Lynchburg in Madison Heights; a traveler can get a spacious room with cable TV, bath, and phone for $28, but it is basic.

The *Comfort Inn-Lynchburg* (☎ 804-847-9041), on Odd Fellows Rd just off Hwy 29, has a pool; the cost for a single/double room in low season is $39/44, in the high season it costs from $45/50. The *Econo Lodge* (☎ 804-847-1045), at 2400 Stadium Drive (off Hwy 29, Exit 4 if southbound, Exit 6 if northbound), has singles and doubles from $45. The *Holiday Inn* (☎ 804-847-4424, 800-465-4329), near the junction of Odd Fellows Rd and Hwy 29, has data ports, an airport bus, and restaurant (The Seasons); singles and doubles are from $65 to $75 in low season, otherwise from $75 to $85. At the *Innkeeper Lynchburg* (☎ 804-237-7771), 2901 Candlers Mountain Rd just off Hwy 29S, breakfast is free and all rooms have cable TV; singles are from $49 to $90 and doubles from $55 to $90.

The top hotel is the *Lynchburg Hilton* (☎ 804-237-6333), at 2900 Candlers Mountain Rd, just off Hwy 29S, with pool, saunas, and restaurant (Johnny Bull's); singles are from $90 to $110, doubles from $100 to $130 (and children stay for free).

B&Bs There are a number of reasonable B&Bs in and close to Lynchburg. Bed & Breakfast Virginia Style (☎ 804-946-7207) is an association of four B&Bs; contact them for locations and prices. Recommended B&Bs include the Georgian Revival mansion *Federal Crest Inn* (☎ 804-845-6155), at 1101 Federal St on Federal Hill; the Spanish Georgian-style *Lynchburg Mansion Inn* (☎ 804-528-5400), at 405 Madison St on Garland Hill (singles/doubles from $84/89); and the cozy antebellum home *Langhorne Manor* (☎ 804-846-4667), at 313 Washington St, Diamond Hill.

Places to Eat

There is an excellent selection of food at the *Lynchburg Community Market – Bateau Landing* (☎ 804-847-1499), on the corner of Main and 12th Sts. The market is open every day from 7 am to 2 pm (as it has been since 1783) and there is a fine selection of baked goods, ethnic foods, meats, and produce (the perfect place to make up a picnic basket). Particularly good is the *Philippine Delight* (☎ 804-384-5654), open Tuesday to Friday from 11 am to 2 pm, Saturday 9 am to 2 pm. Another great place to pick up picnic fare and box lunches is the inexpensive *Farm Basket* (☎ 804-528-1107), at 2008 Langhorne Rd. It also includes a small and always packed restaurant where you can get cucumber sandwiches, three-bean salad, brunswick stew, and delectable gouda cheese biscuits. For sandwiches, hoagies, and homemade salads try the cleverly named *Phila Deli* (☎ 804-384-5972) in the Boonsboro shopping center; it is open Monday to Saturday from 11:30 am to 7 pm.

For made-from-scratch Southern cooking, there is *Morrison's Cafeteria* (☎ 804-237-6549), at 3405 Candler's Mountain Rd in the River Ridge Mall; it is open daily from 11 am to about 8 pm for lunch and dinner and you can dine heartily here for less than $10. *Cattle Annie's* (☎ 804-846-2668), at 4009 Murray Place, is another Southern-style place with smoked meats, salads, and barbecue; it is open Tuesday to Friday for lunch and dinner, Saturday for dinner only, and the club opens daily (except Sunday) at 7 pm for live country music.

There are a number of places for carnivores looking for a huge steak. *TC Trotters* (☎ 804-846-3545), at 2496 Rivermont Ave, is a Tex-Mex place popular with the young professional set. The *Texas Steakhouse* (☎ 804-528-1134), at 4001 Murray Place (behind the Holiday Inn Central), is open on weekdays for lunch and daily for dinner. *The Crown Sterling* (☎ 804-239-7744), at 6120 Fort Ave near the Fort Hill shopping plaza, is open for dinner from Monday to Saturday (they have a great salad bar, a kids' menu and the 'house' dinner of ribeye, salad, rice or potato, a glass of wine, and dessert for $15). The *Landmark Steakhouse & Lounge* (☎ 804-237-1884), at 6113 Fort Ave, serves hickory charcoaled ribs.

Lunch and dinner at *Café France* (☎ 804-385-8989), 3225 Old Forest Rd (in the Forest Plaza West shopping center), are a real delight. The food is not necessarily French but tends to reflect what is available from the adjoining deli. There are also deli take-out and specials menus; dinner mains are from $10 to $20 and the cafe is closed on Sundays. In the same price range is *Cedar St* (☎ 804-384-7118), at 3009 Old Forest Rd, a good choice for seafood, beef, and chicken dishes. It is open weekdays for lunch and daily until about 10 pm for dinner.

There are a number of Asian restaurants. The *China Royal* (☎ 804-385-0011), at 205 Gristmill Drive in the Graves Mill Center, and *King's Island* (☎ 804-384-0066), at 2804 Forest Rd, are both good places; the latter serves dishes with Polynesian flavor. The *Kyoto Fantasy Japanese Steakhouse* (☎ 804-237-9134), at 2160 Wards Rd in the Hills Plaza, is one of those authentic places where chicken, steak, and shrimp dishes are prepared at your table; it is open daily for dinner.

Entertainment

As far as nightlife goes, this is light on! It was only recently that the city and county revoked a long-standing dry law. *Club Gatsby's* (☎ 804-385-5052), at 2034 Lakeside Drive, usually has a band and dancing, Wednesday to Saturday, from 4:30 pm to 2 am. *Cattle Annie's* (see Places to Eat) is a popular nightspot with country bands.

The *Drowsy Poet* (☎ 804-846-6604), at 3700 Candlers Mountain Rd, has folk music and jazz on Wednesday nights, a menu to suit vegetarians, and a selection of books and board games. Across from the community market is *Percival's Isle Coffee & Tea* (☎ 804-847-3059), at 1208 Main St, a popular meeting spot. There is a wonderful ambiance in this old restored building, which is open Monday to Thursday from 7 am to 10 pm, Friday and Saturday to midnight.

The *Lynchburg Fine Arts Center* (☎ 804-846-8451), at 1815 Thomson Drive, is a 500-seat theater where drama, dance, and music are performed regularly. Also, many cultural events are held in the Dillard Fine Arts Building of Lynchburg College. In Amherst County the *Virginia Center for Creative Arts* (☎ 804-946-7236), a retreat for composers, artists, and writers, occasionally holds events where you can meet the writers and artists. The *Randolph-Macon Woman's College* (☎ 804-947-8000) hosts a Blue Ridge Music Festival (jazz, chamber music, and Appalachian melodies) annually.

Getting There & Away

Lynchburg's Regional Airport (☎ 804-847-1632) is on Hwy 29, eight miles south of downtown. Companies serving Lynchburg include USAir Express (☎ 800-428-4322), Atlantic Southeast Air/Delta, and United

Express (☎ 800-241-6522). The taxi/limo service is Airport Limo (☎ 804-239-1777).

The Greyhound/Trailways (☎ 804-846-6614, 800-231-2222) terminal is at the corner of Wildflower Drive and Odd Fellows Rd; there is frequent service to other major centers in Virginia and out of state.

The Amtrak service (☎ 800-872-7245) passes through Lynchburg at really odd hours (the daily 'Crescent' service between New York and New Orleans). Amtrak's station is at the corner of Kemper St and Park Ave.

The Greater Lynchburg Transit Co (☎ 804-847-7771) serves the city and Amherst County; the main terminal is at the Plaza shopping center, Memorial Ave and Lakeside Drive. The office is on Kemper St.

AROUND LYNCHBURG

Bedford

Bedford, tucked away in the foothills of the Blue Ridge Mountains, is on Hwy 460 some 24 miles west of Lynchburg. The **Bedford City/County Museum** (☎ 540-586-4520), at 201 E Main St, is housed in an 1895 Masonic Lodge. It has historical exhibits relating to Bedford and the surrounding county. It's a good place to get information and is open Monday to Saturday from 10 am to 5 pm; admission is $1 for adults, 50¢ for students and children ages six to 18.

The **Bedford Historic Meeting House** (☎ 540-586-8188), at 153 W Main St, is an 1838 Greek Revival building, once used as a meeting house for Methodists in Liberty (later Bedford), and later as an Episcopal church. It is open year round by appointment. The elegant **Avenel**, at 413 Avenel Ave, was built in 1838. It is also open year round by appointment, but its resident ghosts may not show up on cue.

And if you can't make it to Israel, then maybe **Holyland USA** (☎ 540-586-2823) is the next best thing – it's a three-mile trail (no bombs or terrorists) through representations of key Holy Land sites. It is open daily from 8 am to 7 pm. It is three miles south of Bedford – take Route 122S to Dickerson-Neil Rd (Route 746) and turn right; it's just a spit and a holler up the road (follow the star in the east!).

The *Best Western Terrace House Inn* (☎ 804-586-8286), 921 Blue Ridge Ave, has singles from $41 to $50, doubles from $44 to $52.

Appomattox

Civil War buffs will no doubt make a pilgrimage to this region, where the Court House, now an American shrine, is located (it is some 20 miles east of Lynchburg). The Appomattox Depot visitor information center (☎ 804-352-2621), in a restored railroad depot on the main street of downtown Appomattox, has information on a walking tour and carriage rides; it is open daily from 9 am to 5 pm. The **Appomattox County Museum**, housed in an old jail from 1897, has restored rooms and artifacts. It is open May to October on Tuesday, Thursday, and Saturday; admission is $1.

McLean House, where Grant and Lee met in the parlor on April 9, 1865, and where Lee surrendered the Army of Northern Virginia (and effectively ended the Civil War), is now part of the **Appomattox Court House National Historic Park** (☎ 804-352-8987). The 27 buildings of Appomattox village have been restored to their state at the time of the surrender. McLean House, which was torn down in 1893 by a speculator hoping to rebuild it in Washington, DC, has since been reconstructed. (Almost unbelievably, Wilmer McLean had moved here in protest after his farm at Manassas/Bull Run had hosted the first major battle of the war!)

There are self-guided walking tours, audiovisual presentations, and help from rangers at the park; the entrance fee is $2 for adults, and senior citizens and children under 17 are free. The historic park is open daily, June to August, from 9 am to 5:30 pm, September to May from 8:30 am to 5 pm. The courthouse and village are two miles north of Hwy 460 on Route 24.

Surrender at Appomattox

One of the most poignant events of American history was enacted at Appomattox – the surrender of Robert E Lee's Army of Northern Virginia and the end of the bloodiest war ever fought on American soil.

After Grant had taken Petersburg and Richmond, his Army of the Potomac chased Lee's bedraggled Confederate forces. The Union forces destroyed half of the Confederate army at Sayler's Creek, taking many prisoners including General Richard Ewell. General Philip Sheridan's cavalry and a full corps of Union infantry managed to get in front of Lee and block his path. After a sporadic battle Lee sent a soldier through the lines with a white flag and a letter to Grant.

On April 9, 1865 (Palm Sunday), in the modest house of Wilmer McLean at Appomattox Court House, Lee, resplendent in his best uniform with his sword by his side, sat down to talk with Grant, who was dressed in a private's tunic with lieutenant general's stars pinned to its shoulders. Traveller, Lee's horse, munched on the grass outside. Grant, in an attempt at small talk, mentioned to Lee that they had met before, in the Mexican War when Grant was a regimental quartermaster, but Lee could not remember him. After a pause Lee brought Grant back to the matter at hand.

Grant opened his notebook and in straightforward fashion spelled out the terms. These were generous and included the lines that would make it impossible for acts of vengeance to be taken against former Confederate soldiers: Once they had lain down their arms and returned home they were 'not to be disturbed by the United States authorities so long as they observe their paroles and the laws in force where they may reside.' A few changes were made, and after an exchange of military salutes, Lee returned to Traveller and rode away.

When the Union gunners started firing a victory salute, Grant had it stopped immediately. The Confederates were no longer the enemy he retorted and instead he had wagons of Federal supplies moved to the Confederate lines to feed Lee's famished soldiers.

Grant sat down in front of his tent and reminisced about the Mexican War, not outwardly savoring the moment of victory. Lee rode past his troops, many of whom had tears streaming down their faces. In the following days the once-proud Army of Northern Virginia stacked up its arms, formally surrendered, and wandered away to recommence their shattered lives. ■

VIRGINIA

Red Hill National Memorial

About 26 miles south of Appomattox Court House (or 35 miles southeast of Lynchburg) is Red Hill (☎ 804-376-2044), the final and favorite of the many homes of the Revolutionary War patriot Patrick Henry. The house, restored near an original law office, includes many furnishings provided by Henry's family, and there are outbuildings such as a stable and coachman's cabin. The centerpiece of the museum is the PH Rothermel painting *Patrick Henry before the Virginia Houses of Burgesses*.

Henry, who gave the inspiring 'Give me Liberty or give me Death' speech, is buried on the property, two of his seventeen children were born here and two daughters were married here. Patrick Henry died here on June 6, 1799, and the simple inscription on his grave reads 'Fame is his best epitaph.'

To get there from Lynchburg, take Hwy 501 to Brookneal then follow the signs. The house is open daily, April to October, from 9 am to 5 pm, November to February, 9 am to 4 pm, but is closed on major holidays; entry is $3 for adults, $1 for students and children.

Booker T Washington Birthplace

About 20 miles southeast of Roanoke, in the Piedmont, is the restored 224-acre plantation where Booker T Washington was born a slave on April 5, 1856 (see the sidebar in this section). By the end of the Civil War, Washington had lived for nine years as a slave on this former tobacco farm. On this farm you can now experience firsthand the life and landscapes of people who lived as slaves. There are the restored buildings, tools, livestock and crops, and workers in period costume (in summer) relating to the time Booker T was born here.

The birthplace is open daily from 9 am to 4:30 pm and the wheelchair-accessible visitors center (☎ 540-721-2094) has exhibits and a bookstore. They also screen an audiovisual; admission to the whole complex is free.

To get to the birthplace from I-81, take Exit 143 to I-581, which becomes Hwy 220. Follow this south to Rocky Mount, follow park signs, and travel north on Route 122 – the birthplace is six miles east of Burnt Chimney. From Hwy 29 in Lynchburg, take Hwy 460W to Bedford, then Route 122S .

Farmville

This is the town where Robert E Lee met Confederate officials in April 1865, in **Jackson House**, not long before the

Booker T Washington

Booker Talioferro Washington was born on a plantation in Franklin County on April 5, 1856, the son of a slave. He lived on the plantation for nine years and at the end of the Civil War his family moved to Malden, West Virginia. Washington then worked in a salt furnace and coal mines, snatching education whenever he could. From 1872 to 1875 he went to a new school for blacks, today called the Hampton Institute, and paid his tuition by working as a janitor. He taught for two years in Malden after graduation. He returned to the Hampton Institute in 1879 as an instructor and for a time supervised the training of 75 Native Americans, so successfully that he was selected in 1881 as organizer of the Tuskegee Normal School (now Institute) in Alabama.

He developed into a competent public speaker and an important and controversial race leader at a time when racism in the US made it necessary for African Americans to adjust to a new era of oppression. Not all African Americans agreed with Washington's views, especially those expressed in his controversial Atlanta Compromise speech of September 1895, in which he advocated temporary acceptance of his people's inferior social position while they raised their status through vocational training and economic independence.

More importantly, he had the ear of three presidents (William McKinley, Theodore Roosevelt, and William Howard Taft) on educational issues relating to his people. He wrote several books – *The Future of the American Negro* (1899), the autobiographical *Up from Slavery* (1901), and *The Story of the Negro* (1909) – and founded organizations designed to advance the position of his people. He died in 1915, probably the most important spokesperson for African Americans at the time. ■

surrender of the Army of Northern Virginia. There is a 27-stop walking tour, which takes in 19th century warehouse buildings and antebellum churches as well as Jackson House. (It is also a stop on Lee's Retreat Tour.)

You can get brochures from the Farmville Chamber of Commerce (☎ 804-392-3939). Living up to its name, Farmville has a downtown *farmer's market* (☎ 804-392-5686) where you can buy produce from local farms (held every Saturday from June to October).

The **Sailor's Creek Battlefield** (☎ 804-392-3435) is north of Hwy 460 on Route 617. It was the scene of the largest pitched battle during Lee's retreat to Appomattox (tune to 1610 AM for a commentary on the fighting of April 6, 1865). Here General George Meade overtook part of Lee's army and destroyed half of it. The end for the Army of Northern Virginia was near. The restored Hillsman House displays scenes of the fighting.

To the south is **Twin Lakes State Park** (☎ 804-392-3435) which has a loop road running through it. There is also a boat launch and rentals, fishing, and camping (standard sites are $10.50); nearby is the pretty Prince Edward-Gallion State Forest. The park is five miles southwest of Burkeville; take Hwy 360W to County Rds 613 and 629.

SMITH MOUNTAIN LAKE

This extensive state park is on the second largest freshwater body in the state with over 500 miles of shoreline, formed to generate power for the Appalachian Power Company. In addition to many water activities there are hiking trails, bridle trails, primitive camping, picnicking, and a visitors center. When you stop here, consider that the Algonquins were fishing and hunting here long before the advent of electricity.

Smith Mountain Lake Welcome Center (☎ 540-721-1203) is at 2 Bridgewater Plaza, Moneta (on Route 122, between Bedford and Rocky Mount). To get to the park from Hwy 460 take Route 122S to County Rd 608E, then County Rd 626S. If you're interested in **fishing** the humungous striper, contact these guides: Spike Franceschini (☎ 540-297-5611) or Dave Sines (☎ 540-721-5007).

Places to Stay & Eat In addition to primitive sites in the *state park,* which are $7 per night (☎ 540-297-6066), there is the *Crazy Horse Marina & Campground* (☎ 540-721-2792) on Blackwater Cove; the campground is reached by County Rd 616.

There are more 'luxurious' accommodations. In Rocky Mount, there is a *Comfort Inn* (☎ 540-489-4000), at 950 N Main St. *Bernard's Landing* (☎ 800-572-2048), reached by Route 122 and County Rds 616 and 940, is a new resort on the edge of the lake. It has sandy beaches, a pool, health club, and handball and tennis courts. If you want a preview, rent the video *What about Bob?* with Richard Dreyfuss and Bill Murray.

There are a couple of fine restaurants nearby and the most famous, having earned the title of 'Best Restaurant on the Lake,' is *The Landing Restaurant* (☎ 540-721-3028), at Bernard's Landing (see earlier). All of the meals, even the simplest, are cooked with gourmet flair; the restaurant is open daily, and there is an unforgettable Sunday brunch with savory omelets. In Moneta, on Route 122 in Bridgewater Plaza, is *The Anchor House* (☎ 804-721-6540), the place for salads, burgers, tacos, and cocktails.

The nighttime action at Smith Mountain Lake, after a day of fishing and swimming, is found at the *Bridge Club*, 133 Long Island Drive, underneath the Hales Ford Bridge.

There are a couple of **cruise boats**, the 19th century sidewheeler *Virginia Dare* and the motor yacht *Blue Moon*, on which you can enjoy a sunset seafood buffet and live entertainment – a relaxing way to see the lake; contact Paddle Wheel Cruises (☎ 800-721-3273), near Moneta, for costs and times. The departure point is off County Rd 853.

MARTINSVILLE

This small city of 16,000, nestled in the Blue Ridge foothills, is named after General Joseph Martin. It was established in 1871 and, thanks to the railway and an industrial boom, its population increased to over 5000 by 1924. It is now a major manufacturing center of furniture, mirrors, sweatshirts, clocks, and pre-fab homes.

The **Virginia Museum of Natural History** (☎ 540-666-8600), 1001 Douglas Ave, has permanent and traveling exhibits (kids will love the animated triceratops). It is open Tuesday to Saturday from 10 am to 5 pm, Sunday 2 to 5 pm; admission is free.

The **Piedmont Arts Association** (☎ 540-632-3221), at 215 Starling Ave, is an old historical home with five art galleries; the work of national, regional, and local artists is exhibited weekdays from 9 am to 5 pm, Saturday 10 am to 3 pm, and Sunday 1:30 to 4:30 pm; admission is also free.

The **Martinsville Speedway**, on Hwy 220S between Martinsville and the North Carolina border, hosts four annual races on its 0.526 mile asphalt track – the Winston Cup Series (Hanes 500, Goody's 500) and NASCAR double-headers (Miller 500, Winston Classic). The **Martinsville Phillies**, a minor-league affiliate of the Philadelphia Phillies, is the only professional outfit in Henry County. You can see them 'pitch, catch, and foul out' at Hooker Field on Commonwealth Blvd.

The *Super 8 Motel* (☎ 540-666-6835), at 960 Memorial Blvd, 1.5 miles north of town on Hwy 220 Business, is a good economical stalwart; singles/doubles are $36/42. Closer to town, also on Hwy 220 Business, is the *Best Western Martinsville Inn* (☎ 540-632-5611) with a pool, exercise room, and dining room; singles/doubles are from $39/46.

FAIRY STONE STATE PARK

This idyllic little park, minutes from the Blue Ridge Parkway, is known for its lucky 'fairy stones.' These stones, formally known as saurolites, range in size from one-fourth of an inch to an inch and are in the form of a Roman, St Andrews, or Maltese Cross. It is said that when the sad tidings of the crucifixion of Christ was related to the fairies, they began to cry. Their tears on striking the ground crystallized into these tiny crosses.

The park (☎ 540-930-2424) has a lake, beach, pleasure boats, and picnicking. Campsites, with electric/water hook-ups, are $15, one/two bedroom cabins are $62/77 (or $67/82 on the waterfront). To get there, take Route 57W then Route 346 from Bassett (northwest of Martinsville) or Routes 8, 57E, and 346 from the Blue Ridge Parkway.

DANVILLE

Most people would forget Danville if it were not for a train derailment immortalized in a bluegrass music standard, 'The Wreck of the Old 97.' On September 27, 1903, the Southern Railway's Old 97 express jumped the tracks as it crossed a trestle near the Dan River. It hurtled into the ravine killing nine, including the engineer, and injuring seven others. There is a marker on Riverside Drive (Hwy 58W).

Danville (population 56,000) is a real 'southern' industrial town today but not without a certain charm. Originally named Wynnes Falls, after the first settler, it became Danville in 1793. The main street, dominated by late Victorian architecture ('Millionaires' Row'), dates from the 1890s, a period when textiles and tobacco helped the town recover from the ravages of the Civil War.

Information

The Danville Chamber of Commerce (☎ 804-793-5422), at 635 Main St (diagonally across from the post office), is open weekdays from 9 am to 5 pm. Unfortunately it is closed weekends, when most visitors need help! A free pamphlet, *Victorian Walking Tour*, describes the city's fine buildings. The staff of the Science Center and Sutherlin Mansion are very helpful, and fill the weekend void.

The main post office (☎ 804-792-3766) is at 700 Main St. Laundry can be done at

VIRGINIA

the Soap Opera Coin Laundry (☎ 804-797-1645), 743 Colquohoun St.

Museums

Nancy Witcher Langhorne (Astor) hails from Danville. A middle-class Southern gal, she skipped a few rungs on the social ladder when she married Viscount William Waldorf Astor in 1906. In 1919 she became the first woman member of the British House of Commons and served until the end of WWII. Her verbal spars with the great Winston Churchill were legendary.

Nancy Astor's birthplace is at 117 Broad St – she returned to visit it in 1922 and 1946. Stunning Irene Langhorne Gibson, Nancy's sister, was immortalized as the 'Gibson Girl,' the fashion ideal at the turn of the century, by artist husband Charles Dana Gibson. The modest two-story house, being set up as a museum, is open by appointment.

The **Danville Museum of Fine Arts & History** (☎ 804-793-5644), at 975 Main St, is housed in the Sutherlin Mansion built in 1857. It would be just another stately home turned into a regional museum were it not for the fact that it was, for one week in April 1865, the capitol of the Confederacy. As the war neared its end Jefferson Davis and his cabinet fled Richmond for Danville and the dining room of Sutherlin served as the cabinet room. Here Davis penned his eloquent plea to the Confederate states to lay down their arms – the original document is on display. The rooms have been restored to reflect the last days of the Confederacy.

It is open year round Tuesday to Friday from 10 am to 5 pm, weekends from 2 to 5 pm, and entry is free.

The **Danville Science Center** (☎ 804-793-5422), at 700 Craghead St, a great retreat for kids with lots of hands-on activities, is open daily. It is located in a recently restored Victorian train station (the Amtrak depot) in the heart of the warehouse district.

Places to Stay

The *Howard Johnson Hotel* (☎ 804-793-2000, 800-446-4656), at 100 Tower Drive, is a good stalwart with singles/doubles from $59/78. The hotel has a restaurant, bar, and pool and is handicapped accessible. The *Best Western Danville* (☎ 804-793-4000), at 2121 Riverside Drive (on Hwy 58, half a mile east of the junction of Route 86 and Hwy 29), has singles from $50 to $80, doubles from $56 to $80.

The *Stratford Inn* (☎ 804-793-2500), at 2500 Riverside Drive, just east of Hwy 29 Bypass, is the pick of the places to stay and is well known to local travelers. It has a pool, whirlpool, and exercise room; singles are from $42 to $48, doubles from $48 to $52.

Places to Eat

There are plenty of fast food joints and diners scattered along Riverside Drive on the north side of the river and on Hwy 29S on the southern outskirts of town, just before the state border. The *Lobster Pot*, in the Danville Plaza, is a good seafood choice; and the two *Western Sizzlin* restaurants – at 3211 Riverside Drive (in the K-Mart shopping center) and in the Nor-Dan shopping center – have country fare buffets, bakeries, and dessert bars.

Good pasta can be had at *Joe & Mimma's* (☎ 804-799-5763), 3336 Riverside Shopping Center. Lasagna, chicken cacciatore, fettucine, and fresh veal are the daily (except Sunday) specials. The *Golden Dragon* (☎ 804-792-5978), at 2720 W Main St, has a daily lunch buffet with low calorie meals with reduced salt. Try a hearty lunch (the 'apotheosis of Southern cuisine') for $8 at the *Stratford Inn* (see Places to Stay). It caters to kids, seniors, and early birds and you can order carryouts.

Getting There & Away

The Danville Airport, east of the city on Hwy 360/58 and Airport Rd, is served by USAir Express (☎ 800-428-4322). You will need to get a cab into Danville; try Danville Taxi (☎ 804-793-5671).

The Greyhound/Trailways depot (☎ 804-792-4722) is at No 302 on Route 58W, near the intersection with Mt Cross Rd opposite the Danville Plaza. Amtrak has southbound and northbound service stopping at the Science Center at 700 Craghead St. Both of these trains pass through at ungodly hours of the morning.

AROUND DANVILLE

Staunton River State Park

This state park (☎ 804-572-4623), on the banks of Buggs Island Lake (John H Kerr Reservoir), has swimming and wading pools, boat ramps, tennis courts, a children's playground, and a visitors center. A standard campsite is $10.50, one-room/one-bedroom/two-bedroom cabins are $55/62/77 respectively. It is 18 miles east of South Boston; from South Boston, take Hwy 360N for eight miles then Route 344E, via Scottsburg, for nine miles.

The Staunton River Bridge area has been developed into a **battlefield state park** (☎ 804-454-4312) with a Civil War fort, a guided trail, and a museum.

Occoneechee State Park

This park (☎ 540-374-2210) is named after the Native Americans who lived here for many hundreds of years. It is also on Buggs Island Lake and facilities include campsites, picnic areas, an amphitheater, and boat ramps. The campsites cost $10.50, $15 for electric/water hook-ups. From Clarksville, head 1.5 miles east on Hwy 58E. The entrance is near the Hwy 15 intersection. In May, the Native American Heritage Festival and Powwow is held here.

Shenandoah Valley & Ranges

This chapter covers the beautiful Shenandoah Valley and the mountain ranges which the forks of the Shenandoah River lie between – the Blue Ridge to the east of the valley, the Allegheny Mountains to the west, and, in its northern part, Massanutten Mountain – all part of the Appalachian range. The river, the region's dominant feature, starts as a stream near Lexington in the south of the valley; just west of Front Royal the two main forks come together and the Shenandoah 'proper' flows northeast to join with the Potomac River at Harpers Ferry.

The nearly 200-mile-long valley has a rich history. The name 'Shenandoah' has many explanations, but perhaps the most popular is that it is from 'Sherando,' a Native American word meaning 'daughter of the stars' after the reflected light off the broad surface of the river. The first whites to see it were explorers in the mid-1600s, but in the early 1700s larger groups of Scotch-Irish and German families, who migrated south from Pennsylvania and Maryland, settled in the valley. There are many reminders of their coming.

The valley was very important in the war between the states (see Shenandoah Campaigns of 1862 in this chapter). Today there are many reminders of this sad war and two of the great Civil War generals, Robert E Lee and Stonewall Jackson, are buried in Lexington. Just before the war commenced, the great international statesman Woodrow Wilson was born in Staunton.

The natural wonders of the region include: Natural Bridge near Lexington, purportedly one of the 'seven wonders' of the world; the magnificent Shenandoah National Park and incomparable Skyline Drive to the east of the valley; and the Alleghenies, scenic Bath County, and Goshen Pass in George Washington National Forest, to the west. In all of these areas there is scope for outdoor recreation, such as fishing, hiking, biking, camping, and, in winter, snow sports.

The main artery of the Shenandoah Valley is I-81.

HIGHLIGHTS

- Skyline Drive and Shenandoah National Park – probably the state's best attractions
- Lexington and other historic towns showcasing frontier culture and Civil War history
- Sidetrips through the scenic valley's vineyards, caverns, Civil War battlefields, forests, and mountain areas
- The expensive creature comforts of The Homestead or the rustic delights of Bath County's scenic campsites
- Natural Bridge – an awesome natural wonder despite its kitsch surroundings
- The world-famous Appalachian Trail, the largest portion of which is in Virginia

WINCHESTER

This, the first settlement of the American frontier west of the Blue Ridge Mountains, lies in the northern Shenandoah Valley at the intersection of I-81 and I-66, 72 miles from Washington, DC. Initially settled by Scotch-Irish and German settlers in 1732, it played a major part in the French and Indian War. Winchester changed hands 72 times during the Civil War and was the headquarters for both the Confederacy's Stonewall Jackson and the Union's Philip Sheridan.

The town has many associations with the famous. Renowned novelist Willa Cather was born here; country & western singer Patsy Cline spent her childhood here; Revolutionary War hero Daniel Morgan died here; George Washington was elected to his first political office, in 1758, as a member of the House of Burgesses representing Frederick County; and polar explorer Admiral Richard Byrd was also born here.

Winchester (population 22,000) is the self-titled 'apple capital of the world' – there are more than 90 orchards in the surrounding area.

Information

The Winchester-Frederick County Chamber of Commerce & Visitors Center (☎ 540-662-4135, 800-662-1360), at 1360 S Pleasant Valley Rd, has maps for driving and walking tours.

Fiscal needs are satisfied at the F&M Bank (☎ 540-665-4200), 115 N Cameron St, and at the Bank of Clarke County in the Apple Blossom Corners shopping center – both have Cirrus for foreign travelers.

There is a laundromat on Berryville Ave – the Soap Factory Coin-Op is open daily 6 am to 11 pm, Sunday until 9 pm.

For medical needs, the Urgent Care Center (☎ 540-722-0691), next door to the F&M Bank in the Apple Blossom Corners shopping center, is open 9 am to 9 pm; otherwise try the Winchester Medical Center (☎ 540-722-8700), at 1840 Amherst St.

Historic Sites

There are a number of interesting historic and Civil War sites in Winchester.

Stonewall Jackson & the Shenandoah Campaigns of 1862

The Shenandoah Valley was of great strategic significance to both sides in the Civil War. As 'the breadbasket of the Confederacy,' the fertile valley was vital to the food supply. More importantly, it provided a corridor for troop movement that allowed the Confederates to strike north towards Washington, DC, and the Union troops to attempt to outflank Richmond. The valley was one of the most fought over pieces of ground in the Civil War; as control of it changed more than 70 times, about 100,000 soldiers were killed or wounded.

The early battles in the Shenandoah Valley in 1862 were dominated by the brilliant tactics of Thomas 'Stonewall' Jackson, whose army defeated several Union armies. Jackson's 1862 campaign took his troops on a corkscrew path way out into West Virginia, up to Winchester, across to Fort Royal, and down to Port Republic. At the first battle on March 23 at **Kernstown**, Jackson's men lost the battle but did succeed in preventing Union troops from reinforcing McClellan's army, then engaged against the Army of Northern Virginia (in the Peninsula Campaign). On May 8 at **McDowell** (along US Route 250, west of Staunton), where there are still Confederate breastworks to this day, Jackson repulsed an attack by Generals Robert Milroy and Robert Schenck. The Union forces were forced to retreat down the valley.

Jackson swiftly regrouped, moved through the gap in Massanutten Mountain at New Market and down the Luray Valley, then surprised and captured the Federal garrison at **Front Royal** on May 23. Two days later, on May 25, Jackson's army overtook the force commanded by General Nathaniel Banks and defeated them at the Battle of **Winchester**.

In early June three Union columns converged on Strasburg. Jackson retreated quickly up the valley but brilliantly split his force at the same time. He dispatched a force commanded by General Richard S Ewell to oppose the Union troops of General John C Fremont at **Cross Keys**. On June 8, in spite of overwhelming odds, the Confederates were victorious. The following day Jackson's army defeated the advance group of General James Shields' troops at **Port Republic**.

These two battles ended the 1862 Shenandoah Valley Campaign. Jackson was recalled from the valley soon after to join Robert E Lee in the Seven Days Battles around Richmond (see the Richmond chapter). ■

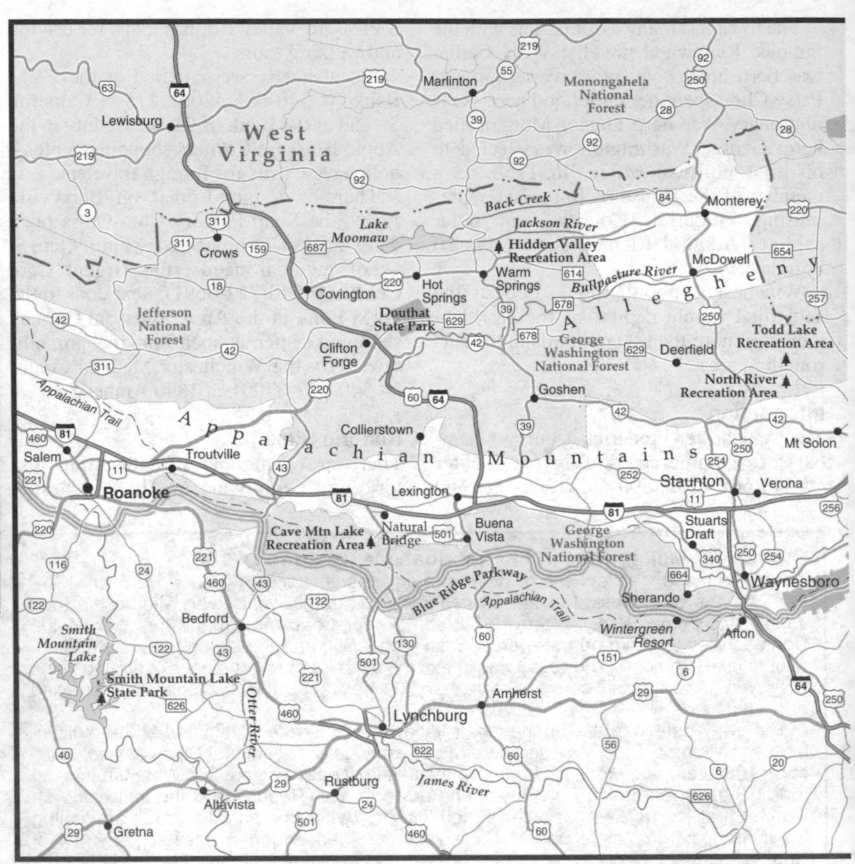

Stonewall Jackson's headquarters for part of 1861–62 was in the small house (☎ 540-667-3242) at 415 N Braddock St. Jackson used this house when he came to Winchester to take command of the Confederate army in the Shenandoah Valley in the winter of 1861–62. Articles relating to Jackson, the cavalry commander Turner Ashby, and the mapmaker Jed Hotchkiss, are on display. (TV star Mary Tyler Moore's great-great-grandfather loaned Jackson the house.) It is open daily April through October, otherwise weekends in March and November from 9 am to 5 pm. Admission is $3.50 for adults, $3 for seniors, and $1.75 for children.

The **Kurtz Cultural Center** (☎ 540-722-6367), at 2 N Cameron St in the heart of the Old Town, has information about most Valley attractions and a permanent exhibit entitled 'Shenandoah, Crossroads of the Civil War.' This has an overview of the fighting, profiles on important battles, and biographical sketches of the commanders. It is open daily from 10 am to 5 pm, Sunday noon to 5 pm; admission is free. Walking tours of the town depart from here at 10 am and 1 pm; these cost $5 per person.

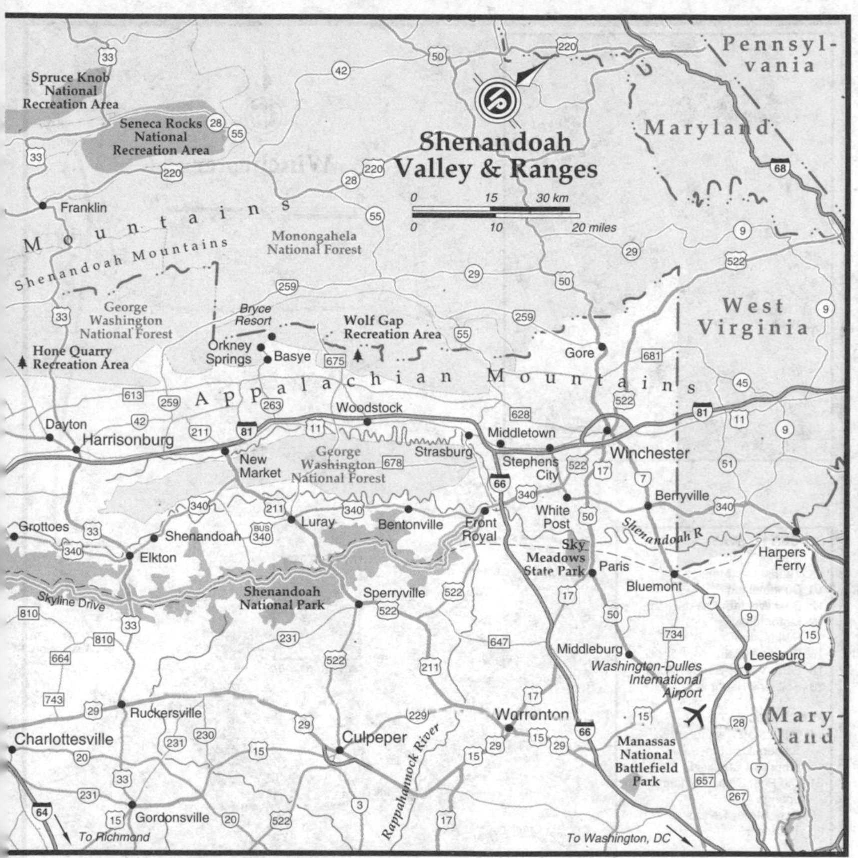

Washington's Office Museum (☎ 540-662-6650), a restored log and stone building at 32 W Cork St, was used by then Colonel Washington when he was building Fort Loudoun during the French and Indian War. It is open daily April to October from 9 am to 5 pm. Admission is $2 for adults, $1.50 for seniors, and $1 for children.

At 1340 S Pleasant Valley Rd is **'Abram's Delight' Museum** (☎ 540-662-6650), a limestone house built in 1754 by a Quaker named Issac Hollingsworth. It has been furnished and restored. The 'Delight' is open daily, April to October, from 9 am to 5 pm. Admission is $3 for adults, $1.50 for children.

Organized Tours

A-Tour Plus (☎ 540-888-3100), PO Box 2142, Winchester, VA 22604, conducts personalized tours. A block entry ticket which includes 'Abram's Delight,' Washington's Office, and Jackson's headquarters is $7.50 for adults, $6 for seniors, and $4 for children.

Special Events

As the self-titled 'apple capital of the world,' Winchester is the natural setting

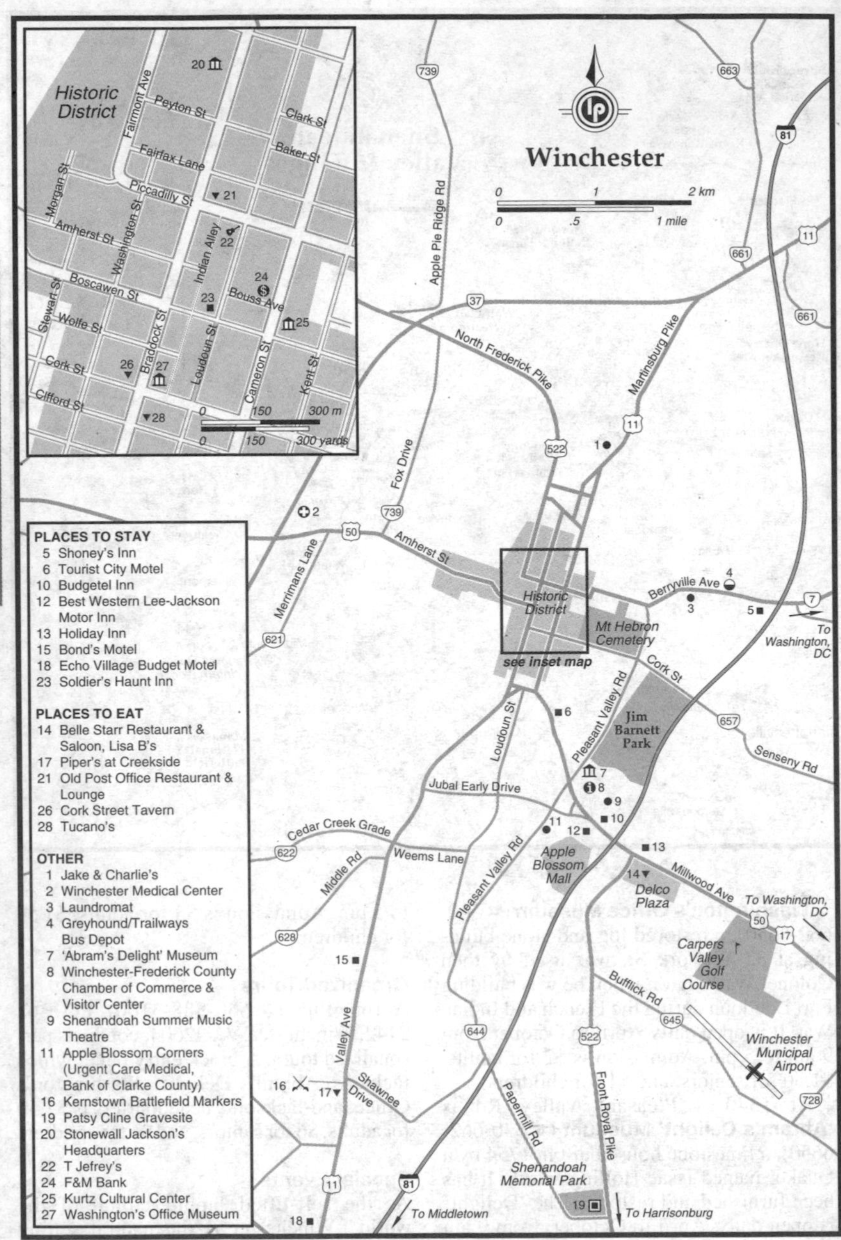
Winchester
0
1
2 km
0
.5
1 mile
Historic District
Peyton St
Clark St
Fairmont Ave
Fairfax Lane
Baker St
Piccadilly St
Morgan St
Washington St
Amherst St
Indian Alley
Boscawen St
Bouss Ave
Stewart St
Wolfe St
Braddock St
Loudoun St
Cameron St
Kent St
Cork St
Clifford St
0
150
300 m
0
150
300 yards
PLACES TO STAY
5 Shoney's Inn
6 Tourist City Motel
10 Budgetel Inn
12 Best Western Lee-Jackson Motor Inn
13 Holiday Inn
15 Bond's Motel
18 Echo Village Budget Motel
23 Soldier's Haunt Inn
PLACES TO EAT
14 Belle Starr Restaurant & Saloon, Lisa B's
17 Piper's at Creekside
21 Old Post Office Restaurant & Lounge
26 Cork Street Tavern
28 Tucano's
OTHER
1 Jake & Charlie's
2 Winchester Medical Center
3 Laundromat
4 Greyhound/Trailways Bus Depot
7 'Abram's Delight' Museum
8 Winchester-Frederick County Chamber of Commerce & Visitor Center
9 Shenandoah Summer Music Theatre
11 Apple Blossom Corners (Urgent Care Medical, Bank of Clarke County)
16 Kernstown Battlefield Markers
19 Patsy Cline Gravesite
20 Stonewall Jackson's Headquarters
22 T Jefrey's
24 F&M Bank
25 Kurtz Cultural Center
27 Washington's Office Museum
Apple Pie Ridge Rd
North Frederick Pike
Martinsburg Pike
Fox Drive
Amherst St
Merrimans Lane
Berryville Ave
Historic District
Mt Hebron Cemetery
see inset map
Cork St
Pleasant Valley Rd
Loudoun St
Jim Barnett Park
Senseny Rd
Jubal Early Drive
Cedar Creek Grade
Weems Lane
Middle Rd
Pleasant Valley Rd
Apple Blossom Mall
Delco Plaza
Millwood Ave
To Washington, DC
To Washington, DC
Carpers Valley Golf Course
Bufflick Rd
Winchester Municipal Airport
Valley Ave
Shawnee Drive
Papermill Rd
Front Royal Pike
Shenandoah Memorial Park
To Middletown
To Harrisonburg

for the annual Shenandoah Apple Blossom Festival (☎ 540-662-3863), held in early May. It includes parades, band competitions, races, lunches, and attracts some 250,000 visitors. And if you believe in finishing what you've started, come back in mid-September for the Apple Harvest Festival.

Places to Stay

Candy Hill Campground (☎ 540-662-8010), at 200 Ward Ave off Hwy 50W, has full hook-ups for $17 to $19; there is also tent camping and showers. It's open from April to November.

Motels are abundant. The *Tourist City Motel* (☎ 540-662-9011), at 214 Millwood Ave, is nothing special but is cheap and close to downtown (I stayed here). The well-maintained *Bond's Motel* (☎ 540-667-8881), at 2930 Valley Ave (Hwy 11), has singles/doubles for $28/32 in the off-season, otherwise $29/35. Another good value is the *Echo Village Budget Motel* (☎ 540-869-1900), on Hwy 11. It is off the road and the rooms have air-conditioning and cable TV; singles/doubles are from $20/27 and an extra person is $3. The *Budgetel Inn* (☎ 540-678-0800), at 800 Millwood Ave, is another functional place with a restaurant nearby; single/double rooms are from $43/50.

There are a few other good reliable hotels/motels in Winchester. *Shoney's Inn* (☎ 540-665-1700), at 1347 Berryville Ave (Exit 315 off I-81), has a bar, restaurant, exercise facilities, and indoor pool; singles/doubles are from $42/47. The *Holiday Inn* (☎ 540-667-3300), at 1017 Millwood Ave, is a comfortable hotel, with restaurant, tennis courts, exercise facilities, and outdoor pool; double rooms are from $49 and an extra person is $6. The *Best Western Lee-Jackson Motor Inn* (☎ 540-662-4154, 800-528-1234), at 711 Millwood Ave (Hwy 50), has a pool and restaurant; singles/doubles are $42/47 in low season, otherwise $49/54.

Good value B&Bs – the price quoted is for doubles – include *Brownstone Cottage* (☎ 540-662-1962), at 161 McCarty Lane (from $65); *The Inn at Vaucluse Spring* (☎ 540-869-9544), at 473 Vaucluse Rd, Stephens City (from $90 to $165); and *Soldier's Haunt Inn* (☎ 540-722-3976), in a historic building at 105–107 N Loudoun St (from $125).

Places to Eat

The old *Cork Street Tavern* (☎ 540-667-3777), at 8 W Cork St, just around the corner from the South Loudoun St pedestrian mall, is a very cozy, casual dining place where a sizable dinner of spare ribs (and other barbecue delights) costs from $11. The *Belle Starr Restaurant & Saloon* (☎ 540-722-2447), in the Delco Plaza on Millwood Ave, has good food such as steaks, sandwiches, fajitas, and 'hot' snake bites. It is open from 11 am to 2 am, daily. Close by, also in the Delco Plaza (No 170–4), is *Lisa B's* (☎ 540-722-0966) for bagels, specialty pizza, and great sandwiches.

A local favorite is the cozy *Cafe Sofia* (☎ 540-667-2950), a Bulgarian and seafood place at 2900 Valley Ave. It is open weekdays from 11 am to 9:30 pm, Saturday from 4 to 10 pm, and is closed Sunday. *Tucano's* 540-722-4557), at 12 S Braddock St, is an excellent Brazilian place popular with locals. Check it out!

At 200 N Braddock St, on the corner of Piccadilly St, is *The Old Post Office Restaurant* (☎ 540-722-9881), for moderately expensive American pasta/seafood dishes; entrees are from $13 to $23. *Pipers at Creekside* (☎ 540-662-2900), at 136 Creekside Lane off Valley Ave, open weekdays for continental meals (dinner only Saturday), is more expensive. Expect to pay from $15 to $20 for a main course, about $50 for a meal for two.

Entertainment

The *Shenandoah Summer Music Theatre* (☎ 540-665-4569), based at 1460 University Drive (Shenandoah University, at the intersection of Hwy 50 and I-81, Exit 313), is a professional theater company, performing four musicals each summer from mid-June to early August. Ask at the visitors

A Forgotten Daughter: Patsy Cline

Virginia Patterson Hensley (Patsy Cline), the country & western legend, was born in Gore, Virginia, on September 8, 1932, but spent most of her life in Winchester where she attended school. She won a talent program in 1957 with the hit *Walkin' After Midnight*, and the following year she performed at the Grand Ole Opry. She went on to receive national awards in 1961 (for No 1 Female Artist) and 1962 (for No 1 Female Artist and for the song *I Fall to Pieces)*.

You can retrace her life in Winchester, where there are many sites associated with her: her home at 608 S Kent St, the house in which she was married at 720 S Kent St, Gaunt's Drug Store at the corner of S Loudoun St and Valley Ave where she was a waitress, WINC Radio at 520 N Pleasant Valley Rd where she often performed, and her grave in the Shenandoah Memorial Park on US Route 522S. Also see the Patsy Cline exhibits in the Kurtz Cultural Center and in the Winchester/Frederick County Chamber of Commerce (where you can also pick up a Patsy Cline Nostalgia tour map).

Patsy Cline was killed in an aircraft accident in Tennessee, at the start of an already brilliant career, on March 5, 1963. She was elected posthumously to the Country Music Hall of Fame in 1973, and long after her death, in 1991, she received a triple platinum award for the album *Patsy Cline's Greatest Hits*.

The Friends of Patsy Cline, a local fan club, lament the fact that she is much forgotten in this city – seemingly, she came from the wrong side of town. ■

center about performances by *Winchester Little Theater*, in the old Pennsylvania Railroad Freight depot, near the kink in Boscawen St.

The very casual *T Jefrey's* (☎ 540-667-0429), at 168 N Loudoun St, has live entertainment on Friday and Saturday evenings. The *Belle Starr* (see Places to Eat) has entertainment nightly, such as rhythm & blues, line dancing, and the dreaded karaoke. *Jake & Charlie's* (☎ 540-722-1017), 821 N Loudoun St, a sports club with entertainment, is open daily from noon to 1 am.

Getting There & Around

Winchester is served by Greyhound/Trailways (☎ 540-662-4161) whose depot is near the junction of Berryville and Atwell Aves. A city transit service (☎ 540-667-1815) operates daily, except Sunday, from outside the Kurtz Cultural Center; the cost of a trip is 50¢ for adults and 35¢ for children.

AROUND WINCHESTER

Millwood & White Post

The small town of Millwood, near the Shenandoah River has the **Burwell-Morgan Mill** (☎ 540-837-1799), at the intersection of Route 255 and County Rd 723. Completed in 1785, it has been restored to the operating condition of a Colonial-era grist mill and is open, May to October, Wednesday to Sunday from 10 am to 5 pm; there is a nominal admission fee.

Out on County Rd 624 is historic **Long Branch** (☎ 540-837-1856), a superbly restored and furnished antebellum mansion, built by Robert Carter Burwell (not of the mill fame – that was Nathaniel). It is open daily, April to October, from 9 am to 5 pm; admission is $5.

White Post, not far from Millwood, has **Dinosaur Land Inc** (☎ 540-869-2222). The kids will deserve a treat after that 'one Civil War site too many' and here are 35 life-sized replicas of dinosaurs (the names of which will be readily known to your children). Positively Jurassic, this park is open daily from 9:30 am to 5 pm in winter, until later in summer; ring to find out costs. The White Post for which the town is named was erected by the young Washington to mark the way to Greenway Court, Lord Fairfax's estate.

The well-known *L'Auberge Provençale* (☎ 540-837-1375, 800-638-1702), in a 1750s farmhouse on Hwy 340, is expensive. It costs from $145 to $195 a double, but you are paying for perfection; deliberately, there are no phones or TVs. The superb five-course French provençal dinner is likely to cost another $55 for each person.

Middletown

This quaint little town on Hwy 11 is near the intersection of I 81 (Exit 302) and I-66.

Most people would deviate off the main drag here to see **Belle Grove** (☎ 540-869-2028), a tasteful stone farmhouse completed in 1794 after Jefferson provided some finishing touches. The farm is still in use today. This was the Union headquarters during the Battle of Cedar Creek in October 1864 and at one stage the battle spilled over onto the farm. The annual reenactment of the battle, staged in October, attracts 2000 bellicose devotees. Belle Grove is open March through December, Monday to Saturday from 10 am to 4 pm, Sunday from 1 to 5 pm; admission is $5 for adults, $4.50 for seniors, and $2.50 for children.

The historic **Wayside Theatre** (☎ 540-869-1776), the second-oldest theater in the state, is just off I-81 on Hwy 11S (Exit 302). A professional theater company, they present a range of musicals, dramas, and comedies, from May to mid-October and in December. Actors who got a start here include Susan Sarandon, Peter Boyle, and Jill Eikenberry. The box office is open Monday and Tuesday from noon to 4 pm, Wednesday to Saturday from 11 am to 9 pm, and Sunday 4 to 8 pm. The Wednesday and Saturday matinee is $15, and it is $17 for evening performances.

The beautifully restored 18th century *Wayside Inn* (☎ 540-869-1797), at 7783 Main St, Middletown, has antique furnished rooms (with four-poster beds) from $75 to $125 in the low season, otherwise $95 to $145. The restaurant serves regional American cuisine and is open daily; a dinner for two will cost about $70.

Lovers of potato chips will probably want to stock up at *Route 11 Potato Chips* (☎ 540-869-0104), at 2325 First St. The chips are made from organically grown potatoes, cooked in peanut and sunflower oil. Tempt yourself, Friday and Saturday from 10 am to 5 pm.

Strasburg

This upper Shenandoah Valley town has a rich history. During the Civil War Stonewall Jackson made a raid on Martinsburg in West Virginia and captured a number of Union army railroad locomotives. These were then pulled down the valley to Strasburg railway station (where the museum is housed today – see below).

For more information on the region contact the Strasburg Chamber of Commerce (☎ 540-465-3187); they also operate an information stand in the Strasburg Emporium.

The **Strasburg Museum** (☎ 540-465-3428) focuses on the town's importance as a trading center. On display are farming tools, Native American artifacts, a colonial kitchen, and industrial arts such as coopering and blacksmithing. It is open daily May to October from 10 am to 4 pm; entry is $2 for adults, $1 for teenagers, and 50¢ for children.

Civil War enthusiasts gravitate to the **Hupps Hill Battlefield Park & Study Center** (☎ 540-465-5884), northwest of Strasburg on Hwy 11, which concentrates on the Shenandoah Valley campaigns. There you'll find a topographical map of the battle of Cedar Creek, remnants of earthworks dug by Union soldiers, and a well-stocked bookstore. Unlike 'don't touch' places, children are encouraged to try on uniforms and sit in Civil War saddles. The helpful and knowledgeable staff will answer any tricky questions you pose. The park is open weekdays from 10 am to 4 pm, weekends from 11 am to 5 pm; admission is $3.50 for adults, $3 for seniors, and $2 for children.

The **America Presidents Museum** (☎ 540-465-4650) is an unusual but worthwhile collection featuring James Madison's desk (upon which the Constitution was written), portraits of the presidents, and documents signed by Jefferson and Washington. It is open Monday to Saturday from 10 am to 5 pm, and Sunday from 2 to 5 pm; admission is $3.50 for adults, $3 for seniors, and $2 for children.

The **Strasburg Emporium** (☎ 540-465-3711), 110 N Massanutten St, which houses over 100 antique dealers, is open daily.

At the *Hotel Strasburg* (☎ 540-465-9191), at 201 Holliday St, you can get antique-furnished Victorian-style single and double rooms from $75 to $165. The adjoining restaurant is open daily for all three meals (delicious salads); main dishes are from $11.

FRONT ROYAL

This sizable town (population 11,500), at the northern end of the Shenandoah National Park/Skyline Drive is, these days, somewhat of an outdoor center.

Front Royal started out as Lehew Town, a stopover on an important packhorse route. In the mid-1700s it became known as 'Helltown' because of its raucous reputation. It featured heavily in the battles of the Civil War and was a base for the famous Confederate spy, Belle Boyd. Today, it is an important commercial center and each May it hosts the **Virginia Mushroom Festival** for those who like things 'kept in the dark and fed on shit.' There is a well preserved historic district along Chester St.

The Front Royal/Warren County visitors center (☎ 540-635-3185, 800-338-2576), in the old Southern Railroad train station at 414 E Main St, is open daily, 9 am to 5 pm.

Belle Boyd Cottage

This cottage (☎ 540-636-1446), at 101 Chester St, was the temporary home of the Confederate spy Belle Boyd, who spent time here with her relatives. On one occasion Belle overheard, through a small hole in the closet floor, a Union general discussing plans with his officers. She wrote the details down in cipher then rode for 15 miles to pass the information on to Stonewall Jackson's Confederate army. The Confederates then moved on Front Royal and captured the town. It is open April to October, weekdays from 10 am to 5 pm, weekends from 1 to 4 pm (the last tour is at 3:30 pm); admission is $2 for adults, $1 for children (eight to 16).

'Warren Rifles' Confederate Museum

Another place with a Civil War theme is this museum (☎ 540-636-6982), at 95 Chester St, which attempts further secular canonization of members of the Confederacy. It is open April through October, weekdays from 9 am to 5 pm, Sunday noon to 5 pm; entry is $2 for adults, children are free.

Wineries

There are a number of vineyards near Front Royal. The 75-acre Oasis Vineyard (☎ 540-635-7627) faces the Blue Ridge Mountains. It is open daily from 10 am to 5 pm for tours and tastings; a tour is $5.

Skyline Caverns

These caverns (☎ 540-635-4545, 800-296-4545) attract visitors because they house unusual anthodites – spiked nodes or 'cave flowers.' These formations, unlike stalactites and stalagmites, which grow straight up and down, seem to defy gravity and grow in all directions. They grow an inch every 7000 years. There is also a stream that plunges over 37-foot falls and chambers with predictable names – Fairytale Lake, Capitol Dome, Cathedral Hall.

The caverns are a mile from the start of Skyline Drive. The caverns are open daily from 9 am; admission is $10 for adults, $9 for seniors, and $4 for children age seven to 13.

Canoeing

Bentonville, being close to the zigzags of the South Fork of the Shenandoah, south of Front Royal, is the place for serious and not-so-serious paddlers and rafters. The Downriver Canoe Co (☎ 540-635-5526), the Front Royal Canoe Co (☎ 540-635-5440, 800-270-8808), and River Rental Outfitters (☎ 540-635-5050, 800-727-4371) offer a number of trips from a three-mile taste of whitewater to ultra-serious trips of 120 miles and longer. A three-mile trip is about $29 per canoe, a day trip about $45, a three-day trip $122, and there are discounts midweek. Tubing is about $15 per person.

These companies operate April to October, weekdays from 9 am to 6 pm, weekends from 7 am to 7 pm. From Skyline Drive (Mile 20) follow Hwy 211 west for eight miles, then head north on Hwy 340 – from here it is 14 miles to Bentonville.

Horseback Riding

The 4200-acre beef cattle Marriot Ranch (☎ 540-364-2627) and Massanutten Trail Rides (☎ 540-636-6061) both offer short and extended trail rides near Front Royal. Costs at the Marriot Ranch are $22.50 per person on weekdays, $27.50 on weekends for a 1½-hour ride, at Massanutten riding lessons are $15 per hour.

Golf

The Bowling Green Country Club (☎ 540-635-2095) and Shenandoah Valley Golf Club (☎ 540-635-3588) cater to those willing to chase elusive white balls around the Shenandoah.

Places to Stay

Camping The *Front Royal KOA* (☎ 540-635-2741, 800-248-0828), near Skyline Drive (Exit 6 off I-81), may advertise that it has a 'civil war nearby,' but you shouldn't hear the guns these days. Instead it is a compact campground with good shady sites, electricity/water hook-ups for $22 for two, a pool, playground, and recreation room.

Motels The cheapest and an OK option is the *Center City Motel* (☎ 540-635-4050), at 416 S Royal Ave (just north of the junction of Hwy 340 and Route 55), with off-season rates of $25 for singles and doubles, otherwise weekday/weekend rates of $28/35. The *Super 8* (☎ 540-636-4888), at 111 South St (Exit 13 off I-66), is a good budget place with off-season singles/doubles for $39/44, otherwise $44/50. The *Pioneer Motel* (☎ 540-635-4784), on Hwy 340 near the north entrance to Skyline Drive at 541 S Royal Ave, is another budget choice.

The *Quality Inn-Skyline Drive* (☎ 540-635-3161), at 10 Commerce Ave, is popular and often full in summer. It has a restaurant with nightly entertainment and a pool. Singles/doubles are $45/50 in the low season, and they rise to $58/75 in the high season.

B&Bs There are a few good B&B choices. *Killahevlin* (☎ 540-636-7335), at 1401 N Royal Ave, is an expensive place (from $100) but it occupies the highest point of Front Royal; and *Chester House Inn* (☎ 540-635-3937), at 43 Chester St, is another stately place with doubles from $65 to $110.

South of Front Royal, off Hwy 522 near Flint Hill, is *Caledonia Farm 1812* (☎ 540-675-3693), a lovely farmhouse with doubles with shared bath/suites from $80/140.

The well-regarded *Inn at Little Washington* (☎ 540-675-3800), on the corner of Middle and Main Sts (Hwy 211), Washington, is one of the best places to stay and dine at if you have the money – B&B rates start at $240 a double and rise to an ultra-costly $450.

Places to Eat

In Front Royal, try *The Feed Mill* (☎ 540-636-3123), at 500 E Main St, a barnlike place in the block up from the visitors center. The huge sandwiches are from $4 and dinner main courses, served with salad, vegetables, and bread, start at $10. It is open daily; in the adjoining lounge there is weekend entertainment.

At the *Inn at Little Washington* (see Places to Stay, above) a fixed price dinner is $78 ($88 on Friday, $98 on Saturday); reserve well in advance.

SHENANDOAH NATIONAL PARK

This park impresses over one million tourists each year. It was authorized by Congress in 1926, established in 1935 as a peaceful refuge for nearby urban populations, and most of it has been restored to the way it would have been found by early settlers. It is said by some that Shenandoah means 'daughter of the stars,' by others 'river of high mountains.' Whatever interpretation, it deserves any such beautiful appellation.

There is something for everyone along the 500 miles of hiking trails, at the 75 overlooks, four campgrounds, seven picnic areas, and in the 30 trout fishing streams. Through its center winds the spectacular 105-mile Skyline Drive.

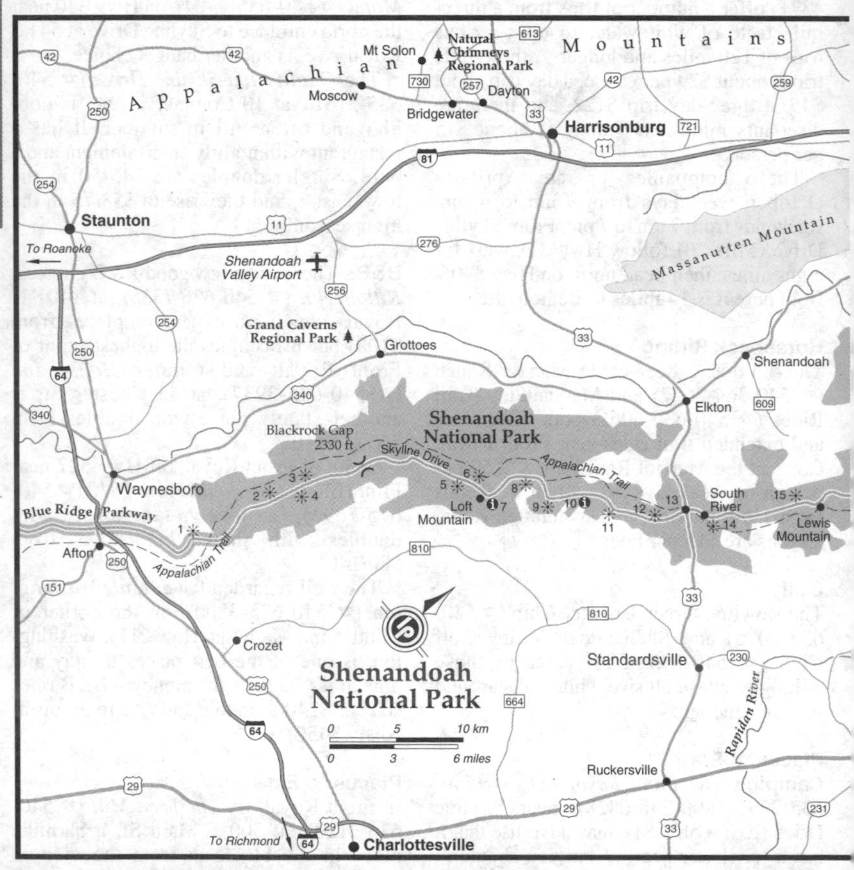

The rocks that form the Blue Ridge, the backbone of the park, are ancient granitic and metamorphic formations, some of which are over one billion years old. Human inhabitation occupies a mere speck on that timeline, about 11,000 years. Primitive food gatherers, and later hunters, used the land but there is little evidence of their passing. Modern settlement of the region began soon after settlers crossed the Blue Ridge in 1716.

Orientation & Information

Skyline Drive (see later) runs through the center of the park. Consequently, most trails and points of interest in the park can be reached from this scenic road.

Visitors can get information by ringing ☎ 540-999-2243 (999-2266 for a 24-hour recorded message) or by writing to The Superintendent, Park Headquarters, Shenandoah National Park, Route 3, PO Box 348, Luray, VA 22835-9051. In an emergency only, call ☎ 800-732-0911.

The Dickey's Ridge Visitors Center

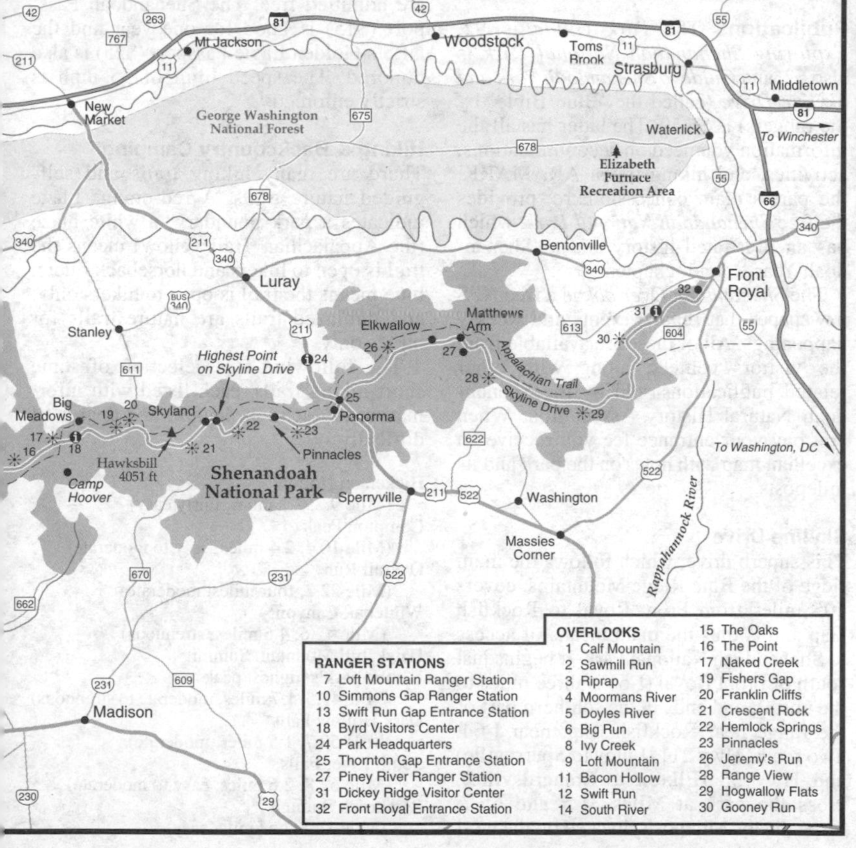

(☎ 540-635-3566), the closest to the northern entrance of the park at Mile 4.6, is open daily, April to November, from 9 am to 5 pm. At Mile 50, in the heart of the park, is the Byrd Visitors Center (☎ 540-999-3283), also open daily, April to October, from 9 am to 5 pm. Both places have exhibits on flora and fauna, pamphlets, weather information, ranger-led activities, and exhibits. Big Meadows, near the Byrd Center, is the park's largest treeless meadow and the place to see wildflowers.

There are additional ranger stations at Piney River (Mile 22.1) and Simmons Gap (Mile 73.2) and a private center at Rockfish Gap, outside the park on Hwy 211.

Publications The *Park Guide* is $2, *Exploring Shenandoah National Park* is also $2, and *Guide to Shenandoah Park and Skyline Drive* (called the 'Blue Bible' by the rangers) is $6.50. The latter has all the information you need on accommodations, activities, and hiking trails. ARAMARK, the park's main concessionaire, provides the free *Shenandoah National Park*, which has an illustrated history and a 'Shenandoah Year-Round' chapter.

The *Shenandoah Overlook* is a free NPS newspaper that reports events and weekly happenings. All of these are available from the visitors centers, along with other related publications sold by the Shenandoah Natural History Association. When you pay your entrance fee you receive an excellent map with notes on the park and its mileposts.

Skyline Drive

This superb drive, which follows the main ridge of the Blue Ridge Mountains, covers 105 miles from Front Royal to Rockfish Gap and is thus the main means of access to Shenandoah National Park. It begins just south of Front Royal (I-66 is three miles to the north), and ends in the southern part of the range near Rockfish Gap, near I-64. Two roads, Hwy 211 (Luray to Sperryville) and Hwy 33 (Elkton to Stanardsville), cross the park at Miles 31.5 and 65.7, respectively. Mileposts, located on the west side of the drive, begin at the northern end of the drive and help you to locate points of interest and facilities.

There are adequate picnic areas along the length of the drive that have fireplaces, tables, water fountains, and comfort stations. These are at Dickey Ridge (Mile 4.6), Elkwallow (Mile 24.1), Pinnacles (Mile 36.7), Big Meadows (Mile 51.3), Lewis Mountain (Mile 57.5), South River (Mile 62.9), and Loft Mountain (Mile 79.5).

The entrance fee to Skyline Drive is $5 per vehicle, $3 for bikers, hikers, and bus passengers, and the pass is good for seven days; disabled people and Golden Age Passport holders (for US citizens over 62) are admitted free. The Shenandoah Passport ($15) is good for one year and the NPS's Golden Eagle Passport ($25) is also honored. The speed limit of 35 mph is strictly enforced.

Hiking & Backcountry Camping

There are many hiking trails and self-guided nature trails. A red-orange blaze indicates a park boundary; a white blaze (the Appalachian Trail yellow) means the trail is open to hikers and horseback riders; blue means the trail is open to hikers only; and unblazed trails are nature trails for hikers only.

The following is a selection of some short hiking trails, each listed with information on location, length, and degree of difficulty:

Hickerson Hollow
(Mile 9.2, 2.2 miles, fairly easy)
Compton Peak
(Mile 10.4, 2.4 miles, easy to moderate)
Overall Run
(Mile 22.2, four miles, moderate)
Whiteoak Canyon
(Mile 42.6, 4.6 miles, strenuous)
Hawksbill Mountain Summit
the park's highest peak
(Mile 45.5, 1.7 miles, moderate to strenuous)
Dark Hollow Falls
(Mile 50.7, 1.5 miles, moderate)
South River Falls
(Mile 62.8, 2.6 miles, easy to moderate)
Blackrock Summit
(Mile 84.8, one mile, easy)

A good guide, *Circuit Hikes in Shenandoah National Park* ($6), describes 32 hikes (ranging from three to 20 miles). There is also the free *Exploring the Backcountry*.

Popular nature trails, all rated easy, include:

Fox Hollow
(Mile 4.6, 1.2 miles)
with the Fox family homesite
Traces
(Mile 22.2, 1.7 miles)
through mature oak forest
Stony Man
(Mile 41.7, 1.6 miles)
follows a portion of the Appalachian Trail
Story of the Forest
(Mile 51, 1.8 miles)
emphasizing natural history
Deadening
(Mile 79.4, 1.3 miles)
which climbs to the top of Loft Mountain

Free **camping** is permitted in the backcountry. Certain rules apply: Campers have to set up out of sight of a road, trail, overlook, cabin, or other campsite, and 25 yards from a water supply. Open fires are prohibited so bring cold food or your own stove – don't light a fire as there is a large fine. Giardia is a problem in some parts of the park, so bring your own water, or a suitable filter, or boil water for the recommended time. It is necessary to get a permit from the park entrances, ranger stations, visitors centers, park headquarters, or by mail (see Orientation & Information in this section); if you haven't registered you may be slapped with a hefty fine. Bicycles and motor vehicles are prohibited on trails. And, importantly, carry out what you carry in.

Horseback Riding

There is riding on designated trails. At Skyland Stables (☎ 540-999-2210), open from May through October, there are guided trail rides (one-hour and two-hour); pony rides are available for children.

Biking

This is only permitted on Skyline Drive and on certain public roads. There is no cycling or mountain-biking on backcountry trails and fire roads. Normal cycling rules apply along Skyline Drive – correct lighting at night, traveling in single file, and keeping to the right.

Fishing

Up to 30 streams, stocked with brook trout, are open for fishing from the third Saturday in March until mid-October. Persons from 16 to 65 must have a valid license, artificial lures with single hook only may be used, and the limit is five trout per day (these must be at least eight inches long).

Other Activities

There are three authorized sites (two in the north and one in the center of the park) from which **hang-gliders** can be launched. You need to obtain a hang-gliding special use permit in advance.

You are allowed to cross-country ski on some trails and fire roads, and on the unplowed shoulder of Skyline Drive. You must have your own equipment and appropriate clothing; there are no equipment rental facilities within the park.

Bird watching and **wildlife spotting** are also popular pastimes. In one of the park programs, 'Birds of Prey,' winged predators, (such as owls and red-tailed hawks) are described in detail. Over 200 species of birds have been recorded in the park. In addition, there are 43 species of mammals, 51 species of reptiles and amphibians, and 22 species of fish.

Places to Stay

Camping & Cabins Three major park service campgrounds, *Big Meadows* (Mile 51.3), *Lewis Mountain* (Mile 57.6), and *Loft Mountain* (Mile 79.5), all have stores, laundries, and showers, but no RV hookups; these are open on a first-come, first-served basis. Lewis, open April through October, is best for tenters ($12 fee); Loft Mountain, open late May through October, has over 50 tent sites and some 160 trailer sites ($12 fee); and Big Meadows, open late May through October, has 40 tent sites and some 160 trailer sites ($14 fee, Memorial

Day to end of October, otherwise $12). For reservations call ☎ 800-365-2267; check site availability at the visitors centers. For backcountry camping, see Hiking & Backcountry Camping in this section.

There are six fully enclosed *cabins* (bunk beds, water, and stoves) in backcountry areas of the park – Range View (Mile 22.1), Corbin (Mile 37.9), Rock Spring (Mile 48.1), Pocosin (Mile 59.5), Doyles River (Mile 81.1), and Jones Mountain (accessible from Criglersville on County Rd 600, not Skyline Drive). These cabins are very popular and should be reserved in advance from the PATC, 118 Park St SE, Vienna, VA 22180 (☎ 703-242-0315). The cost of these, Sunday to Thursday, is $3 per person, Friday to Saturday, $14 per group (one person must be 21 or over). Make sure you bring your own flashlights (torches). They also have seven three-sided *trailside huts* for hikers (see Appalachian Trail in the Southwest & Blue Ridge Mountains chapter).

Lodges There are three lodges; for information and costs contact ARAMARK Virginia Skyline Company (☎ 540-743-5108, 800-999-4714), PO Box 727NP, Luray, VA 22835. *Skyland Lodge*, at the highest point on the drive at 3680 feet (Mile 41.7), is open late March to early December and has rustic cabins that offer magnificent views of the Shenandoah Valley. The cost is from $74 for a single unit on weekdays, $140 for a one-bedroom suite on weekends.

Big Meadows Lodge, at 3640 feet (Mile 51.3), is open early May to late October and has a main lodge and rooms in rustic cabins. A main lodge room, on weekdays, is from $60; a one-bedroom suite on weekends is more than $110. The cabins at *Lewis Mountain* (Mile 57.5), open early May to late October, have fully equipped bedrooms, an adjoining outdoor cooking area, but no phone or TV. The weekday cost for a single-room cabin is $52; on weekends, a two-room cabin is $80.

Places to Eat

At Mile 31.5 is the aptly named *Panorama Restaurant* (☎ 540-999-2265), which serves good traditional Virginia country fare. Sandwiches are from $3 to $5 and entrees are from $7.50. It is open daily April to November 9 am to 5:30 pm. There are also dining rooms at *Skyland Lodge*, open from late March to December, and *Big Meadows Lodge*, open May through October. Both serve all meals; hours are extended at all restaurants in peak season.

The wayside lunch counters and snack bars at Elkwallow (Mile 24.1), Big Meadows, Lewis Mountain, and Loft Mountain serve distinctly ordinary snacks and lunches.

Getting There & Away

There's Greyhound/Trailways service to Waynesboro from Washington, DC ($38), every morning, but there are no buses or trains to Front Royal at the north end of the park. A bicycle or car is essential here; hitching would be difficult.

GEORGE WASHINGTON NATIONAL FOREST

The borders of the George Washington National Forest are not much more than 10 miles both to the southeast and west from Staunton. The forest itself is in three parts: Massanutten Mountain in the north between the North and South forks of the Shenandoah; a larger section that straddles the Blue Ridge Parkway between Charlottesville and Roanoke; and the largest section which skirts the West Virginia border and includes parts of the Shenandoah and Allegheny mountains. It is linked to the Jefferson National Forest on both its southwestern and southeastern extremities – the dividing lines being I-64 in the west and Hwy 501 in the east.

Information

The administrator of this forest is the US Forest Service. The main GWNF headquarters is the Harrisonburg Service Center (☎ 540-564-8300), 101 N Main St, Harrisonburg, VA 22801, good for maps of the entire forest and detailed brochures. Other ranger district offices include:

Deerfield (☎ 540-885-8028),
located west of Staunton on Route 254
Dry River (☎ 540-828-2591),
112 North River Rd, Bridgewater
James River (☎ 540-962-2214),
810-A Madison Ave, Covington
Lee (☎ 540-984-4101),
109 Molineu Rd, Edinburg
Pedlar (☎ 540-261-6105),
2424 Magnolia Ave, Buena Vista
Warm Springs (☎ 540-839-2521),
Hwy 220S, Hot Springs
Massanutten Visitors Center (☎ 540-740-8310),
New Market.

There is talk that the two national forests, George Washington and Jefferson, will be combined in the future.

Ramsey's Draft Wilderness Area

This wilderness was designated by Congress in 1980 to preserve a deeply wooded valley with the last tracts of virgin forest in Virginia. Up in the right prong of the valley are stands of hemlock that have never seen the ax or chainsaw – one that fell had its rings measured and was estimated to be over 450 years old. The valley is a beautiful, quiet, and moody place. There is a picnic area at Ramsey's Draft where interpretative signs relate the first battle (McDowell) of Stonewall Jackson's 1862 Valley campaign. There are Confederate breastworks nearby.

Activities

Covering more than a million acres, the forest offers many activities. There are over 950 miles of **hiking** trails, over 60 miles of the Appalachian Trail, rare wildflowers, waterfalls, and interesting geological formations. Primitive camping is allowed in most of the forest and a permit is not required. The highest point in the forest is the 4458-foot Elliott Knob, to the west of Staunton. The PATC's *Hiking Guide to the Pedlar District of the George Washington National Forest* ($6), an area near Buena Vista, covers many trails.

You can explore the valley along part of the 32-mile **Wild Oak Trail**; get further information from the USFS. There is a great deal of hiking and cross-country skiing in the area but mountain bikes are not permitted. Hunting is permitted, at certain times, so always wear bright clothing. To get to Ramsey's Draft from Staunton take Route 250W; it is well signed.

There is **fishing** with native trout, brook and rainbow trout, small-mouth and large-mouth bass, bluegill, and catfish found in 300 miles of waterways.

Recreation Areas & Camping

Recreation areas are numerous in GWNP; for information check with the USFS headquarters and ranger offices. The major recreation areas are: Todd Lake and North River (near Elk Horn Lake), southwest of Harrisonburg; Wolf Gap to the west of Woodstock; Elizabeth Furnace and Little Fort, southwest of Front Royal on Massanutten Mountain; Sherando Lake (see below); James River and Cave Mountain Lake (see below) near Natural Bridge (covered later in this chapter); and Lake Moomaw, Blowing Springs, and Hidden Valley near Warm Springs and the West Virginia border (off Route 39).

Sherando Lake Recreation Area (☎ 540-564-8300), part of the forest, is east of Staunton at the foot of the Blue Ridge Mountains, approximately 15 miles south of I-64 via County Rd 664. The 24-acre lake has a small beach and bathhouse and a visitors center. The family campsites are available on a first-come, first-served basis. From April to October there is water, otherwise bring your own. The Cliff Trail here takes hikers above the lake. There is also a self-guided nature trail closer to the camping area.

Another great recreation area is **Cave Mountain Lake** (☎ 540-265-6054), an isolated paradise with a seven-acre lake surrounded by hardwoods and pines. It is open daily from 6 am to 11 pm, May to early November, and camping is $8 per site. From I-81, take exits 175 or 180 to Natural Bridge then turn onto Route 130. Follow this road for 3.2 miles to County Rd 759, then take this road for 3.2 miles to County Rd 781. The park is 1.6 miles farther along a paved road.

LURAY

This small town has the good fortune of being situated astride two great wilderness areas – Massanutten Mountain of the George Washington National Forest and Shenandoah National Park. The Luray-Page County Visitors Center (☎ 540-743-3915), 46 E Main St, is open daily from 9 am to 5 pm, until 7 pm in summer.

For the kids there is the **Reptile Center & Dinosaur Park** (☎ 540-743-4113) with its large reptile collection (plus a few life-size dinosaur reproductions).

Luray Caverns

These caverns (☎ 540-743-6551), the eastern US's largest and most popular, are nine miles west of Luray on Hwy 211 (10 minutes from Skyline Drive). Much of their popularity has to do with a most unnatural feature, a stalactite organ, feted as a 'stalacpipe,' which is played electronically on all tours. In addition, the caverns have crystal-clear pools, monumental columns, and walkways; outside there is an antique carriage, car, and coach museum.

The caverns are open daily June 15 to Labor Day from 9 am to 7 pm, Labor Day to mid-November from 9 am to 6 pm, otherwise 9 am to 4 pm on weekdays and 9 am to 5 pm on weekends; entry is $11 for adults, $9 for seniors, and $5 for children aged seven to 13.

Places to Stay

For camping and cabin options, see Shenandoah National Park in this chapter. *Yogi Bear's Jellystone Park* (☎ 540-743-4002) is three miles east of Luray on Hwy 211. It is open from March to November and electric/water hook-ups are from $21 to $26 for two; camping cabins are from $30 to $35, and housekeeping cabins are from $63 to $69.

There are plenty of motels, and Luray is a popular place to stay. The *Luray Caverns Motel East* (☎ 540-743-4531), 831 W Main St, one mile west on Hwy 211 Business, has singles/doubles for $55/70 (an extra person is $7). The older *Luray Caverns Motel West* (☎ 540-743-4536), 1.5 miles west on Hwy 211 Bypass, has the same prices as its eastern counterpart.

The *Ramada Inn Luray/Shenandoah Valley* (☎ 540-743-4521), on Hwy 211 Bypass, 1.7 miles east of the Hwy 340 junction, has a restaurant, pool, and handicapped accessibility. Doubles cost $65 in the low season, otherwise from $85 to $95.

Woodruff House (☎ 540-743-1494), at 330 Mechanic St, is a B&B with a restaurant and outdoor spa (candlelit at night!). Doubles cost from $98 to $115 on weekdays, $125 to $145 on weekends in low season, and about 25% more in the high season.

Six miles to the south of Luray, in Stanley (just off Hwy 340 on County Rd 624), is the *Jordan Hollow Farm* (☎ 540-778-2285). There are good rooms in this 200-year-old building constructed of hand-hewn logs. The farm also has a bar, restaurant, and stables; singles/doubles start at $115/140.

Places to Eat

Near the Luray Caverns is the *Caverns & Coach Restaurant* (☎ 540-743-6551), a barn of a place that serves adequate food. More upmarket is the red-brick *Parkhurst Restaurant* (☎ 540-743-6009), on Hwy 211W, 2.5 miles west of Luray Caverns. It is a pleasant American/Italian place with a dining area in an enclosed veranda with great views. It is open for dinner daily from 4 until 10 pm or later.

The *Guildford Ridge Vineyard*, off Hwy 211 near Luray, has a pavilion where you can enjoy food and wines. In August, they host the outdoor theater and music 'Fête Champêtre'; otherwise the tasting area is open daily, May to November.

NORTH FORK, SHENANDOAH

The North Fork of the Shenandoah River begins west of New Market, in the George Washington National Forest, and flows north (and to the west of Massanutten Mountain) before joining the South Fork near Front Royal. I-81 and Hwy 11 (the original 'Valley Pike') parallel this section of river in a southwest direction.

Woodstock

This little town, 30 miles south of Winchester, is where the Reverend Peter Muhlenberg shouted, 'There's a time to pray and a time to fight' before marching the 8th Virginia Regiment out of his church and off to fight in the Revolutionary War. The Woodstock Chamber of Commerce (☎ 540-459-2542), on N Main St, has information on the region.

The area is also known for the **Shenandoah Valley Music Festival** (☎ 800-459-3396), held on weekends from April to Labor Day at nearby Orkney Springs (15 miles west of I-81 and Mt Jackson on Route 263). Classical, symphony, pops, folk, big band, and jazz performances are held outdoors on the grounds of the historic 19th century Orkney Hotel.

The **Woodstock Museum** (☎ 540-459-5518), at 137 W Court St, features early American furnishings, tools, and farm implements used by early Valley settlers. It is open May to September, Thursday to Saturday from 10 am to 4 pm; entry is by donation.

Just south of Woodstock on I-81 at Edinburgh are the **Shenandoah Vineyards** (☎ 540-984-8699), a boutique winery in a pleasant country setting. They are open 10 am to 6 pm daily; tours are conducted hourly from 11 am to 5 pm.

Places to Stay The *Ramada Inn* (☎ 540-459-5000), at 1130 Motel Drive, has all the trimming you would expect from this chain, plus a good restaurant; singles/doubles are from $44/57.

Country Fare (☎ 540-459-4828), at 402 Main St, is a small and cozy B&B dating from 1772 with rooms from $35/45. The *Inn at Narrow Passage* (☎ 540-459-8000), two miles south of Woodstock on Hwy 11, has been restored to its 18th century appearance with rooms, furnished with antiques, from $65/85 for singles/doubles.

The 25 acres of *River'd Inn* (☎ 540-459-5369), at 1972 Artz Rd by County Rd 663 (off Hwy 11), sit on one of the famous bends of the Shenandoah. It is expensive, with a room for two costing well over $100. A prix fixe dinner is served Wednesday through Sunday.

Bryce Mountain

Picturesque Bryce Mountain Resort (☎ 540-856-2121, 800-296-2121) is in the heart of the Shenandoah Valley near Basye.

Snow skiing is possible from December to early March. There is a vertical rise of 500 feet and the longest run is 3500 feet, served by two chair lifts and three surface lifts. In addition to ski and snowboard rentals there is PSIA and SKIwee instruction. A weekday lift ticket (9 am to 4:30 pm) costs $22 for adults and kids; on weekends it is $35 for adults, $30 for children and seniors. There is night skiing from Tuesday to Saturday from 5:30 to 9:30 pm – this entails additional cost.

Summer activities include horseback riding at the TJ Stables (one hour is $20); mountain-biking ($25 per day); rollerblading ($20 per day); and windsurfing (novice package $32).

Places to Stay Accommodation is in *Stony Court at Bryce Resort* (☎ 800-296-0947), *Hill Condominiums* (☎ 800-307-3938), and *Chalet High on Bryce Resort* (☎ 540-856-2125). The two-bedroom Stony Court townhouses are from $115 per night; Hill condos have a three-night minimum and are from $95; and the Bryce Resort chalets are from $250 to $700 for two nights.

To get there take Exit 273 off I-81 and follow Route 263 for 11 miles west to Basye and Bryce Resort Mountain.

Shenandoah Caverns

These caverns (☎ 540-477-3115) have the usual collection of backlit, colorful stalactites/stalagmites and the ubiquitous Rainbow Lake and Capitol Dome, and a constant temperature of 56°F. One big plus is access for the disabled – there are elevators.

The caverns are open daily from 9 am to 5 pm in winter, and they stay open later in summer; admission is $7 for adults, $6 for senior citizens, $3.50 for children, and 'littlies' under eight are free. To get there from I-81, take the Shenandoah Caverns exit (No 269).

New Market

It is hard to imagine this beautiful valley in the grip of war, but at one time its peaceful serenity was disturbed by the boom of cannon, staccato rifle fire, and the cries of the wounded. You can learn about the terrible fighting in the Shenandoah Valley at the small but informative museum and other buildings in the **New Market Battlefield Historical Park**.

On May 15, 1864, New Market was the scene of the legendary advance by a company of youthful cadets from the Virginia Military Institute in Lexington, 10 of whom were killed on the field of battle. The Hall of Valor commemorates their sacrifice in a simple stained-glass window. Also inside is an excellent chronology of the war. Bushong's farmhouse on the battlefield has been reconstructed and furnished. On the ridge above the Shenandoah River are two spectacular overlooks from which you can see the Alleghenies.

The Hall of Valor (☎ 540-740-3101) is open daily from 9 am to 5 pm; admission is $5 for adults, $2 for children. Entry to the farmhouse is free with Hall of Valor admission; it is open daily 9 am to 5 pm. There is an annual Civil War reenactment in May.

To get to the battlefield park, take I-81 to Route 211W (Exit 264), then take an immediate right and drive for about a mile north into the park, passing two other military museums on the way. Ignore the battery of signs and continue to the VMI museum if you wish to see the main battlefield and best exhibits. Tune in to AM 530 for instructions.

The alternative, eclectic **military museum** (☎ 540-740-8065), on the spot where the battle began, has a facade that resembles Arlington, Robert E Lee's house near Washington, DC. It is open daily, mid-March through November; admission is $6 for adults, $5 for seniors, and $3 for children.

If you have had enough of the Civil War you may wish to visit the **Bedrooms of America Museum** (☎ 540-740-3512), at 9386 Congress St in New Market, just off I-81 at Exit 264. The furnishings of bedrooms from 1650 to 1930 are on display. The chambers are opened from 9 am daily; admission is $2 for adults and $1.25 for children (seven to 14).

North of Hwy 11, two miles south of Mt Jackson, is the **Meems Bottom Covered Bridge**, a 204-foot single span across the North Fork of the Shenandoah. The bridge, originally built in 1893, has been destroyed a few times and was last rebuilt in 1979.

The well-stocked Shenandoah Valley Travel Association center (☎ 540-740-3132) is opposite the battlefield park entrance on Hwy 211W (Exit 264 off I-81).

Places to Stay & Eat In New Market the *Budget Inn* (☎ 540-740-3105), just off I-81 at Exit 264, has singles/doubles from $20/28 to $40/45 depending on the season. The *Quality Inn/Shenandoah Valley* (☎ 540-740-3141, 800-544-4444) is a good-sized place with a restaurant and pool; singles/doubles are $39/52 in low season, otherwise $50/59.

For good traditional, inexpensive Southern food (peanut soup, barbecued beef, and fried chicken) try the *Southern Kitchen* (☎ 540-740-3514) on Hwy 11.

Endless Caverns

These privately owned caverns (☎ 540-896-2283) are not far south of the town of New Market, just off Hwy 11 on County Rd 793. They can also be reached via Exits 264 and 257 off I-81. Colored lighting is used to bring out the best in the calcium carbonate and the 'Snow Drift' is the coup de grace in this subterranean extravaganza.

They are open daily from 9 am; admission is $10 for adults, $5 for children (three to 12).

HARRISONBURG

This market city (population 30,700) was first settled in 1739. It is now an agricultural center (beef, dairy, and poultry) and a college town. In town, there is James

Madison University and the Eastern Mennonite College, and just south of town is the Bridgewater Community College.

You will likely see the incongruous sight of distinctively dressed Mennonites in horse-drawn buggies going about their simple lives in the bustling commercial center of town.

The Harrisonburg-Rockingham County Convention & Visitors Bureau (☎ 540-434-2319) is at 800 Country Club Rd.

Places to Stay & Eat

The *Harrisonburg-New Market KOA* (☎ 540-896-8929) is near the George Washington National Forest. To get there from Harrisonburg take Hwy 11 for nine miles north and then turn east onto County Rd 608 for 3.2 miles. Sites with full hookups are $18 in winter, $21 in summer.

The comfortable *Village Inn* (☎ 540-434-7355) is in a rural setting on Hwy 11, between I-81 exits 240 and 243; singles/doubles are $37/43 and an extra person is $5. Also good is the award-winning *Comfort Inn* (☎ 540-433-6066), 1440 E Market St (Exit 247A off I-81), with tidy, comfortable single/double rooms from $49/59. The *Days Inn Harrisonburg* (☎ 540-433-9353), at 1131 Forest Hill Rd (Exit 245 off I-81), has a nearby restaurant, heated indoor pool, and health club privileges; singles/doubles are from $42/47. The *Ramada Inn* (☎ 540-434-9981), at 1 Pleasant Valley Rd (Exit 243 off I-81) has a number of drive-up rooms, a restaurant, and a pool; singles and doubles are from $50 to $56.

The delightful *Joshua Wilton House Inn & Restaurant* (☎ 540-434-4464), 412 S Main St, is a late–19th century house close to downtown. There is a sun room on the back patio and a restaurant. The good value rooms are furnished with antiques; call for rates.

For an old-fashioned southern-style meal try the *Evers Family Restaurant* (☎ 540-433-0993), on Hwy 11 (Exit 240 off I-81). It is open from 11 am to 8 pm daily, and until 9 pm on Friday and Saturday; a full meal will be less than $10. *El Charro* (☎ 540-564-0386), at 1570 E Market St, is open every day for good Mexican lunches and dinners. The restaurants in the Village Inn and at Joshua Wilton House are recommended, but both are expensive.

Getting There & Away

The Shenandoah Valley Regional Airport (☎ 540-234-8304) is at Weyers Cave, 10 miles south of Harrisonburg and 15 miles north of Staunton. There is scheduled USAir Express service and charter services such as Tri-Star Aviation and Valley Air. Most people traveling in this part of the Shenandoah do so in their own cars.

AROUND HARRISONBURG

Harrisonburg, oft neglected in travel publications, is in a beautiful part of the Shenandoah Valley and close to a number of interesting towns and attractions.

Dayton

This charming little town (population 900), on Route 42 not far south of Harrisonburg, is set in beautiful rural country. Just to the north of town is a fortified frontier home, the **Daniel Harrison House** (☎ 540-879-2280). Built circa 1749, it is being restored and redecorated to look as it would if occupied by a well-to-do frontier family. It is open on weekends from 1 to 5 pm, May to October.

The **Shenandoah Valley Heritage Museum** (☎ 540-879-2681), at 115 Bowman Rd, concentrates on Valley history and folklife (as do a number of museums in the valley). It has an electric wall-sized map of Stonewall Jackson's 1862 Shenandoah Valley campaign (see the sidebar in this chapter). It is open May to October, Monday to Saturday from 9 am to 4 pm, Sunday 1 to 4 pm, otherwise on weekends; entry is $4 for adults, $2 for children.

The traditional **Dayton Farmer's Market** (☎ 540-896-1389) is three miles south of Harrisonburg on Route 42. There are 20 or so shops that sell fresh-baked goods, often prepared by the friendly Mennonite community. It is open Thursday

VIRGINIA

from 9 am to 6 pm, Friday 9 am to 8 pm, Saturday 9 am to 5 pm.

Places to Stay & Eat The *Hone Quarry* (☎ 540-828-2591), 11 miles northwest of Dayton on Route 257, is the cheapest camping ground in the state – it is free. There are only 10 sites and no services but this 'heaven' is nestled below the Shenandoah Mountains, on the fringe of the George Washington National Forest. Nearby is the *North River Campground* (☎ 540-828-2591), another basic facility in GWNP with 16 sites (by Elk Horn Lake) and superb views; sites are $3.

For an inexpensive buffet meal (two will eat here for less than $20) go to *Huyard's Country Kitchen* (☎ 540-879-2613) in the Farmer's Market on Route 42, Dayton. It is open when the market is open.

Massanutten

This ski field (☎ 540-289-9441, 800-207-6277) has 11 slopes, eight of which are lit at night, and the highest (Diamond Jim) has a vertical drop of 1110 feet. There is one quad chairlift and the field has 100% snow-making capacity. The field is known for ski racing and there is a PSIA ski school and SKIwee program. It is open from 9 am to 10 pm daily, usually December to mid-March.

To get to Massanutten from Staunton take I-81 north to Exit 247A in Harrisonburg. Head east on Hwy 33 for 10 miles to County Rd 644; the entrance is on the left. The postal address for information is Massanutten, Box 1227, Harrisonburg, VA 22801. The *Guide to Massanutten Mountain* ($6) has information on USFS trails, including the Big Blue.

Grand Caverns

These caverns (☎ 540-249-5729) are in Augusta County near the appropriately monickered town of Grottoes. They contain one of the largest underground rooms in the East, the Cathedral Hall (70 feet high and 280 feet long). There is some underground graffiti as well, referred to as 'historic signatures' (instead of 'aged vandalism'). Jefferson rode on horseback from Monticello to see the caverns and Stonewall Jackson let his troops sleep here after the Battle of Port Republic.

The caves are open daily April to October from 9 am to 5 pm, in March on weekends from 9 am to 5 pm. Entry is $10 for adults, $6 for children from three to 12. To get there from I-81 take Exit 235 onto Route 256. This meets Hwy 340 at Grottoes; the caverns are nearby on County Rd 844.

A few miles north of Grottoes, just off Hwy 340, is **Port Republic**, the site of one of the last battles of Jackson's 1862 valley campaign (see the sidebar in this chapter).

Natural Chimneys

The Shenandoah Valley was once the floor of a great inland sea. Eons ago, as the sea receded, natural forces sculpted the Natural Chimneys, towers of solid rock which loom as much as 120 feet above the surrounding pastoral terrain. Viewed from one angle they resemble enormous chimneys, from another angle they take on the appearance of a ruined castle or temple. Perhaps their castlelike appearance has something to do with the site being used for the annual Jousting Tournament, held on the third Saturday of August. First held in 1821, it is the oldest continuously held sporting event in North America.

The *Natural Chimneys Regional Park and Campground* (☎ 540-350-2510) is open to visitors for day (9 am to dusk) and overnight use. There are 120 campsites with electric/water hook-ups, hiking and biking trails, picnic shelters, a pool, store, hot showers, laundry, playgrounds, and self-guided tours (the facilities are limited from December through February). Tent/RV sites are $8/17 for four persons from Memorial Day to Labor Day, otherwise $10/18.50. It costs $5 per car to get in for a day visit. The visitors center is open daily May to October from 9 am to 5 pm, November to April 9:30 am to 4 pm.

Stokesville Park (☎ 540-350-2343, 800-626-3948), west of Mt Solon, in George Washington National Forest, has 102 sites and five cabins. The park has a nature trail, playground, swimming, hiking, fishing, and picnicking. Water, electricity, and sewer hook-ups are available year round. The park is 20 miles northwest of Staunton via Hwy 250W, Route 42, and County Rds 760, 747, and 730.

To get to the Chimneys from Harrisonburg travel south on I-81 to Route 42S (Exit 240) and head west to Bridgewater; follow the signs along Route 42S from there. The Upper Valley Regional Park Authority (☎ 540-249-5729), PO Box 428, Grottoes, VA 24441, has more information.

STAUNTON

Staunton (population 25,000) is another old Virginia town exuding history. Pronounced 'Stan-ton' (and don't forget it!), it is on I-81 (or off Hwy 250, 11 miles west of the southern end of Skyline Drive from Waynesboro).

There has long been a pathway through this area, originally traversed by Native Americans as they moved up and down the Shenandoah Valley. In 1732 a Scotch-Irish immigrant named John Lewis and his family built a homestead here, two miles east of present-day Staunton. Later, in 1745, the first log courthouse was built (on the site of today's courthouse) and four years after that Thomas Lewis, son of John, laid out the plans for the town.

It was the seat of government of huge Augusta County, named after the then Princess of Wales. (In 1738 the county included modern-day West Virginia, Ohio, Kentucky, Illinois, Indiana, and the Pittsburgh area of Pennsylvania.) During the Revolutionary War the parish church was briefly, for 17 days in June 1781, capital of Virginia, as Thomas Jefferson and the General Assembly moved here to evade Tarleton's Redcoats.

During the Civil War the Virginia School for the Deaf and Blind was set up as a military hospital and remained as such for the duration. In 1862 Stonewall Jackson, ostensibly leading his men out of the valley to Richmond, took them back over the Blue Ridge Mountains into Staunton by train – probably the world's first use of the railway as a military tactic. During the war Staunton was untouched and today the town has a fine collection of immaculately preserved Victorian buildings.

Staunton is the birthplace of US president Thomas Woodrow Wilson, born here in 1856. There was a huge party in 1912 when the president returned home. Today, Staunton is busily restoring its architectural gems and a visit will be rewarded with engrossing walks.

Orientation & Information

There are five historical districts in town, all easily accessible on foot. **Gospel Hill**, near the corner of Beverley and Coalter Sts, got its name in the late 1790s when religious meetings were held here. Today, it is an area of shady streets and elegant homes. The **North End**, an older neighborhood adjoining Mary Baldwin College (founded in 1842), has lots of historical buildings and steep hills. **Newtown** is the oldest residential area and includes the city's first black church. **Downtown** is a compact area exuding 19th century charm. Most of the buildings date from 1860 to 1920, Staunton's boom period.

The **Wharf Historical District** dates from the time when the Virginia Central Railroad hit town in 1854. The railroad transformed a sleepy rural village into an important commercial center. Warehouses sprang up around the train depot and supplied everything from fresh produce to wagons and harnesses.

The Staunton Welcome Center (☎ 540-332-3971), at Woodrow Wilson's birthplace, 18–24 N Coalter St, has information on nearby attractions. It is open January to March from 10 am to 4 pm, April to November from 9 am to 5 pm.

The Staunton-Augusta County Visitors Center (☎ 540-332-3972, 800-332-5219), at 1303 Richmond Ave, near the junction of I-64, I-81 (Exit 222), and Hwy 250, has lots of information.

The Augusta Medical Center (☎ 540-332-4000), off I-64 in Fishersville, has 24-hour emergency treatment facilities.

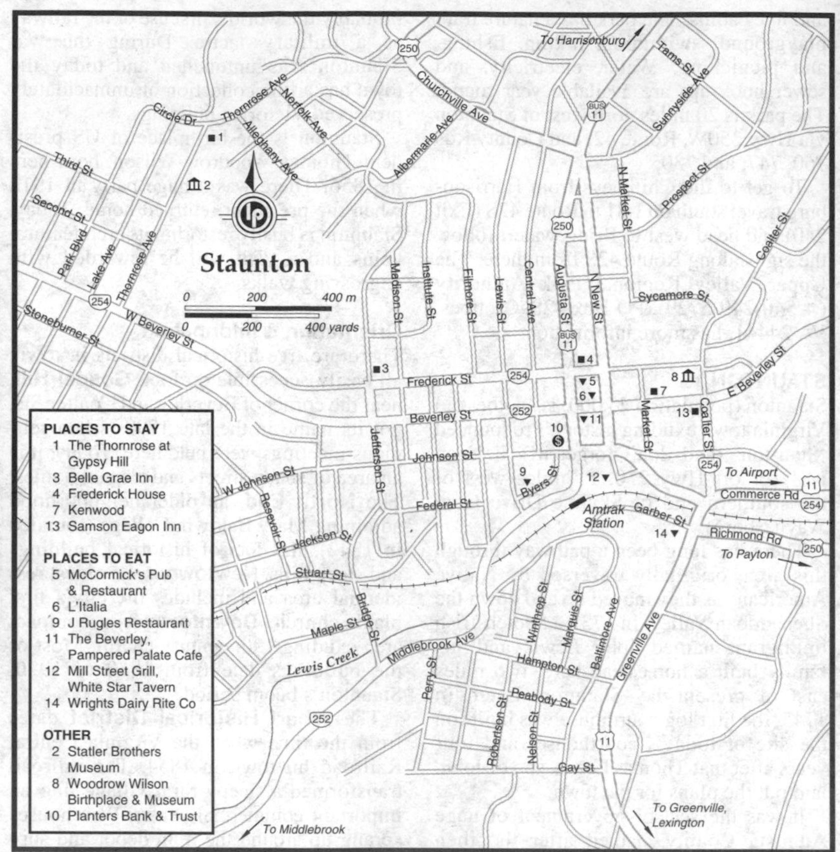

VIRGINIA

There are no foreign currency conversion facilities in Staunton, so have ready cash before you arrive. Planters Bank & Trust (☎ 540-885-1232), on the corner of Augusta and Johnson Sts, has an ATM.

Woodrow Wilson Birthplace & Museum

Thomas Woodrow Wilson was the 28th president of the US and the eighth Virginian-born president. This stately Greek Revival-style house, built in 1846 and occupied by Wilson's Presbyterian minister father from 1855, has been restored to the splendid condition it was in when Woodrow Wilson was born here in 1856.

The museum (☎ 540-885-0897), 18–24 N Coalter St, consists of seven exhibition galleries which outline the accomplishments of Woodrow Wilson, probably the first of the true international American statesmen. Wilson's presidential limousine, a 1919 Pierce-Arrow sedan, is on display. The building is open daily from 9 am to 5 pm (winter hours may vary) and the admission fee of $6 for adults, $5.50 for senior citizens, $4 for students 13 to 18, and $2 for children includes entry to both the birthplace and the museum. There is a gift shop in the gardens and free parking.

Museum of American Frontier Culture
This wonderful folk museum (☎ 540-332-7850), off I-81 at Exit 222 to Hwy 250, presents life on 18th and 19th century farmsteads. Staff in period costume organize demonstrations of daily and seasonal activities such as the tending livestock, planting of fields, and domestic chores.

One of the farms is typical American and the three others are European in origin, representing what the early settler-farmers left in England, Ireland, Scotland, and Germany.

Full attention has been paid to detail – the thatching on the roofs of buildings imported from Ireland was done by master craftspersons and the crops represent, as closely as possible, those planted at the time.

The museum is on the Warriors Path used by Indians traveling up and down the valley. This path later evolved into the County Wagon Road, used by settlers traveling from Pennsylvania to Georgia.

The visitors center includes a museum shop. The museum is open daily from 9 am to 5 pm, December to mid-March from 10 am to 4 pm; admission is $7 for adults, $6.50 for senior citizens, and $3 for children.

Statler Brothers Museum
About two miles from I-81, at 501 Thornrose Ave, is this unusual museum (☎ 540-885-7297), which is dedicated to the Statler Brothers, a group of country singers (four brothers) who hail from Staunton.

It is full of memorabilia including music awards garnered by this popular ensemble in their 25-year career. Who among the older visitors could forget 'Counting Flowers on the Wall?' This museum, housed in the school that the brothers attended, is open weekdays from 10:30 am to 3:30 pm and entry is free. There are free tours on weekdays only at 2 pm.

Places to Stay
Camping There are plenty of camping opportunities in and around Staunton. The *Natural Chimneys Regional Park and Campground* (☎ 540-350-2510) is at the Natural Chimneys (see Natural Chimneys in this chapter); and *Shenandoah Acres Resort* (☎ 540-337-1911) is in Stuarts Draft (see Waynesboro in this chapter).

The *Shenandoah KOA Kampground* (☎ 540-248-2746) is located along Middle River near Verona, just north of Staunton and three miles from I-81. There are 132 shaded campsites, a lake, and electric/water/sewer hook-ups. It is open March through October and sites for two are $20, with sewage hook-ups $22.

Walnut Hills Campground (☎ 540-337-3920), at 391 Walnut Hills Rd, Staunton, accommodates travel trailers, motor homes, and tents. There are level sites for RVs with electric/water/sewer hook-ups; campfires at sites are allowed. In addition there is a pool, playground, volleyball, lake, store, laundry, games room, free showers, and dancing and music on Saturday night. The cost for sites with full hook-ups is $16.

Hotels & Motels There are plenty of reasonably priced places. The *Staunton Budget Motel* (☎ 800-216-6835) is at 816 Greenville Ave near Exit 220 south of the junction of I-81 and I-64 (0.75 mile from the ramp). The room price of $29 includes a hearty breakfast at the cafe across the road. *Shoney's Inn of Staunton* (☎ 540-885-3117) is near the junction of Hwy 250 and I-81 (Exit 222), about half a mile north of I-64 and 2.5 miles east of historic Staunton. The garden-style rooms have sleeping sofas, whirlpool tub, and telephones. There's a lounge, a spa, and a restaurant nearby. Singles/doubles are from $43/50.

Other places include the *Econo Lodge* (☎ 540-885-5158), at 1031 Richmond Ave, on Hwy 250 less than a mile west of I-81 (Exit 222), with singles/doubles from $32/42; the *Super 8 Motel* (☎ 540-886-2888), 1015 Richmond Rd, with off-season singles/doubles for $41/44, and high-season rates of $46/51; and the *Best Western Staunton Inn* (☎ 540-885-1112), on Hwy 250 at I-81 (Exit 222), close to

Rowe's Restaurant, with singles/doubles from $58/65.

The *Comfort Inn* (☎ 540-886-5000), at 1302 Richmond Rd (Hwy 250; take Exit 222 off I-81), has a pool and singles/doubles from $58/65, including breakfast.

There are two golfer-friendly places (even though there is no such thing as a friendly golfer when playing). The *Ingleside Plantation Golf Resort* (☎ 540-248-1201) is off Route 275; and the *Holiday Inn Golf & Conference Center* (☎ 540-248-1201) is on the Woodrow Wilson Parkway (Exit 225 off I-81).

Inns Staunton is well known for its numerous fine old inns. The *Belle Grae Inn* (☎ 540-886-5151), at 515 W Frederick St, is a romantic old place in downtown. The inn comprises closely grouped, carefully restored original Victorian residences each with decorated guest rooms and suites. It is restricted to well-behaved young adults 14 and above and no pets are admitted. The rooms range from $69 to $110 for a double, suites are from $99 to $129 for two. One of the town's best restaurants is attached.

Frederick House (☎ 540-885-4420, 800-334-5575), at the corner of Frederick and New Sts (downtown, two blocks from the Woodrow Wilson birthplace), is a small hotel and tearoom in the European tradition. It has large rooms or suites with big beds, private bath, air-conditioning, TV, phone, and a private entrance; its gourmet breakfasts are prepared year round. Doubles are from $65 to $85 in low season, otherwise $65 to $95.

Kenwood (☎ 540-886-0524), 235 E Beverley St, is a restored turn-of-the-century Colonial Revival home, next to the Woodrow Wilson birthplace and a short walk from historic downtown. It is filled with period furniture and antiques and two of the rooms have private bathrooms. It costs from $66 to $70 for a single, doubles are $15 extra, and it is open year round. The *Samson Eagon Inn* (☎ 540-886-8200, 800-597-9722) is near Kenwood at 238 E Beverley St. This antebellum mansion has spacious rooms with canopied beds, sitting areas, antique furnishings, private bathrooms, queen-sized beds, phones, and TVs. There is no smoking and kids are not allowed. The cost for a double is from $75 to $90 (an extra person is $15) and the price includes a full gourmet breakfast.

The *Thornrose House at Gypsy Hill* (☎ 540-885-7026, 800-861-4338), at 531 Thornrose Ave, is a Georgian Revival brick home with a wraparound veranda. The rooms (infant- and smoke-free) have private baths, air-conditioning, and are furnished with antiques. The highlight here is afternoon tea in the fireplaced parlor. The cost per room of $55 to $70 (extra person $10) includes breakfast and afternoon tea.

Places to Eat

One of my favorite Virginian restaurants is in Staunton. You can get an inexpensive, tasty meal at *Rowe's Family Restaurant* (☎ 540-886-1833), just off I-81 (Exit 222). All the homespun Virginia staples are on offer including mincemeat pies, dishes with Virginia ham, succulent potato soup, salty corned-beef macaroni, bottomless cups of coffee, and wait staff fresh out of the 1950s. I love it.

The Beverley (☎ 540-886-4317), at 12 E Beverley St, a family-owned place, is an old Staunton stalwart. Homemade pies, whipped potatoes, and ham on freshly baked bread are likely to be the basis of a meal under $8.

A local favorite is the drive-in *Wrights Dairy Rite Inc* (☎ 540-886-0435), at 346 Greenville Ave. It has been offering curb service since 1952 and has appeared on the Statler Brothers' album covers (the brothers often pull in for a meal).

McCormick's Pub & Restaurant (☎ 540-885-3111), at the corner of Frederick and Augusta Sts, is open for dinner only for 'not-quite-fine dining.' But the food is good, the place has a casual atmosphere, and occasionally there's live entertainment.

The Pullman Restaurant (☎ 540-885-6612), at the old Staunton C&O train station, has a nutritious lunchtime soup and salad bar six days a week, and brunch on Sunday; it is also open for dinner daily. The

Depot Grille (☎ 540-885-7332), also in the train station, has a 50-foot oak bar where you can enjoy a large selection of beers. Less expensive than the Pullman, it has daily specials and a children's menu.

The *J Rugles Restaurant* (☎ 540-886-4399), at 18 Byers St in an old warehouse, is a hopping place serving a range of pasta, steak, and seafood meals; it is open seven days for dinner. The *Mill Street Grill* (☎ 540-886-0656), at 1 Mill St, is housed in a converted grist mill and serves ribs, steak, seafood, and vegetarian meals. For late night entertainment there's the adjacent *White Star Tavern* with pool tables, a good selection of beers, and a colorful crowd.

The *Pampered Palate Cafe* (☎ 540-886-9463), at 26–28 E Beverley St, is a good choice for vegetarians with a wide range of fresh produce sandwiches. There is also a good selection of coffees and local wines; it is open Monday to Saturday for all three meals and for brunch on Sunday.

At 23 E Beverley St is *L'Italia* (☎ 540-885-0102), a haven for lovers of fine Italian food. It is open Monday to Thursday from 10 am to 11 pm, Friday and Saturday 11 am to 11 pm for tasty pastas, seafood, and homemade pastries.

The *Belle Grae Inn* (see Places to Stay) has an upmarket restaurant that features excellent regional cuisine and beverages. There is a bistro next door, much cheaper, with a good selection of entrees.

Getting There & Away

The Shenandoah Valley Regional Airport (☎ 540-234-8304) is at Weyers Cave, 10 miles south of Harrisonburg, 15 miles north of Staunton (take Exit 235). There is scheduled USAir Express service to Baltimore.

Greyhound-Trailways (☎ 540-886-2424), at 1211 Richmond Rd (Hwy 250), provides daily service to and from New York and throughout the Southern states.

Amtrak (☎ 800-872-7245), on Middlebrook Ave, has trains three times a week to Staunton, on the New York-Cincinnati route (Sunday, Wednesday, and Friday). This train also stops at Clifton Forge rail station for those going to the Homestead resort in Bath County.

WAYNESBORO

The town, settled in 1797 by Irish and German immigrants and named after a Revolutionary War hero, General 'Mad' Anthony Wayne, is well situated eight miles east of the junction of I-81 and I-64. For more information on attractions contact the Waynesboro-East Augusta Chamber of Commerce (☎ 540-949-8203), 310 W Main St, Waynesboro; it is open weekdays from 8:30 am to 5 pm.

There is a visitors center (☎ 540-943-5187) on I-64 at Afton Mountain (Exit 99), open Monday to Saturday from 10 am to 6 pm. There is also the Augusta-Staunton-Waynesboro Travel Information Center (☎ 540-332-3972, 800-332-5219), at 1303 Richmond Ave, Staunton.

The **P Buckley Moss Museum** (☎ 540-949-6473), at 2150 Rosser Ave, is a fine arts museum dedicated to Moss, very much a 'people's artist' whose subject matter includes the Amish and Mennonite communities. It is open daily from 10 am to 6 pm (Sunday from 12:30 to 5:30 pm); admission is free. There are also four galleries in the **Shenandoah Valley Art Center** (☎ 540-942-2428), at 600 W Main St. It is open Tuesday to Saturday from 10 am to 4 pm, Sunday 2 to 4 pm; admission is free.

Shoppers will appreciate the selection at the Waynesboro Village Factory Outlets (☎ 540-949-5000), 601 Shenandoah Drive, where goods ranging from fine crockery to Hanes can be purchased at bargain prices.

In **Stuarts Draft**, to the southwest of Waynesboro on Hwy 340, there are a couple of Mennonite-operated shops such as Kinsinger's Kountry Kitchen (☎ 540-337-2668), on County Rd 651, for bread, cakes, and pies.

Places to Stay

The *Waynesboro North 340 Campground* (☎ 540-943-9573), on Hwy 340 five miles north of Waynesboro off I-64 (Exit 94), has sites from $12 to $17 (most have electricity and water). The *Shenandoah Acres Resort* (☎ 540-337-1911) is on County Rd 660 (off County Rd 608), east of Hwy 340 in Stuarts Draft. It is open from May to September (10 am to 8:30 pm for swimming) and there is mini-golf, playground equipment in the water, basketball, volleyball, and other pursuits to keep you amused. The campsites and cottages are available all year; ring for costs.

The *Deluxe Budget Motel* (☎ 540-949-8253), at 2112 W Main St, 1.5 miles west of town on Hwy 250, has singles/doubles for $25/30 in low season, $30/36 in high season.

The *Iris Inn* (☎ 540-943-1991), at 191 Chinquapin Drive, is a modern B&B with all the trappings of fine Southern living; singles/doubles are $65/75 from Sunday to Thursday, otherwise $80 for two. There is a handicapped-equipped room.

Places to Eat

There are a couple of good cheap places to eat. *Weasie's Kitchen* (☎ 540-943-0500), at 130 E Broad St, is a simple place known for great breakfasts and inexpensive lunches (around $4). It is open daily. If you are craving a vegetable or fruit salad head to *South River: An American Grill* (☎ 540-942-5567), at 2910 W Main St. There are plenty of other dishes on the menu in this no-frills place; it is open daily for lunch and dinner.

The Fox and Hounds Pub & Restaurant (☎ 540-946-9200), housed in a building that dates from 1837, is at 533 W Main St, on Hwy 250. It is the town's best known eatery and has a convivial pub attached. Be warned, the main courses are huge. It is open weekdays for lunch from 11:30 am to 2 pm; for dinner and drinks it's open Monday to Saturday from 5 to 9:30 pm.

WINTERGREEN

This ski resort (☎ 800-325-2200), the oldest in the state and 'the South's single best' (according to *Skiing* magazine), is high in the Blue Ridge Mountains in the beautiful George Washington National Forest, some 43 miles from Charlottesville. Of the 17 trails about 20% are beginner, 40% intermediate, 20% advanced, and 20% expert. A 1000-ft vertical drop is served by one double and four triple chairlifts. Accommodation is in luxury condos and homes. The cost of the ski lift ticket (December to March) includes a round of golf on the same day. There are over 6000 acres of protected forest and a staff biologist who organizes interpretative walks. All year round there are a range of activities to suit active visitors.

Facilities at the *Wintergreen Resort* (☎ 800-325-2200) include restaurants, bar, outdoor pools, indoor pool, tennis courts, two 18-hole golf courses, hiking trails, downhill ski slopes (see earlier), riding center, exercise room and sauna, and 20-acre Lake Monocan for swimming and canoeing. All of this does not come cheap. A double room in the resort costs from $115 in summer and $150 in winter. A round of golf will cost $48 during the week and $59 on the weekend – there are fees for tennis, the Wintergarden spa, guided mountain-bike trips and horseback riding. Bring a swag of money!

Some 3.5 miles up from the Wintergreen Gatehouse, in Devil's Knob Village, is *Trillium House at Wintergreen* (☎ 804-325-9126), a comfortable country inn with weekday rates of $85/90 for singles/doubles, and weekend rates of $100/105.

To get here from the north, follow Hwy 29 south to I-64. Head west on I-64 to Hwy 250 (Exit 107). Take Hwy 250 west to Route 151; Wintergreen is signposted from here and it is 14.2 miles to County Rd 664, then a further 4.5 miles along this road.

Snowboarding

Massanutten, Bryce Mountain, and Wintergreen have tapped into the burgeoning snowboard craze. Eastern adherents ('shredders') of soft boots and radical boards have discovered the pleasures of these three places and the dollar-wise resorts have accordingly added snowboard parks to their slopes. You get a free hour and a half lesson at Wintergreen when you rent a board. The mid-Atlantic snowboard series is held at Massanutten in early February.

LEXINGTON

This relatively small town (population 7000) in the heart of Shenandoah, 36 miles south of Staunton on I-81, has a lot to offer the visitor in the way of grace, charm, history, and attractions. It is a perfect place to relax as the pace of life seems a lot slower here – explore interesting aspects of the Civil War or just wander the streets where there are horse-drawn carriages and many well-preserved homes. It's a place that hardened travelers may find after years of nomadic existence and say, 'I could settle down here.'

It was home to Stonewall Jackson before the Civil War and Robert E Lee after – both of these Confederate generals are buried here (not far from their horses, Sorrel and Traveller). George C Marshall, Nobel Peace Prize winner for his efforts in the reconstruction of Europe after WWII, and the polar explorer Admiral Richard Byrd, both attended the Virginia Military Institute here. More recently the movie *Sommersby*, set in the time of the Civil War, was filmed in and around Lexington and Bath County.

Orientation & Information

The town is hard to miss if you are coming down the valley, as Hwy 11 passes right through it. It is just off I-81 (take Exits 195, 188, or 180). The town is cut into four quarters by the east-west Hwy 60 and the north-south Hwy 11.

The Lexington Visitors Center (☎ 540-463-3777), at 106 E Washington St (Exit 55 off I-64 and Exit 188-B off I-81), is open June through August, daily from 8:30 am to 6 pm, otherwise daily from 9 am to 5 pm. They provide a walking tour map *Historic Lexington* and a directory of accommodations and restaurants. There is a small museum attached and an audiovisual is screened on request. There is a good free quarterly magazine *Visiting Lexington and the Rockbridge Area*, also available from the visitors center.

The First Union Bank (☎ 540-463-7321) is on S Main St, and Crestar (☎ 540-463-2126) is on the corner of Main and Nelson Sts – both have ATMs.

The main post office (☎ 540-463-2822) is on the corner of Nelson St and Lee Ave.

The Stonewall Jackson Hospital (☎ 540-462-1200), off Spotswood Drive, has a 24-hour emergency service.

There is a laundromat on the corner of Randolph and Henry Sts.

Washington & Lee University

This university, with its picturesque colonnaded campus, is the sixth-oldest college in the country. Founded in 1749 as Augusta Academy, it was renamed Washington College after a donation by the first president. Later the 'Lee' was added (from Robert E Lee) following the Civil War, as he was college president for a time. Lee's former office has been preserved as he left it.

The somber-looking **Lee Chapel and Museum** (☎ 540-463-8768), on the campus, has a marble statue of a recumbent and contemplative Lee, surrounded by battle flags and memorabilia; it was sculpted by Edward Valentine. Lee, who died at his university home in 1870, is interred downstairs with members of his family. His horse, Traveller, who was with him throughout the Civil War, is buried outside. The chapel is open, Monday to Saturday, from 9 am to 5 pm, Sunday 2 to 5 pm; admission is free.

There is a statue of inventor and university benefactor Cyrus McCormick on the campus grounds. You can visit **Walnut Grove Farm** (☎ 540-377-2255) where McCormick was born and later developed the first mechanical wheat reaper. It is 18 miles north of Lexington on County Rd 606 (a mile from I-81).

Virginia Military Institute

The huge Gothic campus of this military institute (☎ 540-464-7000; for a cadet guide call 540-464-7325) is just to the east of the Lee Chapel. The institute was founded in 1839 and became famous after 10 of its cadets (including cadet Thomas G Jefferson, son of the third president) were killed in battle at New Market in 1864. The institute was virtually destroyed by Union General David Hunter when his troops

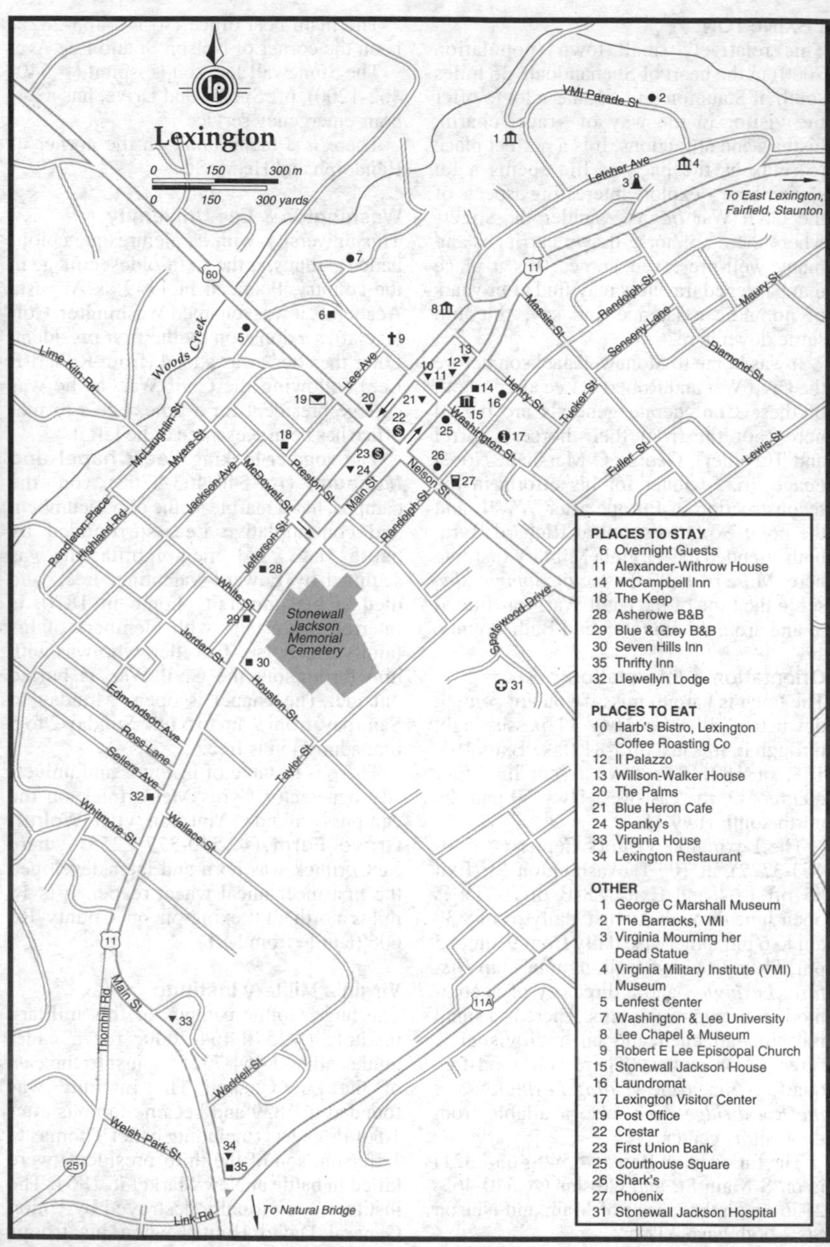
Lexington
0 150 300 m
0 150 300 yards
To East Lexington, Fairfield, Staunton
To Natural Bridge
VMI Parade St
Letcher Ave
Lee Ave
Main St
Nelson St
Washington St
Henry St
Massie St
Randolph St
Tucker St
Fuller St
Lewis St
Maury St
Diamond St
Senseny Lane
Spotswood Drive
Jefferson St
McDowell St
Preston St
Jackson Ave
Myers St
McLaughlin St
Woods Creek
Lime Kiln Rd
Pendleton Place
Highland Rd
White St
Jordan St
Houston St
Taylor St
Edmondson Ave
Ross Lane
Sellers Ave
Whitmore St
Wallace St
Thornhill Rd
Waddell St
Welsh Park St
Link Rd
Stonewall Jackson Memorial Cemetery
PLACES TO STAY
6 Overnight Guests
11 Alexander-Withrow House
14 McCampbell Inn
18 The Keep
28 Asherowe B&B
29 Blue & Grey B&B
30 Seven Hills Inn
35 Thrifty Inn
32 Llewellyn Lodge
PLACES TO EAT
10 Harb's Bistro, Lexington Coffee Roasting Co
12 Il Palazzo
13 Willson-Walker House
20 The Palms
21 Blue Heron Cafe
24 Spanky's
33 Virginia House
34 Lexington Restaurant
OTHER
1 George C Marshall Museum
2 The Barracks, VMI
3 Virginia Mourning her Dead Statue
4 Virginia Military Institute (VMI) Museum
5 Lenfest Center
7 Washington & Lee University
8 Lee Chapel & Museum
9 Robert E Lee Episcopal Church
15 Stonewall Jackson House
16 Laundromat
17 Lexington Visitor Center
19 Post Office
22 Crestar
23 First Union Bank
25 Courthouse Square
26 Shark's
27 Phoenix
31 Stonewall Jackson Hospital

razed Lexington a month after the Battle of New Market.

At 4:30 pm, on most Fridays of the school year, there is a full dress parade, a miniature version of the spectacle at West Point – a great photo opportunity.

At the opposite end of the parade ground is the **George Catlett Marshall Museum** (☎ 540-463-7103), a tribute to the distinguished life of the WWII general and Army Chief of Staff. Marshall was later US Secretary of State and won the 1953 Nobel Peace Prize for his plan for the post-war reconstruction of Europe, the 'Marshall Plan.' The museum follows his career from when he was an aide-de-camp to General John Pershing in World War I through to his acceptance of his peace prize, which is on display. Another item displayed is the Oscar won by Marshall's aide Frank McCarthy, producer of the 1970 WWII epic *Patton*.

The museum is open daily, March to October, from 9 am to 5 pm, otherwise until 4 pm; admission is $3 for adults, $2 for seniors, and $1 for children.

Virginia Military Institute Museum

There is a lot of Jackson memorabilia in this museum (☎ 540-464-7232), on the lower level of the Jackson Memorial Hall on the campus of the military institute. Included is his bullet-pierced coat from Chancellorsville and his now stuffed and mounted horse, Little Sorrel. The history of the military institute, including the story of the 250-odd cadets who fought at the battle of New Market, is also told here. It is open daily Monday to Saturday from 9 am to 5 pm, Sunday from 2 to 5 pm; admission is free.

In the Jackson Memorial Hall, which is the cadet assembly hall, is a painting of the VMI cadet charge at New Market by Benjamin West Clinedinst. It is well worth seeing.

Stonewall Jackson House

This modest brick structure (☎ 540-463-2552), at 8 E Washington St, was built in 1801. It was home to the VMI's philosophy professor, Thomas Jonathan 'Stonewall' Jackson, for two years before his death at Chancellorsville during the Civil War (see the sidebar on Stonewall Jackson in the Northern Virginia chapter).

The house has been restored and includes many of Jackson's possessions and period pieces. There are tours on the hour and half-hour and it is open June through August from 9 am to 6 pm (shorter hours, 9 am to 5 pm, in the off season; always from 1 to 5 pm Sunday). It costs $5 for adults, $2.50 for children.

Jackson is buried among hundreds of fellow Confederates, two Virginia governors, and a number of Revolutionary War soldiers in the **Stonewall Jackson Memorial Cemetery** on S Main St. The statue above his grave was dedicated in 1891. The cemetery is open from dawn to dusk. Park on S Main St and walk up to the statue and gravesite. It is often surrounded by Confederate flags, planted by believers in the chant 'The South will rise again!'

Virginia Horse Center

This $12 million center (☎ 540-463-2194), established by the General Assembly of Virginia in 1985, hosts three-day events, national horse shows, and the annual April Virginia Horse Festival. Entry to most events is free and there are tours of the facilities. To get to the center from I-81 take Exit 191 to I-64W; follow the signs for two miles.

Activities

You can take **horse-drawn carriage tours** conducted by Historic Lexington (☎ 540-463-5647), based at 106 E Washington St. They operate daily April to October from 10 am to 4:30 pm but not if the weather is bad; the horses clatter past most of Lexington's main attractions. It is $10 for adults, $9 for seniors, and $6 for children ($1 for those under three).

Less sedate, but definitely recommended, are **canoe trips** on the James and Maury Rivers with the James River Basin Canoe Livery (☎ 540-261-7334). The daily fee includes all equipment and a trip map.

VIRGINIA

They are located 1.5 miles east of I-81, near Exit 188A on Hwy 60.

There is a good hike on the twelve-mile **Chessie Nature Trail**, a stretch of old Chesapeake & Ohio railbed between Lexington and Buena Vista; it is open daily from dawn to dusk, bicycles are prohibited, and you can get a trail map from the visitors center. Reid's Dam and Lock, two miles down the trail on the Lexington side, was built in the 1850s to allow canal boats to pass rapids in the river.

Places to Stay

Camping & Hostels There are a number of campgrounds around Lexington. *Long's Circle L Campground* (☎ 540-463-7672), on Route 39W (Exit 55 off I-64) close to the Virginia Horse Center, has 45 sites and cabins. In the low/high season sites cost $10/12.50 for three; cabins are $25.

Some 14 miles west of Lexington on the eastern slopes of the Alleghenies is the *Lake A Willis Robertson Recreation Area.* It is open May 20 to Labor Day from 6 am to 10 pm (fall and spring hours are posted, and it is closed in winter); tent/trailer sites are $11/15 per night. To get there take Route 251 to Collierstown and then County Rd 770.

The *Tye River Gap Campground* (☎ 540-377-6168) is 20 miles northeast of Lexington at Vesuvius, one mile from the Blue Ridge Parkway on Route 56. It is open March through November and the sites are from $14 to $17; there are also cabins.

The most economical place to stay in all Virginia, apart from camping, is *Overnight Guests* (☎ 540-463-3075), at 216 W Washington St. Almost unbelievably, it is only $5 a night for a bed in this six-roomed, homey place, and it is only four blocks from the visitors center. It started out as a tourist home for out-of-town VMI and W&L dates.

Hotels & Motels There are plenty of hotels and motels off I-81 and I-64. The cheapest place is the *Thrifty Inn* (☎ 540-463-2151), at 820 S Main St near the junction of Hwy 11S and the bypass. It is about $30 for a very musty single room and a breakfast voucher for McDonald's.

There are several places north of town. The *Econo Lodge* (☎ 540-463-7371) is 1.5 miles north at the intersection of Hwy 11 and I-64 (Exit 55); rooms are from $32 to $64. The *Best Western at Hunt Ridge* (☎ 540-464-1500, 800-464-1501) is not far away; double rooms with great views of the Blue Ridge are from $59 to $79.

The *Howard Johnson Motel* (☎ 540-463-9181) is six miles north of town at the intersection of Hwy 11 and I-81 (Exit 195); singles/doubles are from $39/41 in the low season, otherwise $50/55. Nearby is the *Red Oak Inns* (☎ 540-463-9131) with doubles from $50. Also nearby is the *Ramada Inn* (☎ 540-463-6400), which has some rooms with handicapped facilities; singles/doubles are from $52/60.

B&Bs There are several of this popular type of accommodation in and around Lexington. *Asherowe B&B* (☎ 540-463-4219), at 314 S Jefferson St, is a comfortable place with German-speaking owners. Singles or doubles are $50.

Other good choices are the *Blue and Grey* (☎ 540-463-6260), 401 S Main St, at $105 per couple; the Historic Inns of Lexington (☎ 540-463-2044) – *Alexander-Withrow House*, 3 W Washington St, and the *McCampbell Inn*, 11 N Main St, both with single/doubles from $85/95; *Llewellyn Lodge* (☎ 540-463-3235), 603 S Main St, with singles/doubles from $60/65 (add an extra $5 in high season); *Seven Hills Inn* (☎ 540-463-4715), 408 S Main St, with doubles from $75 to $95, depending on the size of the room; and *The Keep* (☎ 540-463-3560), 116 Lee Ave, with doubles from $80 to $115.

The *Inn at Union Run* (☎ 540-463-9715) is 3.5 miles south of the visitors center on County Rd 674. Nearly all of the rooms have a spa and are filled with Victorian antiques; doubles are from $85 to $115.

About six miles north of Lexington, on Hwy 11N, is the 1850s country inn, *Maple Hall* (☎ 540-463-4666). It is expensive, with the cheapest singles/doubles from $80/95, but there are hiking trails, an outdoor pool, tennis court, and even a trout pond.

Places to Eat

For hearty Southern fare there is the *Virginia House* (☎ 540-463-3643), at 722 S Main St. A good meal of ham, biscuits and corn pudding will cost about $5. Next door to the Thrifty Inn at the southern end of S Main St (No 810) is the *Lexington Restaurant* (☎ 540-463-5844), a favorite with locals who relish their high-cholesterol breakfast; it is open daily from 7 am to 9 pm. Another good reliable place is the *Lee Hi Truck Stop* (☎ 540-463-4666), on Hwy 11, a few miles north of town; it is open 24 hours and is really cheap.

There are a number of places to eat on W Washington St. Across from the Washington and Lee University, at No 110, is the *Blue Heron Cafe* (☎ 540-463-2800) offering a healthy vegetarian alternative to the sometimes stodgy Southern cooking. The owner, self-titled 'goddess of food,' will see to it that you find a personal food nirvana. *Harb's Bistro* (☎ 540-464-1900), at No 19, is a lively place serving salads, soups, big sandwiches, and pasta. It is open most days from 8 am to 9 pm or later, except Sunday and Monday when it closes at 3 pm. If you are just after a good cup of coffee and a snack try the *Lexington Coffee Roasting Co* (☎ 540-464-6586), at No 9, for gourmet coffees, fine teas, pastries, and Italian sodas.

The Palms (☎ 540-463-7911), at 101 W Nelson St, is a local favorite for afternoon drinks; it serves a popular Sunday brunch. They cook great burgers, quiches, and Mexican entrees for around $7 for lunch, $9 for dinner. For traditional Italian fare, *Il Palazzo* (☎ 540-464-5800), at 24 N Main St, has pizza, pasta, and seafood; it is open daily from 11 am to 11 pm.

Willson-Walker House (☎ 540-463-3020), on the corner of N Main and Henry Sts, features creative American cuisine – instead of the regular greasy burger comes a lean patty on a wholegrain bun with caramelized onions, which costs about $7. The restaurant is open Tuesday to Saturday for lunch (the chef's special is $5) and dinner (sunset special is $10). Another popular place of the same style is *Spanky's* (☎ 540-463-3338), at 110 S Jefferson St, which specializes in gourmet sandwiches from its full deli. It is open daily 8:30 to 1:30 am.

Maple Hall (☎ 540-463-4666) – see B&Bs, earlier – is ideal for all extremes of weather. There are fireplaces in the downstairs dining rooms and an outdoor patio for sunny days. The continental fare on the menu is changed monthly and local produce is treated in exciting ways. It's expensive – say $50 for two – but well worth it for excellence and ambiance. It's not open for lunch.

Entertainment

The *Lenfest Center for the Performing Arts* (☎ 540-463-8006), at Washington and Lee University, offers a varied program of theatrical and musical entertainment, including performances by the University of Rockbridge Symphony Orchestra. The season runs from September to May.

The Theater at Lime Kiln (☎ 540-463-3074), set in an outdoor lime quarry off Route 60W, produces original works with Shenandoah Valley and mountain themes. It is open Memorial Day to Labor Day, Tuesday to Sunday, for evening concert performances that commence at 8 pm. The Sunday concerts are primarily musical, with a range of musical styles, from zydeco to bluegrass.

The happening place for nightlife is the *Phoenix* (with its entrance at 20 S Randolph St) where you can play foos ball, sing karaoke style, shoot pool, and drink to the wee small hours. The under-agers are probably found playing pool and sipping sodas at *Shark's* on E Nelson St.

Getting There & Away

There is no local airport – the nearest large airport is at Roanoke. Greyhound/Trailways (☎ 800-231-2222) has daily service that passes through Lexington. The depot is near where Hwy 11N crosses the Maury River, not far from Main St.

By far the best way to get around is in your own car as there are so many good places to visit nearby. If you are staying at a motel or hotel you will need a car to get into town. In winter, check on road conditions before going into the mountains; ring the Department of Highways (☎ 800-367-7623).

There is a reliable taxi service, Tom's Taxi (☎ 540-464-8294).

BATH COUNTY

Route 39 wends its way northwest of Lexington and over scenic Goshen Pass to Bath County, through the majestic George Washington National Forest. This peaceful, relaxing corner of the state is tucked up against the border of West Virginia and town names with the word 'Spring' tell of a time when the good folk of Virginia came to this region 'to take the waters.'

The Bath County Chamber of Commerce (☎ 540-839-5409) has a visitors center on Hwy 220 near the junction with Main St in Warm Springs; it is open weekdays from 9 am to 5 pm.

Goshen Pass in its heyday, before the advent of the railroad, was the principal stagecoach route to Lexington from the interior. Today visitors see the landscape much as the early pioneers did and they can still revel in its beauty, especially in May when a host of plants, including rhododendrons, are in flower. There is a day-use park where you can rubber-raft down the Maury River, fish, swim, or just enjoy a picnic. The oceanographer Matthew Fontaine Maury, who taught at the Virginia Military Institute, thought the pass so beautiful that he requested that when he died, his body be carried through the pass when the rhododendrons were in bloom. VMI cadets complied with their professor's wish, in 1873.

The numerous thermal springs are less popular than they were a century ago, but people still come to Hot Springs and Warm Springs (arrayed along Hwy 220) to bask in the sulfur waters, which range from 77°F to 104°F.

In quaint **Warm Springs**, near the junction of Route 39 and Hwy 220, is **Gristmill Square**, a small complex of historic buildings that includes the Waterwheel Restaurant. The combined smithy's shop and hardware store has been converted into a souvenir shop. Entrance to the clapboard bathhouses of the Warm Springs pools is $7 per person for one hour.

The **Garth Newel Music Center** (☎ 540-839-5018), between Warm Springs and Hot Springs on Hwy 220, hosts chamber music performances in summer. Many people choose to picnic in the grounds before listening to the music in the well-designed Herter Hall.

Three miles west of Covington, just off Hwy 60, is the only surviving trussed arch in America, the very photogenic **Humpback Bridge**; nearby is a pleasant wayside park. What a contrast this provides to the blight of industry that consumes Covington's river.

Places to Stay & Eat

The closest camping is in *Douthat State Park* (☎ 540-862-8100), and RVs are permitted. There is also boat hire, boat ramps, a sandy beach, bathhouse, and picnic areas. Standard sites are $10.50. One-room/one-bedroom/two-bedroom cabins are $55/62/77 respectively, and the lodge (which accommodates 13) is $140.50 per night. The park is near Clifton Forge – take Exit 27 off I-64 to County Rd 629 and head north for seven miles.

For those who want budget motel-style accommodations there is the *Roseloe Motel* (☎ 540-839-5373), halfway between Hot Springs and Warm Springs on Hwy 220; singles/doubles are $34/44. It is almost across the road from the Garth Newel Center.

The *Inn at Gristmill Square* (☎ 540-839-2231) in Warm Springs has some units, in the original miller's house, from $85 to $95 for a double. In addition there is a restaurant, bar, sauna, and outdoor pool.

There are a number of good B&Bs. *Milton House* (☎ 540-965-0196), at 207 Thorney Lane, not far from the Humpback Bridge, is in Covington. Each bedroom (except the center one) has a private bath.

Guests get either a continental or English breakfast and afternoon tea; a double costs from $85.

The 1873 *Longdale Inn* (☎ 540-862-0892) is just across from the ruins of the ironworks on Longdale Furnace Rd in Clifton Forge. There is a range of rooms in this old manor, and depending on the season you can expect to pay from $70 a double. The lovely *Carriage Court* (☎ 540-839-2345) is on Maple Ridge Farm, one mile away from The Homestead (see below) in Hot Springs. There are four neat and tastefully furnished rooms, a restaurant in a converted cow barn, and an outside deck; doubles are from $65 to $100.

The *Waterwheel Restaurant* (☎ 540-839-2231), part of the Inn at Gristmill Square, dates from the 1700s and is an expensive place decorated with tasteful prints. It serves continental cuisine (trout is a specialty) and has a full wine selection. It is open in the evening May to October and for Sunday brunch.

In Hot Springs, the *Sam Snead Tavern* (☎ 540-839-7666), across from The Homestead, is a great place to enjoy an American-style entree and an ale as well as live entertainment in the evenings; it is open daily (except Tuesday) from 5 to 10 pm. Corny menu items include water hazards (fish), handicaps (desserts), and the 19th hole (drinks). The *Cafe Albert* (☎ 540-839-5500), Cottage Row, is a good choice for breakfast, light lunches, and delicious feathery crepes; a light lunch for two will cost about $25.

A popular place to stay in Goshen is the *Hummingbird Inn B&B* (☎ 800-397-3214), on Wood Lane off Route 39 Alt, only five minutes' drive from Goshen Pass. A room is named after the inn's most famous guest, Eleanor Roosevelt. Double rooms are from $70 to $95; a four-course prix fixe dinner is offered to guests for $27.50 but 24 hours advance reservation is required.

Getting There & Away

Ingalls Airport (☎ 540-839-5326), in Hot Springs, has scheduled service with Colgan Airways. Roanoke is the nearest major airport. Woodrum Livery Service (☎ 540-345-7710) has a shuttle to The Homestead.

The closest Amtrak station (☎ 800-872-7245) is in Clifton Forge.

HOT SPRINGS & THE HOMESTEAD

The Homestead is one of the oldest, most famous, luxurious, and expensive resorts in the US. It stands like a Loire Valley castle with the village of Hot Springs arrayed beneath its ramparts. The west wing, east wing, and modern south wing all have rooms furnished in Victorian style with mahogany bedsteads, lounge, writing table, marble bathtubs, and TV (obviously post-Victorian).

This resort (☎ 540-839-1766, 800-838-1776) attracts those intent on getting the maximum out of the many outdoor pursuits offered. There are three 18-hole golf courses, ski slopes, indoor and outdoor pools, over 100 miles of riding trails, tennis courts, bowling alley, trout-stocked streams, spa facilities, and mineral springs. In addition, there are seven restaurants, and one of these has an orchestra and dancing. Again, all of this does not come cheap and for a standard single/double guests can expect to pay upwards of $184/234 in low season to $263/314 in the high season; an extra adult is $90.

A game of golf costs from $40 on the Homestead course in low season, up to $100 on the superb Cascades course in high season. The recommended mountain bike trips include Top of the Mountain for $55 with lunch, and a tour to Warm Springs for $75 with lunch. Living is not cheap here! You can rent mountain bikes and explore on your own; again not cheap at $25 for four hours. Hiking and swimming are 'complimentary.'

The historic *Homestead dining room* (☎ 540-839-5500) has been turned into a lavish palm court that seems to pop from the pages of a Somerset Maugham novel when the orchestra performs. The meal, featuring regional specialties, is six courses; perhaps the cheapest way to dine here is to take a daily meals package (about $50) when you book in. You are expected to dress for dinner; reservations are essential.

To get to The Homestead and Hot Springs take Route 39 through Goshen Pass to Warm Springs. There, turn south on Hwy 220.

NATURAL BRIDGE

This is hardly 'the seventh wonder of the world.' But it is one of the most spectacular sights of the Shenandoah Valley, and rightly elevated into 'must see' status for visitors to the region. The arch, 215 feet high and 90 feet long, has been eroded out of limestone over the centuries by seemingly benign Cedar Creek, a tributary of the James River.

The Native American Monocan tribe worshipped it as the 'Bridge of God;' George Washington surveyed it for Lord Fairfax; Thomas Jefferson at one stage, impressed by its grandeur, purchased it; and, now, it supports a portion of Hwy 11.

JEFF WILLIAMS

An inspiring view from below

Somehow the beautiful, natural structure has been incorporated into a macabre complex entitled the **Natural Bridge Inn & Conference Center** (☎ 540-291-1551, 800-533-1410) which has an attached wax museum, nearby caverns, and lavish accommodations. Commercialism is OK, but only if done tastefully – here one of the US's great attractions is encircled by kitsch.

To see the Natural Bridge from below (the only real photographic angle) will cost $8 for adults and $4 for children (under six get in free). From June to September there is an over-the-top sound and light presentation called 'The Drama of Creation,' held every night at 9 and 10 pm, which justifies the $8 admission if only to see the arch by night.

If you are coming from the south you are probably just beginning to witness 'cavern fever.' It gets worse the further north you go up the valley. The **Natural Bridge Caverns** (☎ 540-291-2121, 800-533-1410) are the equivalent of 34 stories deep. And lurking down below, some 347 feet underground, is the Natural Bridge ghost, a catacomb resident for over 100 years. The caverns are open daily, March to December, from 10 am to 5 pm; hours vary so ring ahead. Entry to the caverns is $7 for adults, $3.50 for children.

If you wish to get into the village (and thus below the arch), and see the wax museum and caverns, it will cost $15 for adults and $7.50 for children. Also, the best overlook, Pulpit Rock, has been closed to the public. If enough of you ask it may be reopened.

The Natural Bridge is 20 miles south of Lexington, just off I-81 (take Exit 180 onto Hwy 11 or Exit 175 onto Route 130). The caverns are to the east of Hwy 11, one mile north of Natural Bridge village.

Places to Stay & Eat

The most beautiful spot in which to camp near Natural Bridge is Cave Mountain Lake (see the George Washington National Forest in this chapter). The *Natural Bridge KOA Kampground* (☎ 540-291-2770), at the junction of Hwy 11 and I-81 (Exits 180 and 180B), has fully serviced sites from $18 to $23.50 for two, and 'kamping kabins' from $32 to $40. The *Campground at Natural Bridge* (☎ 540-291-2727) is off Hwy 11 (Exit 180A) and three miles along on Route 130E; sites are from $14 and there are cabins available.

The *Budget Inn* (☎ 540-291-2896), on Hwy 11 (Exit 180 off I-81), lives up to its name; in low season singles/doubles are from $24/28; in high season they cost from $28/32 Sunday to Thursday and increase to $40/42 on weekends.

The Natural Bridge of Virginia Resort (☎ 540-291-2121) operates the *Natural Bridge Inn & Conference Center* and *Stonewall Inn* – they have a reservations desk at the Natural Bridge ticket office. The rates range from $30 to $70 on weekdays, $40 to $90 on weekends, and three-room suites are from $125 on weekdays, $150 on weekends.

For a quality meal go to the large *Colonial Dining Room* (☎ 540-291-2121), on Hwy 11S, Natural Bridge. They put on a Friday night seafood buffet and a popular Sunday brunch for about $30 for two.

Southwest & Blue Ridge Highlands

VIRGINIA

The Southwest is dominated by the Blue Ridge Mountains, and much of its unique culture stems from its isolation and remoteness. An insensitive observer would label the terrain 'hillbilly country' and yet a nature lover or adventurous outdoor enthusiast would see it as 'God's own playground.' In many guides, this region is added as an afterthought, the descriptions of its attractions are scanty, and it is almost dismissed as being part of its oft forgotten neighbor, West Virginia.

And yet this region is alluring. Roanoke is a surprisingly sophisticated city, Abingdon is a sheer delight, Big Stone Gap is on Virginia's modern frontier, and the many parks of the Appalachians offer myriad outdoor activities. And through much of it runs a scenic part of the Blue Ridge Parkway.

To top it off, the 'mountain people' are among the most friendly you could hope to meet in your travels through Virginia, and when you hear them sing and play bluegrass (and watch them dance into the bargain), you can add 'talented' to the description.

HIGHLIGHTS

- The best hiking in the state – in Mount Rogers National Recreation Area, Jefferson National Forest, Natural Tunnel State Park, and Burke's Garden
- Abingdon – a great little town with the historic Barter Theatre
- The Blue Ridge Parkway, especially the scenic section which cuts through the southwest, with Mabry Mill and sidetrips to unspoiled mountain communities like Floyd
- The sophisticated regional center of Roanoke with its great market, museums, theater, and nightlife

ROANOKE

Roanoke (pronounced 'ROW-an-oak'), with a population of 100,000, is the largest community in western Virginia (and the largest in Virginia west of Richmond) and is easily the main center along the Blue Ridge Parkway. It is a pleasant place to visit, with wide, old streets, a farmer's market, and the Center in the Square mall.

In the 1740s, two Pennsylvania farmers, Mark Evans and Tasker Tosh, took up land near some salt licks where trails used by animals and Native American hunters crossed. In 1834 the area was known as Gainsborough, but it soon became known as the Big Lick. When the railway came in 1852, the town was moved to the tracks and the name went with it. The original town was called Old Lick. The town of Big Lick was chartered in 1874.

When the Shenandoah Valley Railroad came, seven years later, Big Lick was renamed Roanoke to reflect the nearby river and county. The name came from 'rawrenock,' shell beads worn by Native Americans. Another railroad, the Norfolk & Western Railroad, came in 1882. Today, Roanoke is a center for trade, distribution, manufacturing, and health care. It calls itself 'Virginia's festival city' (see Special Events in this section).

Orientation

Arrive in Roanoke at night and you will see the **Star**, a 100-foot high illuminated steel-and-concrete structure that has been a beacon at the top of Mill Mountain for over 40 years. The Center in the Square, a modern mall, is the hub of downtown, with five independent cultural organizations housed there and many nearby restaurants.

Information

The Roanoke Valley Visitor Information Center (☎ 540-345-8622, 800-635-5535), at 114 Market St, is open daily from 9 am to 5 pm. The friendly, enthusiastic staff will screen an eight-minute audiovisual presentation and provide an informative tour map of the city. Also pick up a copy of the free *Roanoke Valley Visitor and Newcomer Guide*. The local daily is the *Roanoke Times* and the area code for the city and Southwest is 540.

There are many banks in town where you can exchange currency. A branch of the First Virginia Bank-Southwest (☎ 540-561-8796) is in Market Square; the main office of the Southwest Virginia Savings Bank (☎ 540-343-0135) is at 302 2nd St SW; and Crestar (☎ 540-985-5231) has many (17 or so) branches throughout the city.

On wet Appalachian days, you can browse at the Dusty Corner Bookstore (☎ 540-362-5042) at 3728 Williamson Rd NW; the Eclectic Bookshop (☎ 540-342-4340) at 110 W Campbell Ave; or Phoenix Rising (☎ 540-985-6886) at 26 Kirk Ave.

And laundry? Try Dirty Duds Inc (☎ 540-982-9530) at 1101 Gus Nicks Blvd and Peters Creek Laundromat (☎ 540-562-2376) at 2392 Peters Creek Rd NW.

For emergency medical treatment, contact the Community Hospital of Roanoke (☎ 540-985-8000) at 101 Elm Ave or Roanoke Memorial Hospital, corner of Belleview Ave and Jefferson St (☎ 540-981-7000).

Center of the Square Museums

Three of Roanoke's museums plus a planetarium can be found in the restored warehouses of the Center in the Square. The **Science Museum of Western Virginia** (☎ 540-342-5710) is one of those great places that focuses on interactive displays for the kids – natural history, energy resources, and plenty of computer games. The Hopkins **planetarium** has daily shows. The museum is open daily from 10 am to 5 pm (Sunday, 1 to 5 pm); admission is $5 for adults, $4 for senior citizens, and $3 for children (3 to 12), plus $1.25 if you wish to visit the planetarium.

The **Roanoke Valley History Museum** (☎ 540-342-5770) has an odd assortment of exhibits, some of which focus on local Native American culture. It is open Tuesday to Friday from 10 am to 4 pm, Saturday 10 am to 5 pm, and Sunday from 1 to 5 pm; entry is $2 for adults, $1 for seniors and children.

Art Museum of Western Virginia

This art museum (☎ 540-342-5760) has a collection of regional works with an emphasis on Appalachian folk art. The museum is in two parts, as there is an annex across an alley connected by a 2nd-floor gallery bridge. The gallery of 19th century American art is particularly good. It is open Tuesday to Saturday 10 am to 5 pm, Sunday 1 to 5 pm (from 6 to 9 pm on the first Friday of the month); admission is free.

Virginia Museum of Transportation

A short walk from Market Square at 303 Norfolk Ave is the Virginia Museum of Transportation (☎ 540-342-5670), a must for those seduced by steam. Roanoke was once a railway town and is still the base for the Norfolk & Western Railway (once the Norfolk Southern). Exhibits on the Nickel Plate locomotive and other trains built in town are worth a look. It has the largest collection of steam and diesel locomotives in the nation. The museum is open Monday to Saturday from 10 am to 5 pm, Sunday from noon to 5 pm (closed Monday in January and February); admission is $5 for adults, $4 for seniors, $3 for students and children.

Harrison Museum of African American Culture

This museum (☎ 540-345-4818), at 523 Harrison Ave NW, is the sponsor of the annual Henry Street Heritage Festival on the last Saturday in September. Lots of exhibits featuring local and regional aspects of African American culture are curated by the friendliest staff you are likely to meet. It is open Tuesday to Friday

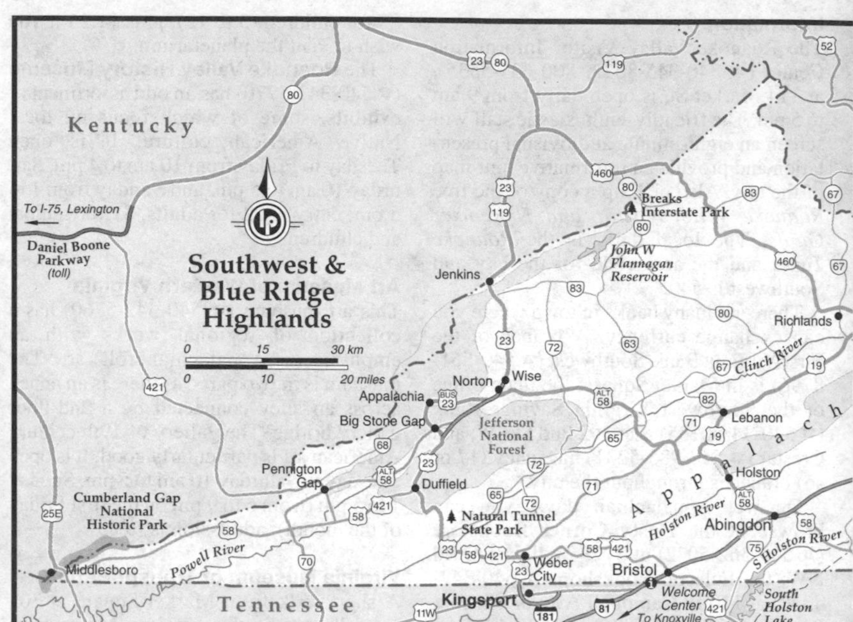

from 10 am to 5 pm and on weekends from 1 to 5 pm; admission is free but donations are welcome.

Dixie Caverns

In nearby Salem, Dixie Caverns (☎ 540-380-2085) will leave you whistling when you see the formations and flows of the Wedding Bell, Turkey Wing, and Cathedral Room. Rock hounds will appreciate the nearby mineral shop. The caverns are at 5753 W Main St (near Exit 132 off I-81, which becomes Hwy 460) and they are open daily from 9:30 am to 5 pm; admission is $5.50 for adults, $3.50 for children (five to 12).

Other Attractions

Other attractions include the **Mill Mountain Zoo** (☎ 540-343-3241), off the Blue Ridge Parkway, which is open daily from 10 am to 5 pm; admission is $4 for adults, $3.60 for seniors, and $2.75 for children under 12. **To the Rescue Museum** (☎ 540-776-0364) in the Tanglewood Mall celebrates the concept of squad rescue, which was developed in Roanoke by Julian Stanley Wise. It is open 10 am to 4 pm Tuesday to Friday, 10 am to 5 pm Saturday, and 1 to 5 pm Sunday; admission is $1. **Virginia's Explore Park** (☎ 540-427-1800), a re-creation of a pioneer village, is at 3900 Rutrough Rd and is open Saturday to Monday from 9 am to 5 pm from April to October; admission is $4 for adults and $2.50 for students six to 18.

Activities

The Roanoke Appalachian Trail Club (☎ 540-387-2347) organizes hikes in the vicinity. Some 28 miles of the Appalachian Trail cuts through the Roanoke Valley. (See the Appalachian Trail section in this chapter.)

The Blue Ridge Bicycle Club (☎ 540-774-4678) organizes rides year round, such as the Rockfish Gap ride, a 100-mile per day trek to Waynesboro and back.

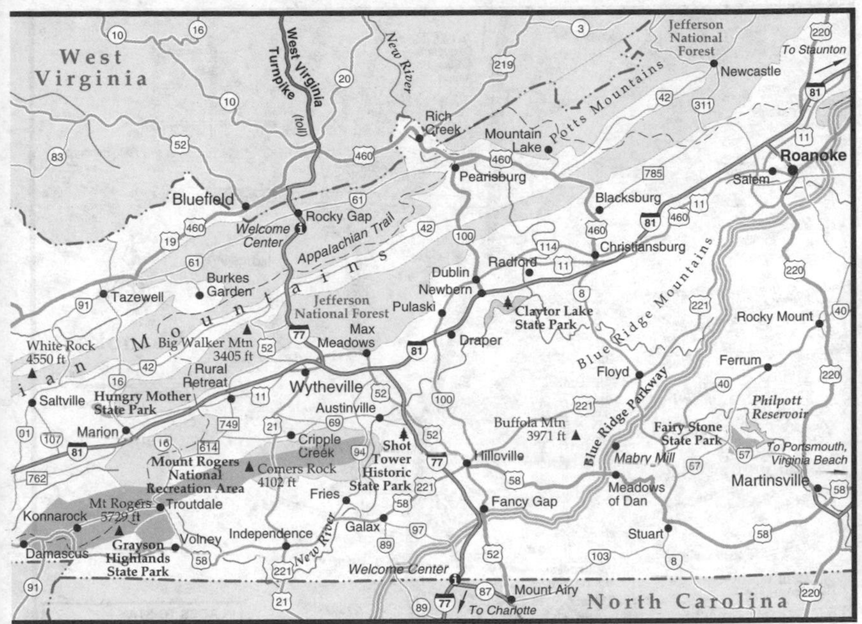

In winter, cross-country skiing options are limited only by your imagination and experience. Perhaps the closest 'known' place is Mountain Lake (☎ 540-626-7121), but skiers will be seen gliding down the Blue Ridge Parkway whenever it's clothed in white.

Special Events

As Virginia's self-styled 'festival city,' Roanoke certainly does live up to its title. Here's a partial list of events to look out for: the Festival in the Park (begins Memorial Day weekend and goes for two weeks), the Downtown Railway Festival (around Columbus Day weekend in October), the Henry St Heritage Festival (late September), Conservation Festival and Roanoke Valley Horse Show (both held in mid-June), Vinton's Dogwood Festival (early May), and a Championship Chili Cook-Off (first Saturday in May). Get more information on these events from the visitors center.

Places to Stay

Camping There is limited camping in and around Roanoke and, unfortunately, there are no cheap hostels. On the city's southern limits at 2551 Mill Mountain Spur Rd in Vinton (Mile 120.4 of the Blue Ridge Parkway) is the *Roanoke Mountain Campground* (☎ 540-857-2490); open from May to October, sites are $9. The *Dixie Caverns Campground* (☎ 540-380-2085), at 5753 W Main St (off I-81 at Exit 132) has grassy, shady sites from $10 to $16 for two; there are also electric/water hook-ups.

Hotels & Motels The *Days Inn Civic Center* (☎ 540-342-4551) at 535 Orange Ave (Exit 4E off I-581) has a pool and tennis courts. The singles/doubles rate of $40/45 includes breakfast. The *Econo Lodge* (☎ 540-343-2413) at 308 Orange Ave (Exit 4E off I-581) has single/double off-season (January to March) rates of $37/39, otherwise $40/45. At 526 Orange Ave NE, across from the Roanoke Civic

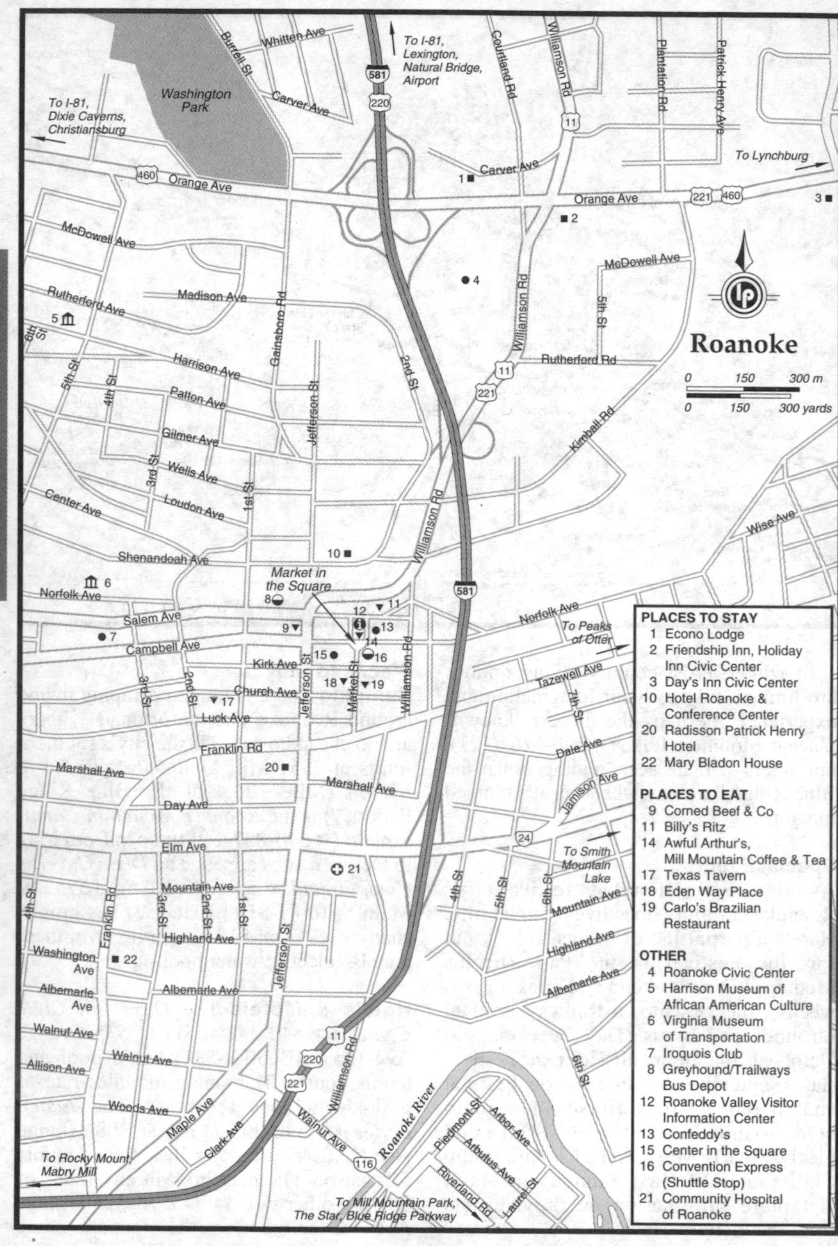

Roanoke
0 150 300 m
0 150 300 yards
To I-81, Lexington, Natural Bridge, Airport
To I-81, Dixie Caverns, Christiansburg
To Lynchburg
Washington Park
To Peaks of Otter
To Smith Mountain Lake
To Rocky Mount, Mabry Mill
To Mill Mountain Park, The Star, Blue Ridge Parkway
Market in the Square
Roanoke River
Whitten Ave
Burrell St
Carver Ave
Orange Ave
McDowell Ave
Rutherford Ave
Madison Ave
Harrison Ave
Patton Ave
Gilmer Ave
Wells Ave
Center Ave
Loudon Ave
Shenandoah Ave
Norfolk Ave
Salem Ave
Campbell Ave
Kirk Ave
Church Ave
Luck Ave
Franklin Rd
Marshall Ave
Day Ave
Elm Ave
Mountain Ave
Highland Ave
Washington Ave
Albemarle Ave
Walnut Ave
Allison Ave
Woods Ave
Maple Ave
Clark Ave
Walnut Ave
Williamson Rd
Courtland Rd
Plantation Rd
Patrick Henry Ave
Rutherford Rd
Kimball Rd
Wise Ave
Tazewell Ave
Dale Ave
Jamison Ave
Gainsboro Rd
Jefferson St
Market St
2nd St
Piedmont St
Arbor Ave
Arbutus Ave
Riverland Rd
Laurel St
PLACES TO STAY
1 Econo Lodge
2 Friendship Inn, Holiday Inn Civic Center
3 Day's Inn Civic Center
10 Hotel Roanoke & Conference Center
20 Radisson Patrick Henry Hotel
22 Mary Bladon House
PLACES TO EAT
9 Corned Beef & Co
11 Billy's Ritz
14 Awful Arthur's, Mill Mountain Coffee & Tea
17 Texas Tavern
18 Eden Way Place
19 Carlo's Brazilian Restaurant
OTHER
4 Roanoke Civic Center
5 Harrison Museum of African American Culture
6 Virginia Museum of Transportation
7 Iroquois Club
8 Greyhound/Trailways Bus Depot
12 Roanoke Valley Visitor Information Center
13 Confeddy's
15 Center in the Square
16 Convention Express (Shuttle Stop)
21 Community Hospital of Roanoke

Center, the *Friendship Inn* (☎ 540-981-9341) has doubles from $40.

There are two Hampton Inns. The *Hampton Inn Airport* (☎ 540-265-2600) at 6621 Thirlane Rd NW at the junction of Peters Creek Rd is close to the airport; singles/doubles are $55/72. The *Hampton Inn Tanglewood* (☎ 540-989-4000) at 3816 Franklin Rd across from the Tanglewood Mall is $55/65; a continental breakfast is included. Also in Tanglewood, at 4468 Starkey Rd (off I-581 at the Franklin Rd/Salem exit) is the *Holiday Inn Hotel Tanglewood* (☎ 540-774-4400); a single or a double is $88. There is a magnificent view of the Blue Ridge Mountains from the bistro.

The *Ramada Inn – River's Edge* (☎ 540-343-0121) at 1927 Franklin Rd just off I-581 is a good solid place. It is reasonable for the price of $42 for singles and doubles in the low season, otherwise $46.

Add to these at varying costs the *Best Western Coachman Inn* (☎ 540-992-1234) just off I-81 at Exit 150B, the *Comfort Inn Roanoke-Troutville* (☎ 540-992-5600, 800-628-1957) at 2654 Lee Highway South, and the *Holiday Inn Airport* (☎ 540-366-8861) at Peters Creek Rd near I-581.

The huge, lavish *Roanoke Airport Marriott* (☎ 540-563-9300) at 2801 Hershberger Rd NW (Exit 3W off I-581) is set on 12 landscaped acres. The single/double rooms have full amenities and 24-hour room service; the cost is from $59 to $129 depending on the size of the room.

The *Clarion Roanoke Airport* (☎ 540-362-4500) – formerly the Sheraton Inn – is at 2727 Ferndale Drive NW (2.5 miles north off I-581 at the Hershberger Rd W exit). There is a restaurant, piano bar, and a club, Miami's. Singles/doubles are from $68/75 and an extra person is $10.

The *Holiday Inn Civic Center* (☎ 540-342-8961) at 501 Orange Ave (near I-581 and Williamson Rd) has a restaurant, lounge, and private outdoor pool with courtyard. The rooms are a good value at $50/67 for singles/doubles.

The *Best Western Inn at Valley View* (☎ 540-362-2400) at 5050 Valley View Blvd (Exit 3E off I-581) is only a mile from Roanoke Regional Airport and right next to Roanoke's largest shopping mall, Valley View. The hotel has full amenities and free continental breakfast; singles/double are from $59/61 to $129/151. More expensive is the *Radisson Patrick Henry Hotel* (☎ 540-345-8811, 800-833-4567) at 617 S Jefferson St, close to downtown. There are antiques and kitchenettes in the spacious rooms, which cost from $55 to $150 per double.

The imposing *Hotel Roanoke & Conference Center* (☎ 540-985-5900) at 110 Shenandoah Ave (Exit 5 off I-581) has been a prominent landmark in Roanoke since it was first built in 1882 by the Norfolk & Western Railroad. It guests have included Joe DiMaggio, Elvis, Jack Dempsey, Amelia Earhart, and a host of presidents. From Monday to Thursday, singles/doubles are from $119/129 to $139/149, and Friday to Sunday from $79.

B&Bs *Mary Bladon House* (☎ 540-344-5361) at 381 Washington Ave SW, in Roanoke's old southwest neighborhood, is a pleasant B&B with singles/doubles for $63/80. *Walnuthill* (☎ 540-427-3312), another B&B at 436 Walnut Ave SE, is slightly cheaper (from $59 to $79) and serves a gourmet Virginian breakfast.

Places to Eat

There is no shortage of places to eat, especially around Market Square. If you are eating on a budget, gravitate to the *Farmer's Market* (☎ 540-342-2028) at 310 1st St SW. Touted as the oldest continuously operated open-air farmers' market, there are many restaurants where you can eat cheaply. Fresh produce is available in abundance.

The Homeplace (☎ 540-384-7252) near Exit 141 off I-81 on Route 311N is, as its title suggests, the place for old-fashioned home-style meals (chicken, green beans, mashed potatoes and gravy). Two people will escape for less than $20. It is open for dinner Thursday to Saturday from 4:30 to 8 pm, Sunday from 11:30 am to 6 pm; no alcohol and no reservations.

If you can manage to get a seat (and there are not many of them), then the tiny *Texas Tavern* (☎ 540-342-4825), also known as the 'Roanoke Millionaires' Club,' at 114 W Church Ave is a real must. The place is usually packed out with locals eager to try (or sample for the thousandth time) the great chili dishes (about $3) on offer. Civility comes a distinct second – when I opened my mouth to order the cook turned to the person next to me and asked 'Whaa'd 'e say?' Still, it's priceless.

The menu is more varied at *Billy's Ritz* (☎ 540-342-3937) at 102 Salem Ave in downtown. The usual surf-and-turf (seafood and steak) and chicken teriyaki are featured on the extensive menu. It is open for lunch on weekdays from 11:30 am to 2:30 pm and for dinner nightly from 5 pm.

Market St, in the market area, has a smattering of reasonable places. Vegetarians will be delighted with the selections at *Eden Way Place* (☎ 540-344-3336), at No 307, a whole-food store with attached cafe. Across the road, at No 310, *Carlo's* (☎ 540-345-7661) serves a variety of international cuisine, including Brazilian dishes (a main course is from $11). *Awful Arthur's Seafood Company* (☎ 540-344-2997) on the corner of Market St and Campbell Ave (No 108) has Roanoke's most extensive raw bar and the freshest of seafood. The crawfish, served by the half-pound and pound, if it features on the specials board, is an absolute must. Also featured in the raw bar are oysters, shrimp, clams, snow crab legs, mussels, and the Captain's Platter (which combines them all).

At 107 S Jefferson St, the excellent *Corned Beef & Co Bar & Grill* (☎ 540-342-3354) is open daily. Lunch is a great value, with 'awesome' salads from $3.95, delicious burgers from $4.15, and blackened chicken and pasta for $5.95. Their sandwich choices fill a full page of their menu.

La Maison du Gourmet (☎ 540-366-2444) – doesn't its name attract the gourmand in us all? – is housed in a labyrinthine Georgian-style colonial mansion at 5732 Airport Rd. In keeping with the marvelous French cuisine, the dining rooms are elegantly outfitted and the ambiance refined. Recommended selections include steak Diane (from $12 to $17) and the lamb entrees. Such presentation, however, does not come cheap. Two will be lucky to escape for less than $45. It is open for lunch from 11 am on weekdays and for dinner from 5 pm daily except Sunday; reservations are advisable.

Even more upmarket is *The Library* (☎ 540-985-0811) at 3117 Franklin Rd SW in the Piccadilly Square shopping center. One of Virginia's finest restaurants, if you weren't here for the tasty seafood or the elegantly presented French cuisine, you could browse through the bookshelves. It is very expensive – dinner for two is likely to be around $50.

Entertainment

Roanoke is very much the cultural center of western Virginia. See the Friday *Roanoke Times* for the entertainment supplement. At 1 Market Square SE in the Center in the Square, the *Mill Mountain Theatre* (☎ 540-342-5740) features professional performances year round as well as a festival of new works and children's productions. The box office is open from 10 am to 6 pm.

The *Roanoke Ballet Theatre* (☎ 540-345-6099) is the focus of performances in spring and fall in town and in other parts of the region. If you are in Roanoke in July or August, try to catch the Summer-in-the-Park Pops performances of the *Roanoke Symphony* (☎ 540-343-6221). There are also monthly classical performances in January, February, May, September, and October at the Roanoke Civic Center just off Williamson Rd. The *Valley Chamber Music Society* (☎ 540-375-2333) performs from October to May at the Olin Theater at Roanoke College, College Lane, Salem.

For a cinema-going experience like few others, the *Grandin Movie Theater* (☎ 540-345-6177) at 1310 Grandin Rd reminds us what it was like to go to the movies before TV; they often have 99¢ specials. Bill Murray, who did a benefit here, reiterated that such places should not be forgotten or destroyed.

If you're tired of highbrow entertainment, try the *Roanoke Comedy Club* (☎ 540-982-5693) at 627 Townside Rd (Fiji Island), where you can eat and laugh (hopefully not at the same time). It is open Thursday to Saturday with local and visiting headliners.

If you like loud music, head-banging, and mixing with an eclectic crowd, then the *Iroquois Club* (☎ 540-982-8879) at 324 Salem Ave is your venue on Friday and Saturday nights.

Another good weekend venue to try is *Confeddy's* (☎ 540-343-9746) at 32 Market St in the heart of downtown. Billy's Ritz (see Places to Eat) also attracts a young crowd, as do Corned Beef & Co and Awful Arthur's.

The *Elephant Walk* (☎ 540-774-4400) in the Holiday Inn Hotel Tanglewood at 4368 Starkey Rd has a DJ from Tuesday to Saturday.

Getting There & Away

Roanoke Regional Airport (☎ 540-362-1999) at 5202 Aviation Drive is 5.5 miles north of downtown. It is served by Delta Connection (ASA and COMAIR), United Express (Atlantic Coast), Northwest Airlink, and USAir/USAir Express. Cab fare from the airport to downtown should be no more than $10. There is no direct airport bus service. All of the major car rentals are represented at the airport.

The Greyhound-Trailways depot (☎ 800-231-2222) is at 17 Campbell Ave (Campbell Court).

If arriving by car on I-81, switch to I-581 (which becomes Hwy 220) and you will arrive in the heart of Roanoke.

Getting Around

Roanoke and its satellites, Vinton and Salem, are served by a good bus service, Valley Metro (☎ 540-982-2222, with TDD available). Buses operate from 5:45 am to 8:45 pm and cost $1.25 for adults and 60¢ for seniors and students; children under five are free. Transfers are free and cash fares require exact change. The main interchange is downtown at Campbell Court.

Taxicab companies include Liberty (☎ 540-560-1776) and, for Salem only, Salem (☎ 540-389-3131).

BLUE RIDGE PARKWAY

The Blue Ridge Parkway traverses the ridge of the southern Appalachians for 469 miles from Shenandoah National Park in Virginia (where it connects with the Skyline Drive) to Great Smoky Mountains National Park in North Carolina. The two-lane, paved motor road is marked by concrete mileposts – these begin in the north at Mile 0 near Shenandoah National Park. With over 17 million visitors per year to various parts of the parkway, it is the most visited site in the US national park system!

Wildflowers are one of the parkway's great attractions. Look out for wild columbine (red and yellow), trailing arbutus (white to pink), yellow lady slipper, white trillium, white Dutchman's breeches, green jack-in-the-pulpit and white bloodroot. A great place to see over 70 species of conspicuous wildflowers (and 20 species of ferns) is along the two-mile Flat Top Trail; it begins at the Peaks of Otter picnic area northeast of Roanoke off Route 43. The parkway is thus seen at its best in spring, when the wildflowers bloom. It is also extremely popular in mid-October, when the change in the color of the leaves is most spectacular.

Information

The parkway can be accessed from several major highways, including I-64, I-81, I-77, I-40, and I-26. There is no fee to enter or use the parkway. The road is sometimes closed in winter by single-digit temperatures, wind, ice, and snow, but in summer the temperatures can soar into the 90s. This is understandable when it is realized that the elevation of the parkway varies from 650 feet to 6000 feet. For emergencies or to learn what to do in the event of a breakdown, call ☎ 808-727-5928. The parkway speed limit is 45 mph, but this drops to 35 mph in developed areas. At this speed, and with stops, you could reasonably expect to spend two days driving the full length.

In Virginia, Roanoke is the main stop-off along the parkway, but there are many other visitors centers, campgrounds, and facilities open from May to October. The main one is Blue Ridge Parkway (☎ 704-298-0398), 400 BB&T Building, Asheville, NC 28801.

There are 11 visitors centers (five in Virginia, six in North Carolina), four concessionaires operating lodges and cabins, seven restaurants, and four service stations along the parkway. There are also a range of activities available – walks vary from simple leg stretchers to extended hikes. In summer and autumn, ranger programs are held at the visitors centers.

Publications Free publications that will make your trip along the Parkway more interesting include *The Blue Ridge Parkway Directory*, complete with a bloom calendar and strip maps; the *Parkway Milepost*; the annual *Blue Ridge Country's Travel Guide*; the quarterly *Blue Ridge Digest*; and the *Blue Ridge Parkway Information Guide*.

Some of the many publications for sale are the *Blue Ridge Almanac*, published six times a year ($3 per issue, ☎ 800-877-6026), *Blue Ridge Parkway Guide* (two volumes, $15.90 a set), *Blue Ridge Parkway: The Story Behind the Scenery* ($8.95), *Bicycling the Blue Ridge* ($10.95), *Inns of the Blue Ridge* ($11.95), *Blue Ridge Range: The Gentle Mountains* ($16) and *Walking the Blue Ridge: A Guide to the Trails of the Blue Ridge Parkway* ($11.95). You can order these books from the Blue Ridge Bookshelf (☎ 800-548-1672), PO Box 21535, Roanoke, VA 24018.

Floyd County

The hills of Floyd County support a counterculture paradise of artists and craftspeople who flourish happily alongside local farming communities. The town of Floyd was once called Jacksonville, after Andrew Jackson, the seventh president, but it was inexplicably named Floyd in the late 1890s. Today, Floyd is a must for those who want to experience the Blue Ridge region as it once was.

The place to go is **Cockram's General Store** (☎ 540-745-4563) at 206 S Locust St, especially on Friday night when they have a Flatfooting Jamboree with locals and guest artists from all over the US. The show starts at 7 pm and entry to the store is free. The rules are: No cussin', no moonshine (or other alcohol), no smokin', and no fightin'.

Great restaurants in Floyd include the cheap *Blue Ridge Restaurant* (☎ 540-745-2147) at 113 E Main St for beans, hotcakes and fried squash; and the ultra-cheap *Three-Legged Cow Cafe* (☎ 540-745-2201) at 110 N Locust St, open for lunch and dinner every day except Wednesday and Sunday. At the 'Cow,' the 'udderly delicious' food is mainly vegetarian. From 5 pm to midnight, Thursday to Saturday, there is live music.

Ferrum

This town, based around Ferrum College, is not exactly on the Blue Ridge Parkway but is easily reached from it. The **Blue Ridge Institute & Farm Museum** (☎ 540-365-4416) is a living history farmstead that illustrates life in the German-American Blue Ridge settlement in 1800. The costumed interpreters explain the livestock breeds, the gardens, and the gallery exhibits. Admission to the museum is free, but farm tours are $3 for adults, $2 for seniors and children. Also in Ferrum College, the **Blue Ridge Dinner Theatre** (☎ 540-365-4335) is open June to July for two daily performances.

Mabry Mill

This sawmill and water-powered gristmill (☎ 540-952-2947) is just north of the Meadows of Dan. It is a magnificent old building in a very picturesque setting and well worth a stop (it has been used on postcards representing a number of other states!).

You can still buy buckwheat flour and cornmeal for those good ol' Southern recipes. It is open daily May to October from 8 am to 6 pm (June to August to 7 pm); admission is free.

Meadows of Dan

Apart from its quaint name, there are a couple of other attractions to this region. Top of the list is Nancy's Homemade Fudge and Candies (☎ 800-328-3834) on County Rd 795 one mile east of the intersection of the parkway and Hwy 58. Here, delectable candies are made, packaged, and consumed; it is open daily from 10 am to 5 pm. Second on the list is the Chateau Morrisette Winery (☎ 540-593-2865) on Winery Rd, off County Rd 726, west of the parkway. The winery, a 'thing of stone and wood,' offers tastings, sales, tours, and a monthly jazz festival. It is open daily, year round, Monday to Saturday from 10 am to 5 pm, Sunday noon to 5 pm.

The **Poor Farmer's Market** (☎ 540-952-2670) is a general store, deli, and gift shop. According to one Roanoke resident, their fried apple pies ($1) are the best ever.

Galax

The name Galax comes from the broad, waxy, green leaf plant that produces a long spiky white bloom resembling a stream of milk (from 'gala,' Greek for milk). If you own a fiddle, chances are you have heard of Galax. In August each year, the **Old Fiddlers' Convention**, the oldest and largest event of its kind in the country, is held here. Rosin up your bow, as there is lots of jollity, dancing, and good music to be had – call ☎ 540-236-8541 for more information. If you miss the festival, you can still attend the Galax Mountain Music Jamboree, held on the third Saturday of each month (except August) at 7 pm at the Grayson St Stage from May to October; otherwise, indoors in the Rex Theatre on Grayson St, Sunday 1 to 4 pm; admission is free.

Just northeast of Galax on Hwy 58/221 in Woodlawn, the **Harmon Museum** (☎ 540-236-4884) displays Native American objects and guns and memorabilia from America's wars. The museum is open year round, Monday to Saturday from 8 am to 6 pm; admission is free.

Places to Stay

The parkway has nine *campgrounds* along its length; four of these are in Virginia and five in North Carolina. The Virginian campgrounds are Otter Creek (Mile 61), Peaks of Otter (Mile 86), Roanoke Mountain (Mile 120), and Rocky Knob (Mile 167). These are open from May to October, except Otter Creek, which is open year round (as is Linville Falls in North Carolina). To make reservations call the state park system (☎ 800-933-7275).

Campground fees vary with the season from $7 to $9 for families or groups with two adults, plus $2 for each additional person over 18. There are no hook-ups or showers. There are also 17 picnic grounds in developed areas and tables at some of the overlooks. In Virginia, the picnic grounds are at Humpback Rocks (Mile 6), Otter Creek, James River (Mile 64), Peaks of Otter, Roanoke Mountain, Smart View (Mile 155), and Rocky Knob. Additionally, there are private campgrounds, restaurants, and hotels in communities and towns along the parkway.

At Mile 86, the *Peaks of Otter Lodge* (☎ 540-586-1081, 800-542-5927) is open year round. At this tranquil location, they have a winter special of $45 per person per night (double occupancy), which includes free dinner every night and free breakfast each weekday morning. They organize tours to the high points of the Peaks of Otter; a bus departs from the lodge hourly May to October from 10 am to 5 pm for the hike to the summit of 3875-foot Sharp Top.

The *Blue Ridge Country HI-AYH* (☎ 540-236-4962) is on the Blue Ridge Parkway at Mile 214.5 (north of Route 89) and is reached by a paved driveway on the eastern side. A quaint 20-bed place with dormer windows and panoramic views, a bed costs $11 for members and $14 for nonmembers. The hostel is open by reservation from November 5 to April 30, with a music room, meeting room, 'clogging' barn, and nearby hiking, canoeing, rafting, horseback riding, skiing, and mountain biking opportunities (there's a bike repair shop in Woodlawn, 12 miles away).

The *Knights Inn Motel* (☎ 540-236-5117) at 312 W Stuart Drive in Galax has doubles from $35 (an extra person is $5). At Mile 189 of the Blue Ridge Parkway near Fancy Gap, the *Doe Run Lodge* (☎ 540-398-2212, 800-325-6189) has rooms from $99/119 for two during the week/weekend in the low season; $109/129 in the high season. The resort has tennis courts, pool, dining room, and lounge bar.

BLACKSBURG

Blacksburg (population 35,000) was formerly known as Draper's Meadow and was the first English-speaking colony west of the Alleghenies. Settlers of German, English, Scottish, and Irish origin established a farming community on the surrounding land. In July 1755, a group of Shawnee killed or captured all but four of the settlers in what has come to be known as the Draper's Meadow Massacre. An outdoor historical drama, *The Long Way Home*, performed every summer in nearby Radford (see Radford, below) tells of these events. Colonel William Preston came to the region in 1772, settled on Draper's farm, and built the imposing Smithfield Plantation.

In the 1990s, Blacksburg became the first fully 'electronic village' in the US with most government services and educational institutions interconnected by the Internet. The town was rated by Rand McNally as one of the nation's top 20 places for quality of life. For more information on regional attractions, visit the Blacksburg Chamber of Commerce (☎ 540-552-4061) at 141 Jackson St.

Blacksburg Transit (☎ 540-961-1185) operates buses from Main St on Monday to Friday only – from spring to fall, the service operates from 7 am until well after midnight. The cost is 50¢ for adults, 25¢ for children.

Museums

There are two interesting museums at Virginia Tech. The first is the **Museum of Geological Sciences** (☎ 540-231-3001) in Derring Hall, which has mineral and fossil displays and a working seismograph. It is open year round, Monday to Friday from 8 am to 4 pm, Saturday 10 am to 2 pm.

The **Museum of Natural History** (☎ 540-231-3001) at 428 N Main St has a number of natural history displays including one on North American mammals. The specimen research collection has over one million insects, mammals, and birds. It is open year round, Wednesday to Saturday from 11 am 5 pm, Sunday 1 to 5 pm. Admission to both museums is free.

Smithfield Plantation

This plantation consists of a 1774 frame house with stockade and was the home of three governors of Virginia. It is furnished with period pieces, and there is a gift shop (☎ 540-951-2060). The buildings, at 1000 Smithfield Plantation Rd, are open April

Audie Murphy Monument

On May 28, 1971, a plane carrying Audie Murphy, the US soldier most decorated in World War II, crashed on the slopes of Brush Mountain in the Jefferson National Forest near Blacksburg. The son of a sharecropper from Kingston, Texas, Murphy died in the crash.

Murphy had joined the infantry at age 18 and served in France. In January 1945, his heroism in action was rewarded with the Congressional Medal of Honor; in all, he was to earn 24 medals from the United States, three from France, and one from Belgium. His high profile led to a film career of over 40 films in which the diminutive actor usually played a tough cowboy. His memoirs were entitled *To Hell and Back*.

The trail to the crash site is an easy loop walk of 1.5 miles. To get there from Blacksburg, follow Main St to Mount Tabor Rd (County Rd 624). Proceed for 12 miles until you pass County Rd 650, then turn left onto a gravel road (Forest Service P188.1). Turn right at the top of Brush Mountain and continue for three miles. The drive is a total distance of 17 miles. For more information, contact the Blacksburg Ranger Station (☎ 540-552-4641). ■

to November, Thursday to Sunday from 1 to 5 pm; entry is $4 for adults, $1.50 for children.

Huckleberry Trail

This six-mile 'rails to trails' is being developed on the old Huckleberry Railroad line in Montgomery County. The Merrimac & Provincial Rail line once served coal mining communities between Blacksburg and Christiansburg. A short section exists as a component of the Blacksburg Bikeway/ Walkway system.

Mountain Lake

This beautiful retreat, northwest of Blacksburg on County Rd 700 just off Hwy 460 (Exit 37), is one of those classy old mountain retreats complete with a picturesque lake. It was the setting for the movie *Dirty Dancing* with Jennifer Grey and Patrick Swayze. There's a hotel and restaurant (see below).

Places to Stay & Eat

The *Holiday Inn* (☎ 540-951-1330) at 3503 S Main St is worth a stay for its railroad-theme restaurant. Travelers will also appreciate the coin-operated laundry, pool, and games room; doubles are from $55.

The *Brush Mountain Inn B&B* (☎ 540-951-7530) at 3030 Mount Tabor Rd is an exquisite place built of cedar and pine on the fringe of Jefferson National Forest. The Audie Murphy monument, where the war hero/actor's plane crashed, is six miles away. Kids are welcome in this place, which has doubles from $65. *The Sycamore Tree* (☎ 540-381-1597), another B&B in a country setting, is at the foot of Hightop Mountain. The rooms, furnished with pieces from the old Hotel Roanoke, start at about $85 a double; children over 12 are welcome.

The Mountain Lake Hotel (☎ 540-626-7121, 800-346-3334) has a restaurant and bar, nightly entertainment, exercise facilities, and tennis courts. A room in the main hotel begins at $165 per double, while those in the gray-clapboard Chestnut Lodge start at $195; rates include breakfast and dinner. (For directions see Mountain Lake above.)

Anchy's (☎ 540-951-2828) at 1600 N Main St is an inexpensive family spot with an eclectic menu. More expensive but consistently good, *Jacob's Lantern* (☎ 540-552-7001) is at the Marriott, 900 Price Fork Rd.

RADFORD

A lot of visitors come to this city (population 16,000), southwest of Blacksburg-Christiansburg, to witness *The Long Way Home*, a romanticized play depicting the story of Mary Draper Ingles' capture by the Shawnee in 1755, her captivity, escape, and subsequent 850-mile journey to freedom from Big Bone Lick, Kentucky. The play is enacted at the Inglesides Amphitheater (☎ 540-639-0679) on Route 232 (Exit 105 off I-81). The amphitheater is open late June to early September from 4 pm, and there are free 30-minute guided tours of the Ingles' property from 7 pm. Performances are held Thursday to Sunday, June through Labor Day, from 8 to 10:30 pm; admission is $7 for adults, $3.50 for children.

A cheap, clean place to stay is the *Executive Motel* (☎ 540-639-1664) on Hwy 11W. All of the rooms have two double beds, air conditioning, phones, and color TV; doubles start at $40. The *Best Western Radford Inn* (☎ 540-639-3000, 800-628-1955) at 1501 Tyler Rd has tremendous views of the Blue Ridge Mountains. Single/ double rooms, colonial in style, are $54/60.

The excellent *Gallery Cafe, Books and More* (☎ 540-731-1555) at 1115 Norwood St is popular with students who drop in to read, sip brewed coffee, and sample the delicious pastries. Downstairs is *Hot Chilies*, where vegetarians will be in heaven, while those who sample the hot chili sauces may think they have gone in the other direction. There's a branch of the local chain *Macado's* (☎ 540-731-4879) at 510 Norwood St.

Claytor Lake State Park

This park (☎ 540-674-5492) is a good place to relax. The historic Howe House has exhibits about the early settlement of the region. Standard campsites are $10.50, electric/water hook-ups are $15, and two bedroom cabins with waterfront views $77/82. To get there from I-81, take Exit 101 near Dublin.

The New River Cruise Co (☎ 540-674-9344, 800-419-0378) based in Claytor Lake State Park, operates two-hour **cruises** up the scenic New River on the *Pioneer Maid*. There is a good commentary, even better food, and great scenery. It operates year round, Tuesday to Saturday at 11 am, 1 and 7:30 pm, and Sunday at 1 pm for a brunch cruise; the cost is $20.50 for lunch, $33 for dinner, and $24.30 for Sunday brunch.

New River Trail State Park

This 57-mile greenway follows an abandoned railroad right-of-way and is a superb hiking/biking/horseback-riding trail. The trail starts in Pulaski in the north, then follows Claytor Lake in its upper reaches before crossing to the true right bank of New River. The direction is then southwesterly across I-77 to the border of the Mount Rogers NRA. Then it's south to either Fries or Galax.

For information contact Shot Tower & New River Trail State Park (☎ 540-699-6778). There is access from Ivanhoe, Galax, Draper, Pulaski, and the shot tower.

PULASKI & NEWBERN

The gritty little town of Pulaski takes its name from a Polish count and Revolutionary War hero. It has a renovated Main St with a number of Victorian-era buildings now housing shops and restaurants. For more information, contact the Pulaski County Chamber of Commerce (☎ 540-480-1991). The *Count Pulaski B&B* (☎ 540-980-1163) at 821 N Jefferson Ave is a moderately expensive place to stay. The furnishings reflect the owners' wide travels and the comfortable, smoke-free rooms are a good value at $75 per double.

The pleasant little town of Newbern on County Rd 611 (just off I-81) and not far from Pulaski has a number of interesting 19th century buildings, of which 26 can be seen from the road. It was a lodging stop for settlers traveling on the Wilderness Road from Pennsylvania and down through the Cumberland Gap to the then unknown. The town was founded in 1810, and the founder's building, used variously as a post office, store, tavern, and home, is now the **Wilderness Road Regional Museum** (☎ 540-674-4835). It has an interesting, if somewhat jumbled, collection of implements that would have been in daily use two hundred years ago. The museum is open Tuesday to Saturday from 10:30 am to 4:30 pm, Sunday 1:30 to 4:30 pm; admission is by donation. Not far away from the museum is an interesting shop where miniature fairground carousel figurines are made.

The family-owned *Valley Pike Inn* (☎ 540-674-1810), just off I-81 at Exit 98, serves inexpensive country fare, including roast beef, fried chicken, and fruit cobblers. It is open May to December from Thursday to Sunday, January to April from Friday to Sunday for dinner; no liquor is served.

JEFFERSON NATIONAL FOREST

This massive area of forest (690,000 acres) in west central Virginia extends from the James River in a southwesterly direction to within 50 miles from the western tip of the state. The forest is mainly Appalachian mixed hardwoods with conifers interspersed, but there are many 'meadow' areas at higher elevation that feature low and flowering vegetation. It is soon to be combined with the George Washington National Forest – the name, and which president will get namesake billing, have yet to be decided.

As a forest managed for its main resource – timber – there are schizophrenic faces to both the region and its administration. Recreational activities (which produce little income), although touted as important, take a definite second place. And this is really apparent when you visit one of the administration centers seeking general information! People come to look at the wildlife and trees in one season, to cut down the trees and shoot the wildlife in another.

The information centers, for what they are worth, are as follows.

Supervisor's Office (☎ 540-265-6054)
5162 Valleypointe Parkway, Roanoke
Blacksburg Ranger District (☎ 540-552-4641)
110 Southpark Drive, Blacksburg
Clinch Ranger District (☎ 540-328-2931)
Route 3, Box 820, Wise
Glenwood Ranger District (☎ 540-291-2189)
Natural Bridge Station
Mount Rogers National Recreation Area
(☎ 540-783-5196)
Route 16, Marion
New Castle Ranger District (☎ 540-864-5195)
County Rd 615, New Castle
Wythe Ranger District (☎ 540-228-5551)
Hwy 11, Wytheville

There are a number of developed campgrounds with over 600 camping units within the forest; all facilities are open from May to September and some remain open in the fishing and hunting season.

There are also noteworthy trails passing through the forest: the Appalachian Trail (300 miles of it pass through the Jefferson); the four-mile Cascades, the four-mile Mount Rogers, 1.5-mile Roaring Run, and nine-mile Hoop Hole national recreation trails; the Virginia Highlands Horse Trail; New River Trail; and the Virginia Creeper Trail. Special areas include the James River Face Wilderness on the northeast end of the forest (see the Shenandoah Valley & Ranges chapter) and the Mount Rogers National Recreation Area.

WYTHEVILLE

This town, at the junction of I-81 and I-77, gateway to the southwest Highlands of the Appalachians, is surrounded by great mountain scenery. The Highlands Gateway Visitor Center (☎ 540-637-6766, 800-446-9670) in Max Meadows east of Wytheville on Route 121 (take Exit 80 off I-81) has a plethora of information on sights and activities in the region. There is a wide choice of accommodations and over thirty restaurants. The Wytheville-Bland Chamber of Commerce (☎ 540-223-3355), on the corner of Monroe and 1st Sts, has information on the town and a historic walking tour pamphlet.

Before doing anything else, drive north of town on Hwy 52 to the **Big Walker Lookout** in Jefferson National Forest, from where you can see five states. There is a cafe and gift shop. From spring to fall, fit visitors can lead a llama on a day hike to the Big Walker Mountain summit; contact Virginia Highlands Llamas (☎ 540-228-6555) for information.

Shoppers should visit the Christmas Carousel (☎ 540-637-6635), where even useless shoppers can find a Christmas present. You can ride the **carousel** for $1. Also try Snoopers Antique & Craft Mall (☎ 540-637-6441), with over 100 shops. Both are at Fort Chiswell, just off I-81.

The architecturally interesting **Haller-Gibboney Rock House Museum** (☎ 540-223-3355), at the corner of Monroe and Tazewell Sts, was built in 1823. Furnished with original pieces, it is open May to September on Sunday from 2 to 4:30 pm; admission is free. Some **old log houses** on Main St (Hwy 11), between 5th and 7th Sts, survived the ravages of the Civil War.

Also reminiscent of times long past, the **shot tower**, near Austinville south of Wytheville off I-77S, was built in 1807 and produced shot for early pioneers. Lead was melted in a kettle at the top of the 75-foot tower and poured through a sieve. It fell through the tower into another 75-foot shaft below, then into a kettle of water.

Nearby are picnic grounds, restrooms and the New River Trail. The tower (☎ 540-699-6778) is open Memorial Day to Labor Day from noon to 5 pm weekdays, 10 am to 6 pm on weekends. Entry is $2 for adults, $1 for children; visitors may climb the tower.

Places to Stay & Eat

There is a good selection of accommodations. The least expensive is the *Econo Lodge* (☎ 540-228-5517) at 1190 E Main St on Hwy 11, a mile west of I-81; singles/doubles are $33/37. More expensive, the

Super 8 Motel (☎ 540-228-6620) is at 130 Nye Circuit near the junction of I-81 and I-77. The *Days Inn* (☎ 540-228-5500) at 150 Malin Drive is moderately sized with 120 rooms at $39/42 for singles/doubles.

The *Holiday Inn* (☎ 540-228-5483, 800-842-7652) on Hwy 11, near the junction of I-77 and I-81, maintains its corporate reliability. There is a restaurant, bar, pool, and handicapped facilities, and a double is $49.

Durham's Restaurant (☎ 540-228-5241) at 150 N 11th St, open from 7 am to 9 pm mid-March to mid-October, has a home-style, kid-friendly menu.

On Holston Rd near the junction of I-81 and Hwy 52 (and in the Comfort Inn), *Scrooges* (☎ 540-228-6622) features English-style entrees from $7 and a 'Tiny Tim' kids' menu. *Peking* (☎ 540-228-5515), open daily at 105 Malin Drive (Exit 73 off I-81), has a Sunday brunch.

HUNGRY MOTHER STATE PARK

Admit it: Like us, you came here because of the name. Ask someone to explain how this place got its name – it's a good icebreaker.

Hungry Mother State Park (☎ 540-783-3422) is known for its beautiful woodlands and peaceful, 108-acre lake, which has a sandy beach, bathhouse, and fishing pier with handicapped access. Camping sites are $10.50, electrical and water hook-ups $15, and one-room/one-bedroom/two-bedroom cabins are $55/67/77 respectively. To get there, go four miles north of Marion on Route 16.

MOUNT ROGERS NATIONAL RECREATION AREA

East of Abingdon, the 115,000-acre Mount Rogers National Recreation Area provides ample hiking and camping opportunities in the hardwood climax forests of the ancient Appalachians. The two highest points in Virginia, Mount Rogers (5729 feet) and White Top (5520 feet) are both within the park.

Outdoor camping is one of the park's attractions (see Places to Stay in this section). Fishing is also popular, and there are introduced trout in the many remote mountain streams; a Virginia license is required.

Mount Rogers NRA is part of the Jefferson National Forest (see Jefferson National Forest in this chapter), so logging still takes place nearby and hunting is permitted in certain areas. Still, there are many unspoiled portions that make the area a good place to spend some time.

Information

Advance information about this very large area – a wise precaution – is available from the Mount Rogers NRA headquarters (☎ 540-783-5196), Route 16, Box 303, Marion, VA 24254, and from the Highlands Gateway Visitor Center (☎ 540-637-6766) at the Factory Merchants Mall (Exit 80) in Max Meadows near Fort Chiswell. Both sell a one-sheet topographic map of the area for $3. The free pamphlets *Campgrounds/Picnic Areas: Mount Rogers NRA* and *Virginia Creeper Multiple-Use Trail* are particularly useful.

The best way to reach the park headquarters is to take Exit 45 off I-81 at Marion, then Route 16, six miles south of Marion. It is open Memorial Day to October, Monday to Friday from 8 am to 5:30 pm, Saturday 9 am to 5 pm, Sunday 8 am to 4:30 pm; otherwise Monday to Friday from 8 am to 4:30 pm. There is no fee to drive through the area, but there are day-use fees for some of the recreational sites.

Hiking

This is the biggest attraction in this wilderness region. There is a 64-mile section of the Appalachian Trail reserved for walkers only, the 51-mile Iron Mountain Trail, and many other trails that interconnect with either of these. A side trail off the Appalachian Trail leads to the summit of Mount Rogers and provides one of the most popular of the short excursions (for those who want to stand on top of Virginia!).

Virginia Creeper Trail The Virginia Creeper Trail began as a Native American footpath; later, European pioneers such as Daniel Boone hiked the trail, but its name stems from the early steam locomotives that wheezed up the steep grades, the last of which ran on March 31, 1977. With 100 trestles and bridges, it was the archetypal mountain railroad. The original creeper engine is in Damascus, near the Straight Creek bridge.

Today, the Creeper is a 34.3-mile, multiple-use trail linking Abingdon, Virginia, with the North Carolina border, 1.1 miles west of White Top Station. It can be used by hikers, cyclists, and horseback-riders, but not by motorized vehicles. About 16 miles of the trail, between Iron Bridge (Mile 18.4) and the state border, is part of the Mount Rogers NRA and Jefferson National Forest. For information, contact the Abingdon Visitor's Bureau (☎ 540-676-2282). Entrance is free.

Mountain Biking & Horseback Riding

It may seem odd to group these two activities under a single heading, but the fact is many of the area's trails are open to mountain-bikers and horseback riders. Cyclists should check with the information center to see which trails are open. A number of bicycle-rental agents serve the region, including Blue Blaze Bike & Shuttle Services (☎ 540-475-5095) at 727 W Laurel Ave, Damascus; Highlands Bike Rentals (☎ 540-628-9672) at 302 Green Spring Rd, Abingdon; and Mount Rogers Outfitters (☎ 540-475-5416, 800-337-5416) at 110 W Laurel Ave, Damascus. Blue Blaze also provides a shuttle service (☎ 540-475-5095, 800-475-5095) for hikers and bikers to the trailheads. Their service for bikers to the top of the Virginia Creeper Trail is $8 from Damascus, $10 from Abingdon; bike rentals are $15 for a half day, $25 for a full day.

The **Virginia Highlands Horse Trail** (66 miles) connects Elk Garden to Route 94 and is the main route for horse riders. There are many other possibilities for riders – nearly 150 miles – connecting to the New River and Iron Mountain trails. There are horse camps at Fox Creek (off County Rd 603), Hussy Mountain (off Forest Route 14 near Speedwell), and Raven Cliff (just south of County Rd 642 and east of Cripple Creek). All of these camps have toilets for the humans and drinking water for the horses.

For more information on horseback-riding, contact Mount Rogers High Country Outdoor Center (☎ 540-677-3900) on County Rd 603 near Troutdale. They also organize day rides and overnight covered-wagon trips by horse and mule.

Cross-Country Skiing

In winter (December to March), the trails of the NRA are great for cross-country skiing, but all precautions must be taken, as the weather in this region can be unforgiving. For more information, contact the Highlands Ski & Outdoor Center (☎ 540-682-9762) on W Main St in Abingdon.

The Forest Service's *Cross-Country Skiing* lists the trails in three regions: four trails in the East End; five in the Feathercamp region; and 18 in the High Country region. These range from easy (along the Highlands Horse Trail) to difficult (those which drop steeply in drainage areas off the easier trails, eg, the five-mile Helton Creek Loop).

Places to Stay

There are five main campgrounds in the NRA; call ☎ 800-933-7275 for information. *Raccoon Branch* is on Route 16 south of Sugar Grove – it has 20 sites, toilets (May to October), and no showers; it's open year round and sites are $4. There's a two-mile trail to Dickey Knob on the Highlands Horse Trail. *Grindstone* is on Route 16, west of Troutdale – it has 188 sites, toilets, warm showers, and a nature trail; it's open May to December and sites are $5. There's a trail to the Mount Rogers summit (six miles). *Beartree* is on Hwy 58, seven miles east of Damascus – it has 113 sites, toilets, showers, year-round fishing, swimming from May to September (10 am to 6 pm in Beartree Lake), and a bathhouse; the day use fee is $2, campsites are $6 (a double unit is $10). *Hurricane* is two miles south of Route 16 on County Rd 650 – it has 29 sites, toilets, showers, and trout fishing; it's open from April to September and sites are

$4. The Hurricane Knob Trail (1.5 miles) is nearby. *Comers Rock* is on Forest Service Road 57 west of Hwy 21 – it has 10 sites, pit toilets, no showers, Hale Lake for trout fishing, and picnic shelters; it's open year round and there are no fees. The Iron Mountain Trail passes through camp.

Right in the shadow of White Top, *Green Cove Cottage* (☎ 540-676-3041) at 1148 Panorama Drive is a remodeled farmhouse with all the amenities; the Virginia Creeper Trail runs directly in front of the property. The *Fox Hill Inn* (☎ 540-677-3313) on Route 16 in Troutdale is a small B&B. A double room, furnished in country style, costs $75, including a country breakfast. Kids will love it, as it is a working farm.

GRAYSON HIGHLANDS STATE PARK

Adjoining Mount Rogers NRA, this park (☎ 540-579-7092) lies near Virginia's highest point, Mount Rogers, and provides expansive views of alpine-like peaks of over 5000 feet. A short section of the Appalachian Trail passes through the park. There are campgrounds with hot showers, stables, a visitors center, and a camp store, but there are no hook-ups. Wild ponies were introduced to keep the grass in the meadows down – you may be lucky enough to spot one as they roam the park. In September, the park hosts the Grayson Highlands Fall Festival. *Campsites* are $10.50.

To get there from I-81, take Exit 45 in Marion, then Route 16S to Volney and go west on Hwy 58 until you see the signed entrance on Route 362.

ABINGDON

Abingdon (population 10,000) is a real delight and, as somewhat of a festival center, has a wide range of accommodations. Many visitors come to see the Barter Theatre, the state theater of Virginia. There is also a 20-block historical district with fine examples of Federal and Victorian architecture.

Information

The Abingdon Convention and Visitors Center (☎ 540-676-2282, 800-435-3440) at 335 Cummings St (about a quarter-mile from Exit 17 on I-81) is open daily from 9 am to 5 pm. Abingdon is Virginia's second electronic village (after Blacksburg); computers are available at the library and the visitors center for public use.

The Washington County Chamber of Commerce (☎ 540-628-8141) at 179 E Main St has information on the local festivals. The free pamphlet *Abingdon: A Walking Tour of Main Street*, available from the visitors center, interprets nearly 40 Abingdon landmarks.

The post office is on Main St. A hospital is on Valley St.

The Barter Theatre

Abingdon's most famous attraction is the Barter Theatre, founded during the Depression by a young, out-of-work actor, Robert Porterfield. It is now the longest running equity theater in the nation. Struggling with fellow actors in New York, Porterfield had the idea to move to his native southwest Virginia, where there was an abundance of food, and to 'barter' admission to performances for local food and produce.

The theater opened on June 10, 1933, and admission was 40¢ or the equivalent in produce; with the slogans like 'with vegetables you cannot sell, you can buy a good laugh,' the concept of trading 'ham for *Hamlet*' caught on quickly. Virginia ham was taken in lieu of play royalties by Tennessee Williams, Thornton Wilder, and Noel Coward, while vegetarian George Bernard Shaw opted for spinach instead. The Barter Theatre has since been a proving ground for emergent actors, eg, Ernest Borgnine, Gregory Peck, Hume Cronyn, Patricia Neal, Ned Beatty, and Barry Corbin (Maurice Minnifield of television's *Northern Exposure*).

Porterfield died in 1971, but the theater he inspired has gone from strength to strength: The original Barter Theatre offers plays in the grand tradition, the Barter Stage II has more exploratory productions, and the First Light Theatre focuses on young audiences. The theater (☎ 540-628-3991, 800-368-3240) at 133 W Main St has live performances, which change every four weeks, late May to late November nightly except Monday. There are performances for children from June to early August. Admission is about $15 (students under 17, $2 off), but you may be able to persuade the door staff to let you in if you offer some pumpkins or a case of Budweiser.

Other Attractions

In addition to many arts and crafts oulets on US 11 between I-81 Exits 10 and 13, the most notable being Dixie Pottery, the 1860 **Fields-Penn House Museum** (☎ 540-676-2282) at 208 W Main St is also worth seeing. It has been set up to show how an average family lived in a small Virginia town just prior to the Civil War. It is open on Thursday, Friday, and Saturday from 11 am to 3 pm; admission is free.

The **William King Regional Arts Center** (☎ 540-628-5005) at 415 Academy Drive is an affiliate of the Virginia Museum of Fine Arts. They offer changing exhibits in two galleries as well as working artists' studios. It is open Tuesday, Wednesday, and Friday from 10 am to 5 pm, Thursday

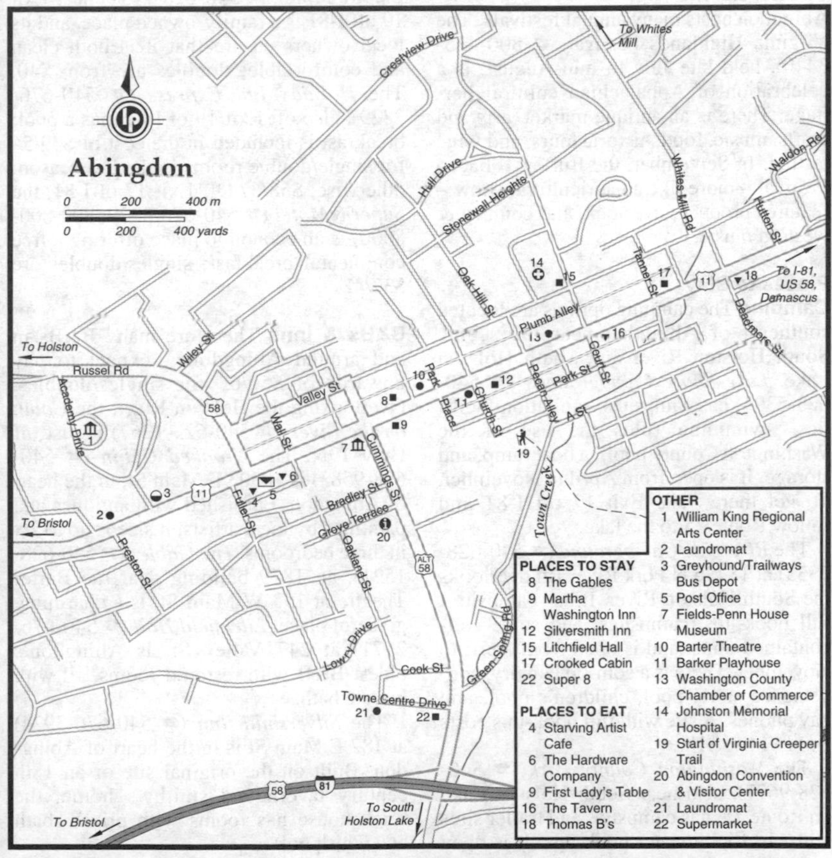

from 10 am to 9 pm, Saturday 10 am to 3 pm, and Sunday 1 to 5 pm; admission is free. In 1996 they had an exhibition of the works of Winslow Homer, Andrew Wyeth, and NC Wyeth.

At 12291 Whites Mill Rd, nestled in the Appalachians 3.5 miles north of Abingdon, is **Whites Mill** (☎ 540-676-0285). Dating from the 1790s, it is the only water-powered grist and flour mill still in operation in the southwest. The mill is open daily year round from 10 am to 5 pm; entry is $2. The nearby general store (1866) sells a range of products.

Special Events

Abingdon hosts many annual festivals. The Virginia Highlands Festival (☎ 800-435-3440), held late July to mid-August, is a celebration of Appalachian cultural heritage. There is an antique market, arts and crafts, music, food, historic tours, and wine tasting. In September, the Burley Tobacco Festival – more like an agricultural show – features produce, livestock, and country & western music.

Places to Stay

Camping The camping options are located southeast of Abingdon near the scenic South Holston River and South Holston Lake. *Lake Shore Campgrounds* (☎ 540-628-5394) has campsites, sanitation facilities, swimming (plus the use of the Washington County pool), a boat ramp, and storage. It is open from April to November. To get there, take Exit 17 off I-81 and follow Route 75 to the lake.

The *Riverside Campground* (☎ 540-628-5333) at 18496 N Fork River Rd overlooks the South Holston River. It has campsites, full hook-ups, campsites, and some self-contained units, and is open from April to November. There is a coin-op laundry, convenience store, pool, children's pool, and pay phones. A site with full hook-ups costs from $14 to $18.

The *Washington County Park* (☎ 540-628-9677), also near South Holston Lake on Route 75, has campsites and trailer sites with electricity/water hook-ups. It is open April to November and sites cost $9, hook-ups from $14.

Hotels & Motels The *Alpine Motel* (☎ 540-628-3178) at 882 E Main St off Exit 19 on I-81 is a small, clean place with nonsmoking rooms and handicapped facilities. In this economical place, popular with families, doubles are $40 in the low season; otherwise, $45. The *Comfort Inn* (☎ 540-676-2222, 800-221-2222) near Exit 14 on I-81 has a heated pool, and continental breakfast is included in the tariff; singles/doubles are $45/60 from Sunday to Thursday, $55/72 on Friday and Saturday. The *Empire Motel* (☎ 540-628-7131) near Exit 19 off I-81 is a family-owned place, and its local owners ensure that it is both clean and comfortable; doubles are from $40. The *Holiday Inn Express* (☎ 540-676-2829), also off Exit 19 of I-81, has a pool; breakfast is included in the cost of $49/54 for single/double rooms in the low season; otherwise, $58/67.Off Exit 17 of I-81, the *Super 8 Motel* (☎ 540-676-3329, 800-800-8000) is an economic place offering a free continental breakfast; singles/doubles are $37/42.

B&Bs & Inns There are many B&Bs in and around Abingdon – expect to pay upwards of $50/65 for singles/doubles. Overlooking the Holston River, the *Cabin on the River* (☎ 540-623-1267) is just off Hwy 19N. The *Crooked Cabin* (☎ 540-628-9583) is at 303 E Main St, in the heart of Abingdon. Furnished with antiques and paintings by local artists, it sleeps up to six in three bedrooms. *The Gables* (☎ 540-628-1521), an 1879 building near the Barter Theatre at 153 W Main St, is a charming, graceful place. *Litchfield Hall* (☎ 540-676-2971) at 247 Valley St, is Abingdon's oldest B&B with restored rooms, all with private bath.

The *Silversmith Inn* (☎ 540-676-3924) at 182 E Main St is in the heart of Abingdon. Built on the original site of an 18th century tavern and smithy's home, the brick house has rooms with private bath and whirlpool.

River Garden (☎ 540-676-0335, 800-952-4296) at 19080 N Fork River Rd is an idyllic place in the foothills of the Clinch Mountains. The private rooms have decks overlooking the Holston River rapids. On the other side of Abingdon, overlooking South Holston Lake at 22131 Sandcastle Rd, are the *Watchtower Cottages* (☎ 540-628-4900). All six cottages, which sleep six, have dishwashers, central heating, air-conditioning, and bathrooms.

The pinnacle of accommodations in Abingdon – and probably in southwest Virginia – is the *Martha Washington Inn* (☎ 540-628-3161, 800-555-8000) at 150 W Main St. This elegantly furnished inn, dating from 1832, is handicapped-accessible. Rooms are expensive (from a rack rate of $135 for a standard to $275 for a premier suite, $270 to $425 for two-bedroom suites), but after a delightful afternoon tea on the porch of the inn it might all seem worth it.

Places to Eat

It's not Alice's, but at *Alison's Restaurant* (☎ 540-628-8002) at 1220 W Main St you can 'get *almost* anything you want.' Known for its ribs, gourmet salads, steaks, and fajitas, it is open daily from 11 am to 9 pm. For a hearty breakfast, try the *Biscuit Connection* (☎ 540-676-2433) at 789 W Main St. Their big biscuits, and big breakfast to match, are served Monday to Friday from 6 am to 3 pm, Saturday from 6 am to 10:30 pm. *Bella's* (☎ 540-628-8101) on Rural Route 8 near Exit 19 off I-81 is open daily from 11 am to 10 pm for the best pizza and subs in town for the price. The *Chick-N-Little Restaurant* (☎ 540-628-1966) at 401 W Main St is a family-owned place; country breakfasts are served anytime.

A favorite is the *Starving Artist Cafe* (☎ 540-628-8445) at 134 Wall St (Depot Square) – you know, 'eat your 'art out.' They have gourmet sandwiches and tasty entrees for lunch and dinner. There is always a selection of the work of local artists on display and outdoor dining in season; the cafe is open Monday from 11 am to 2 pm (lunch only), Tuesday to Saturday from 11 am to 3 pm and from 5 to 9 pm.

The *Harbor House* (☎ 540-676-3500), near Exit 19 off I-81, serves old-fashioned steak, seafood, and chicken dishes (as well as kid's meals) daily at lunchtime from 11 am to 3 pm; dinner is served from 3 to around 10 pm. *Thomas B's* (☎ 540-628-4111), at 414 E Main St, mixes bayou cooking and other traditional tastes. It is open daily for lunch and dinner. *The Tavern* (☎ 540-628-1118) at 222 E Main St is in Abingdon's oldest building (1779). It has been faithfully restored and is open daily for lunch from 11 am to 2 pm and for dinner from 5 to 10:30 pm. Reuben sandwiches and tavern burgers are $6, jambalaya $16, chicken with broccoli $15, and American trout in herb butter with jalapeño/cilantro mayonnaise goes for $14.

Probably the most popular place to meet is the *Hardware Company* (☎ 540-628-1111) on W Main St in the center of town; it stays open late seven days, when the rest of the town is dead quiet, and has a good selection of food (entrees are about $11).

For those who like to mix live entertainment with traditional, hot Mexican cuisine there is *Martin's Taqueria* (☎ 540-623-1520) at 909 W Main St; this popular bar is open nightly until 10 or 11 pm.

The most elegant place in town is the *First Lady's Table at Camberley's Martha Washington Inn* (☎ 540-628-3161, 800-533-1014) at 150 W Main St across the road from the Barter Theatre. Lunch is served from 11 am to 4 pm, dinner from 5 to 10 pm (Sunday brunch from 11 am to 3 pm, dinner from 5 to 9 pm); reservations are needed.

Getting There & Away

Most people arrive here in their own cars. The closest airport is the Tri-Cities Airport, in Tennessee, serving Bristol, Johnson City, and Kingsport.

Greyhound/Trailways has a depot at 465 W Main St with service to Nashville and Washington DC. There is no passenger train.

BRISTOL

This large town is divided through its center (along State and Goodson Sts, the town's main thoroughfares) by the Tennessee-Virginia border. In Virginia the area code is 540 and in Tennessee it is 423 or 615. There is a Virginia Welcome Center (☎ 540-466-2932) at 66 Island Rd (near I-81 at the Tennessee border). The Bristol Convention and Visitors Bureau (☎ 615-989-4850) is at 20 Volunteer Parkway.

On State St you will find the **Paramount Center** (☎ 615-989-4850), a restored Art Deco movie house listed on the National Register of Historic Places. It is open daily and there are tours available. The **Bristol International Raceway** (☎ 423-764-1161), a half-mile racetrack south on Hwy 11E, hosts two races in the NASCAR series.

Entertainment here is likely to be in the form of 'country.' The **Carter Family Fold** (☎ 540-386-9480) has country music concerts every Saturday in Maces Spring just to the north of Hiltons. The barn where the 'electronic-free' performances are held is approximately 20 miles west of Bristol (five miles east of Weber City) off Hwy 58/421 on County Rd 614. The doors open at 6 pm and the concert is from 7:30 to 10:30 pm; admission is $3.50 for adults, $1 for children under 12.

NATURAL TUNNEL STATE PARK

This park is based around an 850-foot-long limestone tunnel, believed to have been formed in the dolostone bedrock one million years ago. There is a picnic area, pool, campground, and hiking trails. A chairlift ($2 per person roundtrip) rises to an overlook from which you get great views of the natural tunnel. Travel through the tunnel is prohibited because of railroad safety regulations.

The park (☎ 540-940-2674) is open daily from 8 am to dusk, and the cable car operates from 10 am to 5 pm. To get there from Duffield, take Hwy 23 south until County Rd 871; it is one mile from the turnoff. In nearby Duffield, the *Ramada Inn-Duffield* (☎ 540-431-4300, 800-228-2828) at Hwys 58 and 23 has a restaurant, bar, and pool; standard singles/doubles are $71/81.

CUMBERLAND GAP NATIONAL HISTORICAL PARK

The Cumberland Gap, a significant break in the Appalachian mountain chain carved by wind and water, is right at the point where Virginia, Tennessee, and Kentucky meet (Virginia's Lee County). It was first crossed by large animals in their major migrations, and later by Native Americans following hunting trails. When the interior was first settled in the late 1700s, some 200,000 pioneers crossed the Gap into 'Kentucke' and beyond. It is still a major thoroughfare.

The national historical park headquarters and visitors center (☎ 606-248-2817) is on Hwy 25E (PO Box 1848, in Middlesboro, KY 40965). The visitor center is open daily mid-June to Labor Day from 8 am to 6 pm, otherwise 8 am to 5 pm; there is no admission fee to the park. There is also a bookstore and museum attached to the visitors center.

There are 70 miles of hiking trails, from a 0.25-mile looped trail to the 21-mile Ridge Trail along the Cumberland Mountains, and mountain biking is permitted in some places. You can camp at the *Wild Road Campground* where there are 170 primitive sites (hot showers within short hiking distance), open year round, which are $10 per site. There are *backcountry campsites* at Gibson Gap, White Rocks, Chadwell Gap, and Martins Fork, for which you require a use permit, available from the visitors center.

Visitors traveling south on I-81 should take the exit onto Hwy 25E at White Pine/Morristown, Tennessee. If traveling on Hwy 23, take the Duffield exit to Hwy 58, which heads to the Cumberland Gap.

BIG STONE GAP

The main attraction in Big Stone Gap (population 5000) is the rugged beauty of the place. Visitors deviating to this far-flung neck o' the woods for a real feel of the

Appalachians won't be disappointed. And for the coal miners' daughters and sons among us, the 'anthracite, lignite, and bituminous' have an irresistible, magnetic power. But choose your weather well as coalfields take on a dismal appearance in the mist and rain.

The tourist center (☎ 540-523-2060) is in the historical 1870 Interstate Railroad car (No 101) on Hwy 23 Business, near the bridge across the Powell River's south fork. It is open Memorial Day to Labor Day, Monday to Wednesday from 10 am to 5 pm, Thursday to Saturday 10 am to 8 pm, Sunday noon to 4 pm; otherwise, weekdays from 9 am to 5 pm.

If you have ventured out here, you will have probably heard of the 20th century novel (and movie) *The Trail of the Lonesome Pine* by John Fox, Jr. Every year, from late June to early September, Thursday to Saturday from 8:15 pm, an **outdoor musical drama** with the same title as the novel is enacted by local performers at the June Tolliver Playhouse (☎ 540-523-1235). The drama depicts the drastic changes in mountain life that followed the Virginia coal boom; otherwise, it is very much a 'local gal meets worldly guy' tale. Admission is $8 for adults, $6 for seniors, and $5 for children. Also on the premises is the historic 1880s **June Tolliver House**, open at intermission during the theater season to sell local crafts, otherwise June to mid-December, Tuesday to Sunday; admission is free.

There are three museums near Big Stone Gap that should be visited if you have made it up this far. The **Southwest Virginia Museum** (☎ 540-523-1322) is housed in a Victorian mansion dating from the coal boom of the 1890s. There are many artifacts and exhibits that relate to the history and culture of southwest Virginia, including furnishings from the mine manager's home. The museum, at the corner of W First St and Wood Ave (just off Alt Route 58), is open daily, March to December, from 9 am to 5 pm; from Memorial Day to Labor Day it is closed on Monday. Admission is $3 for adults and $1.25 for children.

The brown cedar-shingled **John Fox Jr Museum** (☎ 540-523-2747) at 117 Shawnee Ave was the home of the author and is still furnished as it was when the Fox family lived there in the late 19th century. It is open Memorial Day to Labor Day, Tuesday and Wednesday from 2 to 5 pm, Thursday to Sunday from 2 to 6 pm; admission is $3 for adults, $1 for children.

The **Harry Meador Coal Museum** (☎ 540-523-4905) at 505 E 3rd St houses a variety of items that illustrate coal mining, past and present. Especially interesting are the many old photographs. It is open year round, Wednesday to Saturday from 10 am to 5 pm, Sunday 1 to 5 pm; admission is free.

Places to Stay & Eat

The closest *campground* is at Cave Springs Recreation Area, 2.5 miles west on Hwy 58 then six miles south on County Rd 621. It is open from mid-May to mid-October; sites are $8.

The *Country Inn* (☎ 540-523-0374), has singles/doubles for $29/34 and an adjoining camping area. For a hearty country buffet, go to *Stringers' Family Restaurant* (☎ 540-523-5388) at 414 E 5th St. There is an old-fashioned drugstore and cafeteria, *Mutual Drug* (☎ 540-523-1123), on Wood Ave.

NORTON

The city of Norton lies in the center of Wise County, which adjoins the Kentucky border. On Saturday night, 51 weeks of the year (except the second week in September), Appalachian Traditions (☎ 540-523-0891) opens their **country cabin** from 7:30 to 11 pm for performances of traditional and bluegrass music, cakewalks, and brooms dancing. For more information, contact the Wise County Chamber of Commerce (☎ 540-679-0961).

The *Super 8 Motel* (☎ 800-800-8000) at 425 Wharton Way just off Route 58E has queen-sized rooms for one/two people for $43/49. The *Holiday Inn* (☎ 540-679-7000) is on Route 58E; a standard room with two double beds is $73.

BREAKS INTERSTATE PARK

The Breaks is a 4600-acre scenic and recreational park, with a five-mile, 1600-foot-deep gorge, the 'Grand Canyon of the South,' as its centerpiece. Here the Russell Fork River, a tributary of the Big Sandy River, has carved the deepest canyon east of the Mississippi. At one point the river winds around the 1660-foot Towers, a magnificent pyramid of Paleozoic rocks over 250 million years old.

Whitewater rafting and kayaking are popular on the Russell Fork, and the best times for these activities depend on when water is released from the John Flannagan Dam. The Catawba rhododendron is in bloom in mid-May and the rare yellow lady's slipper blooms in early April. There is also scope for fishing, hiking on nature trails, and horseback riding.

The visitors center (☎ 540-865-4413) has exhibits and displays of the natural and historical features of the area. The camping area (122 sites) is open April to October and sites are $7; electricity, water, and sewerage is $1 extra for each service. The park is located not far from where Hwy 460 crosses the Kentucky border. Turn off onto Route 80.

TAZEWELL COUNTY

Near the county seat of Tazewell (once called Jeffersonville) is the **Crab Orchard Museum & Pioneer Park** (☎ 540-988-6755), which depicts the history of the county from prehistoric times to the present. It includes eleven log and two stone structures and a display of horse-drawn equipment.

The museum and park, southwest of Tazewell on Hwy 19/460, are open Monday to Saturday from 9 am to 5 pm, Sunday from 1 to 5 pm (November to March it is closed on Sunday). Admission for adults is $5, seniors $4 and children (13 to 18) $2. To get to Tazewell from I-81, turn off at Marion, near the Mount Rogers NRA, onto Route 16N.

Burkes Garden, northeast of Tazewell on County Rd 623, is 50 sq miles of sylvan farmland encircled by a continuous mountain range with the Appalachian Trail at its edge. It is sometimes referred to as 'God's thumbprint.' Popular myth has it that Cornelius Vanderbilt wanted the 'garden' on which to build an estate (instead, he built the famous Biltmore estate in Asheville, NC), but the proud locals refused to sell him the land. A Fall Festival with produce, arts, and crafts, sponsored by the Burkes Garden Community Association (☎ 540-963-3385), is held here in September.

APPALACHIAN TRAIL

The Appalachian Trail has assumed legendary status among hardy hikers, and those that complete its 2159-mile length (about 150 people each year out of about 1500 that set out) have reason to feel satisfied. Some people mistakenly assume that the trail is an old one, used for centuries by Native Americans and explorers. Certainly parts of it were, but it was really the idea of a Massachusetts regional planner, Benton MacKaye, in 1921, to preserve the Appalachian crests as an accessible, multipurpose wilderness belt, that led to its inception. It was designed, constructed, and marked by volunteer hiking clubs, formed together by the Appalachian Trail Conference, in the 1920s and 1930s.

The trail runs from Katahdin, Maine, to Springer Mountain, Georgia, and about one quarter of its length, some 544 miles, is in Virginia. The direction of the trail through Virginia is southwest-northeast, but it zigzags across I-81 in a number of places. It passes through 14 states, eight national forests, and two national parks, and crosses 15 major rivers. The lowest point is near sea level at the Hudson River in New York, and the highest is the 6642-foot Clingman's Dome in the Great Smokies.

The Virginia section starts at Harpers Ferry, West Virginia, and follows the state border in a southwesterly direction to Bluemount and then to Shenandoah National Park, where it adjoins Skyline Drive. (About 100 miles of the trail pass through Shenandoah National Park, and it crosses Skyline Drive 32 times.) South of Waynesboro, the trail roughly parallels the Blue

Ridge Parkway, passing through George Washington and Jefferson national forests. North of Roanoke, it strikes west across I-81 to Jefferson National Forest then southwest to just south of Tazewell. Here it heads southeast, again across I-81 into the Mount Rogers NRA (where the highest point on the trail in Virginia is the summit of Mount Rogers at 5729 feet) and emerges at Damascus, where it crosses the Tennessee border. At **Damascus**, Trail Days are celebrated every May; contact the Damascus town hall (☎ 540-475-3831) for information.

Information

For general trail information, contact The Appalachian Trail Conference (☎ 304-535-6331), PO Box 807, Harpers Ferry, WV 25425; or the Appalachian National Scenic Trail (☎ 304-535-6278), Harpers Ferry Center, PO Box 50, Harpers Ferry, WV, 25425. The ATC distributes and publishes guidebooks and maps covering every section of the trail, as well as the *Appalachian Trailway News.*

The Potomac Appalachian Trail Club (PATC), 118 Park St SE, Vienna, VA 22180 (☎ 703-242-0315, fax 703-242-0968) sells a great range of books and maps ($3.50 to $5) of the Appalachian Trail and also publishes the *Potomac Appalachian* newsletter. A good book is the *Appalachian Trail: Guide Book 7 – Shenandoah National Park and Side Trails* ($9). One sound reference is Frank and Victoria Logue's *The Appalachian Trail: Backpacker's Planning Guide* ($10.95), which covers all aspects of hiking the Appalachian Trail.

The Roanoke Appalachian Trail Club (RATC), PO Box 12282, Roanoke, VA 24024, maintains 113 miles of the trail. Its friendly, enthusiastic members are always willing to take out-of-towners on hikes.

The trail is marked with 2- by 4-inch vertical white paint blazes; a double blaze indicates that a junction or turn is coming up. Blue blazes mark side trails to shelters and water supplies. In Virginia, a permit is required only if you wish to camp in the Shenandoah National Park.

Places to Stay & Eat

Appalachian Trail hikers can use a number of primitive, open three-sided shelters with stone fireplaces. Placed at approximate day-walk intervals, these shelters are reserved for hikers with three or more nights in different locations stamped in their permits ($1 per night) and are not for casual campers. In the Shenandoah National Park, the following are maintained by the PATC: Gravel Springs (Mile 17.6), Pass Mountain (Mile 31.6), Rock Spring (Mile 48.1), Bearfence (Mile 56.8), Hightop (Mile 68.6), Pinefield (Mile 75.2), and Blackrock (Mile 87.2). The PATC has six fully enclosed cabins in backcountry areas of Shenandoah National Park (see Shenandoah Valley & Ranges chapter).

You should be carrying your own food, eh? There are plenty of towns in Virginia, close to the trail, where you can get a meal if you have tired of 'dehy,' soups, and gorp.

Maryland

Facts about Maryland

For more than three centuries the traditions of English gentry and the independent Bay watermen have governed life here. And while only 20% of Marylanders live the traditional lifestyles of rural gentry, farmers, or watermen, these traditional lifestyles persist in the dreams of Marylanders. They own more thoroughbred horses per capita than people in any other state, and they testify to their romance with the Chesapeake Bay blue crab and the watermen's skipjack by cloning these icons on everything from cocktail napkins to semi-trailers. Their farms, manors, townhouses, public buildings, railroads, and boats – like the oystermen's skipjacks – express those traditions and dreams. Now, nearly obsessed with their heritage, Marylanders have launched into historic preservation of everything from duck decoys to

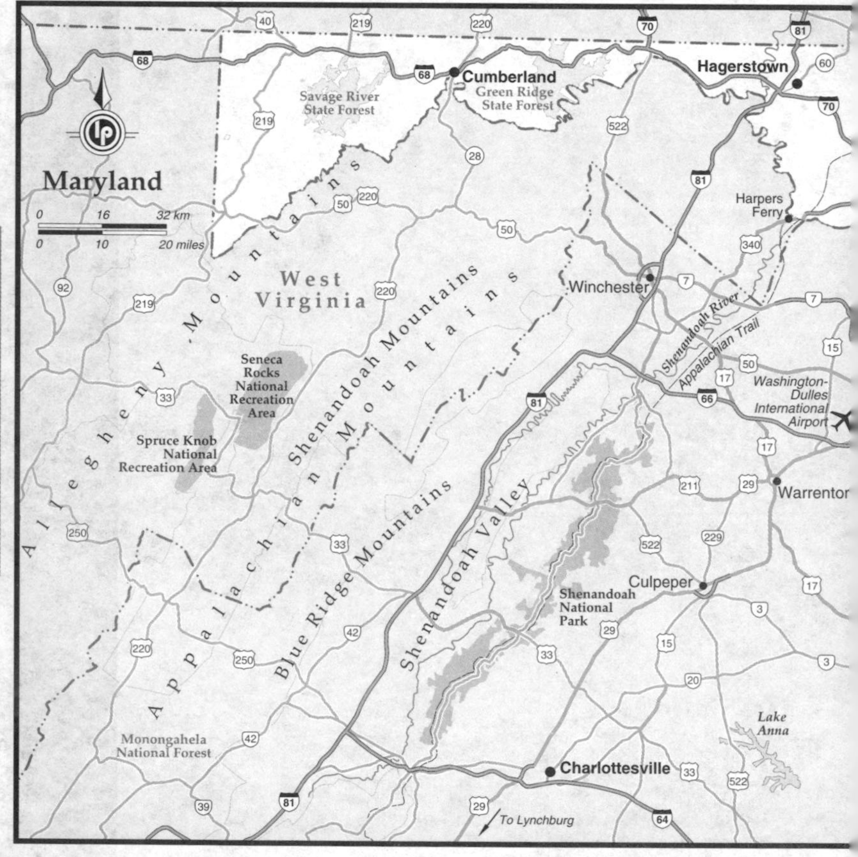

railway locomotives, cannonballs to tall ships and skipjacks. Down to just eight working boats a couple years ago, Maryland's famous fleet of skipjacks, graceful oystering sloops designed 100 years ago, has increased to 13.

The Chesapeake Bay Appreciation Day skipjack races at Sandy Point State Park, the living history interpreters at colonial St Mary's City, and the rebricking of the sidewalks in the historic districts of Annapolis, Chestertown, and Easton are just a few of the more obvious signs of Maryland's preoccupation with its past. Responding to this nostalgia, the number of bed & breakfasts has exploded over the last 10 years to the point where a traveler can tour the state for two weeks, staying in nothing but haunted houses. Today, travelers will find it easy to join an oysterman or crabber on the Bay, or mingle with the high society at horsy affairs like the Marlborough Hunt Races. Best of all, Baltimore, once a seedy industrial port, has emerged as a major cultural center. The city's Inner Harbor has become a tourist destination with more waterfront access and attractions than you can find in Boston, San Francisco, or Miami. For

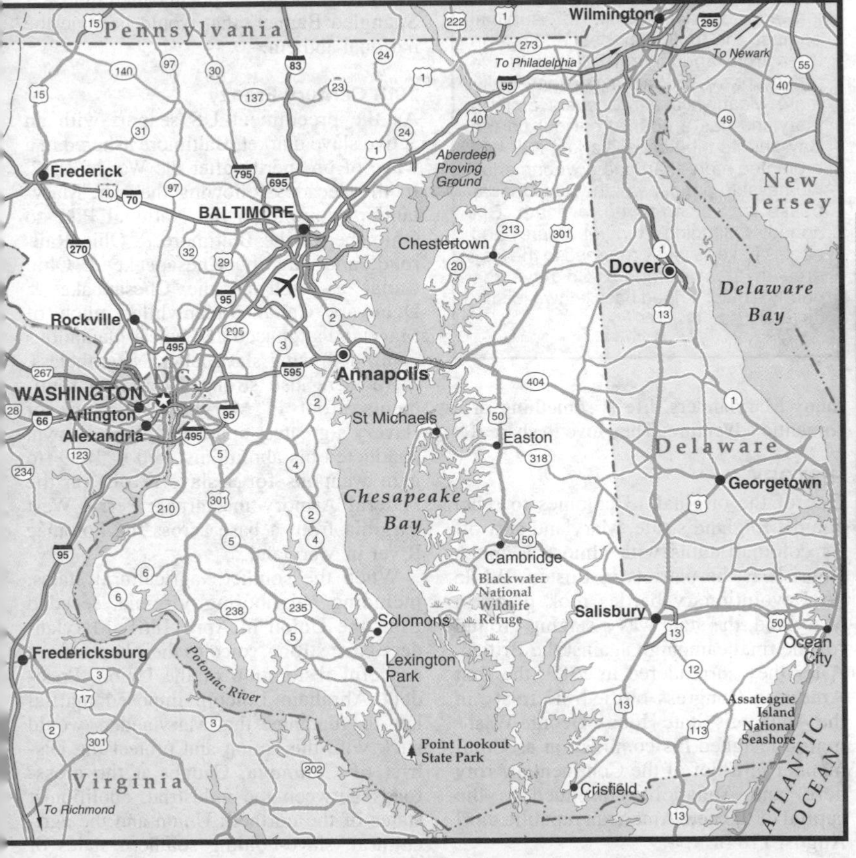

Chesapeake: Loved to Death?

When Marylanders gather to entertain each other with tall tales, a listener will hear stories asserting that in this part of the world people can hardly eat, work, travel, play, worship, or kiss a crab without acknowledging the Bay. Almost 200 miles long and five to 30 miles wide, Chesapeake Bay is the country's largest estuary.

Exploring the Chesapeake and its shores in 1608, Captain John Smith judged, 'Heaven and earth never agreed better to frame a place more perfect for man's habitation.' These days, Smith's remarks ring with irony. Oysters, crabs, and geese of the Chesapeake are fighting an uncertain battle for survival against the pollution descending on them from agricultural runoff and the urban sprawl of Washington and Baltimore. Meanwhile, almost every family in Maryland has a boat to get out on the Bay and its tributaries – a fact that has prompted more than one environmental journalist to ponder whether the Chesapeake isn't being loved to death. But nobody's planning a funeral. Osprey and eagles have recently returned to the Bay area in great numbers. So have the nearly extinct striped bass known locally as 'rock fish.' ■

many Marylanders, life is something of a romantic adventure. They love to share it.

HISTORY

One of the original 13 colonies to rebel against England's rule, Maryland cast off its colonial status with almost as much flourish as the patriots in Boston. While no Revolutionary battles took place in Maryland, the state was a staging ground for the final campaign against the British. After they surrendered in 1783, the first American Congress ratified the treaty in the Annapolis State House. George Washington resigned his commission as Commander in Chief of the Continental Army here, and Annapolis continued as the capital of the new American republic until August 1784.

When a new war with England started in 1812, the British fleet sailed up the Chesapeake Bay, attacking Maryland ports and burning the town of Havre de Grace. In 1814 British troops drove overland from the Patuxent River to burn Washington, DC. That same year the British fleet tried to bring an end to the American fleet of privateers by attacking its base in Baltimore. On the morning of September 14, the tattered remnants of the 30-by-42-foot US flag emerged from the mist and gun smoke over Fort McHenry, thus showing that Americans had repelled the British assault. The event inspired a Maryland lawyer, Francis Scott Key, to write a poem called the 'Star Spangled Banner' that would become the national anthem.

19th Century Frenzy

As the preeminent US seaport with an active slave market, Baltimore ushered in a wave of prosperity after the War of 1812. In the decades following the war, Marylanders completed the National Pike to Ohio, began the Baltimore & Ohio Railroad, and dug the Chesapeake & Ohio Canal as well as the Chesapeake & Delaware Canal. Meanwhile, much of Maryland's tobacco and wheat plantations continued using slave labor. Nevertheless, there were also strong abolitionist sentiments afoot in Maryland, and one of slavery's greatest opponents, John Brown, conducted his abolitionist raid in 1859 (to gain weapons for a slave revolt) on the Federal Armory in Harpers Ferry, West Virginia from a base across the Potomac River in Maryland.

When the southern agricultural states, including neighboring Virginia, seceded from the Union in April 1861, Marylanders gave strong voice to their hopes for a peaceful restoration of the Union. President Abraham Lincoln imposed martial law to guarantee that Marylanders would stick with the Union and protect the District of Columbia. Caught at the crossroads between the industrial, abolitionist states of the northern Union and the agricultural, slave-holding southern states of

John Wilkes Booth, Maryland's Most Infamous Native Son

The man who shot President Abraham Lincoln captured America's imagination with nearly as much vigor as Lincoln himself. Born in 1838 at Bel Air, north of Baltimore, Booth was the son of a respected English actor and seemed destined for celebrity status. As a young man he distinguished himself as an exceptionally talented Shakespearean actor. By the time he was 25 he may have been the most famous actor on the American stage (judged by critics of the time as superior to his brother Edwin who was later considered America's most gifted Shakespearean).

But theatrical fame was not enough for Booth; he became a violent partisan of the South during the Civil War and once organized an unsuccessful conspiracy to abduct President Lincoln. The actor's boldness led him to make the fateful leap (in which he broke his leg) onto the stage at Ford's Theater to take a bow after shooting the President. After the murder Booth spent 12 days trying to attend to his broken leg, hide, and escape through Southern Maryland. He died in Bowling Green, Virginia, of gunshot wounds (possibly self-inflicted) in a barn.

The assassination of Lincoln remains one of the most famous celebrity murder cases in US history. Handsome, charming, and talented, but egocentric and racist, Booth persists as an icon for the consummate American villain.

How to Relive It Flocks of people visit the Surratt House Museum (☎ 301-868-1121) in Clinton (just southeast of DC) and other sites that mark the steps on Booth's path as he attempted to escape punishment for the assassination.

On two Saturdays in the spring and again in the fall, the Surratt Society (named after Mary Surratt who was hung as an accomplice to Booth) sponsors bus trips called the 'John Wilkes Booth Escape Tour,' which spend 12 hours visiting the sites on Booth's flight to Bowling Green, Virginia. ■

the new Confederacy, Maryland became a battleground for the Civil War. The armies of the North and South clashed at Antietam (Sharpsburg). After the smoke cleared, 23,000 soldiers lay dead or wounded, making September 17, 1862, 'the bloodiest day in American history.' When it was over, the North had driven General Robert E Lee's Confederate army back across the Potomac. (See the section on the Civil War in Virginia.)

Lee did not return to Maryland for another year; this time the Union stopped him in another bloodbath outside a village just across the Pennsylvania-Maryland border – Gettysburg. In 1864, Marylanders voted to abolish slavery, several months before the US Congress did the same with the 13th Amendment. The Confederates surrendered on April 9, 1865, but one last scene in the tragedy remained. Five days after the Civil War ended, the respected Maryland actor and Confederate sympathizer John Wilkes Booth shot and killed President Abraham Lincoln. His flight through Maryland to Bowling Green, Virginia, left a trail of accomplices. After the assassination Lincoln's body passed through Maryland on its way back to his home state of Illinois for burial; the train followed the same route the President had traveled to deliver his famous Gettysburg Address.

Riding the Industrial Revolution

Maryland's history after the Civil War is the story of Baltimore's industrialization, waves of immigrant workers from central and southern Europe, and the struggles of African Americans to achieve the status of full citizenship. Because of Baltimore's good highway and railway links to Ohio and the states west of the Appalachian Mountains, the city boomed as a shipping and manufacturing port well into the 20th century. As the westward expansion of American civilization demanded everything from farm fertilizer and steel to spices and refined petroleum products, Baltimore found ways to import or make them. Over the years, enormous factories, like the

Harriet Tubman & the Underground Railroad

Harriet Tubman (c1820–1913) was an abolitionist and former slave who became famous before the Civil War because of her role in the Underground Railroad, which helped slaves escape from the South to the North and Canada.

Escaped slaves in pre-Civil War America were liable to recapture and return to bondage under the federal Fugitive Slave Act of 1793, which was strengthened by the Fugitive Slave Law of 1850. In practice, this meant that under federal law former slaves could be captured in the non-slave North and chained and dragged back to bondage in the South. In opposition to slavery and to fugitive slave laws, some people sought to help slaves to freedom.

One way to free slaves was through the Underground Railroad, which was neither underground nor a railroad. It was 'underground' in the sense of being secret and was a 'railroad' because its members used railroad code words to describe what they did. Routes were 'lines,' stops were 'stations,' guides were 'conductors,' and the fugitives were 'packages' or 'freight.'

The Railroad was a loosely organized network of people including Quakers, Presbyterians, Congregationalists, and, most importantly, free blacks. It was the slaves themselves who often accomplished the most difficult part of the journey from South to North by escaping and then heading north where they were met by Northerners who helped them hide and escape. The most active 'conductors' were northern free blacks and of these Harriet Tubman was the most famous.

Tubman was born in Bucktown, near Cambridge on Maryland's Eastern Shore. As a teenager she was beaten with an iron weight by a brutal overseer and suffered blackouts throughout her life because of it. She escaped in 1849 leaving behind her parents, siblings, and husband. She returned to the south 19 times to lead over 300 slaves, including her parents, to freedom.

Tubman traveled with a pistol and faith in God and said: 'I always told God, I'm going to hold steady onto you, and you've got to see me through.' Her pistol was used to defend the slaves as well as to persuade those who wanted to back out into continuing the journey. At the height of her career as a conductor, Tubman had a $40,000 bounty on her head. She was a friend to abolitionists across the country and helped John Brown plan his raid on Harpers Ferry, West Virginia. Brown called her 'one of the best and bravest persons on this continent – General Tubman as we call her.'

During the Civil War, Tubman worked as a nurse, scout, and spy for the Union Army along the coast of South Carolina. She traveled through enemy territory unnoticed and collected information on the location of cotton warehouses, ammunition depots, and slaves. Tubman was paid only $200 for her work over three years and had to support herself by selling pies, gingerbread, and root beer.

After the war, Tubman settled in Auburn, New York, and helped African Americans there. She made her house into a Home for Indigent and Aged Negroes and financed it by selling copies of her autobiography and giving speeches. She was buried with full military honors on March 10, 1913, and is remembered for her words: 'My people must go free.' ■

Sparrows Point steel mills and oil refineries, grew up along the banks of the Patapsco River. These industries and others created employment for Italian, German, Polish, and Jewish immigrants as well as African Americans fleeing lives as sharecroppers in rural Maryland and the deep South.

Most immigrant groups assimilated into Maryland life through their shared European background and/or Roman Catholic faith. The story was different for blacks: 'Jim Crow' segregation laws kept African Americans as second-class citizens until the 1960s, and racial prejudice went unquestioned among the vast majority of the white population. Perhaps in response, some of the strongest black voices to precipitate social justice in America came from Maryland: in the 19th century abolitionists Harriet Tubman and Frederick Douglass, in the 20th century musical geniuses Eubie Blake and Billie Holiday as well as the first black justice of the Supreme Court, Thurgood Marshall.

ECONOMY

Today, Maryland remains a divided state, not by race or class, not even by the Chesapeake Bay, but by lifestyle. More than half of all Marylanders work in service jobs or manufacturing, which has changed its focus from heavy industries like steel to electronics and communications. Almost 25% of all Marylanders work for the federal or state government, adding over $9 billion to the economy – nearly twice that of manufacturing. Nearly all of these people live in Baltimore or the suburbs between Baltimore, Washington, and Annapolis.

The largest and most valuable estuary in the United States, The Chesapeake Bay produces more food crabs than anywhere else on earth, one quarter of the US oyster harvest, and one half of the country's soft-shell clams.

GEOGRAPHY

About the size of the Netherlands, Maryland is 42nd in land mass among the United States, covering about 10,000 sq miles.

Its odd shape, like a hand grasping the Chesapeake, with the wrist extending into western Maryland, came from a series of border disputes with neighboring colonies. Maryland's northern border is the famous Mason-Dixon Line that has traditionally (and somewhat erroneously) divided the northern industrial colonies from the southern agrarian ones. At its broadest, Maryland extends 250 miles east-west and 90 miles north-south. The state rises from sea level in the east to 3360-foot Backbone Mountain in the west.

Three major topographical regions of the eastern United States exist in Maryland – the Atlantic Coastal Plain, Piedmont Plateau, and Appalachian Region. The bulk of the state lies in the coastal plain, which, along with coastal Virginia is often referred to as the 'Tidewater' area, encompassing all of the land on the Eastern Shore and a lot on the Western Shore of the Chesapeake. English colonists began settling Tidewater Maryland in 1633 where they set up tobacco plantations.

West of the Tidewater is the Piedmont Plateau, an area of low hills and valleys stretching for about 50 miles. The 'fall line,' an area where the land descends 100 feet in several miles, marks the eastern edge of the Piedmont. Here rivers become unnavigable because of waterfalls and rapids. The Piedmont attracted the first non-English settlers – mostly Scotch-Irish and Palatine German. This foothill region remains largely an area of rich farmland, producing corn, soybeans, and hay.

Western Maryland is in the Appalachian Plateau, Ridge, and Valley. Here lie Maryland's share of the Allegheny Mountains and its highest peak. The western portion is the most mountainous, especially near the Pennsylvania border. A 10-mile-wide strip of the Blue Ridge Mountains forms a border between the Appalachian Region and the Piedmont.

The state's soil makes for rich farmland in the Coastal Plain and Piedmont regions. The soil ranges from light sand loam on the Eastern shore to the clay loam of the Piedmont plateau. Silt and clay constitute the

Appalachian Valley. Limestone and sandstone form the soil base in the western Piedmont area.

Maryland has more miles of navigable rivers than any other state. Some of these, like the Savage and the Youghiogheny, offer superb white-water rafting, canoeing, and kayaking. Most of the western rivers drain into the Potomac River, which borders Virginia. Most of the eastern rivers drain into the Chesapeake Bay. Nearly 200 miles long, the Bay covers 8000 miles of shoreline, drains a watershed of 65,000 miles in six states, and claims 150 rivers and tributaries. Ninety percent of the Chesapeake freshwater flows from five rivers – the Susquehanna, Potomac, Rappahannock, York, and James.

POPULATION & PEOPLE

Maryland has nearly 5 million people, placing the state as the 19th most populous. The areas with the greatest concentrations of people are metropolitan Baltimore, and the suburbs surrounding Washington, DC, Annapolis, and Wilmington, Delaware.

A small number of Germans and Scotch-Irish came in the later 1600s, but the largest non-English European population boom – Poles, Russians, Czechs, Italians, etc – came with the 19th century industrialization and transportation revolutions. These people settled primarily in the industrial area around Baltimore. Today, Scotch-Irish and German are strong strains in western Maryland, and the central urban populations of the state are fairly homogenous. The people of the Eastern Shore remain largely of British and African descent, and many of the 7000 persons claiming Native American ancestry in the state also live in this area.

The current ethnic breakdown is white 71%, black 25%, Asian 2.9%, Hispanic 2.6%, and Native American 0.27%. About 95% were born in the US.

ARTS

New York may have its legions of musicians, California its cult of filmmakers, and Massachusetts its galleries of artists, but probably no state in the Union can compare with Maryland for the number of storytellers.

Literature

Maryland's contributions to American literature include the biography written by Reverend Josiah Jensen, a Maryland ex-slave, which inspired Harriet Beecher Stowe to write *Uncle Tom's Cabin*. Edgar Allen Poe wrote, married his 13-year-old cousin, drank himself to death, and got buried in Baltimore. America's most famous journalist, HL Mencken, was a lifelong Baltimorean.

Today, Maryland native and one of the world's most respected novelists, John Barth, author of *The End of the Road* and *The Sotweed Factor*, teaches at Johns Hopkins University, which boasts the most active university press in the US.

The Art of Maryland Folk Tales

Spend more than a few minutes conversing with a Marylander, and you are likely to hear some kind of homespun comical tale of misadventure. Comment to a Chesapeake waterman about the possibility of a thunder squall and a stiff breeze and you might hear him respond: 'Squall? Blow? Why, you ain't seen BLOW. One time down to Hooper Straits, I seen it blow so hard that it sunk five boats, drowned 18 men, and blowed a chicken clean into a bottle.'

Visit the town of Easton, on the Eastern Shore, during the annual fall waterfowl festival and you will find that Marylanders don't just express their folk tales in words. Hundreds of carved duck decoys, traditional boat models, quilts, and paintings depict stories of life and death on the Chesapeake. Folk songs abound throughout the state.

Maryland Folklore by George G Carey (Tidewater Press, 1989) is a compendium of the kinds of stories Marylanders love best. ■

Music

The African American sounds of Eubie Blake's jazz and Billie Holiday's blues have been some of Maryland's greatest contributions to the world of music, but musical expression is hardly limited to the realms of jazz and the blues. Today, native Marylander Mary Chapin Carpenter dazzles pop-country music fans, while classical music lovers find a feast in Maryland. Under the direction of David Zinman, the acclaimed Baltimore Symphony Orchestra performs at the Joseph Myerhoff Symphony Hall. The Annapolis Symphony Orchestra plays in Maryland Hall, Annapolis, and the Maryland Symphony plays in a restored vaudeville house, the Maryland Theater, in Hagerstown.

You can hear chamber music concerts by the National Chamber Orchestra at the F Scott Fitzgerald Theater in Rockville (where the author is buried. There is also chamber music at the University of Maryland in College Park as well as at Goucher College and Loyola University in metropolitan Baltimore. The distinguished Peabody Conservatory of Music at Mount Vernon Square in Baltimore attracts celebrated faculty, guest artists, and students for regular concerts.

Maryland boasts four opera companies and one of the world's greatest gospel ensembles, the predominantly African American Morgan State University Choir. Of course, summer brings a host of local, national, and international musicians to the state for outdoor concerts and music festivals.

Visual Arts

Around the shores of the Chesapeake Bay, a popular specialty handicraft is life-size wooden waterfowl carvings, an art that draws hundreds of collectors to craft festivals each year. And while decoy carving and the other folk arts thrive in rural Maryland, urban Maryland, particularly Baltimore, hosts the fine-arts community. Distinguished art museums like the Baltimore Museum of Art (BMA) and the Walters Art Gallery, along with dozens of other museums across Maryland, developed out of the state's tradition of cultured gentry and industrial fortunes. But the truth is that over the centuries few young artistic dreamers chose Maryland to inspire them and stretch their talents . . . until recently.

During the 1980s, Baltimore's Inner Harbor urban renewal project created a lot of job opportunities for artistic people caught up in the possibilities of redesigning and restoring the heart of a great American city. Many of these young artists and artisans bought derelict row houses in the slums surrounding the Inner Harbor and began restoring the old buildings as studios and galleries. For the last five years, more and more artists from the prestigious Maryland

Billie Holiday

Born Eleanora Holiday in 1915, the singer suffered a poverty-stricken youth in Baltimore's ghetto. But by the late 1920s she escaped the literal misery of her early life and began singing professionally in Harlem clubs. Holiday began recording in the 1930s and eventually became a 'diva,' singing with major orchestras led by figures like Artie Shaw and Count Basie as well as pianist Teddy Wilson and saxman Lester Young.

Holiday's career soared during the 1940s and '50s with hits like 'Lover Man,' 'I'll Look Around,' 'Easy Livin',' and 'God Bless the Child.' But her longtime addiction to heroin undercut later performances, and she died in a New York hospital in 1959 while under arrest for drug possession.

Her 1956 autobiography and the 1972 film called *Lady Sings the Blues* recount the rise and fall of so-called 'Lady Day,' America's best known blues vocalist.

If you want to listen to Billie on compact disc, pick up *Billie Holiday: Complete Decca Recordings 1944–1950* on MHS Jazz Heritage or *Smithsonian Collection of Classical Jazz – Volume II.* ■

Institute of Art and elsewhere have moved into the neighborhoods of Federal Hill and southwest Baltimore to reclaim the ghetto. Now, both neighborhoods have vital communities of working visual artists with annual 'studio days' and fine-arts festivals. The addition of a new modern art wing at the BMA in 1994 testifies to Maryland's growing passion for the fine arts.

Performing Arts

Long before the days when President Lincoln's nemesis John Wilkes Booth interpreted Shakespeare, Marylanders had been going to the theater in hordes. Today, the state boasts four opera companies and more than a dozen dance and theater troupes performing in new or elegantly restored theaters in every major city in the state. Touring Broadway shows play at the Baltimore Center for Performing Arts, but there is a lot more than mainstream theater in Maryland. The Baltimore Theater Project's avant-garde productions and the African American performances of Eva Anderson Dancers are just two of many examples of 'alternative' and ethnic live entertainment in Maryland.

Cinema

Maryland, specifically Baltimore, is currently experiencing a certain celebrity in the filmmaking world. In addition to being the setting for *The Accidental Tourist* and *The Seduction of Joe Tynan*, Baltimore is home to two of the film industry's most respected directors. John Waters' cult classics have introduced viewers to the actor Divine in the off-beat, funny *Pink Flamingos* and *Cry Baby*. Waters also gave us the box-office success *Hairspray*. Barry Levinson, of *Good Morning Vietnam*, *Rain Man*, and *Sleepers* fame, is another native son. He made *Avalon*, *Diner*, and *Tin Man* in Baltimore about life in Baltimore. Fells Point is the set for the weekly TV police drama *Homicide*. Oriole Park (Camden Yard) was a key setting in *Mayor League II* and *Dave*. *Home for the Holidays*, *Boys*, and *12 Monkeys* also have Baltimore sets.

INFORMATION

Area Codes

Maryland has two area codes: 410 and 301. In general 410 is in effect for the more populated areas.

Time

Maryland lies in the Eastern Time Zone of the United States. This is five hours behind GMT and the same as New York City, Washington, DC, and Miami.

Taxes

Maryland sales tax is 5%. Room tax is 10%.

Media

The state's major newspaper is the *Baltimore Sun*, but most people read the *Washington Post* as well. You will find NPR Radio on WJHV, 88.9 FM. Almost everyone in the Baltimore area listens to *Rouse and Co*, a comical morning show on WQRS, 105.7 FM.

Liquor Laws

In Maryland you must 21 to buy or drink alcoholic beverages. Bars generally close at 2 am. Privately owned liquor stores are the only place you can buy alcoholic beverages 'to go.'

Baltimore

A tall ship with a lean black hull and two raked masts, Maryland's new flagship has been sailing into Atlantic ports proclaiming the state's virtues for the last 10 years. Named *Pride of Baltimore II*, the ship is a replica of the famous 'Baltimore Clippers' that made the city, Maryland, and the United States a major maritime power during the early 19th century. In many ways the *Pride* is the perfect symbol for this city – the largest in Maryland and 13th in the nation.

Baltimore's glory has always been rooted in seafaring. Today the signs are everywhere. Visit the Inner Harbor and witness the collection of traditional sailing vessels ranging in size from the 200-year-old battle frigate USF *Constellation* to the *Minnie V*, a turn-of-the-century oystering skipjack. Here, people get out on the water in everything from paddleboats, outboards, and yachts to water taxis and excursion vessels.

Nicknamed 'Charm City' because of its hospitality, Baltimore is every bit as proud as it is welcoming. Pride sparkles in the bold designs of the new skyscrapers and museums surrounding the Inner Harbor and the spit-and-polished restorations of 18th century neighborhoods like Fells Point. You can sense pride in the elaborate descriptions of entrees on the menus in Little Italy and in the beckoning voices of vendors in the city's five markets.

Like the *Pride of Baltimore II*, Baltimore shares a story of rebirth. Some years ago, the original *Pride of Baltimore* sank in a storm off the Bahamas; the new ship was built from the memory of the old. By the early 1980s, Baltimore was slipping beneath a sea of urban blight, until Mayor Donald Schaefer organized a coalition of government, businesses, and citizens to revitalize Baltimore. The project began with the leveling of the industrial slums surrounding the Inner Harbor, and filling the area with parks, galleries of shops, restaurants, a concert pavilion, five-star hotels, new corporate office buildings, a multitude of floating attractions, and continuous musical and cultural events.

HIGHLIGHTS

- People and boat watching along the promenade at the Inner Harbor
- The National Aquarium . . . if you can afford it
- Edgar Allen Poe's grave – eerie, especially around Halloween
- The Fells Point bar scene
- World-class art collection at the Walters Art Gallery
- Great seafood, beer, and camaraderie at the Cross St Market
- Smoke, jazz, and rock 'n' roll at Eight By Ten

Additions to the area include a convention center, the Maryland Science Center, the National Aquarium, and a new baseball stadium for the Baltimore Orioles. The infusion of redevelopment capital and tourist dollars has engendered urban renewal and gentrification in peripheral neighborhoods, attracting a new group of young, talented artists, preservationists and professionals to the city, now hosting a population of some 750,000.

History

When the US declared war on Great Britain in 1812, a British admiral proclaimed that 'Baltimore is a doomed town.' The mariner was speaking specifically of his hopes for shutting down America's most prominent seaport and scattering its fleet of armed merchant ships to the wind. The prophecy summarizes Baltimore's recurring predicament throughout its history: Four different times observers have judged Baltimore doomed, and four times the city has risen, more splendid than before, from its own ruins.

Established as a tobacco and flour-milling center during the 18th century, the settlement took its name in 1729 from George Calvert, Lord Baltimore. The English knight served King Charles I as Secretary of State until Calvert's Roman Catholic religious affiliations barred him from center stage in the royal court. Thereafter, Calvert became a 'New World' real estate developer and the first royal grant holder to the lands of Maryland. The current city, only one of three towns named after Lord Baltimore and his sons, prospered early. With a congenial climate most of the year, a fine harbor, and access to first-rate shipbuilding timber, Baltimore developed rapidly as colonial America's shipping and shipbuilding center. Baltimore ships and sailors made up the bulk of

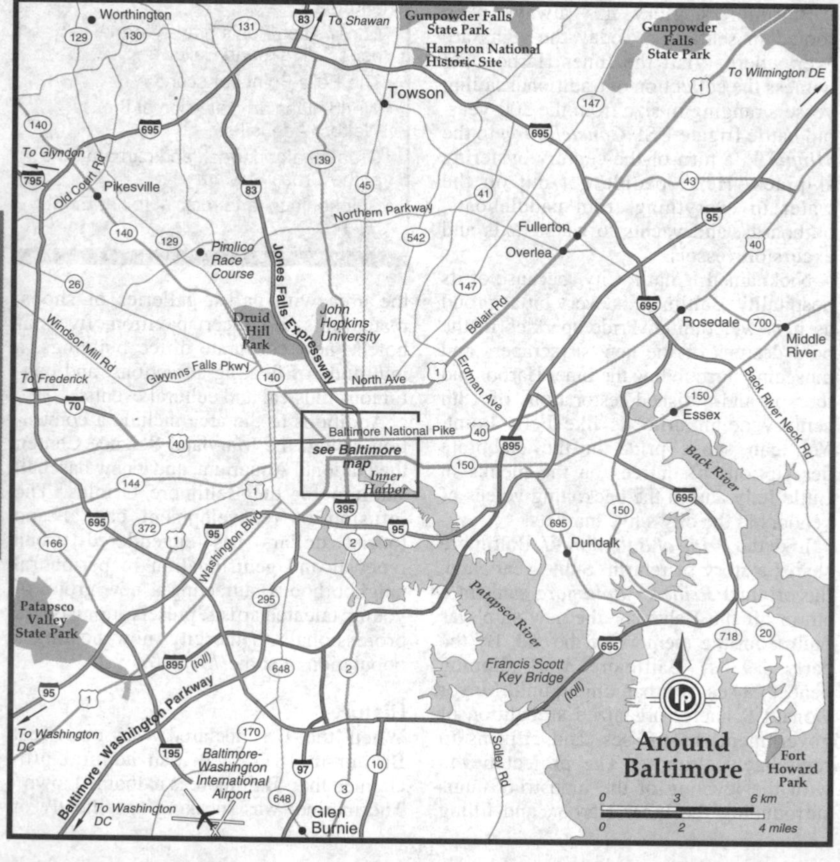

the American privateer fleet that disrupted British supply lines, eventually bringing on the British surrender during the American Revolution.

By the end of the Revolution 45,000 souls lived in Baltimore, and the city's shipyards had begun evolving a new breed of ships – sleek, fast, two-masted schooners with a sharply raked mast – the Baltimore Clippers. But when the British captured scores of merchant vessels from Baltimore, confiscating the ships and cargo as well as impressing the crews as sailors on British warships and whalers, Baltimore shippers suffered great financial loss, and the city suffered.

The worst of Baltimore's suffering came in 1814, two years after the outbreak of the second war with Britain. After the British burned Washington, they moved to close America's biggest shipping port, and Baltimore reeled under British land and sea attack. Many citizens feared that their city would suffer like Washington, but Maryland troops fought valiantly and repelled the British fleet's dramatic assault on Fort McHenry on September 14. The victory here gave rise to the US national anthem, the lyrics of which recount Baltimore's – and all of America's – escape from the English.

With the end of the British conflict, Baltimore rebounded to become the second-largest city in the US. For the next three decades Baltimore prospered as its ships dominated the trade routes to the Caribbean and South America. Meanwhile, Baltimore inventors perfected the steam locomotive and built the Baltimore & Ohio Railroad over the Allegheny Mountains to Pittsburgh, the Ohio River, and the expanding frontier.

Doom struck again with the Civil War. In April 1961, shortly after the Confederate States seceded from the Union, an angry street mob in Baltimore attacked the Sixth Massachusetts Regiment as it marched across the city from one railroad station to another. Four soldiers and 11 citizens died – the first blood letting of the war. Thereafter, President Lincoln imposed military rule over Baltimore. A ring of forts encircled the city with the guns pointed inward. Meanwhile Baltimoreans divided their loyalties between the Union and the Confederacy, and local men fought and died in great numbers for each of the opposing armies. Deprived of free-wheeling commerce, Baltimore withered even after the end of the Civil War as government patronage went to seaports that had been clearly loyal to the Union cause, like Philadelphia, New York, and Boston.

Baltimore eventually bloomed again during the last decades of the 19th century. The railroad brought in massive quantities of grain from the Midwest for milling and shipping, iron and steel factories prospered, the shipbuilding industry flourished, and oyster canning boomed. Then in 1904 a fire broke out in a warehouse and spread before a strong southwest wind. When the conflagration ended, Baltimore's entire business district – 1,500 buildings – lay in ashes and ruins. The devastation caused $125 million in damage. Less than half of the property was insured.

Undaunted, Baltimore's wealthy refinanced the recovery and the city bounced back to be the seventh most productive industrial venue in the country. The boom continued until the Great Depression following the stock market crash in 1929. Thereafter, Baltimore struggled in the doldrums of economic stagnation and growing social problems, bred of a densely packed, undereducated, unemployed population. The city's economy recovered during the industrial boom of WWII and the 1950s, but urban decay grew worse.

By the 1960s citizens fled the city for the suburbs in droves. Crime and sleaze took over; the major downtown tourist attraction became 'The Block,' a neighborhood of striptease palaces, bars, prostitutes, and drug pushers just north of the Inner Harbor. Following the murder of civil-rights leader Martin Luther King, Jr, angry mobs burned and looted the city.

For the fourth time in its history, the city began to rise again during the early 1980s. Plans for renewing the Inner Harbor as an

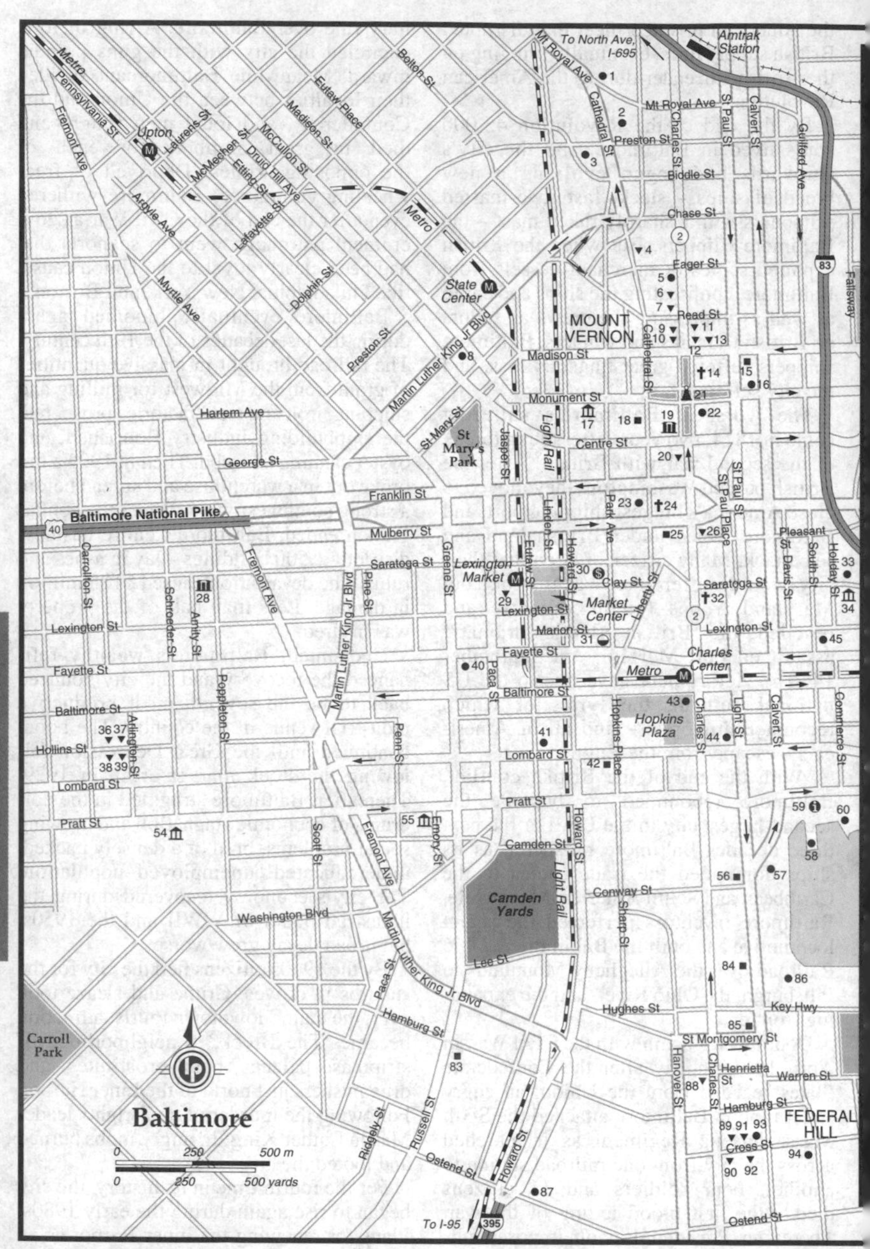
Baltimore
To North Ave, I-695
Amtrak Station
Metro
Upton
State Center
MOUNT VERNON
St Mary's Park
Baltimore National Pike
Lexington Market
Market Center
Charles Center
Hopkins Plaza
Camden Yards
Light Rail
Carroll Park
FEDERAL HILL
To I-95
Mt Royal Ave
Cathedral St
Charles St
St Paul St
Calvert St
Guilford Ave
Fallsway
Preston St
Biddle St
Chase St
Eager St
Read St
Madison St
Monument St
Centre St
Franklin St
Mulberry St
Saratoga St
Clay St
Lexington St
Marion St
Fayette St
Baltimore St
Lombard St
Pratt St
Camden St
Conway St
Lee St
Hughes St
Key Hwy
St Montgomery St
Henrietta St
Warren St
Hamburg St
Cross St
Ostend St
Washington Blvd
Martin Luther King Jr Blvd
Fremont Ave
Pennsylvania St
Laurens St
McMechen St
Druid Hill Ave
McCulloh St
Madison St
Eutaw Place
Bolton St
Etting St
Lafayette St
Argyle Ave
Myrtle Ave
Dolphin St
Harlem Ave
George St
Jasper St
Linden St
Eutaw St
Howard St
Park Ave
Liberty St
Paca St
Greene St
Pine St
Penn St
Emory St
Scott St
Poppleton St
Schroeder St
Amity St
Carrollton St
Arlington St
Hollins St
Hopkins Place
Sharp St
Light St
Hanover St
Pleasant St
Davis St
South St
Holiday St
Commerce St
Ridgely St
Russell St
0 250 500 m
0 250 500 yards
MARYLAND

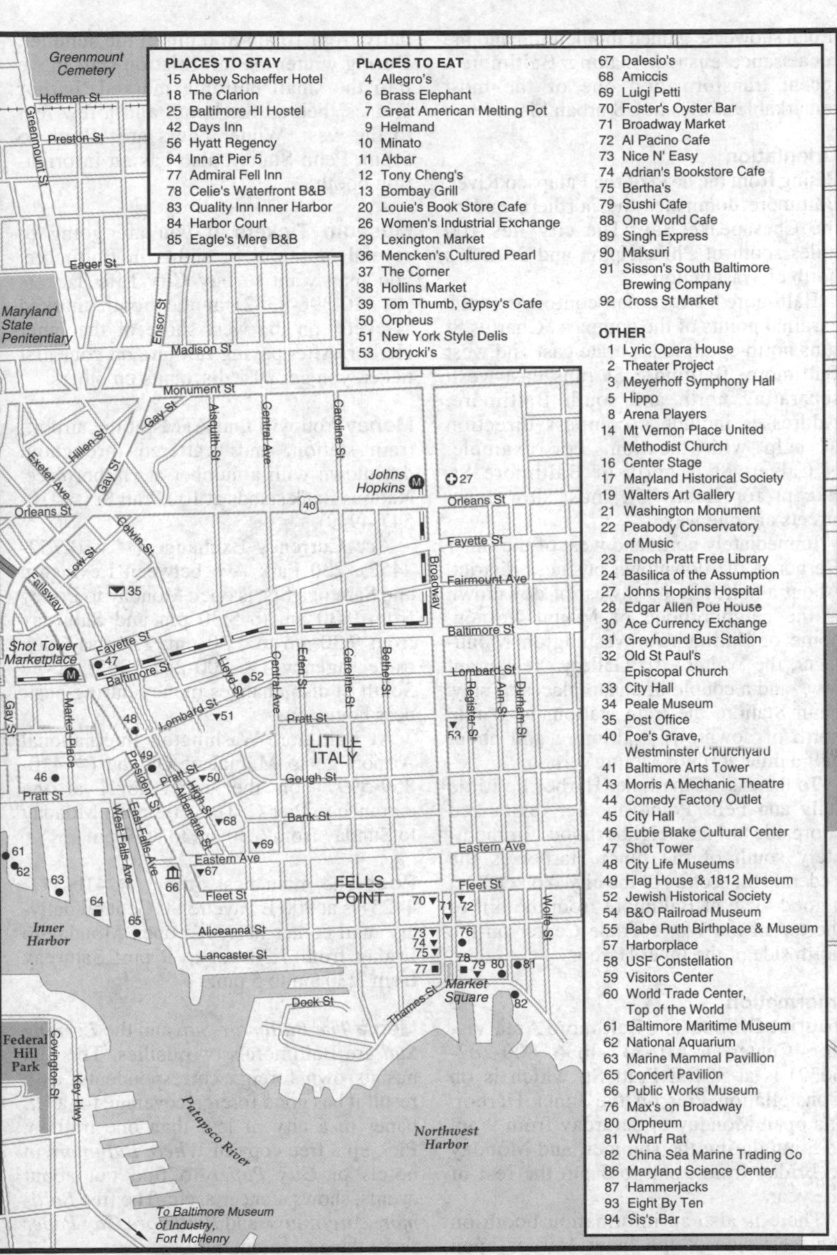
PLACES TO STAY
15 Abbey Schaeffer Hotel
18 The Clarion
25 Baltimore HI Hostel
42 Days Inn
56 Hyatt Regency
64 Inn at Pier 5
77 Admiral Fell Inn
78 Celie's Waterfront B&B
83 Quality Inn Inner Harbor
84 Harbor Court
85 Eagle's Mere B&B
PLACES TO EAT
4 Allegro's
6 Brass Elephant
7 Great American Melting Pot
9 Helmand
10 Minato
11 Akbar
12 Tony Cheng's
13 Bombay Grill
20 Louie's Book Store Cafe
26 Women's Industrial Exchange
29 Lexington Market
36 Mencken's Cultured Pearl
37 The Corner
38 Hollins Market
39 Tom Thumb, Gypsy's Cafe
50 Orpheus
51 New York Style Delis
53 Obrycki's
67 Dalesio's
68 Amiccis
69 Luigi Petti
70 Foster's Oyster Bar
71 Broadway Market
72 Al Pacino Cafe
73 Nice N' Easy
74 Adrian's Bookstore Cafe
75 Bertha's
79 Sushi Cafe
88 One World Cafe
89 Singh Express
90 Maksuri
91 Sisson's South Baltimore Brewing Company
92 Cross St Market
OTHER
1 Lyric Opera House
2 Theater Project
3 Meyerhoff Symphony Hall
5 Hippo
8 Arena Players
14 Mt Vernon Place United Methodist Church
16 Center Stage
17 Maryland Historical Society
19 Walters Art Gallery
21 Washington Monument
22 Peabody Conservatory of Music
23 Enoch Pratt Free Library
24 Basilica of the Assumption
27 Johns Hopkins Hospital
28 Edgar Allen Poe House
30 Ace Currency Exchange
31 Greyhound Bus Station
32 Old St Paul's Episcopal Church
33 City Hall
34 Peale Museum
35 Post Office
40 Poe's Grave, Westminster Churchyard
41 Baltimore Arts Tower
43 Morris A Mechanic Theatre
44 Comedy Factory Outlet
45 City Hall
46 Eubie Blake Cultural Center
47 Shot Tower
48 City Life Museums
49 Flag House & 1812 Museum
52 Jewish Historical Society
54 B&O Railroad Museum
55 Babe Ruth Birthplace & Museum
57 Harborplace
58 USF Constellation
59 Visitors Center
60 World Trade Center, Top of the World
61 Baltimore Maritime Museum
62 National Aquarium
63 Marine Mammal Pavillion
65 Concert Pavilion
66 Public Works Museum
76 Max's on Broadway
80 Orpheum
81 Wharf Rat
82 China Sea Marine Trading Co
86 Maryland Science Center
87 Hammerjacks
93 Eight By Ten
94 Sis's Bar
Greenmount Cemetery
Hoffman St
Preston St
Greenmount St
Eager St
Maryland State Penitentiary
Ensor St
Madison St
Monument St
Gay St
Aisquith St
Central Ave
Caroline St
Hillen St
Exeter Ave
Johns Hopkins
Orleans St
Colvin St
Low St
Fallsway
Fayette St
Fairmount Ave
Broadway
Baltimore St
Shot Tower Marketplace
Lloyd St
Eden St
Bethel St
Lombard St
Register St
Ann St
Durham St
Market Place
Pratt St
LITTLE ITALY
President St
High St
Albemarle St
Gough St
Bank St
West Falls Ave
East Falls Ave
Eastern Ave
Fleet St
FELLS POINT
Wolfe St
Inner Harbor
Aliceanna St
Lancaster St
Thames St
Market Square
Dock St
Federal Hill Park
Covington St
Key Hwy
Patapsco River
Northwest Harbor
To Baltimore Museum of Industry, Fort McHenry
MARYLAND

urban showcase gained momentum and the renaissance ensued, making Baltimore's recent transformation one of the most remarkable stories in US urban history.

Orientation

Rising from the head of the Patapsco River, Baltimore dominates the northern end of the Chesapeake Bay. The city lies 100 miles south of Philadelphia and 25 miles north of Washington.

Baltimore's street plan conforms to the cardinal points of the compass. Charles St runs north-south to separate east and west Baltimore. Baltimore St runs east-west, separating north and south Baltimore. Addresses include a compass direction to help with location. For example, N Calvert St is north of Baltimore St. Except for Eutaw St, most downtown streets are one way.

Immediately north and west of the Inner Harbor is the downtown business district. About a half mile northwest of downtown is the neighborhood of Mount Vernon, home of Baltimore's Washington Monument, the Walters Art Gallery, 'restaurant row,' and a couple of cheap places to stay. Penn Station, the train station, is a mile north of downtown Baltimore and about half a mile north of Mount Vernon.

To the east of the Inner Harbor lie Little Italy and Fells Point, another revitalized shoreside urban neighborhood. Immediately south of the Inner Harbor is the Federal Hill section of the city. You can get a good view of Baltimore from the hill or the top of the World Trade Center on the north side of the Inner Harbor.

Information

Tourist Offices The Baltimore Area Visitors Center (☎ 410-837-4636, 800-282-6632) is at 301 E Pratt St, which is on Constellation Pier on the Inner Harbor. It's open Monday to Saturday from 9 am to 5 pm during the summer, and Monday to Friday from 9 am to 5 pm the rest of the year.

There is also an information booth on the west side of the Inner Harbor open daily from 10 am to 6 pm in the summer. During winter the information staff move into the small building marked 'harbor cruises' behind the booth and a few feet to the west. Winter hours are 10 am to 5 pm. Penn Station also has an information booth.

Museum Tickets If you are going to several museums or sights in Baltimore, you may want to buy City Life Tickets (☎ 410-396-8342) at the booth marked 'Tickets' on the west shore of the Inner Harbor. After paying full fare on your first ticket, you get 20% discounts on others.

Money You will find ATMs at the airport, train station, and scattered throughout downtown with a number at Harborplace. Nations Bank stands at 100 Pratt St (☎ 410-547-4949).

Ace Currency Exchange (☎ 410-752-7452), 230 Park Ave between Lexington and Saratoga Sts, is open Monday to Friday from 9:30 am to 5:30 pm and Saturday from 9:30 am to 1:30 pm. Thomas Cook travel agency (☎ 800-287-7363) at 32 South St also changes money during business hours.

At Baltimore-Washington International Airport go to Mutual of Omaha (☎ 410-859-5997) on the upper level at the entrance to Pier C. They are open Monday to Sunday from 6:30 am to 8:30 pm.

Post The main post office (☎ 410-347-4425) is at 900 E Fayette St. General delivery mail comes here. It's open Monday to Friday from 7:30 am to 9 pm; Saturday from 7:30 am to 5 pm.

Media *The Baltimore Sun* and the *Evening Sun* are Baltimore's two dailies. The Sun has its own foreign correspondents; as a result it has good foreign coverage for a US paper in a city of less than one million. Pick up a free copy of *Where Baltimore* in hotels or *City Paper* to find out about events, shows, concerts, etc. The free *Baltimore Alternative* and *Baltimore Gay Paper* serve the gay community.

Bookstores Louie's Book Store Cafe (☎ 410-962-1224), 518 N Charles St south of the Walters Art Gallery, is one of the better places in town to look for literature and has a cafe and bar with good food in back. Lambda Rising (☎ 410-234-0069) at 241 W Chase St sells gay and lesbian books. For mysteries try Mystery Loves Company (☎ 410-276-6708), 1730 Fleet St in Fells Point. Good general bookstores are B Dalton (☎ 410-659-5846), in the Gallery Mall at the Inner Harbor, and Bibelot (☎ 410-653-5880), at 1829 Reisterstown Rd.

For used books check out BNN Books (☎ 410-243-8559), 10 W 25th St from Thursday to Saturday from 11 am to 6 pm; and the Kelmscott Bookshop (☎ 410-235-6810), 32 W 25th St in northern Baltimore.

Library The Enoch Pratt Free Library (☎ 410-396-5429), 400 Cathedral St between Franklin and Mulberry Sts, is the city's main library. It has exhibits on HL Mencken and Edgar Allen Poe and is open Monday to Wednesday from 10 am to 8 pm, Thursday and Saturday to 5 pm, and Sunday 1 to 5 pm; closed Friday.

Medical Services Johns Hopkins Hospital (☎ 410-955-2280) is at 600 N Wolfe St. Maryland General Hospital (☎ 410-225-8100) is at 827 Linden Ave.

Emergency Travelers Aid (☎ 410-685-3569) operates a 24-hour hotline (☎ 410-685-5874) with desks at Baltimore-Washington International Airport open from Sunday to Friday from 9 am to 9 pm and Saturdays 10 am to 7:30 pm.

Other useful numbers are People Aiding Travelers and the Homeless (☎ 410-685-3569, 410-685-5874); the Grassroots Crisis Intervention Center (☎ 410-531-6677, 410-531-6678); the Sexual Assault and Domestic Violence Hotline (☎ 410-828-6390); and the Gay and Lesbian Hotline & Information (☎ 410-837-8888).

Inner Harbor

The Inner Harbor is the revitalized heart of Baltimore – now a major tourist attraction including the waterfront promenade, museums, tour boats, historic ships, and the National Aquarium. It encompasses both the head of the Northwest Branch of the Patapsco River and the land around it.

National Aquarium This fairly innovative aquarium (☎ 410-576-3800) is two buildings with glass pyramids at the north side of the Inner Harbor. An elevator takes you to the top and you walk down ramps that spiral around large circular tanks filled with over 5000 marine animals. The most popular tanks are those filled with sharks, rays, and porpoises. There is also an Amazon jungle area and a seal area outside on the west side of the main building.

The **Marine Mammal Pavilion** is to the east. Here you can view whale and dolphin shows included with your admission. On weekends and during the summer the aquarium can be extremely crowded; even the adult fee of $11.75 can't keep people away, so get there early. The fee for seniors is $10.50; for children three to 11 it's $7.50. These attractions are open November through February, Saturday to Thursday from 10 am to 5 pm and Friday to 8 pm. From March to October the Aquarium opens Monday to Thursday from 9 am to 5 pm and Friday to Sunday to 8 pm.

Baltimore Maritime Museum The museum (☎ 410-396-3854) is a ship and a submarine docked on the western side of the aquarium. On exhibit are the *Chesapeake*, a floating lightship, the Coast Guard cutter *Roger B Taney*, and the USS *Torsk*, the last submarine to sink a Japanese ship during WWII. At times, other ships join the exhibit.

Maryland Science Center This pink museum (☎ 410-685-5225) at 601 Light St has three floors of interactive attractions. Its exhibits on the Hubble telescope, structures, and weather are great for kids, but adults won't find much to do here. Included with your rather expensive $9 adult or $7 student/senior admission is an IMAX film on a five-story screen. Hours are weekdays from 10 am to 5 pm and weekends from 10 am to 6 pm.

Harborplace This is a shopping development and food complex at the Inner Harbor. The **Light St Pavilion** is on the western side of the Harbor and has a food court inside. The **Pratt St Pavilion** is on the northern side. The Gallery, a collection of clothing and gift shops, is north of Pratt St and connected to the Pratt St Pavilion by a skyway.

USF *Constellation* Normally this ship (☎ 410-539-1797) is docked at the northwest corner of the Inner Harbor. The United States Frigate *Constellation* was the first ship commissioned in the US Navy. It sailed from 1797 to 1945 and along the way fought pirates, the French, and the British. Some interesting American idioms came from the food served to the non-officers on such ships. For example, 'get the bugs out' comes from the practice of sailors tapping the hardtack (years-old biscuits served at meals) on the ship's deck to dislodge insects. As this book goes to press, *Constellation* will begin a $9 million refit and may not be at berth on the Inner Harbor until 1999.

Top of the World There is a good view of Baltimore from the 27th floor of the World Trade Center (☎ 410-837-4515) on the north side of the Inner Harbor. IM Pei designed this building as the world's tallest pentagonal structure. For $2.50 you can go up from Monday to Saturday from 10 am to 5:30 pm and on Sunday from noon to 5 pm.

Concert Pavilion This looks like a white circus tent at the end of Pier Six on the eastern side of the Inner Harbor (☎ 410-752-8632). There are 4338 open-air seats for concerts that feature everything from string ensembles to country music legends.

Public Works Museum The museum (☎ 410-396-5565) is the building with the single smokestack at 751 Eastern Ave at the intersection of President St on the eastern side of the Inner Harbor. You actually enter from the side facing the harbor and the concert pavilion (the western side of the building). It's the first museum devoted to public works – water, waste disposal, and transportation projects – a noble idea, but the museum has very few exhibits. There's a small exhibit on women in public works and an informative, albeit promotional, slide show. Hours are Wednesday to Sunday from 10 am to 4 pm; admission for adults/children is $2.50/1.50.

Downtown

From the area north of the Inner Harbor from Paca St in the west to a few blocks east of I-83 you'll find office buildings, the Lexington Market, City Hall, and a few museums.

Baltimore City Hall This Victorian structure, 100 N Holiday St at Fayette St, was completed in 1875. It's made of local marble, has an iron dome, and mansard roofs. Hours are Monday to Friday from 8:30 am to 4:30 pm; free admission.

Customs House Inside this building (☎ 410-962-2666), at 40 Gay St at Lombard St, is the Call Room where ship captains declared their cargo. Francis Davis Millet painted a mural of the evolution of sea vessels on the ceiling. After his assassination, Abraham Lincoln's body lay in state in the former building on this site, the Merchants Exchange. It's open Monday to Friday from 8 am to 5 pm and is free.

Baltimore Arts Tower This minaret modeled on Florence's Palazzo Vecchio is on the corner of Eutaw and Lombard Sts. Captain Isaac Emerson, the inventor of Bromo Seltzer, paid Joseph Evans Sperry to design the tower. It was completed in 1911 and topped with a 51-foot, 17-ton, lighted, revolving, blue steel Bromo Seltzer bottle. For better or worse, the bottle came down in 1936 because it was causing structural damage. The city bought the tower in 1967 and converted it to an office building for the arts. It's not open to the public.

Prince of Darkness

Poet and scholar Allen Tate put his finger on the enduring appeal of the literature and myth of Edgar Allen Poe when he said that the author is like everyone's distressing American 'cousin' who acts out the deepest arrogant, childish, and violent longings hidden in our selves. In poems like 'The Raven' and 'The Bells,' and stories like 'The Fall of the House of Usher' and 'The Pit and the Pendulum,' Poe gave full voice to the horror that can lurk in the human subconscious.

While a great deal of myth surrounds Poe's life, the truth of his 40 years on earth is quite disturbing enough to have spawned his horrifying literature and self destruction. Poe was born in 1809 in Boston to a pair of touring actors. After his parents died when he was a toddler, Poe spent most of his childhood in the home of his uncle in Richmond, Virginia. During his youth Poe visited Europe once and bounced around private schools. He attended the University of Virginia for a year, but in 1827 Poe's uncle pulled him out of college because he had been leading the life of a gambler and drunk. During the next four years, Poe moved to Boston, published poetry, and served a stint in the US Army. He gained appointment to the Military Academy at West Point, but soon found himself dismissed for neglect of duty.

In 1831 Poe returned to the South and settled in Baltimore with his aunt and her 11-year-old daughter Virginia Climm. Poe began to fall in love with the girl, which inspired a burst of literary energy, and he turned his attention to writing short stories. While living in Baltimore, his 'MS Found in a Bottle' won him a fiction contest in 1832. When Virginia approached the age of 14 Poe married her and moved to Richmond, Virginia. He spent the next decade tending to Virginia's recurrent illnesses (probably tuberculosis). He also perfected the form that would define the modern American short story and drank himself silly. After Virginia died in 1847, Poe's spirit grew even more tortured and haunted (see the autobiographical poem 'Ulalume'). While passing through Baltimore in 1849, Poe got quite drunk and disappeared for days. Someone found him incoherent in a polling place and he died soon thereafter of various causes. In 1875 his remains were moved from a pauper's grave to the catacombs of Westminster Churchyard. ■

Edgar Allan Poe's Grave The author lies in the Westminster Churchyard (☎ 410-706-2072) at the corner of W Fayette and N Greene Sts. If you enter at the gate near the corner, his grave is under a six-foot white obelisk five feet in front of you. An admirer decorates Poe's grave with roses and a bottle of cognac every year on the anniversary of his death (October 7). The churchyard is four blocks north and eight west of the Inner Harbor.

Baltimore City Life Museums Five of these sights (☎ 410-396-3523, tours 410-396-3279) are at 800 E Lombard St a block north and three blocks west of the Inner Harbor. There are holiday events, cooking classes, and overnight stays in the Carroll Mansion and 1840 House. Barring one of these or an interesting changing exhibit, you can skip these museums. The **Carroll Mansion** belonged to Charles Carroll, who signed the Declaration of Independence. It has very barren blue walls and period furniture. **1840 House** (☎ 410-396-3395), next door to the Carroll Mansion, was the home of a mid-19th century craftsman and his family. Guided tours run several times daily. **The Center for Urban Archaeology** has a small one-room display of ceramics, glassware, and other objects from 18th and 19th century Baltimore homes. The **Courtyard Exhibition Center** has changing exhibits about Baltimore and its residents. **Brewers' Park** is across the street from the Carroll Mansion. It's an empty lot with a partial foundation that was an 18th century brewery.

There are also three other City Life museums around the city. The **Peale Museum** (☎ 410-396-1149), half a block north of City Hall at 225 Holiday St, was built in 1814 by Rembrandt Peale in honor of his father Charles Wilson Peale, both portrait painters. It's the oldest museum building in the US, but almost nothing is left of the thousands of curiosities that were originally in the museum. An exception is the dagger used to kill Captain Cook in Hawaii. There is also a reproduction of a mastodon skeleton and several rooms of Peale family paintings. It's open weekends only.

The **Shot Tower** is at 801 E Fayette St, at the intersection of Front and E Fayette Sts, three blocks north of the City Life complex. You can't miss the 215-foot brick tower – it looks like a smokestack. It's called the shot tower because ammunition makers dropped molten lead from the top through perforated pans and into a 'quenching tank' at the bottom. The process shaped, cooled, and solidified the lead into musket shot. In its heyday during the 19th century, this shot tower was one of the largest suppliers of ammunition in the country. The **Mencken House** is worth visiting if you're a fan (see Southwest Baltimore).

All museums except the Peale Museum are open daily from 10 am to 5 pm. Admission for one or all is $6 for adults, $4 for seniors and children.

Flag House & 1812 Museum In this 1793 house (☎ 410-837-1793), 844 E Pratt St at Albemarle St, Mary Pickersgill sewed the 30-by-42-foot flag (with 15 stars and stripes) that inspired Francis Scott Key to write the poem 'Star Spangled Banner.' The flag was the last flag with an equal number of stars and stripes (one each for each state). The two extra stars and stripes beyond the original 13 were for Vermont and Kentucky. After this flag was made, all future flags reverted back to a fixed 13 stripes and a variable number of stars (one for each state).

The house has period pieces, early American art, and an exhibit on the War of 1812. It's open Monday to Saturday from 10 am to 4 pm. Admission is $2.

Jewish Historical Society of Maryland This is a group of three buildings (☎ 410-732-6400) in a marginal neighborhood at 15 Lloyd St between Baltimore and Lombard Sts. It includes the 1845 **Lad St Synagogue**, the 1876 **B'Nai Israel Synagogue**, and the **Jewish Heritage Center**, which is a library and museum of documents, photos, and artifacts of Maryland's

Francis Scott Key & the 'Star Spangled Banner'

Francis Scott Key (1779–1843), a lawyer who dabbled in poetry, had the serendipity to be at the right place during the War of 1812 to receive the proper inspiration to write the 'Star Spangled Banner.'

It was September of 1814, toward the end of the War of 1812. The British had sailed from Washington, DC, having burned it to pay back the Americans for burning York, Canada. They sailed up the Chesapeake to attack Baltimore. On the way north they captured an American physician named William Beanes. Beanes' friends asked Francis Scott Key, then a lawyer with a profitable Georgetown law practice, to intercede with the British and get Beanes released.

Key was allowed aboard a British warship then preparing to attack Baltimore. The British agreed to release Beanes but had to keep Key aboard until they had completed their attack. Through the night of September 13–14 the warship on which he waited bombarded Fort McHenry. Above the fort flew the 30-by-42-foot flag sewn by Mary Pickersgill in Baltimore.

'By dawn's early light' the flag was still flying and the attack on Baltimore had failed. Key was inspired to pen the words to the poem that would later become the national anthem on the back of an envelope. It was soon reprinted and widely distributed as a handbill with the title *Defense of M'Henry*. Within a short time it had been set to music – oddly enough to the tune of the *British* drinking song 'To Anacreon in Heaven.' In 1931 the US Congress declared the notoriously difficult to sing, British drinking-song-poem the National Anthem of the US. ■

Jewish history. It's open Tuesday, Wednesday, Thursday, and Sunday from noon to 4 pm. Admission is $2.

Old St Paul's Episcopal Church Originally built in 1692, the present building opened in 1856 (☎ 410-685-3404) at N Charles and Saratoga Sts, and has stained-glass windows by Louis Tiffany and a fabulous pipe organ. Daily services are given.

Mount Vernon

Mount Vernon is the neighborhood and square about a half mile northwest of the Inner Harbor. Its heart is Baltimore's own Washington Monument at the center of a cruciform park between Madison and Centre Sts. The young brooding folk dressed in black are probably students at the Peabody Conservatory 100 feet southeast of the monument. The Walters Art Gallery, Baltimore's best, is on N Charles St one block south of the monument. So-called 'Restaurant Row' is the stretch of N Charles St in the blocks south and north of the monument. Buses Nos 3 and 31 run north on Charles and south on Cathedral St through Mount Vernon.

Washington Monument Robert Mills, who later designed the Washington, DC monument of the same name, also did this one at Charles St and Monument Place. It's a tall obelisk with a 16-foot Washington statue on top right in the middle of Mount Vernon Square, which divides N Charles St in half for two blocks.

Walters Art Gallery This excellent museum (☎ 410-547-9000), at 600 N Charles St a block south of the Washington Monument, houses in three adjacent buildings the private collection that Henry Walters bequeathed to the city. The collection includes ancient, medieval, Islamic, Renaissance, Asian, and contemporary art – essentially a sampling of pieces from 5000 BC to the present. The original 1904 gallery looks like an Italian palazzo complete with a central courtyard. Admission for adults/seniors is $6/4, students under 18 are free. Admission is free between 11 am and 1 pm on Saturday. Regular hours are Tuesday, Wednesday, Friday from 10 am to 4 pm; Thursday from 10 am to 8 pm; Saturday and Sunday from 11 am to 5 pm.

Peabody Conservatory of Music The conservatory is at the southeast corner of N Charles St and Mount Vernon Place across the street from the Walters Art Gallery. It's the oldest classical music school in the US and is now part of Johns Hopkins University. Famous graduates include pianist Leon Fleisher, composer Dominick Argento, and opera singer Gordon Hawkins. Don't skip going inside the 1878 library (☎ 410-659-8179), with marble floors and a 60-foot atrium, which is surrounded by marble columns and five tiers of balconies holding the books. You can hear free or cheap student recitals (☎ 410-659-8124) on a regular basis.

Mount Vernon Place United Methodist Church This neo-Gothic church (☎ 410-685-5290), 10 E Mount Vernon Place across the street to the north from the Peabody Conservatory, dates from 1872. Its facade, though a bit sooty, includes a lot of green serpentine. In 1843 Francis Scott Key died in a house where the current Asbury House, to the east of the church, now stands. To enter the church ring the Asbury House bell.

Basilica of the Assumption Benjamin Henry LaTrobe, architect of the Capitol in Washington, DC, designed this church – the first Roman Catholic church in the US mixing Greek revival with Eastern elements. It's a few blocks south of the Washington Monument at the corner of Cathedral and Mulberry Sts (the street address is 408 N Charles St). Tours (☎ 410-727-3564) run every Sunday after the 10:45 am Mass.

Maryland Historical Society The museum (☎ 410-685-3750), 201 West Monument St at Park Ave, has the original manuscript of the 'Star Spangled Banner' on display. The society includes the 19th century period rooms of the Enoch Pratt Mansion, the Darnell Young People's Museum and the Radcliff Maritime Museum. The Society is open Tuesday to Friday from 10 am to 5 pm, Saturday from 9 am to 5 pm, and Sunday from 1 to 5 pm. Admission is $3.50.

Federal Hill & South Baltimore

This is the neighborhood around the hill and south of the Inner Harbor not far from the Camden Yards baseball park. Bus No 64 runs from downtown Baltimore south on Light St into Federal Hill.

Federal Hill Park The park is on a hill overlooking the harbor and the city at Battery St and Key Hwy. You can't miss it if you look across the harbor from the north. Around 6 pm the small park fills with dogs and humans trying to meet mates. The covered tunnels around the park, inaccessible to the public, are old iron and clay mining spots.

Fort McHenry National Monument The monument (☎ 410-962-4290) is at the end of E Fort Ave at the eastern end of the peninsula south of Federal Hill. During the War of 1812 the star-shaped fort protected Baltimore harbor against British attack. British warships shelled the fort September 13–14, 1814, but failed to dislodge its defenders. Visitors can walk around the walls of the fort and inside to soldiers quarters, a powder magazine, bomb shelters and some exhibits. The fort is open daily from 8 am to 5 pm. Admission is $2; children under 17 and seniors are admitted free. Bus No 1 runs right to the fort.

Baltimore Museum of Industry The museum (☎ 410-727-4808) is at 1415 Key Hwy in an old oyster cannery. It has a lot of hands-on exhibits that children can operate, like an assembly line and 19th century industrial machines. Other exhibits include a garment-making loft, print shop, and tugboat, all from the 19th century. It is open Memorial Day to Labor Day on Tuesday, Thursday, Friday, and Sunday from noon to 5 pm; Wednesday from 7 to 9 pm; Saturday from 10 am to 5 pm. Admission is $3.50 for adults, $2.50 for students and seniors.

Southwest Baltimore

'SoWeBo,' as locals like to call this area, is a developing bohemian district mostly to the west of Martin Luther King, Jr Blvd. During the last seven years, artists and artisans have moved into the area around Hollins Market (see Places to Eat) to revive the district as something like a clone of New York City's Soho. The renaissance is real but far from complete. Most of SoWeBo remains poverty-stricken and dangerous at night. Bus No 2 goes west on Fayette and Lombard Sts from downtown. Bus No 31 goes west on Lombard St and then south on Gilmore St.

B&O Railroad Museum This museum (☎ 410-752-2490) is in the Mt Clare station at 901 W Pratt St opposite Poppleton St about 10 blocks west of the Inner Harbor. The place is amazing – truly one of the best sights in Baltimore even if you don't like trains. You can see a huge collection of locomotives and passenger cars exhibited in the restored roundhouse, with a cathedral-like ceiling soaring up. You can climb into some of there trains outside in the train yards. B&O was the first railroad to sell tickets for passengers in 1823. Admission is $6 for adults, $5 for seniors, and $3 for those five to 12. Doors open daily from 10 am to 5 pm.

HL Mencken House The house (☎ 410-396-7997) is a City Life Museum, but it's over a mile west of downtown at 1524 Hollins St on a block of restored townhouses facing Union Square Park. This is the place to visit if you're a fan of the witty journalist (1880–1956). The 'sage of Baltimore' lived here for about 70 years – almost his entire life.

Mencken began working for the Baltimore *Morning Herald* when he was 19 and after it closed he moved to the *Sun*, where he remained for 40 years. Mencken also wrote for the *American Mercury*. In his writing he attacked what he saw as the 'genteel tradition' in the US, particularly in literature and politics: 'A good politician, under democracy, is quite as unthinkable as an honest burglar.'

The house has a lot of Mencken memorabilia. Brief, informative, and funny tours run about every hour, but it's only open Saturday from 10 am to 5 pm and Sunday from noon to 5 pm. Like all City Life Museums, admission is $6 which gets you into a half dozen sites. Take bus No 2 to Lombard and Gilmore Sts and walk one block north to Hollins. Better yet, drive.

Babe Ruth Birthplace & Museum This museum (☎ 410-727-1539) is at 216 Emory St off of Pratt between Russell and Penn Sts eight blocks west of the Inner Harbor. It's two blocks east of Martin Luther King, Jr Blvd, but close enough to be included in the SoWeBo section. The museum celebrates the 'Sultan of Swat' and baseball in general. One exhibit describes each of Babe's 714 home runs. There are a few artifacts, but the place is really too small and too expensive; admission is $5 for adults, $3 for seniors, and $2 for kids from five to 16. It's open daily from 10 am to 5 pm.

Edgar Allen Poe House Poe moved into this house in 1832 when he was 23 and wrote *MS Found in a Bottle* here. The house (☎ 410-396-4866) is not within walking distance of the Inner Harbor and is in a dicey area at 203 Amity St off Saratoga St. Take a taxi here if you crave a visit: Your landmark is a black antique lamppost in front of the house. The hours of operation change regularly, and when it is very hot and humid, the house closes early, so call for the current operating schedule. Admission is $3.

North Baltimore

The city grows more residential north of North Ave. Here you will find the Baltimore Museum of Art, the zoo, and Johns Hopkins University. Bus Nos 3, 9, and 11 run to north Baltimore from Inner Harbor.

Johns Hopkins University The college of 4600 students is three miles north of the harbor on N Charles St on land that was the former estate of Charles Carroll, Jr, whose father was a signer of the Declaration of Independence. Founded by a Baltimore financier, Hopkins is one of USA's most distinguished private universities, known worldwide for its contributions to medicine, international relations, and publishing. The Office of Admissions (☎ 410-516-8171) in Garland Hall gives free tours on weekdays.

The school maintains two historic houses on campus. **Homewood** (☎ 410-516-5589), 3400 N Charles St, was Carroll's home, with furnishings from the last two centuries. It's open Monday to Friday from 11 am to 4 pm; Sunday from noon to 3 pm. Admission is $5; free for children under 12.

North of the main campus on N Charles St, **Evergreen House** (☎ 410-516-0895) is on 26 acres including the mansion, theater, and gardens of John Work Garett, ambassador to Italy from 1929 to 1933, and his family. It's open Monday to Friday from 10 am to 4 pm; Sunday from noon to 3 pm, and costs $5/2.50 for adults/students.

Marylanders are fanatic lacrosse players and fans, and they have built a museum honoring the game they adopted from the Native Americans. The **Lacrosse Museum** (☎ 410-235-6882), at 113 W University Pkwy next to the lacrosse field, has exhibits on the evolution of the stick and helmet and photos of players. You can visit it year round, Monday to Friday from 9 am to 5 pm.

Baltimore Museum of Art The museum (☎ 410-396-7100/7101), N Charles and 31st Sts, houses Maryland's largest collection of art, but it isn't as impressive as the Walters. The collection includes Impressionist painting, decorative arts, period rooms, African and Asian art, and sculpture. A new 35,000-sq-ft modern art wing opened in 1995. Hours are Wednesday to Friday from 10 am to 4 pm; weekends from 11 am to 6 pm. They charge $5.50 for adults, $3.50 for seniors and students, and $1.50 for those under 18.

Druid Hill Park The 674-acre park (☎ 410-396-6106) is one of the country's largest city parks. Inside it are the zoo and the **Baltimore City Conservatory**, which is often called the 'Palm House' or the 'Palm Tree Conservancy' because of its collection of tropical plants. The conservatory structure is a Victorian domed greenhouse. To get to the park follow the directions to the Baltimore Zoo.

The **Baltimore Zoo** (☎ 410-366-5466) is in the middle of Druid Hill Park. It includes 1200 animals – many in smallish cages by modern zoo standards. The zoo recently added a six-acre African Watering Hole exhibit with rhinos, zebras, and gazelles. Here, you will also find probably the most innovative children's zoo in the country: Kids can walk through caves, view animals, and pretend they are the animals they see. The zoo costs $7.50 for adults; $4 for seniors and those under 16, and is open daily from 10 am to 4:20 pm.

Because the zoo is in the middle of a large city park, it is difficult to reach by public transportation. From downtown Baltimore take Charles St to I-83 north; take Exit 7A to Druid Park Lake Drive and follow the signs to the zoo. People park in lots near the entrance or along roads in the park near the entrance.

Great Blacks in Wax Museum The museum displays figures of over 100 prominent African Americans (☎ 410-563-3404), 1601 E North Ave at Broadway. Admission is $5.75 for adults; $5.25 for seniors and college students; $3.75 for those 12 to 17; $2.25 for those two to 11. It's open Tuesday to Saturday from 9 am to 6 pm, Sunday from noon to 6 pm from February to mid-October. The rest of the year it closes at 5 pm.

Baltimore Streetcar Museum The museum (☎ 410-547-0264), 1901 Falls Rd near North Ave offers rides in authentic Baltimore streetcars built from the 1890s to the 1940s. The few exhibits are free; rides cost $2 each; $1 for the second, or $4 for all day. It's open year round on Sunday from noon to 5 pm; from June to October on Saturday from noon to 5 pm. The museum is under the North Ave Bridge. Go north on Charles St to Lafayette Ave. Turn left on Lafayette, drive two blocks then turn right on Jones Falls Rd.

Fells Point

Fells Point is the waterfront community located about a mile east of the Inner Harbor along Broadway (which runs from Pratt St to the waterfront) and the streets crossing it. Fells Point is one of the oldest maritime communities in the US. The Fells brothers, from Lancaster, England, settled here in the 1700s; hence the streets named Thames, Shakespeare, Fleet, etc. Fells Point has been a home for the various ethnic communities who worked in the maritime trades. Along the cobblestone streets, you can see the rising tide of gentrification and its accompanying antique shops, vintage-clothing stores, restaurants, and bars.

Most people come here to escape the suburbs, stroll, drink (there are scores of bars) and shop. **Market Square** is a brick plaza at the end of Broadway where it intersects Thames St opposite the water. There are often street festivals in the square and always a host of people watchers. Some of the oldest homes in Baltimore stand along the cobblestone streets.

Take bus No 7 or 10 to Broadway and Eastern Ave and walk south a few blocks into Fells Point. Bus No 21 goes down Caroline St right to Fleet St in Fells Point. Alternatively, you can walk across from the Inner Harbor area on Eastern Ave. If you walk across north of Eastern Ave, you will pass through a large, low-rise, low-income housing project and you should be on guard if you walk here at night.

During the summer the Water Taxi serves Fells Point from stops around the Inner Harbor.

Organized Tours

Land Tours Baltimore Trolley Tours (☎ 410-752-1715) runs a 20-stop trolley around the city. Fares and hours are changing as this book goes to press. Baltimore Rent-A-Tour (☎ 410-653-2998) does a periodic 'Insomniac Tour' (for groups of 15 or more) of Baltimore from about 10 pm to 2 am, starting at $25. The Women's Civic League (☎ 410-837-5424) offers a daily tour of City Hall at 10 am. Zippy Larson's Shoe Leather Safaris (☎ 410-764-8067) makes 30 theme tours of Baltimore for about $25 per person.

Harbor Cruises Buy tickets for the large vessels *Bay Lady* and *Lady Baltimore* (☎ 410-347-5552) at the booth marked 'Harbor Cruises' on the west side of the Inner Harbor. Cruises sail year round and range in price from $10 to $45. The office is open daily from 10 am to 4 pm.

Maryland Tours (☎ 410-685-4288) runs narrated cruises between the Inner Harbor and Fort McHenry from Memorial Day to Labor Day about every half hour from 11 am to 6 pm. The adult roundtrip/one-way fare is $5/3; for children under 12 it's $3.75/2.

The *Baltimore Patriot* (☎ 410-745-9216) has a narrated hour and a half cruise of the harbor for adults/children under 12 at $6.60/3.30.

Ocean World Institute (☎ 410-522-4214) carries group tours on the 1928 oyster 'buy boat' *Half Shell* around Baltimore and to various points on the Eastern Shore.

Sailing The *Clipper City* (☎ 410-539-6277) leaves from the southwest corner of the Inner Harbor near the Science Center. Two-hour sails are $12; three-hour weekend tours are $20; and a three-hour Sunday brunch sail is $30.

The *Nighthawk* (☎ 410-327-7245) sails from Fells Point. A sail with evening buffet or Sunday brunch costs $32.50. The Living Classroom Foundation (☎ 410-685-0295) carries passengers on the oyster skipjack *Minnie V*. Prices for adults/children are $10/3 and $12 for adults on weekends.

Special Events

Baltimore hosts plenty of events, mainly in the summer. Here's a sampling in calendar order starting in May:

Center Plaza Concert Series hosts jazz, blues, salsa, and reggae concerts downtown from May to July. (☎ 800-282-6632)

Friday Nite Alive Concert Series & Summer Sunday Concert Series is held June to August. Big band, swing, jazz and other bands play free concerts at the Inner Harbor Amphitheater. (☎ 410-332-4191)

Fells Point's Market Square (☎ 410-396-9177) hosts the Chesapeake Turtle Derby – a series of turtle heats named after prominent Baltimoreans – and the Hog Calling Contest, which is just what it sounds like.

Artscape, held in July, is an annual celebration of local theater, music, arts, and food in Mount Royal. (☎ 410-396-4575)

Showcase of Nations, which runs August to September is a celebration of multicultural Baltimore; each ethnic group is showcased on different days. (☎ 410-837-4636; 800-282-6632)

Defender's Day Celebration is September 12, the anniversary of the War of 1812's Battle of Baltimore. Military drills, fireworks, and music all happen at Fort McHenry. (☎ 410-962-4290)

Festival on the Hill, in October, is a street fair in Bolton Hill. (☎ 410-669-0220)

Blessing of Baltimore's Work Boats, also in October, is a chance for Baltimore's working boats to parade through the harbor to be blessed. (☎ 410-332-4191)

Places to Stay

Travelers on a budget will find it useful to pick up a copy of *Baltimore, Quick Guide* (☎ 410-783-7520) from one of the tourist offices (see Information). The guide has a good collection of hotel discount coupons and advertisements.

Places to Stay – bottom end

The *Baltimore HI Hostel* (☎ 410-576-8880), 17 W Mulberry St, is between Mount Vernon and downtown in a big old townhouse four blocks from the Greyhound Station. It's large and casual and has a sitting room with piano, TV, and some games. There's a good-size, well-stocked kitchen you can use to prepare your own groceries and you can do laundry in the washer and dryer for $1 each. The four dormitory rooms have a total of 60 metal bunk beds. The bathrooms are shared and everyone helps with chores.

The hostel is open from 10 am to 11 pm, although you can rent a key for $2 if you want to come in late. Locked bag storage is $1. There's no alcohol permitted and only incoming calls for visitors. The rate for members/nonmembers is $13/16. There's often a summer discount of two nights at the regular rate and the third for 25¢, a bargain by any standard. From the bus station walk north on Park Ave for two blocks to Mulberry St, turn right, and the hostel is a block and half up on your right.

The *Abbey Schaeffer Hotel* (☎ 410-332-0405), 723 St Paul St, one block east of the Washington Monument in Mount Vernon, gets overflow from the hostel. It's a bit rundown but serviceable, renting rooms by the hour, day, and week. Rooms with/without bath are $38/49 and weekly rates start at $99. The extra $6 for a private bath makes a good investment; some of the common ones get dirty.

If you have a car and don't mind driving, you can stay 10 miles from downtown at *Duke's Motel* (☎ 410-686-0400), 7905 Pulaski Hwy (Hwy 40) past the eastern city limits in Baltimore County. Duke's has basic, clean motel rooms with air-con and TV for $41/46, single/double, including tax. The downside is that Pulaski Hwy is very sleazy; it's dotted with strip clubs and cheap mini-malls. Although Duke's keeps out the drug and prostitute trade, other motels – which can be $5 or $10 cheaper – don't. So if you are checking them out, be sure to have a thorough look around.

At the western end of town about four miles from downtown is the *Beltway Motel* (☎ 410-242-2363), 3648 Washington Blvd. It's northwest of the intersection of Washington Blvd and I-695. They have over 100 rooms with the usual at $41 for one bed and $46 for two. There is a $3 key deposit.

There are other motels in the $30 to $40 price range in the town of Elk Ridge eight miles west of downtown on Washington Blvd. Some of these have short-time (three hour) rooms, but aren't as sordid as those on Pulaski Hwy. Try the *Terrace Motel* (☎ 410-796-2000), 6260 Washington Blvd, and *Tip Top Motel* (☎ 410-796-0227), 6251 Washington Blvd.

Places to Stay – middle

The *Quality Inn Inner Harbor* (☎ 410-727-3400, 800-221-2222) is actually at 1701 Russell Rd, a highway-like road several blocks east of the harbor. It has standard motel rooms at single/double rates of $58/68, lower from November to April.

Albert J Strubinger rents out two rooms in his 1794 Federal Hill home, *Eagle's Mere B&B* (☎ 410-332-1618), 102 E Montgomery St. One room overlooks the Inner Harbor but most of the view is blocked by the back of the Science Museum across Key Hwy. The other room in the front of the house overlooks Montgomery St and has a working fireplace. Mr Strubinger is a great guy and staying here is more like being a member of the family than a guest. Rooms are $65.

The *Paulus Gasthaus* (☎ 410-467-1688), 2406 Kentucky Ave, has two rooms at a single/double rate of $75/80 in the northern end of the city. Take I-895 north to Erdman Ave. Drive north on Erdman for two miles until you reach Belair Rd. Make a right and go four blocks to Kentucky Ave.

Days Inn Baltimore/Inner Harbor (☎ 410-576-1000, 800-942-7543) is at 100 Hopkins Place near the Inner Harbor. For $89 up to four people get a modern, two-bed standard motel room with TV and air conditioning.

Places to Stay – top end

Mr Mole B&B (☎ 410-728-1179, fax 410-728-3379), 1601 Bolton St, is in the neighborhood of Bolton Hill northwest of Mount Vernon. The B&B is in a renovated 1870s townhouse with high ceilings and extravagantly decorated rooms. Each room is a suite with private bath, telephone, and clock radio. The friendly and knowledgeable hosts are Paul Bragaw and Colin

Clarke. Singles are $87 to $100 and doubles $97 to $125. Colin cooks a large continental-plus breakfast. There is garage parking.

Celie's Waterfront B&B (☎ 410-522-2323, 800-432-0184, fax 410-522-2324) is a recent construction at 1714 Thames St in Fells Point. It's half a block east of the waterfront intersection of Broadway and Thames. You enter through a long stucco corridor, which opens into the main part of the house and a garden. There is also a rooftop deck. Inside there are seven rooms, all with private bath and air-con; some rooms have fireplaces and whirlpools. The only caveat is that Celie's is a 'waterfront' place only in the sense that it's across the street from a large building on the water, sometimes used as a police station in films; Celie's itself is not on the water. Rooms are $125 to $175.

Fells Point's gem is the *Admiral Fell Inn* (☎ 410-522 7377, 800-292-4667, fax 410-522-0707), 888 S Broadway, right at Thames St. This is a historic inn: Once a sailors' hotel, the inn has undergone refurbishment and expansion. The rooms feature Federal-style furniture, four-poster beds, some good views of the area and large baths. The inn's restaurant, Savannah, is a popular upscale dining spot with an original mix of Southern and nouvelle cuisine. Rooms cost $185.

The majority of the most expensive hotels in Baltimore ring the Inner Harbor. The exception is the *Clarion Hotel* (☎ 410-727-7101), 612 Cathedral St in Mount Vernon one block west of the Washington Monument. This hotel is away from the Inner Harbor tourist scene. It has 104 rooms with mini bars, bathroom phones, hair dryers, towel warmers, marble bathrooms, new furniture, and access to a health club. Double rates start at $109 during the week, but there are cheaper weekend packages.

The address for the *Inn at Pier 5* (☎ 410-539-2000) is 711 Eastern Ave, but it's actually on the southern end of Pier 5 across from the aquarium on the Inner Harbor. The hotel was being remodeled at press time. Rates will be high for the new 55 rooms.

The rest of the expensive hotels are around the Inner Harbor. In all cases the harbor view is far superior to the city view, so if these hotels are within your price range, opt for the view. The *Harbor Court* (☎ 410-234-0550, 800-824-0076, fax 410-659-5925), 550 Light St overlooking the western side of the harbor, has the best rooms in Baltimore. The views are excellent, a small window in every room opens, and the rooms have rich fabrics and art. Marble bathrooms have hair dryers and TV. There's a health club with pool, hot tub, tennis and racquetball courts. Singles/doubles with view are $190/260; without $160/220.

If you have the money but can't stay at the Harbor Court, your next bet is the *Hyatt Regency* (☎ 410-528-1234), 300 Light St, a few hundred yards north of the Harbor Court. A standard guest room runs $190; the harbor view costs $215.

Places to Eat

Baltimore's city markets lead the way in cheap eats. The markets sell produce and meat, but also have takeout or counter-seating restaurants that serve everything from seafood to Chinese. The *Baltimore Farmers' Market* sells food underneath the Jones Falls Expressway at Holiday and Saratoga Sts from late June to mid-December.

The city's main restaurant districts have grown up around major attractions and a few distinctive neighborhoods.

Inner Harbor & Downtown Both *Harborplace* complexes have restaurants in them, but the Light St Pavilion is packed with a two-story food court with tables and take-out places. You can eat barbecue, raw bar, pizza, frozen yogurt, burgers, Mexican, Greek, Chinese, candy, etc. This is your best bet for a variety of bargain food. There are also gourmet shops selling everything from imported brie to baguettes and wine. The place is crowded and a lot like a shopping mall, but this is a convenient place to pick up supplies for a picnic along the 7.5 mile promenade that is being built around the Inner Harbor.

The *Women's Industrial Exchange & Restaurant* (☎ 410-685-4388), 333 N Charles St, has been in business since 1882. You enter through a room that sells knit goods, blankets, and pillows. In back of the store is the pale blue and white dining room with its black-and-white linoleum floor. The waitresses are way over 60, and you can get food from a bygone era like chicken aspic or croquettes. They also sell more prosaic sandwich platters and good pie for $2. Lunch costs from $4 to $8.

Lexington Market, Lexington and Eutaw Sts, west of Charles St, is the city's oldest indoor market and has a vast selection of food places. *Faidley's* has the best raw bar in Baltimore, serving oysters at about $1 each, clams, and beer. You can also pick fresh fish and have them cook it, or order crab cakes or something else from the vast selection. Backfin or softshell crab sandwiches are $6.50; fish sandwiches from $3 to $5; fried oysters go for $5. Add a couple of dollars to an order and get two vegetables. There's a large, happy-hour crowd here on Fridays until about 8 pm.

Mount Vernon *Louie's Book Store Cafe* (☎ 410-962-1224), 518 N Charles St south of the Walters Art Gallery is a Baltimore institution. The atmosphere is relaxing and quiet enough to read, and browsers can buy food and liquor at the back of the bookstore. The food is good, fresh, and comes in reasonable portions. Salads are around $6, burgers $5 and sandwiches $4 to $6.

A few restaurants on or near N Charles St offer decent all-you-can-eat lunches. *Minato* (☎ 410-332-0332), 800 N Charles St, on the corner of Madison, has a chicken teriyaki for $10. *Akbar* (☎ 410-539-0944), 823 N Charles St, between Madison and Read Sts, has an all-you-can-eat Indian lunch buffet on weekdays from 11:30 am to 2:30 pm for $7. The *Bombay Grill* (☎ 410-837-2973), 2 E Madison, a few feet east of N Charles St, does an Indian buffet with slightly better food for $9. *Japan* (☎ 410-962-1130), 316 N Charles St, has all-you-can-eat sushi Tuesday from 5 to 9 pm for $24.

Tony Cheng's Szechuan Restaurant (☎ 410-539-6666), 801 N Charles St, has some great spicy entrees for $9 to $12.

The *Helmand* (☎ 410-752-0311), 806 N Charles St, serves good Afghani food in a simple and tasteful environment. Kabuli (lamb and raisins over rice) is $10; most other dishes are under $12.

The Great American Melting Pot (☎ 410-837-9797), 904 N Charles St, has a Roy Lichtenstein-inspired menu with salads for $4 to $7; pastas start at $7.

Highly recommended, the *Brass Elephant* (☎ 410-547-8480), at 924 N Charles St, two blocks north of the monument, is in an 1860s townhouse decorated with brass fixtures, a fireplace, and a few chandeliers. Lunch sandwiches like grilled tuna are around $10.50. Dinner pastas, salmon, sweetbreads, and meats are in the $20 to $25 range.

Federal Hill The *Cross St Market* is at the corner of Cross and Light Sts. The market has delis, Italian, a sushi bar and a raw bar in addition to the usual fresh produce and meat. On Friday and Saturday evenings there is a happy hour from 5 to 8 pm at the raw bar at the western end of the market. It's packed on Fridays with people drinking quarts of draft beer ($2.50), and eating steamed shrimp, raw oysters and clams, crabs, and crab cakes.

Most other places are along Cross St on the north side of the market with a couple on S Light St or S Charles St within a block or so of the market.

Sisson's South Baltimore Brewing Company (☎ 410-539-2093), 36 E Cross St, brews and serves its own beer. The menu has a lot of Cajun dishes like blackened strip steak ($17), chicken étouffée ($14), and jambalaya ($15). The food is good and the atmosphere modern.

Singh Express (☎ 410-752-1895), 1019 S Charles St around the corner from the Cross St Market delivers pizza and other Italian food and Indian food. A 12/16-inch vegetarian pizza is $9/11. The Indian dishes tend to be a tad pricey from $9 to $11 for meat dishes and $7 for vegetarian dishes.

A few doors away (to the south) at 1105 S Charles is *Maksuri* (☎ 410-752-8561) a small, but popular sushi place where a yellowtail roll costs $4.

Barely two blocks north of the Cross St Market you will find one of Baltimore's most trendy cafes, the *One World Cafe* (☎ 410-234-0235) at 904 S Charles. The restored storefront is filled with the smell of pastries and 20 different kinds of coffee. A double espresso costs $1.50, Belgian waffles $3.25. Locals artists shows their work on the wall and there's an upscale pool room on the 2nd floor.

Fells Point The *Broadway Market* has two small buildings (compared to the Lexington Market) in the middle of the Broadway divider north and south of the Aliceanna St intersection. Inside are a couple of diners, a deli, bakery, a few other restaurants, and meat and produce sellers. One seafood vendor sells crab cakes for $4.50.

There are a number of restaurants and more bars, which also sell food, along Broadway. *Foster's Oyster Bar & Restaurant* (☎ 410-558-3600), 606 S Broadway, serves oysters for 50¢ each before 7 pm.

The long-time, local favorite cheap-eats venue in this part of town is the *Nice N' Easy* (☎ 410-782-8821) at 700 S Broadway. Ed and Sue Milburn, an extremely gregarious couple, keep their diner/carryout open 24 hours a day. Here you can get a three-egg breakfast for $1.57 and homemade chili for $2. They have cheap beer, too.

Bertha's (☎ 410-327-5795), at the corner of Broadway and Lancaster St, near the water, is known for its mussels. Large bowls of them are served with a choice of sauces like garlic butter and capers; spinach, tarragon, and garlic; or creamy mustard. All three cost under $8. Bertha's also serves salads, sandwiches, and other seafood dishes. There's live blues most nights.

Sushi Cafe (☎ 410-732-3570), 1640 Thames St east of Broadway, has reasonable deals on sushi. For 10/15/20 pieces they charge $7.50/12.50/17. Sunday to Monday from 5 to 10 pm an all-you-can-gorge is $25.

Al Pacino Cafe (☎ 410-327-0005), 609 S Broadway, has Mediterranean appetizers and pizza with unusual toppings such as pine nuts and squid for $6.35 to $15.

There's a good cafe just down the block toward the harbor called *Adrian's Bookstore Cafe* (☎ 410-732-1048) at 714 S Broadway. There are two floors here, with Adrian's art on the walls, a full selection of new and used books and intimate cafe tables where you can eat salads and sandwiches or just hang for hours while sipping coffee, reading, and watching the eclectic crowd pass through.

Obrycki's (☎ 410-732-6399) is a Baltimore legend at 1727 E Pratt St just east of Broadway above Fells Point. People come here to eat steamed spiced crabs off of tables covered in brown butcher's paper. You buy them by the dozen starting at $22 and going up to near $52 depending on the size.

Southwest Baltimore The area around *Hollins Market*, on Hollins St between Arlington and Carey Sts, has a few restaurants that draw people from other parts of the city. The market, which is closed Monday, has a few food stalls with very fresh food.

On the northwest corner of Hollins and Arlington Sts is *The Corner* coffeehouse. On the southwest corner is the *Tom Thumb* bar. Walk through it past the video poker machines and into *Gypsy's Cafe* (☎ 410-625-9310), 1103 Hollins St. This place is a funky microbrewery where you can get a SoWe Burger made with organically grown beef for around $5, or choose from daily seafood and meat specials.

Across from the north side of the market is *Mencken's Cultured Pearl* (☎ 410-837-1947), a bar and restaurant at 1114 Hollins St that serves Mexican food. Some locals argue it's more expensive and not as good as Gypsy's, others say that it's better and worth the money for the funky atmosphere and bohemian crowd.

Little Italy Little Italy is a quiet neighborhood of row houses immediately east of the Inner Harbor between Pratt St and Eastern Ave. The biggest concentration of its restaurants is along a three-block stretch of S High St. They favor candlelight, ornamental wine bottles, and canned accordion music with entree selections in the $15 to $20 range for meats, less for pasta. If you ask Baltimoreans for a recommendation, you're unlikely to find any agreement. One place with more modern decor and lower prices is *Amiccis* (☎ 410-528-1096), 231 S High St. You can indulge yourself in this small, casual restaurant for $9 to $11. *Luigi Petti* (☎ 410-685-0055), 1002 Eastern Ave on the corner of Exeter St, has a large outdoor patio, something other places lack for about the same money.

Dalesio's (☎ 410-539-1965), 829 Eastern Ave on the corner of Albemarle, has a varied enough menu to include wholewheat pasta and duck-breast ravioli.

Note that finding a parking spot around Little Italy is extremely difficult, and the restaurants employ valet parking guys who can separate you from your money in a hurry.

Elsewhere *Haussner's* (☎ 410-327-8365), 3242 Eastern Ave at S Clinton, serves traditional German dishes in a large room decorated with table-to-ceiling oil paintings, statues, and ceramic sculptures. The bar – where they hide the men's room – is labeled 'strictly stag' and its oil paintings are only of female nudes. The menu has over 80 entrees from seafood to traditional German dishes like the saucy hasenpfeffer (marinated rabbit) for $18 or sauerbraten for $11 and wiener schnitzel for $14. Diners tend to wear jackets and ties even at lunch, but the management doesn't turn away casually dressed clients.

There are three competing New York-style delicatessens along Lombard St between Central Ave and S Exeter St a block north of Little Italy. This is a seedy neighborhood, but this block has parking and is safe. *Lenny's* (☎ 410-327-1177) is a popular cafeteria-style deli closer to Central Ave. The standard corned beef, cole slaw, and Russian dressing sandwich is $3.69; all the other sandwiches are under $4, unless you want them overstuffed in which case they're $4.50 and well worth it.

The competition in the neighborhood is *Weiss Deli*, which has fewer customers, and *Attman's*, which does a huge takeout business.

Entertainment

Bars Baltimore's most active neighborhood for bar-hopping is Fells Point along Broadway, particularly the east side of the street and also on Aliceanna, Lancaster, and Thames Sts to the east of Broadway. One popular bar is the *Wharf Rat* (☎ 410-276-9034), 801 S Ann St in Fells Point. Unlike a lot of the bars that cater to a college-age crowd, the Wharf Rat draws a mix of folks from mariners and bikers to yuppies and artists. The attraction is one of the best jukeboxes in town, a pool table and a selection of nearly 50 microbrews – mostly on tap – including the Rat's own Oliver's Ale. You can try three different drafts for $3. The New York–quality pizza goes for $8.50.

Another lively neighborhood is Federal Hill. The bars along E Cross St next to the Cross St Market give out free and discount drink tickets during happy hour on Friday and Saturday to people at the raw bar in the market. *Sis's Bar* is a genuine south Baltimore, non-tourist place to drink. To get there from the front of Cross St Market, walk one block east on Cross St. Make a right on William St and Sis's is a few feet from the corner downstairs in a townhouse.

Hammerjacks (☎ 410-752-3302) at 1101 S Howard St near the Camden Yard baseball park is the largest gin mill in the city with capacity for 1800 souls. It attracts a singles crowd with a mix of hard rock, alternative and country. Curiously, and extremely rare for Baltimore, the staff cops an attitude toward out-of-towners.

This club is an easy place for a guy to get in a fight, and also the setting for some of the more outlandish scenes in the movie *Serial Mom*.

Gay Nightclubs *Orpheus* (☎ 410-276-5599), 1003 E Pratt St on the corner of S Exeter St, has changing decor and DJs. *Allegro's* (☎ 410-837-3906), 1101 Cathedral St, has a women's night for lesbians every Saturday. *Port in a Storm* (☎ 410-732-5608), 4330 E Lombard St, is another women's bar. The *Hippo* (☎ 410-547-0069), 1 W Eager St, is the largest gay bar in Baltimore with live shows and dancing.

Music *Eight By Ten* (☎ 410-625-2000), 10 E Cross St opposite the north side of the Cross St Market, has live alternative, reggae, blues, and pop music seven nights a week. The place jumps, but you've got to love cigarette smoke and cramped spaces.

The Fells Point bars offer dozens of live acts on weekends. Try *Max's on Broadway* (☎ 410-675-6297), 735 S Broadway, for live progressive, alternative, and jazz seven days a week.

Theater Baltimore has a host of theater companies. The *Arena Players* (☎ 410-728-6500), 801 McCulloh St, is an African American theater group. *Children's Theater Association* (☎ 410-366-6403) plays at 121 McMechen St. *Center Stage* (☎ 410-685-3200), 700 N Calvert St between Monument and Madison Sts, is Maryland's state theater. The *Morris A Mechanic Theater* (☎ 410-837-3913), Hopkins Plaza at Baltimore and Charles Sts, brings Broadway shows to the city. *Theater Hopkins* (☎ 410-516-7159) is the Johns Hopkins University community theater in the Merrick Barn. The *Theater Project* (☎ 410-752-8558), 45 W Preston St, is Baltimore's avant-garde production troupe. The *Eubie Blake Cultural Center* (☎ 410-539-1717) at 34 S Market St is a community arts center.

Performing Arts The *Baltimore Opera Company* performs at the Lyric Opera House (☎ 410-685-5086), which is in northern Baltimore between Mount Royal and Cathedral Sts.

The Meyerhoff Symphony Hall (☎ 410-783-8000) hosts the *Baltimore Symphony Orchestra and Chorus* and touring performances. The *Chamber Music Society of Baltimore* (☎ 410-486-1140), plays at the Meyerhoff Auditorium at the Baltimore Museum of Art at Charles and 31st Sts. The *Peabody Conservatory of Music* (☎ 410-659-8124), 1 E Mount Vernon Place, offers solo, ensemble, and concert performances by students and others.

National and international musical shows are held at the *Pier 6 Concert Pavilion* (☎ 410-725-8632), at Pratt and Market Sts on the Inner Harbor in the summer.

For African and African American dance performances, check out *Sankofa Dance Theater* (☎ 410-448-2345) at 4900 Wetheredsville Rd.

Cinema The *Orpheum* (☎ 410-732-4614), 1724 Thames St east of Broadway in Fells Point, shows revivals and art films.

The *Film House at the Walters Art Gallery* (☎ 410-547-9000) offers an eclectic selection of short films every Friday.

The *Senator* movie theater (☎ 410-435-8338), 5904 York Rd, north of downtown, is a large, beautifully renovated theater in which well known Baltimore directors, such as John Waters and Barry Levinson, have their premieres.

Comedy You're likely to find enough comedians in the people you meet around town to satisfy your appetite for laughter, but Baltimoreans do patronize comedy clubs. The place mentioned most often is the *Comedy Factory Outlet* (☎ 410-576-8558) at Lombard and Light Sts.

Spectator Sports

Baseball Going to a baseball game is a traditional American pastime and one that is particularly enjoyable in Baltimore, though this is more for the enjoyment of the great new Oriole Park at Camden Yards than for watching the sometimes erratic performance of the home team – the Orioles.

Camden Yards, (☎ information: 410-685-9800; tickets: 410-481-7328) west of the Inner Harbor at Eutaw and Pratt Sts, opened in April 1992 to rave reviews, the cleverest being that it offered the 'joyous possibility that a ballpark might actually enhance the experience of watching the game of baseball.' What this means is that Baltimore designed a retro stadium designed to recapture the old joys of going to an idiosyncratic ballpark. Camden Yards is asymmetrical, seats a reasonable 48,000 folks in good-sized seats, none of which are obstructed by support columns as in other stadiums. It also has a selection of good food (not just the $4 hot dogs and $3 soda monopolies at other stadiums).

Baseball season is April to October. The ballpark is walking distance from the Inner Harbor. The Metro stations at Lexington Market and Charles Center are within a 10-minute walk of the ballpark and there is a free shuttle bus from Lexington Market. MARC trains stop right at the park at Camden Station. Buses Nos 27 and 28 also stop at the park.

Horseracing Thoroughbred racing is alive and well at Pimlico Downs (☎ 410-542-9400), 5201 Park Heights. The Preakness Derby, the second jewel in racing's Triple Crown, takes place at Pimlico in mid-May and is a one of the rites of spring for Maryland high society. Post time is 12:35 pm weekdays, 12:15 pm weekends and costs $3 for grandstands, $4 for clubhouse.

MARYLAND

Other Sports The Baltimore Spirits (☎ 410-625-2320) play indoor soccer and the Baltimore Thunder (☎ 410-347-2020) plays lacrosse at the Baltimore Arena (☎ 410-347-2000), 201 W Baltimore St, which also occasionally hosts the Washington Wizards basketball team, concerts, and other shows.

In 1996, the powerful Cleveland Browns professional football team accepted Baltimore's invitation to leave Cleveland and come to Baltimore. In the ensuing legal battles courts approved the team's move to Baltimore but required that the team change its name and uniforms. The team is now called the Baltimore Ravens (☎ 410-261-7283), after Poe's famous poem, and plays its games at Memorial Stadium in North Baltimore.

Things to Buy

Over 50 antique stores are clustered along N Howard St between Read and Monument Sts and nearby along Chase St between Park Ave and Charles St a couple of blocks north of the Washington Monument. If these seem pricey, you can find less expensive antiques in the many shops at Fells Point, particularly on Fleet and Aliceanna Sts east of Broadway.

China Sea Marine Trading Co (☎ 410-276-8220), on the Ann St wharf in Fells Point, has a great selection of nautical equipment salvaged from ships, and other brass items like lanterns. It's open Monday to Friday from mid-afternoon to 7 pm, weekends from noon to 7 pm.

Market Center is a collection of 400 specialty shops bordered to the north and south by Saratoga and Fayette Sts, and to the east and west by Eutaw and Howard Sts.

Harborplace (☎ 410-837-4636) on the Inner Harbor and the connecting Gallery Mall across Pratt St are two of the cornerstones in the Inner Harbor redevelopment. With sunlit atriums, fresh air, and great views, these markets draw hordes of tourists and locals to browse 110 specialty shops that sell everything from sports team T-shirts and toys to fine fashions and ship models. Local artisans sell their products at Sam Smith Market on the upper level of Harborplace's Light St Pavilion.

Getting There & Away

Air Ten miles south of the city center off Route 295, Baltimore-Washington International Airport (BWI; ☎ 410-895-7111) is served by most major airlines. See the listing in the Getting There & Away chapter.

Bus Greyhound (☎ 410-752-1393) has their terminal at 210 W Fayette St three blocks west of downtown.

Train Baltimore's Penn Station is at 1515 N Charles St between Oliver and Lanvale Sts. Buses Nos 3 and 11 pass it going north on Charles St and south on Cathedral St. Bus No 61 goes north on Calvert St and south on St Paul St past the station. MARC (☎ 410-539-5000, 800-325-7245) operates regular train service to/from Washington, DC's Union Station. One-way/roundtrip to DC is $5.25/10.75. Amtrak (☎ 800-872-7245) has service from other cities along the northeast corridor – Washington, Philadelphia, Trenton, Newark, New York and points north.

Car The approach to Baltimore from Washington, DC, is along I-95 north or I-295 north (the Baltimore-Washington Expressway), which becomes Russell Ave, a road that can slowly take you into town west of the Inner Harbor. Depending on unpredictable rush hour traffic, an alternative is to take the I-395 exit from I-95. This spills out as Howard St downtown. Roads from DC to Baltimore can be congested. An alternate route that may add 30 to 45 minutes to the normal 45 minute to one hour trip is to take Hwy 29 north from Washington until it intersects with Hwy 40 east. Then take Hwy 40 east into Baltimore.

From points north, like Wilmington, the route is I-95 south. You can avoid the toll at the Fort McHenry tunnel by taking Exit 59 west (Eastern Ave) into town. Eastern crosses Broadway in Fells Point and then brings you to the Inner Harbor.

From western Maryland and Harpers Ferry, West Virginia, the approach into Baltimore is along Hwy 40 east (the Baltimore National Pike), which leads to Mulberry and Franklin Sts downtown. Don't exit off of Hwy 40 onto I-70 east. Although Hwy 40 and I-70 overlap several times, I-70 ends before it gets to Baltimore. If you end up on I-70 anyway, then take I-695 south (the Baltimore Beltway) to I-95 north to I-395 onto Howard St.

Finally, if you're coming from Annapolis, you're best bet is to take I-97 north to I-695 west to I-95 north to I-395 to Howard St. From points further east, like Ocean City, Maryland, or the Delaware shore, the only approach is across the Chesapeake Bay Bridge (Routes 50 & 301). Go across the bridge and then take Route 2 north right into town where it becomes Hanover St west of the Inner Harbor.

Getting Around

The Metropolitan Transportation Association (☎ 410-539-5000) can tell you how to get anywhere in the city by public transport. The fare system for bus, light rail, and metro systems is identical. You can travel anywhere within the city for $1.35 but make sure you have the exact change. A weekly pass costs $14, permitting unlimited rides within the city from Sunday to Saturday. You can also buy an unlimited one-day pass for $3. You can buy passes at banks and stores throughout the city. The most useful for travel within the city is the bus system. There are about 60 routes throughout the city and into the suburbs. Details on the light rail and metro are outlined below.

To/From the Airport The ground transportation desk (☎ 410-691-2045) is on the ground level at C Pier. You can take the light rail to Cromwell St and then Bus No 17 to the airport for $1.35 plus 10¢ transfer fee. MARC trains (☎ 800-325-7245) run into the city Monday to Friday from 7 am to 10:30 pm, $3.25/6 for oneway/roundtrip.

Amtrak (☎ 800-872-7245) has daily service to/from Penn Station from 7:20 am to midnight for $5/10 for roundtrip. The BWI Super Shuttle (☎ 800-258-3826) runs buses to/from major Baltimore hotels daily every half hour from 6 am to 11 pm. The one-way/roundtrip fare is $10/15.

Private Car (☎ 410-553-8000) runs limousines to/from hotels for $25. Taxis to the city cost about $18.

Light Rail This is a one-line train (☎ 410-539-5000) that runs north-south for 22 miles. It runs back and forth from Timonium north of the city through the city along Howard St to Glen Burnie south of the city. It's most useful for commuting to/from the suburbs, although there are six stops more or less downtown along Howard St and then five more within the city to the north. Trains run Monday to Friday from 6 am to 11 pm; Saturday from 8 am to 11 pm; and Sunday from 11 am to 7 pm.

Metro The Metro runs from Charles St Centre (at the intersection of Baltimore St) downtown out to Owings Mills. Like the Light Rail, it is only useful if you want to go to a limited number of places along one line. The stops downtown are along Eutaw St. The Metro runs weekdays from 5 am to midnight, and Saturday from 8 am to midnight.

Water Taxi Harbor Boating (☎ 410-563-3901, 800-658-8947) runs boats with regularly scheduled stops on the Inner Harbor, Little Italy, and Fells Point. It works like a bus service with a number of boats running continuously on a 14-stop route. The boats run daily from 11 am to 11 pm during the summer, until midnight on weekends, with shorter hours in other seasons. Adults/children under 10 pay $3.50/2.25 for one day's unlimited rides.

Paddle Boats There are paddle-boat rental outlets on the north side of Inner Harbor near the Aquarium. The one to the west, opposite the Pratt St Pavilion of Harborplace, rents them for two/three/four people at $5/6.50/7.50 per hour.

Further east, opposite the World Trade Center, Trident Electric Boat (☎ 410-539-1837) has electric boats for two/three people at $10/15 per half hour.

Taxi Local companies include Diamond (☎ 410-947-3333); Sun (☎ 410-235-0300) and Yellow Cab (☎ 410-685-1212).

Pedicab Destination Baltimore (☎ 410-732-2378) will take you around in a pedicab; you negotiate the fare with your driver.

MARYLAND

HORSE COUNTRY

North of Baltimore on either side of I-83 to York, Pennsylvania, lies over 100 sq miles of Piedmont fields and forest divided by hedges, white rail fences, and stone walls. Sometimes called the Worthington and Greenspring Valleys after creeks that divide the terrain, this area is a huge collection of fancy horse farms watched over by stately, ancestral manors. Many of Maryland oldest and wealthiest families have lived on these manors for centuries, and the place is thick with legendary figures, including Olympic riders, world champion horses, and Baltimore baseball titan Cal Ripken who owns an estate here. Sagamore Farms, the former Vanderbilt estate, is the birthplace of Secretariat, a Triple Crown winner and the highest-earning thoroughbred stud in history.

There are only a few chances to see a collection of the celebrity owners, riders, and horses. One of the premier events for the horse crowd is the **Maryland Hunt Cup Race**, held in Glyndon on the third weekend in April. This is America's most-challenging steeplechase: Contestants face

Hampton: Not Your Ordinary Horse Farm

To get a taste of life on a Maryland manor, you can stop at Hampton (☎ 410-962-0688) just off the Beltway (I-695) at Exit 27B in Towson. One of the largest late Georgian houses in Maryland, Hampton is a national park on 60 acres of land. The Ridgely family began building the house as the family seat for its horse farm in 1783 and the site for genteel entertainment on a grand scale. Nine rooms in the house are decorated to represent the different periods of Ridgely habitation and include significant antiques and portraits by major painters like Rembrandt Peale and Thomas Sully. The grounds have exotic trees, shrubs, and flowers including 200-year-old catalpas. Hampton is free and open 9 am to 4 pm daily, except in foul weather. Tours run hourly. ■

wooden fences, and the nine-minute race attracts thousands. Spectators arrive around noon dressed in their spring finery – which may include linen dresses and formal attire – to enjoy lavish tailgate parties that have a tendency to put almost everybody in a euphoric state by the late afternoon race. If you fancy cherry blossoms, mint juleps, and rubbing shoulders with Maryland's aristocracy as well as some of Washington's senators and congressional representatives, the Maryland Hunt Cup may be worth some effort to reserve a parking space. For a parking ticket you must call the Maryland Hunt Cup Association (☎ 410-833-4188) or write them at 3302 Belmont Rd, Glyndon, MD 21071. The ticket to park your car costs $30, which entitles you to bring as many people as you can fit in your vehicle; $50 will get you 'patron' parking in a field full of Benzes, Beamers, and Rollses where the in-crowd parties and the chauffeurs do the driving.

Other horsey events that draw a crowd are the **Blessing of the Hounds** on the green in front of St James Episcopal Church in Monkton. Call the Hunt Cup Association for the spring date. The **Timonium State Fair** runs for 10 days over the last week of August and features thoroughbred sales that draw a lot of beautiful animals and beautiful people. Of course, the **Preakness Derby** in mid-May (see Spectator Sports) is a social event of grand proportions as well as one of the jewels in the Triple Crown of thoroughbred racing.

But even if attending one of the horsey events is not in your schedule, you might just want to explore the country roads. As they wind through the villages of Worthington, Glyndon, and Shawan to the west of I-83 – and Monkton, Madonna, and My Lady's Manor to the east – these roads make for refreshing cycling or motor touring and take you past a host of impressive horse farms. The place is awash with colors and scents in April and May when all the trees and flowers around the manors are in blossom. Sagamore Farms is on the road between Worthington and Shawan.

Annapolis & Southern Maryland

ANNAPOLIS

Thirty-five miles south of Baltimore and an equal distance east of Washington on the Western Shore of the Chesapeake, Annapolis has been the capital of Maryland since colonial times and now has a population of 33,000. A national landmark, the city has one of the largest concentrations of 18th century homes and public buildings (many open to the public) in the country. Although Annapolis is the seat of the state bureaucracy, no modern office buildings mar the skyline or the narrow brick streets.

Home of the US Naval Academy since 1845, Annapolis Harbor and its connecting tidal creeks shelter dozens of marinas where thousands of cruising and racing sailboats tie up. This concentration of recreational sailing vessels, probably the largest fleet of any city or town in America, has earned Annapolis the title of 'Sailing Capital of the United States.' In response to the onshore appetites of the sailing crowd and the tourists who come to immerse themselves in history and the nautical scene, an extensive collection of restaurants, bars, and inns has grown up around the city's waterfront. Today, Annapolis has a well-deserved reputation as a party town.

HIGHLIGHTS

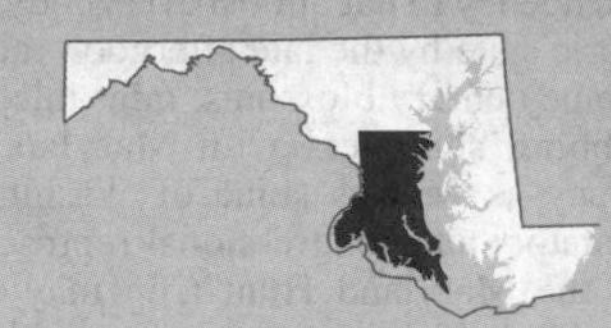

- The grounds, of the Naval Academy and St John's College
- State House Circle
- People watching at City Dock, especially from the porch of the Middleton Tavern
- The US Sailboat Show in October
- Skipjack races at Chesapeake Bay Appreciation Day at Sandy Point in late October
- Crabbing at Chesapeake Beach or the Solomons
- Traditional oyster shucking operation at the JC Lore Oyster House, Solomons
- Fossil-hunting at Calvert Cliffs State Park
- Point Lookout State Park
- Colonial Maryland at St Mary's City

History

Puritans from Virginia settled Annapolis in 1649 and named their community after Princess Anne Arundel, who became Queen of England. From its inception Annapolis proved an important port and quickly won the distinction of being the seat of government for the Maryland colony. Following the Revolutionary War, Annapolis served as the US capital from November 1783 to August 1784.

With Baltimore eclipsing Annapolis as a commercial center during the next two hundred years, the city settled into genteel obscurity for all but Maryland's politicians, naval midshipmen coming to learn the trade of their hero Captain John Paul Jones, and local watermen. Rediscovered as an architectural treasure by the masses fleeing Baltimore and Washington in the 1960s, Annapolis was one of the first municipalities in the state to enthusiastically champion historic preservation. Some of the early efforts lacked finesse, but during the last 30 years, the city's historic center has been fastidiously buffed and polished several times. Today, Annapolis blends its historic ambiance with a contemporary enthusiasm for high-tech sailing craft of all shapes and sizes.

Orientation

Annapolis sits on a small peninsula between College and Spa Creeks. The US Naval Academy takes up the northeastern half of the peninsula and the city constitutes the rest. It's a very compact town, so compact, in fact, that you can walk from one end to the other easily. At the center in State Circle is the State House and west of that one block is Church Circle. Running southeast to the City Dock from Church Circle is Main St, the major commercial street. Duke of Gloucester St runs southeast from Church Circle to the drawbridge to the Eastport, a collection of marinas and residences across Spa Creek.

Information

Tourist Offices The Annapolis & Anne Arundel County Conference & Visitors Bureau (☎ 410-280-0445, fax 263-9591), 26 West St, is open daily from 9 am to 5 pm. From April to October there is an information booth at the City Dock open from 10 am to 5 pm.

There's a Maryland state visitors center (☎ 410-974-3400) in the lobby of the State House open daily from 9 am to 5 pm.

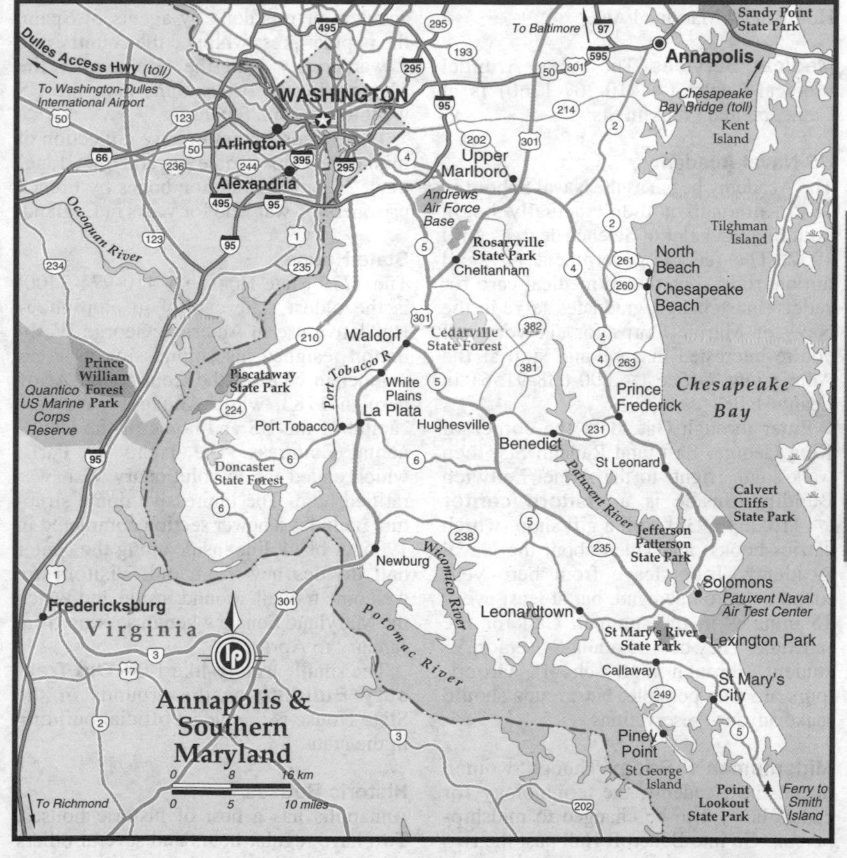

Post The post office (☎ 410-263-9292) is on Church Circle at Northwest St.

Media The daily newspaper is the *Capital*. Pick up a copy of the giveaway *Inside Annapolis* for information on things happening in town.

Bookstores Super Crown Books (☎ 410-268-7670) is the most complete bookstore in Annapolis, 176 Main St. It's open from 10 am to 10 pm Monday to Saturday, and 10 am to 6 pm Sunday.

Laundry Locals swear by Self-Service Laundry (☎ 410-297-9092) near the State House at 74 Maryland Ave.

Medical Services The Anne Arundel Medical Center (☎ 410-267-1260) is at Cathedral and Franklin Sts.

US Naval Academy

The Academy began as the Naval School in 1845, although it didn't actually begin awarding Bachelor of Science degrees until 1932. The federal government pays all tuition, room, board, and medical care for cadets. In exchange, graduates serve in the Navy or Marine Corps for six years. If you're interested in applying, stop at the Admissions Office (☎ 800-638-9156) in Leahy Hall.

Enter through Gate 1 at the corner of King George, East, and Randall Sts, then walk south (right) to the Armel Leftwich Building. Inside is a **visitors center** (☎ 410-263-6933) with a gift shop (which carries books) and video about the Naval Academy. Tours leave from here year round based on demand, but at least every 15 minutes in the summer. Call for the schedule. They cost $5 adult, $4 senior, $3 student (through high school). Groups tours are also possible, but groups should make advance reservations.

Midshipman's Room Though women attend the Academy, the terminology for cadets has yet to be changed to midship*person*. Go into Bancroft Hall past the two cannons aiming at you and down the hallway to the left to find the designated 'typical midshipman's room.' However, if you want to see a real midshipman's room, look in the windows before you go through the gate into the Bancroft courtyard. Real rooms have computers and stereos.

Preble Hall This hall has a museum of naval history, swords, silver settings, a raft on which three men floated for 34 days before being rescued, and artifacts from the battleship *Maine*. On February 15, 1898 the *Maine* blew up in Havana's harbor killing 266 on board. Although it has never been established whether the explosion was an accident or was done by agents of Spain, the popular press whipped the country into a war frenzy with the 'Remember the Maine' slogan. Two months later the US went to war with Spain.

There is also an impressive collection of miniature ships (some several feet long) made of beef and mutton bones by French prisoners-of-war held for years in England.

State House

The 1779 State House (☎ 410-974-3400) is the oldest state capitol in continuous legislative use in America. George Washington resigned his commission as commander in chief of the Continental Army here in 1783, while Annapolis was the capital of the US and home of the Continental Congress. The Treaty of Paris, which ended the Revolutionary War, was ratified here. The impressive dome structure includes a newer section completed in 1905. A black line inside along the center hall divides new from old. Visitors are welcome to walk around inside and watch the Maryland Senate when in session from January to April.

The small, armory-like 1735 **Old Treasury Building** on the grounds of the State House is the oldest official building in the state.

Historic Houses

Annapolis has a host of historic houses. Two have regular hours and several others

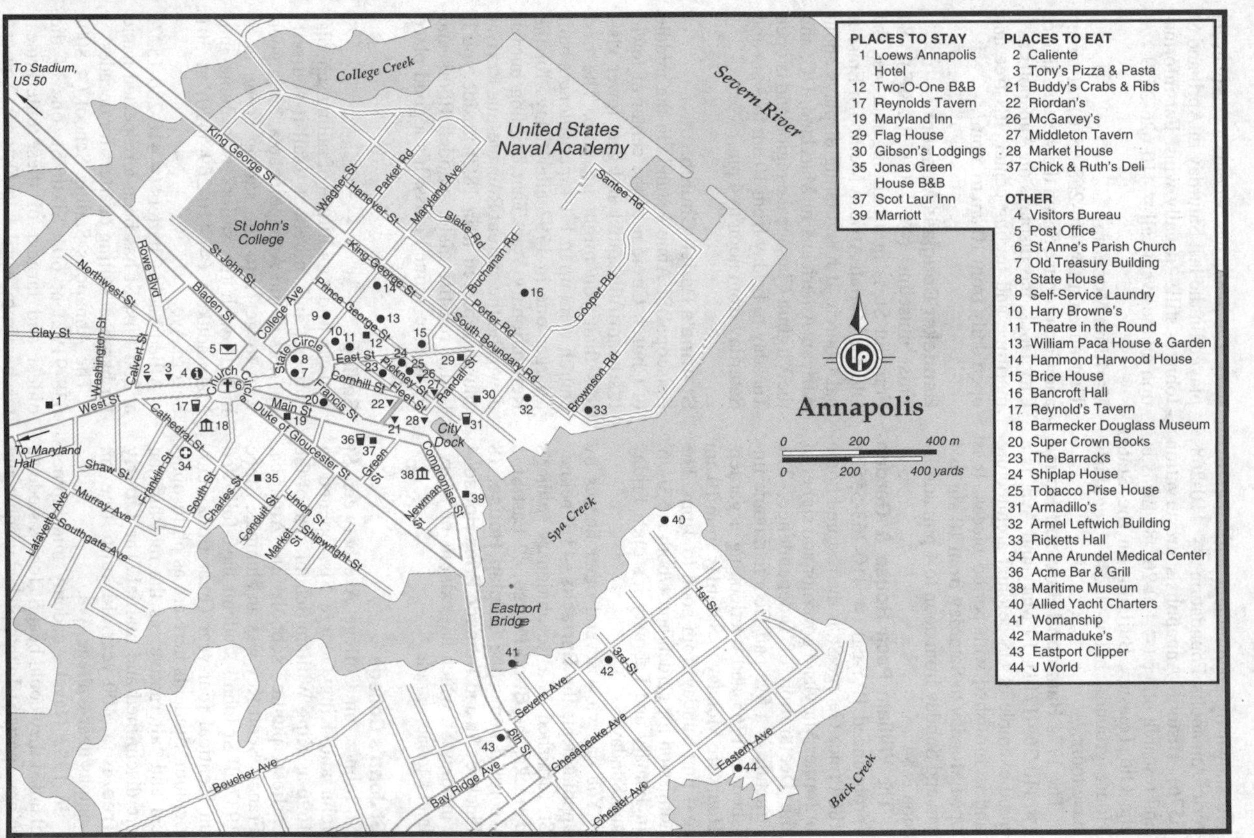
PLACES TO STAY
1 Loews Annapolis Hotel
12 Two-O-One B&B
17 Reynolds Tavern
19 Maryland Inn
29 Flag House
30 Gibson's Lodgings
35 Jonas Green House B&B
37 Scot Laur Inn
39 Marriott
PLACES TO EAT
2 Caliente
3 Tony's Pizza & Pasta
21 Buddy's Crabs & Ribs
22 Riordan's
26 McGarvey's
27 Middleton Tavern
28 Market House
37 Chick & Ruth's Deli
OTHER
4 Visitors Bureau
5 Post Office
6 St Anne's Parish Church
7 Old Treasury Building
8 State House
9 Self-Service Laundry
10 Harry Browne's
11 Theatre in the Round
13 William Paca House & Garden
14 Hammond Harwood House
15 Brice House
16 Bancroft Hall
17 Reynold's Tavern
18 Barmecker Douglass Museum
20 Super Crown Books
23 The Barracks
24 Shiplap House
25 Tobacco Prise House
31 Armadillo's
32 Armel Leftwich Building
33 Ricketts Hall
34 Anne Arundel Medical Center
36 Acme Bar & Grill
38 Maritime Museum
40 Allied Yacht Charters
41 Womanship
42 Marmaduke's
43 Eastport Clipper
44 J World
Annapolis
0 200 400 m
0 200 400 yards
To Stadium, US 50
College Creek
Severn River
United States Naval Academy
St John's College
King George St
Wagner St
Hanover St
Parker Rd
Maryland Ave
Blake Rd
Buchanan Rd
Porter Rd
South Boundary Rd
Cooper Rd
Santee Rd
Brownson Rd
Rowe Blvd
Northwest St
Bladen St
St John St
College Ave
Prince George St
Clay St
Washington St
Calvert St
State Circle
Church Circle
East St
Cornhill St
Pinckney St
Fleet St
Randall St
Francis St
Main St
West St
Cathedral St
Duke of Gloucester St
Green St
City Dock
Compromise St
Newman St
To Maryland Hall
Shaw St
Franklin St
South St
Charles St
Conduit St
Union St
Market St
Shipwright St
Murray Ave
Southgate Ave
Lafayette Ave
Spa Creek
Eastport Bridge
1st St
3rd St
6th St
Severn Ave
Chesapeake Ave
Eastern Ave
Boucher Ave
Bay Ridge Ave
Chester Ave
Back Creek

MARYLAND

are shown by appointment with the Historic Annapolis Foundation (☎ 410-268-5576). Historic Annapolis's preservation and research office (☎ 410-267-8149) is in the Old Treasury Building on the State House grounds, but it doesn't regularly have tours.

The 1774 **Hammond Harwood House** (☎ 410-269-1714), 19 Maryland Ave, is a good example of US colonial architecture and is furnished with period pieces. It is open Monday to Saturday from 10 am to 4 pm and Sunday from noon to 4 pm; admission is $4.

The **William Paca House & Garden** (pronounced PAY-ca) (☎ 410-263-5553), 186 Prince George St, is the restored home of former Maryland governor and signer of the Declaration of Independence. The structure is a five-part Georgian home finished in 1765 and overlooking a garden. Hours are Monday to Saturday from 10 am to 4 pm; Sunday from noon to 4 pm. The admission for garden/house/both is $3/4/6. In January and February it's open Friday and Sunday.

You can view several other houses by appointment: the **Barracks**, 43 Pinckney St, furnished as a Revolutionary soldier's barracks; the **Brice House**, 42 East St, a Georgian home; the **Shiplap House**, 18 Pinckney St; and **Tobacco Prise House**, 4 Pinckney St, which has exhibits on Maryland's tobacco trade.

MARYLAND

St John's College

St John's, on College Ave between St John and King George Sts, opened in 1696 as King William School, one of the earliest public schools in America. Francis Scott Key was an alumnus. Since 1937 all St John's students have followed an identical four-year Great Books curriculum. Students here are as philosophical and 'alternative' as the midshipmen are disciplined and martial. The **Liberty Tree** is a 400-year-old tulip tree on campus near College Ave.

In 1982 Naval Academy midshipmen claimed they could beat St John's students at any sport; St John's picked croquet and won. The match has become a yearly event played on the last Saturday in April and St Johns – still – usually wins. For information on the event call ☎ 410-626-2539.

Maritime Museum

The museum (☎ 410-268-5576), at Green and Compromise Sts on the western side of City Dock, has displays on Annapolis as a maritime and trading center. It's free and open daily from 10 am to 5 pm.

Banneker Douglass Museum

This museum (☎ 410-974-2893), 84 Franklin St, is in a building that was the Old Mt Moriah African Methodist Episcopal Church. It has rotating displays about African Americans in Maryland, DC, and the Virginia Chesapeake region and is open Tuesday to Friday from 10 am to 3 pm and Saturday from noon to 4 pm.

St Anne's Parish Church

Episcopal St Anne's stands in the middle of Church Circle near the center of town. It's beautifully quiet and gets fewer visitors than you might imagine. The first church went up in 1704; parishioners built a larger one in 1792 after delays for the Revolutionary War. That building burned down and the current Romanesque Revival church replaced it in 1859. Inside you'll find a red-tile aisle, wooden floors and some nice stained glass. It's a good place to relax.

Sailing

You can find a multitude of sailing schools, cruises, and bareboat (sail-it-yourself) charters in the Annapolis area, but a good way to get into the sailing scene is to mingle with the sailors who come into Marmaduke's (☎ 410-269-5420) at 301 Severn Ave.

Allied Yacht Charters (☎ 410-280-1522) at 236 First St has been a respected name for bareboat sailing charters for decades.

The Annapolis Sailing School (☎ 800-638-9192) at 601 Sixth St, one of the oldest and largest of these enterprises, teaches from April 1 to October. You can get two hours of instruction on a 24-foot sloop for $25.

J World (☎ 800-966-2038; 280-2040), 213 Eastern Ave, teaches sailing aboard high-tech sloops in two- to five-day courses.

Womanship (☎ 410-267-6661, 800-342-9295) at 410 Severn Ave, a sailing school for and by women, advertises 'No Shouting' aboard (a stereotypical male behavior) and gets raves from its clients.

The schooner *Woodwind* (☎ 410-263-7837) is a 74-foot yacht that sails from in front of the Marriott Hotel four times daily at 11 am, 1:30, 4, and 6:45 pm. Cruises last about two hours and cost $20. You can also rent a berth to sleep overnight aboard.

Beginagain (☎ 410-626-1422) leaves the City Dock for three-hour cruises three times a day at 9 am, 1, and 5 or 6 pm. The rate is $50 per person.

Bicycling

The Baltimore & Annapolis Trail Park (☎ 410-222-6244) is a 13.3-mile linear trail that follows the old Baltimore & Annapolis Railroad route from Annapolis to Glen Burnie. The southern end of the trail is just north of Annapolis at the intersection of Hwy 50 and Hwy 450. Downtown Cycle (☎ 410-268-5794), 6 Dock St, rents bicycles.

Organized Tours

Chesapeake Marine Tours (☎ 410-268-7600) has 40- and 90-minute harbor cruises from Memorial Day to October. Cruises cost $5 or $10. From Memorial Day to Labor Day there is a daylong cruise around the harbor and to St Michaels for $33, or $28 in advance.

At the Maritime Museum (☎ 410-268-5576), you can get recorded tours of the city narrated by Walter Cronkite for $7.

Three Centuries Tours (☎ 410-263-5401) does a two-hour walking tour of town and the Naval Academy from April 1 to October 31; tours cost $7/3 for adults/students.

Historical Tours Pedicabs (☎ 410-841-6235) pedals folk around town. You can call for a pickup or find them in front of the Annapolis Marriott.

Special Events

You can count on plenty of activity throughout the year in Annapolis. Here's a list of the main events. See also the sidebar on Marlborough Hunt Races at the end of this chapter.

Chesapeake Bay Bridge Walk & Bayfest (☎ 410-288-8405) is held the first Sunday in May. One span of the 4.3-mile bridge is closed for a day and about 50,000 people walk, ride, skateboard, and wheelchair across. Buses take people over to the Eastern Shore for free and then people make their way back. The event can tie up traffic on US Hwy 50 for miles.

Rotary Club Crab Feast (☎ 410-761-6603), held in late July, is the world's largest crab feast so big they have it in the Navy-Marine Corps Stadium.

Kunta Kinte Festival in mid-September commemorates the arrival of Alex Haley's slave ancestor who figures in Haley's book/film *Roots*, at City Dock – the site of a booming slave market in the 17th to 18th century.

Maryland Renaissance Festival (☎ 410-266-7304; 800-296-7304) is eight weekends of jousting, theater, taverns, buskers, artisans, and food taking place from late August to October in nearby Crownsville. Tickets are about $13.

US Sailboat & Powerboat Shows (☎ 410-268-8828) are the city's equivalent of Mardi Gras, held the first two weekends in October. City Dock and surrounding wharves fill with a fleet of new boats, vendors, food stalls, and what seems like half the world's Jimmy Buffett fans. The streets, bars, restaurants and inns overflow with crowds of happy – but not totally sober – folk. Traffic and parking can be something of a challenge. There is another boat show in April to herald the beginning of the sailing season. The spring show is slightly saner.

Chesapeake Bay Appreciation Day (☎ 410-269-6622), the last weekend of October at Sandy Point State Park, showcases Maryland arts, crafts, and music. Watermen bring their skipjacks here to race and test their vessels and crews before the oyster dredging season begins the following Monday. This is the best time and place to see working skipjacks under sail.

First Night Annapolis turns the entire city into a stage on December 31 with 250 indoor performances of classical, jazz, blues, folk, dance, and drama. Midnight fireworks announce the new year, and the crowds party till sunrise.

Places to Stay – bottom end to middle

Camping *Capitol KOA Campground* (☎ 800-638-2216, 923-2771), 768 Cecil Ave, in Millersville 12 miles away is the closest camping. Take Hwy 50 West to I-97 North then Exit 10 (Benfield Blvd); make a right onto Veterans Hwy and follow the signs. Sites are $18 to $20. The grounds are open April 1 to November 1.

Hotels The cheapest hotels are a couple of miles out of town on a commercial strip. *Econo Lodge* (☎ 410-224-4317), 2451 Riva Rd, has singles/doubles for $69/79. *Days Inn* (☎ 410-224-2800, 800-638-5179, fax 410-266-5539), 2520 Riva Rd, has rooms starting at $69. Take Exit 22 from US Hwy 50 and drive north for half a mile on Riva Rd.

The *Scot Laur Inn* (☎ 410-268-5665) is at 165 Main St above Chick & Ruth's Delly. The very friendly deli folk rent 10 rooms with TV, air-con, phones, and private bath on the two upper floors. Room rates include a full breakfast at the restaurant. Room rates are $58 to $78. If no one answers the phone, just go to the Delly and ask.

Gibson's Lodgings (☎ 410-268-5555), 110 Prince George St, is two houses and an annex with a total of 21 guest rooms. One building is an 18th century Federal-Georgian house with a newer facade; the other is a 19th century one, the third is a modern annex. You will find the interior more modern than the facade suggests. The prices are good, rooms clean and tasteful. Singles cost $58 to $110 and doubles are $68 to $125; both are with shared bath.

The *Jonas Green House B&B* (☎ 410-263-5892) at 124 Charles St is one of the two oldest houses in Annapolis and claims the same family in residence since 1738. Air-conditioned with period furnishings, this B&B welcomes children and pets. Rates are $65 to $95.

Places to Stay – top end

The *Flag House* (☎ 410-280-2721, 800-437-4825), 26 Randall St, has seven rooms in two connected townhouses; look for the row of international flags out front. Rooms are large with fans, TVs, king-size beds, central air and heat, quilts, and wood furniture. There are two gas fireplaces in the common rooms. Rates are $90 to $120, including breakfast.

Two-O-One B&B (☎ 410-268-8053), 201 Prince George St, is a Georgian townhouse a block from the City Dock. It is impeccably furnished with period pieces and has a sun deck and a fridge stocked with Evian and Coke for guests. There are two bright rooms, the larger with a fireplace. The rooms are $120 and $150 with a full English breakfast.

Harborview Boat & Breakfast (☎ 410-268-9330) offers berths on a choice of 20 different boats with a continental gourmet breakfast delivered to your vessel. Rates run $150 to $200 per couple.

The *Loews Annapolis Hotel* (☎ 410-263-7777), 126 West St, is a large corporate place with over 200 rooms, a seven-story atrium, ballrooms, and good-sized rooms with refrigerators and hair dryers. The single/double rate is $105/145 with lower rats during the week.

The *Historic Inns of Annapolis* (☎ 410-263-2641, 800-847-8882) is a collection of four inns built in historic structures renovated to modern standards. Traditional furnishings retain a sense of an earlier era. The inns are the *Maryland Inn*, the *Governor Calvert House*, the *State House Inn*, and the *Robert Johnson House*. The Maryland Inn, 16 Church Circle, seems to be the most popular choice. Rates are $105 to $185, but the inns run specials that include dinner, free entrance to hear music at the King of France Tavern in the Maryland Inn, and breakfast.

More authentic is the *Reynolds Tavern* (☎ 410-626-0380), 7 Church Circle. William Reynolds operated The Beaver and Lac'D Hat, a tavern and hat business, here in the mid-18th century. After a number of uses, the building came into the hands of the Historical Annapolis Society and it's now run as a restaurant and inn. There are three suites for $125 each and a double room for $90, including continental breakfast. They have broad-planked wooden floors, rugs (but not carpet), antique furniture, and modern bathrooms.

Places to Eat

Chick & Ruth's Delly (☎ 410-269-6738), 165 Main St, is an Annapolis institution run by the second generation of the Levitt family. The service is genuinely friendly. The deli's open 24 hours and it tends to be full of regulars who come to sit in the wooden booths and eat sandwiches named after national and local politicians.

Tony's Pizza & Pasta (☎ 410-268-1631), 36 West St, has slices, subs, spaghetti, lasagna, eggplant parmigiana, etc. You can spend $4 or $5 for a sandwich or around $7.50 on an entree.

The *Market House* right at City Dock is an indoor food complex with raw bar, sandwiches, and seafood. Six oysters on the half-shell cost $3.95.

The *Middleton Tavern* (☎ 410-263-3323), 2 Market Square across from the City Dock has a raw bar and serves oyster shooters – oysters with a shot of beer – for 95¢. Lunch includes fried oysters, burgers,

The Art of Eating a Steamed Crab

More than a few connoisseurs have compared eating a Chesapeake Bay blue crab to exploring the mysteries of sex. But for the uninitiated, figuring out how to eat Marylanders' favorite food can be a daunting, clumsy enterprise. Learning the secret sources of the crab's sweet meat is something like a rite of passage in Bay Country.

The key to getting started is having a paring knife in one hand and a small wooden mallet nearby. Your table should be broad and covered with paper to absorb the drips and eventually wrap the fragments. Eating crabs is a messy business, so roll up your sleeves.

Dainty eaters and strangers to Bay Country have a habit of beginning by snapping the legs off the body of their crab. They then make a career out of cracking open the claws with their mallets or knife handle and prying and sucking the meat out of the broken appendages. The initiated know that such pursuits yield little meat for all the effort and simply delay the main event – the attack on the body. Leave the claws and legs for later when appetite is in the wane.

If you want to eat a crab like a seasoned waterman or waterwoman, start first with the body. With thumb or knife point, pry off the 'apron' flap on the belly of the crab. The apron covers the crab's reproductive organs and opens the way to get inside the crab's shell.

Second, use your thumb or knife point to pry the top shell off the body and discard it. Break off the toothed claws and set them aside for later.

Third, now that you have exposed the body, use the knife edge to scrape off the gills – called 'dead men' – and the mustard-colored fat. You will see a semitransparent membrane covering the meat which is divided into chambers. These chambers fan out to the root of each leg.

Fourth, hold the crab's body on each side and break it apart at the center. Discard the legs.

Fifth, take your knife and slice lengthwise through the center of each body half. Now you have exposed succulent chunks of meat which you can push out of the chambered shell with you fingers or knife. Eat the meat as is or dip it in some vinegar and Old Bay spice. Depending on the size of the crabs and your staying power, you will repeat the ritual five or 10 times before you feel totally satiated.

Cold beer and corn on the cob complement the feast. ■

and crab cakes for around $7. Dinners are more expensive pastas, fish, and seafood for $12 to $16. Horatio Middleton opened the tavern in 1740 for the 'seafaring man.' George Washington, Thomas Jefferson, and Ben Franklin found the pub to their liking. You'll find warming hearth fires in cold weather; tables on the porch offer the best people-watching in the city.

Riordan's Saloon & Restaurant (☎ 410-263-5449) at 26 Market Space offers a changing variety of food and drink specials. Checkered tablecloths, a big window on City Dock, and the scent of steamed shrimp and beer make Riordan's a popular Sunday brunch place. You can pick up a big bowl of chili for $4.25 and five small beers for $4. The bar has a lively pick-up scene for the upscale under-35 crowd at night.

McGarvey's Saloon & Oyster Bar (☎ 410-263-5700) at 8 Market Space is pretty much a Riordan's clone where some of the sailing crowd hangs out. *Buddy's Crabs & Ribs* (☎ 410-626-1100), 100 Main St, has combination meals of ribs with shrimp or softshell crab or chicken strips for $15 to $16.

If you can't stay away from Mexican, try *Caliente* (☎ 410-268-8548) a California-style *taqueria* at 50 West St. The portions of all the usual entrees are huge, and the service is fast and friendly.

Entertainment

Bars Annapolis has dozens of watering holes, and pub crawling is a favorite night-time sport of Annapolitans from Wednesday through Sunday afternoon. To keep the throngs of veterans engaged and challenged, the pubs offer endless promotions – like extended happy hour, dollar beers, free hors d'oeuvres, sports paraphernalia, you name it – and draw a lot of musical talent from Washington and Baltimore. On most nights a survey will turn up at least a score of live acts playing the bars and restaurants around City Dock.

The *King of France Tavern* (☎ 410-263-2641) in the Maryland Inn on Main St hosts nationally prominent jazz and folk acts. Downstairs in the *Reynolds Tavern* (☎ 410-626-0380), 7 Church Circle, you can hear acoustic music most nights.

Head for the *Acme Bar & Grill* (☎ 410-280-6486) at 163 Main St to join the under-25 crowd for serious rock. *Armadillo's* (☎ 410-268-6680) at 132 Dock Square has slightly mellower music and people pushing 35.

Wednesday night is a wild and crazy sailors' scene at *Marmaduke's* (☎ 410-269-5420) at 301 Severn Ave in Eastport. The management videotapes the major drama and bloopers from the Wednesday evening sailboat races and plays back the tape so everyone can relive the agony and ecstasy. This is the place to come if you're looking for a way to get on the Bay. Boat skippers are always seeking a racing crew, and you may get lucky enough to be invited for a cruise across the Bay to some of the scenic Eastern Shore anchorages. The karaoke fad draws a crowd to the *Eastport Clipper* (☎ 410-280-6400) at 400 Sixth St.

Harry Browne's (☎ 410-263-4332) has a quiet bar above its posh restaurant at 66 State Circle where a gay and straight crowd mingle.

Performing Arts *Maryland Hall for the Creative Arts*, 801 Chase St, is the main center of performing arts. It hosts the opera (☎ 410-267-8135, 410-263-2710) when in town; the Annapolis Chorale (☎ 410-263-1906), a 150-person chorus and chamber orchestra that performs September to May; the Ballet Theater (☎ 410-263-8289); and the Annapolis Symphony Orchestra (☎ 410-296-1132). To find Maryland Hall head out of town on West St for about a mile and look for the signs.

Annapolis Summer Garden Theater (☎ 410-268-9212) presents Broadway musicals out of doors during the summer months at City Dock.

Colonial Players (☎ 410-268-7373) puts on five productions, including *A Christmas Carol*, each year at *Theater in the Round*, 108 East St.

Cinema *Apex Cinemas* (☎ 410-224-1145) has two multiplex locations at the Eastport

Shopping Mall and the Annapolis Mall. Neither is within walking distance of downtown.

Getting There & Away

Air The nearest airport is Baltimore-Washington. Super Shuttle (☎ 410-724-0009) operates a shuttle to/from the airport and the larger Annapolis hotels and the Naval Academy. Fares change but are in the range of $14/22, one-way/roundtrip.

Bus Baltimore Mass Transit Administration (☎ 800-543-9809) runs bus No 210 from downtown Baltimore to Annapolis.

Greyhound (☎ 800-231-2222) has service to/from Washington for $7.50/15 one-way/roundtrip. You will find the bus stop at the Metro sign near the football stadium at Rowe Blvd and Taylor Ave.

Car Annapolis is about 35 miles east of Washington, DC, and 35 miles south of Baltimore. From Washington take I-495 (the Beltway) to Hwy 50E and you will come right into town. From Baltimore take I-695 to Hwy 2S to Hwy 50W.

Coming from anywhere on the Eastern Shore, like Delaware or Ocean City, you approach via Hwy 50 or Hwy 301 (they overlap) across the Chesapeake Bay Bridge and into Annapolis.

The Marlborough Hunt Races

MD I

One of the best places to get a sense of Maryland's love affair with the thoroughbred horse, have a spring picnic, join a world-class tailgating party, and mingle with some of the state's high society is at the Marlborough Hunt Races held on the last Sunday of March in Davidsonville, about 10 miles southwest of Annapolis. The races take place in the rolling countryside of a classic Maryland horse farm, Roedown. There are nine races starting at noon and ranging from junior/pony class races over flat courses under a mile, to major competitions on two- to three-mile courses over hurdles and timber. More than a 100 riders and horses compete each year.

Gates open for parking at 10 am, and the heart of the sophisticated tailgating party takes place on a hilltop overlooking the race courses. The atmosphere at the Marlborough Races really does have something of the feel of the film *National Velvet*. Everywhere you look you will see magnificent horses and elegant riders in sparkling boots, jodhpurs, and silks. Here you will find an exceptional collection of classic cars – mostly from the British shops of Rolls, Bentley, Austin Healey, and Jaguar – and classic high society dressed in tweeds and lace. Caviar and champagne are the essential ingredients of the picnic lunches that emerge from the trunks of the cars to spread themselves among the silver on linen-covered tables and under tents brought by spectators. At noon there is a 'tailgating competition' awarding prizes to the tailgate setups with the most panache.

Parking in this area costs $95 to $200 for four people per vehicle, no RVs. Slightly cheaper 'rail parking' costs $40 to $80. If you don't feel the need to park with the upper crust, you can pay $5 for general parking and $5 per person for general admission. To reserve a parking place or tickets you must write the Marlborough Hunt Races, PO Box 277, Upper Marlboro, MD 20773. For race information call ☎ 301-627-1817.

From Annapolis go south on Hwy 2 through the Hwy 214 intersection. Continue on Hwy 2 for about five miles. Turn right on Harwood Rd to Roedown Farm. ■

Getting Around

Annapolis is compact and best navigated on foot. Annapolis Transit (☎ daytime: 410-263-7964; evenings, weekends: 410-263-7994) runs a bus or trolley for 75¢ from the Naval Academy stadium parking lot south on Rowe Blvd and Duke of Gloucester St to the City Dock from 6:30 am to 7 pm. There are also bus routes out of town.

Parking This can be difficult, especially during the summer. Most streets have meters, and most spots are occupied. You're better off using a lot. There is free parking inside the Naval Academy from 9 am to sundown. This is technically for visitors to the Academy but people wander out into town as well. Enter at Gate 3 on Maryland Ave.

There are several commercial lots in town. The state lots on Rowe Blvd and Calvert St cost money on weekdays, but are free weekends; Hillman Garage is just behind Main St about a block up from the City Dock; Gotts Court Garage is at Calvert and Northwest Sts; the West St Lots are several lots on Calvert St, Clay St, and City Gate Lane west of Church St off of West St. The Naval Academy stadium lot is northwest of downtown on Rowe Blvd and Taylor Ave. Annapolis Transit runs a trolley or bus from the stadium to the City Dock downtown from 6:30 am to 7 pm.

SANDY POINT STATE PARK

This bayside park sits near the foot of the Chesapeake Bay Bridge just off Hwy 50/301. Sandy Point (☎ 410-974-2149) is the closest place to Annapolis where you can try to beat the summer heat and humidity. There's a broad beach overlooking an offshore lighthouse and the Bay's main shipping lanes. The state provides changing facilities, a vending area, boat ramps, and fishing jetties. Note: This place can be packed in July and August, and the Chesapeake's infamous stinging jellyfish, sea nettles, can make you wish you were in Alaska. Fees are $2 per adult from Memorial Day to Labor Day and $1 per car at other times.

Southern Maryland

South of Annapolis lies one of the least-explored areas of the state. Calvert, St Mary's, and Charles Counties compose a rural mix of farms, forest, marsh, and hundreds of miles of tidewater shore. The primary destination in this area is a major yachting, fishing, and weekend oasis known as the Solomons. But Southern Maryland has other charms as well including the small resort of Chesapeake Beach. You will also find the archeological sites of some of the state's oldest Native American communities as well as historic St Mary's City, the first European colony in Maryland. The scenery and lack of people make this area perfect for exploring by bicycle and small boat. The shoulders on most roads are wide to accommodate the horse-drawn buggies of Amish and Mennonite farmers who shun the conveniences of modern technology.

CHESAPEAKE BEACH

This small resort lies 25 miles south of Annapolis on the Chesapeake's Western Shore. In 1900 a tourist railroad called the Chesapeake Beach Railway Company completed a rail line from the District of Columbia to 'CB' and opened Chesapeake Beach to hordes of Washington, DC's middle class looking for an affordable escape from the capital's heat and humidity during the summer months.

CB reached its prime during the Roaring Twenties when tens of thousands took the train to the beach to stroll the boardwalk, bathe, go fishing on party boats, listen to concerts at the casino, catch some thrills at an amusement park, and spend a few nights in the Grand Hotel.

The Depression of the 1930s, and improved access to the superior Atlantic beaches like Ocean City, sent the resort into a decline that lasted until the 1980s; all of the old attractions except the railway station vanished while the cottage community grew ramshackle and populated with a seedy crowd of year-rounders looking for cheap rents.

With the recreational boating boom of the 1980s, sailors and anglers rediscovered Chesapeake Beach, its two sheltered harbors, and the rare (for the Chesapeake) sandy strand. Since this rediscovery, gentrification has reclaimed much of Chesapeake Beach, bringing a yacht basin, an extensive sportfishing charterboat fleet, condos, good restaurants, two new boardwalks, and a small, but lively night scene. Gentrification has also begun to overtake CB's cottage community of North Beach, but many of the homes remain modestly constructed and casually maintained. For travelers who like poking into unsophisticated backwaters, fishing enthusiasts, and cyclists exploring the woods and farm country of rural southern Maryland, CB is worth a stop.

Information

For a brochure on all of CB's points of interest, stop by the Calvert County Tourism office (☎ 410-535-6355) at the courthouse in Prince Frederick, 10 miles south of Chesapeake Beach on Route 2, or write to them at Prince Frederick, MD 20678.

Things to See

The two new **boardwalks** at North Beach and CB are great places to cool off, and you can fish or crab from the pier at North Beach, but you need to bring your own equipment. The beach here is narrow by most standards, but it has surprisingly fine sand and is far less crowded than the Bay beach at Sandy Point. Of course, stinging sea nettles can be a problem here during the summer months as they are in most of the Chesapeake.

In the heart of CB is the **Chesapeake Beach Railway Museum** (☎ 410-257-3892). Housed in the old depot overlooking the Bay, this museum includes a passenger car, locomotive cabs, and a collection of photos and memorabilia depicting CB in its halcyon years. The museum is free and open daily from 1 to 4 pm May to September; same hours on weekends April and October.

Around the general area of the museum you will find the heart of the commercial village which includes a couple of **art galleries** and antique shops, a water park, and the docks with dozens of **sportfishing** boats for hire at $300 plus for a half day.

How to Catch a Blue Crab

Blue crabs scavenge the bottom of Chesapeake Bay for pungent morsels. Raw clams (out of their shells) or – better – uncooked chicken necks are ambrosia to a crab. So . . . if you want to catch a crab, get one or the other for bait.

Before you head to the dock or pier to start crabbing, go to a hardware store or borrow your tools – a ball of twine (your fishing line), a long handled dip net to land your catch, and a bucket to store your catch.

Once you are at the pier, tie a piece of bait to your line and drop the line into the water until you feel the bait touch the bottom. Pay out an additional two feet of line, then cut the line and tie it off a railing or the edge of the dock. To be efficient you should deploy about a half dozen lines in this fashion.

Next watch your lines until they go taut. When you see a taut line, it means a crab has latched onto the bait with its claws and is trying to make off with the food.

Slowly reel in the line by hand. Grab your dip net and ease the net's basket about a foot beneath the surface of the water. You will see the crab hanging onto the bait as you reel the line to the surface. Before the crab and bait break the surface of the water, scoop up the crab with the dip net in one fluid swipe and lift the crab out of the water. Shake the net over the bucket and the crab will drop in.

If you must pick up the crab, grab it at the joint between the backfin (paddle-shaped leg) and the shell so the crab can't give you a painful nip with its claws.

Store the crabs in a shady place or cover the bucket with a wet cloth to keep your catch alive until you can steam them in a pot with Old Bay Spice and beer. ■

Places to Stay

Breezy Point Campgrounds (☎ 410-535-1600, ext 225) on Breezy Point Rd has 13 campsites with Bay views costing $25 with electricity, $20 without. All sites have water and a picnic table; there is a bathhouse and places for swimming, fishing, and crabbing.

Angels in the Attic (☎ 301-855-2607) is a restored 1903 B&B at 9200 Chesapeake Ave, North Beach. You can get a room with a Bay view and Victorian tea for $65.

Tidewater Treasures (☎ 410-257-0785) is a contemporary B&B on the beach at 7315 Bayside Rd. There are four rooms with queen-size beds, two of which overlook the Bay. This is a nonsmoking inn with family pets, which include a dog, cats, and a cockatoo. Innkeeper Sharon Oldham is welcoming and knowledgeable about the area. Rooms including full breakfast run $74 to $99.

The *Herrington Inn* (☎ 410-741-5100) is a one-story Caribbean-style inn with 29 rooms, three efficiencies, and a restaurant attached to the marina about a mile north of the cottage community of North Beach on Route 261. Standard rooms cost from $59 to $85 during the April to September 'season'; for a patio and Jacuzzi you pay $99 to $130. There is a private beach, paddleboat rentals for $5 per half hour and bike rentals for $4 a day.

Places to Eat

The *Rod N Reel* (☎ 410-257-2735) is a restaurant and lounge overlooking the Bay from a spot poised between the Railway Museum and the docks where the charter-boat fleet ties up. This place is the social hub of CB. Not only can you get a panoply of Bay Country dishes like rock fish and crab cakes, but the restaurant runs a host of special events like oyster, pig, and bull roasts to complement the $25 weekend buffet, which includes entertainment. *GW's Bay Club*, which is the back lounge of the Rod N Reel, packs in a crowd of all ages (over 21) for dancing to cover bands most weekends.

Next door to the Rod N Reel you will find *Smokey Joe's Grill* (☎ 410-257-2427) with a casual dining room and bar overlooking the charter boats. A lot of the captains hang out here for beers after work, and you can hear some great fish stories if you catch this place around 5 pm. Chili is a deal at $3 a bowl; spicy chicken wings run $5.

Getting There & Away

Take Route 2 south from Annapolis for about 30 miles, then turn east on either Route 261 (scenic) or Route 260 (direct).

FLAG PONDS NATURE PARK

With the Solomons as a base, you can find several undeveloped beaches and hiking trails for day trips, such as those at this park. Flag Ponds (☎ 410-586-1477) has 327 acres of woods, marsh, and hay fields, including a three-mile hiking trail, observation towers for bird watching, two ponds, extensive wildflowers like the blue flag iris, a fishing and crabbing pier, indoor exhibits on wildlife, and the remnants of an active watermen's 'pound net' community that thrived here until the 1950s. If you come by car it will cost you $6 to park for the day from April to October and $4 for other months. Flag Ponds lies halfway (about 10 miles) between the town of Prince Frederick (see Solomons Island for details on the nearby campground) and the Solomons on Route 2/4.

CALVERT CLIFFS STATE PARK

Slightly closer to the Solomons, a few miles south of Flag Ponds on Route 2/4, lies Calvert Cliffs State Park (☎ 301-872-5688). There are over 500 acres in this bayside park, and considering the size of the park and its 40- to 100-foot cliffs, you might conclude that this is a place to come for a quiet walk on the beach. You would be mistaken. The actual beach at the park is quite small and prohibits swimming. Visitors come to here to sift through the sand in search of fossils from the deep-sea creatures that got buried here during the

Miocene Epoch 10 to 20 million years ago. Huge shark teeth are a common find, but over 600 different kinds of fossils have been discovered here. If you ask a park ranger for advice, odds are you will find your own fossil. There are 13 miles of hiking trails, closed to bikes and horses. The walk to the beach is two miles from the parking lot and a hot trip at the height of summer. Much of the park is open to hunters after October 1, and some of the trails are closed. The park is open most days from 10 am to 6 pm. Entrance costs $2 per person.

JEFFERSON PATTERSON STATE PARK

If you like archeology or harbor an interest in Native American life in Chesapeake country, you ought to visit this park on the Patuxent River. Given to the state in 1983 by Mrs Jefferson Patterson, and listed on the National Register of Historic Places, Jefferson Patterson (☎ 410-586-0050, 410-586-0055) has 512 acres, 2.5 miles of riverfront, and over 70 archeological sites, with some currently under excavation. Follow the archeological trail to see the evolution of native culture over the last 12,000 years along the Patuxent, from hunting-gathering to a relatively sophisticated plantation community. There are also nature trails, and the park **museum** displays artifacts from all of the periods of human habitation. The park is open from 10 am to 5 pm, Wednesday to Sunday, April 15 to October 15. Admission is free. To get here from either the Solomons or Annapolis, take Route 2/4 to Port Republic, then follow Route 264 about three miles south of Prince Frederick. Take Route 264 for two miles. Turn left on Route 265 and proceed six miles to the park entrance.

SOLOMONS ISLAND

The primary destination for many travelers headed south from Annapolis, Solomons Island sits at the point where the broad Patuxent River joins the Chesapeake Bay. About 25 years ago, Solomons Island was a sleepy watermen's town with a marine research station at the end of Route 2. Separated from the mainland by a small tidal creek spanned by a very short highway bridge, and sheltering a snug harbor, Solomons Island attracted the attention of the yachting crowd who proclaimed the town and harbor the Western Shore's equivalent to the quaint Eastern Shore village of St Michaels.

Marinas, restaurants, inns, and charter fishing boats began moving in. A bridge over the Patuxent opened up Solomons Island to traffic headed to/from the large Patuxent River Naval Air Test Station across the river at Lexington Park. Washington gentry built vacation and retirement homes on the mainland side of the harbor, and a huge Holiday Inn was built. Now, the community is much more than the island itself, and people call the place 'The Solomons' to acknowledge the island (which forms the southwest side of the harbor) as well as the rest of the surrounding development. The postal service has settled on 'Solomons.' Whatever you call it, this community rates high as a romantic getaway spot for Washingtonians and suburbanites and can be jammed with visitors on warm weekends.

Information

You can learn about Solomons Island through the Calvert County Tourism office (see Information in Chesapeake Beach) or visit the Solomons Information Center (☎ 410-326-6027) just off Route 2/4 at the north end of the Patuxent River bridge.

Things to See

The most popular attraction in the Solomons is the **Calvert Marine Museum** (☎ 410-326-2042) right across the street from the information center. The museum is open daily 10 am to 5 pm, except some holidays. For a nominal fee visitors can view a collection of traditional watermen's vessels, see displays about the changing environment and creatures of the Patuxent River and Chesapeake Bay, learn about the

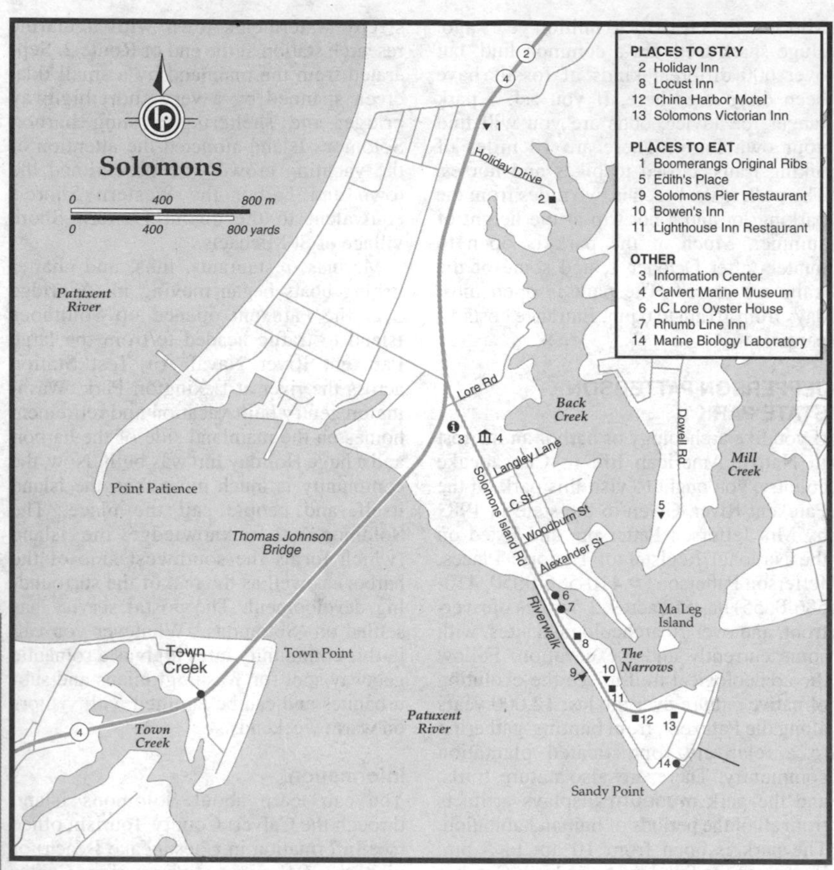

Miocene Epoch when 50-foot sharks and crocodiles populated the Chesapeake, take a cruise aboard a converted (to power) 19th century bugeye schooner, and watch river otters at play.

From the museum it's a short walk down Solomons Island Rd (so-called 'Main St') across the bridge to the island proper where you can visit the **JC Lore Oyster House**, which is also part of the museum. This building is an old-time 'shucking house' where tens of thousands of oysters were removed from their shells daily in season. Once, almost every village on the Chesapeake had a shucking house like this employing thousands of people, mainly poor and black women. Today, almost all of the shucking houses have disappeared.

Across the street from the oyster house, the **Solomons Riverwalk** begins. This boardwalk is a good place for a picnic or to catch the cool breeze off the broad river.

The Riverwalk parallels Solomons Island Rd. This is obviously the main street on the island, and it leads you on a one-mile circuit along the shores of the island. On your way you will see a fishing and crabbing pier and a number of small boat rentals where you can get 14-foot boats with small outboards for $40 to $75 depending on whether you rent for a half day, whole day, or the week. You will also find a collection of restaurants, shops, and marinas that range from homey operations to slick tourist traps. Perhaps the best part of this walk is simply the uninterrupted changing vistas of tidewater. No town on the Chesapeake offers a pedestrian better access to the water.

Places to Stay

Patuxent River Campsites (☎ 410-586-9880) at 4770 Williams Wharf Rd in Broomes Island is about eight miles by water and 15 miles north by highway (take Routes 2/4, then follow Route 264) from Solomons Island. Here you will find 125 campsites, many on the river, with electricity and water, bathhouse, pier, and boat ramp. Tent sites are $18 a night, sites for trailers/RVs are $20. The boat ramp costs $5, and there is a good convenience store two miles up the road. It's open May 1 to October 15.

The least expensive place to stay on the island is the former Island Manor Motel, now called *China Harbor Motel* (☎ 410-326-3700). The rate is $45 a night, but you might get a better deal for multiple days if you bargain. This small '50s-style motel is attached to the China Restaurant. Right next door is the Tiki Bar on the edge of the harbor. The outdoor bar draws an overflowing crowd of the young and single with loud music and cheap beer most nights during the summer, and unless you're part of the action, you'll hate this place as the noise persists long after midnight.

One quiet, moderately priced alternative is the *Locust Inn* (☎ 410-326-0454) right across the street from the Riverwalk. The innkeeper, Mrs English, is a mature Southern lady full of local lore. She has eight rooms starting at $52.50 for one double bed. Rooms are air-conditioned, and guests can use a small pool near the harbor.

The *Solomons Victorian Inn* (☎ 410-326-4811) is also on the island overlooking the harbor, and offers six rooms and a loft suite furnished with period antiques. Rooms start at $90 and go to $165 for the suite with a spa. All rooms include private baths, air-conditioning, and elaborate Bay Country breakfasts.

The *Holiday Inn* (☎ 410-326-6311), off the island on Route 2/4 at the head of the harbor, is a cut above what you might expect from this chain. While it is an extensive complex, the two-story dark-stone structure does its best not to look like a hospital and to blend with the surrounding woods. There is an extensive marina, tennis courts, a large pool, active outdoor bar, and a fitness center with sauna. A room for two costs $89, and there are weekend packages.

Places to Eat

The undisputed local favorite breakfast stop in the Solomons is *Edith's Place* (☎ 410-326-1036), across the harbor from the island at the Calvert Marina on Dowell Rd. You have to drive around the harbor to get here, but the 1.5-mile drive is worth it. Run by Edith Taylor whose husband is a local charterboat captain, the restaurant opens at 6 am and has both indoor and patio seating. Edith serves up 'country-size' portions of everything from eggs and sausage to grits and pancakes for $2 to $4. Lots of patrons show up for lunch and dinner by private boat. Some bargains on the menu include a turkey club sandwich for $5, and a bowl of crab soup for $3.25. You can also get soda, beer, wine, and ice to go if you are planning a boating picnic.

Bowen's Inn (☎ 410-326-9814) at 14630 Solomons Island Rd is one of the oldest restaurants in town and claims to have the best crab cakes in the Solomons. Not everyone agrees, but everybody seems to be a fan of Bowen's fare, especially on Thursdays when $5 gets you all the tacos you can eat.

The *Lighthouse Inn Restaurant* (☎ 410-236-2444) at 14640 Solomons Island Rd stands out among the half-dozen on-the-water places where you can eat seafood under the stars. Built with weathered wood and expanses of glass to resemble a Chesapeake lighthouse and boat shed, this restaurant – where the bar is a fully rigged skipjack – draws yachts to its wharf and a collection of polished European town cars to its lot. In addition to the view of the harbor and the candlelit ambiance, the Lighthouse draws an upscale clientele by virtue of its first-class service and the attention the chef brings to seasoning his offerings. The average entree costs $19, surf and turf $27. This is the place to come if you want to dress up and blow your allowance.

If you've had enough seafood, *Boomerangs Original Ribs* (☎ 410-326-6050) near the Holiday Inn is a popular lunch and dinner stop for BBQ from the grill. Four racks of ribs with potato and side dishes cost $13 at dinner and can feed two. Small rib dishes run about $7 at lunch, but this could easily count as the main meal in your day.

Entertainment

This is a Maryland resort, so of course there is a bar scene. The *Tiki Bar* (☎ 410-326-4300) in China Harbor Motel (see Places to Stay) rocks out most nights with the under-25 crowd hooting, dancing, collecting promising phone numbers, consuming an ocean of beer, and stealing off for moonlit walks around the harbor.

A slightly older crowd mingles with the yachties at the *Rhumb Line Inn* (☎ 410-326-3261) where there's a dance club, sports bar and food until 1 am on Friday and Saturday.

Couples gather to toast the sunset at the *Solomons Pier Restaurant & Lounge* (☎ 410-326-2424) looking west from the Riverwalk.

Getting There & Away

Solomons Island lies 60 miles south of Annapolis and Washington on Route 2/4, which is a low-traffic four-lane highway except on warm-weather weekends when traffic can be intense.

SOTTERLY PLANTATION

Just four miles up the Patuxent River from the Solomons, on the western bank, sits Sotterly (☎ 301-373-2280) an elegant colonial plantation. You can come in your own private boat and tie up at the plantation pier . . . or take the 10-mile drive. While Sotterly's manor house, built in 1717, is not on the scale of George Washington's Mount Vernon, the building does have its peculiar charms, which include being the oldest post-and-beam style house in the US. The plantation is still a working farm, and the slave quarters, house, and furnishings give a strong sense of pre-Revolutionary America. Admission is $5 adults, $4 seniors, $2 children, and it is currently open by appointment. To reach Sotterly from the Solomons, cross the Solomons Island bridge to the western shore of the Patuxent; take Route 235 north three miles; turn right (east) on Route 245 and proceed to Sotterly Rd.

NAVAL AIR TEST & EVALUATION MUSEUM

This is not a stop for everyone, but if you are curious about how the US Navy spends citizens' tax dollars, love military aircraft, or want a behind-the-scenes look into the best test pilot school in the world, you might want to visit this museum. Located at the North Gate of the Patuxent River Naval Air Station on Route 235 five miles south of the Solomons in Lexington Park, the Naval Air Test & Evaluation Museum (☎ 301-863-7418), has a good collection of aircraft, hardware, and memorabilia to profile the test pilot school from which celebrated astronauts like Glenn, Shepard, Schirra, and Carpenter graduated. You can examine a number of warbirds, climb aboard an F-4 Phantom simulator, or look at failed prototypes like an inflatable rubber airplane. Hours are from 11 am to 4 pm Friday to Saturday, and Sunday from noon to 5 pm. Admission is free.

Lexington Park is a typical military base town. This means it has an extensive collection of tract housing, shopping malls, fast-food franchises, and traffic lights (on Route 235). Weekday rush hours present significant traffic jams. Simply put, the base and Lexington Park seem to appear in the middle of rural Maryland like a mirage out of *Fear and Loathing in Las Vegas*.

POINT LOOKOUT STATE PARK

At the very southern tip of Maryland lies Point Lookout on a long peninsula jutting out between the Chesapeake and the Potomac River. This state park (☎ 301-872-5688), on over 1000 acres of wetlands and forest, is one of the best – and most-overlooked – camping and recreation sites in the state. In addition to 143 campsites, Point Lookout has nature trails, a swimming beach, fishing and crabbing pier, inexpensive boat and canoe rentals, boat ramp, and an excursion ferry to Smith Island in the middle of the Bay (see Smith Island in the Eastern Shore chapter). Furthermore, there always seems to be a breeze along the shores even when the rest of Bay Country swelters under a midsummer heat wave.

During the Civil War, Point Lookout was the site of Fort Lincoln (some of the ramparts are still here), one of the largest Union prisons for captured Confederate soldiers. Cramped quarters, unsanitary conditions, and mosquitoes spread cholera, dysentery, and malaria killing 3364 Confederates here. Two monuments in the park honor the men who died in sight of their homeland: Virginia lies just across the Potomac. Over the years park rangers, campers, and psychics have reported regular sightings of Confederate ghosts.

The park stays open year round, and day admission is free. From Memorial Day to Labor Day tent sites cost $12 a day from Monday to Thursday; sites with electricity cost $14; full hookup is $20. Add $2 to the price on Friday, Saturday, and Sunday. Rates are slightly less in the off season. Rowboats and canoes rent for $3 an hour at the camp store; motor boats cost $8. For weekend and holiday stays during the summer, you should call ahead for a reservation. The park is 20 miles south of Lexington Park on Routes 235 and 5.

ST MARY'S CITY

Maryland's first capital overlooks Horseshoe Bend on the St Mary's River from a promontory capped with historic buildings, stately trees and lush fields. While hardly the size of Virginia's colonial capital at Williamsburg, St Mary's City (☎ 301-862-0990, 800-762-1634) is like Williamsburg in that it is a living history museum with recreated colonial buildings and costumed, role-playing historic interpreters. Near this spot in 1634, about 200 of Maryland's first colonists, led by Lord Baltimore's brother Leonard Calvert, stepped ashore St Clements Island and celebrated a thanksgiving mass. Thereafter, this mix of Catholic and Protestant colonists sailed to Horseshoe Bend aboard their ships the *Ark* and the *Dove* where they established St Mary's City on the site of a former Native American village. Here the colonists enjoyed peaceful relations with local Native Americans and formed the first European community in North America to guarantee all citizens the right to practice whatever religion they chose. The settlement was, nonetheless, a commercial venture, and it prospered, remaining the capital of Maryland until 1695 when the capital moved to Annapolis. The town all but vanished in subsequent centuries, but during the 1970s archeologists began exploring the site and reconstructing the city.

Exploring the 800 acres of the museum, you will see active archeological digs and a building in which artifacts highlighting the town's history are on display. On the property you can visit the reconstructed State House of 1675, the working Godiah Spray Tobacco Plantation, a freeman's house, Farthing's Ordinary serving food and drink, and a sailing replica of the *Dove*, the small square-rigger that carried the supplies for the first colonists to this shore. At the **Chancellor's Point Natural History Area** there's a Native American longhouse. Adjacent to the historic 'city' is St Mary's College, a state-run liberal-arts institution with handsome colonial and Georgian buildings and friendly flocks of students.

Historic St Mary's City lies on Route 5 seven miles south of Lexington Park via Route 246. The museum is open March to late November, Wednesday to Sunday from 10 am to 5 pm. Admission is $6.50 for adults, $3.25 children.

PINEY POINT & ST GEORGE ISLAND

If you are looking for a truly 'far out' place, fancy a warm-weather sail on a skipjack, yearn for a crab feast, or picture yourself scuba diving on the wreck of a German submarine, follow Route 249 south from Route 5 at Callaway. The road passes through Piney Point where there is a merchant seamen's academy, and then deadends at the small community of St George Island. There are plenty of bigger and rowdier communities dominated by the independent watermen (whose families have fished the Bay for centuries) on the Bay's Eastern Shore, but none of them look more rural, less touched by mainstream America than narrow, mile-long St George Island.

If you are curious about the mysterious, sunken German sub, visit the **Piney Point Lighthouse Museum & Park** (☎ 301-769-2225), open May to October on weekends from noon to 5 pm. The lighthouse was the summer retreat of James Madison, the fourth President of the United States (1809–17) and other Washington notables, and the small museum has an exhibit. A mile offshore lies the wreck buoy marking the Maryland's first Historic Shipwreck Diving Preserve. The WWII **German submarine *U-1105*** lies upright and more or less intact in about 70 feet of water. The sub was a war prize that the US Navy scuttled here in secret in 1949 after failing to understand the ship's 'stealth' rubber coating that made it invisible on sonar. The wreck was rediscovered by sport divers in 1985 and now is fully protected under law. Diving on the wreck is considered an 'advanced dive' with generally low visibility. If you are interested in making the dive or learning more about the sub's history, contact the St Clements Island Museum (☎ 301-769-2222).

Captain Jackie Russell will take you sailing on his working **skipjack** the *Dee of St Mary's* (☎ 301-994-0897). There are a number of sailing options, but the best deal is a two-hour dinner sail up the St Mary's River, which includes an all-you-can-eat crab feast for $25.

MARYLAND

Places to Stay & Eat

You can camp at attractive *Camp Merryelande* (☎ 301-862-3301, 800-382-1073), on 25 acres of forest with 500 yards of sandy beach. This camp has all the amenities with 30 tent sites, six cottages and a bunkhouse. Mike Evans charges $20 a day for the tent sites during the summer months. One-bedroom cottages cost $65 a day from Monday to Thursday, $125 Friday to Sunday, and $400 a week. If you have five or more people you can rent the bunkhouse for $10.50 per person, $100 minimum. It's just off the only road (Route 249) on St George Island.

If you're in the mood for seafood and a visit to an absolutely authentic Maryland crab house on a watermen's pier, head for *Evans Seafood Restaurant* (☎ 301-994-2299) just a quarter of a mile from the bridge on the main road. This place tells the truth when it claims that it 'looks like a collection of fishermen's shacks.' Ronnie Evans, his wife Carol, and their kids serve up mammoth portions of clams, oysters, shrimp, and crab dishes. Try a dozen steamed, local soft clams for $6.25 or a soft-crab sandwich for $5.50. Beer costs $1.60 a mug. This place is popular, so come early or be prepared to wait for a table.

WALDORF

With a Piscataway longhouse as its centerpiece, the **Maryland Indian Cultural Center** (☎ 301-782-7622) at 16816 Country Lane is the only reason for visiting the sprawling town of Waldorf, 25 miles south of Washington on Hwy 301. Nearly lost among the traffic and shopping malls that have overwhelmed this once-tranquil country town, the small museum houses displays that illustrate Piscataway arts and crafts as well as highlight the lifestyles of Maryland's largest tribe of indigenous people. Currently the museum is open by appointment only, except during the first weekend in June and September when the Piscataway community gathers here for spring and harvest **powwows** (☎ 301-372-1932). During powwows you can visit the

Bass Fishing in Charles County

During the last few years national television and outdoor magazine coverage has brought a lot of attention to the environmental revival of the Potomac River. Just a few years ago this river was so polluted environmentalists suggested that the Potomac's nickname be changed from 'National River' to 'National Disgrace.' Since those sad days, better sewage treatment facilities and attention to agricultural runoff have improved the river's water quality dramatically. In addition, biologists have planted more than 40 miles of grass beds in the river, which have drawn such huge schools of rock fish (striped bass) that Maryland's Charles County, with more than 100 miles of coastline along the tidal Potomac and its tributaries, is now recognized as a world-class fishing hole. Charles County is the site of the annual Bass Anglers Sportsman Society's multimillion-dollar bass fishing tournament.

Boat ramps, marinas, restaurants, and camping and fishing complexes have opened along the river to meet the needs of anglers. One such facility is *Goose Bay Marina* (☎ 301-934-3812) in Welcome on Route 6 west of La Plata. Campsites cost $16, boat ramp use is $7. There is a ships' store with groceries, ice, fishing tackle, and marine supplies for sale.

For a complete list of marina facilities, professional guides, and accommodations geared toward anglers, call the Charles County Tourism Office, Department of Community Services (☎ 800-766-3386). ■

museum, see how the Piscataway lived in their longhouses, watch demonstrations of Piscataway music and dance, and shop for Native American arts and foods.

PORT TOBACCO

While small by comparison to the reconstructed colonial settlement at St Mary's City, Port Tobacco (☎ 301-934-4313) is worth a stop if you're caught up in the romance of revisiting colonial America while touring or boating along the country roads and backwaters of Charles County. When English traders arrived at the head of the Port Tobacco River in 1642, they found a thriving Piscataway settlement here. The English quickly usurped the land with wily real estate transactions and turned the deep-water river into a naval port of entry for the British Crown. The English colony thrived for 150 years, but faded with the decline in tobacco trade and the growing importance of Washington, DC, at the beginning of the 19th century.

When Port Tobacco had become all but ruins, preservationists moved in to start historic restorations in the 1930s. Some of the houses on the town square are private, but you can visit the Catslide House and the Courthouse, which features exhibits on the history of the town and the local tobacco industry. It is open July and August on weekends, from noon to 4 pm; donations accepted.

To reach Port Tobacco from Washington or Annapolis, take Hwy 301 south to La Plata, then go three miles west on Route 6. This site is only about 10 miles south of Waldorf, and you can easily visit all the sites in this area in one day.

Western Maryland & the Alleghenies

Known to few people except locals, Civil War enthusiasts, and outdoor adventurers, western Maryland and the Alleghenies are a region ripe for 'backcountry' exploration. The rugged foothills and mountains that compose this territory isolate western Maryland from the rest of the state as well as from suburban Washington. And yet anyone heading from DC to the foothills passes the Washington suburb of Bethesda. For folks heading to DC from the mountains, Bethesda offers a good spot to transition from a rural and scenic setting to a frenetic, urban one.

The meandering Potomac River forms the south and west borders of this region, the Mason-Dixon Line marks where Maryland meets Pennsylvania to the north, and central Maryland lies to the east. Interstate Hwys 70/270 run northwest and southeast along the dividing line between western Maryland's hill country and central Maryland's Piedmont.

West of I-70/270 family farms mix with vast wilderness, and mountain rivers like the Youghiogheny, Savage, Potomac, and Shenandoah carve out deep, narrow 'hollows' between the peaks. When the National Road, the Chesapeake & Ohio Canal, and the Baltimore & Ohio Railroad pushed through these hollows, small towns emerged as outposts along the primary route through the Appalachians to America's western frontier. Controlling these trade routes meant much to the Union and Confederate forces during the Civil War, and some of the war's fiercest fighting unfolded here at the Battle of Antietam and elsewhere. Not far from Antietam at Harpers Ferry in West Virginia (on the border with Maryland), the abolitionist John Brown waged his legendary pre-Civil War raid on the federal armory with hopes of inciting a national slave revolt. The famous Appalachian Trail traverses the Blue Ridge Mountains of western Maryland and passes right through Harpers Ferry.

HIGHLIGHTS

- Antietam Battlefield, a sobering experience
- Harpers Ferry, and a hike along Maryland Heights Trail for a vista of the Potomac and Shenandoah Rivers
- C&O Canal National Historical Park in Cumberland for hikes along the towpath
- The Rocky Gap Music Festival in August, near Cumberland – the Woodstock of bluegrass music
- Rafting or kayaking the white waters of the Youghiogheny River

Today, Antietam, Harpers Ferry, and the C&O Canal are national parks where travelers come face to face with dramatic moments in America's past in settings of extraordinary natural beauty. In western Maryland you will find world-class hiking, cycling, kayaking, and canoeing three seasons a year. During the winter western Maryland offers cross-country and downhill skiing. When the tidewater basin overheats with summer humidity, the mountain climate of western Maryland remains cooler and drier.

Tourist Offices Four state information centers meet visitors entering western Maryland along all the major highways: I-70 eastbound at South Mountain, 10 miles from Frederick near Boonsboro (☎ 301-293-2526); I-70 westbound (☎ 301-293-

4161); Route 15 S near Emmittsburg just south of the Pennsylvania border (☎ 301-447-2553); and the seasonal Catoctin Mountains Visitors Center (☎ 301-271-3285) on Route 15 south of Thurmont.

Beltway Maryland

BETHESDA

Until relatively recently a quiet Maryland town, Bethesda has grown to one of the largest, most influential, and most affluent suburban communities in the nation. Connected to DC along the cosmopolitan stretch of Wisconsin Ave from Georgetown and with a handy Metro station downtown, Bethesda is one of the most accessible suburbs for Washington visitors.

Despite its sophisticated modern trappings, some of Bethesda's most appealing spots remain its old-time attractions, such as its old movie theater, classic diner, and renowned crab shacks. Bethesda is also home to the National Institutes of Health and the Bethesda Naval Hospital.

Things to See & Do

The **Bethesda Theatre Cafe** (☎ 301-656-3337), 7719 Wisconsin Ave, presents second-run films and family matinees in its huge old movie house outfitted with cafe tables and swivel chairs. Order pitchers of beer and nachos in the dark (servers dial it in on lit computer pads) while the kids get wieners and chips.

The Kenwood district has enough **cherry trees** to rival the Tidal Basin in spring. In late March to early April, drive out to Kenwood via Wisconsin Ave to River Rd west, then north on Brookside Drive.

The affluent suburb has many **bookstores**, as you'd expect. Travel Books & Language Center (☎ 301-951-8533), 4931 Cordell Ave (off Wisconsin Ave), maintains a large selection of guidebooks, travel literature, language instruction sets, and maps. The staff is quite knowledgeable. You might also check the Rand McNally Map & Travel Store (☎ 301-365-6277) in the Montgomery Mall (7101 Democracy Blvd).

Hear literary readings at the **Writers Center** (☎ 301-656-1638 for schedule), 4508 Walsh St near Wisconsin Ave.

The Bethesda Metro Center Plaza (☎ 301-652-4988) sponsors **big-band dances** in the summer and free **ice skating** in the winter.

Places to Stay

The *Hyatt Regency Bethesda* (☎ 301-657-1234, 800-233-1234), 1 Bethesda Metro Center near Wisconsin Ave, is a deluxe suburban hotel atop Bethesda's Metro station (weekdays $175/200 single/double, weekends $105 single or double).

Generally Bethesda isn't the place to look for budget accommodations, but a cheaper option is the *American Inn* (☎ 301-656-9300, 800-323-7081) at 8130 Wisconsin Ave, a short walk from the Metro. Standard weekday room rates from $90 drop to $58 on weekends (add $10 for doubles), continental breakfast included.

Places to Eat

Bish Thompson's seafood restaurant (☎ 301-656-2400), 7935 Wisconsin Ave at West Virginia Ave, and the *Bethesda Crab House* (☎ 701-652-3382), 4958 Bethesda Ave near Arlington Rd, both offer a typical crab-house experience; expect newsprint for tablecloths and hammers and chisels to crack-your-own.

The *Tastee Diner* (☎ 301-652-3970), 7731 Woodmont Ave, is a classic chrome diner offering meat loaf and all the trimmings, open 24 hours.

The *Bean Bag* (☎ 301-530-8090), in the shopping center at Woodmont Ave and Old Georgetown Rd, sells gourmet coffee beans by the pound or cup, along with pastries, sandwiches, and soups.

You can also find suburban branches of favorite Georgetown restaurants: try *Booeymonger* (☎ 301-718-9550) at 4800 East-West Hwy at Wisconsin (open daily), or *La Posada* (☎ 301-656-9588) a Mexican grill at 8117 Woodmont Ave.

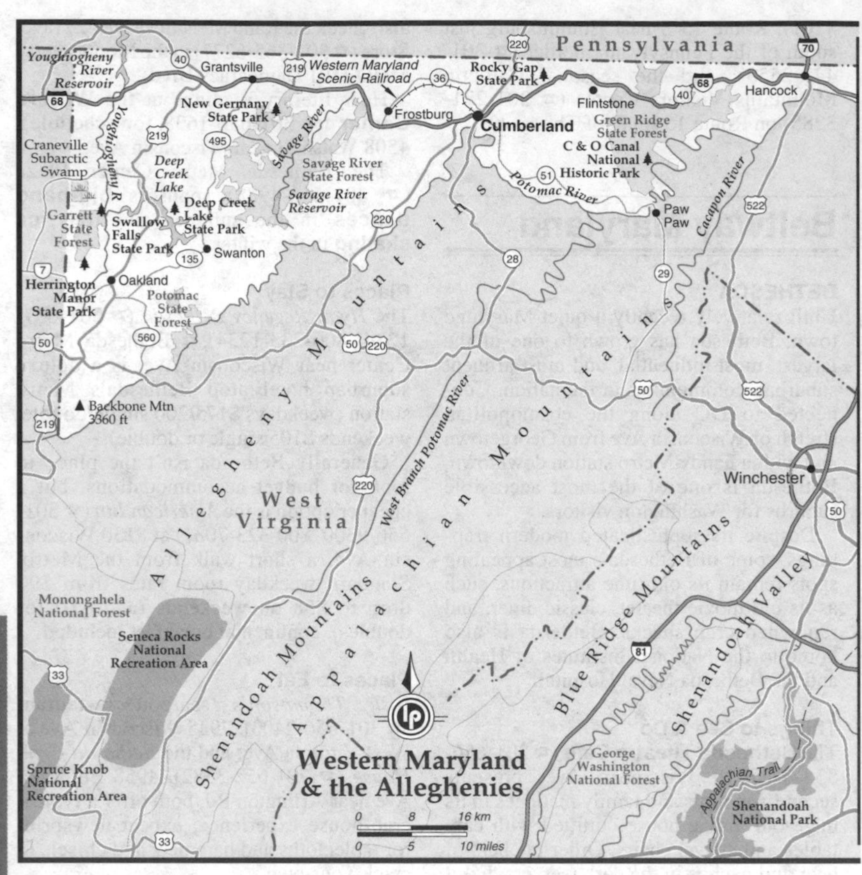

THE PAUL GARBER FACILITY

This is the Smithsonian's Air & Space restoration and storage facility. Here specialists have restored the controversial *Enola Gay*, the B-29 bomber that dropped the atomic bomb on Hiroshima. More than 90 other historic aircraft at the facility include warbirds from WWI and WWII along with spacecraft. Just about anyone who visits here will tell you the Garber Facility is a haunting place – an odd mix of aircraft cemetery and Dr Frankenstein's lab. You can find the Garber Facility (☎ 202-357-1400) on Silver Hill Rd in Suitland. Tours are by reservation only. No fee.

SURRATT HOUSE

Once a post office and tavern, this building on Brandywine Rd in Clinton gained its infamy after the assassination of Abraham Lincoln. Proprietor Mary Surratt was the mother of a co-conspirator of John Wilkes Booth, Lincoln's assassin. Surratt's son John and Booth hid weapons and hatched their murder plot here. Although Mary

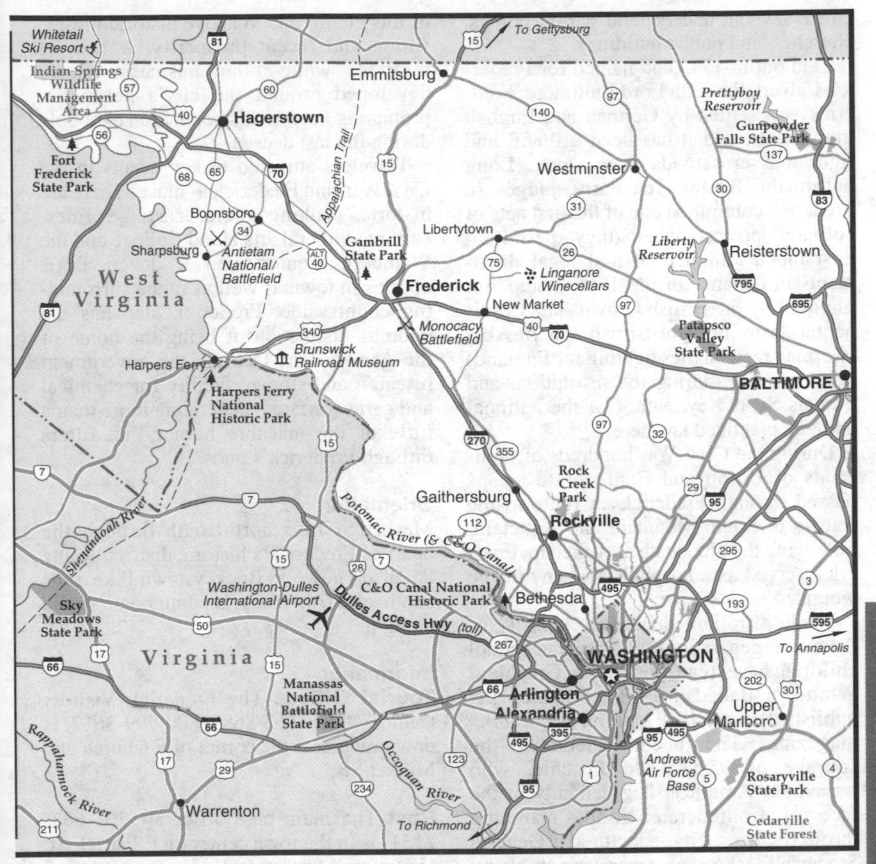

Surratt probably had no idea what her son and Booth were up to, a military court judged her an accomplice in the Presidential assassination and ordered her to be hanged. Mary Surratt was the first woman to die of such punishment in the US. Curiously, her son John, the true Wilkes accomplice, escaped execution.

The Surratt House (☎ 301-868-1121) is open March to mid-December 11 am to 3 pm Thursday to Friday, noon to 4 pm Saturday and Sunday. Half-hour guided tours cost $3, $2 seniors, $1 children under 18.

Western Foothills

FREDERICK

Thirty-five miles north of the District of Columbia, Frederick (population 45,000) is a gateway to the far western reaches of the state. South of Frederick sprawl a hundred permutations of the capital's suburbs. But if you get off I-270 and head into downtown Frederick, you will discover a 33-block historic core of restored 18th and 19th century Italian Renaissance,

Greek revival, and Federal period homes, churches, and public buildings.

Laid out in 1745 and named for Frederick Calvert, the sixth Lord Baltimore, Frederick was settled by German and English immigrants, and it has been a literal and figurative crossroads ever since. Long before the Boston Tea Party, judges in Frederick committed one of the first acts of colonial protest when they permitted unstamped commercial and legal documents in defiance of the 1765 Stamp Act imposed by the British Crown. The Continental Army brought British and Hessian (German mercenaries fighting for England) prisoners here during the revolution, and Francis Scott Key, author of the national anthem, practiced law here.

During the Civil War hundreds of thousands of Union and Confederate troops passed through Frederick en route to the Battles of South Mountain and Antietam. Following the bloodbath at Antietam, Frederick served as a hospital for many of the wounded.

While historians debate the veracity of the event, generations of American school children have read poet John Greenleaf Whittier's 'Ballad of Barbara Fritchie,' first published in an 1863 edition of *Atlantic* magazine. The poem celebrates the courage of 95-year-old Fritchie, who waved her American flag defiantly in the face of Confederate troops marching through her city, lectured General Stonewall Jackson on American patriotism, and challenged the 'rebel hordes' to 'shoot if you must this old gray head.' Hoping to avoid a public relations nightmare, the Confederates left the old lady in peace, but Fitchie's legend grew to haunt the South.

Shortly after the Battle of Antietam, America's famous jurist and author Oliver Wendell Holmes traveled to Frederick to visit his son wounded in the battle. Surveying the town, Holmes wrote: 'How graceful, how charmingly its group of steeples nestles among the Maryland hills. The town had a poetical look from a distance, as if seers and dreamers might dwell there.' Today, the core of Frederick retains much of this charm due to active historic preservation and recent prosperity. A host of midsize, white-collar businesses have developed around the city's perimeter, prompting Frederick's population to double during the last decade.

Travelers attracted to key events in the Civil War find Frederick a 'must.' There are historic walking tours, carriage rides, culture at liberal arts Hood College and the Weinberg Center, and a dozen B&B options in town as well as in the surrounding countryside. Frederick also has the dubious distinction of being the home of the Army's Fort Detrick, the government research and storage facility for chemical and germ warfare – generating more than a little of the macabre humor that filters through Frederick's pubs.

Orientation

Market St runs north/south through the heart of Frederick's historic district. Route 85, also known as Buckeystown Pike, runs south of I-70; many accommodations lie along it.

Information

Tourist Offices The Frederick Visitors Center (☎ 301-663-8687, 800-999-3617) is downtown near the corner of E Church and Market Sts.

Post The main post office (☎ 301-662-2131) is in the town center on E Patrick St. Hours are Monday to Friday 8:30 am to 5 pm, Saturday 8:30 am to 2 pm.

Bookstores Wonderbook & Video (☎ 301-694-5955), 1306 W Patrick St, has the city's most complete selection. The Curious Traveler (☎ 301-696-8660), 35 N Market, specializes in books for wayfarers.

Laundry 7th Street Laundry is in the shopping plaza near the intersection of Route 15 and 7th St.

Medical Services Frederick Memorial Hospital (☎ 301-698-3200) is at 400 W 7th St.

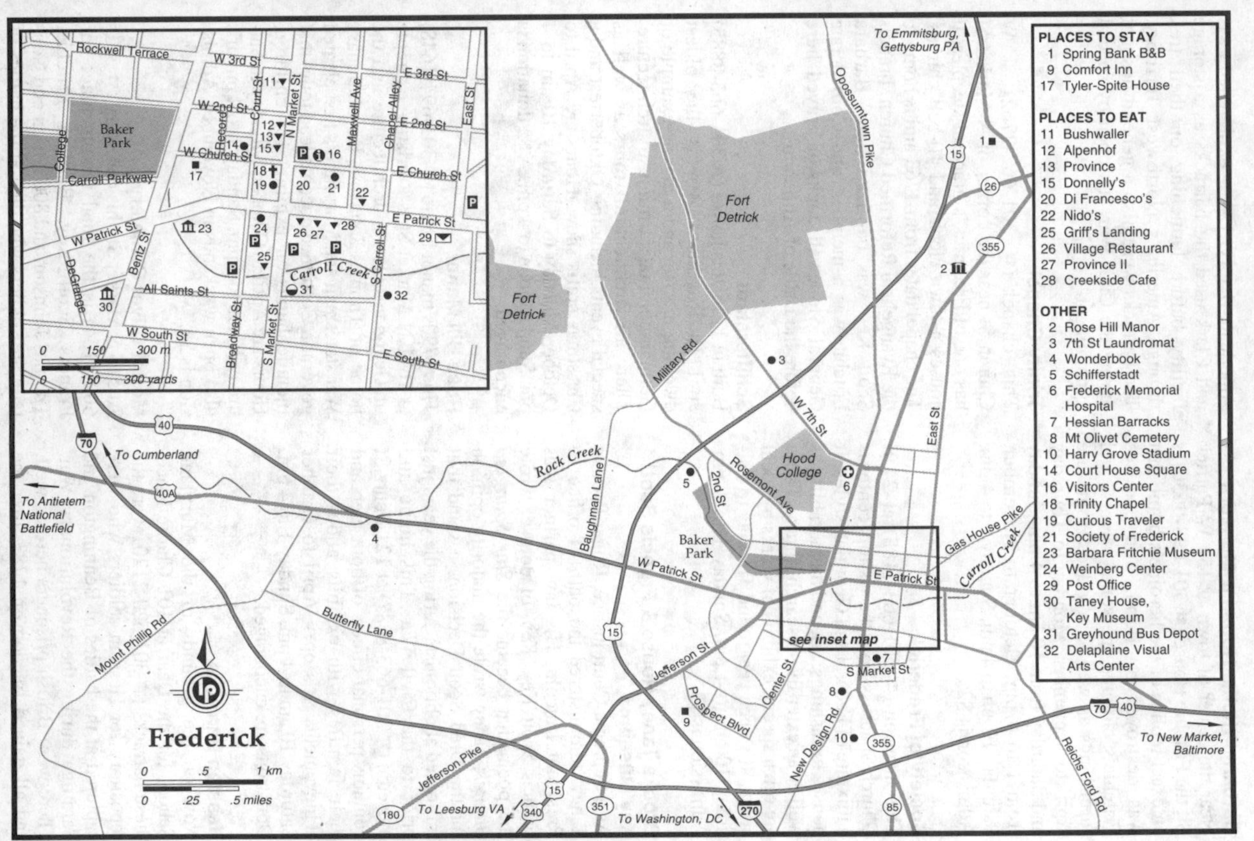
PLACES TO STAY
1 Spring Bank B&B
9 Comfort Inn
17 Tyler-Spite House
PLACES TO EAT
11 Bushwaller
12 Alpenhof
13 Province
15 Donnelly's
20 Di Francesco's
22 Nido's
25 Griff's Landing
26 Village Restaurant
27 Province II
28 Creekside Cafe
OTHER
2 Rose Hill Manor
3 7th St Laundromat
4 Wonderbook
5 Schifferstadt
6 Frederick Memorial Hospital
7 Hessian Barracks
8 Mt Olivet Cemetery
10 Harry Grove Stadium
14 Court House Square
16 Visitors Center
18 Trinity Chapel
19 Curious Traveler
21 Society of Frederick
23 Barbara Fritchie Museum
24 Weinberg Center
29 Post Office
30 Taney House, Key Museum
31 Greyhound Bus Depot
32 Delaplaine Visual Arts Center
Frederick
To Emmitsburg, Gettysburg PA
To New Market, Baltimore
To Washington, DC
To Leesburg VA
To Cumberland
To Antietam National Battlefield
Opossumtown Pike
Reichs Ford Rd
Gas House Pike
Carroll Creek
East St
E Patrick St
S Market St
New Design Rd
Center St
Prospect Blvd
Jefferson St
Jefferson Pike
W Patrick St
W 7th St
Military Rd
Rosemont Ave
2nd St
Baughman Lane
Butterfly Lane
Mount Phillip Rd
Rock Creek
Hood College
Fort Detrick
Baker Park
see inset map
Rockwell Terrace
College
Carroll Parkway
W 3rd St
W 2nd St
W Church St
Record St
Court St
N Market St
Chapel Alley
Maxwell Ave
E 3rd St
E 2nd St
E Church St
E South St
Carroll St
Broadway St
All Saints St
W South St
Bentz St
DeGrange
0 150 300 m
0 150 300 yards
0 .5 1 km
0 .25 .5 miles

MARYLAND

Barbara Fritchie House & Museum

Near the center of town at 154 W Patrick St, the Fritchie House (☎ 301-698-0630) is an exact replica of the heroine's home that was destroyed by flood. You can see Fritchie's clothing, personal effects, and furnishings as well as a video. Hours are April to September, Monday to Thursday and Saturday from 10 am to 4 pm, Sunday from 1 to 4 pm; October to November, Saturday 10 am to 4 pm, Sunday 1 to 4 pm. Admission is $2.

Society of Frederick

This mansion (☎ 301-663-1188) at 24 E Church St across from the visitors center is a mixture of Federal and Georgian styles. It houses furnishings, art, and memorabilia as well as an extensive research library. There are often special exhibits of works by local artists. It's open year round Tuesday to Saturday 10 am to 4 pm, Sunday 1 to 4 pm. Admission is $2.

Brooke Taney House & Francis Scott Key Museum

As a Supreme Court justice, Roger Brooke Taney administered the oath of office to President Lincoln. His law partner was Francis Scott Key. Key, of course, wrote the poem that became the *Star Spangled Banner*; Taney wrote the majority opinion for the Dred Scott Decision, a stand that infuriated abolitionists during the years just prior to the Civil War. This home and museum (☎ 301-663-8687) at 121 Bentz St contains personal effects of both men and their families with exhibits about their achievements. It's open April to October Saturday 10 am to 4 pm, Sunday 1 to 4 pm. Donations are encouraged.

Hessian Barracks

Now on the grounds of the Maryland School for the Deaf at 101 Clarke Place, these barracks (☎ 301-620-2120) were the repository for Hessian soldiers who were captured at the battles of Bennington and Saratoga during the Revolutionary War. There were British prisoners here as well, and all gained freedom in 1783 after the American victory. Later, explorers Lewis and Clark used the barracks as a storage facility before launching on their trek through America's Northwest Territory. The barracks were also a general hospital during the Civil War. It's open by special appointment.

Trinity Chapel

This chapel (☎ 301-662-2762) at W Church St near the corner of N Market St has one of Frederick's graceful steeples. It houses a town clock and 10-bell chimes. The chapel dates from 1763 and is home to the Evangelical Reformed Church. Francis Scott Key was baptized here, Barbara Fritchie was a member, and Confederate General Stonewall Jackson prayed here before the Battle of Antietam.

Schifferstadt

Built in 1756, this house (☎ 301-663-3885) at 1110 Rosemont Ave is the oldest dwelling in town and a classic example of German-colonial farmhouse architecture. There are architectural tours as well as special events including Oktoberfest and a Christmas crafts show. Hours are April to October Monday to Saturday 10 am to 4 pm, Sunday noon to 4 pm. A $2 donation is encouraged.

Rose Hill Manor

This 1790s manor house (☎ 301-694-1648) at 1611 N Market St is a pristine example of Georgian colonial architecture and the home of Thomas Johnson, Revolutionary War statesman and Maryland's first elected governor. Costumed docents lead tours that include hands-on exhibits for children. Hours are April to October, Monday to Saturday 10 am to 4 pm, Sunday 1 to 4 pm; it's also open weekends in November. Admission is $3.

Mount Olivet Cemetery

At 515 S Market St, this cemetery (☎ 301-662-1164) is the final resting place for Francis Scott Key, Barbara Fritchie, Thomas Johnson, and 800 Union and Confederate soldiers who died at the battles of

Antietam and Monocacy. You could make some good tombstone rubbings here.

Delaplaine Visual Arts Center

At 40 Carroll St, the Delaplaine (☎ 301-698-0656) is a lively regional museum with regularly changing exhibits of works by national and regional artists. It's open Thursday to Saturday from 10 am to 5 pm, Sunday 1:30 to 4 pm. It's free.

Weinberg Center for the Arts

This theater (☎ 301-694-8585) at 20 W Patrick St produces a continuous program of music, dance, and visual-art offerings. It's also home to the Fredericktowne Players. Most tickets cost between $15 and $20.

Frederick Brewing Company

Brewing 'Blue Ridge' beer since 1992, this microbrewery (☎ 301-694-7899), 4607 Wedgewood Blvd, has revived the rich brewing tradition in Frederick. There are tours and tastings. Call for current hours.

Cross-Country Skiing

Winter visitors will find cross-country skiing in New Germany State Park (west of Cumberland) or Blackwater Falls State Park in West Virginia, both west of Harpers Ferry. River & Trail Outfitters (☎ 301-695-5177) in Knoxville just outside of Harpers Ferry hosts weekend ski tours from mid-January to mid-March. The Blackwater Falls tour costs $199 per person and includes lessons, skiing, equipment, five meals, and two nights' accommodations. The New Germany overnight tour includes lessons, skiing, three meals, and one night's accommodations for $99 per person.

Organized Tours

Guided walking tours of Frederick depart from the visitors center (see Information), 19 E Church St, on Saturday, Sunday, and occasional Monday holidays. Historic district tours start at 1:30 pm; Civil War walking tours begin at 3 pm. They cost $4.50 for adults ($3.50 for seniors).

You can also take carriage tours of the historic district. Prices and hours vary. Call ☎ 301-694-7433 for reservations.

Special Events

Frederick sees several events of note each year: the Maryland Civil War Show in late April; the Frederick Festival of the Arts in late June; Commemoration of the Battle of Monocacy during the second week in July; and New Market Days, one of the largest antique fairs in the country in late September.

Places to Stay – bottom end

Camping *Gambrill State Park* (☎ 301-271-7574) is five miles northwest of Frederick on Route 40. Encompassing more than 1000 acres, this park has three scenic overlooks, hiking/nature trails, fishing, picnic sites, and 35 sites for tent and RV camping. Tent sites cost $10 on weekdays, $14 on weekends; RV hookups are $5 extra. It's open May to October.

Motels The *Comfort Inn* (☎ 301-695-6200), 420 Prospect Blvd, is your standard two-story brick motel built at a highway interchange (Jefferson St Exit off I-270/Route 15 south of town). Although the property is nothing special, you do get a pool, laundry, and exercise room. Rates are $60 single, $65 double with a Continental breakfast.

Slightly cheaper *Days Inn* (☎ 301-694-6600) at 5646 Buckeystown Pike (near I-270 and Route 85) is another generic chain motel. Rooms run $56 to $61.

The *Hampton Inn* (☎ 301-698-2500), 5311 Buckeystown Pike, is a six-story high-rise on the commercial strip near the Days Inn. It has an artificial lake with an outdoor crab restaurant, plus pool, exercise room, and Jacuzzi. Rooms start at $69 with a continental breakfast.

Places to Stay – middle

Catoctin Inn & Antiques (☎ 301-874-5555) at 3613 Buckeystown Pike (Route 85) is in the rural village of Buckeystown four miles south of Frederick's historic district.

Decorated in country antiques and featuring fireplaces in some rooms, the inn offers its guests a full country breakfast and afternoon tea. The inn also has several independent cabins for rent as well. There is a shop with 30 antique dealers on the property. This is a good place to stay if you want to avoid the traffic of greater Frederick. Rooms cost $95 in the inn, $125 for one of the cottages.

The *Morningside Inn* (☎ 301-898-9147), 7477 McKaig Rd, is10 minutes east of town off Route 26 near Mount Pleasant. This new inn has eight rooms in a converted and restored hay barn on a 300-acre farm. All rooms have a private bath. The rate is $95 and includes a full country breakfast.

The *Spring Bank B&B* (☎ 301-694-0440) at 7945 Worman's Mill Rd is a large brick Italianate/Gothic revival inn listed on the National Register of Historic Places. The inn sits on 10 acres north of the historic district on Route 15. The owners have decorated Spring Bank with 19th century antiques and William Morris wallpaper. Most rooms share baths and cost $75; $90 gets you a private bath.

MARYLAND

Places to Stay – top end

The *Tyler-Spite House* (☎ 301-831-4455), 112 W Church St, is the only B&B in the historic district. Opulently decorated in a 19th century style, this Federal mansion has a parlor, library, music room, garden, and swimming pool. Guests are served high tea and given a horse-drawn carriage ride. Rooms cost $150 to $250.

Places to Eat

The *Province II* (☎ 301-663-3315) at 12 E Patrick St sells fresh baked goods, sandwiches, soups, and salads. This can be a great stop for breakfast or lunch or for a takeout picnic. Breakfasts cost under $4.

Just two doors away at 16 E Patrick St is the *Creekside Cafe* (☎ 301-698-1845). The menu features healthy fare including homemade soups and desserts, and there are mounds of veggies on the sandwiches. Try the Hawaiian chicken salad for $6.50.

The *Village Restaurant* (☎ 301-662-1944) at 4 E Patrick St is a breakfast spot popular with the locals. An all-you-can-eat pancake breakfast costs $4.

Donnelly's (☎ 301-695-5388) at 103 N Market St has a pub atmosphere with lots of upscale sandwich and salad choices for lunch. You can get a chicken caesar salad for under $7.

Griff's Landing (☎ 301-694-8696) at 43 S Market is a nautical-theme restaurant with huge trophy fish hung on the walls. The chef specializes in seafood. The popular Cajun steak and barbecue shrimp will cost you $18, but you can find entrees under $11.

Nido's (☎ 301-694-5939), 111 E Patrick, is a small Italian oasis with candlelight and Chianti bottles on the tables. The entrees run to $15, but you can get pasta dishes for under $10.

Alpenhof Restaurant (☎ 301-662-2866) at 137 N Market St recalls Frederick's early history as a new home for many German colonists. If you like good Wiener schnitzel, sauerbraten, or wurst, and dark brews from overseas, this is the place to stop. Many substantial dinner entrees run less than $12.

Bushwaller's (☎ 301-694-5697), 209 N Market St, is another downtown restaurant in a historic setting – this one in a former drugstore. Decorated with photos, political cartoons, and newspaper front pages from the turn of the century, Bushwaller's revives a sense of the Gay Nineties. The menu is international. This is a good place for a big lunch for under $6 (the burgers and chili are memorable), but dinner can get pricey.

Province (☎ 301-663-1441) spreads out through one of the city's oldest homes (1767) at 131 N Market St. The decor is eclectic with a strong emphasis on crafts and shows by local artists. With a changing menu, the restaurant offers creative French cuisine. Filet mignon broiled with herbs from the restaurant garden is a popular entree. Most meals cost over $15.

Tauraso's (☎ 301-663-6600) is on Everedy Square at 6 East St in part of a shopping complex. Tauraso's is a popular spot for upscale lunches and dinners. The outdoor patio has a great casual atmosphere. You can get frittatas for under $6, while buck à l'orange could cost you over $20.

The *Brown Pelican* (☎ 301-695-5833) is a basement restaurant close to the visitors center at 5 E Church St. Amid nautical antiques you can eat Southern tidewater dishes like stuffed shrimp with crab imperial for $16.

Di Francesco's (☎ 301-695-5499) is in the heart of the historic district at 26 N Market St. With its whitewashed walls, candlelight, and soft music, Di Francesco's offers classic Italian ambiance and cuisine. Top-end entrees include veal saltimbocca and shrimp scampi, but you can eat from a selection of pasta dishes for under $12.

Entertainment

Bushwaller's, Donnelly's, and *Griff's Landing* (see Places to Eat) all have live bands on weekends that draw in the Hood College students and under-30s crowd. Frederick has a small-town feel, and you are likely to get a mix of ages and lifestyles in these bars. Griff's has comedy on Thursday.

Legends (☎ 301-698 2600) is an oldies disco at the Hampton Inn (see Places to Stay) where an over-30 crowd gathers.

Spectator Sports

The Frederick Keys (☎ 301-662-0013) are the city's popular minor-league-baseball Class A farm team for the Baltimore Orioles. The Keys play at Harry Grove Stadium from April to September. Tickets cost $5.

Things to Buy

During the last 50 years, Frederick and the surrounding townships have been quietly developing a vital art scene. Today, there are 16 studios and galleries in and around the city for shopping and browsing.

Less than 10 miles east of Frederick off I-70 is the Federal-era village of New Market. During the past 20 years, antique dealers by the dozens have reclaimed New Market's main street. Collectors now claim that this little village is among the very best places to browse for antiques in all of America. There is an exceptional restaurant here as well. *Mealey's* (☎ 301-865-5488), 8 W Main, serves moderately priced Maryland cuisine throughout a maze of rooms furnished with country antiques.

Getting There & Away

Bus Greyhound (☎ 301-663-3311) stops at the depot at E All Saints St. From Monday to Thursday you pay $11 to/from Baltimore, $12 to/from DC; it costs an extra $1 on Friday, Saturday, and Sunday.

Train MARC trains (☎ 800-325-7245) stop 15 miles southwest of town at Brunswick (near Harpers Ferry) on weekdays, but plans are in the works to bring MARC trains to downtown and suburban Frederick stations in the near future.

Car Frederick is at the junction of I-70, I-270, and Route 15. Any of the exits from the interstate highways lead to the historic district, but for travelers coming from Baltimore or DC the Route 85 N Exit is the most direct.

Getting Around

There are four parking lots just south of the intersection Patrick and Market Sts, which cross at the center of town. There is also a parking lot next to the downtown visitors center on E Church St. Transit Service of Frederick County (☎ 301-694-2065) runs buses within the city as well as to satellite communities. The fare is $1.

The Frederick Cab (☎ 301-662-2250) is an alternative to driving to sites across town.

AROUND FREDERICK

National Shrine of St Elizabeth Ann Seton

In 1991 Pope John Paul II designated this chapel/shrine a 'minor basilica' (☎ 447-6606 Monday to Friday, ☎ 447-3121 weekends). At 333 S Seton St in Emmittsburg near the Pennsylvania border, the serene grounds include a 1770s farm house and the larger 'White House' from which

America's first saint led her heroic life of charity. There's a daily mass. It's open 10 am to 5 pm with abbreviated hours in December and January.

Brunswick Railroad Museum

If you like elaborate HO-scale model railroads, take a trip to the village of Brunswick near Harpers Ferry. At 40 W Potomac St (☎ 301-834-7100) you will find the B&O rail lines, the station, round house, and museum interpreting life in a railroad town at the turn of the 20th century. It's open April to December Saturday 10 am to 4 pm, Sunday 1 to 4 pm; in summer, there are additional hours on Thursday and Friday 10 am to 2 pm. Admission is $3.

Linganore Wine Cellars

This 230-acre vineyard (☎ 301-831-5889) is open for tours, tastings, and picnics. Linganore specializes in fruit and berry wines as well as estate-bottled versions of popular grape varietals like Chardonnay. About 12 miles east of Frederick on I-70, you will find Exit 62; head north on Route 75 N and turn right at Glisans Mill Rd.

Monocacy Battlefield

In early July 1864, 5000 Union soldiers delayed 18,000 Confederates here, three miles south of Frederick on Route 355 (4801 Urbana Pike). This delaying tactic on the part of General Lew Wallace gave the Union's General Grant a chance to reinforce his regiments at Fort Stevens to protect Washington, DC, and head off the Confederate attempts to overrun the national capital. At the battlefield (☎ 301-662-3515) you will find artifacts and an electronic map presenting details of the conflict. The surrounding farmland is virtually unchanged since the days of the battle. It's open every day from Memorial Day to Labor Day 8 am to 4:30 pm, September to June Wednesday to Sunday only.

ANTIETAM NATIONAL BATTLEFIELD

The hilly farmland on the extreme western edge of the Piedmont marks the site of the bloodiest single day in the Civil War and US history – some people claim the corn still grows red. Northerners call this site Antietam (Ann-TEE-tum) after the creek that flows here. Southerners call it Sharpsburg after the nearby town. On September 17, 1862, over 23,000 Union and Confederate soldiers fell dead or wounded, or went missing during General Robert E Lee's first invasion of the North, which ended as a tactical draw. Clara Barton, who later founded the American Red Cross, treated the battle's wounded.

Information

The Park Service Visitors Center (☎ 301-432-5124) is on State Rd 65 north of Sharpsburg. There is a $2/4 single/family admission fee. The center is open June to August from 8:30 am to 6 pm; 8:30 am to 5 pm the rest of the year. With the price of admission, visitors get a pamphlet with a driving tour that leads you through the battle. The park rangers also offer free talks and walks during the summer months. The visitors center rents tour tapes for $4. If you want a more in-depth tour, ask the rangers for a list of private guides who come with you in the car and talk about the battle in depth. The going rate is $20 per vehicle.

The Park Service shows a 26-minute film, *Antietam Visit*, which re-creates the events of the battle and Lincoln's visit to Union commander General George B McClellan. The film includes an actor's rendering of Lincoln's purported reflections on the battle and the war. You can also see *Antietam Victory*, an 18-minute slide show on the tactical aspects of the battle every hour on the half hour.

The Battlefield

The battlefield and surrounding area are surprisingly uncluttered, save for historic plaques and statues honoring the units that fought here. Antietam is a remarkable contrast to Gettysburg, where a string of fast-food restaurants mark the main entrance to the battlefield. There are no wax museums, trinket shops, or tourist

The Battle of Antietam

The Battle of Antietam occurred when Confederate General Robert E Lee first attempted to take the Civil War to the North. Lee's 41,000 troops marched north from Virginia hoping to surprise Union General George B McClellan's encampment of 87,000. In addition to being on home turf, McClellan enjoyed a further advantage when, eight days before the battle, a Union soldier found a copy of the Confederate battle plan, known as 'Lee's Lost Dispatch' or 'Lee's Special Order No 191.'

The battle took place on September 17, 1862, over 12 sq miles and in three phases – early morning, midday, and afternoon. From about 6 am to 9 am, Union troops attacked and drove back Confederate troops dug in north of the current-day visitors center. Some of the most horrendous slaughter took place in the Miller cornfield (about half a mile north of the visitors center) as fighting raged back and forth across it for three hours. Union General Joseph Hooker noted, 'At the time I am writing every stalk of corn in the northern and greater part of the field was cut as closely as could have been done with a knife and the slain lay in rows precisely as they had stood in their ranks a few moments before.'

During the midday phase, Union and Confederate infantry fought over the sunken road between the Roulette and Piper farms from 9:30 am to 1 pm. The road (about half a mile southeast of the visitors center) became known as 'Bloody Lane' because of the 5000 casualties sustained there.

In the afternoon phase Union General Burnside attacked across the Lower Bridge (a mile southeast of the town of Sharpsburg), but Confederate General AP Hill drove Burnside's men back to the bridge.

Lee's failure to bring the war successfully into the North probably prevented England from recognizing the Confederacy. The war continued for another two years, due in part to McClellan's extreme caution in committing his reserve troops and refusal to pursue the Confederates back into Virginia. Had he acted decisively, he might have achieved an early end to the conflict. ■

traps here. Antietam seems a solemn, haunting place – as it should – when you drive along the roads past split-rail fences and monuments.

Special Events

Living history reenactments of different elements of the Antietam conflict take place several times a month July to December. Sharpsburg Heritage Festival is three days of Civil War living history, music, crafts, and workshops organized on the weekend closest to the battle anniversary. In early December there is an Antietam National Battlefield Memorial Illumination at which 23,110 candles are lit to honor the battle's casualties.

Getting There & Away

From Frederick take Hwy 40 Alt about 17 miles north to Boonsboro, and then head west on Hwy 34 toward Sharpsburg and follow the signs to the battlefield.

INDIAN SPRINGS WILDLIFE MANAGEMENT AREA

This 6500-acre site (☎ 301-842-2702) is in Clear Spring, 12 miles west of Hagerstown. The top of Fairview Mountain was a Civil War signal post where messages were flashed to South Mountain across the Cumberland Valley. Visitors come here to fish and hunt for deer, turkey, grouse, rabbits, quail, and some waterfowl. There is also a nature trail and two lakes stocked with trout. During the spring and fall birddog clubs hold field trials for their canines.

FORT FREDERICK STATE PARK

Fort Frederick lies in the heart of the park (☎ 301-842-2155) in Big Pool, 16 miles west of Hagerstown. It was built in 1756 to defend English settlers against the French and Indians during the French and Indian War. The fort is unique among frontier forts of the period for its size and stone stockade wall. The only time the fort ever actually saw battle was on Christmas 1861 when Union troops inside fought off a small party of Confederate troops. There is hiking, fishing, and boating in the park, and muzzle loader shoots and military reenactments take place in the fort. It's one mile south of I-70 on Route 56.

WHITETAIL SKI RESORT (PA)

Whitetail (☎ 717-328-9400) is about 18 miles northwest of Hagerstown just across the border in Pennsylvania. The resort has some good trails and it is less crowded than many other regional ski areas. Lift tickets are $30 on weekdays; $39 on weekends, $25 for night skiing (4 to 10 pm). On off-peak days there are general discounts and special discounts for beginners, seniors, and families. To get there take I-70 west to Route 68 (Exit 18). Go through the traffic light in Clear Spring, and follow the snowflake signs to the mountain. The slopes are open from 8:30 am to 10 pm.

SIDELING HILL ROAD CUT

This is an unusual tourist destination but well worth a look if you're in the area and you like geology. The cut, which was begun in 1983, is where I-68 goes through Sideling Hill and exposes a 600-foot section of tightly folded 330-million-year-old rock. The strata run in color from tan to green to gray to red. The visitors center (☎ 301-842-2155) is open daily from 9 am to 5 pm. Take I-70 west to I-68 west to Sideling Hill.

HARPERS FERRY NATIONAL HISTORIC PARK (WV)

Harpers Ferry is a small town at the confluence of the Shenandoah and Potomac Rivers in West Virginia just across the river border from Maryland. About 20 miles from Frederick, Harpers Ferry draws many visitors from Washington, DC. The town's notoriety began with abolitionist John Brown's raid on the federal armory here in 1859. Brown had hoped to gain weapons to arm the slaves and spark a national rebellion. Not long after the raid, Harpers Ferry was in the thick of conflict during much of the Civil War.

Although people still live and work in Harpers Ferry, much of the town is a 'national historic park' spanning the Maryland and West Virginia sides of the Potomac. The easternmost section along the river has three major streets where the town as it was on the eve of the Civil War is re-created.

Harpers Ferry is well situated for commerce at the intersection of the Potomac and Shenandoah Rivers, with the Baltimore & Ohio Railroad and the C&O Canal providing transport between Washington and Baltimore and the western frontier. The town takes its name from Robert Harper, who took over an already established ferry operation in 1747. George Washington convinced Congress to establish a federal armory here in the late 18th century. Eventually the armory, with its 20 buildings and 400 workers, became the industrial anchor for the town. Before the Civil War, over 3000 people lived in Harpers Ferry; today there are about 400.

John Brown's October 1859 raid brought the town national recognition. During the Civil War Confederate and Union troops moved through town repeatedly; they burned the armory, and the town suffered heavy war damage. Flooding damaged the town further in the late 1800s. One post-war high point was the establishment of Storer College, founded to educate freed blacks, but the college closed in the mid 1950s.

History is not the town's only draw. The longest and most-famous hiking path in the US, the Appalachian Trail, passes through Harpers Ferry. Day hikers as well as backpackers seek out the dramatic vistas on hills overlooking the confluence of two of the country's most historic rivers.

Orientation

The majority of park buildings are at the base of a steep hill along three streets at the eastern end of town near the intersection of the Potomac and Shenandoah Rivers. The buses from the visitors center let you off on Shenandoah St, which runs northeast and

MDT

The teams line up for introductions on opening day at Oriole Park in Camden Yards, Baltimore.

ROBERT DE GAST

Pride of produce at Lexington Market, Baltimore

RICK GERHARTER

The chapel at the US Naval Academy in Annapolis, MD

MDT

The Annapolis waterfront

RICK GERHARTER

Midshipman maneuvers in Annapolis

ROBERT DE GAST

Tobacco drying shed in southern Maryland

MDT

Western Maryland Scenic Railroad in Cumberland

MDT

Herds of wild ponies have roamed Assateague Island for centuries. Be careful – they bite!

ends right in front of John Brown's fort. Potomac and High Sts run northwest towards Camp Hill to the Storer College buildings.

Information

The visitors center (☎ 304-535-6298) is on a hill above the town. A seven-day pass for park buildings is $5 per vehicle or $3 for walk-ins and cyclists. Since the entire town is not a national park, you could walk the streets and enter any non-park building. The park is open daily from 8:30 am to 5 pm and from 8:30 am to 6 pm from Memorial Day to Labor Day, although the town is always open. There is also a park information center on Shenandoah St in town.

There is almost no parking at all in Harpers Ferry. Everyone who drives parks at the visitor center and takes the free bus down to the town. If you come in the off season, you may be able to park along Potomac St next to the train station, but there are fewer than 20 spots.

The Harpers Ferry Historical Association (☎ 800-821-5206) on Shenandoah St has an excellent bookstore with a wide selection of titles on the Civil War, John Brown, and Harpers Ferry.

The Appalachian Trail Conference Headquarters (☎ 304-535-6331) is at the corner of Washington and Jackson Sts. The headquarters has books and hiking equipment and is open seven days a week April to October.

Master Armorer's House

This structure on Shenandoah St, built in 1858, was the home for the chief gunsmith of the armory. Inside are a few rooms with information on the armory and a display of muskets and rifles. Here you learn that Armorer John Hall's creation of a standard-size rifle with interchangeable parts revolutionized the firearms industry. Mechanically produced parts could fit any and all rifles, and standardized production resulted in better, cheaper weapons. Hall's technology made possible the wholesale carnage of the Civil War and brought the price of firearms within the range of all Americans wishing to emulate Billy the Kid.

John Brown's Fort

Brown and his men barricaded themselves in this building after attacking the armory. The 'fort' was the armory's fire engine house and originally stood north of Potomac St across from Whitehall Tavern, but it has been reconstructed and moved to its present location on Arsenal Square (the empty plot of land with the foundations of two buildings burned in 1861 when Federal troops evacuated Harpers Ferry).

Storer College

This institution (now closed) was primarily a teacher's college for freedmen and other African Americans. Storer resided in various armory homes and in Anthony Hall, now a Park Service building, on Camp Hill, above the main part of Harpers Ferry. The college buildings are part of the park and are open to the public.

Storer began when Reverend NC Brackett of the Freewill Baptist Home Mission Society of New England set up a one-room schoolhouse for freedmen. The school was part of a nationwide effort by blacks, northern philanthropists, and the Freedmen's Bureau to educate the thousands of Americans freed by the end of slavery.

In 1867 John Storer of Maine gave $10,000 to the Freewill Baptists to establish a 'colored school' in the South under several conditions. These included that the school be open to all who applied regardless of ethnicity or sex, that it eventually become a college, and that the Baptists also raise $10,000 for the effort. They did and in 1868 Storer College opened. It continued to educate students until the 1955 *Brown v the Board of Education* Supreme Court ruling ended legal segregation, and West Virginia cut off funding. Storer closed in June 1955.

Jefferson Rock

Take the stairs up from High St past St Peter's Catholic Church to the footpath up to the rock. Here Thomas Jefferson

John Brown & the Raid on Harpers Ferry

John Brown was an abolitionist born in Connecticut and raised in Ohio, where he worked in his father's leather tanning business. From his 20s to his 40s, Brown tried his luck as a tanner, wool merchant, farmer, and land speculator in various places from Pennsylvania to Massachusetts. A ne'r-do-well who took satisfaction in being a social rebel, Brown was fanatically convinced of the evils of slavery and actively supported the abolitionist cause throughout his life. In 1849, he and his family settled in an African-American community in North Elba, New York, where his home was a station on the Underground Railroad. Brown spent very little time at his farm; his wife Mary Ann Day and some of his children kept it running.

In 1854 Brown and several of his sons moved to Kansas to join the fight to keep it a free (non-slave) territory. They settled in Osawatomie, and Brown organized a guerrilla band to fight pro-slavery settlers. In 1856 Brown and his guerrillas murdered in cold blood five reputed pro-slavery settlers at Pottawatomie Creek. After this incident, 'Old Osawatomie Brown' became a particularly feared figure.

With backing from northern abolitionists and a band of 21 men, black and white, Brown attacked the arsenal at Harpers Ferry on October 16, 1859. However, they never gained the firearms they sought, nor did their raid incite a national uprising of slaves. Brown's army barricaded themselves in the armory fire engine and guard house – 'John Brown's fort.' On October 18, Colonel Robert E Lee and Lieutenant JEB Stuart, serving then in the US Army, stormed the building, killed 10 of Brown's men, including two of his sons, and captured Brown. Brown was tried for murder, treason, and conspiring with slaves to create an insurrection. A court found him guilty and sentenced him to death by hanging on December 2, 1859.

Despite the raid's quick end, it inspired many people in the North and outraged many in the South. On the day of his death Brown wrote a note and gave it to his jailer. It read, 'I, John Brown, am now quite certain that the crimes of this guilty land will never be purged away but with blood. I had, as I now think, vainly flattered myself, that without very much bloodshed it might be done.' A year later, in April 1861, the Civil War began. ■

claimed the view of three states was 'worth a voyage across the Atlantic.'

The Appalachian Trail

The trail runs 2144 miles along Appalachian ridge lines from Maine in the north to Georgia in the south. Constructed and marked during the 1920s and '30s, the trail traverses state and federal lands along 96% of its course. In 1968 the national Trails System Act made the AT a linear national park and authorized funds to buy up the remaining private lands along the trail. Backpackers and day hikers use the trail by the tens of thousands each year.

The AT descends from South Mountain, follows the C&O Canal towpath along the Potomac River, crosses the footbridge appended to the railroad bridge near the river junction, passes through the center of town, heads south over the Hwy 340 bridge across the Shenandoah River, and climbs into the Blue Ridge Mountains of Virginia.

Maryland Heights Trail

This trail covers the area of major Union fortification during the Civil War and also leads hikers to vistas of the river gorges known as the Harpers Ferry Water Gap. You join this trail by following the AT across the Potomac River footbridge at the end of Shenandoah St and then along the towpath to cliffs that overlook the river and Harpers Ferry (3.9 miles). You can continue up to Stone Fort, built by Union troops (another 1.2 miles). The trail circles back from there to the towpath and railroad tracks. The trail is well marked, but you can also obtain maps at the visitors center.

The Point
This is the spit of land east of Shenandoah St on the two rivers. Stand here and you can look across the rivers to Virginia, Maryland, and more of West Virginia.

Other Sights
The **John Brown Museum** is a museum devoted to the events of the raid. **Black Voices from Harpers Ferry** has information on the African-American population of Harpers Ferry. There are other historic buildings along Potomac, Shenandoah and High Sts, including a confectionery, tavern, dry goods store, and some homes.

Organized Tours
Nighttime ghost tours popular with Marylanders are available from Friday to Sunday from early May to early November for $2 per person (☎ 304-725-8019).

The Park Service gives public walking tours from Memorial Day to Labor Day.

Places to Stay
Harpers Ferry KOA (☎ 304-535-6895) has over 200 sites for $26 for two people and $4 for each additional person. It's open all year. Take US 340 southwest from the Shenandoah River Bridge for one mile, and then follow the signs.

John Brown's Body
Within two years of Brown's death, people all over the Union were singing the song 'John Brown's Body' to the tune of what is now used for the 'Battle Hymn of the Republic.'

Ironically, the song was originally about another John Brown. Sergeant John Brown was a Scottish immigrant from Boston and a member of the Boston Light Infantry of the Massachusetts Volunteer Militia. He was also a tenor in his battalion's chorus. The chorus used to improvise lyrics to a Methodist song that went like this:

Say brothers will you meet us,
On Canaan's happy shore.

As a joke, they sang the following words to the same tune:

John Brown's body lies a-moldering in the grave,
But his soul goes marching on.

In the summer of 1861 the Massachusetts Twelfth Regiment marched down Broadway in New York singing their version. The crowd loved the song and it soon swept the country, with some different variations. Part of one of the most popular versions about John Brown of Harpers Ferry fame runs:

Old John Brown's body lies a-moldering in the grave,
While weep the sons of bondage whom he ventured all to save,
But though he lost his life in struggling for the slave,
His truth is marching on.
Glory, glory, hallelujah!
Glory, glory, hallelujah!
Glory, glory, hallelujah!
His truth is marching on!
He captured Harpers Ferry with his nineteen men so few,
And he frightened Old Virginny 'til she trembled through and through,
They hung him for a traitor, themselves a traitor crew,
But his truth is marching on.

After President Abraham Lincoln's assassination, Julia Ward Howe changed the words and kept the tune in her haunting 'Battle Hymn of the Republic,' a tribute to the fallen national leader who had accomplished what Brown had failed to do – free the slaves. ■

A good place to stay is the *Harpers Ferry HI* (☎ 301-834-7652) in Knoxville, Maryland, just east of Harpers Ferry (the MARC train stops here on its run from DC). The hostel has a stone fireplace, kitchen, and 39 beds. Lockout is from 9:30 am to 5 pm. The rate is $11/14 members/nonmembers. To get there from Maryland take Route 340 west. Go half a mile and make a left on Keep Tryst Rd. Go one-third of a mile and make a right on Sandy Hook Rd (which is also labeled Harpers Ferry Rd). The hostel is on your left about 100 yards up the road. From Harpers Ferry take Route 340 across the Potomac into Maryland and make a right on Kemp Tryst Rd and continue as above.

The *Hillside Motel* (☎ 301-834-8144), 19105 Kemp Tryst Rd, is two miles east of Harpers Ferry in Maryland. It's open all year with standard motel rooms with one/two beds for $25/32. It's near the hostel.

There are several B&Bs, each with two rooms, above town in the historic district. Almost all are priced between $60 and $75. *Between the Rivers* (☎ 304-535-2768) is at the corner of Gilmore and Ridge Sts. It has a balcony room and a separate cottage room. Rates, including full breakfast, are $75 to $90. The *Harpers Ferry Guest House* (☎ 304-535-6955) is on Washington St across from the Appalachian Trail Conference Headquarters. It has two large rooms with private bath. Weekday/weekend rooms are $63/85 with full breakfast.

MARYLAND

Places to Eat

The *Coffee Mill* and the *Back Street Cafe* are burger and sandwich places on Potomac St. There are chocolate stores all over town.

Little Ponderosa BBQ (☎ 304-535-2168) is in an old railway car opposite the train station. Bruce and Thelma Stallings cook up the meat. A BBQ beef or pork sandwich costs $3.75. A ⅓-lb burger with cheese costs $3.75, but a ¼-lb one is only $2.25.

Getting There & Away

Train There are commuter trains, but the schedule meets the needs of people who live in Harpers Ferry and commute to/from DC, not travelers. You can't go to Harpers Ferry from DC and return to DC the same day.

Amtrak (☎ 800-872-7245) train No 30 departs Harpers Ferry at 12:15 pm and arrives in DC at 1:35 am daily. Train No 29 leaves Washington, DC, at 4:05 pm and arrives in Harpers Ferry at 5:09 pm.

MARC (☎ 800-325-7245) runs commuter train service between DC and Harpers Ferry from Monday to Friday. MARC trains take about 1½ hours. Trains to DC leave at 5:55 and 7 am. Trains from DC leave at 4:55, 5:30, and 6:50 pm.

Car Coming from Frederick, take Hwy 340 about 20 miles west from I-70 to the village of Sandy Hook on the edge of the national park, and then follow the signs to the visitors center. You'll cross attractive hilly landscape on the drive.

Free buses run from the visitors center to the town from 6 am to 5 pm from November to May and until 7:30 pm from April to October. The trip takes five minutes. See Information for details about parking.

The Alleghenies

Maryland's mountain recreation areas occupy hundreds of square miles of wilderness west of Cumberland along I-68 and Route 40. Although the Allegheny Mountains can't match the Rockies or Cascades for height or extensive wilderness, the mountains and their hiking trails can take you a long way from civilization into pristine mountains and valleys. Venturing west of Cumberland, you will find 70,000 acres of public wilderness including the Savage River State Forest south of Grantsville. The Potomac and Garrett State Forests also offer plenty of backcountry exploration.

Camping

Extreme western Maryland has some of the best camping facilities in the state. The state parks at New Germany, Deep Creek Lake, Swallow Falls, and Herrington

Manor have campsites and water. Tent sites run $10 during the week, $14 on weekends. For hookups add $5. Cabin rates are $65 to $85; reservations are accepted up to a year in advance. Primitive camping in the state forest carries a $2 per night fee.

Glen Acres (☎ 301-387-9596) in Swanton on Route 135 is open May to October. Tent sites are $17, RV sites $19.

Double G Ranch (☎ 301-387-5481) in McHenry on Route 219 is open year round with bathhouse, store, playground, laundry, and video games. The fee is $17; for $19.50 you get water, electricity, sewer, and cable TV.

Sssss – A Word about Poisonous Snakes

The Allegheny Mountains are home to the eastern (timber) rattlesnake and the copperhead. Both species are large vipers with enough venom to kill a human. Watch for these serpents in the vicinity of bolder piles and fallen trees where they like to nest. Hikers in the Alleghenies should always carry a walking staff to parry snakes, wear leather hiking boots (and possibly leg protection), and carry a snake-bite kit and/or an antitoxin vaccine. ■

Whitewater Rafting & Kayaking

The Youghiogheny River presents a variety of world-class whitewater experiences. The Upper Yough has class V+ rapids near Friendship; it has been the site of numerous national and international kayaking events. The lower parts of the river are tamer as is the nearby Savage River. For regulations and water releases on the Yough, call Youghiogheny River Management (☎ 301-387-4111).

Outfitters in Ohiopyle, Pennsylvania, can help you plan a rafting adventure. At White Water Adventurers (☎ 412-329-8850, 800-982-7238) you can rent a four-person inflatable boat for as little as $40 a day or inflatable kayaks for $25. Guided trips down 11 miles of continuous rapids on the Upper Yough cost $99 to $150 a day.

Mountain Streams (☎ 800-723-8669) advertises rafting trips for as little as $20 per person and runs expeditions into West Virginia's whitewater streams like the wild Cheat River.

Laurel Highlands River Tours (☎ 800-472-3846) meets the competition's prices with two-day expeditions that include guided and unguided trips.

Skiing

Both cross-country and downhill skiing are possibilities. Nordic skiers use the trails in all of the state parks, but head for New Germany State Park if you want trails that are cleared and marked specifically for Nordic skiing. Wisp Resort at Deep Creek Lake is Maryland's only ski resort and just one of a handful of places for downhill skiing within day-tripping range of DC.

Fishing

The lakes and slow-moving streams of western Maryland have a healthy stock of largemouth bass. The faster streams have pike, walleye, and trout. To inquire about seasons and limits, check with the Maryland Department of Natural Resources (☎ 410-974-3771. The so-called 'Three Sisters' rivers – the Youghiogheny, Casselman, and North Branch of the Potomac – have been featured in four national TV shows about fly-fishing. For a list of stocked streams and regulations, consult the *Maryland Sportfishing Guide* available from sellers of fishing licenses.

Swimming

There are four good public swimming sites west of Cumberland. Deep Creek Lake has an 800-foot sandy beach with lifeguards during the summer (scuba-diving lessons are also given here; see Deep Creek Lake below). New Germany State Park has 600-feet of beach on its 13-acre lake. You will find a 700-foot beach at the Broadford Recreation Area near Mountain Lake Park right in the town of Oakland. The lake at Herrington Manor State Park is substantial (53 acres), but the beach is short at 400 feet.

CUMBERLAND

Originally called 'Fort Cumberland' this small city (population 24,000) has been a frontier outpost since young George Washington and General Braddock used Cumberland as their spearhead into the wilderness during the French and Indian War. Cumberland sits in Maryland's western 'wrist,' about 135 miles from Washington and Baltimore on the north shore of the Potomac River, surrounded by the thick forests of the rugged Allegheny Mountains that long divided America's civilized colonies from the western territories.

Generations of explorers and pioneers followed the Potomac to Cumberland and took the mountain trails across the Allegheny watershed westward to Pittsburgh, Pennsylvania, where the Ohio River led the way to the frontier. The first national pike (Route 40 Alt) and the C&O Canal ended here, and the western Maryland Railroad grew up to carry manufactured goods and imports from Baltimore over the mountains. Cumberland boomed as a shipping center in the 19th century and later found greater prosperity when miners began exploiting the rich bituminous coal fields beneath the surface of the Alleghenies.

With improved routes to the west through Pennsylvania, and a decline in demand for soft coal for homes and industries, Cumberland slipped into depression after WWII. The little city with its stock of once-elegant Victorian homes and public buildings became a place time seemingly forgot until the mid-1970s when a new generation of explorers turned to the Allegheny wilderness as an oasis from the crowds, pollution, and crime of places like Washington and Baltimore. Today, the Cumberland area has become the center for a thriving outdoor tourist industry where outfitters have made the forbidding Alleghenies accessible to hikers, campers, mountain bikers, skiers, boaters and whitewater enthusiasts. While hardly gentrified, Cumberland is steadily pursuing historic preservation that is reclaiming many public buildings as well as many Victorian homes.

With attractive neighborhoods, some good restaurants, and major attractions like the C&O Canal National Historic Park and the steam-driven Western Maryland Scenic Railway, Cumberland is inviting in its own right, and it's also a gateway to outdoor adventure.

Many younger travelers find themselves drawn to the nearby town of Frostburg where the country-village setting gains texture and vitality from a significant young, intellectual population associated with Frostburg State University. On the first week in August tens of thousands of people – many young – descend on the Cumberland area for the Rocky Gap Music Festival – the 'Woodstock' of traditional bluegrass music – held in nearby Rocky Gap State Park.

Orientation

The intersection of Baltimore St and Centre Sts mark the heart of town where there is now a pedestrian shopping mall. Sixteen miles west of Cumberland is the college town of Frostburg, where there are decent restaurants, hotels, and bars.

Information

Tourist Offices Take your questions to the Allegany County Visitors Bureau in Western Maryland Station Center (☎ 301-777-5905, 800-508-4748), Canal St. It's open Monday to Friday 9 am to 5 pm, weekends 10 am to 4 pm. See also Western Maryland Station Center.

Post The post office (☎ 301-722-8190) stands at 215 Park St. Hours are weekdays from 8:00 am to 4:30 pm; Saturday from 9:00 am to noon.

Bookstores The Book Center (☎ 301-722-2284) at 15-17 N Centre St is a large full-line, independent bookstore with a local-history section and a good supply of out-of-town newspapers.

Laundry In downtown Cumberland you will find the Sunshine Central Laundromat (☎ 301-759-9711) at 401 Green St.

Medical Services There are three hospitals in the Cumberland area. Memorial Hospital (☎ 301-777-4000) at 600 Memorial Ave is the largest. But you will also find complete emergency service at Sacred Heart Hospital (☎ 301-759-4200) at 900 Seton Drive. In Frostburg the hospital (☎ 301-689-3411) is at 48 Tam Terrace.

Western Maryland Station Center

Any stop in Cumberland should begin here. This restored depot at 13 Canal St houses the Canal Visitors Center, the Scenic Railroad offices, the county visitors bureau, and the Council for the Arts. Restored to its 1913 elegance, the depot is a superb example of Victorian-style public architecture.

C&O Canal National Historic Park

The 184½-mile canal that begins in DC ends here (see C&O Canal sidebar in the DC chapter). To understand the scale and historical significance of the canal visit the exhibits in the Canal Visitors Center (☎ 301-722-8226) at trackside in the Western Maryland Station Center at 13 Canal St. This is a good place to get maps and information in preparation for an excursion along the towpath built in 1850. The tow path leads southeast along the Potomac all the way to Washington, and touring it in part or in total makes for a low-stress outdoor adventure for hikers, bikers, and campers. The towpath trail through western Maryland plumbs the heart of the Green Ridge State Forest and leads to attractions like the Paw Paw Tunnel and the Canal boat replica. The park visitors center is open Tuesday to Sunday 9 am to 5 pm. Admission is free.

Five miles south of Cumberland off Route 51 on the North Branch of the canal park, you will find the fully restored **Lock 75** (☎ 301-729-3136). Tied near the log lockhouse is a 93-foot replica of one of the **canal freight boats** complete with a furnished captain's cabin, hay house, and stable for the mule that towed the boat. You can go aboard for a tour June to August on Sunday from 1 to 4 pm, but you can see the boat from shore any time you hike the trail. There's no fee.

Lying 28 miles downstream from Cumberland, the **Paw Paw Tunnel** (☎ 301-22-8226) goes 3118 feet through a mountain, permitting the canal and towpath to pass right through. You can hike through the tunnel and return overland via the two-mile Tunnel Hill Trail. The tunnel lies near Route 51 and makes a good place for hikes and bikers to join or leave the towpath on a day trip to/from Cumberland.

Victorian Historical District

Placed on the National Register of Historic Places in 1973 and constantly restored and polished since then, the private homes and public buildings along Washington St on the west side of town reflect Cumberland's prosperity in the years before 1924 when the canal, the railroads and King Coal made fortunes for the citizens. You can get walking tour maps at the visitors center in the railroad station.

The 18-room mansion at 218 Washington St (☎ 301-777-8678) was once the home of the president of the C&O Canal following the Civil War. The county historical society now owns the property and has restored the house and furnished it with period antiques. From May to October it's open Tuesday to Saturday from 11 am to 3 pm, Sunday 1:30 to 4 pm; from November to April, hours are Tuesday to Saturday 11 am to 3 pm. Admission is $3.

Western Maryland Scenic Railroad

Rising from the ashes of the old mountain freight line to Frostburg, this railroad (☎ 301-759-4400, 800-872-4650) re-creates the boomtown days of Cumberland. A steam locomotive pulls a train of coaches 1300 feet uphill to Frostburg as it threads through ravines, forests, and a tunnel. In the Depot Center where the scenic railway stops, **Tharsher Carriage Museum** (☎ 301-777-5905) has the largest collection of horse-drawn carriages in the US. A bequest of collector James R Thrasher, the collection includes President Theodore Roosevelt's inaugural carriage. Passengers can also sightsee in Frostburg.

After an hour and a half the train crew turns their engine on a turntable and heads back down to Cumberland. The trip lasts about three hours. Trains run May to December everyday except Monday and can be packed during the fall color season (in October). Trains depart Cumberland Station Center in late morning. Adult fares are usually about $14 but can run higher during color season. Reservations are a good idea.

Transportation & Industrial Museum

This museum (☎ 301-724-4398) is housed in the Station Center at 13 Canal St. Here you can see displays pertaining to the railroad, canal, and industries that launched Cumberland's economic boom. It's open May to October daily (closed Monday) from 10 am to noon and 2 to 4 pm. Donations are encouraged.

George Washington's Headquarters

George Washington used this log cabin as his quarters during the French and Indian War. It's the last remaining structure from Fort Cumberland. You will find the cabin (☎ 301-777-8214) in Riverside Park at Green St, and you can look through a window to view the period furnishings. There is a push-button tape recording that informs visitors about the history. The headquarters is open on some holidays. No fee.

Emanual Episcopal Church

Built over the earthworks of Fort Cumberland and containing a model of the fort, this church (☎ 301-777-3364) dates to the 1850s and contains Tiffany stained glass. Tours are by appointment.

Activities

Lots of people come to the Cumberland area to hike, bike, camp, canoe, and kayak in the surrounding mountains and waterways. The Potomac River east of Paw Paw and Cacapon River attract the car-top-boat folk. The C&O Canal towpath is the most popular hiking venue, and Rocky Gap State Park (see below) is another attractive choice. Bolder outdoor adventurers head into the 38,000-acre Green Ridge State Forest (see below). There are also some good technical climbs and excellent caving in the Cumberland area. There's good cross-country skiing in New Germany State Park (see below).

If you are planning some outdoor adventuring, you could get up to speed on sites and itineraries, stock up on provisions, and find equipment by calling an outfitter/guide service. Two good ones in the Cumberland area are Allegany Adventures (☎ 301-729-9708) at 14419 National Highway (Route 40) LaVale or Allegheny Expeditions (☎ 301-722-5170, 800-819-5170) on Route 2 in Cumberland.

Special Events

Cumberland sees several interesting events during the summer. During Heritage Days in early June you can buy arts and crafts and watch historical reenactments. In the second weekend in July there's the C&O Canal Boat Festival. In the first weekend in August, folks come from throughout the region to hear top-notch bluegrass music at the Rocky Gap Music Festival (see Rocky Gap State Park below). During the Street Rod Roundup on Labor Day weekend, hundreds of classic hotrods descend on the town.

Places to Stay

Camping There are tent and RV sites at Rocky Gap State Park (see below) about 15 miles east of town.

Motels & Hotels *Charlie's Motel* (☎ 301-689-6557) at 220 W Main St in Frostburg, across from the Tasty Freeze, is your best bet for cheap digs in all of western Maryland. There are 10 basic motel rooms with TV and air conditioning. A single bed costs $25, two beds $30.

The *Super 8 Motel* (☎ 301-729-6265) is closer to Cumberland at 1301 National Hwy (Route 40 Alt) in LaValle. This is a no-frills modern motel with TV and air conditioning. Singles go for $45, doubles $55.

For just a little more money than you would spend in one of the Route 40 motel chains, you can stay in Old-World hotel comfort at *Failinger's Hotel Gunter* (☎ 301-698-6511) at 11 W Main St in Frostburg. Failinger's is a turn-of-the-century Victorian hotel with 17 rooms that has been fully restored with private baths and an elevator while retaining the original oak interiors with brass trim. In the basement you can see the remains of an old jail. The pit used for cock fights is now a popular bar. Rooms feature canopy beds, unique decor, and period antiques. Rates are $55 to $80 per night.

B&Bs The *Inn at Walnut Bottom* (☎ 301-777-0003, 800-286-9718) at 120 Green St has 12 rooms – most with private bath – in these restored Victorian Cowden and Dent houses just a block off historic Washington St. Rooms sport period decor and furnishings including four-poster beds. The Oxford House restaurant (see Places to Eat) is on the property. Rooms with air conditioning and TV run $69 to $160 with a full breakfast.

The Castle (☎ 301-264-4645) on Route 36, about 10 miles from Cumberland at Mount Savage, is the area's premier B&B. This 1840 Gothic-revival stone mansion is a National Historic Landmark that was once the personal estate of a Scottish industrialist. Today Lisa and Bob Miller have six rooms with air conditioning, four with bath. Old English antiques dominate the decor, which includes a mix of four-poster and canopy beds. Rates are $70 to $125 and include full breakfast and afternoon tea.

Places to Eat – Cumberland

Locals say you haven't experienced the city until you've had a hot dog from the place that has been serving them since 1918. *Coney Island and Curtis* (☎ 301-759-9707) with two locations at 15 & 35 N Liberty St claims the 'secret is in our sauce.' A Coney Island hotdog with sauerkraut or chili costs $1.05. You can eat in or take it out.

Pennywhistle's (☎ 301-724-6626) at 25 N Centre St is a popular soup, salad, and sandwich stop near Cumberland's downtown pedestrian mall. Try the smoked turkey with cranberry relish on a croissant for $4.

The *Oxford House* (☎ 301-777-7101) is at 118 Greene St in the Inn at Walnut Bottom. This formal dinner restaurant specializes in international cuisine. The popular chicken Annapolis (breasts stuffed with ham and crab meat) costs $16. The owners of the Oxford House have recently opened *Tivoli* (☎ 301-777-2885), a deli-style sandwich, dinner, or takeout place, at 30 N Centre St. The Philadelphia cheesesteak sub costs you $6.

East of Cumberland's town center off of I-68 at Exit 46 and then on Ali Ghan Rd, you will find *L'Osteria* (☎ 301-777-3553), operating in a former 19th century tavern. This is a dinner-only restaurant specializing mostly in continental cuisine. If the European offerings don't interest you, try the Cajun-style blackened red fish. You could easily spend over $20 here.

Places to Eat – Frostburg

The *Princess Restaurant* (☎ 301-689-1680) at 12 W Main St is the preferred cheap-eats venue for the college folk from Frostburg State University. This is a good place to get the inside scoop on the area from friendly locals as well as the college crowd. At lunch you can get a steak burger with fries for $3.

A new coffee and sandwich spot, the *Tombstone Cafe* (☎ 301-689-5254) at 60 E Main St is getting a lot of attention. For starters you can get strong espresso for $1.50. The kitchen specializes in healthy sandwiches: try the havarti cheese and Granny Smith apple on multigrain bread for $3.75. The cafe has imported beer and wine at reasonable prices as well.

Lots of tourists who ride the Scenic Railroad to Frostburg eat their lunch at the *Old Depot* (☎ 301-689-1221), 19 Depot St. This is a railroad-theme restaurant that includes restored dining cars, baker, ice cream stand, and shops. Try the burgers or chicken wings for less than $5.

Gandolf's (☎ 301-689-2010), 16 W Main St, draws something of a bohemian crowd with lots of crunchy sandwiches and 12 microbrews on tap. Pita chips and hummus costs $2.25, Thai red curry rice $8. It's open 5 pm to 2 am.

Guiseppe's (☎ 301-689-2220) at 11 Bowery St gets a lot of local votes as the best place to eat Italian. This restaurant is just off the university campus and is staffed with a lot of college students. Pizza, pasta, and chicken cacciatore are the bargains for under $11.

Frostburg's top-end restaurant, *Au Petit Paris* (☎ 301-689-8946), 86 E Main St, has bistro-style decor and furnishings including murals of French landscapes. The menu ranges from coq au vin to Châteaubriand. Some entrees run over $30.

Entertainment

At 110 Johnson St sits the *Cumberland Theatre* (☎ 301-759-4990), western Maryland's only regional professional theater. First-class drama and music occasionally takes place here June to November. Tickets cost between $12 and $16.

L'Osteria (see Places to Eat – Cumberland) has a basement bar called the *Winecellar* which brings in jazz and live bands on weekends. This is a lively place for an upscale, mixed crowd.

If you like things a little younger and wilder, head for the *Clarysville Inn* (☎ 301-722-3900) halfway between Cumberland and Frostburg on Old Route 40. This roadhouse bar rocks out with live music, particularly on weekends.

In Frostburg you will find the college crowd at *Gandolf's*. On Saturday nights there are rock bands and sometimes serious foot-stompin' bluegrass. There's rarely a cover charge.

Getting There & Away

USAir Commuter (☎ 800-428-4322) flies in and out of Cumberland Regional Airport on Route 28 over the border in West Virginia.

Greyhound (☎ 301-722-6226) runs regular buses that stop at 201 Glenn St. Amtrak (☎ 301-724-8890, 800-872-7245) offers limited passenger service to Cumberland. The trains stop at the station on E Harrison St.

The only sensible way to approach Cumberland from the east or west is I-68. Follow the signs to downtown.

AROUND CUMBERLAND

Rocky Gap State Park

Surrounding 243-acre Lake Habeeb about 15 miles east of Cumberland (off I-68 at Exit 50 in Flintstone), this state park (☎ 301-777-2139) encompasses the natural saddle formed by Evitt's and Martin's Mountains. This park is a good place to stop if you want a relatively tame outdoor adventure. In addition to hiking trails and campsites, Rocky Gap has launch ramps for boats, a swimming beach, and a bathhouse.

During the **Rocky Gap Music Festival** (☎ 301-724-2511, 800-424-2511) in August the park is a world-class party for the Capital Region's youth and lovers of the Scotch-Irish-derived, foot-stomping fiddle and fife bluegrass music of Appalachian Mountain folk. If you want to attend the festival, book your camping reservations six months in advance and come early. Traffic can be heavy.

There are 278 *campsites*. Tent sites cost $15 weekdays, $19 weekends; hookups are $3 extra. The park is open year round, but campsites are available April through November only.

Green Ridge State Forest

At Exit 64 off I-68 south of Flintstone you will find this vast mountain wilderness with 38,811 acres of mountain forest (☎ 301-478-3124). Wildlife is plentiful with lots of turkey, deer, and black bear. Trails are long and bushy, but the payoff comes with scenic overlooks, wild streams, and pristine campsites. This is not a place for the unfit, inexperienced, or ill-prepared. Always carry up-to-date topographic maps, compass, and perhaps a hand-held GPS when hiking on any of Green Ridge's backcountry trails. The state mountain-biking championship is sometimes held here in early October.

YOUGHIOGHENY RIVER & RESERVOIR

The 'Yough' (pronounced 'Yock'), threading between the mountains of western Pennsylvania and western Maryland, is one of the wildest and most scenic rivers in the eastern US. The river flows from southern Garrett County, curls north through southern Pennsylvania, and feeds into the Youghiogheny Reservoir – an Army Corps of Engineers recreational and flood-control project – near Friendship.

The Youghiogheny River presents a variety of world-class whitewater experiences. Working with outfitters in Ohiopyle, Pennsylvania, you can plan a **whitewater rafting** adventure to meet your personal skills and courage (for specific operators, see Whitewater Rafting & Kayaking above). The Upper Yough has class V+ rapids near Friendship; it has been the site of numerous national and international kayaking events. The lower parts of the river are tamer.

DEEP CREEK LAKE & STATE FOREST

Twelve miles long with 65 miles of shoreline, Deep Creek Lake is the heart of western Maryland's outdoor recreation area. Originally created as a hydroelectric reservoir in 1925, the lake is now under the management of the Maryland State Forest and Park Service. A good many vacation homes line the shores and recreational boats fill the waters during the summer. The busy state park (☎ 301-387-5563) at 868 State Park Rd (off Route 219, 10 miles northeast of Oakland) is on the eastern side of the lake. It has 112 campsites and a long sandy beach (see Camping in the introduction to The Alleghenies section).

The Deep Creek Lake-Garrett County Promotion Council (☎ 301-334-1948) is at 200 S 3rd St in Oakland. From mid-May to mid-October you can also get visitor's information at the Information Booth on Route 219 south of the Deep Creek Lake Bridge.

Boating & Sailing

Mile for mile, Deep Creek Lake seems more populated with watercraft than Chesapeake Bay. Water-skiing is probably the most popular activity on the lake, but small-boat sailing comes in a close second – the lake was home to the late Sandy Douglas, the designer and builder of the Olympic-class Flying Scot sloop.

Deep Creek Sailing School (☎ 301-387-4497) has sailing lessons in a variety of high-performance craft.

You can rent motorboats at a number of marinas. Try Blue Anchor Rental (☎ 301-387-5677) if you want to ski or just part the waters in a fast runabout.

Horseback Riding

Western-style riding is one of the most popular ways to see western Maryland. The Deep Creek Lake area has three stables with trail rides: Small Oaks Riding Stables in Deer Park (☎ 301-334-5733, 301-334-4991); Sunny Slopes Stables in Oakland (☎ 301-334-8434), which has horses and cabins; and Western Trails Riding Stables (☎ 301-387-6155) off Route 219 near Deep Creek Lake, which offers a bathhouse and camping options.

Mountain Biking

Wisp Resort (see Skiing below) has good mountain biking in summer. To bike at Wisp, call Rudy's Outdoor Adventures (☎ 301-387-4640) for rentals, maps, and trail access. Another outfitter to try is High Mountain Sports (☎ 301-387-2113) at two locations around Deep Creek Lake: Route 219 and Sang Run Rd, and Route 219 at Trader's Landing.

Skiing

Wisp Resort (☎ 301-387-4911) at 290 Marsh Hill Rd, Deep Creek Lake, has a summit elevation of over 3000 feet and gets plenty of snow, but the vertical drop is only 610 feet. Wisp has big-mountain prices ($38 on weekends), and there are more than enough skiers willing to pay to ride four chair lifts and ski 23 trails.

SAVAGE RIVER STATE FOREST

With 53,000 acres of forest land, Savage River State Forest (☎ 301-895-5759) is the largest of Maryland's public forests. It occupies part of the Appalachian Plateau in Garrett County. Backcountry campers should check in at the headquarters (349 Headquarters Lane in Grantsville) to pay $2 usage fee and collect a trail map and etiquette guide and to get reports on conditions. Currently all trails are open to mountain bikers.

Located five miles southeast of Grantsville in the heart of the Savage River Forest, the 462-acre **New Germany State Park** (☎ 301-974-3683) is a popular place for hikers and bikers to stay. There are 39 *campsites* and 11 furnished cabins open year round (see Camping in the Allegheny Mountains introduction above). The park's 10 miles of groomed Nordic ski trails are a big attraction during winter months (see Cross-Country Skiing under Frederick for ski tours).

POTOMAC & GARRETT STATE FORESTS

These two forests (☎ 301-334-2038) in southeastern Garrett County comprise 18,000 acres of wilderness, including a number of attractions for hikers – the highest point in the state (Backbone Mountain), Lost Run, Cascade Falls, and the Potomac Overlook. Herrington Manor and Swallow Falls State Parks are part of this wilderness. (For information on camping in the forests see the introduction of The Alleghenies section.)

Five miles northwest of Oakland on Herring Manor/Swallow Falls Rd, **Herrington Manor State Park** (☎ 301-334-9108) attracts the outdoor crowd with its 53-acre lake stocked with trout. There are also boat rentals and 20 furnished cabins open year round.

Swallow Falls State Park (☎ 301-387-6838) is nine miles north of Oakland past Herrington Manor State Park on the same road. The attractions here are the tall hemlock forest and a number of substantial waterfalls. The largest is 63-foot Muddy Creek Falls. Swallow Falls and Lower Falls are on the Youghiogheny. The park has 65 campsites.

CRANESVILLE SUBARCTIC SWAMP

The Nature Conservancy, a nonprofit foundation that buys up wilderness areas to protect them for habitat and limited public use, owns and protects 500 acres of this boreal bog formed during the Ice Age. A boardwalk allows visitors to pass through the swamp and observe rare flora and fauna usually seen north of the Arctic Circle.

To reach the swamp from Oakland follow Liberty Ave out of town; this becomes Herrington Manor Rd. Go six miles and turn left on Cranesville Rd. Continue four more miles, turn left on Lake Ford Rd, and follow the signs. The site is open daily. For more information, contact the Nature Conservancy (☎ 301-656-8673), 2 Wisconsin Circle, Chevy Chase.

MARYLAND

Maryland's Eastern Shore

The Eastern Shore, also called the Delmarva Peninsula (for Delaware, Maryland, Virginia) juts south from Wilmington, Delaware, to form the eastern border of Chesapeake Bay and a long stretch of Atlantic beaches. Maryland's portion is about 100 miles long by 65 miles wide. The state of Delaware takes up the upper northeastern wedge of the peninsula and Virginia its southern tip. But Maryland has most of the choice Chesapeake Bay waters.

Before 1952 and the construction of the William Preston Lane Memorial Bridge (Hwy 50) from Annapolis to Kent Island and the Eastern Shore, this long peninsula remained isolated from mainstream America. Because of this isolation, the descendants of shoremen (farmers) and watermen from the west coast of England, who settled the Eastern Shore 300 years ago, have held tight to their traditional lifestyles. On the Eastern Shore you will find some of Maryland's oldest towns and earliest ports, a vital seafood industry ('Maryland is for crabs'), pristine beaches, herds of wild horses, and one of the country's biggest beach resorts – Ocean City.

The Eastern Shore is flat farm country. Its beauty is almost impossible to see from the main highway (Hwy 50/301), which was designed to force-feed Ocean City with millions of tourists each year. You need to get onto the backroads and/or out on the tidal Chesapeake waterways to find the substantial charms that lurk here.

HIGHLIGHTS

- Historic Chestertown and beer and conversation at Andy's
- The Chesapeake Bay Maritime Museum, St Michaels, for an overview of the watermen's culture
- Steamed crabs at the Crab Claw, St Michaels
- Tilghman Island – a classic watermen's community, home port to most of the last working skipjacks
- Biking around Oxford/St Michaels; take the Oxford-Bellevue Ferry
- Bird watching for bald eagles and waterfowl at Black Water National Wildlife Refuge
- Backcountry camping in the land of wild horses, Assateague Island

CHESTERTOWN

Most visitors coming to Chestertown are professional people in search of a place to unwind and escape hectic lives and pressures in Washington, Baltimore, Philadelphia, or New York. Put one way, travelers who come to Chestertown are clearly not seeking overstimulation; they come to find a place to kick back and pursue simple pleasures. The historical setting, romantic accommodations, and imaginative restaurants are at the heart of the Chestertown experience. Lying on the upper Eastern Shore just 40 miles northeast across the Chesapeake from Annapolis, Chestertown (population 4000) is an architectural and historic gem. What makes it doubly attractive is that it is frequently overlooked by tourists in a hurry to get to the Eastern Shore's better-known destinations.

When you first see Chestertown on a summer morning from the Hwy 213 bridge over the Chester River, the facades of the red-brick mansions on the banks of the meandering Chester give the impression of a place in a dream. The morning mist lies

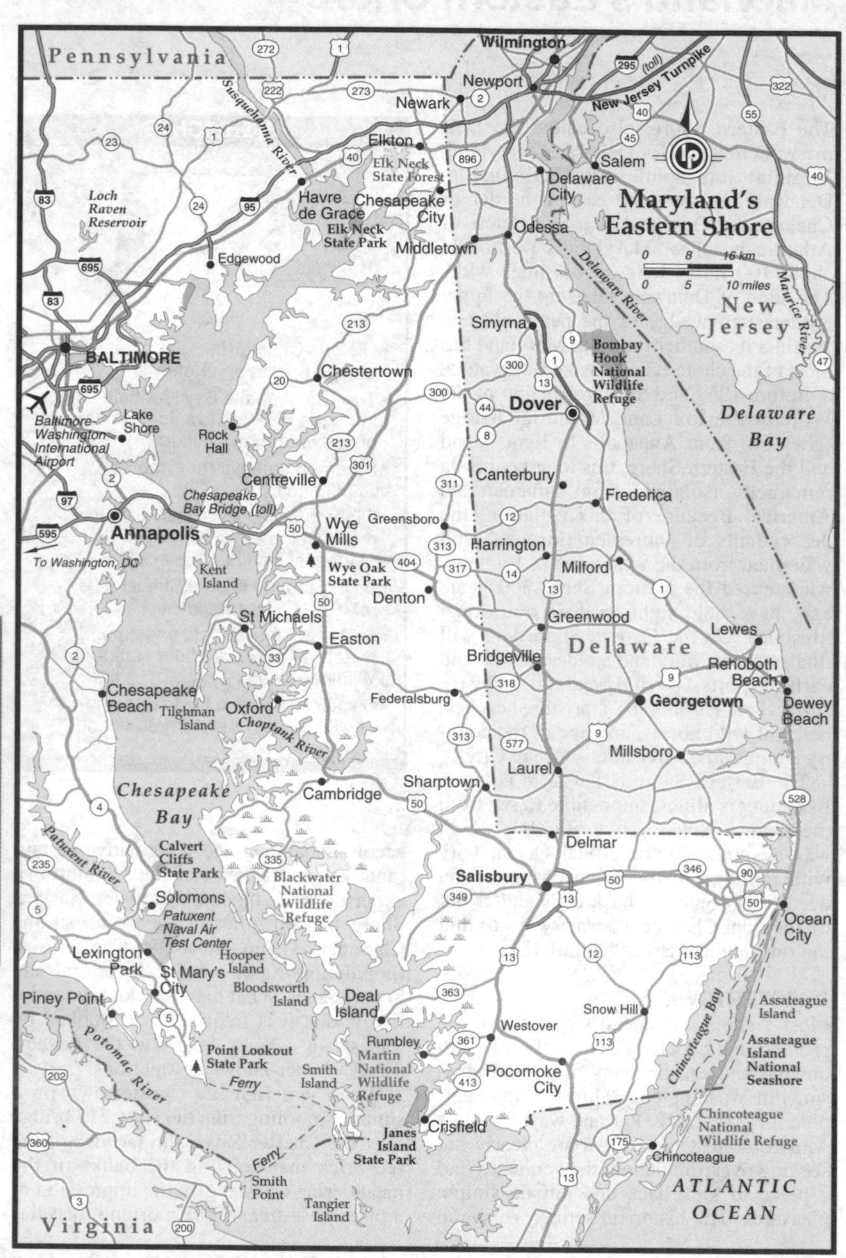
Maryland's Eastern Shore
Pennsylvania
New Jersey
Delaware
Virginia
MARYLAND
Wilmington
Newport
Newark
New Jersey Turnpike
(toll)
Salem
Elkton
Elk Neck State Forest
Havre de Grace
Chesapeake City
Elk Neck State Park
Delaware City
Odessa
Middletown
Edgewood
Loch Raven Reservoir
Susquehanna River
Delaware River
Maurice River
BALTIMORE
Chestertown
Smyrna
Bombay Hook National Wildlife Refuge
Dover
Delaware Bay
Baltimore-Washington International Airport
Lake Shore
Rock Hall
Centreville
Canterbury
Frederica
Chesapeake Bay Bridge (toll)
Annapolis
To Washington, DC
Wye Mills
Wye Oak State Park
Greensboro
Harrington
Milford
Kent Island
Denton
St Michaels
Easton
Greenwood
Lewes
Bridgeville
Rehoboth Beach
Dewey Beach
Georgetown
Federalsburg
Chesapeake Beach
Tilghman Island
Oxford
Choptank River
Millsboro
Laurel
Sharptown
Cambridge
Chesapeake Bay
Delmar
Salisbury
Calvert Cliffs State Park
Patuxent River
Blackwater National Wildlife Refuge
Solomons
Patuxent Naval Air Test Center
Ocean City
Lexington Park
Hooper Island
St Mary's City
Bloodsworth Island
Piney Point
Deal Island
Snow Hill
Assateague Island
Westover
Assateague Island National Seashore
Chincoteague Bay
Rumbley
Martin National Wildlife Refuge
Point Lookout State Park
Potomac River
Smith Island
Pocomoke City
Ferry
Crisfield
Chincoteague National Wildlife Refuge
Janes Island State Park
Chincoteague
Smith Point
Tangier Island
ATLANTIC OCEAN
0 8 16 km
0 5 10 miles

like a cloud over the river, casting a golden haze over the tall oaks and cedars, 18th-century church steeples, and the Georgian cupolas of the courthouse and Washington College.

Visiting Chestertown in 1774, a young traveler and graduate of Princeton University by the name of Philip Vickers Fithian judged, 'A delightful part of the country . . . Chester-Town – this is a beautiful small Town on a River out of the Bay navigable by Ships.' In the same year Englishman George Chalmers toured Chestertown and remarked on the magnificent Queen Anne and Georgian mansions that stood as symbols of the town's trading wealth.

Chartered in 1706 as one of Maryland's 'ports of entry,' Chestertown had grown to a town of 200 houses when Fithian and Chalmers passed through. Here colonists prospered through the exportation of corn and wheat from surrounding plantations. Meanwhile, Chestertown mariners and ships excelled in trade with the West Indies. Patriots stormed aboard the brigantine *Geddes* on May 13, 1774, and staged their own 'tea party' by dumping the vessel's cargo of tea into the river as a symbol of support for the Boston Tea Party patriots.

Today, the town's grand houses, along with some churches and public buildings, constitute a collection of restored colonial architecture to rival that of Annapolis. But Chestertown remains a quiet country town, with culture that derives from its traditional place as the seat of Kent County government, centuries of well-traveled citizens, and Washington College. Visitors come here to explore Kent County's 280 miles of Bay shores, stay in a vast selection of historic B&Bs, and feel like they have escaped into a carefree past. During colonial times Chestertown's Hynson-Ringgold House was known as a 'home of the cavaliers' where young English gentlemen ignored the troubles of the world at large and made Chestertown 'one of the gayest places in Maryland.' The spirit persists, particularly if you visit 'C-town' on a Friday or Saturday night.

Orientation

Most travelers approach Chestertown from Annapolis and points south. From this direction, Hwy 213 crosses a bridge over the Chester River and becomes Maple Ave in Chestertown. Planners laid out the municipality in a rectangular grid, with the heart of the town one block southwest of Maple Ave on High St. This main thoroughfare – High St – butts against the river to the southeast and stretches northwest about a mile to Washington College. Kent County Courthouse marks the center of town, overlooking the small Fountain Park on High St between Cross and Court Sts.

Information

The Kent County Chamber of Commerce & Visitor's Center (☎ 410-778-0416) is at 400 S Cross St, next to the defunct railroad station. It has good maps for town walking tours as well as driving tours of Kent County. Hours are Monday to Friday from 9 am to 4 pm, Saturday 9 am to 2 pm, May to December; closed the rest of the year.

The post office (☎ 410-778-0690) is at 200 Spring Ave. A well-stocked, popular bookstore is the Compleat Bookseller (☎ 410-778-1480) at 301 High St. You will find Kent Laundry (☎ 410-778-3278) at the west end of town at 607 High St. The nearest hospital is Memorial Hospital (☎ 410-778-0603) 40 miles south in Easton. Call ☎ 911 for an ambulance.

Walking Tour

Begin with Chestertown's most-famous landmark, the **Hynson-Ringgold House** at the corner of Cannon and Water Sts in the southwest corner of town. Built in stages between 1735 and 1772, the mansion with its antler staircase is a good example of the evolution of Georgian-style architecture (named after England's four monarchs who ruled America from 1714 until the Revolution). In its early days the house was a party site for young English gentry. Since 1944 the presidents of Washington College have lived here.

The **Customs House** sits a block north on Water St. Constructed in 1746 and

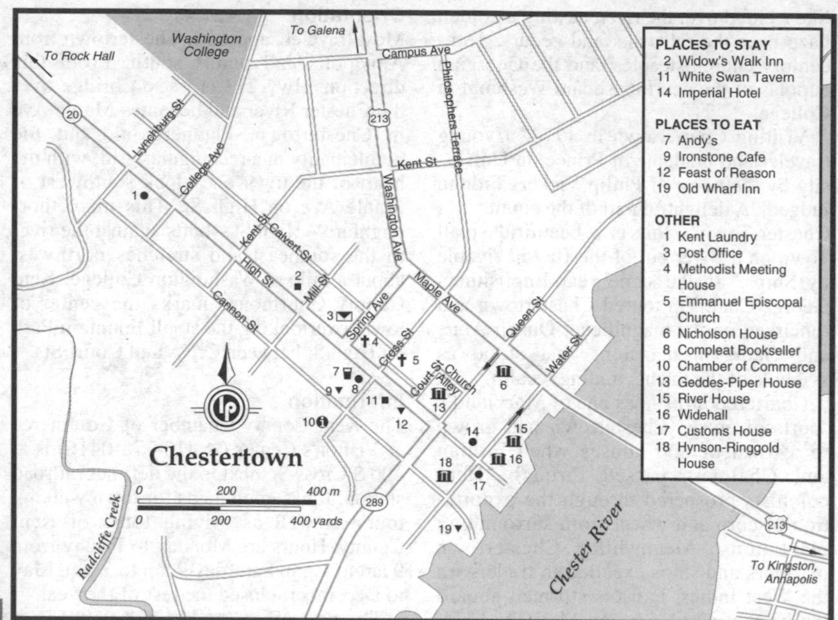

embellished with Flemish Bond brickwork, this building served as both the customs office and private residence in the days when the Chestertown Tea Party took place along a nearby river wharf.

Just across High St at No 101 sits one of Chestertown's most elaborate townhouses, **Widehall**. Kent County's wealthiest merchant, Thomas Smythe, built this house in 1770. Smythe became the head of Maryland's Revolutionary Provisional Government for the two years preceding the framing of the state constitution in 1776. His home is an example of the symmetry characteristic of Georgian architecture.

A few houses farther northeast along Water St, you find the **River House** at No 107, built by Richard Smythe between 1784 and 1787. This 'English basement house' is an example of Federal-style architecture. Houses like this one, one room deep with no windows on the side, are characteristic of Philadelphia townhouses.

One block inland you find Queen St running parallel to Water St. There are many fine Federal townhouses on this street. A particularly attractive example is **Nicholson House** at No 111, which belonged to Captain John Nicholson who skippered the revolutionary sloop of war *Hornet* and the frigate *Deane*. The *Deane* took the last naval prizes of the American Revolution and was the only frigate held by the Navy at the end of the war.

The **Geddes-Piper House** (☎ 410-778-3499) at 101 Church Alley (off Queen St) is the current home of the Historical Society of Kent County. This Philadelphia-style townhouse is open Saturday and Sunday from 1 to 4 pm, May to October. Admission is $2.

Heading back to High St and another block inland, you come to Fountain Park. Here, on the corner of Park Row and Cross St, you will see **Emmanuel Episcopal Church** built from 1767 to 1772. The rector of this parish in 1780, Dr William Smith, founded Washington College and the Protestant Episcopal Church of the United States.

At the north end of Fountain Park stands the **Methodist Meeting House**. Built between 1801 and 1803, this meeting house attracted the attention of the first Methodist bishop of America. After his visit, Bishop Francis Ashbury judged Chestertown a 'very wicked place.' Apparently, the bishop had a different standard for conduct than the dominant sect of Episcopalians. Some of the town's most lively taverns were right across High St from the meeting house.

One of the places that would have scandalized the bishop was the **White Swan Tavern** at 231 High St. Built as a residence in the 1730s, entrepreneurs expanded the building into an ale house in the 1790s. After almost two centuries of rough treatment, and a zillion kegs of brew, the Swan reopened as a fully restored B&B in 1981.

Washington College

In 1782 George Washington gave his name to this college, Maryland's first school of higher education. Washington was one of the school's first distinguished visitors and served with the governors who chose the designs for the original buildings and drafted a lottery to finance them: Washington sold the tickets around his home, Mount Vernon, in Alexandria, Virginia.

Washington College stands as the 10th-oldest college in America. A longtime all-male liberal arts institution, the college has been coed for two decades. There are 950 students, many preparing for careers in law, medicine, business, and Chesapeake Regional Studies. Lacrosse and crew are distinctive sports at the college and draw sizeable crowds to competitions. ■

Auctions

Every Wednesday people come from all over the East Coast to go to Dixon's Furniture Auction (☎ 410-928-3006) in nearby Crumpton, one of the largest auctions of antique and country-estate furniture in the US.

Bicycling

In recent years bicycling has become a popular pastime along the rural broad-shouldered roads that fan out from Chestertown. The chamber of commerce in Chestertown publishes an excellent cycling-tour guide with nine great rides. Most cyclists bring their own, but Bikeworks (☎ 410-778-6940) at 208 S Cross St has touring and mountain bikes for rent.

Boating

Even more popular than cycling, recreational boating has drawn a lot of people to Chestertown/Kent County and introduced them to the region's charms. Many people come to charter cruising sailboats and to explore the Chesapeake from the multitude of charter operations located around Rock Hall's harbor. But much of Kent County's 280 miles of shoreline border sheltered creeks and rivers, perfect places for exploring and fishing by canoe, kayak, or a trailer boat three seasons a year.

Kent County has more than 30 public landings. But beware: If you park or launch a trailer boat at one of these landings, you need a $35 'Landing Permit,' available at the Public Works Office (☎ 410-778-7439). Most out-of-staters with boats pay a small fee to use one of the marina's launching ramps. Eastern Neck Boat Rentals (☎ 410-639-7680) in Rock Hall rents aluminum rowboats for $22 from 6 am to 6 pm. You can put your own small outboard on one.

If you want to get out on the water to experience the waterman's life, Echo Hill Outdoor School (☎ 410-348-5880) in Worton has a working skipjack, oyster 'buy' boat, and an oyster tonger's bateau. For $58 per person the watermen/teachers will take you down the Chester River for a day of oystering (from November to March).

Organized Tours

Friendly and knowledgeable, Margaret Fallaw at Historic Chestertown & Kent

County Tours (☎ 410-778-2829) conducts 1½-hour walking tours by arrangement and charges $7 for one or two people.

Special Events

A good way to get inside Chestertown's historic homes is the Maryland House and Garden Tour held every other May. The Chestertown Tea Party Festival, also in May, takes place along the waterfront and High St. The Chester River Sailing Regatta in July features graceful three-sail-rigged log canoes and one-time oyster tonging boats. In October, the Candlelight Walking Tour lights up the streets with columns of history lovers parading from house to house by the light of you-know-what. Also in October, the Kent House Tour actually opens private homes to the public, while the Jazz Extravaganza brings musicians and audiences together for finger snapping sessions in the town inns and restaurants.

Places to Stay – bottom end

Camping *Duck Neck Camp* (☎ 410-778-3070) is on the Chester River nine miles from Chestertown. Go north on Hwy 213 from Chestertown, turn left on Route 544 towards Millington for four miles, and then go left on Double Creek Rd for one mile. Finally, turn left on Double Creek Point Rd. The arches to the camp are a quarter mile farther. There are 10 tent sites for $17.50 and 20 full hookups for $19.50. The camp, which has a beach with nettle-free swimming, is open April to October.

You will find 80 transient sites with hookups for $18 and 100 tent sites for $16 at *Ellendale Campsite* (☎ 410-639-7485) off Route 20 in Rock Hall. Take Route 445 south from Rock Hall toward Eastern Neck. The camp is three miles down the road on the right. There is a sand beach, boat ramp, and store. Many campers bring canoes.

Motels *Foxley Manor Motel* (☎ 410-778-3200) north of Chestertown behind Buzz's Restaurant (see Places to Eat) on Washington Ave (Hwy 213) has standard motel rooms for $43 single, $47 double.

Comfort Suites (☎ 410-810-0555) is the first hotel chain to hit Chestertown (and the local historical society is ripped). The motor inn is behind the Chestertown Plaza north of town. Rooms start at $60 and include a microwave and fridge. Some have Jacuzzis.

Places to Stay – middle

Widow's Walk Inn (☎ 410-778-6455) at 402 High St is a mammoth Victorian right in the heart of the historic district with shops and restaurants two minutes away. Furnished in period antiques, this B&B stands out for its enormous country breakfasts and its reputation for having a friendly ghost: We ourselves witnessed a staircase door open and close on its own. Rates are generally $85 to $110 but less during the week.

Farther up High St, perched on a gentle hill at the edge of town is the *Lauretum Inn* (☎ 410-778-3236) at No 954. This is a Victorian manor with five air-conditioned guest rooms, costing from $75 to $150, with two nights for the price of one during the winter.

Jim and Tracy Stone have six rooms in their 1743 brick manor house overlooking Stoneybrook Pond, a 10-minute drive from Chestertown on Route 21 to Tolchester. All rooms at the *Inn at Mitchell House* (☎ 410-778-6500) have colonial furnishings and most have a private bath. Rates are $75 to $110. This is a good place to come if you're looking for a manor house experience without breaking the bank.

Places to Stay – top end

Great Oak Manor (☎ 410-778-5943) overlooks the Chesapeake, eight miles north of Chestertown on Route 514. Built with bricks from ships' ballast in the 1700s, this 25-room mansion on 12 acres is regal with its circular staircase, library, and hunt room. Swimming, tennis, and golf are possible next door, and guests can rent bikes. Rooms have private baths and cost $95 to $135.

Dating back to 1733 the *White Swan Tavern* (☎ 410-778-2300) at 231 High St is no longer a tavern but a B&B right in the center of the historic district. The public rooms are museum-quality showcases of 18th-century furnishings and decor. Guests and walk-in visitors can take sweet tea ($3 for transients) here daily at 4 pm.

Closer to the river on High St stands the *Imperial Hotel* (☎ 410-778-5000). This small Victorian gem has won a prestigious preservation award. With period decor, heated towel racks, and antique armoires to conceal cable TV, the hotel really does preserve the feel of a Victorian pleasure dome. Rooms range from $98 to $285.

Places to Eat

Andy's (☎ 410-778-6779) at 337½ High St (see Entertainment) has pub food after 4 pm. Try the baked sausage and mozzarella stuffed into French bread – a small sandwich costs $3.15.

Farther down High St toward the river is *Feast of Reason* (☎ 410-778-3828) at No 203. This is an upscale lunch place with 10 tables and takeout. The owner bakes his own breads, and you can get large beef, turkey, salmon, or vegetarian sandwiches for $4.25.

For inexpensive home-style cooking local residents favor *Buzz's Restaurant & Cafe* (☎ 410-778-1214) at 601 Washington Ave on the way north out of town. Chicken teriyaki with two veggies, rice, and mushrooms costs $6.95.

The *Bay Wolf* (☎ 410-778-6855) on Rock Hall Ave offers Austrian and Eastern Shore cuisine. Most entrees run $12 to $15. The house specialty, Wiener schnitzel (veal cutlet and parsley potatoes), costs $15.95.

At the foot of Cannon St you will find the *Old Wharf Inn* (☎ 410-778-3566) with a great view of the river. People favor the wharf as a Sunday brunch place, when you can get a bowl of vegetable crab soup for $2.95 or the extensive salad bar for $6.25. Dinners are in the $14 range.

For fancier cuisine head to the *Ironstone Cafe* (☎ 410-778-0188) in the heart of town at 236 Cannon St. The menu changes all the time, but at lunch look for the quiche of the day with salad for $5.50. Sautéed veal sweetbreads with lemon and capers for dinner costs $18.

The *Imperial Hotel* (see Places to Stay) recently placed third out of 650 restaurants in the Washington-Baltimore area for 'Best American Cuisine.' This is a crystal and linen dining room with formal service. Plan on spending $18 or more for delicacies like grilled mahi mahi with tomato marjoram sauce. The Cellar coffee bar is an attractive breakfast or brunch stop if you like espresso and want to sample the pastry chef's creations.

Entertainment

Gone are the colonial days when every inn on High St was also a pub. But don't dismay. Washington College alumna Andy Goddard runs a world-class saloon, with a distinct woman's touch. *Andy's* (see Places to Eat) attracts a crowd ranging from watermen and college students to travelers and older gentry.

Andy always wanted to run a pub like Miss Kitty's Long Branch Saloon in the TV series *Gunsmoke*. From the moment you look over the bar and see the oil painting of Andy clad in a satin teddy and draped on a divan with a dreamy look in her eyes, you know how strongly she has stamped her personality on this establishment. In the front room Andy has exotic brews on tap, current papers and magazines for browsing, shuffleboard, and light fare until midnight.

The pub's back room looks like an elegant, country living room built around a fireplace, but one corner of the room has a dance floor and stage attracting the best of acoustical, rock, and bluegrass from the Washington-Baltimore area. Andy's opens at 4 pm and has music almost every night. There's a $3 cover except Thursday (when it gets packed), but Andy offers so many specials – ladies' night, men's night, extended happy hour – that the cover seems insignificant. This is a place where single women can feel welcome and comfortable.

Getting There & Away

Coming from Annapolis you approach Chestertown via the Chesapeake Bay Bridge (Hwy 50). Five miles after crossing the bridge you take Route 213 north about 20 miles. From the north follow I-95 around the Bay until it crosses 213. Take 213 south, then west at Galena and follow 213 into Chestertown.

ROCK HALL

Calling itself the 'pearl of the Chesapeake,' this onetime ferry terminal and waterman's village on Route 20 about 13 miles west of Chestertown, now has 12 marinas, six real-estate offices, and hundreds of vacation condos. If you like to look at wharves full of sailboats, eat in pricey restaurants, and watch suburban Americans pretend they are country folk or mariners, Rock Hall is the place to come. Along with Kent Island, which you passed over (all those mini-malls) after crossing the Bay Bridge from Annapolis, Rock Hall stands as a warning to other Chesapeake communities as to what will happen when unrestricted development descends on their serene harbor and village.

EASTERN NECK NATIONAL WILDLIFE REFUGE

Fortunately, Rock Hall is not the only place to visit on Hwy 20. This refuge (☎ 410-639-7056) lies just a few miles down the road after you pass Rock Hall village. At the confluence of the Chester River and the Bay, Eastern Neck is a 2285-acre island refuge for migratory and wintering waterfowl. The island is also home to the endangered Delmarva fox squirrel and the southern bald eagle. Staff have documented peaks of more than 40,000 waterfowl on the island. Common species include Canada geese, tundra swans, canvasbacks, mallards, widgeons, and lesser ducks. There are also many species of wading birds like great blue heron, killdeer, sandpiper, and woodcock. Deer, beaver, red fox, raccoon, muskrat, and other indigenous mammals roam free.

You will find six miles of roads and trails to explore, including three wildlife trails and an observation tower. This tower is one of the best places to get a sense of the vast wilderness that still remains typical of the Eastern Shore. The Ingleside Recreation Area within the refuge has facilities for crabbing and car-top boat launching from May 1 to September 30. There are also picnic tables. Many people fish from the bridge at the entrance to the refuge.

EASTON

Established around a 17th century Quaker meeting house and the 18th century Talbot County Courthouse, both of which are still in use, Easton (population 9937) sits about halfway down the Eastern Shore. The town has traditionally called itself the 'Colonial Capital of the Eastern Shore' because the Maryland General Court met here during the Federal period. Travelers often view Easton as the gateway to nearby tourist destinations like St Michaels and Oxford. But Easton is much more. It has remained the county seat as well as the commercial and cultural center of wealthy Talbot County for 200 years. Easton has a national reputation for its Waterfowl Festival that takes place every November. Sport-hunters from around the globe know that Easton, Maryland, is the place to go if you want world-class duck hunting. But when they get here, they discover a town with an 18th-century center that looks every bit as traditional as Annapolis or Chestertown.

The gentle climate and the subtle landscapes of corn fields, pine forests, and twisting tidal tributaries charm visitors. During the last two decades, Easton's historic architecture and the surrounding manors along the Tred Avon, Miles, and Wye Rivers have drawn a lot of wealthy refugees from mainstream America. The yachtsmen and the travelers on bicycles are here too from April through Thanksgiving. But despite the boom in tourism, the area still has a bedrock of ancestral farms, working watermen, great seafood, and small towns worth exploring. Finding cheap places to stay is another matter.

Orientation

Easton lies south of the Chesapeake Bay Bridge from Annapolis, 65 miles from Baltimore, and about 40 miles south of

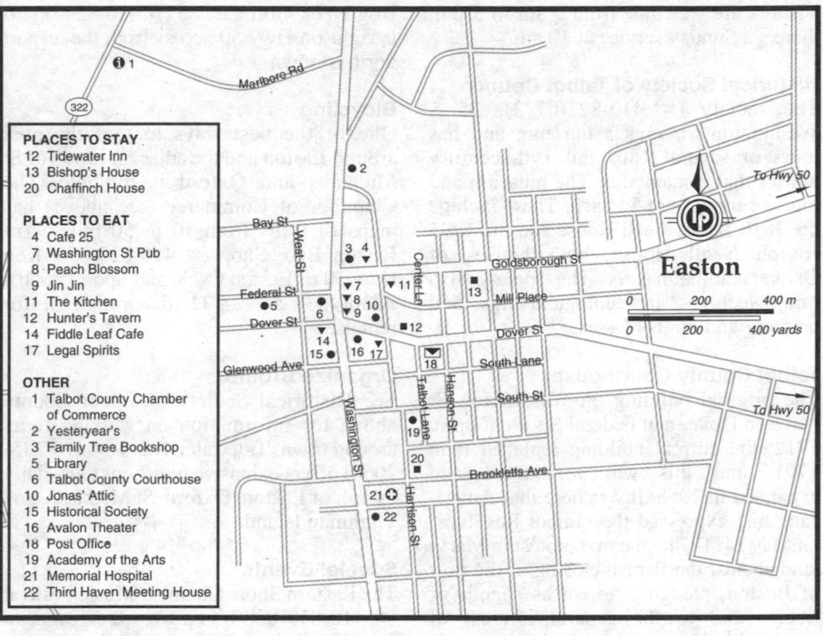

Chestertown on Hwy 50. The highway, with its motels, gas stations, and fast-food franchises, skirts the town's eastern edge. The heart of Easton's historic district is six blocks west of the half-dozen streets laid out in a perfect grid around the colonial courthouse.

Information

Tourist Offices The Talbot County Chamber of Commerce (☎ 410-822-4606, fax 410-822-7922), 805 Goldsborough St, is in the Tred Avon Plaza at the intersection of Route 322 and Marlboro Rd on the west side of Easton. The office stays open from 9 am to 5 pm daily and has information on Easton, St Michaels, Oxford, Tilghman Island, and surrounding towns.

Post The post office (☎ 410-822-0491) stands at 116 E Dover St.

Bookstores You can find a good selection of local and best-selling titles at Family Tree Bookshop (☎ 410-820-5252) at 9 Goldsborough St. Jonas' Attic (☎ 410-820-8266) has books at 39 E Dover St.

Library The Talbot County Free Library (☎ 410-822-1626), at 100 W Dover St, has an extensive local history collection where author James Michener researched his blockbuster *Chesapeake*.

Laundry Easton Plaza Laundry (☎ 410-820-8919) is a drive from the center of town to the intersection of Glebe and Marlboro Rds.

Medical Services The Memorial Hospital (☎ 410-822-1000) is at 219 S Washington St.

Third Haven Meeting House

This 1682 structure built by Quakers is probably the oldest frame building used for religious meetings in the States. It's still peaceful and quiet, set off from S Washington St. William Penn preached here.

MARYLAND

Visitors are welcome from 9 am to 5 pm; there's a Sunday service at 10 am.

Historical Society of Talbot County

The society (☎ 410-822-0773), 25 S Washington St, runs a museum and has tours of several 18th and 19th century houses that it maintains. The museum and tours of homes are $4 each. These include the 1810 James Neall House and the 1795 Joseph Neall House, both houses of Quaker cabinetmakers. The society also offers lectures, archaeological digs, and painting and crafts classes.

Talbot County Courthouse

The original building on Washington St between Dover and Federal Sts went up in 1712; the current building replaced it in 1791, and this was remodeled and expanded in 1958. It was here that Americans first expressed the 'Talbot Resolves' on May 24, 1774 – the first protest in Maryland against the British closing of the port of Boston, pledging 'to act as friends of liberty and to the general interest of mankind.' These same sentiments later found their way into the American Declaration of Independence.

Academy of the Arts

The academy (☎ 410-822-0455), 106 South St, has a good collection of 19th- and 20th century art and also sponsors concerts and art classes. It is open year round Monday to Saturday from 10 am to 4 pm.

No Corner for the Devil

Four Protestant denominations built this hexagonal structure in 1881 and shared it on alternating Sundays. Its wide-angle design is so 'the devil would have no corner in which to sit and hatch evil.' The building is on Hwy 50 West about three miles south of Easton between mile markers 67 and 68.

Golf

Easton attracts a lot of golfers to its championship courses. Easton Club Golf Course (☎ 410-820-9100) is on the road to Oxford. Hog Neck Golf Course (☎ 410-822-6079) is right on Hwy 50 across from the airport north of town.

Bicycling

One of the best ways to tour the area around Easton and the adjacent towns of St Michaels and Oxford is by bike. The Chamber of Commerce (see above) has maps of trails from 10 to 50 miles. Try Easton Bike Shop (☎ 410-822-8580) on Hwy 50 or Easton Cycle and Sport (☎ 410-822-7433) at 723 Goldsborough St for rentals.

Organized Tours

See Historical Society of Talbot County above for information on walking tours around town. Tidewater Tours (☎ 410-745-2060) offers extensive four-hour tours daily by van of Easton, Oxford, St Michaels, and Tilghman Island.

Special Events

The Eastern Shore Chamber Music Festival (☎ 410-819-0380) is a two-week event in June featuring concerts at the Avalon Theater and other spots around the town. The Talbot County Fair in mid-July is three days of games, exhibits, and food at the Talbot Agricultural Center in Easton. The Waterfowl Festival (☎ 410-822-4567), held in mid-November is a three-day event including a decoy auction, retriever-dog demonstrations, a shooting exhibition, and a lot of arts and crafts exhibits.

Places to Stay

Rates for Easton and nearby towns are highest in the summer and during prime waterfowl hunting season (October to January). Unless noted, all rates are high season.

Places to Stay – bottom end

The cheapest places to stay are along Ocean Gateway (Hwy 50) near the intersection with Goldsborough Rd, mixed in with the fast-food places at the eastern edge of town. The *Econolodge* (☎ 410-820-5555, fax 410-820-7466), 8175 Ocean

Gateway, has singles/doubles for $45/50. They're standard chain motel rooms with beds, desk, bathroom, TV, and phone.

Country B&B (☎ 410-822-0587), 5991 Ocean Gateway, is a few miles south of downtown Easton. There's a sign in the yard and the mailbox has the address on it. It has two comfortable rooms for $50 each with breakfast.

Places to Stay – middle

The *Bishop's House* (☎ 410-820-7290, 800-223-7290), 214 Goldsborough St, is in a nicely restored home, built by a local steamboat captain for the former governor of Maryland. Later it was the home of the bishop of Easton. The house has high ceilings, good old oak, walnut, and mahogany furniture, and fireplaces in most rooms. Prices for all rooms, including a full breakfast, are $75 during the week and $80 to $120 on weekends.

The *Chaffinch House* (☎ 410-822-5074) at 132 S Harrison St is a huge Queen-Anne Victorian with a turret and porches on every floor. The 'wedding room' is actually a suite decorated like a Victorian bridal chamber complete with a bride's gown on a dressmaker's mannequin. There's also a sleeping porch for warm weather and bicycles for the borrowing if you like. Innkeeper Laura Brandt seems like a gracious Victorian herself. Rooms start at $65.

Places to Stay – top end

The *Tidewater Inn* (☎ 410-822-1300, 800-237-8775) at 101 E Dover St is the replica of a brick inn in the Queen-Anne style that led the way for historic preservation in downtown Easton. Rooms are modern but with traditional mahogany furnishings like four-poster beds. Diners and guests can get a free carriage tour of the town from the livery man waiting at curbside. Doubles cost $139 to $160, but you can get weekend packages that include dinner, breakfasts, and champagne for $295.

Manor Houses Some of the best top-end places in the state are 18th-century manor houses on former estates north of town. They're invariably located on one or more creeks or rivers, have spacious, tree-covered grounds, and every amenity.

If you want to splurge for a manor-house experience without pretension, the best is *Gross' Coate 1658* (☎ 410-819-0802, 800-580-0802, fax 410-819-0803). The original part of the current 15,000-sq-foot house was built in 1760. The manor has had only three families of owners since the Grosses built their coate (cottage). The owners for the longest period of time – several hundred years – were the Tilghmans of Revolutionary War and Maryland history fame.

Gross' Coate sits on Hwy 50 bordering Lloyd Creek, Gross Creek, and the Wye River. The house has 16 fireplaces, an 18-hole golf course, pool, stables (bring your own horse), and a dock. Outbuildings include a working smokehouse and a small tavern stocked with liquor, cigars, and smoking supplies. The hosts rent five suites with fireplaces. The suites are large and airy with views of the grounds and furnished in a casual mix of styles. Guests may bring children and pets, a marked contrast to the staid museum-piece feeling of the usual manor home. Suites are $295 to $495, including complimentary liquor, a continental breakfast at 7 am, and a full seafood breakfast at 11 am.

Ashby 1663 (☎ 410-822-4235) is another manor house; its earliest foundations date to 1663. The house is well decorated and has been used as a movie set. Inside you'll find chandeliers, fireplaces, a piano, panoramic views through wide glass doors, and other luxuries. Room rates are from $265 to $595.

Places to Eat

Cafe 25 (☎ 410-822-9360), 25 Goldsborough St, has an Italian deli alongside the dining room. The cafe dining room is a favorite with the local dinner crowd in search of creative Italian entrees like gourmet shrimp pizza for about $10. The *Fiddle Leaf Cafe* (☎ 410-822-4353) on West Dover St is a good place to pick up carryout for a picnic. Large sandwiches run about $4, and they have fresh pies and cheesecake. The *Kitchen* (☎ 410-819-6780) at 22 Harrison St is another great place to pick up sandwiches for a picnic.

Jin Jin (☎ 410-820-0011), 6 N Washington St, has Chinese lunch specials from $4 to $5. Dinner entrees are in the $6 to $10 range.

Peach Blossom (☎ 410-822-5220) at 14 N Washington St has a reputation for fine dining on California-style entrees like crab cakes served on garlic mashed potatoes. Entrees run in the $12 to $15 range.

You can get moderately priced pub food – burgers and sandwiches – for around $5 to $6 and more expensive seafood dinners from $14 at the *Washington St Pub* (☎ 410-822-9011), 20 N Washington St.

The hot place with locals is *Legal Spirits* (☎ 410-820-0033) at 42 E Dover St. The pub looks like a 1920s speakeasy, and the chef likes to add things like portobello mushrooms to his quesadillas. Pastas are under $10.

The *Hunter's Tavern* (☎ 410-822-1300) in the Tidewater Inn, 101 Dover St, is a casual, wood-floored restaurant with burgers around $6 and dinners like scallops, seafood Thermidor, and lobster for $14 to $28.

MARYLAND

Entertainment

The bar at the *Washington St Pub* (see Places to Eat) is a lengthy brass-rail affair with high ceilings and a 'Gay '90s' feel. Here you will find the biggest singles scene in town; the place rocks out with a variety of live acts and dancing on Thursdays. *Yesteryears* (☎ 410-822-2433) in the Talbottown Shopping Center offers a packed, smoky dancing scene with a DJ for the under-30 crowd every Friday.

Getting There & Away

Air Maryland Airlines (☎ 410-822-0040) has charter flights from DC ($230) and BWI ($190) to Easton. Prices are per flight, not per person. To get from the airport in Easton D&S Family Taxi (☎ 410-819-0331) charges $5.

Bus Trailways (☎ 410-822-3333) stops at the Fast Stop Texaco station and convenience store on Hwy 50 across from the Easton Airport north of town. The fare to Washington, DC, is $22.

Car Coming from Annapolis, you approach Easton via the Bay Bridge and Hwy 50. Coming south from Chestertown, take Route 213 and join Hwy 50 at the town of Wye Mills. Hwy 50 is also your artery between Ocean City and the Eastern Shore of Virginia if you are coming from the south.

AROUND EASTON

Wye Mill

The Wye Mill (☎ 410-827-6909, 410-827-2886) on Route 662 off Hwy 50 north of Easton is the oldest commercial building in continuous use in Maryland. Built in 1671 and rebuilt in 1720 and 1840, the mill provided flour for American troops during the Revolutionary War. The water-driven mill still grinds grist and is open April to mid-November from 11 am to 1 pm on weekdays, and weekends from 10 am to 4 pm. The mill pond makes a great picnic site in fair weather, and you can get fresh 'beaten' biscuits from *Orrell's Bakery* (☎ 410-822-8090) just up the street.

Wye Oak

The Wye Oak is also on Route 662 off Hwy 50 near the Wye Mill and south of the town of Wye Mills. This 400-year-old white oak is Maryland's official tree. It's 95 feet high, 21 feet around, and spreads out across 165 feet. The tree takes up most of Wye Oak State Park, the only one-tree state park in the country. Maryland residents can buy Wye Oak seedlings (acorns planted and grown for a few years).

Annual Jousting Tournament

Every August since 1868 a jousting tournament (☎ 410-822-6910) takes place in Cordova near Wye Mills. It is a benefit for St Joseph's Catholic Church – the oldest Catholic church on the Eastern Shore, founded as a mission in 1765. This is a good place to see the state sport that plays itself out with humans and horses in armor just like in movies about England in the Middle Ages. Due to blunted tips on the lances, no one gets impaled these days . . . just dumped off a horse in a thrilling manner.

ST MICHAELS

Bay Hundred Peninsula thrusts into the Chesapeake like a crab claw from the Bay's Eastern Shore near Easton. Along Bay Hundred's shores lie the sweeping manors and productive fishing ports that have typified Chesapeake life for three centuries. St Michaels, the so-called 'Town That Fooled the British,' lies nine miles west of the Easton on Route 33. The nickname comes from events during the War of 1812. St Michaels citizens rigged a forest with lanterns to decoy British naval gunners into bombarding the wilderness while the actual town lay safe under a cloak of darkness.

St Michaels warrants exploration by boat, bike, and foot. From the water, St Michaels looks like a maze of coves. Beyond the town center dominated by the lighthouse and spire on St Mary's Church, the shore is a mix of forest and a scattering of wharves leading to stately manor houses. Sometimes a fleet of the tall, three-sail log canoes will race out from the yacht club on Long Haul Creek like ghosts.

Thickly settled around a trio of coves on the Miles River, St Michaels (population 1200) has been a vital port on the Chesapeake since the 1700s. Today, the town maintains its colonial feel with red-brick Georgian buildings, bed & breakfast inns, and historic water craft tied at the wharf of the Chesapeake Bay Maritime Museum. Less than 30 years ago St Michaels was a backwater where many of the citizens earned a living as watermen harvesting the Bay's oysters from fall through winter and blue crabs from spring through summer. Landed gentry maintained vast manors outside the town and brought a patina of sophistication to the area with their fox hunts and sailboat racing. People measured time in seasons, not by days or hours.

Bay Hundred

The term Bay Hundred comes from the English division of Maryland into 'hundreds' for administrative and military purposes. Anglo Saxon hundreds were 10 families, 10 estates, or 100 fighting men. Colonists used the distinction of 'hundreds' in Maryland until after the American Revolution. ■

Life changed in St Michaels during the 1980s when James Michener's novel *Chesapeake* popularized the area. The town is no longer one of those undiscovered gems of colonial America: The influx of outside money has given a bit of spit and polish to a lot of historic homes and businesses that had been settling into decrepitude. The shops along Talbot St have become self-consciously quaint, and a fleet of vacationing yachts from all over the Atlantic now mix with the watermen's boats in the harbor. But the shady byways of the village still smell of tidewater, crabs, and oysters. The watermen still unload their catches at harborside. Hunters, or as they say on the Eastern Shore 'gunners,' come here in season. Pickup trucks and retrieving dogs remain cultural icons, and the population is a funky mix of watermen, old money, 'arrivistes,' the young, and the restless.

Orientation

Route 33 runs right into the heart of St Michaels where it becomes Talbot St, the main commercial thoroughfare. Many of the most popular restaurants and B&Bs lie on Talbot St or on side streets between this thoroughfare and the harbor two blocks to the east. The Chesapeake Bay Maritime Museum, wharfage for the watermen, inns, and restaurants surround the three small coves that form the harbor.

Information

Information describing St Michaels is available through the Talbot County Chamber of Commerce in Easton. The post office (☎ 410-745-8616) stands at the corner of Talbot and Mulberry Sts.

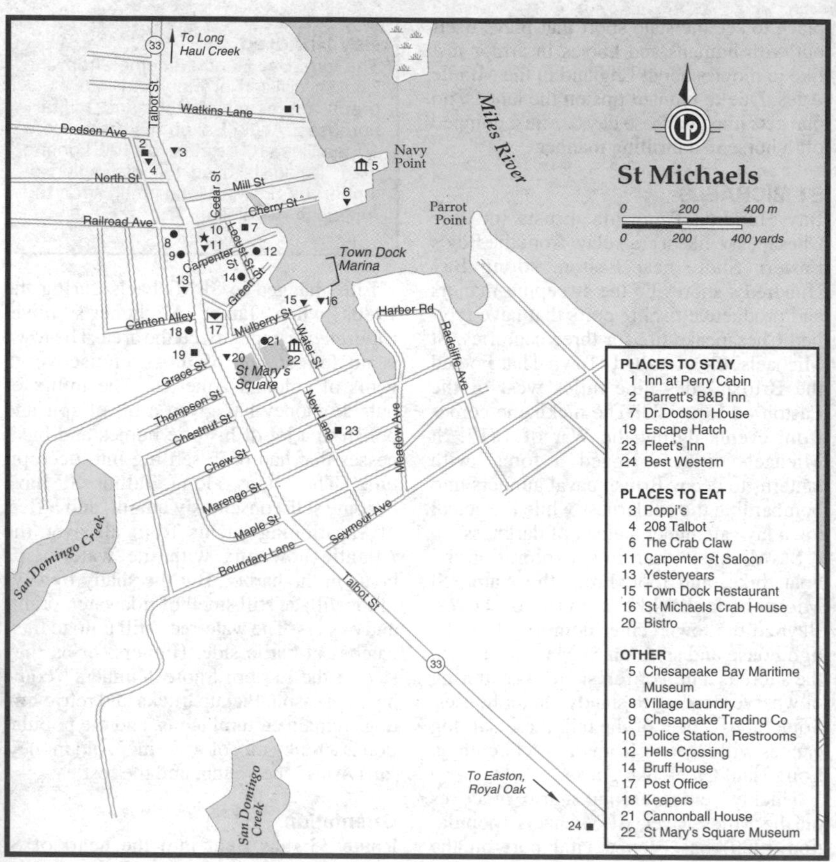

The Chesapeake Bay Maritime Museum Store (☎ 410-745-2098) on the museum grounds at Navy Point offers a complete selection of books on local history, maritime subjects, and the Chesapeake Bay. In town the Chesapeake Trading Company (☎ 410-745-9797) at 102 N Talbot is an espresso bar selling books, antiques, music, jewelry, clocks, and apparel. It stays open from 9 am to 8 pm every day Monday through Saturday and from noon to 5 pm on Sunday.

Village Laundry (☎ 410-745-9293) at 106 Railroad Ave is hot and busy, but it's a great place to make friends and get answers to questions you never even thought to ask about St Michaels and Bay Hundred. The Memorial Hospital at Easton (☎ 410-822-1000) is nine miles down Route 33. St Michaels Police Station (☎ 410-745-9500) is in the center of town on Talbot St, and the public restrooms are behind the station.

Chesapeake Bay Maritime Museum

Overlooking the harbor from Navy Point, the historic Hooper Straits octagonal lighthouse has become the image most people associate with Chesapeake Bay and is the focal point for the Maritime Museum (☎ 410-745-2916). Surrounding the lighthouse on the museum grounds are historic homes, a working boat shop, steamboats, and a prodigious collection of the Chesapeake's historic sailing craft including a bugeye schooner, a skipjack, and log canoes. The museum sponsors frequent seminars on marine topics and Chesapeake heritage as well as races for traditional sailing craft. The museum is open from 9 am to 5 pm March through December, weekends only during January and February. Admission is $7.50.

St Mary's Square Museum

This building (circa 1800) on St Mary's Square was part of a steam grist mill. The building serves as a gallery for furnishings, tools, and artifacts from St Michaels' Colonial and Federal periods. The museum is open 10 am to 4 pm Saturday and Sunday from May through September.

Cannonball House

During the War of 1812 a cannonball smashed through the roof of this house on Mulberry St, rolled across the attic floor, and down the staircase. Legend has it that the dame of the house, one Mrs Merchant, felt that the Devil himself pursued her as she fled from the house.

Hells Crossing

The intersection of Locust and Carpenter Sts takes the name Hell's Crossing. Some legends assert that the nickname arose in the 19th century because of the noise from the shipyards as well as the fire and fog bell near here. Others claim that the name comes from the quantities of sin smoldering in the brothels that sprung up here.

Bruff House

This 'southern marine'-style house on Locust St dates to 1791 and is a good example of recent historic preservation in the town.

Bicycling

In addition to the bikes available to guests at some of the B&Bs, St Michaels Town Dock Marina (☎ 410-745-2400) at 305 Mulberry St rents touring bikes for $4 an hour, $14 a day. Keepers (☎ 410-745-6388) at 300 S Talbot St has fancy mountain bikes for $13.50 for two hours, $24 a day.

Chesapeake Bay Log Canoes

Looking nothing like their name, log canoes are tall, slender traditional racing sailboats with three sails, needle-bow sprits, and at least a half-dozen crew members. Before the mid-19th century, Chesapeake watermen built their oystering skiffs by clamping together two to five big logs, then hollowing them out to make the hull of a boat. The results were narrow, sail-propelled vessels that could carry one or two men out to the shell-fishing bars to tong for oysters. Over the years the boats grew to over 30 feet in length and a second mast was added, which allowed boats to carry more oysters and achieve more speed in racing home to get the best price from the oyster buyers. Racing log canoes for sport began in St Michaels in 1859, as an obsession with speed consumed Eastern Shore builders and watermen.

By 1925 gasoline engines had replaced the sails on the oyster tongers' boats, but the watermen and – increasingly – local gentry continued their obsession with these log canoes that, from a distance, look like majestic tall ships. To keep these narrow boats from upsetting under a press of sail in strong wind, captains recruit six to 10 crew members to help trim sails and ride like acrobats on staging planks that stretch out 10 feet on the windward side of the boat. Hence, watching the crew scampering to keep their sleek antique vessels upright in shifty winds is a spectacle that draws huge spectator fleets of pleasure craft generally filled with plenty of foodstuffs and beer. The log canoes race most weekends during July and August around St Michaels, Oxford, and Chestertown, and spawn a carnival atmosphere on the water and ashore after the races when the crews tie up or beach their boats for cookouts and keg parties. ■

Boating
You can rent 15-foot runabouts with 40 horsepower engines at the St Michaels Town Dock Marina (☎ 410-745-2400) for $99 for a half day. Chesapeake Bay Kayaks (☎ 410-886-2855) has guided eco-tours for $20 an hour. The *Patriot* (☎ 410-745-3100) leaves the Crab Claw dock four times a day for one-hour narrated cruises along the historic shores of the Miles River. Tickets are $7.

Special Events
See the sidebar on log canoes to find out about races. In September you can watch the Traditional Boat Race/Festival. The Mid-Atlantic Small Craft Festival takes place in October.

Places to Stay – bottom end
'Bottom end' is quite relative. There are no rooms under $40 a night in this town. *Best Western St Michaels Motor Inn* (☎ 410-745-3333) lies a mile east of town on Route 33. This is a typical two-story modern motel with 93 rooms, two pools and free continental breakfast. It seems totally out of character with the rest of St Michaels, but at $58 per room you get a lot of amenities.

Fleet's Inn (☎ 410-745-9678) is a block off Talbot St near the harbor at 200 E Chew St. With only three rooms with shared bath in this private residence, it's an intimate stop. Four-poster beds add to the atmosphere as does the entertaining housekeeper who seems to know everyone and everything in the town. At $75 per room this is the cheapest B&B in the village.

If you have a bike or a car, *Pasadena Inn* (☎ 410-745-5053) is the best bargain in the St Michaels area. About four miles out of town on the road to the village of Royal Oak, the inn is a 1748 plantation house set among massive oaks on a tidewater slough. This is not a cutesy restored B&B; the Pasadena has the feel of a working plantation. Rooms in the main house start at $65 and there are cottages (former slave quarters?) that go for over $110.

The Wades Point Inn (☎ 410-745-2500) lies five miles west of town on a lane leading from Route 33. This is really a manor house set on a 120-acre farm overlooking Chesapeake Bay. Staying here is like joining the landed gentry. Betsy and John Feiler offer some rooms for as little as $75.

MARYLAND

Places to Stay – middle
Dr Dodson House (☎ 410-745-3691), a one-time tavern set in a restored Federal brick house at 200 Cherry St, offers private baths, canopy beds, antiques, and individual fireplaces. The B&B also provides free evening hors d'oeuvres, gourmet breakfast, and bikes. Prices start at $115.

The Getaway (☎ 410-745-2094) lies a mile west of town on Long Haul Creek. Overlooking the Miles River Yacht Club and some of the most historic manors on the river, this inn has the look and feel of an English guesthouse. Rooms all with private baths cost $125 to $175. Shade trees, hammocks, and dock add to the ambiance.

The *Harbourtowne Golf Resort* (☎ 800-446-9066) lies near Long Haul Creek as well, and its 111 rooms look out on the broad reaches of Eastern Bay. This is a hotel with a country club atmosphere, including Robert Dye golf course, pool, and tennis courts. Some rooms are as little as $70 off season, but cost $145 from spring to fall.

Places to Stay – top end
Barrett's Bed & Breakfast Inn (☎ 410-745-3322) is right at the heart of the action at 204 N Talbot St. Rooms with a double Jacuzzi in front of the fireplace, private baths, full breakfast, and homemade bread cost from $140 to $195 a night.

Above Saltbox Antiques on Talbot St, the *Escape Hatch* (☎ 410-745-6360) offers a two-bedroom suite with kitchen, living room, and porch. You get cable, VCR, telephone, and a welcome basket of edibles for $155.

The *Inn at Perry Cabin* (☎ 410-745-2200) on Watkins Lane is fashioned after an English country home overlooking the Maritime Museum. Sir Bernard Ashley built this 'showpiece' inn with docks, gardens, and gazebo bar a dozen years ago to give St Michaels aristocratic accommodations. 'Pretentious' is the adjective that comes to many local minds when they consider both the structure and the price of a room – $175 to $525.

Places to Eat

Recently, fancy eateries have bloomed along the three-block business strip on Talbot St. *Poppi's* (☎ 410-745-3158) at 207 N Talbot St serves breakfast and lunch, and advertises beer, wine, and ice cream in the same sentence. Poppi's also claims to serve the best burger in town, but many locals swear by the grill at the *Carpenter St Saloon* (☎ 410-745-5111) on the corner of Carpenter and Talbot Sts.

Gourmet diners head to *208 Talbot* (☎ 410-745-3838) for the lamb and nouvelle cuisine, or to chef David Stein's *Bistro* (☎ 410-745-9111) where Toulouse sausage with polenta and spinach costs $17. At *Town Dock Restaurant* (☎ 410-745-5577) at 125 Mulberry St you can get the crab cake and Bloody Mary Sunday brunch served al fresco on the harborside deck.

Two restaurants catering to the throngs of weekend tourists are *Yesteryears* (☎ 410-745-6206) at 200 S Talbot St, specializing in prime rib and broiled rock fish, and the *St Michaels Crab House* (☎ 410-745-3737), serving you-know-what at the water end of Mulberry St.

Good as they may be, none of these newer restaurants compare to the grand mammy of them all. Perched on Navy Point like an annex to the Maritime Museum, *The Crab Claw* (☎ 410-745-2900) has served two generations of locals and travelers . . . and was the vehicle for putting St Michaels on the tourist trail 30 years ago. Eating on the 2nd-floor deck, with its view of the entire town and harbor, is close to a religious experience, or at least a cultural ritual, for anyone caught up in the romance of the Chesapeake. You can feast for hours on trays mounded with blue crabs steamed in tangy Old Bay sauce and beer. The air fills with the swish and fizz of beer poured from pitchers, the slaps of crab mallets cracking open hundreds of shells, and the scent of plump meat from 'jimmy' (male) crabs. The price of crabs varies by season and availability, but you can plan on spending at least $20 for your feast.

Entertainment

A meeting place for restless gentry, watermen, and youth is the *Carpenter St Saloon* (see Places to Eat). In recent years, the management has tried to make the bar a little more tourist-friendly by jazzing up the decor in the dining room and adding hanging ferns in the windows. But the 'C St' can still be a wild and woolly place on a Friday night when St Michaels steps out – or as the locals say, 'goes down the road' – for a good time. The juke box cranks out Garth Brooks and Reba McEntire anthems to a barroom overflowing with laughter, dart throwers, tall tales, and draft beer. Police generally hover right outside the door (the police station is the adjacent building) to break up fights and subdue the intoxicated.

On weekends *The Inn at Perry Cabin* and *The Town Dock Restaurant* have dancing to live bands covering mainstream rock music.

TILGHMAN ISLAND

Tilghman is a three-by-1½-mile island at the end of Route 33 – 't'end o' the road,' as the locals say – 14 miles southwest of St Michaels. This low Bay island marks the northern juncture of the Bay and the broad Choptank River. Connected to the mainland across Knapps Narrows by a counterbalance drawbridge, Tilghman is a thriving watermen's community. Here you will find hundreds of oystering, clamming, fishing, and crabbing boats along with the rough-and-ready men and women who, as they say, 'follow the water.'

Tilghman is the home port for at least eight of the remaining working skipjacks still dredging for Chesapeake oysters. It has become a cliché to say that Tilghman Islanders (along with residents of other remote Eastern Shore islands) speak with the Elizabethan English accents of their ancestors. That's stretching the case, but the watermen and their families do have a distinctive way of speaking that one recent visitor from Cornwall, England, said reminded him of the fisherfolk from home. On Tilghman, you'll hear some of the toughest men you've ever met call each other 'honey.' Tilghman Island has had various names in its history, including Great Choptank Island. Gentleman William Tilghman inherited the island in 1775 and his family name remains.

For information on the island, go to the Talbot County Chamber of Commerce in Easton.

Boating, Oystering & Crabbing

Many captains have begun taking visitors out on the Bay aboard their work boats. Most of the skipjacks sail from **Dogwood Harbor** on the north end of the island. After crossing the drawbridge, drive for half a mile past the Fire Hall and Country Store; then look for the harbor about 100 yards ahead on your left.

The *Tilghman Lady* (☎ 410-886-2141) sails from the drawbridge; Captain Ed Farley (☎ 410-745-6080) takes people out under sail on his working skipjack the *HM Krentz*, which carries up to 32 passengers on summer sails. Tickets are $25 a person or $300 for two-hour charters.

Captain Wade Murphy (☎ 410-886-2176) owns the *Rebecca T Ruark*, the oldest skipjack on the Chesapeake; parts of the boat date from 1886. For a price, Captain Murphy will take people oystering or just for a sail around the Bay. Captain Murphy usually leaves at around 5 am to 'drudge' oysters during the season – November 1 to March 15. You will pay around $50 a head for oystering. From April to the end of October, you can go crabbing and take home a bushel to eat for $60 a person.

If you're fit, eager, and dressed to work, you might find a waterman who will take you out on the Bay in exchange for your labor. Be respectful, and ask one of the local bartenders to help you out with meeting watermen when they come ashore in the afternoons. Expect a long, hard day, but the rewards can be the freshest seafood you will ever eat, shared beers after work, and lifelong friendships.

Special Events

Tilghman Island Seafood Festival in late June is a one-day celebration of music, crab races, crab picking, and a fireman's parade. Tilghman Island Day, in late October, is an islandwide celebration of seafood, boat races, watermen, music, boat docking contests, and other activities.

Places to Stay

Norma's Guest House (☎ 410-886-2395) is right across from Dogwood Harbor. Norma has a couple of efficiencies for rent; the smaller has a microwave oven and the larger one a washer/dryer and full kitchen. Outside there's a barbecue, crab cooker, and fish cleaning table. The places rent for $65/75 for single/double occupancy.

Harrison's Chesapeake House (☎ 410-886-2121, 886-2109), is a motel-like affair owned and run by Buddy Harrison. It's on the east side of Route 33 towards the north end of the island. Rooms with a view are $75 and $85; others are $65 and $80, and there's an annex with $50 and $65 rooms. Single rooms are $10 less and most rooms are around $50 from January to May. There are 14 boats in Captain Buddy's navy, so if you want to fish and need a boat, come here. Fishing rates alone are $50 Sunday to Friday and $60 Saturday, or you can charter your own boat with a maximum of six people for $300/350. They also have 'buddy plan fishing packages' for $115 to $130 including room, meals, and fishing.

The *Black Walnut Point Inn* (☎ 410-886-2452, fax 410-886-2053) is on the southern tip of Tilghman Island in a 50-acre wildlife preserve. The house and cottages sit on a small point surrounded on three sides by water. There are four rooms in the main

The Chesapeake Bay Skipjack

The undisputed icon for the tradition and romance of the Chesapeake is the skipjack – the graceful two-sail white sloops the watermen use for dredging (or as they say, 'drudging') oysters from the Bay. These V-bottomed beauties with raked masts evolved during the 1880s as cheap and easy-to-build platforms for towing large dredges that scoop up oysters as the boats sail back and forth over the shellfish bars. More than 2000 of these vessels once sailed the Bay for oysters. With colorful names like *Ruby G Ford, Rosie Parks, Lena Rose, Rebecca T Ruark*, or *Nellie Bird*, the skipjacks continue to ply the Maryland section of the Chesapeake Bay for oysters long after power work boats replaced sailboats in the rest of the country.

The skipjacks survive due to a Maryland conservation law that only permits dredging for oysters from a sailboat the size and shape of which define the skipjack. The average skipjack is about 45 feet long on deck and 15 feet wide. A 15-foot needlenose bowsprit juts forward from the bows. The vessel hoists more than 1200 sq feet of sail and carries its load of oysters on deck. There is a small cabin aft with a stove where the crew of four to six 'drudgers' can escape the weather and eat meals.

Old age and continuing poor oyster harvests, due to oyster blights, have steadily shrunk the ranks of the working skipjacks. While you may still see skipjacks tied at the wharves in Baltimore, Annapolis, or Chestertown, these boats now carry passengers. Only about a dozen skipjacks are still what the watermen call 'drudge boats,' ships that actually go out on the Bay to catch a 'fair living' of oysters during the season that runs from November through March.

Today, most of the working skipjacks sail from Tilghman Island where the tradition of independent watermen persists in spite of hard times, attempts to gentrify the island, and the lure of safer, better-paying jobs in the tourist industry. If you visit Tilghman during the winter season, you will hear the watermen's trucks roll up to the skipjacks at four in the morning, the bluster of the pushboat motors, and the call 'away' as the watermen slip their lines and head out through the gloam to arrive on the drudging bars at sunrise. Bart Murphy, captain of the skipjack *Nellie Bird*, says, 'I wouldn't trade this life with no man, not the President or no man.' Murphy's son Little Bart, the mate on his father's drudge boat, says the same. ■

house and three cottages for $105 and one larger cottage for $135. The Point also has a pool, and the innkeepers have Chesapeake Bay retrievers, which spend part of every day swimming in the Bay.

The *Wood Duck Inn* (☎ 410-886-2070) on Gibsontown Rd overlooking the skipjack fleet in Dogwood Harbor is a onetime sailors' boarding house and bordello that has been restored as an elegant Victorian B&B. This is a six-room inn for romantics and discriminating travelers. Gourmet breakfasts include fresh fruits, Tilghman omelet puffs, and sherry crab quiche. Owner Dave Feith is a part-time waterman who can hook you up with people who might share their days on the Bay with you. Rooms start at $115.

Places to Eat

The *Bay Hundred* (☎ 410-886-2622) is on the west side of Route 33 immediately before the drawbridge. It has good fresh seafood such as crab soup for $5, sandwiches from $5 to $9, and entrees for around $9. The dining room overlooks Knapps Narrows and the Bay. Bartenders here are a wealth of local information.

The *Osprey* ☎ 410-886-2330) is a less expensive and more casual version of the Bay Hundred on Tilghman Island across the drawbridge. You'll find a lot of watermen in here for coffee, pizza, and beer once they have sold their catches at the seafood buyers wharves that line the channel through Knapps Narrows. You can get half a pound of shrimp steamed in beer for $6.95.

OXFORD

Travelers come to Oxford to absorb the feel of the Eastern Shore's genteel past and ride its historic ferry. The village lies on the third peninsula or 'neck' south of Easton jutting into the Tred Avon River. Route 333 (Oxford Rd) runs nine miles south from Easton past the estates and plantations of Talbot County's landed gentry and dead-ends in Oxford village.

European settlers arrived here in the early 1660s. In 1683 the Maryland General Assembly named Oxford as a seaport, and planners laid out a town. Meanwhile, English gentry developed tobacco plantations in the rich soil along the Tred Avon in response to England's voracious demand for the 'sot weed.' Ten years later the General Assembly named Oxford as one of only two 'Ports of Entry' in Maryland, and the town thrived with its markets for tobacco and slaves. Many of the ancestors of the Eastern Shore's African Americans passed through the Oxford slave market and former tobacco plantations.

The town's prominence faded as other towns like Baltimore grew after the Revolutionary War and other regions usurped the tobacco trade. During the late 19th and early 20th centuries, Oxford boomed as a center for oyster buying, shucking, canning, and shipping until overfishing exhausted local oyster beds. The town's long periods of dormancy have left it free from the ravages of extensive development; a collection of Federal-style homes under majestic shade trees overlooks the Tred Avon and Choptank Rivers. A grassy knoll above the Choptank called 'the Strand,' is the most prestigious address on the Eastern Shore. 'Old Money' families from the tobacco plantations, 'New Money' from the oystering days a century ago, and newcomer wannabes have protected their community from development and commercialism. The only dramatic changes in the town during the last hundred years is around the harbors on Town Creek and Bachelor's Point. With no fewer than nine yacht yards or marinas, Oxford's biggest business is pleasure boating, but unlike Rock Hall and St Michaels, Oxford remains almost strictly residential. Morris St, an extension of Hwy 333, runs north right through the center of the village to the Oxford-Bellevue Ferry landing at the intersection with the Strand.

Oxford had some famous early residents. Robert Morris, Jr, helped finance the American Revolutionary War and was one of only two men to have signed the Declaration of Independence, the Articles of Confederation, and the Constitution. Other famous figures are Reverend Thomas Bacon, who compiled the first laws of Maryland; and Colonel Tench Tilghman, George Washington's aide-de-camp and the man who brought word of Cornwallis' surrender to the Continental Congress.

The Talbot County Chamber of Commerce in Easton has information on the town.

MARYLAND

Things to See & Do

The **Oxford-Bellevue Ferry** (☎ 410-745-9023), begun in 1683, is the oldest continuously running ferry operation in the US. It runs across the Tred Avon River to Bellevue; from Bellevue you can drive or cycle seven miles to St Michaels. The crossing takes less than 10 minutes and the small boat runs every 20 minutes. Daily trips run from 7 am to 5:15 pm with longer hours midsummer. There's always a cooling breeze and good view of Oxford's historic houses as well as the manor houses on the farms farther up the river. Car and driver cost $4.50/6.25 one way/roundtrip; bikes are $1.50; walk-ons 75¢.

The small **Oxford Museum** (☎ 410-226-0191) is at the corner of Morris and Market Sts. It shows exhibits on the town's history Friday to Sunday from 2 to 5 pm. There is a replica of the 1694 **Oxford Customs House** at the foot of Morris St near the ferry.

If you want to go **bicycling**, Oxford Mews (☎ 410-820-8222), 105 Morris St, rents bikes by the hour/day/week for $3.50/14/75.

For **sailing** Skylark Sailing Yachts (☎ 410-226-5656) at Shaws' Boat Yard, Myrtle St, has 16-foot Bullseye sloops;

MDT

Maryland blue crab, a gastronome's delight

ROBERT DE GAST

Harvesting oysters

MDT

Watermen have been known to play scales on their catches.

ROBERT DE GAST
A fine display of duck decoys

RICO ALLEN
Snow geese migrating at Bombay Hook, DE

RICO ALLEN
At Cape Henlopen State Park in Delaware you can almost see the 'walking dunes' on the move.

RICO ALLEN
Mansions on The Strand in New Castle, DE

RICO ALLEN
The Delaware River from Battery Park in New Castle, D

Choptank Sailing Society (☎ 410-226-5571), 202 Bank St, rents day sailers with electric motors to get you home if the wind quits; and, also on Bank St, Eastern Shore Yacht Charters (☎ 410-226-5000) maintains a fleet of yachts up to 39 feet as well as day sailers that qualified sailors can take out on their own.

Places to Stay

The *Robert Morris Inn* (☎ 410-226-5111) is at the end of Morris St opposite the ferry landing. Ship carpenters built the original part of the structure before 1710. Rooms are spread around three buildings – the original inn, the Sandaway (a mansion one block away), and a more modern annex. Prices for rooms range from $70 to $220 depending on view and amenities. In 1750 Robert Morris, Sr, was hit in the arm by wadding flying out of a cannon fired in his honor. Morris died from his infected injuries and may be the only person to have ever been killed by a salute in his honor.

The *Oxford Inn* (☎ 410-226-5220), on S Morris St, has 11 rooms, a sitting room with TV, and stamped-tin ceilings. Rooms with shared bath are $70 to $100, with private bath $95 to $135, including continental breakfast.

The *1876 House* (☎ 410-226-5496) at 110 N Morris St is a Queen-Anne Victorian house with wide plank floors and Oriental carpets. Rooms are $90 to $100.

Places to Eat

The *Robert Morris Inn* (see Places to Stay) serves sandwiches for $5 to $6. Dinner dishes like crab cakes, oyster sandwiches, and scallops served with crystal and linen are $14 to $20. The restaurant is closed in winter.

Sally's Deli (☎ 410-226-5615) does a steady breakfast and lunch business at 103 Mill St. This is a good place to provision for a picnic or stop for a sub or deli sandwich while on a cycling tour.

Local gentry and yachties favor *Latitude 38* (☎ 410-266-5303) just as you enter town on Route 333. It features such nouvelle cuisine dishes as shrimp and pasta salad for $6.95. Dinner entrees are not cheap: crab imperial costs $19.

Set on the water at the foot of Tilghman St near the entrance to the yacht basin at Town Creek, *Schooner Landing* (☎ 410-226-0160) is a rambling restaurant built in an old oyster shucking house with indoor and outdoor decks. The decor of nautical memorabilia and antiques comes on strong, but a lot of lunches are under $6, the service is friendly, and the view overlooks the parade of yachts in and out of Town Creek. The made-to-order oyster stew ($5.25) is as good as it comes. For entertainment, the tables are pushed back for dancing and live music on Friday nights. You can listen to acoustic music on the outdoor deck on weekends during warm weather.

BLACKWATER NATIONAL WILDLIFE REFUGE

This 17,000-acre refuge (☎ 410-228-2677), 20 miles south of Easton, is mostly made up of tidal marshes set aside for migrating waterfowl. The **visitors center** on Key Wallace Drive is open from 8 am to 4 pm Monday to Friday and from 9 am to 5 pm on weekends, but it remains closed on summer weekends (Memorial Day to Labor Day). The entrance fee is $3 per car and $1 for bikers or pedestrians.

The best time for bird watching is mid-October to mid-March. The refuge is one of the major stopping points for Canada geese and has the greatest density of bald eagles in the eastern US north of Florida. You can also see snow geese, peregrine falcons, blue herons, ospreys (nesting platforms are provided), and 20 duck species.

Blackwater also has raccoons, otters, opossums, skunks, muskrats, red foxes, and fox squirrels. You might see white-tailed deer and Asian sika deer in the remaining wooded areas.

There is a five-mile road in the park. It runs past ponds, woods, fields, and marshland. There are also several short walking trails. You can get interpretive leaflets at the visitors center. The refuge is rife with insects in July and August, so bring repellent.

To get there, drive south on State Rd 335 from Cambridge. At the intersection of Key Wallace Drive make a left and follow the signs to the entrance.

CRISFIELD

Crisfield (population 2900) is a flat, plain-looking town with few historical buildings, on the southern tip of Maryland's Eastern Shore about 75 miles south of Easton. Ocean City lies 55 miles to the east. Come here if you love hanging around commercial fisherfolk, you can't resist seeing the annual Labor Day Hard Crab Derby, or you want to take a boat to Smith or Tangier Islands in the Chesapeake.

History

Local citizens like to say that Crisfield was built on oystering, literally and figuratively. A quiet fishing village known as Somers Cove for 200 years before the railroad arrived in 1867, Crisfield took its current name from a local entrepreneur who brought the railroad and turned the tiny village into a boomtown.

As oysters became the preferred delicacy among America's upper-crust during the final decades of the 19th century, the Chesapeake's skipjack fleet grew to thousands of vessels. In response to the millions of bushels coming ashore from the 'drudge boats,' Crisfield turned into a maze of buyers' wharves, with shucking houses (for cleaning oyster meat from the shells) sprawled throughout the town. The railroad shipped trainloads of canned and fresh oysters to diners in Washington, Baltimore, Philadelphia, New York, and Boston. Empty oyster shells were used to fill in the marshes to make room for more wharves and seafood buyers as well as to pave the roads.

More recently, with the continuing decline in the oyster harvest over the last 50 years, Crisfield likes to call itself the 'crab capital of the world' because its seafood buyers have all but cornered the market on Maryland's hard and soft-shell crabs, packing and shipping in excess of 125,000 bushels a year.

MARYLAND

Information

The Somerset County Tourism Office (☎ 410-651-2968, 800-521-9189) is in a rest area at mile marker 19 on Hwy 13 north of Crisfield. The Crisfield Chamber of Commerce & Visitors Center (☎ 410-968-1380) is in the J Millard Tawes Museum off of W Main St in town. It's open from 10 am to 4 pm weekdays, and daily from Memorial Day to Labor Day.

Things to See & Do

Just off of Main St close by Eighth St is **J Millard Tawes Museum** (☎ 410-968-2501). Tawes, a Crisfield native, was once a Maryland governor. The museum traces his career in public service and has his papers. Unless you're a J Millard Tawes fan, you might want to skip this one. On the other hand, learning about one of the region's favorite sons can really shed light on the culture. It's open from 10 am to 4 pm, and admission for adults/children is $1/50¢.

For charter and 'head' boats (on which you pay per-person/'head') contact the Somers Cove Marina (☎ 410-968-0925, 800-967-3474).

Special Events

The Annual Hard Crab Derby & Fair (☎ 410-968-2682, 800-782-3913) on Labor Day weekend has events like crab races with competing crabs from many species, crab-picking contests, and crabs cooked in every possible way for consumers. Hotels hike their rates and are usually booked for this weekend.

Places to Stay

The *Pines Motel* (☎ 410-968-0900) on N Somerset Ave has 40 clean standard motel rooms with a pool. Most of the rooms are on ground level with large windows in front overlooking the motel grounds. Rates are $40 to $45, and it's open year round.

Paddlewheel Motel (☎ 410-968-2220), 701 W Main St, is a slightly worn motel near the center of town. Efficiency rooms are $42 to $57. It's open from March to November. The *Somers Cove Motel* (☎ 410-968-1900), RR Norris Drive on the southern end of the Somers Cove Marina, is a two-story place that overlooks the marina. No surprises, but it's clean and has a pool. Rates are $45 to $75, open year round. *Leonora's Crisfield Inn* (☎ 410-968-2181) at 209 W Main St has three rooms and a continental breakfast in the $80 range.

My Fair Lady B&B (☎ 410-968-3514), 38 Main St, is a large restored wooden home with four rooms for guests. It's a Victorian place (rare in Crisfield) with country antiques, a rosewood piano, and a sun porch. The hosts are very friendly and helpful. Rooms with continental breakfast are $85.

Places to Eat

The *Dockside* (☎ 410-968-3464) on W Main St near 10th St has diner food. The captains who run the boats to Smith and Tangier Islands come here for breakfast. At the north end of town on Maryland Ave (Route 413), just past the intersection with Standard St, is the *Big Belly Deli*, a modern sandwich place with no atmosphere but decent sandwiches.

The two seafood restaurants to try are the *Captain's Galley* (☎ 410-968-1636), 1101 W Main St, and the *Watermen's Inn* (☎ 410-968-2119), Ninth and W Main Sts. Watermen's is run by culinary school graduates. Seafood dishes are in the $10 to $15 range.

Getting There & Away

Crisfield is at the southern end of Route 413. Take Hwy 13 south until you see signs for 413 and the town of Westover. Follow 413 about 15 miles south right into Crisfield.

SMITH ISLAND

Twelve miles west of Crisfield in the middle of the Chesapeake lies Smith Island, actually several islands (due to the rise in Bay waters during the last four centuries) and a marsh forming a ragged archipelago eight miles long and four miles wide. Smith is the only island in Maryland that can be reached only by boat. There are three villages – Ewell and Rhodes Point (which are on opposite sides of the largest island), and Tylerton. Passenger boats from Crisfield generally stop at Ewell but will stop at Tylerton on request.

Smith Islanders are exceptionally friendly and speak with an archaic Cornish accent that is even stronger than what you hear on Tilghman. Often described as 'historic' or 'rustic,' Smith Island has a tendency to disappoint day-trip visitors. Smith is important in soft-shell crab production and many watermen live here, but the villages are not well-swept troves of historic architecture. Similar to Tilghman Island, Smith is a place dedicated to the 'water business,' not to looking good for travelers. Nondescript houses, aluminum siding, telephone wires, and abandoned cars (it's difficult to get dead vehicles off the island) are commonplace. So are beer cans and plastic litter along the Smith Island Rd, which runs between Ewell and Rhodes Point.

The joys of Smith Island can hardly be perceived, let alone explored, during an afternoon visit. The vast meadows of chartreuse marsh grass, stands of loblolly pine, and gatherings of waterfowl really deserve exploration by water. One person who took her kayak to Smith spent a week paddling around, camping on a remote islet one night. She said she thought she had found heaven until one of the Chesapeake's legendary thunder squalls ripped across the Bay.

The island takes its name from Captain John Smith, who explored the Chesapeake in 1608, stopped here, and gave the site his name. For him, this place was an oasis.

Places to Stay

Bernice Guy's B&B (☎ 410-425-2751), 4017 Tyler Rd in Ewell, has two rooms with a shared bath. Mrs Guy gives you breakfast, dinner, and the room for $45 per person. Get off at the dock, walk north on Jones Rd, and make a left on Tyler Rd; the B&B is the only gray house with white shutters on the block. The nearby *Ewell Tide Inn* (☎ 410-425-2141), 4063 Tyler Rod, has four rooms for $65 in a modern setting with bike rentals. *Tourist Home* (☎ 410-425-2751), at 2 Tyler Rd, is a small bungalow with two rooms for rent. You get the room with a home-cooked dinner and breakfast for $45.

Places to Eat

The *Bayside Inn Restaurant* (☎ 410-425-2771) and *Harbor Side Restaurant* (☎ 410-425-2201) are next to each other on the water. Some boats dock in front of them. They serve standard seafood dishes for tourists. *Ruke's Seafood Deck* (☎ 410-425-2311) is up the block from the City Dock in Ewell. It sells soda and sandwiches.

Getting There & Away

Smaller boats, including one that carries mail, run year round from City Dock at the end of W Main St in Crisfield. You just show up and pay the captain. If you want to call ahead, try the *Captain Jason I & II* (☎ 410-425-5931, 410-425-4471) and the *Island Belle II* and *Island Princess* (☎ 410-968-3206). The trip to Smith Island costs $10 per person, half price for those from six to 12. It takes about 35 minutes. Boats generally leave Crisfield at 12:30 pm and return from Smith Island at 3:30 pm. There are sometimes afternoon boats that stay overnight during the summer.

Larger cruise boats generally run from Crisfield to Smith Island from May to October. They leave from both the City Dock and the dock behind the Tawes Museum. The *Captain Tyler II* (☎ 410-425-2771), departing from behind the Tawes Museum, is a large modern boat and costs $18 roundtrip. You can get a bus tour of the island in an old yellow school bus for an additional $2.

During the summer, travelers will find two interesting alternatives for returning to Crisfield on one of the ferries. Excursion boats run between Smith Island and Point Lookout or Reedsville, Virginia, on the Western Shore. The Point Lookout boat (☎ 410-425-2771) leaves the Western

MARYLAND

The Story of Jimmy & Sook

Although blue crabs live along most of the Atlantic Coast of the US, they prefer estuaries where salt and fresh water mix. The Chesapeake Bay is ideal. The crab's Latin name is *Callinectes sapidus Rathbun*. The first two words translate as 'tasty beautiful swimmer.' The third, Rathbun, is from Dr Mary Rathbun, a Smithsonian carcinologist, who identified and described 1000 new crab species.

Blue crabs have an elaborate mating ritual. In autumn a courting jimmy (male) approaches a mature sook (female) and raises himself on his legs weaving back and forth and waving his swimming legs. To make sure he gets the female's attention, he'll also dig up a storm of sand with his legs. The jimmy then grabs the sook and pulls her, right side up and face forward, under himself. He then cradle-carries her for at least two days, usually swimming for miles until she molts, which is the only time she may be fertilized. The pair, called 'doublers,' swims along the surface of the water and can easily be scooped up with a dip net that has a chicken-wire basket. After the female molts, the male carefully flips her over on her back and inserts his two pleopods into her genital pores. Coitus lasts five to 12 hours. When the lovemaking is over the female saves the sperm until next spring and then uses it to fertilize the eggs she carries.

Sooks lay their eggs in the lower parts of the Bay, generally from June to August, but the time and place vary. At hatching, crabs – called zoea – are 1/25 of an inch long and look like an insect. Only one in a million eggs produces an adult crab. The zoea sheds its carapace several times and begins to look like an adult crab, at which point it's called a 'megalops.' These young crabs begin to move north in the Bay during the fall and keep molting – a total of about 20 times – until cold weather sets in and they bury themselves in the mud through the winter. When spring comes, the crabs continue migrating northward. In the few hours after molting, a crab is a softshell crab (a delicacy when pan-fried with spices and a few bread crumbs). The softshell crab is only about a third as large as its discarded shell. ■

Shore at 10 am and departs Ewell at 2 pm; roundtrip fare for adults/children is $20/10. The Virginia boat (☎ 804-453-3430) leaves Smith Point (Reedsville) at 10 am and departs Ewell at 4 pm. Fares are $18.50; kids cost half.

TANGIER ISLAND

Tangier Island, in Virginia, lies 14 miles south of Crisfield, and 10 miles south of Smith Island in the middle of the Chesapeake. It is barely a mile wide and three miles long, and has the same unscrubbed ambiance you find on Smith Island, although there are no vehicles. There are gift shops, a couple of restaurants, and watermen's homes, however. You can eat home-cooked crab cakes, clam fritters, and country ham at *Hilda Crockett's Chesapeake House* (☎ 757-891-2331) for $11.25 (all you can eat). Hilda's also has rooms for $45 a night including breakfast, dinner, tax, and tip. The *Islander Seafood Restaurant* (☎ 757-891-2249) has seafood in the $8 to $13 range.

Tangier Island Cruises (☎ 410-968-2338) runs trips to the island from the wharf behind the Dockside Diner near 10th and W Main Sts in Crisfield. Other boats leave from in back of the Tawes Museum or from City Dock. The ride costs $18; it's free for those under 12. It takes 1½ hours.

OCEAN CITY

Founded as a vacation community just four years after the end of the Civil War, Ocean City ('OC') is Maryland's mammoth Atlantic shore resort. It sprawls southward from the Delaware border along 10 miles of barrier beach. Ocean City sits on the same strip of coast as the Delaware towns of Bethany Beach and Fenwick Island, but the change from the tranquil Delaware state parks and beach-house communities to Ocean City can provoke culture shock. Route 1, the main north-south coastal road in Delaware, becomes Maryland's Coastal Highway 528 (known as Philadelphia Ave from about 33rd St south) in Ocean City. Along its length are high-rise condos, fast-food franchises, beach-gear stores, restaurants, and motels of every size and price. The southern end of town, called 'the Inlet,' has a hint of Victorian flavor and is the place where OC started as a resort. Hurricane Hazel carved the actual inlet between the Atlantic and the saltwater bays on the inshore side of the island in 1933. South of the inlet lies Assateague Island, 37 miles of undeveloped state park and National Seashore extending into Virginia. On Assateague, herds of wild horses have roamed free for centuries.

Ocean City gets a wide range of visitors from working class to wealthy. The town has an extraordinary mix (OC invites expansive adjectives) of boardwalk attractions, amusement parks (two large ones), water slides, bars, condos, and motels, without being hopelessly tacky. Then again, it has 23 miniature golf courses, bars named 'Bearded Clam' and 'Big Pecker's,' and go-kart racing. While most Maryland towns claim a host of historical heroes as their celebrity visitors, OC claims Spiro Agnew, Bobby Baker, and Marvin Mandel, three infamous political characters from the '60s and '70s.

With only about 6000 people claiming OC as home, the city seems like a ghost town from November through mid-April, but during the summer, particularly on weekends, the population balloons to around 300,000, making this beach Maryland's second-largest city. During June, Ocean City fills with recent high school graduates and college students (who come to work in the resort businesses), and the city takes on many aspects of a world-class fraternity party. July and August temper the scene a bit with tens of thousands of families trying to beat the Mid-Atlantic heat waves with one- or two-week vacations. As one veteran of OC's summer scene put it, 'You either love it or hate it, but OC is America at leisure.' If you are a traveler with some skills in the restaurant or hotel business, you can always find work during the summer in OC if you want to supplement your traveling funds.

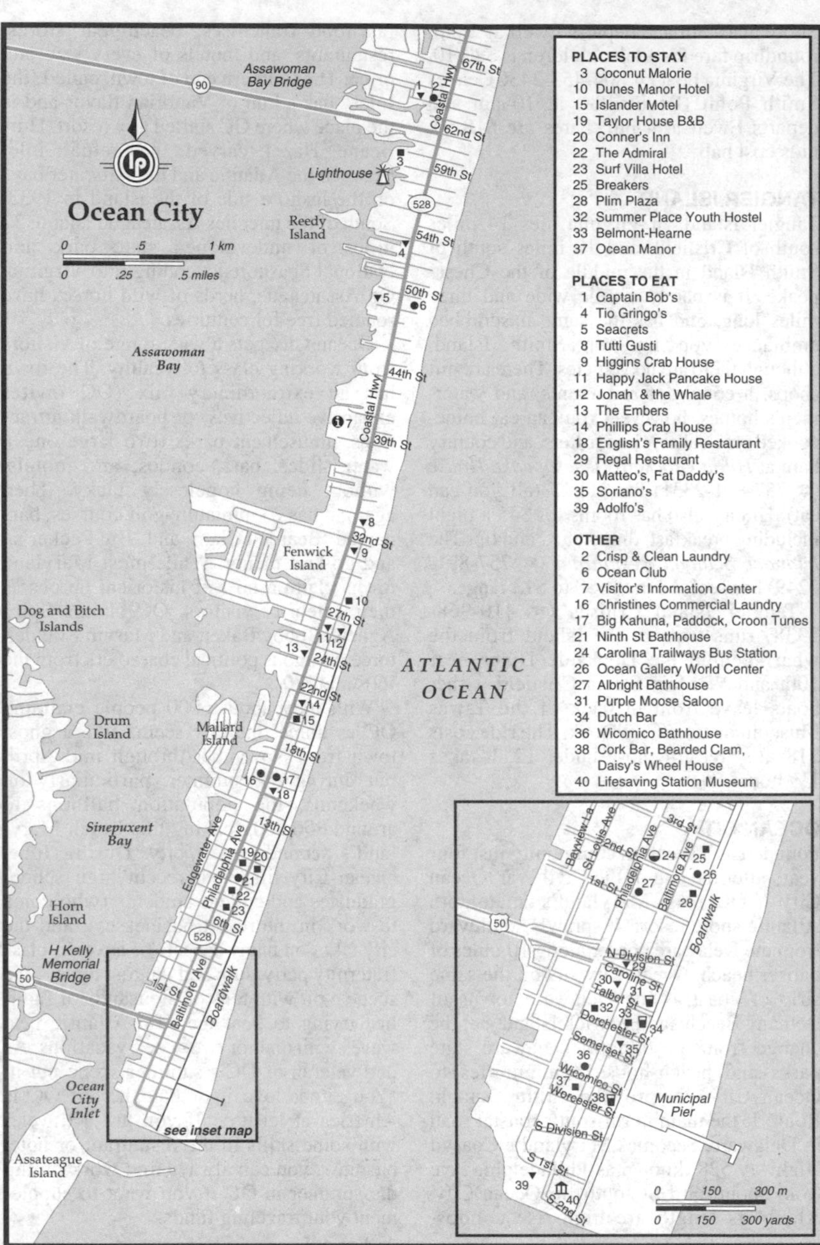
Ocean City
0 .5 1 km
0 .25 .5 miles
PLACES TO STAY
3 Coconut Malorie
10 Dunes Manor Hotel
15 Islander Motel
19 Taylor House B&B
20 Conner's Inn
22 The Admiral
23 Surf Villa Hotel
25 Breakers
28 Plim Plaza
32 Summer Place Youth Hostel
33 Belmont-Hearne
37 Ocean Manor
PLACES TO EAT
1 Captain Bob's
4 Tio Gringo's
5 Seacrets
8 Tutti Gusti
9 Higgins Crab House
11 Happy Jack Pancake House
12 Jonah & the Whale
13 The Embers
14 Phillips Crab House
18 English's Family Restaurant
29 Regal Restaurant
30 Matteo's, Fat Daddy's
35 Soriano's
39 Adolfo's
OTHER
2 Crisp & Clean Laundry
6 Ocean Club
7 Visitor's Information Center
16 Christines Commercial Laundry
17 Big Kahuna, Paddock, Croon Tunes
21 Ninth St Bathhouse
24 Carolina Trailways Bus Station
26 Ocean Gallery World Center
27 Albright Bathhouse
31 Purple Moose Saloon
34 Dutch Bar
36 Wicomico Bathhouse
38 Cork Bar, Bearded Clam, Daisy's Wheel House
40 Lifesaving Station Museum
Assawoman Bay Bridge
67th St
62nd St
59th St
54th St
50th St
44th St
39th St
32nd St
27th St
24th St
22nd St
18th St
13th St
6th St
1st St
Coastal Hwy
Lighthouse
Reedy Island
Assawoman Bay
Fenwick Island
Dog and Bitch Islands
Drum Island
Mallard Island
Sinepuxent Bay
Horn Island
H Kelly Memorial Bridge
Ocean City Inlet
Assateague Island
ATLANTIC OCEAN
Edgewater Ave
Philadelphia Ave
Baltimore Ave
Boardwalk
see inset map
Bayview La
St Louis Ave
3rd St
2nd St
N Division St
Caroline St
Talbot St
Dorchester St
Somerset St
Wicomico St
Worcester St
S Division St
S 1st St
S 2nd St
Municipal Pier
0 150 300 m
0 150 300 yards
MARYLAND

Orientation

Most travelers enter OC at the south end of town via Hwy 50 from Easton and Salisbury. The commercial development and summer weekend traffic jams begin miles before you cross the bridge over Sinepuxent Bay to the city. 'City' really is the right word for this resort: Except for the broad beach, there is almost no 'green' space but plenty of sunburned people in season. Once you are off the beach and boardwalk and away from the sea breeze, the summer heat can make the place feel as sticky and smoldering as Bangkok.

The two main north-south thoroughfares are Philadelphia and Baltimore Aves. Baltimore Ave runs closest to the beach. Endless traffic lights make travel along both streets slow during the summer season.

At the south end of town, you pass through blocks of east-west streets named after Eastern Shore counties like Talbot. Continuing north toward the Delaware border, you will find the east-west streets numbered 1st to 146th St. The town is generally just two or three blocks wide, although there are condo developments on pieces of land that jut out into the bay. A second bridge accesses the mainland (Route 90) at 62nd St.

Information

Tourist Offices The Convention and Visitors Bureau (☎ 410-289-8181, 800-OC-OCEAN) is in the Convention Center at 40th St and Coastal Hwy. Look for the sign that says 'Information' in the window of the Convention Center. There is also an information office in an old railway car next to the boardwalk on Worcester St and an information center on Route 50 about a quarter of a mile before you cross over the bridge to the Inlet.

Post The main post office (☎ 410-289-7819) is on Philadelphia Ave and 5th St. There is a satellite office (☎ 410-524-6039) in the north end of town at Montego Bay.

Media The most useful papers for travelers are free: Check out the *Ocean City Today* and the *Maryland Coast Dispatch*. If you are just looking for food and entertainment, pick up *Oceana* or the *Beachcomber*.

Bookstores There is a great collection of used paperbacks as well as out-of-print titles at the Mason Collection (☎ 410-213-0041), across the Hwy 50 bridge in Shantytown, West OC.

Bookworld (☎ 410-289-7466), at the heart of the action at 1st St and the boardwalk, has used and rare books as well. O'sea Books (☎ 410-213-1440) in the Phillips Beach plaza hotel at 13th St and the boardwalk is the resort's biggest discount vendor of current trade books for adults and kids.

Laundry Surprisingly, there are only two self-service laundries in OC. You will find Christine's Commercial Laundry (☎ 410-289-2269) at 1607 N Philadelphia Ave. The Crisp & Clean Laundromat (☎ 410-524-5410) is at 106 64th St.

Medical Services OC has a number of medical centers: 63rd St Medical Center (☎ 410-534-9355); 75th St Medical Center (☎ 410-524-0075); and 125th St Medical Center (☎ 410-250-8000). Atlantic General Hospital (☎ 410-641-1100) is five miles from OC on Healthway Drive in the town of Berlin.

Emergency Call 911 for police, fire, or ambulance. The Coast Guard number is ☎ 410-289-7579.

The Boardwalk

Residents built the first removable boardwalk in 1879. They laid it out to protect their tender feet from the burning sand on July 4 and packed it up in September for use again the next year. The city built the first permanent boardwalk in 1912, and the current one extends from the Inlet to 27th St. It is cement at the lower end near the Inlet but wood for most of its length. Lined with food vendors, trinket stores, arcades, and hotels, the boardwalk becomes a mob scene on hot summer

Ocean City Activities

Boat Rentals, Water-Skiing & Jet Skiing

The following places rent equipment:

Island Watersports (☎ 410-289-2896), 308-A N 1st St and the Bay at BJ's South. Jet ski rentals and parasailing.

Advanced Marina (☎ 410-723-2124) on the Bay between 66th and 67th Sts.

Bahia Marina (☎ 410-289-7438) on the Bay between 21st and 22nd Sts. Boat rentals.

Bay Sports (☎ 410-289-2144), Bahia Marina. Jet ski rentals

54th St Marina (☎ 410-723-5454), 54th St and the Bay.

Waterways Jet Ski (☎ 410-723-4227), 5307 Coastal Hwy.

Fishing – head boats & charters

Bahia Marina (☎ 410-289-7438) on the Bay between 21st and 22nd Sts.

Bay Queen (☎ 410-213-0926), Shantytown Pier on the Bay across the Hwy 50 Bridge from Ocean City.

Talbot St Pier (☎ 410-289-9125, 289-3503), Talbot St and the Bay.

Angler (☎ 410-289-7424), Talbot St and the Bay next to the Talbot St Pier.

Captain Bunting (☎ 410-289-6720), Dorchester St and the Bay.

OC Guide Service (☎ 410-289-5520). Pairs visitors with local experienced anglers.

Sailing

Therapy (☎ 410-213-0018) docks at the Ocean City Fishing Center across the Hwy 50 Bridge next to Shantytown Marina. A three-hour trip is $30 per person, with a minimum of two and maximum of six people.

Vivacious (☎ 410-213-2725), 12636 Selsey Rd. Take Hwy 50 to Keyport Point Rd. Cruises of 2 to 3½-hours are $25/35 per person with a four-person minimum. Take Hwy 50 across the bridge and go to the fourth traffic light, which will be Keyser Point Rd. Make a right and follow it for 1.4 miles until it dead-ends at Selsey Rd. Take a right on Selsey and go a third of a mile until it dead-ends at the Bay. The boat is at the Spanish-style house with the red-tile roof at 12636 Selsey Rd.

Parasailing

Island Parasail (☎ 410-213-2740),1st St and the Bay next to BJ's South. 400-, 800-, and 1200-foot parasailing for $40/50/65; tandem rides for an adult and child for $20. Jet ski rentals.

OC Parasail (☎ 410-723-1464), 54th St and the Bay. 400- and 600-foot rides for $40/50.

Watercraft Rental (☎ 410-250-2777, 302-539-8666), Sharks Cove. 400- to 1000-foot rides from $60 to $90.

Windsurfing

Sailing Etc (☎ 410-723-1144), 54th St near the Bay, teaches windsurfing to six-person groups for 2½ hours for $45 per person. It also rents windsurfers, kayaks, and catamarans.

nights. You can see the largest marlin and shark caught in Ocean City waters on display in Plexiglas cases at the southern end of the boardwalk, but watching the volume and variety of *Homo sapiens* flowing up and down the promenade can be a lot more fun.

The entire 10 miles of beach are open to the public from 6 am to 10 pm. The sands are widest in front of the parking lot between the jetty at the inlet and the pier on Wicomico St. The waves can get big here, so this is the place you will often find the surfers congregating. Although the beach narrows as you follow it north from the pier, it is still broad enough to accommo-

Cruises

Bay Queen (☎ 410-213-0926), Shantytown Pier, West Ocean City on the other side of the Hwy 50 Bridge, $7.

OC Princess (☎ 410-213-0926), Shantytown Pier, West Ocean City. Three-hour 'nature cruise' for $18.

Captain Bunting (☎ 410-289-6720), Dorchester St and the Bay. One-hour cruise $7; free if you eat dinner at AT Lantic's restaurant, 10 Talbot St.

Angler (☎ 410-289-7424), Talbot St and the Bay. One-hour evening cruises $6; free if you eat dinner at the Angler restaurant at the dock.

Judith M (☎ 410-289-7438), Bahia Marina, 21st St and the Bay. Half day of fishing $25.

Miss Ocean City (☎ 410-213-0489), N 1st St and the Bay. Half day of fishing $20.

Speedboats

Patriot Missile (☎ 410-289-0017), a 75-foot speedboat, makes 50-minute trips ($9) in the Bay, along Assateague Island, and on the ocean. It leaves from Dorchester St and the Bay.

Surfing

From May to September, the city allows surfing on only two beaches per day, one each in northern and southern Ocean City. To find out which beaches, call the beach patrol (☎ 410-289-7556) or one of the surf shops. Off-season, you can surf anywhere. *Cloud Break* (☎ 410-723-0010) at 58th St and Coastal Hwy, is one of the friendliest and most helpful. The others are listed below.

Endless Summer (☎ 410-289-3272), 38th St and Coastal Hwy; 118th St and the Bay.

K-Coast (☎ 410-789-6602), 78th St and Coastal Hwy.

Ocean Atlantic (☎ 410-289-3803), 35th St and Coastal Hwy.

Sundancer (☎ 410-289-7797), N Division St and Baltimore Ave.

Sunshine House (☎ 410-524-6004), 63rd St and Coastal Hwy.

Bicycling

Along the boardwalk, you will find an abundance of bike rentals. Some rental places aren't shops at all but just a vendor with a fleet of bicycles lined up for your inspection. You can expect to pay an hourly/daily/weekly rate of around $3/10/35 for a single-speed bike and around $4/15/50 for mountain bikes, but prices fluctuate.

Bike World (☎ 410-289-2587), 10 Caroline St.

Continental Cycle (☎ 410-524-1313), 73rd St and Coastal Hwy.

Eden Roc (☎ 410-289-6022), 20th St and Baltimore Ave.

Darlene's on the Boardwalk (☎ 410-289-6035), 12th St and the boardwalk.

Jo's Bikes (☎ 410-289-5298), 2nd St and the boardwalk.

Mike's Bikes (☎ 410-289-4637), 5 N 1st St. ■

date hundreds of thousands of sunbathers and swimmers without being even close to as crowded as, say, St Tropez, France, in August. Beach sports including Frisbee and volleyball are prohibited from 9 am to 5:30 pm. Pets, alcoholic beverages, and motor vehicles are always taboo. Lifeguards are on station daily and the beach is well groomed every night after 10 pm. The beach patrol will arrest you if they find you here after hours.

If you want to get away from the masses, try spreading out your blanket in front of one of the hotels near the northern end of the strand. In spite of the crowds, you can walk for hours every morning along the edge of the sea without seeing anyone except the occasional surf anglers.

Bathhouses

Albright Bathhouse (☎ 410-289-7349) is on N 1st St a few feet back from the boardwalk. It's very musty but clean. For $5 you are allowed one shower, but everything else is extra – soap (25¢), a towel (50¢). They store your stuff in bins for free.

The other bathhouses are Ninth St Bathhouse (☎ 410-289-9189), Baltimore Ave and 9th St, and Wicomico Bathhouse (☎ 410-289-5025) on Wicomico next to the laundry a block back from the boardwalk.

Lifesaving Station Museum

The museum (☎ 410-289-4991) is in the 1891 Lifesaving Station building on the boardwalk almost at the Inlet. It has exhibits of items recovered from the sea by divers, photos of storms that have battered Ocean City, an exhibit on the lifesaving stations of the Delmarva coast, and small models of the city's early hotels. It's open June to September daily from 11 am to 10 pm; May and October daily from 11 am to 4 pm; and in winter on weekends from noon to 4 pm. Adults/kids cost $2/1.

Delmarva Downs

This harness-racing track (☎ 410-641-0600) is about five miles from Ocean City at the intersection of Hwy 50 and Route 589. The season is from spring to Labor Day. Grandstand/clubhouse admission is $2/3.

Special Events

Ward World Championship Wildfowl Carving in April is the largest and most prestigious wildfowl carving competition in the world. There are a thousand carvers and almost $100,000 in cash prizes.

Sunfest in September is a four-day festival of food, crafts, music, and a huge kite festival with cash prizes.

Places to Stay

The Ocean City Hotel-Motel-Restaurant Association (☎ 410-289-6733, fax 410-289-5645) in the Convention Center and Visitor's Bureau on 40th St and Philadelphia Ave can be very helpful in finding you a place to stay. The staff knows the price ranges and styles and will call the hotels for you. You can also get an *Accommodations & Restaurant Guide*, which lists addresses and phone numbers of association members but no prices.

The other visitors guide, *Sea for Yourself*, lists all places that are members of the chamber of commerce, describes them, and gives some prices, although these aren't always accurate.

The cheapest places are at the southern end of town in the Inlet section. There is a seamless line of motels along Baltimore Ave from the Inlet to 33rd St. More motels line Philadelphia Ave (Coastal Hwy). The more expensive ones are farther north, particularly along 'Condo Row' between 94th and 118th Sts.

Places to Stay – bottom end

Camping In addition to the campgrounds listed here, check out the facilities at Assateague Island, 12 miles from Ocean City (see Assateague Island later in this chapter).

Ocean City Travel Park (☎ 410-524-7601) is a year-round campground right in the middle of the strip at 70th and Coastal Hwy. Most of the sites are for vehicles, but the park has about 30 tent sites. Sites, including water and sewage, are $37 from May to September and $32 other months. You might be able to bargain for cheaper rates if you have a tent, but the campground is really geared for RVs, and it is not a bucolic wonderland.

Frontier Town Campground (☎ 410-641-0880, 800-228-5590) is four miles from Ocean City. Sites without/with water and electricity are $22.50/31.50; $35 with sewage hookup; $45 for a waterfront site. The place has a pool, showers, stores, and miniature golf. From Hwy 50, just before entering Ocean City at its southern end, go south on Route 611 for about four miles and the campground is on your left.

Bali-Hi RV Park (☎ 410-352-5477) is about four miles from the center of Ocean

City. Sites with hookups are $30 and up; there are no tent sites. Take the 62nd St Bridge across the Bay from Ocean City onto Route 90. Make a right at the first blinking light, which is St Martin's Neck Rd. Go two miles and you'll see it on your left. It's open May 1 to November 1.

Hostel *Summer Place Youth Hostel* (☎ 410-289-4542), 104 Dorchester St, between Baltimore and Philadelphia Aves, is the cheapest place in town at $15 a night or $80 to $150 a week. It's really a cross between a mellow rooming house and a hostel. Kimberleigh and Van Duzee Flynn rent 10 rooms of varying sizes in their house – seven singles and three doubles. Guests have use of the kitchen, a barbecue, a sun deck, and, if you're real nice, a hot tub. The place can fill up with folks working in town for the season, so your best bet is to come in April or May.

Places to Stay – middle

If you want the true Ocean City boardwalk-Inlet experience, there is only one place to stay: the *Belmont-Hearne* (☎ 410-289-8344, 800-638-2758) at 4 Dorchester St, a few feet from the boardwalk and beach. Friendly 'Kate' Jones Bunting and family run the operation. The hotel is actually three buildings, one of which has served as a hotel since early in the century, although it has been remodeled and redivided many times since. Kate was born and raised on her block and knows the history of Ocean City inside and out. Weekday/weekend singles with sink and shared bath are $50/60; doubles are $70/80. Weekday/weekend singles with private bath are $60/70; doubles are $80/90. Efficiencies are $65 to 80 weekdays or $325 to $455 weekends. If you want a Saturday night only, the rates are higher, but they also go down a lot for longer stays. All rooms have air conditioning, and most include TV.

In September, Kate hosts weekend seafood (spiced crab, shrimp, oyster, clam), prime rib, and pig roast specials. You get two dinners and two breakfasts and a room for the weekend for around $86 per person, including tax.

Ocean Manor (☎ 410-289-9050), 107 Wicomico St between Philadelphia and Baltimore Aves, has 20 rooms and a number of efficiencies and apartments. The rooms are small, neat, and clean and go for $50/315 daily/weekly. Efficiencies are $450 a week. Off-season rates are 25 to 30% less.

The *Surf Villa Hotel* (☎ 410-289-9434), 705 N Baltimore Ave, has 25 rooms with air conditioning and TV and access to a kitchen, which is a boon in a town where eating out can be costly and/or disappointing. This hotel is a sunny, airy, and immaculate retreat a block from the beach. Double rooms cost $39 from May to September, $59 in June, and $69 July and August. Add $6 to $10 for each extra person and $10 to $20 for weekends. There are a few rooms with shared baths; these are $5 to $10 less.

Conner's Inn (☎ 410-289-7721) is at 2 N 10th St half a block from the ocean. It has about 25 rooms that rent between $50 and $125 depending on size and month. The house is clean and airy but packed with rooms, all of which have air conditioning and TVs. There are three large porches with ocean views. You get breakfast and use of bicycles and beach umbrellas.

Among the hundred or so motels, check out the *Admiral* (☎ 410-289-6280, 800-292-6280). It takes up the entire square block between 8th and 9th Sts and Baltimore and Philadelphia Aves. It's one four-story hotel and a series of one-story motel buildings and a pool. The hotel rates are cheapest at $65 to $75; the motel costs $80 and up. The rooms are average size with air conditioning and TVs, and the furniture is slightly worn.

The *Breakers* (☎ 410-289-9165), 3rd St and boardwalk, has 35 rooms in various sizes. Double rates start at $75 with ocean front at the upper end. Rooms are clean and sport newish motel furniture and some attempts at Victorian touches. It's a pretty good deal for the size and location.

The *Islander Motel* (☎ 410-289-9179) is at 20th St and Philadelphia Ave. Motel rooms are $55 to $70, and efficiency rates are $65 to $85 throughout the summer and less in May and September.

The *Plim Plaza* (☎ 410-289-6181, 800-638-2106) is on the boardwalk at 2nd St. The hotel sets up rockers on a porch next to the boardwalk. This is clearly a place for ardent Christians to stay. On the beach in front of the hotel, guests sometimes build larger-than-life sand sculptures of a crucified Jesus, Jesus's face, and religious aphorisms which are lit-up at night. Weekday/weekend doubles, which feature pink and blue veneer furniture, TV, air conditioning, and refrigerators, are $104/119 for no view and $111/126 for oceanview in season. Off-season rates are $56 for no view and $59 for oceanview.

Places to Stay – top end

Fager's Island (☎ 410-723-6100, 800-767-6060, fax 524-9327) has two hotels offering the most distinctive ambiance in town. You will find the *Lighthouse* at 56th St on the bay (literally) and the *Coconut Malorie* on adjacent property at 60th St and Coastal Hwy, bay side. The Malorie has a white-marble lobby. The rooms are all suites with Jacuzzis, marble bathrooms, refrigerators, and TVs. The Lighthouse is a large replica of the octagonal lighthouses that used to sit on shoals in the Chesapeake. The hotel has 23 rooms arranged in a circle on two floors, most with good bay views. They also have marble bathrooms with Jacuzzis. Rates at both hotels range from $129 to $299 in season , slightly less off season.

Taylor House B&B (☎ 410-289-1177), 1001 Baltimore Ave, has four rooms furnished in antiques and reproductions. The house is a former casino and speakeasy. A lot of the rooms have cypress paneling, and the fireplace in the living room is made of stones from the old lighthouse in Cape Henlopen, Delaware. In-season rates for rooms with shared/private bath are $95/130, including full breakfast. Off-season they are $50 to $60 for shared bath and $65 to $90 for private bath. It's open year round.

The *Dune's Manor Hotel* (☎ 410-289-1100, 800-523-2888), at 28th St and Baltimore Ave, is the large pink high-rise that looks like a mix of Victorian and Bauhaus. All of its rooms face the ocean. The hotel has an indoor-outdoor pool, a porch with rockers, and daily tea. Summer rooms are from $125 to $189. With off-season rates from $79 to $95, the Dunes can be a value.

The *Sheraton Fontainebleau Hotel* (☎ 410-524-3535, 800-638-2100) is on condo row at 101st St and Coastal Hwy. The hotel has a health spa and balconies, but the rooms have a generic architecture and decor. All rooms face north or south with only partial ocean view. Summer double rates are $179 to $199 – too much for what you get.

The *Princess Royale* (☎ 410-524-7777), 91st St and Coastal Hwy, is a condo-hotel complex. Many rooms overlook the four-story indoor atrium and pool. The rooms on the same level as the pool look out at the people walking past your sliding-glass door. All of the furniture is new and all rooms have kitchens and electronic safes. Off-season rates are $124 to $169, in-season rates $199 to $259.

Places to Eat

The visitors guide advertises that there are over over 22,000 restaurant seats in Ocean City. Here, both purveyors and customers seem to judge dining by quantity. You will find a lot of seafood on the menus, and you will discover that most larger restaurants serve all-you-can-eat meals. In addition, OC's boardwalk tenders a plethora of burgers, hot dogs, pizza, ice cream, and candy. As you can imagine, quality varies immensely, not just according to your choice of eatery but also according to how the day has been going for the college students preparing or serving your meal. There are few professionals in OC's food service industry.

If you're looking for cheap eats, *Matteo's* (☎ 410-289-6409) at Baltimore Ave and Talbot St, has $1 to $1.35 tacos, burritos for $3.75, and wings in 6/12/24 count at $3/5/10.50.

Soriano's is a diner on Baltimore Ave between Dorchester and Somerset Sts. *Fat Daddy's Sub Shop* serves cheese steaks and sandwiches at the corner of Talbot St and Baltimore Ave. *Regal Restaurant*, corner of Caroline St and Baltimore, is another diner. It advertises the best coffee in town, but the service can be slow.

Captain Bob's (☎ 410-524-7070) is a family restaurant at 64th on the bay. OC veterans flock there for steaks, chicken and side dishes like peas, cole slaw, potato salad, and mashed potatoes. A half chicken, two sides, and a roll is under $8.

La Hacienda (☎ 410-524-8080), 80th St and Coastal Hwy, has economic, authentic Mexican fare from 5 pm on. Most dishes cost under $10. Another is *Tio Gringo's*, Coastal Hwy between 53rd and 54th Sts.

Seacrets (☎ 410-524-4900), 49th St and the Bay, has good Caribbean dishes in a great atmosphere – sand-covered pathways, tables on the bay, and several bars. You can get jerk chicken ($6.25), a Jamaican burger with green and red onions and spices ($6), Jamaican pizza ($5.50 plus $1 per topping), and ribs with jerk spices ($10 and $15.50). There always two-for-one food deals and early-bird specials (before 6:30 pm).

The *Hobbit* (☎ 410-524-8100), 81st St and the Bay, is one of OC's better restaurants with no all-you-can-stuff deals. Tables overlook the Bay and seafood entrees are in the $20 range.

In search of all-you-can-eat breakfasts, head for *English's Family Restaurant* (☎ 410-289-7333) at 15th or 137th Sts and Coastal Hwy ($5), and *Embers* (☎ 410-289-3322) at 24th St and Philadelphia Ave ($6.50), which also has a lunch buffet for $19. The *Princess Royale* hotel (☎ 410-524-7777), 91st St and Coastal Hwy, serves a brunch buffet on Sundays for $11, and a lunch buffet for $18.

For crabs try *Higgins Crab House* (☎ 410-289-2581), 31st and Coastal Hwy. Your money goes a little further here than it does in many crab houses: Eat all-you-want steamed crabs, fried chicken, Alaskan crab legs, spiced shrimp, crab soup, and corn on the cob for about $13. The oldest crab house is *Phillips Crab House* (☎ 410-289-6821), 21st St and Philadelphia Ave. Phillips started as a shack and now, after countless additions, seats around 1500. All-you-can-inhale crabs are $19 ($17 before 5:30 pm).

Other places with buffets, which usually include seafood, are *Happy Jack Pancake House* (☎ 410-289-7377), 26th St and Coastal Hwy ($8), and *Jonah & the Whale* (☎ 410-524-2722), 26th St and the boardwalk ($16).

An all-you-can-eat Chinese buffet is available at the *Bonfire* (☎ 410-524-7171), 71st St and Coastal Hwy ($14).

Adolfo's (☎ 410-289-4001), at the Inlet end of Baltimore Ave, serves all-you-can-eat spaghetti and meatballs for $7. You can find upscale northern Italian at *Tutti Gusti* (☎ 410-289-3318) at 33rd St and Coastal Hwy. You can whet your appetite on homemade bread served with olive oil and a garlic clove. Servings are substantial enough to split, and many cost under $12.

Entertainment

Dutch Bar (☎ 410-289-5557), on the boardwalk, stands a few doors north of Dorchester St near the Belmont-Hearne Hotel. The place is narrow, just wide enough for the bar and some stools, but widens at the back to accommodate a couple of pool tables and a juke box stocked with heavy metal music. All the beer is in bottles or cans. Most clients are under 25.

A block up the boardwalk from Dutch Bar is the *Purple Moose Saloon* (☎ 410-289-6953). The Moose has loud live music at the back and looks to be the clubhouse for the University of Maryland men's and women's lacrosse teams.

Lined up on Wicomico St right off the boardwalk and the pier are the *Cork Bar*, the *Bearded Clam*, and *Daisy's Wheel House*. These are three popular and rather sleazy local bars that offer a host of happy-hour deals to pack in an eclectic crowd – including a lot of day-trippers who park in the nearby public lot and take to the highways after tanking up. OC and state police are vigilant for speeders and drunk drivers, but in this party town the bad guys outnumber the good guys by thousands.

Seacrets (☎ 410-524-4900), 49th St and the Bay, has the best atmosphere of any bar in town. The place is constructed on and around the Bay and has five bars, including one in a wooden boat on the beach. Tables overlook the Bay, and there are lots of palm trees (which are replaced every summer). During the day you can drink while sitting on small floating tubes in the shallow part of the Bay. There is live music five nights a week in the summer and three nights in winter. Bands cover perennial OC favorites like Jimmy Buffett and Bruce Hornsby (a good ole Tidewater boy from Virginia). You can also hear some great reggae with Jamaican bands out of Baltimore and DC.

The *Big Kahuna*, *Paddock*, and *Croon Tunes* (☎ 410-289-6331, 289-6335) are three connected nightspots at 18th St and Philadelphia Ave. If there is a cover, $3 to $5 gets you into all of them. Kahuna's has a surf-bar atmosphere, and the Paddock is a large dance floor with half a Volkswagen embedded in the wall. Croon Tunes draws in some uninhibited karaoke singers.

Fager's Island (☎ 410-524-5500) is at 60th St and the Bay behind the Coconut Malorie hotel (the one with the blue neon sign that says 'Suite Hotel' on top). Fager's has five bars on the bay and a boardwalk across the water to a gazebo offshore. They've got rock music on weekends with no cover.

A slightly older crowd drinks at the *Ocean Club* (☎ 410-524-7500), at 49th St on the ocean. It has live rock bands as well as piano or acoustic music seven days a week inside and an outdoor bar above the restaurant ('crow's nest bar') from which you can look out onto the ocean.

Gay Nightlife At first it seems strange that a resort the size of OC has no gay bars or entertainment, but OC has a distinctly 'hetero' character. Gays and lesbians prefer the open, tolerant atmosphere at Rehoboth Beach, Delaware, a few miles north of OC where there are a lot of gay-owned businesses and a substantial gay community.

Things to Buy

Joe Kroart runs the Ocean Gallery World Center (☎ 410-289-5300) at 2nd St and the boardwalk. Billed as the gallery with the most paintings per sq foot in the world, Ocean Gallery is a two-story building where a lot of framed reproductions and poster art are piled on top of each other in a maze of passages. Mr. Kroart does showcase local and regional artists, who often come to openings, but individual paintings outside of the shows lose their impact in the clutter.

Kite Loft stores sell a broad selection of kites and flying accessories. They are on boardwalk at 5th St (☎ 410-289-6852); 45th St and Coastal Hwy (☎ 410-524-0800); and 131st and Coastal Hwy (☎ 410-250-4970). These folks sponsor the dramatic kite-flying events that take place at the Sun Festival in September every year.

Cloud Break surf shop (☎ 410-723-0010), 58th St and Coastal Hwy, sells a T-shirt with a picture of Charles Manson on the front. On the back of the shirt are the words 'Charlie Don't Surf' for cognoscenti who think Robert Duvall's line in *Apocalypse Now* codifies the American character with a healthy sense of irony. This sense of irony seems to grow in people the longer they spend among OC excesses.

Getting There & Away

Air The Ocean City Municipal Airport (☎ 410-213-2471) is three miles west of town on Route 611 if you come by charter or private plane. There is a fair amount of traffic around OC, and it is not unreasonable to consider hitching a ride with a private pilot to new destinations. Weekends are good days to meet pilots in transit.

USAir (☎ 800-428-4322) services the Salisbury-Wicomico County Regional Airport with flights to Washington, Baltimore, and Philadelphia. The airport is 20 miles away from OC.

Bus The Carolina Trailways Station (☎ 410-289-9307) is at 2nd St and Philadelphia Ave. There is regularly scheduled service to/from major cities in the region.

Car Most people coming from the west take Hwy 50 from the Baltimore-Washington area across the Delmarva Peninsula and right into Ocean City at the Inlet. You can also exit Hwy 50 onto Route 90 about 12 miles before entering Ocean City. This will bring you into OC at 62nd St and avoid some traffic.

Coming south on the Delmarva coast from the Delaware beaches stay on Route 1, which enters Ocean City at 146th St and becomes Coastal Hwy/Philadelphia Ave.

If you're coming north from Virginia, take Route 13 to Route 113 in Maryland and follow this to Hwy 50, which will then lead you into the Inlet.

Getting Around

Parking Meters are in effect 24 hours a day and parking can be a problem on summer weekends. There are some lots along Philadelphia Ave. You can park for free at the Convention Center at 40th St, but this is a long walk from everything. Luckily, most places to stay give guests a parking space.

Buses City buses (☎ 410-723-1607) run daily from the Inlet to the Delaware state line. They run south from the state line along Coastal Hwy/Philadelphia Ave to S Division St and north from the Inlet along Baltimore Ave to 17th St, and then go west one block and continue north on Coastal Hwy/Philadelphia Ave. Buses run about every 10 minutes during the summer and every half hour otherwise. You can ride all day for $1.

Boardwalk 'Train' This is a train of connected golf-cart-like cars pulled by a Jeep. The train runs up and down the boardwalk from south to north about every 20 minutes from Easter to the first weekend in October. The fare is $1.50. You can buy a ticket at either end of the boardwalk or hail the train and pay the conductor sitting at the end of the last car exact change.

Water Taxi Water Taxi of Ocean City (☎ 410-213-0126) connects 14 points (actually 14 restaurants at these points) on the mainland and along the Bay in Ocean City below 14th St. The fare is $1 to $3. Call the pager (☎ 410-546-8800) and enter a code number (one to 14); the taxi boat will pick you up.

ASSATEAGUE ISLAND

Just across the ocean inlet at the south end of OC lies Assateague, the 37-mile-long barrier island that is as wild in fact as Ocean City is in spirit. Assateague is a national park (the Assateague Island National Seashore) in which there is also a small state park (Assateague State Park). One of the biggest attractions of the island are the herds of wild horses that live there. The name 'Assateague' is a corruption of an Indian name for 'marshy place across' – as in across from the mainland. Before Hurricane Hazel carved out the inlet in 1933, Assateague was part of OC. In the minds of nature lovers, the hurricane was nothing short of an act of divine intervention.

Orientation & Information

The lower third of Assateague is in the state of Virginia and can be visited via the town of Chincoteague (see Virginia's Eastern Shore). From Ocean City it's 11 miles by road.

The Barrier Island Visitor Center (☎ 410-641-1441) is on Route 611 before you enter the park. There are a few exhibits here, and you can pick up maps and information. It costs $4 per vehicle to enter the national park; cyclists and walk-in visitors pay $2. This price is a good deal since you get a permit good for a week with your payment. The fee-collection booth is on the island after you drive through the state park. The official national park handbook, *Assateague Island*, by the renowned marine

Wild Horses

Although most people use the word 'ponies' to describe the herds of wild hooved animals roaming Assateague, they are, in fact, horses. Folklore claims that the Assateague horses are the descendants of the four-legged cargo of a shipwrecked Spanish galleon. More likely the herds' progenitors escaped from domestic stock grazing on the island during the 17th century. Livestock owners kept animals here to circumvent colonial laws requiring livestock to be fenced and taxed.

ROBERT DE GAST

There are two herds of about 150 animals each on the island separated by a fence at the Maryland-Virginia border. The National Park Service manages the Maryland herd and the Volunteer Fire Department in Chincoteague, Virginia, owns and manages the Virginia herd. Every year on the last Wednesday and Thursday of July the fire department rounds up the Virginia herd and swims it across to Chincoteague where a number of the foals and yearlings are auctioned off to pay the fire department's operating expenses. The rest of the horses swim back. The story of one such foal, *Misty of Chincoteague* by Marguerite Henry, is a classic of American children's literature. The tale is largely responsible for canonizing Assateague's wild horses as symbols of mystery and freedom.

The highest bid so far for a pony was $3000 (in 1994), but the average is around $600. A carnival atmosphere pervades the week preceding 'pony penning.' There are pony races and other events. Many of the locals quip that the ponies are treated much better than the locals are, not only in July but at all times of the year.

You can see the Maryland herd roaming almost anywhere on Assateague, especially along the roads, in the parking areas, and near the beach in the summer. In other seasons, look in the salt marsh.

Note: Every year several people get bitten or kicked because they ignored warnings not to approach the horses or try to feed or pet them. Leave these animals in peace! ■

MARYLAND

biologist William H Amos may be purchased at the visitors centers.

Wildlife

Assateague is a good place for bird watching. You can see snowy egrets, dunlins, great blue herons, and black-crowned night herons. The island is also one of the primary winter roosts for the endangered snow goose. The large waterfowl wing here from Labrador by the tens of thousands. When they take flight in early spring the sky fills with their haunting calls and the hum of beating wings.

The island also has red foxes, white-tailed and sika deer, opossums, bats, river otter, and the Delmarva Peninsula fox squirrel, which you might spot in wooded areas of the Chincoteague Wildlife Refuge in Virginia.

Fishing

Many visitors come to Assateague to go crabbing and collect shellfish. Surf fishing for mackerel, blue fish, and striped bass (rock fish) is popular along the beaches.

Camping

There are three camping areas in the park: national park backcountry sites, and national park and state park sites that you pay for.

The National Park Service maintains six backcountry camping areas: State Line and

Little Levels on the beach, and the bayside sites of Pope Bay, Jims Gut, Pine Tree, and Tingles Island. The oceanside sites are open year round, the bayside sites from February 1 to October 31. The sites have only picnic tables and a chemical toilet. All the sites are wild and attractive, although they don't have access to fresh water. The oceanside sites are among the dunes, and the bayside sites are in pine tree groves (except the Pope Bay site, which has only limited shade). They are from two to 14 miles from the end of the road in the park. You have to be self-sufficient, with tent, food, and an adequate supply of water. You must register with the ranger station/campground registration office in the *national* park after you drive through the state park. Permits are issued a maximum of 24 hours in advance and will cost $5 on top of the $4 entrance fee. Don't forget insect repellent, sturdy shoes for sand walking, and hard soled shoes for wading in the bay.

The National Park Service also has an oceanside and a bayside campground with 104 and 49 sites respectively near the parking areas along the access road in the National Seashore area. These sites have access to toilets, drinking water, and outdoor showers. The oceanside campground is open year round and the bayside one from spring to fall. You can reserve a spot from May 15 to October 15 by calling ☎ 800-365-2267. When they answer, punch in the letters 'ASSA' and respond to the prompts. Sites cost $12 a night, $10 off season. If you have questions, call the Sinepuxent Ranger Station/Campground Office (☎ 410-641-3030).

The Assateague State Park (☎ 410-641-2120) has 311 campsites with hot showers and bathrooms at $20 per night. These sites are rather close together in the state park, which you enter first as you come across the bridge onto the island. About half of the sites may be reserved; the others are kept open on a first-come, first-served basis.

Getting There & Around

Take Route 611 from Hwy 50 to Assateague. It's 11 miles south of Ocean City. The Chincoteague National Wildlife Refuge is the southern Virginia half of the island. To get there take Hwy 50 west from Ocean City to Route 113 south to Route 13 south. Five miles after you cross the Virginia state line take State Road 175 east to the park. It's 55 miles south of Ocean City by road.

You may drive off-road vehicles along the beach from the end of the paved road to the Virginia border, but you have to buy a yearly permit for $40 issued at the ranger station to do so. There are 16 parking areas along the beach.

Delaware

Facts about Delaware

What a difference a bay makes. Like Maryland and Virginia, Delaware is one of America's original 13 colonies, sharing strong roots with other Tidewater states; the three states also share the Delmarva Peninsula. But unlike its southern and western neighbors, Delaware does not face the sheltered meanders of the Chesapeake and its tributaries.

Instead, tucked into the northeast corner of the peninsula, Delaware faces the rougher waters of the Atlantic and the Delaware Bay, an estuary that lies exposed to the open Atlantic. A tugboat captain who tows barges through both the Delaware and the Chesapeake offered this perspective on the difference between the two bodies of water: 'The Chesapeake is a milk run in almost any weather – you can kick back and relax; the Delaware – when the wind comes hard against a tide – can be a test. This is not a place for your common Joe or the faint of heart.'

The captain might have been speaking of the state of Delaware as well. The wind and waves that have whipped the sand into the huge dunes at Cape Henlopen have all but hewn Delaware's 100 miles of coast, Atlantic and bay alike, into one weathered piece. In keeping with the tough climes and landscapes, the state has long been a locus for rugged individualism, courage, extraordinary accomplishment, and – occasionally – sheer madness.

An often-told legend asserts that ancient Egyptians visited Delaware and brought the state's lotus plants with them, but most evidence points to Native Americans as the earliest residents. Recent archaeological finds indicate that the first people may have been Owascos, who migrated from near the Finger Lakes in New York. The first Native Americans that European immigrants encountered were Algonquin people. The Lenni-Lenape ('the people'), called the 'Delaware' by Europeans, lived on both shores of the northern Delaware River. The best-known southern peoples were the Nanticoke and Assateague. Although European real estate trickery and disease forced most Native Americans out of the state by the mid-18th century, a small but strong community of Nanticoke people continues to live about 12 miles west of Rehoboth Beach along the Indian River and holds a yearly powwow in September.

Dutch, Swedes, and English began arriving in the 17th century, as did Africans who were brought as slaves. A hundred years later a wave of Scotch-Irish immigrants descended on Delaware along with some Welsh and French. Central and southern Europeans came in the 19th century. Most immigrants went to northern New Castle county, which had the port of Wilmington, industry, and proximity to jobs in the rapidly developing metropolis of Philadelphia just up the river.

Although Delaware received its initial groups of immigrants from Europe, most recent immigrants have actually migrated from within the United States – from Pennsylvania or the Eastern Shore of Maryland. Today only about half of Delaware's population was actually born in the state, with almost two thirds living in northern New Castle county.

Ranking as America's second-smallest state (after Rhode Island), Delaware is often overlooked by all but shoppers searching for tax-free bargains (no sales tax) and entrepreneurs incorporating their businesses here to take advantage of the state's tax incentives and liberal incorporation laws. Immigrants and travelers have all but forgotten about Delaware Bay, even though it is the second largest estuary on the Atlantic coast. And Delaware is better known for being the headquarters of chemical giant Du Pont (as well as half the other Fortune 500 corporations) than as a destination for the wild at heart.

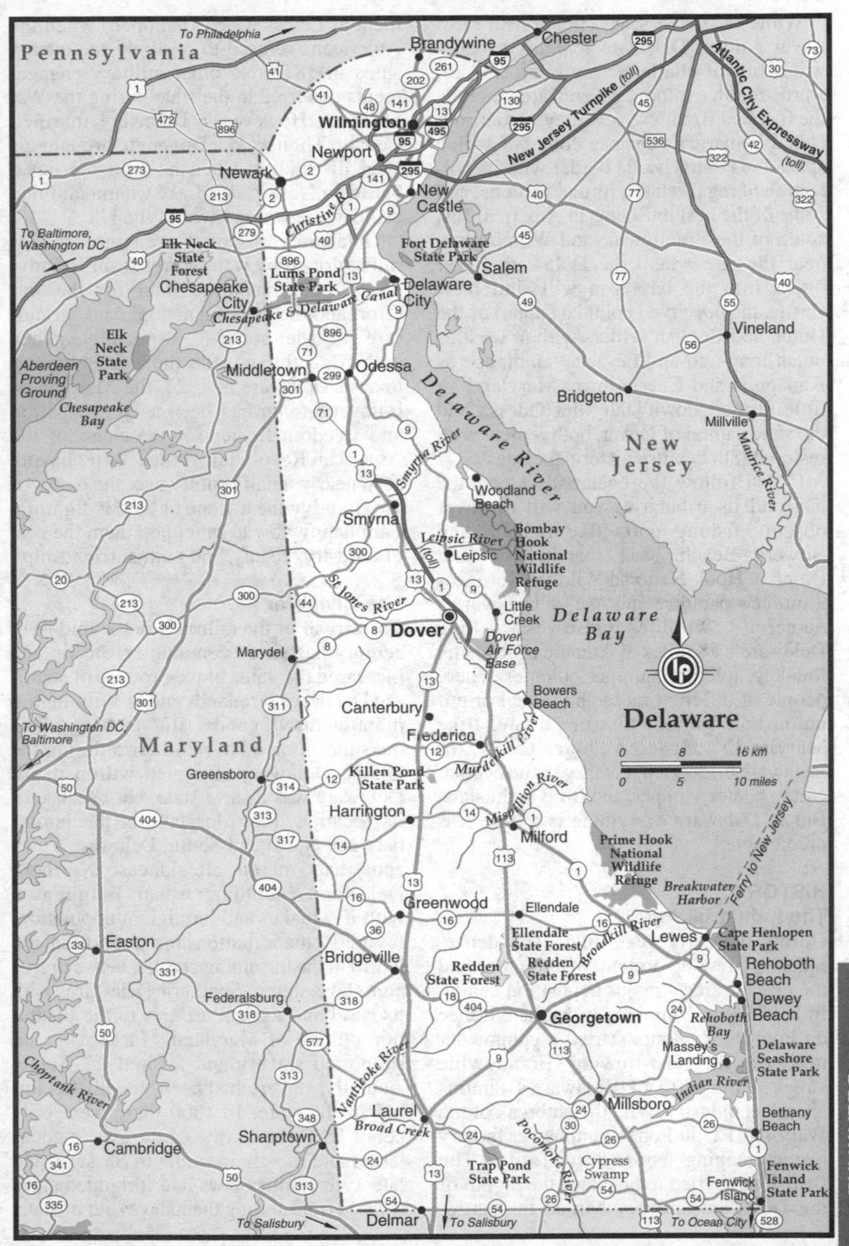
To Philadelphia
Pennsylvania
Brandywine
Chester
Atlantic City Expressway
(toll)
New Jersey Turnpike (toll)
Wilmington
Newport
Newark
New Castle
Christine R
To Baltimore, Washington DC
Elk Neck State Forest
Chesapeake City
Lums Pond State Park
Fort Delaware State Park
Salem
Delaware City
Chesapeake & Delaware Canal
Elk Neck State Park
Aberdeen Proving Ground
Chesapeake Bay
Middletown
Odessa
Vineland
Bridgeton
Millville
Maurice River
Delaware River
New Jersey
Smyrna River
Woodland Beach
Smyrna
Leipsic River
(toll)
Leipsic
Bombay Hook National Wildlife Refuge
St Jones River
Little Creek
Delaware Bay
Dover
Dover Air Force Base
Marydel
Bowers Beach
To Washington DC, Baltimore
Canterbury
Frederica
Murderkill River
Maryland
Delaware
0 8 16 km
0 5 10 miles
Greensboro
Killen Pond State Park
Mispillion River
Harrington
Milford
Prime Hook National Wildlife Refuge
Breakwater Harbor
Ferry to New Jersey
Greenwood
Ellendale
Ellendale State Forest
Broadkill River
Lewes
Cape Henlopen State Park
Easton
Bridgeville
Redden State Forest
Redden State Forest
Rehoboth Beach
Dewey Beach
Federalsburg
Georgetown
Rehoboth Bay
Massey's Landing
Delaware Seashore State Park
Choptank River
Nanticoke River
Indian River
Laurel
Millsboro
Broad Creek
Pocomoke River
Bethany Beach
Sharptown
Cambridge
Trap Pond State Park
Cypress Swamp
Fenwick Island
Fenwick Island State Park
To Salisbury
Delmar
To Salisbury
To Ocean City

While receiving scant attention in most travel guides, Delaware remains a backwater full of challenge, mystery, and rewards for an explorer. The rewards include the forested Brandywine Valley, sometimes called 'America's chateau country,' which spans the Pennsylvania border with its collection of regal estates, formal gardens, and some of the best museums in America. Just south of the Brandywine and Wilmington, near the site where the Delaware River opens into the bay, you will find New Castle, the preserved colonial capital of the Dutch and English settlers with at least as much long-ago-and-far-away ambiance as Annapolis and Chestertown, Maryland. A little further 'down state' lies Odessa and the state capital of Dover, both replete with restored l8th century historical centers.

If you follow the backroads along the bay and its tributaries you will discover obscure fishing ports like Leipsic and Bowers Beach, vast marshlands, and Bombay Hook National Wildlife Refuge – a birder's paradise and one of Delaware's numerous wildlife preserves. Along Delaware's 28 miles of Atlantic beaches lie low-key, tolerant summer colonies where people of different races and sexual orientation mix without fuss or fanfare. Like Maryland's Eastern Shore, most of Delaware offers rich territory to the cyclist, cartop boater, camper, and B&B enthusiast. But in Delaware everything is a little less predictable.

HISTORY

The Industrial Age

During the early years of independence, industry grew up around Wilmington, and the city became a major population center. In 1802 French immigrant Eleuthère Irénée du Pont de Nemours started a gunpowder mill on the fast-flowing Brandywine Creek – the birth of Delaware's famous chemical industry. With the outbreak of the War of 1812, du Pont's gunpowder factory began reaping enormous profits. The British navy tried to blockade the mouth of the Delaware and bombarded the settlement at Lewes (Cape Henlopen) when the Americans refused to resupply the enemy ships in 1813. No other military engagements occurred in the state during the War of 1812. However, a Delaware mariner, Captain Thomas MacDonough, brought his state distinction when he won the naval battle on New York's Lake Champlain that decided the war in favor of the US.

Delaware prospered even more as its mills, driven by waterpower from Brandywine Creek, supplied flour for the war effort and the growing nation. And agriculture in the south – especially peach orchards – thrived after the war. Returning to visit Delaware in 1824, the Marquis de Lafayette, who had been a French patron and freedom fighter for the cause of the American Revolution, wrote, 'After having seen nearly a half century ago, the banks of the Brandywine a scene of bloody fighting, I am happy now to find upon them the seat of industry, beauty, and mutual friendship.'

The Civil War

The arrival of the railroads in the mid-19th century hastened economic expansion and increased the value of the produce of southern Delaware farmlands and of Wilmington manufactured goods. But as the 'slave question' loomed over America during the 1850s, Delaware struggled within itself. Delaware was a slave state, but because of its location, like Maryland at the border between North and South, Delaware's citizens had mixed allegiances. Northern Delaware, including urban Wilmington with its Quaker and immigrant population, favored emancipation and supported the North in the unfolding conflict between free and slave states. Southern Delaware, with its rural and agriculture ties to the plantation culture of Maryland's Eastern Shore, supported slavery and favored the South. Actually, slavery had been steadily declining in the state. In 1860 there were only about 1800 slaves (8% of the state's population and mostly in southern Sussex), and late 17th century laws had forbidden slave owners from selling their slaves out of state.

Tall Tales

If you take the time to explore the secondary roads or tidal streams of Kent and Sussex Counties that run to the remote and marshy fringes of Delaware and Assawoman Bays, you may come across a solitary character known locally as a 'progger.' A progger is like a waterman; he makes a living from the bay fishing, catching turtles, crabbing, oystering, or trapping muskrats. But unlike a waterman, a progger is not much interested in earning more than a subsistence living. He often lives in a primitive shack along the tidewater and works only when he needs money, the weather is 'right,' or he just feels the urge. Proggers are notorious for two things – ignoring fish and game laws . . . and telling elaborate tall tales full of the mystery and hard times that typify the literature of Delaware. On the bay's shores, tale telling and the poaching of game often go hand in hand.

One day while exploring the marshland in Bombay Hook National Wildlife Refuge by canoe, we came across a progger splashing around in an old boat on the edge of a tidal creek that feeds into the Leipsic River. He might have been setting an illegal net across the creek to catch fish on the ebb tide, but we had no time to look for the evidence. Eyeing us like we might be conservation or game officers, the progger, who claimed he would be 82 the next month, paddled his boat alongside our canoe, grabbed our gunwales and trapped us with a serio-comic tale of hard times down the road:

'Gave up perch fishin'. Several reasons. Got tired of the expense. Then I was fool enough to catch a lot of fish; had to clean 'em. Then I got to deliver 'em. Ones I had left someone took from my refrigerator. So no more of that. I quit bein' everybody's fool. Besides weather's hot, and I can't take this here heat. Anyway I don't like fish. Wouldn't give you a dime for three of 'em.'

As the yarn unraveled, the progger switched the subject away from fishing and for several minutes he blasted the federal government for the high cost of construction:

'Why I can't even build a doghouse without a permit. All our natural privileges is gone. Them dirty culprits down in Washington ought to be hung by the neck at sunrise . . . '

At last the progger took his hands off the gunwale of our canoe, and we paddled away feeling somehow more informed, or at least less alone in the swamp, than we had before our encounter. The progger gave us a smile and a wave. As we turned a bend in the creek and started to lose sight of him, he began thrashing around with something beneath the stern of his boat that had all the markings of a perch net. ■

Although many Delaware residents supported the right of the Southern states to secede, Delaware itself did not secede. To ensure loyalty the federal government took actions in Delaware similar to those imposed on Maryland, suspending of the writ of habeas corpus, disarming questionable militia units, and supervising elections. Quaker residents and their allies helped escaped slaves make it to the North on the Underground Railroad, smuggling many blacks across Delaware Bay to Quaker free state outposts like Greenwich, New Jersey. During the Civil War, the state contributed proportionally more men under arms than any other Union state . . . and paid heavily. More than half of the Delaware troops at the bloody Battle of Antietam died in combat. (For more on that battle site, see the Western Maryland chapter.) Meanwhile du Pont's gunpowder factories grew rich on the war effort, and 12,500 Confederate prisoners filled the Union prison at Fort Delaware on Pea Patch Island near the bay head at Delaware City. Before the fighting ended, 2700 of these prisoners had died from cholera, malaria, and other diseases spread by unsanitary conditions and the bay's fierce mosquitoes.

After the war, the federal government instituted various Reconstruction efforts to ensure African Americans' suffrage and equality. However, beginning in 1873

Delaware's post-war Democratic government disenfranchised blacks through state tax and literacy laws. The Democratic party said it was not 'morally bound' by any of the new national constitutional amendments that empowered blacks. African Americans' struggle to ensure the right to vote continued well into the 20th century, and racial segregation remained a fact of life in Delaware's two southern counties until the 1950s.

The 20th Century

Out-of-state corporations took over many Delaware companies in the latter 19th and early 20th centuries. But the Du Pont corporation's phenomenal growth kept the state's economy tracking at the forefront of the Industrial Revolution. By the outset of WWI, Du Pont, known as the 'powder trust,' produced 90% of America's gunpowder, and heirs of the fortune were building chateaux in the style of French royalty all over the Brandywine Valley. Delaware prospered during WWI, largely due to du Pont and other munitions manufacturers, who expanded into the field of chemicals, fertilizers, and synthetic products like nylon.

Several of Delaware's du Pont millionaires spent money on improvements to the state. Coleman du Pont built a highway and donated it to the state (from 1911 to 1924), Alfred I du Pont set up a pension fund for the aged (1931), and Pierre S du Pont spent $2 million for African American schools when the state balked at doing so (1920s). Henry F du Pont built his fabulous estate Winterthur, filled it with the largest and best collection of early American antiques in the country and

Delaware Bay

South of the Chesapeake & Delaware Canal, the Delaware River opens into Delaware Bay. This broad, shallow bay covers over 1000 sq miles. Like the Chesapeake, Delaware Bay is the basin for a glacial river that once opened into the Atlantic at the edge of the Continental Shelf during the last ice age 10,000 years ago. Shaped like the prehistoric horseshoe crab that breeds here by the hundreds of thousands, the bay sees more than 3000 ships a year – many of them oil tankers and auto carriers – pass through its waters. Currently, Wilmington-Philadelphia-Camden constitutes the second busiest port in America.

But before this almost endless parade of ships filled the bay, it was a productive fishing ground to rival the Chesapeake. During the early part of the 20th century mile-long nets stretched across the bay's shallows to catch sturgeon that yielded the bulk of the world's caviar.

Until the 1950s hundreds of schooners, twice the size of Chesapeake skipjacks, dredged for oysters in the Maurice River Cove and on the bars off the mouths of the Smyrna, Leipsic, and Mispillion Rivers. But the Russians usurped the caviar business, a strange disease called MSX ravished the oyster beds, and the watermen dragged their schooners into the marshes to die. Today, after twenty-five years of environmental protection, Delaware Bay supports a small group of diehard watermen who crab and catch oysters from small boats. A handful of the old oyster schooners remain, but all of them have been converted to power, their masts and sails long gone.

Today few people experience the bay waters although local anglers know that Delaware Bay is once again a great place to fish for weak fish (sea trout), shad, and rock fish (striped bass). Unlike the Chesapeake, with its dozens of charming harbors and bayside villages, Delaware Bay remains a much wilder place with a coastline of broad marshlands, tidal creeks, and isolated beaches. Wading birds, turtles, and waterfowl love it. During the midsummer full moon, thousands upon thousands of horseshoe crabs – one of the earth's most primitive species – come ashore to lay their eggs. Watermen harvest the creatures for bait in eel and crab traps. ■

ultimately set up Winterthur as the nation's foremost museum of Americana.

In January 1996 another of the du Pont heirs, John E, brought international attention to his celebrated family. In a fit of paranoia he allegedly murdered an Olympic wrestling champion who was his friend and a guest at du Pont's Brandywine Valley manor just across the border in Pennsylvania. Subsequent to the murder, du Pont, an able sharp shooter and gun collector, held local police at bay for three days before being captured. The murder and standoff created a media circus with network TV newscasters raising questions about whether du Pont (who had apparently been delusional for some time) had been protected by his prominent family and tolerated by local law enforcers because of his wealth and connections.

Beyond the world of the du Ponts, advances in technology, particularly refrigeration, allowed the southern part of Delaware to become increasingly integrated into the regional economy. Kent and Sussex counties shipped poultry, dairy products, and vegetables widely. But, as in most parts of the US during the 20th century, farm employment declined, and more workers moved to Du Pont, International Latex, and other firms. Production for WWII continued Delaware's prosperity with huge oil refineries developing along the bay at places like Delaware City.

While few people were noticing, pollution from Delaware, Pennsylvania, and New Jersey industry choked Delaware River and Bay, killing off the shad and sturgeon that had once made Delaware Bay the caviar capital of the world. Watermen on the bay continued to eke out a living fishing for crabs, clams, and oysters, but the days when fleets of oystering and fishing schooners plied the bay had passed. So had the days when excursion steamers carried thousands of city folk down bay from Camden, Philadelphia, and Wilmington for summer holidays at bay beaches. Once-thriving Delaware Bay fishing ports and resort beaches became virtual ghost towns. The bay had become an industrial sewer and a sea road for thousands of ships a year traveling to and from the industries lining the Delaware River.

In the 1950s Delaware finally began integrating its public schools, but not without resistance from rural areas down state. This resistance presented a problem since most political power in the state rested with southern legislators until the US Supreme Court ordered that the state legislature to reapportion itself to fairly reflect the population. It did so in the 1960s and most legislators are now elected by voters from more urban and liberal New Castle County, which has the largest population.

Delaware's indebtedness increased from 1950 to 1980 as rapid population growth necessitated greater spending for schools, transportation, and government services. But Delaware has been reluctant to raise taxes and it still has no state sales, real estate, or personal property tax. Many banks and companies continue to incorporate in the state because of its low taxes and central location.

Judging by the state's low 4% unemployment and the ever-expanding Wilmington-Newark suburbs, Delaware continues to ride the waves of chemical and commercial booms, but in recent years the voices of environmentalists and preservationists have caught the attention of the state government and general citizenry. Environmental legislation has reversed trends of pollution: Shad, for example, have returned to Delaware Bay in sizable numbers, and coastal zoning has protected hundreds of square miles of wetlands from development by petroleum companies seeking deep-water refineries along the southern coast of the bay. Once-shabby, forgotten towns like New Castle, Odessa, and Lewes have embraced historic preservation. And downtown Wilmington, a victim of urban decay, has been revitalized with the Market St Mall, five blocks of the city's heart closed to all but pedestrian traffic. Plans are in the works for a vibrant Avenue of the Arts on the banks of the Christina River.

GEOGRAPHY

Delaware's northern edge abuts Pennsylvania (the border is actually the arc of a perfect circle with a 12-mile radius centered on the court house in New Castle); its western border splits the Delmarva Peninsula in half with Maryland, which lies to the south as well. The eastern border has 28 miles of beaches on the Atlantic, but most of the state's coast lies along 70 miles of Delaware Bay, with New Jersey on the opposite shore.

Delaware has a land mass of just 2044 sq miles with over 100 sq miles of inland water areas, excluding Delaware Bay. The state stretches 96 miles north to south and 35 miles at its widest from east to west. Delaware's highest natural point, in Centreville in the northwestern corner of the state, is just 442 feet.

The northern tip of the state lies on the Piedmont Plateau, but the rest of the state is on the Atlantic Coastal Plain, or Tidewater. The Christina River that runs through Wilmington separates the Piedmont from the Tidewater. The Piedmont contains many of the streams that powered early mills. The coastal plain is fairly flat, almost never higher than 80 feet above sea level, with marshes and beaches along the coast.

Delaware's soil is fertile but somewhat sandy. In northern New Castle the soil is a two-layered clay and sand-gravel mixture. Moving south the surface clay can be a sandy loam or a silt loam. Because the soils have been cultivated for over 200 years, many farmers rely heavily on fertilizers.

Most of the state's rivers rise in a watershed near the western border and flow east to the Delaware River and Bay (which link the state to New York, New Jersey, and Pennsylvania) or west to the Chesapeake. The largest of the important tributaries are the Christina River and Brandywine Creek. The Chesapeake & Delaware Canal crosses the state about 15 miles south of Wilmington and connects the Delaware River and Bay to the Chesapeake. Local lore maintains that the South begins below the canal.

ECONOMY

European settlers began planting tobacco in the late 17th century, but they had largely abandoned it for other products by the beginning of the Revolution. Initially shipbuilders lumbered the state for its extraordinary stands of white oak until they had all but depleted the forests; today, a small lumber industry still produces shingles, keels, and bark for tanning. Because of Delaware's waterfront, shipbuilding was common in early Delaware. As late as WWII a single Wilmington shipyard was the state's largest employer. By the latter part of the 18th century, flour mills on the northern Brandywine Creek were well known.

Today there are 360,000 people in Delaware's labor force, and they are primarily employed in five sectors: service (21%), manufacturing (21%), sales (20%), trade (18%), and government (12%).

Although farmland covers half the state, agriculture accounts for under 2% of the state's gross state product. In the 19th century Delaware was known as the 'Peach State,' but after disease decimated the trees, the crop declined to almost nothing. As in Maryland, broilers (five-week to 12-week-old chickens) are the state's most important agricultural products, followed by dairy items. Soybeans are the leading crop. Some commercial fishing fleets work out of Lewes and small bay ports, with crabs their most important catch.

Chemicals rank first on the list of the state's manufactured products; specific items include nylon, drugs, plastics, and industrial chemicals. The largest producers are EI du Pont de Nemours & Co, Hercules, and ICI. Wilmington is the center of manufacturing in Delaware and is one of the largest chemical centers in the world (due more to research and corporate headquarters than to production). Newark has a huge auto assembly plant for General Motors. Delaware's favorable tax laws and fees regarding corporations have encouraged over 200,000 companies to incorporate here.

Delaware's most famous corporation, Du Pont, became so large that in 1912 the federal government forced the company to split into three companies to avoid monopolization. In spite of this, Du Pont still maintains its monopoly in the production of smokeless gunpowder for national security reasons.

POPULATION & PEOPLE

Only Alaska, Vermont, and Wyoming have fewer residents than Delaware, which has 680,000. The population is about 70% urban and 30% rural. Wilmington, with 72,000 residents, is the only large city; none of the others have more than 30,000 residents.

The ethnic breakdown is white (80%); black (17%); Hispanic (1.5%); Asian (1.3%); and Native American (0.30%). About 96% of all the state's residents are native-born US citizens.

ARTS

Delawareans are proud of the vigor and sophistication that characterizes their arts scene – and they should be. As Delaware rode the crest of the Industrial Revolution its entrepreneurs amassed extraordinary wealth. And in the tradition of wealth begetting and attracting wealth, the Brandywine Valley spanning the Delaware-Pennsylvania border ranks with Florida's Palm Beach as one of America's most financially and socially exclusive addresses. Eschewing nearby Philadelphia and its populous traditions, the Brandywine's elite and wannabe elite have made Delaware – particularly Wilmington – their playground. First-class musicians, dramatists, and painters have recognized the possibilities for patronage in Delaware and heeded the call. For most of the 20th century, the performing and visual arts have flourished in Wilmington . . . and the momentum continues to build. Down state simpler pleasures prevail. Like Maryland's Eastern Shore, Kent and Sussex counties are a region of storytellers.

Visual Arts

The Brandywine Valley's landscapes and light have inspired artists for generations and given birth to one of America's best-known styles of painting, the so-called 'Brandywine School.' Hailed as the 'Father of American Illustration' at the turn of the 20th century, Wilmington's Howard Pyle pioneered the super-realistic, nostalgic, haunting style of painting. The definitive collection of Pyle's masterpieces is on display at the Delaware Art Museum in Wilmington. The DAM also features the work of other 20th century masters like Hopper and Lichtenstein as well as the USA's largest collection of English pre-Raphaelite art.

While Pyle began the Brandywine School, it was his pupil NC Wyeth, and Wyeth's son Andrew and grandson Jamie, who made the Brandywine School world-famous. Their works hang at the Brandywine River Museum in Chadds Ford, Pennsylvania, along with the works of Maxfield Parrish (another celebrated Pyle protégé), Edward Moran, Asher Durand, and Thomas Nast.

The Delaware Center for the Contemporary Arts in Wilmington showcases the work of local, national, and international modern artists. Wilmington also has an active gallery scene with many new openings.

In addition to supporting and collecting great art, Delaware's art patrons have provided two of the most spectacular sites for viewing art in America, as well as a world-class center of the horticultural arts. All three sites are Brandywine Valley estates. Nemours Mansion and Gardens is a Louis XVI-style mansion on 300 acres that preserves Alfred I du Pont's collections of antiques, carpets, tapestries, paintings, and automobiles. The celebrated Winterthur Museum (the country estate of another du Pont) displays the world's premier collection of American antiques and decorative arts in period room settings. And 30-acre Longwood Gardens contains 11,000 types of plants and flowers displayed in conservatories and throughout the estate.

Music & Performing Arts

Comparable to the grandeur of Winterthur and Nemours, the Grand Opera House in the heart of Wilmington is America's finest remaining example of cast-iron architecture. Built in 1871 on the model of French Second Empire designs, the Grand is home to the nationally renowned Delaware Symphony Orchestra with Maestro Stephen Gunzenhauser. Barely two blocks from the Grand, the Playhouse Theatre in the Hotel du Pont has been hosting traveling Broadway productions for more than 80 years. Near the Christina River waterfront, the Delaware Theatre Company stages classic and contemporary serious drama.

Regional theater troupes include the Wilmington Drama League often staging Broadway shows, the University of Delaware Center for Black Culture in Newark showcasing African American arts, and the Media Theatre for the Performing Arts in nearby Media, Pennsylvania, where you can see musicals. Two dinner theaters thrive as well: the Candlelights Music Dinner Theatre and Three Little Bakers Dinner Theatre. The Russian Ballet Theatre of Delaware in Rockland (Greater Wilmington) stages four classic and contemporary masterpieces each year and features dancers trained in Russia's finest academies.

Literature

A collection of mysteries by Wade B Fleetwood has been published locally. The novels include *Murder at the Henlopen*, *Murder in Bethany Beach*, *Murder in Rehoboth*, and *Murder on the Ocean City Pier*. JP Marquand's novels do a good job prying into the private lives of Delaware's socialites.

For enthusiasts of sea stories or pirates, there are *Shipwrecks, Sea Stories & Legends of the Delaware Coast* (1989) and *Ghost Stories of the Delaware Coast* (1990), both by David Seibold and Charles Adams, available from Exeter House, Box 8134, Reading, Pennsylvania. Another author in this vein is Jack Beach, *Pirates on the Delmarva* (Lewes: Media Associates, 1985).

Film

Most people who have seen the exceedingly popular *Dead Poets Society* starring Robin Williams believe the film takes place in New England as the script contends. The truth is otherwise: The production crew shot the entire movie in Delaware. St Andrews School in Middletown is the major location. But the crew shot the drama scenes in the Middletown Theater. Lots of the exterior town scenes took place in New Castle, and Wilmington also provided a number of sets.

Historic Delaware towns like New Castle and Dover have 'doubled' for colonial New England in other films as well. Most recently they appeared in a documentary about the Revolutionary War, because the Georgian architecture, rolling countryside, family farms, and brilliant fall foliage replicate images of New England that hardly exist any longer in places like Boston.

Southern Delaware, around Assawoman Bay and Fenwick Island, starred in *Violets Are Blue* with Sissy Spacek and Kevin Cline.

INFORMATION

Area Codes

The area code for all of Delaware is 302.

Time

Delaware lies in the Eastern Time Zone of the United States. This is five hours behind GMT, as are New York City, Washington, DC, and Miami.

Taxes

Delaware has no sales tax. The room tax in hotels is 8%.

Media

In northern Delaware most people read *The News Journal*. From Dover south the most popular paper is *The Delaware State News*. You can find NPR in the Wilmington area on WHYY(Philadelphia) at 91.0 FM.

Liquor Laws

You must be 21 to buy or drink alcoholic beverages in Delaware. Bars generally close at 1 am. Privately owned liquor stores are the are the only places to buy alcohol 'to go.' Sunday sales start at noon.

Wilmington

Although Delaware's largest city (population 72,000) claims a long, proud history, Wilmington lacks a reputation as an architectural treasure like Annapolis or as a major destination of day trippers like Baltimore. And frankly, viewed from an Amtrak train sliding along the Northeast Corridor, or from the interstate highways that bound the city, Wilmington can look about as thrilling as Trenton, New Jersey. Hence, most of the world tends to dismiss Wilmington as little more than the home of corporations, banks, and industry, flooded with a sea of lawyers. But this small city can be well worth a stop, particularly if you are the kind of traveler who likes to get off the beaten path. Furthermore, Wilmington serves as a gateway to the chateau country of the Brandywine Valley and historic New Castle.

HIGHLIGHTS

- The green space, river, and breezes in Brandywine Park
- The Delaware Art Museum – showcasing American realists Homer, Eakin, and Wyeth
- Tubing through the historic sites on the Brandywine River
- The restaurant and bar scene at Trolley Square on the weekend
- Dancing at Renaissance, with a mix of gays and straights

Wilmington offers some impressive historical buildings, a very good art museum, progressive art galleries, a zoo, and an expansive riverside park. There are also some exceptional restaurants, many well-attended bars with live music, dance spots, a popular professional baseball team, and an extremely active theater scene.

By day Wilmington is a bustling working city with more than its share of modern banks and corporate headquarters. Legions of professionals in pinstriped suits and Gucci shoes give downtown Wilmington a palpable vitality. But after work the professional crowd trickles back to the suburbs leaving the business district a bluesy sort of place for tavern-goers, the theater crowd, and business travelers staying in four major downtown hotels. The streets are well-lighted, and public safety officers wearing orange vests patrol the Market St Mall area. But almost all the shops and many restaurants in the mall area close at sunset, and the streets are virtually deserted after dark.

Because Wilmington is a small city with extensive industrial zones, there are some impoverished neighborhoods with desperate people where a traveler probably should not venture. Enjoying Wilmington depends on knowing where and when to walk. By night the town is safest and most lively in the West End at Trolley Square (14th and Du Pont Sts). Little Italy has some good restaurants along the western end of Lancaster Ave. And there is an up-and-coming sports/nightclub scene in the south end of town around Frawley Stadium where the Wilmington Blue Rocks play baseball. Neighborhoods grow more prosperous as you move north and west across the city. The area east of Walnut St downtown is not safe. This area includes the attractive Christina and Fort Christina Parks, which in recent years have become havens for the homeless.

History

Sailing aboard the 220-ton pinnace *Kalmar Nyckel*, 22 Swedish traders and soldiers rode a fair tide up Delaware Bay and ghosted into the deep, sheltered mouth of the Christina River. The Europeans stepped ashore on an outcropping of blue rocks that made a natural wharf at present-day

Wilmington and almost immediately began trading for the furs the Lenni-Lenape brought by canoe to the European encampment. Here on the Christina's natural harbor, the Swedes quickly built palisades and ramparts of earth as well as log houses for shelter and storing the furs. They named this site Fort Christina after their young queen.

Subsequent expeditions to Fort Christina brought more Swedes who prospered as traders and small-scale grain farmers. In 1655 the Dutch governor of New Amsterdam (New York City) arrived at Fort Christina with ships and soldiers and claimed the flourishing settlement for Holland. The English ousted the Dutch nine years later, but barely disturbed the lives of the settlers, who encouraged more waves of immigration from their homelands, especially Sweden.

For the next 50 years the settlement at Christina Harbor thrived as a center for trade and shipping grain milled at water works poised along the steep descents of Brandywine Creek. By 1730 real estate developers, including one Thomas Willing, mapped out an extended street plan for the village, divided up 10 acres of land into house lots, and named the first in a succession of Delaware subdivisions 'Willingtown.' Over the years the name evolved into the present 'Wilmington.' Recognizing the potential for real estate profits, a Quaker entrepreneur named William Shipley slipped into Willingtown in 1735, bought all of the land west of Market St, subdivided it, and doubled the number of houses in the town within a year. The settlement boomed as Shipley built a market house, wharf, and – to most people's delight – a brewery. Quakers from Pennsylvania moved here by the hundreds. The port gained momentum as a trading center where rigging gangs fitted out ships for the exportation of flour, butter, meat, and barrel staves for trade with the West Indies.

As America's troubles with England sharpened during the years just before the American Revolution, Wilmington became a center of patriotic sympathies. Locals feared that the English would close their port as they had done in Boston . . . and the citizens' fears proved well-founded. In May 1776 the English frigates *Roebuck* and *Liverpool* positioned themselves in the Delaware River to blockade the entrance to the Christina River and the port of Wilmington. In one of the first naval battles of the Revolution, the fast and more maneuverable American schooner *Wasp*, together with several armed rowing galleys, thwarted the blockade. But Wilmington's independence proved short-lived. The war returned to Wilmington on August 25, 1777, when British General Howe landed his army of 18,000 men less than 20 miles away on the Elk River at the head of the Chesapeake. Fearing that Howe planned to capture the all-important grain mills in the Brandywine Valley and then move on to attack the Revolutionary capital at Philadelphia, General George Washington moved 11,000 soldiers, the main force of the Continental Army, to the southwest edge of the town to protect the port and the mills. Washington set up his headquarters in the home of Captain Joseph Bennett, a mariner, at 303 West St.

On September 11 Howe attacked and outflanked Washington's Continentals, driving them back to Chester, Pennsylvania. The next day British forces took possession of Wilmington and engaged the citizens in tending to the needs of hundreds of wounded. The following day the British captured Delaware's Revolutionary President John McKinly aboard a sloop in the river with state funds and crucial documents.

Following the Revolution, Wilmington mills and shipping once again prospered and the town quickly grew to a population exceeding 5000. Before the Civil War, Wilmington's mills diversified to produce textiles, paper, and – of course – EI du Pont's gunpowder. By midcentury Wilmington was building iron-hulled ships and railway cars to facilitate America's economic development. Wave after wave of immigrants arrived: first came the Irish, then the French, then the Italians and Jews. Blacks arrived as a consequence of the

Underground Railroad run by Wilmington's ardent abolitionist Quakers. Free-flowing money financed new neighborhoods of substantial brick town houses.

A place of divided loyalties – as was Baltimore – during the Civil War, Wilmington suffered the same kind of isolation with federal troops 'protecting' the city's crucial industries like the gunpowder mills. But after the war Wilmington prospered again with steel mills, the ever-growing du Pont empire, and a marine terminal to handle larger ships right on the Delaware River. The city reached its industrial peak as its mills ran 24 hours a day to supply the military needs of WWI and the population ballooned for a time over 100,000.

Wilmington's heavy industry suffered during the Depression of the 1930s and has never regained its former vigor. But, led by the various permutations of the du Pont chemical empire, Wilmington has evolved into something like an American Zurich. Delaware's tax incentives and liberal incorporation laws have transformed Wilmington into a commercial and banking capital that is trying to imitate Baltimore in revitalizing the heart of the city. Not only are the Market St Mall and the nascent Avenue of the Arts a start to reviving downtown, but in 1996 the city forged a deal with New York's prestigious Pratt Institute and DC's Corcoran School of Art to locate a professional college of art and design at 600 Market St in the former Delmarva Light and Power Building. Called the Brandywine College of Art and Design, the school plans to begin (in September 1997) bringing talented art students into the heart of Wilmington. When this campus becomes a reality, the art students will no doubt add just what Wilmington is currently missing, downtown residents and a bohemian youth scene.

Orientation

Wilmington stands at the confluence of Brandywine Creek, the Christina River, and the Delaware River and rises from former marsh land in the east to a series of hills in the west. Planners laid out the streets in a roughly north-south, east-west grid on the delta of land between Brandywine Creek to the north and the Christina River to the south. Market St, running north-south, is the main artery bisecting the town and the locus for historical sites, daytime restaurants, shopping, and theater. Old Town Hall at 512 Market St marks the heart of the city.

Pennsylvania Ave and its off-shoot Delaware Ave are the main arteries leading to the upscale restaurant/gallery/bar scene at Trolley Square in the West End. Little Italy's restaurants lie just south of Pennsylvania Ave on Lincoln St in the West End. Pennsylvania Ave becomes Route 52 as it leaves the city and is the main route to the sites in the chateau country of the Brandywine Valley.

Interstate 95 bisects the city and basically divides the city into the business district to the east and residential neighborhoods to the west.

Information

Tourist Offices The best source for information is the Greater Wilmington Convention & Visitors Bureau's Visitor Information Center (☎ 302-737-4059) on I-95, just south of Wilmington between Rts 896 and 273. The travel counselors here are extremely helpful. Another reason to pay them a visit is that you can save money on several local motels when you book them at the center. It's open daily from 8 am to 8 pm.

In downtown Wilmington, the Greater Wilmington Convention & Visitors Bureau (☎ 302-652-4088, 800-422-1181) is at 1300 Market St, Suite 504.

Acting as an unofficial tourist office, Cavanaugh's bar and restaurant (☎ 302-656-4067), at 703 Market St (see Places to Eat), keeps a good selection of printed tourist information and current events.

Post Office Wilmington has a number of postal stations due to the large volume of business mail flowing to and from the city. You will find the central post office (☎ 302-656-0196) at 1101 King St, on Rodney Square in the center of town.

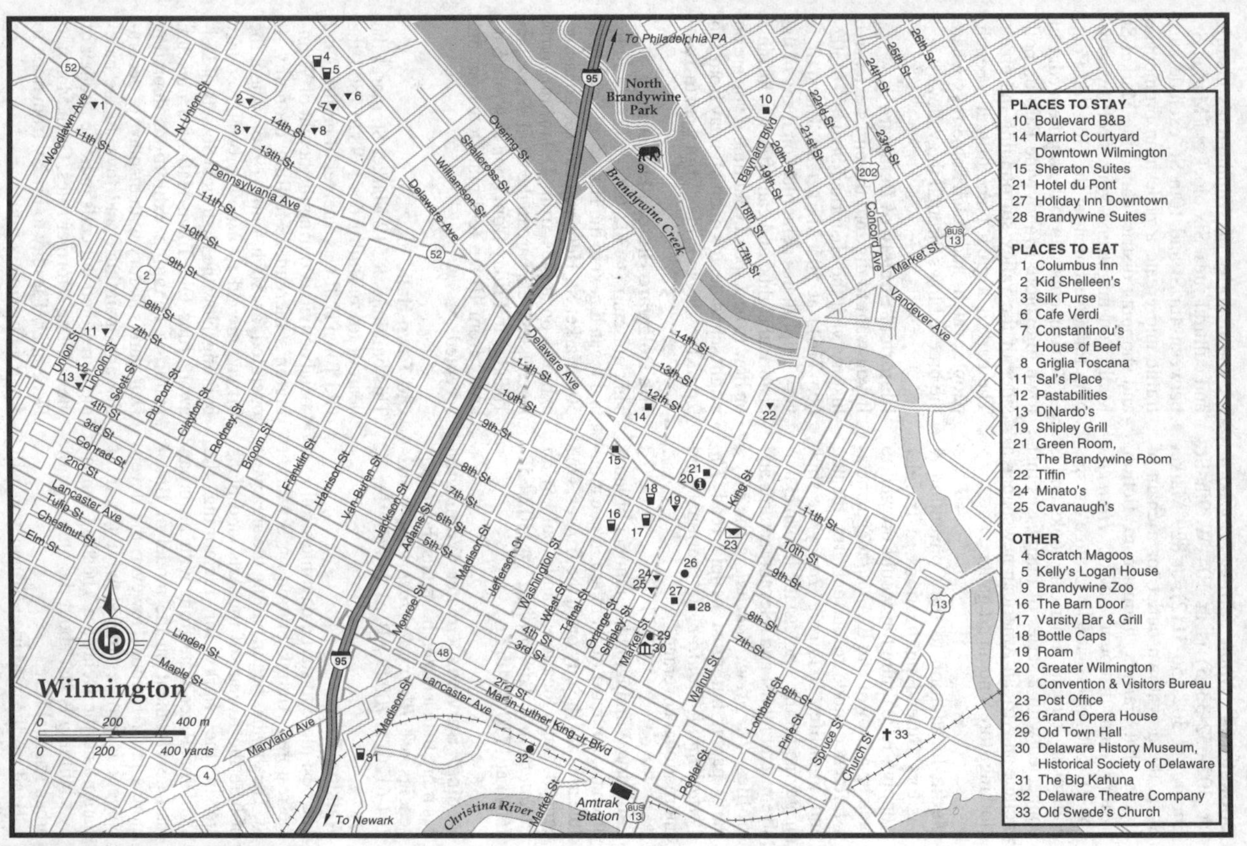
Wilmington
PLACES TO STAY
10 Boulevard B&B
14 Marriot Courtyard Downtown Wilmington
15 Sheraton Suites
21 Hotel du Pont
27 Holiday Inn Downtown
28 Brandywine Suites
PLACES TO EAT
1 Columbus Inn
2 Kid Shelleen's
3 Silk Purse
6 Cafe Verdi
7 Constantinou's House of Beef
8 Griglia Toscana
11 Sal's Place
12 Pastabilities
13 DiNardo's
19 Shipley Grill
21 Green Room, The Brandywine Room
22 Tiffin
24 Minato's
25 Cavanaugh's
OTHER
4 Scratch Magoos
5 Kelly's Logan House
9 Brandywine Zoo
16 The Barn Door
17 Varsity Bar & Grill
18 Bottle Caps
19 Roam
20 Greater Wilmington Convention & Visitors Bureau
23 Post Office
26 Grand Opera House
29 Old Town Hall
30 Delaware History Museum, Historical Society of Delaware
31 The Big Kahuna
32 Delaware Theatre Company
33 Old Swede's Church
To Philadelphia PA
North Brandywine Park
Brandywine Creek
Christina River
Amtrak Station
To Newark
Martin Luther King Jr Blvd
Delaware Ave
Pennsylvania Ave
Lancaster Ave
Maryland Ave
Concord Ave
Vandever Ave
Baynard Blvd
Market St
King St
Orange St
Shipley St
Tatnall St
West St
Washington St
Jefferson St
Madison St
Monroe St
Adams St
Jackson St
Van Buren St
Harrison St
Franklin St
Broom St
Rodney St
Clayton St
Du Pont St
Scott St
Lincoln St
Union St
N Union St
Woodlawn Ave
Overing St
Shallcross St
Williamson St
Walnut St
Lombard St
Pine St
Spruce St
Church St
Poplar St
Linden St
Maple St
Tulip St
Chestnut St
Elm St
Conrad St
0 200 400 m
0 200 400 yards
DELAWARE

Bookstores *Ninth Street Bookstore* (☎ 302-652-3315) is at 104 W 9th St. *Encore* (☎ 302-656-3112), at 829 Market St, is the downtown outlet for a chain of stores that carries mainstream fiction, history, and discount books. *Haneef's* (☎ 302-656-4193), at 911 Orange St, specializes in African American books and is connected with a series of businesses that include an African American newspaper, a clothing store, and an art gallery.

Media In addition to the Convention & Visitors Bureau publications, a traveler stopping in Wilmington would do well to pick up a copy of *Out & About* magazine as a reference guide to current arts, theater, and nightlife. *Delaware Today*, a slick magazine for the whole state, has an extensive restaurant list and relevant features and profiles. *The News Journal* is the city's daily paper, but most people read *The Philadelphia Inquirer* for national and international coverage.

Laundry Wilmington has number of laundromats, but most of them are in questionable areas of the city or on the fringes. One central, safe location stands out: *Swan Cleaners and Laundromat* (☎ 302-652-7607) at 1710 W 4th St.

Medical Services Greater Wilmington has more than a dozen hospitals. For emergencies use *Riverside Hospital* (☎ 302-764-6120) at 700 Lea Blvd; or call 911.

Walking Tour

The best place to start a daytime stroll is at the restored Amtrak Station on S Market St. The city has begun calling the area west of here the Avenue of the Arts, and plans are in the works for reclaiming the Christina River waterfront with an urban mall development on the model of Baltimore's Inner Harbor. However, the development is progressing slowly; the train station and the Delaware Theatre Company's building is just about the only sign of urban renewal here.

Head north on Market St and you will see the majority of Wilmington's historic and cultural sites. Six blocks of Market St, between 4th St and 10th St, exclude auto traffic and create a pedestrian promenade and shopping district called the Market St Mall. You might end your stroll by stopping for refreshment at the Hotel du Pont. Or you can continue to the northern edge of town to explore Brandywine Park on both sides of the valley surrounding the creek. The park is a great place to find a bench, people watch, and catch some rays where the breeze blows through the valley.

Historical Society of Delaware

If you want to dig into the city's extensive history, visit the Historical Society (☎ 302-655-7161) at 505 Market St. The staff is very helpful, has pamphlets on many of the historical sights, and can offer you insights on how to best spend your time if you are on a tight schedule. It's open Monday from 1 to 9 pm, Tuesday to Friday from 9 am to 5 pm.

The Delaware History Museum

This museum (☎ 302-656-0637) is run by and located next to the Historical Society at 504 Market St. Here you can see changing exhibits on topics from Delaware sports legends to Delaware in the Civil War. Open Tuesday to Friday from noon to 4 pm; Saturday from 10 am to 4 pm. Donations are accepted.

Old Town Hall

This building, at 512 Market St, marks the heart of town. Built from 1798 to 1800, the Old Town Hall was a center of political and social activities during the height of Wilmington's mercantile-milling economy. It operated as such until 1916, when the offices moved to a new city and county building. Now the Historical Society of Delaware runs Old Town Hall as a museum featuring changing exhibitions depicting Delaware's history with displays of decorative arts, paintings, and toys. In the basement, restored jail cells indicate another of the building's former roles. Open March to December, Tuesday to Friday from noon to 4 pm; admission is free.

Willingtown Square
This collection of four stately 18th century homes surrounds a courtyard of cobblestone and brick at 506 Market St. Not open to the public, these buildings were moved here from other areas of the city by the Historical Society.

Grand Opera House
The Grand Opera House (☎ 302-658-7898), 818 Market St, is the architectural showpiece of Wilmington. Built in 1871 and originally a Masonic temple, the Grand lives up to its name as a superb example of cast-iron architecture. Listed on the National Historic Register, the interior is perhaps even grander than the facade, with ceiling frescoes, winding staircases, box seats, and felt and brass decor. Home to the Delaware Symphony Orchestra, the Grand opens its doors to visitors on Thursdays from 11:30 am to 1:30 pm.

Christina Cultural Arts Center
You will find the lively Christina Cultural Arts Center (☎ 302-652-0101) at 705 Market St, between 7th and 8th Sts. The center is the Delaware Valley's premier community school of the arts celebrating African American culture. In addition to the variety of classes offered, the CCAC also features a schedule of theatrical, dance, and musical performances and art exhibitions.

Old Swede's Church
This simple chapel (☎ 302-652-5629) rises near the Christina River at 606 Church St. Built in 1698 – one of the country's oldest churches – Old Swede's still has regular Episcopal services. Free guided tours are offered Monday, Wednesday, Friday, and some Saturdays, between 1 and 4 pm.

Delaware Art Museum
Home to a renowned collection of American art, the Delaware Art Museum (☎ 302-571-9590) is at 2301 Kentmere Pkwy. Dating from 1840 to the present, the collection includes the works of Winslow Homer, Thomas Eakins, Howard Pyle, NC Wyeth, Frank Schoonover, Andrew Wyeth, and John Sloan. America's largest collection of English pre-Raphaelite art can also be seen here. The museum is open Tuesday from 10 am to 9 pm, Wednesday to Saturday from 10 am to 5 pm, and Sunday from noon to 5 pm. Admission is free.

Mellon Bank Center
This gallery is an extension of the Delaware Art Museum at 10th and Market Sts with changing exhibits often featuring national traveling shows that sometimes complement the DAM's collection of Brandywine artists and pre-Raphaelites. The center opens Monday to Friday from 9 am to 5 pm.

Brandywine Park
Listed in the National Registry of Historic places and inspired by Frederick Law Olmstead, creator of New York's Central Park, Brandywine Park is a long narrow band of greenery lining both banks of the Brandywine Creek for about a mile and a half. Beginning at the Market St crossing of the Brandywine, just north of downtown, the park climbs from the lowlands to the steeps of the city and provides a relaxing escape from the traffic and concrete of the surrounding streets.

Brandywine Zoo
You will find Delaware's only zoo (☎ 302-571-7747) at 1001 N Park Drive. The zoo stands on 180 acres of Brandywine Park and features 140 animals native to North and South America. It's open daily from 10 am to 4 pm. Admission from April to October is $3; from November to March it's free.

Kalmar Nyckel Foundation
The Kalmar Nyckel Foundation (☎ 302-429-7447) is a working 17th century shipyard at the extreme east end of 7th St. Shipwrights here are building a replica of the 110-foot ship that brought the original Swedes to Delaware, and a similar project is underway to recreate the Delaware Valley's first permanent European settlement. Tours are offered Tuesday through Saturday from 10 am to 4 pm.

Lincoln Collection of the University of Delaware

Over 2000 items pertaining to Abraham Lincoln's private and public life are presented here at the Goodstay Center (☎ 302-573-4468), 2600 Pennsylvania Ave (Route 52). Open October to May on Tuesdays, from noon to 4 pm. Admission is free.

Steam Train

Wilmington & Western Tourist Railroad (☎ 302-998-1930), Greenbank Station on Route 41, three blocks north of the junction with Route 2, features a ride through Red Clay Creek Valley aboard vintage steam trains. In July and August it runs on Saturdays; at other times from May to November it runs on Sundays. Admission is adults $7, children $4.

Canoeing

Wilderness Canoe Trips (☎ 302-654-2227), at 2111 Concord Pike in the Fairfax Shopping Center, offers two- to six-hour canoe and tube trips down Brandywine Creek.

Brew Tour

Rockford Brewing Company (☎ 302-575-1640), at 15 St James Court, is Delaware's first microbrewery, established in 1952. The family-run business makes full-bodied beers in the European tradition. You can tour the brewery, taste the merchandise and purchase quantities of beer to go.

Special Events

Wilmington has its share of annual celebrations. An event you might catch no matter what time of year you are in town is an Art on the Town Loop. Occurring the first Friday of every month except January and August, these popular events take the name 'loops' because free bus service loops around the city to connect the various galleries, restaurants, theaters, and bars hosting art openings and music. Several annual events are held in spring and summer:

Tour du Pont, May. Wilmington is the official starting point for America's premier cycling event.

Winterthur Point to Point, the first Sunday of May. This festival of amateur steeplechase racing is held on the museum grounds.

Clifford Brown Jazz Festival, the week after Memorial Day. Named for the great trumpet player, this festival brings five days of entertainment to Rodney Square during.

LPGA McDonald's Championship, May or June. The LPGA tour stops in Wilmington.

Holy Trinity Greek Festival, first week in June.

St Anthony's Italian Festival, second week in June.

Rockwood Ice Cream Festival, July

Places to Stay

When visiting Wilmington, you can choose from staying in a downtown hotel, B&B, or a moderately priced motel off I-95, in New Castle or in Newark. To save money, visit the Greater Wilmington Convention & Visitors Bureau's Visitor Information Center (☎ 302-737-4059) on I-95, just south of Wilmington between Routes 896 and 273. You can enjoy special lower rates at certain properties when making reservations here (see Information).

Places to Stay – camping

The nearest campground is 17 miles south of Wilmington via Route 13. *Lums Pond State Park* (☎ 302-368-6989) is two miles south of Kirkwood on Route 71. There are 72 tent sites and a bathhouse, no electricity or water at individual campsites. Tent sites are open from April through October and cost $11 a night. The Oceanmart, two miles away from the park in Kirkwood, is the closest place to shop.

Places to Stay – middle

A 10-minute drive south of downtown, the *Economy Inn* (☎ 302-656-9431, fax 302-654-6039), 1015 S Market St (Route 13), is a bit sleazy with, for example, a free Playboy channel promotion. However, it is inexpensive with singles/doubles for $28/37.

The lovely *Boulevard B&B* (☎ 302-656-9700), 1909 Baynard Blvd (between 19th and 20th Sts), is located in one of Wilmington's tree-lined historic districts. Built in 1913 and listed on the National Register of Historic Places, the Boulevard is within walking distance of the downtown business district. Singles/doubles with shared bath are $55/60, with private bath $65/75; full breakfast is included.

Brandywine Suites (☎ 302-656-9300), 707 King St, features two-room suites for $99 with complimentary buffet breakfast.

Holiday Inn Downtown (☎ 302-655-0400, 800-777-9456) at 700 King St has an indoor swimming pool. Singles/doubles cost $69/85.

Places to Stay – top end

Wilmington boasts a hotel whose architecture and interior design make it one of the world's most impressive hotels. The *Hotel du Pont* (☎ 302-594-3100, 800-441-9019), 11th and Market Sts, opened in 1913 to rival Europe's finest hotels. After undergoing a major renovation in 1993, its rooms have won a major design award. Even if you do not plan to stay or eat here, you should make a point of visiting just to see the lobby's hand-crafted furniture, oriental carpets, walnut reception desk, and paneling. Check out the Gold Ballroom, a testament to craftsmanship and artistry that prevails in Delaware quarters where money is no object. Singles/doubles run from $175 to $209. Busy during the week with business travelers, the hotel offers good value packages for weekends and holidays. These can include dining certificates, welcome gifts, and admission to museums or special events.

The *Sheraton Suites* (☎ 302-654-8300), 422 Delaware Ave, is an all-suite property with an indoor pool, sauna, and exercise room. Singles/doubles cost $120 on weekdays, but drop to $90 on weekends.

The *Marriott Courtyard Downtown Wilmington* (☎ 302-429-7600), at 1102 West St, has rooms for $94. The hotel offers such amenities as an exercise facility, an extensive continental breakfast, and microwave ovens in the rooms.

Places to Eat

West End & Little Italy An extensive collection of restaurants has grown up along Lincoln St in this longtime Italian neighborhood. This area is one of the best places to examine a large number of restaurants.

Pastabilities (☎ 302-656-9822), at 415 N Lincoln, is a newcomer to the scene and has to be Wilmington's most romantic place to eat. You enter through the kitchen where chef-owner Luigi Vitrone sings along with the opera on the sound system as he dances between his coolers, chopping blocks, and burners. In the back of the building are eight tables under a funky starlit ceiling. Northern Italian entrees like stuffed prawns cost $16. Pastas are under $10; a glass of Chianti runs $3.50.

Rossis (☎ 302-655-8584), at 1835 W 4th St, is a longtime favorite for Wilmington residents. You can get good veal and chicken for under $14.

Sal's Place (☎ 302-656-1200), at 603 N Lincoln St, serves candlelit French and Continental cuisine with entrees running about $16.

DiNardo's (☎ 302-652-9503), located at 405 N Lincoln St, is legendary for its crabs, but also serves other seafood with an Italian touch.

Another landmark restaurant is *Constantinou's House of Beef* (☎ 302-652-0653), 1616 Delaware Ave, renowned for its beef and seafood.

The colonial-style *Columbus Inn* (☎ 302-571-1492), at 2216 Pennsylvania Ave, is in one of the city's oldest buildings (1798). Set on a hill overlooking the main road to the Brandywine Valley, the Columbus Inn specializes in fresh seafood. It's open for lunch and dinner (jackets required for men in the evening).

Trolley Square The north end of Lincoln St runs into a four-block area of gentrified town houses just north of Pennsylvania Ave known as Trolley Square. Here you will find the most popular places in the city to window-shop among upscale boutiques, art galleries, cafes, and restaurants. While many of these restaurants look like they are quartered within the walls of old houses, most of them actually have backyard decks and patios that offer *al fresco* dining.

One spot in this area stands out for great cheap eats. Try *Cafe Verdi* (☎ 302-656-5411) right in the Trolley Square shopping plaza. On Mondays and Tuesdays you can get a large pizza for $5.

Silk Purse (☎ 302-654-7666), at 1307 N Scott St, is hidden on a quiet residential block and retains the feel of a private home. Serving international cuisine with a Mediterranean emphasis, the owners also operate the simpler bistro *Sow's Ear* (☎ 302-654-7848) in the same building.

Michele's (☎ 302-655-8554), 1828 W 11th St, prepares American cuisine with French and Italian influences in a converted row house and has won a devoted following since opening in 1993. Downstairs looks like a hip, funky bar, while the upstairs dining room is Victorian with floral-print decor.

Griglia Toscana (☎ 302-654-8001), at 1412 N Dupont St, is a popular Northern Italian bistro with an open kitchen and extensive wine list. The place appeals to upscale suburbanites.

Kid Shelleen's (☎ 302-658-4600), on the corner of 14th and Scott Sts, is a charcoal house featuring grilled seafood and chicken, homemade soups, and a yuppie crowd. Entrees cost under $10.

Downtown In addition to the standard choice of fast food outlets, there are two good old-fashioned budget choices on Market St, on either side of 8th St: *Leo & Jimmy's Deli* (☎ 302-657-7151), at 728 N Market St, is a traditional delicatessen serving great sandwiches made to order. *Govato's* (☎ 302-652-4082), at 800 N Market, is an old-style candy store and restaurant. Across the street, *Olympic Subs Steaks Deli* (☎ 302-652-46770), at 813 N Market St, serves good-sized sandwiches.

Gennelle's Restaurant and Bakery (☎ 302-654-5322), at 730 N Market St, has exceptional Guyanese-Caribbean cooking. The oxtail curry chicken and curried goat will knock your socks off. Prices run from $6 to $9.

Minatos (☎ 302-655-4322), 101 W 8th St between Shipley and Market Sts, is a popular, small sushi bar with a friendly older proprietor.

The Hotel du Pont (see Places to Stay) boasts two award-winning restaurants: *The Brandywine Room*, serving American-Continental cuisine, is open for dinner Sunday to Thursday. The ornate *Green Room*, Wilmington's ultimate fine-dining experience, is open for lunch daily (around $30 per person), and for dinner on Friday and Saturday only ($60 to $80) with a harpist playing from the balcony. You can get a superb Sunday brunch here for $26.50. You can also take afternoon tea ($10.25) here with Brandywine Valley matrons in the hotel's *Lobby Lounge* from 2:30 to 4:30 pm.

Tiffin (☎ 302-571-1133), 1208 N Market St, is a popular power-lunch spot for downtown lawyer and banker types, serving California-style entrees.

Shipley Grill (☎ 302-652-7797), 913 Shipley St (between 9th and 10th Sts), is one of the city's nicest restaurants. You can enjoy lunch here for about $15 per person.

Pubs Many of Wilmington's watering holes offer tasty, inexpensive food, as well as the usual liquid attractions and evening entertainment.

Cavanaugh's (☎ 302-656-4067), 703 Market Street (at 7th St), occupying the former Reynold's candy company building, is open seven days a week from 11 am to 1 am. The pub offers draft beer, wines, and a wide variety of food all day: sandwiches, salads, pasta, seafood, steaks, and snacks. There is a daily happy hour from 5 to 7 pm, including complimentary or cheap snacks. They also offer customers free parking at the Holiday Inn lot.

Bottlecaps (☎ 302-427-9119), 216 9th St between Orange and Tatnal Sts, features '99 bottles of beer and great food' with a daily happy hour from 4 to 8 pm. Sandwiches cost about $4 with some entrees in the $12 range. You will find pool tables here and live music Thursday to Saturday with a $2 to $3 cover. It's closed Sunday. Bottlecaps hosts a monthly block party, the

'9th Street Outdoor Cabaret,' with eight or so local bands playing on two stages from 8 pm to 1 am. The cover is $5.

Varsity Grill (☎ 302-656-8827), at 837 Orange St (on the corner of 9th St), has live music or a DJ Thursday to Saturday, usually with no cover. There are seven pool tables, with a satellite TV showing major sports events. It's a little more laid back than Bottlecaps.

The Barn Door (☎ 302-655-7749), at 845 Tatnal St between 8th and 9th Sts, features daily live music – they book 'bands that nobody else will book.' Virtually all of the local bands get their start here. No draft beer is available.

The *Green Room* is the Hotel du Pont's bar (see Places to Stay), where the business travelers and lawyers network.

Churchill's Beef and Beer (☎ 302-655-2116), at 914 N Orange St, is the place to go if you're between the ages of 30 and 50 and looking for a good deli menu or seafood. The atmosphere is clubby with a hip clientele. Nights feature jazz, comedy, karaoke, and mystery theater.

Entertainment

Music In addition to the annual jazz festival, jazz loops, and bar scene, Wilmington stages a mix of concerts.

The *Grand Opera House* (☎ 302-658-7897), at 818 Market St, is Wilmington's restored Second Empire theater seating 1100 and hosting world-class classical, jazz, and popular artists. Director Stephen Gunzenhausen and the *Delaware Symphony Orchestra* (☎ 302-656-7374) perform at the Grand.

Opera Delaware (☎ 302-658-8063), at 4 S Poplar St, has a reputation for bold productions mixing new works with a classical repertory.

The *Christina Cultural Arts Center* (see individual entry above), features live jazz with a jam session on Thursdays at 7 pm; admission is $3.

Theater The *Playhouse Theatre* (☎ 302-656-4401), part of the du Pont Building (Hotel du Pont) at 10th and Market Sts, has been hosting traveling Broadway shows since the 1920s.

On the Avenue of the Arts the *Delaware Theatre Company* (☎ 302-594-1100) faces the Christina River and plays classic and contemporary drama in a state-of-the-art facility.

Wilmington Drama League (☎ 302-764-1172), at 10 W Lea Blvd, is the oldest community theater in town with over 60 years of experience.

A company of Russian-trained dancers called the *Russian Ballet Theatre of Delaware* (☎ 302-888-2900) mounts four major productions a year.

Three Little Bakers Dinner Theatre (☎ 302-368-1616), 3540 Foxcroft Drive, near Pike Creek Shopping Center off Route 7, has buffet with Broadway shows.

In the village of Arden, another dinner-play option is the *Candlelight Music Dinner Theatre* (☎ 302-475-2313), Miller Rd off I-95.

Bars & Discos *The Big Kahuna* (☎ 302-571-8401), 550 S Madison St (south of downtown across from Legends Stadium), is currently Wilmington's most popular club and a major-league strut, wiggle, and pickup scene for the 'big hair' crowd. Kahuna's has an outdoor deck overlooking the river, which attracts a mellower crowd with national acts like the Charlie Daniels Band.

Renaissance (☎ 302-652-9435), on the corner of 6th and Shipley Sts, is gay but attracts a sizable straight crowd and everybody in Wilmington except the homophobic raves about the dancing there.

Roam, upstairs from the Shipley Grill at 913 Shipley St (between 9th and 10th Sts), is predominantly gay, as is the *814 Club*, a block away on Shipley St. Both charge $5 cover.

If you're into bar hopping and in the mood for good jazz and rock & roll, head for Trolley Square. While the place does not jump on the same scale as similar venues in Baltimore or Annapolis, Trolley Square's bars attract thousands on weekend nights and have entertainment playing all week long.

On Friday nights *Kelly's Logan House* (☎ 302-655-6426), at 1701 Delaware Ave, draws a crowd of over a thousand people, spreading out over two floors and a huge patio to listen to a really whacked mix of blues, reggae, alternative, and rock.

Virtually next door to Kelly's, *Scratch Magoos* (☎ 302-651-9188), at 1709 Delaware Ave, is another popular place for cheap beer, music, and lots of company.

Spectator Sports

Baseball Wilmington sports fans harbor much enthusiasm for their Class A baseball club, the Wilmington Blue Rocks (☎ 302-888-2015), a feeder team for the Kansas City Royals. Named after those blue rocks at Fort Christina where the first Swedish settlers landed, and competing in the Carolina League, the team plays three or four home games a week at Legends Stadium, from mid-April to early September.

Horseracing Delaware Park Race Course (☎ 302-994-2521) is in Stanton, on Route 7 off I-95, Exit 4N. One of the country's most picturesque sports settings, this track features daytime thoroughbred racing from mid-April to November. Post time is 12:45 pm Tuesday, Wednesday, Saturday, and Sunday. Adults pay $2 admission.

Things to Buy

The city's primary shopping district runs along the six-block pedestrian concourse of the Market St Mall in the heart of town, and spills over into the three-block 9th St Plaza west of Market. Artisan's III (☎ 302-656-7370), corner of 9th and Shipley Sts, sells gifts and clothing from Africa, Asia, and South America. Check out Nzinga's (☎ 302-657-2103), at 911 Orange, for Africana. You might find terrific used clothing at the Goodwill Boutique (☎ 302-654-6926), 7th and Market Sts.

Wilmington has two major malls if you need to escape a heat wave, hurricane, or blizzard. The huge Christiana Mall is on Route 7 at Exit 4S, in Newark. Concord Mall sprawls north of the city on Hwy 202N.

Delaware Memorial Bridge – The World's Largest Twin Span

Carrying I-295 traffic over the Delaware River, the Delaware Memorial Bridge links the states of Delaware and New Jersey just south of Wilmington. Among the many highways that feed into the bridge are Hwys 13 and 40, the New Jersey Turnpike, and the Delaware Turnpike. It is part of the direct route from Maine to Florida.

Its main spans of 2150 feet make it the world's largest twin-suspension bridge. The original bridge, the New Jersey-bound span, opened in August 1951. The Delaware-bound bridge opened in September 1968. Tolls are collected in one direction only: Motorists pay $2 as they enter Delaware. ■

Getting There & Away

Air Philadelphia International Airport (PIA; ☎ 215-492-3181) is just 30 minutes' drive away. The following airlines serve PIA:

Atlantic Air	☎ 215-365-7270
British Airways	☎ 800-247-9297
Continental Airlines	☎ 215-592-8005
Delta Air Lines	☎ 215-928-1700
Midway Airlines	☎ 215-492-4200
USAir	☎ 215-563-8055
United Airlines	☎ 800-241-6522

There's an information desk and an ATM in every terminal, while Terminals A, B, and C each have a currency-exchange office.

Bus Greyhound/Trailways provides daily service into the Wilmington Transportation Center (☎ 302-655-6111), at 318 Market St. As usual, the neighborhood is not wonderful and is not too safe at night.

Train The handsome, restored Wilmington Amtrak station (☎ 302-658-1515) sits at Martin Luther King Blvd and King St. The city is on the main East Coast corridor between New York and Baltimore, with service to Philadelphia and Washington, DC.

Car Interstate 95 cuts right through the center of Wilmington, running through DC and Maryland to the south, and through New Jersey to the north. The Delaware Memorial Bridge connects the city to the New Jersey Turnpike. Hwy 13 links the city to southern Delaware and Virginia.

Getting Around

To/From PIA Delaware Express (☎ 302-454-7634) and Super Shuttle (☎ 302-655-8878) run small shuttle buses between PIA and Wilmington. You must make reservations. Fares run from $21 to $23 per person.

In Town Beyond the Market St attractions, which can be easily covered on foot, you will need transportation to get around.

Wilmington's local bus network is known as DART (Delaware Administration for Regional Transit). Blue-and-white signs indicate DART stops throughout the city. The buses can take you to major sites outside the city, like the Brandywine Valley attractions and New Castle. For information about routes, call ☎ 302-577-3278. Fares are $1.15 for travel within one zone, $1.90 for two zones; transfers cost an additional 10¢.

If you have a car there are a number of commercial lots for you in the center of town. But you will save some money by parking at the Holiday Inn at Market and W 8th Sts (see Places to Stay) and visiting Cavanaugh's for a drink or snack to get your parking validated (see Places to Eat).

Northern Delaware

The northern region of Delaware – New Castle County beyond Wilmington – includes the important tourist attractions of New Castle and the Brandywine Valley's chateau country. New Castle County holds the bulk of Delaware's population, most of its historical buildings, a vital visual and performing arts scene, museums, and the state's best selection of accommodations, including a number of attractive B&Bs. You will also find a lot of heavy industry marring beautiful landscapes (check out the Getty Oil refinery at Delaware City for an eyesore), maddening traffic, and a proliferation of housing developments. Depending on what roads you travel and where you stop, New Castle County will either seduce you or repulse you.

If you are a cyclist or get nauseous at the sight of mini-malls, fast food franchises, and filling stations, *avoid* Hwy 202 running north of Wilmington to West Chester, Pennsylvania; Route 2 between Wilmington and Newark is just as bad; Hwy 40 south of these two towns also makes for a hideous trip. But Delaware's Ugly Highway Award goes to Hwy 13, running from the Pennsylvania state line in the north to Delaware's southern border with Maryland. When Coleman du Pont bankrolled this highway back in the 1910s, it was a lovely, straight thoroughfare traversing farm country and linking historic towns. Today, after 80 years of no apparent zoning, Hwy 13 is a commercial corridor plagued with an endless array of traffic lights causing backups not only in Greater Wilmington, but in minuscule towns along the route. Currently, the state is completing the final stretch of a parallel, limited-access highway, Route 1, to bypass the congestion on Hwy 13 between Greater Wilmington and Dover. Take Route 1 if you are headed north or south in a hurry, but realize that during the summer this road is packed with cars headed to/from the Atlantic beaches.

HIGHLIGHTS

- Winterthur, one of the great castles of the world
- The grounds at Nemours, which will make you feel like you're lost in France
- Picnicking in Longwood Gardens
- The Brandywine River Museum for generations of Wyeth paintings
- Historic Newcastle's streets for a trip back to the 18th century
- Rock concerts at the famous Stone Balloon in Newark

Fortunately, you can escape these nightmares. Try exploring Routes 52, 82, and 100 as they wind through the Brandywine Valley area north of Wilmington. If you're heading south, follow Route 9 into New Castle then through the corn and soybean farms and along the marshy fringes of Delaware Bay. Bound east or west between Wilmington and Newark, your best bet by car is to take I-95 and just get the trip over with. Cyclists will like the secondary roads that network through places like Mermaid, Pleasant Hill, and Milford Crossing.

BRANDYWINE VALLEY

You don't have to go far out of your way to take in the best sights of the Brandywine Valley, such as Winterthur and Hagley Museum. If time permits, also stop in at Nemours, Longwood Gardens, Rockwood, and the Brandywine River Museum.

Orientation

Straddling the Delaware-Pennsylvania state line, the Brandywine Valley's chateau country is Northern Delaware's primary tourist destination. Most of the attractions

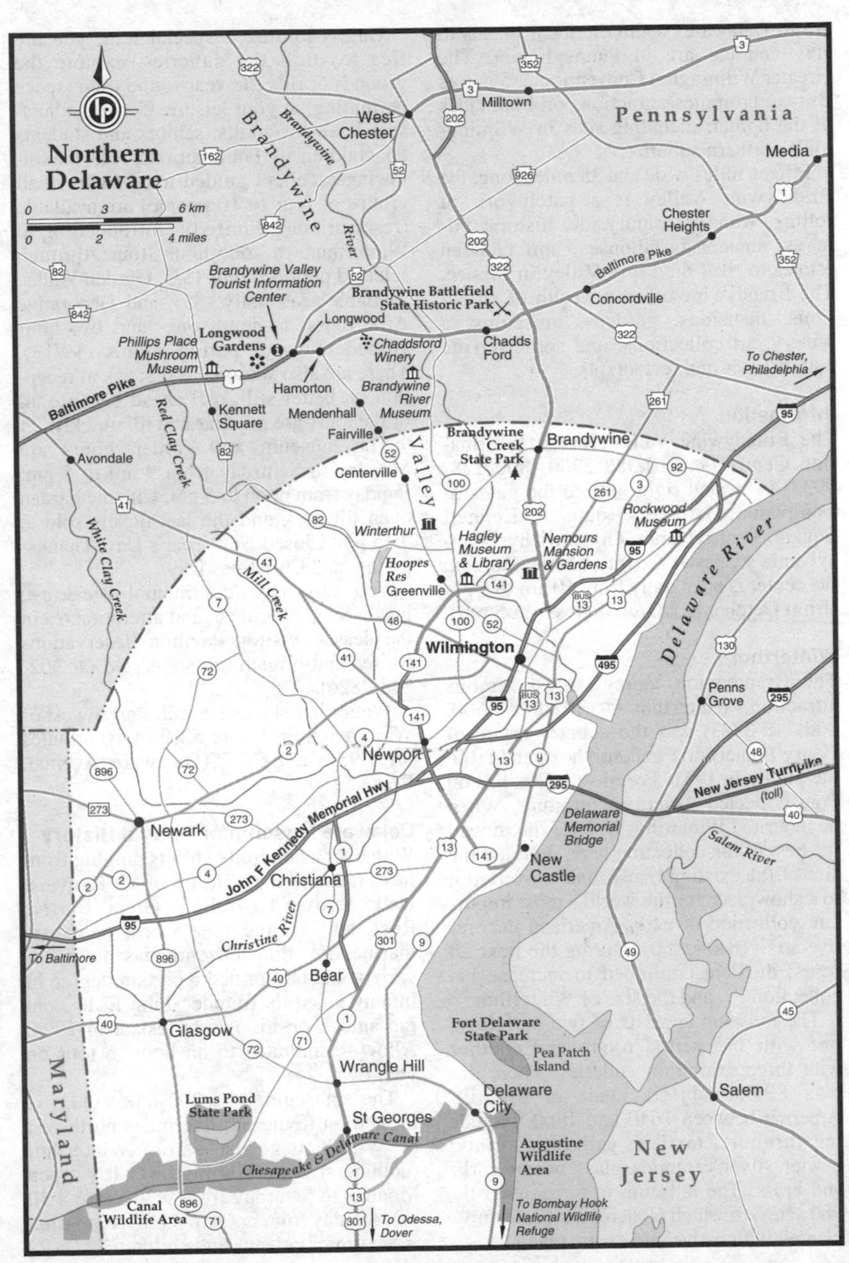
Northern Delaware
0 3 6 km
0 2 4 miles
Pennsylvania
Brandywine
Brandywine River
West Chester
Milltown
Media
Chester Heights
Baltimore Pike
Concordville
Brandywine Valley Tourist Information Center
Brandywine Battlefield State Historic Park
Longwood
Longwood Gardens
Phillips Place Mushroom Museum
Chaddsford Winery
Chadds Ford
To Chester, Philadelphia
Hamorton
Brandywine River Museum
Baltimore Pike
Kennett Square
Mendenhall
Fairville
Red Clay Creek
Brandywine Creek State Park
Brandywine
Avondale
Centerville
Valley
Rockwood Museum
White Clay Creek
Winterthur
Hagley Museum & Library
Nemours Mansion & Gardens
Delaware River
Hoopes Res
Greenville
Mill Creek
Wilmington
Penns Grove
Newport
New Jersey Turnpike (toll)
John F Kennedy Memorial Hwy
Newark
Delaware Memorial Bridge
Salem River
New Castle
Christiana
Christine River
To Baltimore
Bear
Glasgow
Fort Delaware State Park
Pea Patch Island
Maryland
Wrangle Hill
Salem
Lums Pond State Park
Delaware City
St Georges
Chesapeake & Delaware Canal
Augustine Wildlife Area
New Jersey
Canal Wildlife Area
To Odessa, Dover
To Bombay Hook National Wildlife Refuge
DELAWARE

are in Delaware, while the local places to stay and eat are in Pennsylvania. The Greater Wilmington Convention & Visitors Bureau promotes attractions on both sides of the border, including sites in Wilmington's northern suburbs.

Fifteen miles wide and 35 miles long, the Brandywine Valley is a patchwork of rolling, wooded countryside, historic villages, ancient farmhouses, and chateau estates to rival the Loire Valley in France. The Brandywine offers a wealth of attractions: mansions, gardens, museums, a winery, art collections, and some terrific country inns and restaurants.

Information

The Brandywine Valley Tourist Information Center (☎ 610-388-2900, 800-228-9933) is located right outside the gates of Longwood Gardens, Route 1, Kennett Square, Pennsylvania. Operated by Pennsylvania's Chester County Tourist Bureau, the center is open daily from 10 am to 6 pm (from October to March it closes at 5 pm).

Winterthur

The Brandywine Valley's most famous attraction, Winterthur (☎ 302-888-4600, 800-448-3883) was the country estate of Henry Francis du Pont until he opened it to the public in 1951. For most of his life du Pont collected American furniture. When he inherited Winterthur in 1927, he moved the best of his collection here, doubled the size of the existing house, and converted it to a showplace for the world's most important collection of early American decorative arts (1640–1860). During the next 20 years, du Pont continued to increase his collection . . . and the size of Winterthur.

The museum consists of two buildings, one with 175 period rooms and another with three exhibition galleries. There are over 89,000 objects made or used in America between 1640 and 1860, including furniture, textiles, paintings, prints, pewter, silver, ceramics, glass, needlework, and brass. The museum is surrounded by 980 acres, of which 60 acres are beautifully planted with native and exotic plants.

Unless joining a special tour, you are free to stroll the galleries, explore the grounds or ride the year-round tram (space permitting) at your leisure. General admission is $8 for adults, seniors and students $6, children $4. For additional fees, the following excellent guided tours (with small groups of four to 10 people) are available (reservations required): Introduction to Winterthur, a one-hour tour through selected period rooms ($5); Garden Walks, available seasonally ($5); and Decorative Arts Tours, in-depth one- and two-hour guided tours of period rooms ($9/13). There are also seasonal tours; ask at reception or, better still, call ahead because all of the tours are popular and fill quickly.

The museum and garden hours are Monday to Saturday from 9 am to 5 pm; Sunday from noon to 5 pm, with the garden open till dusk and the last tickets sold at 3:45 pm. Closed New Year's Day, Thanksgiving, and Christmas Day.

You can have continental breakfast, lunch, Sunday brunch, and afternoon tea in the pleasant Visitors Pavilion. Reservations for tea and brunch are suggested (☎ 302-888-4826).

Winterthur stands six miles northwest of Wilmington on Route 52, just 10 minutes off I-95 via Exit 7 (Delaware Avenue, Route 52N).

Delaware Museum of Natural History

With over a hundred exhibits ranging from local fauna to the wildlife of Mt Kenya, a walk across Australia's Great Barrier Reef, and an undersea world of exotic marine life, this museum has plenty of variety and has gained a certain degree of infamy since its founder John E du Pont ran amuck on his nearby estate in 1996. Allow 45 minutes to an hour to tour on your own.

The museum (☎ 302-658-9111) is located on Route 52, five miles northwest of Wilmington, just before Winterthur (coming from Wilmington). It's open Monday to Saturday from 9:30 am to 4:30 pm; Sunday from noon to 5 pm. Admission is $4, senior citizens and children $3.

Hagley Museum & Library

Beautifully situated on the banks of the Brandywine River, Hagley – like Winterthur – should be a must-see for visitors to the area. This 240-acre outdoor museum on the site of the birthplace of the Du Pont company tells the story of the du Ponts as part of the broader history of America's Industrial Revolution.

Du Pont started operations here as a gunpowder manufacturer in 1802. You can explore the ruins of the original mills, tour Eleutherian Mills, the 1803 residence of EI du Pont, see the French-style garden, and visit restored buildings with exhibits, models, and live demonstrations.

Allow at least three to four hours for your visit. Hagley is a large site with great natural beauty and lots of things to see and do. Hagley's hours are: March 15 through January 1, open daily from 9:30 am to 4:30 pm; January 2 through March 14, open Saturday and Sunday from 9:30 am to 4:30 pm; Monday to Friday ticket sales at 1 pm with one guided tour of the site from 1:30 to 4 pm. It's closed Thanksgiving, Christmas, and New Year's Eve Days. Admission is $9.75; students and senior citizens $7.50.

The museum (☎ 302-658-2400) is on Route 141, Wilmington. From I-95, take Exit 7 to Route 52N, to Route 100N, to Route 141N; or take Exit 8 from I-95 (Route 202N) to Route 141S, and follow the signs to Hagley Museum.

Nemours Mansion & Gardens

This is the estate of Alfred I du Pont, named after the site of the family's ancestral home in north-central France. Surrounded by 300 acres of gardens and natural woodlands, the Louis XVI–style chateau was built in 1909–1910 and has

Mr Gunpowder

The biography of Eleuthère Irénée du Pont de Nemours is not your average American immigrant rags-to-riches story. Du Pont arrived on the shores of Delaware with a bundle of money; after he got here, he just made plenty more – enough to make the state of Delaware his family's virtual principality for generations to come. The keys to his success were an uncommon education, plenty of investment capital, and a legacy of entrepreneurial skills which put him in a position to deliver to Americans something they crave like hamburger.

Born into the wealthy family of a French economist and publisher in 1771, EI du Pont grew up on the ancestral estate in Nemours and had the good fortune to study with the noted chemist Antoine Lavoisier. From Lavoisier, du Pont learned the secrets of making gunpowder and perfected his talents working in the royal powder mills in Essone. While gunpowder was what du Pont loved, he felt a filial duty to work in his father's printing business during the 1790s until the French Revolution made things too hot for royalists such as the du Ponts. Like political refugees the world over, du Pont and his father grabbed what they could of the family fortune and split for America.

It didn't take the young du Pont long to see that while Americans loved their shooting irons, their gunpowder was just as bad as the local wine. Figuring he had a better shot at improving the gunpowder situation – rather than the American viniculture industry – du Pont returned to France, appropriated plans and models of superior French gunpowder machinery, secured some additional financial backing, and returned to the USA to start EI du Pont de Nemours and Co.

The rest, as they say, is history. Du Pont made gunpowder that went snap-bang when guys like Daniel Boone required it – without huge clouds of sulfurous smoke. And Americans got themselves into an endless series of armed conflicts (including an obsession to tame the frontier) that made du Pont's gunpowder a household word. By the time du Pont died in 1834, he had monopolized the American gunpowder industry and might have taken some credit for the deaths of hundreds of thousands of his fellow Homo sapiens and a whole lot more lions and tigers and bears. ■

102 rooms. Today it contains fine examples of antique furniture, oriental rugs, tapestries, and paintings dating back to the 15th century. Nemours exhibits items illustrating the du Ponts' lavish lifestyle, including vintage cars, a billiard room, a bowling alley, and rooms for making ice and bottling sparkling water. The French gardens, stretching almost one third of a mile along the main vista from the mansion, are generally considered to be among the finest of their kind in America.

Located on Rockwood Rd, Wilmington, Nemours (☎ 302-651-6912) is open from May through November with the following guided tour schedule: Tuesday through Saturday at 9, 11 am, 1, and 3 pm; Sunday at 11 am, 1, and 3 pm. Admission is $8. Nobody under 16 is admitted. Tours take a minimum of two hours and include a guided tour through a series of rooms on three floors of the mansion, followed by a bus tour through the gardens. Visitors need to arrive at reception a good 15 minutes before the start of the tour. Reservations are recommended for individuals; the office is open Monday to Friday from 8:30 am to 4:30 pm.

Longwood Gardens

For many fans of horticulture, Longwood is America's ultimate garden, with 1050 outdoor acres and 20 indoor gardens presenting 'a never-ending cavalcade of exquisite bloom.' There are 11,000 different kinds of plants, roses, and orchids in bloom year round, an indoor Children's Garden with a maze, an Idea Garden for home gardeners, the historic Pierce–du Pont House, and one of the world's mightiest pipe organs. Each season brings another range of colors, while the heated conservatory and seasonal festivals and concerts add dimensions to the spectacle. At night, displays of illuminated fountains in the summer, and festive lights at Christmas, are breathtaking. It's open daily; the outdoor gardens from 9 am, conservatories from 10 am. They all close at 6 pm from April to October, and at 5 pm from November to March. Admission is $10, under 21 years old $6, children $2. On Tuesdays, adults are charged $6. Longwood Gardens (☎ 610-388-6741) lies along Route 1, Kennett Square, Pennsylvania.

DELAWARE

Rockwood Museum

This 19th century country estate owes its inspiration to the English country house. Built in the gothic style of architecture in 1851 by the merchant-banker Joseph Shipley, and standing on 72 of its original 300 acres, the museum consists of the porter's lodge, gardener's cottage, barn, and sundry outbuildings. A collection of English, Continental, and American decorative arts from the 17th to 19th centuries fill the manor house, while the grounds contain six acres of exotic foliage. The Rockwood Museum (☎ 302-761-4340) is located at 610 Shipley Road, Wilmington. It's open Tuesday to Saturday from 11 am to 3 pm. Admission is $5, seniors $4, children $1. Guided tours run every 30 minutes, and you can walk the grounds on your own.

Brandywine River Museum

A renowned showcase of American art, this museum presents a fine collection of works by three generations of the Wyeth family. Housed in a 19th century grist mill, the galleries also feature other American artists like Howard Pyle, Maxfield Parrish, William Trost Richards, and Horace Pippin, amongst hundreds of others. It's located at Hwy 1 and Route 100, Chadds Ford, Pennsylvania, (☎ 610-388-2700) and is open daily from 9:30 am to 4:30 pm. Admission for adults is $5; senior citizens and students pay $2.50.

Phillips Place Mushroom Museum

A unique collection of exhibits explaining the history, lore, and mystique of mushrooms (mushroom farming is a local tradition), Phillips Place features film, slides, and nutritional charts. It's located half a mile south of Longwood Gardens on Hwy 1, Kennett Square, Pennsylvania (☎ 610-388-6082), and it's open daily from 10 am to 6 pm. Admission is $1.25.

Chaddsford Winery

If the Brandywine Valley is really chateau country, then there must be a winery . . . and here it is. Operating from a renovated 18th century barn, this boutique winery (☎ 610-388-6221) is located on Hwy 1, in Chadds Ford, Pennsylvania (five miles south of Hwy 202). Producing small lots of varietal wines with grapes imported from the surrounding area, Chaddsford offers free guided and self-guided tours to see the grapes being crushed, fermented, barrel-aged, and bottled. For $5 you can taste seven or eight of the wines (and you get to keep your logo glass). Their white wines include Chardonnay, sauvignon blanc, and vidal blanc. For reds, Chaddsford offers cabernet sauvignon, merican (a cabernet sauvignon–cabernet Franc blend), and some chambourcins. There are tables for picnics outside around the barn. It's open Monday to Saturday from 10 am to 5:30 pm and on Sunday from noon to 5 pm.

John Chadds House

Located on Route 100 in Chadds Ford, Pennsylvania (☎ 610-388-7376), this was the home of John Chadds, ferryman, farmer, and tavern keeper. There is a demonstration of baking in a beehive oven. Built around 1725, the home is open from

The Battle of Brandywine Creek

The English army nearly ended the American Revolution when it attacked and overwhelmed the Continental forces at Brandywine Creek on September 11, 1777.

Weeks before the actual battle, General George Washington knew that a confrontation of major proportions was brewing. In late August Washington learned that British General William Howe had landed 13,000 British troups and 5000 Hessian mercenaries at the head of the Chesapeake Bay and had been advancing slowly through Delaware, gathering intelligence and securing supply lines, for an attack on Philadelphia, the new capital of the rebellious United States.

In defense of Philadelphia, Washington moved 11,000 Continentals to the Wilmington area. Realizing that the Brandywine presented a geographical obstacle to Howe, Washington and his French supporter the Marquis de Lafayette set up the bulk of their defenses along the high ground east of the creek at Chadds Ford, the most likely place for the British to cross the Brandywine. In addition, American troops covered two other fords on the Brandywine in hopes of forcing Howe to fight at Chadds Ford.

Howe anticipated Washington's plans and, using intelligence from local British sympathizers, sent the bulk of his troops on a long march to the north to round Washington's right flank under the cover of darkness and fog on September 11. Meanwhile, when the fog lifted at Chadds Ford, Howe's generals made a decoy attack and marched a few columns back and forth among the hills to give Washington's scouts the impression that the main British force was gathering at Chadds Ford for a charge. Preoccupied at Chadds Ford, Washington did not realize until midafternoon that Howe and 11,000 Redcoats had rounded the Continental right flank and nearly encircled the Americans. After brutal fighting, the remains of the American force escaped to Chester, Pennsylvania. British troops suffered 600 dead and wounded; the Continentals had 900 casualties and lost 400 men as prisoners of war.

Fifteen days later, Howe's troops marched into Philadelphia unopposed, but Washington was regrouping to fight again. Although Washington's attack on Howe at Germantown in October failed, and he had to suffer a long, cold winter encamped at Valley Forge, history shows that Washington's escape from the near catastrophe at Brandywine Creek gave the United States the hope and manpower to continue the revolution. As Washington reported to Congress following the Battle of Brandywine, 'Notwithstanding the misfortune of the day, I am happy to find the troops in good spirits; and I hope another time we shall compensate for the losses now sustained.' ■

May to September on Saturday and Sunday, from noon to 6 pm. Admission is $2.

Barns-Brinton House

Located on Hwy 1, Chadds Ford, Pennsylvania (☎ 610-388-7376), this house was originally built as a tavern in 1714 and has been restored to its original appearance by the Chadds Ford Historical Society. It is open May to September on Saturday and Sunday, from noon to 6 pm. Admission is $2.

Brandywine Battlefield Park

This park (☎ 610-459-3342), which includes the farmhouses that served as headquarters for George Washington and his French comrade the Marquis de Lafayette, lies on the north side of Hwy 1 just after you cross the Chadds Ford Bridge heading east. The chief reason to stop here is to pick up pamphlets on the battle that took place on farms north of the park, to see a reenactment of the battle, or to visit the restored headquarters of the Revolutionary generals who came close to losing their bid for American independence at Brandywine. Hours are Tuesday through Saturday from 9 am to 5 pm, Sunday from noon to 5 pm. It's closed on Monday. Park visits are free, but tours of the headquarters cost $3.50.

Special Events

From January to April Longwood Gardens holds its Welcome Spring Indoors celebration, with fragrant bulbs, acacias, orchids, and organ concerts. From April to May, Longwood celebrates Acres of Spring with daffodils, flowering cherries, tulips, irises, and wisterias.

In May Brandywine River Museum holds an antiques show. During the same month, the Point to Point Race is staged in Winterthur.

From June to September, Longwood Gardens holds its annual Festival of Fountains, with evening fountain displays, fireworks, outdoor concerts, roses, and water lilies. In July a Country Pride pops concert is offered at Winterthur.

From September through December the Brandywine River Museum features its Harvest Market & Christmas Shops. Held in mid-September, the Revolutionary Times at Brandywine is a reenactment of the Battle of Brandywine; there are crafts and food, too.

In October Longwood Gardens celebrates Autumn's Colors with chrysanthemums, fall foliage, and organ concerts. Delaware Museum of Natural History stages its annual Hoots, Howls & Haunts Halloween Carnival.

In November Winterthur has an antiques show, while Longwood Gardens holds a Chrysanthemum Festival, with 15,000 mums indoors. From Thanksgiving through New Years, Christmas exhibitions and events are held at most Brandywine Valley museums.

Places to Stay

Accommodations in Wilmington and New Castle, and even Philadelphia, are within easy reach of the Brandywine Valley. However, there are also some options that are even closer. Hwy 202 (Concord Pike) has a larger selection of accommodations, whereas there is only one on Route 52 (Kennett Pike). Most motels and hotels offer good value packages (especially on weekends) that include admission to Brandywine Valley museums.

On Hwy 202, the *Best Western Brandywine Valley Inn* (☎ 800-537-7772), is at 1807 Concord Pike, one mile north of Exit 8 on I-95, with rooms starting at $69. In the same area and similarly priced is the *Holiday Inn of Wilmington – North* (☎ 302-478-2222), at 4000 Concord Pike. Further north, the *Radisson Hotel Wilmington* (☎ 302-478-6000), 4727 Concord Pike, has singles from $60 to $90 and doubles from $85 to $109. Right before the Pennsylvania border, the cheaper *Tally-Ho Motor Lodge* (☎ 302-478-0300), 5209 Concord Pike, has singles/doubles for $45/60.

In Pennsylvania there is a selection of country-style inns and B&Bs. The 1987-built *Brandywine River Hotel* (☎ 610-388-1200), Hwy 1 and Route 100, Chadds Ford, has 40 rooms with double rooms from $109, and suites for $130. This hotel is not a piece of antiquity, but it is nicely designed to blend in with the surroundings and has a colonial-style interior.

Pace One (☎ 610-459-3702), Thornton and Glen Mills Rds, is a combination restaurant (see Places to Eat) and B&B in a 250-year-old restored barn. Doubles are $65 to $85. All seven rooms are decorated in different colors, with Lancaster oak queen beds, original watercolors of local scenes and private bath/shower. From Route 52 near Chadds Ford, head east on Hwy 1 and then left on Thornton Rd. The inn is on your right.

The luxurious *Fairville Inn* (☎ 610-388-5900) on Route 52, Mendenhall, is a delightful establishment, run by Ole and Patricia Retlev. The main house was built in 1826, and there is a rear carriage house and barn. Seven of the 15 rooms have fireplaces and the entire place is beautifully decorated. Prices range from $100 to $150, with two suites for $180. A substantial continental breakfast and light but delicious afternoon tea are included. From Hwy 1 west of Chadds Ford, take Route 52S to Mendenhall; the Fairville is almost a mile past Mendenhall on the left side.

Places to Eat

In Greenville, on Route 52 and convenient for many of the Brandywine attractions, there are a couple of nice establishments in the Powder Mill Square shopping complex. *Brew ha ha!* (☎ 302-658-6336) is an espresso cafe serving soup, sandwiches, and salads along with the coffee. *Cromwell's* (☎ 302-571-0561) is an upscale tavern serving such specialties as crab cakes, chicken winglets, and daily specials. It's open daily from 11 am to 1 am (closing at 10 pm on Sunday).

Buckley's Tavern (☎ 302-656-9776), 5812 Kennett Pike, Route 52, Centreville, is one of the region's most popular drinking spots. There is a small pub with a dining room and garden room at the back. Locals of all stripes, from gentry to farmers, are regulars here, and the place is usually packed. There is a small menu featuring good food, dishes ranging from $5 to $15. It's open daily.

Chadds Ford Inn (☎ 610-388-7361), Hwy 1 and Route 100 in Chadds Ford, Pennsylvania, dates back to the 1700s. The house was built by Francis Chadsey, an English Quaker who had bought the land from William Penn's commissioner of land grants. In 1736, his eldest son turned the house into a tavern which through the centuries has evolved into a popular restaurant, furnished with antiques and colonial memorabilia. The international cuisine served is up to date, though, as are prices, with lunch costing $10 to $15 and dinner costing $25 to $40. It's open daily.

Another popular historic restaurant is *Dilworthtown Inn* (☎ 610-399-1390), Old Wilmington Pike at Brinton Bridge Rd, Dilworthtown, Pennsylvania. Open daily for dinner ($30 to $50), this wood, stone, and brick structure with fireplaces and gas lamps dates back to 1758 and serves French cuisine. To find the inn, head north on Hwy 1 from the junction with Hwy 202. After a mile and a half, turn left at the second traffic light and continue for another mile and a half. Go straight when you reach the stop sign and the restaurant is the second on your right.

Pace One (see Places to Stay) has a restaurant that is open daily (no lunch Saturday, extensive brunch on Sunday). Lunch costs about $15 and dinner costs about $30. Artwork and vases of fresh flowers decorate a dimly lit interior room with stucco walls, bare floors, and a low ceiling. There is also a brighter porch-like outer room.

Things to Buy

Concord Mall, on Hwy 202N, is home to the Strawbridge & Clothier department store, Sears, Boscov's, and over 90 specialty stores. Most of the region's museums operate gift shops offering a wide range of gifts and souvenirs. Winterthur also has a popular mail order catalogue. There are several attractive upscale shopping options along Route 52, from Fairville, through Centreville to Greenville.

Getting There & Away

Route 52 and Hwy 202 form the general eastern and western borders of the Brandywine Valley, accessible from Wilmington. If you're coming from Philadelphia, take I-95 to join either road.

FORT DELAWARE STATE PARK

In the Delaware River, Pea Patch Island lies a mile from the shore of Delaware City. Here Fort Delaware State Park (☎ 302-834-7941) surrounds a granite fortress that served as a detention center during the Civil War. Of the 12,500 prisoners incarcerated here during the war, 2700 perished from cholera and other diseases spread by unsanitary conditions and mosquitoes. Visitors can see 19th century cells in the museum here, along with other artifacts from the period. There is also an audiovisual presentation. The park itself is popular with birders as the island is a nesting spot for egrets, herons, and other marsh fowl. There is an observation tower for bird watchers, along with nature trails, fishing, and picnic facilities. It's open daily from 11 am to 6 pm.

The only way to reach Pea Patch Island is via a 10-minute ride on the passenger ferry *Delafort* from Delaware City. The ride costs $3.50; there is no additional charge to enter the park or museum. The park is open May to September. Delaware City can be reached via Route 9.

NEW CASTLE

Historic New Castle (population 4800), the longtime colonial capital of Delaware, lies seven miles south of Wilmington on the Delaware River, near the spot where the river begins to widen into the bay. With rough, cobblestone streets and unbroken blocks of 18th century townhouses and public buildings, the heart of New Castle remains much as it was in colonial times. The oldest courthouse in the United States is here, and surveyors Mason and Dixon measured the arc of Delaware's northern boundary with Pennsylvania from the courthouse cupola.

Historic New Castle is the real thing. Beyond visiting the museums, admiring the architecture, exploring the shops, taking in the view of the Delaware River, and enjoying a drink, snack, or meal in one of the pleasant establishments found here, what truly completes the picture is the air of authenticity provided by all the little touches the residents have contributed in their private homes. As you look around, notice the heraldic flags and banners hanging from numerous homes, the painted signs, the lamp fixtures, the window frames, and other period details. Due to a strict code controlling these items, the town truly does allow you to step back in time. Architectural examples of the Dutch, Colonial, French, Georgian, Federal, and Empire periods exist here. If you can, be sure to visit A Day in Old New Castle (see Special Events), held every year in May, when residents open up their homes to visitors and the town celebrates the rites of spring.

Surprisingly, there are no hordes of tourists here, and New Castle can be just the antidote for the nearby bustle of traffic racing along the highways of America's Northeast Corridor. You can come to New Castle for the day, or you can check into one of the town's B&Bs and disconnect from the modern world indefinitely. The Visitors Bureau has dubbed it 'The Little Williamsburg on the Delaware River,' and New Castle actually lives up to its billing.

History

Originally named Fort Casimir by the Dutch, Peter Stuyvesant founded the settlement in 1651 to provide a position from which to command river traffic. Due to its strategic location on the Delaware River, the Dutch, Swedish, and English all fought and gained control of the town at one time or another. After defeating the Dutch, the English renamed the settlement and gave the town to William Penn. In 1682, Penn came ashore at the foot of Delaware St to take possession, adding the three counties of what is now Delaware to his lands in America. Dissatisfied with life under Penn, these counties won the privilege of electing

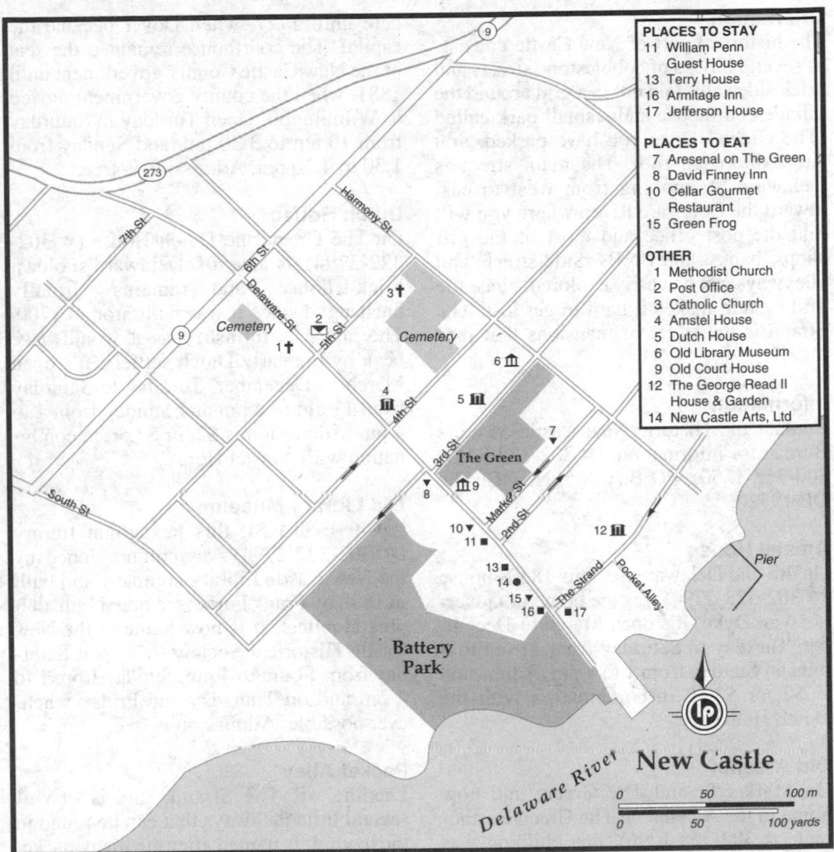

their own legislature in 1704, and New Castle became the colonial capital of Delaware. The town also served as the first state capital until its vulnerability to British naval attack caused the government to move to Dover in 1777.

An ideal transfer point for trips up and down the coast, New Castle thrived during the 1700s and early 1800s. The courts and general assembly that functioned here attracted numerous judges, lawyers, and government officials who built grand homes, many of which have been restored today. Five signers of the Declaration of Independence – George Read, George Ross, Jr, Thomas McKean, Charles Thompson, and Francis Hopkin – were New Castle citizens. Although the great fire of 1824 destroyed many of the inns and warehouses on The Strand, some were rebuilt and the rest of the village has remained intact.

New Castle today has two identities. It is both the historical center and the sprawling modern town that virtually surrounds it. Most passersby do not make a point of stopping and only see the thoughtless commercial development along Hwy 13.

Orientation
The historical part of New Castle consists of several blocks of cobblestone streets and brick sidewalks laid out in a grid around the village courthouse and a small park called 'The Green.' Once you have parked, you can explore on foot. The main street is Delaware St, running from west to east toward the Delaware River, where you will find the post office and most of the gift shops, banks, and B&Bs. Side streets and alleyways can be easily explored, since the grid system makes it hard to get lost. The Strand is the street of mansions that face the river.

Information
Contact the Historic New Castle Visitors Bureau for information: (☎ 302-322-8411, 800-758-1550), PO Box 465, New Castle, DE 19720.

Amstel House
On 4th and Delaware Sts, this 1830s house (☎ 302-322-2794) was the home of Governor Van Dyke. It's open March to December, Tuesday to Saturday from 11 am to 4 pm and Sunday from 1 to 4 pm. Admission is $2, or $3.50 in combination with the Dutch House.

Old Arsenal
On Market St and The Green, and now home to the Arsenal on The Green Restaurant (☎ 302-328-1290), this building was built by the federal government in 1809 in preparation for the war of 1812. Note the bas-relief of an American eagle perched on a gun on the south wall.

Old Churches & Graveyards
On The Green in the center of the village are two early 18th century churches and their cemeteries, which date from the 1600s. They are usually open every day and admission is free.

Old Court House
On Delaware St, this is the oldest surviving courthouse (☎ 302-323-4453) in the US, built in 1732. The colonial assembly met here until 1777, when Dover became the capital. The courthouse remained the seat of the New Castle County government until 1881, when the county government moved to Wilmington. Open Tuesday to Saturday from 10 am to 3:30 pm, and Sunday from 1:30 to 4:30 pm. Admission is free.

Dutch House
On The Green, the Dutch House (☎ 302-322-2794) is one of Delaware's oldest brick houses and remains virtually unchanged since it was built around 1700. The house is furnished as it would have been by the early Dutch settlers. It's open March to December, Tuesday to Saturday from 11 am to 4 pm and Sunday from 1 to 4 pm. Admission is $2, or $3.50 in combination with Amstel House.

Old Library Museum
At 40 E 3rd St, this hexagonal library (☎ 302-322-2794) was commissioned by the New Castle Library company and built in 1892 by Frank Furness, a noted Philadelphia architect. It is now home to the New Castle Historical Society. It's open Saturday from 11 am to 4 pm, Sunday from 1 to 4 pm and on Thursday and Friday whenever possible. Admission is free.

Packet Alley
Leading off The Strand, this is one of several little pathways that can be found in the town. It is named after the many packet boats that traveled to New Castle in the late 1700s and early 1800s. On the side wall next to the alley is one of the oldest surviving Ivory Soap billboards.

George Read II House & Garden
On The Strand, at No 42, this beautiful Federal mansion (☎ 302-322-8411) is furnished in the early 19th century style. The surrounding gardens still maintain much of the original 1840s plan. In January and February it's open Saturday from 10 am to 4 pm and Sunday from noon to 4 pm; from March to December it's open Tuesday to Saturday from 10 am to 4 pm, and Sunday from noon to 4 pm. Admission is $4.

Riverfront & Battery Park

At the foot of Delaware St, be sure to enjoy the cooling breezes and lovely views of the Delaware River from the wharf. There is a children's playground, a 2.5-mile jogging and bicycle trail, and picnic tables.

Organized Tours

The Historical Society of Delaware offers guided walking tours of historic New Castle. Lasting about one hour, tours cost $2 per person and are available every day except Monday. Reservations are required. Contact the Society at George Read II House & Garden (☎ 302-322-8411) as far in advance as possible.

Special Events

During the first weekend in May the May Market – a plant and flower sale – takes place in the Market Square. New Castle's biggest event, A Day in Old Newcastle, falls on the third Saturday in May. Some 60 private homes open up to the public and such special events as Maypole dancing, carriage rides, music performances, and bell-ringing can be enjoyed. Thousands of visitors enjoy this special day. Tickets cost $10 and are available on the day from the Old Court House, with proceeds going toward the preservation and continued restoration of the site.

Separation Day is celebrated on the first or second Saturday in June. It's a daylong celebration of Delaware's separation from England, ending with fireworks. A large antique show is held on Battery Park on the last Sunday in August.

On the fourth Saturday in September arts, crafts, and music are celebrated in Art on The Green.

Candlelight tours happen during the second and fourth weekends in December. The tours celebrate Christmas by visiting decorated museums, churches, and public buildings, and they often include live performances by musical ensembles.

Places to Stay

Historic District The best way to soak up the slow-paced congeniality of historic New Castle is to spend a night or two here at a B&B. As space is limited, reservations are recommended to secure preferred weekend dates (usually a month or so in advance, but for the Day in New Castle weekend up to a year before). As this guide goes to press, new B&Bs are in the works, and travelers might want to consult the New Castle Visitors Bureau (see Information) for listings.

The Terry House (☎ 302-322-2505), 130 Delaware St, is a Federal townhouse (1869) overlooking Battery Park and the Delaware River. With 12-foot-high ceilings and Chippendale or Queen Anne furniture (some of it authentic), the four spacious rooms each have private baths, air-con, cable TV, and queen-sized beds. Rates are $80 per room Friday and Saturday, $60 to $70 the rest of the week, depending on the season. Continental breakfast is included. Visa, MasterCard, and Discover are accepted.

The *William Penn Guest House* (☎ 302-328-7736), 206 Delaware St, offers a less expensive alternative. Dating from 1682, William Penn actually slept here. The four rooms share two bathrooms. Rates are $50 Friday to Sunday and $45 the rest of the week, with continental breakfast included. They accept cash or checks only.

The *Jefferson House* (☎ 302-325-1025), at No 5 on The Strand, offers three rooms with full breakfast served at the nearby *Cellar Gourmet Restaurant*. Rates are $54 for a 1920s basement apartment with antique oak furnishings, iron and brass bed, and full kitchen; $75 for a ground floor bedroom unit with an iron and brass bed and its own screened-in porch overlooking the river; and $85 for a spacious room with a working 19th century fireplace, full kitchen, and antique cherry Victorian furniture. Each room has private bath, and there is an outdoor Jacuzzi.

The *Armitage Inn* (☎ 302-328-6618), at No 2 on The Strand, has the grandest location, fronting right on the park with the river vistas just 100 yards away. Steve and Rina Marks recently restored this colonial townhouse built in 1732 to its original splendor and beyond. The public rooms are a treasure trove of antiques, family heirlooms, and an eclectic collection of original art. The four guest rooms feature elegant colonial reproductions, canopy beds, and private baths. The homemade kugel (a sweet noodle pudding) and carefully brewed gourmet coffee make for a rich breakfast. Rates are $105 to $135.

Du Pont Hwy If you are unable to find a vacancy in the historic district, or want something else, head two miles west of the village to Hwy 13 (Du Pont Hwy) where you will find a variety of motels. Among the cheapest is *Hollywood Motel* (☎ 302-322-3070), at 145 S Du Pont Hwy, with singles or doubles for $25, and a two-bedded room for $35.

Next door, *Super 8 Motel* (☎ 302-322-9480) at 215 S Du Pont Hwy, has singles/doubles for $40/45.

Rodeway Inn (☎ 302-328-6246), at 111 S Du Pont Hwy, is probably the nicest motel along this stretch.

Across the highway, the *Econo Lodge* (☎ 302-322-4500), at 232 S Du Pont Hwy, has singles/doubles for $38/48.

Places to Eat & Drink

The *Cellar Gourmet Restaurant*, 208 Delaware St, is the place to go for a cup of coffee, or for a variety of light meals like quiches, salads, sandwiches, ice creams, waffles, and other desserts from $3 to $7. It's open daily.

For something grander, try the *Arsenal on The Green* (☎ 302-328-1290) on Market St. Housed in the 1809 Arsenal, this restaurant offers an elegant but informal setting. Afternoon tea is served on Friday and Saturday from 2:30 to 4:30 pm. Sunday brunch is served from 11:30 am to 2:30 pm. Lunch (around $20 per person) and dinner ($30 to $50) are served daily.

The *Green Frog* (☎ 302-322-8898), 114 Delaware St, is the town's English pub (built in 1724). The pub takes its name from the early cast-iron frog doorsteps used in the 18th century. Open Monday to Saturday from 9 to 1 am, the Frog is a friendly place for a game of darts, a drink, or tasty bar food like chili or crab soup for under $4. On Monday and Tuesday the Frog has personal pizzas and beers for $1 each. Wednesday they offer all-you-can-eat pasta for $6.25. There is a lively mixed crowd here on weekend nights.

On Hwy 13, *Lone Star Steakhouse & Saloon* (☎ 302-322-3854), 113 S Du Pont Hwy, has become a popular spot with locals and visitors alike. This casual, cowboy-theme restaurant with sawdust on the floor serves up burgers, ribs, and steaks. Meal prices vary from $10 to $20 per person. Along this same busy stretch of Hwy 13, you will find an array other chain and fast food restaurants.

Things to Buy

Eight or 10 attractive shops along Delaware St justify a browse. You will find few bargains, but you might discover something you like for yourself or as a gift. Look for New Castle Arts, Ltd (☎ 302-322- 9191) at No 116, Antique Co-op of New Castle (☎ 302-325-2510), next to the Green Frog, and the Read House Gift Shop (☎ 302-322-8411), at the museum at No 42 on The Strand.

Getting There & Away

Car Approaching from the south on I-95, take Exit 5, Route 141S toward New Castle. Continue past the overpass of Hwys 13 and 40. At the intersection of Route 9 and 273, turn left onto Route 9N. Go half a mile to the next light and bear right onto Delaware St to enter historic New Castle (look for the River Plaza shopping center to your left).

Approaching from the north on I-95, follow I-295 toward New Jersey. Take the last exit before paying the toll, Route 9 south to New Castle. Follow Route 9S for about two miles. At the first stop sign, go straight ahead into New Castle and turn left onto Delaware St at the first light (look for the River Plaza Shopping Center to your right).

Approaching from New Jersey on I-295 and the NJ Turnpike, take the Delaware Memorial Bridge into Delaware. At the first exit after paying the toll, take Route 9S to New Castle as detailed above.

Bus Wilmington's DART bus system provides a service to/from New Castle. Call ☎ 800-652-3278 for information.

NEWARK

Pronounced 'New Ark,' this is the home of the University of Delaware's main campus, along with auto assembly plants, and New Castle County's second-largest city. Newark (population 25,000) is primarily a college town and has little else to justify a visit. However, you might find that this is a great a place to stay if you crave the strong coffee, heady conversations, cheap beer, and great rock & roll that go along with thousands of bright, young adults trying to squeeze excitement out of every moment.

The University of Delaware began here in 1765 and has bloomed into a 1000-acre campus with over 16,000 full-time undergraduate and graduate students. You can find everything you might expect in the way of a university education here . . . as well as some things you might not expect – like an experimental farm and a program in ice skating science for Olympic hopefuls. Dozens of fraternities and sororities enroll 16% of the student body. More than half the students come from out of state; 89% are white; women outnumber men, seven to six.

Orientation

Main St east of the university is a one-way thoroughfare (westbound traffic) and the heart of Newark's commercial life. Along this stretch of town lie stores, a post office, several banks, a shopping mall (the Newark Shopping Center with a cinema), and various eating, drinking, and live music venues. There is also an inexpensive motel here.

Places to Stay

Allowing you to step outside and stroll along Main St makes the *Travelodge* (☎ 302-737-5050), 268 E Main St, attractive. Standard motel-type singles/doubles are $30/40.

Two other motels in Newark are less centrally located. *Howard Johnson* (☎ 302-368-8521), 1119 S College Ave, is just off the intersection of I-95 at Exit 1B (Route 896). Singles/doubles cost $49/59. Across the road, the *Comfort Inn* (☎ 302-368-8715), 1120 S College Ave, has singles/doubles for $54/62.

Places to Eat & Drink

The popular *Klondike Kate's Saloon & Restaurant* (☎ 302-737-6100), 158 E Main St, serves a wide-ranging selection plus specials; meat loaf, pastas, pizza, burgers, and salads run from $6 to $20. It's open daily from 11 am to 1 am.

Try the *Post House Restaurant* (☎ 302-386-3459) on E Main St for breakfasts under $3 and lunches for less than $5.50. It's not open for dinner.

Deer Park Tavern (☎ 302-731-5315), 108 W Main St, has a history of its own. On this site, a log cabin was built in 1747. Called the St Patrick's Inn, it existed for nearly one hundred years and served, among others, the surveyors Mason and Dixon (1764) and the writer Edgar Allan Poe (1843). The present building went up in 1851 and was named after the surrounding farm land, known as Deer Park. It was home to a women's seminary, a ballroom, a polling place, a barbershop, and also one of the region's finest hotels. This was the site of women's suffrage movements in 1913 and became a forum for student activists in the 1960s. Today's students still flock here, along with others who enjoy the somewhat rundown surroundings, the bar, and the primarily Mexican menu. Meals cost from $2 to $7, and the very good Sunday brunch is $6 to $10. It stays open daily from 9 am to 1 am. You can hear live music here most nights.

East End Cafe (☎ 302-738-0880), 270 E Main St next to the Travelodge, specializes in grilled burgers, chicken, and tuna sandwiches for under $6, and live entertainment. It's closed Sunday.

Crab Trap, 57 Elkton Rd, claims to

feature Newark's largest selection of draft beers, sandwiches from $4 to $5, and seafood entrees from $6 to $10. It's open daily from 11 am to 1 am.

Entertainment

The Stone Balloon Tavern & Concert Hall (☎ 302-368-2000), 115 E Main St, just celebrated its 25th anniversary. This is one of the Capital Region's top music venues with nationally renowned bands regularly featured here. Tickets vary from $5 to $12 depending on the artist.

Other places for live music along Main St are *Deer Park* (never a cover charge) and the *East End*.

Getting There & Away

Newark is best reached by car. From I-95 take Exit 1B to Newark.

To get there by bus, take the DART bus No 6 from Wilmington. The fare is $1.90.

Central Delaware

South of the Chesapeake & Delaware Canal lies the heart of Delaware Bay country. Largely ignored by tourists rushing to and from Delaware's Atlantic beaches, Central Delaware is a quilt of family farms and marshes. Amish people travel the roads by horse and buggy; bayside fishing communities endure; spartina swamps spread to the edge of the bay; tidal rivers snake through the countryside; and important wildlife refuges shelter tens of thousands of migratory Canada and snow geese. Here you will discover funky fishing ports as well as historic settlements including the Brigadoon-like Odessa and the state capital of Dover with its village Green and 18th-century public buildings.

Life in Central Delaware is distinctly slower, more rural, and more conservative than you will find at either end of the state. Here in bay country, a soft drawl similar to that heard on Maryland's Eastern Shore (clearly a kindred region) replaces the Pennsylvania twang you heard in the speech of people living north of the canal. The traditional lifestyles of waterman, farmer, and progger persist. For fun, people head to country fairs, hunt all types of beasts and fowl, or go fishing. But the 21st century is never far away. Dover has a NASÇAR raceway and an active air-transport base flying gigantic C-5 Galaxies.

Much like Southern Maryland, Central Delaware has a hundred curious back-waters unknown to all but local citizens . . . and they're ripe for exploration by cycle or small boat.

HIGHLIGHTS

- Biking along the Heritage Greenway to discover coastal wilderness and funky ports
- Eating steamed crabs at Sambo's on the Leipsic River
- Bird watching during the fall or spring migration at Bombay Hook

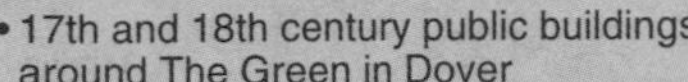

- 17th and 18th century public buildings around The Green in Dover

COASTAL HERITAGE GREENWAY

This is a spectacular backroad tour of bayside Delaware which essentially follows Route 9, also known as the River Rd, south from New Castle. The Greenway is well marked with signs that plot your course along a narrow, blacktop road that winds through farmland, marsh meadows, and wildlife refuges. Along the way you will see historic farmhouses, watermen's wharves, and a whole village that is on the National Registry of Historic Places. Currently the Coastal Heritage Greenway ends in Dover, but the trail will eventual guide motorists and cyclists along the bay's coast all the way to the Atlantic beaches.

For an excellent 27-page collection of maps and narratives relevant to the Greenway, call the Department of Natural Resources and Environmental Control (☎ 302-739-5282) or stop by the Greater Wilmington Convention Center and Visitors Bureau Information Center at milepost No 6 on I-95 between Wilmington and Newark.

ODESSA

About halfway between Wilmington and Dover, the village of Odessa, with its concentration of 18th and early 19th century buildings, can on a foggy morning appear like a mirage from another century. All of the village is on the National Registry of Historic Places, and while most of the homes are private, Winterthur Museum owns three sites and opens them to the public. Odessa is a great retreat for cyclists, birders, and cartop boaters exploring the

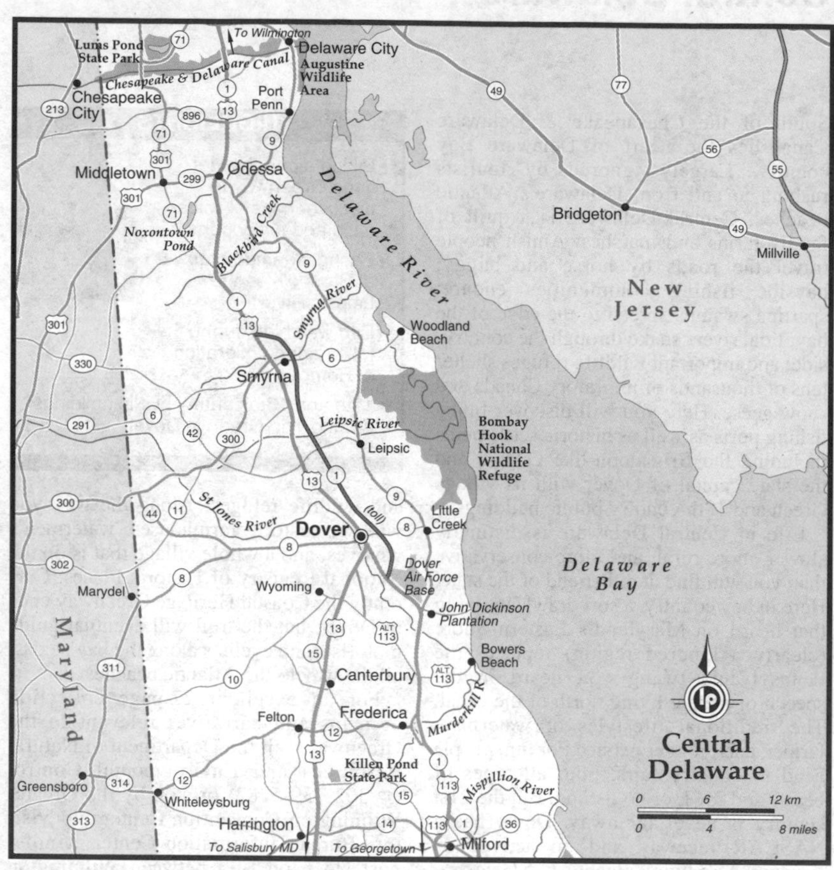

Greenway, tidewater creeks, and vast marshlands that stretch all the way from Delaware Bay to doorsteps of Odessa's citizens.

Historic Houses

Originally settled by the Dutch and known in the 18th century as Cantwell's Bridge, Odessa was a busy grain-shipping port. In an effort to give the community world prominence as a grain port, citizens renamed their town in 1885 after the Ukrainian seaport which enjoyed international celebrity as a grain center. The public relations maneuver did not work, and Odessa became another Delaware Bay port that time forgot until preservationists began to reclaim the decaying trove of historic buildings in the 1930s. Today you can stroll along the quiet tree-lined streets and admire examples of Colonial, Federal, and early 19th century architecture. Three buildings (☎ 302-378-4098) are open to the public: Wilson-Warner House, Corbit-Sharp House, and the Brick Hotel Gallery. They're open from March to December, Tuesday to Saturday from 10 am to 4 pm, Sunday from 1 to 4 pm. Admission is $4 for one property, $6 for two, $7 for three.

The Chesapeake & Delaware Canal

Spanning the narrow neck of the Delmarva Peninsula for about 12 miles between Elkton, Maryland, and Delaware City, Delaware, the C&D Canal is one of the oldest and most heavily trafficked canals in the US.

As early as 1654, enterprising leaders like Delaware's Swedish governor Rising saw the advantage to trade that would accrue once the colonies on the Delaware were linked by canal to those on the Chesapeake. Work to connect St Georges Creek to Back Creek did not begin until after the Revolutionary War, in 1804. The job stalled for decades due to a lack of funds, but in 1829 private investors opened the canal to provide an all-water route between the swelling cities of Philadelphia and Baltimore. As originally built, the canal was a shallow 10 feet deep and less than 50 feet wide. Three sets of locks in the canal compensated for the tidal differences between the waters of the Chesapeake and the Delaware Bays. In spite of the canal's limitations, it shortened the boat trip from Philadelphia to Baltimore by as much as a week while adding the safety of a purely inland passage to the trip. To get a sense of the dimensions of the old canal, you can look at a remnant that serves as a boat basin in Delaware City today.

In 1919 the federal government bought the canal and began a 17-year project to widen and deepen the ditch. Today's canal is 450 feet wide with a controlling depth of 33 feet. Thousands of ships, seagoing tugs, and tows pass through the C&D every year. A good place to watch the action is at Schaefer's Canal House (☎ 410-855-2200) on Bank St in North Chesapeake City, Maryland (like Delaware City, this place is really a village). At Schaefer's you will see launches racing alongside passing ships to pick up and drop off pilots to guide the ships through the Chesapeake and Delaware Bays. The C&D Canal Museum (☎ 410-885-5622), at 2nd St and Bethel Rd in Chesapeake City, features the old lock pumphouse and historical exhibits. It's open Easter to Thanksgiving, Monday to Saturday from 8 am to 4:15 pm, Sunday from 10 am to 6 pm; closed on holidays and Sundays in winter. Admission is free. ■

Special Events

On July 4, US Independence is celebrated with fireworks. During October's Decoy & Carving Festival, nature enthusiasts can enjoy waterfowl and other art exhibitions by local artists and swap and sell decoys. There are also craft stalls and music performances. At the end of the month, Halloween is celebrated with a hayride, bonfire, hot dog roast, and family entertainment.

Yuletide in Odessa takes place from the third week in November through December featuring candlelight tours, performances of The Nutcracker, and historic homes opened to the public.

Places to Stay

The sole choice in Odessa is a remarkable B&B, *Cantwell House* (☎ 302-378-4179), 107 High St. It's a restored 1840 three-story house with four rooms, owned and operated by Carole Coleman. These vary in size and just one has a private bathroom. They cost from $55 to $85 depending on the room and day of the week. A continental breakfast with homebaked items is included. Cantwell House is usually closed for July and August. High St is one block up the hill from the historic properties on Main St, and Cantwell House is the second house down from the library.

Getting There & Away

Odessa is about 23 miles south of Wilmington and 26 miles north of Dover. Hwy 13 runs past the western edge of the village; the historic houses lie a few blocks to the east. Route 299 makes a short link from Odessa to Route 9 and the Greenway.

LEIPSIC

Further south on Route 9 is another small village that is home to a legendary eating place. *Sambo's Tavern* (☎ 302-674-9724) on Front St in Leipsic is one of the East

Coast's most renowned crab houses. This place is friendly and informal with newspaper-covered tables overlooking the meanders of the Leipsic River. There are also a few stools at the bar, a pool table, and a jukebox. A map of the world on one wall allows visitors to hang name and place tags to illustrate that people from far and wide continue to eat here. Crabs served in the shell are the main event. Expect to spend about $20. The menu also features crab cakes, platters, shrimp, oysters, and various sandwiches, ranging from as little as $2.50 to $16.

Sambo's is open from April to the Saturday before Thanksgiving, Monday to Saturday from 9 am (the kitchen is ready by 11 am) to 11 pm with last orders at 10 pm. The place can fill up during the summer and whenever there is a major speedway event at Dover Downs or bird watching at Bombay Hook, so make reservations. Heading north six miles from Dover, Leipsic's one main street veers east off Route 9.

BOMBAY HOOK NATIONAL WILDLIFE REFUGE

This beautiful 15,918-acre site (☎ 302-653-9345) is a haven for migrating and resident waterfowl, primarily ducks and geese. Three quarters of the refuge is tidal salt marsh. A visitors center encourages the public to visit the refuge for wildlife observation, nature study, and photography throughout the year. Very well organized with informative signs posted throughout, the refuge is a joy to explore. You will find an auto tour route, observation towers, and nature trails. Call ahead to inquire about special events. Birders travel from all over the country, even the world, to watch the Canada and snow geese, heron, eagles, and other species that migrate or nest here.

Admission is $4 per vehicle, $2 per person without a vehicle. The visitors center is open Monday to Friday from 8 am to 4 pm. During spring Bombay Hook is open on Saturday and Sunday from 9 am to 5 pm. The refuge is sometimes closed on summer and winter weekends.

To reach Bombay Hook Headquarters go about a mile north of the village of Leipsic on Route 9, then head east on Whitehall Neck Rd for two miles and look for the signs.

Standing on the northern edge of the refuge beside Route 9, **Allee House** is one of the best-preserved 18th century brick farmhouses in the state. Believed to have been built in 1753, the house was restored in the 1960s and is now open to the public on Saturday and Sunday from 2 to 5 pm. Admission is free and the house can be reached via the refuge auto tour or from Route 9, which is north of the entrance to the visitors center.

LITTLE CREEK

Reached by the Greenway (Route 9), Little Creek is a tiny village, home to the popular seafood restaurant *Village Inn* (☎ 302-734-9724). Look for it just to the west side of the road, south of a bridge crossing the Mahon and Little Rivers. Lunch costs $15 and dinner costs $30.

DOVER

In the midst of Central Delaware's farm country, Dover (population 30,000), the state capital, is an attractive town with a historical center and a collection of small museums. It is also a potential jumping-off point for historical and natural sights nearby. But in spite of the attractions, Dover does not draw flocks of tourists except during a few key weeks each year when it is totally overwhelmed. These moments of chaos coincide with NASCAR racing events at the local speedway and the State Fair in nearby Harrington.

During the rest of the year the coming and going of Air Force personnel to Dover AFB accounts for the bulk of Dover's transient clientele. Despite being a state capital with 30,000 people, Dover remains something of a farm town with the feel of one of those rural all-American communities where almost everyone knows everybody and life is just a little simpler than it is in the rest of the USA. It is not uncommon to hear the state governor and a police officer greet each other by their first names.

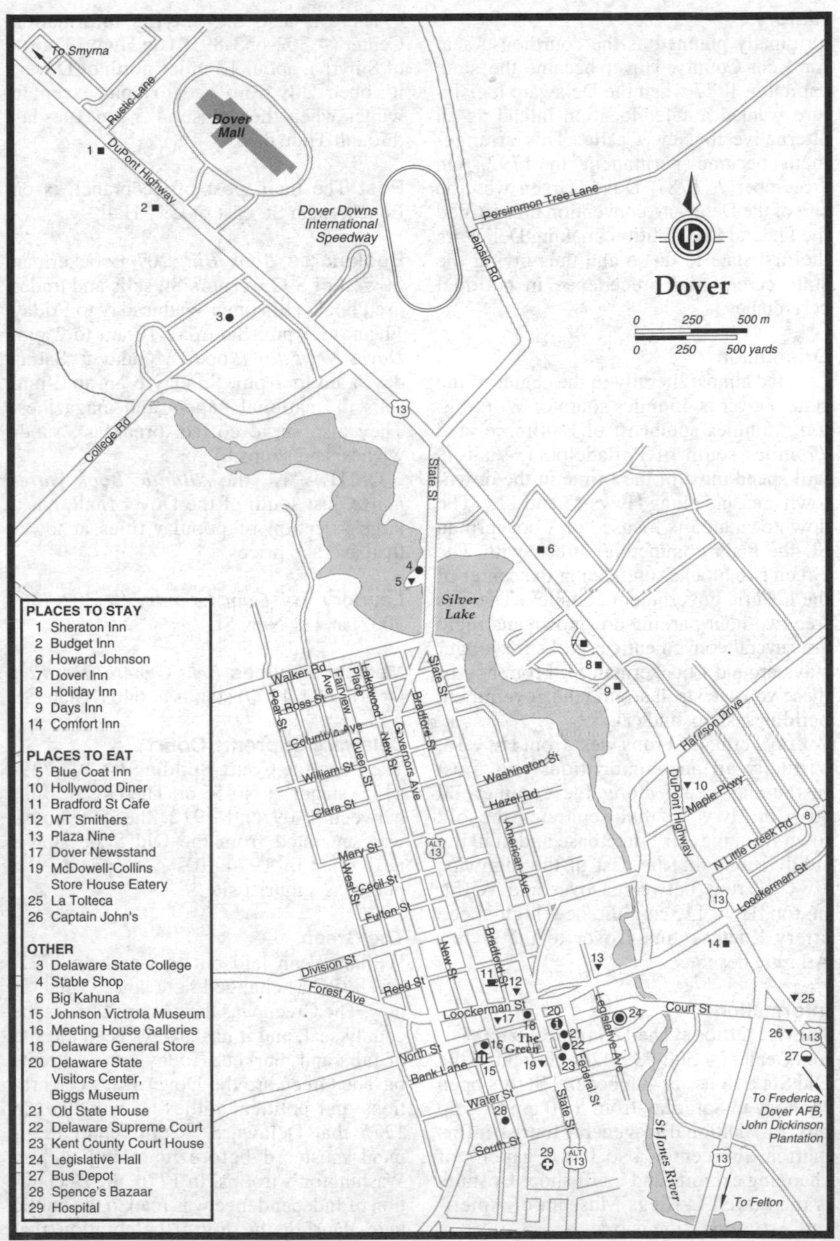
Dover
0 250 500 m
0 250 500 yards
To Smyrna
Rustic Lane
DuPont Highway
Dover Mall
Dover Downs International Speedway
Persimmon Tree Lane
Leipsic Rd
College Rd
State St
Silver Lake
Walker Rd
Ross St
Pearl St
Fairview Ave
Lakewood Place
Bradford St
Columbia Ave
Queen St
New St
Governors Ave
William St
Clara St
Washington St
Hazel Rd
American Ave
Mary St
West St
Cecil St
Fulton St
Division St
Forest Ave
Reed St
Loockerman St
The Green
North St
Bank Lane
Water St
South St
Federal St
Legislative Ave
Court St
Harrison Drive
Maple Pkwy
N Little Creek Rd
Loockerman St
St Jones River
To Frederica, Dover AFB, John Dickinson Plantation
To Felton
PLACES TO STAY
1 Sheraton Inn
2 Budget Inn
6 Howard Johnson
7 Dover Inn
8 Holiday Inn
9 Days Inn
14 Comfort Inn
PLACES TO EAT
5 Blue Coat Inn
10 Hollywood Diner
11 Bradford St Cafe
12 WT Smithers
13 Plaza Nine
17 Dover Newsstand
19 McDowell-Collins Store House Eatery
25 La Tolteca
26 Captain John's
OTHER
3 Delaware State College
4 Stable Shop
6 Big Kahuna
15 Johnson Victrola Museum
16 Meeting House Galleries
18 Delaware General Store
20 Delaware State Visitors Center, Biggs Museum
21 Old State House
22 Delaware Supreme Court
23 Kent County Court House
24 Legislative Hall
27 Bus Depot
28 Spence's Bazaar
29 Hospital

History

Originally planned as the courthouse seat for Kent County, Dover became the state capital in 1777 when the Delaware legislature wanted a safer location inland as an alternative to New Castle. This arrangement became permanent in 1792. On December 7, 1787, Dover Green was the site of the Delaware convention that ratified the Federal Constitution, making Delaware the first state to do so and thus giving the state ceremonial precedence in national ceremonies.

Orientation

Located almost literally in the center of the state, Dover is 45 miles south of Wilmington, 86 miles southeast of Baltimore, and 77 miles south of Philadelphia. Visitors will spend most of their time in the downtown area and along Hwys 13 and 113. The downtown area is focused on Loockerman St, the main commercial street, with The Green two blocks south being the center of the historic government complex. There is free two-hour parking downtown and there are several convenient car parks for longer stays around Loockerman St. From any of these you can stroll around the government buildings, shop, and eat.

Loockerman St runs west from Hwy 13. Virtually all accommodations and most restaurants stand along the commercial strip of Hwy 13 that separates the old town from the Air Force base and housing subdivisions that lie east of the highway. Hwy 13 runs between Dover and Wilmington. Hwy 113 and the new high-speed artery Route 1 link Dover to the state's Atlantic beaches.

Information

Tourist Offices The Delaware State Visitors Center (☎ 302-739-4266) is behind the Old State House at 406 Federal St. It's open Monday to Saturday from 8:30 am to 4:30 pm. In additional to general tourist information, the center also has a gallery of changing exhibits and a gift shop. Upstairs is the Sewell C Biggs Museum of American Art. Admission is free.

There is also the Smyrna Information Center (☎ 302-653-8910) on Hwy 13 north of Smyrna, about 12 miles north of Dover; it's open daily from 7 am to 8 pm, except in winter when they close at 5 pm Tuesday through Thursday.

Post The main post office branch is on Loockerman St, east of City Hall.

Bookstores *Book Bin*, 207 Loockerman St west of S Governors St, sells and trades used books. It's open Wednesday to Friday 11 am to 5 pm, Saturday 10 am to 2 pm. *Dover Newsstand*, open Monday to Saturday 6 am to 7 pm, Sunday 6 am to 2 pm, sells the national papers and magazines. They also serve coffee, breakfast, sandwiches, and soups to go.

On Hwy 13, the *Atlantic Book Warehouse*, just south of the Dover Mall, has a large selection of popular titles at lower than average prices.

Laundry Try *Coin Laundry* (☎ 302-736-5002) at 431 New St.

Medical Services *Kent General Hospital* (☎ 302-674-4700) stands at 640 S State St.

Delaware Supreme Court

The Supreme Court Building (☎ 302-739-4155) stands at No 55 on The Green. Built between 1909 and 1912, the courthouse was separated from the Old State House next door in 1974. It's not open to the public as a tourist site.

The Green

William Penn laid out this park in 1722, and little has changed here since. Then, as now, The Green was the center of life as the county seat, and it has always been the site of fairs and markets. Today's main events on The Green are the Dover Days celebrations and political rallies. It was here in 1775 that Delaware's Continental Regiment mustered before marching to join Washington's troops. In 1776, the Declaration of Independence was read to the public here. During the joyful celebration that immediately followed, there was a public burning of King George III's portrait.

Kent County Court House

At No 38 on the Green, this building was erected in 1874 on the site of the Court House of 1691. That was itself a replacement of an even earlier version that the court had ordered 'Burnt to get ye naiules [nails].' From about 1722 to 1863 a tavern occupied this site. A legend claims that the tavern had a portrait of King George III on its sign until patriotic yearnings caused the king's portrait to be painted out and replaced with a likeness of George Washington. It's not open to the public.

Legislative Hall

Standing on Legislative Ave and built in 1932, this is where Delaware's General Assembly, made up of the Senate and House of Representatives, meets on the first floor. The governor's offices are on the second floor. It's open Monday to Friday from 8:30 am to 4:30 pm. Admission is free.

Old State House

On S State St and The Green you will find the country's second-oldest state house in continuous use, built in 1792. Guided tours provide information about legislative and judicial activities and the period and reproduction furnishings and accessories on display. Visitors can also see an 18th century courtroom and legislative chamber. It's open Tuesday to Saturday from 10 am to 3:30 pm. Admission is free. For a free guided tour, inquire at the Visitors Center.

Johnson Victrola Museum

Located on Bank Lane and New St, this museum is a very interesting tribute to Eldridge R Johnson, who grew up in Dover and became a leading pioneer in the development of the talking machine and subsequently the record business. He founded what is today RCA. (See the sidebar 'The RCA Legend' for more on Johnson.) Set up like a 1920s Victrola dealer's store, the museum has an extensive collection of talking machines, early recordings (by the likes of Enrico Caruso), and an exhibit with Johnson's famous company trademark 'His Master's Voice,' featuring Nipper the dog. There is a small gift shop. It's open Tuesday to Saturday from 10 am to 3:30 pm. Admission is free.

The RCA Legend: Eldridge R Johnson

Born in Wilmington and raised in Dover, Eldridge R Johnson (1867 – 1945) became one of America's greatest individual business success stories. While it was Thomas Edison who invented the talking machine, Johnson invented many patented improvements on the basic design. Johnson is remembered today for his business acumen and vision, which greatly contributed to bringing music to the masses via records. He founded the Victor Talking Machine Co in Camden, New Jersey, the forerunner of today's RCA. The company's famous 'His Master's Voice' trademark featuring Nipper the dog became recognized around the world.

Johnson received a posthumous Grammy in 1985 and was cited for his contribution to the record industry with his invention of the first motor that allowed a disc talking machine to operate at uniform speed. The Academy said that Johnson transformed the talking machine 'from a scientific toy to a commercial article of great value.' ■

Meeting House Galleries

Located in a 1790s Presbyterian church at 316 S Governors Ave is Meeting House Gallery I, with an exhibition of 12,000 years of Dover's archaeological heritage. It's open Tuesday to Saturday from 10 am to 3:30 pm. Admission is free.

Right next door to the former church, in an 1880s Sunday school, is Meeting House Gallery II, presenting a look at 'Main Street Delaware' – an exhibit on small town life. With authentic displays incorporating original fixtures, you can see recreations of a post office, a general store, a drugstore, a printshop, and carpentry from the 18th and 19th centuries. Both Meeting Houses are open Tuesday to Saturday from 10 am to 3:30 pm. Admission is free.

Biggs Museum of American Art

If you go to 406 Federal St (upstairs from the Visitors Center), you will find this museum housing a personal collection devoted to local artists. It's open Wednesday to Saturday from 10 am to 4 pm and Sunday from 1:30 to 4:30 pm. Admission is free.

Delaware Agricultural Museum

You can see two centuries of life on the farm portrayed here. An indoor display of farmer Americana includes a Swedish log house, vintage farm equipment and vehicles, dairy paraphernalia, and numerous other objects. Outside, behind the exhibit hall, are life-sized recreations of an 1890s village and a 19th century farmstead. The village includes a barbershop, general store, train station, school, and blacksmith and wheelwright's shop. The farmstead includes a farmhouse, garden, henhouse, privy, granary, animal pen, and cornhouse.

Located at 866 N Du Pont Hwy (Hwy 13), the museum (☎ 302-734-1618) is open Tuesday to Saturday from 10 am to 4 pm, Sunday from 1 to 4 pm. Admission is $3.

Dover Air Force Base & Museum

Dover AFB is the second-largest industry in town (after state government). The base is the home for squadrons of the Military Airlift Command's giant C-5 Galaxy, one of the world's largest operational aircraft, and while in Dover you will most likely see one of these monsters lumbering to or from the airfield. But as impressive as the C-5 is, it is not the feature that distinguishes the base in the minds of most Americans. Dover AFB is the US military morgue – and as such it is known to hundreds of millions of TV watchers as the place seen on the evening news every time the US government reclaims a dead American's body. It is the home of the flag-draped coffin, the sound of a rifle salute, and the trumpet dirge of 'Taps.' Victims of Guyana's Jonestown Massacre ended up here (in storage for months), as have political hostages, Gulf War casualties, and the bones of MIAs uncovered in Vietnam. Hang around with local citizens long enough, and you are sure to hear about all sorts of ghostly sightings.

The base museum (☎ 302-677-5938), however, is not a house of horrors. Here you will find an expanding collection of vintage planes, WWII and Vietnam War memorabilia, and related artifacts. The volunteer staff are very enthusiastic Air Force veterans who are more than happy to guide you around the exhibits. It's open Monday to Saturday from 9 am to 3 pm. Admission is free.

To get there, take Hwy 113 two miles south of Dover and follow signs to the main base gate. The security police will give you directions from there.

John Dickinson Plantation

John Dickinson was one of Delaware's leading statesmen during the Revolutionary and Federal periods. Built around 1740, his boyhood home is furnished with family pieces and antiques. Farm outbuildings and a log dwelling have been built to present an 18th century plantation of the region. The museum (☎ 302-732-1808) is located east of Hwy 113, four miles south of Dover. It's open Tuesday to Saturday from 10 am to 4 pm, Sunday from 1 to 4 pm. Admission is free.

Organized Tours

Dover Heritage Trail, Inc (☎ 302-678-2040), PO Box 1628, Dover, DE 19903, operates two very good two-hour walking tours: Old Dover Historic District and Victorian Dover. Each costs $2 per person; call ahead for reservations.

Special Events

Old Dover Days takes place in May. It's two days of celebrating Dover's heritage with a parade, Maypole dancing, arts and crafts, a Civil War military encampment, historic house tours, country dancing, a costume ball, and a recreation of 19th century baseball – a great time to visit! In June, NASCAR racing comes to Dover Downs International Speedway.

Independence Day celebrations are held on or during the week of July 4. Also in July are the African Festival & Parade and the Delaware State Fair (in Harrington).

NASCAR racing returns to Dover Downs International Speedway in September. In October, the Woodburn Fall Festival is held at the Governor's mansion. The Bombay Hook Annual Field Day takes place in November.

Places to Stay

All of Dover's accommodations are located along Hwy 13.

If you will be coming to Dover while a speedway event is being staged at Dover Downs, make reservations as far ahead as possible to be sure of getting a place to stay. The major speedway races take place during the first weekend in June and the third weekend in September.

Among the cheapest motels is the very basic *Kent Budget Motel* (☎ 302-674-2211) with singles/doubles for $30/35.

You get a much nicer room with singles/doubles for around $35/45 at any of the following: the *Relax Inn* (☎ 302-734-8120); *Dover Inn* (☎ 302-674-4011); or the *Budget Host* (☎ 302-678-0161).

With singles/doubles at $40/50 and more modern facilities, four motels stand out: *Budget Inn* (☎ 302-734-4433); *Comfort Inn* (☎ 302-674-3300); *Howard Johnson* (☎ 302-678-8900); and *Days Inn* (☎ 302-674-8002).

Holiday Inn (☎ 302-734-5701), 348 N Du Pont Hwy (Hwy 13) near Delaware State University, has singles/doubles for $50/60.

The *Sheraton Inn – Dover* (☎ 302-678-8500) has singles/doubles for $70/77. Facilities include an indoor pool, health club, and a hot tub.

Places to Eat – budget

Dover Newsstand, on Loockerman St, serves coffee, breakfast, sandwiches, and soups to go, with items costing under $3.

McDowell-Collins Store House Eatery, 408 S State St by the Green, is open weekdays. The Store House has just two tables and serves breakfast, bagels, and various snacks, mainly to go.

Hollywood Diner is an authentic 1950s diner run by an efficient team of women on the east side of Hwy 13, north of Junction 8. Breakfast runs about $4; the standard diner menu offers dishes mainly in the $3 to $6 range. It's open 24 hours.

Places to Eat – middle

The *Bradford St Cafe* (☎ 302-736-6200), at 150 S Bradford St, is a well-tended, attractive cafe in the heart of town. Marianne and Tony Panicola give their personal attention to a clientele that ranges from rastamen in dreads to state senators and grandmothers. The menu is healthful with items like turkey burgers and Middle Eastern salad. The low-fat chili is a tasty bargain at $4.95.

Captain John's (☎ 302-678-8166), on Hwy 113, is open daily from 6 am to 10 pm. The Captain's has a reputation for its all-you-can-eat buffets: breakfast for $4.25, weekdays from 7:30 to 11:30 am; lunch for $6.95, weekdays from 12:45 to 2 pm. Hot and salad buffets for $6.95, Wednesday to Thursday from 5 to 8 pm. The seafood, salad, and roast meats buffet costs $14.95, Friday to Sunday from 5 to 8 pm. The weekend brunch and salad buffet costs $5.95, Saturday and Sunday till 2 pm. There is also an extensive à la carte menu. The coffee here is very good.

WT Smithers (☎ 302-674-8875), 140 S State St, is named after the man whose childhood home this bar now occupies. William T Smithers (1876–1948) apparently lived an interesting life as an orphan, sportsman, politician, soldier, lawyer, husband, investor, and used car salesman. Draft beer, wine, and a wide variety of food are available all day—anything from various appetizers, sandwiches, salads, and pizza to seafood, steaks, and chicken. Sandwiches run $5 to $9, dinner entrees cost $10 to $19. There is a Sunday jazz brunch from noon to 3 pm.

If you want to see how Central Delaware does Mexican, try *La Tolteca* (☎ 302-734-3444), at 245 S Du Pont Hwy, where Tex-Mex cuisine is served in a hacienda-style dining area. A chicken chimichanga for lunch costs $4.75; you can get two for dinner for $8.

Places to Eat – top end

Plaza Nine (☎ 302-736-9990), Treadway Building, 9 E Loockerman St, is a popular lunch spot for the state legislators from across the street. The restaurant specializes in seafood, steak, and veal. Lunch usually runs $9, dinner $18.

The posh colonial-style *Blue Coat Inn* (☎ 302-674-1776), 800 N State St, is beautifully situated overlooking Silver Lake and its food tastes just as good as the place looks. Set in a former colonial home with stone fireplaces and antiques, the inn serves delicacies like stuffed lobster tail for lunch ($11) and shrimp Rockefeller ($18) for dinner.

Some diners claim that Harry and David at *The Nuts* (☎ 302-678-0988), 1068 S State St, serve up the best steaks in Dover. The restaurant stands just before the spot where State St joins Hwy 13, south of downtown. With specialties like Norwegian salmon and beef Wellington, dinner prices can exceed $18. It's open for lunch weekdays, and for dinner Monday to Saturday.

Entertainment

Bars *WT Smithers* (see Places to Eat – middle) has a daily happy hour from 4:30 to 7 pm, with complimentary food Wednesday and Friday. Smithers brings in a variety of cover bands on Thursday to Saturday nights with a $3 cover. The place is very popular with a mixed crowd.

Dancing *The Big Kahuna* (☎ 302-678-8118), at the Howard Johnson on Hwy 13, is currently one of Dover's hottest nightspots. It's open from 9 pm to 1 am; $7 cover with $1.50 drinks.

Arizona (☎ 302-735-8226) is a country and western roadhouse that has become extremely popular. Sunday is Family Day with everyone from children to seniors turning out from noon to 5 pm. It's open Tuesday to Sunday evenings from 11 am to 1 am. On Friday and Saturday night they charge a $4 cover. During the week the cover varies. There are occasional live performances here featuring nationally known artists. On most nights between 8 and 9 pm you can take dance lessons here. When driving down Hwy 113 from Dover, stay to the left and follow the Route 10W signs. The club is on the left just after the overpass (look for the pizza sign). Be sure to turn off at the small exit road before the club. The next exit leads to another highway with no exits for miles.

Spectator Sports

The Dover Downs International Speedway (☎ 302-674-4600), east of Hwy 13 and just north of the city center, is the host of popular NASCAR racing events in June and September. The raceway currently has 190,000 seats and is in the process of adding even more. Nevertheless, you need to plan far ahead (a year is not unreasonable) to get good seats and a place to stay on these weekends.

Harness racing runs from November to March at Dover Downs.

Things to Buy

Spence's Bazaar on New and Queen Sts is a wonderful flea/farmers'/antique market. Established half a century ago, it operates each Tuesday and Friday from around 8 am to 4 pm. Some of the local Amish community participate. On Tuesday evenings there are auctions, starting at around 5:30 pm and lasting until 9 pm. Items found here range from furniture, antiques, and farm produce to tools, cars, and farm equipment.

Delaware General Store (☎ 302-736-1419) is located in a delightful 18th century house at 214 S State St. A showcase for local manufacturers, the store specializes in Delaware-made products.

Stable Shoppe on S State St is a lovely country store crammed with a wide selection of gifts and collectibles.

Beyond Dimensions (☎ 302-674-9070), 59 S Governors Ave in a residential block, is a gift shop specializing in American-made hand-crafted items. The shop has a slight New Age emphasis, but some traditional styles, too.

Rose Valley Quilt Shop is an Amish craft shop west of Dover. Take Route 8 (head west along Loockerman St) for about five miles. Turn left on Route 198 immediately after Byler's Store. After a mile or so you will see the shop on your left. It's open Monday to Wednesday and Friday from 9 am to 6 pm, Saturday from 9 am to 5 pm.

Dover Mall on Hwy 13, the capital's largest, is home to stores like JC Penney and Sears.

Getting There & Away

Bus Greyhound/Trailways (☎ 302-734-1417, 800-231-2222) has two buses a day to/from Wilmington and the beaches. The bus station is at 650 Bay Court Plaza.

DART (☎ 800-652-3278) runs a number of buses between Dover and Wilmington and the beaches. At $4 for a Dover-Wilmington ticket the fare is about half what you would pay for Greyhound.

Car Hwy 13 from the north and Hwy 113 from the south are the major roads to/from the state capital.

BOWERS BEACH

About eight miles south of Dover off Hwy 113 at the end of Bowers Beach Rd lies one of the most unforgettable fishing ports in the Capital Region. Bowers Beach squats at the mouth of the Murderkill River like a town dreamed up by Alfred Hitchcock. Rows of tilted, weathered Victorian structures line the main street, Hubbard Ave. Fifty-passenger party-fishing boats tie up along rickety wharves. And when the boats return after seven-hour trips into the bay for 'weakfish' (sea trout), bluefish, and flounder, the long rows of cleaning tables that overlook the wharves get packed with what the local captains call 'meat hunters.' Mostly men, these people are generally a mix of African Americans and Amish farmers who come with 50-pound coolers to catch anything and everything – from toadfish to sharks – that the bay will provide.

> **Delaware's Amish**
> Kent County has been home for a community of Old Order Amish since 1915. Not as well known as their Pennsylvania counterparts, the present population is an estimated 1200. Increased development west of Dover has impinged on Amish land and families have been slowly relocating further west to Kentucky, Missouri, and Kansas. ■

When all the fish have been cleaned, and the whole town smells like fish guts, a fair percentage of the crowd retires to the *Bay View Inn* (☎ 302-335-4201) at the end of Hubbard Ave, which looks like a cantina from a David Lynch film. Inside, the light is orange and draft beer costs 75¢. Men in jeans and women in tight sweaters shoot pool, tell fish stories, drink beer, and listen to Elvis Presley on the juke box until there is not a care in the world.

If you want to do some cheap fishing or escape into a world you thought only existed in *film noir*, do not miss Bowers Beach. Some of the most popular party boats run from Faulkner's Pier (☎ 302-335-5706). A day of fishing will cost about $22. Rod rentals run $5.

Tony Cadiz is a friendly guy with the cheapest rooms within 75 miles at his *Bowers Old Inn* (☎ 302-335-3085), 46 Hubbard Ave. Tony has 10 simple rooms with a double bed and shared bath for $30 a night.

ISLAND FIELD MUSEUM

This museum, just south of Bowers Beach, is adjacent to ancient burial pits containing as many as 140 Native American bodies turned up here in 1967 after the state brought in archaeologists to investigate artifacts surfacing in a farmer's field along the Murderkill River and Delaware Bay. The remains and artifacts date from 700 to 1000 AD and represent a sacred cemetery of a civilization known as the Webb Phase People. The museum (☎ 302-335-5395) displays many tools found at the site, like fish hooks, scrapes, mortars, and pestles. The human remains have been reburied at the request of Delaware's living Native Americans.

You can find the museum by following the signs that lead off Hwy 113 south of Bowers Beach. Hours are Tuesday through Saturday from 10 am to 4:30 pm, Sunday from 1:30 to 4:30 pm. Admission is free.

BARRATT'S CHAPEL & MUSEUM

Eleven miles south of Dover, on the east side of Hwy 113 and north of Frederica, this chapel (☎ 302-335-5544) is the 'cradle of Methodism' in America. Built in 1780 by a local landowner, Philip Barratt, the chapel is where the Methodists established the New World chapter of their congregation in 1784. It's open Tuesday to Saturday from 10 am to 3:30 pm, Sunday from 1:30 to 4:30 pm; in January and February it's closed on Sundays. Admission is always free.

Delaware Seashore

Delaware has 28 miles of sandy beaches on the Atlantic Ocean, running south from Cape Henlopen State Park at the junction of the Delaware River and the Atlantic Ocean to the Maryland border. State parks protect nearly half of the coastline from development, distinguishing the Delaware seashore from the New Jersey coastline to the north and Maryland's crowded Ocean City just down the coast to the south. Delaware's beach towns – Lewes, Rehoboth Beach, Bethany Beach, and Fenwick Island – each have a distinctive character. While it would be stretching the case to call these towns quaint, Delaware's resorts seem like something of an oasis in comparison to the huge New Jersey and Maryland resort towns.

Many of Washington's more affluent and celebrated citizens have summer homes on the Delaware coast, and you will also find the small but proud Nanticoke tribe of Native Americans living on the fringe of the inshore bays here. During recent years Rehoboth Beach has become popular with gay and lesbian vacationers, and an atmosphere of open-mindedness and respect has taken root. While families on one or two week vacations constitute half the resorts' visitors during the summer, Delaware's beaches have become romantic getaways for couples during the spring and fall. Lewes and Rehoboth have exceptional restaurants that far exceed the standard offerings of most American beach resorts. Like Ocean City, Maryland, Delaware's resorts, particularly Rehoboth Beach, are good places for a traveler with working papers to stop and get some seasonal employment to refill the kitty.

HIGHLIGHTS

- Shops, restaurants, and cafes in Lewes
- The dunes and beaches of Cape Henlopen
- La Rosa Negra for great Italian food in Lewes
- Breezes on the Rehoboth Boardwalk
- Cheap eats and brew at Dogfish Head Brewing, Rehoboth
- The nonstop college/yuppie party scene at the Rusty Rudder, Dewey
- The Renegade in Rehoboth, for the gay/lesbian dance scene
- Miles of empty beach at Delaware Seashore State Park

LEWES

Long considered by vacationers as simply the southern terminus of the Cape May-Lewes ferry and a gateway to Delaware and Maryland's Atlantic beaches, Lewes (pronounced LOO-iss; population 2600) is an often overlooked waterside retreat for upscale travelers and people who eschew populous beach resorts and like to surround themselves with a sense of history. The town has a good beach on Delaware Bay, a number of historic buildings, some attractions, and a small but inviting eating and shopping district with shady Bradford pear trees – all within a half-mile radius of the center. Unlike the neighboring beach resorts, Lewes has the feel of a town that was here long before tourism: For centuries Lewes has been the home of mariners and Delaware Bay pilots who guide ships up and down the bay and river. In the same maritime spirit, Lewes is the site of the College of Marine Studies of the University of Delaware, which maintains a coastal park, harbor, and research vessels here. There are good marinas for yachts, and sport fishing boats that stage billfishing tournaments every summer.

History

The Dutch began to dispossess the resident Lenni-Lenape with a whaling settlement at

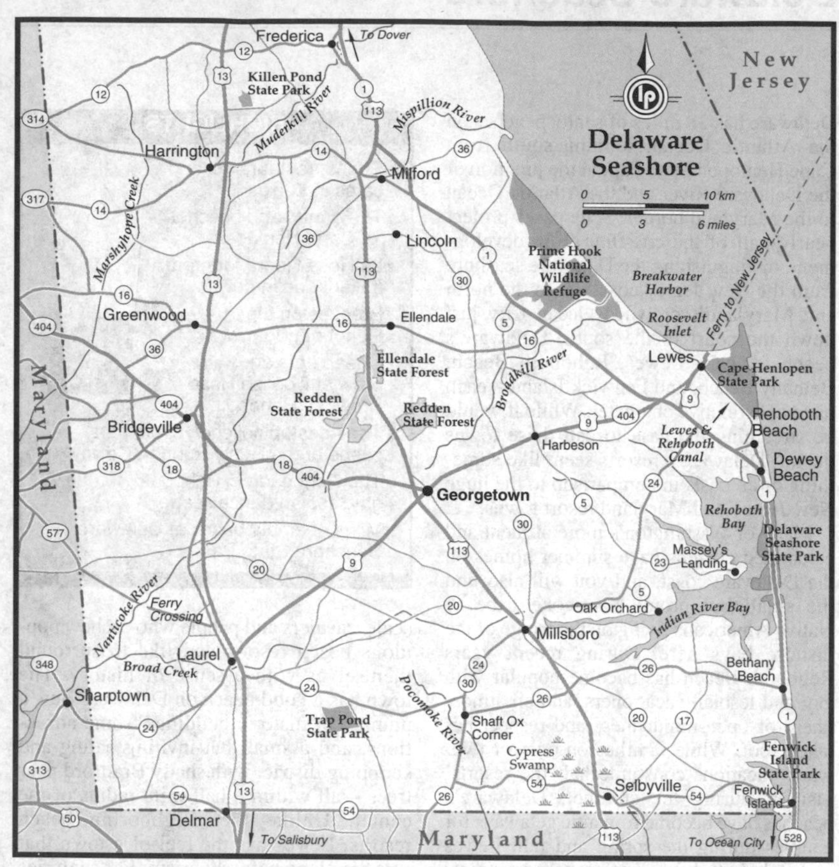

Lewes in 1631. The Native Americans massacred the first settlers, but other Europeans followed to take advantage of the good natural harbor here behind the dunes of Cape Henlopen. Lewes is called the 'First Town in the First State' because of the original Dutch settlement, Zwaanendael (Valley of the Swans). Mariners have sought shelter here ever since. For awhile the port bore the name 'Whorekill,' testimony to rough and ready days here.

Information

Tourists Offices The Lewes Chamber of Commerce and Visitors Bureau (☎ 302-645-8073), at 120 Kings Hwy in the 1730 Fisher-Martin house behind the Zwaanendael Museum, distributes a useful guide to the town's buildings and businesses. They also provide a walking tour map. The chamber is open year round on weekdays from 10 am to 4 pm; during the summer it's also open on Saturday from 10 am to 2 pm.

Post The post office takes up a small block in the commercial center of town on Front St between Bank St and Neil Alley.

DELAWARE

Bookstores Books by the Bay (☎ 302-645-2304), 130 Second St, is a small store owned by John Allwood that sells new books and has a good selection of Delaware history.

Media The *Daily Whale* is the newspaper for the shore towns of Lewes and Rehoboth Beach. There are a number of free weeklies distributed up and down the coast, with the usual entertainment information and ads from restaurants, motels, and every other business. You can pick these up in most stores, restaurants, and motel lobbies along the coast. Papers – which come and go – include the *Beachcomber*, the *Coast Press*, *Delaware Beach Guide*, and the *Delaware Wave*, whose content has more news than restaurant and activity information.

Laundry You can find Quick Wash (☎ 302-645-8542) at 411 Kings Hwy.

Medical Services Beebe Memorial Hospital (☎ 302-645-3300) is located at 424 Savannah Rd.

Zwaanendael Museum

This museum (☎ 302-645-9418), at the intersection of Kings Hwy and Savannah Rd, is a 1931 replica of the town hall in Hoorn, Holland. The small museum has several professionally curated exhibits, the largest of which is a collection of items retrieved from the sunken treasure brig *deBraak*, which went down in 1798 and was excavated in 1984. The museum also has a collection of period household items. It's open Tuesday to Saturday from 10 am to 4:30 pm; and Sunday from 1:30 pm to 4:30 pm. Admission is free.

Nassau Vineyards

If you wind your way to 36 Nassau Commons (take Route 1N to the Nassau Bridge, then follow Route 14B and the signs) you will find the vineyard (☎ 302-645-9463) cellars and sales building surrounded by an orchard and picnic tables. This is a great place to bring a picnic: You can get a tour and tasting of five wines including Chardonnay and rosé for free. Bottles run from $7 to $12. Hours are Tuesday through Saturday, 11 am to 5 pm, Sunday noon to 5 pm.

Historic Buildings

There are six structures built during the 17th and 18th centuries collected at the **Lewes Historical Complex** (☎ 302-645-7670), Shipcarpenter and Third Sts. They include a farmhouse, a store, and a doctor's office. There is also a reading room with material on Delaware history. Admission is $4, or $5 for a guided tour. It's open Tuesday to Friday from 10 am to 3 pm and Saturday from 10 am to 12:30 pm.

The **Ryves Holt House**, Second and Mulberry Sts, built in 1665, is probably the oldest house in the state. The **Cannonball House**, Front and Bank Sts, is celebrated because the British fired a cannonball into it during the War of 1812. (A lot of towns celebrate their cannonball houses.) It now has a marine museum inside.

Steam Train

Queen Anne's Railroad (☎ 302-644-1720), 730 Kings Hwy, runs 90-minute daytime excursions over 18 miles of track and two and a half hour dinner trips with their steam powered locomotive and coaches. Excursions run four days a week and cost $9 for adults, $7 for children (bring a picnic lunch). Dinner trains with full dining service, plus murder mystery theater or swing band, cost $100 per couple and run most weekend nights during the summer, Saturdays through November.

Fishing

Party and charter boats leave from Fisherman's Wharf (☎ 302-645-8862, 645-8541). The marina also rents small fishing boats at $65 and $75 a day.

Biking

If you didn't bring a bike, you can get one at *Lewes Cycle Sports* (☎ 302-645-4544). Bikes cost $9 to $14 per day and are a better deal at $23 to $39 a week. The town streets and paths make for quiet and scenic touring.

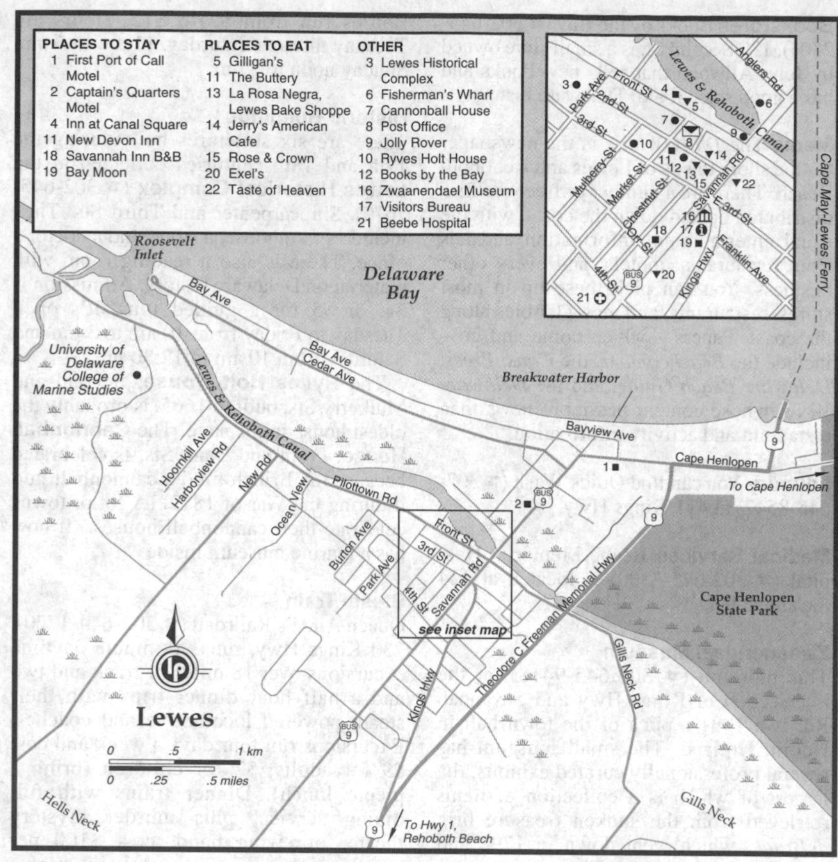

Sailing

The *Jolly Rover* (☎ 302-644-1501) sails in Delaware Bay. The boat leaves from Lewes Memorial Park at the corner of Front and Savannah Sts. The child/adult fare for a two-hour sail is $13/15; for a three-hour sail it's $15/18.

Organized Tours

Blue Cricket Tours (☎ 302-645-4545) provides a one-hour bus tour in and around Lewes. The tour starts and ends at the ferry terminal and goes around town and Cape Henlopen State Park. The cost for the tour is $6 for adults and $3 for children under 12.

Special Events

On the first weekend in November, thousands come to Lewes to watch the World Championship Punkin' Chunkin' (☎ 800-515-9095). Contestants propel pumpkins as far as possible by any means. In 1995 the winner chunked a pumpkin 2655 feet (using a compressed-air cannon). In December, the annual house tour occurs. For $10 you can participate in a daylong tour of famous houses in town.

Places to Stay – middle

The *Savannah Inn* (☎ 302-645-5592), 330 Savannah Rd, is a seven-room year-round inn near the center of town. Dick and Susan Stafursky, the vegetarian owners, rent simple but comfortable rooms. Breakfast is a large fruit salad and home-baked goods. Rooms, all with shared bathrooms, run from $45 to $60 in season and are about $10 less in the off season.

First Port of Call Motel (☎ 302-645-7266), in a not very enticing location across from the ferry terminal, rents small, standard motel rooms with air-conditioning and television for $54 in season. They also sell sandwiches and bait and tackle. The management here is so laid back that they don't always answer knocks on the office door.

The pleasant *Kings Inn* (☎ 302-645-6438), 151 Kings Hwy, is a 100-year-old house with porches, a backyard, and a Jacuzzi. Rooms are $55 to $75.

Captain's Quarters Motel (☎ 302-645-7924), 406 Savannah Rd on the way into town from the ferry terminal, rents larger rooms that are clean but musty and not worth the $70/80 weekday/weekend rates in season. The off-season rates are more reasonable at $30/40.

Places to Stay – top end

The *Wild Swan* (☎ 302-645-8550), 525 Kings Hwy, is a turn of the century Queen Anne house a few blocks from the center of town. The house is furnished with nice Victorian pieces and has a pool. Mike and Hope Tyler rent four rooms with air-conditioning and private bath for $105 each mid-May until the end of October, $75 the rest of the year.

The *New Devon Inn* (☎ 302-645-6466, 800-824-8754) is a restored 1920s brick hotel with 24 rooms on the corner of Second and Market Sts. The rooms are in three sizes, decorated with antiques (no televisions, but there is a TV room), with private modern bathrooms. Rates include a bed turndown with cordials and breakfast. In-season rates are $85 to $135; off-season rates are $45 to $110.

The *Inn at Canal Square* (☎ 302-645-8499, 800-222-7902), 122 Market St, overlooks the marina. The inn has 19 large rooms with queen- or king-sized beds. Although this inn was built recently, it has a traditional country feel with its decor incorporating plants, pretty fabrics, and well chosen furniture. Despite the charm of the location, architecture, and decor, the soundproofing in this hotel leaves a lot to be desired. Rooms, with continental breakfast, are $130 to $165 in season and $75 to $135 off season. There is also a two-bedroom houseboat moored in the marina.

Bay Moon (☎ 302-644-1802), at 128 Kings Hwy, is the newest B&B on the scene. This eclectic Victorian inn near the Zwaanendael Museum and the commercial district offers guests complimentary wine and hors d'oeuvres. Rates are $105 to $125 with discounts off season and for longer stays.

Places to Eat

La Rosa Negra (645-1980), at 128 Second St, is a romantic Italian bistro whose chef gets raves from the locals. The menu constantly evolves, but try the broiled rockfish with crab meat in sherry sauce ($17) if you can get it.

Exel's (☎ 302-645-7458), 329 Savannah Rd across from the Savannah Inn, is a neighborhood diner with high-quality homestyle cooking. The menu offers breakfast all day, lima-bean soup made with large, locally grown beans, and sandwiches and subs ($2.75 to $5). Their pies are good, too.

There are several places to eat among the shops on Second St. *Jerry's American Cafe* (☎ 302-645-9733), 115 Second St, is an upscale sandwich ($6) and entree place ($10 to $20).

The *Rose & Crown* (☎ 302-645-2373), 108 Second St, is a modern bar and restaurant that looks like something out of the Gay Nineties with gold-painted tin ceiling, brass rails, and etched glass. Sandwiches run $5 to $7. Dinner prices seem a bit steep for what you get: cottage pie ($11), fish and chips ($12), and crab cakes ($16).

The Buttery (☎ 302-645-7755) is a bistro-style restaurant with nouvelle cuisine in the New Devon Inn. There are prix-fixe dinner specials for $13 if you come before 6:30 pm.

The *Lewes Bake Shoppe*, at 124 Second, is a small coffee shop selling coffee beans and a few baked goods.

Gilligan's (☎ 302-645-7866), on the canal at the end of Market St, has sandwiches and salads for lunch ($6 to $8); pasta, seafood, and meat for dinner ($11 to $19).

Taste of Heaven (☎ 302-644-1992), at 115 Savannah Rd, is the most popular breakfast spot and cafe in town. They offer cappuccino, bagels, and sandwiches in a French baguette ($6).

Entertainment

The *Rose & Crown* (see Places to Eat) has live rock on weekends with a youngish but mixed crowd. Usually there is no cover.

Getting There & Away

Ferry Travelers going up and down the Mid-Atlantic coast take the Cape May-Lewes Ferry (☎ 800-643-3779 for schedules, 800-717-7245 for car reservations) to save themselves the hours it takes to drive around Delaware Bay from the beaches of Cape May, New Jersey, to the Delaware beaches. The ferry has daily year-round service between the two points. The trip lasts 70 minutes and can have the pitching and rolling associated with an ocean voyage because the ferries transit the often rough, open mouth of Delaware Bay: If you are prone to seasickness you may want to consider a morning passage when the wind and seas are generally at their calmest. The five enormous ferries can carry 800 passengers and 100 cars.

Passengers pay $4.50 for adults, $2.50 for kids under 12. Vehicles pay $18 to $64 according to length; bikes and motorcycles are less. All rates decrease from December to March.

The Lewes ferry terminal (☎ 302-664-6030) is next to the Cape Henlopen State Park entrance, a mile from the center of Lewes; follow the signs.

Car Lewes is tucked right behind Cape Henlopen at the entrance to Delaware Bay. It is accessible by Routes 1 or 9.

Getting Around

The Jolly Trolley (☎ 302-645-6800) runs people from the ferry terminal in and around Lewes for $2 May to September.

Delaware Resort Transit (DRT; ☎ 302-226-2001, 800-553-3278) runs buses from Lewes to Rehoboth and Dewey Beaches along Business Route 9, and Routes 1 and 1A. The buses run from around 7 or 8 am to around 10 or 11 pm from Memorial Day to Labor Day. For $1 you get a pass good for riding from 7 am to 4 pm.

CAPE HENLOPEN STATE PARK

This 3143-acre park is on the Atlantic coast east of Lewes. In the 19th century part of Cape Henlopen served as a quarantine station for immigrants. Later the cape was a major coastal defense to protect Delaware Bay from attack by German submarines, particularly during WWII. There was no state park here until the Department of Defense gave the land to the state in 1964; consequently the park is festooned with abandoned bunkers, gun emplacements, buildings, and other military fixtures. Some small active Navy buildings still remain.

Most of the cape is now a park, but the overall effect is of a reclaimed place, rather than of an eternally pristine one. The landscape includes a lot of small pine trees, high dunes, and dune grass. In addition to the unpopulated bay and sea shores, some of the park's most interesting geographical features are the so-called 'walking dunes,' which are actually migrating through the pine forest. Gordon's Pond Wildlife Area has a big lagoon at its heart that is a good place for bird watching. The park is open daily from 8 am to dusk. Fees ($2.50 for Delaware license plates, $5 for others) are collected from Memorial to Labor Day and on weekends in April, September, and October.

Visitors Center

You can pick up information at the park office (☎ 302-645-8983) about 800 feet south of the fee-collection booth on the way in. The office is open daily from April to October, 8 am to 4:30 pm; weekdays only the rest of the year.

Nature Center

The Nature Center (☎ 302-645-6852) is on the left side of the road running straight past the fee booth. The center has an extensive series of educational programs, hikes, and courses for visitors. The staff also sponsor concerts, a Halloween spook trail, and bird watching and they distribute pamphlets for self-guided trails.

Great Dune

On the coast near the shore is this huge sand dune, one of the tallest on the Atlantic coast. You can climb the 105 steps of the observation tower in the middle of the park for a view of Cape May, New Jersey, across the bay, the Atlantic, and the beach resorts.

Swimming

There are swimming areas with lifeguards, bathrooms, etc at the northern and southern ends of the park. Each end also has a food concession.

Fishing

The park has a fishing pier with a bait and tackle shop, Hoss's Pier One (☎ 302-645-2612), right next to it.

Camping

The campground (☎ 302-645-2103) has 159 sites rented on a first-come, first-served basis at the center of the park at $16 per site. There is also a 'primitive' youth camping area, with minimal services.

REHOBOTH BEACH & DEWEY BEACH

Delaware's most popular beach, Rehoboth is a small coastal town eight miles south of Lewes that swells to become the state's second largest city each summer, when its permanent population of 4000 explodes to 50,000. Starting in June, vacationers arrive from Washington, Baltimore, Wilmington, Philadelphia, and central Pennsylvania. By comparison to Ocean City, Maryland, 20 miles south of here, Rehoboth is still small enough to have some charm. The town can be a great place to stroll or bike with tree-lined streets, duck ponds, lagoons, and green spaces among neighborhoods of beach houses trimmed in clapboard and cedar shingles. There are small neat yards and lots of flowers. Modern ocean-front resort motels and hotels break some of Rehoboth's spell as you get closer to the waterfront. The commercial strip along Rehoboth Ave has something of a honky-tonk feel with T-shirt emporiums, fast food stands, and a thousand short-term parking spaces. However, a 'Main Street Restoration Project' is underway with hopes of restoring Rehoboth Ave to its appearance of a hundred years ago.

Rehoboth's clientele is a genial mix of white families and a sizable gay community. (See the sidebar 'Gay Rehoboth.')

Rehoboth also gets a lot of high school graduates and college students to work in the hotels and restaurants, although not nearly as many as Ocean City, Maryland. Add to this mix a lot of yuppies from DC, Wilmington, and Philadelphia who get groups of soulmates together and rent condos for a month or the season.

The under-30 scene focuses on the narrow strand called Dewey Beach, south of Rehoboth where Route 1 threads along the sandbar between the ocean and Rehoboth Bay. Beach houses, condos, restaurants, bars, and motels – most erected within spitting distance of each other in recent decades – line both sides of Route 1 in Dewey and make this strand the Capital Region's version of Margaritaville. The Bay at Dewey is a popular place for windsurfing, water-skiing, and jet skiing.

The beach is the main attraction in both Rehoboth and Dewey, but people-watching comes in a close second.

History

Rehoboth (named for the third in a series of wells dug by Isaac, as told in the book of Genesis) started as a camp meeting convened by the Methodist Episcopal Church in 1872, and a village of Victorian summer cottages grew quickly in the following decade. Methodists held religious revival meetings at this 'Christian seaside resort' until 1881. Soon a rail line arrived making

Gay Rehoboth

Rehoboth rivals Fire Island, New York, for the distinction of being the largest gay-friendly Atlantic resort between Provincetown, Massachussetts, and Key West, Florida. Popular gay beaches are Poodle Beach, at the south end of the boardwalk, and North Beach, in Cape Henlopen State Park. Women generally prefer North Beach. *Letters from Camp Rehoboth* has a list of businesses, restaurants, and accommodations that advertise as gay and lesbian friendly.

The Rehoboth Police actively guard against harassment and hate crimes. If you are a witness or victim, call ☎ 302-227-2577. The University of Delaware Lesbian, Gay, and Bisexual Community has a very useful information line (☎ 302-831-4114). ■

Rehoboth the closest Atlantic Beach to Washington, and when the secular influence (politicians) slipped into town Christian activities subsided, leaving Rehoboth a summer resort for many of America's most famous and powerful lawmakers. At the beginning of the 20th century, people commonly referred to Rehoboth as the 'Nation's Summer Capital.'

Orientation

Route 1 bypasses the heart of town, which covers the land between the Lewes and Rehoboth Canal and the ocean. Rehoboth's main east-west avenue is called Rehoboth Ave (Route 1A); it crosses a bridge over the canal, passing through the heart of town before ending at the boardwalk. The two streets running parallel to the north of Rehoboth Ave are Baltimore and Maryland Aves, and the two running parallel to the south are Wilmington and Delaware Aves. Baltimore Ave has a lot of the shopping, particularly antiques. It is connected to Rehoboth Ave between First and Second Sts by a series of small pedestrian malls. Second St/Bayard Ave is the main north-south artery, the continuation of Route 1A south to Dewey beach.

Information

Tourist Offices The Chamber of Commerce and Visitors Center (☎ 302-227-2233, 800-441-1329) is just across the canal bridge in the restored 1879 railway station on your left at 501 Rehoboth Ave. The center has brochures and maps and is open year round on weekdays from 9 am to 5 pm. From Memorial Day to Labor Day it's also open on Saturday from 9 am to 2 pm and on Sunday from 9 am to 1 pm.

Post The post office (☎ 302-227-8406) is at 179 Rehoboth Ave between First and Second Sts.

Media In addition to the giveaway shore papers, *Letters from Camp Rehoboth* is a free paper with more than 32 pages put out by members of Rehoboth's gay community. It has articles and advertisements and 'seeks to create a more positive environment of cooperation and understanding among all people.'

Bookstores Lambda Rising (☎ 302-227-6969), 39 Baltimore Ave, stocks gay and lesbian books, periodicals, and videos. Browseabout Books (☎ 302-227-0905), at 133 Rehoboth Ave, has a complete stock of mainstream fiction and nonfiction.

Laundry Try the centrally located Rehoboth Laundromat (☎ 302-227-4744) at 5 First St.

Medical Services You will find Beebe Hospital (☎ 302-645-3300) located at 424 Savannah Rd, Lewes.

Anna Hazzard Museum

The museum (☎ 302-226-1119) is in a former camp meeting tent that was moved to its present location at the fork of Christian St and Wilmington Ave. The museum has items from the history of Rehoboth. It's open Memorial Day to Labor Day on the first and third Saturdays of each month. Donations are accepted.

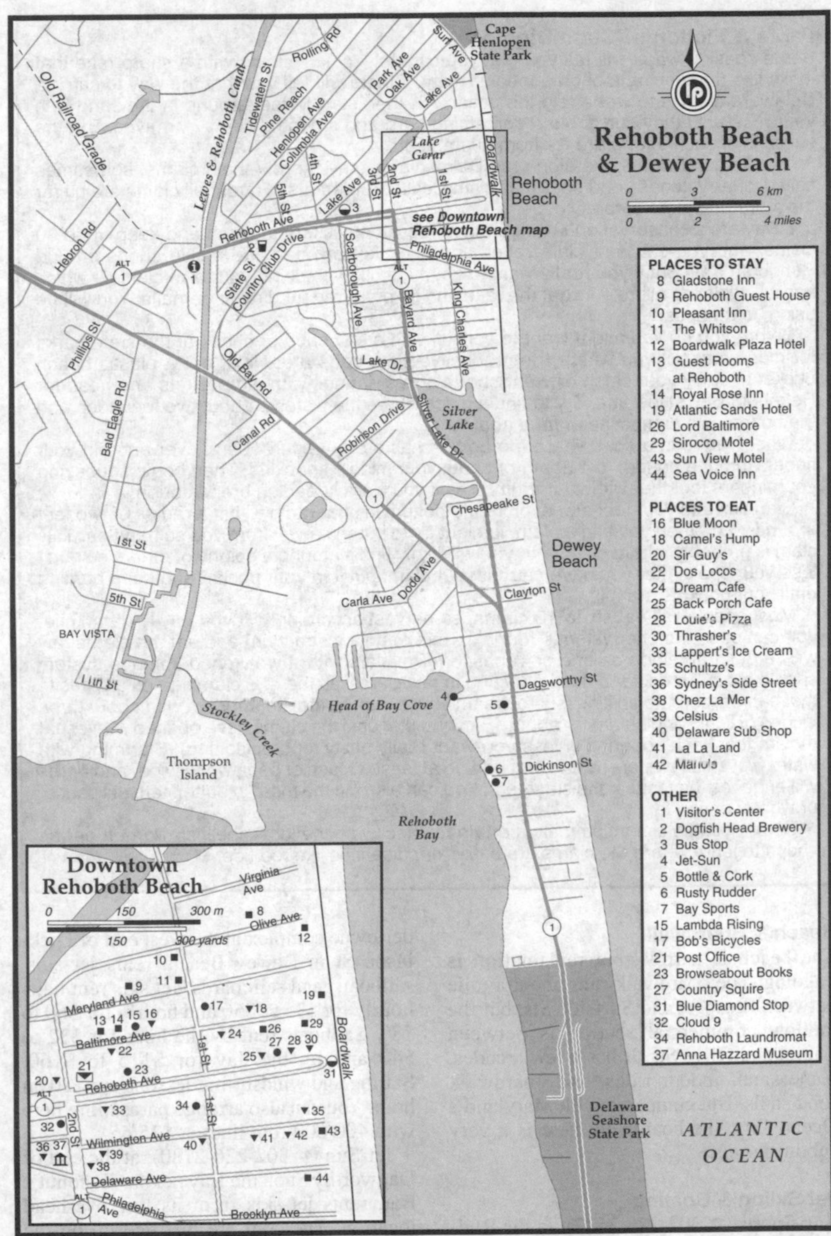
Rehoboth Beach & Dewey Beach
0 3 6 km
0 2 4 miles
PLACES TO STAY
8 Gladstone Inn
9 Rehoboth Guest House
10 Pleasant Inn
11 The Whitson
12 Boardwalk Plaza Hotel
13 Guest Rooms at Rehoboth
14 Royal Rose Inn
19 Atlantic Sands Hotel
26 Lord Baltimore
29 Sirocco Motel
43 Sun View Motel
44 Sea Voice Inn
PLACES TO EAT
16 Blue Moon
18 Camel's Hump
20 Sir Guy's
22 Dos Locos
24 Dream Cafe
25 Back Porch Cafe
28 Louie's Pizza
30 Thrasher's
33 Lappert's Ice Cream
35 Schultze's
36 Sydney's Side Street
38 Chez La Mer
39 Celsius
40 Delaware Sub Shop
41 La La Land
42 Mano's
OTHER
1 Visitor's Center
2 Dogfish Head Brewery
3 Bus Stop
4 Jet-Sun
5 Bottle & Cork
6 Rusty Rudder
7 Bay Sports
15 Lambda Rising
17 Bob's Bicycles
21 Post Office
23 Browseabout Books
27 Country Squire
31 Blue Diamond Stop
32 Cloud 9
34 Rehoboth Laundromat
37 Anna Hazzard Museum
Cape Henlopen State Park
Old Railroad Grade
Lewes & Rehoboth Canal
Tidewaters St
Rolling Rd
Pine Reach
Henlopen Ave
Columbia Ave
Park Ave
Oak Ave
Surf Ave
Lake Ave
Lake Gerar
Boardwalk
Rehoboth Beach
4th St
5th St
3rd St
2nd St
1st St
see Downtown Rehoboth Beach map
Rehoboth Ave
Hebron Rd
State St
Country Club Drive
Scarborough Ave
Philadelphia Ave
Bayard Ave
King Charles Ave
Phillips St
Old Bay Rd
Lake Dr
Bald Eagle Rd
Silver Lake
Silver Lake Dr
Canal Rd
Robinson Drive
Chesapeake St
Dewey Beach
1st St
Dodd Ave
Carla Ave
Clayton St
5th St
BAY VISTA
11th St
Dagsworthy St
Head of Bay Cove
Stockley Creek
Thompson Island
Dickinson St
Rehoboth Bay
Delaware Seashore State Park
ATLANTIC OCEAN
Downtown Rehoboth Beach
0 150 300 m
0 150 300 yards
Virginia Ave
Olive Ave
Maryland Ave
Baltimore Ave
1st St
Rehoboth Ave
Boardwalk
2nd St
Wilmington Ave
Delaware Ave
Philadelphia Ave
Brooklyn Ave
ALT 1
DELAWARE

Facts & Fiction of Clam Digging

Some seaside wags will tell you that you can only 'catch' clams with a sharp rake that looks like a trenching tool on a moonlit night. Others will tell you that the way to catch a Delaware clam is to wade into the ocean . . . then start to feel around in the sand with your toes until they curl around something hard and smooth. Well . . . maybe. But the success of such efforts are far from guaranteed.

Two kinds of clams live along the Delmarva coast – 'hard' (shell) clams, sometimes called 'cherrystones,' and soft-shell clams, called 'steamers.' Hardshell clams are by far the more prevalent of the two.

Delaware's conservation laws permit nonresident visitors to catch and keep up to 50 clams, and you can rent clam rakes and buckets from bait and tackle shops around Rehoboth Bay. But if you really want to get the thrill of catching your own clams – which has an addicting allure – forget the rake and be prepared for dirty fingernails: You will be using your hands.

Before you go you might want to consult with a bait shop or check at the state parks for maps that tell you where the productive clam beds are. Next, get a plastic beach bucket to carry your catch or wear shorts or a swim suit with big pockets and head for Rehoboth Bay at low tide. Try to find a place where the water is about two feet deep and the bottom is a composite of mud and sand.

When you're in a spot where the bottom has a silty texture, bend over and dig your fingers into the bottom to a depth of about your middle knuckles. Then begin squeezing your fingers together with your thumbs as if you were kneading bread dough.

Start close to your feet and explore the bottom in quadrants within a radius of two feet around you. When you find a clam, it might try to burrow away from you so hang on. This clam is probably a hard clam, and you will likely find it among a colony of others so don't lose your spot. After you have caught your clam, put it in your pocket and keep hunting until your pockets are full.

Most people will eat six to 12 clams, so harvest accordingly. If you buy a clam knife, you can open the cherrystones (don't try this without instruction) and eat the clams raw with a dash of lemon or lime or Tabasco. (Travelers with a weakened immune system should consult a doctor before indulging in raw clams, as the rare clam carries a parasite that can exacerbate an illness.) To steam your catch, fill the steamer pot with about three inches of liquid and steam for about 15 minutes or until the clams have opened (*never* eat a clam that hasn't opened unless you want really nasty food poisoning). Steaming with water – even seawater – is fine, but adding at least a touch of beer, white wine, and herbs will enhance the taste of the steamers. You can also dip the meat in butter, teriyaki sauce, or whatever you fancy.

Before you go clamming make certain to check with the local shellfish warden or bait shops to learn where the clams are safe from diseases like red tide. ■

Beach & Boardwalk

The beach is narrow, but reclamation is ongoing. The boardwalk runs about a mile between Prospect and Surfside Sts, but the mellow commercial section is between Laurel and Olive Sts. It has a few arcades, some small indoor rides, and boardwalk food stalls. But compared with Maryland's Ocean City, the boardwalk here is a very subdued scene.

Jet Skiing & Boating

Bay Sports (☎ 302-226-2677), in the Ruddertowne complex at the west end of Dickinson St in Dewey Beach, rents jet skis, sailboats, and sailboards. Jet skis rent half-hourly for $35 to $50 and hourly for $60 to $80. Sailboats rent by the hour for $32 to $40 and by the day for $115 to $160. Sailing and windsurfing lessons are $20 an hour. You can also arrange parasailing here with 400/600-foot lines at $35/45.

Jet-Sun (☎ 302-226-2780), at the end of Dagworthy St on the Bay next to Coconut's Bar, rents jet skis from its low overhead location. The craft are just tied up on the sand at the end of the road. Rates are $40 to $45 per half hour on weekends and $40 for 40 minutes during the week.

Biking

Bob's Bicycles (☎ 302-227-7966), on First St between Baltimore and Maryland Aves, rents adult bikes by the hour ($2), day ($7), and week ($20); mountain bikes are $2.50 to $3 by the hour, $8 to $10 by the day, and $22 to $27 by the week. They also have tandems and one- and two-seat surreys.

Organized Tours

Jolly Trolley (☎ 302-227-1197) offers narrated trolley tours of Rehoboth. The trolley leaves from the boardwalk at Rehoboth Ave and costs about $3.

Special Events

During much of the summer, concerts are held on weekend evenings as well as some weekdays at the bandstand on Rehoboth Ave. They start at 8 pm – check local papers for listings. In early July the Rehoboth Art League Tour of Homes takes place.

Rohoboth's Jazz Festival takes place during a four-day weekend in October. At the end of October Halloween is celebrated at the Sea Witch Festival, with activities for children and a parade.

Places to Stay – camping

The *Big Oaks Campground* (☎ 302-645-6838) is three miles from Rehoboth. It's open May 1 to October 1. Daily/weekly sites are $19.50/117. Take Route 1N from Rehoboth to Road 270 (just before Route 24). Go right and the campground is on your left. Coming south on Route 1, go past Route 24, make a U-turn onto Route 1N, and then go right on Road 270.

Places to Stay – middle

James and Doris Downs have run the *Lord Baltimore* (☎ 302-227-2855), 16 Baltimore Ave, for over 30 years. The front portion of the building dates to the latter half of the 19th century. They rent 12 rooms in a large white building with plenty of parking half a block from the beach at the center of town. Rates are $25 to $50 off season, $35 to $65 in season – small rooms with air-conditioning, television, and shared bath are at the low end; larger rooms with private bath at the upper. The Downses also rent apartments and efficiencies. It's open year round and very friendly.

The *Whitson* (☎ 302-227-7966), 30 Maryland Ave, has basic rooms with sink and shared bath for $40 on the first floor. As you ascend to the floors above, prices go up to $60 for rooms with refrigerators and private bath. All rates include a continental breakfast. It's open from mid-May to the end of September.

The *Gladstone Inn* (☎ 302-227-2641), 3 Olive Ave, is one building away from the beach. Some guests find the furniture cheesy, but it's serviceable. Eight rooms with air-conditioning and shared baths or outside showers go for $55. Apartments that sleep six are $525 to $575 a week.

The *Sea Voice Inn* (☎ 302-226-9435, 800-637-2862), 14 Delaware Ave, is a B&B and retreat house. A group of 30 women who had been coming to the beach to stay at a YWCA cottage bought the house in 1926. They formed a corporation called the Bettie Neumann Girls Club – named after the social secretary of the YWCA cottage. Men could come for vacation, but could not become members of the club. The club disbanded in 1984 and the house was sold, although former members still come for vacation. Jeff and Susie Bond rent 11 rooms in the house at rates from $55 to $90. Call ahead to make sure a retreat group is not in residence.

Rehoboth Guest House (☎ 302-227-4117), 40 Maryland Ave, is a gay owned and operated beach house open year round. The floors and walls are painted wood, there is a mix of beach furniture, a roof sundeck, and two outdoor showers. All rooms have air-conditioning. Rates include a continental breakfast, and the owners stage a wine and cheese gathering in the backyard Saturday nights in season. Off-season rates are $30 to $50, in-season rates are $55 to $90. The cheapest room is a small one up on the dormered top floor.

The *Pleasant Inn* (☎ 302-227-7311) is on a small hill at 31 Olive Ave and lives up to its name. Rooms with air-conditioning and private bath are $65 to $75. They also rent a studio from $85 and a one-bedroom apartment from $550 a week. The friendly owner will help you find a place elsewhere if he's full.

The *Royal Rose Inn* (☎ 302-226-2535), 41 Baltimore Ave, is another nice place. A beach bungalow with eight air-conditioned rooms, rates include a continental breakfast with home-baked food. In-season rates are $50 to $95 weekdays, $80 to $115 weekends. The lower rates share baths.

The *Sun View Motel* (☎ 302-227-3651, 800-777-1293), at Wilmington Ave and the boardwalk, was built in 1963 after the 1962 hurricane wiped out the coast. Not much has changed since then – walls are paneled and the carpet is thick. This place is not fancy, but it's clean and right on the ocean. All 18 rooms have air-conditioning, TV, microwaves, and refrigerators. Summer rates are $75 to $90; off-season (until June 24) rates are $35 to $60. Ocean-view rooms are only $5 extra. It's open from May 1 to the end of September.

Places to Stay – top end

The Ramshead (☎ 302-226-9171), at Road 2, Box 509 on Route 275 (off Route 1, two miles from town), is a small upscale resort for men only. There are nine rooms in a restored, expanded farmhouse with bath. Also featured are a heated pool, a cabana service bar, a gazebo with hot tub, a gym, and a 10-person sauna. Nudity on the deck is accepted. Rooms run $100 to $140, seasonal.

Guest Rooms at Rehoboth (☎ 302-226-2400), 45 Baltimore Ave, is a gay owned and operated inn. You will find antiques, a sun porch, a small workout room with weights, and a stair machine. There are five rooms, most with shared baths. In-season rates are $95 to $125; off-season (after October 1) rates are $55 to $95.

Every one of the eight rooms in the *Sirocco Motel* (☎ 302-227-9324), on Baltimore Ave and the boardwalk, faces the ocean. The furnishings are older motel – paneling, veneer furniture, and dropped ceilings. Take a room on the 3rd floor; those on the 2nd have an overwhelming view of the asphalt roofs of boardwalk shops. All rooms have TVs and refrigerators but no phones. In-season rates are $106 weekdays, $116 weekends; off season they're between $60 and $88.

The *Atlantic Sands Hotel* (☎ 302-227-2511, 800-422-0600) is on the north side of Baltimore Ave and the boardwalk. You will find unexciting rooms with a pool, hot tub, and gas grills. In-season rates are from $112 to $180.

The *Boardwalk Plaza Hotel* (☎ 302-227-7169, 800-332-3224), at Olive Ave and the boardwalk, opened in 1991. The hotel has an indoor-outdoor Jacuzzi, fitness room, and sundeck. Rooms have antique or reproduction furniture, microwaves, coffee makers, and air-conditioning. A camera near the boardwalk beams oceanfront views to the TVs in rooms without a view. Rates are from $55 in the very low season to $250 during the summer.

Places to Eat – budget

The boardwalk has a few sandwich places, candy stores, and other fast food purveyors.

Louie's Pizza (☎ 302-227-6002) is at 11 Rehoboth Ave. A slice costs $2.

Thrasher's is at Nos 7 and 26 Rehoboth Ave. These stands sell fries to go with vinegar and salt only – no catsup. There are several other imitators on the block that are just as good, but Thrasher's is 'the original' resort chip vendor, having been around for more than 80 years and still drawing long lines in season.

Lappert's Ice Cream & Gourmet Coffee, at 162 Rehoboth Ave, sells Walter Lappert's Hawaiian ice cream concoctions. Check out the Kauai pie, a mix of Kona coffee ice cream, fudge, macadamia nuts, and coconut. A basic cone costs $2.25.

Dos Locos (☎ 302-227-5626), on the south side of Baltimore Ave between First and Second Sts, is a small Mexican place. The cooks make their own sauces, taco shells, and tortilla chips and the food tastes better because of it. Quesadillas, tacos, burritos, and chimichangas, including vegetarian, cost less than $6.

The *Delaware Sub Shop* (☎ 302-227-0440), at First St and Wilmington Ave, makes overstuffed subs (you can't close the bread because there is so much meat) in the $6 to $7 range.

Dream Cafe (☎ 302-226-3233), 26 Baltimore Ave, has good coffee, muffins, and French breads. They also serve lunch salads and sandwiches for around $5. The only drawback is that you sit below street level and have to look up for natural light.

Places to Eat – middle

Mano's (☎ 302-227-6707), 10 Wilmington Ave, has seafood from $11 to $13. The crabcakes are especially good – lumpy with crab meat, not flour. Mano's also has a bar, and a real mix of people hang out here.

Schultze's (☎ 302-227-7660), 1 Wilmington Ave, has wiener and jaegerschnitzel ($13) and smoked pork chops ($11) for dinner. For lunch they have reubens ($6) and corned beef sandwiches ($5).

The *Camel's Hump* (☎ 302-227-0947), at 21 Baltimore Ave across the street from the Lord Baltimore Hotel, has Middle Eastern food in a converted beach house. If you aren't averse to paying $9 for a gyro or $10 for falafel, this is the place.

Dogfish Head Brewing & Eats (☎ 302-226-2739), at 320 Rehoboth Ave, is the beach's new microbrewery. You can get hickory-smoked pizza for under $10.

Places to Eat – top end

Although there are restaurants on the other avenues, Wilmington Ave between Second St and the boardwalk has the best eateries in Rehoboth. Rehoboth's top-end restaurants have a well-deserved reputation for catering the best food on the Delmarva coast. It is just about the only place to go for something more imaginative than the standard broiled fish, potato, and veggie meals that you will find at most of the shore's innumerable seafood places, where they rope you in with a good view and slap the 'catch of the day' on your plate.

The *Back Porch Cafe* (☎ 302-227-3674), 59 Rehoboth Ave, has a brunch menu if you want to escape from the bacon and eggs breakfast routine. The menu includes salmon and cream omelet ($7.50) and shirred eggs with ham and asparagus ($8.50). Dinner choices include mahi mahi ($21), jerk pork ($17), and Indian-spiced salmon ($22). They also have a bar and serve wine by the glass.

The *Blue Moon* (☎ 302-227-6515) is a beach house converted into a restaurant at 35 Baltimore Ave. The restaurant has an extensive wine list and entrees like swordfish with pesto ($21), duck with coconut curry ($16), and tuna with ginger sauce ($21). The bar is popular in the evenings.

Chez La Mer (☎ 302-227-6494), 201 Second St (corner of Wilmington Ave), has a changing menu that includes appetizers like baked brie with roasted garlic puree topping ($6) and shallot and wild mushroom soup ($4). Entrees include rack of lamb ($23), duck with Indian spices ($21), and seafood variations.

La La Land (☎ 302-227-3887), 22 Wilmington Ave, is one of the best restaurants in the state. You sit in chairs painted gold, green, purple, and blue. It's elegant without being stuffy. The entrees are in the $18 to $25 range: Thai-spiced swordfish, lamb tamales, teriyaki catfish, and salmon lasagna with dill and black pepper pasta.

La La Land's rival is *Celsius* (☎ 302-227-5767), at 50C Wilmington Ave. The chef cooks American cuisine with a California flare, featuring dishes like grilled calamari salad and chops from naturally raised lambs. You'll probably spend over $25 here.

Entertainment

In addition to the bars at restaurants like *Mano's*, *Back Porch Cafe*, and *Blue Moon*, there are a few places with live music.

The *Country Squire* (☎ 302-227-3985), 19 Rehoboth Ave, has live music Friday to Sunday in season. It varies from progressive rock to blues and oldies and there is no cover. Other nights they have open mike and karaoke. The place has one long bar and the band plays at the back. The Squire also serves food in the under $10 range.

Sir Guy's Restaurant & Pub (☎ 302-227-7616), 243 Rehoboth Ave, has live music on weekends year round, without any cover. It's generally reggae on Saturdays and variations on rock other nights. The crowd tends to be in their mid-20s and up.

Sydney's Side Street (☎ 302-227-1339) is a small bar-restaurant, at 25 Christian St just before it runs into Rehoboth Ave. Sydney brings in live music nightly during the summer and on weekends in the off season. The music is always jazz or blues and the cover, if any, is $5 or under. Sydney's also offers wine and liquor tastings, and you can order entrees in small ('grazing') portions.

The *Bottle & Cork* (☎ 302-227-8545), Route 1 in Dewey Beach, bills itself as 'the greatest rock & roll bar in the world.' Having passed its 60th anniversary, this ersatz Tudor-style roadhouse must be doing something right. The rock is continuous, the dance floors are a mob scene, and the crowd is mostly over 30.

The *Rusty Rudder* (☎ 302-227-3888) sits right on the edge of the bay at 113 Dickinson St in Dewey Beach. This place is a big Southern California kind of place with a deck that holds 500 people. The Rudder does a quick change every night from restaurant to club. The after-beach crowd shows up for drinks and steel drums everyday from 4 to 9 pm. Wednesday through Friday top regional bands play a mix of oldies, progressive, and rock. Saturday night separate DJs work the indoor and deck venues. The crowd here includes plenty of tan, young hardbodies – mostly straight – with few inhibitions: college kids during the week, yuppies on the weekends. This is the place to come if you like to dance or wish to pursue a torrid but brief romantic adventure.

The Renegade (227-4713) on Route 1 is a huge nightspot with a pool, and multiple bars and dance floors. This is Rehoboth's premier gay entertainment site for both men and women. There is live music and dancing every night in season as well as occasional drag revues.

Cloud 9 (☎ 302-226-1999), located at 234 Rehoboth Ave, is a bistro next to Sydney's with a lively happy hour. It has a DJ and dancing on weekends. The Cloud is popular with a mix of gay, lesbian, and straight people. There is a tea dance on some Sundays.

Things to Buy

There are a lot of resort-wear shops in the pedestrian walkways between Baltimore and Rehoboth Aves. Rehoboth Ave from Second St to the boardwalk has a lot of shops selling 'family' items like T-shirts, jewelry, toys, T-shirts, Christmas ornaments, candy, T-shirts, clothing, and T-shirts.

The big thrill for the shopping crowd is the ever-growing Ocean Outlets (☎ 302-227-6860) shopping malls outside of town on Route 1. At this writing, there are more than 100 factory outlet stores in these complexes and the number is growing. Almost all of the big apparel manufacturers are here, including Izod, LL Bean, Eddie Bauer, and Reebok. Whether you like these kinds of malls or not, Ocean Outlets is the closest one to a major travelers' attraction in all of the Capital Region. You really can get some good deals, saving up to 40% off the normal prices on clothing and everyday accessory items.

Getting There & Away

Bus Greyhound Carolina Trailway (☎ 800-231-2222) stops in front of the Wilgus Glamorama dry cleaners (☎ 302-227-7223), 251 Rehoboth Ave near Fourth St. There is one bus a day to/from DC; the cheapest weekend rate is $25. Two daily buses go to Wilmington for $16.

DART (☎ 302-577-6686, 800-652-DART) runs weekday service to Wilmington by way of Dover. The bus stops at Rehoboth Ave and the boardwalk.

Car Route 1 runs straight from Wilmington and continues down the coast to Ocean City, Maryland.

Getting Around

Bus Delaware Resort Transit (DRT; ☎ 302-226-2001, 800-553-3278) runs buses between Lewes, Rehoboth Beach, and Dewey Beach along Business Route 9 and Routes 1 and 1A. The buses run from Memorial Day to Labor Day from around 7 am to around 11 pm. For $1 you get a pass good for riding from 7 am to 4 pm.

Ruddertowne Transit Trolley Service (☎ 302-227-3888) runs a free shuttle from Rehoboth Ave and the boardwalk to Dewey Beach.

Car Despite Route 1 expanding to six lanes in the vicinity of Rehoboth, stoplights as well as beach and outlet traffic make for slow driving during the summer and sunny weekends year round.

Pedicabs Kangaroo Kabs cruise the streets and take people around on a negotiated fare or a tip-only basis. The average in-town fare is around $5 but you pay more to go to Dewey Beach.

NANTICOKE INDIAN MUSEUM

The Nanticokes are the last remaining Native American people in Delaware. The museum (☎ 302-945-7022) is in a schoolhouse at the intersection of Route 24 and Road 297 about 12 miles west of Rehoboth. Inside is one large room of exhibits including artifacts and replicas from the Nanticokes and other Native American peoples. The museum is open Tuesday to Thursday from 9 am to 4 pm and Saturday from noon to 4 pm and costs $1.

The **powwow** occurs yearly in September, usually the first weekend after Labor Day, at a wooded site near the museum. The gathering includes two days of singing, dancing, drumming, and storytelling. There are a lot of booths selling silver and turquoise jewelry and feather items. You can also buy 'fry bread' on which you sprinkle confectionery sugar or honey (Italian zeppole is a rounder version of this bread). The powwow gets crowded. Parking is in a large field near the site, but the traffic backs up nearby. Parking and admission costs $5, walk-ins are $1.

Take Route 1N from Rehoboth to Route 24. Take Route 24 heading southwest about nine miles to the intersection with Road 297 and look for the signs directing you to parking.

DELAWARE SEASHORE STATE PARK

Delaware Seashore State Park is a 10-mile long and half-mile wide peninsula stretching along the coast between the towns of Dewey Beach to the north and Bethany Beach to the south. The beach on the ocean side is long, straight, and clean – and, unlike Cape Henlopen, it is unmarred by abandoned military installations. The park takes up the entire thin peninsula, with Route 1 running down its center.

The park office (☎ 302-227-2800) is at the southern end of the park on the west side of Route 1, north of the Indian River Inlet Bridge. It's open daily year round from 8 am to 4:30 pm. Usage fees are charged if you want to stop and use the park, but you can drive through for free. The fee for Delaware-registered vehicles is $2.50, for all others it's $5. The fee is collected daily from Memorial Day to Labor day, and in May, September, and October it's collected on weekends and holidays.

Hiking

You will find a looping 1.5-mile hike onto Burton's Island west of the marina. There are 13 points on the trail marked to correspond with an interpretive pamphlet that you can pick up at the park office.

Swimming

Guarded swimming areas are on the ocean at the north end of the park (Tower Road Ocean) and at the southern end (Southeast Day Area). There are also access roads to unguarded beaches in between.

Fishing

The Indian River Inlet Marina (☎ 302-227-3071) is west of the park office. Over 30 charter fishing boats run out of the marina. Book one by calling ☎ 302-947-1924.

Camping

There are three campgrounds (☎ 302-539-7202), all around the Indian River Inlet. The New Camp south of the inlet has sites with water, electricity, and sewage for $21. The Old Camp, next to it, has sites without hookups for $14. There is also Overflow Camp on the north side of the inlet, without hookups for $14. This is used when the others fill up.

The land on both sides of the inlet is crowded with the campgrounds, park office, a coast guard station, picnic and swimming areas, and the marina. There are also power lines overhead, and the view of the highway bridge from below doesn't add much to one's sense of getting back to nature. But once you get to the ocean, you can forget about the camping conditions and walk in virtual privacy for miles.

BETHANY BEACH & FENWICK ISLAND

These two beach towns bill themselves together as the 'quiet resorts.' Bethany Beach is the first community on the coast south of Delaware Seashore State Park. Immediately south of Bethany is Fenwick Island State Park (which runs for three miles along the coast). Next comes the town of Fenwick Island. If you look at a map, you'll see what appears to be a long barrier peninsula with the two towns and the park on it. You will also see that the Assawoman Canal runs north-south behind Bethany Beach, and that the towns are actually on an island because the canal separates the beach communities from the mainland.

Bethany is a popular upper-middle class summer resort (the town's permanent population of 350 balloons to 4000 in summer) with several thousand expensive beach houses, many built on stilts to withstand hurricanes. But while the homes are large and lovely, the lots are tiny, creating a visual contradiction and undermining Bethany's pretensions. Nevertheless, Bethany is exclusive enough to draw vacationers the likes of actor Denzel Washington, Vice President Al Gore, and many other prominent government officials and media celebrities.

Bethany Beach remains quiet because it is a community of housing developments with few places for travelers to stay. Nonetheless, Bethany Beach has evolved quite a bit from its origins as a camp meeting town of 'seaside assembly for the Christian churches of this country.' (The Biblical town of Bethany was the home of Lazarus, who Jesus raised from the dead.) Fenwick Island is something of a small-scale Bethany, with fewer glitzy homes. The center of the village of Fenwick Island along Route 1 is more commercial but seems almost like an oasis when compared with Ocean City, just across the border in Maryland. Parking is difficult, but there are metered lots just north and south of Garfield Pkwy near the beach along Atlantic Ave.

Information

The Bethany-Fenwick Area Chamber of Commerce (☎ 302-539-2100, 800-962-7873) is in a large wooden beach house on stilts on the eastern side of Route 1, at the line between Fenwick Island and Fenwick Island State Park. From June to November the Chamber is open weekdays from 9 am to 5 pm and on weekends from 10 am to 2 pm. In the off season the weekday hours are 10 am to 4 pm.

Things to See

There isn't much besides the quiet beach and largely noncommercial boardwalk in Bethany. Garfield Pkwy off of Route 1 is the main road and leads to the center of the boardwalk. There are some beach clothing stores, a market, and a few places to eat along Garfield.

Fenwick Island doesn't have a boardwalk, but the beach has clean, hard sand that's good for walking. **Fenwick Lighthouse** is at the south end of town just west of Route 1 before you enter Maryland. You can see it from the highway and drive up to look at it, but you can't go up.

Activities
Steen's Beach Service (☎ 302-539-9160), on the beach near the boardwalk, rents umbrellas and chairs. Bethany Rental Service (☎ 302-539-6244/2244), at 201 Central Ave, a part of Harry's Bait & Tackle, rents all kinds of beach equipment, from bicycles and boats to microwaves, blenders, and typewriters. The Fenwick Islander bike shop (☎ 302-537-2021), Route 1 and Virginia Ave, rents bikes.

Places to Stay – Bethany Beach
Camping *Sandy Cove Campsite* (☎ 302-539-6245) is in Ocean View four miles inland from Bethany. Sites with water and electricity cost $22.

Tuckahoe Acres (☎ 302-539-1841) is six miles inland from Bethany Beach on the Indian River Bay; prices are slightly less.

B&Bs & Motels The cedar-shingle house *Journey's End* (☎ 302-539-9502) is on Atlantic Ave near the corner of Parkwood St. The house was built for John Addy, a plumber and one of the original founders of Bethany Beach. It was the first house to have indoor plumbing in town and used to sit closer to the shore but was moved back to avoid erosion. It's a pleasant, airy beach house thanks to its 67 doors and 100 windows. Most rooms have two single beds and rent for $40 in June and September and $60 in July and August. Guests share bathrooms and must take showers outside.

The *Addy Sea* (☎ 302-539-3707) sits right on the beach at the end of Ocean View Pkwy, although it was moved back from its original location to escape the surf. This inn has been a guest house since 1935; the rates are $60 to $80.

The *Blue Surf Motel* (☎ 302-539-7531) is at the ocean end of Garfield Pkwy. It has reasonably large rooms with low-end but unworn furniture and deck-like wood floors outside between the rooms that give it an earthy motel feeling. In-season rates are $85 to $95, more for an oceanfront view. Off-season rates are between $50 and $80.

The *Bethany Arms Motel* (☎ 302-539-9603) is at Hollywood St and the ocean. It has five buildings – two ocean front, one with ocean view, and two with no view. Some rooms are a little musty so look at a couple. The furniture is 1950s motel. In-season rates are $80 to $90, $110 to $125 with a view. Off-season rates run from $40 to $85.

Places to Stay – Fenwick Island
Camping In Fenwick Island, *Treasure Beach RV Park & Campground* (☎ 302-436-8001) is on Route 54. There are 80 sites. Tent sites cost $15, full hook-ups $25. You'll probably need reservations here in season.

Motels There are a few motels with unsurprising decor on Route 1 in Fenwick Island. The *Sands Motel* (☎ 302-539-7745, 302-539-8200) has some very '70s furnishings and a beach view partially obscured by houses. Get a room on the second floor, because the lower rooms look out on a weedy lot. Rooms are clean and come without phones. The cheapest rates are $29 off season, $60 in season. Larger rooms go up to about $100; add $15 for weekends.

The *Fenwick Islander* (☎ 302-539-2333), on Route 1 and South Carolina Ave, was built in 1985 and is one of the newer ones around. Off-season rates are $74 to $89, in-season rates are $29 to $59. Add 10% to 20% for weekends. The lowest rates are for October.

Places to Eat
Bethany Beach Neither Bethany nor Fenwick Island may excite you with delicious food; they're a particular letdown if you've come south from Rehoboth.

The *Coyote Beach Cafe* (☎ 302-539-9343) is at the eastern end of Garfield Pkwy in the small pedestrian mall on the southern side of the street. Enchiladas, burritos, and seafood are on the menu, costing anywhere from $3 to $8. The cafe also serves burgers, hot dogs, and sandwiches.

La Pizzeria is at 109 Garfield. *Tim's Aloha Stand*, also on Garfield near the beach, serves shaved ice and typical beach-style fast food.

If you are in the mood for a cheap feast you might consider driving two miles west on Route 26 (which is Garfield Pkwy in town) to get to *Bootsie's Bar-B-Q* (☎ 302-539-9529). This restaurant is a small, brown, wooden building standing alone on your right. The chicken and pork ribs are good, but ignore the chopped pork barbecue unless you like Sloppy Joes. Half a barbecued chicken with potato salad, cole slaw, and roll costs $5. A rack of ribs is $7.50; sandwiches are under $5. Take out only.

Fenwick Island A 'family restaurant,' *Warren's Station* (☎ 302-539-7156), is on Route 1 across from the Sands Motel. It serves diner-style sandwiches (under $5) and fish and meat dishes ($6 to $12).

There are a few large seafood places in Fenwick serving up the usual. *Harpoon Hanna's* (☎ 302-539-3095), just west of Route 1 before Ocean City (watch for the signs), serves shrimp and chicken dishes ($14) and fish ($13 to $18). The *Fenwick Crab House* (☎ 302-539-2500) is on Route 1 near Delaware Ave. The crab house offers the usual seafood plus crab imperial and crab cakes ($14), Alaskan snow crab legs ($16), and jambalaya ($13).

Getting There & Away

Bus The Delaware Department of Transportation (☎ 800-652-3278) runs buses that connect cities on the coast with inland Northern Delaware. The stop in Bethany is at Central Blvd at Pennsylvania Ave.

Greyhound Carolina Trailway (☎ 800-231-2222) stops at Harry's Bait & Tackle at the corner of Central Blvd and Pennsylvania Ave in Bethany Beach (see Rehoboth).

In Fenwick Island, DRT (☎ 800-553-3278) runs buses to stops at the state park entrance and at Ocean Hwy (Route 1) at the corner of Lighthouse Rd (Route 54) on the southern end of town. Buses also go into Ocean City, just across the state line in Maryland, where they stop at Ocean Hwy and 145th St.

Car Bethany Beach and Fenwick Island lie along the Route 1 beach highway between Rehoboth and Ocean City, Maryland. During the summer season this route can be packed with slow-moving traffic. If you are coming from the west and just want to get to one of these quiet resorts, try taking a couple of back roads. Route 26 runs through swamp country to Bethany; Route 54 will bring you to the coast a few miles further south at Fenwick Island.

FENWICK ISLAND STATE PARK

Fenwick Island State Park (☎ 302-539-9060, 302-539-1055) is a three-mile strip bordered on the east by the Atlantic Ocean and on the west by Little Assawoman Bay. As with Delaware Seashore State Park, you can drive through on Route 1 without paying a usage fee. However, if you pull off at the southern end's guarded swimming beach, you will have to pay $2.50 if you have Delaware license plates and $5 if you don't. The park has a good three-mile Atlantic beach, although the only access if you're driving is at the southern end, and you'll have to pay. There are a couple of surf-fishing access points, but to drive onto the beach at these, you need a surf-fishing permit. The charge for Delaware-registered vehicles is $50; for out-of-state ones, $100.

Bay Sports (☎ 302-539-7999), on the bay side of the park across Route 1 from the guarded beach, rents water sports equipment. Jet skis go half hourly for $35 to $50, hourly for $60 to $80. Sailboats rent by the hour for $32 to $40 and by the day for $115 to $160. Sailing and windsurfing lessons are $20 an hour. There is parasailing, too, with 400/600-foot lines at $35/45.

Index

ABBREVIATIONS

DE - Delaware
MD - Maryland
PA - Pennsylvania
VA - Virginia
WV - West Virginia

MAPS

TEXT

LONELY PLANET PRODUCTS

Lonely Planet is known worldwide for publishing practical, reliable and no-nonsense travel information in our guides and on our web site. The Lonely Planet list covers just about every accessible part of the world. Currently there are eight series: *travel guides, shoestring guides, walking guides, city guides, phrasebooks, audio packs, travel atlases* and *Journeys*–a unique collection of travelers' tales.

EUROPE

Austria • Baltic States & Kaliningrad • Baltic States phrasebook • Britain • Central Europe on a shoestring • Central Europe phrasebook • Czech & Slovak Republics • Denmark • Dublin city guide • Eastern Europe on a shoestring • Eastern Europe phrasebook • Finland • France • Greece • Greek phrasebook • Hungary • Iceland, Greenland & the Faroe Islands • Ireland • Italy • Mediterranean Europe on a shoestring • Mediterranean Europe phrasebook • Paris city guide • Poland • Prague city guide • Russia, Ukraine & Belarus • Russian phrasebook • Scandinavian & Baltic Europe on a shoestring • Scandinavian Europe phrasebook • Slovenia • St Petersburg city guide • Switzerland • Trekking in Greece • Trekking in Spain • Ukrainian phrasebook • Vienna city guide • Walking in Switzerland • Western Europe on a shoestring • Western Europe phrasebook

NORTH AMERICA

Alaska • Backpacking in Alaska • Baja California • California & Nevada • Canada • Florida • Hawaii • Honolulu city guide • Los Angeles city guide • Mexico • Miami city guide • New England • New Orleans city guide • New York, New Jersey & Pennsylvania • Pacific Northwest USA • Rocky Mountain States USA • San Francisco city guide • Southwest USA • Washington, DC & the Capital Region

CENTRAL AMERICA & THE CARIBBEAN

Central America on a shoestring • Costa Rica • Cuba • Eastern Caribbean • Guatemala, Belize & Yucatán: La Ruta Maya • Jamaica

SOUTH AMERICA

Argentina, Uruguay & Paraguay • Bolivia • Brazil • Brazilian phrasebook • Buenos Aires city guide • Chile & Easter Island • Colombia • Ecuador & the Galápagos Islands • Latin American Spanish phrasebook • Peru • Quechua phrasebook • Rio de Janeiro city guide • South America on a shoestring • Trekking in the Patagonian Andes • Venezuela

Travel Literature: Full Circle: A South American Journey

AFRICA

Arabic (Moroccan) phrasebook • Africa on a shoestring • Cape Town city guide • Central Africa • East Africa • Egypt & the Sudan • Ethiopian (Amharic) phrasebook • Kenya • Morocco • North Africa • South Africa, Lesotho & Swaziland • Swahili phrasebook • Trekking in East Africa • West Africa • Zimbabwe, Botswana & Namibia • Zimbabwe, Botswana & Namibia travel atlas

ISLANDS OF THE INDIAN OCEAN

Madagascar & Comoros • Maldives & Islands of the East Indian Ocean • Mauritius, Réunion & Seychelles

Also Available: Antarctica • Bermuda • Travel with Children • Traveller's Tales

MAIL ORDER

Lonely Planet products are distributed worldwide. They are also available by mail order from Lonely Planet, so if you have difficulty finding a title please write to us. North American and South American residents should write to Embarcadero West, 155 Filbert St, Suite 251, Oakland CA 94607, USA; European and African residents should write to 10 Barley Mow Passage, Chiswick, London W4 4PH; and residents of other countries to PO Box 617, Hawthorn, Victoria 3122, Australia.

NORTH-EAST ASIA

Beijing city guide • Cantonese phrasebook • Central Asia • China • Hong Kong city guide • Hong Kong, Macau & Canton • Japan • Japanese phrasebook • Japanese audio pack • Korea • Korean phrasebook • Mandarin phrasebook • Mongolia • Mongolian phrasebook • North-East Asia on a shoestring • Seoul city guide • Taiwan • Tibet • Tibet phrasebook • Tokyo city guide

Travel Literature: Lost Japan

MIDDLE EAST & CENTRAL ASIA

Arab Gulf States • Arabic (Egyptian) phrasebook • Central Asia • Iran • Israel • Istanbul city guide • Jordan & Syria • Middle East • Turkey • Turkish phrasebook • Trekking in Turkey • Yemen

Travel Literature: The Gates of Damascus

INDIAN SUBCONTINENT

Bengali phrasebook • Bangladesh • Delhi city guide • Hindi/Urdu phrasebook • India • India & Bangladesh travel atlas • Indian Himalaya • Karakoram Highway • Kashmir, Ladakh & Zanskar • Nepal • Nepali phrasebook • Pakistan • Rajasthan • Sri Lanka • Sri Lanka phrasebook • Trekking in the Indian Himalaya • Trekking in the Karakoram & Hindukush • Trekking in the Nepal Himalaya

Travel Literature: Shopping for Buddhas

SOUTH-EAST ASIA

Bali & Lombok • Bangkok city guide • Burmese phrasebook • Cambodia • Ho Chi Minh city guide • Indonesia • Indonesian phrasebook • Indonesian audio pack • Jakarta city guide • Java • Laos • Lao phrasebook • Malay phrasebook • Malaysia, Singapore & Brunei • Myanmar (Burma) • Philippines • Pilipino phrasebook • Singapore city guide • South-East Asia on a shoestring • Thailand • Thai phrasebook • Thailand travel atlas • Thai audio pack • Thai Hill Tribes phrasebook • Vietnam • Vietnamese phrasebook • Vietnam travel atlas

AUSTRALIA & THE PACIFIC

Australia • Australian phrasebook • Bushwalking in Australia • Bushwalking in Papua New Guinea • Fiji • Fijian phrasebook • Islands of Australia's Great Barrier Reef • Melbourne city guide • Micronesia • New Caledonia • New South Wales & the ACT • New Zealand • Northern Territory • Outback Australia • Papua New Guinea • Papua New Guinea phrasebook • Queensland • Rarotonga & the Cook Islands • Samoa • Solomon Islands • South Australia • Sydney city guide • Tahiti & French Polynesia • Tasmania • Tonga • Tramping in New Zealand • Vanuatu • Victoria • Western Australia

Travel Literature: Islands in the Clouds • Sean & David's Long Drive

THE LONELY PLANET STORY

Lonely Planet published its first book in 1973 in response to the numerous 'How did you do it?' questions Maureen and Tony Wheeler were asked after driving, bussing, hitching, sailing and railing their way from England to Australia.

Written at a kitchen table and hand collated, trimmed and stapled, Across Asia on the Cheap became an instant local best seller, inspiring thoughts of another book.

Eighteen months in South-East Asia resulted in their second guide, South-East Asia on a shoestring, which they put together in a backstreet Chinese hotel in Singapore in 1975. The 'yellow bible', as it quickly became known to backpackers around the world, soon became the guide to the region. It has sold well over half a million copies and is now in its 8th edition, still retaining its familiar yellow cover.

Today there are 200 titles, including travel guides, walking guides, language kits & phrasebooks, travel atlases and travel literature. The company is one of the largest travel publishers in the world. Although Lonely Planet initially specialized in guides to Asia, we now cover most regions of the world, including the Pacific, North America, South America, Africa, the Middle East and Europe.

The emphasis continues to be on travel for independent travelers. Tony and Maureen still travel for several months of each year and play an active part in the writing, updating and quality control of Lonely Planet's guides.

They have been joined by over 50 authors and 155 staff at our offices in Melbourne (Australia), Oakland (USA), London (UK) and Paris (France). Travelers themselves also make a valuable contribution to the guides through the feedback we receive in thousands of letters each year.

The people at Lonely Planet strongly believe that travelers can make a positive contribution to the countries they visit, both through their appreciation of the countries' culture, wildlife and natural features, and through the money they spend. In addition, the company makes a direct contribution to the countries and regions it covers. Since 1986 a percentage of the income from each book has been donated to ventures such as famine relief in Africa; aid projects in India; agricultural projects in Central America; Greenpeace's efforts to halt French nuclear testing in the Pacific; and Amnesty International.

'I hope we send the people out with the right attitude about travel. You realize when you travel that there are so many different perspectives about the world, so we hope these books will make people more interested in what they see. These are guidebooks, but you can't really guide people. All you can do is point them in the right direction.'

– Tony Wheeler

LONELY PLANET PUBLICATIONS

Australia
PO Box 617, Hawthorn 3122, Victoria
☎ (03) 9819 1877 fax (03) 9819 6459
e-mail talk2us@lonelyplanet.com.au

USA
Embarcadero West, 155 Filbert Street,
Suite 251, Oakland, CA 94607
☎ (510) 893 8555, (800) 275 8555
fax (510) 893 8563
e-mail info@lonelyplanet.com

UK
10 Barley Mow Passage, Chiswick,
London W4 4PH
☎ (0181) 742 3161 fax (0181) 742 2772
e-mail 100413.3551@compuserve.com

France
71 bis rue du Cardinal Lemoine, 75005 Paris
☎ 1 44 32 06 20 fax 1 46 34 72 55
e-mail 100560.415@compuserve.com

World Wide Web: http://www.lonelyplanet.com